HANDBOOK OF DEPRESSION
Second Edition

HANDBOOK OF DEPRESSION

Second Edition

Edited by
E. EDWARD BECKHAM
WILLIAM R. LEBER

THE GUILFORD PRESS
New York   London

Library of Congress Cataloging-in-Publication Data

Handbook of depression / edited by E. Edward Beckham, William R.
Leber. — 2nd ed.
      p.   cm.
   Includes bibliographical references and index.
   ISBN 0-89862-841-5
   1. Depression, Mental.   I. Beckham, Ernest Edward.   II. Leber,
William R.
   [DNLM: 1. Depressive Disorder.   WM 171 H2366 1995]
RC537.H338   1995
616.85'27—dc20
DNLM/DLC
for Library of Congress   94-49600
                                                               CIP

Contributors

AARON T. BECK, MD, Department of Psychiatry, University of Pennsylvania Medical School, Philadelphia, Pennsylvania

E. EDWARD BECKHAM, PhD, Department of Psychiatry and Behavioral Sciences, Oklahoma University Health Sciences Center, Oklahoma City, Oklahoma

JULES R. BEMPORAD, MD, Department of Psychiatry, Cornell University Medical College, White Plains, New York; Present address: School Consultation Services, New York Medical College, Valhalla, New York

CHRISTIANE BREMS, PhD, Department of Psychology, University of Alaska, Anchorage, Alaska

DENNIS P. CANTWELL, MD, Department of Psychiatry and Biobehavioral Sciences, UCLA Neuropsychiatric Institute, Los Angeles, California

DAVID C. CLARK, PhD, Department of Psychiatry, Rush Medical College, Chicago, Illinois; Institute for Mental Well-Being, Rush–Presbyterian–St. Luke's Medical Center, Chicago, Illinois

RUTH C. CRONKITE, PhD, Center for Health Care Evaluation, Department of Veterans Affairs and Stanford University Medical Centers, Palo Alto, California

MARY E. FARMER, MD, MPH, Epidemiology and Psychopathology Research Branch, Division of Epidemiology and Services Research, National Institute of Mental Health, Rockville, Maryland

MAURIZIO FAVA, MD, Depression Research Program, Department of Psychiatry, Massachusetts General Hospital, Boston, Massachusetts; Department of Psychiatry, Harvard Medical School, Boston, Massachusetts

ROBERT FERRIS, BA, Department of Psychology, Holy Cross College, Worcester, Massachusetts

ANDREW FUTTERMAN, PhD, Department of Psychology, Holy Cross College, Worcester, Massachusetts

DOLORES GALLAGHER-THOMPSON, PhD, Department of Veterans Affairs Health Care System, Palo Alto, California; Division of Gerontology, Endocrinology, and Metabolism, Stanford University School of Medicine, Palo Alto, California

IAN H. GOTLIB, PhD, Department of Psychology, Northwestern University, Evanston, Illinois

HARRY GWIRTSMAN, MD, Department of Psychiatry, Vanderbilt University Medical School, Nashville, Tennessee; Psychiatry Service, Department of Veterans Affairs Medical Center, Nashville, Tennessee

SHARON HIRSCH, MD, Department of Psychiatry and Behavioral Sciences, Northwestern University Medical School, Chicago, Illinois; Department of Child and Adolescent Psychiatry, Children's Memorial Hospital, Chicago, Illinois

ROBERT H. HOWLAND, MD, Department of Psychiatry, Western Psychiatric Institute and Clinic, University of Pittsburgh School of Medicine, Pittsburgh, Pennsylvania

THOMAS A. INCK, PhD candidate, Adelphi University, Garden City, New York

NEIL S. JACOBSON, PhD, Department of Psychology, University of Washington, Seattle, Washington

ROBIN B. JARRETT, PhD, Department of Psychiatry, University of Texas Southwestern Medical Center at Dallas, Dallas, Texas

CHARLES T. KAELBER, MD, DPH, Epidemiology and Psychopathology Research Branch, Division of Epidemiology and Services Research, National Institute of Mental Health, Rockville, Maryland

AMY S. KAISER, MA, MEd, Department of Psychology, The Toronto Hospital, Toronto, Ontario, Canada

RANDY KATZ, PhD, CPsych, Department of Psychology, The Toronto Hospital, Toronto, Ontario, Canada; Department of Psychiatry, University of Toronto, Toronto, Ontario, Canada

DOREEN KOTIK-HARPER, PhD, Department of Family Practice and Community Medicine, University of Texas Health Sciences Center, Houston, Texas

HOWARD M. KRAVITZ, DO, MPH, Department of Psychiatry, Rush–Presbyterian–St. Luke's Medical Center, Chicago, Illinois; Department of Psychiatry, Rush North Shore Medical Center, Skokie, Illinois

WILLIAM R. LEBER, PhD, Department of Psychiatry and Behavioral Sciences, Oklahoma University Health Sciences Center, Oklahoma City, Oklahoma; VA Medical Center, Oklahoma City, Oklahoma

PETER M. LEWINSOHN, PhD, Oregon Research Institute, Eugene, Oregon

JOHN C. MARKOWITZ, MD, Department of Psychiatry, Cornell University Medical College, New York, New York

JACK D. MASER, PhD, Anxiety and Somatoform Disorders Program, National Institute of Mental Health, Rockville, Maryland

KARIN MENDELBAUM, MD, Department of Psychiatry, Free University Clinics of Brussels, Erasme Hospital, Brussels, Belgium

JULIEN MENDLEWICZ, MD, PhD, Department of Psychiatry, Free University Clinics of Brussels, Erasme Hospital, Brussels, Belgium

JAMES R. MERIKANGAS, MD, Genetic Epidemiology Research Unit, Yale University School of Medicine, New Haven, Connecticut

KATHLEEN RIES MERIKANGAS, PhD, Genetic Epidemiology Research Unit, Yale University School of Medicine, New Haven, Connecticut

THEODORE MILLON, PhD, DSc, Department of Psychology, University of Miami, Coral Gables, Florida; Department of Psychiatry, Harvard Medical School, Boston, Massachusetts

RUDOLF H. MOOS, PhD, Center for Health Care Evaluation, Department of Veterans Affairs and Stanford University Medical Centers, Palo Alto, California

DOUGLAS E. MOUL, MD, MPH, Epidemiology and Psychopathology Research Branch, Division of Epidemiology and Services Research, National Institute of Mental Health, Rockville, Maryland

ALAN J. NEWMAN, Department of Psychiatry, Rush–Presbyterian–St. Luke's Medical Center, Chicago, Illinois

J. CHRIS NORDGREN, PhD, Disaster Mental Health Institute, University of South Dakota, Vermillion, South Dakota

STACEY E. PRINCE, BS, Department of Psychology, University of Washington, Seattle, Washington

JERROLD F. ROSENBAUM, MD, Outpatient Psychiatry Division, Department of Psychiatry, Massachusetts General Hospital, Boston, Massachusetts; Department of Psychiatry, Harvard Medical School, Boston, Massachusetts

WILLIAM P. SACCO, PhD, Department of Psychology, University of South Florida, Tampa, Florida

JEREMY D. SAFRAN, PhD, Clinical Psychology Program, Graduate Faculty, New School for Social Research, New York, New York

SERGE SEVY, MD, Department of Psychiatry, Free University Clinics of Brussels, Erasme Hospital, Brussels, Belgium

BRIAN F. SHAW, PhD, CPsych, Department of Psychology, The Toronto Hospital, Toronto, Ontario, Canada; Department of Psychiatry and Behavioural Sciences, University of Toronto, Toronto, Ontario, Canada

DONALD L. SHERAK, MD, Adolescent and Family Treatment Program, Taunton State Hospital, Charles River Health Management, Taunton, Massachusetts

PATRICIA L. SPEIER, MD, Child and Adolescent Outpatient Service, Department of Psychiatry, University of California at San Francisco, San Francisco, California

DENISE E. STEVENS, PhD, Genetic Epidemiology Research Unit, Yale University School of Medicine, New Haven, Connecticut

MICHAEL E. THASE, MD, Department of Psychiatry, Western Psychiatric Institute and Clinic, University of Pittsburgh School of Medicine, Pittsburgh, Pennsylvania

LARRY THOMPSON, PhD, Department of Veterans Affairs Health Care System, Palo Alto, California; Division of Gerontology, Endocrinology, and Metabolism, Stanford University School of Medicine, Palo Alto, California

T. MICHAEL VALLIS, PhD, CPsych, Department of Psychology, Camp Hill Medical Centre, Halifax, Nova Scotia, Canada

RICHARD WEISE, MEd, Psychosocial Factors Program, National Institute of Mental Health, Rockville, Maryland

MYRNA M. WEISSMAN, PhD, Department of Psychiatry, Columbia University College of Physicians and Surgeons, New York, New York; Division of Clinical–Genetic Epidemiology, New York State Psychiatric Institute, New York, New York

DIANE J. WILLIS, Child Study Center, Oklahoma University Health Sciences Center, Oklahoma City, Oklahoma

LORRAINE K. YOULL, PhD, Department of Psychology, University of Central Oklahoma, Edmond, Oklahoma

Preface

We are very pleased to publish this second edition of the *Handbook of Depression*. The original edition had become dated and in some areas had been made obsolete by the rapid accumulation of new acknowledge. So much information continues to be discovered in the area of mood disorders that handbooks of this sort must be updated at least every 10 years. In fact, the growth of knowledge is so rapid that some might even question the feasibility of such a handbook at all. But comprehensive reviews such as this one continue to be very important to mental health professionals. In fact, they become important precisely because of the information explosion in mental health. No one can stay abreast of all of the relevant information by reading journal articles. Even many books on depression focus on a narrow area, so that a comprehensive understanding of the disorder might require many different volumes. In conducting workshops on depression, we have found that professionals feel a great need to understand more about mood disorders. Both new graduates and experienced practitioners show a desire for more knowledge and additional techniques. Given the crowded curricula of graduate schools and professional schools, there is not always an opportunity for students to learn about the full scope of mood disorders, including the different kinds of depression, the variety of theoretical explanations, and the numerous types of treatment. On the other hand, it is impossible for the working professional to stay abreast of all of the developments in this area. In fact, it is difficult even for the academician and researcher to do so because of the very wide variety of disciplines involved. Thus, for the researcher, this book offers an opportunity to gain an overview of how other disciplines are investigating depression. For the student, it provides the opportunity to gain an initial all-encompassing view. For the practicing clinician, it provides a wealth of useful information in the areas of diagnosis and treatment, as well as a theoretical grounding in the rationale behind treatments.

The interplay of psychological, biological, and social factors is a major emphasis of this book. An especially useful task for a handbook of depression is to present information on biological theories and psychological understandings within the same volume. As researchers, teachers, and clinicians, we have been especially interested and intrigued by the important but still unclear relationship between psychological and biological processes. Both types of treatments have proven their worth, just as biological and psychological theories have had their validity demonstrated. For both the researcher and the clinician, it is important to grasp the interplay between the two areas, even if a full understanding lies well into the future.

In acknowledging the persons who have been most instrumental in brining this book to fruition, there is one person we would most like to mention. Seymour Weingarten, editor-in-chief of The Guilford Press, has been extremely helpful. His assistance has been critical in the extensive task of editing this book, which has taken years to complete. The importance of his patience, knowledge, and ability to work both with us and with contributing authors cannot be overstated. Two secretaries have been instrumental in managing the correspondence and manuscripts, and we extend our appreciation to them. They are Dee Wagner at the Oklahoma University Health Sciences Center and Rosemary Mills at Psychiatric Associates. Without their assistance, this project could not have been completed.

E. Edward Beckham
William R. Leber

Contents

I

DEFINING THE BOUNDARIES OF DEPRESSION

1

Epidemiology of Depression

CHARLES T. KAELBER
DOUGLAS E. MOUL
MARY E. FARMER

METHODOLOGICAL CONSIDERATIONS

The Purpose and Strategy of Epidemiology

Epidemiology contributes to the investigation of mental and behavioral disorders by studying their distribution and determinants. Epidemiology has both descriptive and analytic components. Describing the variations in disease frequency in population subgroups over time and in different locations permits epidemiologists to assess whether the occurrence of diseases is stable, increasing, or decreasing, and in what locations—critical information in attempts to measure illness in the community, as well as to understand stability and changes in disease frequency. This descriptive task can serve a public health purpose in providing reliable and unbiased information that can permit planners and policy makers to make informed choices among policy alternatives. But in addition, analyzing the frequency of disorders in populations also permits the unbiased identification of risk factors, and thereby provides critical information in discovering causal mechanisms, both behavioral and biological. The ultimate goal for

epidemiology is to control, if not to prevent entirely, the occurrence of new disease. Understanding the distribution and causes of diseases is essential to provide a basis for developing strategies for the prevention and control of these disorders.

The frequencies of disorders in a population are expressed as "prevalence estimates," "incidence rates," and "mortality rates." Prevalence estimates are based on identifying persons who have the disorder in a period that might vary from as short as a day to as long as a lifetime. Studies of incidence rates focus on the development of new cases during a defined period and provide the most unbiased information for identifying etiological risk factors. Studying persons when they first become ill sharpens the focus on antecedent factors that influenced the onset of the illness, and minimizes the bias of factors that only prevent the illness from abating (or causing death) once it is initiated. In studies of prevalence, illness-initiating factors may not be distinguishable from illness-maintaining factors when the data are analyzed. This problem confounds the search for causal factors in cross-sectional studies. Unfortunately, determining incident cases is often difficult in psychiatric epidemiology. Because of the unreliability of self-reports, information from at least two different points in time is required to identify more clearly those persons becoming newly affected with a disorder.

The views expressed in this chapter are our own and do not necessarily reflect those of the National Institute of Mental Health.

When studying mental disorders in a population survey, epidemiologists focus on a defined population group, define operationally what a "case" of a specific disorder is in as objective and reliable a manner as possible, and then find persons in the population who meet the operational criteria. Epidemiological analysts then compare those persons with and without the disorder, and seek to find factors or exposures that the two groups have not experienced in common. Another useful tactic, called "ecological analysis," is to identify population subgroups that have differences in incidence and prevalence. In both these strategies, any described differences in disorder frequency between subgroups permit estimation of the strength and certainty of association between hypothesized causal factors and the disorder being investigated. When the strength and certainty of an association are both high, then such an association becomes a candidate for more detailed scientific investigation.

Although psychiatric epidemiology is sometimes thought to concern only finding the incidence and prevalence of disorders, providing these statistics is just part of the epidemiological strategy. "Case–control studies" compare individuals having an illness with a control group hypothesized to be comparable, in an attempt to uncover whether the cases have experienced exposures or factors differing from those of the controls. "Cohort studies," on the other hand, follow groups with and without a particular factor or exposure, to see whether they have different outcomes. The "clinical trial" is a specialized type of cohort study in which the investigators determine exposure assignment for study volunteers. In all these kinds of studies, the goal is to isolate how a specific exposure or antecedent condition is related to a psychiatric outcome. Although disagreements exist about exposure determinations, the problem for psychiatric research in general, and psychiatric epidemiology in particular, has often been that there has been disagreement about what constitutes the measure of outcome—namely, the occurrence of the disorder. This is nowhere more true than it is in the area of depression.

Defining Depression and Its Boundaries

Case description in psychiatry can follow one of two kinds of approaches. The first, called the "idiographic approach," is one in which a person's disturbance is examined in depth in all its contextual detail. This approach places a premium on understanding the individual's problems, and is well suited to individualizing treatment. Examples of idiographic approaches for depression might be the detailed understanding of a person's losses or of a person's depressive cognitions. The idiographic approach may facilitate such detailed understanding, but may not be as good at facilitating prediction of clinical course or comparisons between patients. The second approach, called the "nomothetic approach," is one in which various persons' clinical illnesses are examined for features that can be constructed into putative lawful classifications and relationships summarizing the type of illness across patients. Even though the nomothetic approach alone is inadequate as a basis for understanding individual patients and their life circumstances, this approach is integral to developing consensual formal diagnostic criteria.

Current formal diagnostic systems—the 10th revision of the *International Classification of Diseases* (ICD-10; World Health Organization, 1992), and the third, revised third, and fourth editions of the *Diagnostic and Statistical Manual of Mental Disorders* (DSM-III, DSM-III-R, and DSM-IV, respectively; American Psychiatric Association, 1980, 1987, 1994)—use clinical criteria (i.e., symptoms and behavioral signs) to classify subtypes of depressive experience and functional impairment. The DSM-III, DSM-III-R, and DSM-IV acknowledge that depression, like many mental disorders, has no currently obvious natural classes. DSM-IV conceptualizes each disorder "as a clinically significant behavioral or psychological syndrome or pattern that occurs in an individual and that is associated with present distress (e.g., a painful symptom) or disability (impairment in one or more important areas of functioning)" (American Psychiatric Association, 1994, p. xxi), rather than strictly requiring the presence of specific symptoms and disabilities. If natural classes of depression exist, then their nosology awaits the discovery of distinct and reliable genetic, biological, clinical, or other predictors of risk, severity, or clinical course. Clinicians have a tradition of separating depressions into subtypes; however, this subtyping has not yet led to clear-cut delineations of syndromes in populations. Perhaps these subtypes are in fact the "natural classes" of depression. Unfortunately, the development of psychiatry and of its epidemiology has not yet progressed to the point where these clinical delineations can be confirmed or ruled out in population terms. Nonetheless, even if depression may not come in natural "kinds," it is still possible to understand the causes of depression if one understands that conventional boundaries for depression, although sometimes vague and historically variable, can still permit some conclusions about etiology. To assume otherwise would risk abandoning research into the causes of depression.

Depressive affect is common if not ubiquitous in the general population and may be considered normal under some circumstances, as in grieving over loss of a loved one or over other significant psychological losses (e.g., loss of a job). It is meaningful to assert that depressed affect and functioning may exist on a continuum. Speaking conventionally, however, depressive disorders are distinguished from more ordinary fluctuations in affect by the severity and duration of symptoms and by the effect of these symptoms on functioning.

In both the DSM and ICD classification systems, depressed mood or affect is described as part of a number of disorders. Broadly speaking, a depressive syndrome is characterized by a cluster of signs and symptoms, including depressed mood; loss of interest; disturbances in sleep, appetite, and psychomotor activity; lack of energy; thoughts of worthlessness or guilt; and difficulties in concentrating. Depressive affect may occur independently of any other identified disorder, or it can occur in association with other forms of psychopathology (e.g., psychosis, substance-related disorders, anxiety disorders) and/or other forms of medical pathology (e.g., cerebrovascular accidents, infectious diseases). Depressive affect can occur acutely and remit; can occur chronically without remitting; can occur in the absence of other alterations in affect (e.g., mania or hypomania); or can occur in association with these other alterations.

In DSM-III, DSM-III-R, DSM-IV, and ICD-10, disorders that involve depressive affect occurring in cyclic association with elevations in affect are conceptualized differently (e.g., bipolar I and II disorders, cyclothymia) from disorders involving depressive affect only. Furthermore, in the spectrum of psychiatric disorders, the number, severity, and duration of these various symptoms and signs are conceptualized as distinguishing the various syndromes or disorders. Whether these various specific syndromes involving depressed affect are truly distinct entities is not resolved in the DSM classification; however, conceptualizing them as distinct permits the development of specificity for case identification, prognosis, and treatment. The specific etiological relevance of the syndromal definitions remains to be determined. Despite these complexities in the classification of disorders involving depression, in this chapter only the epidemiology of conventionally defined unipolar depressive syndromes (depression without mania, and dysthymia) in adults is being considered.

Even when attention is limited to depressive episodes, another difficulty is that the symptomatology, duration, and severity of these episodes can be quite variable. Recently developed evidence suggests that severe recurrent depressive disturbances can be comparatively brief (Angst & Dobler-Mikola, 1985; Angst, Merikangas, Scheidegger, & Wicki, 1990; Montgomery & Montgomery, 1992), and this evidence has added to an older controversy regarding whether it is appropriate to draw a distinction between major depressive episodes that meet formal criteria for major depression and "minor" depressive episodes that only meet criteria for the milder dysthymic disorder (Angst & Wicki, 1990). Obviously, individuals can meet criteria for both formal diagnoses; this has led to questions about whether major depression and dysthymia are etiologically distinct, whether there are "depressive personalities," and whether one syndrome serves as a prodrome for the other.

To some extent, the controversy surrounding depressive diathesis is a reminder of past work on the relationship among neuroticism, anxiety, and depression. Although there are undoubtedly virtues in considering both anxiety and depression as existing on a spectrum of distress, current nosologies have attempted to distinguish these commonly associated kinds of syndromes—partly to sharpen conceptualization (Klerman, Endicott, Spitzer, & Hirschfeld, 1979), and partly for empirical reasons (Jorm, 1987b). Similarly, some past and current clinical and community studies attempt to quantify the occurrence of depressive signs and symptoms in a nondiagnostic fashion, without emphasis on explicit diagnostic criteria. To the extent that difficulties in the dimensional scaling of depression are similar to those of the dimensional scaling of psychological distress, similar difficulties have arisen in distinguishing between depressive disorders as previously arose in distinguishing between depression and anxiety. Resolution of these questions will determine the diagnostic nomenclatures of the future. Even so, which approach will turn out to be the more useful in the study of etiology remains to be determined.

The Impact
of Formal Diagnostic Criteria

The study of the epidemiology of depression (and most other mental disorders) has been hampered by the lack of consensus on case definitions. When investigators do not agree that similar cases are being identified in surveys or studies of a disorder, then alternative hypotheses about the "disorder" in question have no clear way of being resolved in ways that investigators can agree about, and the prospects for a common understanding of the "disorder" are seriously limited by the variability in diagnostic practice. Early attempts to define and describe the occurrence of psychopathology in general populations were not based on specific diagnostic criteria, since widely accepted criteria to define cases did not exist until relatively recently. Investigators avoided the notion of diagnostic criteria and assessed only symptoms in clinical and community samples. The Center for Epidemiologic Studies Depression Scale (CES-D Scale) of the National Institute of Mental Health (NIMH) is one well-known example of this approach (Radloff, 1977; Radloff & Locke, 1986). Even when surveys inquired about symptoms alone, investigators developed their own operational definitions of "caseness" (e.g., Leighton, Harding, Macklin, MacMillan, & Leighton, 1963; Srole, Langner, Michael, Opler, & Rennie, 1962), although this was slightly less true for the "score of 16" criterion for the CES-D Scale (Aneshensel, Frerichs, & Clark, 1981; Boyd, Weissmann, Thompson, & Myers, 1982; Comstock & Helsing, 1976; Radloff & Rae, 1979).

An important development in helping to standardize case definition was the decision by the architects of DSM-III to promote the use of more objective criteria in making diagnoses for mental and behavioral disorders (American Psychiatric Association, 1980). The DSM-III, DSM-III-R, and DSM-IV disclaim assumptions about the discontinuous distribution of disorders in populations, in recognition that a continuum of severity may exist in natural populations, making differentiation difficult. None-

theless, devising more objective diagnostic criteria was a major goal in the formulation of DSM-III, and was intended to improve interrater reliability among practitioners and investigators. Improving interrater reliability is a prerequisite step in the scientific investigation of psychiatric disorders, because investigators can then use a common terminology to communicate findings. Because no natural classes of depression have been demarcated, and because of new information, diagnostic criteria have changed with each new edition of the DSM; this has made the conduct of epidemiological surveys difficult, especially because such surveys often take many years to complete. This is likely to be a continuing problem for survey research. For this reason, one cannot be too confident about precise incidence or prevalence estimates of disorders or syndromes, since even small changes in criteria may alter these estimates significantly, or may alter their extant meaning. Nonetheless, psychiatric epidemiology has benefited from having a defined nosology that can be related to conventionally defined clinical syndromes.

The necessary task of developing high-specificity criteria for case definitions remains unfinished. In the United States, the work toward this goal has continued with the publication of the DSM-III-R and DSM-IV (American Psychiatric Association, 1987, 1994). The need to improve interrater diagnostic reliability has also found wide international acceptance, and the ICD-10 reflects the influence of this growing consensus as well (World Health Organization, 1991). Although more objective criteria for defining specific disorders are now available, operationalizing these criteria in clinical and epidemiological investigations remains inexact for most mental and behavioral disorders, including depressive disorders.

Case Identification Instruments
and Assessment Methods

Clinical and epidemiological investigators have come to recognize the importance not only of specificity of case definition, but also of systematic assessment in mental and behavioral disorders. When studies disagree, differences may arise from differing methodologies, rather than from different risks of disease occurrence and/or persistence.

Use of semistructured clinical interviews represents one alternative to studying individuals in the community. This approach is typically conducted with the understanding that the interviewer has specialized training in assessing psychopathology. The interviewer uses the semistructured interview as a guide to ensure that there is consistent topic coverage. The ability of the interviewer to probe at length when necessary regarding the context of reported signs and symptoms permits the assessments conducted to reflect better the contextual elements of the interviewee's reported symptomatology. This has the virtue of permitting a nomothetic classification pertinent to the DSM or ICD categories, while making use of idiographic, individualized interpretations of the subject's circumstances. In some studies, the possibility of interviewer idiosyncrasy in diagnostic interpretation is addressed to some extent through review of each interview by a panel of peers, or through reinterview, to yield a consensus diagnosis. Consensus diagnoses are particularly important in psychiatric genetic studies, where it is especially important that diagnoses be as specific as possible.

In keeping with the capacity to probe for the temporal and intensional context of symptoms, this semistructured methodology seems better suited to specifying the nature of ethnographic factors, adverse life events and statuses, timing of events and experiences, and their possible relationship to depressive disorder. The clinical interview can be individualized to be most sensitive to the psychological impact of an event—something that cannot be as easily done with more rigid, fully structured interviewing protocols. One disadvantage of this idiographic method is that it is more theory- or nosology-dependent than a rigid, questionnaire-based method of assessment, so that one's confidence in the results depends more upon one's confidence in the theory, nosology, and investigative procedures used than is the case for the more rigid method. One further disadvantage of the use of semistructured interviews is its expense, since the assessment is usually long and usually requires highly paid professional assessors. Despite questions about whether such methods provide consistent sensitivity and specificity across studies, these kinds of methods continue to have value and importance because they provide a more intuitive link to clinical studies, where assessments are more idiographic in nature.

A number of diagnostic assessment instruments enable epidemiologists to provide a thorough review of symptoms and to evaluate the occurrence (past and present) of depressive episodes according to standardized criteria. One example is the Schedule for Clinical Assessment in Neuropsychiatry (SCAN; Wing et al., 1990). This instrument has been based on previous editions of the Present State Examination (PSE), which itself has been widely used in clinical and epidemiological studies (Wing, Cooper, & Sartorius, 1974). The SCAN also has been extensively tested internationally, and is designed to lead toward case identification according to DSM-III-R and ICD-10 diagnostic criteria when administered by clinically trained interviewers. Standard diagnoses can be computed from the interviews, and this has strengthened the standardization of assessments done with these interviews. These instruments are a partial solution to the problem of generalizability across studies utilizing highly trained assessors, because they enforce a common systematic structure upon the diagnostic interviews.

Further generalizability may be possible if the structure of an assessment is completely specified. In this approach, questions are asked verbatim, with no alterations or allowances for individualized questioning. Here the assessment is done not by an assessor, but by the questions themselves. This circumstance makes it possible for interview administration to be conducted by lay interviewers or via computer. An instrument that is designed to be administered by lay interviewers is the Composite International Diagnostic Interview (CIDI). This instrument is the successor to the Diagnostic Interview Schedule (DIS; Robins, Helzer, Croughan, & Ratcliff, 1981), an instrument developed for use in the Epidemiologic Catchment Area (ECA) study, sponsored by the NIMH (see next section). The DIS and CIDI lend themselves easily to computerization of diagnosis—a process that has been used in many publications from the ECA program. The DIS was designed to identify cases meeting DSM-III criteria for selected major psychiatric disorders. The CIDI has also been extensively tested internationally and is designed to identify cases meeting DSM-III-R and ICD-10 criteria (Robins et al., 1988). Recent work has also proceeded to computerize the administration of the DIS and CIDI.

These highly structured interviewing protocols have the advantage of making the diagnostic process in surveys as thoroughly objective as possible. Investigators know completely what questions were asked, even if they do not agree that the questions were the correct ones to ask. Problems with this method include cases where diagnoses may be appropriate, but are not captured by a fixed set of questions. Although the questions may be stringently specified, their meaning may vary, depending upon how the question is interpreted by the interviewee. This may be part of the nature of differences in prevalences among age groups, language groups, or ethnic groups. A second difficulty is that this kind of questioning does not capture well the individualized components of a person's situation, which may influence the reporting or causation of psychiatric morbidity. This is a particular problem for psychotic patients and for the role of recent life events, where qualitative and intensional elements are considered relevant to understanding the nature of the patient's problems.

The development, testing, and utilization of these diagnostic instruments are expected to play an important role in the epidemiological investigation of psychiatric disorders, including the most common syndromes of depression.

DESCRIPTION OF PREVALENCE AND INCIDENCE

General Populations

Epidemiologic Catchment Area Study

Methods Used. One of the most important data sources available to describe the epidemiology of selected major mental disorders in adults is the ECA study (Regier & Robins, 1991), in which over 20,000 persons aged 18 and older were interviewed. A fully structured interview containing the DIS was used. As noted above, the DIS had been specifically developed to standardize the method of identifying specific DSM-III psychiatric disorders (including major depression and dysthymia) in community samples (Robins et al., 1981). The interview was given by specially trained lay interviewers. Although not intended as literal clinical diagnoses, DIS assessments by trained lay interviewers in clinical settings compared reasonably well with assessments made by clinicians (Helzer et al., 1985; Robins, Helzer, Ratcliff, & Seyfried, 1982). This standardization of assessment, coupled with probability-based sampling of unusually large samples at five sites (New Haven, Connecticut; Baltimore, Maryland; Durham,

North Carolina; St. Louis, Missouri; and Los Angeles, California), made this a landmark study and provided a new level of description for the incidence and prevalence of selected major psychiatric disorders. At each site, the probability samples were carefully selected to yield population-based frequency data. The study samples were deliberately community-based in order to avoid clinic and other selection biases, such as might occur in studies of first hospital admissions (Der & Bebbington, 1987). Two major biases this strategy avoided were the bias that persons who actually seek treatment may be unrepresentative of those who are unwilling or unable to seek treatment, and the bias that those who actually seek treatment are likely to have greater comorbidity.

Survey data were obtained in two waves. Wave I was a cross-sectional survey, from which the prevalence for the prior month, year, and lifetime periods were estimated. One year later, the Wave II survey was conducted; this permitted additional estimates of prevalence, as well as 1-year incidence rates when cross-referenced with Wave I data. In assessing the accuracy of the information collected in this and similar studies, one must remember that recall biases undoubtedly occur in retrospective self-reports. People may underreport mild and long-forgotten episodes. This tendency can be especially true of older persons who are reporting a lifetime's experience: An elderly person may well forget symptoms or episodes he/she had early in life, particularly if subsequent experiences made the symptoms and episodes seem mild, transient, or embarrassing. These potential biases might mean that the statistically significant associations observed would apply only to severe forms of depression, or only to recent episodes. One of the methodological strengths of the ECA program was that two survey waves were obtained on the initial sample, which enabled calculation of incidence rates (Eaton et al., 1989) and some assessment of respondent recall effects. Therefore, the ECA data provide one of the most comprehensive community-based surveys of depression in existence. More details about the sample selection procedures and characteristics are provided elsewhere (Eaton & Kessler, 1985; Leaf, Myers, & McEvoy, 1991).

Prevalence estimates from the ECA study can be described for various time periods—1 month, 1 year, and lifetime. Computerized case definition algorithms classified responses to DIS questions as meeting or not meeting diagnostic criteria for selected DSM-III disorders.

Prevalence of Depressive Symptoms, Episodes, and Disorders. Table 1.1 displays the lifetime prevalence of depressive symptoms lasting 2 weeks or longer by age, gender, and ethnicity (adapted from Weissman, Bruce, Leaf, Florio, & Holzer, 1991). Nearly 30% of persons in this survey reported experiencing "dysphoria" lasting at least 2 weeks at some point during their lifetime. Other symptoms were less frequently reported, although some symptoms (appetite change, sleep change, and thoughts of death) occurred in about a quarter of the population. In their scoring, these symptoms were reported as unrelated to physical illness or to the use of illicit drugs, alcohol, or medications. The prevalence of depressive symptoms was highest for the age group 30–44 years, and lowest among those aged 65 years and older. Women reported more of all symptoms than men. Whites reported more dysphoria, sleep changes, fatigue, guilt, diminished concentration, and thoughts about death, whereas blacks reported more appetite change and psychomotor agitation or retardation, relative to other ethnic groups. Greater than 5% percentage differences were observed for dysphoria (white > black) and fatigue (white > Hispanic).

Even though depressive symptoms lasting 2 weeks or longer are fairly common, contemporaneous collections of symptoms meeting the 2-week duration criteria for a diagnosis of depressive disorder were less frequent (see the portion of Table 1.2 adapted from Weissman et al., 1991). Less than 4% of the sample met criteria for a major depressive episode within 1 year, and only 6.3% met criteria for at least one major depressive episode over a lifetime. As with the prevalence of symptoms, the highest frequency of depressive episodes occurred among those aged 30–44 years for both time periods, while those aged 65 years and older had the lowest reported prevalence. The prevalence among women was more than twice that among men for both time periods. Whites had higher lifetime prevalence estimates than the other two ethnic groups, whereas Hispanics reported slightly higher estimates than whites for a 1-year period.

Having a depressive episode is not sufficient for a diagnosis of major depression, and among those with a lifetime depressive episode in the ECA study, only 77% also met diagnostic criteria for major depression in their lifetimes. The remaining 23% had one of three other diagnoses (bipolar I, 8.5%; bipolar II, 7.3%; and short-term grief, 6.9%). For major depression, the mean age of onset was 26.5 years, and the mean duration between first and most recent episode was 8.7 years. However, age of onset also appeared to increase with age of the respondent, possibly reflecting either a historical cohort effect or a recall bias.

TABLE 1.1. Depressive Symptoms: Lifetime Prevalence by Age, Sex, and Ethnicity in the ECA Study (Percentage Reporting These Symptoms as Lasting 2 Weeks or Longer)

	Dysphoria	Appetite change	Sleep change	Psychomotor change	Loss of interest	Fatigue	Guilt	Diminished concentration	Thoughts of death
Total	29.9	23.8	22.9	9.1	5.2	15.9	10.5	13.9	28.2
Age									
18–29	30.7	27.3	24.2	9.6	4.4	16.1	12.1	16.4	30.2
30–44	33.6	27.4	26.0	11.0	8.1	20.7	13.9	16.8	32.4
45–64	27.9	20.5	20.3	8.0	4.8	14.0	8.5	11.4	25.1
65+	25.0	16.2	19.4	6.6	2.2	10.6	4.7	7.8	21.6
Sex									
Men	23.5	18.8	18.3	7.9	3.4	11.6	8.6	10.8	22.8
Women	35.7	28.5	27.0	10.2	6.8	19.9	12.3	16.7	33.0
Ethnicity									
White	30.6	23.8	23.4	9.1	5.2	16.6	10.9	14.2	28.9
Black	24.7	25.4	19.0	9.9	5.3	13.1	7.5	12.2	24.0
Hispanic	28.9	21.2	22.9	7.2	4.3	11.1	9.8	12.5	24.9

Note. Adapted from Weissman, Bruce, Leaf, Florio, & Holzer (1991). Copyright 1991 by Lee N. Robins and Darrel A. Regier. Adapted by permission of The Free Press, an imprint of Simon & Schuster.

TABLE 1.2. Major Depressive Episode, Major Depression, Dysthymia, and All Affective Disorders: Lifetime and 1-Year Prevalence (%) by Age, Sex, and Ethnicity in the ECA Study and the National Comorbidity Survey (NCS)

ECA study[a]

	Major depressive episode		Major depression		Dysthymia (lifetime)	All affective disorders (lifetime)
	Lifetime	1-year	Lifetime	1-year		
Total	6.3	3.7	4.9	2.7	3.2	7.8
Age						
18–29	6.7	4.2	5.0	2.9	3.0	
30–44	9.5	5.1	7.5	3.9	3.8	
45–64	5.0	2.9	4.0	2.3	3.6	
65 or over	2.0	1.4	1.4	0.9	1.7	
Sex						
Men	3.6	2.2	2.6	1.4	2.2	5.2
Women	8.7	5.0	7.0	4.0	4.1	10.2
Ethnicity						
White	6.6	3.7	5.1	2.8	3.3	
Black	4.5	3.3	3.1	2.2	2.5	
Hispanic	5.6	3.9	4.4	3.3	4.0	

NCS[b]

	Major depressive episode		Major depression		Dysthymia (lifetime)	All affective disorders (lifetime)
	Lifetime	1-year	Lifetime	1-year		
Total	17.1	10.3	14.9	8.6	6.4	
Age						
15–24	15.7	12.8				
25–34	16.5	9.9				
35–44	19.2	10.4				
45–54	16.7	7.4				
Sex						
Men	12.7	7.7	11.0	6.1	4.8	14.7
Women	21.3	12.9	18.6	11.0	8.0	23.9

[a]Adapted from Weissman, Bruce, Leaf, Florio, & Holzer (1991). Copyright 1991 by Lee N. Robins and Darrel A. Regier. Adapted by permission of The Free Press, an imprint of Simon & Schuster.

[b]Adapted from Kessler, McConagle, Swartz, Blazer, & Nelson (1993); Kessler et al. (1994); and Kessler et al. (in press). Copyright 1993 by Elsevier Science B.V.; copyright 1994 by the American Medical Association; and copyright by the Royal College of Psychiatrists. Adapted by permission.

The lifetime prevalences of major depression and dysthymia from the ECA program are also shown in Table 1.2. Overall, nearly 5% of the sample met criteria for past or current major depression, while 3.2% met criteria for past or current dysthymia. As with the prevalence of reported symptoms, the age group 30–44 had the highest lifetime prevalence for both disorders, whereas persons aged 65 years and older reported the lowest lifetime prevalence for both, even though the variation by age for dysthymia seemed less. Lifetime prevalence among women was more than twice that among men. One-year prevalence estimates for major depression were lower than lifetime prevalence estimates, but the associations with age and gender were similar (Weissman et al., 1991).

In the ECA study, ethnic variability in prevalence of major depression was not dramatic. Among ethnic groups, however, the lifetime prevalence of major depressive disorder was highest for whites, while that for dysthymia was highest among Hispanics. Blacks had lower estimates of major depression and dysthymia than other ethnic groups, even though they had higher estimates for some depressive symptoms (Somervell, Leaf, Weissman, Blazer, & Bruce, 1989). Hispanics had the highest 1-year prevalence for major depressive disorder (Table 1.2).

Persons can have both major depression and dysthymia (so-called "double depression"). In DSM-III, the classification of those persons who met criteria for both major depression and dysthymia was confusing and difficult to implement. This was later modified in DSM-III-R, which specified that when a major depressive episode occurs during the first 2 years of an otherwise dysthymic period, the dysthymic period should be regarded as the prodromal phase of a major depression. The typical absence of an abrupt onset for either of these disorders complicates their separation in both clinical and population settings. This practical problem illustrates the difficulties in being able to identify the "natural class" boundaries of these depressive disorders. With the use of the DSM-III-based DIS in the ECA study, however, it was observed that of those who ever met criteria for dysthymia, only 42% also met criteria for past or current major depression. Conversely, of those with current major depression, only 28% also met criteria for dysthymia (Weissman et al., 1991). Despite any difficulties in separating major depression and dysthymia as unique disorders, it is clear from other analyses that these disorders are often comorbid with anxiety and substance-related disorders (Regier et al., 1990a; Regier, Narrow, & Rae, 1990b; Weissman, Leaf, Bruce, & Florio, 1988).

Incidence Rates of Major Depression. In addition to measuring baseline prevalence estimates, the ECA study resurveyed previously interviewed persons 1 year later in order to estimate annual incidence rates (Eaton et al., 1989), as noted above. Annual incidence rates of about 1 case of major depression per 100 person-years in men and 2 cases per 100 person-years in women were consistent with prevalence estimates, making it seem that women's episodes of major depression were as long as men's. In men, the highest rate was among young men, and the lowest rate was among middle-aged men (see Table 1.3, adapted from Eaton et al., 1989). In women, the annual incidence rate remained about 2 per 100 person-years among adult women up until retirement age, then declined slightly among elderly women.

Data on incidence rates are especially noteworthy, since few data sets are available to provide community-based incidence rates for depression. Analysis of the ECA resurvey also highlighted the difficulties of recall bias in surveys of this type. Some persons reported the occurrence of symptoms and met diagnostic criteria at Wave I, yet at Wave II they reported no prior lifetime symptoms (Eaton et al., 1989)—a logical inconsistency. These and similar inconsistencies are not unique to the ECA study (Aneshensel, Estrada, Hansell, & Clark, 1987; Bromet, Dunn, Connell, Dew, & Schul-

TABLE 1.3. Annual Incidence of DIS/DSM-III Major Depressive Disorder per 100 Person-Years of Risk, by Gender and Age

	Males	Females	Both sexes
Age at first interview (years)			
18–29	1.40	2.01	1.72
30–44	1.22	2.18	1.73
45–64	0.64	2.02	1.44
65+	0.90	1.48	1.25
All ages	1.10	1.98	1.59

Note. Adapted from Eaton et al. (1989). Copyright 1989 by Munksgaard International Publishers Ltd. Adapted by permission.

berg, 1986); they reflect the limitations of a person's ability to remember and his/her current motivation to report.

Sociodemographic Correlates of Depression. In addition to providing information on the frequency of depressive disorders by age, gender, and ethnicity in these community population samples, the ECA program also collected information on a number of other social and economic measures, in an effort to provide comparisons with other studies and to identify new risk factors. In the ECA study, divorced and separated men and women had the highest estimates for major depression. Regarding marital history, for the married with no divorces, the 1-year prevalence of major depression was 1.5%; for the never-married, 2.4%; for those divorced once, 4.1%; for those divorced twice, 5.8%; and for those cohabiting, 5.1% (Weissman et al., 1991). Regarding current marital status, for the currently married, the 1-year prevalence was 2.1%; for the widowed, 2.1%; for the separated/divorced, 6.3%; and for the never-married, 2.8%. One plausible hypothesis for the increased prevalence of depression among single persons (i.e., the never-married, widowed, separated, or divorced) was that marriage provides the type of social support that is protective against depression. However, the ECA data suggested that the disruption of previous marital bonds was more closely associated with higher prevalence of major depression than simply being unmarried. This may not be a refutation of the social support hypothesis, but only an indication that it is easier to measure social support disruptions than it is to measure social support qualities. The aspects possibly affecting the relationship between social support and depression are probably more complex than can be simply captured by determining marital status alone (Dean, Lin, & Ensel, 1981).

In the ECA data, the 1-year prevalence of major depression in persons currently employed was 2.2%, whereas it was 3.4% among those who were unemployed. For those who were not unemployed for 6 months or more in the previous 5 years, the rate of major depression was 2.0%; it was 6.1% among those who were unemployed for more than 6 months in that period. Causal linkages for this association between depression and unemployment remain to be clarified. Other studies have suggested that men and women may experience different risks

of depression, depending on such factors as marital status (Ensel, 1982; Gove & Tudor, 1973), kind of employment (Brown & Bifulco, 1990), number of children (Brown & Harris, 1978; Cleary & Mechanic, 1983), social class (Bebbington, Sturt, Tennant, & Hurry, 1984; Brown & Harris, 1978; Dohrenwend et al., 1992), social mobility (Dohrenwend et al., 1992), age (Ensel, 1982), education (Dohrenwend et al., 1992), and quality of marital relationship (Brown & Bifulco, 1990; Brown & Harris, 1978). Admittedly, all these factors could plausibly interact with employment status to alter one's risk of being depressed. However, the ECA data set could not address many of these questions, because its focus was more descriptive than analytic.

Although previous studies reported an association between lower socioeconomic status and depression, the ECA study provided only weak evidence for this association. In the ECA data, the prevalence of major depression was slightly higher among white-collar workers (2.5%) than among other employed persons (1.7%); higher among persons with 12 years of education or more (2.8%) than among those with less (2.6%); but higher among persons with annual incomes under $15,000 (2.9%) than among those with higher annual incomes (1.8%) (Weissman et al., 1991). However, in keeping with the socioeconomic hypotheses, the clinical reappraisal substudy at the Baltimore site did provide clear evidence that persons receiving public financial support were much more likely to suffer from major depression (Romanoski et al., 1992).

Two sites in the ECA program included subsamples from rural settings, the results from which could be used to explore urban–rural differences in depressive disorders. Curiously, one site (St. Louis) reported higher estimates of major depression among its rural population (1-year prevalence of 3.5% vs. 2.5% among the urban section), whereas the other site (Durham) reported higher estimates of major depression among its urban subsample (2.3%) than its rural (1.0%) (Weissman et al., 1991). It has been suggested that one reason for this inconsistency could be that the St. Louis "rural" subsite may have had a "suburban" contaminant (Weissman et al., 1991).

Using conditional logistic regression methods on constructed risk sets (with neighborhood matching) from the ECA data, two studies utilized a case–control methodology, exploring incident cases of depression for potential risk factors influencing disease onset (Anthony & Petronis, 1991; Gallo, Royall, & Anthony, 1993). Among adults 18–44 years old, the relative risks for major depression were as follows: 1.5 for women versus men, 1.9 for the separated/divorced versus other and 0.6 for employed versus unemployed. For this group, depressive syndrome risk was lower for Hispanics (relative risk = 0.3). Women were increasingly at risk for incident depressive syndrome up to age 44 in this logistic model. In the group of incident cases older than age 44, the logistic model did not find a difference in risk of major depression in unemployed persons. On the other hand, having fewer than 12 years of education increased risk (relative risk = 2.2), especially for older women (relative risk = 3.3). Gallo et al. (1993) have pointed to this finding as implicating a delayed effect of low education, occurring many decades after schooling was completed.

National Comorbidity Survey

A second recently reported epidemiological study is the National Comorbidity Survey (NCS; Kessler, McGonagle, Swartz, Blazer, & Nelson, 1993; Kessler et al., 1994; Blazer, Kessler, McGonagle, & Schwartz, 1994; Kessler et al., in press). Building on the experience from the ECA study, Kessler and associates administered a modified version of the CIDI to a probability-based sample of the U.S. population between the ages of 15 and 54. They paid special attention to encouraging respondents to review their past carefully, and to report accurately any past episodes of psychiatric illness. Their intention was to increase the sensitivity of lifetime reporting of psychiatric disorders and substance use. These methodological changes were designed to overcome potential gender-based and age-based recall biases, as well as to obtain a sample that would be more generalizable to the entire United States than the five sites of the ECA program were. Like the ECA study, however, the NCS had the special virtue of avoiding the biases encountered in sampling only those who are willing or able to seek treatment. Both studies thus involved less bias in estimating the prevalence of many psychiatric disorders than might have resulted from the use of other sampling methods.

Overall, the NCS found substantially higher estimates of dysthymia, major depressive episodes, and other psychiatric disorders than did the ECA study. Substantial methodological differences between the two surveys (e.g., assessment instrument differences, diagnostic criteria, and age range of the samples) may account for these discrepancies. As noted earlier, the ECA used the DIS to assess DSM-III disorders, whereas the NCS used a modified version of the CIDI, which incorporated DSM-III-R criteria. The NCS found that the lifetime prevalence of major depressive episode was 17.1% overall: 12.7% in males and 21.3% among females (see Table 1.2). The prevalence estimates for the most recent 12-month period was 10.3% overall: 7.7% among males and 12.9% among females. For major depressive disorder, the lifetime prevalence was 14.9% overall: 11.0% among males and 18.6% among females. The prevalence estimates for 12-month prevalence of major depressive disorder was 8.6% overall: 6.1% among males and 11.0% among females. For dysthymia, the overall lifetime rate within this age group was 6.4%: 4.8% among males and 8.0% among females. The prevalence of persons meeting criteria for dysthymia during the preceding 12-month period was 2.5% overall: 2.1% among males and 3.0% among females. For both males and females, lifetime estimates of major depressive episodes appeared to increase up to age 35–44 years and to decline thereafter (Kessler et al., 1993). Explanations for this apparent anomalous finding of decreasing lifetime estimates with advancing age include unfavorable differential mortality among the depressed (less likely), age-related selection bias among those participating in surveys (less likely), a cohort effect (possible), and age-related differences in recalling and/or reporting symptoms (more likely).

The noteworthy differences between the ECA and NCS findings pose a problem not only for interpretation of prevalence estimates, but also for risk factor research (Helzer et al., 1985). It seems improbable that the ECA or NCS statistical weighting procedures were grossly in error, or that there was a massive increase in psychiatric morbidity from 1983 to 1992 (the years the respective surveys ended their data collection). It is clear that any differences in risk factor findings between the two surveys will need to be interpreted in the context of the apparent differences in the studies' sensitivities and specificities, which may constrain generalizability from one or both studies.

Association of Depression with Female Gender

One of the most consistent findings in the epidemiology of mental disorders has been the higher prevalence of depression in females compared to males. This finding has been replicated in numerous national and international studies, including the ECA study, the NCS, and others (Kessler et al., 1993; Kessler et al., 1994; Paykel, 1991; Weissman et al., 1991; Weissman & Klerman, 1977; Wittchen, Essau, von Zerssen, Krieg, & Zaudig, 1992). Generally, reported prevalence among women is about 1.5 to 3.0 times that among men. Recently, Kessler et al. (1993) tried to explore aspects of this gender difference in more detail, using data from the NCS. In the NCS, men not only reported less depressed mood or diminished interest, but also reported fewer of the symptoms that make up the symptom cluster of a major depressive episode. Kessler et al. also noted that the ratio of 12-month prevalence estimates to lifetime prevalence estimates (an approximation of the chronicity of the disorder) was almost the same for men (60.1%) and women (60.5%). The mean age of onset of the first depression episode among women was only slightly less than that in men (23.5 years in women vs. 24.0 years in men). This analysis of the NCS data indicated that the overall course of depression did not differ between the genders. Women had an increased risk of first onset of major depression, but their risk of chronicity or recurrence did not appear to be substantially greater than for men.

Depression in the Elderly

Table 1.4 shows international prevalence estimates of major depression by age, as ascertained by several diagnostic instruments. These included the Schedule for Affective Disorders and Schizophrenia together with the Research Diagnostic Criteria (SADS-RDC); the DIS; the Geriatric Mental State using the computerized diagnostic system Automated Geriatric Examination for Computer Assisted Taxonomy (GMS-AGECAT); and the PSE. Current prevalence estimates based on a GMS diagnosis were in general much higher than those based on a DIS or SADS-RDC diagnosis.

One would expect that the prevalence of depression would increase with age. With age comes a greater probability of different kinds of losses, including loss of family and friends due to death, loss of health and physical function due to medical illnesses, and loss of financial income and social status due to retirement (Klerman, 1988). Awareness of mortality must certainly be greater in the elderly, and may negatively influence their attitudes about their personal future. However, in the ECA study, lifetime prevalence estimates of major depression were significantly higher in the younger age groups (5.0% for ages 18–29, 7.5% for ages 30–44, 4.0% for ages 45–64) and decreased with age, with the lowest estimates among those aged 65 or older (1.4%) (see Table 1.2; Weissman et al., 1991). One-month prevalence estimates of major depression in the ECA study mirrored this pattern: The highest 1-month prevalence rate was in the 25–44 age group (3.0%), whereas the lowest was in those 65 years and older (0.7%) (Regier et al., 1993). Even after adjustment for gender, ethnicity, marital status, and socioeconomic status, the odds ratio of the 1-month prevalence of major depression was 0.27 in those aged 65 years and older, compared to those aged 18–24 years (Regier et al., 1993). Clinical reappraisals of the ECA sample in Baltimore found an "inverted-V" shape to the current prevalence curve for DSM-III major depression (0% for those aged 18–24 years, 1.2% for those aged 25–44 years, 2.0% for those aged 45–64 years, and 0.5% for those aged 65 and over) (Romanoski et al., 1992). The shape of this curve is similar to those for psychiatrist-ascertained severe depression found in other studies (Romanoski et al. 1992; Sorenson & Stromgren, 1961). These findings would suggest that old age is protective against depression. However, when the prevalence estimates of all categories of current depression were totaled in the clinical reappraisal of the ECA sample in Baltimore (including DSM-III major depression, DSM-III depressive disorders other than major depression, and no DSM-III depressive disorder but actively depressed), the prevalence of any active depressive mood disturbance, regardless of category, etiology, or severity, was highest among the elderly (Romanoski et al., 1992). This finding is consistent with other studies (Blazer, 1989; Dovenmuehle, Reckless, & Newman, 1970; Gurland, Dean, Cross, & Golden, 1980; Romanoski et al., 1992). It may be that the elderly suffer more than do younger persons from milder or atypical forms of depression that do not meet diagnostic criteria for DSM-III major depression.

Henderson (1994) has reviewed possible reasons for the observed decrease in prevalence

TABLE 1.4. Prevalence of Major Depression in Elderly Samples

Study	n	Instrument/ criteria	Population	Age	Time reference	Prevalence of major depression (%)
Weissman & Myers (1978)	938	SADS-RDC	New Haven, CT	26–45	Current	1.9
				46–65	Current	6.3
				≥65	Current	5.4
Regier et al. (1993a)	18,571	DIS	U.S. ECA sites	18–24	Current	2.2
				25–44	Current	3
				45–64	Current	2
				≥65	Current	0.7
Kramer, German, Anthony, Von Korff, & Skinner (1985)	3,332	DIS	Baltimore, MD (ECA)	18–64	6-month	2.5
				65–74	6-month	0.7
				75+	6-month	1.3
Madianos, Gournas, & Stefanis (1992)	251	DSM-III	Athens, Greece	65+	Current	1.6
Saunders et al. (1993)	5,222	GMS-AGECAT	Liverpool, England	65+	Current	10
Copeland et al. (1987a)	1,070	GMS-AGECAT	Liverpool, England	65+	Current	11.3
Copeland et al. (1987b)	396	GMS-AGECAT DSM-III depression	London	65+	Current Current	19.4 12.7
Copeland et al. (1987b)	445	GMS-AGECAT	New York	65+	Current	16.2
Kua (1992)	612	GMS-AGECAT	Singapore	65+	Current	5.7
				65–69	Current	3.9
				70–74	Current	5.9
				75–79	Current	8.7
				80–84	Current	4.5
				85+	Current	7.4
Kay et al. (1985)	274	DSM-III	Hobart, Australia	70–79	Curernt	6.3
				80+	Current	15.5
				70–79	Current	13.9
				80+	Current	14.8
Ben-Arie, Swartz, & Dickman (1987)	139	PSE	Cape Town, South Africa	65+	Current	13.7

estimates of major depression in the elderly. Although nonresponse bias due to depression, physical illness, or frailty in the elderly could contribute to the observed differences by age, Henderson has pointed out that underrepresentation of the physically ill should make elderly samples more like younger adults. A bias in case-finding instruments could be resulting in the observed differences. For example, the DIS may underestimate depressive symptoms by excluding those that could be attributed to physical illness or medication—factors that are usually higher in the elderly. This possibility has received some support from a study by Knauper and Wittchen (1994), who found that the frequency of depressive symptoms in the elderly was similar to that of younger respondents, but that depressive symptoms were more frequently attributed to comorbid physical illness. Instrument bias could also result if the depressed elderly were less likely to acknowledge certain symptoms such as lowered mood.

Henderson (1994) has proposed several testable explanations for the validity of the finding of decreased prevalence of depression in the elderly. The elderly may have many depressive symptoms, but may not fulfill all the diagnostic criteria necessary to be a case. A higher mortality rate in the depressed elderly may lead to a reduced prevalence. The elderly may have a similar incidence rate but a shorter duration of illness, thereby reducing the observed prevalence. The elderly may experience a reduced number of adverse life events, and social supports may become stronger. Finally, exposure to stress over a lifetime may help the elderly build up a resistance to depression. Which among these alternatives is correct may tell us a great deal about the general nature of depression as individuals proceed through the life cycle.

George (1992) used data from the Duke University ECA site to look at the impact of various social factors in relation to depression, with particular focus on the influence of age as a direct effect on the onset of depression, as well as on the impact of age through other social variables. George included 10 factors in a multivariate statistical model (age, gender, race, urban vs. rural residence, marital status, education, income, physical illnesses, stressful life events, and subjective perceptions of social support). Her analysis was limited to data from the Durham ECA sample, of which about half came from rural counties in north central North Carolina. Persons aged 60 years and older were also oversampled, in order to permit more detailed assessment of mental and behavioral disorders in this age group. Consistent with the main ECA findings, the prevalence of major depression was highest among youths and young adults (ages 18 through 39 years) and lower at older ages. As independent variables, younger age, female gender, urban residency, physical illness, stressful life events, and less subjective social support were all associated with higher estimates of major depression, whereas ethnicity, marital status, education, and income were not. When the interactive effects of age with the other variables were considered, significantly increased prevalence of major depression among women, blacks, and those with urban residency occurred only among the youngest group (aged 18 to 39 years). Those who were married had a significantly lower prevalence of major depression for those aged 65 years and older (but not for younger ages), whereas those who were never married had a significantly increased risk of major depression among those aged 40 and older (but not those younger). Educational level and physical illness were as-

sociated with increased risk only for those aged 18 to 39, but stressful life events increased the risk of depression at all ages, and subjective social supports decreased the risk at all ages. Paradoxically, George observed that persons aged 60 years or more seemed to have low estimates of major depressive disorder, while at the same time they had depressive symptoms with a frequency as high as or higher than that of younger persons.

International Estimates of Depression and Dysthymia

In recent years, with the development of cross-cultural survey instruments, it has been possible to develop internationally comparable estimates of depression. A number of international studies have published prevalence estimates of major depression in community-based samples. Table 1.5 gives information on recent studies that used a standardized diagnostic instrument to assess major depression. These surveys differed in various respects (e.g., assessment instruments, age range covered, urban–rural differences, temporal differences). There were fairly wide differences among the various studies in prevalence estimates of current, 6-month, 1-year, and lifetime major depression. Prevalence estimates of current major depression ranged from 1.1% in Italy to 12.4% in Africa. Six-month prevalence estimates were more consistent across the four studies that assessed it; they ranged from 3.0% to 3.2%. Lifetime prevalence estimates, however, varied considerably across studies, ranging from 3.3% in Seoul to 17.1% in the NCS. These prevalence differences might be explained to a large extent by methodological factors, such as cultural differences in the sensitivity and specificity of the diagnostic instruments used, age compositions of the samples studied, different methods of weighting, and different diagnostic systems used. Because these studies were conducted at different times over the span of more than a decade, differences in prevalence estimates could also be due in part to period or cohort effects. Another likely hypothesis to explain differences in prevalence might be that there are true differences in the frequency of major depression among countries. Estimates for both major depression and dysthymia in women were generally greater than those for men in all of these countries (Weissman et al., 1993).

TABLE 1.5. Prevalence of Major Depression in Community-Based Samples

Study	n	Instrument/ criteria	Population	Age	Time reference	Prevalence of major depression (%)
Dean, Surtees, & Sashidharan (1983)	576	RDC	Women in Edinburgh	18–65	Episode-based	7.0
Mavreas, Beis, Mouyias, Rigoni, & Lykefsos (1986)	489	PSE	Athens, Greece	18–74	Current	5.4
Vásquez-Barquero et al. (1987)	452	140-item PSE	Cantabria, Spain	17+	Current	3.8 (ICD-9 dx. of 300.4)
Canino et al. (1987)	1,513	Spanish DIS	Puerto Rico	17–64	6-month Lifetime	3.0 4.6
Regier et al. (1988)	18,571	DIS	U.S. ECA sites	18+	1-month 6-month Lifetime	2.2 3.0 5.8
Bland, Orn, & Newman (1988)	3,258	DIS	Edmonton, Canada	18+	6-month Lifetime	3.2 8.6
Hwu, Yeh, & Chang (1989)	5,005 3,004 2,995	DIS-CM (Chinese-modified)	Taipei Taiwan (small town) Rural Taiwan Taipei Taiwan (small town) Rural Taiwan	18+	Lifetime Lifetime Lifetime 1-year 1-year 1-year	8.8 16.8 9.7 6.4 11.4 8.1
Wells, Bushnell, Hornblow, Joyce, & Oakley-Browne (1989)	1,498	DIS	New Zealand	18–64 18–24 25–44 45–64	Lifetime Lifetime Lifetime Lifetime	12.6 9.7 15.1 10.8
Faravelli, Degl'Innocenti, Aiazzi, Incerpi, & Pallanti (1990)	1,000	DSM-III DSM-III DSM-III-R single episode DSM-III-R recurrent DSM-III-R single episode DSM-III-R recurrent	Italy	15+	1-year Current 1-year 1-year Current Current	6.3 2.8 2.1 4.1 1.1 1.7
Lehtinen et al. (1990)	7,217	PSE	Finland	30+	Current	4.6
Lee et al. (1990)	1,966 3,134	DIS DIS	Rural Korea Seoul		Lifetime Lifetime	3.5 3.3
Hollifield, Katon, Spain, & Pule (1990)	356	DIS (abridged)	Africa	19–93	Current	12.4
Wittchen, Essau, von Zerssen, Krieg, & Zaudig (1992)	483	DIS	Germany	18–55	6-month Lifetime	3.0 9.0
Regier et al. (1993b)	20,291	DIS	U.S. ECA sites	18+	1-year new 1-year prevalence	3.2 5.0
Kessler et al. (1994)	8,098	CIDI (University of Michigan version)	U.S. NCS	15–54	12-month Lifetime	10.3 17.1

Special Population Groups

Depression among African-Americans and Hispanic-Americans

Although depressive symptoms have been reported to be higher in blacks than in whites (Somervell et al., 1989), 1-month prevalence estimates of major depression in the ECA study did not differ significantly by race/ethnicity (2.2% for those in the nonblack, non-Hispanic group, 2.5% for blacks, and 2.6% for Hispanics) (Regier et al., 1993). Lifetime prevalence estimates of major depression in the ECA study, however, were significantly lower in blacks than in whites (3.1% for blacks vs. 5.1% for whites and 4.4% for Hispanics) (Weissman et al., 1991). Clinical reappraisals of the ECA sample in Baltimore also found that neither form of clinically appraised depression (current DSM-III major depression and current "nonmajor depression," a term for the other depressive disorder categories in DSM-III) was influenced strongly by race (Romanoski et al., 1992). It may be that blacks suffer more from mild forms of distress than whites, but less from clinical depression (Weissman et al., 1991), or perhaps blacks did not respond to the DIS in the same way that whites did.

Using data obtained as a part of the Hispanic Health and Nutrition Examination Survey (HHANES), Narrow, Rae, Mościcki, Locke, and Regier (1990) reported findings from the Cuban-American population included in that survey. The HHANES was a large-scale health interview and examination of three major Hispanic populations in the United States. As a part of the evaluation, interviewed persons reported on their depressive symptoms by responding to the CES-D Scale, as well as to the section of the DIS dealing with depression. About 10% of the Cuban population was found to score 16 or higher on the CES-D Scale—a measure of "caseness." Lifetime, 6-month, and 1-month prevalence estimates for major depression were 3.2%, 2.1%, and 1.5%, respectively. Because of the small sample size and rather low case rate, only a lifetime diagnosis of major depression was found to be independently associated with an income level of less than $10,000, according to a multiple-regression analysis.

From the same HHANES, Mościcki, Locke, Rae, and Boyd (1989) reported on the results of the CES-D Scale administered to Mexican-Americans. Results from the depression section of the DIS were not given. "Caseness," again defined as a CES-D score of 16 or greater, was judged to overlap with cases of major depression and dysthymia, and perhaps with some instances of depressive symptoms not sufficient to reach threshold levels for any diagnostic category. A caseness prevalence of 13.3% was reported. Higher levels of depressive symptoms were associated with female gender, low educational achievement, low income, and U.S. birth compared with Anglo-oriented acculturation. The CES-D prevalence estimates overall were lower in comparison to estimates for other Hispanic groups.

Other Studies of the Epidemiology of Depression

Cross-sectional data, focusing on prevalence, need to be supplemented with cohort studies to determine incident cases of depressive symptoms, episodes, and disorders. Persons who are initially free of depression are followed through time for the development of symptoms. This study design reduces the likelihood of selective recall, and has a higher probability of identifying more mild episodes as well.

Coryell, Endicott, and Keller (1992) looked at risk factors for first onset of major depression in a nonclinical sample. Their study sample of 3,119 persons (including 2,306 first-degree relatives, 469 controls matched to characteristics of these first-degree relatives, and 344 spouses of affectively ill persons) were examined 6 years apart to establish the onset of first episodes of depression. Clinicians used semistructured interviews to generate diagnoses of depression according to the RDC (Spitzer, Endicott, & Robins, 1978). Nearly 12% of Coryell et al.'s sample developed at least one episode of major depression during this 6-year period. Persons who were under age 40 were three times more likely than those over 40 to become ill, and women became ill at twice the rate of men. Persons who experienced marital discord, who were raised in a farm setting, or who had high educational achievement had significantly increased incidence compared to others. Twenty-nine percent of persons with other, nonaffective mental illness at the outset of the period of observation developed major depression during the follow-up period. The "nonaffectively ill" were defined in this study as persons who reported one or more illnesses considered by the RDC as causes for secondary depression, such as panic disorder, Briquet's syndrome, antisocial personality disorder, alcohol-related and other substance-related disorders, and phobic disorders. Among the nonaffectively ill, associations with younger age and female gender were noted. The prognosis for those with "secondary" depressions having presumed causes seemed more severe than for those who had depressions without identifiable causes.

ANALYSIS OF SELECTED TOPICS ON DEPRESSION IN POPULATIONS

Birth Cohort Analysis: Is the Frequency of Depression Changing?

Lifetime prevalence estimates of depression have been reported as being higher among younger persons than among older persons, suggesting that the frequency of depression may have been increasing in recent decades (Warshaw, Klerman, & Lavori, 1991). Findings from clinical studies (Rice et al., 1984), cross-sectional and longitudinal epidemiological surveys (Weissman & Myers, 1978), and family studies (Price et al., 1985; Klerman et al., 1985; Cross-National Collaborative Group, 1992) suggest a progressive increase in prevalence and incidence of major depression in successive birth cohorts through the 20th century. Other longitudinal studies have not found such a striking cohort effect over this same time period (Murphy, Sobol, Neff, Olivier, & Leighton, 1984; Roberts, Lee, & Roberts, 1991; Srole et al., 1962).

Klerman and Weissman (1989) reviewed several large epidemiological studies that reported using similar diagnostic criteria (RDC, ICD, and DSM-III) and similar assessment methods to assess the frequency of depression in community populations. Klerman and Weissman argued that lifetime prevalence estimates for major depression should increase as cohorts age, yet some community data do not show this. The authors used life table methodology to support the conclusion that the age of onset has become earlier and the prevalence for succeeding birth cohorts has increased in birth cohorts born after World War II. They also noted, however, that community studies in Puerto Rico, Los Angeles, and Korea did not find an increasing prevalence in younger cohorts (Karno et al., 1987; Lee, Kovak, & Rhee, 1987). In their discussion, Klerman and Weissman considered other alternatives to account for the data, such

as an increased mortality among older persons with depression, increased institutionalization among older persons with depression, selective migration of younger persons with depression into urban areas, changing diagnostic criteria for depression to include persons with more mild symptoms, changing attitudes among both mental health professionals and in society at large, and biases of recall and memory.

The possibility of significant temporal change must be kept in mind, because such changes may provide important clues to etiology. Overall, however, the documentation that significant changes have occurred needs to be strengthened by prospectively gathered data from community studies that utilize unchanging diagnostic criteria and assessment methods across many decades.

Life Events and Socioeconomic Status

One extensive study utilizing a semistructured interview approach was the Camberwell study in the mid-1970s (Brown & Harris, 1978). In that study, intensively trained clinicians carefully interviewed a representative sample of women from a borough of London, and found clear associations among recent adverse life events, lower socioeconomic class, past life losses, and recently initiated depression as defined by the PSE. These plausible findings were more in keeping with a social causation model for depression. Even within the ECA project itself, similar results were reported from the clinical reappraisal at the Baltimore site (Romanoski et al., 1992). The clinical reappraisal also found a clear relationship between being on public assistance and suffering from major depression. In a related way, a recently reported study from Israel (Dohrenwend et al., 1992), using a semistructured interviewing protocol, found a relationship between socioeconomic status and major depression. The ECA study did not find as clear-cut a relationship among life events, socioeconomic status, and major depression, but it was not as well suited to discovering such relationships. It seems likely that there is a relationship. The problem of the relationship among socioeconomic status, life events, and major depression in highly structured protocol studies probably rests in part with difficulties in measuring the subjective significance of the first two factors (Dohrenwend, 1990). It will be necessary to classify events and statuses in more specific ways before a better understanding can be obtained from findings regarding the etiological roles of life events and socioeconomic status.

Depression in Women

In recent years, some research has helped to define more clearly the processes that may be at work to yield a greater incidence and prevalence of depression in women. The first question investigators have asked has been whether the ratio of 2:1 is due to methodological confounding. Although this ratio may seem small, it reflects a very large population excess of depression in women. There appear to be real gender differences in willingness to seek treatment (Kessler, Brown, & Broman, 1981; Padesky & Hammen, 1981), propensity to be prescribed a medication (Uhlenhuth, Balter, Mellinger, Cisin, & Clinthorne, 1983), permission to cry when depressed (Hammen & Padesky, 1977), mechanisms of coping with depressed mood (Funabiki, Bologna, Pepping, & FitzGerald, 1980; Nolen-Hoeksema, 1987; Ruble, Greulich, Pomerantz, & Gochberg, 1993), and depressive symptom profiles (Clark, Aneshensel, Frerichs, & Morgan, 1981; Ernst & Angst, 1992; Funabiki et al., 1980; Hammen & Padesky, 1977; Padesky & Hammen, 1981; Young, Fogg, Scheftner, Keller, & Fawcett, 1990a; Young, Scheftner, Fawcett, & Klerman, 1990b). None of these factors are of sufficient magnitude to explain the gender ratio (Kessler et al., 1981; Weissman & Klerman, 1977; Young et al., 1990a), particularly when formal criteria for major depression have been utilized. Methodological confounding may be somewhat more arguable when one considers minor depression, considering that depressive and related symptoms are common to women during the late luteal phase of the menstrual cycle (Andersch, Wendestam, Hahn, & Öhman, 1986; Hallman, 1986; Hargrove & Abraham, 1982; Johnson, McChesney, & Bean, 1988; Kessel & Coppen, 1963), and so may conceivably be contaminating estimation of minor depressions. Nonetheless, the gender ratio does not appear to be due to methodological confounding for major depression.

The next analytic question becomes whether physiological state changes associated with female reproductive function are responsible for the increased prevalence in women. As just mentioned, depressed affect is a well-known concomitant of the premenstrual period in a significant minority of women. However, studies of women seeking treatment of menstrual problems have found that women with severe premenstrual problems also tend to have lifetime histories of major depression and other psychiatric disorders (DeJong et al., 1985; Endicott, 1993; Endicott, Halbreich, & Nee, 1986; Graze, Nee, & Endicott, 1990; Halbreich & Endicott, 1985; Kashiwagi, McClure, & Wetzel, 1987; Mackenzie, Wilcox, & Baron, 1986; Perlstein et al., 1990; Rivera-Tovar & Frank, 1990; Warner, Bancroft, Dixson, & Hampson, 1991). This suggests that women with more severe forms of premenstrual sadness are experiencing a period when liability to major depression is greater, given a coincidental sadness. From this, it appears more likely that a bout of mildly sad mood before menses may kindle the development of a major depressive episode that the individual is likely to have anyway, than that a separable, natural class of depressive disorder is causally unique to late luteal phase physiological changes. Having a menstrual period is not a unique risk for major depression among women, even though it is a risk for sadness unique to women. This interpretation is consistent with the results of Schmidt et al. (1991), who prospectively diagnosed women with late luteal phase dysphoric disorder, and then prospectively manipulated the hormonal patterns of the menstrual cycle to see whether the hormonal manipulations could alter the cycling in depressed mood. That the mood and menstrual cycles were dissociable argues more strongly that the menstrual cycle is merely a "zeitgeber" (literally, "time giver") for the mood cycle in some women than that changes in hormone levels as such cause major, persistent mood disturbances.

In a related vein, recent epidemiological reviews of the menopausal process indicate that the menopausal period is not a time when women are particularly prone to depression in great numbers, as had been proposed in the older psychiatric literature (Ballinger, 1990; Greene, 1980). This also argues that hormonal changes associated with the menopause do not increase risk of major depression in large numbers of women. Women who seek treatment for menopausal complaints do appear to have a higher number of comorbid psychiatric disorders (Stewart & Boydell, 1993). When estimates are examined, it appears more likely that increases are associated with the years before menopause, but these are more likely to be related to life cycle developmental issues than to hormonal factors (Greene, 1980).

The postpartum period is well known as a time when women are likely to feel fatigue and sadness (Richards, 1990). For most women, this transient period of sadness and fatigue subsides in a few days to weeks and does not require psychiatric intervention. One investigation found that those women who did go on to develop major depression had subtle differences in estriol levels (O'Hara, Schklechte, Lewis, & Wright, 1991). In that study, however, women developing "postpartum blues" were also more likely to have personal and family histories of depression, stressful life events, and other psychosocial factors present, which may serve to explain more parsimoniously the depth and persistence of these "blues." There is some evidence that the postpartum period is associated with increases in thyroid hormone changes, possibly explaining depressive symptomatology in a subset of postpartum women (Walfish, Meyerson, Provias, Vargas, & Papsin, 1992). Nonetheless, it is not clear that hormonal changes are specifically causal for women who develop severe postpartum sadness, and it seems that more severe postpartum major depressions are more likely to be causally related to pre-existing vulnerabilities to major depression or to coincidental psychosocial circumstances.

Taken together, the literature on mood changes associated with the menstrual cycle, the menopause, and the postpartum period does not provide strong support for the role of acute changes in gonadal steroids in causing major depressive episodes. This conclusion places life events in greater focus as causally influential in initiating episodes, and also relates to socioeconomic influences over probability of experiencing a major depressive episode. Women do experience more life events, by virtue of their having wider social networks than men (Kessler & McLeod, 1984). Several studies have reported that working-class women and middle-class women have different risks of depression (Brown & Harris, 1978; Bebbington et al., 1984). Not only may women have adverse risk factors or adverse social event exposures differing from those of men; their impact may be conditioned by women's life circumstances in ways that do not occur for men. This would explain the gender ratio as due to a kind of confounding caused by the interaction of mutable social differences between the genders with

distributions of socioeconomic conditions. Alternatively, there may be comparatively immutable trait differences between adult men and women, which may explain the difference in prevalence.

Trait differences could be the result of neuroanatomical and neurophysiological differences between the sexes, or they could be the product of culturally mediated, gender-predominant psychological traits resulting from gender training early in development. That the gender ratio of unipolar depressive disorders appears first in adolescence (Garrison, Addy, Jackson, McKeown, & Waller, 1992; Kandel & Davies, 1982; Lewinsohn, Hops, Roberts, Seeley, & Andrews, 1993) suggests that the relevant trait differences appear at or before puberty. Since epigenetic changes are culturally influenced and potentially changeable, we here consider "biological" in the strict sense of "genetic," rather than also encompassing epigenetic influences occurring after birth. For the biological hypothesis regarding the gender ratio to be plausible, gender differences should be observed in most studies of gender ratio, especially in studies where the social conditions of the genders are comparable. In some studies where this has been done, the gender ratio has been 1:1 or reversed (Jenkins, 1985; Parker, 1979; Rosenfield, 1980; Wilhelm & Parker, 1989). Certainly, general population surveys have found that women report more symptoms than men (e.g., Weissman et al., 1991; Kessler et al., 1993). However, some studies utilizing clinician interviews have found severe depressions as frequently in men as in women, suggesting that the excess prevalence in women lies in the less severe grades of depressive disorder (Romanoski et al., 1992). The studies finding a 1:1 gender ratio may be subject to Type II error, but they do tend to argue against the biological hypothesis for the gender difference.

Since review of gender ratios across cultures reveals that women are more likely to have depression across the cultures sampled (Weissman & Klerman, 1977; Weissman et al., 1993), this apparent transcultural stability of gender ratio makes the biological hypothesis more plausible. However, it is not clear that the existing literature measures depression in all possible cultural settings. Furthermore, such a transcultural generalization faces the difficult task of interpreting variability in estimates in different genders, age groups, and cultures. Understanding the relationship of masculinity and femininity within each sex is needed to determine the extent to which the psychological gender "software," as opposed to the genetic "hardware" differences between the sexes, influences vulnerability to major depression. Since one cannot randomly assign individuals to their sex, this research would, of necessity, use only observational studies; because of this, it would never be absolutely free of the risk of confounding. Despite this possibility, these kinds of epidemiological studies are vital if we are to understand and to prevent the excess of major depression among women. Such a project should pay particular attention to mutable risk factors. Understanding the causes and effectively preventing the onset of major depression may not be helpful in devising treatments for a depressive episode, once it has occurred. This assessment may also not apply if "depression" represents a collection of numerous disorders, or if particular gender-specific subtypes of depression have very low prevalence.

Genetic Factors

Many studies have found that major depression is familial (Tsuang & Faraone, 1990). Twin and adoption studies (Gershon et al., 1982; Kendler, Neale, Kessler, Heath, & Eaves, 1993d; Tsuang, Winokur, & Crowe, 1980; Weissman, Kidd, & Prusoff, 1982) have found differing results with regard to the degree to which familial aggregation of major depression is due to genetic or familial-environmental factors. Only one of three major adoption studies found significant genetic effects for major depression (Wender et al., 1986); the other two found more evidence for environmental effects (Cadoret, O'Gorman, Heywood, & Troughton, 1985; von Knorring, Cloninger, Bohman, & Sigvardsson, 1983). Three twin studies of major depression published since 1990 found varying results (Kendler, Neale, Kessler, Heath, & Eaves, 1993d); Andrews, Stewart, Allen, and Henderson (1990) found little evidence for an etiological role for genetic factors in major depression. Kendler, Neale, Kessler, Heath, and Eaves (1992) estimated the heritability of liability to lifetime depression in a sample of female twins at 42%, but found no evidence for a contribution of familial-environmental factors to the liability to depression. McGuffin, Katz, and Rutherford (1991) found that both genetic factors and shared family environment made substantial and significant contributions to the familiality of

major depression, with an estimated heritability of liability to major depression of about 50%. Many of the major twin studies of affective illness have been methodologically flawed in the following ways (Kendler, Kessler, Neale, Heath, & Eaves, 1993b; Tsuang & Faraone, 1990): (1) unrepresentative samples; (2) small sample sizes that precluded rigorous statistical evaluation; (3) nonblind evaluation and diagnosis; (4) use of indirect diagnostic information; (5) nonblind or potentially inaccurate zygosity evaluation; (6) questionable reliability and validity of the assessment of lifetime major depression by a structured psychiatric interview; and (7) the cross-sectional nature of the studies, which limited information about temporal stability of risk factors for major depression.

Kendler et al. (1993d) assessed the 1-year prevalence of major depression, using DSM-III-R criteria, at two time points a minimum of 1 year apart in both members of 938 adult female–female twin pairs ascertained from the population-based Virginia Twin Registry. Interviewers at Time 1 and Time 2 interviews of each twin were "blind" to the psychopathological status of the cotwin. Zygosity was determined blindly by standard questions, photographs, and (when necessary) DNA analysis. Through model fitting, it was estimated that the liability to 1-year prevalence of major depression was due to additive genes and individual specific environment, with a heritability of 41% to 46%. Over a 1-year time period, genetic effects on the liability to 1-year prevalence of major depression were entirely stable, whereas environmental effects were entirely occasion-specific. This suggests that genetic factors play a moderate etiological role in major depression. It also suggests that environmental factors play a major role in the etiology of major depression, but that their effects are transitory and do not lead to permanent changes in the liability to illness. Kendler et al. (1993d) have concluded that the persistence of liability to major depression in adult women is largely genetic in origin.

In another study of 680 female–female twin pairs of known zygosity from the population-based Virginia Twin Registry, Kendler et al. (1993b) developed an exploratory, integrated etiological model for the prediction of episodes of major depression. The best-fitting model predicted 50% of the variance in the liability to major depression. The strongest predictors of this liability were (ranked in descending order) (1) stressful life events, (2) genetic factors, (3) previous history of major depression, and (4) neuroticism. The model suggests that at least four major and interacting risk factor domains are needed to understand the etiology of major depression: traumatic experiences, genetic factors, temperament, and interpersonal relations. Kendler and colleagues' studies need to be replicated and extended to studies of singletons and men. Nonetheless, it seems likely that understanding the etiology of major depression will necessitate investigation of environmental as well as genetic and temperamental risk factors.

RISK FACTOR OVERVIEW

Although we have presented data from two well-known community surveys of mental disorders, it is important to place them in a broader context. Only against the background of psychiatric knowledge and of other surveys can one evaluate the relative significance of differences in prevalence and incidence in any one study. Even though estimates of prevalence and incidence may reflect the true prevalence and incidence in the population reasonably well, risk factor assessment is undoubtedly more insecure, because of the nature of measurement errors in measuring both disorders and exposures (Helzer et al., 1985). This implies that any factor found to be statistically significant may have more likelihood of being misidentified as etiologically important than would be the case for a clinical or laboratory study, where the conditions of observation are better controlled. On the other hand, clinical and laboratory studies undoubtedly have sampling biases.

To some extent, how one interprets a risk factor depends in part upon notions one may have about the general nature of a disorder. We adopt the view that since surveys often do not delineate clear symptom boundaries—either in number, in kind, or in temporal contiguity—populations may not readily evince discontinuous distributions of depressive disorders. This means that depression may be a spectrum of symptomatically related syndromes that do not occur in a "yes–no" fashion. Although it is not possible to be a "little bit pregnant," it probably is possible to be a "little bit depressed." A second point to make in regard to putative risk factors is that they are merely factors or exposures associated with the disorder; they may be causative, certainly, but they also may be only associated epiphenomena or even just consequences of the disorder. This point is especially important when interpreting cross-sectional surveys, where one cannot be certain about the temporal relationships between the factors and the disorder. This is much less true in studies of the incidence of a disorder, where the temporal order is more plausibly obtained. Even in studies of incidence of psychiatric disorders, however, methodological problems involving reporting accuracy and sample attrition create additional difficulties. These complexities demand that some informed judgment be used in forming a picture of depression in populations.

As can be seen in Table 1.6, numerous risk factors for depression have been proposed. Some of these factors, such as gender and socioeconomic status, have been rather consistent across studies of depression. However, three aspects of risk factor research in depression and other disorders make the direct generalization and clinical application of these factors difficult. The first aspect is that, as in the case of gender differences, there may be many issues of confounding even when a factor is easily measured. Although we can readily determine a person's sex (and, by implication, his/her gender), we may have much greater difficulty separating the factor from other factors with which it is associated. Second, a factor may be measurable to some extent, as is socioeconomic or marital status, but may be difficult to relate mechanistically and specifically to the onset of the disorder. Using such variables relies heavily upon theory-dependent suppositions about their etiological significance in populations. Third, a factor may be operative, but only in particular contexts. Here, the risk of disorder is conditional; thus, the risk factor cannot be termed a universal risk, but only a virtual risk in the setting of other factors. The determination of risk factors undoubtedly suffers from some probability of false positives. A collection of risk factor studies such as that in Table 1.6 may give the impression of vagueness or imprecision in the studies, when the difficulty may lie more in problems specific to unmeasured personal, cultural, historical, or socioeconomic contexts, the effects of which the studies do capture and measure. This might be taken as support for the traditional, idiographic approach to treating depression, rather than a nomothetic approach. In an idiographic approach, risk factors are less determinative in diagnosis, since the approach emphasizes extensive, individualized case formulation, However, without some overarching theoretical and em-

TABLE 1.6. Risk Factors, Protective Factors, and Consequences of Major Depression

Highly plausible	Risk (causative) factors for major depression		Discounted
	Plausible	Possible	
Being female in gender (4; 7; 31; 35; 41; 60; 73; 96; 98; 99; 101; 105; 114; 122–124)	Being never-married (34; 44; 74; 81;101)	Genetic (68; 69; 86; 113)	Menopause (5; 112; 130)
Prior depression (66)	Being unmarried (6; 74; 81; 101)	Living in a city (10)	Elective abortion
Being divorced or separated (20; 34; 44; 101)	Having one or more small children in home (2; 17; 26; 34; 46)	Ethnicity (4; 105)	Luteal phase estrogen/progesterone changes (110)
Other psychiatric disorder	Family history (105)	Configuration of role in family	Neuroticism in women per se (61)
Poor general health (3; 39; 65)	Loss of mother before age 11 (17)	Historical cohort membership (78; 79)	Proximity to electric power lines (87)
Major adverse life events (17; 105)	Being a member of an oppressed minority	Pollutants	Postpartum period (23; 93; 103)
Being institutionalized	Spontaneous miscarriage	Neuroanatomical features (50)	Global gender-determined reporting bias (25; 35; 40; 52; 95; 129; 130)
Being abused or tortured	Social isolation (63)	Doing housework chronically (12; 94)	
Smoking history (14; 15; 43; 71)	Physical environment of domicile	Having a stroke (90)	
Low socioeconomic status (9; 17; 29; 91; 105; 117)	Genetics in female twins (67; 68; 69; 70)	Therapy with beta-blockers	
Comorbid anxiety or dysthymia (102; 125)	Experiencing a natural disaster with losses	Residential mobility (63)	
Being widowed (6; 19; 81; 105)	Girlhood education and socialization (55; 92; 99; 108)	Infertility	
Substance abuse (100)	Larger subjective social network of women (8; 75)	Nurturant role (45)	
Comorbid dysthymia (85; 125)	Specific occupations (30)	Greater empathy for others (32)	
Other medical illness (3; 63; 111; 115)	Menstrual cycle phase (1; 28; 33; 47; 49; 51; 53; 59; 72; 84; 97; 104; 118)	Being an unmarried vs. married male (44)	
Concurrent psychosis	Time of year (11; 36; 48; 54; 64; 83; 109)	Geographic site (31; 121)	
Hypothyroidism		Protestant denomination (88)	
Cushing's syndrome			

Migraine headaches (13; 89)
Having a myocardial infarction (38; 126)
Certain occupations (30)
Entering adolescence (42; 62; 82)
Unemployment (63; 81; 115)
Low education (63; 105)
Chronic fatigue syndrome (80; 127)
Cost of antidepressant medications
Traditional feminine role (55; 92; 106–108; 128)
Low social support (21; 22; 27)
Having poor intimate relationship (16)
Receiving public assistance (105)
Age between 20 and 50 (31; 34; 105)

Protective factors against major depression

Highly plausible	Plausible	Possible	Discounted
Extended education (29; 41)	Social support available	Exercise (37)	Vitamins
Being employed (2; 7; 16; 46; 76; 77; 105; 119)	Having a close intimate relationship (18; 24; 56)	Ethnicity	Neuroleptic treatments in the absence of psychosis
Financial stability and prosperity	Antidepressant or psychotherapy compliance (58)	Normal body weight	
Effective health care delivery systems	Religious attendance	Car ownership	
Education of MDs regarding depression	Completion of planned education	Geographic	
	Recreational activities	Being physically attractive or tall	
	Being a married male	Genetic factors	
	"Intolerance" of depression (92; 120)	Old age	
	Spouse with depression (57)	Fixed role (45)	
	Certain occupations (30)		
	Acute sleep deprivation		

(continued)

TABLE 1.6. (Continued)

Medical	Psychological	Plausible consequences of major depression	
		Social	
Suicide	Impaired general social skills	Lower socioeconomic status	
Myocardial infarction (38)	Negative view of self, world,	Divorce	
Autoimmune disease (116)	and future	Unemployment	
Nicotine dependence	Lowered optimism and motivation	Social stigma	
Comorbid psychiatric disorder	Impaired concentration and	Impaired fertility	
Impaired nutrition	creativity	Impaired education	
Substance abuse/dependence	Decreased enjoyment of	Lowered financial security	
Poorer general health	pleasurable activities	Victimization	
Functional gastrointestinal illness (116)	Impaired empathy for others		
Use of psychotropic medications (114)	Decreased competence		
	in intimate relationships		
	Decreased awareness		
	of environment		
	Fatigue		

Note. Numerals in parentheses designate the following references: (1) Andersch, Wendestam, Hahn, & Öhman (1988); (2) Aneshensel, Frerichs, & Clark (1981); (3) Aneshensel, Frerichs, & Huba (1984); (4) Anthony & Petronis (1991); (5) Ballinger (1990); (6) Bebbington (1987); (7) Bebbington, Hurry, Tennant, Sturt, & Wing (1981); (8) Bebbington et al. (1988); (9) Bebbington, Sturt, Tennant, & Hurry (1984); (10) Blazer et al. (1985); (11) Booker (1983); (12) Boulton (1983); (13) Breslau, Kilbey, & Andreski (1991); (14) Breslau, Kilbey, & Andreski (1993a); (15) Breslau, Kilbey, & Andreski (1993b); (16) Brown & Bifulco (1990); (17) Brown & Harris (1978); (18) Brown, Harris, & Copeland (1977); (19) Bruce, Kim, Leaf, & Jacobs (1990); (20) Bruce & Kim (1992); (21) Brugha et al. (1987); (22) Brugha et al. (1990); (23) Campbell & Cohn (1991); (24) Champion (1990); (25) Clark, Aneshensel, Frerichs, & Morgan (1981); (26) Cleary & Mechanic (1983); (27) Dean, Lin, & Ensel (1981); (28) DeJong et al. (1985); (29) Dohrenwend et al. (1992); (30) Eaton, Anthony, Mandel, & Garrison (1990); (31) Eaton et al. (1989); (32) Eisenberg & Lennon (1983); (33) Endicott (1993); (34) Ensel (1982); (35) Ernst & Angst (1992); (36) Faedda et al. (1993); (37) Farmer et al. (1988); (38) Fielding (1991); (39) Frerichs, Aneshensel, Yokopenic, & Clark (1982); (40) Funabiki, Bologna, Pepping, & FitzGerald (1980); (41) Gallo, Royall, & Anthony (1993); (42) Garrison, Addy, Jackson, McKeown, & Waller (1992); (43) Glassman et al. (1990); (44) Gove (1972); (45) Gove (1984); (46) Gove & Geerken (1977); (47) Graze, Nee, & Endicott (1990); (48) Haggag, Eklund, Linaker, & Götestam (1990); (49) Halbreich & Endicott (1985); (50) Halbreich & Lumley (1993); (51) Hallman (1986); (52) Hammen & Padesky (1977); (53) Hargrove & Abraham (1982); (54) Harris & Dawson-Hughes (1993); (55) Hartley (1966); (56) Hickie, Parker, Wilhelm, & Tennant (1991); (57) Holte, Bjoru, Sorvig, & Brahamsen (1990); (58) Isacsson, Boëthius, & Bergman (1992); (59) Johnson, McChesney, & Bean (1988); (60) Jorm (1987a); (61) Jorm (1987b); (62) Kandel & Davies (1982); (63) Kaplan, Roberts, Camacho, & Coyne (1987); (64) Kasper, Wehr, Bartko, Gaist, & Rosenthal (1989); (65) Katon & Sullivan (1990); (66) Keller, Lavori, Rice, Coryell, & Hirschfeld (1986); (67) Kendler, Heath, Neale, Kessler, Heath, & Eaves (1993a); (68) Kendler, Neale, Kessler, Heath, & Eaves (1993c); (69) Kendler, Neale, Kessler, Heath, & Eaves (1993d); (70) Kendler, Neale, Kessler, Heath, & Eaves (1993e); (71) Kendler et al. (1993f); (72) Kessel & Coppen (1963); (73) Kessler, McGonagle, Swartz, Blazer, & Nelson (1993); (74) Kessler et al. (1994); (75) Kessler & McLeod (1984); (76) Kessler & McRae (1981); (77) Kessler & McRae (1982); (78) Klerman et al. (1985); (79) Klerman & Weissman (1989); (80) Lane, Manu, & Matthews (1991); (81) Leaf, Weissman, Myers, Holzer, & Tischler (1986); (82) Lewinsohn, Hops, Roberts, Seeley, & Andrews (1993); (83) Lingiaede & Reichborn-Kjennerud (1993); (84) Mackenzie, Wilcox, & Baron (1986); (85) Markowitz, Moran, Kocsis, & Frances (1992); (86) McGuffin, Katz, & Rutherford (1991); (87) McMahan, Ericson, & Meyer (1994); (88) Meador et al. (1992); (89) Merikangas, Merikangas, & Angst (1993); (90) Morris, Robinson, & Raphael (1990); (91) Murphy et al. (1991); (92) Nolen-Hoeksema (1987); (93) O'Hara, Schlechte, Lewis, & Wright (1991); (94) Oakley (1974); (95) Padesky & Hammen (1981); (96) Paykel (1991); (97) Perlstein et al. (1990); (98) Radloff (1975); (99) Radloff & Rae (1979); (100) Regier et al. (1990a); (101) Regier et al. (1993); (102) Regier, Narrow, & Rae (1990b); (103) Richards (1990); (104) Rivera-Tovar & Frank (1990); (105) Romanoski et al. (1992); (106) Rosenfield (1980); (107) Rosenfield (1989); (108) Ruble, Greulich, Pomerantz, & Gochberg (1993); (109) Sakamoto, Kamo, Nakadaira, Tamura, & Takahashi (1993); (110) Schmidt et al. (1991); (111) Stallones, Marz, & Garrity (1990); (112) Stewart & Boydell (1993); (113) Tsuang & Faraone (1990); (114) Uhlenhuth, Balter, Mellinger, Cisin, & Clinthorne (1983); (115) Vázquez-Barquero et al. (1992); (116) Vogt, Pope, Mullooly, & Hollis (1994); (117) Warheit, Holzer, Bell, & Arey (1976); (118) Warner, Bancroft, Dixson, & Hampson (1991); (119) Warr & Parry (1982); (120) Warren (1983); (121) Weissman, Bruce, Leaf, Florio, & Holzer (1991); (122) Weissman et al. (1993); (123) Weissman & Klerman (1977); (124) Weissman & Klerman (1985); (125) Weissman, Leaf, Bruce, & Florio (1988); (126) Wells, Rogers, Burnam, & Camp (1993); (127) Wessely & Powell (1989); (128) Wilhelm & Parker (1989); (129) Young, Fogg, Scheftner, Keller, & Fawcett (1990a); (130) Young, Scheftner, Fawcett, & Klerman (1990b).

pirical basis, even an idiographic approach must depend upon drawing analogies across patients for any generalizability. It is probably in this way that tables such as Table 1.6 can be useful to practitioners.

METHODOLOGICAL CHALLENGES FOR FUTURE STUDIES

A few depressive syndromes that have come to be recognized in the past decade probably deserve further scrutiny from psychiatric epidemiologists. These syndromes are winter depression, brief recurrent depression, atypical depression, and chronic fatigue syndrome. By one report, winter depression affects 7% of populations in temperate latitudes (Kasper, Wehr, Bartko, Gaist, & Rosenthal, 1989). Although the seasonal epidemiology has been uneven (Booker & Hellekson, 1992; Faedda et al., 1993; Haggag, Eklund, Linaker, & Götestam, 1990; Hansen, Jacobsen, & Husby, 1991; Kasper et al., 1989; Rosen et al., 1990; Wicki, Angst, & Merikangas, 1992), the potential public health significance justifies further epidemiological studies focusing on the effect of seasons on mood. Brief recurrent depression is of unknown exact prevalence, owing to the circumstance that the sample in which it was first described was pathology-enriched; nonetheless, the severity of the disorder appears to be great, with implied risk of suicide for sufferers. Since risk of suicide is of obvious public health relevance, brief recurrent depression warrants further study. Atypical depression appears to occur more often in women, and may relate to developmental or genetic explanations for the excess prevalence of depression in women; it should be studied in community-based research. Lastly, chronic fatigue syndrome bears a strong resemblance to depression and should be studied to discern similarities and differences with depressive disorders, if only for the reason of improving the specificity of survey instruments. These disorders are of clear and present relevance for psychiatrists and other primary care physicians.

Although there has not been much research into work environment risks for major depression, at least one study using incident cases in a community setting (Eaton, Anthony, Mandel, & Garrison, 1990) has suggested that certain kinds of work environment transmit a risk for depression, whereas other confer protection. Even in such a study of incident cases, selection factors may bias interpretation of any biopsychosocial or physical mechanisms at work. Certainly an older literature describing problems with housework (Boulton, 1983; Oakley, 1974) and liability to depression faced the same problem. Nonetheless, there is a good rationale for exploring this area of potential influence over mood and functioning, as there may be ways to alter the work environment to reduce depression, anxiety, and burnout. One problem to be surmounted will be to define the general nature of "work" (Stacey, 1981) so as to include aspects of paid employment, unpaid housework, parenting, and educational activities during late adolescence and adulthood. Such an expansion of perspective will acknowledge that individuals' effortful activities serve to define their environment, and that these activities influence mood and emotional functioning. In addition, although some studies have explored how social support and intimate relationships protect against depression, further research needs to explore in more detail how this effect works.

Many depressive syndromes are defined in relation to their timing and period. For example, seasonal and premenstrual depressive episodes are defined as beginning in relation to either environmental or physiological events. In addition, brief recurrent depression and late luteal phase depression occur for a few days, whereas dysthymia is defined as lasting for a prolonged time. A major depressive episode is defined as lasting 2 weeks or longer. When the errors of recall are examined in medical studies, it has been observed that people can forget entire hospital admissions. In studies where investigators have changed their manner of querying for lifetime prevalence, as was done in the NCS, they have obtained results differing from those of other well-established studies, such as the ECA study. These kinds of interstudy differences in querying temporal information pose significant problems for the accurate determination of prevalence and incidence of specific depressive syndromes. Further work needs to be done on improving the questioning about the timing and duration of depressive syndromes if surveys of depressive disorders are to have greater reliability and validity. This is particularly true when syndromes are defined according to temporal criteria. Further consensus needs to be developed not only for sharp symptomatological definition, but also for improved quality standards for temporal data in population surveys of psychological and behavioral morbidity.

SUMMARY OF MAJOR RISK FACTORS FOR DEPRESSIVE DISORDERS

Major depressive disorder occurs more frequently among youths and young adults, with the frequency declining at older ages in the absence of secondary causes of depression (which tend to increase at older ages). (We assume that depressive disorders with identified "secondary" causes represent different disorders from depressive disorders that occur "spontaneously.") First onset seems highest in youths and young adults, but it occurs at more advanced ages as well. It is not clear whether depressive symptoms may be associated with maturational problems in relation to choosing an occupation, life companionship, gender identity, and other major developmental factors more closely associated with youths and young adults.

One of the most robust findings has been that depressive disorders are more common in females than in males by a factor of perhaps 2:1, making gender one of the most important risk factors. Some explanations that have been advanced include the following: (1) Women may self-report depressive symptoms more openly than men; (2) men may deal with their depressive affects through antisocial behaviors and substance use (behaviors more prevalent in men than in women); and (3) women, because of long-standing societal bias, may feel devalued and more prone to depressive symptoms.

Reports of ethnic variation tend to show somewhat higher estimates among whites, followed by Hispanics and blacks, but these associations do not seem especially robust. Studies of marital status typically show that persons who are married have the lowest levels of risk, followed by those who are widowed, separated, and divorced, but the variation in risk levels does not seem substantial. Depression does not seem especially closely associated with specific occupational groups or socioeconomic groups. In sum, the major demographic variables provide only limited clues to identify groups at especially high or low risk.

REFERENCES

American Psychiatric Association. (1980). *Diagnostic and statistical manual of mental disorders* (3rd ed.). Washington, DC: Author.

American Psychiatric Association. (1987). *Diagnostic and statistical manual of mental disorders* (3rd ed., rev.). Washington, DC: Author.

American Psychiatric Association. (1994). *Diagnostic and statistical manual of mental disorders* (4th ed.). Washington, DC: Author.

Andersch, B., Wendestam, C., Hahn, L., & Öhman, R. (1986). Premenstrual complaints: I. Prevalence of premenstrual symptoms in a Swedish urban population. *Journal of Psychosomatic Obstetrics and Gynaecology, 5,* 39–49.

Andrews, G., Stewart, G., Allen, R., & Henderson, A. (1990). The genetics of six neurotic disorders: A twin study. *Journal of Affective Disorders, 19,* 23–29.

Aneshensel, C. S., Estrada, A. L., Hansell, M. J., & Clark, V. A. (1987). Social psychological aspects of reporting behavior: Lifetime depressive episode reports. *Journal of Health and Social Behavior, 28,* 232–246.

Aneshensel, C. S., Frerichs, R. R., & Clark, V. A. (1981). Family roles and sex differences in depression. *Journal of Health and Social Behavior, 22,* 379–393.

Aneshensel, C. S., Frerichs, R. R., & Huba, G. J. (1984). Depression and physical illness: A multiwave, nonrecursive causal model. *Journal of Health and Social Behavior, 25,* 350–371.

Angst, J., & Dobler-Mikola, A. (1985). The Zurich study—a prospective epidemiological study of depressive, neurotic and psychosomatic syndromes: IV. Recurrent and Nonrecurrent brief depression. *European Archives of Psychiatry and Neurological Sciences, 234,* 408–416.

Angst, J., Merikangas, K., Scheidegger, P., & Wicki, W. (1990). Recurrent brief depression: A new subtype of affective disorder. *Journal of Affective Disorders, 19,* 87–98.

Angst, J., & Wicki, W. (1990). The Zurich study: XI. Is dysthymia a separate form of depression? Results of the Zurich cohort study. *European Archives of Psychiatry and Neurological Sciences, 240,* 349–354.

Anthony, J. C., & Petronis, K. R. (1991). Suspected risk factors for depression among adults 18–44 years old. *Epidemiology, 2,* 123–132.

Ballinger, C. B. (1990). Psychiatric aspects of the menopause. *British Journal of Psychiatry, 156,* 773–787.

Bebbington, P. (1987). Marital status and depression: A study of English national admission statistics. *Acta Psychiatrica Scandinavica, 75,* 640–650.

Bebbington, P. E., Brugha, T., MacCarthy, B., Potter, J., Sturt, E., Wykes, T., Katz, R., & McGuffin, P. (1988). The Camberwell collaborative depression study: I. Depressed probands: Adversity and the form of depression. *British Journal of Psychiatry, 152,* 754–765.

Bebbington, P., Hurry, J., Tennant, C., Sturt, E., & Wing, J. K. (1981). Epidemiology of mental disorders in Camberwell. *Psychological Medicine, 11,* 561–579.

Bebbington, P. E., Sturt, E., Tennant, C., & Hurry, J. (1984). Misfortune and resilience: A community study of women. *Psychological Medicine, 14,* 347–363.

Ben-Arie, O., Swartz, L., & Dickman, B. J. (1987). Depression in the elderly living in the community: Its presentation and features. *British Journal of Psychiatry, 150,* 169–174.

Bland, R. C., Orn, H., & Newman, S. C. (1988). Lifetime prevalence of psychiatric disorders in Edmonton. *Acta Psychiatrica Scandinavica*, *77*, 24–32.

Blazer, D. G. (1989). The epidemiology of depression in late life. *Journal of Geriatric Psychiatry*, *22*, 35–52.

Blazer, D. G., George, L. K., Landerman, R., Pennybacker, M., Melville, M. L., Woodbury, M., Manton, K. G., Jordan, K., & Locke, B. (1985). Psychiatric disorders: A rural/urban comparison. *Archives of General Psychiatry*, *42*, 651–656.

Blazer, D. G., Kessler, R. C., McGonagle, K. A., & Swartz, M. S. (1994). The prevalence and distribution of major depression in a national community sample: The National Comorbidity Survey. *American Journal of Psychiatry*, *151*(7), 979–986.

Booker, J. M., & Hellekson, C. J. (1992). Prevalence of seasonal affective disorder in Alaska. *American Journal of Psychiatry*, *149*(9), 1176–82.

Boulton, M. G. (1983). *On being a mother*. New York: Tavistock.

Boyd, J. H., Weissmann, M. M., Thompson, W. D., & Myers, J. K. (1982). Screening for depression in a community sample: Understanding the discrepancies between depression symptom and diagnostic scales. *Archives of General Psychiatry*, *39*, 1195–1200.

Breslau, N., & Davis, G. C. (1993). Migraine, physical health and psychiatric disorder: A prospective epidemiologic study in young adults. *Journal of Psychiatry Research*, *27*(2), 211–221.

Breslau, N., Kilbey, M. M., & Andreski, P. (1993a). Nicotine dependence and major depression: New evidence from a prospective investigation. *Archives of General Psychiatry*, *50*(1), 31–35.

Breslau, N., Kilbey, M. M., & Andreski, P. (1993b). Vulnerability to psychopathology in nicotine-dependent smokers: An epidemiologic study of young adults. *American Journal of Psychiatry*, *150*(6), 941–946.

Bromet, E. J., Dunn, L. O., Connell, M. M., Dew, M. A., & Schulberg, H. C. (1986). Long-term reliability of diagnosing lifetime major depression in a community sample. *Archives of General Psychiatry*, *43*(5), 435–440.

Brown, G. W., & Bifulco, A. (1990). Motherhood, employment, and the development of depression: Replication of a finding? *British Journal of Psychiatry*, *156*, 169–179.

Brown, G. W., & Harris, T. (1978). *Social origins of depression: A study of psychiatric disorder in women*. New York: Free Press.

Brown, G. W., Harris, T., & Copeland, J. R. (1977). Depression and loss. *British Journal of Psychiatry*, *130*, 1–18.

Bruce, M. L., & Kim, K. M. (1992). Differences in the effects of divorce on major depression in men and women. *American Journal of Psychiatry*, *149*, 914–917.

Bruce, M. L., Kim, K. M., Leaf, P. J., & Jacobs, S. (1990). Depressive episodes and dysphoria resulting from conjugal bereavement in a prospective community sample. *American Journal of Psychiatry*, *147*(5), 608–611.

Brugha, T., Bebbington, P. E., MacCarthy, B., Potter, J., Sturt, E., & Wykes, T. (1987). Social networks, social support and the type of depressive illness. *Acta Psychiatrica Scandinavica*, *76*, 664–673.

Brugha, T. S., Bebbington, P. E., MacCarthy, B., Sturt, E., Wykes, T., & Potter, J. (1990). Gender, social support and recovery from depressive disorders: A prospective clinical study. *Psychological Medicine*, *20*, 147–156.

Cadoret, R. J., O'Gorman, T. W., Heywood, E., & Troughton, E. (1985). Genetic and environmental factors in major depression. *Journal of Affective Disorders*, *9*, 155–164.

Campbell, S. B., & Cohn, J. F. (1991). Prevalence and correlates of postpartum depression in first-time mothers. *Journal of Abnormal Psychology*, *100*, 594–599.

Canino, G. J., Bird, H. R., Shrout, P. E., Rubio-Stipec, M., Bravo, M., Martinez, R., Sesman, M., & Guevara, L. M. (1987). The prevalence of specific psychiatric disorders in Puerto Rico. *Archives of General Psychiatry*, *44*, 727–735.

Champion, L. (1990). The relationship between social vulnerability and the occurence of severely threatening life events. *Psychological Medicine*, *20*, 157–161.

Clark, V. A., Aneshensel, C. S., Frerichs, R. R., & Morgan, T. M. (1981). Analysis of effects of sex and age in response to items on the CES-D Scale. *Psychiatry Research*, *5*, 171–181.

Cleary, P. D., & Mechanic, D. (1983). Sex differences in psychological distress among married people. *Journal of Health and Social Behavior*, *24*, 111–121.

Comstock, G. W., & Helsing, K. J. (1976). Symptoms of depression in two communities. *Psychological Medicine*, *6*, 551–563.

Copeland, J. R. M., Dewey, M. E., Wood, N., Searle, R., Davidson, I. A., & McWilliam, C. (1987a). Range of mental illness among the elderly in the community: Prevalence in Liverpool using the GMS-AGECAT package. *British Journal of Psychiatry*, *150*, 815–823.

Copeland, J. R. M., Gurland, B. J., Dewey, M. E., Kelleher, M. J., Smith, A. M. R., & Davidson, I. A. (1987b). Is there more dementia, depression, and neurosis in New York? A comparative study of the elderly in New York and London using the computer diagnosis AGECAT. *British Journal of Psychiatry*, *151*, 466–473.

Coryell, W., Endicott, J., & Keller, M. (1992). Major depression in a nonclinical sample: Demographic and clinical risk factors for first onset. *Archives of General Psychiatry*, *49*, 117–125.

Cross-National Collaborative Group. (1992). The changing rate of major depression: Cross-national comparisons. *Journal of the American Medical Association*, *268*, 3098–3105.

Dean, A., Lin, N., & Ensel, W. M. (1981). The epidemiological significance of social support systems in depression. *Research in Community and Mental Health*, *2*, 77–109.

Dean, C., Surtees, P. G., & Sashidharan, S. P. (1983). Comparison of research diagnostic systems in an Edinburgh community sample. *British Journal of Psychiatry*, *142*, 247–256.

DeJong, R., Rubinow, D. R., Roy-Byrne, P., Hoban, C., Grover, G. N., & Post, R. M. (1985). Premenstrual mood disorder and psychiatric illness. *American Journal of Psychiatry*, *42*, 1359–1361.

Der, G., & Bebbington, P. (1987). Depression in inner London: A register study. *Social Psychiatry*, *22*, 73–84.

Dohrenwend, B. P. (1990). Socioeconomic status (SES) and psychiatric disorders: Are the issues still compelling? *Social Psychiatry and Psychiatric Epidemiology*, *25*, 41–47.

Dohrenwend, B. P., Levav, I., Shrout, P. E., Schwartz, S., Nevah, G., Link, B. G., Skodol, A. E., & Stueve, A. (1992). Socioeconomic status and psychiatric disorders: The causation–selection issue. *Science*, *255*, 946–952.

Dovenmuehle, R. H., Reckless, J. M., & Newman, G. (1970). Depressive reactions in the elderly. In E. Palmore (Ed.), *Normal aging: Results from the Duke longitudinal study* (pp. 90–97). Durham, NC: Duke University Press.

Eaton, W. W., Anthony, J. C., Mandel, W., & Garrison, R. (1990). Occupations and the prevalence of major depressive disorder. *Journal of Occupational Medicine*, 32, 1079–1087.

Eaton, W. W., & Kessler, L. G. (Eds.). (1985). *Epidemiologic field methods in psychiatry: The NIMH Epidemiologic Catchment Area program*. New York: Academic Press.

Eaton, W. W., Kramer, M., Anthony, J. C., Dryman, A., Shapiro, S., & Locke, B. Z. (1989). The incidence of specific DIS/DSM-III mental disorders: Data from the NIMH Epidemiologic Catchment Area program. *Acta Psychiatrica Scandinavica*, 79, 163–178.

Eisenberg, N., & Lennon, R. (1983). Sex differences in empathy and related capacities. *Psychological Bulletin*, 94, 100–131.

Endicott, J. (1993). The menstrual cycle and mood disorders. *Journal of Affective Disorders*, 29, 193–200.

Endicott, J., Halbreich, U., & Nee, J. (1986). Mood and behavior during the normal menstrual cycle. In L. Dennerstein & I. Fraser (Eds.), *Hormones and behavior* (pp. 113–119). New York: Elsevier.

Ensel, W. M. (1982). The role of age in the relationship of gender and marital status to depression. *Journal of Nervous and Mental Disease*, 170, 536–543.

Ernst, C., & Angst, J. (1992). The Zurich study: XII. Sex differences in depression: Evidence from longitudinal epidemiological data. *European Archives of Psychiatry and Clinical Neuroscience*, 241, 222–230.

Faedda, G. L., Tondo, L., Teicher, M. H., Baldessarini, R. J., Gelbard, H. A., & Floris, G. F. (1993). Seasonal mood disorders: Patterns of seasonal recurrence in mania and depression. *Archives of General Psychiatry*, 50(1), 17–23.

Faravelli, C., Degl'Innocenti, B. G., Aiazzi, L., Incerpi, G., & Pallanti, S. (1990). Epidemiology of mood disorders: A community survey in Florence. *Journal of Affective Disorders*, 20, 135–141.

Farmer, M. E., Locke, B. Z., Mościcki, E. K., Dannenberg, A. L., Larson, D. B., & Radloff, L. S. (1988). Physical activity and depressive symptoms: The NHANES I epidemiologic follow-up study. *American Journal of Epidemiology*, 128, 1340–1351.

Fielding, R. (1991). Depression and acute myocardial infarction: A review and reinterpretation. *Social Science and Medicine*, 32, 1017–1027.

Frerichs, R. R., Aneshensel, C. S., Yokopenic, P. A., & Clark, V. A. (1982). Physical health and depression: An epidemiologic survey. *Preventive Medicine*, 11, 639–646.

Funabiki, D., Bologna, N. C., Pepping, M., & FitzGerald, K. C. (1980). Revisiting sex differences in the expression of depression. *Journal of Abnormal Psychology*, 89, 194–202.

Gallo, J. J., Royall, D. R., & Anthony, J. C. (1993). Risk factors for the onset of depression in middle age and later life. *Social Psychiatry and Psychiatric Epidemiology*, 28, 101–108.

Garrison, C. Z., Addy, C. L., Jackson, K. L., McKeown, R. E., & Waller, J. L. (1992). Major depressive disorder and dysthymia in young adolescents. *American Journal of Epidemiology*, 135, 792–802.

George, L. (1992). Social factors and the onset and outcome of depression. In K. Schall, D. Blazer, & J. House (Eds.), *Aging, health behaviors, and health outcomes* (pp. 137–159). Hillsdale, NJ: Erlbaum.

Gershon, E. S., Hamovit, J., Guroff, J. J., Dibble, E., Leckman, J. F., Sceery, W., Targum, S. D., Nurnberger, J. I., Goldin, L. R., & Bunney, W. E. (1982). A family study of schizoaffective, bipolar I, bipolar II, unipolar, and normal control probands. *Archives of General Psychiatry*, 39, 1157–1167.

Glassman, A. H., Helzer, J. E., Covey, L. S., Cottler, L. B., Stetner, F., Tipp, J. E., & Johnson, J. (1990). Smoking, smoking cessation, and major depression. *Journal of the American Medical Association*, 264(12), 1546–1549.

Gove, W. R. (1972). The relationship between sex roles, marital status, and mental illness. *Social Forces*, 51, 34–44.

Gove, W. R. (1984). Gender differences in mental and physical illness: The effects of fixed roles and nurturant roles. *Social Science and Medicine*, 19, 77–91.

Gove, W. R., & Geerken, M. R. (1977). The effect of children and employment on the mental health of married men and women. *Social Forces*, 56, 66–76.

Gove, W. R., & Tudor, J. F. (1973). Adult sex roles and mental illness. *American Journal of Sociology*, 78, 812–835.

Graze, K. K., Nee, J., & Endicott, J. (1990). Premenstrual depression predicts future major depressive disorder. *Acta Psychiatrica Scandinavica*, 81, 201–205.

Greene, J. G. (1980). Life stress and symptoms at the climacterium. *British Journal of Psychiatry*, 136, 486–491.

Gurland, B. J., Dean, L., Cross, P., & Golden, R. (1980). The epidemiology of depression and dementia in the elderly: The use of multiple indicators of these conditions. In J. O. Cole & J. E. Barret (Eds.), *Psychopathology of the aged* (pp. 37–62). New York: Raven Press.

Haggag, A., Eklund, B., Linaker, O., & Götestam, K. G. (1990). Seasonal mood variation: An epidemiological study in northern Norway. *Acta Psychiatrica Scandinavica*, 81(2), 141–145.

Halbreich, U., & Endicott, J. (1985). Relationship of dysphoric premenstrual changes to depressive disorders. *Acta Psychiatrica Scandinavica*, 71, 331–338.

Halbreich, U., & Lumley, L. A. (1993). The multiple interactional biological processes that might lead to depression and gender differences in its appearance. *Journal of Affective Disorders*, 29, 159–173.

Hallman, J. (1986). The premenstrual syndrome—an equivalent of depression? *Acta Psychiatrica Scandinavica*, 73, 403–411.

Hammen, C. L., & Padesky, C. A. (1977). Sex differences in the expression of depressive responses on the Beck Depression Inventory. *Journal of Abnormal Psychology*, 36(6), 609–614.

Hansen, V., Jacobsen, B. K., & Husby, R. (1991). Mental distress during winter: An epidemiologic study of 7759 adults north of the Arctic Circle. *Acta Psychiatrica Scandinavica*, 84, 137–141.

Hargrove, J. T., & Abraham, G. E. (1982). The incidence of premenstrual tension in a gynecologic clinic. *Journal of Reproductive Medicine*, 27, 721–724.

Harris, S., & Dawson-Hughes, B. (1993). Seasonal mood changes in 250 normal women. *Psychiatry Research*, 49, 77–87.

Hartley, R. (1966). A developmental view of female sex role identification. In B. J. Biddle & E. T. Thomas

(Eds.), *Role theory: Concepts and research* (pp. 354–361). New York: Wiley.

Helzer, J. E., Robins, L. N., McEvoy, L. T., Spitznagel, E. L., Stoltzman, R. K., Farmer, A., & Brockington, I. F. (1985). A comparison of clinical and diagnostic interview schedule diagnoses: Physician reexamination of lay-interviewed cases in the general population. *Archives of General Psychiatry, 42,* 657–666.

Henderson, A. S. (1994). Does aging protect against depression? *Social Psychiatry and Psychiatric Epidemiology, 29,* 107–109.

Hickie, I., Parker, G., Wilhelm, K., & Tennant, C. (1991). Perceived interpersonal risk factors of non-endogenous depression. *Psychological Medicine, 21,* 399–412.

Hollifield, M., Katon, W., Spain, D., & Pule, L. (1990). Anxiety and depression in a village in Lesotho, Africa: A comparison with the United States. *British Journal of Psychiatry, 156,* 343–350.

Holte, A., Bjoru, E., Sorvig, B. S., & Brahamsen, P. (1990). Simultaneous depression. *Acta Psychiatrica Scandinavica, 81,* 463–467.

Hwu, H.-G., Yeh, E.-K., & Chang, L.-Y. (1989). Prevalence of psychiatric disorders in Taiwan defined by the Chinese Diagnostic Interview Schedule. *Acta Psychiatrica Scandinavica, 79,* 136–147.

Isacsson, G., Boëthius, G., & Bergman, U. (1992). Low level of antidepressant prescription for people who later commit suicide: 15 years of experience from a population-based drug database in Sweden. *Acta Psychiatrica Scandinavica, 85,* 444–448.

Jenkins, R. (1985). *Sex differences in minor psychiatric morbidity.* New York: Cambridge University Press.

Johnson, S. R., McChesney, C., & Bean, J. A. (1988). Epidemiology of premenstrual symptoms in a nonclinical sample: I. Prevalence, natural history and help-seeking behavior. *Journal of Reproductive Medicine, 33,* 340–346.

Jorm, A. F. (1987a). Sex and age differences in depression: A quantitative synthesis of published research. *Australian and New Zealand Journal of Psychiatry, 21,* 46–53.

Jorm, A. F. (1987b). Sex differences in neuroticism: A quantitative synthesis of published research. *Australian and New Zealand Journal of Psychiatry, 21,* 501–506.

Kandel, D. B., & Davies, M. (1982). Epidemiology of depressive mood in adolescents: An empirical study. *Archives of General Psychiatry, 39,* 1205–1212.

Kaplan, G. A., Roberts, R. E., Camacho, T. C., & Coyne, J. C. (1987). Psychosocial predictors of depression: Prospective evidence from the Human Population Laboratory studies. *American Journal of Epidemiology, 125,* 206–220.

Karno, M., Hough, R. L., Burnam, A., Escobar, J. I., Timbers, D. M., Santana, P., & Boyd, J. H. (1987). Lifetime prevalence of specific psychiatric disorders among Mexican Americans and non-Hispanic whites in Los Angeles. *Archives of General Psychiatry, 44,* 695–701.

Kashiwagi, T., McClure, J. N., & Wetzel, R. D. (1987). Premenstrual affective syndrome and psychiatric disorder. *Diseases of the Nervous System, 37,* 116–119.

Kasper, S., Wehr, T. A., Bartko, J. J., Gaist, P. A., & Rosenthal, N. E. (1989). Epidemiological findings of seasonal changes in mood and behavior: A telephone survey of Montgomery County, Maryland. *Archives of General Psychiatry, 46*(9), 823–833.

Katon, W., & Sullivan, M. D. (1990). Depression and chronic medical illness. *Journal of Clinical Psychiatry, 51*(6, Suppl.), 3–11.

Kay, D. W. K., Henderson, A. S., Scott, R., Wilson, J., Rickwood, D., & Grayson, D. A. (1985). Dementia and depression among the elderly living in the Hobart community: The effect of the diagnostic criteria on the prevalence rates. *Psychological Medicine, 15,* 771–788.

Keller, M. B., Lavori, P. W., Rice, J., Coryell, W., & Hirschfeld, R. M. A. (1986). The persistent risk of chronicity in recurrent episodes of nonbipolar depressive disorder: A prospective follow-up. *American Journal of Psychiatry, 143,* 24–28.

Kendler, K. S., Heath, A. C., Neale, M. C., Kessler, R. C., & Eaves, L. J. (1993a). Alcoholism and major depression in women: A twin study of the causes of comorbidity. *Archives of General Psychiatry, 50*(9), 690–698.

Kendler, K. S., Kessler, R. C., Neale, M. C., Heath, A. C., & Eaves, L. J. (1993b). The prediction of major depression in women: Toward an integrated etiologic model. *American Journal of Psychiatry, 150,* 1139–1148.

Kendler, K. S., Neale, M. C., Kessler, R. C., Heath, A. C., & Eaves, L. J. (1992). A population-based twin study of major depression in women: The impact of varying definitions of illness. *Archives of General Psychiatry, 29,* 257–266.

Kendler, K. S., Neale, M. C., Kessler, R. C., Heath, A. C., & Eaves, L. J. (1993c). The lifetime history of major depression in women: Reliability of diagnosis and heritability. *Archives of General Psychiatry, 50,* 863–870.

Kendler, K. S., Neale, M. C., Kessler, R. C., Heath, A. C., & Eaves, L. J. (1993d). A longitudinal twin study of 1-year prevalence of major depression in women. *Archives of General Psychiatry, 50,* 843–852.

Kendler, K. S., Neale, M. C., Kessler, R. C., Heath, A. C., & Eaves, L. J. (1993e). A longitudinal twin study of personality and major depression in women. *Archives of General Psychiatry, 50,* 853–862.

Kendler, K. S., Neale, M. C., MacLean, C. J., Heath, A. C., Eaves, L. J., & Kessler, R. C. (1993f). Smoking and major depression: A causal analysis. *Archives of General Psychiatry, 50*(1), 36–43.

Kessel, N., & Coppen, A. (1963). The prevalence of common menstrual symptoms. *Lancet, i,* 61–64.

Kessler, R. C., Brown, R. L., & Broman, C. L. (1981). Sex differences in psychiatric help-seeking: Evidence from four large-scale surveys. *Journal of Health and Social Behavior, 22,* 49–64.

Kessler, R. C., McGonagle, K. A., Swartz, M., Blazer, D. G., & Nelson, C. B. (1993). Sex and depression in the National Comorbidity Survey: I. Lifetime prevalence, chronicity and recurrence. *Journal of Affective Disorders, 29,* 85–96.

Kessler, R. C., McGonagle, K. A., Zhao, S., Nelson, C. B., Hughes, M., Eshleman, S., Wittchen, H.-U., & Kendler, K. S. (1994). Lifetime and 12–month prevalence of DSM-III-R psychiatric disorders in the United States: Results from the National Comorbidity Survey. *Archives of General Psychiatry, 51,* 8–19.

Kessler, R. C., & McLeod, J. D. (1984). Sex differences in vulnerability to undesirable life events. *American Sociological Review, 49,* 620–631.

Kessler, R. C., & McRae, J. A. (1981). Trends in the relationship between sex and psychological distress: 1957–1976. *American Sociological Review, 46,* 443–452.

Kessler, R. C., & McRae, J. A. (1982). The effect of wives' employment on the mental health of married men and women. *American Sociological Review, 47,* 216–227.

Kessler, R. C., Nelson, C. B., McGonagle, K. A., Liu, J., Swartz, M., & Blazer, D. G. (in press). Comorbidity of DSM-III-R major depressive disorder in the general population: Results from the U.S. National Comorbidity Survey. *British Journal of Psychiatry*.

Klerman, G. L. (1988). The current age of youthful melancholia: Evidence for increase in depression among adolescents and young adults. *British Journal of Psychiatry*, 152, 4–14.

Klerman, G. L., Endicott, J., Spitzer, R., & Hirschfeld, R. M. A. (1979). Neurotic depressions: A systematic analysis of multiple criteria and meanings. *American Journal of Psychiatry*, 136, 57–61.

Klerman, G. L., Lavori, P. W., Rice, J., Reich, T., Endicott, J., Andreasen, N. C., Keller, M. B., & Hirschfeld, R. M. A. (1985). Birth-cohort trends in rates of major depressive disorder among relatives of patients with affective disorder. *Archives of General Psychiatry*, 42, 689–693.

Klerman, G. L., & Weissman, M. (1989). Increasing rates of depression. *Journal of the American Medical Association*, 261(15), 2229–2235.

Knauper, B., & Wittchen, H. U. (1994). Diagnosing major depression in the elderly: Evidence for response bias in standardized clinical interviews? *Journal of Psychiatric Research*, 28, 147–164.

Kramer, M., German, P. S., Anthony, J. C., Von Korff, M., & Skinner, E. A. (1985). Patterns of mental disorders among the elderly residents of eastern Baltimore. *Journal of the American Geriatrics Society*, 33, 236–245.

Kua, E. H. (1992). A community study of mental disorders in elderly Singaporean Chinese using the GMS-AGECAT package. *Australian and New Zealand Journal of Psychiatry*, 26, 502–506.

Lane, T. J., Manu, P., & Matthews, D. A. (1991). Depression and somatization in the chronic fatigue syndrome. *American Journal of Medicine*, 91, 335–344.

Leaf, P., Myers, J., & McEvoy, L. (1991). Procedures used in the Epidemiological Catchment Area study. In L. Robins & D. Regier (Eds.), *Psychiatric disorders in America* (pp. 11–32). New York: Free Press.

Leaf, P. J., Weissman, M. M., Myers, J. K., Holzer, C. E., & Tischler, G. L. (1986). Psychosocial risks and correlates of major depression in one United States community. In J. E. Barrett & R. M. Rose (Eds.), *Mental disorders in the community* (pp. 47–67). New York: Guilford Press.

Lee, C. K., Kwak, Y. S., Yamamoto, J., Rhee, H., Kim, Y. S., Han, J. H., Choi, J. O., Lee, Y. H. (1990). Psychiatric epidemiology in Korea: Part II. Urban and rural differences. *Journal of Nervous and Mental Disease*, 178, 247–252.

Lee, K. C., Kovak, Y. S., & Rhee, H. (1987). The national epidemiological study of mental disorders in Korea. *Journal of Korean Medical Science*, 2, 19–34.

Lehtinen, V., Joukamaa, M., Lahtela, K., Raitasalo, R., Jyrkinen, E., Maatela, J., Aromaa, A. (1990). Prevalence of mental disorders among adults in Finland: Basic results from the Mini Finland Health Survey. *Acta Psychiatrica Scandinavica*, 81, 418–425.

Leighton, D., Harding, J., Macklin, D., MacMillan, A., & Leighton, A. (1963). *The character of danger*. New York: Basic Books.

Lewinsohn, P. M., Hops, H., Roberts, R. E., Seeley, J. R., & Andrews, J. A. (1993). Adolescent psychopathology: I. Prevalence and incidence of depression and other DSM-III-R disorders in high school students. *Journal of Abnormal Psychology*, 102(1), 133–144.

Lingjaede, O., & Reichborn-Kjennerud, T. (1993). Characteristics of winter depression in the Oslo area (60°N). *Acta Psychiatrica Scandinavica*, 88, 111–120.

Mackenzie, T. B., Wilcox, K., & Baron, H. (1986). Lifetime prevalence of psychiatric disorders in women with perimenstrual difficulties. *Journal of Affective Disorders*, 10, 15–19.

Madianos, M. G., Gournas, G., & Stefanis, C. N. (1992). Depressive symptoms and depression among elderly people in Athens. *Acta Psychiatrica Scandinavica*, 86, 320–326.

Markowitz, J. C., Moran, M. E., Kocsis, J. H., & Frances, A. J. (1992). Prevalence and comorbidity of dysthymic disorder among psychiatric outpatients. *Journal of Affective Disorders*, 24, 63–71.

Mavreas, V. G., Beis, A., Mouyias, A., Rigoni, F., & Lyketsos, G. C. (1986). Prevalence of psychiatric disorders in Athens: A community study. *Social Psychiatry*, 21, 172–181.

McGuffin, P., Katz, R., & Rutherford, J. (1991). Nature, nurture, and depression: A twin study. *Psychological Medicine*, 21, 329–335.

McMahan, S., Ericson, J., & Meyer, J. (1994). Depressive symptomatology in women and residential proximity to high-voltage transmission lines. *American Journal of Epidemiology*, 139, 58–63.

Meador, K. G., Koenig, H. G., Hughes, D. C., Blazer, D. G., Turnbull, J., & George, L. K. (1992). Religious affiliation and major depression. *Hospital and Community Psychiatry*, 43(12), 1204–1208.

Merikangas, K. R., Merikangas, J. R., & Angst, J. (1993). Headache syndromes and psychiatric disorders: Association and familial transmission. *Journal of Psychiatry Research*, 27, 197–210.

Montgomery, S. A., & Montgomery, D. (1992). Features of recurrent brief depression. *L'Encéphale*, 18, 521–523.

Morris, P. L. P., Robinson, R. G., & Raphael, B. (1990). Prevalence and course of depressive disorders in hospitalized stroke patients. *International Journal of Psychiatry in Medicine*, 20, 249–364.

Mościcki, E. K., Locke, B. Z., Rae, D. S., & Boyd, J. H. (1989). Depressive symptoms among Mexican Americans: The Hispanic Health and Nutrition Examination Survey. *American Journal of Epidemiology*, 130, 348–360.

Murphy, J. M., Olivier, D. C., Monson, R. R., Sobol, A. M., Federman, E. B., & Leighton, A. H. (1991). Depression and anxiety in relation to social status. *Archives of General Psychiatry*, 48, 223–229.

Murphy, J. M., Sobol, A. M., Neff, R. K., Olivier, D. C., & Leighton, A. H. (1984). Stability of prevalence: Depression and anxiety disorders. *Archives of General Psychiatry*, 41, 990–997.

Narrow, W. E., Rae, D. S., Mościcki, E. K., Locke, B. Z., & Regier, D. A. (1990). Depression among Cuban Americans: The Hispanic Health and Nutrition Examination Survey. *Social Psychiatry and Psychiatric Epidemiology*, 25(5), 260–268.

Nolen-Hoeksema, S. (1987). Sex differences in unipolar depression: Evidence and theory. *Psychological Bulletin*, 101(2), 259–282.

O'Hara, M. W., Schklechte, J. A., Lewis, D. A., & Wright, E. J. (1991). Prospective study of postpartum blues: Biologic and psychosocial factors. *Archives of General Psychiatry*, 48, 801–806.

Oakley, A. (1974). *The sociology of housework*. New York: Pantheon Books.

Padesky, C. A., & Hammen, C. L. (1981). Sex differences in depressive symptom expression and help-seeking among college students. *Sex Roles*, *7*, 309–320.

Parker, G. (1979). Sex differences in non-clinical depression. *Australian and New Zealand Journal of Psychiatry*, *13*, 127–132.

Paykel, E. S. (1991). Depression in women. *British Journal of Psychiatry*, *158*(Suppl. 10), 22–29.

Perlstein, T. B., Frank, E., Rivera-Tovar, A., Thoft, J. S., Jacobs, E., & Mieczkowski, T. A. (1990). Prevalence of Axis I and Axis II disorders in women with late luteal phase dysphoric disorder. *Journal of Affective Disorders*, *20*, 129–134.

Price, R. A., Kidd, K. K., Pauls, D. L., Gershon, E. S., Prusoff, B. A., Weissman, M. M., & Goldin, L. R. (1985). Multiple threshold models for the affective disorders: The Yale–NIMH Collaborative Family Study. *Journal of Psychiatry Research*, *19*, 533–546.

Radloff, L. (1975). Sex differences in depression: The effects of occupation and marital status. *Sex Roles*, *1*(3), 249–265.

Radloff, L. (1977). The CES-D Scale: A self-report scale for research in the general population. *Applied Psychological Measurement*, *1*, 385–401.

Radloff, L., & Locke, B. Z. (1986). Community mental health survey and the CES-D Scale. In M. M. Weissman, J. Myers, & C. Ross (Eds.), *Community surveys of psychiatric disorders* (pp. 177–189). New Brunswick, NJ: Rutgers University Press.

Radloff, L. S., & Rae, D. S. (1979). Susceptibility and precipitating factors in depression: Sex differences and similarities. *Journal of Abnormal Psychology*, *88*(2), 174–181.

Regier, D. A., Boyd, J. H., Burke, J. D., Rae, D. S., Myers, J. K., Kramer, M., Robins, L. N., George, L. K., Karno, M., & Locke, B. Z. (1988). One-month prevalence of mental disorders in the United States: Based on five Epidemiologic Catchment Area sites. *Archives of General Psychiatry*, *45*, 977–986.

Regier, D. A., Farmer, M. E., Rae, D. S., Locke, B. Z., Keith, S. J., Judd, L. L., & Goodwin, F. K. (1990a). Comorbidity of mental disorders with alcohol and other drug abuse: Results from the Epidemiologic Catchment Area (ECA) study. *Journal of the American Medical Association*, *264*, 2511–2518.

Regier, D. A., Farmer, M. E., Rae, D. S., Myers, J. K., Kramer, M., Robins, L. N., George, L. K., Karno, M., & Locke, B. Z. (1993a). One-month prevalence of mental disorders in the United States and sociodemographic characteristics: The Epidemiologic Catchment Area study. *Acta Psychiatrica Scandinavica*, *88*, 35–47.

Regier, D. A., Narrow, W. E., & Rae, D. S. (1990b). The epidemiology of anxiety disorders: The Epidemiologic Catchment Area (ECA) experience. *Journal of Psychiatry Research*, *24*(Suppl. 2), 2–14.

Regier, D. A., Narrow, W. E., Rae, D. S., Manderscheid, R. W., Locke, B. Z., & Goodwin, F. K. (1993b). The de facto U.S. mental and addictive disorders service system: Epidemiologic Catchment Area prospective 1-year prevalence rates of disorders and services. *Archives of General Psychiatry*, *50*, 85–94.

Regier, D. A., & Robins, L. (1991). Introduction. In L. Robins & E. Regier (Eds.), *Psychiatric disorders in America* (pp. 1–10). New York: Free Press.

Rice, J., Reich, T., Andreasen, N. C., Lavori, P. W., Endicott, J., Clayton, P. J., Keller, M. B., Hirschfeld, R. M. A., & Klerman, G. L. (1984). Sex-related differences in depression: Familial evidence. *Journal of Affective Disorders*, *71*, 199–210.

Richards, J. P. (1990). Postnatal depression: A review of recent literature. *British Journal of General Practice*, *40*, 472–476.

Rivera-Tovar, A. D., & Frank, E. (1990). Late luteal phase dysphoric disorder in young women. *American Journal of Psychiatry*, *147*, 1634–1636.

Roberts, R. E., Lee, E. S., & Roberts, C. R. (1991). Change in prevalence of depressive symptoms in Alameda County. *Journal of Aging and Health*, *3*, 66–86.

Robins, L. N., Helzer, J. E., Croughan, J., & Ratcliff, K. S. (1981). National Institute of Mental Health Diagnostic Interview Schedule: Its history, characteristics, and validity. *Archives of General Psychiatry*, *38*(4), 381–389.

Robins, L. N., Helzer, J. E., Ratcliff, K. S., & Seyfried, W. (1982). Validity of the Diagnostic Interview Schedule, Version II: DSM-III diagnoses. *Psychological Medicine*, *12*, 855–870.

Robins, L. N., Wing, J., Wittchen, H. U., Helzer, J. E., Babor, T. F., Burke, J., Farmer, A., Jablenski, A., Pickens, R., Regier, D. A., Sartorius, N., & Towle, L. H. (1988). The Composite International Diagnostic Interview: An epidemiologic instrument suitable for use in conjunction with different diagnostic systems and in different cultures. *Archives of General Psychiatry*, *45*(12), 1069–1077.

Romanoski, A. J., Folstein, M. F., Nestadt, G., Chahal, R., Merchant, A., Brown, C. H., Gruenberg, E. M., & McHugh, P. R. (1992). The epidemiology of psychiatrist-ascertained depression and DSM-III depressive disorders: Results from the Eastern Baltimore Mental Health Survey clinical reappraisal. *Psychological Medicine*, *22*(3), 629–655.

Rosen, L. N., Targum, S. D., Terman, M., Bryant, M. J., Hoffman, H., Kasper, S. F., Hamovit, J. R., Docherty, J. P., Welch, B., & Rosenthal, N. E. (1990). Prevalence of seasonal affective disorder at four latitudes. *Psychiatry Research*, *31*, 131–144.

Rosenfield, S. (1980). Sex differences in depression: Do women always have higher rates? *Journal of Health and Social Behavior*, *21*, 33–42.

Rosenfield, S. (1989). The effects of women's employment: Personal control and sex differences in mental health. *Journal of Health and Social Behavior*, *30*, 77–91.

Ruble, D. N., Greulich, F., Pomerantz, E. M., & Gochberg, B. (1993). The role of gender-related processes in the development of sex differences in self-evaluation and depression. *Journal of Affective Disorders*, *29*, 97–128.

Sakamoto, K., Kamo, T., Nakadaira, S., Tamura, A., & Takahashi, K. (1993). A nationwide survey of seasonal affective disorder at 53 outpatient university clinics in Japan. *Acta Psychiatrica Scandinavica*, *87*, 258–265.

Saunders, P. A., Copeland, J. R. M., Dewey, M. E., Gilmore, C., Larkin, B. A., Phaterpekar, H., & Scott, A. (1993). The prevalence of dementia, depression, and neurosis in later life: The Liverpool MRC-ALPHA Study. *International Journal of Epidemiology*, *22*, 838–847.

Schmidt, P. J., Nieman, L. K., Grover, G. N., Muller, K. L., Merriam, G. R., & Rubinow, D. R. (1991). Lack of effect of induced menses on symptoms in women with premenstrual syndrome. *New England Journal of Medicine*, *324*, 1174–1179.

Somervell, P. D., Leaf, P. J., Weissman, M. M., Blazer, D. G., & Bruce, M. L. (1989). The prevalence of major depression in black and white adults in five United States communities. *American Journal of Epidemiology, 130*(4), 725–735.

Sorenson, A., & Stromgren, E. (1961). Frequency of depressive states within geographically delimited population groups (the Samso investigation). *Acta Psychiatrica et Neurologica Scandinavica*, Suppl. 162.

Spitzer, R. L., Endicott, J., & Robins, E. (1978). Research Diagnostic Criteria: Rationale and reliability. *Archives of General Psychiatry, 35,* 773–782.

Srole, L., Langner, T., Michael, S., Opler, M., & Rennie, T. (1962). *Mental disorders in the metropolis.* New York: McGraw-Hill.

Stacey, M. (1981). The division of labour revisited or overcoming the two Adams. In P. Abrams, R. Deem, J. Finch, & P. Rock (Eds.), *Practice and progress: British sociology 1950–1980* (pp. 172–190). London: George Allen & Unwin.

Stallones, L., Marx, M., & Garrity, T. (1990). Prevalence and correlates of depressive syndromes among older U.S. adults. *American Journal of Preventive Medicine, 6,* 295–303.

Stewart, D. E., & Boydell, K. M. (1993). Psychologic distress during menopause: Associations across the reproductive life cycle. *International Journal of Psychiatry in Medicine, 23*(2), 157–162.

Tsuang, M. T., & Faraone, S. V. (1990). *The genetics of mood disorders.* Baltimore: Johns Hopkins University Press.

Tsuang, M. T., Winokur, G., & Crowe, R. R. (1980). Morbidity risks in schizophrenia and affective disorders among first-degree relatives of patients with schizophrenia, mania, depression, and surgical conditions. *British Journal of Psychiatry, 137,* 497–504.

Uhlenhuth, E. H., Balter, M. B., Mellinger, G. D., Cisin, I. H., & Clinthorne, J. (1983). Symptom checklist syndromes in the general population: Correlations with psychotherapeutic drug use. *Archives of General Psychiatry, 40*(11), 1167–1173.

Vázquez-Barquero, J. L., Diez-Manrique, J. F., Muñoz, J., Arango, J. M., Gaite, L., Herrera, S., & Der, G. J. (1992). Sex differences in mental illness: A community study of the influence of physical health and sociodemograpic factors. *Social Psychiatry and Psychiatric Epidemiology, 27,* 62–68.

Vázquez-Barquero, J. L., Diez-Manrique, J. F., Pena, C., Aldama, J., Rodriguez, C. S., Arango, J. M., & Mirapeix, C. (1987). A community mental health study in Cantabria: A general description of morbidity. *Psychological Medicine, 17,* 227–241.

Vogt, T., Pope, C., Mullooly, J., & Hollis, J. (1994). Mental health status as a predictor of morbidity and mortality: A 15-year follow-up of members of a health maintenance organization. *American Journal of Public Health, 84,* 227–231.

von Knorring, A. L., Cloninger, C. R., Bohman, M., & Sigvardsson, S. (1983). An adoption study of depressive disorders and substance abuse. *Archives of General Psychiatry, 40,* 943–950.

Walfish, P. G., Meyerson, J., Provias, J. P., Vargas, M. T., & Papsin, F. R. (1992). Prevalence and characteristics of post-partum thyroid dysfunction: Results of a survey from Toronto, Canada. *Journal of Endocrinologic Investigation, 15,* 265–272.

Warheit, G. J., Holzer, C. E., Bell, R. A., & Arey, S. A. (1976). Sex, marital status, and mental health: A reappraisal. *Social Forces, 55,* 459–470.

Warner, P., Bancroft, J., Dixson, A., & Hampson, M. (1991). The relationship between perimenstrual depressive mood and depressive illness. *Journal of Affective Disorders, 23,* 9–23.

Warr, P., & Parry, G. (1982). Paid employment and women's psychological well-being. *Psychopharmacology Bulletin, 91*(3), 498–516.

Warren, L. W. (1983). Male intolerance of depression: A review with implications for psychotherapy. *Clinical Psychology Review, 3,* 147–156.

Warshaw, M. G., Klerman, G. L., & Lavori, P. W. (1991). Are secular trends in major depression an artifact of recall? *Journal of Psychiatry Research, 25,* 141–151.

Weissman, M. M., Bland, R., Joyce, P. R., Newman, S., Wells, J. E., & Wittchen, H.-U. (1993). Sex differences in rates of depression: Cross-national perspectives. *Journal of Affective Disorders, 29,* 77–84.

Weissman, M. M., Bruce, M., Leaf, P., Florio, L., & Holzer, C. (1991). Affective disorders. In L. Robins & E. Regier (Eds.), *Psychiatric disorders in America* (pp. 53–80). New York: Free Press.

Weissman, M. M., Kidd, K. K., & Prusoff, B. A. (1982). Variability in rates of affective disorders in relatives of depressed and normal probands. *Archives of General Psychiatry, 39,* 1397–1403.

Weissman, M. M., & Klerman, G. L. (1977). Sex differences and the epidemiology of depression. *Archives of General Psychiatry, 34,* 98–111.

Weissman, M. M., & Klerman, G. L. (1985). Gender and depression. *Trends in Neuroscience, 8,* 416–420.

Weissman, M. M., Leaf, P. J., Bruce, M. L., & Florio, L. (1988). The epidemiology of dysthymia in five communities: Rates, risks, comorbidity, and treatment. *American Journal of Psychiatry, 145,* 815–819.

Weissman, M. M., & Myers, J. K. (1978). Affective disorders in a U.S. urban community: The use of Research Diagnostic Criteria in a community survey. *Archives of General Psychiatry, 35,* 1304–1311.

Wells, J. E., Bushnell, J. A., Hornblow, A. R., Joyce, P. R., & Oakley-Browne, M. A. (1989). Christchurch Psychiatric Epidemiology Study, Part I: Methodology and lifetime prevalence for specific psychiatric disorders. *Australian and New Zealand Journal of Psychiatry, 23,* 315–326.

Wells, K. B., Rogers, W., Burnam, M. A., & Camp, P. (1993). Course of depression in patients with hypertension, myocardial infarction, or insulin-dependent diabetes. *American Journal of Psychiatry, 150,* 632–638.

Wender, P. H., Kety, S. S., Rosenthal, D., Schulsinger, F., Ortman, J., & Lunder, I. (1986). Psychiatric disorders in the biological and adoptive families of adopted individuals with affective disorders. *Archives of General Psychiatry, 43,* 923–929.

Wessely, S., & Powell, R. (1989). Fatigue syndromes: A comparison of chronic "postviral" fatigue with neuromuscular and affective disorders. *Journal of Neurology, Neurosurgery and Psychiatry, 52,* 940–948.

Wicki, W., Angst, J., & Merikangas, K. R. (1992). The Zurich Study: XIV. Epidemiology of seasonal depression. *European Archives of Psychiatry and Clinical Neuroscience, 241,* 301–306.

Wilhelm, K., & Parker, G. (1989). Is sex necessarily a risk factor to depression? *Psychological Medicine, 19,* 401–413.

Wing, J., Babor, T., Brugha, T., Burke, J., Cooper, J., Giel, R., Jablensky, A., Regier, D., & Sartorius, N. (1990).

SCAN: Schedule for Clinical Assessment in Neuro-psychiatry. *Archives of General Psychiatry, 47,* 589–593.

Wing, J., Cooper, J., & Sartorius, N. (1974). *Measurement and classification of psychiatric symptoms: An instruction manual for the PSE and CATEGO program.* Cambridge, MA: Harvard University Press.

Wittchen, H. U., Essau, C. A., von Zerssen, D., Krieg, J. C., & Zaudig, M. (1992). Lifetime and six-month prevalence of mental disorders in the Munich follow-up study. *European Archives of Psychiatry and Clinical Neuroscience, 241,* 247–258.

World Health Organization. (1992). *International classification of diseases* (10th rev.): *Clinical descriptions and diagnostic guidelines.* Geneva: Author.

Young, M. A., Fogg, L. F., Scheftner, W. A., Keller, M. B., & Fawcett, J. A. (1990a). Sex differences in the lifetime prevalence of depression: Does varying the diagnostic criteria reduce the female/male ratio? *Journal of Affective Disorders, 18,* 187–192.

Young, M. A., Scheftner, W. A., Fawcett, J., & Klerman, G. L. (1990b). Gender differences in the clinical features of unipolar major depressive disorder. *Journal of Nervous and Mental Disease, 178*(3), 200–203.

2

The Diagnostic Classification of Depression

E. EDWARD BECKHAM
WILLIAM R. LEBER
LORRAINE K. YOULL

Despite our increased understanding of mood disorders late in the 20th century, a suitable system for the classification of depressive disorders continues to be elusive. It is not hard to find criticisms of the current system and frustration that a more precise nosology has not been developed (e.g., van Praag, 1989). The sophistication and the complexity of classification systems for depression have increased. The dichotomizing by Kraepelin (1913/1921) of mental illness into "manic–depressive insanity" and "dementia praecox" was followed by a succession of systems delineating a variety of subtypes of depression. The latest version of the diagnostic system prevailing in the United States, the fourth edition of the *Diagnostic and Statistical Manual of Mental Disorders* (DSM-IV; American Psychiatric Association, 1994), lists seven separate depressive and manic disorders in the section on mood disorders, as well as various episode and course specifiers. Moreover, there are categories in the manual for normal grief reaction (uncomplicated bereavement); for the mild depressive reaction of a normal individual to a significant stressful event (adjustment disorder with depressed mood); for depression resulting biologically from general medical disorders (mood disorder due to a general medical condition); for depression resulting from substance use (substance-induced mood disorder); and for mood disorder not otherwise specified (NOS).

The once fashionable view that the diagnosis of mental disorders is not a useful or appropriate activity (Szasz, 1957) now appears to be a dead issue. Szasz asserted that depression and other mental disorders are not illnesses, but patterns of behavior that deviate from prevailing legal, moral, or social norms. In his view, diagnosis obscures the individual's responsibility for his/her behavior by placing the patient in a passive role, making resolution of the problem unlikely. Actually, the act of informing a patient of his/her diagnosis may have both positive and negative effects. There has been little research into this area, and much needs to be done. However, that has nothing to do with the scientific legitimacy of diagnosis itself. The purpose of diagnosis should not be confused with its misuse. Current research demonstrates that there are subtypes of depression (e.g., unipolar and bipolar), which vary in etiology, course, treatment response, and so on. There is massive evidence that several forms of depression are in fact illnesses or diseases resulting from genetic and biological dysfunction. Distinctions between depression and schizophrenia, unipolar and bipolar depression, and psychotic and non-

Some portions of this chapter were originally contributed by Pamela Danker-Brown, PhD, for the 1985 edition of the *Handbook of Depression*.

psychotic depression have made successful treatment of these conditions more likely and have thereby alleviated much suffering. Other forms of depression may not be biological in origin or nature, but they still have definable symptoms, course, risk factors, and response to treatment.

THE DIAGNOSTIC INTERVIEW AS A POTENTIALLY THERAPEUTIC PROCESS

The usefulness of diagnosis is not necessarily limited to clinicians and researchers. It can also serve as a map for patients to understand their disorder. Individuals with major depression have entered a new territory. They don't understand at first what is happening to them. They may misinterpret the nine possible DSM-IV symptoms of major depression as nine different problems rather than as aspects of one single syndrome. It is not unusual for patients to attribute their physical symptoms to one or more physical disorders. For example, one depressed individual returning from a trip abroad was first suspected to have contracted a parasite; this was the explanation given the patient by her primary care physician. The patient saw absolutely no connection between her weight loss and her feelings of depression. Thus, it is important for clients to have a cognitive map.

The diagnostic interview can be used as an early intervention. Understanding the disorder can give a patient a sense of control and eliminate some of the anxiety over not understanding what is happening. The diagnostic process can be used to reassure the patient that a professional recognizes his/her disorder and is likely to be able to successfully treat it. The interview can also be used to deal with any feelings of shame regarding the depression. Patients may believe (or may have been told by their families) that they are "weak," "crazy," or the like. Thus, the diagnostic interview can be a process of both gathering information from patients and sharing with them the emerging pattern and its implications.

Another aspect of the diagnostic/educational process is helping patients understand that severe depression is as much a physical disorder as a psychological one. This point can be made fairly easily by reviewing with patients the symptoms of major depression:

"Physical symptoms"	"Psychological symptoms"
Appetite or weight change	Depressed mood
	Feelings of worthlessness/guilt
Sleep change	Loss of interest
Psychomotor changes	Decreased concentration/memory
Fatigue	Suicidal ideation

The "physical" and "psychological" nature of these symptoms should not be taken too literally, so as to assume that these symptom lists reflect on the etiology of depression. This chart is also not meant to indicate symptoms of melancholic and nonmelancholic depression. Symptoms can be misleading in this regard, since guilt is clearly one of the symptoms of melancholic/endogenous depression. However, this chart can have an instructive or pedagogical value for patients, demonstrating that the effects of depression are both psychological and physical. It can be useful to compare clinical depression with an illness patients are familiar with, such as influenza. Patients with the flu can do things that a physician suggests will hasten recovery, but they cannot will the flu away. Nor did they contract the illness because they were weak. Analogies such as this can provide patients with a framework that appeals to common sense and competes with shame-inducing explanations of their depression.

THE PURPOSES OF CLASSIFICATION

The field of psychopathology has not yet reached a level of knowledge that would allow identification of the best system of classification for depression. Some authors have even argued that classification systems are no more than convenient creations constructed for our own purposes, and that they do not necessarily have any true basis in reality. According to Zigler and Phillips (1961), "a diagnostic system cannot be described as true or false, but only as useful or not useful in attaining prescribed goals" (p. 614). A more balanced view, however, is that classification systems can be either "natural" or "artificial" (Brill, 1974). A natural classification system reflects "some deeper underlying pattern or reality" (p. 1123), whereas an artificial system "is purely arbitrary and synthetic and is developed for utilitarian purposes" (p. 1123). For example, we ourselves believe that the diagnosis of major depression, as it currently exists, reflects the presence of an actual disorder (or a group of related disorders) present in many patients. The reality of the disorder is reflected in its having a distinct genetic history, biology, course, symptom cluster, and response to treatment. On the other hand, the level of severity that it designates could be made more or less stringent, and the label of "major depression" would still serve a useful purpose. In this sense, it is synthetic. The diagnosis of melancholia, on the other hand, should be less arbitrary, in that it attempts to reflect the presence of certain biochemical processes not present in non-melancholic depressions.

Most authors appear to agree that the fundamental purposes of diagnosis are to provide (1) a common language that facilitates communication about mental disorders; (2) descriptive systems for classifying persons, for the purpose of conducting research on the causes and correlates of mental disorder; and (3) information useful to clinicians in making decisions regarding treatment and prevention(Blashfield & Draguns, 1976a; Caveny, Wittson, Hunt, & Herrman, 1955; Goodwin & Guze, 1984; Spitzer & Williams, 1980).

Communication

The most fundamental purpose of diagnosis is to be a basis for communication. Stengel (1959) noted that without a common international classification system, the exchange of information—and thus progress in the understanding of mental disorders—is hindered. This can be clearly seen in the field of depression, where estimates of worldwide incidence and prevalence have been hindered by use of different terminology and diagnostic criteria (Boyd & Weissman, 1981).

Research Classification

Diagnosis serves a simplifying function by allowing a complex set of symptoms to be characterized as one concept and by promoting research on correlates of such a syndrome. This makes possible the study of extremely complex psychological phenomena. The main alternative—examining correlates of individual symptoms—not only is impractical, but generally fails to lead to knowledge about etiology and treatment response.

Clinical Prediction

The third goal is often cited by clinical practitioners as the most important reason for classification. Clinicians make diagnoses of depression primarily because of the belief that those diagnoses will help predict treatment response and other clinically relevant information, such as which patients will respond to tricyclic medication or will be most susceptible to depressive relapse.

MAJOR DEPRESSION AS PHENOTYPE AND GENOTYPE, AND MISTAKES IN CLINICAL DIAGNOSIS

The category of major depression causes a great deal of confusion, because it implies both an underlying disorder and a set of criteria. Clinicians sometimes hesitate to apply the diagnosis of major depression because of the following clinical reasons:

Insufficient severity
Lack of a family history of depression
Rapid treatment response
Presence of features of histrionic or other personality disorders
Presence of a clear precipitant

The criteria of DSM-IV may lead to the diagnosis of major depression in persons whom a particular clinician does not think of as severely or endogenously depressed. When DSM-III was first published (American Psychiatric Association, 1980), false negatives in the diagnosis of major depression occurred for just such a reason. However, the DSM-III criteria for major depression were not necessarily only for endogenous depression, and a subcategory was used (melancholia) to capture individuals with such symptoms. Thus, technically, major depression merely means that a person technically satisfies the criteria as set forth. Nevertheless, many clinicians are uncomfortable with applying the term "major depression" to certain individuals. In some cases, this is because the depression is very short-lived or is rather mild. This issue can be partially circumvented by use of the modifier "mild" after "major depression." However, as someone has commented, this solution to the problem would appear to involve a contradiction in terms ("mild" vs. "major").

Problems of this sort can be circumvented to a degree if "major depression" is understood as a label for a set of criteria rather than as an underlying disorder. By keeping clear in our own minds and in our communications with others whether we are referring to a phenotype (surface symptom patterns) or a genotype (distinct types of underlying disorders), we can reduce frustration and confusion.

DECISIONS IN DIAGNOSTIC CLASSIFICATION

Diagnostic classification is a process of ordering complex phenomena into categories by a specified set of criteria. This superficially simple task encounters numerous complexities when applied to depression and other mental disorders. One must begin with the question of what is to be classified—types of depressed persons, patterns of depressive symptoms, or etiologies of depression. Second, there is the question of whether psychiatric/psychological problems such as depression are best viewed as "diseases," "disorders," "dysfunctions," or some other construct. Decisions on nomenclature strongly imply certain views regarding etiology and treatment, and hence can ultimately affect social attitudes, patients' willingness to seek help, and even insurance reimbursement for treatment. (For example, if dysthymia, an Axis I disorder, were to be replaced by depressive personality, an Axis II disorder, insurance companies might refuse to reimburse patients for treatment. This might suddenly lead to a dramatic reduction in the clinical diagnosis of chronic mild depression.)

The term "mental disorder" is the currently agreed-upon term, but there has been considerable disagreement over its definition. Various authors have offered proposals (Klein, 1978; Spitzer & Endicott, 1978) for defining the term "mental disorder"; these were carefully examined by the Task Force on Nomenclature and Statistics of the American Psychiatric Association for inclusion in DSM-III. Neither definition was included, because "no definition would be satisfactory and therefore any attempt to formulate one was doomed to failure" (Spitzer & Williams, 1980, p. 1054). Spitzer and Williams articulated what they believed to be the basic assumptions "necessarily implicit in a classification of mental disorders" (p. 1035), which are paraphrased as follows:

1. That one can identify behavioral signs or symptoms that do not occur randomly but occur in meaningful patterns that can be identified as syndromes.
2. That these patterns of behavior are undesirable because they are associated with distress or disability.
3. That underlying these patterns is a dysfunction within the individual.
4. That these patterns of behavior are systematically related to other variables, such as etiology, prognosis, and treatment response.
5. That inclusion of certain nonbehavioral correlates of syndromes, such as information about etiology, in the definition of the syndrome, provides more useful information than behavioral description alone.
6. That diagnostic classes can be organized into a hierarchy such that a disorder high in the hierarchy may include all of the characteristics found in disorders lower in the hierarchy but the reverse is not true.

These assumptions generally appear valid regarding classification of depression, although it is not at all clear that the total locus of all types of depression (or other mental disorders) is "within the individual." For example, because of the interpersonal origins and context of many cases of depression, the etiology of depression may in these cases be within the family system just as much as it is within the individual. Relapse has been shown to be hastened by family criticism. It is also not clear that all depressions can be assigned a fixed place in a hierarchy.

CRITERIA FOR EVALUATING CLASSIFICATION SYSTEMS

There are at least four criteria by which diagnostic systems may be evaluated: reliability, validity, feasibility, and utility.

Reliability

"Reliability" refers to the likelihood that a patient will be given the same diagnosis by different persons, and/or at different times. Lack of reliability was a major criticism of DSM-I and DSM-II (Blashfield & Draguns, 1976b; Zigler & Phillips, 1961). Low reliability necessarily means that a system will have poor validity, although high reliability does not necessarily mean that a system will have high validity.

There are several possible sources of variance in making descriptive diagnoses, including differences in level of training of diagnosticians; poorly operationalized diagnostic categories; intradiagnostician inconsistency; use of different sources of information (self-report, behavioral observation, information from significant others); and, most importantly, use of different diagnostic systems. Research with the DSM-III and with descriptive diagnostic systems upon which the DSM-III was based showed that reliability was improved by the use of operational definitions of disorders with specific inclusion and exclusion criteria (Helzer et al., 1977a, 1977b; Spitzer & Williams, 1980). Reliability statistics for major mood disorders in the two DSM-III field trials were kappa = .68 and .80 (American Psychiatric Association, 1980).

Validity

Classification systems may be examined with regard to several types of validity. "Face validity" is simply the extent to which clinicians agree upon the description of a class of diagnostic categories. This is sometimes, but not always, the easiest type of validity to demonstrate.

"Descriptive validity" refers to the degree of homogeneity among individuals within a given class. There are two problems with measurement of this type of validity. First, no symptoms (not even sad mood) are found in *all* depressed patients, although some symptoms are found in most depressives. Second, homogeneity is a relative concept and there is no agreed-upon statistical test for homogeneity, although Wilk's lambda has been cited by Blashfield and Draguns (1976b) as perhaps the most useful statistic for describing homogeneity.

"Predictive validity" means that a diagnosis predicts characteristics other than those included in the definition of the class. Studies that assess family background, treatment response, complications, and course of different diagnostic subtypes address issues of predictive validity.

"Construct validity" signifies a network of consistent empirical relationships between the diagnosis on the one hand, and other diagnoses and other aspects of depression on the other. Because of this "nomological net," the construct can be inferred to have some basis in reality. For example, for "endogenous depression" to have validity as a construct, it must be shown to explain or to relate to a variety of other variables in logical, predictable ways. A finding that "endogenous" and "nonendogenous" depressions differ in symptoms, genetic background, medication response, physiology, and personality characteristics would support the construct validity of the two subtypes.

Feasibility

Even a very reliable system that has good validity will not be put to use if it is not practical. A system that requires elaborate training, time-consuming procedures, or expensive equipment may be useful for researchers but not for clinicians. For that reason, a biological classification requiring expensive tests, such as sleep studies or positron emission tomography, would hardly gain wide acceptance as a standard system of diagnosis.

Utility

A diagnostic system may have absolute reliability. It may be perfectly valid in measuring or predicting certain aspects of disorders. And it may be feasible to be administered by any trained mental health professional without exorbitant costs in money or time. However, it may still lack utility. Until depressions can be defined by their characteristics at a molecular/cellular level, the primary criterion by which depressive diagnostic systems are likely to be judged is their utility. A diagnostic system with good utility assists professionals in achieving their desired goals. "Utility" may refer to clinical utility (most generally, predicting course and optimal treatment) or to usefulness in research (such as identifying homogeneous populations).

If a system were good at predicting whether a particular variant of depression would go on to involve somatization or anxiety disorders at a later point in time, it would be of some clinical interest but would have a fairly low level of utility. On the other hand, if a system predicted whether a person would respond to psychotherapy or to particular classes of antidepressants, it would have a much higher level of clinical utility.

Some of the important types of information that may be provided by a diagnostic system of depression are the following:

1. Distinguishing etiologically distinct disorders from each other
2. Providing prognoses for individual patients

3. Describing underlying biological processes
4. Guiding clinicians in the selection of acute treatment
5. Helping clinicians to decide on longer-term maintenance treatments
6. Predicting the course of a disorder in a patient over time

Reliability, Validity, Feasibility, and Utility of DSM-III-R and DSM-IV

As stated above, the interrater reliability of DSM-III criteria for major depression was quite good. Since the DSM diagnostic system has generally relied primarily on information obtainable in interviews, it is clearly feasible for use in most settings.

There is no ultimate criterion by which to judge the validity of DSM-III-R (American Psychiatric Association, 1987) and DSM-IV criteria for major depression, since the term "major" is relative in meaning. However, considerable data support the validity of the diagnosis as representing a construct distinct from other types of psychopathology (e.g., schizophrenia, anxiety disorders). A wealth of research has compared persons with major depression to nondepressed persons and to persons having other types of psychopathology. The validity of the subtypes of major depression in DSM-III-R and DSM-IV is slowly being established. However, there remain questions about the utility of some of the DSM categories, especially the subtype categories. That is, it is not clear how much clinical information is gained about patients, once it is known that they are of the melancholic subtype or the atypical subtype. At this writing, several studies support the utility of the atypical subtype as a predictor of preferential response to monoamine oxidase inhibitors (MAOIs) as opposed to tricyclic antidepressants. The validity and utility of the diagnosis of the melancholic subtype are discussed later in the chapter.

TRADITIONAL CLASSIFICATIONS OF DEPRESSION

Emil Kraepelin included the manifestations of what are now called "unipolar depression" and "bipolar depression" within the overall rubric of "manic–depressive insanity." This broad category included "certain slight and slightest colorings of mood, some of them periodic, some of them continually morbid, which on the one hand are to be regarded as the rudiment of more severe disorders, on the other hand passing over without sharp boundary into the domain of personal predisposition" (Kraepelin, 1913/1921, p. 1). The array of affective manifestations included in this description encompasses the full range of affective disorders, from major depression and mania to depressive personality. Kraepelin perceived the basic causes of manic–depressive insanity as "permanent, internal changes which very often, perhaps always, are innate" (1913/1921, p. 3). In addition to the likelihood of a biologically based etiology, he also believed manic–depressive insanity to be characterized by a good short-term prognosis with a high likelihood of recurrence, and he viewed the manic and depressive manifestations of the disorder as opposite poles of the same underlying process.

As alternatives to this unitary concept, a number of suggested subtypes of depressive disorders have been advanced. Certain dichotomies in classification have found widespread acceptance because of their clinical utility. Among these have been the "neurotic–psychotic," the "reactive–endogenous," the "primary–secondary," and the "unipolar–bipolar" distinctions.

The Neurotic–Psychotic Distinction

The neurotic–psychotic dichotomy has traditionally been one of the most widely used and most confusing classifications of depression. "Psychotic depression" has been used to mean endogenous depression, severe depression, or depression accompanied by hallucinations or delusions. "Neurotic depression" has been a synonym for reactive depression, characterological depression, chronic depression, nonendogenous depression, mild depression, depression secondary to characterological disorders, and depression unaccompanied by hallucinations or delusions. Because of this multiplicity of meanings, Klerman, Endicott, Spitzer, and Hirschfeld (1979) suggested that the term "neurotic depression" is too vague to have any further clinical usefulness. Debate continues on this issue. Neurotic depression has been included in editions of the *International Classification of Diseases* (ICD), but it has been essentially deleted from DSM-III, DSM-III-R, and DSM-IV.

Whether "neurotic depression" has any clinical usefulness and validity depends to a great degree on how it is defined. Simply defining it as any depression that is *not* melancholic or *not* endogenous does not appear to be as useful as specifying more delimiting criteria of what it *is*. Winokur, Black, and Nasrallah (1987) showed that neurotic depressives were younger, had made more suicide attempts, showed fewer memory deficits, were less likely to have delusions, and were less likely to meet criteria for melancholia than non-neurotic depressives. There was also a tendency for neurotic depressives to be less likely to be markedly improved at discharge. Neurotic depressives were defined by Winokur et al. as having a pre-existing diagnosis (such as substance abuse, an anxiety disorder, somatization disorder, or a personality disorder), or a family history of alcoholism.

DSM-III, as well as ICD-9 (World Health Organization, 1978), clearly preserved the diagnosis of psychotic depression. Within the diagnosis of major depression, "psychotic features" may be noted when hallucinations or delusions occur. This, of course, only refers to one of the traditional meanings of the term, but this refinement of the definition should actually make the category a more useful one. The issue of psychotic depression is discussed further below.

The Reactive–Endogenous Distinction

Another significant attempt to dichotomize depressive disorders has been the reactive–endogenous distinction. Theoretically, an endogenous depression has generally been assumed to have a biological etiology and an independence from precipitating life events (an "autonomous" quality). However, the term "endogenous depression" has been increasingly limited to describing depressions with a particular cluster of symptoms (e.g., loss of weight, terminal insomnia, psychomotor retardation, guilt, etc.), without consideration of whether precipitating events appear to have triggered the depression (see, e.g., the Research Diagnostic Criteria [RDC]; Spitzer, Endicott, & Robins, 1978).

"Reactive depression" has generally denoted a depression that follows an environmental event that would be stressful for most persons, or an event that is particularly stressful for reasons idiosyncratic to a particular patient. The appearance of this distinction in the late 1920s (Gillespie, 1929) was consistent with the increase in attention being paid to the environment and its effects on behavior. The label has enjoyed a certain amount of face validity, since clinicians frequently feel able to identify the events that precipitated their patients' depressions. However, despite the face validity of the concept of reactive depression, considerable disagreement has arisen as to the sufficiency of an environmental event to cause a major affective disorder. Paykel et al. (1969) found that nearly all depressive episodes were preceded by "stressful events," and that there was no consistent relationship between the severity of the stress and the severity of the depression.

In a study of the diagnosis of "situational depression," Hirschfeld (1981) found mixed evidence for the validity of the construct. On the one hand, persons with situational depression were more likely to recover in 6 months than persons with nonsituational depression. Symptomatically, situational depressives had more depressed mood, more suicidal ideation and behavior, more anger and self-pity, and more alcohol and drug abuse. But, surprisingly, there was no overall difference between "situational" and "nonsituational" groups in their amount of recent stress, their endogenous factor scores, or their personality scores. Benjaminsen (1981) studied endogenous and nonendogenous primary depressives and found no significant differences between groups in the number of stressful events preceding the episode. Hirschfeld, Klerman, Andreasen, Clayton, and Keller (1985) showed that situational and nonsituational major depressives did not differ along certain important theoretical dimensions, such as clinical characteristics and family history. Moreover, when the statistical relationship between stressors and depression has been studied, only about 10% of the variance of depression can be accounted for by environmental events (Warheit, 1979).

On the other hand, studies have shown that stressful events are clearly more common among depressed persons than among nondepressed persons (Billings, Cronkite, & Moos, 1983; Brown & Harris, 1978; Costello, 1982). The issue is further complicated by the finding that in addition to discrete stressful events, chronic strain (e.g., an ongoing financial or marital problem) is associated with depressive symptoms (Pearlin & Schooler, 1978). Thus, it remains unclear whether the reactive–nonreactive distinction has sufficient reliability and validity to be useful for either clinicians or researchers.

Although the reactive and endogenous subtypes were thought to be somewhat different in their symptomatology, studies over the past 20 years attempting to show differences among patients categorized into endogenous and reactive groups have shown mixed results. Prusoff, Weissman, Klerman, and Rounsaville (1980) found that situational depressives were less likely to have endogenous symptomatology than were nonsituational depressives. Thus, it remains unclear whether reactive and endogenous depressions are opposites or represent two orthogonal dimensions. The evidence for the validity of the concept of reactive depression is weak; the endogenous subtype clearly has more evidence for its validity at present. Recent studies have thus not attempted to compare endogenous depression to reactive depression, but have compared endogenous depression to nonendogenous depression.

The concept of reactive depression was prominent until the development of DSM-III. In DSM-II (American Psychiatric Association, 1968), reactive depression might be classified under depressive neurosis, psychotic depressive reaction, or adjustment reaction of adult life, depending on the concomitant symptomatology. The concept of a psychosocial precipitant triggering depression was also incorporated in the RDC, which includes a situational subtype of major depressive disorder. However, it has not been included in DSM-III, DSM-III-R, or DSM-IV except to the degree that it is reflected in the Axis IV severity of psychosocial stressors.

It is clear that although the concept of reactive depression may be somewhat related to (i.e., opposite to) melancholia, the relationship is so weak and undependable (as with neurotic depression and melancholia) that the utility of the concept of reactive depression and of the concept of endogenous/melancholic depression must be considered separately.

There is considerable evidence for the validity of an endogenous syndrome. Parker, Hadzi-Pavlovic, and Boyce (1989), for example, examined a number of factor-analytic studies and concluded that a factor is typically found that corresponds to the endogenous–reactive dimension. By applying quantitative methods to data already reported in other studies, they concluded that the most characteristic features of the endogenous syndrome are severity; psychomotor retardation; lack of a precipitant; failure to react to pleasant events; older age; absence of an immature/hysterical character structure; adequate personality, lack of hypochondriasis; distinct quality of mood; lack of variability; delusions/paranoid features; and guilt. Some of the vegetative symptoms normally associated with

endogenous depression—terminal insomnia, agitation, diurnal variation, and weight loss—received lower rankings in their review.

In another review, Nelson and Charney (1981) examined factor, cluster, and discriminant analyses of the symptomatology, physiology, and treatment response of depressed patients, and identified a recurring concept of "major depressive illness characterized by a depressive syndrome unaffected by environmental change, associated with alterations of neurochemistry and requiring biological treatment" (p. 1). They labeled this type of depression "autonomous." The symptoms found to be most frequently associated with autonomous depression were psychomotor retardation and agitation, severe depressed mood, and lack of reactivity. A review of all of the studies documenting the existence of an endogenous type of depression is beyond the scope of this chapter. However, further evidence for the concept of endogenous depression continues to be generated in studies using factor-analytic, cluster-analytic, and discriminant-analytic techniques (e.g., Andreasen & Grove, 1982; Davidson, Turnbull, Strickland, & Belyea, 1984; Feinberg & Carroll, 1982, 1983; Matussek, Soldner, & Nagel, 1981).

Rush and Weissenburger (1994) recently surveyed studies regarding melancholic/endogenous depressions and concluded that melancholic features are associated with particular biological signs and clinical features. Specifically, melancholia appears to be associated with shorter rapid-eye-movement (REM) latency and nonsuppression of cortisol during the dexamethasone suppression test.

It is often assumed that endogenous depression represents a distinct biological group and therefore constitutes a category of patients for whom genetic, familial transmission of depression is occurring. However, attempts to demonstrate this have not succeeded (Andreasen et al., 1986).

There is some evidence that endogenous depressives do not respond to placebo as well as nonendogenous depressives do (Fairchild, Rush, Vasavada, Giles, & Khatami, 1986). In Fairchild et al.'s research, 20 of 37 nonendogenous patients responded to placebo, but only 1 of 18 endogenous patients did so. Further evidence that the placebo response rate is better for nonmelancholic depressives comes from Peselow, Sanfilipo, Difiglia, and Fieve (1992). The two groups differed in their response to the two treatments (i.e. antidepressant and placebo). The difference in response was greatest for patients with moderate depressions; there was less difference for those with severe depressions. This was attributed to a poorer response to medication among the patients with severe melancholic depressions, rather than to a better response to placebo among those with severe nonmelancholic depressions.

Abou-Saleh and Coppen (1983) evaluated the usefulness of the Newcastle Diagnostic Scale (a scale meant to measure endogenicity) in estimating the response rate of patients with unipolar depression to antidepressant therapies. Patients with middle-range scores (4–8) on the Newcastle Scale showed more improvement with both electroconvulsive therapy (ECT) and antidepressant medication than did patients with either lower or higher Newcastle scores. Patients with higher Newcastle scores responded better to lithium prophylaxis than did patients with lower scores. In their review of the literature, Rush and Weissenburger (1994) concluded that endogenous depressives, especially the most severely depressed, are most likely to be responsive to tricyclic antidepressants and ECT.

Yet studies have not uniformly supported the idea that endogenous/melancholic depressives are more medication-responsive than other depressives. Georgotas et al. (1987) examined whether or not elderly patients with different subtypes of depression responded differently to antidepressants. Patients were categorized as experiencing either endogenous or nonendogenous depressions and major depression with or without melancholia. There were no significant differences between the responses of endogenous and nonendogenous depressives to nortriptyline and phenelzine in this sample. Nor were there any significant differences in the response rate of patients with major depression with or without melancholia to these antidepressants. The authors concluded that they were unable to find any strong predictors of differential response to antidepressants in a geriatric population.

The Primary–Secondary Distinction

Still another diagnostic distinction that has been used is that between primary and secondary depression (Robins & Guze, 1972). "Secondary depression" was originally defined by the Washington University (St. Louis) group as meaning that the first episode of depression for an individual occurred after a pre-existing, nonaffective psychiatric disorder or after life-threatening or incapacitating medical illnesses (Feighner, Robins, Guze, Woodruff, Winokur, & Munoz, 1972). The St. Louis group eventually removed life-threatening illness as a pre-existing condition. Secondary depression, as defined in the RDC, was determined for each episode of illness within an individual rather than for the overall course of the disorder, and one episode could be primary with a later episode being secondary (e.g., if an anxiety disorder occurred in between). The RDC included anxiety disorders, schizophrenia, alcoholism, drug dependency, antisocial personality, and preferred homosexuality as pre-existing psychiatric disorders.

The theoretical conceptualization of secondary depression overlaps greatly with that of neurotic depression. Both concepts emphasize the nonprimacy of affective processes, as well as the instability or weakness of the personality prior to the onset of depression. The rationale behind the distinction was that depression resulting as a reaction to another illness should follow a course similar to the initial illness (Andreasen, 1982). Some support for the reliability of the distinction between primary and secondary depressions has been found in the stability of these diagnoses over time (Murphy, Woodruff, Herjanic, & Fischer, 1974; Faravelli & Poli, 1982).

The utility of the primary–secondary distinction has thus far been primarily in its research applications. Research carried out using only patients with primary depression has the advantage of employing a more homogeneous population unaffected by the wide variety of psychiatric symptoms and possible biological dysfunctions that may accompany the other psychiatric disorders. This conclusion is supported by research showing that patients with other psychiatric disorders often have secondary depression, and that the demographic characteristics of secondary depressives can differ considerably from those of primary depressives. Patients with secondary depression tend to have less severe depressions, tend to have their first episode at a younger age, and tend to have histories of more psychiatric illness in their families (Weissman et al., 1977). The concept has not been widely used in clinical practice, however, because of generally low utility in clinical contexts.

The Unipolar–Bipolar Distinction

Leonhard (1957) proposed that depressions with and without manic periods should be viewed as two different types of depression. Since then, researchers have vigorously pursued this thesis with a variety of types of studies. The question has not been one of whether the overall course of bipolar disorder is different from unipolar disorder, since the phenomenology of the two disorders is distinctly different. Manic periods involve clear elation or excessive irritability, heightened energy and activity, expansive self-esteem (which may even reach delusions of grandeur), talkativeness and/or racing thoughts, distractibility, decreased need for sleep, and impulsive behavior. At issue has been whether the depressive phase of bipolar disorder is different in any fundamental way from unipolar depression. Research into the distinction has primarily examined seven different areas: genetics, demographic characteristics, course of illness, psychosocial differences, symptomatology, biological processes, and response to treatment.

Genetic Transmission

Studies have left no doubt that bipolar disorder is strongly determined by genetic factors. The evidence is also clear for unipolar depression, but the effect is stronger for bipolar disorder. Various studies (e.g., Winokur, Clayton, & Reich, 1969, Trzebiatowska-Trzeciak, 1977; Winokur, Coryell, Endicott, & Akiskal, 1993a; Andreasen et al., 1987) have found an elevated incidence of bipolar relatives in the pedigrees of bipolar patients. Relatives of unipolar patients do not show such an increased incidence of bipolar disorder (Angst, 1966; Perris, 1966). This suggests that at least two different genotypes may be present. On the other hand, relatives of bipolar patients show crossover between the two diagnoses, in that there is a significant incidence of unipolar disorder among them—approximately 10% (Angst, 1966; Perris, 1966).

Another type of evidence supporting a distinction between bipolar disorder and unipolar disorder comes from data showing that identical twins tend to be concordant for bipolar disorder or unipolar disorder, rather than manifesting different disorders. Zerbin-Rudin (1969) found that monozygotic twins had a 71% concordance rate for mood disorder, and that out of those who were concordant, 81% were also concordant for the type of disorder. This ten-dency toward concordance for type of affective disorder has been confirmed by Bertelsen, Harvald, and Hauge (1977).

Demographic Characteristics

Whereas in unipolar depression women typically outnumber men by approximately a 2:1 ratio (Weissman & Klerman, 1977), the sex distribution in bipolar disorders is approximately equal between males and females (Angst, 1966; Perris, 1966). This difference has been shown repeatedly by different investigators (Winokur et al., 1993a).

Course of Illness

Age of onset for bipolar depression is typically in the late 20s, whereas the mean age of onset for unipolar depression has been found to be in the early 40s (Angst, 1966; Carlsson, Kotin, Davenport, & Adland, 1974; Perris, 1966; Winokur et al., 1969). Bipolar patients not only have an earlier age of onset on average; they also tend to have a more acute onset (Winokur et al., 1993a). Prospective studies have shown that bipolar patients have a greater number of episodes over time (Winokur, Coryell, Keller, Endicott, & Akiskal, 1993b). There appears to be no difference in the degree to which bipolar and unipolar patients experience stressors prior to the onset of their depressive episodes (Rice et al., 1984).

Psychosocial Differences

Painful childhood experiences have been found to be elevated among several psychiatric groups relative to the normal population. However, no differences have been found between bipolar and unipolar patients on this variable (Perris & Perris, 1978).

There are definite residual social problems in the lives of both bipolar and unipolar patients. For example, there tends to be a decline in income and job status (Coryell et al., 1993). In general, these psychosocial deficits are similar between the two groups of patients and persist for years following episodes of illness, even when there has been symptomatic recovery. Some differences between unipolar and bipolar depression have been found but need to be replicated. In one study, unipolar depressed mothers interacted more negatively with their offspring than did bipolar depressed mothers (Gordon et al.,

1989). In another, marriages of bipolar patients were found to end in divorce more often than those of unipolar patients (Perris, 1966).

Symptomatic Differences

There is some evidence that bipolar and unipolar depressions may differ in minor ways in their symptomatology. Compared to unipolar depressives, bipolar patients are more likely to have hypersomnia rather than insomnia (Akiskal et al., 1983; Detre et al., 1972). Unipolar patients may be more likely to have lessening of appetite (Casper et al., 1985) and loss of weight (Gurpegui, Casanova, & Cervera, 1985). Bipolar patients have been found in some studies to have more somatic complaints and to be less likely to experience subjective anxiety (Beigel & Murphy, 1971; Katz, Robins, Croughan, Secunda, & Swann, 1982). On the other hand, there is mixed evidence as to whether there is a difference between unipolar and bipolar patients in proneness to suicide (Black, Winokur, & Nasrallah, 1988; Dunner, Gershon, & Goodwin, 1976).

Biological Processes

There has been no consistent evidence that bipolar and unipolar depressions differ in their underlying biology. Once a bipolar patient enters a depressed phase, the physiological processes appear to be much the same as for unipolar depression (Perris, 1992).

Response to Treatment

Both bipolar and unipolar patients often show a beneficial response to lithium, although there is some evidence that depressed bipolar patients respond better than persons with unipolar depression (see review by Coppen, Metcalfe, & Wood, 1982). Katz et al. (1982) found that depressed bipolar patients responded somewhat more poorly to tricyclics than did unipolar depressives. With regard to ECT, some evidence suggests that unipolar patients require more treatments than bipolar patients (Perris, 1966, pp. 153–165), whereas other studies indicate a similar response rate between the two disorders (Strömgren, 1973).

The Issue of Bipolar II Disorder

Mild forms of bipolar disorder with less than full episodes of mania have in the past been called either bipolar II disorder (as in the RDC), atypical bipolar disorder, or bipolar disorder NOS. Bipolar II disorder has been included as a clinical diagnosis by DSM-IV. Bipolar II requires only an episode of hypomania rather than mania. Hypomania in turn may last a shorter period of time (4 days as compared to the required 7 days for full mania). In addition, mania is specified as severe enough "to cause marked impairment in occupational functioning or in usual social activities or relationships with others, or to necessitate hospitalization to prevent harm to self or others" (American Psychiatric Association, 1994, p. 335). Hypomania is less impairing and simply causes an "unequivocal change in functioning that is uncharacteristic of the person when not symptomatic" (American Psychiatric Association, 1994, p. 338).

In establishing this new diagnosis, it becomes important to show that it is a separate entity from both bipolar I disorder and unipolar depression. Although Dunner (1987) has noted that there is no biological factor to indicate that bipolar II is a stable and independent subtype of the bipolar affective disorder, bipolar II patients have more frequent suicide attempts than patients with other mood disorders, and more completions than either bipolar I patients or patients with unipolar depression. About 11% of bipolar II patients in one study went on to develop bipolar I disorder in a 5-year period, compared to only 4% of unipolar patients (Coryell, Endicott, Reich, Andreasen, & Keller, 1984). Despite the fact that some bipolar II patients may go on to develop or manifest bipolar I illness, the two groups tend to remain diagnostically stable across time (Coryell et al., 1989). Coryell et al. also found that relatives of bipolar II probands were significantly more likely to have bipolar II disorder.

On the other hand, Gershon et al. (1982) proposed that schizoaffective, bipolar I, bipolar II, and unipolar disorders occur on a familial continuum. They proposed a continuum of genetic vulnerability, in which the type of illness depends on the capacity of the illness to be transmitted familially. They suggested that bipolar illness is manifested when genetic vulnerability is highest, followed by unipolar disorder when vulnerability is lower, and other diagnoses when vulnerability is lowest. Their data indicated a genetic overlap among these disorders. Fieve, Go, Dunner, and Elston (1984) also concluded on the basis of their data that bipolar illness may occur on a continuum instead of in dichotomous categories, and may be caused by many factors. If that is the case, then the use of a bipolar II category may be useful for practical reasons (e.g., describing bipolar patients who have not typically had to be hospitalized), but may be confusing theoretically.

With regard to the diagnosis of hypomania, Rush (1993) noted that a duration criterion (4 days) is needed to assure that "major depressive disorder is not artificially converted into a bipolar disorder variant" (p. 190). Rush further noted that false-positive diagnoses are a clear danger with a bipolar II diagnosis. Unipolar depressives may feel elated when they are adequately treated, leading to the possibility of a misdiagnosis of hypomania. Furthermore, patients with borderline personality disorder often tend toward marked emotional lability, which may appear to be a hypomanic episode at times. It is also not clear whether lithium has a prophylactic effect in preventing hypomania, as it does with mania, and/or whether this effect is more powerful than preventing recurrent unipolar depressive episodes (Dunner, Stallone, & Fieve, 1982; Kane et al., 1982).

As noted above, DSM-IV includes categories for hypomania and bipolar II disorder. A hypomanic episode is defined similarly to a manic episode, requiring "elevated, expansive, or irritable mood" (American Psychiatric Association, 1994, p. 338) as well as at least three symptoms out of a list of seven. Again, the time period required for hypomania is only 4 days, compared to 7 for mania; there need only be an "unequivocal change in functioning" rather than marked impairment in social or occupational functioning; and hospitalization is not needed.

HISTORY OF U.S. CLASSIFICATIONS OF MAJOR DEPRESSION

The two predominant classification systems currently used in the United States have their roots in the research criteria for primary affective disorder developed by the St. Louis group (Feighner et al., 1972). The work of the St. Louis group was refined by Spitzer et al. (1978) in their development of the RDC. The development of the RDC was motivated by a need for a "consistent set of criteria for the description or selection of samples of subjects with functional psychiatric illnesses" (Spitzer et al.,

1978, p. 190). The RDC, in turn, became the skeleton for a major part of the DSM-III, which was adopted by the American Psychiatric Association and published in 1980. The intent of the task force charged with the development of DSM-III was to produce an atheoretical diagnostic system (American Psychiatric Association, 1980, p. 7). The rationale for this goal was that the diagnostic system would presumably be used by clinicians from a variety of theoretical orientations, and that for most disorders there was not yet conclusive evidence regarding etiology. The goal has remained the same for DSM-III-R and DSM-IV.

The concept of major depression is central to both the RDC and DSM-IV categorizations of mood disorders. Feighner et al. (1972) cited a series of 11 articles as the basis for the St. Louis criteria for depression. However, the exact rationale behind the selection of each of the specific criteria has never been fully set forth for any of the three systems. It is reasonable to wonder how the particular set of symptoms was selected, and why certain other frequent symptoms associated with depression, such as feelings of hopelessness or social withdrawal, were not included. In addition, it is reasonable to ask on what basis the RDC requires depressed mood plus five other symptoms (DSM-IV, five symptoms total), rather than some other number, for a diagnosis of major depression. A third question has to do with the rationale behind the duration requirement for the diagnosis of major depression. DSM-IV and the RDC require 2 weeks, whereas the St. Louis criteria (Feighner et al., 1972) require 4 weeks.

One way to approach these questions would be to study false positives and negatives, and true positives and negatives, for different combinations of the various sets of criteria. Unfortunately, such research requires an external criterion for major depression, which currently does not exist. There are several possible criteria, none of which is entirely satisfactory. Research on criteria for major depression might be carried out by comparing clearly impaired patients to depressed persons who are not clearly impaired, or by comparing hospitalized to nonhospitalized depressives. The diagnosis of major depression, as currently defined by DSM-IV, is a heterogeneous category and is not meant to include only medication-responsive or biologically based depressions, although these qualities are thought to apply to the melancholic subtype (see below). As it currently exists, the category of major depression has clear but somewhat arbitrary boundaries.

Despite the lack of a published rationale for individual symptoms and criteria, the concept of major depression as it is variously (and similarly) defined in the criteria of the St. Louis group, the RDC, and the DSM-IV is a step forward, because it allows for the reliable selection of relatively homogeneous samples of patients for research. The use of distinct guidelines for rating symptomatology (such as those offered in the Schedule for Affective Disorders and Schizophrenia or the Structured Clinical Interview for DSM-III-R) has been an important step in the refinement of criteria.

OTHER TYPES AND SUBTYPES OF DEPRESSION IN DSM-III-R AND DSM-IV

Atypical Depression

Klein (1974) proposed that depressions could be classified as "endogenomorphic depressions," "acute dysphoria," or "chronic overreactive dysphoria." Endogenomorphic depressions were hypothesized to result from a biological defect that inhibits the experience of pleasure. Acute dysphoria was the term Klein applied to reactive depression, defined as "a sudden dysphoric reaction of frustration in a normal personality" (p. 449). Chronic overreactive dysphoria referred to "chronic overreactions to disappointment and demoralization" (p. 449). Klein hypothesized that the capacity for pleasure is maintained in the dysphoric disorders.

A special diagnostic subgroup proposed by Klein within chronic overreactive dysphoria was "hysteroid dysphoria." Patients in this category were characterized as very responsive to external praise and support, and as very susceptible to depression when disappointed in romantic relationships. Symptoms of the syndrome were said to be "atypical"—that is, to include oversleeping and overeating. MAOIs were suggested as the treatment of choice (Liebowitz & Klein, 1981). Various investigators (Liebowitz et al., 1984; Thase, Carpenter, Kupfer, & Frank, 1991) have since shown that MAOIs are superior to tricyclics for treating atypical depressions.

There is some difference of opinion as to whether hysteroid dysphoria (now being termed

"atypical depression") should be considered a subtype of major depression or a variant of dysthymia. Akiskal and Weise (1992), for example, consider it to be the latter. Atypical depression tends to occur at younger ages than does endogenous depression. Atypical depressives also have fewer symptoms of melancholia.

The DSM-IV mood disorders committee found sufficient evidence for the validity of the atypical concept to include "with atypical features" as a cross-sectional modifier, similar to the way that "with melancholic features" is a modifier of the diagnosis of major depression in DSM-III-R. Moreover, the "atypical" modifier can be applied not only to major depressive disorder, but to bipolar I disorder, bipolar II disorder, and dysthymia. DSM-IV criteria for the classification of a depression as "with atypical features" are as follows:

A. Mood reactivity (i.e., mood brightens in response to actual or potential positive events)
B. Two (or more) of the following features: [Note: These are present most of the time for at least two weeks.]
  (1) significant weight gain or increase in appetite
  (2) hypersomnia
  (3) leaden paralysis (i.e., heavy, leaden feelings in arms or legs)
  (4) long-standing pattern of interpersonal rejection sensitivity (not limited to episodes of mood disturbance) that results in significant social or occupational impairment
C. Does not meet criteria for With Melancholic Features (or With Catatonic Features during the same episode. (American Psychiatric Association, 1994, p. 386)

Melancholia

"Melancholia" was the name given to endogenous depression by DSM-III to keep the DSM category separate from other definitions and meanings of the subtype. Findings regarding the validity and utility of the concept of endogenous depression have already been reviewed. Criteria for melancholia have changed with each version of the DSM, and this was a source of concern for the DSM-IV mood disorders committee. They noted that "there is considerable concern that the definition of Melancholia has been changed so frequently (based on insufficient evidence), that it may be best to retain the current system in the interest of continuity" (American Psychiatric Association, 1991, p. G:22). Nevertheless, the final decision was to revise the criteria again by deleting from DSM-IV the DSM-III-R criteria that are not symptoms of the current episode, such as previous good response to somatic treatment, lack of significant personality disturbance prior to the first depression, and good recovery following previous episodes.

Although clinicians have traditionally believed melancholic patients to be more responsive to medication than nonmelancholic patients, hard data have been lacking. Studies regarding endogenous/melancholic depression have already been discussed above, but there is evidence that melancholic depression is less responsive to placebo than are other types of depression (Peselow et al., 1992). The evidence that melancholic depression responds better than nonmelancholic depressions to medication is less clear, but there is evidence that melancholic symptom features predict good response to ECT and to tricyclic antidepressants among severely depressed patients (Rush & Weissenburger, 1994).

Psychotic Depression

The distinction between depression with and without accompanying psychotic symptomatology is a dichotomy particularly attractive to clinicians, because of the dramatic differences in presentation and because of the important implications for treatment. Moreover, there appears to be more diagnostic stability for psychotic depression across episodes than for some other subtypes (e.g., anxious/retarded and endogenous) (Coryell et al., 1994). In addition, patients with delusional depression tend to respond less well to traditional treatment for depression (Parker, Roy, Hadzi-Pavlovic, & Pedic, 1992); are much less likely to experience spontaneous remission (Roose and Glassman, 1988); and tend to have a poor short-term outcome, regardless of the type of treatment they have received (Coryell & Tsuang, 1982). Finally, their depression tends to be only weakly associated with significant life events (Paykel & Cooper, 1992).

There has been some confusion over the terminology used to describe psychotic depression. For example, "endogenous depression" and "psychotic depression" have been sometimes used synonymously to describe the presence of severe but not necessarily psychotic symptoms

of depression (Coryell & Winokur, 1992; Kendall, 1976). The trend recently, especially in the United States, has been toward focusing on hallucinations and delusions to make a diagnosis of psychotic depression (Parker et al., 1991a, 1991b).

In addition, there is considerable debate in the literature about whether psychotic depression is a form of severe melancholia or a separate disorder (Bellini, Gatti, Gasperini, & Smeraldi, 1992; Fink, 1993; Parker et al., 1991a, 1991b, 1992). The unitary view of depression regards all depressive disorders as occurring on a single continuum with varying degrees of severity. The binary view of psychotic depression holds that it should be considered a separate diagnostic entity, largely because of its poor response to antidepressant treatment approaches alone (Parker et al., 1991b; Roose & Glassman, 1988). Until the use of tricyclic antidepressants emerged as an effective treatment of depression, psychotic features present during depression were simply considered to be another set of depressive symptoms (Coryell & Winokur, 1992).

In spite of the controversy over diagnostic criteria and terminology, the distinction as to whether delusions or hallucinations are mood-congruent or not contributes valuable clinical information. The presence of mood-congruent delusions or hallucinations suggests that a psychotic illness is a mood disorder, such as psychotic depression. However, mood-incongruent delusions tend not to resolve with the treatment of an affective disorder. For that reason, the presence of mood-incongruent delusions suggests a diagnosis of schizoaffective disorder or schizophrenia (Roose & Glassman, 1988).

In an attempt to empirically delineate the diagnosis of psychotic depression, several researchers have investigated demographic variables. When delusional and nondelusional depressive patients were compared (Bellini et al., 1992; Glassman & Roose, 1981), no significant demographic variables were identified that distinguished the two groups. Nor have any significant gender differences have been established (Fennig, Bromet, & Jandorf, 1993).

Treatment response, however, appears to differ between psychotic and nonpsychotic depressives. Some researchers have concluded that delusional depression has a poor response rate to tricyclics alone (Parker et al., 1992; Roose & Glassman, 1988; Spiker et al., 1985). Kocsis et al. (1990) found that a group of moderately depressed nonpsychotic patients responded better to a 4-week regimen of tricyclic antidepressants than did a group of severely depressed patients. In turn, the severely depressed group of patients responded better than did a group of patients with psychotic depression.

Spiker et al. (1985) found that the combination of amitriptyline and perphenazine was a more effective treatment than was either type of drug alone in the treatment of psychotic depression. Parker et al. (1992) also concurred that combination drug therapy was more effective than either type of drug alone. However, Parker and his colleagues further concluded as a result of a meta-analysis of the literature that ECT was of comparable efficacy to a combination drug treatment and was more effective than tricyclics alone. Roose and Glassman (1988) suggested that if combination drug therapy is not effective in treating psychotic depression, ECT is recommended as the next treatment step.

Dysthymic Disorder

"Dysthymia," or long-term mild depression, is a poorly understood form of depressive disorder. Often having its first symptomatic development in childhood or adolescence, it is usually not an aberration occurring in the midst of a patient's normal personality; it is instead generally woven into the patient's personality. It often occurs early enough that social skill development and identity are thoroughly intermixed with it. As a result, dysthymic individuals' normal way of seeing themselves and their world is very negative. Their social abilities are impaired. Treatment does not involve helping these persons return to their normal selves; instead, it involves creating new "normal" selves. It would be logical to hypothesize that whereas major depression may be treated with one of a variety of psychotherapeutic approaches, dysthymia may need a multimodal approach, since all spheres of a dysthymic person's life have been affected and entrenched patterns are likely to be present.

There is no clear agreement as to whether there is a depressive personality distinct from dysthymic disorder. Indeed, there is controversy as to whether early-onset dysthymia is a depressive disorder or a personality disorder. Some authors have argued that the DSM-III-R category of dysthymic disorder requires too great a level of symptomatology to capture persons with depressive personality (Klein, 1990). However, the inclusion of a separate category of depressive personality in addition to dysthymia would create new problems. Klein (1990) noted three possible options:

1. To keep both categories.
2. To combine early-onset dysthymia with the category of depressive personality, and limit dysthymia to adult-onset mild chronic depression.
3. To eliminate the category of dysthymia and create a new subtype of major depression— "double depression"—which would subsume many of the more symptomatic dysthymics.

Dysthymic disorder tends to have a poor response to pharmacological treatment and has a long-term course, even with psychotherapy (Keller, Lavori, Endicott, Coryell, & Klerman, 1983; Kocsis, Voss, Mann, & Frances, 1986; McCullough et al., 1988). Thus, dysthymic disorder and major depression differ in a variety of ways: Dysthymic disorder tends to have an earlier age of onset and to last many years; dysthymic disorder does not respond well to antidepressants; and treatment of it generally takes longer than treatment of major depression. Major depression is not totally separate from dysthymic disorder, however, because dysthymic disorder usually results in the development of major depression at some point (Keller & Lavori, 1984). When major depression is thus superimposed on dysthymic disorder, the resulting complex is sometimes termed "double depression," as noted above. Double depression has been found in some studies to predict greater likelihood of relapse into major depression following successful treatment (e.g., Keller et al., 1983). There is some controversy, however, about whether double depression in fact represents a distinct disorder or is purely a definitional construct (Frances et al., 1989).

The DSM-IV committee members chose not to include a diagnosis of depressive personality in the main body of the manual, and considered separating dysthymic disorder more distinctly from major depression. They considered eliminating some of the vegetative symptoms that had been included in DSM-III-R, such as changes in appetite and sleep, and adding mild symptoms such as low self-esteem, social withdrawal, irritability and anger, and decreased effectiveness and productivity. However, there was not sufficient agreement on these points, and the DSM-III-R criteria for dysthymic disorder were retained.

Seasonal Affective Disorder

Considerable research has appeared in recent years dealing with the concept of seasonal affective disorder (SAD). The relationship between season and certain aspects of depression has also been studied. For example, there is a relationship between incidence of suicide and various times of the year (Lester, 1971; Souetre et al., 1987). Extensive controlled studies of SAD began to appear too late for inclusion of the disorder in DSM-III, but it was included in the DSM-III-R as a modifier called "with seasonal pattern," applicable to bipolar disorder, recurrent major depression, or depressive disorder NOS. (In DSM-IV, it can be applied to bipolar II disorder as well.) The criteria for seasonal pattern differ somewhat from the criteria used by SAD researchers (Bauer & Dunner, 1993), with the SAD researchers' criteria being somewhat more inclusive. The differences relate to the exact specification of the time window for the development and remission of successive episodes, the number of required episodes, and the existence of other Axis I disorders.

Although consideration has been given to designating SAD as a discrete disorder, a number of issues cloud the distinction between SAD and nonseasonal affective disorders. Among these is the fact that research suggests that there may be seasonal variations in mood and behavior in the general population, as well as those diagnosed with affective disorders (Rosen & Rosenthal, 1991). Also, within the families of SAD patients there is a greater prevalence of affective disorders, but not necessarily SAD (Allen, Lam, Remick, & Sadovnick, 1993). Bauer and Dunner (1993) reviewed various criteria for the validity of psychiatric syndromes in general and then evaluated the evidence for SAD as a valid, discrete syndrome. They concluded that because of the overlap in symptomatology between SAD and other subtypes of depression, the lack of evidence for differential specificity of treatment response, and the poor understanding of the processes underlying SAD, it is still too soon to identify it as a distinct disorder. As an example of the lack of specificity in treatment response, early studies using phototherapy found some improvement even in those patients whose depression did not have a seasonal pattern. Conversely, patients with SAD have been shown to respond to treatment with an MAOI (Dilsaver, Del Medico, Quadri, & Jaeckle, 1990). Perhaps in the future, however, research will definitively demonstrate the specificity and uniqueness of the disorder, and it will merit a diagnosis of its own.

Organic Mood Disorder/ Mood Disorder Due to a General Medical Condition

The concept of a disorder that meets some or all of the criteria for a mood disturbance, and that has its onset rather abruptly following brain dysfunction, has existed in many classification schemes. Lipowski (1990) attributes the first use of this concept to Stahl in 1707. In the earlier versions of the DSM, the term "organic" referred to disorders that included global intellectual impairment. More recently, in DSM-III-R, organic mental disorders included a variety of cognitive, affective, and personality changes thought to have their etiological base in some form of brain dysfunction. Of particular interest here is that organic mood disorder encompassed a range of affective symptoms, including persistent depressed mood, that might be attributed to "a specific organic factor." The DSM-IV work group proposed dropping the term "organic," and instead categorized this disorder as a "mood disorder secondary to a nonpsychiatric medical condition" (Tucker, Popkin, Caine, Folstein, & Grant, 1990). DSM-IV thus uses the categorical description of "mood disorder due to a general medical condition" (American Psychiatric Association, 1994).

The DSM-IV work group's proposal sparked a lively debate concerning the importance and utility of the term "organic." The work group maintained that the organic–nonorganic dichotomy was "obsolete" (Tucker et al., 1990). Other authors (Spitzer, Williams, First, & Kendler, 1989; Spitzer et al., 1992), took the position that the organic–nonorganic distinction was inextricably tied to an outmoded mind–body dualism. In addition, they pointed to advances in knowledge of the relationship between central nervous system function and psychiatric disorders, and correctly pointed out that many of the traditional functional disorders (such as schizophrenia) have biological elements as a major part of their etiology.

Fogel (1990) raised similar issues with respect to the fact that diagnosis of major depression versus organic mood disorder required the exclusion of causal organic factors. He pointed out that rules for weighing various causes of depression were not specified, and that the distinction between causal and contributory factors was arbitrary. Fogel also suggested eliminating the category of organic mood disorder.

Lipkowski (1990, 1991) took issue with the "premature" burial of the term "organic." He adopted the formulation found in the 1989 draft of ICD-10, which characterizes organic syndromes as those that can be attributed to an "independently diagnosable cerebral or systemic disease" (World Health Organization, 1989, p. 30). Lipowski maintained that a true dichotomy exists between these disorders and those for which the etiology, biological or otherwise, is not yet clear. Moreover, emphasizing the etiology in this way places priority on the diagnosis and treatment of the underlying disorder (Lipowski, 1990; Fava, 1992).

Whether one prefers the description "organic mood disorder" or "mood disorder due to a general medical condition," a number of issues demand attention. Of interest in this chapter is whether or not depression occurs as a result of brain dysfunction, and if so, whether that type of disorder differs in any important ways from other depressive disorders. Put another way, is a depression related to a physiological event, such as stroke or traumatic brain injury, phenomenologically different from a major depression or dysthymic disorder that occurs in a different context? It is difficult to distinguish for a particular individual between the depressive reaction to disability or other aspects of the brain injury, and depression more directly resulting from the physiological insult.

This issue has been addressed in studies of the presentation of depression in patients following brain injury and strokes. Depression may be the most common emotional complaint identified in patients with neurological dysfunction (Messner & Messner, 1988). A depressive or catastrophic reaction is commonly observed in patients with left-hemisphere brain damage, especially those with aphasia, and a significant inverse relationship has been found between the severity of depression and distance of lesion from the frontal pole (Robinson, Kubos, Starr, Rao, & Price, 1983; Starkstein, Robinson, & Price, 1988). Other researchers, however, have found that depression per se is not common among stroke survivors. House et al. (1991) did not find depression to be a common sequela to stroke; instead, they found a high incidence of emotional lability, which they have stated may

be the basis for others' reports of poststroke depression. Thus, there seems to be some disagreement as to whether a depressive syndrome, as opposed to intermittently depressed mood, occurs as a result of physiological insult.

Jorge, Robinson, and Arndt (1993a) studied the presence of vegetative and psychological symptoms of depression in 66 patients with traumatic brain injury, and conducted 6-month and 1-year follow-up evaluations. They found that both vegetative and psychological symptoms were more frequent in the group with depressed mood, and that the DSM-III-R criteria for major depression correctly identified the depressed group. Jorge et al. (1993b) have suggested that the depressive symptoms in the acute stage of recovery may be attributable to biological factors, whereas depression occurring in the late stage may be attributable to psychological factors. If this is the case, then the differentiation of "organic" and "nonorganic" depressions in the same individual becomes more difficult.

Federoff, Starkstein, Parikh, Price, and Robinson (1991) examined the presence of depressive symptoms in acute stroke patients. As Jorge et al. (1993a) found with their brain-injured patients, both autonomic (vegetative) and psychological symptoms were found more often in stroke patients with depressed mood, and patients without depressed mood reported only an average of one autonomic symptom. The results of Federoff et al.'s study also indicate that the presentation of depression that may be physiologically based may not be differentiable from the more spontaneously occurring depressions. The causal factors of depression may change over the course of the episode as well. Location of lesion and severity of depression are highly correlated during the first few months following brain trauma, suggesting a possible biological link. However, as the time after the trauma increases, the location becomes much less important, and factors such as social adjustment and degree of disability account for more of the variance in depression levels.

In addition to the symptomatic presentation and course of illness, the response to treatment must be considered in comparing spontaneously occurring depression and depression that may be physiologically based. Tricyclic antidepressants have been shown to be effective in reducing depression in stroke patients (Lipsey, Robinson, Pearlson, Rao, & Price, 1984; Reding et al., 1987; Gualtieri, 1988). Moreover, psychotherapy is being increasingly used for depression, as well as other mood disorders, in brain-injured patients (Jenkins, 1993; Leber & Jenkins, in press). Although outcome studies specifically aimed at delineating the mood symptoms that respond to particular interventions have not been carried out, it is clear that a combination of psychological interventions improves the emotional and social functioning of individuals who have suffered brain trauma. Considerable work is still required to determine whether depression that may be linked to a readily identifiable physiological cause is different from other depressions.

THE MINOR VARIATIONS OF MOOD DISORDERS

The classification of depression requires categories for lesser forms of mood disorder. For example, chronic (2-year) cycling between hypomania and episodes of depression, but without major depression is classified as cyclothymic disorder. Short-term forms of mild depression that occur within 3 months of an identifiable stressor are labeled in DSM-IV as adjustment disorder with depressed mood or adjustment disorder with mixed anxiety and depressed mood. Depressive disorder NOS includes premenstrual dysphoric disorder, minor depressive disorder, and recurrent brief depressive disorder (as well as three other groups of depressive symptoms). Each of these three disorders is also listed, with specific criteria, in the appendix "Criteria Sets and Axes Provided for Further Study." For further information on these, the reader is referred to DSM-IV. DSM-IV chose not to include depressive personality disorder as an accepted Axis II diagnostic category, but it also is listed among the diagnoses for further study. DSM-IV remarks, "It remains controversial whether the distinction between depressive personality disorder and Dysthymic Disorder is useful" (American Psychiatric Association, 1994, p. 732).

DSM-IV AND ICD-10

ICD-10 has been developed by the World Health Organization (1992), and its preparation has overlapped in time with the preparation of DSM-IV. However, considerably different principles underlie the DSM and ICD systems. One major criterion of classification of affective disorders in the ICD is the occurrence of a single episode of depression or mania versus the presence of multiple or bipolar episodes. This principle has been adopted for only some DSM-IV disorders (e.g., major depression and bipolar I disorder). The second major classificatory principle in ICD-10 is severity of the disorder, which was chosen because different treatments will probably be used for various levels of severity, and because different levels of health care service must be planned for and made available. DSM-IV tends toward classification of different disorder, rather than levels of severity. A third ICD-10 principle does resemble one in DSM-IV: ICD-10 notes the presence or absence of somatic (melancholic) symptoms with depressive and bipolar disorders, and includes this as an additional modifier. Finally, the number of categories in DSM-IV is greater than in ICD-10, partially because of the presence in DSM-IV of cross-sectional symptom features and course specifiers.

As mentioned earlier, DSM-IV and ICD-10 differ in the classification of mood disorders related to cerebral or systemic disease. DSM-IV implicitly classifies these as secondary mood disorders by using the categorical descriptor "mood disorder due to a general medical condition." By classifying this type of disorder within the mood disorders section and by emphasizing "mood disorder" in the diagnostic title, DSM-IV relies on the symptoms observed as the primary factor in diagnosis. ICD-10 bases its classification primarily on the identified or presumed etiology, and thus classifies these mood disorders with such other disorders as dementia and post-concussional syndrome. ICD-10 also includes a hybrid category: "mixed anxiety and depressive disorder." Although this category is included with anxiety disorders, the description indicates that if only one diagnosis can be used, depression should be given precedence.

The importance of differences between DSM-IV and ICD-10 has been minimized by Spitzer and his colleagues (Spitzer et al., 1992), and emphasized by others (Lipowski, 1990). DSM-IV has the appearance of being a more complex system, which may be due to the fact that it was developed to be used by professionals specializing in mental health. The mental disorders section of ICD-10 has been designed for use by primary care professionals, as well as specialists. ICD-10 has also attempted to take into account the implications of a diagnostic system for health care planning on a large scale. Because ICD-10 allows and requires much more clinical judgment than DSM-IV, it may appear somewhat vague to U.S. mental health professionals, who are by now accustomed to more highly operationalized criteria. Nevertheless, it should still be possible for a clinician using it to classify any particular case within the appropriate ICD category without contradiction.

PROBLEMS WITH DSM-III-R AND DSM-IV

DSM-III-R has been criticized as relying excessively on phenotypic considerations; this reliance has been said to result in overlapping syndromes that have little to do with distinguishing underlying biological disorders (van Praag, 1989). Along those lines, van Praag points out that there are no symptoms that *must* be diagnosed for a diagnosis of major depression or dysthymic disorder. Instead, there are groups of symptoms with a requirement that a certain *number* be present. This can, he points out, result in a variety of underlying disorders' being diagnosed. Yet the problem may not be, as van Praag points out, with the criteria themselves. The problem may lie in the symptomatic approach to diagnosing underlying depression. The situation is something like attempting to determine types of pollution on the earth from color satellite photos. One may be too far removed from the problem to be able to diagnose the problem fully. On the other hand, biological markers of types of depression have thus far proved elusive and expensive. For the time being, a symptomatic approach to diagnosis appears to be the only feasible approach.

Another problem is that DSM-IV has now enumerated at least 15 types and subtypes of mood disorders. There are over 50 different code combinations for mood disorders. This is likely to be both a strength and a weakness for DSM-IV. The specific description of so many variations allows for better communication regarding the particular disorder being diagnosed or treated. On the other hand, the increased specificity will require increased information and time spent on diagnosis. It will be inaccurate or useless unless clinicians are fully familiar with the diagnostic system and accurately elicit and process the required information for diagnosis. From a theoretical point of view, the

multiplying of diverse categories may obscure underlying similarities between or among various symptom pictures, and may lead to excessively descriptive diagnosis. However, it is unlikely that the DSM-IV authors would have been able to find a compromise to this issue that would please everyone.

Third, it is not clear why some symptoms clearly related to major depression are not part of DSM-IV criteria for the disorder. Most important among these symptoms are hopelessness and social withdrawal.

A fourth area that has not been addressed well enough in the DSM criteria is the differentiation of grief and depression. Normal grief experienced when a loved one dies is categorized under the nondiagnostic "V codes" as uncomplicated bereavement. Clayton, Halikas, and Maurice (1972) reported that 35% of a sample of widowed subjects experienced symptomatology sufficient in severity and quality to meet criteria for major depression in the month following the spouse's death. Accordingly, DSM-IV notes that normal bereavement may include much of the symptomatology of major depression, with certain explicit exceptions (American Psychiatric Association, 1994, pp. 684–685). Thus, it is the occurrence of a death that mainly differentiates major depression from uncomplicated bereavement. The ironic result of this is that, for example, if a woman's husband dies and she experiences depression, it is not considered a disorder; however, if her husband leaves her and she never sees him again, the same symptomatology could qualify as major depression. Although the events are quite similar in their effects—that is, loss of a major part of the social support system—they lead to very different diagnoses.

Another problem is that adjustment disorder with depressed mood is classified outside of the mood disorders. This diagnosis may include some depressions of moderate severity not quite meeting the criteria for major depression. Some of the depressions classified in this category would have more in common with mood disorders than with the other adjustment disorders.

A final limitation of the DSM subtypes of depression is their relative lack of demonstrated predictive validity for psychotherapeutic intervention. The DSM subtypes tend to be more focused on categories that have some predictive validity regarding pharmacological treatment. Currently, research has not been published that indicates that the DSM categories of depression provide for differential prediction of psycho-therapeutic success. At the time DSM-III was published, it was proposed that a sixth axis would be necessary—one that could be labeled "psychodynamic evaluation" (Karasu & Skodol, 1980). The purpose of this axis would be to provide additional information in the diagnosis that would be useful in formulating psychothera-peutic intervention. Any attempt to develop such an axis, however, would certainly run into difficulty, since it would require agreement on a theoretical system. Still, the fact remains that DSM's atheoretical approach often provides little direction regarding appropriate nonsoma-tic, psychological intervention.

FUTURE DIRECTIONS IN CLASSIFICATION

A Biological Classification of Depression?

An approach that differs from the descriptive diagnostic systems discussed in this chapter—one that uses laboratory diagnostic procedures to distinguish biologically based depressions from nonbiologically based depressions—may eventually be possible. Such a diagnostic pro-cedure might well have the advantage of being able to predict relative treatment response to psychotherapy and somatic therapies. The clas-sification systems already discussed attempt to achieve this by using descriptive criteria, call-ing biological depression "primary," "endog-enous," "melancholic," "endogenomorphic," and so forth. A biological classification based on laboratory data might well prove to be more valid. However, such techniques seem to be even further away than when the first edition of the present book was published in 1985. The dexamethasone suppression test, REM latency measures, and other tests have lacked either the sensitivity or the specificity needed to be use-ful clinical measures.

A Classification Based on Psychosocial Processes?

The classification of depression need not be lim-ited to biological processes, treatment response, and so on. Another important dimension for diagnostic classification that has yet to be uti-lized is the nature of the psychological and so-cial factors that may precipitate or maintain depression. Study of depressed patients might reveal subgroups of different psychological dy-namics, each amenable to a particular type of psychotherapeutic intervention.

A prototype of such a diagnostic classification is present in the formulation of "interpersonal psychotherapy" (IPT; see Markowitz & Weiss-man, Chapter 13, this volume). Klerman, Weiss-man, Rounsaville, and Chevron (1984) concep-tualize depression as arising from one of four sources: unresolved grief, interpersonal role disputes, interpersonal deficits, and role tran-sitions. Specific strategies of IPT are employed to deal with each of these problem areas. The problem areas outlined by Klerman et al. (1984) are obviously theorized to describe certain groups of patients and to have utility in the ap-plication of IPT (although, to our knowledge, no studies have yet been done to assess the impor-tance of such classification and its impact on IPT outcomes).

Beck (1983) has suggested that there are two types of depressed patients: those with autono-mous schemas, and those whose depressions are more sociotropic and reflect a high need for approval and positive reinforcement from others. There is evidence that such categories provide useful information about what types of events may trigger depressions for individuals (i.e., events relating to autonomy for autono-mous depressives, and events relating to inter-personal rejection and loss for sociotropic in-dividuals) (Robins, 1990; Hammen, Ellicott, Gitlin, & Jamison, 1989). Beck also views the autonomous type of depression as having simi-larities to endogenous depression.

Other psychological categories for defining "subtypes" of depression could include loss of positive social reinforcers, uncontrollable envi-ronmental stress, early abuse, attachment diffi-culties, or chronic characterological features (e.g., emotional lability). Depressions concep-tualized as arising from each of these sources may be need to be approached in a different psychotherapeutic manner. The development of a diagnostic system that would allow for the specification of such factors, followed by appro-priate research, could greatly assist clinicians in quickly identifying differential treatments for various depressions. The major obstacle to the development of such a system is the lack of a widely held, common theoretical understand-ing of the etiology of depression. However, within specific theoretical systems such catego-ries could be readily developed, as has been done with IPT.

CONCLUSION

The diagnosis of depressive disorders has advanced considerably since Kraepelin's time, and its evolution is continuing. Diagnostic processes are currently based primarily on description of overt symptoms, and diagnostic understandings based on underlying processes are progressing more slowly. An ideal diagnostic system would separate depressions into homogeneous categories that could be differentiated from one another on the basis of symptoms, biology, and/or psychosocial features. Diagnostic categories within such a system would need to provide considerable information regarding the etiology, course, prognosis, and treatment response of different groups. The system would also need to use decision criteria that would not require expensive or overly time-consuming procedures. The present diagnostic categories may be considered marginally adequate by comparison with this ideal.

REFERENCES

Abou-Saleh, M. T., & Coppen, A. (1983). Classification of depression and response to antidepressive therapies. *British Journal of Psychiatry, 143,* 601–603.

Akiskal, H. S., Walker, P., Puzantian, V. R., King, D., Rosenthal, T. L., & Dranon, M. (1983). Bipolar outcome in the course of depressive illness: Phenomenologic, familial and pharmacologic predictors. *Journal of Affective Disorders, 5*(2), 115–128.

Akiskal, H. S., & Weise, R. E. (1992). The clinical spectrum of so-called "minor" depressions. *American Journal of Psychotherapy, 46,* 9–22.

Allen, J. M., Lam, R. W., Remick, R. A., & Sadovnick, A. D. (1993). Depressive symptoms and family history in seasonal and nonseasonal mood disorders. *American Journal of Psychiatry, 150,* 443–448.

American Psychiatric Association. (1968). *Diagnostic and statistical manual of mental disorders* (2nd ed.). Washington, DC: Author.

American Psychiatric Association. (1980). *Diagnostic and statistical manual of mental disorders* (3rd ed.). Washington, DC: Author.

American Psychiatric Association. (1987). *Diagnostic and statistical manual of mental disorders* (3rd ed., rev.). Washington, DC: Author.

American Psychiatric Association. (1991). *DSM-IV options book: Work in progress.* Washington, DC: Author.

American Psychiatric Association. (1994). *Diagnostic and statistical manual of mental disorders* (4th ed.). Washington, DC: Author.

Andreasen, N. C. (1982). Concepts, diagnosis and classification of depression. In E. S. Paykel (Ed.), *Handbook of affective disorders* (pp. 24–44). New York: Guilford Press.

Andreasen, N. C., & Grove, W. M. (1982). The classification: Traditional versus mathematical approaches. *American Journal of Psychiatry, 139,* 45–52.

Andreasen, N. C., Rice, J., Endicott, J., Coryell, W., Grove, W. M., & Reich, T. (1987). Familial rates of affective disorder: A report from the National Institute of Mental Health collaborative study. *Archives of General Psychiatry, 44,* 461–469.

Andreasen, N. C., Scheftner, W., Reich, T., Hirschfeld, R. M. A., Endicott, J., & Keller, M. B. (1986). The validation of the concept of endogenous depression: A family study approach. *Archives of General Psychiatry, 43,* 246–251.

Angst, J. (1966). Zur Atiologie and Nosologie endogener depressiver Psychosen. *Monographien aus dem Gesamtgebiete der Neurologie and Psychiatrie, 76,* 489–500.

Bauer, M. S., & Dunner, D. L. (1993). Validity of seasonal pattern as a modifier for recurrent mood disorders for DSM-IV. *Comprehensive Psychiatry, 34,* 159–170.

Beck, A. T. (1983). Cognitive therapy of depression: New perspectives. In P. J. Clayton & J. E. Barrett (Eds.), *Treatment of depression: Old controversies and new approaches* (pp. 265–290). New York: Raven Press.

Beigel, A., & Murphy, D. L. (1971). Unipolar and bipolar affective illnesses: Differences in clinical characteristics accompanying depression. *Archives of General Psychiatry, 24,* 215–220.

Bellini, L., Gatti, F., Gasperini, M., & Smeraldi, E. (1991). A comparison between delusional and non-delusional depressives. *Journal of Affective Disorders, 25,* 129–138.

Benjaminsen, S. (1981). Primary endogenous depression and features attributed to reactive depression. *Journal of Affective Disorders, 3,* 245–259.

Bertelson, A., Harvald, B., & Hauge, M. (1977). A Danish twin study of manic–depressive disorders. *British Journal of Psychiatry, 130,* 330–351.

Billings, A. G., Cronkite, R. C., & Moos, R. H. (1983). Social-environmental factors in unipolar depression: Comparisons of depressed patients and nondepressed controls. *Journal of Abnormal Psychology, 92,* 119–133.

Black, D. W., Winokur, G., & Nasrallah, A. (1988). Effect of psychosis on suicide risk in 1,593 patients with unipolar and bipolar affective disorders. *American Journal of Psychiatry, 145,* 849–852.

Blashfield, R. K., & Draguns, J. G. (1976a). Evaluation criteria for psychiatric classification. *Journal of Abnormal Psychology, 85,* 151–155.

Blashfield, R. K., & Draguns, J. G. (1976b). Toward a taxonomy of pathology: The purpose of psychiatric classification. *British Journal of Psychiatry, 129,* 574–583.

Boyd, J. H., & Weissman, M. M. (1981). Epidemiology of affective disorders. *Archives of General Psychiatry, 38,* 1039–1046.

Brill, H. (1974). Classification and nomenclature of psychiatric conditions. In S. Arieti (Ed.), *American handbook of psychiatry* (2nd ed., Vol. 1, pp. 1121–1137). New York: Basic Books.

Brown, G. W., & Harris, T. (1978). *Social origins of depression: A study of psychiatric disorder in women.* New York: Free Press.

Carlsson, G. A., Kotin, J., Davenport, Y. B., & Adland, M. (1974). Follow-up of 53 bi-polar manic depressive patients. *British Journal of Psychiatry, 124,* 134–139.

Casper, R. C., Redmond, D. E., Jr., Katz, M. M., Schaffer, C. B., Davis, J. M., & Koslow, S. H. (1985). Somatic symptoms in primary affective disorder: Presence and relationship to the classification of depression. *Archives of General Psychiatry, 42,* 1098–1104.

Caveny, E. L., Wittson, C. L., Hunt, W. A., & Herrman, R. S. (1955). Psychiatric diagnosis: Its nature and function. *Journal of Nervous and Mental Disease, 121,* 367–373.

Clayton, P. J., Halikas, J. A., & Maurice, W. L. (1972). The depression of widowhood. *British Journal of Psychiatry, 120,* 71–78.

Coppen, A., Metcalfe, M., & Wood, K. (1982). Lithium. In E. S. Paykel (Ed.), *Handbook of affective disorders* (pp. 276–285). New York: Guilford Press.

Coryell, W., Endicott, J., Reich, T., Andreasen, N., & Keller, M. (1984). A family study of bipolar II disorder. *British Journal of Psychiatry, 145,* 49–54.

Coryell, W., Keller, M., Endicott, J., Andreasen, N., Clayton, P., & Hirschfeld, R. (1989). Bipolar II illness: Course and outcome over a five-year period. *Psychological Medicine, 19,* 129–141.

Coryell, W., Scheftner, W., Keller, M., Endicott, J., Maser, J., & Klerman, G.L. (1993). The enduring psychosocial consequences of mania and depression. *American Journal of Psychiatry, 150,* 720–727.

Coryell, W., & Tsuang, M. T. (1982). Primary unipolar depression and the prognostic importance of delusions. *Archives of General Psychiatry, 39,* 1181–1184.

Coryell, W., & Winokur, G. (1992). Course and outcome. In E. S. Paykel (Ed.), *Handbook of affective disorders* (2nd ed., pp. 89–110). New York: Guilford Press.

Coryell, W., Winokur, G., Shea, T., Maser, J. D., Endicott, J., & Akiskal, H. S. (1994). The long-term stability of depressive subtypes. *American Journal of Psychiatry, 141,* 199–204.

Costello, C.G. (1982). Social factors associated with depression: A retrospective community study. *Psychological Medicine, 12,* 329–339.

Davidson, J., Turnbull, C., Strickland, R., & Belyea, M. (1984). Comparative diagnostic criteria for melancholia and endogenous depression. *Archives of General Psychiatry, 4,* 506–511.

Detre, T., Himmelhoch, J., Swartzburg, M., Anderson, C. M., Byck, R., & Kupfer, D. J. (1972). Hypersomnia and manic–depressive disease. *American Journal of Psychiatry, 128,* 1303–1305.

Dilsaver, S. C., Del Medico, V. J., Quadri, A., & Jaeckle, S. (1990). Pharmacological responsiveness of winter depression. *Psychopharmacology Bulletin, 26,* 303–309.

Dunner, D. L. (1987). Atypical bipolar disorders: Stability of bipolar II affective disorder as a diagnostic entity. *Psychiatric Annals, 17,* 18–20.

Dunner, D. L., Gershon, E. S., & Goodwin, F. K. (1976). Heritable factors in the severity of affective illness. *Biological Psychiatry, 11,* 31–42.

Dunner, D. L., Stallone, F., & Fieve, R. R. (1982). Prophylaxis with lithium carbonate: An update [Letter to the editor]. *Archives of General Psychiatry, 39,* 1344–1345.

Fairchild, C. J., Rush, A., Vasavada, N., Giles, D. E., & Khatami, M. (1986). Which depressions respond to placebo? *Psychiatric Research, 18,* 217–226.

Faravelli, C., & Poli, E. (1982). Stability of the diagnosis of primary affective disorder: A four-year follow-up study. *Journal of Affective Disorders, 4,* 35–39.

Fava, G. A. (1992). Comments on the proposal to eliminate the organic mental disorders category in DSM-IV. (Letter to the editor). *American Journal of Psychiatry, 149,* 429–430.

Federoff, J. P., Starkstein, S. E., Parikh, R. M., Price T. R., & Robinson, R. G. (1991). Are depressive symptoms nonspecific in patients with acute stroke? *American Journal of Psychiatry, 148,* 1172–1176.

Feighner, J. P., Robins, E., Guze, S. B., Woodruff, R. A., Winokur, G., & Munoz, R. (1972). Diagnostic criteria for use in psychiatric research. *Archives of General Psychiatry, 26,* 57–63.

Feinberg, M., & Carroll, B. J. (1982). Separation of subtypes of depression using discriminant analysis: I. Separation of unipolar endogenous depression from nonendogenous depression. *British Journal of Psychiatry, 140,* 384–391.

Feinberg, M., & Carroll, B. J. (1983). Separation of subtypes of depression using discriminant analysis: II. Separation of bipolar endogenous depression from nonendogenous ("neurotic") depression. *Journal of Affective Disorders, 5,* 129–139.

Fennig, S., Bromet, E., & Jandorf, L. (1993). Gender differences in clinical characteristics of first-admission psychotic depression. *American Journal of Psychiatry, 150*(11), 1734–1736.

Fieve, R. R., Go, R., Dunner, D. L., & Elston, R. (1984). Search for biological/genetic markers in a long-term epidemiological and morbid risk study of affective disorders. *Journal of Psychiatric Research, 18,* 425–445.

Fink, M. (1993). Catatonic and psychotic (delusional) depression, distinct syndromes in DSM-IV [Letter to the editor]. *American Journal of Psychiatry, 150*(7), 1130–1131.

Fogel, B. (1990). Major depression versus organic mood disorder: A questionable distinction. *Journal of Clinical Psychiatry, 51,* 53–56.

Frances, A., Kocsis, J., Marin, D., Manning, D., Markowitz, J., Mason, B., & Widiger, T. (1989). Diagnostic criteria for dysthymic disorder. *Psychopharmacology Bulletin, 25,* 325–329.

Georgotas, A., McCue, R. E., Cooper, T., Chang, I., Mir, P., & Welkowitz, J. (1987). Clinical predictors of response to antidepressants in elderly patients. *Biological Psychiatry, 22,* 733–740.

Gershon, E. S., Hamovit, J., Guroff, J. J., Dibble, E., Leckman, J. F., Sceery, W., Targum, S. D., Nurnberger, J. I., Goldin, L. R., & Bunney, W. E. (1982). A family study of schizoaffective, bipolar I, bipolar II, unipolar, and normal probands. *Archives of General Psychiatry, 39,* 1157–1167.

Gillespie, R. D. (1929). Clinical differentiation of types of depression. *Guy's Hospital Reprints, 79,* 306–344.

Glassman, A. H., & Roose, S. P. (1981). Delusional depression: A distinct entity? *Archives of General Psychiatry, 38,* 424–427.

Goodwin, D. W., & Guze, S. B. (1984). *Psychiatric diagnosis.* New York: Oxford University Press.

Gordon, D., Burge, D., Hammen, C., Adrean, C., Jaenicke, C., & Hiroto, D. (1989). Observations of interactions of depressed women with their children. *American Journal of Psychiatry, 146,* 50–55.

Gualtieri, C. T. (1988). Pharmacotherapy and the neurobehavioural sequelae of traumatic brain injury. *Brain Injury, 2,* 101–129.

Gurpegui, M., Casanova, J., & Cervera, S. (1985). Clinical and neuroendocrine features of endogenous unipolar and bipolar depression. *Acta Psychiatrica Scandinavica, 72*(Suppl. 320): 30–37.

Hammen, C., Ellicott, A., Gitlin, M., & Jamison, K. R. (1989). Sociotropy/autonomy and vulnerability to specific life events in patients with unipolar depression and bipolar disorders. *Journal of Abnormal Psychology, 94,* 154–160.

Helzer, J. E., Clayton, P. J., Pambakian, R., Reich, T., Woodruff, R. A., & Reveley, M. A. (1977a). Reliability of psychiatric diagnosis: II. The test/retest reliability of diagnostic classifications. *Archives of General Psychiatry, 34,* 136–141.

Helzer, J. E., Robins, L. N., Taibelson, M., Woodruff, R. A., Reich, T., & Wish, E. D. (1977b). Reliability of psychiatric diagnosis: I. A methodological review. *Archives of General Psychiatry, 34,* 129–133.

Hirschfeld, R. M. A. (1981). Situational depression: Validity of the concept. *British Journal of Psychiatry, 139,* 297–305.

Hirschfeld, R. M. A., Klerman, G., Andreasen, N., Clayton, P., & Keller, M. (1985). Situational major depressive disorder. *Archives of General Psychiatry, 42,* 1109–1114.

House, A., Dennis, M., Mogridge, L., Warlow, C., Hawton, K., & Jones, L. (1991). Mood disorders in the first year after stroke. *British Journal of Psychiatry, 158,* 83–92.

Jenkins, M. R. (1993). Individual therapy with brain-injury survivors. In W. R. Leber (Chair), *Psychotherapy with brain-injured clients and their families.* Symposium presented at the 101st Annual Convention of the American Psychological Association, Toronto.

Jorge, R. E., Robinson, R. G., & Arndt, S. (1993a). Are there symptoms that are specific for depressed mood in patients with traumatic brain injury? *Journal of Nervous and Mental Disease, 181,* 91–99.

Jorge, R. E., Robinson, R. G., Arndt, S. V., Starkstein, S. E., Forrester, A. W., & Geisler, F. (1993b). Depression following traumatic brain injury: A one-year longitudinal study. *Journal of Affective Disorders, 27,* 233–243.

Kane, J. M., Quitkin, F. M., Rifkin, A., Ramos-Lorenzi, J. R., Nayak, D. D., & Howard, A. (1982). Lithium carbonate and imipramine in the prophylaxis of unipolar and bipolar II illness. *Archives of General Psychiatry, 39,* 1065–1069.

Karasu, T. B., & Skodol, A. E. (1980). VIth Axis for DSM-III: Psychodynamic evaluation. *American Journal of Psychiatry, 137,* 607–610.

Katz, M. M., Robins, E., Croughan, J., Secunda, S., & Swann, A. (1982). Behavioural measurement and drug response characteristics of unipolar and bipolar depression. *Psychological Medicine, 12,* 25–36.

Keller, M. B., & Lavori, P. W. (1984). Double depression, major depression, and dysthymia: Distinct entities or different phases of a single disorder? *Psychopharmacology Bulletin, 20,* 399–402.

Keller, M. B., Lavori, P. W., Endicott, J., Coryell, W., & Klerman, G. L. (1983). "Double depression": Two-year follow-up. *American Journal of Psychiatry, 140,* 689–694.

Kendall, R. E. (1976). The classifications of depression: A review of contemporary confusion. *British Journal of Psychiatry, 129,* 15–28.

Klein, D. F. (1974). Endomorphic depression: A conceptual and terminological revision. *Archives of General Psychiatry, 31,* 447–454.

Klein, D. F. (1978). A proposed definition of mental illness. In R. L. Spitzer & D. F. Klein (Eds.), *Critical issues in psychiatric diagnosis.* New York: Raven Press.

Klein, D. N. (1990). Depressive personality: Reliability, validity, and relation to dysthymia. *Journal of Abnormal Psychology, 99,* 412–421.

Klerman, G. L., Endicott, J., Spitzer, R., & Hirschfeld, R. M. A. (1979). Neurotic depressions: A systemic analysis of multiple criteria and meanings. *American Journal of Psychiatry, 136,* 57–61.

Klerman, G. L., Weissman, M. M., Rounsaville, B. J., & Chevron, E. S. (1984). *Interpersonal psychotherapy for depression.* New York: Basic Books.

Kocsis, J. H., Croughan, J. L., Katz, M. M., Butler, T. P., Secunda, S., Bowden, C. L., & Davis, J. M. (1990). Response to treatment with antidepressants of patients with severe or moderate nonpsychotic depression and of patients with psychotic depression. *American Journal of Psychiatry, 147,* 621–624.

Kocsis, J. H., Voss, C., Mann, J. J., & Frances, A. (1986). Chronic depression: Demographic and clinical characteristics. *Psychopharmacological Bulletin, 22,* 192–195.

Kraepelin, E. (1921). *Textbook of psychiatry* (8th ed.): Vol. 3. *Manic–depressive insanity and paranoia* (R. M. Barclay, Trans.; G. M. Robertson, Ed.). Edinburgh: E. & S. Livingstone. (Original work published 1913)

Leonhard, K. (1957). *Aufteilung der Endogenen Psychosen.* Berlin: Akademieverlag.

Leber, W. R., & Jenkins, M. R. (in press). Psychotherapy with brain-injured patients and their families. In O. A. Parsons, R. L. Adams, & J. Culbertson (Eds.), *Neuropsychology for the clinical psychologist.* Washington, DC: American Psychological Association.

Lester, D. (1971). Seasonal variation in suicidal deaths. *British Journal of Psychiatry, 118,* 627–628.

Liebowitz, M. R., & Klein, D. (1981). Interrelationship of hysteroid dysphoria and borderline personality disorder. *Psychiatric Clinics of North America, 4,* 67–87.

Liebowitz, M. R., Quitkin, F. M., Stewart, J. W., McGrath, P. J., Harrison, W., Rabkin, J., Tricamo, E., Markowitz, J. S., & Klein, D. F. (1984). Phenelzine versus imipramine in atypical depression: A preliminary report. *Archives of General Psychiatry, 41,* 669–677.

Lipowski, Z. J. (1990). Is "organic" obsolete? [Editorial]. *Psychosomatics, 31,* 342–344.

Lipowski, Z. J. (1991). Reply to R. Spitzer: Organic mental disorders and DSM-IV [Letter to the editor]. *American Journal of Psychiatry, 148,* 396–397.

Lipsey, J. R., Robinson, R. G., Pearlson, G. D., Rao, K., & Price, T. R. (1984). Nortriptyline treatment of post-stroke depression: A double-blind study. *Lancet, i,* 297–300.

Mattussek, P., Soldner, M., & Nagel, D. (1981). Identification of the endogenous depressive syndrome based on the symptoms and the characteristics of the course. *British Journal of Psychiatry, 138,* 361–372.

McCullough, J. P., Kasnetz, M. D., Braith, J. A., Carr, K. F., Cones, J. H., Fielo, J., & Martelli, M. F. (1988). A longitudinal study of an untreated sample of predominantly late onset characterological dysthymia. *Journal of Nervous and Mental Disease, 176,* 658–667.

Messner, M., & Messner, E. (1988). Mood disorder following stroke. *Comprehensive Psychiatry, 29,* 22–27.

Murphy, G. E., Woodruff, R. A., Herjanic, M., & Fischer, J. R. (1974). Validity of the diagnosis of primary affective disorder: A prospective study with a five-year follow-up. *Archives of General Psychiatry, 30,* 751–756.

Nelson, J. C., & Charney, D. S. (1981). The symptoms of major depressive illness. *American Journal of Psychiatry, 138,* 1–13.

Parker, G., Hadzi-Pavlovic, D., & Boyce, P. (1989). Endogenous depression as a construct: A quantitative analysis of the literature and a study of clinician judgements. *Australian and New Zealand Journal of Psychiatry, 23,* 357–368.

Parker, G., Hadzi-Pavlovic, D., Hickie, I., Boyce, P., Mitchell, P., Wilhelm, K., & Brodaty, H. (1991a). Distinguishing psychotic and non-psychotic melancholia. *Journal of Affective Disorders*, 22, 135–148.

Parker, G., Hadzi-Pavlovic, D., Hickie, I., Mitchell, P., Wilhelm, K., Brodaty, H., Boyce, P., Eyers, K., & Pedic, F. (1991b). Psychotic depression: A review and clinical experience. *Austrialian and New Zealand Journal of Psychiatry*, 25, 169–180.

Parker, G., Roy, K., Hadzi-Pavlovic, D., & Pedic, F. (1992). Psychotic (delusional) depression: A meta-analysis of physical treatments. *Journal of Affective Disorders*, 24, 17–24.

Paykel, E. S., Myers, J. K., Dienelt, M. N., Klerman, G. L., Lindenthal, J. J., & Pepper, M. P. (1969). Life events and depression: A Controlled study. *Archives of General Psychiatry*, 21, 753–760.

Paykel, E. S., & Cooper, Z. (1992). Life events and social stress. In E. S. Paykel (Ed.), *Handbook of affective disorders* (2nd ed., pp. 149–170). New York: Guilford Press.

Pearlin, L. I., & Schooler, C. (1978). The structure of coping. *Journal of Health and Social Behavior*, 19, 2–21.

Perris, C. (1966). A study of bipolar and unipolar recurrent depressive psychoses. *Acta Psychiatrica Scandinavica*, 42(Suppl. 194): 172–188.

Perris, C. (1992). Bipolar–unipolar distinction. In E. S. Paykel (Ed.), *Handbook of affective disorders* (2nd ed., pp. 57–75). New York: Guilford Press.

Perris, C., & Perris, H. (1978). Status within the family and early life experiences in patients with affective disorders and cycloid psychoses. *Psychiatria Clinica*, 11, 155–162.

Peselow, E. D., Sanfilipo, M. P., Difiglia, C., & Fieve, R. R. (1992). Melancholic/endogenous depression and response to somatic treatment and placebo. *American Journal of Psychiatry*, 149, 1324–1334.

Prusoff, B. A., Weissman, M. M., Klerman, G. L., & Rounsaville, B. J. (1980). Research Diagnostic Criteria subtypes of depression: Their role as predictors of differential response to psychotherapy and drug treatment. *Archives of General Psychiatry*, 37, 796–801.

Reding, M. J., Orto, L. A., Winter, S. W., Fortuna, I. M., Di Pontee, P., & McDowell, F. H. (1986). Antidepressant therapy after stroke: A double-blind study. *Archives of Neurology*, 43, 763–765.

Rice, J., Reich, T., Andreasen, N. C., Lavori, P. W., Endicott, J., Clayton, P. J., Keller, M. B., Hirschfeld, R. M., & Klerman, G. L. (1984). Sex-related differences in depression: Familial evidence. *Journal of Affective Disorders*, 7, 199–210.

Robins, C. J. (1990). Congruence of personality and life events in depression. *Journal of Abnormal Psychology*, 99, 393–397.

Robins, E., & Guze, S. B. (1972). Classification of affective disorders: The primary–secondary, the endogenous–reactive, and the neurotic–psychotic concept. In T. A. Williams, M. M. Katz, & J. A. Shield (Eds.), *Recent advances in the psychobiology of the depressive illnesses* (DHEW Publication No. HSM 79–9053, pp. 283–293). Washington, DC: U.S. Government Printing Office.

Robinson, R. G., Kubos, K. L., Starr, L. B., Rao, K., & Price, T. R. (1983). Mood changes in stroke patients: Relationship to lesion location. *Comprehensive Psychiatry*, 24, 555–566.

Roose, S. P., & Glassman, A. H. (1988). Delusional depression. In A. Georgotas & R. Cancro (Eds.), *Depression and mania* (pp. 76–85). New York: Elsevier.

Rosen, L. N., & Rosenthal, N. E. (1991). Seasonal variations in mood and behavior in the general population: A factor-analytic approach. *Psychiatry Research*, 38, 271–283.

Rush, A. J. (1993). Mood disorders in DSM-IV. In D. L. Dunner (Ed.), *Current psychiatric therapy* (pp. 189–195). Philadelphia: W. B. Saunders.

Rush, A. J., & Weissenburger, J. E. (1994). Melancholic symptom features and DSM-IV. *American Journal of Psychiatry*, 151, 489–498.

Souetre, E., Salvati, E., Belugou, J. L., Douillet, P., Braccini, T., & Darcourt, G. (1987). Seasonality of suicides: Environmental, sociological and biological covariations. *Journal of Affective Disorders*, 13, 215–225.

Spiker, D. G., Weiss, J. C., Dealy, R. S., Griffin, S. J., Hanin, I., Neil, J. F., Perel, J. M., Rossi, A. J., & Soloff, P. H. (1985). The pharmacological treatment of delusional depression. *American Journal of Psychiatry*, 142(4), 430–436.

Spitzer, R. L., & Endicott, J. (1978). Medical and mental disorder: Proposed definition. In R. L. Spitzer & D. F. Klein (Eds.), *Critical issues in psychiatric diagnosis*. New York: Raven Press.

Spitzer, R. L., Endicott, J., & Robins, E. (1978). Research Diagnostic Criteria: Rationale and reliability. *Archives of General Psychiatry*, 35, 773–782.

Spitzer, R. E., First, M. B., Williams, J. B. W., Kendler, K. S., Pincus, H. A., & Tucker, G. (1992). Now is the time to retire the term "organic mental disorders." *American Journal of Psychiatry*, 149, 240–244.

Spitzer, R. L., & Williams, J. B. W. (1980). Classification of mental disorders and DSM-III. In H. I. Kaplan, A. M. Freedman, & B. J. Sadock (Eds.), *Comprehensive textbook of psychiatry* (3rd ed., Vol. 1, pp. 1035–1072). Baltimore: Williams & Wilkins.

Spitzer, R. E., Williams, J. B. W., First, M. B., & Kendler, K. S. (1989). A proposal for DSM-IV: Solving the "organic/nonorganic" problem [Editorial]. *Journal of Neuropsychiatry and Clinical Neurosciences*, 1, 126–127.

Starkstein, S. E., Robinson, R. G., & Price, T. R. (1988). Comparison of patients with and without post-stroke major depression matched for size and location of lesion. *Archives of General Psychiatry*, 45, 247–252.

Stengel, E. (1959). Classification of mental disorders. *Bulletin of the World Health Organization*, 32, 601–621.

Strömgren, L. S. (1973). Unilateral versus bilateral electroconvulsive therapy: Investigations into the therapeutic effect in endogenous depression. *Acta Psychiatrica Scandinavica*, 49(Suppl. 240), 8–65.

Szasz, T. S. (1957). The problem of psychiatric nosology. *American Journal of Psychiatry*, 114, 405–413.

Thase, M. E., Carpenter, L., Kupfer, D. J., & Frank, E. (1991). Atypical depression: Diagnostic and pharmacologic controversies. *Psychopharmacology Bulletin*, 27, 17–22.

Trzebiatowska-Treciak, O. (1977). Genetical analysis of unipolar and bipolar endogenous affective psychoses. *British Journal of Psychiatry*, 131, 478–485.

Tucker, G., Popkin, M., Caine, E., Folstein, M., & Grant, I. (1990). Reorganizing the "organic" disorders. *Hospital and Community Psychiatry*, 41, 722–724.

van Praag, H. M. (1989). Moving ahead yet falling behind: A critical appraisal of some trends in contemporary depression research. *Neuropsychobiology*, 22, 181–193.

Warheit, G. J. (1979). Life events, coping, stress, and depressive symptomology. *American Journal of Psychiatry, 136,* 502–507.

Weissman, M. M., & Klerman, G. L. (1977). Sex differences in the epidemiology of depression. *Archives of General Psychiatry, 34,* 98–111.

Weissman, M. M., Pottenger, M., Klebver, H., Reuben, H. L., Williams, D., & Thompson, W. D. (1977). Symptom patterns in primary and secondary depression. *Archives of General Psychiatry, 34,* 98–111.

Winokur, G., Black, D. W., & Nasrallah, A. (1987). Neurotic depression: A diagnosis based on preexisting characteristics. *European Archives of Psychiatry and Neurological Sciences, 236,* 343–348.

Winokur, G., Clayton, P., & Reich, T. (1969). *Manic–depressive illness.* St. Louis: C. V. Mosby.

Winokur, G., Coryell, W., Endicott, J., & Akiskal, H. (1993a). Further distinctions between manic–depressive illness (bipolar disorder) and primary depressive disorder (unipolar depression). *American Journal of Psychiatry, 150,* 1176–1181.

Winokur, G., Coryell, W., Keller, M., Endicott, J., & Akiskal, H. (1993b). A prospective follow-up of patients with bipolar and unipolar affective disorder. *Archives of General Psychiatry, 50,* 457–465.

World Health Organization. (1978). *Mental disorders: Glossary and guide to their classification in accordance with the ninth revision of the* International Classification of Diseases. Geneva: Author.

World Health Organization. (1989). *World Health Organization 1989 draft of chapter 5: Mental and behavioral disorders.* Geneva: Author.

World Health Organization. (1992). *ICD-10 classification of mental and behavioural disorders: Clinical description and diagnostic guidelines.* Geneva: Author.

Zerbin-Rudin, E. (1969). Zur Genetik depressiver Erkrankungen. In Hippius & Selbach (Eds.), *Das Depressive Syndrom* (pp. 37–56). Munich: Urban & Schwarzenberg.

Zigler, E., & Phillips, L. (1961). Psychiatric diagnosis: A critique. *Journal of Abnormal and Social Psychology, 63,* 607–618.

3

The Assessment of Severity and Symptom Patterns in Depression

RANDY KATZ
BRIAN F. SHAW
T. MICHAEL VALLIS
AMY S. KAISER

This chapter is concerned with the assessment of psychological variables related to depression (specifically major depressive disorder [MDD]). Depression involves psychological (e.g., self-criticism, anhedonia), biological (e.g., weight loss, insomnia), and social (e.g., avoidance, passivity) symptoms that impair an individual's ability to function normally. The emphasis of this review is on methods for assessing the severity and symptom pattern of depression, with particular attention to the reliability, validity, and clinical utility of these measures.

Reliability and validity are important in the assessment of depression (or any construct) for at least three reasons. First, in order to design an appropriate intervention strategy, an accurate descriptive classification or diagnostic system needs to be established. Beutler, Wakefield, and Williams (1994) highlight the importance of psychological tests and instruments for treatment planning. As the number of psychological interventions for depression increases, the question of the efficacy of specific treatments with specific types of individuals will receive more attention. For instance, traditional clinical thinking posits that pharmacological or physiological interventions are particularly effective with certain subtypes of depression (e.g., tricyclic antidepressants for patients with endogenous depression without hypochondria), whereas almost by exclusion psychological interventions are frequently considered more effective for individuals not exhibiting these features. These treatment decisions place a heavy emphasis on accurate assessment and subtyping. Second, without a reliable and valid assessment, it becomes very difficult to select appropriate targets for intervention for a given individual's treatment. Some depressed patients, for example, exhibit pervasive anhedonia and require careful planning of daily activities. Others exhibit social skills deficits and benefit from skill acquisition programs. Third, in order to evaluate the effectiveness of therapy, some metric of symptom severity is required. If this metric lacks adequate reliability and/or validity, evaluation is impaired, if not prevented.

In our evaluation of the major psychological methods for assessing depression, we consider both interview methods and self-report methods of assessment. The review is not intended to be exhaustive; instead, it is designed for relatively easy use as a reference by the clinician. Assessment techniques can be categorized into those that screen for the *presence* of depression (i.e., diagnostic assessments concerned with inclusion and exclusion criteria) and those that assess the *severity* of depression (not directly relevant for diagnostic purposes). It is important not to confuse the types of information provided by these two types of tests.

When considering the assessment of depression, the clinician must always remain aware of the fact that depression is a multifaceted condition. Despite numerous efforts, work on subtyping this disorder has generally been unrewarding. Nevertheless, we can expect that in time research will provide clinically meaningful classifications (see Skinner & Blashfield, 1982). At present, one surprising error that can still be observed involves confusing the syndrome of depression with one of its symptoms (most frequently mood; see Beck, 1967). Thus, when an individual's mood changes, there is a tendency to think that all other symptoms will also change. A positive change in mood that sometimes precedes a suicide attempt is but one example of why one should not equate symptoms with the syndrome. Adequate assessment of depression should not be restricted to a single dimension such as mood, but should sample the range of relevant factors, including psychological, biological, and social functioning.

Before we begin our discussion of the psychological assessment of depression, a further word about subtypes of depression is in order. As a result of systematic research (e.g., Depue & Monroe, 1979), as well as the advent of the Research Diagnostic Criteria (RDC; Spitzer, Endicott, & Robins, 1978) and the revised third edition of the *Diagnostic and Statistical Manual of Mental Disorders* (DSM-III-R; American Psychiatric Association, 1987), attention to the value of classifying the depression has been renewed. Techniques reviewed in this chapter are most frequently used with the DSM-III-R categories of depressive disorders. One might question how psychological assessment fits with such categorization. Do all of the assessment measures apply to all categories, or only to certain subtypes? Our position is that regardless of the type of depression, it is essential to assess the severity and pattern of the depressive symptomatology. By classifying, we anticipate descriptive and prognostic differences between groups. An empirical emphasis on assessment will help determine the relevant differences. Please note that this chapter deals with the severity and symptom pattern of a depressive episode, not with differential diagnosis of depression. We focus mainly on the depressive aspect of affective disorders. Also, we include a discussion of relevant issues in assessing depression in the medically ill. Finally, for completeness, we review two selected measures of mania.

INTERVIEWING THE DEPRESSED PATIENT

Among the most frequently used interview methods are the Hamilton Rating Scale for Depression (HRSD; Hamilton, 1960; Hamilton & White, 1959), the depression subsection of the Schedule for Affective Disorders and Schizophrenia (SADS; Endicott & Spitzer, 1978), and the depression subsection of the Present State Examination (PSE; Wing, Birley, Cooper, Graham, & Isaacs, 1967; Wing, Cooper, & Sartorius, 1974; Wing et al., 1990). Prior to reviewing these methods, however, we consider some of the more practical issues involved in interviewing a depressed patient. These issues (common to all interviews) include the interviewer's knowledge of the disorder and of the behavioral correlates of depression, as well as the interviewer's clinical demeanor.

The task of interviewing a depressed patient can be a difficult and frustrating one, frequently accompanied by irritability and negative affect on the part of the interviewer (Beck, 1967). Depressed individuals may experience marked difficulties maintaining an interpersonal interaction, particularly when they are under pressure to produce information. They may be unresponsive, have difficulty following questions, or be nondisclosing, all of which can contribute to the interviewer's frustration.

Before the beginning of an interview, several factors need to be considered. It is assumed that the interviewer is familiar with the range of depressed symptomatology. Despite problems with and objections to the system (e.g., Smith & Kraft, 1983), familiarity with the latest edition of DSM (currently DSM-IV; American Psychiatric Association, 1994) is recommended. Interviewers should also be aware of the paradoxical reports of depressed patients. Beck (1967) discusses some of these paradoxes. For example, a successful businesswoman may portray her level of functioning as inefficient, when she has in fact experienced only a small change in an otherwise highly efficient manner. The reports of depressed patients are often stated in absolutes or extremes. It is important for the interviewer to have the necessary skills (i.e., warmth, empathy, ability to reflect content, feeling, or process) to be sensitive to a patient's verbal and nonverbal communication. These skills understandably increase the completeness and validity of the information obtained by increasing self-disclosure. For example, a patient may be seriously considering suicide and yet may be reluctant on first contact to tell this information to the interviewer. The probability of disclosure is increased if the clinician is perceived as understanding, warm, and concerned. Instructional texts, such as those by Evans, Hearn, Uhlemann, and Ivey (1984) or Othmer and Othmer (1989), are useful in developing these interviewing skills.

In terms of the actual content of the information obtained, the interviewer should obtain a relevant and complete history. This history should definitely include information about the current episode, past episodes, significant medical history, and family history. It is often useful to have the patient make an initial report on the Life History Questionnaire (Lazarus, 1971). Any additional relevant information on known markers or risk factors for depression (e.g., history of depression in first-degree relatives) should also be obtained. Kupfer and Rush (1983) have outlined the specific factors relevant to depression that should be included in scientific reports. This outline can also serve as a guide to the types of information clinicians should obtain from depressed patients and include in clinical reports.

When interviewing a depressed individual, it is important to work toward an understanding of the patient's phenomenology (i.e., the situation *from his/her perspective*). Although a patient's descriptions may seem implausible or exaggerated to the interviewer (e.g. "I am hollow inside," "I think I must be the devil, I'm so evil"), they are understandable in that they may be based on a negative view of the self, the world, and the future (Beck, 1967; Beck, Rush, Shaw, & Emery, 1979). Discussion of a diagnosis is reassuring to most patients who are confused about their symptomatology. However, diagnostic formulations should not be presented without a clear opportunity to answer questions. It is important that the interviewer avoid using the term "depressive" to describe the patient, as this may imply an unchangeable trait and thus may reinforce the notion that the patient will remain depressed. Most patients experience episodes of depression, and although they may remain vulnerable to depression, few are chronically depressed. Clinicians should also be aware that discussing diagnosis may increase a patient's sadness as a result of the labeling process (i.e., "I'm depressed because I'm depressed"). For these reasons, it is important to obtain feedback from patients as to their reactions to the interview and interviewer. De-

pressed patients may misinterpret an interviewer's comments in a negative way. For example, if an interviewer interrupts the patient in an attempt to structure the interview, the patient may interpret this behavior as an indication that the interviewer doesn't respect him/her, or is not really interested in what he/she has to say. Thus, it is useful to explain the constraints of the interview with respect to limited time, necessary information to be gathered, and the importance of direction at the onset of the interview before the patient may develop such negative reactions. Patients may be informed that their task is to let the interviewer see the full extent of their current feeling, thinking, and behavior. Some patients react self-critically if they cry, and a supportive, encouraging response is required. The clinician should avoid pejorative labeling of the patient and an attitude that the patient may *want* to be depressed. (Like defense lawyers, clinicians would be wise to assume that their patients want to be free—in this case, of depression.)

The clinician must always be sensitive to possible suicidal ideation or behavior when interviewing a depressed individual. Although a few novice clinicians may endorse the myth that questioning about suicide may increase its likelihood, this belief has *not* been supported by research or experience. An open, frank, and matter-of-fact discussion of suicide is essential for an accurate assessment of suicidal potential (Linehan, 1981). Several suicide scales may be useful guides to the clinician's questioning: the Scale for Suicide Ideation (Beck & Kovacs, 1979) and the Reasons for Living Inventory (Linehan & Chiles, 1983).

In addition to the content of the patient's reports, nonverbal characteristics may be useful indicators of depression. Speech rate and quality of voice are often associated with depressed affect. A depressed individual will often speak in a slowed manner, and his/her voice is frequently a monotone. A change in activity level is another nonverbal behavior associated with depression. Depressed individuals may be slowed in their physical movements as well as their speech rate (psychomotor retardation). Conversely, agitation (increased activity, noted by such things as pacing, wringing of the hands, and shifting in a chair) may be a feature of the depressed individual's presentation. The posture of a depressed individual may also give clues to depression. Depressed individuals commonly sit with their heads down and their shoulders slumped forward, avoid eye contact, and smile rarely (see work on nonverbal behavior by Fisch, Frey, & Hirsbrunner, 1983; Ekman & Friesen, 1974; Waxer, 1974).

It must be stressed that the above-described verbal and nonverbal indicants are not always differentially diagnostic of depression. These behaviors are frequently observed in psychiatric conditions other than depression (e.g., anxiety states, schizophrenia). It is important nonetheless to be sensitive to these features, as they are readily observable and are clear signs of disordered functioning; their absence may be equally important as an indication of improvements in the patient's condition.

More formal techniques to assess the overt behavior and speech qualities of depressed individuals have been developed, and are worthy of mention. Williams, Barlow, and Agras (1972) have developed the Ward Behavior Checklist for use with hospitalized patients. This scale has been demonstrated to have excellent interrater reliability and has been shown to relate to other measures of depression. Lewinsohn (1976) and Howes and Hokanson (1979) assessed the verbal behavior of depressives as it relates to the construct of social skills, and have developed an elaborate coding scheme for speech content. Assessment techniques such as those developed by Williams et al. (1972), Lewinsohn (1976), and Howes and Hokanson (1979) have not been widely employed when assessing depression in the clinic. Also, the extent to which these assessment systems are appropriate for nonhospitalized patients (or to patients with less severe depressions) is not clear. Nonetheless, these techniques are available and can be developed.

INTERVIEW METHODS FOR ASSESSING DEPRESSION

In this section we review the SADS, the Structured Clinical Interview for DSM-III-R (SCID), the HRSD, and the PSE. We realize that this review is not exhaustive; we have chosen to consider in detail several of the most common methods rather than presenting limited reviews of numerous methods.

Schedule for Affective Disorders and Schizophrenia

To facilitate the reliability of interviews used to establish RDC diagnoses, Endicott and Spitzer

(1978) designed the SADS. The SADS was developed in an attempt to reduce the variance between interviewers in the type and amount of information available from which to make a diagnosis. To reduce the variance in the criteria (both inclusion and exclusion criteria) required to make a diagnosis, the RDC were also specified by this group (Spitzer et al., 1978). Alternatively, the DSM classification system (which was developed after the RDC) may be used, but there are some differences between RDC and DSM diagnostic criteria. It is noteworthy that the SADS is not restricted to the assessment of depression, but covers a wide variety of psychiatric categories, including MDD, dysthymic disorder, schizophrenia, anxiety disorders, and personality disorders.

Three versions of the SADS are available: the regular version, the lifetime version, and the change version. The regular version is composed of two parts. Part I assesses the symptomatology (and severity) of the current episode. The current episode is evaluated both at its worst point and over the week prior to the interview. Part II assesses past psychiatric disturbances and relevant historical information (e.g., schooling, adolescent social patterns). The lifetime version of the SADS is similar to Part II of the regular version, except that the current episode is included within the time frame of the interview (i.e., historical information up to and including the present). As a result, less consistent and detailed information is provided about the current episode in the lifetime version. Also, the lifetime version does not allow for assessment of the severity of the current episode. The change version of the SADS involves those questions from Part I of the regular version that assess severity. Obtaining severity judgments over time (e.g., before and after treatment) provides a measure of change.

The SADS is highly structured and involves the use of a detailed guide. The interviewer progresses through a series of specific questions that cover a variety of psychiatric conditions. Depending on the answers to the questions, the interviewer can explore in greater detail specific symptoms and characteristics related to a particular disorder (e.g., if a patient has had a period of at least 1 week where the predominant mood was sadness, then the specific relevant symptomatology of a major depressive episode is explored in detail). Interviewers are encouraged to use all sources of information available in making their decisions. It is recommended that the SADS be employed only by highly trained individuals with extensive clinical knowledge. In our experience, the average interview requires 2 hours to complete.

In addition to diagnostic decisions, the SADS allows the calculation of summary scale scores. These summary scales were developed on the basis of clinical knowledge and on factor analyses of types of psychopathology. Summary scales for depression include Depressive Mood and Ideation, Endogenous Features, Depressive Associative Features, and Suicidal Ideation and Behavior.

Reliability estimates for the depression section of the SADS are impressive. Endicott and Spitzer (1978) report interrater reliability coefficients (intraclass coefficients) of at least .95 for the depression summary scales. These data were based on 150 interviews. As well, the internal consistency of the summary scales was high (at least .95), and the scales were moderately intercorrelated (.40 to .90). Finally, the summary scales were shown to correlate moderately (.42 to .68) with the depression scales of the Katz Adjustment Scale (Katz & Lyerly, 1963) and the Symptom Checklist-90 (SCL-90; Derogatis, Lipman, & Covi, 1973).

In terms of the reliability of diagnoses made through SADS interviews, Spitzer et al. (1978) report a kappa of .90 for the diagnosis of MDD and .81 for minor depressive disorder (the RDC were used). Clearly, these data indicate that the RDC and the SADS can be employed in a highly reliable manner. In addition to having high reliability, the SADS reduces the variance in information obtained by different interviewers and can be adapted to DSM diagnoses. This latter point suggests that the SADS can be a widely applicable method for both clinicians and researchers.

Perhaps the weakest feature of the SADS is that it is time-consuming, and therefore costly, to administer. It requires the efforts of a skilled clinician familiar with psychopathology. This requirement may restrict its use, since there are numerous settings where experienced clinicians do not have sufficient time to administer a 2-hour interview. A related concern has to do with the fact that the SADS addresses the issue of establishing a diagnosis more than it does the issue of formulating of the most appropriate treatment plan. A clinician with limited time might choose to perform a functional assessment (e.g., Hersen, 1976) that would yield information with more direct treatment implica-

tions, although in time it is hoped that specific descriptive diagnoses will be more useful to the prediction of treatment response. More recently, other structured interview formats that yield DSM-III or DSM-III-R diagnoses have been developed for use by unskilled interviewers: the Diagnostic Interview Schedule (DIS; Robins, Helzer, Croughan, & Ratcliff, 1981); the SCID (Spitzer, Williams, Gibbon, & First, 1992); and the Composite International Diagnostic Interview (CIDI; Robins et al., 1988).

The DIS, for instance, has been developed for use by laypersons. Like the SADS, the DIS assesses a wide variety of psychiatric conditions in addition to depression. Interviewers proceed through the highly structured interview guide, recording answers to closed-ended questions. Probes are required for some questions, and these are indicated in the guide. The actual probes to be used are specified in the guide; thus, very little is left to the discretion of the interviewer. Questions are designed to yield decisions on a lifetime basis as well as more currently (last 2 weeks, last month, last 6 months, last year). In addition, the information generated is consistent with both RDC and DSM-III criteria. Robins et al. (1981) compared interviews by laypeople with 1 week of training to those by psychiatrists, with favorable results. For instance, kappas of .63 and .64 resulted for DSM-III and RDC diagnoses of depression, respectively. Furthermore, laypersons identified 80% of depression cases and 84% of noncases (no depression diagnosis) that were identified by psychiatrists. Thus, the possibility of using nonclinician evaluation for the assessment of depression (and other psychiatric disorders) is very real indeed.

Structured Clinical Interview for DSM-III-R

There are some problems associated with using nonclinical interviewers for the assessment of psychiatric illness, however. As noted by Spitzer in his presidential address at the 1983 annual meeting of the American Psychopathological Association (cited in Spitzer et al., 1992), the most valid diagnostic assessment still requires the skills of a clinician with experience in evaluating a range of psychopathology. An experienced clinician can tailor an interview by phrasing questions to fit the subject's understanding, asking additional questions that clarify differential diagnosis, challenging inconsistencies in the patient's account, and judging whether the patient's description of an experience conforms to the intent of a diagnostic criterion. As an attempt to remedy problems inherent in the other structured interviews, Spitzer and his colleagues developed the SCID, a clinical assessment procedure that was consistent with the specific criteria outlined in DSM-III-R and included features not present in previous clinical diagnostic instruments.

The SCID is organized into modules, each generally corresponding to a major DSM-III-R diagnostic class. This feature allows researchers and clinicians who are primarily interested in depression, for example, to eliminate the other modules. The module for mood disorders includes bipolar disorder, MDD, dysthymia (past 2 years), other bipolar disorder (includes bipolar disorder not otherwise specified [NOS] and cyclothymia), and psychotic disorder (diagnosed as depressive disorder NOS in DSM-III-R). SCID interviewers should be individuals who have enough clinical experience and knowledge of psychopathology and psychiatric diagnosis to conduct a diagnostic interview without an interview guide. They should then further be trained in specific SCID interviewing techniques (Spitzer et al., 1992).

In terms of the reliability of diagnoses of depression made through SCID interviews, the data are somewhat inconsistent. Williams et al. (1992) conducted studies in North America and Germany, and found kappa values to range from .37 for subjects in a substance abuse treatment unit to .82 for a patient population in Munich, Germany. For MDD, kappas for current and lifetime diagnoses in the patient samples were above an acceptable .60, with a mean kappa of .64 for current, and .69 for lifetime diagnoses for the combined samples. Agreement was often considerably lower for the nonpatient samples, with a mean kappa of .42 for current and .49 for lifetime diagnoses. The results from this series suggest that the SCID may be an acceptable instrument for the assessment of patient samples where substance abuse is not an issue, but would not be the instrument of choice for nonpatient population studies. Further evidence in favor of using the SCID as a clinical interview for patient samples comes from a study conducted in Norway (Skyr, Onstad, Torgersen, & Kringlen, 1991). In this study, good interrater agreements were observed for both MDD (.93) and dysthymia (.88), suggesting that the SCID yields highly reliable diagnoses.

Hamilton Rating Scale for Depression

The HRSD is historically the most common interview measure of depression. It was devised by Hamilton (1960) to improve on other measures available at the time. According to Hamilton (1960), the major disadvantages with depression measures existing in the 1950s included the following: The measures were often developed with a normal population, and therefore were not sensitive to qualitative and quantitative differences from clinical depression; self-report measures had low reliability and were of limited use with semiliterate patients; and measures of general psychopathology did not assess depression with sufficient precision.

Hamilton's original scale involved 21 items, 17 of which were scored. The remaining four (diurnal variation, depersonalization, paranoia, obsessive–compulsiveness) either were considered unrelated to the severity of depression or were too infrequent to be included in the scoring. The HRSD was intended to be used as an index of severity with individuals already diagnosed as suffering from depression (i.e., it is not a diagnostic measure). The scale is completed following a clinical interview (Hamilton estimated 30-minute interviews as typical). Although some rough interview guidelines were presented by Hamilton, there is often considerable variability in the type and amount of information obtained by different interviewers (see Sotsky & Glass, 1983). Hamilton acknowledged that "its value depends entirely on the skill of the interviewer in eliciting the necessary information" (1960, p. 56). Interviewers are encouraged to use all sources of information available to them, in addition to the actual interview.

There have been two modifications to the HRSD since the original version. First, specific descriptive anchor points were developed for each of the values for each item. This was intended to objectify the ratings. Second, "cognitive" items assessing hopelessness, helplessness, and worthlessness have been added. Even though there are up to 24 items in the scale, most researchers score only the assigned 17 items. Thus, the value of the additional items is questionable (i.e., if they are not included in the total score for the severity of the disorder, they serve only as descriptors). Of the 17 scorable items, 9 are rated on 5-point (0–4) scales, and 8 on 3-point (0–2) scales (total scores range from

0 to 52). The 0–2 items are limited to judgments of whether the symptom is present or absent, with a score of 1 reserved for judgments that the symptom is trivial or doubtful. No evaluation is made as to the degree of severity on these items (M. Hamilton, personal communication to E. Beckham, February 1984). The 0–4 items reflect a symptom that is either absent or present to a trivial, mild, moderate, or severe degree (scores of 1, 2, 3, or 4, respectively). Hamilton (personal communication to E. Beckham, February 1984) states that "the rater should not hesitate to record if the symptom is severe, even though he recognizes that other patients are even worse." This introduces ambiguity into the ratings, since a given rating may represent different things for two different patients. It was originally suggested that two raters complete the HRSD for each interview and their scores be summed. This procedure enhances the reliability of ratings (see Epstein, 1979). In lieu of two raters, Hamilton (1960) recommended that the score of a single rater be doubled. Although this method makes the score comparable to when two raters are involved, it in no way enhances reliability. It would avoid confusion if the number of raters were clearly reported in clinical or scientific documents.

Scores on the HRSD (based on a single rater) of 6 or below are considered to reflect normal, nondepressed functioning; scores of 7–17 are considered to reflect mild depression; scores of 18–24 are considered to reflect moderate depression; and scores of 25 or more are considered to reflect severe depression. In several major multisite collaborative psychotherapy studies (e.g., the National Institute of Mental Health [NIMH] Treatment of Depression Collaborative Research Program), a score of 14 or greater was required for outpatients to be entered into the study (Sotsky & Glass, 1983). A cutoff score of 17 has frequently been used as the criterion for entry into many drug outcome studies (see Endicott, Cohen, Nee, Fleiss, & Sarantakos, 1981).

The HRSD is perhaps the most frequently used severity measure of depression, particularly with inpatients and in drug outcome studies. There has been some variation in the scoring of the scale (e.g., some investigators score the helplessness, hopelessness, and worthlessness items; see Hedlund & Vieweg, 1979). Although these modifications have not markedly influenced the reliability and validity coefficients of the HRSD (Hedlund & Vieweg, 1979;

Sotsky & Glass, 1983), they do impair the comparability of the scale to the original 17-item version. If summary scores are used, it is important to note whether any modifications have been made to the original scale. To minimize misinterpretation of data, it would be possible for clinicians who use some modification of the scale to report the 17-item score also.

Very few data are available on the internal consistency of the HRSD. Schwab, Bialow, and Holzer (1967) report item–total correlations ranging from .45 to .78 for medical patients. Bech, Bolwig, Kramp, and Rafaelsen (1979) reported item–total correlations ranging from −.02 to .81 (median = .47). Thus, the scale demonstrates only moderate homogeneity. For a scale to assess the range of depressive symptomatology adequately, however, low to moderate internal consistency may not be a major problem—a point considered more fully below.

Data on the interrater reliability of the HRSD are impressive. Hedlund and Vieweg (1979) reviewed nine studies that report interrater reliability coefficients of .84 or above (the exception was one study reporting a coefficient of .52). It is important to note that these investigators conducted a systematic search of all available research reported on the HRSD from 1967 to 1979. Therefore, the high reliabilities reported above are not likely to have been a function of selective reporting.

The HRSD is most frequently used by experienced clinicians; as such, it may be expensive, particularly if Hamilton's recommendations are followed and two raters are used. Notably, O'Hara and Rehm (1983) found that with only 5 hours of training, undergraduates could reach acceptable interrater reliability ($r = .76$). Each of the three trained undergraduate students' ratings correlated at least .82 with the mean rating of four expert judges. Ziegler, Meyer, Rosen, and Biggs (1978) examined the reliability of the HRSD when ratings were made from a videotape of an interview. Rating made by psychiatric residents (via videotape) correlated .97 with ratings made by two experienced psychiatrists (via actual interview). Together, these data are encouraging, in that they suggest that experienced professionals may not be required for the HRSD to be employed in a reliable manner. Nonetheless, caution should be used when interpreting data from inexperienced raters. Reliability of nonprofessional raters must be systematically assessed and documented; it cannot be assumed.

High interrater reliability of the HRSD may be partly a function of the shared background, experience, and attitude that exist when raters from the same setting are used (Sotsky & Glass, 1983). Different raters from different settings are less likely to be similar on these factors and may therefore attenuate reliability. Furthermore, Sotsky and Glass (1983) suggest that the range of scores may be restricted when the HRSD is employed with moderately depressed outpatients. This possibility relates to the heavy loading of somatic items on the HRSD, relative to mood or cognitive items. Outpatients may experience fewer somatic symptoms than inpatients. Restriction of range of scores would be expected to lower the reliability coefficient. Sotsky and Glass's (1983) position is bolstered by data from their pilot study, which revealed only moderate interrater reliability (.52) when raters were from different sites and moderately depressed outpatients were evaluated.

On the basis of the data from their pilot study, Sotsky and Glass (1983) propose specific guidelines for scoring items. These guidelines are more highly operationalized than those provided by Hamilton. They focus on the following dimensions: severity, frequency, objectivity, specificity, and activity. Once raters were trained in the use of these guidelines, interrater reliability increased to .78. Clearly, further interest in the use of these guidelines is warranted. Increased specificity in the scoring criteria will facilitate the use of this scale. This development is particularly exciting, given that the HRSD can be used reliably by relatively nonexperienced raters.

In terms of validity, the HRSD has been shown to differentiate depressed individuals from well individuals, and to differentiate depressed individuals from nondepressed psychiatric patients (Hedlund & Vieweg, 1979). In addition, HRSD scores are related to global severity ratings by clinicians, and moderately related to several of the major self-report measures of depression (see below).

Although concurrent validity estimates are acceptable, data on discriminant validity are less available. Sotsky and Glass (1983) report a study by Giser, which found that scores were as highly correlated to the Depression scale of the SCL-90 (Derogatis et al., 1973) as they were to the Anxiety and Obsessive–Compulsive scales of the SCL-90, which calls into question the discriminative validity of the scale.

In addition to being correlated with other scales, the HRSD has repeatedly been shown to be sensitive to change in the severity of depression, as measured by global ratings and other tests. Several factor analyses have been conducted on the HRSD. Although numerous factors (up to six) have been extracted, only two consistent factors emerge across studies. One factor taps the general severity of depression, on which all items tend to load positively. The second factor can be labeled "agitated–retarded," in that symptoms of anxiety and retardation load highly (and in opposite directions) on this factor.

Endicott et al. (1981) report a procedure for deriving HRSD ratings from the SADS. They present a specific algorithm whereby SADS scores on specific items can be converted to HRSD scores on corresponding items. In a few cases, several items from the HRSD are collapsed into one item in the SADS. When raters completed the HRSD and SADS on 48 depressed inpatients, the correlation between extracted HRSD scores (i.e., extracted from the SADS) and actual scores was .92. Endicott et al. (1981) point out that agreement between extracted and actual scores is about the same as the agreement between actual scores from more than one rater.

In conclusion, the HRSD is an interview measure that appears to be reliable, demonstrates moderate associations with other depression measures, and is sensitive to change. Data suggest that specific steps can be taken to increase reliability, and that there is potential for the scale to be used by trained but relatively nonexperienced individuals (e.g., undergraduates). The HRSD can also be extracted reliably from the SADS. Although the scale is generally useful, there are some additional problems with the scale that should be noted. First, the anchor points for some items are unclear. For instance, the anchor points for the psychic anxiety item mix objective observation (scale value 3—apprehensive attitude apparent in face or speech) with self-reported concern not necessarily limited to the present (e.g., scale value 2—worrying about minor matters). This raises a second problem with the scale: Ratings include two time periods, the immediate situation and the past week. There are no guidelines for resolving discrepancies between these two time frames. Finally, it should be noted that one item, insight, is rarely scored in an outpatient setting. Such a low-frequency item would contribute little to the scale. Future work with this scale should address these issues. Also, future research should focus on the use of the HRSD with moderately depressed outpatients, as well as on the discriminative validity of the HRSD.

Present State Examination

Another interview method used to assess depression, and psychopathology in general, is the PSE (Wing et al., 1967, 1974, 1990). This measure is a semistructured interview designed to assess the presence of a variety of psychopathological conditions present over the preceding month. The interview was designed as a clinician rating scale and not simply as a verbal questionnaire. The interviewer asks questions that probe various areas of psychopathology. Once an area of pathology is suspected, the interviewer begins a process that Wing et al. (1967) label "cross-examination." The task is to obtain sufficient information with which to make specific decisions about the presence, absence, or severity of a particular symptom. This decision is made by the examiner, not by the respondent. For most symptoms a form of questioning is suggested, although the interviewer is free to depart from this and from the order of questioning if necessary to obtain clarity. The time period recommended for the PSE is limited, usually to 1 month, because results of experiments suggested that recall of subjective experience over a longer period was often not satisfactory (Wing et al., 1990). However, clinicians and researchers are free to depart from this practice if they wish, provided that they specify the period used when reporting their results.

One of the greatest advantages of the PSE is the corresponding CATEGO system of computer programs that can be used with the full PSE or with the PSE syndrome checklist, a technique for systematically formulating diagnostic criteria from case records. The CATEGO system of computer programs was designed to produce from each interview a classification that could be conflated into 10 classes, each approximately equivalent to an *International Classification of Diseases*, ninth revision (ICD-9) diagnosis. The CATEGO programs include a program called the Index of Definition for specifying eight levels of confidence that sufficient clinically significant PSE symptoms are present to allow a classification into one of the main ICD-9 categories.

Ten editions of this interview have been constructed. The most recent version, PSE-10, is incorporated within the Schedules for Clinical Assessment in Neuropsychiatry (SCAN; Wing et al., 1990). The SCAN system allows for the assessment of three distinct time periods: present state, present episode, and lifetime. The SCAN system is relatively new, and few data are available to establish its overall reliability. However, the depression section is similar to that of PSE-9 (with some modification for DSM-III-R criteria), and reliabilities for have been found to range from .72 to .90 in several studies. On the basis of PSE information only, two independent examiners reached agreement 80% of the time on diagnoses of psychotic depression and nonpsychotic depression (Wing et al., 1974). Reliability of ratings of the presence of specific symptoms of depression was also acceptable. In contrast to the data on reliability, few data pertaining to validity are available.

The PSE appears to be a reliable instrument. It has not been used very frequently (particularly in North America); thus, accumulated experience with this scale is not great. In the earlier versions the interviewer focused only on the past month, and this format was a limiting factor, since historical information is essential for diagnoses such as bipolar disorders and dysthymic disorder. Finally, as discussed by Wing et al. (1967), the use of the PSE by a wide variety of interviewers has not been systematically examined. The PSE-10, incorporated within the SCAN system, has managed to overcome most of the problems associated with using the PSE in North America. This interview therefore promises to be valuable for the assessment of depression for both clinicians and researchers.

SELF-REPORT METHODS OF ASSESSMENT

In this section we describe and evaluate the following self-report tests: the Beck Depression Inventory (BDI), the Minnesota Multiphasic Personality Inventory's Depression scale (MMPI-D), the Carroll Rating Scale for Depression (CRS), the Zung Self-Rating Depression Scale (SDS), the Center for Epidemiologic Studies Depression Scale (CES-D), the Lubin Depression Adjective Checklists (DACL), and visual analogue scales. Note that with the exception of the MMPI-D, none of these scales were originally designed to diagnose depression; rather, they were meant to measure depressive symptomatology or severity. Even though diagnosis was the original aim of the MMPI-D, this goal has not been attained. A comprehensive list of other self-report tests that assess symptoms of depression can be found in Appendix 3.1.

Beck Depression Inventory

The BDI (Beck, Ward, Mendelson, Mock, & Erbaugh, 1961) is the most frequently used self-report method of assessing severity of depression. The scale is essentially clinically derived and designed to measure both "attitudes and symptoms which appeared to be specific for depression and those which were consistent with descriptions in the psychiatric literature," while not intending "to reflect any theory regarding the etiology of depression" (Beck & Beamesderfer, 1974, p. 155). This 21-item scale was originally intended to be interviewer-assisted, but common practice at present is to have the patient complete the test in an unassisted self-report manner. Each item in the inventory consists of four self-evaluative statements scored 0 to 3, with increasing scores indicating greater severity of depression. Responses are added to yield a total score ranging from 0 to 63. One item that assesses weight loss is not scored if the individual indicates that he/she has been attempting to lose weight. BDI scores are generally categorized into levels of depression in the following manner: 0–9 indicates a normal nondepressed state, 10–15 reflects mild depression, 16–23 reflects moderate depression, and 24–63 reflects severe depression. In many clinical settings, posttreatment scores between 0 and 9 are considered to indicate depression in remission; scores between 10 and 15 are considered to indicate partial remission; and scores between 16 and 63 are considered to indicate that the individual remains symptomatic. Easy administration facilitates the use of the scale in clinical applications. Repeated administration allows assessment of between-session change and quick evaluation of suicidal ideation.

Extensive examination of the internal consistency of the scale has been reported in the literature. Split-half reliability coefficients have been reported in the range of .58 to .93 (Beck & Beamesderfer, 1974; Gallagher, Niles, & Thompson, 1982; Reynolds & Gould, 1981; Strober, Green, & Carlson, 1981). Item–total correlations ranged from .22 to .86, with the average being .68 (Strober et al., 1981). Test–retest reliability, although suggested to be a poor evaluative criterion because of the expected fluctuation of symptom severity during a depressive episode, ranged from .69 to .90 (Gallagher et al., 1982; Strober et al., 1981).

The BDI has been reported to have good concurrent validity. Beck, Steer, and Garbin (1988) cited 35 studies where correlations were reported between the BDI and other well-established instruments that measure depression, including the HRSD (Hamilton, 1960), the Zung SDS (Zung, 1965), the MMPI-D (Hathaway & McKinley, 1943), the Multiple Affect Adjective Checklist's Depression scale (Zuckerman & Lubin, 1965), and clinicians' ratings of depth of depression (Beck, Rial, & Rickels, 1974; Salkind, 1969; Strober et al., 1981; Nussbaum, Wittig, Hanlon, & Kurland, 1963). The correlation coefficients between the BDI and these measures ranged from a relatively modest .33 with DSM-III major depression (Hesselbrock, Hesselbrock, Tennen, Meyer, & Workman, 1983) to a more substantial .86 with the Zung SDS (Turner & Romano, 1984) and the HRSD (Steer, McElroy, & Beck, 1982). However, the most significant relationship was found between clinicians' ratings and the BDI, where the correlation coefficient was reported at .96 (Beck, Rial, & Rickels, 1974). This is not surprising, because the BDI was developed on the basis of clinical observation of patients suffering from depression. Taken together, the data show that the BDI correlates well with most other self-report measures of depression.

The BDI is also a useful instrument, as it has been demonstrated to be applicable across a variety of cultures. Cross-cultural applicability has been tested in subjects from Switzerland, France, Finland, and Czechoslovakia (Blaser, Low, & Schaublin, 1968; Delay, Picot, Lemperiere, & Mirouze, 1963; Stenback, Rimon, & Turunen, 1967). Moreover, various forms of the BDI, including an abridged version (13 items; Beck & Beck, 1972) and a modified version (the scoring key was removed to avoid possible response bias due to the number beside each of the self-evaluative statements; statements were randomized; and respondents were instructed to pick the most representative statement), have been used and demonstrated to be adequately reliable and valid (Beck & Beamesderfer, 1974; May, Urquart, & Taran, 1969; Reynolds & Gould, 1981; Scott, Hannum, & Ghirst, 1982). The abridged version has also been shown to be an effective tool for clinicians requiring a quickly administered test, devised to screen for depression (Beck & Beck, 1972), although the 21-item BDI takes only 10 to 15 minutes to complete.

The BDI has been criticized as being a measure of a social undesirability response set and not a measure of depression (Langevin & Stancer, 1979). Although Beck and Beamesderfer (1974) addressed this issue and suggested that social undesirability may in itself be diagnostic of depression, Langevin and Stancer (1979) viewed this explanation as unacceptable. They maintained that depression is a "unitary concept," and as such should have only one factor in a factor-analytic study. In fact, more than one factor is usually identified. However, depression has always been identified as a varied, diverse problem with affective, physiological, behavioral, and cognitive symptoms associated with it. Thus, on a scale designed to measure many aspects of depressive symptomatology, it is predictable that more than one factor would be extracted in a factor analysis. In fact, social desirability, as measured by the Marlowe–Crowne Social Desirability Scale (Crowne & Marlowe, 1960), has only been weakly correlated with the BDI ($r = -.26$; Reynolds & Gould, 1981). As other researchers (e.g., Nevid, 1983) have pointed out in a similar controversy involving the Hopelessness Scale (Beck, Weissman, Lester, & Trexler, 1974), a scale's covariation with social desirability should not make it invalid as long as the covariation is consistent with theory, and overlap between the two constructs is not completely redundant. Similarly, although many factors are extracted in factor-analytic studies of the BDI (e.g., Weckowicz, Muir, & Cropley, 1967), as long as they are in line with depressive symptomatology and/or theory, the scales should not be viewed as useless or simply measuring another concept. The position that there is only one factor in depression runs counter not only to the use of the BDI but to a multidimensional notion of depression. The fact that many depression scales, including the BDI, are designed to assess the variety of factors involved in depression has implications for the internal-consistency estimates. Low estimates may not reflect a poor scale; rather, they may suggest a multifactored scale. Factor analyses of the BDI clearly support this notion.

Another criticism of the BDI has been reported in a study of 170 undergraduate psychology students reported by Meites, Lovallo, and Pishkin (1980). These authors found the correlation between the BDI and the Taylor Manifest Anxiety Inventory ($r = .64$) to be greater than the correlation between the BDI and the SDS ($r = .60$). Thus, the BDI may be as highly related to anxiety measures as depression measures. Future work on the discriminant validity of the BDI is required, particularly with clinical samples including anxiety disorders.

The BDI was developed as a symptom inventory, not as a diagnostic instrument. Therefore, inappropriate use of the BDI as a diagnostic instrument can lead to misleading information, which may overestimate the prevalence of depressive illness. For instance, Ennis, Barnes, Kennedy, and Trachtenberg (1989) examined a series of 71 consecutive admissions to an inpatient psychiatric crisis service following the patients' deliberate attempts at self-harm. Although 80% of those admitted to the hospital scored within the moderate to severe range of depression as measured by the BDI, only 31% met DSM-III-R criteria for a major depressive episode. Ennis and his colleagues reported a dramatic reduction in BDI scores within a few days following admission, even though these patients did not receive any significant treatment for depression. Similar findings were reported by Newson-Smith and Hirsh (1979), using the General Health Questionnaire (GHQ) and the PSE, and by van Praag and Plutchik (1987), using subjective recollections of distress. These findings suggest that for patients in a current state of acute emotional distress, high BDI scores may not necessarily reflect clinical depression, but may be interpreted as general psychological distress.

Minnesota Multiphasic Personality Inventory, Depression Scale

The MMPI (Hathaway & McKinley, 1943) was originally designed to be an objective pencil-and-paper method of deriving psychodiagnostic labels for individuals. Due to the unreliability of the nosological system (see Hersen, 1976) and high intercorrelations between scales, however, this purpose has largely failed. Current procedures for interpretation include descriptions of the person's likely behaviors and attitudes, based on a profile analysis rather than on the interpretation of individual scale scores. Overlap between scale items makes such a profile interpretation of questionable validity. The restandardization of the MMPI resulted in the MMPI-2 (Butcher, Dahlstrom, Graham, Tellegen, & Kaemmer, 1989), which was designed to replace the MMPI. The only change in the items of the standard validity and clinical scales of the MMPI-2 was the deletion of 13 items with objectionable or outdated content (Butcher, Dahlstrom, et al., 1989). New content scales (Butcher, Graham, Williams, & Ben-Porath, 1989) were developed for the MMPI-2, so that clinicians still have empirically and rationally derived scales available for interpretation. The MMPI-2 consists of 567 true–false items. As with the MMPI, scoring of the MMPI-2 proceeds by counting the client's deviant responses to each of the items on a particular scale. The items are not weighted in the scoring process. Because the most significant research to date has utilized the MMPI, the following discussion is based on the original scales.

The MMPI is an empirically derived scale whose items were selected not necessarily on the basis of face or construct validity principles, but on the basis of their ability to discriminate between normal and patient groups. Thus, the validity of the scales is dependent on the validity of the diagnosis of the criterion group. The resultant scale contains 566 self-referent items, including 4 validity scales and 10 clinical scales. Other scales have been developed in addition to these, but are not typically used in standard clinical practice. Items of the MMPI are answered in a forced-choice true–false format, and scale scores are standardized (T-scores; mean = 50, standard deviation = 10). T-scores greater than 70 are interpreted as clinically significant, and, as noted earlier, the pattern of the scale elevations is an important consideration.

The Depression scale, the MMPI-D, consists of 60 items and was originally designed to measure symptomatic depression. The items cover aspects of depression such as low self-worth, psychomotor retardation, withdrawal, lack of interest, and physical complaints. Although high scores (above 80 T) may suggest clinical depression, more moderate scores tend to be indicative of low morale and lack of involvement (Graham, 1977). Since the MMPI-D is a good indicant of distress, high scores (above 70 T) may suggest a need for psychotherapy or counseling (Graham, 1977).

In terms of internal consistency, split-half reliability coefficients have been reported in the range of .58 to .84 (Gilliland & Colgin, 1951; Winfield, 1952). Test–retest reliability coefficients with a delay of 1 day to 2 weeks have been reported in the range of .69 to .96 in college students (Butcher & Dahlstrom, 1964; Faschingbauer, 1972; Windle, 1955) and .72 to .89 in psychiatric patients (Eichman, 1973; Jurjevich, 1966; Newmark, 1971, 1973).

The MMPI-D has also been shown to have acceptable concurrent validity. Correlation coefficients with other self-report measures (e.g., the BDI, the SDS) fall in the moderate to good range (r = .56 to .80; Biggs, Wylie, & Ziegler, 1978; Brown & Zung, 1972; Nussbaum et al., 1963; Zung, 1967, 1968, 1969; Zung, Richards, & Short, 1965). Also, comparisons between clinicians' ratings of depression and MMPI-D scores have shown moderate correspondence (r = .51; Endicott & Jortner, 1966).

Factor-analytic studies of the internal structure of the MMPI-D have consistently shown multiple factors, many of which are not consistent with depression (Comrey, 1957; O'Connor, Stefic, & Gresock, 1957). Both Comrey (1957) and O'Connor et al. (1957) have suggested that the scale should be interpreted in component parts based on their factor-analytic studies, rather than being used to provide one score for depression. Dempsey (1964) shortened the 60-item scale to 30 items (D-30) in an attempt to increase its homogeneity. Using contextual analysis (Dempsey & Baumoff, 1963), he calculated a coefficient of dimensionality for each item. Only those items best correlating to a depressive dimension were retained. This resulted in a significant improvement in the split-half reliability of the test, despite its being shortened by 30 items. Dempsey (1964) proposed that the 30 items more accurately measure depression, and that the 30 excluded items actually contributed more to error variance than to depression score variance.

Another study attempting to refine the MMPI-D was reported by Burkhart, Gynther, and Fromuth (1980). These authors categorized MMPI-D items as "obvious," "neutral," and "subtle" in their relationship to depression. They found that the correlation between the MMPI-D obvious items and the BDI was greater (r = .60) than the correlation between the BDI and the full scale (r = .49). It was also seen that the subtle items were *negatively* correlated with BDI scores (r = –.22). Burkhart et al. (1980) suggest that "practitioners may want to give more weight to D-O [obvious, face-valid item scores] than to the standard D scores because the former predict the criterion [BDI scores] more powerfully than the latter" (p. 751).

The fact that it was developed for diagnostic purposes clearly limits the applicability of the MMPI-D. Nevertheless, it is frequently used to index severity, and these two purposes should not be equated. High MMPI-D scores may not necessarily reflect the severity of depression, since the various MMPI scales are highly correlated. Thus, elevations on the other scales (e.g., Psychasthenia or Hypochondriasis) might account for MMPI-D elevations (due to item overlap). This problem, in conjunction with the difficulty in criterion validation of the MMPI-D (i.e., scale items were not necessarily chosen to tap relevant aspects of depression, but simply to differentiate depressed from nondepressed groups), leads us not to recommend this test. Other instruments described in this chapter have more to recommend them as measures of depressive symptomatology.

Carroll Rating Scale for Depression

Carroll, Feinberg, Smouse, Rawson, and Greden (1981) developed the CRS to obtain a self-report instrument closely following the item content of the HRSD. Because the BDI is concerned mostly with psychological and cognitive features, whereas the HRSD is more concerned with behaviorial and somatic features, the BDI in itself was not seen as an adequate self-report inventory (Carroll et al., 1981).

The CRS consists of 52 statements, each written in a self-descriptive format (e.g., "I feel in good spirits"). Individuals respond to each question in a forced-choice yes–no format, based on their feelings over the past few days. To partially control for possible acquiescent response sets, 40 statements are keyed yes while the remaining 12 statements are indicative of depression if answered no.

The CRS translates the HRSD into a self-report format, and, like the HRSD, has a total score range of 0 to 52. HRSD items scored 0 to 4 are represented by four statements in the CRS; items scored 0 to 2 on the HRSD are represented in the CRS by two statements. The cutoff indicating clinically significant depression is a score of 10.

Internal consistency has been reported by Carroll et al. (1981) in the form of split-half correlation coefficients (r = .87) and item–total correlations (median r = .55, range = .05 to .78). A correlation matrix involving items of the CRS and the HRSD indicated that corresponding item correlations ranged from –.06 to .73 (median = .60). This would indicate that a direct match between CRS and HRSD items was not obtained, although the diagonal of the matrix showed that 13 of 17 CRS items were correlated most strongly with their HRSD counterparts.

Items measuring retardation, agitation, somatic anxiety, and loss of insight were correlated more strongly with other HRSD items than with their intended counterparts.

In terms of concurrent validity, total score correlations between the HRSD and the CRS range from .71 to .80 (Carroll et al., 1981; Feinberg, Carroll, Smouse, & Rawson, 1981); the BDI and the CRS correlated .86; and the CRS correlated .67 with a clinician's 4-point global rating of depression. The CRS also correlated .68 with patients' global self-ratings on a visual analogue scale (to be described later) (Feinberg et al., 1981).

The CRS was able to distinguish severity of depression at a level comparable to that of the HRSD for a low-severity group. As severity of depression increases, the CRS scores no longer match the HRSD scores (scores on the CRS are greater than scores on the HRSD with increased severity; Feinberg et al., 1981).

Thus, the CRS relates well to the HRSD. There may be some tendency for CRS scores to be inflated as severity of depression increases. As well, there seems to be a tendency for nonendogenous patients (patients with a primary diagnosis of neurotic depression) to overrate the severity of their symptoms. Overall, the utility of this measure is good, in that it is comparable to the HRSD while not requiring the clinician to interview the patient.

Zung Self-Rating Depression Scale

Zung (1965) developed the SDS, which was intended to be a short, comprehensive, and reliable instrument for measuring severity of depression. Items were developed to tap features of depression that had been identified in previous factor-analytic studies (e.g., Friedman, Cowitz, Cohen, & Granick, 1963; Grinker, Miller, Sabshin, Nunn, & Nunnally, 1961; Overall, 1962). Twenty items were generated by following this method. Items assess mood (e.g., feeling down-hearted and blue, crying spells), psychological factors (e.g., hopelessness, irritability, suicidal ideation), and psychomotor factors (e.g., agitation, retardation). Each item is rated on a 4-point continuous scale, with scale anchors ranging from "a little of the time" to "most of the time." Half of the 20 items are worded in a depressed tone (e.g., "I feel down-hearted and blue"), and half are worded in a nondepressed tone (e.g., "I feel that I'm useful and needed").

The scale is presented in an easy-to-administer booklet and requires minimum time (10–15 minutes) to complete. Each item is assigned a weight from 1 to 4, with 4 referring to the most depressed alternative. A depression index is then generated by summing the item scores and dividing by 80. This index yields a value from .25 to 1.00, with 1.00 being the maximum.

Very little work has been conducted to investigate the reliability of this scale. We are unaware of data that address the stability of the SDS (i.e., test–retest reliability) or its internal consistency (i.e., split-half and item–total coefficients), although Knight, Waal-Manning, and Spears (1983) report an alpha coefficient of .79 for the SDS. One might argue that a scale designed to measure the severity of depression does not require test–retest reliability (see the discussion in the section on the BDI), but the paucity of other reliability studies is notable.

More effort has been devoted to issues of validity. Zung et al. (1965), Zung (1969), and Zung and Wonnacott (1970) have demonstrated that the SDS discriminates depressed patients from nondepressed psychiatric patients and normal subjects (nondepressed patients had diagnoses such as anxiety reactions, personality disorders, and psychological disturbances).

Although the SDS appears to differentiate depressed from nondepressed individuals, its ability to discriminate severity of depression is less clear. Carroll, Fielding, and Blashki (1973) found that the SDS did not discriminate severity of depression among patients, whereas Biggs et al. (1978) reported that SDS scores differed significantly among four groups of depressed outpatients classified in terms of severity by clinicians' global ratings. Zung and Wonnacott (1970) attempted to establish whether the SDS could discriminate responders to electroconvulsive therapy (ECT) or pharmacotherapy. This was done in an attempt to predict treatment response on the basis of SDS scores. This study was poorly designed for this purpose, however, and instead attempted to discriminate the ECT group from the drug-treated group on specific SDS items.

Accumulated data on concurrent validity indicates that the SDS correlates moderately to highly with the HRSD, the MMPI-D, the BDI, and clinicians' estimates of the severity of depression (Biggs et al., 1978; Brown & Zung, 1972; Zung, 1967, 1969; Zung et al., 1965; Beck et al., 1988). Raft, Spencer, Toomey, and Brogan (1977) found that general medical out-

patients who were diagnosed as having "masked depression" (i.e., individuals whose primary complaint was somatic illness) were not identified by the SDS. These authors conclude that the SDS should not be used in a general medical setting because of this possible misclassification. Finally, Zung (1967) demonstrated that the SDS is not influenced by a variety of demographic factors, including age, sex, marital status, education, financial status, and intellectual level.

One of the useful features of the SDS is that it has been translated into 10 different languages. Zung (1969) demonstrated that the scale discriminated diagnostic groups (depressed from nondepressed and normal) for most of these translated versions. The availability of translated versions clearly facilitates the use of this scale with a variety of populations.

In summary, the SDS is an easy-to-administer and widely applicable scale. It is lacking, however, in data on psychometric qualities (particularly reliability). The test was initially constructed to measure the severity of depression, but the available validity data provide only weak evidence that this goal has been achieved. The scale appears more useful for the identification of depressed individuals than it does for the accurate assessment of the severity of depression. Also, there is some evidence that it is not adequate for use in a general medical setting. It should be noted, however, that the SDS has been shown to be responsive to decreased depression as a function of successful treatment (Zung, 1965, 1968).

Center for Epidemiologic Studies Depression Scale

The CES-D was developed to measure depressive symptomatology in the general population (Radloff, 1977). The scale consists of 20 items obtained from other previously validated scales (the MMPI-D, BDI, and SDS; Gardner, 1968; Raskin, Schulterbrandt, Reatig, & McKeon, 1969). Items were selected from areas of depressive symptomatology previously described and validated. The items tap areas of depressed mood, feelings of guilt and worthlessness, feeling of helplessness and hopelessness, psychomotor retardation, loss of appetite, and sleep disturbance. Although previous scales have been designed to assess severity, the CES-D was intended to assess depressive symptomatology with emphasis on the affective component, depressed mood (Radloff, 1977). This goal was partially accomplished, as a factor analysis of the CES-D revealed four factors, with the largest factor being depressed mood. This factor accounted for only 16% of the variance, however.

Individuals respond to each item based on the frequency of occurrence during the past week (0 = rarely or none of the time [less than 1 day], 3 = most or all of the time [5 to 7 days]). Four of the items are worded in a positive manner, to partially control for response bias. The range of the scores on the CES-D is 0 to 60, with higher scores indicating more symptom presence, weighted by frequency of occurrence. A suggested cutoff score of 16 is indicative of significant depressive symptomatology (Craig & Van Natta, 1978). Husaini, Neff, Harrington, Hughes, and Stone (1980) suggest cutoffs of 17 and 23 for "possible" and "probable" depression. The scale has been used in both interviewer-assisted and self-report formats (Boyd, Weissman, Thompson, & Myers, 1982; Radloff, 1977).

Internal consistency of the CES-D is good. Split-half correlations were .85 for patient groups and .77 for normal groups. Coefficient alpha and Spearman–Brown coefficients were .90 and .92 for patient groups, and .85 and .87 for normal groups. Test–retest reliability (time interval 6 months), with no intervening life events to disrupt scores, was .54 (Radloff, 1977).

In terms of concurrent validity, the CES-D has correlated moderately with other measures of depression (e.g., the HRSD). The CES-D and the DACL (see below) correlated .37 to .51 in normal groups, while a correlation of .70 was found in patient groups (Radloff, 1977). Correlations of .81 with the BDI and .90 with the SDS have been reported for recovered depressed patients (Weissman, Prusoff, & Newberry, 1975). Interviewer ratings of depression and the CES-D correlated moderately at .46 to .53 (Radloff, 1977). As well, it was demonstrated that the CES-D was responsive to change in patients' severity of depression. Low negative correlations with social desirability, as measured by the Marlowe–Crowne scale, add further to the scale's usefulness.

Even though a factor analysis revealed four factors (depressed affect, positive affect, somatic and retarded activity, and interpersonal factors), they were all consistent with depression. For this reason, as well as the high internal consistency across groups, Radloff (1977) suggests that only a total score should be calculated. Boyd

et al. (1982) found that of the persons who had scores of 16 or more, only one-third were diagnosed by the RDC as depressed, while 36% of those people diagnosed as having MDD had scores of less than 16. Boyd et al. suggest that these errors could be explained by nay-saying response sets, by the exclusion criteria of the RDC, or by the presence of other medical illnesses. They suggest methods of overcoming these problems, such as changing cutoff scores, incorporation of the test in an interview format, screening for other psychiatric or medical illness, and defining the construct of "role impairment" in the RDC. In a similar study, Lewinsohn and Teri (1982) compared the CES-D to the SADS. Only 34% of those scoring above the cutoff score of 17 met criteria for depression in the SADS. The authors attribute the discrepancy to the fact that scales such as the CES-D represent tabulations of symptoms or complaints (regardless of etiology), rather than assessment of an independent syndrome. Together, these data suggest that the scale should not be used as a clinical diagnostic instrument (e.g., Boyd et al., 1982; Myers & Weissman, 1980), although these authors suggest that lowering the cutoff scores and thereby reducing false negatives could make this scale useful as a rough screening instrument. The scale may also be useful in nonpsychiatric settings to screen for depressive illness (Katz et al., 1995).

Depression Adjective Checklists

The DACL were designed to measure "transient depressed mood, feeling, or emotion," as the BDI and MMPI-D were "available for the measurement of more chronic enduring depression" (Lubin, 1965, p. 57). The author decided on a checklist format, due to ease of administration and high face validity. Seven lists (four of 32 adjectives each and three of 34 each) were developed. Each of the four lists of 32 adjectives contains 22 positive adjectives (those adjectives checked more often by depressed patients) and 10 negative adjectives (those adjectives checked more often by normal subjects). The remaining three lists each contain 34 adjectives, 22 positive and 12 negative. Responses are scored such that higher scores indicate greater depressed mood. Internal consistency of the lists is high, with split-half correlations ranging from .82 to .93 for the seven lists and correlations between the seven lists ranging from .80 to .93 (Lubin, 1965). Unfortunately, validity coefficients are rather disappointing. Concurrent validity coefficients with the MMPI-D were low to moderate (.25 to .53), although correlations with the BDI were somewhat better, in the range of .38 to .66 (Christenfeld, Lubin, & Satin, 1978; Lubin, 1965). The Zung SDS correlated .41 with the DACL form E in one study (Christenfeld et al., 1978) and in the range of .51 to .64 in another study (Marone & Lubin, 1968). These latter authors also reported a correlation between clinicians' global ratings and the DACL. Social desirability effects seem negligible, in that Christenfeld et al. (1978) found a correlation of .08 between the DACL and the Marlowe–Crowne Social Desirability Scale. The DACL also seems responsive to changes in severity of depression. Lubin, Hornstra, and Lowe (1974) found that patients' scores lowered from a pretreatment interview to a posttreatment 3-month follow-up.

Clinical utility of the DACL is good in reference to administration time (2 to 3 minutes), but the ability to discriminate between diagnostic groups has been shown to be less than adequate (Lubin, 1965). Also, the issue of sex differences between lists has not been addressed. Users are informed of differences and are told to choose lists for use with reference to these differences (Lubin, 1965). A possible explanation for low concurrent validity coefficients with other instruments is that the DACL was designed to measure only a depressed mood, compared with the syndrome of depression. Depression is a complex state involving cognitive, motivational, behavioral, and affective components. Thus, although the DACL is easy to administer, it is not recommended for clinical use unless a sophisticated method of measuring change is developed.

Visual Analogue Scales

The Visual Analogue Mood Scale (VAMS), a modification of the scale proposed by Aitken (1969), is simply a 100-mm line. Individuals are asked to respond to the question "How is your mood right now?" by making a mark at some point on the line that best describes their mood. Anchors are "worst" at the left edge and "best" at the right edge. The score is the distance in millimeters from the left edge of the line; thus, higher scores indicate better mood. As a result, it is likely that correlations with measures of depression will be negative. In fact, negative correlations of $-.61$ to $-.67$ between the VAMS and the SDS have been reported (Folstein &

Luria, 1973; Luria, 1975). In a comparison of the Clyde Mood Scale (Clyde, 1950) to the VAMS, it was found that the VAMS consistently reflected depression but not other moods such as aggression. Test–retest correlations have been reported in the range of .61 to .73 (Folstein & Luria, 1973). The Visual Analogue Scale for Depression (Aitken, 1969) has been compared to the HRSD, BDI, and SDS, and correlations of .51 to .88 have been reported by Davies, Burrows, and Poynton (1975).

The VAMS is reasonably related to depressed mood as indicated above, but it is not suggested for uses other than obtaining only a rough estimate of depressed mood. Visual analogue scales in general seem reasonably related to depression and other depression measures, but they are seriously lacking in the amount of information that they offer. As well, it is virtually impossible to compare two respondents' scores, as they may use different criteria to place themselves at various points on the line.

Comparative Value of Self-Report and Interview Measures

Given the multifaceted nature of depression, a consideration of the advantages and disadvantages of self-report versus interviewer rating scales is in order. Interviewer rating scales are thought to have higher validity than self-report scales, because of the extent of information available to the interviewer from both the patient and other sources. Kazdin (1981, p. 361), in a review of the measures to assess childhood depression, states that "the interview not only allows the child to report on his or her perceptions of the problem but also permits the clinician to draw conclusions about areas the patient may not explicitly address. Thus, the sources of data available in an interview include, but also suppress, the information available from self-report measures."

The advantage of higher validity is potentially offset by the lower reliability of interview-based measures. Test–retest reliability of the instruments is generally seen as impractical because of the changing nature (particularly the severity) of the disorder. Interrater reliability may be reduced by the varied ways of applying the rating scale. As we have seen, *with training* many of these interview-based scales have good interrater reliability; however, the emphasis is on the training, and many clinicians have not had this type of training.

Self-report scales, on the other hand, may suffer from problems with validity despite strong reliability. Most of the scales have high face validity; therefore, responses can be easily distorted by individuals who are operating with a social undesirability set for reasons other than depression. Individuals who want to "fake good" will also encounter little challenge. For this reason, these tests, like any psychometric instruments, require careful interpretations. We still know very little about the validity of the tests when we subject them to repeated applications (e.g., weekly testing with the BDI). Nonetheless, from a clinical position, it is most important to look for discrepancies in the endorsement of specific items from week to week. If a treatment is targeted to a specific aspect of the syndrome, then these items deserve special scrutiny. For example, if a cognitive therapist directs an intervention toward a patient's sense of failure, he/she can check for changes in the patient's written as well as oral self-report.

SPECIAL CONSIDERATIONS

Two issues in the assessment of the severity and symptom patterns of depression have direct clinical relevance and deserve special consideration: relevant subtypes, and medical or other conditions that may interfere with or cloud our judgments of depression.

Relevant Subtypes

"Depression" is a ubiquitous term. The concept has been used in a variety of ways over the years. Members of the general public speak of "being depressed" when they are referring to their sad moods. For most clinicians, however, the term is reserved for a syndrome or disorder that in turn can be divided into various subtypes. We have earlier commented on our preference at this time for following the DSM categorization. Although the DSM system has some difficulties, it is based on relatively clear criteria that serve as a good foundation for future work.

The introduction of dysthymic disorder (previously categorized as neurotic depression) is one hallmark of the DSM-III as a descriptive nosology. Akiskal (1981; Akiskal et al., 1980) has reported relevant research with these patients. He subdivides dysthymic patients into those with "character spectrum disease" (individuals who have characterological depression; early onset of

symptoms) and those with "subaffective" disorder (those patients who have never really recovered from an episode of major depression; typically, later onset of symptoms). Further research is required to evaluate the prognostic value on preferred treatments of these conditions.

The differentiation of anxiety disorders from depression, and a subtyping of anxious depressed patients (see Fowles & Gersh, 1981; Gersh & Fowles, 1979), remain uncertain and deserve comment. Whenever one is assessing depression, it is useful to obtain a concomitant assessment of anxiety. Anxiety states are clinically important in that a number of depressed patients report concomitant anxiety, particularly as the severity of the depression lessens. Riskind and Beck (1983) reported using the Hamilton Rating Scale for Anxiety (Hamilton, 1959) to distinguish among generalized anxiety disorder, MDD, and "mixed" disorder (an amalgam of anxiety and depression symptoms). They found that clusters of symptoms rather than total scores were effective in discriminating the groups. This study is but one example of a line of research using multivariate statistical methods to discriminate diagnostic groups. The emphasis is on the grouping of symptoms from standard assessment instruments, and the procedure emphasizes the importance of a careful selection of measures used to subtype patients.

Another subtyping distinction within depression is the endogenous–nonendogenous distinction. Endogenous symptoms have been described by a number of investigators (e.g., Klein, 1974; Carroll et al., 1980). The previous endogenous– reactive or endogenous–exogenous categorizations, which were dependent upon judgments of etiology (e.g., Kiloh & Garside, 1963), are no longer viewed as useful. The new endogenous classifications are thought to be predictive, with recent research pointing to their value when antidepressants are being used. Notably, however, studies using some forms of psychological interventions such as cognitive–behavioral therapy (Beck et al., 1979) have not found the endogenous–nonendogenous classification to be useful in the prediction of treatment response (e.g., Blackburn, Bishop, Glen, Whalley, & Christie, 1981). Other subtypings such as hysteroid dysphoria (Klein, 1974; Williams & Spitzer, 1984) may prove to be useful in the future, but at present there is little support for their value.

Still other subtypes of depression deserve further consideration. Paykel (1971) reported on four categories of depressed patients (psychotic, anxious, and hostile depressed patients, and young depressed patients with personality disorder). Similarly, Overall and colleagues (e.g., Overall & Zisook, 1980) have also reported on a phenomenological classification system using the Brief Psychiatric Rating Scale (Overall & Gorham, 1962) and other scales to classify patients into four subtypes: anxious, hostile, retarded, or agitated. With the advent of microprocessors, clinicians may be able to make better use of the complex information available to the field. In particular, the prediction of which types of patients will respond to which therapeutic interventions may require an assessment of subtypes. Following the initial assessment to detect depression, to measure its severity, and to determine the appropriate subtype, the clinician will be in a better position to plan treatment. At present, clinicians tend not to use statistically derived subtypes (e.g., factor scores), due in part to technological limitations; yet many of the measures previously reported may require factor or cluster analysis to derive treatment-relevant predictions.

Assessment of Depression in the Medically Ill

From a clinical perspective, it is important to differentiate conditions in which the symptoms of depression are concomitants of another disorder rather than a primary diagnosis. In fact, depression as a symptom is widely found in a number of disorders. Even more confusing is the tendency of some investigators to speak of "depressive equivalents" or "masked depression." Depression may appear as a symptom in many disorders, ranging from schizophrenia to phobic disorders. The term "secondary depression" was coined to describe individuals who have a primary medical or psychiatric diagnosis other than MDD, and yet who also exhibit signs and symptoms of depression. At this time, it is difficult to assess differential treatment responses of primary versus secondary depressions, and we can only make note of the distinction and its potential usefulness.

A number of medical disorders are accompanied by symptoms of depression, and these disorders should be ruled out. Two conditions are mentioned in this context as examples. Patients who are dependent upon alcohol or drugs frequently experience physiologically based symptoms of sleep disturbance, appetite loss, de-

creased libido, and a general apathy *during withdrawal*. These symptomatic changes are a function of the state of withdrawal rather than of depression (Steer, Shaw, Beck, & Fine, 1977). Similarly, patients with anorexia nervosa may also experience symptoms of depression under conditions of starvation. Of course, some drug-dependent patients and some patients with anorexia nervosa do meet the criteria for a depressive disorder (Garner & Bemis, 1984). A repeated observation is that somatic symptoms used to diagnose depression are frequently reported by patients in general medical settings (Moffic & Paykel, 1975; Clark, Cavanaugh, & Gibbons, 1983) and with specific medical conditions, including cancer (Bukberg, Penman, & Holland, 1984), end-stage renal disease (Smith, Hong, & Robinson, 1985; Craven, Rodin, Johnson, & Kennedy, 1987), diabetes mellitus with metabolic dyscontrol (Lustman, Griffith, Clouse, & Cryer, 1986), rheumatoid arthritis (Frank et al., 1988), Parkinson's disease (Starkstein & Robinson, 1989), and multiple sclerosis (Krupp, Alvarez, LaRocca, & Scheinberg, 1988).

Over the past decade, a substantial body of research has been devoted to identifying features that discriminate major depression from somatic symptoms associated with different physical illnesses. Attempting to untangle the relationship between depressive symptoms and those symptoms that are more direct manifestations of physical disease is complicated by the facts that there is often a realistic basis for feelings of sadness and loss associated with serious medical conditions (Rodin, Craven, & Littlefield, 1991), and that the most common vegetative symptoms characteristic of depression are often the results of a physical illness itself. The assessment of depression in the physically ill is a difficult task even for experienced clinicians, and the interested reader should consult the recent text by Rodin et al. (1991), which deals specifically with these issues.

SELECTED MEASURES TO ASSESS MANIA

Minnesota Multiphasic Personality Inventory, Hypomania Scale

The MMPI's hypomania scale (MMPI-Ma) is a 46-item self-report scale developed to identify hypomanic symptomatology in psychiatric patients (McKinley & Hathaway, 1944). Common characteristics of mania include overactivity, elevated (but unstable) mood, and flight of ideas. Although the scale items are very heterogeneous, the more face-valid items reflect these areas. Sample items include "I have periods of such great restlessness that I cannot sit long in a chair," "At times I have fits of laughing and crying I cannot control," and "At times my thoughts have raced ahead faster than I could speak them." The scale was developed using a criterion group of psychiatric patients suffering from hypomania and mild acute mania. Patients suffering from severe symptoms of mania are typically unable to concentrate sufficiently to complete this measure, and were therefore left out.

Scores on the MMPI-Ma are related to age and race. Young subjects often score in the range of 55 to 65 T, while it is not uncommon for older subjects to score below 50 T. Black subjects typically score higher (range of 60 to 70 T) than white subjects. Scores above 90 T are clinically significant and may suggest that a patient is in the manic phase of manic–depressive disorder (Graham, 1977).

Internal-reliability estimates reported in Dahlstrom, Welsh, and Dahlstrom (1975) indicate that split-half reliability estimates range from .55 to .64. Test–retest reliability coefficients (psychiatric patients, interval 1 day to 2 weeks) range from .71 to .81.

Thus, the MMPI-Ma appears acceptably reliable. No comment on the validity of this scale can be made, as we are unaware of any relevant data. Finally, it is important to note that acute manic patients are often unable to complete this self-report scale; therefore, it is suggested that a more appropriate observer-rated scale be used, as discussed in the following section.

Manic-State Rating Scale

In response to the increase in interest in mania that accompanied the use and availability of lithium carbonate, Beigel, Murphy, and Bunney (1971; see also Beigel & Murphy, 1971) constructed an observer-rated scale. The rating scale contains 26 items derived from interviews with five nurses who had considerable experience working with manic inpatients. The interviews were structured around 16 comprehensive issues that were considered relevant to mania. From the transcripts of the interviews, items judged to reflect the affect, behavior, and cognition of mania were selected. Nurses' own words were used as much as possible, since they were the intended raters. Examples of the resulting items include the following: looks depressed (item 1), moves from one place to another (item 3), is irritable (item 11), has diminished impulse control (item 20), and jumps from one object to another (item 26). It is important to note that items do not appear to be independent in their content (e.g., is sexually preoccupied [item 25] and talks about sex [item 26]).

Beigel et al. (1971) had nurses complete the rating scale following an 8-hour period of observation. The authors did not state whether this was a continuous observation period; differential observation time across raters might be a source of error variance. Raters evaluated each item on two dimensions, frequency and intensity. Both ratings are made on a 5-point Likert scale, and the product of two raters (range 0–25) is used as the item score. Beigel et al. (1971) reported on the reliability of the scale. Twelve nurses rated a group of 13 patients (seven were unipolar depressives, six bipolar depressives). At least two raters evaluated each patient, and different raters were used for different patients. Since raters were not consistent from patient to patient, the intraclass correlation coefficient might be biased if it was based on a single analysis of variance for a crossed design, rather than the appropriate balanced incomplete block design. No information is provided in the paper to clarify this, however. Despite this methodological question, Beigel at al. reported extremely high item reliability coefficients (ranging from .86 to .99). Reliability was equally high when the small sample of manic patients was considered alone. Thus, the scale appears to have high reliability when used by experienced nurses who are trained in the use of the scale and granted an extended observation period.

In addition to reliability, Beigel et al. (1971) also reported on the concurrent validity of the scale. They correlated the nurses' ratings with a global mania rating (15-point scale) made by staff psychiatrists. The validity coefficients for 22 of the 26 items were highly significant (ranging from .86 to .93). Beigel et al. also reported the correlation between the Manic-State Rating Scale and a checklist of manic symptoms completed by the nurse raters. However, each item in the checklist corresponded to one or more items in the rating scale. Since there was almost total item overlap and the same raters completed both scales, information on the correlation between scales has little meaning and therefore is not reported here.

Thus, the Manic-State Rating Scale was developed specifically for use with bipolar depressives and has demonstrated adequate reliability and concurrent validity. The scale has been used as an outcome measure to evaluate change (e.g., Beigel & Murphy, 1971; Janowsky et al., 1978) and is worthy of future examination. Additional evaluation of the scale would be worthwhile.

CONCLUSION

In this chapter we have reviewed the psychological assessment of depression. A large number of specific psychometric scales have been included. The number of methodological criteria, in combination with the number of measures examined, makes the task of integrating the information difficult. On the basis of our experience in working with depressed patients, we have developed what we consider a useful assessment battery. Although some of these measures are not covered in the present chapter, readers may find this information useful. Table 3.1 outlines our recommended assessment battery.

The major emphasis in this chapter has been on the psychometric properties and the clinical utility of the measures discussed here. Advances in our field are often preceded by (and dependent on) advances in the measurement of our constructs. In the past 20 years the assessment of depression has progressed, and it is hoped that this chapter will serve as an encouragement to clinicians to employ these readily available, well-researched instruments while continuing

to investigate the variations in this most interesting disorder.

APPENDIX 3.1. INSTRUMENTS FOR ASSESSING DEPRESSION

Self-Report Tests That Assess Symptoms of Depression

An asterisk indicates a test designed for assessment of depression with a special population.

Inventory of Depressive Symptoms
Inventory to Diagnose Depression
Beck Depression Inventory (BDI)
Geriatric Depression Scale°
Zung Self-Rating Depression Scale (SDS)
Weissman–Rick Elation–Depression Scale
Center for Epidemiologic Studies Depression Scale (CES-D)
Lee's Self-Rating Scale for Depression
Comprehensive Psychopathological Rating Scale for Depression
Kellner and Sheffield Self-Rating Test
Wittenborn Psychometric Rating Scale
Depression Adjective Checklists (DACL)
Wakefield Self-Assessment Depression Inventory
Multiscore Depression Inventory
Depression Self-Rating Scale for Children°
Children's Depression Inventory°
Carroll Rating Scale for Depression (CRS)
Weinberg Screening Affective Scale°
Childhood Depression Assessment Tool°
Costello–Comrey Scale
QD2 Questionnaire
Depression Rating Scale for Children°
Clyde Mood Scale
Wang Self-Assessing Depression Scale
Institute for Personality and Ability Testing Depression Scale
Rockliff Self-Rating Questionnaire
Plutchik–van Praag Self-Report Depression Scale
Depression Questionnaire
Depression Symptom Inventory
Popoff Index of Depression
Rimon's Brief Depression Scale
Hospital Anxiety and Depression Scale
Levine–Pilowsky Questionnaire
Vietnamese Depression Scale
The Anxiety and Depression Scale
Irratibility, Anxiety and Depression Scale

Projective Tests Used in the Assessment of Depression

Rorschach
Thematic Apperception Test
Family Drawing Depression Scale
Bender Gestalt Test
Picture Projective Test

TABLE 3.1. Recommended Assessment Battery

Session	Recommended measures
First session	Structured Clinical Interview for DSM-III-R (SCID) Hamilton Rating Scale for Depression (HRSD) Beck Depression Inventory (BDI) Symptom Checklist-90 (SCL-90) Hopelessness Scale (HS)
Weekly	BDI
Monthly	HRSD
Termination	SCID HRSD BDI SCL-90 HS

Tests That Assess General Psychopathology or Mood, Including Depression

General Health Questionnaire
Symptom Checklist-90-R (SCL-90-R)
Hopkins Symptom Checklist
Newcastle Anxiety and Depression Diagnostic Index
Middlesex Hospital Questionnaire
Multiple Affect Adjective Checklist
Profile of Mood States
General Behavior Inventory
Mental Health Inventory
Eight State Questionnaire
Differential Emotions Scale

Tests That Assess Personality Related to Depression

There are many tests that assess various aspects of theories of depression; these tests are not listed here.

Minnesota Multiphasic Personality Inventory (MMPI) and MMPI-2
Manifest Depression Scale
Millon Clinical Multiaxial Inventory
Eysenck Personality Questionnaire
Marke–Nyman Temperament Scale

REFERENCES

Aitken, R. C. B. (1969). Measurement feelings using visual analogue scales. *Proceedings of the Royal Society of Medicine, 62*, 989–993.

Akiskal, H. (1981). Subaffective disorders: Dysthymic, cyclothymic and bipolar II disorders in the "borderline" realm. *Psychiatric Clinics of North America, 4*, 25–46.

Akiskal, H., Rosenthal, T., Haykal, R., Lemmi, H., Rosenthal, R., & Scott-Strauss, A. (1980). Characterological depressions: Clinical and sleep EEG findings separating "subaffective dysthymias" from "character spectrum disorders," *Archives of General Psychiatry, 33*, 777–783.

American Psychiatric Association. (1987). *Diagnostic and statistical manual of mental disorders* (3rd ed., rev.). Washington, DC: Author.

American Psychiatric Association. (1994). *Diagnostic and statistical manual of mental disorders* (4th ed.). Washington, DC: Author.

Bech, P., Bolwig, T., Kramp, P., & Rafaelsen, O. (1979). The Bech–Rafaelsen Mania Scale and the Hamilton Depression Scale. *Acta Psychiatrica Scandinavica, 59*, 420–430.

Beck, A. T. (1967). *Depression: Clinical, experimental and therapeutic aspects*. New York: Harper & Row.

Beck, A. T., & Beamesderfer, A. (1974). Assessment of depression: The depression inventory. In P. Pichot (Ed.), *Modern problems in pharmacopsychiatry: Vol. 7. Psychological measurement in psychopharmacology*. Basel: Karger.

Beck, A. T., & Beck, R. W. (1972). Screening depressed patients in family practice: A rapid technique. *Postgraduate Medicine, 52*, 81–85.

Beck, A. T., & Kovacs, M. (1979). Assessment of suicidal intention: The Scale for Suicide Ideation. *Journal of Consulting and Clinical Psychology, 47*, 343–352.

Beck, A. T., Rial, W. Y., & Rickels, K. (1974). Short form of depression inventory: Cross validation. *Psychological Reports, 34*(3), 1184–1186.

Beck, A. T., Rush, A. J., Shaw, B. F., & Emery, G. (1979). *Cognitive therapy of depression*. New York: Guilford Press.

Beck, A. T., Steer, R. A., & Garbin, M. A. (1988). Psychometric properties of the Beck Depression Inventory: Twenty-five years of evaluation. *Clinical Psychology Review, 8*, 77–100.

Beck, A. T., Ward, C. H., Mendelson, M., Mock, J., & Erbaugh, J. (1961). An inventory for measuring depression. *Archives of General Psychiatry, 4*, 561–571.

Beck, A. T., Weissman, A., Lester, D., & Trexler, L. (1974). Measurement of pessimism: The Hopelessness Scale. *Journal of Consulting and Clinical Psychology, 42*, 861–865.

Beutler, L. E., Wakefield, P., & Williams, E. (1994). Use of psychological tests/instruments for treatment planning. In M. E. Maruish (Ed.), *The use of psychological testing for treatment planning and outcome assessment*. Hillsdale, NJ: Erlbaum.

Beigel, A., & Murphy, D. (1974). Assessing clinical characteristics of the manic state. *American Journal of Psychiatry, 128*, 44–50.

Beigel, A., Murphy, D., & Bunney, W. (1971). The Manic State Rating Scale: Scale construct, reliability, and validity. *Archives of General Psychiatry, 25*, 256–262.

Biggs, J. T., Wylie, L. T., & Ziegler, V. E. (1978). Validity of the Zung Self-Rating Depression Scale. *British Journal of Psychiatry, 132*, 381–385.

Blackburn, I., Bishop, S., Glen, A., Whalley, L., & Christie, J. (1981). The efficacy of cognitive therapy in depression: A treatment trial using cognitive therapy and pharmacotherapy each alone and in combination. *British Journal of Psychiatry, 131*, 181–189.

Blaser, R., Low, D., & Schaublin, A. (1968). Die Messung der depressionstiefe mit einmen Fragebogen. *Psychiatric Clinics, 1*, 299–319.

Boyd, J. H., Weissman, M. M., Thompson, W. D., & Myers, J. K. (1982). Screening for depression in a community sample: Understanding the discrepancies between depression symptom and diagnostic scales. *Archives of General Psychiatry, 39*, 1195–1200.

Brown, G. L., & Zung, W. W. K. (1972). Depression scales: Self- or physician rating? A validation of certain clinically observable phenomena. *Comprehensive Psychiatry, 13*, 361–367.

Bukberg, J., Penman, D., & Holland, J. C. (1984). Depression in hospitalized cancer patients. *Psychosomatic Medicine, 46*, 199–212.

Burkhart, B. R., Gynther, M. D., & Fromuth, M. E. (1980). The relative predictive validity of subtle versus obvious items on the MMPI Depression scale. *Journal of Clinical Psychology, 36*, 748–751.

Butcher, J. N., & Dahlstrom, W. G. (1964). *Comparability of the taped and booklet versions of the MMPI*. Unpublished manuscript, University of North Carolina.

Butcher, J. N., Dahlstrom, W. G., Graham, J. R., Tellegen, A. M., & Kaemmer, B. (1989). *MMPI-2: Manual for administration and scoring*. Minneapolis: University of Minnesota Press.

Butcher, J. N., Graham, J. R., Williams, C. L., & Ben-Porath, Y. (1989). *Development and use of the MMPI-2 content scales*. Minneapolis: University of Minnesota Press.

Carroll, B. J., Feinberg, M., Greden, J. F., Haskett, R. F., James, N., Steiner, M., & Tarika, J. (1980). Diagnosis of endogenous depression: Comparison of clinical, research and neuroendocrine criteria. *Journal of Affective Disorders, 2*, 177–194.

Carroll, B. J., Feinberg, M., Smouse, P. E., Rawson, S. G., & Greden, J. F. (1981). The Carroll Rating Scale for Depression: I. Development, reliability, and validation. *British Journal of Psychiatry, 138*, 194–200.

Carroll, B. J., Fielding, J. M., & Blashki, T. G. (1973). Depression rating scales: A critical review. *Archives of General Psychiatry, 28*, 361–366.

Christenfeld, R., Lubin, B., & Satin, M. (1978). Concurrent validity of the Depression Adjective Checklist in a normal population. *American Journal of Psychiatry, 135*, 582–584.

Clark, D. C., Cavanaugh, S. V. A., & Gibbons, R. D. (1983). The core symptoms of depression in medical and psychiatric patients. *Journal of Nervous and Mental Disease, 171*, 705–713.

Clyde, D. (1950). *Construction and validation of an emotional association test*. Unpublished doctoral dissertation, Pennsylvania State College.

Comrey, A. (1957). A factor analysis of items on the MMPI Depression scale. *Educational Psychological Measurement, 17*, 578–585.

Craig, T., & Van Natta, P. (1978). Current medication use and symptoms of depression in a general population. *American Journal of Psychiatry, 135*, 1036–1039.

Craven, J. L., Rodin, G. M., Johnson, L., & Kennedy, S. H. (1987). The diagnosis of major depression in renal dialysis patients. *Psychosomatic Medicine, 49*, 482–492.

Crowne, D., & Marlowe, D. (1960). A new scale of social desirability independent of psychopathology. *Journal of Consulting Psychology, 24*, 349–354.

Dahlstrom, W., Welsh, G., & Dahlstrom, L. (1975). *An MMPI handbook: Vol. 2. Research applications*. Minneapolis: University of Minnesota Press.

Davies, B., Burrows, G., & Poynton, C. (1975). A comparative study of four depression rating scales. *Australian and New Zealand Journal of Psychiatry, 9*, 21–24.

Delay, J., Pichot, P., Lemperiere, T., & Mirouze, R. (1963). La nosologie des états depressifs: Rapports entre l'étiologie et la sémiologie. II. Résultats du questionnaire de Beck. *Encephale, 52*, 497–505.

Dempsey, P. (1964). A unidimensional depression scale for the MMPI. *Journal of Consulting Psychology, 28*, 364–370.

Dempsey, P., & Baumoff, M. (1963). The statistical use of artifact distributions to establish chronological sequence. *American Antiquity, 28*, 496–509.

Depue, R. A., & Monroe, S. M. (1979). The unipolar-bipolar distinction in the depressive disorders. *Psychological Bulletin, 85*, 1001–1029.

Derogatis, L. R., Lipman, R. S., & Covi, L. (1973). SCL-90: An outpatient psychiatric rating scale—preliminary report. *Psychopharmacology Bulletin, 9*, 13–25.

Eichman, W. J. (1973). *A short-term retest study of female psychiatric cases*. Unpublished manuscript, University of North Carolina.

Ekman, P., & Friesen, W. (1974). Nonverbal behavior and psychopathology. In R. Friedman & M. Katz (Eds.), *The psychology of depression: Contemporary theory and research*. Washington, DC: V. H. Winston.

Endicott, J., Cohen, J., Nee, J., Fleiss, J., & Sarantakos, S. (1981). Hamilton Depression Rating Scale, extracted from regular and change versions of the Schedule for Affective Disorders and Schizophrenia. *Archives of General Psychiatry, 38*, 98–103.

Endicott, J., & Spitzer, R. (1978). A diagnostic interview: The Schedule for Affective Disorders and Schizophrenia. *Archives of General Psychiatry, 35*, 837–844.

Endicott, N. A., & Jortner, S. (1966). Objective measures of depression. *Archives of General Psychiatry, 15*, 249–255.

Ennis, J., Barnes, R. A., Kennedy, S., & Trachtenberg, D. D. (1989). Depression in self harm patients. *British Journal of Psychiatry, 154*, 41–47.

Epstein, S. (1979). The stability of behavior: I. On predicting most of the people much of the time. *Journal of Personality and Social Psychology, 37*, 1097–1126.

Evans, D., Hearn, M., Uhlemann, M., & Ivey, A. (1984). *Essential interviewing: A programmed approach to effective communication* (2nd ed.). Monterey, CA: Brooks/Cole.

Faschingbauer, T. R. (1972). *A short written form of the group MMPI*. Unpublished doctoral dissertation, University of North Carolina.

Feinberg, M., Carroll, B. J., Smouse, P. E., & Rawson, S. G. (1981). The Carroll Rating Scale for Depression III. Comparison with other rating instruments. *British Journal of Psychiatry, 138*, 205–209.

Fisch, J., Frey, S., & Hirsbrunner, H. (1983). Analyzing nonverbal behavior in depression. *Journal of Abnormal Psychology, 92*, 307–318,

Folstein, M. F., & Luria, R. E. (1973). Reliability, validity and clinical application of the Visual Analogue Mood Scale. *Psychological Medicine, 3*, 479–486.

Fowles, D. C., & Gersh, F. (1979). Neurotic depression: The endogenous–neurotic distinction. In R. A. Depue (Ed.), *The psychology of depressive disorders: Implications for the effects of stress*. New York: Academic Press.

Frank, R. G., Beck, N. C., Parkerm J. C., Kashani, J. H., Elliott, T. R., Haut, A. E., Smith, E., Atwood, C., Brownlee-Duffeck, M., & Kay, D. R. (1988). Depression in rheumatoid arthritis. *Journal of Rheumatology, 15*, 920–925.

Friedman, A. S., Cowitz, B., Cohen, H. W., & Granick, S. (1963). Syndromes and themes of psychotic depression. *Archives of General Psychiatry, 9*, 504–509.

Gallagher, D., Niles, G., & Thompson, L. W. (1982). Reliability of the Beck Depression Inventory with older adults. *Journal of Consulting and Clinical Psychology, 50*, 152–153.

Gardner, E. (1968). *Development of a symptom check list for the measurement of depression in the population*. Unpublished manuscript.

Garner, D., & Bemis, K. (1984). Cognitive therapy for anorexia nervosa. In D. M. Garner & P. E. Garfinkel (Eds.), *Handbook of psychotherapy for anorexia nervosa and bulimia*. New York: Guilford Press.

Gersh, F. S., & Fowles, D. C. (1979). Neurotic depression: The concept of anxious depression. In R. A. Depue (Ed.), *The psychology of depressive disorders: Implications for the effects of stress*. New York: Academic Press.

Gilliland, A. R., & Colgin, R. (1951). Norms, reliability and forms of the MMPI. *Journal of Consulting Psychology, 15*, 435–438.

Graham, J. R. (1977). *The MMPI: A practical guide*. New York: Oxford University Press.

Grinker, R. R., Miller, J., Sabshin, M., Nunn, R., & Nunnally, J. C. (1961). *Phenomena of depressions*. New York: Harper & Row.

Hamilton, M. (1959). The assessment of anxiety states by rating. *British Journal of Medical Psychology, 32*, 30–55.

Hamilton, M. (1960). A rating scale for depression. *Journal of Neurology, Neurosurgery and Psychiatry, 12*, 56–62.

Hamilton, M., & White, J. (1959). Clinical syndromes in depressive states. *Journal of Mental Science, 105*, 985–987.

Hathaway, S. R., & McKinley, J. C. (1943). *The Minnesota Multiphasic Personality Inventory* (rev. ed.). Minneapolis: University of Minnesota Press.

Hedlund, J., & Vieweg, B. (1979). The Hamilton Rating Scale for Depression: A comprehensive review. *Journal of Operational Psychiatry, 10*, 149–162.

Hersen, M. (1976). Historical perspectives in behavioral assessment. In M. Hersen & A. Bellack (Eds.), *Behavioral assessment: A practical handbook*. Elmsford, NY: Pergamon Press.

Hesselbrock, L. C., Hesselbrock, V. M., Tennen, H., Meyer, R. E., & Workman, K. L. (1983). Methodological considerations in the assessment of depression in alcoholics. *Journal of Consulting and Clinical Psychology, 51*, 399–405.

Howes, M., & Hokanson, J. (1979). Conversational and social responses to depressive interpersonal behavior. *Journal of Abnormal Psychology, 88*, 625–634.

Husaini, B. A., Neff, J. A., Harrington, J. B., Hughes, M. D., & Stone, R. H. (1980). Depression in rural communities: Validating the CES-D scale. *Journal of Community Psychology, 8*, 20–27.

Janowsky, D., Judd, L., Huey, L., Rochman, N., Parker, D., & Segal, D. (1978). Naloxone effects on manic symptoms and growth-hormone levels. *Lancet, 320*.

Jurjevich, R. M. (1966). Short interval test–retest stability of MMPI, CPI, Cornell Index, and Symptom Check List. *Journal of General Psychology, 74*, 201–206.

Katz, M. M, & Lyerly, S. B. (1963). Methods for measuring adjustment and social behavior in the community: Rationale, description, discriminative validity and scale development. *Psychological Reports, 13*, 503–535.

Katz, R., Stephen, J., Shaw, B. F., Mathew, A., Newman, F., & Rosenbluth, M. (1995). The East York Health Needs Study: I. Incidence and prevalence of DSM-III-R psychiatric disorder in a sample of Canadian women. *British Journal of Psychiatry, 166*, 100–106.

Kazdin, A. E. (1981). Assessment techniques for childhood depression: A critical appraisal. *Journal of the American Academy of Child Psychiatry, 22*, 157–164.

Kiloh, L. G., & Garside, R. F. (1963). The independence of neurotic depression and endogenous depression. *British Journal of Psychiatry, 109*, 451–463.

Klein, D. F. (1974). Endogenomorphic depression. *Archives of General Psychiatry, 31*, 447–454.

Krupp, L. B., Alvarez, L. A., LaRocca, N. G., & Scheinberg, L. C. (1988). Fatigue in multiple sclerosis. *Archives of Neurology, 45*, 435–437.

Knight, R. G., Waal-Manning, H. J., & Spears, G. F. (1983). Some norms and reliability data for the State–Trait Anxiety Inventory and the Zung Self-Rating Depression Scale. *British Journal of Clinical Psychology, 22*, 245–249.

Kupfer, D., & Rush, A.J. (1983). Recommendations for specific reports on depression. *American Journal of Psychiatry, 140*, 1327–1328.

Langein, R., & Stancer, H. (1979). Evidence that depression rating scales primarily measure a social undesirability response set. *Acta Psychiatrica Scandinavica, 59*, 70–79.

Lazarus, A. (1971). *Behavior therapy and beyond*. New York: McGraw-Hill.

Lewinsohn, P. (1976). Manual of instruction for behavior ratings used for observation of interpersonal behavior. In E. Mash & L. Terdal (Eds.), *Behavior therapy assessment*. New York: Springer.

Lewinsohn, P., & Teri, L. (1982). Selection of depressed and nondepressed subjects on the basis of self-report data. *Journal of Consulting and Clinical Psychology, 50*, 590–591.

Linehan, M. (1981). A social–behavioral analysis of suicide and parasuicide: Implications for clinical assessment and treatment. In J. Clarkin & H. Glazer (Eds.), *Depression: Behavioral and directive intervention strategies*. New York: Garland Press.

Linehan, M., & Chiles, J. (1983). Reasons for staying alive when you are thinking of killing yourself: The Reasons for Living Inventory. *Journal of Consulting and Clinical Psychology, 51*, 276–286.

Lubin, B. (1965). Adjective checklists for measurement of depression. *Archives of General Psychiatry, 12*, 57–62.

Lubin, B., Hornstra, R. K., & Lowe, A. (1974). Course of depressive mood in a psychiatric population upon application for service and at 3- and 12-month reinterview. *Psychological Reports, 34*, 424–426.

Luria, R. E. (1975). The validity and reliability of the Visual Analogue Mood Scale. *Journal of Psychiatric Research, 12*, 51–57.

Lustman, P. J., Griffith, L. S., Clouse, R. E., & Cryer, P. E. (1986). Psychiatric illness in diabetes mellitus: Relationship to symptoms and glucose control. *Journal of Nervous and Mental Disease, 174*, 736–742.

Marone, J., & Lubin, B. (1968). Relationships between set 2 of the Depression Adjective Check Lists (DACL). and Zung Self-Rating Depression Scale (SDS). *Psychological Reports, 22*, 333–334.

May, A. E., Urquart, A., & Taran, J. (1969). Self-evaluation of depression in various diagnostic and therapeutic groups. *Archives of General Psychiatry, 21*, 191–194.

McKinley, J., & Hathaway, S. (1944). The MMPI: V. Hysteria, Hypomania, and Psychopathic Deviate. *Journal of Applied Psychology, 28*, 153–174.

Meites, K., Lovallo, W., & Pishkin, V. (1980). A comparison of four scales for anxiety, depression, and neuroticism. *Journal of Clinical Psychology, 36*, 427–432.

Moffic, H. S., & Paykel, E. S. (1975). Depression in multiple sclerosis. *General Hospital Psychiatry, 9*, 426–434.

Myers, J. K., & Weissman, M. M. (1980). Use of a self-report symptom scale to detect depression in a community sample. *American Journal of Psychiatry, 137*, 1081–1084.

Nevid, J.S. (1983). Hopelessness, social desirability and construct validity. *Journal of Consulting and Clinical Psychology, 51*, 139–140.

Newmark, C. S. (1971). MMPI: Comparison of the oral form presented by a live examiner and booklet form. *Psychological Reports, 29*, 797–798.

Newmark, C. S. (1973). *Brief retest stability with female psychiatric cases*. Unpublished manuscript, University of North Carolina.

Newson-Smith, J. G. B., & Hirsh, S. R. (1979). Psychiatric symptoms in self-poisoning patients. *Psychological Medicine, 9,* 493–500.

Nussbaum, K., Wittig, B. A., Hanlon, T. E., & Kurland, A. A. (1963). Intravenous nialamide in the treatment of depressed female patients. *Comprehensive Psychiatry, 4,* 105–116.

O'Connor, J., Stefic, E., & Gresock, C. (1957). Some patterns of depression. *Journal of Clinical Psychology, 13,* 122–125.

O'Hara, M., & Rehm, L. (1983). Hamilton Rating Scale for Depression: Reliability and validity of judgements of novice raters. *Journal of Consulting and Clinical Psychology, 51,* 318–319.

Othmer, E., & Othmer, S. C. (1991). *The clinical interview using DSM-III-R.* Washington, DC: American Psychiatric Press.

Overall, J. E. (1962). Dimensions of manifest depression. *Psychiatric Research, 1,* 239–245.

Overall, J. E., & Gorham, D. R. (1962). The Brief Psychiatric Rating Scale. *Psychological Reports, 10,* 799–812.

Overall, J. E., & Zisook, S. (1980). Diagnosis and the phenomenology of depressive disorders. *Journal of Consulting and Clinical Psychology, 48,* 626–634.

Paykel, E. S. (1971). Classification of depressed patients: A cluster analysis derived grouping. *British Journal of Psychiatry, 118,* 275–288.

Radloff, L. S. (1977). The CES-D Scale: A self-report depression scale for research in the general population. *Applied Psychological Measurement, 1,* 385–401.

Raft, D., Spencer, R. F., Toomey, T., & Brogan, D. (1977). Depression in medical outpatients: Use of the Zung scale. *Diseases of the Nervous System, 38,* 999–1004.

Raskin, A., Schulterbrandt, J., Reatig, N., & McKeon, J. (1969). Replication of factors of psychopathology in interview, ward behavior, and self-report ratings of hospitalized depressives. *Journal of Nervous and Mental Disease, 148,* 87–96.

Reynolds, W. M., & Gould, J. W. (1981). A psychometric investigation of the standard and short form Beck Depression Inventory. *Journal of Consulting and Clinical Psychology, 49,* 306–307.

Riskind, J., & Beck, A. T. (1983). *Phenomenology of emotional disorder: Symptoms that differentiate between generalized anxiety disorder, major depressive disorder, and mixed disorder.* Paper presented at the World Congress on Behaviour Therapy, Washington, DC.

Robins, L. N., Helzer, J. E., Croughan, J., & Ratcliff, K. S. (1981). National Institute of Mental Health Diagnostic Interview Schedule: Its history, characteristics and validity. *Archives of General Psychiatry, 38,* 381–389.

Robins, L. N., Wing, J., Wittchen, H. U., Helzer, J. E., Babor, T. F., Burke, J., Farmer, A., Jablenski, A., Pickens, R., Regier, D. A., Sartorius, N., & Towle, L. H. (1988). The Composite International Diagnostic Interview: An epidemiologic instrument suitable for use in conjunction with different diagnostic systems and in different cultures. *Archives of General Psychiatry, 45,* 1069–1077.

Rodin, G., Craven, J., & Littlefield, C. (1991). *Depression in the medically ill: An integrated approach.* New York: Brunner/Mazel.

Salkind, M. R. (1969). Beck Depression Inventory in general practice. *Journal of the Royal College of General Practice, 18,* 267–271.

Schwab, J., Bialow, M., & Holzer, C. (1967). A comparison of two rating scales for depression. *Journal of Clinical Psychology, 23,* 94–96.

Scott, N. A., Hannum, T. E., & Ghirst, S. L. (1982). Assessment of depression among incarcerated females. *Journal of Personality Assessment, 46,* 372–379.

Skinner, H., & Blashfield, R. (1982). Increasing the impact of cluster analysis research: The case of psychiatric classification. *Journal of Consulting and Clinical Psychology, 50,* 727–735.

Skyr, I., Onstad, S., Torgersen, S., & Kringlen, E. (1991). High interrater reliability for the Structured Clinical Interview for DSM-III-R Axis I (SCID-I). *Acta Psychiatrica Scandinavica, 184,* 167–173.

Smith, D., & Kraft, W. (1983). DSM-III: Do psychologists really want an alternative? *American Psychologist, 38,* 777–785.

Smith, M. D., Hong, B. A., & Robinson, A. M. (1985). Diagnosis of depression in patients with end-stage renal disease: Comparative analysis. *American Journal of Medicine, 79,* 160–166.

Sotsky, S., & Glass, D. (1983). *The Hamilton Rating Scale: A critical appraisal and modification for psychotherapy research.* Paper presented at the annual convention of the Society for Psychotherapy Research, Sheffield, England.

Spitzer, R., Endicott, J., & Robins, E. (1978). Research Diagnostic Criteria: Rationale and reliability. *Archives of General Psychiatry, 35,* 773–782.

Spitzer, R., Williams, J. B. W., Gibbon, M., & First, M. (1992). The Structured Clinical Interview for DSM-III-R (SCID): I. History, rationale, and description. *Archives of General Psychiatry, 49,* 624–636.

Starkstein, S. E., & Robinson, R. G. (1989). Depression and coexisting disease. In R. G. Robinson & P. V. Rabins (Eds.), *Assessment of depression.* New York: Igaku-Shoin.

Steer, R. A., McElroy, M. G., & Beck, A. T. (1982). Structure of depression in alcoholic men: A partial replication. *Psychological Report, 50,* 723–728.

Steer, R. A., Shaw, B. F., Beck, A. T., & Fine, E. W. (1977). Structure of depression in black alcoholic men. *Psychological Reports, 41,* 1235–1241.

Stenbeck, A., Rimon, R., & Turunen, M. (1967). Validitet av Taylor Manifest Anxiety Scale. *Nordisk Psykiatrisk Tidsskrift, 21,* 79–85.

Strober, M., Green, J., & Carlson, G. (1981). Utility of the Beck Depression Inventory with psychiatrically hospitalized adolescents. *Journal of Consulting and Clinical Psychology, 49,* 482–483.

Turner, J. A., & Romano, J. M. (1984). Self report screening measures for depression in chronic pain patients. *Journal of Clinical Psychology, 40,* 909–913.

van Praag, H., & Plutchik, R. (1987). Interconvertability of five self-report measures of depression. *Psychiatry Research, 22*(3), 243–256.

Waxer, P. (1974). Nonverbal cues for depression. *Journal of Abnormal Psychology, 53,* 318–322.

Weckowicz, T. E., Muir, W., & Cropley, A. J. (1967). A factor analysis of the Beck Inventory of Depression. *Journal of Consulting Psychology, 31,* 23–28.

Weissman, M. M., Prusoff, B., & Newberry, P. B. (1975). *Comparison of CES-D, Zung, Beck self-report depression scales* (Tech. Report No. ADM 42–47–83). Rockville, MD: Center for Epidemiology Studies, National Institute of Mental Health.

Williams, J. B. W., Barlow, D., & Agras, W. (1972). Behavioral assessment of severe depression. *Archives of General Psychiatry, 72,* 303–337.

Williams, J. B. W., Gibbon, M., First, M., Spitzer, R., Davies, M., Borus, J., Howes, M., Kane, J., Pope, H., Rounsaville, B., & Wittchen, H. (1992). The Structured Clinical Interview for DSM-III-R (SCID): II. Multisite test–retest reliability. *Archives of General Psychiatry, 49,* 630–637.

Williams, J. B. W., & Spitzer, R. (Eds.). (1984). *Psychotherapy research: Where are we and where should we go?* New York: Guilford Press.

Windle, C. (1955). Further studies of test–retest effect on personality questionnaires. *Educational and Psychological Measurement, 15,* 246–253.

Winfield, D. L. (1952). An investigation of the relationship between intelligence and the statistical reliability of the MMPI. *Journal of Clinical Psychology, 8,* 146–148.

Wing, J. K., Babor, T., Brugha, T., Burkem, J., Cooper, J. E., Giel, R., Jablenski, A., Regier, D., & Sartorius, N. (1990). SCAN: Schedules for Clinical Assessment in Neuropsychiatry. *Archives of General Psychiatry, 47,* 589–593.

Wing, J. K., Birley, J., Cooper, J., Graham, P., & Isaacs, A. (1967). Reliability of a procedure for measuring and classifying "present psychiatric state." *British Journal of Psychiatry, 113,* 499–515.

Wing, J. K., Cooper, J. F., & Sartorius, N. (1974). *Measurement and classification of psychiatric symptoms: An instructional manual for the PSE and CATEGO program.* New York: Cambridge University Press.

Ziegler, V., Meyer, D., Rosen, S., & Biggs, J. (1978). Reliability of videotaped Hamilton ratings. *Biological Psychiatry, 13,* 119–122.

Zuckerman, M., & Lubin, B. (1965). Normative data for the Multiple Affect Adjective Check List. *Psychological Reports, 16,* 438.

Zung, W. W. K. (1965). A self-rating depression scale. *Archives of General Psychiatry, 12,* 63–70.

Zung, W. W. K. (1967). Factors influencing the Self-Rating Depression Scale. *Archives of General Psychiatry, 16,* 543–547.

Zung, W. W. K. (1968). Evaluating treatment methods for depressive disorders. *American Journal of Psychiatry, 124,* 40–48.

Zung, W. W. K. (1969). A cross-cultural survey of symptoms of depression. *American Journal of Psychiatry, 126,* 154–159.

Zung, W. W. K., Richards, C. B., & Short, M. J. (1965). Self-rating depression scale in an outpatient clinic. *Archives of General Psychiatry, 13,* 508–515.

Zung, W. W. K., & Wonnacott, T. H. (1970). Treatment prediction in depression using a self-rating scale. *Biological Psychiatry, 24,* 321–329.

4

Depression and Its Boundaries with Selected Axis I Disorders

JACK D. MASER
RICHARD WEISE
HARRY GWIRTSMAN

THE NATURE OF COMORBIDITY

The present chapter considers the relationship between the depressive disorders and other selected Axis I disorders. Although the revised third edition of the *Diagnostic and Statistical Manual of Mental Disorders* (DSM-III-R; American Psychiatric Association, 1987) is the primary definitional source for much of this chapter, we have attempted to update to the fourth edition (DSM-IV; American Psychiatric Association, 1994) where possible. The reader may also wish to read Lehmann's (1985) chapter on the same subject, which appeared in the first edition of this handbook (Beckham & Leber, 1985). A related, complementary perspective on boundaries and comorbidity of psychiatric disorders generally may be found in Klein and Riso (1993).

In this chapter we consider the meaning of the term "comorbidity," and point out that major depression is itself one of the most frequent comorbid disorders, if not the most frequent one. For reasons to be brought out later, recognition of depression in the clinic and its formal assessment are made more difficult by comorbidity. In

order to diagnose a person as depressed, and in addition as having a separate disorder (such as dysthymia or anorexia nervosa), one must distinguish the two disorders from each other and conclude that the observed mixture is not a third, separate disorder. In so doing, we are faced with a number of topics that need resolution, or at least recognition as problem areas. How are disorders defined? Is the primary–secondary distinction a means of assigning priority with regard to etiology? What is the impact of symptom and syndrome instability? We then bring these issues to bear on depressions that are comorbid with dysthymia; schizophrenia and schizoaffective disorder; anxiety disorders; eating disorders; somatization disorder; and substance abuse/dependence. Throughout the chapter, we discuss numerous instances of comorbidity between depression and other Axis I disorders. However, a mere listing of such instances would be of limited interest.

The term "comorbidity" does not appear in the subject index of the 1985 edition of this handbook (although Lehmann mentions "comorbidity" on p. 669). Even though "comorbidity" was coined in 1970 by Alvin Feinstein, a computer search of the literature does not reveal the use of the word in the psychological or psychiatric literature prior to 1986. After 1986, the use of "comorbid" for describing the presence of coexisting disorders increased dramati-

The opinions or assertions expressed in this chapter are our own and are not to be considered as official or as reflecting the views of the National Institute of Mental Health.

cally. (On the basis of this increasing frequency, "comorbidity" was introduced as a medical subject heading in the National Library of Medicine's Medlars system in 1989.)

Feinstein (1970) defined "comorbidity" as "any distinct additional clinical entity that has existed or that may occur during the clinical course of a patient who has the index disease under study" (pp. 456–457). Several types of comorbidity are described, but these may be more applicable to other medical specialties than they appear to be at this time for mental illness.

Others have used the concept in a different manner or have preferred an alternative term. Epidemiologists in psychiatry have defined "comorbidity" as the relative risk of developing another disorder. Relative risk can be assessed by a statistic called the "odds ratio." "Odds" is defined as the probability of the occurrence of an event divided by the probability of its non-occurrence. An odds ratio, in a comorbidity sense, is the odds of a second disorder's occurring in the group already having one disorder divided by the odds of the second disorder's occurring in a group without the first disorder. For example, the mood disorders have a high lifetime prevalence in the population—8.3%. Mood disorders are frequently associated with substance abuse, and the National Institute of Mental Health (NIMH) Epidemiologic Catchment Area (ECA) study has revealed that this association occurs in 32% of individuals with at least one mood disorder. Comparing the probabilities of individuals with both a mood disorder and substance abuse to individuals with substance abuse but no mood disorder, we find the odds ratio to be 2.6 (Regier et al., 1990).

A person with one mental illness is likely to have more than one (Boyd et al., 1984; Sturt, 1981). The additional disorders may be concurrently comorbid, or (especially in psychiatric illnesses) comorbid over a lifetime. Many, if not most, disorders listed in the DSM-IV are considered lifetime disorders—for example, schizophrenia, recurrent mood disorders, most anxiety disorders, personality disorders, substance abuse/dependence (at least from the time of addiction), mental retardation, sleep disorders, and others. Even in times of remission, clinicians can usually observe subclinical or low-grade signs and symptoms. If all symptoms of the primary disorder are completely in remission, one does not speak of comorbid disorders, except over the patient's lifetime.

Without the discrete, categorical entities of the DSM-IV, comorbidity would not be an issue of importance. In a dimensional system of classification, the problem of comorbidity—the coexistence of disorders—is minimized, and the patterning of covariation among dimensions becomes important.

Coexistence of disorders can take several forms. They can be of independent origin, but occur together; they can be of different origins, and confound diagnosticians with a mixed presentation; and they may appear to have a primary–secondary relationship to each other. Moreover, the *symptoms* of one or more disorders may occur in the presence of a *syndrome*. Winokur (1990) correctly argues that in the absence of known pathogens for major depression, panic disorder, or schizophrenia, the proper term should be "cosyndromal" rather than "comorbid." The use of "comorbid," however, is widespread, and its acceptance by the clinical community is not likely to be challenged by the more technically accurate "cosyndromal."

DEPRESSION AND COMORBIDITY

Major depression and dysthymia have the potential to coexist with every illness, physical and mental. Indeed, major depression probably co-occurs with other disorders more often than any other psychiatric disorder (Moldin et al., 1993; Wells, Rogers, Burnan, Greenfield, & Ware, 1991; Mezzich, Ahn, Fabrega, & Pilkonis, 1990). By comparison to major depression, bipolar I disorder (i.e., depression and mania) is relatively rare as either a single or a comorbid disorder.

If someone learns that he/she has a terminal illness or is going blind or must have a limb amputated, we would not expect this information to result in schizophrenia, obsessive-compulsive disorder, bulimia nervosa, or mania; however, few would deny the possibility of depression. Similarly, it is not unexpected that chronic psychiatric illnesses, such as schizophrenia or multiple personality disorder, are often accompanied by depression. Major depression as a coexisting disorder is so pervasive that in multiple personality disorder it may be expected to appear in at least one of the personalities. Caddy (1985) reports the psychologically curious case of Audrey H., one of at least three personalities in the same individual. Audrey H. was clinically depressed and began to suffer phobic reactions after a (single?) panic attack. The other personalities were neither depressed nor phobic. Depression can even be present during the manic phase of bipolar disorder—a condition known as "dysphoric" or "mixed" mania (see McElroy et al., 1992, for a review). Clues to the evolution and origins of psychopathology may be found in the very pervasiveness of depression and those disorders with which it most frequently coexists.

Comorbidity of depression with some other disorder raises the practical problem of recognizing the presence of each disorder. Clinicians often miss the symptoms of depression when the presenting complaints focus on another disorder. It is well known that primary care physicians are usually the first health care professionals to see depressed and anxious patients (Watts, 1947; Blacker & Clare, 1987), but are these disorders recognized when seen? Depression was frequently missed by physicians when they were presented with hypochondriacal patients. The patients themselves were usually well aware that they felt dysphoric most of the time; however, because the clinician's attention was focused on the hypochondriasis, the depression went unrecognized and untreated (Barsky, Wyshak, & Klerman, 1991).

Ormel, Koeter, van den Brink, and van de Willige (1991) studied recognition of psychiatric disorders by general-practice physicians in the Netherlands. These physicians recognized anxiety or depression in only 47% of the sample. Physicians tended to recognize patients with depression and comorbid anxiety–depression more frequently than other psychiatric disorders. Less dramatic presentations of anxiety and depression were seldom recognized.

CASENESS AND DIAGNOSIS

How does one define a "case" of depression? At first blush we can say that the diagnostic criteria in the DSM-IV might serve this purpose. Each category in the DSM provides for a binary decision process: A patient either has the disorder or does not. There is no opportunity for a probabilistic statement. However, several factors complicate this easy solution.

First, the objective criteria of DSM-III (American Psychiatric Association, 1980) improved reliability of diagnoses, but agreement among trained clinicians is still below 100%.

There is room for improvement, and this fact means that the nomenclature needs continued verification and change.

Second, testing the validity of DSM categories is a more difficult problem than testing their reliability. There is so much heterogeneity among patients seen by clinicians that it is hardly surprising that even the best diagnosticians come to conceptualize their limited samples in diverse ways. Yet in regard to the core features of various disorders there is broad agreement, and one result of this consensus is the DSM-IV. The process is slow, but research data do affect clinical perspective and allow new hypotheses to emerge.

A third factor complicating total reliance on the DSM-IV for defining a case is that most patients have more than one disorder (Boyd et al., 1984; Sturt, 1981). Clinicians are frequently uncertain whether two disorders are independent of each other; whether one is occurring because of the presence of the other; or whether a third, unknown factor is influencing clinical presentation.

Fourth, the reader is referred to an excellent discussion by Blacker and Tsuang (1992) of the weaknesses of the DSM-III-R (and, by logical extension, of DSM-IV) as a binary, categorical system of classification. These authors review the problems in differential diagnosis of bipolar disorder, and suggest that at this stage in our knowledge a dimensional, probabilistic model may prove more useful.

While not using the term "comorbidity," successive editions of the DSM were forced to deal with its obvious presence. DSM-III did so in part by setting out hierarchical exclusionary rules for the classification system, the effects of which were to restrict dual diagnoses and thereby to bring premature closure to questions of shared vulnerability. Anxiety and depression co-occur so often that they are thought to share some etiological factor(s); however, prior to the removal of most hierarchies, a more accurate prevalence of anxiety disorders was obscured by depression, which ranked higher than anxiety and was therefore the disorder of record.

Multiple diagnoses were made possible in DSM-III through the use of Axis II (personality disorders and developmental disorders) and Axis III (physical disorders or conditions). The presence of an Axis II condition was not meant to imply a fundamental difference in pathogenesis between such a condition and the disorders coded on Axis I. Rather, Axis II was meant to draw attention to these somewhat less florid but more stable, trait-like conditions thought to begin early in development.

Axis III was meant to identify coexisting physical conditions that are potentially relevant to the understanding or management of the case. Some diagnosticians assumed that Axis III implied that disorders listed on Axes I and II did not have a physical component. Such an interpretation can be quickly seen as false because of the presence of many somatic diagnostic criteria in Axis I disorders. For example, somatic changes related to weight, sleep, and activity are frequently observed in major depressive episode; in panic disorder, the clinician can observe dyspnea, dizziness, tachycardia, trembling, sweating, choking, nausea, paresthesia, and other somatic symptoms.

THE PRIMARY–SECONDARY DISTINCTION

The term "secondary depression" is frequently used, yet it is not mentioned in DSM-IV except by implication. If we speak of a "primary" and a "secondary" disorder, clearly we are referring to coexisting or comorbid disorders. The concept of a secondary disorder has an interesting history that dates back to Munro (1966), who proposed the distinction between primary and secondary disorders at about the same time as the Washington University group did so (Woodruff, Murphy, & Herjanic, 1967; Robins & Guze, 1972). The goal of the Washington University investigators was to increase clinical homogeneity in research samples. Woodruff et al. (1967) defined secondary affective disorder as a "current affective syndrome occurring in a patient who has a pre-existing, diagnosable, non-affective, *psychiatric* illness" (emphasis added). This definition is clearly too narrow by today's standards. There is no reason why an affective disorder cannot be secondary to a pre-existing medical condition, and if the primary illness must be "non-affective," we exclude the primary–secondary relationship between chronic dysthymia and major depressive episode, called "double depression" by Keller and Shapiro (1982). Nevertheless, the notion that "secondary" refers to the temporal sequence of syndromes became entrenched in the Feighner criteria (Feighner et al., 1972); in the Research Diagnostic Criteria of Spitzer, Endicott, and Robins (1978a, 1978b); and in

common clinical usage. Here, we present six definitions of "secondary."

1. *As mentioned above, the most frequent reference is to time or chronology: A depressive episode occurs second in time to some pre-existing or primary illness or disorder.* For example, without concluding that a causal relationship exists, a clinician may observe that after years of debilitating anxiety an afflicted individual becomes depressed. Because depression is seen as coming after anxiety attacks, the depression is called "secondary." This meaning is also the one given to "secondary" by Winokur (1990), who holds the primary–secondary distinction to be preferable to that of comorbidity.

2. *A secondary disorder can be "due to the presence of a primary disorder."* Thus, a terminally ill cancer patient may be depressed due to an incurable disease. In this example, the primary disorder, cancer, appeared first and depression second. This differs from the purely temporal definition in that a causal relationship is inferred. DSM-IV states that if a person has a disease like cancer, "the diagnosis is Mood Disorder Due to a General Medical Condition" (American Psychiatric Association, 1994, p. 343).

3. *"Due to" may also mean that the symptoms of the secondary disorder are incorporated in the primary disorder. As the course of the primary illness reaches its most complete expression, many of the symptoms of the secondary disorder follow along.* An example can be found in DSM-III, where the symptoms of anxiety were considered part of the emergent syndrome of depression, and therefore due to depression; hence, they were eliminated as a separate disorder by the application of hierarchical rules.

4. *Another definition of "secondary" is used informally among practitioners to indicate a syndrome or disorder with relatively less severity or predominance than an index disorder.* For example, depression is highly prevalent among schizophrenics, but schizophrenia is seen as the more pervasive and severe condition. Using high treatment rates and lifetime suicide attempts as measures of severity, Vollrath and Angst (1989) found mixed panic and depression to be a more serious illness than depression alone. For this reason, we would call the mixed condition primary and depression secondary.

5. *The primary–secondary distinction has also been used to specify which of several disorders has most severely impaired a patient's functioning. The most impairing disorder is called*

primary; the disorder that produces the lesser impairment in functioning is secondary. Jane Murphy (1990) has analyzed the Stirling County epidemiological data to show that depression is a more seriously disabling disorder than anxiety, carrying a greater burden of risk for death and poor clinical outcome. Depression, by the functional-impairment definition, thus becomes the primary disorder.

Does the use of a temporal definition produce a different grouping of patients than a definition based on impaired functioning? In a well-designed study of a Dutch sample, de Ruiter, Rijken, Garssen, van Schaik, and Kraaimaat (1989) replicated the work of Barlow, DiNardo, Vermilyea, Vermilyea, and Blanchard (1986), but took the original finding of comorbidity among anxiety and depressive disorders one interesting step further. Whereas Barlow et al. used only interference with functioning to define the primary disorder, de Ruiter et al. compared the temporal definition to the interference-with-functioning definition. In the Dutch study, 113 patients were assigned a primary diagnosis of anxiety or depression. By the interference-with-functioning method of distinguishing primary from secondary disorders, the most frequent primary DSM-III-R diagnoses were panic disorder, panic disorder with agoraphobia, generalized anxiety disorder, dysthymia, and major depression. Simple phobia was easily the most frequent additional diagnosis. Social phobia, dysthymia, and major depression were also observed as additional diagnoses, but much less so than simple phobia. According to the temporal or chronological procedure for making the primary–secondary distinction, however, simple phobia was by far the most frequently assigned primary diagnosis. Panic disorder with agoraphobia and panic disorder were also assigned as primary, but in many fewer instances. The most frequent secondary or additional disorder by the temporal method was panic disorder with agoraphobia (31 instances), followed by dysthymia (10), and major depression and panic disorder alone (9 each).

6. *Our last primary–secondary distinction finds its meaning in clinical course. Here the secondary disorder is defined by its influence on the clinical course of the primary disorder.* In mental illness, one is hard pressed to think of a secondary disease or disorder that has no effect on the primary one. The course of depression is potentially influenced by all Axis I, II, and III comorbid conditions, but the extent of that in-

fluence on clinical course is probably not uniform. The idea that this form of secondary illness can have a graded effect on the primary illness may be seen in a study by Coryell, Endicott, and Winokur (1992). These investigators reported a high frequency of recurrence among depressed patients with coexisting obsessions or compulsions, panic attacks, or phobias. All of the anxiety disorders influenced the clinical course of depression; that is, their presence led to recurrence. However, the manner in which they did so was not uniform: Obsessions or compulsions had a greater effect than panic attacks, and phobias had the least effect of the three secondary disorders.

These six definitions are not mutually exclusive. It is possible to use the influence-on-clinical-course definition in combination with any of the other definitions of "secondary." A secondary depression, for example, may occur after a primary anxiety (temporal definition), yet may still influence the course of the anxiety. Secondary depression may also have a lesser influence on functioning or may not represent the preponderance of symptoms, but it may still influence the clinical course of the primary anxiety disorder.

Angst, Vollrath, Merikangas, and Ernst (1990) found that 62% of a purely anxious sample later developed depression, compared to 18% of purely depressed subjects who later developed anxiety. Several clinical investigators have considered the meaning of this preponderance in directionality, taking their start from the biphasic monkey response to separation. Alloy, Kelly, Mineka, and Clements (1990) see it in terms of a revised helplessness–hopelessness theory (Abramson, Seligman, & Teasdale, 1978). A person who is uncertain of his/her degree of helplessness in controlling some important future event will experience pure anxiety. As conviction about being helpless grows and the likelihood of a negative event's occurring becomes certain, a mixed anxiety–depression syndrome results. The syndromes of anxiety and depression share an expectation of uncontrollability, but differ in their expectation of negative outcome. The hopelessness subtype of depression occurs when helplessness turns to hopelessness.

Akiskal (1990) observes that the most common life stressors are losses or threat of loss. The usual reaction to acute stress is an anxiety–depression admixture, which DSM-IV calls adjustment disorder with mixed anxiety and depressed mood. As the adjustment disorder persists, symptoms of generalized anxiety and major depressive episode meet the criteria for these two disorders. Other patterns are described that also take into account the anxiety-to-depression sequence.

MULTIFORMITY IN A DISEASE

The concept of "multiformity in a disease" was introduced by Winokur (1990) to explain why disorders may express themselves with different signs and symptoms and with varying sequences and timing of symptom appearance. If "multiformity" means that some forms of comorbidity may represent alternative expressions of the same underlying diathesis, then it has links to earlier, similar formulations (see Akiskal, 1990, p. 605). Multiformity may have value in helping to conceptualize comorbid conditions (or, as Winokur would prefer, cosyndromal conditions).

Since psychiatric etiologies are unknown, we can presume that two broad classes exist: multiformity, in which a single process is somehow expressed in different yet similar clinical forms; and etiological heterogeneity, in which multiple processes underlie similar clinical phenomena. For our purposes, it is enough to know that in spite of this variability, there are limits to the forms of these disorders seen by clinicians. The physical and psychological limits placed on the range of human experience, action, and reaction constrict the number of possible signs and symptoms, no matter how numerous the causal factors may be.

We extend Winokur's idea of multiformity by linking it to the polythetic diagnostic rules found in the DSM-III and later editions. The rules for diagnosing major depressive episode in DSM-IV require at least five of nine symptoms for this diagnosis. Thus, two patients diagnosed with major depressive episode may present with at least four different symptoms. Further support for the notion that the nomenclature is reflecting multiformity is evident from the introduction of fifth-digit diagnostic code numbers for severity and the presence or absence of psychotic features. Moreover, specifying melancholic features of a major depressive episode introduces two symptoms from which set only one is necessary, and six symptoms of which only three are necessary. The possibility of seasonal patterns, postpartum onset, and the presence of such associated symptoms or comorbid disorders as panic, anxiety, obsessive rumination, and

phobias, add to the picture of clinical complexity and instability. The struggle to develop a classification system that places homogeneous groups of core symptoms together in one category is conceivably made more difficult by temporal patterning, inconsistent symptom expression, a large range of symptoms, associated features, and apparent comorbidity caused by multiple etiologies.

SYMPTOM STABILITY AND CLINICAL COURSE

The concept of multiformity, and the polythetic system of classification now in general use (i.e., the DSM-IV), are tied to assumptions of symptom stability and clinical course. In discussing this issue, we focus on the relationship between anxiety disorders and depression, both of which are now recognized to be lifetime. What is the clinical course of depressive symptoms? Are they stable within a given episode? Are the same symptoms present at each episode of recurrence and relapse?[1] Do our diagnostic systems predict clinical course? And to what extent is course altered by treatment? These are interesting questions for which there are few answers and few data.

Tyrer, Alexander, Remington, and Riley (1987) addressed many of these questions in a 2-year study of the course of illness among three categories of patients classified according to the ninth revision of the *International Classification of Diseases* (ICD-9; World Health Organization, 1978): depressive neurotics, anxiety neurotics, and phobic neurotics. These groups correspond roughly to patients with dysthymia, panic with agoraphobia, and specific phobia, respectively. All patients were assessed four times over the 2-year period. The null hypothesis—no symptomatic differences among the groupings over the four assessments—was rejected: "At different times one symptom may predominate, but such preponderance rarely lasts." Tyrer et al. concluded that the symptoms of anxiety and depression are not consistent enough over time to result in an accurate, discrete, categorical diagnosis.

Symptom instability frustrates efforts to construct a stable, internally consistent categorical system of classification for mental illness. As Tyrer et al. (1987) pointed out, neither the DSM nor the ICD predicts such instability in clinical course. The DSM-IV does suggest that symptom (and syndrome) instability exists through its use of polythetic diagnostic criteria, but it has little to say about prediction of clinical course in depression and the role that one or more comorbid disorders may play in that course. If prediction were possible (e.g., that phobia consistently antedates panic, which antedates depression), it might then be possible to intervene and break the cycle. In the following sections, beginning with major depression and dysthymia, we consider the co-occurrence of depression with various other disorders; in so doing, we consider clinical course and many of the other issues discussed above.

DEPRESSION AND DYSTHYMIA

Dysthymia is both within the spectrum of depressive disorders and comorbid with other disorders within the spectrum. According to Akiskal and Simmons (1985), dysthymia begins insidiously in late childhood or early adolescence in the absence of an episode of major depression. Early onset results in dysthymia's being incorporated in the personality structure of the individual. Adults most often evidence chronic, low-grade depression or dysthymia as a residuum of incompletely remitted unipolar major depression (see Akiskal & Simmons, 1985, for an overview).

Akiskal, King, Rosenthal, Robinson, and Scott-Strauss (1981) established in clinical samples that a large percentage (90%) of adult dysthymics go on to develop depression, while the residua of chronic depressions coalesce into the next recurrence. Lewinsohn, Rohde, Seeley, and Hops (1991) replicated the finding in a community sample, showing a large predominance (91.3%) of adolescents who went on to develop unipolar depression and a smaller percentage (64%) of adults with a similar temporal pattern. The reverse sequence (i.e., dysthymia following depression for the first time) was relatively rare.

Markowitz, Moran, Kocsis, and Frances (1992) found dysthymia preceding other diagnoses; in cases where it did not, an anxiety disorder was the primary illness. For these latter cases, the authors raise the interesting possibility that early-onset anxiety is *prodromal* to dysthymia. The existence of this smaller group would be in accord with the assertion of Cloninger, Martin, Guze, and Clayton (1990) that dysthymia follows anxiety disorders.

Dysthymics have comorbidity beyond depression, and the degree of coexisting disorders is not uniform across the lifespan. Dysthymic patients have a greater frequency of comorbid diagnoses than nondysthymic psychiatric patients. Markowitz et al. (1992) found that dysthymics were more likely to meet criteria for major depressive disorder, social phobia, and Axis II disorders; 88% of the dysthymic sample had one to three comorbid disorders, and 6% had four or five other diagnoses. In a community sample of adults and adolescents, Rohde, Lewinsohn, and Seeley (1991) found an elevated rate of other mental disorders, particularly among adolescents. However, the comorbidity of major depression with dysthymia was so prevalent that it was discussed in a separate paper (Lewinsohn et al., 1991): The degree of current comorbidity among adolescents was about 20 times greater than that expected by chance, and among adults it was over four times greater than chance.

Many of the issues of clinical course could be resolved with a longitudinal study that started literally at the time of conception. Researchers would enroll young couples in which one or both partners were diagnosed as having a depressive-spectrum disorder. The real focus of the study would be on their offspring, who would be at risk for a similar disorder because of genetic and/or environmental reasons. If we had the knowledge or wisdom to choose the appropriate measures at each stage of development, then we would presumably observe the natural course of depression and related disorders.

MOOD DISORDERS
AND SCHIZOPHRENIA

A sizable percentage (15–57%) of schizophrenic outpatients report the presence of depressive mood disorders, and Bleuler mentioned depressive symptoms to be one of the most frequent acute disturbances in schizophrenia (Johnson, 1991). ECA data show that schizophrenics have 28.5 times greater odds of having major depressive disorder than someone who is not schizophrenic (Boyd et al., 1984). Depressed schizophrenics tend to live alone, to have either one or no living parent, to have been previously treated for depression, to have made attempts to harm themselves, to have encountered more aversive life events, and to have had more hospital admissions than schizophrenics who are not depressed.

Depression in schizophrenic patients is most often considered a secondary disorder, etiologically distinct from the schizophrenic syndrome. This contention is supported by three findings. First, the observed depression is not recurrent (as in primary major depressive disorder); second, this type of depression is responsive to neuroleptic treatment; third, in at least two well-designed family studies, no significant comorbidity was observed (Frangos, Athenassenas, Tsitourides, Katsanou, & Alexandrakou, 1985; Prusoff, Weissman, Merikangas, Leckman, & Harding, 1984).

Nevertheless, there are enough instances of nonspecific affective symptoms prodromal to a relapse of schizophrenia to suggest that some depression may be a part of the schizophrenia spectrum. A recent selective review of family, twin, and adoption studies concluded that in some families these disorders coexist, and that a continuum model could be supported (Taylor, 1992). In this model, a shared genotype would have its expression modified by the environment to produce persons who are either unaffected, affectively ill, schizoaffective, or schizophrenic.

Until the publication of DSM-III in 1980, it was clinical lore that the presence of Bleulerian or Schneiderian symptoms was all that the diagnostician needed to establish the presence of schizophrenia. Manic–depressives were assumed to have few or none of these symptoms, and where they did occur, they were secondary. Pope and Lipinski (1978) noted that delusions, visual and auditory hallucinations, thought broadcasting, experiences of influence, and other Schneiderian first-rank symptoms were relatively common (20–50%) in the literature on well-validated cases of bipolar disorder (Pope, 1983). This observation meant that the presence of such symptoms could not be diagnostic of schizophrenia, but could only establish that the patient was psychotic.

More recently, Blacker and Tsuang (1992) have provided a thorough review of the contested boundaries of bipolar disorder. Among the DSM-III-R disorders comorbid with bipolar disorder, making differential diagnosis difficult, are schizophrenia, cyclothymia, borderline personality disorder, adult attention deficit disorder with hyperactivity, and instances of mania where mania is secondary to endocrine dysfunction and brain organicity. The problem in differential diagnosis is almost always the manic phase. For example, delusions, hallucinations, catatonia, and verbal incoherence can be found in both schizophrenia and bipolar disorder. Attempting to distinguish between schizophrenia and mania on the basis of inappropriate affect, flight of ideas, and loose associations will quickly demonstrate the subtlety of symptom presentation.

Lithium's efficacy in treating many bipolar patients is well documented, and it is also well documented that lithium is a poor treatment for schizophrenia. (However, see Coryell et al., 1995, and Himmelhoch, 1994, for limitations of lithium therapy.) Chronicity (as opposed to the episodic nature of classic manic–depressive illness), the absence of a full bipolar syndrome, a family history of poor prognosis, and a positive response to lithium may be the most useful distinctions between pure schizophrenia and bipolar disorder with psychotic features. These links between schizophrenia and mood disorders bring us to schizoaffective disorder.

MOOD DISORDERS AND SCHIZOAFFECTIVE DISORDER

In considering the relationship between the mood disorders and schizoaffective disorder, we are confronted with distinguishing differential diagnosis and comorbidity. Comorbidity forces diagnosticians to re-evaluate their assumptions about how diseases (or disorders) are categorized, and to seek replicable ways to differentiate disease entities. The problem is especially difficult for psychiatric illnesses, where few laboratory tests exist. Kraepelin fell victim to this problem as he grappled with the problem of classification.

Kraepelin (1913/1921) divided mental illness into two broad categories: "manic–depressive illness" (circular psychoses and simple mania) and "dementia praecox" (schizophrenia). In making this division, Kraepelin left some patients in a diagnostic limbo. These patients, usually young, with good premorbid adjustment, experience a rapid onset of a psychosis marked by emotional turmoil and false sensory impressions. Their illness often appears in response to stress, and the course is one of chronic deterioration of social function. Are they to be considered schizophrenic, manic–depressive, or both?

The crux of the problem is the presence of delusions or hallucinations that may accompany mania and give the manic patient the appearance of schizophrenia. Symptoms not meeting full criteria for both bipolar I disorder and schizophrenia are present, but the patients are neither schizophrenic nor bipolar. Patients whose symptoms, course, and outcome lie somewhere between these two categories of disorders challenge the Kraepelinian dichotomy. In other words, mixed symptomatology was as troublesome for Kraepelin in his day as it is today for neo-Kraepelinians. The question of whether schizoaffective disorder is a subtype of schizophrenia, a condition prodromal to schizophrenia (Piotrowski & Lewis, 1950), a comorbid presence of two separate illnesses, or a heterogeneous disorder from which homogeneous subtypes wait to be identified constitutes a debate that began decades ago and continues to the present (Goodwin & Jamison, 1990). The creation of schizoaffective disorder is a modern compromise.

The results of these attempts to make difficult clinical distinctions without the benefit of laboratory tests are diagnostic uncertainty and error. Akiskal and Puzantian (1979) list 14 diagnostic pitfalls that commonly lead to the misdiagnosis of an affective disorder as schizophrenia. Five of these pitfalls that seem particularly relevant to the present topic are the following:

1. Mistaking emotional blunting in schizophrenia for the anhedonia and depersonalization of depression.
2. Mistaking paranoid ideation for schizophrenia.
3. Mistaking the formal thought disorder of schizophrenia for the flight of ideas seen in mania.
4. Always equating bizarre ideation with schizophrenia.
5. Relying too heavily on incidental Schneiderian criteria in making differential diagnostic assignment of psychotic patients.

From these five sources of error, the reader can see how even experienced, skillful clinicians are often perplexed by patients who present with these comorbidities.

DSM-IV emphasizes the temporal relationship of schizophrenic and mood disorders in providing a route for the clinician to follow in making a diagnosis of schizoaffective disorder. At one point in time a patient must have presented with both a schizophrenic and a mood disturbance, and at a different time he/she must have presented with psychotic symptoms but no mood symptoms.

Nevertheless, DSM-III-R considers the differential diagnosis of schizoaffective disorder "far from definitive" (American Psychiatric Association, 1987, p. 208), especially for the bipolar subtype, and DSM-IV states that "Distinguishing Schizoaffective Disorder from Schizophrenia and from Mood Disorder with Psychotic Features is often difficult" (American Psychiatric Association, 1994, pp. 294–295).

In summary, schizoaffective disorder is a compromise to which most diagnosticians have agreed. The category was created for those patients who have mixed symptomatology for affective and schizophrenic disorders. It represents a model for at least one other current debate on comorbidity, that involving mixed anxiety–depression. Readers who wish to pursue the history and problems of differential diagnosis of schizoaffective disorder with bipolar disorder, schizophrenia, borderline personality disorder, brief reactive psychosis (brief psychotic disorder in DSM-IV), and other disorders are referred to Chapter 5 of Goodwin and Jamison (1990).

DEPRESSION AND ANXIETY DISORDERS

The odds ratios for finding both depression and anxiety disorders in the same patients are rather high: 18.8, 9.0, and 10.8 for DSM-III panic disorder, simple phobia, and obsessive–compulsive disorder (Boyd et al., 1984). This means, for example, that the odds that a person diagnosed with an episode of major depression will have panic disorder are 18.8 times greater than the odds that someone without depression will have panic disorder. Moreover, there is a much stronger trend for anxiety alone to evolve into depression with anxiety than for depression alone to develop into comorbid anxiety–depression (e.g., Angst et al., 1990). Anxiety subjects in the Angst et al. (1990) Zurich longitudinal study were less likely (10%) to have pure anxiety at follow-up than were the depressives to remain purely depressed (28%). Both pure-disorder groups were about equally likely to switch to the pure form of the other disorder (anxiety only to depression only, 13%; depression only to anxiety only, 14%). The directionality that seems to exist for pure anxiety is mostly to a mixed condition of anxiety plus depression.

Modern epidemiology has only recently confirmed in community samples what clinicians have long observed. But these observations have been interpreted in different ways. Lewis argued many years ago that there is only one affective disorder, anxiety plus depression, and that severity of one or the other produces the appearance of two separate illnesses (Lewis, 1934a, 1934b). Roth and Mountjoy (1982) have contended, however, that the two disorders are qualitatively as well as quantitatively different phenomena. Akiskal (1990) takes the position that etiologically heterogeneous clinical conditions underlie the comorbidity of anxiety and depressive disorders. While arguing for a mixed condition, Akiskal would nevertheless say that pure depressions and anxiety disorders exist, as evidenced at least in part by their need for different treatments (Van Valkenburg, Akiskal, Puzantian, & Rosenthal, 1984), and more tentatively because of different sleep patterns in polysomnographic studies (Akiskal et al., 1984).

There are key differences between the presenting somatic symptomatology of depressed and anxious patients:

> Depressed patients have more conspicuous vegetative symptoms (such as anorexia, loss of weight, and impairment of libido), whereas some other bodily symptoms, particularly those caused by sympathetic nervous system over-activity, are more characteristic of anxiety (such as tachycardia, sweating, and symptoms induced by hyperventilation). Other symptoms, such as abdominal discomfort and various sensations in the chest, tend to occur in both classes of disorders. (Kellner, 1990b, p. 243)

The comorbidity of anxiety and depression raises a number of issues for their clinical assessment. It has been known for a number of years that instruments originally designed to measure anxiety *or* depression generally measure anxiety *and* depression (Bystritsky, Linn, & Ware, 1990; Dobson & Cheung, 1990; Rehm, 1990; Wetzler & Katz, 1989). Often such measures (e.g., the Beck Depression Inventory or the Center for Epidemiologic Studies Depression Scale) were designed before the objective diagnostic criteria of DSM-III became an integral part of clinical assessment. Therefore, these measures sought to reveal depression as a dimension of psychopathology.

Instruments more closely tied to the disorder-specific symptoms of the DSM-III and later editions of the DSM tend to focus directly on those symptoms. This narrow approach treats comorbid disorders and co-occurring symptoms

as noise—interference with the primary task of matching symptoms to the DSM's diagnostic criteria. One result of linking assessments to the DSM only is a severe restriction on the opportunity to learn something novel about the phenomenology of the disorder.

Watson and Clark (1984) make the astute observation that patients may not be able to distinguish anxiety from depression when the overlap is substantial. From a patient's perspective, these may not be two concepts, but one—not two distinctive disorders, as a nosologist might prefer, but one global source of suffering. A patient who cannot distinguish anxiety from depression may well assign ratings on self-report tests randomly or according to the symptoms he/she feels to be most prominent at the time. Moreover, it is not clear that patients can identify the cognitive and somatic symptoms of anxiety and depression with similar ease (or difficulty). For example, Dobson and Shaw (1986) recorded depressive cognitions from patients with relative ease, whereas during panic attacks patients often reported that their thoughts were frozen. Rachman (1988) found significant cognitive *consequences* of panic, but the cognitions reported *during* panic were both few in number and restricted in content.

A provocative conceptual contribution to the debate over the interpretation of anxiety–depression comorbidity has been Akiskal's (1990) introduction of the "panic–depressive" versus "manic–depressive" dichotomy. He envisions a triphasic "panic–depressive" disorder (composed of panic, depression, and anxious–depressive states) that is analogous to manic–depressive disorder (with its manic, depressive, and mixed phases). The dichotomy has implications for symptom overlap, treatment, and prognosis. To further explore the foregoing complex relationships between anxiety and depressive disorders, we review below relevant data bearing on them.

A sample of 57 social phobics was studied for lifetime prevalence of other psychiatric disorders by Van Ameringen, Mancini, Styan, and Donison (1991). For this sample, 96.5% had a generalized social phobia (defined as social anxiety and avoidance in more than two social situations). The most common additional diagnosis found in the sample were the mood disorders. Forty-seven out of the 57 patients (or 82.5%) had a lifetime diagnosis of mood disorders; of these 47, 40 had major depressive disorder. When the investigators asked (retrospectively) about the temporal course of the two disorders, they found that 81.7% of the time social phobia preceded any mood disorder, and social phobia predated major depression in 90% of those cases. This study has now increased its number of social phobic subjects to 78 and replicated the original findings (M. Van Ameringen, personal communication, February 28, 1992).

Precise knowledge of the temporal relationship between social phobia and depression is unknown and would require a longitudinal investigation of course. The problem is that the data are accurate only to the degree that individuals can retrospectively recall events that may have occurred many years ago. For example, Stein, Tancer, Gelernter, Vittone, and Uhde (1990) found that 91% of their sample reported the onset of major depression to be, on average, 13.2 (± 7.9) years after the onset of social phobia. DiNardo and Barlow (1990) reported a lower percentage (38%) of social phobics to be depressed, and Stein et al. (1990) reported that 35% of social phobics had experienced one or more depressive episodes.

There are several possible explanations for the observed relationship between depression and anxiety. First, several disorders may result from a single disorder that expresses both sets of symptoms concurrently or over time separately. The factors leading to a diverse clinical presentation may include the individual's past history of reinforcement, life stressors, social support, and personality. Second, depression and anxiety may both have a high frequency in the population of mentally ill people, resulting in a tendency for them to occur together by chance alone. Third, having one disorder may make it highly likely that the other disorder will occur, even though the two disorders are of independent origin. Fourth, there may be minimal biological similarities, but the range of human experience may be sufficiently restricted that the clinical expression of diverse biological events is equally restricted.

The observed relationship between anxiety and depression raises a host of interesting questions regarding assessment, symptom stability, clinical course, biological underpinnings, treatment strategies, and classification. We cannot hope to do justice to these topics when two books have already covered them in considerable detail from different perspectives (Maser & Cloninger, 1990; Kendall & Watson, 1989).

DEPRESSION AND EATING DISORDERS

Depressive disorders have long been associated with problems in eating. Significant weight loss when not dieting, weight gain, or change in appetite is considered to be subsumed under one of the DSM-IV criteria for major depressive episode. Weight loss is specifically associated with melancholic features (American Psychiatric Association, 1994). Anorexia nervosa and bulimia nervosa are eating disorders described in the DSM-IV. These disorders are discussed here because they have significant overlap on a number of characteristics with depressive disorders.

Clinical studies of eating-disordered populations have found that many patients with anorexia and bulimia nervosa exhibit signs and symptoms of depression. Multiple depressive features have been observed in 25–50% of patients with anorexia nervosa (Swift, Andrews, & Barklage, 1986). One study estimated that major depression is found in 56% of anorexia patients (Hendren, 1983), and this estimate is further strengthened by long-term follow-up studies of the disorder, which find lifetime prevalence rates for affective disorder ranging from 36% to 68% (Halmi et al., 1991). This large percentage has led certain investigators to propose that anorexia nervosa represents an atypical affective disorder occurring in females during adolescence, when body image issues are predominant (Cantwell, Sturzenberger, Burroughs, Salkin, & Green, 1977; Hsu, 1988). Such an assertion is further strengthened by family studies showing a twofold or higher risk of morbidity for affective illness among first-degree relatives of anorexia probands (Szmukler, 1987).

However, some other studies do not support such a model. For example, there is the well-known observation that starvation alone can result in the elaboration of a number of dysfunctional psychological symptoms, including depression (Keys, Brozek, Henschel, Mickelsen, & Taylor, 1950), and that these symptoms improve with nutritional rehabilitation (Eckert, Goldberg, Halmi, Casper, & Davis, 1982; Channon & De Silva, 1985). Furthermore, family studies indicate that affective disorder is more common in the relatives of anorexics who have concurrent bulimia than in anorexia probands who have no bulimic episodes (Strober, Salkin, Burroughs, & Morrell, 1982). Similarly, a higher prevalence of affectively ill relatives has been reported in anorexia probands who have concurrent major depression than in anorexics who are not depressed (Biederman et al., 1985), and there does not appear to be an increased prevalence of eating disorders in the first-degree relatives of probands with affective disorders (Strober, Lampert, Morrell, Burroughs, & Jacobs, 1990).

Descriptive studies indicate rates of coexisting affective disorder ranging from 27% to 75% among bulimic patients. When more rigorous methods are applied, the current rate of major depression is only 24–33%, but lifetime history of depression is over 75% (Walsh, Roose, Glassman, Gladis, & Sadik, 1985). Standardized psychological tests such as the Minnesota Multiphasic Personality Inventory, the Hopkins Symptom Checklist, and the Beck Depression Inventory demonstrate that the level of depression is in the moderate range (Swift et al., 1986). Furthermore, both subjective observations (Russell, 1979) and objective investigations have found that the depressive symptoms in bulimia nervosa are more highly reactive, unstable, short-lived, and temporally related to bingeing and purging episodes (Cooper & Fairburn, 1986), with low rates of "endogenous" features. Finally, a follow-up study of bulimic patients did not indicate persistence of depression, even though more than 85% continued to exhibit significant bulimic pathology (Swift, Kalin, Wamboldt, Kaslow, & Ritholz, 1985).

Family studies in general indicate a higher prevalence of affective disorders in first-degree relatives of bulimics (Hinz & Williamson, 1987), though there is still some disagreement among the best-controlled investigations (Stern et al., 1984; Kassett et al., 1989). Arguing against a common genetic spectrum is a study that failed to find increased rates of eating disorders among relatives of depressed, manic, and schizophrenic patients (Strober & Katz, 1987). We now discuss biological and pharmacological studies of possible links between affective and eating disorders.

Biological Studies

The most cogent investigations of biological markers involve (1) neuroendocrine probes of the hypothalamic–pituitary–adrenal (HPA) and hypothalamic–pituitary–thyroid (HPT) axes, and (2) catecholamine metabolism.

HPA axis findings common to both anorexia nervosa and affective disorders include the following: increased cortisol secretion (Gwirtsman et al., 1989b); failure to suppress cortisol by dexamethasone (abnormal dexamethasone suppression test [DST] results) (Gerner & Gwirtsman, 1981); blunting of adrenocorticotropic hormone (ACTH) response to corticotropin-releasing hormone (CRH) (Gold et al., 1986); and increased levels of CRH in the cerebrospinal fluid (CSF) (Kaye et al., 1987). Although these biological similarities appear compelling, there are still some important distinctions to be made. First, cortisol production and DST abnormality begin to normalize with early refeeding, well before the psychological state of the patient has undergone much rehabilitation (Abou-Saleh, Oleesky, Crisp, & Lacey, 1986; Doerr, Fichter, Pirke, & Lund, 1980). Furthermore, the DST abnormalities and increased cortisol are seen in normal individuals who fast (Fichter, Pirke, & Holsboer, 1986), as well as in obese subjects who lose weight (Edelstein, Roy-Byrne, Fawzy, & Dornfeld, 1983). Thus, certain HPA abnormalities appear to be more related to nutritional state than to the psychiatric illness. Of note also is the observation that patients whose DST abnormalities persist after weight restoration seem to be those with clinically significant depressive symptoms (Brambilla et al., 1985).

With respect to monoamine function in urine, plasma, and CSF, underweight patients with anorexia nervosa generally have decreased metabolite levels, and these return to normal following weight correction (Weiner, 1985). However, patients with anorexia nervosa who have been weight-recovered for 1 year or more appear to have low plasma and CSF norepinephrine levels (Kaye, Jimerson, Lake, & Ebert, 1985). In contradistinction, endogenously depressed patients have either higher (Roy, Pickar, Linnoila, & Potter, 1985) or more variable (Gwirtsman et al., 1989a) levels of norepinephrine and 3-methoxy-4-hydroxyphenyl glycol (MHPG). Platelet monoamine oxidase (MAO) activity is lower in anorexia patients with coexisting depression, according to one study (Biederman et al., 1984).

HPA axis disruption in bulimia nervosa is not as extensive, with normal cortisol production (Gwirtsman et al., 1989b) and normal ACTH responses to CRH (Gold et al., 1986), as well as normal CSF CRH levels (Gwirtsman et al.,

1990b). Furthermore, the DST abnormalities also appear to be correlated with lowered dexamethasone levels (Walsh et al., 1987). This abnormality of dexamethasone metabolism has also been noted in patients with major depression.

Abnormalities in HPT function have been noted in both anorexia and bulimia nervosa. The low levels of thyroxine (T_4) and triiodothyronine (T_3) observed in anorexia nervosa appear to be largely attributable to the effects of weight loss and carbohydrate restriction. The blunted responses of thyroid-stimulating hormone (TSH) to thyrotropin-releasing hormone (TRH), observed in some bulimic patients, may represent hypothalamic dysfunction, but may also be accounted for by caloric restriction and other metabolic factors (Hudson & Hudson, 1984; Altemus et al., 1991; Spalter, Gwirtsman, Demitrack, & Gold, 1993). Overall, the evidence is weak for a primary hypothalamic disturbance of the HPT axis in eating disorders.

To summarize, although biological studies have demonstrated a great number of similarities between affective and eating disorders, there are sufficient differences and confounds due to inadequate nutrition to permit a fair degree of skepticism with regard to acceptance of the hypothesis that anorexia nervosa represents an affective-spectrum disorder. Rather, the data appear to indicate that the two disorders are distinct, but have a reasonable amount of biological overlap and clinical comorbidity.

Pharmacological Studies

Although the phenomenological, family, and biological data point toward an important overlap between anorexia nervosa and affective illness, attempts to treat this illness with standard antidepressant pharmacotherapeutic agents have met with little success (Weltzin, Gwirtsman, Jimerson, & Kaye, 1990). Some improvements in adherence to traditional behavioral weight-gaining programs, and better results with weight maintenance, have been achieved with use of adjunctive fluoxetine (Gwirtsman, Guze, Yager, & Gainsley, 1990a; Kaye, Weltsin, Hsu, & Bulik, 1991). It remains to be seen whether or not the newer generation of antidepressants will be more useful for this disorder than tricyclics and MAO inhibitors, which can only be utilized with great caution in severely undernourished, medically compromised patients.

In recent years, multiple controlled studies have demonstrated the efficacy of treatment with antidepressants such as tricyclics, MAO inhibitors, and fluoxetine for patients with bulimia nervosa (Weltzin et al., 1990; Fluoxetine Bulimia Nervosa Collabortive Study Group, 1992); psychotherapies such as cognitive–behavioral therapy have also been found to be quite effective (Fairburn, 1984; Mitchell et al., 1990). Besides their action against concurrent depression, antidepressants also appear to have specific "antibulimic" effects, since nondepressed bulimic patients have been found to exhibit significantly decreased binge frequency (Walsh, 1988). The limited available long-term follow-up data suggest that pharmacotherapy merely suppresses bulimic symptoms while it is applied, and relapse rates after medication discontinuation are high (Pope, Hudson, Yurgelun-Todd, & Jonas, 1985).

Although the data above support the notion that bulimia and depression are variants of a common disorder, it may be overzealous to embrace this view. It should be noted that not all illnesses that improve with an antidepressant are necessarily depression; obsessive–compulsive disorder, other anxiety disorders, and certain types of cardiac arrhythmias also appear to be responsive to these agents (Chaitin, 1988; Hinz & Williamson, 1987).

In conclusion, a large body of data from phenomenological, family, biological, and pharmacological investigations suggests that depression is a common and significant problem for eating-disordered patients. Without accepting the premise that eating disorders are variants of affective disorder, one can still conclude that these disorders exhibit a high degree of comorbidity. Furthermore, when the eating disorder improves the depression improves, and vice versa. The astute clinician should maintain a high index of suspicion about, and should be prepared to treat aggressively, a concurrent affective disorder in a patient with an eating disorder who also exhibits symptoms of mood instability and has a family history of affective illness.

DEPRESSION AND SOMATIZATION DISORDER

DSM-IV (American Psychiatric Association, 1994) describes the essential feature of somatoform disorders as the presentation of physical symptoms suggestive of a general medical condition, but without the involvement of a general medical condition, the direct effects of a substance, or another mental disorder. The symptoms must cause clinically significant distress or impairment in functioning. Since the etiology and presentations of these disorders are presumably psychologically linked, they are classified as mental disorders. Somatoform disorders are differentially diagnosed from psychological factors affecting medical condition in that there is no diagnosable medical condition to fully account for the physical symptoms. Somatoform disorders are further differentiated from disorders in which the symptom production is intentional. Somatization disorder, characterized by recurrent and multiple somatic complaints over several years' duration, is one of the seven somatoform disorders. In the remainder of this section, we focus on somatization disorder.

The symptoms of somatization disorder are commonly encountered in general practice (Katon et al., 1991; Smith, 1990) and present in various forms, including gastrointestinal complaints, various types of pain, cardiopulmonary symptoms, pseudoneurological complaints, and complaints related to sexual dysfunction or the reproductive system (Rasmussen & Avant, 1989). The NIMH ECA study (Regier et al., 1988) found a low 1-month prevalence (0.01%, almost exclusively female) in the general population, using the full DSM-III-R criteria. Nonetheless, reviews of somatization disorder imply that symptomatic presentations are so common in family practice that a physician may very likely encounter one every day he/she sees patients (Rasmussen & Avant, 1989; Kaplan, Lipkin, & Gordon, 1988).

Regarding comorbidity with depression, strong associations have been found in the ECA data between the symptoms of somatization disorder and of depression or dysthymia (Simon & Von Korff, 1991; Escobar, Burnam, Karno, Forsythe, & Golding, 1987). The odds ratio for the coexistence of depression and somatization disorder was reported to be 26.8 (Boyd et al., 1984). In a Washington State health maintenance organization study, Dworkin, Von Korff, and LeResche (1990) found that subjects with multiple pain complaints were at an elevated risk for a diagnosis of major depression. The number of pain conditions cited in this study was a better predictor for depression than was severity or persistence of pain. These findings of high comorbidity with depression in the general population are paralleled by observations and investigations conducted in psychiatric settings (Orenstein, 1989; Fabrega, Mezzich, Jacob, & Ulrich, 1988; Morrison & Herbstein, 1988; Akiskal, 1983).

The association between somatization disorder and depression is so marked that Lipowski (1990) recommends that when a diagnosis of somatization disorder or any other somatoform disorder is made, one should always look for evidence of depression or panic in order to ensure adequate treatment. Theories to explain this close relationship between affective disorder and somatization disorder symptomatology abound. The best-supported, however, are the theories regarding masked depression and the manifestation of anxiety (Kellner, 1990a), as discussed below.

Fisch (1987) states that about half of all depressions seen by family physicians initially present with somatic symptoms, and that many of these depressions are misdiagnosed and mistreated. In the Lundby study, conducted in Sweden, individuals who developed endogenous depression and later committed suicide had mostly presented with somatic complaints that masked their mood disorder (Hagnell & Rorsman, 1978). Some of these patients undoubtedly were aware of their mood dysfunction, but selectively chose to focus on their physical complaints. Others may have lacked the ability to distinguish between their mood dysfunction and physical problems, as Watson and Clark (1984) described for depression and anxiety (see above), or for some reason may have been unable or unwilling to discuss their emotional distress. In an earlier study, Kellner, Simpson, and Winslow (1972) found somatic symptoms to be more strongly associated with anxiety than with depression. They described a vicious circle of illness in which an affective disorder induces somatic symptoms, followed by selective attention to those symptoms with fear of further disease, resulting in higher anxiety, and so on in an escalating cycle.

In summary, the high prevalence of comorbidity between depression and anxiety (Maser & Cloninger, 1990), and their many somatic diagnostic criteria, complicate their relationship to somatization disorder symptomatology. The manifestations of somatization disorder differ substantially from case to case, leading to the hypothesis that they exist along a continuum. As the number of medically unexplained symptoms increases, so also do the rates of coexisting psychiatric disorders (Katon et al., 1991). This comorbidity is so common that Katon et al. (1991) suggested that in addition to somatization disorder, the DSM-IV should include a new classification to describe the combination of an abridged definition of somatization disorder with anxiety–depression. However, this was not incorporated into the DSM-IV.

DEPRESSION AND SUBSTANCE ABUSE/DEPENDENCE

Alcohol abuse and dependence have a strong association with all of the mood disorders that far exceeds what we would expect from chance (Regier et al., 1990). Lifetime ECA data show that 21.8% of persons with any affective disorder (8.3% of the population) also have an alcohol-related diagnosis. Patients with bipolar disorder carry the greatest burden of this average, with 43.6% having an alcohol-related diagnosis. If any substance abuse or dependence is considered, comorbidity with bipolar disorder jumps to 56.1%. Unipolar major depressives and dysthymics carry a lighter share, at 14.5% and 20.9%, respectively. All figures are somewhat lower for any drug-related diagnosis other than alcohol. The ECA data reveal that 19.4% of persons with any affective disorder suffer from any other drug abuse/dependence. Bipolar patients again carry the greatest weight of this average at 40.7%; unipolar major depressives and dysthymics have an essentially equal comorbidity prevalence (18% and 18.9%, respectively).

A major question raised by these patterns regards the secondary or causal relationship of mood disorders to abuse of or dependence on alcohol and/or other substances. That is, is the substance-related disorder due to the mood disorder, or is depression an outgrowth of the substance-related disorder? The causal direction proposed by Vaillant (1983) in connection with alcoholism is from alcoholism to psychopathology. Shuckit (1986) surveyed the literature and found five reasons underlying the diagnostic confusion between primary alcoholism and primary affective disorder. Three of these seem to support the hypothesis that alcoholism leads to psychopathology: (1) Alcohol can cause depressive symptoms in anyone; (2) signs of temporary serious depression can follow prolonged drinking; and (3) depressive symptoms and alcohol problems occur in other psychiatric disorders. Shuckit

concluded that alcoholism and affective disorder have independent etiologies, but that some of their clinical symptoms overlap.

Winokur has long argued that alcoholism and mood disorder are different forms of the same disease. In his view, this disease is more likely to produce alcoholism in males and depression in females (Winokur & Clayton, 1967). This hypothesis leads to the prediction of a sex-linked gene for depressive-spectrum disorder. One approach to studying this hypothesis may be found in family pedigree studies. Mirin, Weiss, Sollogub, and Michael (1984) studied the relatives of substance abusers and found the prevalence of alcoholism and/or depression (among the relatives) to be highly correlated with alcoholism and/or depression in the proband. Alcoholism in the proband did not increase the probability that the relative would be depressed, however. On the other hand, early-onset depression and bipolar disorder in the proband does appear to increase the probability that alcoholism aggregates in the first-degree relatives (Taylor & Abrams, 1981; Behar, Winokur, Van Valkenburg, & Lowry, 1980).

In another study of relatives, Puig-Antich et al. (1989) examined the adult relatives of prepubertal children with major depression. They found the following:

1. Prepubertal children who developed major depressive disorder had families with significant levels of major depressive disorder, alcoholism, and anxiety disorders. However, there was a low prevalence of mania in these families.

2. Children who had separation anxiety, but who were never depressed, had relatives with as high a prevalence of major depression and anxiety disorders as relatives of depressed children.

3. The levels of alcoholism in the relatives of children who had separation anxiety, but were never depressed, were in the "normal" range.

It would appear that prepubertal onset of major depression is likely in families with a high aggregation of affective disorders when these families *also* have a high prevalence of alcoholism. The sex distributions of psychopathology in the relatives were in accord with Winokur's theory.

Other theorists, like Khantzian (1985), have proposed a self-medication hypothesis, whereby the substance of abuse/dependence treats the psychopathology and enhances well-being. Addicts with psychiatric problems do not select drugs randomly, but rather for the drug's ability to relieve distress associated with depression.

We may ask whether one or more of the mood disorders have an addiction aspect embedded in the underlying disease, or whether people with these disorders are using drugs that make them feel better. There is a paucity of information on this question, but self-medication probably leads to abuse/dependence by an independent process of addiction. Paradoxically, alcohol, especially in high doses and during detoxification, often depresses rather than elevates mood.

Like comorbidity of other illnesses, comorbidity of depression and substance abuse/dependence results in a greater likelihood of seeking treatment. The ECA lifetime figures for substance abuse comorbid with unipolar major depression, dysthymia, bipolar I disorder, and bipolar II disorder, are 27.2%, 31.4%, 60.7%, and 48.1%, respectively (Regier et al., 1990). Clearly, with such high percentages, many clinicians (especially those in addiction clinics and prisons) will be treating patients with more than one disorder.

Kranzler and Liebowitz (1988) advise the clinician to distinguish between whether the alcoholism is the primary or secondary disorder "based on the persistence of symptoms" (p. 870), and to conduct a "detailed inquiry into the temporal relationship between substance use and co-morbid symptoms" (p. 870). Persistence of symptoms may be a seventh definition of the primary–secondary distinction (see above). Patients present for treatment in either a *transient* or a *persistent* symptom state. The symptoms of the transient state may be quite intense, but they nevertheless will pass within a few days or weeks. Depression and anxiety may be present and may be secondary to withdrawal. They may also occur as a reaction to psychosocial stressors into which a person has been drawn by substance use (e.g., divorce, bankruptcy). Persistent symptoms may be intense and last for weeks or months, with less variability for intensity than in the transient state. The symptoms of alcoholism become chronic when left untreated, creating vulnerability to depression, and in the presence of continued drinking depression tends to persist. This tendency may explain why alcoholics face increased risk for suicide (Murphy, 1988; Murphy, Wetzel, Robins, & McEvoy, 1992).

SUMMARY

Depression, in addition to being a focal primary illness, is a common companion to other Axis I disorders. In this chapter, we have discussed the implications of this comorbidity from both a general theoretical and a context-specific perspective. The general discussion has covered the difficulty that practitioners and researchers experience in the recognition, diagnosis, and assessment of comorbid depression. Diagnostic concerns such as establishing the primary–secondary distinction, and the effects of multiform etiology and symptom stability, have been considered. Contextually, we have discussed comorbidity with dysthymia, schizophrenia, schizoaffective disorder, anxiety disorders, eating disorders, somatization disorder, and substance abuse/dependence. Increased research attention to these issues and their further refinement may well herald the beginning of new understanding, diagnostic approaches, and methods of clinical care.

Acknowledgments. We thank Drs. Hagop Akiskal, Mary Blehar, Daniel Klein, and Peter Lewinsohn for their critical comments on early drafts of this chapter.

NOTE

1. "Recurrence" is defined as the appearance of a new episode during recovery. "Relapse" is defined as a return of symptoms satisfying the full DSM-III-R syndrome criteria for an episode that occurs during the period of remission, but before recovery. "Recovery" is defined as a remission of criterion symptoms from an index episode that lasts for 8 consecutive weeks. The NIMH Clinical Research Branch Collaborative Program in the Psychobiology of Depression set 8 consecutive weeks with no more than one or two criteria symptoms present to a mild degree as an arbitrary period for recovery (Coryell, Andreasen, Endicott, & Keller, 1987). Relapse required a preceding period of recovery and the reappearance of symptoms sufficient to satisfy criteria at the "definite" level. Quitkin, Rifkin, and Klein (1976) defined relapse as a worsening of symptoms that occurs *within* 6 months following remission, and recurrence as a worsening of symptoms that occurs *after* 6 months of remission. (See Prien, 1988, and Prien, Carpenter, & Kupfer, 1991, for more complete discussions of these terms.)

REFERENCES

Abou-Saleh, M. T., Oleesky, D., Crisp, A. H., & Lacey, J. H. (1986). Dexamethasone suppression and energy balance in eating disorders. *Acta Psychiatrica Scandinavica, 73,* 242–251.

Abramson, L. Y., Seligman, M. E., & Teasdale, J. D. (1978). Learned helplessness in humans: Critique and reformulation. *Journal of Abnormal Psychology, 87,* 49–74.

Akiskal, H. S. (1983). Diagnosis and classification of affective disorders: New insights from clinical and laboratory approaches. *Psychiatric Developments*, *1*, 123–160.

Akiskal, H. S. (1990). Toward a clinical understanding of the relationship of anxiety and depressive disorders. In J. D. Maser & C. R. Cloninger (Eds.), *Comorbidity of mood and anxiety disorders* (pp. 597–607). Washington, DC: American Psychiatric Press.

Akiskal, H. S., King, D., Rosenthal, T. L., Robinson, D., & Scott-Strauss, A. (1981). Chronic depressives: Part I. Clinical and familial characteristics in 137 probands. *Journal of Affective Disorders*, *3*, 297–315.

Akiskal, H. S., Lemmi, H., Dickson, H., King, D., Yerevanian, B., & Van Valkenburg, C. (1984). Chronic depressions, Part 2: Sleep EEG differentiation of primary dysthymic disorders from anxious depressions. *Journal of Affective Disorders*, *6*, 287–295.

Akiskal, H. S., & Puzantian, V. R. (1979). Psychotic forms of depression and mania. *Psychiatric Clinics of North America*, *2*(3), 419–439.

Akiskal, H. S., & Simmons, R. C. (1985). Chronic and refractory depressions: Evaluation and management. In E. E. Beckham & W. R. Leber (Eds.), *Handbook of depression: Treatment, assessment, and research* (pp. 587–605). Homewood, IL: Dorsey Press.

Alloy, L. B., Kelly, K. A., Mineka, S., & Clements, C. M. (1990). Comorbidity of anxiety and depressive disorders: A helplessness–hopelessness perspective. In J. D. Maser & C. R. Cloninger (Eds.), *Comorbidity of mood and anxiety disorders* (pp. 499–543). Washington, DC: American Psychiatric Press.

Altemus, M., Hetherington, M. M., Flood, M., Licinio, J., Nelson, M. L., Bernat, A. S., & Gold, P. W. (1991). Decrease in resting metabolic rate during abstinence from bulimic behavior. *American Journal of Psychiatry*, *148*(8), 1071–1072.

American Psychiatric Association. (1980). *Diagnostic and statistical manual of mental disorders* (3rd ed.). Washington, DC: Author.

American Psychiatric Association. (1987). *Diagnostic and statistical manual of mental disorders* (3rd ed., rev.). Washington, DC: Author.

American Psychiatric Association. (1994). *Diagnostic and statistical manual of mental disorders* (4th ed.). Washington, DC: Author.

Angst, J., Vollrath, M., Merikangas, K. R., & Ernst, C. (1990). Comorbidity of anxiety and depression in the Zurich cohort study of young adults. In J. D. Maser & C. R. Cloninger (Eds.), *Comorbidity of mood and anxiety disorders* (pp. 123–137). Washington, DC: American Psychiatric Press.

Barlow, D. H., DiNardo, P. A., Vermilyea, B. B., Vermilyea, J., & Blanchard, E. (1986). Comorbidity and depression among the anxiety disorders: Issues in diagnosis and classification. *Journal of Nervous and Mental Disease*, *174*, 63–72.

Barsky, A. J., Wyshak, G., & Klerman, G. L. (1991, September). *Hypochondriacal patients, their physicians, and their medical care*. Paper presented at the Fifth Annual NIMH International Research Conference on the Classification, Recognition and Treatment of Mental Disorders in General Medical Settings, Bethesda, MD.

Beckham, E. E., & Leber, W. R. (Eds.). (1985). *Handbook of depression: Treatment, assessment, and research*. Homewood, IL: Dorsey Press.

Behar, D., Winokur, G., Van Valkenburg, C., & Lowry, M. (1980). Familial subtypes of depression: A clinical view. *Journal of Clinical Psychiatry*, *41*, 52–56.

Biederman, J., Rivinus, T. M., Herzog, D. B., Ferber, R. A., Harper, G. P., Orsulak, P. J., Harmatz, J. S., & Schildkraut, J. J. (1984). Platelet MAO activity in anorexia nervosa patients with and without a major depressive disorder. *American Journal of Psychiatry*, *141*, 1244–1247.

Biederman, J., Rivinus, T., Kemper, K., Hamilton, D., MacFadyen, J., & Harmatz, J. (1985). Depressive disorders in relatives of anorexia nervosa patients with and without a current episode of nonbipolar major depression. *American Journal of Psychiatry*, *142*, 1495–1497.

Blacker, C. V., & Clare, A. W. (1987). Depressive disorder in primary care. *British Journal of Psychiatry*, *150*, 737–751.

Blacker, D., & Tsuang, M. T. (1992). Contested boundaries of bipolar disorder and the limits of categorical diagnosis in psychiatry. *American Journal of Psychiatry*, *149*(11), 1473–1483.

Boyd, J. H., Burke, J. D., Gruenberg, E., Holzer, C. E. III, Rae, D. S., George, L. K., Karno, M., Stoltzman, R., McEvoy, L., & Nestadt, G. (1984). Exclusion criteria of DSM-III: A study of co-occurrence of hierarchy-free syndromes. *Archives of General Psychiatry*, *41*, 983–959.

Brambilla, F., Cavagnini, F., Invitti, C., Poterzio, F., Lampertico, M., Sali, L., Maggioni, M., Candolfi, C., Paneria, A. E., & Muller, E. E. (1985). Neuroendocrine and psychopathological measures in anorexia nervosa: Resemblances to primary affective disorders. *Psychiatry Research*, *16*, 165–176.

Bystritsky, A., Linn, L. S., & Ware, J. E. (1990). Development of a multidimensional scale of anxiety. *Journal of Anxiety Disorders*, *4*, 99–115.

Caddy, G. R. (1985). Cognitive behavior therapy in the treatment of multiple personality. *Behavior Modification*, *9*(3), 267–292.

Cantwell, D. P., Sturzenberger, S., Burroughs, J., Salkin, B., & Green, J. K. (1977). Anorexia nervosa: An affective disorder? *Archives of General Psychiatry*, *34*, 1087–1093.

Chaitin, B. F. (1988). The relationship of the eating and affective disorders. In B. J. Blinder, B. F. Chaitin, & R. Goldstein (Eds.) *The eating disorders: Medical and psychological bases of diagnosis and treatment* (pp. 345–355). New York: PMA.

Channon, S., & De Silva, W. P. (1985). Psychological correlates of weight gain in patients with anorexia nervosa. *Journal of Psychiatric Research*, *19*, 267–272.

Cloninger, C. R., Martin, R. L., Guze, S. B., & Clayton, P. J. (1990). The empirical structure of psychiatric comorbidity and its theoretical significance. In J. D. Maser & C. R. Cloninger (Eds.), *Comorbidity of mood and anxiety disorders* (pp. 439–462). Washington, DC: American Psychiatric Press.

Cooper, P. J., & Fairburn, C. G. (1986). The depressive symptoms of bulimia nervosa. *British Journal of Psychiatry*, *148*, 268–274.

Coryell, W., Andreasen, N. C., Endicott, J., & Keller, M. (1987). The significance of past mania or hypomania in the course and outcome of major depression. *American Journal of Psychiatry*, *144*, 309–315.

Coryell, W., Endicott, J., Maser, J. D., Mueller, T., Lavori, P., & Keller, M. B. (1995). The likelihood of recurrence in bipolar affective disorder: The importance of episode recency. *Journal of Affective Disorders*, *33*, 201–206.

Coryell, W., Endicott, J. & Winokur, G. (1992). Anxiety syndromes as epiphenomena of primary major depression: Outcome and familial psychopathology. *American Journal of Psychiatry, 149,* 100–107.

de Ruiter, C., Rijken, H., Garssen, B., van Schaik, A., & Kraaimaat, F. (1989). Comorbidity among the anxiety disorders. *Journal of Anxiety Disorders, 3,* 57–68.

DiNardo, P. A., & Barlow, D. H. (1990). Syndrome and symptom co-occurrence in the anxiety disorders. In J. D. Maser & R. C. Cloninger (Eds.), *Comorbidity of mood and anxiety disorders* (pp. 205–230). Washington, DC: American Psychiatric Press.

Dobson, K. S., & Cheung, E. (1990). Relationship between anxiety and depression: Conceptual and methodological issues. In J. D. Maser & R. C. Cloninger (Eds.), *Comorbidity of mood and anxiety disorders* (pp. 611–632). Washington, DC: American Psychiatric Press.

Dobson, K. S., & Shaw, B. F. (1986). Cognitive assessment with major depressive disorders. *Cognitive Therapy and Research, 10,* 13–29.

Doerr, P., Fichter, M., Pirke, K. M., & Lund, R. (1980). Relationship between weight gain and hypothalamic-pituitary–adrenal function in patients with anorexia nervosa. *Journal of Steroid Biochemistry, 13,* 529–542.

Dworkin, S. F., Von Korff, M., & LeResche, L. (1990). Multiple pains and psychiatric disturbance: An epidemiologic investigation. *Archives of General Psychiatry, 47,* 239–244.

Eckert, E. D., Goldberg, S. C., Halmi, K. A., Casper, R. C., & Davis, J. M. (1982). Depression in anorexia nervosa. *Psychological Medicine, 12,* 115–122.

Edelstein, C. K., Roy-Byrne, P., Fawzy, F. I., & Dornfeld, L. (1983). Effects of weight loss on the dexamethasone suppression test. *American Journal of Psychiatry, 140,* 338–341.

Escobar, J. I., Burnam, M. A., Karno, M., Forsythe, A., & Golding, J. M. (1987). Somatization in the community. *Archives of General Psychiatry, 44,* 713–718.

Fabrega, H., Jr., Mezzich, J., Jacob, R., & Ulrich, R. (1988). Somatoform disorder in a psychiatric setting: Systematic comparisons with depression and anxiety disorders. *Journal of Nervous and Mental Disease, 176,* 431–439.

Fairburn, C. G. (1981). A cognitive behavioral approach to the treatment of bulimia. *Psychological Medicine, 11,* 707–711.

Feighner, J. P., Robins, E., Guze, S. B., Woodruff, R. A., Jr., Winokur, G., & Munoz, R. (1972). Diagnostic criteria for use in psychiatric research. *Archives of General Psychiatry, 26,* 57–63.

Feinstein, A. R. (1970). The pre-therapeutic classification of co-morbidity in chronic disease. *Journal of Chronic Disease, 23,* 455–468.

Fichter, M. M., Pirke, K. M., & Holsboer, F. (1986). Weight loss causes neuroendocrine disturbances: Experimental study in healthy starving subjects. *Psychiatry Research, 17,* 61–72.

Fisch, R. Z. (1987). Masked depression: Its interrelations with somatization, hypochondriasis and conversion. *International Journal of Psychiatry in Medicine, 17,* 367–379.

Fluoxetine Bulimia Nervosa Collaborative Study Group. (1992). Fluoxetine in the treatment of bulimia nervosa. *Archives of General Psychiatry, 49,* 139–147.

Frangos, E., Athanassenas, G., Tsitourides, S., Katsanou, N., & Alexandrakou, P. (1985). Prevalence of DSM-III schizophrenia among first-degree relatives of schizophrenic probands. *Acta Psychiatrica Scandinavica, 72,* 382–386.

Gerner, R. H., & Gwirtsman, H. E. (1981). Abnormalities of dexamethasone suppression test and urinary MHPG in anorexia nervosa. *American Journal of Psychiatry, 138(5),* 650–653.

Gold, P. W., Gwirtsman, H. E., Avgerinos, P. C., Nieman, L. K., Gallucci, W. T., Kaye, W. H., Jimerson, D. C., Ebert, M., Rittmaster, R., Loriaux, D. L., & Chrousos, G. P. (1986). Abnormal hypothalamic–pituitary–adrenal function in anorexia nervosa: Pathophysiologic mechanisms in underweight and weight-corrected patients. *New England Journal of Medicine, 314(21),* 1335–1342.

Goodwin, F. K., & Jamison, K. R. (1990). *Manic–depressive illness.* New York: Oxford University Press.

Gwirtsman, H. E., Guze, B. H., Yager, J., & Gainsley, B. (1990a). Treatment of anorexia nervosa with fluoxetine: An open clinical trial. *Journal of Clinical Psychiatry, 47(9),* 378–382.

Gwirtsman, H. E., Halaris, A. E., Wolf, A. W., DeMet, E., Piletz, J. E., & Marler, M. (1989a). Apparent phase advance in diurnal MHPG in depression. *American Journal of Psychiatry, 146* (11), 1427–1433.

Gwirtsman, H. E., Kaye, W. H., George, D. T., Berrettini, W. H., Jimerson, D. C., & Gold, P. W. (1990b). CSF beta-endorphin decreased in abstinent bulimics. *American Psychiatric Association Annual Meeting New Research,* NR494, p. 236. (Abstract)

Gwirtsman, H. E., Kaye, W. H., George, D. T., Jimerson, D. C., Ebert, M. H., & Gold, P. W. (1989b). Central and peripheral ACTH and cortisol in anorexia nervosa and bulimia. *Archives of General Psychiatry, 46(1),* 61–69.

Hagnell, O., & Rorsman, B. (1978). Suicide and endogenous depression with somatic symptoms in the Lundby study. *Neuropsychobiology, 4,* 180–187.

Halmi, K. A., Eckert, E., Marchi, P., Sampugnaro, V., Apple, R., & Cohen, J. (1991). Comorbidity of psychiatric diagnoses in anorexia nervosa. *Archives of General Psychiatry, 48,* 712–718.

Hendren, R. I. (1983). Depression in anorexia nervosa. *Journal of the American Academy of Child Psychiatry, 22,* 59–62.

Himmelhoch, J. M. (1994). On the failure to recognize lithium failure. *Psychiatric Annals, 24(5),* 241–250.

Hinz, L. D., & Williamson, D. A. (1987). Bulimia and depression: A review of the affective variant hypothesis. *Psychological Bulletin, 102(1),* 150–158.

Hudson, J. I., & Hudson, M. S. (1984). Endocrine dysfunction in anorexia nervosa and bulimia: Comparison with abnormalities in other psychiatric disorders and disturbances due to metabolic factors. *Psychiatric Developments, 4,* 237–272.

Hsu, L. K. G. (1988). Classification and diagnosis of the eating disorders. In B. J. Blinder, B. F. Chaitin, & R. Goldstein (Eds.), *The eating disorders: Medical and psychological bases of diagnosis and treatment* (pp. 235–246). New York: PMA.

Johnson, D. A. W. (1991). Depression in chronic schizophrenia. In G. Racagni, N. Brunello, & T. Fukuda (Eds.), *Biological psychiatry* (Vol. 1, pp. 556–559). Amsterdam: Elsevier.

Kaplan, C., Lipkin, M., Jr., & Gordon, G. H. (1988). Somatization in primary care: Patients with unexplained and vexing medical complaints. *Journal of General Internal Medicine, 3,* 177–190.

Kassett, J. A., Gershon, E. S., Maxwell, M. E., Guroff, J. J.,

Kazuba, D. M., Smith, A. L., Brandt, H. A., & Jimerson, D. C. (1989). Psychiatric disorders in the first-degree relatives of probands with bulimia nervosa. *American Journal of Psychiatry*, 146(11), 1468–1471.

Katon, W., Lin, E., Von Korff, M., Russo, J., Lipscomb, P., & Bush, T. (1991). Somatization: A spectrum of severity. *American Journal of Psychiatry*, 148, 34–40.

Kaye, W. H., Gwirtsman, H. E., George, D. T., Ebert, M. H., Jimerson, D. C., Tomai, T. P., Chrousos, G. P., & Gold, P. W. (1987). Elevated cerebrospinal fluid levels of immunoreactive corticotropin-releasing hormone in anorexia nervosa: Relation to state of nutrition, adrenal function, and intensity of depression. *Journal of Clinical Endocrinology and Metabolism*, 64(2), 203–208.

Kaye, W. H., Jimerson, D. C., Lake, C. R., & Ebert, M. H. (1985). Altered noradrenergic metabolism following long-term weight recovery in patients with anorexia nervosa. *Psychiatry Research*, 14, 333–342.

Kaye, W. H., Weltzin, T. E., Hsu, L. K. G., & Bulik, C. M. (1991). An open trial of fluoxetine in patients with anorexia nervosa. *Journal of Clinical Psychiatry*, 52(11), 464–471.

Keller, M. B., & Shapiro, R. W. (1982). "Double depression": Super-imposition of acute depressive episodes on chronic depressive disorders. *American Journal of Psychiatry*, 139, 438–442.

Kellner, R. (1990a). Somatization: Theories and research. *Journal of Nervous and Mental Disease*, 178, 150–160.

Kellner, R. (1990b). Somatization: The most costly comorbidity? In J. D. Maser & C. R. Cloninger (Eds.), *Comorbidity of mood and anxiety disorders* (pp. 239–252). Washington, DC: American Psychiatric Press.

Kellner, R., Simpson, G. M., & Winslow, W. W. (1972). The relationship of depressive neurosis to anxiety and somatic symptoms. *Psychosomatics*, 13, 358–362.

Kendall, P. C., & Watson, D. (1989). *Anxiety and depression: Distinctive and overlapping features*. San Diego: Academic Press.

Keys, A., Brozek, J., Henschel, A., Mickelsen, O., & Taylor, H. L. (1950). *The biology of human starvation*. Minneapolis: University of Minnesota Press.

Khantzian, E. J. (1985). The self-medication hypothesis of addictive disorders: Focus on heroin and cocaine dependence. *American Journal of Psychiatry*, 142(11), 1259–1264.

Klein, D. N., & Riso, L. P. (1993). Psychiatric disorders: Problems of boundaries and comorbidity. In C. G. Costello (Ed.), *Basic issues in psychopathology* (pp. 19–66). New York: Guilford Press.

Kraepelin, E. (1921). *Textbook of psychiatry* (8th ed.): *Vol. 3. Manic–depressive insanity and paranoia* (R. M. Barclay, Trans.; G. M. Robertson, Ed.). Edinburgh: E. & S. Livingstone. (Original work published 1913)

Kranzler, H. R., & Liebowitz, N. R. (1988). Anxiety and depression in substance abuse: Clinical implications. *Medical Clinics of North America*, 72(4), 867–885.

Lehmann, L. (1985). The relationship of depression to other DSM-III Axis I disorders. In E. E. Beckham & W. R. Leber (Eds.), *Handbook of depression: Treatment, assessment, and research* (pp. 669–699). Homewood, IL: Dorsey Press.

Lewinsohn, P. M., Rohde, P., Seeley, J. R., & Hops, H. (1991). Comorbidity of unipolar depression: I. Major depression with dysthymia. *Journal of Abnormal Psychology*, 100(2), 205–213.

Lewis, A. (1934a). Melancholia: A clinical survey of depressive states. *Journal of Mental Science*, 80, 277–378.

Lewis, A. (1934b). Melancholia: Historical review. *Journal of Mental Science*, 80, 1–42.

Lipowski, Z. J. (1990). Somatization and depression. *Psychosomatics*, 31, 13–21.

Markowitz, J. C., Moran, M. E., Kocsis, J. H., & Frances, A. J. (1992). Prevalence and comorbidity of dysthymic disorder among psychiatric outpatients. *Journal of Affective Disorders*, 24, 63–71.

Maser, J. D., & Cloninger, C. R. (Eds.). (1990). *Comorbidity of mood and anxiety disorders*. Washington, DC: American Psychiatric Press.

McElroy, S. L., Keck, P. E., Pope, H. G., Jr., Hudson, J. I., Faedda, G. L., & Swann, A. C. (1992). Clinical and research implications of the diagnosis of dysphoric or mixed mania or hypomania. *American Journal of Psychiatry*, 149, 1633–1644.

Mezzich, J. E., Ahn, C. W., Fabrega, H. Jr., & Pilkonis, P. A. (1990). Evidence for comorbidity: Treated samples and longitudinal studies. In J. D. Maser & C. R. Cloninger (Eds.), *Comorbidity of mood and anxiety disorders* (pp. 189–204). Washington, DC: American Psychiatric Press.

Mirin, S. M., Weiss, R. D., Sollogub, A., & Michael, J. (1984). Psychopathology in the families of drug abusers. In S. M. Mirin (Ed.), *Substance abuse and psychopathology* (pp. 80–106). Washington, DC: American Psychiatric Press.

Mitchell, J. E., Pyle, R. L., Eckert, E. D., Hatsukami, D., Pomeroy, C., & Zimmerman, R. (1990). A comparison study of antidepressants and structured intensive group psychotherapy in the treatment of bulimia nervosa. *Archives of General Psychiatry*, 47(2), 149–160.

Moldin, S., Scheftner, W. A., Rice, J. P., Nelson, E., Knesevich, M. A., & Akiskal, H. S. (1993). Association between major depressive disorder and physical illness. *Psychological Medicine*, 23(3), 755–761.

Morrison, J., & Herbstein, J. (1988). Secondary affective disorder in women with somatization disorder. *Comprehensive Psychiatry*, 29, 433–440.

Munro, A. (1966). Parental deprivation in depressive patients. *British Journal of Psychiatry*, 112, 443–457.

Murphy, G. (1988). Suicide and substance abuse. *Archives of General Psychiatry*, 45(6), 593–594.

Murphy, G., Wetzel, R. D., Robins, E., & McEvoy, L. (1992). Multiple risk factors predict suicide in alcoholism. *Archives of General Psychiatry*, 49, 459–463.

Murphy, J. M. (1990). Diagnostic comorbidity and symptom co-occurrence: The Stirling County study. In J. D. Maser & R. C. Cloninger (Eds.), *Comorbidity of mood and anxiety disorders* (pp. 153–176). Washington, DC: American Psychiatric Press.

Orenstein, H. (1989). Briquet's syndrome in association with depression and panic: A reconceptualization of Briquet's syndrome. *American Journal of Psychiatry*, 146, 334–338.

Ormel, J., Koeter, M. W., van den Brink, W., & van de Willige, G. (1991). Recognition, management, and course of anxiety and depression in general practice. *Archives of General Psychiatry*, 48, 700–706.

Piotrowski, Z. A., & Lewis, N. D. (1950). An experimental Rorschach diagnostic aid for some forms of schizophrenia. *American Journal of Psychiatry*, 107, 360–366.

Pope, H. G., Jr. (1983). Distinguishing bipolar disorder from schizophrenia in clinical practice: Guidelines and case reports. *Hospital and Community Psychiatry*, 34(4), 322–328.

Pope, H. G., Jr., Hudson, J. I., Yurgelun-Todd, D., &

Jonas, J. M. (1985). Antidepressant treatment of bulimia: A two-year follow-up study. *Journal of Clinical Psychopharmacology*, 5, 320–327.

Pope, H. G., Jr., & Lipinski, J. F. (1978). Diagnosis in schizophrenia and manic–depressive illness: A reassessment of the specificity of "schizophrenic" symptoms in the light of current research. *Archives of General Psychiatry*, 35, 811–828.

Prien, R. F. (1988). Somatic treatment of unipolar depressive disorder. In A. J. Frances & R. E. Hales (Eds.), *Review of psychiatry* (Vol. 7, pp. 213–234). Washington, DC: American Psychiatric Press.

Prien, R. F., Carpenter, L. L., & Kupfer, D. J. (1991). The definition and operational criteria for treatment outcome of major depressive disorder: A review of the current research literature. *Archives of General Psychiatry*, 48, 796–800.

Prusoff, B. A., Weissman, M. M., Merikangas, K. R., Leckman, J. F., & Harding, P. S. (1984). Psychiatric illness in relatives of probands with delusional depression. *Psychopharmacological Bulletin*, 20, 358–361.

Puig-Antich, J., Goetz, D., Davies, M., Kaplan, T., Davies, S., Ostrow, L., Asnis, L., Twomey, J., Iyengar, S., & Ryan, N. D. (1989). A controlled family history study of prepubertal major depressive disorder. *Archives of General Psychiatry*, 46, 406–418.

Quitkin, F. M., Rifkin, A., & Klein, D. F. (1976). Prophylaxis of affective disorders. *Archives of General Psychiatry*, 33, 337–341.

Rachman, S. (1988). Panics and their consequences: A review and prospect. In S. Rachman & J. D. Maser (Eds.), *Panic: Psychological perspectives* (pp. 259–303). Hillsdale, NJ: Erlbaum.

Rasmussen, N. H., & Avant, R. F. (1989). Somatization disorder in family practice. *American Family Physician*, 40, 206–214.

Regier, D. A., Boyd, J. H., Burke, J. D., Jr., Rae, D. S., Myers, J. K., Kramer, M., Robins, L. N., George, L. K., Karno, M., & Locke, B. Z. (1988). One-month prevalence of mental disorders in the United States based on five Epidemiologic Catchment Area sites. *Archives of General Psychiatry*, 45, 977–986.

Regier, D. A., Farmer, M. E., Rae, D. S., Locke, B. Z., Keith, S. J., Judd, L. L., & Goodwin, F. K. (1990). Comorbidity of mental disorders with alcohol and other drug abuse. *Journal of the American Medical Association*, 264(19), 2511–2518.

Rehm, L. P. (1990). Extracting comorbidity for self-report instruments: A cognitive perspective. In J. D. Maser & R. C. Cloninger (Eds.), *Comorbidity of mood and anxiety disorders* (pp. 633–648). Washington, DC: American Psychiatric Press.

Robins, E., & Guze, S. B. (1972). Classification of affective disorders: The primary–secondary, the endogenous–reactive, and the neurotic–psychotic concepts. In T. A. Williams, M. M. Katz, & J. A. Shield (Eds.), *Recent advances in the psychobiology of the depressive illnesses* (DHEW Publication No. HSM 79-9053, pp. 283–293). Washington, DC: U.S. Government Printing Office.

Rohde, P., Lewinsohn, P. M., & Seeley, J. R. (1991). Comorbidity of unipolar depression: II. Comorbidity with other mental disorders in adolescents and adults. *Journal of Abnormal Psychology*, 100(2), 214–222.

Roth, M., & Mountjoy, C. Q. (1982). The distinction between anxiety states and depressive disorders. In E. S. Paykel (Ed.), *Handbook of affective disorders* (pp. 70–92). New York: Guilford Press.

Roy, A., Pickar, D., Linnoila, M., & Potter, W. Z. (1985). Plasma norepinephrine level in affective disorders. *Archives of General Psychiatry*, 42, 1181–1185.

Russell, G. F. M. (1979). Bulimia nervosa: An ominous variant of anorexia nervosa. *Psychological Medicine*, 9, 429–448.

Shuckit, M. A. (1986). Genetic and clinical implications of alcoholism and affective disorder. *American Journal of Psychiatry*, 143(2), 140–147.

Simon, G. E., & Von Korff, M. (1991). Somatization and psychiatric disorder in the NIMH Epidemiologic Catchment Area study. *American Journal of Psychiatry*, 148, 1494–1500.

Smith, G. R., Jr. (1990). *Somatization disorder in the medical setting*. Washington, DC: U.S. Government Printing Office.

Spalter, A. R., Gwirtsman, H. E., Demitrack, M. A., & Gold, P. W. (1993). Thyroid function in bulimia nervosa. *Biological Psychiatry*, 33, 408–414.

Spitzer, R. L., Endicott, J., & Robins, E. (1978a). *Research Diagnostic Criteria*. New York: Department of Biometrics Research, Evaluation Section, New York State Psychiatric Institute.

Spitzer, R. L., Endicott, J., & Robins, E. (1978b). Research Diagnostic Criteria: Rationale and reliability. *Archives of General Psychiatry*, 35, 773–782.

Stein, M. B., Tancer, M. E., Gelernter, C. S., Vittone, B. J., & Uhde, T. W. (1990). Major depression in patients with social phobia. *American Journal of Psychiatry*, 147, 637–639.

Stern, S. L., Dixon, K. N., Nemzer, E., Lake, M. D., Sansone, R. A., Smeltzer, D. J., Lantz, S., & Schrier, S. S. (1984). Affective disorder in the families of women with normal weight bulimia. *American Journal of Psychiatry*, 141, 1224–1227.

Strober, M., & Katz, J. L. (1987). Do eating disorders and affective disorders share a common etiology? A dissenting opinion. *International Journal of Eating Disorders*, 6(2), 171–180.

Strober, M., Lampert, C., Morrell, W., Burroughs, J., & Jacobs, C. (1990). A controlled family study of anorexia nervosa: Evidence of familial aggregation and lack of shared transmission with affective disorders. *International Journal of Eating Disorders*, 9, 239–254.

Strober, M., Salkin, B., Burroughs, J., & Morrell, W. (1982). Validity of the bulimia–restrictor distinction in anorexia nervosa: Parental personality characteristics and family psychiatric morbidity. *Journal of Nervous and Mental Disease*, 170, 345–351.

Sturt, E. (1981). Hierarchial patterns in the distribution of psychiatric symptoms. *Psychological Medicine*, 11, 783–794.

Swift, W. J., Andrews, D., & Barklage, N. E. (1986). The relationship between affective disorder and eating disorders: A review of the literature. *American Journal of Psychiatry*, 143, 290–299.

Swift, W. J., Kalin, N. H., Wamboldt, F. S., Kaslow, N., & Ritholz, M. (1985). Depression in bulimia at 2- to 5-year followup. *Psychiatry Research*, 16, 111–122.

Szmukler, G. I. (1987). Some comments on the link between anorexia nervosa and affective disorder. *International Journal of Eating Disorders*, 6(2), 181–189.

Taylor, M. A. (1992). Are schizophrenia and affective disorder related? A selective literature review. *American Journal of Psychiatry*, 149(1), 22–32.

Taylor, M. A., & Abrams, R. (1981). Early- and late-onset bipolar illness. *Archives of General Psychiatry*, 38, 58–61.

Tyrer, P., Alexander, J., Remington, M., & Riley, P. (1987). Relationship between neurotic symptoms and neurotic diagnosis: A longitudinal study. *Journal of Affective Disorders, 13*, 13–21.

Vaillant, G. (1983). *The natural history of alcoholism.* Cambridge, MA: Harvard University Press.

Van Ameringen, M., Mancini, C., Styan, G., & Donison, D. (1991). Relationship of social phobia with other psychiatric illness. *Journal of Affective Disorders, 21*, 93–99.

Van Valkenburg, C., Akiskal, H. S., Puzantian, V., & Rosenthal, T. (1984). Anxious depressions: Clinical, family history, and naturalistic outcomes. Comparisons with panic and major depressive disorders. *Journal of Affective Disorders, 6*, 67–82.

Vollrath, M., & Angst, J. (1989). Outcome of panic and depression in a seven-year follow-up: Results of the Zurich study. *Acta Psychiatrica Scandanivica, 80*, 591–596.

Walsh, B. T. (1988). Antidepressants and bulimia: Where are we? *International Journal of Eating Disorders, 7*(3), 421–423.

Walsh, B. T., Lo, E. S., Cooper, T., Lindy, D. C., Roose, S. P., Gladis, M., & Glassman, A. H. (1987). Dexamethasone suppression test and plasma dexamethasone levels in bulimia. *Archives of General Psychiatry, 44*, 797–800.

Walsh, B. T., Roose, S. P., Glassman, A. H., Gladis, M., & Sadik, C. (1985). Bulimia and depression. *Psychosomatic Medicine, 47*(2), 123–131.

Watson, D., & Clark, L. A. (1984). Negative affectivity: The disposition to experience aversive emotional states. *Psychological Bulletin, 96*, 465–490.

Watts, C. A. H. (1947). Endogenous depression in general practice. *British Medical Journal, 1*, 11–14.

Weiner, H. (1985). The physiology of eating disorders. *International Journal of Eating Disorders, 4*, 347–388.

Wells, K. B., Rogers, W., Burnam, A., Greenfield, S. & Ware, J. E., Jr. (1991). How the medical comorbidity of depressed patients differs across health care settings: Results from the Medical Outcomes Study. *American Journal of Psychiatry, 148*, 1688–1696.

Weltzin, T., Gwirtsman, H., Jimerson, D. C., & Kaye, W. H. (1990). Anorexia and bulimia: Pharmacotherapy. In A. S. Bellack & M. Hersen (Eds.), *Handbook of comparative treatments for adult disorders* (pp. 371–388). New York: Wiley.

Wetzler, S., & Katz, M.M. (1989). Problems with the differentiation of anxiety and depression. *Journal of Psychiatric Research, 23*(1), 1–12.

Winokur, G. (1990). The concept of secondary depression and its relationship to comorbidity. *Psychiatric Clinics of North America, 13*, 567–583.

Winokur, G., & Clayton, P. J. (1967). Family history studies: II. Sex differences and alcoholism in primary affective illness. *British Journal of Psychiatry, 113*, 973–979.

Woodruff, R. A., Jr., Murphy, G. E., & Herjanic, M. (1967). The natural history of affective disorders: I. Symptoms of 72 patients at the time of index hospital admission. *Journal of Psychiatric Research, 5*, 255–263.

World Health Organization. (1978). *International classification of diseases: Clinical modification* (9th revision). Ann Arbor, MI: Edwards Brothers.

5

The Relationship of Depression to Disorders of Personality

THEODORE MILLON
DOREEN KOTIK-HARPER

Historically, the relationship between personality attributes and vulnerability to depression has received extensive coverage from a diverse range of clinical theorists. The introduction of Axis II personality disorders in the third edition of the *Diagnostic and Statistical Manual of Mental Disorders* (DSM-III; American Psychiatric Association, 1980) further heightened the awareness of potential interactions between psychiatric syndromes (including depression) and characterological features. The elucidation of the comorbidity of personality traits/disorders and affective disorders is of both theoretical and clinical importance. Major depression is among the most common reasons for seeking psychiatric help and hospitalization in the general population. Clarification of the interrelationship between personality and affective symptomatology can have important implications in psychotherapeutic and psychopharmacological interventions. An increased understanding of this relationship can also help clarify the heterogeneous nature of affective illness and can better delineate the ways in which depression and personality interact and modify each other.

ALTERNATIVE HYPOTHESES

Despite the recent upsurge of relevant research, the relationship between personality features and affective disorders remains a persistent issue warranting further clarification. Although the structure of DSM-III and its successors suggests quasi-independence of personality and depression (Farmer & Nelson-Gray, 1990), continued research in this area has generated controversy about this proposition and resulted in alternative hypotheses about such a relationship (Akiskal, Hirschfeld, & Yerevanian, 1983; Hirschfeld & Cross, 1987; Widiger, 1989). A summary of these possible relationships follows, drawn from the comprehensive works of Klein, Wonderlich, and Shea (1993), Farmer and Nelson-Gray (1990), Hirschfeld and Cross (1987), Phillips, Gunderson, Hirschfeld, and Smith (1990), and Hirschfeld and Shea (1992). For a more exhaustive treatment of the models of relationships between personality and depression, the reader should refer to the work of Klein et al. (1993).

Characterological-Predisposition Hypothesis

The most popular approach in both theory and research, the characterological-disposition hypothesis—also described by Klein et al. (1993) as the "vulnerability model"—suggests that characterological disorders are primary, with depression being a secondary feature of character pathology. It is postulated that particular

107

features of a personality style (e.g., ineffective coping mechanisms; maladaptive, self-defeating behaviors; or alienation of others) may render an individual vulnerable to specific psychosocial stressors (e.g., abandonment, rejection, or loss of prestige).

Complication Hypothesis

Opposite to the characterological-predisposition hypothesis, the complication theory, also known as the "scar model" (Klein et al., 1993), postulates that the experience of a depressive disorder influences personality. Such changes in personality may be limited to the duration of the depressive episode, may appear only as a short-term alteration immediately following the episode, or (in the case of recurring depressive episodes) may develop into a long-term or chronic alteration. These changes in personality may include changes in the person's perception of self and the environment, and/or the person's style of interacting with others (Hirschfeld & Cross, 1987). Commonly recognized postmorbid personality features include resignation, insecurity, or pessimism (Phillips et al., 1990).

Attenuation Hypothesis

Also known as the "subclinical approach" (Hirschfeld & Cross, 1987) or "spectrum model" (Klein et al., 1993), the attenuation hypothesis presumes that personality disorders are an attenuated or alternative expression of the disease process underlying the depressive disorder. As such, certain personality traits (e.g., cyclothymia) may be viewed as milder manifestations of the full-blown affective disorder. Both the personality disorder or set of traits and the depression are seen to rise from the same genetic or constitutional origins.

Coeffect Hypothesis

The coeffect hypothesis, also known as the "common-cause hypothesis" (Klein et al., 1993), is that depression and personality disorder may occur together as a result of a common third variable (e.g., a traumatic childhood), even though they do not share a common psychobiological origin. In this sense, neither the personality disorder nor the depressive disorder gives rise to the other.

Modification Hypothesis

Also known as the "pathoplasty approach" (Hirschfeld & Cross, 1987; Paykel, Klerman, & Prusoff, 1976), and the "exacerbation model" (Klein et al., 1993), the modification hypothesis puts etiology and pathogenesis aside, proposing instead that personality features may substantially influence the clinical presentation, treatment responsivity, and prognosis of the depressive episode. Depending on the premorbid personality, depressive symptoms such as hopelessness, helplessness, and self-deprecation may serve a variety of goals. Among the secondary gains of depression are the eliciting of nurturance from others, an excuse for avoiding unwanted responsibilities, a rationalization for poor performance, or a method of safely (albeit indirectly) expressing anger toward others. Partly determined by the gains received, depressive symptoms may take the form of dramatic gestures, irritable negativism, passive loneliness, or philosophical intellectualizations.

The effects of personality traits and depression on treatment response have been particularly well researched, with the findings being fairly consistent that personality pathology is correlated with a decreased responsivity to pharmacological and psychotherapeutic interventions (Tyrer, Casey, & Gall, 1983; Charney, Nelson, & Quinlan, 1981; Pfohl, Coryell, Zimmerman, & Stangl, 1987; Pilkonis & Frank, 1988; Shea, Glass, Pilkonis, Watkins, & Docherty, 1987). In other studies where populations with mixed personality and affective symptomatology improved with medication, it has been argued that the personality symptomatology may have been secondary to the affective pathology or the result of the same underlying neurochemical cause (e.g., Akiskal et al., 1985; Frank, Kupfer, Jarrett, & Jacob, 1987).

Orthogonal Hypothesis

The orthogonal hypothesis suggests that although personality disorders and depression are independent entities, their frequent co-occurrence results from the fact that they are both common conditions. This theory relates to the influence of base rates, in that it suggests that separate conditions with high probabilities of occurring in a given population or setting will tend to be diagnosed together more often than ones that are infrequently encountered within that setting (Widiger, 1989; Frances, Widiger, & Fyer, 1990).

Overlapping-Symptomatology Hypothesis

According to the overlapping-symptomatology hypothesis, the observed comorbidity of personality disorders and depression is largely artifactual as a result of overlapping criteria sets used to define each of the disorders. The influence of classification methods on comorbidity has been the subject of much recent research (Frances et al., 1990; Widiger, 1989; Hirschfeld & Cross, 1987; Akiskal et al., 1985; Gunderson & Elliott, 1985). Proponents of this hypothesis cite the frequent inclusion of maladaptive affectivity as being diagnostically relevant to a number of personality disorders, particularly those from DSM's "dramatic, erratic" personality cluster (Farmer & Nelson-Gray, 1990). Such overlap may result in the assignment of two or more independent diagnoses on multiple axes for what is in fact a single disorder.

Heterogeneity Hypothesis

The final hypothesis postulates that several different sources contribute to the signs and symptoms of depression and personality disorders. Various configurations of genetic/constitutional factors in conjunction with environmental variables may combine to produce differing vulnerabilities to expressions of depression or personality pathology. A heterogeneous population, which includes a subset of individuals who evidence both symptoms of personality disorder and depression, arises from these various combinations. The heterogeneity hypothesis is most consistent with Millon's (1969, 1981, 1986) biopsychosocial conceptualization of personality and psychopathology.

COMORBIDITY RATES AND GENERAL CHARACTERISTICS

The comorbidity rate of personality disorders and depression as estimated by Farmer and Nelson-Gray (1990) in their review article falls between 30% and 70%. The presence of personality disorder complicates a depressive episode, as evident from more frequent suicidal

ideation and attempts (Charney et al., 1981; Pfohl, Stangl, & Zimmerman, 1984; Shea et al., 1987), poorer treatment response (Weissman, Prusoff, & Klerman, 1979; Charney et al., 1981; Frank et al., 1987; Pilkonis & Frank, 1988), and greater risk for hospitalization (Zimmerman, Coryell, Pfohl, Stangl, & Corenthal, 1988). It has been further suggested that depressives with concurrent personality disorder also have an earlier age of onset for their first depressive episode (Charney et al., 1981; Pfohl et al., 1984), a longer duration of the depressive episode (Pfohl et al., 1984; Shea et al., 1987), and a greater tendency to experience recurring depressive episodes (Shea et al., 1987). Farmer and Nelson-Gray (1990) also contend that their review suggests a higher incidence of the "dramatic, erratic" personality disorders in inpatient samples of depressives, whereas outpatient depressive populations are more frequently characterized by the "anxious, fearful" cluster of personality disorders (Shea et al., 1987; Pilkonis & Frank, 1988).

PROBLEMS WITH THE COMORBIDITY RESEARCH

Before we proceed further with this discussion on personality disorders and depression, it is important to emphasize that research in this area is fraught with methodological pitfalls, much as would be the case for the study of comorbidity in any two diagnostic entities. Hirschfeld and Cross (1987) have grouped the methodological problems that characterize much of the research in this area into three general categories: "specificity of patient samples; specificity of independent and dependent variables; and the effect of clinical state on assessment of personality" (p. 320). With respect to patient characteristics, depression encompasses an enormous, heterogeneous group of disorders with different etiologies, clinical courses, and treatments. As such, the role of personality may differ significantly among the various affective subtypes. In certain subtypes personality features may be seen as predisposing, whereas in other subtypes such personality features may be irrelevant. The difficulty here lies in the frequent inability to differentiate among these various subtypes. This should prove to be an increasingly difficult task, as DSM-IV (American Psychiatric Association,

1994) and recent literature on depression suggest the addition of such affective states as bipolar I and II disorders, minor depressive disorder, primary versus secondary dysthymic disorders, and double depression (Miller, Norman, & Dow, 1986). The heterogeneity of such affective subtypes may contribute considerable imprecision to a study design. Furthermore, personality studies may vary considerably if age ranges or sex ratios of the samples differ, since both these factors may affect the personality attributes. Finally, others (Frances et al., 1990; Farmer & Nelson-Gray, 1990) remind us that different patient characteristics may be expected according to different settings (e.g., inpatient vs. outpatient).

The next difficulty encountered relates to assessment issues and the specificity with which the variables are defined and measured. This includes the need for both operational criteria and objective, reliable measures for determining both depressive disorders and personality characteristics. As noted earlier, overlapping diagnostic criteria complicate the differentiation of depression from personality, as well as the differentiation of specific depressive subgroups or specific personality subtypes. The problem of shared diagnostic criteria among personality types is notorious (Farmer & Nelson-Gray, 1990; Pfohl et al., 1984), resulting in multiple personality diagnoses for any given patient. Similar difficulties involve item overlap between affective disorders and such entities as borderline personality disorder or the depressive personality disorder, which is described in Appendix B of DSM-IV (American Psychiatric Association, 1994).

A review of the extant literature on depression and personality reveals the need for operational criteria for the definition of important variables in both depression and personality—for example, "orality," "dependency," "neurotic depression," and "extraversion" (Hirschfeld & Cross, 1987). The multifarious characteristics of personality and depressive subtypes have resulted in the development and utilization of a vast number of assessment instruments, both self-report and interview-based. As such, study findings may often be inconsistent or uninterpretable, and cross-study comparisons may be virtually impossible.

Even differentiating personality from depression in terms of operational criteria can be quite difficult. In his excellent review, Widiger (1989) notes that such indicators as biological markers,

treatment responsivity, phenomenology, and course can no longer infallibly differentiate the two diagnostic entities. Previously, the biogenetic–psychosocial distinction between depression and personality was acceptable. It is clear now, however, that affective disorders have not only a biogenetic basis but cognitive, behavioral, and interpersonal contributants as well (Beck, 1981; Lewinsohn, 1974; Abramson, Seligman, & Teasdale, 1978). Similarly, personality disorders are not limited to environmental or psychosocial etiologies, but also may be associated with specific genetic and biological markers, as well as physiological correlates (Siever, Klar, & Coccaro, 1985; Siever et al., 1987; Marin, DeMeo, Frances, Kocsis, & Mann, 1989; Shader, Scharfman, & Dreyfuss, 1986; Guerrera, 1990). To the extent that personality disorders may be due in part to abnormal neurochemical functioning, it cannot then be assumed that all personality-disordered depressive states will be unreactive to a pharmacological intervention. In addition, although many subgroups of depressives with personality disorders do not respond to pharmacological treatment, they have been shown to respond to other forms of therapy (Hoberman & Lewinsohn, 1985; Akiskal & Simmons, 1985). It is becoming increasingly clear that affective disturbance is not limited to a disorder of mood, but, like personality disorder, can be pervasive in its effects on behavior, cognition, and interpersonal relations. Similarly, the course of depression, like the course of a personality disorder, may be chronic and lifelong. This is especially clear in the case of dysthymia, which may become apparent in childhood and continue throughout a person's life (Widiger, 1989).

Moreover, it is notable that low reliability is certainly associated with the assessment of personality disorders in particular (Farmer & Nelson-Gray, 1990), varying significantly among patient self-report, report of a knowledgeable informant, and the report of a trained clinician (Zimmerman et al., 1988; Frances et al., 1990).

A final methodological problem that is very much related to the assessment issues of reliability and validity is the need to minimize bias in personality assessment by reducing the influence of the depressive state on the measurement of personality traits (Hirschfeld & Cross, 1987). It has been well documented that depressed patients do not provide valid reports of their premorbid personality functioning, despite the instructional set to do so. Specifically, during periods of depression, patients may rate themselves as significantly more impaired (e.g., dependent, irritable, labile, neurotic, introverted, etc.) than they may when their depression has abated (Hirschfeld, Klerman, Clayton, & Keller, 1983; Liebowitz, Stallone, Dunner, & Fieve, 1979; Libb et al., 1990). Such findings emphasize the need to obtain personality ratings during a premorbid or intermorbid symptom-free period. Farmer and Nelson-Gray (1990), however, remind us that assessing a patient following the remission of a depressive episode may result in ratings of personality that are qualitatively different from those that might have been obtained during baseline levels (Akiskal et al., 1983; Hirschfeld et al., 1989).

OUR CONCEPTS OF DEPRESSION AND PERSONALITY

It is our task in this chapter to provide a more extensive review of the interaction between depression and personality characteristics, drawing upon theoretical deduction as well as upon the recent clinical and empirical literature. A "continuum" conceptualization of depression is employed in this evaluation, rather than a clearly demarcated typology.

"Depression" is viewed here as a multifaceted syndrome that manifests affective, cognitive, behavioral, and vegetative symptoms. The most prominent feature, of course, is a disturbance of mood, in which the individual feels sad, blue, apathetic, or helpless. Expressions of discouragement, self-deprecation, and guilt are frequently present, along with somatic disturbances; the latter include loss of energy, social interests, and sexual desire, as well as disruptions in sleeping, eating, and ability to concentrate. Relationships with others may be affected as a result of heightened interpersonal sensitivity, irritability, clinging dependency, or demandingness. In severe cases, preoccupation with suicidal ideation is often present.

Personality, like depression, may best be conceived as falling on a continuum of severity. The concept of "personality" employed here refers to deeply etched characteristics that pervade all aspects of the individual's functioning. Derived from the complex and progressive interactions of constitutional and experiential factors, these patterns (including perceptions, attitudes, and behaviors) tend to persist with little change throughout an individual's lifetime, regardless

of the adaptive level of the individual's functioning. Pathological personality patterns or personality disorders are distinguished from normal, healthy patterns by their adaptive inflexibility, their tendency to foster vicious circles of inefficient and self-defeating behaviors, and their tenuous stability under conditions of stress (Millon, 1969, 1981, 1986).

Although the interpretations offered here may be extended to include the more adaptive and "healthy" personality traits and patterns, the focus of this chapter is on the relationships between depression and the 10 disorders of personality included on Axis II of the DSM-IV, as well as the two personality disorders included in Appendix B of the DSM-IV for further study (American Psychiatric Association, 1994).

THE DEPENDENT PERSONALITY

Distinguished by their marked need for social approval and affection, and by their willingness to live in accord with the desires of others, dependent personalities are among the most likely individuals to become depressed. Characteristically, these individuals are docile, noncompetitive, and passive. Apart from requiring signs of belonging and acceptance, dependent personalities make few demands on others. Their own needs are subordinated and their individuality denied, as these individuals assume a submissive, self-sacrificing, and placating role in relation to others. Social tension and interpersonal conflicts are carefully avoided, while troubling events are smoothed over or naively denied. Beneath their warm and affable presentation, however, may lie a plaintive and pessimistic quality. Dependent individuals perceive themselves as weak, fragile, and ineffective. The recognition of their helplessness and utter reliance upon others may result in self-effacement and denigration. In addition, they may become excessively conciliatory in relationships, to the point of submitting themselves to intimidation and abuse (Millon, 1981, 1986).

Given their pronounced susceptibility to separation anxiety, dependent personalities are quite likely to experience any number of affective disorders. Frequently, the underlying characterological pessimism of these individuals lends itself to a chronic but mild depression or dysthymia (Kocsis & Frances, 1987). When they are faced with possible abandonment or the actual loss of a significant other, a major depression may ensue. Initially, these individuals may react with clinging helplessness and pleas for reassurance and support. Expressions of self-condemnation and guilt are also likely, as such verbalizations serve to deflect criticisms and evoke sympathetic reactions. Feelings of guilt can also act as a defensive maneuver to check outbursts of resentment or hostility. Fearful that their underlying feelings of anger might cause further alienation or retribution, dependent individuals typically turn their aggressive impulses inward, discharging them through a despondency colored by self-derisive comments and contrition. On occasion, dependent personalities may make a desperate attempt to counter or deny emerging feelings of hopelessness and depression, through a temporary reversal of their typical passive, subdued style to one of hypomanic activity, excitement, and optimism. Such dramatic shifts in affective expression may resemble a bipolar disorder.

The dependent personality corresponds to the psychoanalytic "oral character," and more specifically to what has been termed the "oral-sucking" or "oral-receptive" character. According to both Abraham (1911/1968) and Freud (1917/1968), the orally fixated depressive or melancholic individual has great oral needs, manifested by sucking, eating, and insatiable demands for oral expressions of affection. Abraham and Freud also emphasized the affectional frustrations occurring during the pre-Oedipal period. In essence, the melancholic person has experienced a pathological introjection, or identification with the ambivalently regarded love object through the process of oral incorporation. Thus, an interpersonal conflict is transformed into an intrapsychic conflict, with the angry desire to devour the frustrating love object being turned inward and experienced as depression. As psychoanalytic theory developed, the concept of orality was extended to include the general feelings of affection, support, nourishment, and security. It was thought that the dependent personality's reliance on external approval and support for maintenance of self-esteem makes the individual particularly vulnerable to depression resulting from the loss of a significant other. Rado (1968) described melancholia as a "despairing cry for love," while Fenichel (1968) described the orally dependent depressive as a "love addict."

A theory of depressive subtypes, based on attained level of object representation, has been developed by Blatt (1974). Of the two depressive subtypes offered, "anaclitic" and "introjective," anaclitic depression corresponds most closely to dependent depression. Individuals with this form of depression have histories of impaired object relations at the primitive, oral level of development. Anaclitic depression is associated with intense dependency on others for support and gratification, vulnerability to feelings of deprivation, and considerable difficulties in managing anger expression for fear of alienating the love object. Blatt, D'Afflitti, and Quinlan (1976) provided empirical support for the division of depression into anaclitic and introjective subtypes. A Depressive Experiences Questionnaire was constructed to tap phenomenological experiences (rather than observed symptoms) of depression. Three stable factors emerging from this questionnaire included dependency, self-criticism, and efficacy. Corresponding with anaclitic depression is the dependency factor, which consists of items reflecting feelings of loneliness and helplessness, reliance on others, needs for closeness, fears of rejection and abandonment, and uneasiness about anger expression. Further empirical support was provided for Blatt's depressive subtypes in a study by Blatt, Quinlan, Chevron, McDonald, and Zuroff (1982). Here clinical judges successfully predicted type of depression based on the case records of psychiatric patients. In the high-dependency patients, clinical records contained evidence of oral excesses (i.e., alcohol, food, and drug abuse), a history of early object loss or deprivation, and issues of abandonment and loneliness.

Bemporad (1971), as reviewed by Hirschfeld, Klerman, Chodoff, Korchin, and Barrett (1976), suggests that there are three attributes to what he terms "pathological dependency." First is "dependency on a dominant other" who provides meaning to the activities of the depressive person's life. Related to this is "fear of autonomous gratification." Rather than deriving pleasure from their successes and professional accomplishments, depressives use these achievements as bartering agents to win love and acceptance by the dominant other. The depressive's denial or sacrifice of autonomous satisfaction in return for nurturance from the dominant other is reflected in Bemporad's third feature of pathological dependency: the "bargaining relationship." Arieti and Bemporad (1980) offer a depressive typology similar to that of Blatt (1974). Depression is characterized as resulting from a "limitation of alternate ways of thinking and as self-inhibition from new experiences" (p. 1360). On the basis of clinical experience (i.e., long-term psychoanalytic therapy with 40 depressed patients), the three following premorbid types of depressive personality were proposed: (1) the "dominant-other" type; (2) the "dominant-goal" type; and (3) the "chronic character structure," or personality disorder. Akin to the dependent or anaclitic depressive personality, the dominant-other depressive personality is characterized by "clingingness, passivity, manipulativeness, and avoidance of anger" (p. 1361). Depression in such individuals may be precipitated by the loss of an esteemed other.

In a study examining the themes of both dependency and autonomy in depressive personalities, Pilkonis (1988) utilized a modified prototype methodology, in which experienced clinicians provided detailed descriptors of the two constructs. Descriptors of excessive autonomy clustered into three subtypes, whereas descriptors of excessive dependency clustered into two distinct subtypes. The first prototype described the excessive dependency and "anxious attachment" hypothesized to be characteristic of many unipolar depressives (e.g., depending too much on other people, loss of confidence when rejected by another, feelings of helplessness). The second cluster contained items most often associated with borderline personality (i.e., affective lability, limited tolerance for frustration, and aberrant and manipulative attempts to maintain the involvement of significant others).

In his comprehensive review of the relationship between dependency and depression, Birtchnell (1984) has proposed three distinct components to dependency. "Affectional dependency" relates to the psychoanalytic concept of the oral personality and concerns regarding the uncertainty of being loved. It corresponds with Blatt's (1974) anaclitic depression and with Blatt et al.'s (1976) dependency factor, as well as the concept of "anxious attachment." The second component, "ontological dependency" (Laing, 1965), relates to the state of incomplete separation from the parent and, in consequence, a poorly established identity. Survival of the ontologically dependent person is based on becoming fused with a person who is at a similar level of differentiation. Depression ensues if the balance of such an arrangement is disrupted. The third component is termed "deferential dependency" and corresponds to Blatt's (1974) introjective depression and Blatt et al.'s (1976) self-criticism factor. It relates to an inclination toward self-effacement, humility, pessimism, and self-blame.

The emphasis on premorbid dependency in depressive individuals is also apparent in the constructive–developmental model of depression, offered by Kegan, Rogers, and Quinlan (1981). On the basis of Kohlberg's (1976) sociomoral developmental stages, Kegan et al. (1981) have generated three subtypes of depression, relating to (1) egocentricity and control issues, (2) issues of interpersonal dependency, and (3) issues of self-definition and evaluation. Kegan et al.'s interpersonal-dependency subtype correlates closely with depression in the dependent personality, in that feelings of dysphoria are directly related to the establishment and breaking of social bonds. Individuals with this form of depression often feel abandoned, unloved, betrayed, alienated, and unworthy of attention and regard. Again, problems with the expression of anger are common, as anger might threaten the stability of an established dependent relationship.

Although agreeing that depressives are typically orally dependent personality types, Bibring (1953) offered a slightly different emphasis from the traditional psychodynamic focus on orality in depression. He argued that depression is a basic ego state reflecting feelings of helplessness about fulfilling needs critical to the maintenance of self-esteem. According to Bibring, the infant's recurrent experiences of frustrated helplessness and ensuing depression result in the formation of a prototypical reaction pattern that is reactivated by similar events in the future. Thus, with the loss of a significant object or with the perception of inability to control an aversive event, a reactivation of the helpless ego state (rather than a regression due to oral fixation) results in passivity, inhibition, and the belief that striving is meaningless.

In their review of self-esteem and dependency as they relate to clinical depression, Hirschfeld et al. (1976) suggest that depressives' self-esteem differs in two important ways from that of normal personalities. First, their interpersonal-dependency needs for support and approval are greater, as are their feelings of anxiety about being alone or abandoned. These individuals have fragile feelings and low self-confidence, as well as difficulty in making decisions on their own. They are in essence unable ever to get enough care and attention. Perceived loss of support will lead to a fallen self-esteem, which in turn contributes to the onset of depression. Second, depressives' self-esteem even in intermorbid states relies mostly on the satisfaction of interpersonal dependencies; other self-esteem determinants are of little importance. For example, being successful in business or athletics, improving one's appearance, or doing something well is not sufficient to maintain a reasonable level of self-esteem. The lack of diversity in the determinance of self-esteem renders it quite unstable and vulnerable in such individuals.

Considerable overlap can be seen among the different depressive and dependent subtypes. The relationship of depression to dependency, self-esteem, and self-efficacy is also heavily emphasized by the cognitive–behavioral theorists. Seligman's (1974) behavioral theory of depression, for example, hypothesizes that reactive depression is essentially a state of learned helplessness, characterized by the perception of noncontrol. A reformulation of Seligman's theory (Abramson et al., 1978) proposes that the severity and chronicity of depression are related to the attributions made to account for the perceived lack of control. If an individual assumes personal responsibility for his/her inability to control events, and further assumes that inner deficiencies are likely to continue to result in feelings of helplessness in future situations, then a rather chronic state of depression associated with lowered self-esteem is likely to occur. The individual is then more likely to behave more helplessly, initiating fewer responses to control reinforcement, and having more difficulty in recognizing the successful responses that result in reinforcement. A related behavioral theory of depression has been offered by Lewinsohn (1974), who has proposed that a low rate of response-contingent positive reinforcement causes depression. Insufficient reinforcement can result from at least three causes: Few events are reinforcing to the individual; few potentially reinforcing events are available in the environment; and/or the instrumental behaviors emitted by the individual elicit reinforcement infrequently (Blaney, 1977; Lewinsohn, 1974).

Both Seligman's (1974) and Lewinsohn's (1974) models of depression are relevant to the experience of depression in dependent personalities. Such individuals, with their self-perceptions of inadequacy and ineffectiveness, perpetuate behavioral helplessness by relying almost totally upon others for their support and reinforcement. By passively clinging to one or two individuals for nurturance, dependent personalities restrict their interpersonal and activity range, which in turn limits their exposure to alternate sources of reinforcement and diminishes the probability of their learning more appropriate coping skills.

Critical in dependent personalities' propensity toward depression are their beliefs that they are ineffective, inferior, and unworthy of regard. This negative cognitive set—that is, poor self-concept, disparaging view of the world, and the projection of continued hardships and frustrations in the future—is central to Beck's (1974) conception of the cognitive set in depression. Beck (1981) later extended his cognitive formulation to include other predisposing and precipitating factors, including personality attributes that may lead to depression. He has proposed two basic personality modes, the "autonomous" and the "socially dependent," and described the respective depressive symptom patterns of each. Individuals within the socially dependent cluster depend on others for safety, help, and gratification, and are characterized by passive receiving. Such individuals require stability, predictability, and constant reassurance in relationships. Because they consider rejection worse than aloneness, they take no risks that might lead to alienation from sources of nurturance (e.g., asserting themselves with others). Similarly, socially dependent individuals avoid making changes and exposing themselves to novel situations, as they feel ill equipped to cope with the unexpected. Depression in these individuals is usually precipitated by the experience of interpersonal rejection or loss, and is accompanied by diminished confidence and self-esteem. The socially dependent depressive personality is more likely than the autonomous depressive personality to cry, complain of sadness and loneliness, and make demands for help. Such individuals evidence greater emotional lability and are more likely to experience an "anxious depression." They are also more optimistic about the benefits of help, and respond better (at least temporarily) to support and reassurance.

A considerable amount of research lends support to the relationship among interpersonal dependency, "orality," and depression, especially in outpatient populations. Earlier studies on personality features of depressives refer to such traits as submissive dependency and family attachment (Paykel & Weissman, 1973); low self-confidence, dependence on the opinions of others, and the tendency to deny anger or avoid confrontation (Wittenborn & Maurer, 1977); low self-esteem, helplessness, lack of confidence, unhappy outlook, and narcissistic vulnerability (Altman & Wittenborn, 1980; Cofer & Wittenborn, 1980); and lack of autonomy and assertiveness, conformity, passive submissiveness, dependency on others, and avoidance of responsibility (Matussek & Feil, 1983).

More recently, several clinical studies have arisen out of the Collaborative Research Program on the Psychobiology of Depression, sponsored by the National Institute of Mental Health (NIMH). In these studies multiple measures of affective distress were utilized to evaluate depression, while personality functioning was assessed through a 436-item self-report battery taken from five other measures: the Guilford–Zimmerman Temperament Survey (GZTS), the Interpersonal Dependency Inventory (IDI), the shortened version of the Lazare–Klerman–Armor Personality Inventory (LKAPI), the Maudsley Personality Inventory (MPI), and the Minnesota Multiphasic Personality Inventory (MMPI) (Hirschfeld et al., 1983). In one of the first studies, three groups were compared: 26 female patients who had completely recovered from a primary nonbipolar major depressive disorder; 134 first-degree female relatives who also had completely recovered from a primary nonbipolar major depressive disorder; and 272 first-degree female relatives without current or past psychiatric illness. Among other findings, Hirschfeld et al. (1983) noted that scores reflecting emotional reliance on another person were greatest in the recovered depressives, reflecting an increased need for recognition and approval, excessive vulnerability to being hurt, and extreme dependency on a significant other.

Reich, Noyes, Hirschfeld, Coryell, and O'Gorman (1987) examined personality differences among three subject groups; 36 patients with panic disorder, 66 patients with major depression, and 124 control subjects. Assessment instruments included the LKAPI, the IDI, and the GZTS. Recovered patients scored significantly lower than the controls on "emotional stability" and "objectivity," while they scored significantly higher on "orality," "emotional reliance" on another person, and "lack of social self-confidence." The authors suggest that anxiety and depression may share a common diathesis, with certain personality traits making an individual more vulnerable to either anxiety or depression; or, alternatively, that acutely ill patients with either affective or anxiety disorders display similar alterations in personality while ill.

Boyce et al. (1990) examined 75 outpatients with remitted depression characterized as either melancholic/endogenous or nonmelancholic/nonendogenous depression. The testing included the IDI, as well as the Eysenck Personality Inventory (EPI), the author's own Interpersonal Sensitivity Measure (ISM), and a locus of control inventory. Patients with nonmelancholic/nonendogenous depression were generally rated as having more vulnerable personality styles, with the specific differences depending on the particular diagnostic system utilized. A principal-components analysis isolated three underlying personality constructs: dependency, introversion, and timidity. Patients with nonmelancholic/nonendogenous depression scored as significantly more dependent.

A number of studies have reported a greater representation of Cluster III or Cluster C ("anxious, fearful") patients in outpatient depressive populations. Shea et al. (1987) investigated personality functioning in a sample of 249 outpatients with major depressive disorder, using the Personality Assessment Form (PAF). The PAF was developed by the NIMH Treatment of Depression Collaborative Research Program (Shea et al., 1987) and consists of 11 dimensions corresponding to the DSM-III Axis II disorders. The interviewer rates the patient on each dimension on a 6-point scale, utilizing a descriptive paragraph emphasizing the salient features of the personality disorder in question. Employing stringent criteria, Shea et al. (1987) found that 35% of the sample had at least one personality disorder; using the probable criteria resulted in another 40% with personality disorders. The most frequently occurring personality disorders were those in the "anxious, fearful" cluster of Axis II, which includes the avoidant, dependent, and obsessive–compulsive disorders. Pilkonis and Frank (1988) evaluated 119 treatment-responsive patients with recurrent unipolar depression, utilizing the PAF as well as the Hirschfeld–Klerman personality battery. Nearly half the patients showed personality disturbance, with the most common features being avoidant, obsessive–compulsive, and dependent.

Similar results were achieved by Mezzich, Fabrega, and Coffman (1987) in their evaluation of a large population of patients presenting for evaluation and care at a university-affiliated 24-hour clinic. These included 3,455 depressive and 7,837 nondepressive patients of all ages and both sexes. Members of a psychiatric evaluation team jointly completed the Initial Evaluation Form, a semistructured clinical interview procedure that organizes information with all five axes of the DSM-III. The depressive patients presented a differentially higher frequency of dependent personality disorder and the other personality disorders in the "anxious, fearful" cluster.

Comparable findings were reported in a study conducted by Libb et al. (1990), who examined 73 depressed psychiatric outpatients 1 week prior to treatment with an experimental antidepressant medication and 12 weeks following treatment. The Millon Clinical Multiaxial Inventory (MCMI; Millon, 1983) was utilized for the assessment of personality functioning. The MCMI is a 175-item self-report questionnaire consisting of 20 clinical scales derived from Millon's theory of personality and psychopathology, most of which correlate directly with the DSM-III-R. The MCMI is constructed in a way that allows for correction of test-taking attitudes, which may superficially elevate or deflate scales; it is also measured in terms of actuarial "base rate" data, so that it may be comparable to representative clinical prevalence rates. Pretreatment personality data suggested a high frequency (85%) of personality disorders among the depressed patients, concentrated in the passive–aggressive, dependent, borderline, avoidant, and/or schizoid personality disorders. Consistent with literature suggesting an elevated and amplified presentation of certain personality traits among acutely depressed patients, the prevalence of most of these personality disorders declined significantly following 12 weeks of treatment. A lesser and nonsignificant decrease was found in the prevalence of dependent personality disorder.

In a study of late-life depression, Thompson, Gallegher, and Czirr (1988) assessed personality disorder and treatment outcome among 79 outpatients. Axis II formulations were obtained using the Structured Interview for DSM-III Personality Disorders (SIDP; Pfohl et al., 1984). This interview includes highly structured questions in 16 topical sections, along with the DSM-III criteria to be rated on the basis of these questions. Patients were instructed to respond to the SIDP with respect to how they usually felt, as well as how they felt at the time they first sought help for depression. Personality disorder

was diagnosed in one-third of the patients according to how they typically viewed themselves, whereas more than two-thirds of the sample reported evidence of personality disorder when actually in an episode. When patients were describing their typical selves, the dependent and avoidant categories combined accounted for 16% of the total sample, while the compulsive and passive–aggressive disorders occurred at an incidence of roughly 5% and 4%, respectively. Patients diagnosed with dependent or avoidant personality disorder had more successes than failures in treatment, whereas those with compulsive or passive–aggressive personality disorder had fewer successes than failures.

THE HISTRIONIC PERSONALITY

Histrionic personalities, like dependent personalities, are characterized by intense needs for attention and affection. In contrast to the passive, receptive stance of dependent individuals, however, histrionic individuals actively solicit the interest of others through seductive, immaturely exhibitionistic, or self-dramatizing behaviors. For the purposes of assuring a constant receipt of the admiration and esteem they require, histrionic personalities develop an exquisite sensitivity to the desires and moods of those they wish to please. Although others may perceive them as less than genuine or as shallow, they are nonetheless typically viewed as gregarious, entertaining, and superficially charming. Their extreme other-directedness and approval seeking result in a capricious and fickle pattern of personal relationships. Unlike dependent individuals, with their blind loyalty and attachment to one significant other, histrionic individuals are lacking in fidelity and dissatisfied with single attachments. Their interpersonal relationships tend to be characterized by demandingness and manipulation, and at times by childish dependency and helplessness. These behaviors are particularly pronounced in sexual relationships, where histrionic personalities demonstrate a marked appetite for fleeting romantic encounters (Millon, 1981, 1986).

Histrionics tend to be emotionally overreactive and labile. Frustration tolerance is quite low, and there is a proneness toward immature stimulation seeking and impulsive responsiveness. These individuals crave excitement, pleasure, and change, and become easily bored with normal routines. A well-developed sense of inner identity is typically lacking. Their perception of themselves is conceptualized in terms of their relationships and their effect upon others. In contrast to their hypersensitivity to the thoughts and moods of others, histrionic individuals lack insight into their own feelings. They are oriented toward external stimuli and pay only fleeting, impressionistic attention to details. Their cognitive style is marked with difficulties in concentration and logical thinking. Experiences are poorly integrated and learned; consequently, judgment is often lacking. In part, their cognitive flightiness results from their attempts to avoid potentially disrupting ideas and urges (e.g., recognition of their ravenous dependency needs and their resultant vulnerability to loss or rejection). Consequently, histrionic personalities will simply seal off, repress, or dissociate large segments of their memories and feelings.

Recent research on core psychobiological predispositions and vulnerabilities in the development of personality disorders has suggested several features that may be associated with the "dramatic, erratic" cluster of personality disorders, including the histrionic personality. Siever et al. (1985) have suggested that two primary features may be associated with this cluster: impulsivity and affective instability. Impulsivity has been associated with lowered cortical arousal and disinhibited motoric responses to internal or external stimuli. Affective instability may be conceived of as an excessive emotional responsiveness to environmental stimuli. It has been speculated that such individuals may have heightened sensitivity (e.g., an exaggerated tendency toward disappointment in the face of losses) and experience their internal affective states as outside their own control. Instead, emotions may seem determined by shifts in their interpersonal environment (e.g., separations, frustrations, or perceived rejection). As such, the environment may become the major regulator of self-esteem and well-being, with boundaries between the self and the external environment becoming blurred. Such individuals may attempt to regulate their own internal states by acting upon their environments (e.g., attempting to manipulate or control the behavior of others).

Guerrera (1990) has reviewed the literature on biological and behavioral features associated with personality types and concluded that there is supporting evidence for the existence of two personality prototypes, reflective of individual differences in central serotonin and/or catecholamine activity. The prototype that corresponds to the histrionic personality as well as to other "dramatic, erratic" types is labeled the "action-oriented" prototype and is associated with the following features: high stimulation seeking, elevated scores for Extraversion and Psychoticism on the EPI, low harm avoidance, high novelty seeking, an augmenting pattern of evoked potentials, and a low level of platelet monoamine oxidase (MAO) activity.

Histrionic personalities' virtually insatiable needs for attention and approval make them quite prone to feelings of dejection and anxiety, should they fail to evoke the recognition they desire. Signs of indifference or neutrality on the part of others are frequently interpreted as rejection, and result in feelings of emptiness and unworthiness. Unlike the flat and somber symptom picture of dependent personalities, dysthymia in histrionic personalities is characteristically overplayed in dramatic and eye-catching gestures, characteristic of their exhibitionistic display of mood. Episodes of the milder forms of depression are usually provoked less by fear of abandonment than by a sense of emptiness and inactivity. Such dysphoria is likely to occur when histrionics find themselves stranded between one fleeting attachment and another, or between one transitory excitement and the next. At such times of noninvolvement, these individuals sense their lack of inner substance and direction, and begin to experience fears of an empty life and aloneness.

Depressive complaints in histrionic personalities tend to be expressed in current, fashionable, or intellectualized terms (e.g., "existential neurosis" or "chronic fatigue"). Expressing their distress in this manner enables histrionics to rationalize their personal emptiness and confusion; perhaps more importantly, it provides them with a bridge to others, at a time when they feel most isolated from the social life they so desperately seek. Histrionics are also among the personalities who may "mask" an underlying depression through psychosomatic disorders, through hypochondriacal syndromes, or through acting-out behaviors such as substance abuse, overeating, or sexual promiscuity (Akiskal, 1983; Lesse, 1974).

Major depression in histrionic personalities is primarily precipitated by anticipated losses in dependency security and is more likely to be evidenced in an agitated than in a retarded form (Millon, 1981). In the hope of soliciting support and nurturance, histrionics may wail aloud and make well known their feelings of helplessness and abandonment. Suicidal threats or gestures are not uncommon at such times. Major depression may also be colored with irritability and anger, although reproving reactions, especially from significant others, will cause histrionics to withdraw and substitute dramatic declarations of guilt and contrition for their anger.

It might be theorized that histrionic personalities would be particularly susceptible to bipolar and cyclothymic disorders, as these syndromes are consistent with their characteristic socially gregarious and exuberant style. Severe separation anxieties or the fear of losing social approval may intensify histrionics' habitual behavior pattern until it reaches the forced and frantic congeniality of hypomania. To stave off the growing feeling of depressive hopelessness, tension may be released through hyperactivity and a frenetic search for attention. One of the affective personality subtypes presented by Akiskal (1989) is reminiscent of these qualities in the histrionic personality. The "hyperthymic temperament" (akin to the "hypomanic") is described as exuberant, people-seeking, stimulus-seeking, and deficient in both insight and judgment. Akiskal (1989), however, also describes an overlap in this personality with the "anancastic" (compulsive) personality, in that such an individual may be driven and ambitious, with an inordinate capacity for work.

Many of the psychoanalytic writings concerning the depressed orally dependent personality's pronounced affectional needs are equally applicable to depression in the histrionic personality. Freud (1932/1950) wrote that a "dread of loss of love" governs the behavior of hysterics, and Rado (1951) referred to the predepressive individual's strong cravings for narcissistic gratification and low tolerance of affectional frustration. In addition, the active manipulative qualities of the histrionic personality have been stressed. Bemporad (1971), it will be recalled, described some depressives as engaging in "bargaining relationships" to ensure fulfillment of dependency needs. Chodoff (1972) described the low frustration tolerance of oral depression-prone individuals, as well as the various techniques—for example, "submissive, manipulative, coercive, piteous, demanding and placating" (p. 670)—that they employ to satisfy their narcissistic needs. Finally, whereas Blatt (1974) characterized anaclitic depressives as typically being more passive and helpless, many case history

studies of these patients also revealed evidence of histrionic features, such as impulsive behavior, suicidal gestures, and acting out through substance abuse (Blatt et al., 1982).

Considerable attention has been paid to the clinical presentation of depression in histrionic personalities. Although some have argued that the dramatic behavioral styles of histrionics may obscure a clear view of an underlying depression (Akiskal et al., 1983), others believe that histrionics' "high spirits" and gregariousness protect against or mitigate the emergence of depressive feelings. Lazare and Klerman (1968) studied a small group of hospitalized depressed women who also carried the diagnosis of "hysterical personality." Assessment during the time of their illness revealed that hysterical patients, as compared to depressed patients without hysterical features, showed less intense feelings of depression, hopelessness, and worthlessness; less psychomotor retardation; fewer paranoid and obsessional symptoms; and more somatic complaints. Hysterical depressed patients also differed in their behavioral presentation while hospitalized, in that they were described as irritable, demanding, manipulative, and more hostile than patients without hysterical features. Follow-up studies (Paykel & Prusoff, 1973; Paykel et al., 1976), utilizing clinical interviews, self-report inventories, and ratings by relatives, supported the initial findings. Neurotic depressives showed more orally dependent traits; depressed patients with hysterical personalities tended to be less severely ill, showing patterns of depression mixed with hostility and irritability, but little evidence of anxiety.

Such studies suggest that a key component in histrionic personalities' apparent resistance to severe depression is their ability to express hostility. Classical psychodynamic formulations emphasize the depressive individual's turning of aggression against the self in punishment of the internalized, frustrating love object. Other studies (Gershon, Cromer, & Klerman, 1968; Schless, Mendels, Kipperman, & Cochran, 1974) have challenged the universality of aggression turned inward as the depressive mechanism, arguing that depression is seen in those who overtly express hostility, as well as in individuals where hostility remains covert. Some evidence, however, does appear to suggest that hostility expressed outward may be associated with less severe depression, as well as hysterical features. In a rather extensive study of a very small group of hospitalized depressives, Gershon et al.

(1968) found that whereas "hostility-in" was positively correlated with depressive symptoms, "hostility-out" appeared to be associated with depression only in the few subjects described as having hysterical personalities. For these patients, significantly fewer verbalizations of depression were noted, while the degree of hostility expressed appeared to be closely and positively related to the severity of depression.

Schless et al. (1974), in their study group of 37 depressed patients, found that although the degree of turning hostility inward appeared to be related to the severity of depression, the most severely depressed patients had an increase in both inwardly and outwardly directed hostility. The authors proposed that depression, hostility, and anxiety are all signal emotions, with hostility sometimes serving as a secondary defense to depression. The portrayal of hostility as a secondary defense in depression gains some support from Lazare and Klerman's (1968) study, where hostility was quite pronounced in hysterical personalities during the time of their clinical depression, but diminished as the patients' depressive symptoms abated. Grinker, Miller, Sabshin, Nunn, and Nunnally's (1961) early factor-analytic work also generated a depressive subtype with features conforming to those of the histrionic depressive. Patients corresponding to "Factor Pattern C" evidenced less than average depressed affect, guilt, or anxiety. Their behavior was marked by agitated, demanding, hypochondriacal complaints, associated with psychosomatic symptoms. In contrast to the irrational, complaining attitudes noted in these patients was the very low loading on dismal and hopeless affect.

In general, the histrionic personality as well as the other "dramatic, erratic" personalities has been associated with nonmelancholic inpatient populations (Charney et al., 1981; Pfohl et al., 1984; Davidson, Miller, & Strickland, 1985) and with chronic, mild, characterological depressions (Akiskal et al., 1980; Paykel, 1971; Charney et al., 1981; Liebowitz & Klein, 1981). The characterological depression that tends to occur among this cluster of personality disorders warrants special attention.

Akiskal (1983), one of the most prominent and prolific of the theorists and researchers in this area, has proposed a classification scheme that differentiates mild, chronic depression or dysthymia into three subgroups, one of which is a characterological depressive subgroup. Akiskal further divides this subgroup into sub-

affective dysthymic disorders and character-spectrum disorders. The subaffective dysthymia is presumed to share a biogenic association with primary depressive disorders, as suggested by the following: a favorable or sometimes hypomanic response to tricyclic antidepressants, MAO inhibitors (MAOIs), or lithium; shortened rapid-eye-movement (REM) sleep latency; and family histories of affective disorders (both unipolar and bipolar). Such individuals are also more likely to have unremarkable developmental histories and classic "depressive personality" features (e.g., pessimistic, self-doubting, brooding, and overly duty-bound). Akiskal suggests that dysthymia with later onset and more severe dysthymia be placed on Axis I, and that the medication-responsive, characterological dysthymia be considered a depressive personality pattern and be placed on Axis II.

In comparison, character-spectrum disorder is viewed as a nonaffective disorder with a remarkably different profile: poor response to antidepressant drugs; normal REM latency; onset in childhood or adolescence; a greater prevalence among females; and a family history of alcoholism, sociopathy, or parental assortative mating. Such individuals are also more likely to be characterized by unstable personality features (e.g., immature and manipulative behaviors, impulsivity, interpersonal instability, and a high incidence of substance abuse) and a greater prevalence of histrionic, borderline, antisocial, and dependent personality disorders. Finally, these individuals are more likely to have experienced childhood parental loss, separation, or divorce (Akiskal et al., 1980).

Liebowitz and Klein (1981) describe another subgroup of depression, which they refer to as "hysteroid dysphoria" or "rejection-sensitive dysphoria"; this subtype shares some of the features of an atypical depression. Described as consisting of chronic, repetitive, nonpsychotic depressed moods, this disturbance appears to occur more frequently in women with pronounced needs for attention, approval, and praise, especially within a romantic relationship. Extreme intolerance of personal rejection is the hallmark of this disorder. Depression in these individuals is usually of short duration and is manifested symptomatically in overeating or craving for sweets, oversleeping, or extreme fatigue. Substance abuse during episodes of depression may also be common. Described as "attention junkies" with "addictions" for approval, hysteroid dysphorics also evidence "unstable" features (e.g., proneness toward angry outbursts, impulsive acting out, and physically self-damaging acts), which are suggestive of a more severe histrionic personality or a border-line personality. Unlike character-spectrum depressives, hysteroid dysphorics are reported to be responsive to MAOIs, which seem to temper both their depression and some of their maladaptive behaviors. As such, the underlying affective disorder appears to be more primary in this subgroup (Shader et al., 1986).

Research relevant to these characterological depressions includes Winokur's research on the depressive-spectrum disorder subtype, which is defined to include patients with primary depression and at least one first-degree relative with alcoholism or antisocial personality (Winokur, 1979). This subtype appears to occur more frequently in females, has an earlier onset of depression, and generally responds less well to treatment. Finally, Paykel (1971) presented two personality subtypes relevant to this discussion, derived from a cluster analysis of 35 variables in a population of 165 depressed patients from varied treatment settings. The first of these subtypes consisted of "hostile depressives," who were relatively young patients with moderately severe depression, flavored with hostility and self-pity. "Young depressives with personality disorder" were the youngest group and evidenced relatively mild depression with situationally reactive mood fluctuations. These two subgroups overlapped somewhat, and while being high on neuroticism, also evidenced disturbed social relations suggestive of personality disorder with hysterical features.

THE SCHIZOID PERSONALITY

The essential features of the schizoid personality are a profound defect in the ability to form social relationships and an underresponsiveness to all forms of stimulation. Such individuals exhibit an intrinsic emotional blandness—an imperviousness to joy, anger, or sadness. Seemingly unmoved by emotional stimuli, schizoid personalities appear to possess a generalized inability to be aroused and activated, a lack of initiative and vitality. Their interpersonal passivity is not intentional or self-protective, but stems from a fundamental imperceptiveness to the moods and needs of others (Millon, 1981).

Schizoid personalities typically prefer limited interpersonal contact and play only peripheral roles in social and family relationships. They tend to choose interests and vocations that will allow them to maintain their social detachment. Colorless and lacking in spontaneity, they are usually perceived as unresponsive, boring, or dull in relationships. Their speech tends to be characterized by emotional flatness, vagueness, and obscurities, and they seem unable to grasp the emotional components of human interactions and communications. They seem indifferent to both praise and criticism. Consistent with their interpersonal style, schizoids possess little awareness of themselves and employ only minimal introspection. Lacking in insight and relatively untroubled by intense emotions or interpersonal conflicts, these individuals possess limited and uncomplicated intrapsychic defenses.

Schizoid personalities' pervasive imperviousness to emotions puts them among the personalities least susceptible to depression or other affective distress. Having failed to develop an "appetite" for social stimulation (including affection and attachment), these individuals are not vulnerable to dejection resulting from "object loss." In addition, since schizoids derive only limited pleasure from themselves, they are not particularly susceptible to loss of self-esteem or self-deprecation. Emotional distress may develop, however, when these personalities are faced with unusual social demands or responsibilities, or when their stimulation levels become either excessive or drastically curtailed. In addition, their inner barrenness and interpersonal isolation may occasionally throw them into a fear of nonbeing or petrification.

On rare occasions, schizoids may exhibit brief, frenzied episodes of manic-like excitement in an attempt to counter the anxieties of depersonalization. A fleeting and erratic course of frantic and rather bizarre conviviality may then temporarily replace their characteristic impassive, unsociable pattern. More frequently, however, schizoids react to disequilibrium with increased withdrawal and dissociation. Lacking investment and interest in themselves, as well as in external events, they fail to acquire a coherent and well-integrated inner identity. Disruptions to the consistency of the schizoid lifestyle, such as those resulting from unwanted social overstimulation or prolonged periods of social isolation, may consequently result in a kind of splitting or disintegration. During such periods of self-estrangement, schizoids may experience irrational thinking and compounding of their typical emotional poverty. Behaviorally, this may be manifested in profound lethargy, lifeless facial expressions, and inaudible speech, simulating but not reflecting a depressive mood.

Empirical data on affective disorders in schizoid personalities is quite scant. Those studies providing data on the incidence of schizoid personalities and/or the "odd, eccentric" cluster of personality disorders suggest that such personality patterns are infrequent among depressive populations (Mezzich et al., 1987; Zimmerman et al., 1988; Black, Bell, Hulbert, & Nasrallah, 1988). Although the disorders in the "odd, eccentric" cluster were rated present for 20% of the depressed patients in one of the NIMH treatment studies (Shea et al., 1987, 1990), the authors note that this group in this study consisted primarily of patients with paranoid personality disorder rather than the schizoid or schizotypal patterns.

Schizoid and schizotypal traits occurred frequently among dysthymic patients, and to a lesser extent among patients with major depression and cyclothymia, as assessed by the MCMI in a study by Alnaes and Torgersen (1991). Libb et al. (1990), however, demonstrated that although the MCMI suggested a relatively high incidence of schizoid personality as well as other personality disorders in depressed patients initially, posttreatment retesting (12 weeks later) revealed a significant decline in such personality traits. It was speculated that there may have been difficulties in distinguishing the schizoid from the avoidant personality disorder, or, alternatively, that the "hit rate" for certain personality disorders (as well as the test–retest reliability for the MCMI) might be somewhat limited. Finally, some of the characteristics associated with the schizoid personality might also be expected to occur as a result of a depressive disorder (e.g., lack of a sense of humor; social anxiety or social withdrawal; blunted affect and anhedonia).

THE AVOIDANT PERSONALITY

Although the schizoid and avoidant personalities may appear superficially rather similar, they differ in several important ways, including their susceptibility to depression. Both types of personalities may appear withdrawn, emotionally flat, and lacking in communicative and social skills. The affective flatness of the avoidant personality, however, is typically a defensive maneuver against underlying emotional tension and disharmony. Similarly, the apparent detachment and interpersonal withdrawal of avoidant individuals develop in response to a fear of intimacy and a hypersensitivity to rejection and ridicule. Strong desires for affection and acceptance exist in these individuals, but are denied or restrained out of apprehension and fearful mistrust of others. Not infrequently, avoidants have had experiences of painful social derogation, which have resulted in an acute sensitivity and alertness to signs of ridicule and humiliation. This hypersensitivity and vigilance often cause these individuals to misperceive innocuous social comments or events as critical rejection (Millon, 1981).

For the most part, avoidant personalities engage in self-imposed isolation and social withdrawal. They will, however, enter into relationships with a limited number of people, if provided with strong guarantees of uncritical acceptance. Avoidants may become quite dependent on the one or two people they do allow into their lives. However, they are likely to remain rather cautious in relationships, engaging in frequent, subtle testing of their partners' sincerity.

Although avoidant personalities may view people in general as critical, betraying, and humiliating, they are usually very dissatisfied with the peripheral social roles they feel forced to play, and experience painful feelings of loneliness and alienation. Avoidants tend to be excessively self-critical, blaming themselves for their social undesirability. Consequently, they may become estranged from themselves as well as from others. They tend to resort to extreme defensive coping strategies to deal with the chronic feelings of interpersonal ambivalence and affective distress that they experience. In addition to active avoidance and withdrawal from threatening social situations, they may attempt to block and interfere with their own troubling cognitions; this may result in a fragmentation of their thoughts and disjointed verbal communications, as well as the appearance of being emotionally confused or socially irrelevant.

Avoidant types are among the personalities most vulnerable to psychiatric symptom disorders. Perhaps most frequently, they will suffer from feelings of anxiety and ruminative worry. Also, as with schizoid personalities, prolonged estrangement from self and others can result in varied forms of dissociative disorders. Further-more, avoidants are quite prone to feelings of deep sadness, emptiness, and loneliness. Frustrated yearnings for affection and approval, coupled with the self-deprecation they experience for their unlovability and ineffectuality, may result in a chronic melancholia. Depression may nonetheless be difficult to detect in avoidant personalities, given their characteristic affective flattening and their typical presentation of slowness of speech and movement. Moreover, avoidants will attempt to hide and contain their feelings of inner despair, for fear that overt expressions of such weakness and suffering may render them even more vulnerable to social ridicule, humiliation, and rejection. Although the symptoms of major depressive episodes in these individuals may be similar to the symptomatic presentation of depressed schizoids (i.e., psychomotor retardation, extreme social withdrawal, and apathy), avoidants may also experience anxiety or obsessive ruminations with their depression.

The avoidant personality's susceptibility to depression can be readily explained from a cognitive–behavioral framework. First is the avoidant's tendency to view things pessimistically—that is, contempt directed at the self, fear and suspicion of others, and a sense of future despair. Next are the avoidant's limited possibilities for experiencing reinforcing events. Characteristically, these individuals tend to be inflexible, confining themselves to a small range of potentially reinforcing experiences. Although they possess the innate capacity to experience pleasure, the interpersonal anxiety they feel may cause them to deny themselves the satisfaction they could derive from others, and to discount praise, compliments, and other social reinforcers. Similarly, their distorted view of themselves as ineffectual and unlovable precludes the possibility of pleasure coming from within.

Although the avoidant personality is a relatively new concept in psychiatric nosology (Millon, 1969), the characteristics of this pattern have frequently been cited in the literature on depression. Arieti and Bemporad (1980), in their proposal of three premorbid types of depressive personality, described a depressive personality structure characterized by constant feelings of depression lurking in the background, and by an inhibition of nearly any form of gratification. Additional features of this form of chronic character structure are as follows:

> A chronic, mild sense of futility and hopelessness which results from a lack of involvement in everyday activities . . . emptiness because they do not develop deep relationships for fear of being exploited or rejected . . . harsh, critical attitude towards themselves and others. (Arieti & Bemporad, 1980, p. 1362)

According to these authors, such depressive subtypes experience episodes of clinical depression when they are forced by some event to re-evaluate their mode of existence, and are confronted with the barrenness and meaninglessness of their lives.

Bowlby (1977) discussed both "compulsively self-reliant" and "anxiously attached" individuals and their predisposition to depression. He described the latter as individuals who are eager for interpersonal contact but at the same time are inhibited from soliciting it. When they do finally establish relationships, such people become excessively dependent on attachment figures. Boyce et al. (1990) related three underlying personality constructs in their population of nonmelancholic/nonendogenous depressive patients: dependency, introversion, and timidity. The authors noted that the personality scales best discriminating types of depression included the Interpersonal Awareness, Separation Anxiety, and Fragile Inner-Self subscales of the ISM, and, to a lesser extent, the Emotional Reliance on Another subscale of the IDI and the Neuroticism scale of the EPI. They noted that these findings support Bowlby's observations regarding difficulties associated with the formation and maintenance of affectional bonds in the genesis of depression.

Avoidant personality disorder, along with the other "anxious, fearful" personality disorders, has frequently been cited in studies on affective disorders, including major depression with and without melancholia, dysthymia, and depression mixed with panic disorder (Davidson et al., 1985; Mezzich et al., 1987; Alnaes & Torgersen, 1990). Pilkonis and Frank (1988) found that avoidant personality disorder occurred most frequently in their population of recurrent unipolar depressive patients, while Shea et al. (1990) cited it as the second most frequently occurring personality disturbance in their outpatient population of depressives. Some studies suggest that individuals with avoidant personality features are among those who respond most favorably to treatments of depression

(Pilkonis & Frank, 1988; Pfohl et al., 1987; Thompson et al., 1988).

In a critical review of research on personality factors in affective disorders, Akiskal et al. (1983) suggested that introversion and low sociability have emerged as consistent and relatively robust premorbid features of nonbipolar depressive disorders. Among the studies cited in their review at that time was that of Hirschfeld et al. (1983), in which recovered depressed patients and their formerly depressed relatives were shown to be more passive and dependent, but also far less extraverted. The recovered depressives in this study were described as very introverted, "shy, withdrawn, reserved, restrained, serious, deliberate, and controlled" (Hirschfeld et al., 1983, p. 997). While these individuals showed an extreme dependence on one significant other, they tended not to be very sociable or to enjoy company. The authors concluded that social introversion is "the most powerful personality characteristic associated with primary nonbipolar depression," whereas heightened interpersonal dependency is a "modest second factor" (p. 997). A second study by Hirschfeld et al. (1989), which tracked high-risk subjects and their controls from the onset of depression, found that lower emotional strength and resiliency characterized the affected subjects. Overall differences were not found on measures of either interpersonal dependency or extraversion. The onset of depression in older subjects, however, was associated with decreased emotional strength, increased thoughtfulness, and increased interpersonal dependency. In both of these studies, the authors suggested that avoidant features, like dependent features, may be a function of a depressive episode. Consistent with this, Libb et al. (1990) found avoidant personality features to be among those that declined most significantly following remission of a depressive episode.

There also appears to be some association between avoidant personality disorder and the newly proposed depressive personality disorder (conceptualized as an Axis II personality disorder linked to Axis I depressive disorders) (Phillips et al., 1990; Klein, 1990). Akiskal (1983) modified Schneider's (1923/1958) criteria for the depressive personality to include the following traits: (1) quiet, introverted, passive, and nonassertive; (2) gloomy, pessimistic, serious, and incapable of fun; (3) self-critical, self-reproaching, and self-derogatory; (4) skeptical, hypercritical, and hard to please; (5) conscientious, responsible, and self-disciplined; (6) brooding and given to worry; and (7) preoccupied with negative events, feelings of inadequacy, and personal shortcomings. The Axis II diagnoses that seem to exhibit the greatest overlap with the depressive personality include the obsessive–compulsive personality, the dependent personality, and (to a lesser extent) the avoidant personality. Interestingly, Klein's (1990) own study of 177 outpatients suggested that the relationship between the depressive personality and the dependent and obsessive–compulsive personalities may be relatively weak. In contrast, significant differences appeared between patients with and without depressive personality on the following set of traits: quiet, introverted, passive, and indecisive. Klein notes that this apparent overlap of the depressive personality and the avoidant personality are consistent with the finding of Standage (1986) that the avoidant personality was the DSM-III Axis II condition most closely related to Schneider's (1923/1958) construct of the depressive personality.

THE SCHIZOTYPAL PERSONALITY

The hallmark of the schizotypal personality is a variety of peculiarities of behavior, speech, thought, and perception that are not severe enough to warrant the diagnosis of schizophrenia. There is considerable variability in the presentation of this syndrome (e.g., magical thinking, ideas of reference or suspiciousness, illusions, depersonalization, and hypersensitivity with undue social anxiety), and no single feature is invariably present. It is our contention that the schizotypal syndrome should be viewed as an advanced dysfunctional personality (akin in severity to the borderline or paranoid types), and that it is best understood as a more pathological version of the schizoid and avoidant patterns. Such a framework allows a greater appreciation of the schizotypal characteristics of social impoverishment and the tendency toward distant rather than close interpersonal relationships. In fact, the observed oddities in behavior and thought, such as paranoid ideation, magical thinking, and circumstantial speech, stem in part from the schizotypal personality's withdrawn and isolated existence. Without the stabilizing influences and repetitive corrective experiences that come with frequent human contact and social interactions, these individuals may lose their sense of behavioral judgment and gradually begin the process of acting, thinking, and perceiving in peculiar and eccentric ways. In the advanced stages of this dysfunctional progression, they may merely drift aimlessly from one activity to another, leading meaningless and ineffectual existences, and remaining on the periphery of society.

Depending on which of the detached patterns (i.e., schizoid or avoidant) that schizotypal individuals resemble, they may be emotionally flat, sluggish, and apathetic, or hypersensitive, anxious, and socially apprehensive. In a similar fashion, schizotypal personalities' vulnerability to depression or other symptom disorders is in part dependent upon whether they are more like the sensitive and suffering avoidants or the innately bland, unfeeling schizoids.

Very little empirical or theoretical literature exists on the relationship of affective disorders to the schizotypal personality. Alnaes and Torgersen (1991) found the schizotypal personality to be among the personality disorders most frequently associated with dysthymia. Klein, Taylor, Dickstein, and Harding (1988b) also cited the schizotypal personality, along with the borderline personality, as occurring more frequently among early-onset than among late-onset dysthymics. This study, however, assessed only three personality disorders: borderline, antisocial, and schizotypal. To gain a greater appreciation of affective disorders in the schizotypal personality, the reader is referred to the preceding sections on the depressive experience in schizoid and avoidant personalities.

THE ANTISOCIAL PERSONALITY

On the basis of data reanalysis, literature reviews, and field trial results, the DSM-IV has condensed and slightly altered the criteria for the antisocial personality disorder. Two items (irresponsible parenting and failure to sustain a monogamous relationship) have been deleted, while two other items tapping irresponsibility have been collapsed into one. However, in our opinion, the DSM-IV and its predecessors have focused on the delinquent, criminal, and socially undesirable behaviors that may be found among antisocial personalities, while paying scant attention to the personality characteristics from which such antisocial behaviors stem. We feel that insufficient attention has been paid to persons with similar propensities and basic traits who have managed to avoid criminal involvement (Millon, 1981).

It is our contention that antisocial personalities are characterized primarily by hostile affectivity, excessive self-reliance, interpersonal assertiveness, callousness, and a lack of humanistic concern or sentimentality. Such individuals exhibit rebelliousness and social vindictiveness, with particular contempt being directed toward authority figures. Irascible and pugnacious, antisocial personalities exhibit frequent verbal abuse, and at times even physically cruel behaviors. Other notable features include a low tolerance for frustration, impulsivity, and an inability to delay gratification. Consistent with this is a tendency to become easily bored and restless with day-to-day responsibilities and social demands. Not only are such individuals seemingly undaunted by danger and punishment; they appear attracted to it, and may actually seek it out or provoke it. Our portrayal of antisocial personalities is more consistent with the concept of sociopathic or psychopathic personalities as depicted in the incisive writings of Cleckley (1941). These individuals are most notable for their guiltlessness, incapacity for object love, impulsivity, emotional shallowness, superficial social charm, and an inability to profit from experience. Psychobiological predispositions to this personality disorder are hypothesized to be similar to those for the histrionic and/or borderline personalities—that is, the action-oriented prototype (Guerrera, 1990) of high stimulation seeking, low harm avoidance, high novelty seeking, and lowered cortical arousal with disinhibited motoric responses.

An argument may also be made for a "non-antisocial" variant of the sociopathic personality. Such individuals may view themselves as assertive, energetic, self-reliant, and hard-boiled, but as realistic, strong, and honest. In a competitive society, these traits tend to be commended and reinforced. Consequently, such individuals may achieve positions of authority and power, which provide socially sanctioned avenues for expressing their underlying aggressiveness.

Antisocial individuals tend to be finely attuned to the feelings, moods, and vulnerabilities of others, and they take advantage of this sensitivity to manipulate and control. However, they typically evidence a marked deficit in self-insight and rarely exhibit foresight. Although inner tensions, frustrations, and dysphoria may occur, such discomforts are not tolerated for very long, being discharged through acting out rather than through intrapsychic mechanisms. Perry (1985), for example, found that subjects with both antisocial and borderline personality disorders had fewer symptoms of depression and anxiety than did subjects with pure borderline personality disorder. Perry attributes this finding to the protective role of acting out as a defense against depression. Frequent references are made to the antisocial personality's active avoidance of, and inability to tolerate, awareness of depression (Reid, 1978). From this framework, conscious feelings of depression are viewed as a failure of the defensive mechanisms that permitted the previous involvement in antisocial behaviors (Cormier, 1966; Reid, 1978).

An appreciation of the antisocial individual's resistance to depression can be drawn from the psychoanalytic conceptualization of depression as a turning of hostility inward (Gershon et al., 1968; Paykel & Prusoff, 1973; Schless et al., 1974); in this view, the inherent hostile affectivity, resistance to social dependency, and interpersonal forcefulness of the antisocial person all serve as safeguards against depression. This position is also consistent with cognitive–behavioral formulations. Seligman (1974), for example, has proposed that the individuals most resistant to depression (and helplessness) are those whose lives (especially their childhoods) have been filled with mastery and extensive experience in controlling and manipulating sources of reinforcement. Similarly, Beck (1974) has written:

> The satisfactory expression of hostility seems to be a very powerful means of increasing a person's subjective feeling of effectiveness, thus increasing his self-esteem and combating the negative cognitions which I hold to be so important in the generation of depression. (p. 21)

Although antisocial personalities' active independence, internal locus of control, and appetite for stimulating change may mitigate the impact of life stressors, these same characteristics can also make the individuals vulnerable to occasional major depressive episodes. Precipitants for depression may include situations of forced interpersonal submissiveness or curtailed personal freedom (e.g., incarceration or required military service), as well as internal conditions (e.g., medical illness or age-related physical decline) that result in incapacitation, passivity, or immobility. It has also been suggested (Reid, 1978) that depression may ensue when antisocials are forced to confront their inner emptiness, emotional void, and tenuous object relations. Again, this forced recognition is most likely to occur when such persons are made to feel inadequate or weakened in a way that strips from them their "resilient shell of narcissism" (Reid, 1978, p. 499).

Although the evidence is rather meager in comparison to the attention paid to the dependent, introversive, and obsessive characteristics of depressives, a growing body of literature argues for a depressive subtype whose salient features are autonomy, self-control, and aggressiveness. In addition to his "socially dependent" mode of depression, Beck (1981) has proposed an "autonomous" mode characterized by a great investment in "preserving and increasing his independence, mobility and personal rights" (p. 272). For such action-oriented individuals, their well-being is dependent on their ability to maintain their autonomy and direct their own activities without external constraint or interference. There is little sensitivity to the needs of others, with a corresponding lack of responsiveness to external feedback and corrective influences. It should be noted that the autonomous individuals described by Beck are also characterized by excessively high internalized standards and criteria for achievement—features that may be more indicative of the compulsive character structure, or the noncriminal variant of the antisocial personality. Such individuals tend to experience a hostile depression, characterized by social withdrawal, rejection of help, self-criticism, resistance to crying, and "active" or violent forms of suicide attempts.

Of particular relevance to the experience of depression in the antisocial personality is the "self sacrificing depressive" included among the three subtypes in Kegan et al.'s (1981) sociomoral developmental formulation of depression. Characterized by egocentricity and control issues, these depressives experience dysphoria and discontent when unable to satisfy their desires because of external forces that constrain their freedoms or deprive them of the opportunity to act as they choose. To such individuals, issues of control, power, and influence are central. In a sense, they are victims of their own impulses and desires. They view other people as either possible instruments or possible obstacles to achieving their needs.

The fear is that to relinquish living in the flux of each moment and satisfying each want is to relinquish the self, to compromise away the core experiences of self. Where "guilt" is expressed or experienced, it is not a matter of self-punishment but of anxious anticipation that other parties will punish or curtail. (Kegan et al., 1981, p. 4)

When depression does occur in the antisocial personality, and it is not "masked" through an exaggeration of acting-out behaviors, it is likely to be colored by bitterness, angry complaints, and accusations. Periods of self-loathing may occur at the perception of inner weakness and ineffectualness, and the sympathy of others is often actively shunned. Such features may be consistent with the "Factor Pattern D" depressive subtype described by Grinker et al. (1961). Demonstrating the traits of gloom, hopelessness, and anxiety with some guilt feelings, these patients do not cling or demand attention, nor do they evidence hypochondriacal symptoms. Described as the "angry depressives," these patients typically exhibit demanding, provocative behavior, and are most likely to have had narcissistic and overaggressive premorbid personalities. Because they have traditionally assumed the role of authority and power at home and in business, their depression may be precipitated by frustration at the inability to continue this pattern due to external factors. Such patients are difficult to treat, as they resist psychotherapy in their constant struggle to remain "on top," and may express their rage eruptions through serious suicide attempts. A similar, empirically derived depressive subtype is offered by Overall and Hollister (1980), whose "hostile depressive" is characterized by anxiety, irritable complaining, and anger, with suspiciousness sometimes accompanying the feelings of hostility. Recent research has found antisocial personality disorder to be associated more frequently with nonmelancholic depressions (Davidson et al., 1985), cyclothymic disorders (Alnaes & Torgersen, 1990), and perhaps the "unstable" character-spectrum disorder (Akiskal et al., 1980).

THE NARCISSISTIC PERSONALITY

The essential features of the narcissistic personality style are an overvaluation of self-worth and a grandiose sense of self-importance and uniqueness. In seeming contradiction to the inflated self-concept is an inordinate need to be loved and admired by others. Unlike the ravenous affectional needs of histrionic and dependent personalities, however, is narcissists' belief that they are entitled to tribute and praise by virtue of their "specialness." These personalities also share the antisocial features of egocentricity, interpersonal exploitation, and exaggerated needs for power and success. In contrast to the anger and vindictiveness of antisocials, however, narcissists are characterized by a benign arrogance and a sense that they are "above" the conventions and reciprocity of societal living. There is little real empathy for others, but rather a tendency to use people for self-enhancement and for indulging their desires. Those who satisfy their needs are idealized, while others who can serve no immediate purpose are devalued and even treated contemptuously. This shifting of overvaluation and denigration may occur frequently within the same relationship. There is an expectation of preferential treatment and special favors, without any assumption of reciprocal responsibilities.

Narcissistic personalities are cognitively expansive, enjoying fantasies of unrealistic goals, with a tendency to overestimate their abilities and achievements. However, these exaggerated feelings of personal importance can leave narcissists quite vulnerable to injuries of self-esteem and pronounced feelings of unworthiness, should their grandiose self-expectations not be met. Although they are characteristically imperturbable and insouciant, repeated failure and social humiliations may result in uncertainty and a loss of self-confidence. Over time, with the growing recognition of inconsistencies between their self-perception and their actual performance, self-disillusionment, feelings of fraudulence, and in some cases a chronic state of dysthymia may result. In other instances, a psychic blow generated from a single event (e.g., a humiliating defeat or a public criticism) may precipitate a brief but severe major depressive episode. Such states rarely endure for extended periods, because depression is not experienced as consonant with narcissists' self-image. The symptomatology of the narcissistic depression may be quite variable, shifting between dramatic expressions of worthlessness and self-deprecation to irritable demandingness and criticism of others. Although feelings of helplessness may accompany their depression, such perceptions tend to be attributed to external, "universal" causes rather than to personal inner inadequacies (Abramson et al., 1978). Consistent with this formulation, narcissists may subtly accuse others of not supporting or caring for them enough. At other times, hostility may be directly expressed, as narcissists become enraged at others' being witnesses to their shame and humiliation.

Owing to the infrequency of long-lasting major depression in these individuals, little mention has been made of premorbid narcissistic characteristics in depressed patients. There appears to be some overlap in the psychoanalytic literature, however, between the "oral" depressive's pronounced affectional needs and the "narcissistic" depressive's craving for admiration. Rado (1928) characterized the depressive personality as having a low tolerance for narcissistic frustrations, with even trivial disappointments precipitating a marked loss of self-esteem. According to Rado, after actively courting and securing the affection and devotion of a love object, the predepressive individual may then proceed to treat this other person with a "sublime nonchalance" or tyrannical domination. Characteristically, unaware of this mistreatment of the love object, the predepressive may react with "embittered vehemence" should the object withdraw or retaliate (1928, p. 422). In a theoretical review of depressive neurosis, Sacks (1986) discusses the more recent psychoanalytic emphasis on the narcissistic grandiosity and vulnerability of the predepressive individual, noting that the inflated self-image and aspirations of such an individual are easily punctured or frustrated. Sacks refers to Kohut's (1977) self-psychological focus on narcissists' attachments in determining their self-esteem and vulnerability to depression. Such individuals may react with depression when the valued objects (or "selfobjects") fail to provide "mirroring" or external confirmation of the depressives' grandiose self-image, or fail to live up to an expected idealized state.

Klerman (1974) described depression as a response to fallen self-esteem, a signal of discrepancies within the self system between "ideal expectations and practical reality" (p. 139). In a similar fashion, Salzman (1970, 1972) described predepressives as individuals characterized by exceptionally high standards and an unwillingness to accept compromises. Depression in such individuals follows the inability to maintain the unreasonable expectations they set for themselves and others. The premorbidly independent depressive described by Salzman (1970)

shares features of Beck's (1981) "autonomous" mode, depressive, Kegan et al.'s (1981) "self sacrificing" depressive, and the "angry" depressive reported by Grinker et al. (1961). While possessing many features of the obsessive–compulsive personality, the independent depressive overvalues autonomy and personal abilities in a way that is reminiscent of the depressive experience in the narcissistic personality:

> While he feels helpless and dependent, he is loath to accept any help, since his standards require total independence and omnipotence. He frequently rejects or distorts any sympathetic reassurance or aid, even while he needs and asks for it, insisting that it is insufficient or patronizing. (Salzman, 1970, p. 115)

Kernberg (1975) provides perhaps the most relevant and eloquent description of the process of self-disillusionment and depression in narcissists:

> For them, to accept the breakdown of the illusion of grandiosity means to accept the dangerous, lingering awareness of the depreciated self—the hungry, empty, and lonely primitive self surrounded by a world of dangerous sadistically frustrating and revengeful objects. (p. 311)

THE PARANOID PERSONALITY

The paranoid personality style may be viewed as a more dysfunctional variant of the antisocial and narcissistic patterns; the three patterns share an independent orientation and preoccupation with matters of adequacy, power, and prestige. Among the more prominent features of paranoid personalities are a pervasive and unwarranted mistrust of others, hypersensitivity to signs of deception or malevolence, and restricted affectivity. These individuals are fearful of external sources of influence, and may be resistant to forming intimate relationships for fear of being stripped of their power of self-determination. In spite of their air of self-importance, invincibility, and pride, paranoid personalities tend to experience extreme jealousy and envy at the "good fortune" (actual or perceived) of others. To justify these feelings of resentment, they constantly search for signs of deception and actively construct situations to "test" the sincerity of others. Inevitably, their provocative and abrasive behaviors elicit the very signs of malice that they project upon others. Even the slightest, most trivial cues are seized upon and magnified to justify their preconceptions. Data that contradict their perceptions are ignored, with the paranoids accepting no responsibility or blame for their role. This distortion of events, though personally logical, is irrational and at times verges on the delusional.

In their attempts to remain constantly on guard and mobilized, paranoid personalities may exhibit an edgy tension, irritability, and rigid defensive posture. To protect themselves from the sadistic treatment and betrayal that they anticipate, these individuals maintain an interpersonal distance, and attempt to desensitize themselves from tender and affectionate feelings toward others. They become hard and insensitive to the suffering of others, as well as alienated from their own emotions and inner conflicts.

Although dysfunctionally rigid, this stance of social withdrawal, callousness, and projection of personal malevolence and shortcomings onto others provides paranoid personalities with a glorified self-image and relative freedom from intrapsychic distress. Under circumstances of real or imagined threats to their autonomy or challenges to their competence, however, their tenuous sense of self-determination and superiority can be badly shaken. Initially, these individuals may construct new "proofs" to fortify their persecutory fantasies, while vigorously struggling to re-establish their former autonomy and esteem.

During the course of their self-assertion, paranoid personalities may unleash considerable hostility upon others. In paranoids with prominent narcissistic features, threats to their illusion of omnipotence and superiority may elicit a self-exalted and pompous variant of a manic episode. With an exaggerated cheerfulness, excitement, and buoyancy, reminiscent of their former state of complacency, these individuals are frantically driven to recover their lost exalted status. In some instances, their previous sense of self-determination and confidence cannot be easily reconstructed. Time and again, their competence has been shown to be defective, and they have been made to look foolish. Defeated and humiliated, with their past arrogance and self-assurance now submerged, the individuals may experience a deep sense of helplessness and major depression. As with the other independently oriented personalities (i.e., the narcissist and antisocial), the weakness and dependency associated with depression are perceived as unacceptable and humiliating. Consequently, the depression may be colored with anger, agitation, and a suspicious mistrust that precludes the acceptance of outside help. Many of these behavioral features would correspond to Grinker et al.'s (1961) Factor Pattern D, the "angry depressive" pattern, as well as with Overall and Hollister's (1980) "hostile depression," which is described as "anxiety combined with depressive mood, but in this type irritable complaining, or angry feelings are also significantly present. Suspiciousness may accompany hostility in the hostile depression type which could suggest a mild paranoid-like syndrome" (p. 376).

Because depression is relatively infrequent in paranoid personalities, little has been written on the depressive experience in these personalities. In recent literature, Shea et al. (1990) cited the paranoid disorder as among the four most frequently occurring personality disorders in their study of outpatients with major depression (preceded only by the "anxious, fearful" disorders). Alnaes and Torgersen (1990) found that paranoid personality features were more frequently associated with mixed anxiety–depression conditions than with either condition alone.

THE BORDERLINE PERSONALITY

The term "borderline" has been rightfully criticized for its overinclusiveness and failure to convey a behavioral pattern with distinctive stylistic features (Akiskal, 1981; Millon, 1981; Perry & Klerman, 1978). Depending upon the theoretical orientation taken, the label has been used to connote the following:

1. A character organization existing at a level of personality cohesion midway between neurotic and psychotic (Kernberg, 1970; Knight, 1953).
2. An incipient precursor of schizophrenia.
3. A set of personality variants within the spectrum of affective disorders (Akiskal, Khani, & Scott-Strauss, 1979; Stone, 1979).
4. A relatively stable and moderately severe level of functioning that encompasses a variety of different personality subtypes (Grinker, Werble, & Drye, 1968; Millon, 1969).

The borderline label is employed by the DSM-IV to reflect a discrete syndromal entity—a pervasive pattern of instability of mood, interpersonal relationships, and self-image. In addition, the DSM-IV has considered the cognitive distortions frequently experienced by borderline personalities by adding a new item for transient, stress-related paranoid ideation or severe dissociative symptoms. As described by Akiskal (1981), the borderline personality is characterized by an unstable sense of self, stemming from disturbances in the separation–individuation phase of development:

> The disorder is conceptualized in characterologic terms and defined by impulsivity, drug-seeking behavior, polymorphous sexuality, affective lability (i.e., display of unmodulated affects such as rage and panic), boredom, anhedonia, bizarre attempts at self-harm and "micropsychotic episodes." (p. 25)

From our perspective, the borderline concept is best used to represent a moderately severe level of functioning that may occur in virtually any of the personality disorders (perhaps with the exception of the schizoid and antisocial styles). Most frequently, however, the borderline personality appears as an advanced dysfunctional variant of the dependent, the histrionic, the obsessive–compulsive, or (most commonly) the passive–aggressive personality. Regardless of the background personality history, borderlines are characterized by intense, variable moods and irregular energy levels, both of which frequently appear to be unrelated to external events. The characteristic affective state may be either depressed or excited, or marked by recurring periods of dejection and apathy, interspersed with episodes of anger, anxiety, or euphoria. There is a notable fear of separation and loss, with considerable dependency reassurance required to maintain psychic equilibrium. The dependency upon others is colored with strong ambivalent feelings, such as love, anger, and guilt. Chronic feelings of anxiety may be present as borderlines struggle between feelings of anger and shame at being so dependent, and fears that self-assertion will endanger the security and protection they so desperately seek. In an attempt to secure their anger and constrain their resentment, borderlines often turn against themselves in a self-critical, condemnatory manner, which at times may lead to self-mutilating and suicidal thoughts as well as self-damaging behaviors. Relevant to this is Pilkonis's (1988) work on differentiating excessive dependency types in unipolar depressives. In addition to the anxious attachment subtype, a cluster of descriptors emerged that were thought to be very consistent with the borderline personality (i.e., affective lability, limited tolerance of frustration, and aberrant manipulative attempts to ensure the availability of others).

As a result of their instability of both affect and behavior, borderline personalities are prone to rather checkered histories in their personal relationships and in their school and work performance. Most exhibit repeated setbacks, a lack of judgment and foresight, tendencies to digress from earlier aspirations, and failures to utilize their natural aptitudes and talents. For the most part, despite their setbacks, borderlines manage to recoup and regain their equilibrium before slipping into a more pernicious and serious decompensation. At times, however, when they are overwhelmed with mounting internal pressures, their tenuous controls may break down, resulting in an eruption of bizarre behaviors, irrational impulses, and delusional thoughts. These minipsychotic episodes tend to be brief and reversible, and seem to assist borderlines in regaining their psychic balance. Afterward, such episodes are usually recognized by the individuals as being peculiar or deviant.

As noted earlier, overt and direct expressions of hostility in borderlines tend to be exhibited only impulsively, for fear that such actions may result in abandonment or rejection. A characteristic form of anger control in these individuals is to turn feelings of resentment inward into hypochondriacal disorders and mild depressive episodes. Borderlines tend to overplay their helplessness and anguish, employing their depression as a means of avoiding responsibilities and placing added burdens upon others. Their exaggerated plight causes guilt and discomfort among family and friends, as they try to meet the borderlines' "justified" need for attention and care. As with passive–aggressive personalities, the dour moods and excessive complaints of borderline personalities may evoke exasperation and rebuke from others. In this event, borderlines may turn their anger upon themselves even more intensely, voicing a flood of self-deprecatory comments about their worthlessness, evilness, and inordinate demands upon others. This self-derision may be accompanied by thinly veiled suicidal threats, gambling, substance abuse, or other impulsively self-damaging acts; these not only serve to discharge anger, but often succeed in eliciting forgiveness and reassurance (if not compassion) from others.

Although some of the antisocial, acting-out features of borderline personalities may serve to defend against depression (Perry, 1985), the overall chaotic integration of these personalities suggests that they may frequently succumb to affective disorders. The literature on the comorbidity of borderline personality disorder and depression is extensive, with the rate of major depression in this personality type typically ranging between 25% and 65% (Gunderson & Elliott, 1985; Docherty, Fiester, & Shea, 1986; Farmer & Nelson-Gray, 1990).

Although the symptomatic features of borderlines' affective episodes tend to be rather mixed or erratic, varying in quality and focus according to the individuals' specific vulnerabilities, an episode typically consists of some composite of depression, impulsivity, hostility, and anxiety. Agitated depressions may be common, with borderlines exhibiting an apprehensive and tense despondency, accompanied by a querulous irritability and hostile depressive complaints. Some borderlines may demonstrate a more intropunitive, self-deprecatory depression, manifested by expressions of self-doubt, feelings of unworthiness, delusions of shame and sin, and suicidal thoughts. In still other borderlines, a retarded form of depression is expressed, in which guilt and self-disparagement are accompanied by lethargy, feelings of emptiness, boredom, and "deadness."

At times borderlines may display a scattering of ideas and emotions, and a jumble of disconnected thoughts and aimless behaviors, that are similar to cyclothymic or bipolar disorder presentations. Because borderlines' moods are quite changeable and inconsistent with their thoughts and actions, it is virtually impossible for others to comprehend or empathize with their experiences. In their more euphoric moments, borderlines' zestful energy and joviality may temporarily engage and entertain others. However, the irrational, self-expansive quality of the borderlines' forced sociability, along with their lapses into irritability, eventually exasperate and drain others, destroying any patience or goodwill that was previously evoked.

In Grinker et al.'s (1968) landmark study of the borderline syndrome, depression was mentioned in each of the four borderline subtypes. The Group I patients were characterized by inappropriate and negative behaviors, as well as hostile, angry depression; the Group II or "core" borderlines exhibited a vacillating involvement with others and acted out expressions of anger,

alternating with a lonely, hopeless depression; the Group III patients, similar to DSM-III-R's schizoid personality, demonstrated a withdrawn, affectless depression; and the Group IV borderlines were characterized by gross defects in self-esteem and confidence, and a depressive quality not associated with anger or guilt feelings. Although borderline personality characteristics occur in outpatient populations, they are seen most frequently in inpatient populations (Shea et al., 1990). Libb et al. (1990) did find a high incidence of borderline personality disorder in their outpatient population (especially before treatment and symptom resolution). The authors have suggested that this personality disorder may have been overdiagnosed, however, because both MCMI and DSM-III diagnostic criteria may inadequately attend to three essential borderline features: unstable object relations, identity disturbance, and affective instability. Recent studies suggest a relationship between borderline personality disorder and unipolar nonmelancholic depressions (Gunderson & Elliott, 1985; McGlashan, 1987), dysthymia or chronic depression (Perry, 1985; Klein, Taylor, Dickstein, & Harding, 1988a; Akiskal, 1981), cyclothymic disorder (Akiskal et al., 1979; Alnaes & Torgersen, 1991), character-spectrum disorders (Akiskal, 1981), and hysteroid dysphoria (Liebowitz & Klein, 1981).

The association between unstable borderline features and treatment-resistant, characterological depressions such as hysteroid dysphoria and character-spectrum disorder (Akiskal, 1981; Charney et al., 1981, Winokur, 1979) has frequently been cited in the affective disorders literature. On the basis of differential responsiveness to pharmacological agents, Klein and colleagues (Klein, 1975; Liebowitz & Klein, 1981) have asserted that the borderline designation subsumes several heterogeneous subtypes that all share a vulnerability to affective dysfunction. Of the three borderline personality subtypes that Klein has proposed—the phobic–anxious, the emotionally unstable, and the hysteroid dysphoric—the hysteroid dysphoric syndrome has generated the most attention and controversy (Spitzer & Williams, 1982; Stone, 1979). This chronic, "rejection-sensitive" atypical depression is seen most frequently among unstable individuals with a marked need for attention. According to Liebowitz and Klein (1981),

> These vulnerabilities often give rise to a lifelong pattern of affective instability, difficulty being

alone, and feelings of chronic emptiness, as well as to unstable or chaotic interpersonal and vocational functioning and a proneness toward angry outbursts, impulsive behavior, and physically self-damaging acts. In essence, the vulnerabilities that we posit as the core of hysteroid dysphoria may be sufficient to produce many of the features of borderline personality disorder. (p. 73)

Stone (1979) concurs with these authors, reporting that in his own experience hysteroid dysphorics almost invariably met the traditional borderline criteria, and in many cases had at least one first-degree relative with a serious affective disorder. It has been suggested that the responsiveness of hysteroid dysphorics to MAOIs reflects the primality of the underlying affective disorder (Shader et al., 1986).

Although stressing the heterogeneity of the borderline category and its overlap with various other disorders (e.g., bulimia nervosa, somatization disorder, substance abuse, sociopathy), Akiskal suggests that many borderlines (perhaps 50%) exhibit "atypical, chronic and complicated forms of affective disorder with secondary personality dysfunction" (1981, p. 31; see also Akiskal et al., 1985; Akiskal, 1983). He and his colleagues suggest that the comorbidity of borderline personality disorder with subaffective disorders may be an artifactual result of misdiagnosis (Akiskal et al., 1985). The differential diagnosis of borderline personality and cyclothymia is noted to be especially difficult because of shared characteristics of irritability, dysphoric restlessness, impulsivity, obstructiveness, and tempestuous lifestyle (Akiskal, 1989).

It can be seen that Akiskal and Klein tend to conceptualize borderline symptomatology as a secondary or concurrent manifestation of primary affective disorder (Farmer & Nelson-Gray, 1990). In support of this hypothesis are studies suggesting biological markers for borderline personality disorder, including lowered cortical arousal, an augmenting pattern of evoked potentials, low platelet MAO activity, dysregulation of the central serotonergic system, abnormal dexamethasone suppression and thyrotropin-releasing hormone tests, and electroencephalographic (EEG) abnormalities (Marin et al., 1989; Siever et al., 1985, 1987; Guerrera, 1990). Akiskal et al. (1985) have emphasized the neuroendocrine and sleep EEG characteristics and pharmacological hypomania shared by borderline and affective disorders, whereas Liebowitz and Klein (1981) have referred to the shared family history and medication responsivity of their hysteroid dysphorics and depressives.

Psychoanalytic formulations have also been offered to account for the association between borderline personality and depression. Gunderson and Elliott (1985) and Farmer and Nelson-Gray (1990), in their reviews of this literature, note two specific hypotheses. The first, known as "abandonment depression" as described by Masterson (1972), suggests that borderline patients use anger and other types of acting-out behaviors to defend against an anaclitic-like depression arising from traumatic separations during early development. The second formulation emphasizes the sense of "inner badness" and dissociated anger in borderlines. Depressive self-condemnation defends against aggressive impulses toward others, while maladaptive acting-out behaviors help avoid recognition of the evil self-image. A third theory of association between borderline and affective disorders postulates that the two are unrelated, with each having a relatively high incidence in psychiatric populations. Overlapping symptomatology of these independent disorders may account for the artifactual comorbidity (Widiger, 1989; Gunderson & Elliott, 1985).

Despite the number of similarities between the two disorder types, mounting evidence suggests that depressive disorders and borderline personality disorder may be differentiated on a number of dimensions. For example, borderlines tend to demonstrate a normal REM latency and a poor response to tricyclic antidepressant therapy (Akiskal et al., 1980). In addition to affective disorders, they may also share diagnostic borders with a number of other Axis II as well as Axis I disorders; moreover, relatives of borderlines as compared to depressives show a greater incidence of personality disorders (Rosenthal, Akiskal, Scott-Strauss, Rosenthal, & David, 1981; Akiskal et al., 1985; Fyer, Frances, Sullivan, Hurt, & Clarkin, 1988). Snyder, Sajadi, Pitts, and Goodpaster (1982) found that features such as anger, affective instability, impulsiveness, and suspiciousness were "strikingly" more common in borderline patients than in dysthymic patients, whereas McGlashan (1987) found that pure unipolar patients differed from borderline and mixed unipolar–borderline patients with respect to sexual promiscuity and deviation, devaluation, manipulation and hostility in relationships, and impulsivity. McGlashan also found that borderline personality features were more frequently associated with histories of substance abuse.

A recent study by Weston et al. (1992) offered empirical support for a phenomenonologically distinct depressive experience in borderline patients. A small number of borderline inpatients with and without major depressive disorder were compared to a small group of nonborderline inpatients with major depression. Utilizing the Hamilton Rating Scale for Depression (Hamilton, 1960) to assess depression severity and the Depressive Experiences Questionnaire (Blatt et al., 1976) to assess depression quality, this group found that borderlines both with and without major depression evidenced a qualitively distinct, interpersonally focused "borderline depression," even when severity of depression was controlled for. This borderline depressive experience was characterized by emptiness, loneliness, diffuse negative affectivity (including anger, fear, and desperation in relation to attachment figures), inconsistent self-concept and self-esteem, dependency, and fears of abandonment.

These findings are consistent with Gunderson and Elliott's (1985) reports that the depressive experience of borderlines is more frequently marked by loneliness, emptiness, and boredom than by guilt, remorse, and acute failures in self-esteem. On the basis of their review, these authors suggest that the observed concurrence of affective and borderline symptoms reflects a heterogeneity of this population, in which biophysiological vulnerabilities increase the risk of becoming psychologically impaired. As such, early traumas can create vulnerability to either or both disorders, with the actual presentation varying as a function of later physiological and psychological reactions to environment and temperament. This formulation is not inconsistent with the positions of Widiger (1989), Siever et al. (1985, 1987), and Akiskal (1985; Akiskal et al., 1979), which suggest that the borderline personality disorder is perhaps best conceptualized as a characterological variant of impulsive/affective pathology.

THE OBSESSIVE–COMPULSIVE PERSONALITY

The most prominent features of the obsessive–compulsive personality include excessive emotional control and interpersonal reserve; preoccupation with matters of order, organization,

and efficiency; indecisiveness; and a tendency to be overly conscientious, moralistic, and judgmental. It is our belief that much of the personality organization of the obsessive–compulsive individual arises in reaction to marked underlying feelings of interpersonal ambivalence. Like negativistic/passive–aggressive personalities, obsessive–compulsive personalities are torn between their leanings toward submissive dependency on the one hand and defiant autonomy on the other (Millon, 1981). In contrast to the overt emotional lability and chronic vacillation of passive–aggressives, however, obsessive–compulsive personalities bind and submerge their rebellious and oppositional urges through a rigid stance of overcompliance, conformity, and propriety. By clinging grimly to rules of society and insisting upon regularity and uniformity in relationships and life events, these individuals help restrain and protect themselves against their own aggressive impulses and independent strivings. Although this behavioral and cognitive rigidity may effectively shield the individuals from intrapsychic conflict as well as social criticism, it may also preclude growth and change, cause alienation from inner feelings, and interfere with the formation of intimate and warm relationships.

To others, obsessive–compulsives appear to be industrious and efficient, but lacking in flexibility, imagination, and spontaneity. They may also be viewed as stubborn or stingy and picayune, with a tendency to get lost in minutiae rather than to appreciate the substance of everyday life. Obsessive–compulsives are easily upset by the unfamiliar or by deviations from their accustomed routines. Their perfectionistic standards and need for certainty may result in a tendency toward indecisiveness and procrastination. Although the social behavior of obsessive–compulsives is typically polite and formal, there is a definite tendency to relate to others on the basis of their rank or status. Obsessive–compulsives require considerable reassurance and approval from their superiors, and consequently may relate to them in a deferential, ingratiating, and even obsequious manner. In contrast, these individuals may be quite autocratic and condemnatory with subordinates, using their authority and the rules they represent to justify the venting of considerable hostility and criticism.

Obsessive–compulsives devalue self-exploration and exhibit little or no insight into their motives and feelings. Beset with deep ambivalence and contrary feelings, they must employ extensive defensive maneuvers to transmute or seal off frightening urges from conscious awareness. Although rigid moralism and behavioral conformity bind many of their hidden feelings of defiance and anger, these individuals also find it necessary to compartmentalize or isolate their emotional responses to situations. They may particularly attempt to block or otherwise neutralize reactions to stressful events, for fear that signs of emotional weakness may become apparent and lead to embarrassment or disapproval.

Despite their elaborate defensive strategies, obsessive–compulsives tend to be among the personalities most troubled by psychiatric symptoms. Their cognitive and behavioral organization makes them particularly susceptible to affective disorders of virtually every type (Shea et al., 1990; Mezzich et al., 1987; Thompson et al., 1988). Plagued by their own exacting standards, as well as the high expectations that they perceive others to hold for them, obsessive–compulsives frequently feel as though they have fallen short of their criteria for acceptable performance. Although angry at themselves for being imperfect, and resentful toward others for their unyielding demands, these individuals dare not expose either their own shortcomings or their hostility toward others. Rather than voicing their defiance or venting their resentment and thereby becoming subject to social rebuke, they turn their feelings inward, discharging their anger toward themselves. In this regard, obsessive–compulsives' propensity toward experiencing guilt, expressing self-reproval, and acting contrite serves as a form of expiation for hidden, unacceptable feelings while preventing humiliation or condemnation from others. The "anger, guilt, self-degradation" sequence may occur quite frequently in obsessive–compulsives, resulting in a chronic, mild depression or in dysthymic disorder.

Major depressive states may be quite common among obsessive–compulsives in later life, usually following a period of reflection and self-evaluation. At such times, these individuals are confronted with the realization that their lofty life goals and long-held standards of excellence have not been attained; furthermore, their rigid conformity to external values has yielded a rather barren existence, with the denial of a multitude of potentially satisfying experiences. Severe depression in obsessive–compulsives tends to have an agitated and apprehensive quality, marked by feelings of guilt and a tendency to complain about personal sin and unworthiness. The tense and anxious coloring of their depression may be a reflection of their struggle to contain their hostility and resentments, as well as their fear that contrition and despondency will prompt derision and condemnation from others. On occasion, in an exaggerated portrayal of their premorbid drive and achievement strivings, obsessive–compulsives will attempt to counter a melancholic depression with brief periods of accelerated activity directed toward some unrealistic goal. Such manic-like episodes of grandiosity and self-assertion tend to be short-lived, however, as they may generate considerable anxiety.

The obsessive–compulsive personality (also known as the "anancastic obsessive" or "conforming" personality) is undoubtedly the most frequently cited personality in the depression literature. Its psychoanalytic counterpart, the "anal character," has often been described in association with neurotic depression, manic depression, and involutional melancholia. Abraham (1924/1966), noting marked similarities between obsessive–compulsives and melancholics, suggested that both syndromes arise from fixations in the anal stage of psychosexual development, with obsessive–compulsives emerging from the more advanced anal-retentive phase and melancholics arising from complications in the more primitive anal-expulsive phase. Abraham cited a number of shared anal character traits in these two groups, including excessive punctuality, orderliness, obstinacy, parsimony, and marked feelings of ambivalence in interpersonal relationships.

A number of other theorists with analytic leanings have offered depressive subtypes akin to the anal-obsessive. A "subvalid" personality has been proposed by Swedish psychiatrist Sjobring (1973) in his multidimensional theory of personality. The subvalid individual is described as cautious, reserved, precise, industrious, and scrupulous. Numerous researchers (Coppen, 1966; Nystrom & Lindegard, 1975; Perris, 1966) employing the Nyman–Marke Temperament Scale, which objectifies Sjobring's concepts, found depressed individuals (especially of the unipolar endogenous type) to exhibit a significant tendency toward subvalidity. As used in the Nyman–Marke instrument, the subvalid concept has a somewhat broader meaning, referring to individuals who are bound to routine, easy to fatigue, cautious, tense, neurasthenic, and meticulous (Akiskal et al., 1983). Using a different Swedish personality inventory, Perris, Eisemann, von Knorring, and Perris (1984) studied 208 recovered depressive patients of all types and found that despite some intergroup differences, the main personality characteristics exhibited by the depression-prone individuals seemed to be anxiety, psychasthenia (covering such traits as orderliness, conscientiousness, and being bound to routine), suspicion, and guilt. Depression-prone individuals also showed a higher level of inhibited aggression and a lower level of manifest aggression than healthy controls. Chodoff (1970) focused upon the interpersonal ambivalence and unexpressed hostility of premorbid depressives. He noted that some depressives denied their dependency needs and internalized unrealistic self-standards. Chodoff (1970) suggested that this might lead to the development of a "perfectionistic, neurotically prideful obsessive" (p. 58).

In Blatt's (1974) depressive typology, which is based on the level of object representation achieved, he has described a depression subtype associated with issues of "superego formation and the relatively advanced and complex phenomenon of guilt" (p. 109). The "introjective depression" is characterized by intense feelings of inferiority, guilt, and worthlessness. On the basis of a factor-analytic study employing the Depressive Experiences Questionnaire, Blatt et al. (1976) identified a "self-criticism" factor that relates closely to the concept of introjective depression. According to the authors, the self-criticism factor, in comparison with the other two factors identified, had the highest correlation with traditional psychometric measures of depression. This factor consisted of items relating to

> concerns about feeling guilty, empty, hopeless, unsatisfied, and insecure, having failed to meet expectations and standards, and being unable to assume responsibility, threatened by change, feeling ambivalent about self and others, and tending to assume blame and feel critical toward self. (Blatt et al., 1976, p. 385)

A later study (Blatt et al., 1982), involving the identification of depressive subtypes on the basis of psychiatric case histories, showed clinical records of the self-criticism group to be characterized by "social isolation, intense and self-critical involvement in work, professional and/or academic strivings, feelings of worthlessness and failure, a history of a very critical or ideal-

ized parent, obsessive and paranoid features, anxiety and agitation" (Blatt et al., 1982, p. 120).

In a similar fashion, Arieti and Bemporad (1980) have proposed a "dominant-goal" predepressive among their three premorbid types of depressive personalities. Described as "usually seclusive, arrogant, and often obsessive" (p. 1361), this form of personality organization is reported to be more common in men. According to Arieti and Bemporad (1980), dominant-goal individuals have learned from their parents that achievement is rewarded with support and acceptance. Consequently, these individuals come to derive their sense of meaningfulness, satisfaction, and self-esteem from fantasies about obtaining some lofty objective. In pursuing their goals, they may shun other activities as a diversion from their quest. For such individuals, the realization that a selected goal is unobtainable may threaten not only their sense of self-esteem, but the very structure upon which the meaning of their lives is based.

The two basic depressive personality modes described by Beck (1981) have already been discussed. The "autonomous" mode shares several features of the obsessive–compulsive, including internalized standards, goals, and criteria for achievement that tend to be higher than the conventionally accepted norms; an emphasis on independence, control, and action; and a tendency to be direct, dogmatic, and authoritarian. Individuals operating within the autonomous mode are vulnerable to depression when they feel they have failed in their attempts to reach a crucial goal. Beck (1981) has described autonomous depression as being permeated with the theme of defeat or failure, as the individual "blames himself continually for falling below his standard (self-attribution), and excoriates himself for his incompetence (self-punishment)" (p. 276). Beck has also noted that such individuals experience a striking behavioral shift when depressed, from having been "self-sufficient, inner-directed, and active" to appearing "powerless, devoid of initiative and self-control" (p. 276).

In his study of the relationship of dependency and depression, Birtchnell (1984) has identified a "deferential" dependency, which he feels corresponds to Blatt's introjective depression and the self-criticism factor. In this dependent subtype, Birtchnell includes both deference and abasement; the first refers to humility, respectfulness, and a reluctance to be outspoken or complaining, and the latter involves self-judgment, self-accusation, and self-punishment. He feels that these two aspects of dependency have the most in common with depression and overlap most clearly with the enduring negative attitudes of Beck's depression-prone personality. Similarly, Pilkonis's (1988) prototypes of dependency and autonomy in depressives include an excessive-autonomy cluster characterized by obsessive–compulsive features, including rigidity, perfectionism, lack of spontaneity, and an emphasis on productivity, intellectuality, and self-control. The second excessive-autonomy cluster, "defensive separation," also appears to relate to the obsessive–compulsive individual as described here, as well as the compulsively self-reliant prototype discussed by Bowlby (1977). Descriptors in this category include insistence on being self-sufficient, maintenance of strong personal boundaries, and avoidance of close relationships because of the obligations they entail.

From a slightly different theoretical perspective (i.e., sociomoral development), Kegan et al. (1981) have proposed a "self-evaluative depression," in which "dysphoria and discontent are described in terms of the failure to live up to one's own hopes for oneself, falling short of one's standards" and "negative self-evaluation" (p. 6). In this form of depression, there may also be a sense of not being whole, as "the price of self-determination and control has been the exclusion of important parts of oneself," and "self-imposed isolation, and the inability to experience true intimacy" (Kegan et al., 1981, pp. 6–7).

As mentioned earlier, the obsessive–compulsive personality has been frequently cited in association with involutional melancholia. Although the syndrome of involutional depression has been the subject of considerable debate (Chodoff, 1972), the concept of an endogenous unipolar or psychotic depression, occurring for the first time in middle age, has received widespread clinical recognition. In association with this syndrome, a melancholic personality has been proposed that is characterized by some "oral" features but predominantly by "anankastic" features. Von Zerssen (1977), in his review of the international literature, found the clearest association between affective disorders and personality traits to be that between unipolar depressive psychosis (including involutional melancholia) and the melancholic personality. His description of the "melancholic type" includes the features of "orderliness, conscientiousness, meticulousness, high value achieve-

ment, conventional thinking and dependency on close personal relationships" (Von Zerssen, 1977, pp. 97–98). The association of late-onset endogenous depression with anankastic, obsessional traits has been reported by a number of other researchers. Paykel et al. (1976) found older depressed patients in their study group to be significantly less neurotic, hysterical, and oral, but more obsessive. On symptomatic measures, these patients also evidenced a more severe endogenous pattern of depression, accompanied by a greater level of anxiety than seen in younger patients. Cadoret, Baker, Dorzab, and Winokur (1971), employing Cattell's personality inventory, found that scores on the factor denoting "superego strength" were highest in depressive patients whose illness began after the age of 40. Scores on this factor were also higher in their healthy first-degree relatives, as compared to the relatives of early-onset depressive patients. On the basis of such studies, Yerevanian and Akiskal (1979) concluded:

> There appears little reason to dispute the classic notion that portrays the late-onset (usually psychotic) depressive as a self-critical, conscientious, hard-working, and well integrated (into the dominant culture) individual who has responded to losses and life reverses with self-punitive and self-denigrating cognitions. (p. 603)

In recognition of studies that have failed to confirm the age association between obsessionalism and unipolar depression (e.g., Snaith, McGuire, & Fox, 1971; Kendell & Discipio, 1970), Chodoff (1972) drew the more conservative conclusion that "among individuals suffering depressive breakdowns for the first time in middle life, there exists a certain well defined subgroup, among men as well as women, who display premorbid obsessional personality characteristics" (p. 667).

Interpretation of the apparent age effect upon personality and depressive features is not straightforward. As mentioned earlier, midlife reflection and self-evaluation may confront conforming, "obsessive" individuals with the realizations that (1) idealized internal standards have rarely been met; (2) productivity and the capacity to achieve are likely to decline sharply with advanced age; and (3) the choice of an industrious, conforming lifestyle has been made at the expense of interpersonal intimacy and emotional fulfillment. An alternate explanation for these age-associated features is that personality traits may actually be altered with age, leading to the development of "more obsessive, less hysterical, less dependent and less emotionally labile patterns" (Paykel et al., 1976, p. 332).

Like involutional melancholia, anankastic, obsessive–compulsive personality traits have held a prominent place in the psychoanalytic literature on manic–depressive illness. Kolb, in his 1973 revision of Noye's original text, provides the following description of the premorbid personality of a depressed-type manic–depressive:

> Many have been scrupulous persons of rigid ethical and moral standards, meticulous, self-demanding, perfectionistic, self-depreciatory, prudish, given to self-reproach, and sensitive to criticism. Their obsessive–compulsive tendency have doubtless been defensive mechanisms for handling hostility, which characteristically they cannot express externally. (Kolb, 1973, pp. 372–373)

A number of empirically based studies have suggested that bipolar disorders are not necessarily associated with cyclothymic, hyperthymic, or unstable characterological features (Hirschfeld, Klerman, Keller, Andreasen, & Clayton, 1986). Rather, there is evidence to suggest that the illness may occur most frequently among individuals who, except for "obsessive" features, are otherwise unremarkable (Alnaes & Torgersen, 1991; Donnelly, Murphy, & Goodwin, 1976; Hirschfeld & Klerman, 1979; Perris, 1971). Consistent with this is the factor-analytic study of Matussek and Feil (1983), which identified a "hypomanic success and achievement" factor that differentiated endogenous bipolar patients from "normals," as well as from other types of depressed patients. The authors reported that this factor reflects a personality substructure characterized by "hypomanic drive for success, high aspiration level, anankastic features, pedantry, subordinate to authority, perseverance in difficult tasks, and detachment for achievement" (Matussek & Feil, 1983, p. 787). The authors noted that the strong achievement orientation, exaggerated aspiration level, pronounced sense of duty, and scrupulousness of the endogenous bipolar patients all served to make these individuals exquisitely vulnerable to feelings of inadequacy and failure, whereas reaching a lofty goal might trigger a mania if it subjectively represented a great success after hard work.

In earlier writings, Akiskal and his colleagues (Akiskal et al., 1979, 1983) noted similarities between the ambitious, driven, hyperthymic individual with an inordinate capacity for work, and the duty-bound and work-addicted obsessive–compulsive individual. Comparisons were also made between the premorbid adjustment of bipolar patients and the "Type A" coronary-prone behavior pattern, which is characterized by extremes of competitiveness, achievement striving, time urgency, and aggressiveness. It was suggested that future research might well be directed at detecting the incidence of frank bipolar disorders in the families of people displaying the Type A pattern. Akiskal et al. (1979) also suggested similarities between obsessive–compulsive personalities and manic–depressive patients in terms of pharmacological treatment response. They noted the ample number of anecdotal reports suggesting favorable and sometimes dramatic effects of lithium carbonate upon the compulsive drivenness of bipolar patients during intermorbid periods, as well as the drivenness, indecisiveness, and anxious worry seen in several obsessive–compulsive personalities.

In his 1989 work on affective personality types, Akiskal has noted that in addition to driven ambitiousness, the hyperthymic temperament also has many unstable features, including impulsivity and poor judgment. He suggests that this temperament may be more prone to bipolar II disorder, which is characterized by recurrent retarded depressions plus hypomanic symptoms. Bipolar I disorder, which is characterized primarily by mania, is thought to arise from a depressive temperament. Akiskal argues that the subaffective dysthymic pattern is one type of depressive personality. It will be recalled that Akiskal has portrayed the subaffective dysthymic as sharing many of the features of Schneider's depressive psychopath. Although he notes the depressive personality's features of overdedication to work, selfless devotion, and much attention to detail, Akiskal has also described these individuals as having intense attachment needs and displaying some overlap with the psychoanalytic construct of the masochistic or self-defeating personality. Phillips et al. (1990) have also noted some overlap between the obsessive–compulsive and the depressive personality as suggested by both psychoanalytic and German theorists, although the depressive personality also overlaps significantly with the self-defeating personality and (to a lesser extent) the dependent personality. Consistent with this, Klein's (1990) evaluation of Schneider's construct of the depressive personality (as formalized by Akiskal) has suggested that the relationship of the obsessive–compulsive and dependent personalities to the depressive personality may be relatively weak. In this instance, the overlap between the avoidant personality and the depressive personality is emphasized.

At this point in the literature review, an important distinction must be made between obsessive–compulsive personality traits and obsessive–compulsive symptoms as they occur in depression. Although there is some evidence that obsessions, ruminative worry, and compulsive behaviors are more likely to occur in individuals with "obsessional" or compulsive premorbid personalities (Vaughn, 1976; Videbech, 1975), these same symptoms are frequent accompaniments of depressive episodes in a variety of other personality types. Studies that have attempted to carefully tease apart depressive symptomatology from enduring characterological traits, however, have revealed considerable differences with respect to the intensity and duration of obsessive–compulsive symptoms in depression.

Wittenborn and Maurer's (1977) investigation of characterological traits among depressives (reviewed earlier in this chapter) found two traits, worried moodiness and obsessionalism, to be persistent features among only a subgroup of the depressed patients. In other patients, these features appeared as part of the prodromal intensification of the episode, remitting with the development of the depression. Kendell and Discipio (1970) found that on measures of obsessionalism, recovered unipolar depressives had scores intermediate between those of obsessional neurotics and two "normal" groups. Comparisons between neurotic and psychotic depressives found neurotic depressives to be more obsessional premorbidly, while psychotic depressives developed more new obsessional symptomatology during their depressive illness. Contrary to other reports (Gittelson, 1966; Videbech, 1975), obsessional traits did not appear to intensify during the depressive episode among premorbidly obsessional individuals. Vaughn (1976) found obsessive symptoms to occur more frequently in depression among a group of patients with obsessional personalities. He further reported that premorbidly obsessive patients evidenced less anxiety during their illness, while the presence of obsessive symptoms in other depressed patients tended to be associated with an agitated and anxious form of depression.

Of particular interest is the suggestion among some of these studies that obsessional symptoms and traits serve as a defense against depression. Wittenborn and Maurer (1977) hypothesized that intensification of obsessionalism and denial of anger at the onset of the depressive episode may serve a defensive function among individuals feeling overwhelmed by environmental stressors and sensing an impending loss of control. Kendell and Discipio (1970) suggested that marked premorbid obsessionalism may offer protection against the development of manic episodes. Von Zerssen (1977, 1982), in his review of the literature, postulated that many of the traits of the "melancholic type" result from the tendency to build defenses against the negative emotions involved in depression. He cites as an example the melancholic's strivings toward self-confirmation in performance, as a strategy to avoid a lack of self-esteem. Consistent with this line of thought and in summary, Yerevanian and Akiskal (1979) have noted that "the psychoanalytical literature has suggested that the anankastic traits of orderliness, guilt and concern for others are a defense against the depressive's tendency for disorganization, hostility and self-preoccupation" (p. 604).

PERSONALITY DISORDERS CONSIDERED FOR FURTHER STUDY

The Passive–Aggressive Personality (Negativistic Personality)

In DSM-IV, the passive–aggressive personality disorder has been deleted from classification on Axis II, with the revised version being moved to Appendix B. In the past, concerns have been raised that the passive–aggressive disorder might be too narrowly defined, too situation-specific, and more of a symptom or dynamic than an actual personality disorder (American Psychiatric Association, 1991). The characterization of the passive–aggressive personality as depicted in DSM-IV places greater emphasis on the negativistic attitudes and sullen, resentful temperament that underlie these passive, resistant behaviors. This portrayal of the negativistic personality is more consistent with our position, in that it offers a more comprehensive concept to reflect the general contrariness and disinclination to doing as others wish. Beyond the passive resistance of negativistic personalities are a capricious impulsiveness, an irritable moodiness, and an unaccommodating, fault-finding pessimism (Millon, 1981).

The broader formulation of the passive–aggressive or negativistic personality taken here is consistent with that of the "oral-sadistic melancholic" described in the writings of early psychoanalysts. Characterized by deep-seated and pervasive ambivalence, consequent to difficulties arising in the "oral-biting" stage, these individuals have been described as spiteful, petulant, and overdemanding, with a pessimistic mistrust of the world (Menninger, 1940). More recently, Small, Small, Alig, and Moore (1970), in a study of 100 patients diagnosed as passive-aggressive personalities, suggested that these individuals were characterized by "interpersonal strife, verbal (not physical) aggressiveness, emotional storms, impulsivity and manipulative behavior. Suicidal gestures and lack of attention to everyday responsibilities commonly accompanied this intensive style of relating" (p. 978).

On the basis of the characteristics most frequently reported in both the theoretical and the research literature, we propose the following to be among the most essential features of the passive–aggressive or negativistic personality: (1) irritable affectivity (e.g., quick temper and moodiness); (2) behavioral contrariness (e.g., passive–aggressive, obstructive, and sulking behaviors); (3) discontented self-image (e.g., feelings of being misunderstood, unappreciated, and disillusioned about life); (4) deficient regulatory controls (e.g., capricious and poorly modulated emotional expression); and (5) interpersonal ambivalence (e.g., conflicts concerning dependency and self-assertion, as well as unpredictable and exasperating social behaviors).

The characteristic vacillation, discontentment, and socially maladaptive behaviors of passive-aggressive personalities almost inevitably result in varying states of interpersonal conflict and frustration, as well as emotional confusion and distress. Consequently, such individuals are highly susceptible to psychiatric symptomatology, including anxiety, somatoform disorders, and especially depression. Although major depressive episodes are not uncommon, passive-aggressive personalities are probably most likely to experience chronic forms of dysthymic disorder. Typically, these individuals display an agitated form of dysphoria, shifting from states of anxious futility, self-deprecation, and despair to demanding irritability and bitter discontent. They may struggle between their desire to act out defiantly and their social sense that they must curtail their resentments. Although passive–aggressive personalities are accustomed to venting their feelings directly, anger will be restrained and turned inward if they sense that such expression may result in rejection or humiliation. Their grumbling, moody complaints, and sour pessimism, however, serve as vehicles of tension discharge, relieving them periodically of mounting inner- and outer-directed anger. A secondary but important function of these behaviors is to intimidate others and induce guilt, which provides the passive–aggressives with some sense of retribution for the miseries others have caused them in the past. After a time, however, the sullen moodiness and complaining of these individuals may tend to annoy and alienate others. Although their piteous distress may inhibit others from directly expressing their frustration and annoyance, the others' exasperation is readily perceived by the hypersensitive passive–aggressives and taken as further evidence of the low esteem in which they are held.

The dynamics of the passive–aggressive personality's depressive cycle are well formulated in Salzman's (1972) interpersonal theory of depression, as well as Coyne's (1976) interactional description of depression. Both theorists describe a downward depressive spiral that starts with the depressive's initial expression of helplessness and hopelessness, which successfully engages others and elicits support. Questioning the sincerity of the attention received or dissatisfied with the extent of it, the depressive may then proceed to test others or complain of their lack of caring. Although irritated, the increasingly guilt-ridden and inhibited members of the social environment may continue at first to provide gestures of reassurance and support. The continuing abnegating tendencies and bemoaning of the depressive may ultimately, however, cause others to replace their sympathy with annoyance and their compassion with contempt. As noted earlier, the downward depressive spiral is especially consistent with the broader formulation of the negativistic/passive–aggressive personality, who, in Lewinsohn's (1974) terms, lacks the social skills necessary to elicit and sustain consistent positive response from others.

Much of the theoretical and research literature on young, hostile, unstable, and characterological depressives (Akiskal, 1983; Charney et al., 1981; Overall & Hollister, 1980; Paykel, 1972) is pertinent to the depressive experience in passive–aggressive personalities. In a study of characterological traits among a large group of depressed women, Wittenborn and Maurer (1977) noted that the following features persisted before and after depressive episodes: a tendency to blame others, a demanding and complaining attitude, and low self-confidence. Rosenthal and Gudeman (1967), in a factor-analytic study of depressed women, described two factors, one of which was associated with self-pity, hypochondriasis, complaining and demanding behavior, irritability, hostility, and anxiety. This factor bears a resemblance to two of Paykel's (1972) depressive subtypes: the hostile depressives, characterized by verbal belligerence and self-pity, and the young personality-disordered depressives, who evidenced negativism and persisting disturbances in social and interpersonal relationships. Two additional empirically derived depressive subtypes appear to be descriptive of the depressive experience in passive–aggressive personalities. The first is the "agitated depression" reported by Overall and Hollister (1980). This profile is characterized as an anxious depression, accompanied by tension, excitement, and psychomotor agitation. The second subtype that shares some of the features of the passive–aggressive depressive pattern is the "Factor Pattern C" generated by Grinker et al. (1961), which is characterized by agitation, demandingness, complaining, and hypochondriasis.

Finally, similarities can be drawn between characteristics of the passive–aggressive personality and the "autodestructive–neurotic" factor of depression reported by Matussek and Feil (1983). As described by the authors, this factor is associated with withdrawal tendencies and contact disturbances, but is characterized primarily by "mistrust (suspicion), dissatisfaction, a negative attitude toward life, anger, reproaches towards self and others, vulnerability and being easily hurt by petty matters" (p. 787). It will be recalled that Matussek and Feil reported unipolar nonendogenous depressives to share many of the features previously reported to be associated with neurotic depressives, including chronic pessimism, loneliness, dissatisfaction, hostility, guilt feelings, and low frustration tolerance.

Although the negativistic personality has not been specifically mentioned in the empirical literature on depression, reference has been made to the passive–aggressive personality along with the others in the "anxious, fearful" cluster (Mezzich et al., 1987). Davidson et al. (1985) noted the passive–aggressive personality disorder to occur within both nonmelancholic and melancholic depressions, while Thompson et al. (1988) found passive–aggressive personalities to be among the poor responders in their later-life depressive patients. Alnaes and Torgersen (1991), utilizing both the MCMI and the DSM-III, found passive–aggressive personality disorder to occur in patients with major depression, cyclothymia, and dysthymia. They have suggested that the higher incidence of passive–aggressive disorder in their patient population probably reflects the MCMI's broader category of negativistic personality disorder rather than the more focal passive–aggressive disorder. Libb et al. (1990) reported similar conclusions in their study of outpatient depressives, where passive–aggressive disorder was the most frequently occurring personality disorder prior to medical interventions. Following 12 weeks of treatment, however, the incidence of passive–aggressive personality disorder decreased significantly, which to them suggested an overlap between the clinically depressed state and the negativistic/passive–aggressive personality traits.

The Depressive Personality

The depressive personality disorder is proposed in Axis B of the DSM-IV as a diagnostic category needing further study. Features of the depressive personality as described in the DSM-IV Options Book and DSM-IV Appendix B (American Psychiatric Association, 1991, 1994) show some overlap with the self-defeating or masochistic personality as proposed in Appendix A in the DSM-III-R and considered by the DSM-IV Task Force (Grinspoon, 1990; Fiester, 1991; Klein, 1990; Phillips et al., 1990; Asch, 1986; Akiskal, 1989). The self-defeating personality was characterized by a pervasive pattern of self-defeating behaviors occurring in a variety of contexts in more than one area of functioning, such as work, school, social relationships, or close interpersonal relationships. Examples of such self-defeating behavior included choosing people or situations that lead to disappointment and failure, inciting angry or rejecting responses from others and then feeling hurt or defeated, and rejecting opportunities for pleasure or responding to positive personal events with dysphoric mood or guilt.

Originally, this diagnostic category was labeled "masochistic personality disorder" until multiple objections and concerns were raised, especially by women's groups. The concept of masochism was thought to be too closely identified with psychoanalytic theory, which in its most familiar version implies two ideas about self-defeating behavior: that its roots are often in some sense sexual, and that it involves unconscious pleasure in suffering (Grinspoon, 1990). The term "masochism" has been used to mean any inward turning of aggression, self-punishment for forbidden wishes, or attempts to wreak revenge through martyrdom. Analytic theory has made it synonymous with any suffering that seems unnecessary or self-induced, or with passivity in general. Freud (1932/1950) theorized that masochism derives from the death instinct—a theory that is rarely used today. His term "moral masochism," however, continues to be widely used. It refers to the personal conflict within the masochistic individual created by various aspects of the personality (especially the superego) that require him/her to restrict his/her gratifications (Asch, 1986). It also proposes that masochism has an especially important role in the emotional lives of women because of the suffering they endure in relation to their biological functioning. Opponents of this theory have cautioned that economic and social subordination or training in patience and selflessness may cause women to behave in ways that may be labeled as "masochistic," with the implication that they unconsciously enjoy being mistreated. Such critics were especially concerned that the label of masochism would be misapplied to victims of domestic violence.

Another controversy about the self-defeating personality disorder was that it really was a disorder on the affective spectrum, not a personality disorder (Fiester, 1991). Asch (1986) noted the close dynamic relationship between the masochistic personality pattern and dysthymic or major depressive disorders. He noted that many masochistic personalities do manifest depression at various times and may even progress to clinical depression later in life; conversely, some depressive disorders may merge into a masochistic lifestyle when the affective disorder is in remission. It was noted that self-defeating personalities and depressive patients share such diagnostic criteria as guilty responses to positive events, rejection of opportunities for pleasure, failure to accomplish tasks, and negative, pessimistic cognitions (Fiester, 1991; Grinspoon, 1990). Akiskal (1989) noted a great deal of overlap between his depressive temperament type and the self-defeating or masochistic personality, while researchers such as Klein (1990), Fiester (1991), and Phillips et al. (1990) referred to the concept of a depressive–

masochistic personality as posited by Kernberg (1988). The dominant traits of depressive–masochistic individuals include (1) overconsciousness, humorlessness, and self-criticism; (2) excessive dependency and demandingness, which may induce guilt and rejection by others; and (3) inappropriate expression of anger, which may also trigger rejection or be directed toward the self in the form of depression and guilt.

Simons (1987) argued that although masochistic and depressive personalities certainly coexist, many features of the two disorders are quite distinct. He referred to the two behaviorally distinct constellations within the masochistic personality: the "masochistic personality disorder" and "moral masochism." The former, as Simon defines it, refers to behavior that provokes punitive, rejecting responses by others, while the latter refers to intrapunitive behavior such as self-criticism and guilt. Simons noted that moral masochism overlaps with the depressive personality, whereas self-defeating personality disorder as defined by DSM-III-R and the DSM-IV Options Book reflected a masochistic personality disorder constellation, with few if any of the moral masochistic traits. In their review of Simon's theory, Phillips et al. (1990) wrote that patients with masochistic personality disorder unconsciously torture and blackmail others; in contrast, patients with depressive personality disorders and its moral masochism equivalent internalize the conflict, leading to self-torture and self-defeat in the absence of provoked retaliation from others. Compatible with this viewpoint was Fiester's (1991) observation that although there was confusion regarding the nature of the relationship of self-defeating personality to the affective disorders, it did not appear that the self-defeating personality disorder could be satisfactorily subsumed under a depressive personality category. It was our contention that this proposed diagnostic category actually represented a heterogeneous mixture of personality traits, including those associated with the dependent, avoidant, and borderline personality disorders, and especially with the negativistic/passive–aggressive personality disorder. Ultimately, the self-defeating personality disorder was dropped altogether in DSM-IV because of the extensive criticism with which it was associated, as well as the questionable utility of the concept. Conversely, the depressive personality seems to be generating continued and growing interest, and as such has been included in DSM-IV as a criteria set warranting further study.

The history of the depressive personality is extensive with respect to both clinical and theoretical literature, especially that by psychoanalytic and German phenomenological authors. Although a brief overview of this literature is presented here, the reader is referred to the exhaustive review offered by Phillips et al. (1990). The Germanic concept of the depressive personality emphasizes the inherited subaffective depressive temperament (a genetically attenuated form of major depressive disorder), as evidenced in the writings of Kraepelin, Tellenbach, and especially Schneider. As noted previously, Schneider's depressive psychopath has many features in common with the obsessive–compulsive and avoidant personality disorders (e.g., gloomy pessimism, skepticism and worry, and overresponsibility). The psychoanalytic view of the depressive character, as expressed in the works of Berliner, Arieti, Bemporad, and Kernberg, is that it is developmentally determined; certain premorbid personality traits (e.g., persistent low self-esteem, helplessness, self-depreciation, and guilt) predispose an individual toward depression. As noted in the description of Kernberg's depressive–masochistic personality, the analytic theorists have identified a great deal of overlap between the depressive personality and the masochistic personality, in addition to the passive-dependent (oral) and the obsessive (anal) personality.

The early versions of the DSM reflected the influence of psychoanalytic theory, in that depressive reaction was listed under psychoneurosis and cyclothymia was listed under personality disorders. In addition, DSM-II (American Psychiatric Association, 1968) introduced both the neurasthenic neurosis, related to the depressive personality and characterized by chronic weakness and easy fatigability, and the asthenic personality disorder, also defined by fatiguability, low energy level, lack of enthusiasm, incapacity for enjoyment, and oversensitivity to stress. With the development of several new classification schemes for depressive disorders (Klein & Davis, 1969; Akiskal, Bitar, Puzantian, Rosenthal, & Walker, 1978; Kendell, 1976), dissolution of the depressive neurosis was proposed because of its diagnostic and prognostic heterogeneity and the potential for underutilization of antidepressant medications. With the development of DSM-III in 1980, the depressive neurosis was moved to Axis I, where it was called dysthymic disorder and encompassed all chronic, mild depressions (including those with both affective and characterological variants). Other affective personality types were dropped at this time, including the neurasthenic neurosis and asthenic personality, while cyclothymic disorder was moved to Axis I. Continued criticism of the dysthymic disorder category as being too heterogeneous resulted in the creation of more homogeneous subgroups, including primary versus secondary and early-onset versus late-onset dysthymia, as well as a separate subtype for chronic major depression. The primary early-onset type of dysthymia corresponds most closely to characterological depression/depressive personality. To provide a place for patients with a depressive character structure and less severe or persistent symptoms, self-defeating personality disorder was also introduced.

Significant problems continued to remain, however, because of the overlapping constructs of depressive personality, neurotic depression, and chronic depression/dysthymia. More researchers have provided data to suggest that despite the conceptual overlap between dysthymia and the depressive personality, there may be important differences between these constructs (Klein, 1990; Akiskal, 1989). Klein, for example, utilized Akiskal's modification of Schneider's construct of the depressive personality, along with multiple structured diagnostic and family history reviews, an extensive battery of inventories, and a 6-month follow-up; he found that despite significant overlap between the depressive personality and the diagnosis of dysthymia, the majority of patients did not meet the criteria for dysthymia and appeared to exhibit a more symptomatic condition, with a weaker familial relation to nonbipolar depression.

After reviewing the clinical, theoretical, and research history of the concept of the depressive personality, Phillips et al. (1990) suggest that this personality type should be differentiated from dysthymia in several ways. First, the depressive personality should have an early onset (which is not required for dysthymia) and should be more trait-like than state-like (e.g., more stable, durable, and resistant to change across situations and time than dysthymic symptoms). Medication-induced change in the depressive personality should not be rapid or dramatic, or affect all domains of the disorder (e.g., behaviors, relationships, cognitions, and self-concept). They further suggest that the core psychopathology of the depressive personality may be primarily cognitive, whereas dysthymia may be affective and somatic.

Diagnostic criteria for the depressive personality disorder as provided for further study in Appendix B of DSM-IV (American Psychiatric Association, 1994) include the following: (1) usual mood dominated by dejection, gloom, and unhappiness; (2) prominent self-concept centering around feelings of inadequacy, worthlessness, and low self-esteem; (3) critical, blaming, derogatory, and punitive attitude toward oneself; (4) tendency to brood and worry; (5) negativistic, critical, and judgmental attitude toward others; (6) pessimism; and (7) proneness to guilt. These features should not occur exclusively during major depressive episodes in order for the diagnosis of depressive personality disorder to be considered. It is our feeling once again that this proposed diagnosis encompasses several existing personality subtypes that are all especially prone to affective disorders; as such, it may not prove to be a particularly useful construct in diagnosis and treatment. As noted by Phillips et al. (1990), empirical evaluation is necessary to assess the possible redundancies between the putative depressive personality and other Axis II disorders. Similarly, Klein (1990) notes the need for further work to determine whether the depressive personality and dysthymia represent qualitatively different (albeit overlapping) conditions, or whether the depressive personality is best conceptualized as a milder, less symptomatic form of dysthymia. Klein feels that the data support the latter view, and suggests that it may be useful to extend the concept of the affective spectrum to include less symptomatic, more trait-based conditions, such as the depressive personality, particularly in family/genetic and high-risk studies.

REFERENCES

Abraham, K. (1966). A short study of the development of the libido, viewed in the light of mental disorders. In B. D. Lewin (Ed.), *On character and development* (pp. 67–129). New York: Norton. (Original work published 1924)

Abraham, K. (1968). Notes on the psychoanalytical investigation and treatment of manic–depressive insanity and allied conditions. In W. Gaylin (Ed.), *The meaning of despair* (pp. 26–50). New York: Science House. (Original work published 1911)

Abramson, L. Y., Seligman, M. E., & Teasdale, J. (1978). Learned helplessness in humans: Critique and reformulation. *Journal of Abnormal Psychology, 87,* 49–74.

Akiskal, H. S. (1981). Subaffective disorders: Dysthymic, cyclothymic and bipolar II disorders in the "borderline" realm. *Psychiatric Clinics of North America, 4*(1), 25–46.

Akiskal, H. S. (1983). Dysthymic disorder: Psychopathology of proposed chronic depressive subtypes. *American Journal of Psychiatry, 140*(1), 11–20.

Akiskal, H. S. (1989). Validating affective personality types. In L. Robins & J. Barrett (Eds.), *The validity of psychiatric diagnosis* (pp. 217–227). New York: Raven Press.

Akiskal, H. S., Bitar, A.H., Puzantian, V. R., Rosenthal, T. L., & Walker, P. W. (1978). The nosological status of neurotic depression: A prospective three to four-year follow-up examination in light of the primary–secondary and unipolar–bipolar dichotomies. *Archives of General Psychiatry, 40,* 801–810.

Akiskal, H. S., Chen, F., Davis, G., Puzantian, B., Kashgarian, M., & Bolinger, J. (1985). Borderline: An adjective in search of a noun. *Journal of Clinical Psychiatry, 46,* 41–48.

Akiskal, H. S., Hirschfeld, R. M. A., & Yervanian, B. (1983). The relationship of personality to affective disorders. *Archives of General Psychiatry, 40,* 801–810.

Akiskal, H. S., Khani, M. K., & Scott-Strauss, A. (1979). Cyclothymic temperamental disorders. *Psychiatric Clinics of North America, 2*(3), 527–554.

Akiskal, H. S., Rosenthal, T. L., Haykal, R. F., Lemmi, H., Rosenthal, R. H., & Scott-Strauss, A. (1980). Characterological depressions: Clinical and sleep EEG findings separating "subaffective dysthymias" from "character-spectrum disorders." *Archives of General Psychiatry, 37,* 777–783.

Akiskal, H. S., & Simmons, R. (1985). Chronic and refractory depressions: Evaluation and management. In E. E. Beckham & W. R. Leber (Eds.), *Handbook of depression: Treatment, assessment, and research* (pp. 587–605). Homewood, IL: Dorsey Press.

Alnaes, R., & Torgersen, S. (1990). DSM-III personality disorders among patients with major depression, anxiety disorders, and mixed conditions. *Journal of Nervous and Mental Disease, 178,* 693–698.

Alnaes, R., & Torgersen, S. (1991). Personality and personality disorders among patients with various affective disorders. *Journal of Personality Disorders, 5*(2), 107–121.

Altman, J. H., & Wittenborn, J. R. (1980). Depression-prone personality in women. *Journal of Abnormal Psychology, 89,* 303–308.

American Psychiatric Association. (1968). *Diagnostic and statistical manual of mental disorders* (2nd ed.). Washington, DC: Author.

American Psychiatric Association. (1980). *Diagnostic and statistical manual of mental disorders* (3rd ed.). Washington, DC: Author.

American Psychiatric Association. (1987). *Diagnostic and statistical manual of mental disorders* (3rd ed., rev.). Washington, DC: Author.

American Psychiatric Association. (1991). *DSM-IV options book: Work in progress.* Washington, DC: Author.

American Psychiatric Association. (1994). *Diagnostic and statistical manual of mental disorders* (4th ed.). Washington, DC: Author.

Arieti, S., & Bemporad, J. R. (1980). The psychological organization of depression. *American Journal of Psychiatry, 137,* 1360–1365.

Asch, S. (1986). The masochistic personality. In A. M. Cooper, A. J. Frances, & M. H. Sacks (Eds.), *Psychia-*

try: Vol. 1. The personality disorders and neuroses (pp. 291–299). Philadelphia: J. B. Lippincott.

Beck, A. T. (1974). The development of depression: A cognitive model. In R. J. Friedman & M. M. Katz (Eds.), The psychology of depression: Contemporary theory and research (pp. 3–19). Washington, DC: V. H. Winston.

Beck, A. T. (1981). Cognitive therapy of depression: New perspectives. In P. Clayton & J. Barrett (Eds.), Treatment of depression: Old controversies and new approaches (pp. 265–284). New York: Raven Press.

Bemporad, J. (1971). New views on psychodynamics of the depressive character. In S. Arieti (Ed.), World biennial of psychiatry and psychotherapy (Vol. 1, pp. 219–243). New York: Basic Books.

Bibring, E. (1953). The mechanism of depression. In P. Greenacre (Ed.), Affective disorders (pp. 14–47). New York: International Universities Press.

Birtchnell, J. (1984). Dependence and its relationship to depression. British Journal of Medical Psychology, 57, 215–225.

Black, D., Bell, S., Hulbert, J., & Nasrallah, A. (1988). The importance of Axis II and patients with major depression: A controlled study. Journal of Affective Disorders, 14, 115–122.

Blaney, P. H. (1977). Contemporary theories of depression: Critique and comparison. Journal of Abnormal Psychology, 86, 203–223.

Blatt, S. J. (1974). Levels of object representation in anaclitic and introjective depression. Psychoanalytic Study of the Child, 29, 426–427.

Blatt, S. J., D'Afflitti, P., & Quinlan, D. M. (1976). Experiences of depression in normal young adults. Journal of Abnormal Psychology, 85, 383–389.

Blatt, S. J., Quinlan, D. M., Chevron, E. S., McDonald, C., & Zuroff, D. (1982). Dependency and self-criticism: Psychological dimensions of depression. Journal of Consulting and Clinical Psychology, 50, 113–124.

Bowlby, J. (1977). The making and breaking of affectional bonds. British Journal of Psychiatry, 130, 201–210.

Boyce, P., Parker, G., Hickie, I., Wilhelm, K., Brodaty, H., & Mitchell, P. (1990). Personality differences between patients with remitted melancholic and nonmelancholic depression. American Journal of Psychiatry, 147, 1476–1483.

Cadoret, R., Baker, M., Dorzab, J., & Winokur, G. (1971). Depressive disease: Personality factors in patients and their relatives. Biological Psychiatry, 3, 85–93.

Charney, D. S., Nelson, J. C., & Quinlan, D. M. (1981). Personality traits and disorder in depression. American Journal of Psychiatry, 138, 1601–1604.

Chodoff, P. (1970). The core problem in depression: Interpersonal aspects. In J. Masserman (Ed.), Depression: Vol. 17. Theories and therapies, science and psychoanalysis (pp. 56–65). New York: Grune & Stratton.

Chodoff, P. (1972). The depressive personality: A critical review. Archives of General Psychiatry, 27, 666–673.

Cleckley, H. (1941). The mask of sanity. St. Louis, MO: C. V. Mosby.

Cofer, D. H., & Wittenborn, J. R. (1980). Personality characteristics of formerly depressed women. Journal of Abnormal Psychology, 89, 309–314.

Coppen, A. (1966). The Marke–Nyman Temperament Scale: An English translation. British Journal of Medical Psychology, 39, 55–59.

Cormier, B. M. (1966). Depression and persistent criminality. Canadian Psychiatric Association Journal, 11, 208–220.

Coyne, J. C. (1976). Toward an interactional description of depression. Psychiatry, 39, 28–40.

Davidson, J., Miller, R., & Strickland, R. (1985). Neuroticism and personality disorder and depression. Journal of Affective Disorders, 8, 177–182.

Docherty, J., Fiester, S., & Shea, T. (1986). Syndrome diagnosis in personality disorder. In A. J. Frances & R. E. Hales (Eds.), American Psychiatric Association annual review (Vol. 5, pp. 315–355). Washington, DC: American Psychiatric Press.

Donnelly, E., Murphy, D., & Goodwin, F. (1976). Cross-sectional and longitudinal comparisons of bipolar and unipolar depressed groups on the MMPI. Journal of Consulting and Clinical Psychology, 44, 233–237.

Farmer, R., & Nelson-Gray, R. (1990). Personality disorders in depression: Hypothetical relations, empirical findings, and methodological consideration. Clinical Psychology Review, 10, 453–476.

Fenichel, O. (1968). Depression and mania. In W. Gaylin (Ed.), The meaning of despair (pp. 108–154). New York: Science House.

Fiester, S. (1991). Self-defeating personality disorder: A review of data and recommendations for DSM-IV. Journal of Personality Disorders, 5(2), 194–209.

Frances, A., Widiger, T., & Fyer, M. (1990). The influence of classification methods and comorbidity. In D. Maser & R. Cloninger (Eds.), Comorbidity of mood and anxiety disorders (pp. 41–61). Washington, DC: American Psychiatric Press.

Frank, E., Kupfer, G., Jarrett, D., & Jacob, M. (1986). Self-rating of personality characteristics and their relationship to treatment response in recurrent unipolar depressives: A pilot study. Psychopharmacology Bulletin, 22(1), 196–199.

Freud, S. (1950). Libidinal types. In Sigmund Freud: Collected papers (Vol. 5). London: Hogarth Press. (Original work published 1932)

Freud, S. (1968). Mourning and melancholia. In W. Gaylin (Ed.), The meaning of despair (pp. 50–70). New York: Science House. (Original work published 1917)

Fyer, M., Frances, A., Sullivan, T., Hurt, S., & Clarkin, J. (1988). Comorbidity of borderline personality disorder. Archives of General Psychiatry, 45, 348–352.

Gershon, E., Cromer, M., & Klerman, G. (1968). Hostility and depression. Psychiatry, 31, 224–235.

Gittelson, N. L. (1966). The effect of obsessions on depressive psychosis. British Journal of Psychiatry, 112, 253–259.

Grinker, R. R., Miller, J., Sabshin, M., Nunn, R., & Nunnally, J. (1961). The phenomenon of depressions. New York: Hoeber.

Grinker, R. R., Werble, B., & Drye, R. C. (1968). Borderline syndrome. New York: Basic Books.

Grinspoon, L. (1990). Self-defeating behavior and masochism. Harvard Medical School Mental Health Letter, 6(9), 1–4.

Guerrera, R. (1990). Some biological and behavioral features associated with clinical personality types. Journal of Nervous and Mental Disease, 178, 556–566.

Gunderson, J., & Elliott, G. (1985). The interface between borderline personality disorder and affective disorder. American Journal of Psychiatry, 142(3), 277–288.

Hamilton, M. (1960). A rating scale for depression. Journal of Neurology, Neurosurgery and Psychiatry, 23, 56–62.

Hirschfeld, R. M. A., & Cross, C. (1987). The measurement of personality in depression. In A. J. Marsella,

R. M. A. Hirschfeld, & M. M. Katz (Eds.), *The measurement of depression* (pp. 319–343). New York: Guilford Press.

Hirschfeld, R. M. A., & Klerman, G. L. (1979). Personality attributes and affective disorders. *American Journal of Psychiatry, 136,* 67–70.

Hirschfeld, R. M. A., Klerman, G. L., Chodoff, P., Korchin, S., & Barrett, J. (1976). Dependency–self–esteem–clinical depression. *Journal of the American Academy of Psychoanalysis, 4*(3), 373–388.

Hirschfeld, R. M. A., Klerman, G. L., Clayton, P. J., & Keller, M. B. (1983). Personality and depression. *Archives of General Psychiatry, 40,* 993–998.

Hirschfeld, R. M. A., Klerman, G. L., Keller, M. B., Andreasen, N. C., & Clayton, P. J. (1986). Personality of recovered patients with bipolar affective disorder. *Journal of Affective Disorders, 11,* 81–89.

Hirschfeld, R. M. A., Klerman, G. L., Lavori, P., Keller, M. B., Griffith, P., & Coryell, W. (1989). Premorbid personality assessment of first onset of major depression. *Archives of General Psychiatry, 46,* 345–350.

Hirschfeld, R. M. A., & Shea, M. T. (1992). Personality. In E. S. Paykel (Ed.), *Handbook of affective disorders* (2nd ed., pp. 185–194). New York: Guilford Press.

Hoberman, H., & Lewinsohn, P. (1985). The behavioral treatment of depression. In E. E. Beckham & W. R. Leber (Eds.), *Handbook of depression: Treatment, assessment, and research* (pp. 39–81). Homewood, IL: Dorsey Press.

Kegan, R., Rogers, L., & Quinlan, D. (1981). Constructive–developmental organizations of depression. In *New approaches to depression.* Symposium conducted at the annual meeting of the American Psychological Association, Los Angeles.

Kendell, R. E. (1976). The classification of depression: A review of contemporary confusion. *British Journal of Psychiatry, 129,* 15–28.

Kendell, R. E., & Discipio, W. J. (1970). Obsessional symptoms and obsessional personality traits in patients with depressive illness. *Psychological Medicine, 1,* 65–72.

Kernberg, O. F. (1970). A psychoanalytic classification of character pathology. *Journal of the American Psychoanalytic Association, 18,* 800–822.

Kernberg, O. F. (1975). *Borderline conditions and pathological narcissism.* New York: Jason Aronson.

Kernberg, O. F. (1988). Clinical dimensions of masochism. *Journal of the American Psychoanalytic Association, 36,* 1005–1029.

Klein, D. F. (1975). Psychopharmacology and the borderline patient. In J. E. Mack (Ed.), *Borderline states in psychiatry* (pp. 75–101). New York: Grune & Stratton.

Klein, D. F. (1990). Depressive personality: Reliability, validity, and relation to dysthymia. *Journal of Abnormal Psychology, 4,* 412–421.

Klein, D. F., & Davis, J. N. (1969). The diagnosis of affective disorders. In D. F. Klein & J. N. Davis (Eds.), *Diagnosis and treatment of psychiatric disorders* (1st ed.). Baltimore: Williams & Wilkins.

Klein, D. F., Taylor, B., Dickstein, S., & Harding, K. (1988a). Primary early-onset dysthymia: Comparison with primary nonbipolar nonchronic major depression on demographic, clinical, familial, personality, and socioenvironmental characteristics and short-term outcome. *Journal of Abnormal Psychology, 97*(4), 387–398.

Klein, D. F., Taylor, B., Dickstein, S., & Harding, K. (1988b). The early–late onset distinction in DSM-III-R dysthymia. *Journal of Affective Disorders, 14,* 25–33.

Klein, M. H., Wunderlich, S., & Shea, M. T. (1993). Models of relationships between personality and depression: Toward a framework for theory and research. In M. H. Klein, D. J. Kupfer, & M. T. Shea (Eds.), *Personality and depression* (pp. 1–54). New York: Guilford Press.

Klerman, G. L. (1974). Depression and adaptation. In R. J. Friedman & M. M. Katz (Eds.), *The psychology of depression: Contemporary theory and research* (pp. 129–145). Washington, DC: V. H. Winston.

Knight, R. P. (1953). Borderline states. *Bulletin of the Menninger Clinic, 17,* 1–12.

Kocsis, J., & Frances, A. (1987). A critical discussion of DSM-III dysthymic disorder. *American Journal of Psychiatry, 144*(12), 1534–1542.

Kohlberg, L. (1976). Moral stages and moralization: The cognitive developmental approach. In T. Lickona (Ed.), *Moral development and behavior.* New York: Holt, Rinehart & Winston.

Kohut, H. (1977). *The restoration of the self.* New York: International Universities Press.

Kolb, L. C. (1973). *Modern clinical psychiatry* (8th ed.). Philadelphia: W. B. Saunders.

Laing, R. D. (1965). *The divided self.* Harmondsworth, England: Penguin Books.

Lazare, A., & Klerman, G. L. (1968). Hysteria and depression: The frequency and significance of hysterical personality features in hospitalized depressed women. *American Journal of Psychiatry, 11,* 48–58.

Lesse, S. (1974). Depression masked by acting-out behavior patterns. *American Journal of Psychotherapy, 28,* 352–361.

Lewinsohn, P. M. (1974). A behavioral approach to depression. In R. J. Friedman & M. M. Katz (Eds.), *The psychology of depression: Contemporary theory and research* (pp. 156–185). Washington, DC: V. H. Winston.

Libb, W., Stankovic, S., Freeman, A., Sokol, R., Switzer, P., & Houck, C. (1990). Personality disorders among depressed outpatients as identified by the MCMI. *Journal of Clinical Psychology, 46*(3), 277–283.

Liebowitz, M. R., & Klein, D. F. (1981). Interrelationship of hysteroid dysphoria and borderline personality disorder. *Psychiatric Clinics of North America, 4*(1), 67–87.

Liebowitz, M. R., Stallone, F., Dunner, D. L., & Fieve, R. F. (1979). Personality features of patients with primary affective disorder. *Acta Psychiatrica Scandinavica, 60,* 214–224.

Marin, D., DeMeo, M., Frances, A., Kocsis, J., & Mann, J. (1989). Biological models and treatments for personality disorders. *Psychiatric Annals, 19*(3), 143–146.

Masterson, J. S. (1972). *Treatment of the borderline adolescent: A developmental approach.* New York: Wiley–Interscience.

Matussek, P., & Feil, W. (1983). Personality attributes of depressive patients. *Archives of General Psychiatry, 40,* 783–790.

McGlashan, T. (1987). Borderline personality disorder and unipolar affective disorder. *Journal of Nervous and Mental Disease, 175*(8), 467–473.

Menninger, K. (1940). Character disorders. In J. F. Brown (Ed.), *The psychodynamics of abnormal behavior.* New York: McGraw-Hill.

Mezzich, J., Fabrega, H., & Coffman, G. (1987). Multiaxial characterization of depressive patients. *Journal of Nervous and Mental Disease, 175*(6), 339–346.

Miller, I., Norman, W., & Dow, M. (1986). Psychosocial

characteristics of "double depression." *American Journal of Psychiatry, 143*(8), 1042–1044.

Millon, T. (1969). *Modern psychopathology*. Philadelphia: W. B. Saunders.

Millon, T. (1981). *Disorders of personality: DSM-III, Axis II*. New York: Wiley.

Millon, T. (1983). *Millon Clinical Multiaxial Inventory manual* (3rd ed.). New York: Holt, Rinehart & Winston.

Millon, T. (1986). Personality prototypes and their diagnostic criteria. In T. Millon & G. Klerman (Eds.), *Contemporary directions in psychopathology* (pp. 671–712). New York: Guilford Press.

Nystrom, S., & Lindegard, B. (1975). Depression: Predisposing factors. *Acta Psychiatrica Scandinavica, 51*, 77–87.

Overall, J., & Hollister, L. (1980). Phenomenological classification of depressive disorders. *Journal of Clinical Psychology, 36*(2), 372–377.

Paykel, E. S. (1971). Classification of depressed patients: A cluster analysis derived grouping. *British Journal of Psychiatry, 118*, 275–288.

Paykel, E. S. (1972). Correlates of a depressive typology. *Archives of General Psychiatry, 27*, 203–210.

Paykel, E. S., Klerman, G. L., & Prusoff, B. A. (1976). Personality and symptom pattern in depression. *British Journal of Psychiatry, 129*, 327–334.

Paykel, E. S., & Prusoff, B. A. (1973). Relationships between personality dimensions: Neuroticism and extraversion against obsessive, hysterical and oral personality. *British Journal of Social and Clinical Psychology, 12*, 309–318.

Paykel, E. S., & Weissman, M. M. (1973). Social adjustment and depression. *Archives of General Psychiatry, 24*, 659–663.

Perris, C. (1966). A study of bipolar (manic–depressive) and unipolar recurrent depressive psychosis. *Acta Psychiatrica Scandinavica, 42*(Suppl. 194), 68–82.

Perris, C. (1971). Personality patterns in patients with affective disorders. *Acta Psychiatrica Scandinavica, 47*(Suppl. 221), 43–51.

Perris, C., Eisemann, M., von Knorring, L., & Perris, H. (1984). Personality traits in former depressed patients and in healthy subjects without past history of depression. *Psychopathology, 17*, 178–186.

Perry, J. C. (1985). Depression in borderline personality disorder: Lifetime prevalence at interview and longitudinal course of symptoms. *American Journal of Psychiatry, 142*, 15–21.

Perry, J. C., & Klerman, G. L. (1978). The borderline patient. *Archives of General Psychiatry, 35*, 141–150.

Pfohl, B., Coryell, W., Zimmerman, M., & Stangl, D. (1987). Prognostic validity of self-report and interview measures of personality disorders in depressed inpatients. *Journal of Clinical Psychiatry, 48*, 468–472.

Pfohl, B., Stangl, D., & Zimmerman, M. (1984). The implications of DSM-III personality disorders for patients with major depression. *Journal of Affective Disorders, 7*, 309–318.

Phillips, K., Gunderson, J., Hirschfeld, R. M. A., & Smith, L. (1990). A review of the depressive personality. *American Journal of Psychiatry, 147*, 830–837.

Pilkonis, P. (1988). Personality prototypes among depressives: Themes of dependency and autonomy. *Journal of Personality Disorders, 2*(2), 144–152.

Pilkonis, P., & Frank, E. (1988). Personality pathology in recurrent depression: Nature, prevalence, and relationship to treatment response. *American Journal of Psychiatry, 145*, 435–441.

Rado, S. (1928). The problem of melancholia. *International Journal of Psycho-Analysis, 9*, 420–438.

Rado, S. (1951). Psychodynamics of depression from the etiologic point of view. *Psychosomatic Medicine, 13*, 51–55.

Rado, S. (1968). Psychodynamics of depressive from the etiologic point of view. In W. Gaylin (Ed.), *The meaning of despair* (pp. 96–108). New York: Science House.

Reich, J., Noyes, R., Hirschfeld, R. M. A., Coryell, W., & O'Gorman, T. (1987). State and personality in depressed and panic patients. *American Journal of Psychiatry, 144*, 181–187.

Reid, W. H. (1978). The sadness of the psychopath. *American Journal of Psychotherapy, 32*, 496–509.

Rosenthal, S., & Gudeman J. (1967). The self-pitying constellation in depression. *British Journal of Psychiatry, 113*, 485–489.

Rosenthal, T. L., Akiskal, H., Scott-Strauss, A., Rosenthal, R. H., & David, M. (1981). Familial and developmental factors in characterological depressions. *Journal of Affective Disorders, 3*, 183–192.

Sacks, M. H. (1986). Depressive neurosis. In A. M. Cooper, A. J. Frances, & M. H. Sacks (Eds.), *Psychiatry: Vol. 1. The personality disorders and neuroses* (pp. 395–408). Philadelphia: J. B. Lippincott.

Salzman, L. (1970). Depression: A clinical review. In J. Masserman (Ed.), *Depression: Vol. 17. Theories and therapies, science and psychoanalysis* (pp. 109–119). New York: Grune & Stratton.

Salzman, L. (1972). Interpersonal factors in depression. In F. Flach & S. Draghi (Eds.), *The nature and treatment of depression* (pp. 43–56). New York: Wiley.

Schless, A., Mendels, J., Kipperman, A., & Cochrane, C. (1974). Depression and hostility. *Journal of Nervous and Mental Disease, 159*, 91–100.

Schneider, K. (1958). *Psychopathic personalities* (M. W. Hamilton, Trans.). London: Cassell. (Original work published 1923)

Seligman, M. E. (1974). Depression and learned helplessness. In R. J. Friedman & M. M. Katz (Eds.), *The psychology of depression: Contemporary theory and research* (pp. 83–109). Washington, DC: V. H. Winston.

Shader, R., Scharfman, E., & Dreyfuss, D. (1986). A biological model for selected personality disorders. In A. M. Cooper, A. J. Frances, & M. H. Sacks (Eds.), *Psychiatry: Vol. 1. The personality disorders and neuroses* (pp. 41–51). Philadelphia: J. B. Lippincott.

Shea, T., Glass, D., Pilkonis, P., Watkins, J., & Docherty, J. (1987). Frequency and implications of personality disorders in a sample of depressed outpatients. *Journal of Personality Disorders, 1*(1), 27–42.

Shea, T., Pilkonis, P., Beckham, E., Collins, J., Elkin, I., Sotsky, S., & Docherty, J. (1990). Personality disorders and treatment outcome in NIMH Treatment of Depression Collaborative Research Program. *American Journal of Psychiatry, 147*, 711–718.

Siever, L., Klar, H., & Coccaro, E. (1985). Psychobiologic substrates of personality. In H. Klar & L. Siever (Eds.), *Biologic response styles: Clinical implications* (pp. 37–65). Washington, DC: American Psychiatric Press.

Siever, L., Coccaro, E., Zemishlany, Z., Silverman, J. S., Klar, H., Losonczy, M., Davidson, M., Friedman, R., Mohs, R., & Davis, K. (1987). Psychobiology of personality disorders: Pharmacologic implications. *Psychopharmacology Bulletin, 23*(3), 333–335.

Simons, R. C. (1987). Psychoanalytic contributions to psychiatric nosology: Forms of masochistic behavior. *Jour-*

nal of the American Psychoanalytic Association, 35, 583–608.

Sjobring, H. (1973). Personality structure and development: A model and its applications. Acta Psychiatrica Scandinavica, 49(Suppl. 244), 1–20.

Small, I., Small, J., Alig, V., & Moore, D. (1970). Passive–aggressive personality disorder: A search for a syndrome. American Journal of Psychiatry, 126, 973–983.

Snaith, R. P., McGuire, R. J., & Fox, K. (1971). Aspects of personality and depression. Psychological Medicine, 1, 239–246.

Snyder, S., Sajadi, C., Pitts, W. M., & Goodpaster, W. A. (1982). Identifying the depressive border of the borderline personality. American Journal of Psychiatry, 139, 814–817.

Spitzer, R. L., & Williams, J. B. W. (1982). Hysteroid dysphoria: An unsuccessful attempt to demonstrate its syndromal validity. American Journal of Psychiatry, 139, 1286–1291.

Standage, K. (1986). A clinical and psychometric investigation comparing Schneider's and the DSM-III typologies of personality disorders. Comprehensive Psychiatry, 27(1), 35–46.

Stone, M. H. (1979). Contemporary shift of the borderline concept from a subschizophrenic disorder to a subaffective disorder. Psychiatric Clinics of North America, 2(3), 577–593.

Thompson, L., Gallagher, D., & Czirr, R. (1988). Personality disorder and outcome in the treatment of late-life depression. Journal of Geriatric Psychiatry, 21, 133–146.

Tyrer, P., Casey, P., & Gall, J. (1983). Relationship between neurosis and personality disorder. British Journal of Psychiatry, 142, 404–408.

Vaughn, M. (1976). The relationships between obsessional personality, obsessions in depression and symptoms of depression. British Journal of Psychiatry, 129, 36–39.

Videbech, T. (1975). A study of genetic factors, childhood bereavement, and premorbid personality traits in patients with anancastic endogenous depression. Acta Psychiatrica Scandinavica, 52, 178–222.

Von Zerssen, D. (1977). Premorbid personality and affective psychoses. In G. D. Burrows (Ed.), Handbook of studies on depression (pp. 79–103). Amsterdam: Excerpta Medica.

Von Zerssen, D. (1982). Personality and affective disorders. In E. S. Paykel (Ed.), Handbook of affective disorders (pp. 212–228). New York: Guilford Press,

Weissman, M. M., Prusoff, B. A., & Klerman, G. L. (1979). Personality and the prediction of long-term outcome of depression. American Journal of Psychiatry, 136, 555–558.

Weston, D., Moses, J., Silk, K., Lohr, N., Cohen, R., & Segal, H. (1992). Quality of depressive experience in borderline personality disorder and major depression: When depression is not just depression. Journal of Personality Disorders, 6(4), 382–393.

Widiger, T. (1989). The categorical distinction between personality and affective disorders. Journal of Personality Disorders, 3(2), 77–91.

Winokur, G. (1979). Unipolar depression: It is divisible into autonomous subtypes. Archives of General Psychiatry, 36, 47–52.

Wittenborn, J. R., & Maurer, H. A. (1977). Persisting personalities among depressed women. Archives of General Psychiatry, 34, 968–971.

Yerevanian, B. L., & Akiskal, H. S. (1979). Neurotic, characterologic and dysthymic depressions. Psychiatric Clinics of North America, 2, 595–617.

Zimmerman, M., Pfohl, B., Coryell, W., Stangl, D., & Corenthal, C. (1988). Diagnosing personality disorder in depressed patients. Archives of General Psychiatry, 45, 733–737.

6

Comorbidity of Depression and Other Medical Conditions

DENISE E. STEVENS
KATHLEEN RIES MERIKANGAS
JAMES R. MERIKANGAS

BACKGROUND

A strong association between depression and numerous physical diseases has been consistently reported in clinical studies of patients with specific medical disorders, as well as among persons in treatment for depression. Estimates of the prevalence of depression in patients with medical disorders range from 20% to 83% (Editorial, 1979), and approximately 12% to 36% meet diagnostic levels of depressive symptoms (Rodin & Voshart, 1986). Conversely, 10% of depressed patients manifest a medical disorder as the underlying precipitant or cause of depression (Hall, 1980). Regardless of the index disorder for which such individuals have sought treatment, the accurate classification of comorbidity between these conditions has major implications for diagnosis, treatment, and course of both depression and the associated medical disorder.

The term "comorbidity," introduced by Feinstein (1970), refers to the presence of any additional coexisting ailment in a patient with a particular index disease. Failure to classify and analyze comorbid diseases can create misleading medical statistics and may suggest spurious associations during the planning and evaluation of treatment for patients. Comorbidity can alter the clinical course of patients with the same diagnosis by affecting the time of detection, prognostic anticipations, therapeutic selection, and posttherapeutic outcome of an index diagnosis (Kaplan & Feinstein, 1974).

This chapter reviews the studies of comorbidity between depressive disorders/symptoms and a broad range of somatic conditions. The specific disorders reviewed herein are limited to those for which there are sufficient number of studies from which to draw at least suggestive evidence regarding an association with depression. Methodological issues, risk factors, possible mechanisms, and implications of comorbidity are described. Finally, recommendations are made for future studies to address the gaps identified in this review.

METHODOLOGICAL ISSUES AND COMORBIDITY

Elucidation of evidence for comorbidity of affective disorders and physical illnesses is complicated by numerous methodological inconsistencies across studies. The most salient issues that must be considered are the definitions of both depression and the somatic disorder; the method of assessment of the two conditions; sources of the samples; comparability of the samples; inclusion of an appropriate control or comparison group; and incorporation of procedures to minimize bias, such as "blindness" of the interviewers with respect to the study hypotheses. Nevertheless, if the aggregate data across studies suggest associations despite methodological differences, preliminary conclusions regarding comorbidity may be drawn.

Definitions

Depression

In common usage, "depression" refers to a normal human emotion that can range from a period of sorrow in response to a disappointment or loss, to a severe and incapacitating disorder accompanied by delusional thoughts. In a clinical sense, "depression" can be said to occur when the subject passes a particular threshold on an underlying continuum, beyond which depressive symptoms are so severe or incapacitating that depression becomes a disorder. In the context of this review, it is particularly important to discriminate between short-lived, acute dysphoric reactions to a diagnosis and clinical depression. The present review is limited to studies that defined depressive disorders and symptoms according to standardized diagnostic criteria, including the eighth or ninth revisions of the *International Classification of Diseases* (ICD-8 or ICD-9; World Health Organization, 1970, 1977); the Research Diagnostic Criteria (RDC; Spitzer, Endicott, & Robins, 1978); or the third or revised third editions of the *Diagnostic and Statistical Manual of Mental Disorders* (DSM-III or DSM-III-R; American Psychiatric Association, 1980, 1987).

Somatic Disorders

In addition to the issues regarding measurement of depression, studies of comorbidity must include reliable and valid measures of somatic conditions as well. In general, ICD-8 or ICD-9 criteria were employed in most of the studies reviewed herein. However, evaluation of the consistency and validity of the definitions was precluded by the failure of most studies to provide information on diagnostic and assessment methods.

Classification of Depression and Comorbid Disorders

There are numerous approaches to the classification of concomitant psychiatric and medical conditions. The St. Louis school introduced the primary–secondary distinction, in which the disorders are classified according to their order of onset (Woodruff, Murphy, & Herjanic, 1967; Feighner et al., 1972). "Primary depression" refers to a depressive syndrome that occurs either in the absence of, or prior to the onset of, another medical illness, whereas "secondary depression" occurs after the onset of a physical illness. Both primary and secondary depression have been differentiated on the basis of a number of risk factors, including age, sex, family history, number of depressive symptoms, and biological parameters (for a review, see Kathol & Petty, 1981). However, despite its utility, there is little evidence for the validity of the primary–secondary distinction; it has been shown to lack sensitivity and specificity because of the lack of reliability of retrospective dating of the order of onset of the conditions in question, as well as the insidious onset of depression and many of the associated physical disorders. Neither DSM-III-R nor ICD-9 has a separate diagnostic category for depression concomitant with a medical illness. Although there is a category for an organic affective syndrome in DSM-III and DSM-III-R, the requirement of only the symptom of depression rather than the full symptomatic manifestation does not adequately cover the spectrum of disease in terms of severity, nor is it helpful in determining treatment regimens (Cassem, 1990). However, the introduction of the multiaxial system in the DSM-III was designed to provide a description of the individual beyond that of symptoms alone. Separate axes were incorporated for the classification of personality disorders, adaptive functioning, and psychosocial stressors; concomitant medical conditions were likewise recorded on a separate axis (i.e., Axis III for physical disorders and conditions).

A separate category for "mood disorder due to a general medical condition" has now been included in the DSM-IV criteria (American Psychiatric Association, 1994). Although this appears to be a progressive step, the validity of distinguishing depression as a true effect of a medical disorder requires sophisticated study designs that will not be available to most clinicians attempting to employ this category. It is particularly noteworthy that the term "organic" has been omitted, because of the implication that other disorders within the domain of the diagnostic system do not have an organic basis (Spitzer, Williams, First, & Kendler, 1989).

The ICD-10 has also included a category for organic disorders associated with depression and/or mania, entitled "other disorders due to brain damage and dysfunction and to physical disease" (World Health Organization, 1992). A recent review identifies several problems with this category (Lewis, 1994). The major criticism is based on the lack of reliability of the category, for which there are no standardized and universally accepted definitions and procedures. In addition, detection of concomitant medical illnesses may vary, according to the specialty; the local standards regarding the comprehensiveness of clinical evaluation; the level of diagnostic sophistication of the clinician; and the availability of laboratory technologies with which to detect comorbid conditions. Moreover, the temporal relationship between the onset of depression and the diagnosis of the index disease may be highly variable. In summary, although there is general agreement that depression arising from specific disorders should be so designated, limited knowledge regarding the nature of the interrelationships between disorders and depression, and the lack of widely applicable methods of measurement with acceptable levels of sensitivity and specificity, preclude the derivation of an appropriate classification at this time.

Characteristics of Depression in the Medically Ill

Several issues must be considered in evaluating the co-occurrence of depression (especially major depressive disorder) and a somatic disorder. First, the assessment of depression in the medically ill is often complicated by an overlap in the vegetative symptoms of the illness with those that are characteristic of depression, such as fatigue, anorexia, and disturbances of sleep, eating, and appetite. Second, pain and disability induced by the somatic illness may also be confounded with symptoms of depression. Third, depressed mood may be a direct psychological effect of a diagnosis of a life-threatening disorder, or one that will lead to major life changes, such as cancer or heart disease. Finally, depression may be an iatrogenic effect of the treatment of the index medical illness; cardiovascular disease is a leading example of such an illness. A substantial proportion of the antihypertensive drugs, such as alpha-methyl dopa, propranolol, and reserpine (which is no longer in general use) (Paykel, Fleminger, & Watson, 1982); the glucocorticoids (Pope & Katz, 1988);

and the antiparkinsonian agents, such as levodopa and amantadine, are associated with depressive reactions (Klerman, 1987). Therefore, assessment of current and past treatment for a somatic disorder is essential to determine whether a depressive disorder has been induced by the treatment of an index condition.

Depressive features that characterize patients with medical illness include age above 40; late onset of depression; and *absence* of the following: crying, a history of suicide attempts, diminished social interest, feelings of being punished, and a sense of failure (Clark & Gibbons, 1983; Winokur & Nasrallah, 1988). Other factors that have been reportedly associated with depression among the medically ill include premorbid personality; degree of pain and disability associated with the medical disorder; and impairment in cognitive function, which can impede accurate measurement of the depression as well (Silverstone, 1992).

Measures

Depression

In the majority of studies of depression and somatic illness, the chief measures of depression are self-report symptom checklists (Table 6.1). Although all of these instruments have been widely standardized in numerous settings, they generally lack adequate specificity to distinguish true cases of depression from those with high levels of symptoms not attributable to depressive states. Moreover, the time period of assessment of most of these symptom scales is limited to the current state. The symptom rating scales may be designed for self-administration or for administration by a trained rater.

Structured and semistructured diagnostic interviews—such as the Schedule for Affective Disorders and Schizophrenia (SADS; Endicott & Spitzer, 1978); the Structured Clinical Interview for DSM-III (SCID) and its successors for DSM-III-R and DSM-IV (Spitzer & Williams, 1985; Spitzer, Williams, Gibbon, & First, 1992; Spitzer, 1994); the Present State Examination (PSE; Wing, 1970); and the Schedule for Clinical Assessment in Neuropsychiatry (SCAN; Wing & Blair, 1990)—provide more valid classifications of the syndrome of depression and other psychiatric disorders, particularly when administered by a clinically experienced interviewer. These interviews assess the inclusion and exclusion criteria for each diagnostic cat-

TABLE 6.1. Self-Report Instruments Used in Depression Research

Abbreviation	Title	Author	Rater	Threshold for depression
BDI	Beck Depression Inventory	Beck, Ward, Mendelson, Mock, & Erbaugh (1961)	Self-rated	Range = 0–63; >21 = severely depressed; >13 = moderately depressed
CES-D	Center for Epidemiologic Studies Depression Scale	Radloff (1977)	Self-rated/ clinician	Range = 0–60; >16 = depressed
GHQ	General Health Questionnaire	Goldberg (1972)	Self-rated	No standard cutoff
HRSD	Hamilton Rating Scale for Depression	Hamilton (1960)	Clinician	Range = 0–50; >25 = severely depressed; 18–24 = moderately depressed
MMPI	Minnesota Multiphasic Personality Inventory	Hathaway & McKinley (1951)	Self-rated	Mean = 50; >2 *SD* from mean = depressed
SCL-90	Symptom Checklist 90	Derogatis (1977a, 1977b)	Self-rated	Factor score based on 13 items
SDS	Zung Self-Rating Depression Scale	Zung (1965)	Self-rated	Range = 25–100; >69 = severe depression; 60–69 = moderate depression

egory of standardized diagnostic systems; hence, diagnoses derived from such interviews are generally highly reliable and far more specific in excluding noncases of depressive disorders than the checklists described in Table 6.1. More structured diagnostic interviews designed for use by lay interviewers include the Diagnostic Interview Schedule (DIS; Robins, Helzer, Croughan, & Ratcliff, 1981), which assesses the diagnostic criteria for DSM-III disorders, and the Composite International Diagnostic Interview (CIDI; Wittchen et al., 1991), which elicits criteria simultaneously for DSM-III-R and ICD-10.

Medical Disorders

Structured assessments of somatic disorders have not been as well developed as those of psychiatric disorders. In general, medical disorders are diagnosed according to chronological course of clusters of symptoms, along with confirmatory laboratory studies. The classes of disorders reviewed herein include cancer, which is diagnosed by specific pathological findings; heart disease, which is assessed via measures of blood pressure, blood studies, electrocardiography, ultrasound, and angiography; and immunological/endocrine disorders, the diagno-

sis of which is based upon the results of a physical examination and serological studies. Ascertainment of the diagnostic criteria for the neurological diseases is more variable, depending on the degree to which classification is based upon specific clinical and laboratory findings. Whereas the diagnosis of stroke is based on confirmatory laboratory studies (including computed tomography [CT], magnetic resonance imaging [MRI], and angiography), migraine, Parkinson's disease, and multiple sclerosis are clinically based categories that rely principally on the clinical interview, as do their counterparts in psychiatry.

Study Designs and Samples

The two major study designs for investigating comorbidity are case–control studies and community surveys. Case–control studies compare the prevalence of a comorbid disorder in a series of subjects with an index condition to that in a series of controls who are similar to the cases on all relevant factors except the disease of interest. Studies that employ a case–control design may incorporate retrospective assessment of the comorbid condition, or may follow the cases and controls prospectively to assess the incidence of the comorbid disease of interest.

Few of the studies included in the present review have employed adequate control groups for assessing comorbidity between depression and somatic disorders. Instead, the studies have relied on the expected frequency of the comorbid disorder derived from previous community surveys. However, very large sample sizes are required to yield an excess of expected depression, in light of the high prevalence rate of depression in the general community. Moreover, investigation of comorbidity in samples selected from clinical settings, which are non-representative of persons with an index disease in the general population (i.e., "Berkson's paradox"; Berkson, 1946), may yield spurious associations because of the increased tendency for persons with two or more conditions to enter treatment. In order to avoid this bias, samples should be selected from a range of treatment settings and from the general community as well.

Studies of unselected samples of the general population provide an ideal mechanism with which to investigate comorbidity, because they avoid the bias associated with treated samples. However, the size of community surveys must be extremely large to yield sufficient power to detect associations for rare disorders, such as the majority of those considered in this chapter. In general, the epidemiological studies reviewed herein had insufficient statistical power to detect associations between depression and rare diseases. Indeed, the negative associations in the smaller samples of both the clinical and case–control studies may often have resulted from β-type errors, rather than from a true lack of association between depression and other diseases.

Another methodological limitation of the designs of the majority of studies of depression comorbidity was the failure to incorporate confounding risk factors that could explain the association between depression and the index disease. Moreover, the majority of studies failed to control for the interrelationships between the comorbid disorders themselves in multivariate analyses, thereby possibly yielding spurious associations.

Case–control studies have investigated comorbidity between depression and medical illness by examining the prevalence of medical illness in patients presenting with psychiatric illness and by examining the rates of depression in medically ill patients. Choice of an index sample should be based on the prevalence of a medical disorder in the general population. If the condition is rare, it is necessary to obtain a sample of persons with the rare condition and evaluate the prevalence of depression to obtain sufficient power to detect an association. Selection of the index sample should also be based upon the clinical sophistication required for diagnosis of the medical disorder, since many of the somatic disorders reviewed herein require expertise outside the realm of psychiatry.

In contrast, sampling subjects with a particular somatic disorder may restrict the range of demographic and other potentially confounding factors associated with the index disease. In order to control for such factors, a comparison group that is comparable to the index patients on all relevant confounding characteristics, with the exception of the somatic condition, must be employed. This may require substantially greater effort and expense than using a restricted sample of controls.

The vast majority of studies of comorbidity of depression and somatic disorders have been based on the application of symptom checklists among persons diagnosed with a particular somatic disorder. Few studies have employed control groups, or incorporated adequate measures of depression as a disorder.

COMORBIDITY OF DEPRESSION AND NONSPECIFIC MEDICAL DISORDERS

In general, the range of depression in medical outpatients is from 12% to 36%, and depression is present in approximately 33% of medical inpatients (Cavanaugh, 1983; Cavanaugh & Gibbons, 1983). Most studies of comorbidity of depression and medical disorders in general have been based on treated samples of persons with the index disorders of interest. One of the largest such studies examined the degree of well-being among a group of patients with chronic diseases (arthritis, renal diseases, cancer, diabetes, dermatological conditions), compared to that among a group of depressed patients (Cassileth & Strouse, 1984). These findings suggested that the emotional sequelae of a chronic illness are similar across groups and not unique to any particular disease. Cassileth and Strouse also examined the data by diagnostic subtypes (e.g., type of arthritis), and found no differences among the groups. They did not however, rule out severity of disease as a predictor of psychological function. Stewart and Winokur (1965) contrasted three groups of patients: (1) severely ill medical patients; (2) moderately ill medical patients; and (3) bipolar patients. They found that 26.7% of the severely ill medical patients had major depressive disorder that tended to be characterized by mood reactivity.

Two large-scale studies have investigated the association between depression and somatic disorders (Wells, Golding, & Burnam, 1988; Moldin & Rice, 1993). The former study employed data from a large population-based study (the Epidemiologic Catchment Area study) in the United States to compare the prevalence of depression among 841 subjects with chronic medical conditions with that among 1,711 subjects with no medical disorder. The results revealed that there was only a slight difference between the prevalence in the medically ill community subjects (i.e., 42.4%) and that in the community (i.e., 33%). The other major study of the association between major depressive disorder and a variety of medical disorders in both treated and untreated samples of depressives was that of Moldin and Rice (1993). The only conditions associated with depression in both the treated and untreated depressives were stomach ulcer and migraine. Diabetes was also associated with major depression, but only among those with a history of treatment for depression. However, the power of the analyses of cardiovascular disorder and immunological disorders was limited by the low base rates of these conditions in their sample.

SUMMARY OF MAJOR AREAS OF CO-OCCURRENCE OF MEDICAL AND PSYCHIATRIC DISORDERS

In the following sections, we review studies of the association between depression and several types of disorders within specific specialty areas of medicine. This chapter focuses on those medical conditions that have been associated with depression in previous studies. The review is limited to those conditions for which there were at least seven studies, in order to employ aggregate data to draw conclusions regarding this association. The major classes of disease investigated here include cancer; cardiovascular disorders; neurological disorders; endocrine disorders; and immunological diseases.

Cancer

Prevalence

The notion that cancer may be perceived as a psychosomatic illness is not new. As early as 1893, Herbert Snow reported on the comorbidity of the "depressive character" and malignancies of the breast and uterus. Although there have been numerous investigations of the "cancer-prone personality," there is little evidence thus far to substantiate this claim. However, there is evidence to suggest that depressive disorders are strongly associated with cancer (Table 6.2). Indeed, depressive disorders are the most prevalent psychiatric disorder in cancer patients, ranging from 5% to 85% (compared to population-based norms of 2–4%). The substantial variability in rates is largely attributable to methodological problems, including varied diagnostic criteria, utilization of symptom checklists that lack specificity, disparate cancer types with various degrees of severity, and lack of appropriate control groups. Only 1 of the 21 studies reported in the literature collected data prospectively and included a patient control group (Hinton, 1963). Otherwise, all of the previous studies collected data retrospectively, and if they included control groups, these were often other hospitalized patient groups or psychiatric controls. The majority of the studies included hospitalized patients with cancers of various types, stages, and degree of severity, as compared with 17.4% of the studies utilizing outpatients, who were ambulatory and usually less severely ill. The most common symptom checklists employed were the MMPI, the BDI, and the HRSD. Of all of the reported studies, perhaps only two are noteworthy. Bukberg, Penman, and Holland (1984) employed a structured diagnostic interview and used specific diagnostic criteria. The rates of depression were highest in patients with severe, advanced cancer (77%), compared to 23% in ambulatory patients. Derogatis et al. (1983), who examined a randomly selected population of inpatients, found the prevalence rate of depressive disorders to be 24%, and that of adjustment disorder to be 32%.

A number of risk factors have been identified that may predispose cancer patients to develop depression. These have been reviewed by the Depression Guideline Panel (1993) and include a positive family history of depressive disorders, social isolation, pessimistic outlook, socioeconomic pressures, recent losses, alcohol or other

TABLE 6.2. Prevalence of Depressive Disorders/Symptoms in Cancer

Author(s)	n	Basis for depression diagnosis	Source of patients	Type of cancer	Severity of cancer	Results
Hinton (1963)	102	Interview	Hospital	Mixed	Severe	17% depressive disorders (45% mild/moderate depression)
Koenig, Levin, & Brennan (1967)	36	MMPI	Hospital	Bowel	Advanced	25% depressive symptoms
Peck (1972)	50	Interview	Outpatient	Mixed	Mixed	2% reactive depression
Craig (1974)	30	SCL-90	Hospital	Mixed	Mixed	50% depressive disorders
Greer & Morris (1975)	160	Interview	Hospital	Breast	Early	35% depressive disorder
Plumb (1977)	97	BDI	Hospital	Mixed	Advanced	23% depressive disorder
Levine, Silberfarb, & Lipowski (1978)	100	Interview	Hospital	Mixed	Mixed	56% depressive disorder
Massie & Mastrovito (1979)	334	Interview	Hospital	—	—	25% depressive disorder
Plumb & Holland (1981)	80	CAPPS[a]	Hospital	Mixed	Advanced	45% depressive disorders (78% mild depression)
Fava, Pilowsky, Pierfederici, Bernardi, & Pathak (1982)	325	CES-D	Hospital	Mixed	Mixed	34% depressive disorders
Cain et al (1983)	60	HRSD	Hospital	Gynecological	Mixed	37% depressive disorders
Derogatis et al. (1983)	215	DSM-III	Hospital/ outpatient	Mixed	Mixed	6% major depression; 18% depressive disorders; 32% adjustment disorder
Bukberg, Penman, & Holland (1984)	62	DSM-III	Hospital	Mixed	Mixed	42% major depression (56% depressive disorders)
Hopwood & Maguire (1984)	26	Interview	Hospital	—	—	35% depressive disorder
Lansky et al. (1985)	505	HRSD	Outpatient	Mixed	Mixed	5.3% major depression
Holland & Tross (1986)	200	DSM-III	Hospital	Gastric vs. pancreatic	Advanced	Pancreatic > gastric
Joffe & Denicott (1986)	21	DSM-III	Hospital	Gastric vs. pancreatic	Mixed	33.3% pancreatic > 0 % gastric
Evans et al. (1986)		DSM-III	Hospital	Gynecological	Mixed	23% major depression; 24% adjustment disorder
Pedicini, Veltno, & Vincenti (1987)	20	MMPI	Outpatient	Mixed	Ambulatory	85% depressive symptoms
Hardman, Maguire, & Crowther (1989)	126	Interview	Hospital	—	—	23% depressive disorder
Kathol & Williams (1990)	808	DSM-III, DSM-III-R	Hospital	Mixed	Severe	38.2% major depression (DSM-III); 29.6% major depression (DSM-III-R)

[a]CAPPS, Current and Last Psychopathology Scales.

153

substance abuse, previous suicide attempts, and poorly controlled pain.

Incidence

An important goal of prospective studies is to establish the temporal relationship between disease and their putative risk factors. A primary hypothesis in prospective studies of the relationship between cancer and depressive illness is that depression is a risk factor in the development of cancer. A review of these studies is presented in Table 6.3. In a previous review of the literature, Noyes and Kathol (1986) noted that previous studies were flawed because they often began after the onset of the malignant disease. However, most of the studies presented in Table 6.3 revealed that depression began before the onset of disease. Interestingly, there is little evidence to suggest that depression is a risk factor for cancer. Of the nine prospective studies, only Shekelle and Ostfeld (1981) reported positive findings. They followed a total of 2,000 subjects over 17 years and found that the development of cancer was associated with elevated MMPI depression scores at baseline. Depression was a significant predictor of cancer mortality even after adjustment for age, smoking status, alcohol use, socioeconomic status, and family history.

Methodological Challenges

A number of methodological issues are important in determining whether or not a true association exists between depression and cancer. First, clinicians and researchers need to be aware of the significant degree of symptom overlap between the two conditions. For example, breast cancer has been shown to lead to hyperparathyroidism, which in turn is related to hypercalcemia (Gordon, 1974), and both have been linked to depression. Second, the severity of disease (in terms of progression and prognosis) may be related to the risk for development of depression. Massie and Holland (1990) reported that cancers in the advanced stages, with central nervous system (CNS) involvement, are associated with an increased risk for severe depression. Therefore, it is essential that studies include a combination of inpatients and outpatients in order to control for severity (the prevalence of depression is lower in outpatient studies). Third, persons who have a history of depression before the onset of cancer may be at increased risk for the development of depression after being diagnosed. Hence, it is important to be aware of any premorbid psychiatric characteristics. Fourth, the chronic pain so often experienced in severe cancer may be associated with the development of depression (Ahles & Ruckdeschel, 1984). An appropriate combination of medications may often alleviate both conditions. Fifth, depression may be a response to treatment. A number of pharmacological and radiological agents have produced depressive symptoms in cancer patients (for a review, see Lesko & Holland, 1988). In more extreme cases, pharmacological treatment has led to the development of organic affective disorder (Maguire & Brook, 1980; Cooper & Russell, 1979; Siverfarb, 1988; Peterson & Popkin, 1980). Disfigurement as the result of surgical treatments (e.g., mastectomy, laryngec-

TABLE 6.3. Prospective Studies of the Association between Depressive Symptoms and Cancer

Author(s)	n	Basis for depression diagnosis	Follow-up (years)	Results (relative risks)
Watson & Schuld (1977)	40	MMPI	4–7	n.s.
Dattore & Coyne (1980)	75	MMPI/interview	3–4.5	Depression > cancer
Shekelle & Ostfeld (1981)	2,020	MMPI	17	2.3
Weissman et al. (1986)	515	DIS	6	n.s.
Persky, Kempthorne-Rawson, & Shekelle (1987)	2,020	MMPI	20	2.3
Kaplan & Reynolds (1988)	6,801	—	17	0.83–1.19
Hahn & Petitti (1988)	8,932	MMPI	11–14	1.4
Zonderman & McCrae (1989)	2,586	CES-D	10	n.s.
Linkins & Comstock (1990)	2,264	CES-D	12	n.s. (except as related to smoking)

tomy, maxillofacial surgery, hair loss) has also been associated with the development of depression. Finally, the use of symptom inventories should be discouraged in the diagnosis of depression in cancer patients, because of a high false-positive rate elicited by such checklists.

Putative Causal Associations

Several possible causal relationships have been advanced to explain the association between cancer and depression (Whitlock, 1979). First, tumors that originate in the CNS—for example, temporal lobe tumors—are known to cause depressive symptoms (Brown, 1982). Depression often appears as an early manifestation of a frontal lobe tumor (Gelasko & Thal, 1988), a left fronto-temporal tumor, or a right parieto-occipital tumor (Lohr, 1987). Second, tumors that originate in the periphery may metastasize to the CNS, or may have a paraneoplastic effect and produce depressive symptoms. Perhaps the best-understood paraneoplastic syndrome is pancreatic cancer, where depression is often the first presenting symptom (Yaskin, 1931; Rickles, 1945). Fras and Pearson (1967) reported that 50% of their pancreatic cancer patients presented with signs of psychiatric illness. Third, there may be a subclass of persons genetically predisposed to the development of both disorders. Fourth, certain types of cancer may induce biochemical changes that cause depressive symptoms. For example, tumors that increase plasma cortisol levels are associated with depression. In addition, paraneoplastic syndromes may affect the CNS directly and cause depression, possibly through mechanisms that affect peptide secretion (e.g., methionine enkephalin) (Pullan, 1980) or immune dysfunction (Corsellis, 1969). Fifth, depression may occur as the result of a compromised immune system. There is some compelling evidence for a relationship between stress, depression and the immune system. For example, stress and depression have similar hormonal effects (Selye, 1956; Yuwiler, 1976) and immunological effects (Amkraut & Solomon, 1975). Stress has been shown to lead to a release of hormones, which increases the levels of corticosteroids and produces immune suppression (Linkins & Comstock, 1990). Sixth, depression may be the result of treatment of cancer. Cycloserine is an anticancer agent that is known to produce symptoms of depression. Although the role of biogenic amines in the etiology of depression remains unclear, these same compounds have been associated with cancer of the pancreas (Jacobson & Ottosson, 1971).

Treatment of Depression and Cancer

A number of pharmacological agents have been proven to be efficacious in the treatment of cancer patients with concommitant depressive disorders. However, there have been relatively few well-designed placebo-controlled studies. In a random placebo-controlled clinical trial of mianserin, 73 depressed women with cancer showed a superior response to the drug when compared with controls matched on tumor location, stage, and duration of depression (Costa, Mosos, & Toma, 1985). The usual first-line agents for the treatment of depression (e.g., tricyclics) should only be recommended when a cancer patient does not have cardiac complications. Otherwise, monoamine oxidase inhibitors (MAOIs), fluoxetine, trazodone, and buproprion, among others, should be considered. In very severe cases, electroconvulsive therapy (ECT) may be recommended.

Cardiovascular Disease

Myocardial Infarction

Prevalence. Myocardial infarction (MI) is the end result of blockage of the coronary arterial flow, leading to death of the cardiac muscle and necrosis. MI affects as many as 500,000 patients annually (Ross, 1973), many of whom experience significant psychological and emotional distress during hospitalization and for months afterwards.

The psychosocial consequences of coronary artery disease, particularly MI, have been widely recognized and can be as debilitating as the illness itself. Generally, the patient feels heightened anxiety the first few days after the MI, followed shortly by depressed mood. Although anxiety may be predominant, a review of the literature suggests that depression may be a common manifestation (Table 6.4). Of the 11 studies reported in the literature, only 1 utilized standardized diagnostic criteria for depression; this study found the overall rate of affective disorders to be 45%, and the specific rate of major depressive disorder to be 18%, when assessed at 1 week post-MI (Schleifer et al., 1989). Symptom checklists revealed rates of depression ranging from 15% to 34%. Interestingly, the same rate of major depressive disorder was

TABLE 6.4. Prevalence of Depressive Disorders/Symptoms in Myocardial Infarction

Author	n	Basis for depression diagnosis	Source of patients	Controls	Results
Wynn (1967)	400	Clinical interview	Inpatient	None	40% depression
Bruhn, Chandler, & Wolf (1969); Bruhn & Wolf (1971)	30	MMPI	Inpatient	Normal	n.s.
Hellerstein & Friedman (1970)	48	MMPI	—	Coronary-prone	Elevated scores on depression, hysteria, hypochondriasis
Cay, Vetter, Philip, & Dugard (1972)	131	Clinical interview	Inpatient	None	42% depression
Kavanagh, Shepherd, & Tuck (1975)	101	MMPI	—	None	34% depressive symptoms
Cassem & Hackett (1977)	445	Clinical interview	Inpatient	None	9.9% depression
M. J. Stern, Pascale, & Ackerman (1977)	68	SDS	Inpatient	None	22% depressive symptoms
Lloyd & Cawley (1982)	100	SPI[a]	Inpatient	None	35% depressive symptoms
Schleifer et al. (1989)	283	SADS/HRSD	Inpatient	None	45% depression; 18% major depressive disorder
Silverstone (1990)	211	MADRS[b]	Inpatient	None	37% depressive symptoms
Ladwig, Roll, Breithardt, Budde, & Borggrefe (1994)	552	SDS	Inpatient	None	37% moderate/severe depressive symptoms

[a]Standardized Psychiatric Interview.

[b]Montgomery and Asberg Depression Rating Scale.

found (using the RDC) in a sample of patients with coronary artery disease who had never had an MI and who were candidates for cardiac catheterization surgery (Carney et al., 1987). In further support of depression's commonly preceding MI is Lloyd and Cawley's (1982) finding that 16% of their sample of inpatients had been diagnosed with depression before their MI. This suggests that depression may precede the development of MI; however, in general, the rates of major depression are not convincingly higher in subjects at risk for MI than are population base rates of depression. Bruhn and colleagues (Bruhn, Chandler, & Wolf, 1969; Bruhn & Wolf, 1971) followed a cohort of MI patients for 9 years and found that mortality as the result of MI was significantly related to elevated depression scores, compared to those of MI survivors; this finding implicates more than one mechanism in the pathogenesis of MI and depression.

Incidence. There have been no incidence studies on the association between depression

and MI. However, in a 15-year follow-up of the Stirling County study, Murphy, Monson, Olivier, and Sobol (1987) found that presence of depression was associated with increased mortality from cardiovascular disease by at least twofold, particularly in men (e.g., the standardized mortality ratio was 2.1).

Methodological Challenges. Unlike other disorders discussed in this review, MI is a disorder generally characterized by an acute onset and extreme pain; it is thereby subject to its own unique set of limitations. Anxiety, denial, and depression are almost universal in people who unexpectedly experience a life-threatening situation. The sudden pain and fear of death associated with MI precipitate a feeling of extreme insecurity, especially given the possibility of a recurrence.

Several studies have reported rates of depression at varying intervals post-MI. These variable follow-up lengths have led to a great deal of confusion regarding the actual rates of major depressive disorder. In general, these studies tend to support a reduction in rates of depression over time (M. J. Stern, Pascale, & Ackerman, 1977; Bruhn et al,, 1969; Bruhn & Wolf, 1971). For example, M. J. Stern et al. (1977) reported rates of 22% immediately post-MI, 18% at 3 months, and 16% at 1 year. Further evidence for the transient nature of depressive symptoms has been reported by Goldberg and Blackwell (1970), who found that two-thirds of their patients initially had mild depressive symptoms that resolved within 6 months, and Tennant and Bebbington (1981), who found that such symptoms in 50% of their patients remitted within 1 month post-MI. Only one study suggested that depression was mild and did not require treatment (Lloyd & Cawley, 1983).

Putative Causal Mechanisms. Several risk factors have been identified that may be associated with an increased risk of developing depression following an MI, including previous psychiatric history, concomitant medical disorder, and increased stressful life events (Carney et al., 1987; Schleifer et al., 1989).

One possible mechanism by which an MI may be associated with depressive symptoms is that of altered brain metabolism, resulting from the abrupt reduction of cardiac output and the associated drop in blood pressure and cerebral perfusion. Cerebral thrombosis in small arteries may also cause minute infarcts (possibly undetected by the patient or physician) in the basal ganglia, thalamus, and other regions that have been implicated in the pathogenesis of depression. If the internal carotid artery is blocked and circulation to the frontal lobe falls, depressive symptoms may predominate, with generalized "slowing" and decreases in spontaneous activity (i.e., abulia).

Treatment of Depression and Myocardial Infarction. Because of the risk of serious cardiac anomalies associated with tricyclic antidepressants, it may be preferable to employ other classes of drugs in treating persons with MI, such as the serotonin reuptake inhibitors (e.g., buproprion) or the MAOIs (Glassman & Johnson, 1983; Dalack, Roose, & Glassman, 1991; Ellison, Milofsky, & Ely, 1990). These agents may be used to treat depression secondary to some of the drugs used to prevent reinfarction (e.g., beta-blockers).

Hypertension

Prevalence. Hypertension is generally a chronic condition characterized by a persistent high arterial blood pressure, with the usual thresholds of 140–150 mm Hg systolic pressure and 90-100 mm Hg diastolic pressure. Hypertension may be a symptom of an underlying disorder or may stand on its own. It is commonly associated with renal failure, visual problems, and heart disease. Epidemiological studies reveal that hypertension afflicts 10–15% of the population. The risk increases with age and is greater in blacks and males. Personality traits, such as "Type A" behavior, are often recognized as risk factors (Drummond, 1982). As early as 1898, an association was observed between depression and hypertension (Craig, 1898). Interestingly, Craig reported that hypertension increased during episodes of depression and returned to baseline with remission—a finding observed in several subsequent studies (Bruce & Alexander, 1901; Alexander, 1902; Guirdham, 1950; Altschule, 1953).

The association between emotional status and hypertension is poorly understood. Although it is well established that a rise in blood pressure is a physiological response to acute emotional distress, it is undetermined whether prolonged emotional disturbances can lead to an irreversible increase in blood pressure. Numerous studies have examined this relationship—in particular, how anger inhibition, anxiety, stress, and personality traits affect blood pressure changes (Wheatley, Balter, & Levine, 1975; Harburg et al., 1973; Cochrane, 1973; Davies, 1971; Robinson & Wood, 1968). Depression, however, has not been a major focus except as a potential side effect of antihypertensive drug therapy. Most of the studies reviewed have examined depression only within the context of personality traits such as "neuroses," or in conjunction with anxiety and stressful situations.

Several studies have examined the association between depression and hypertension, and have reported the range of depressive symptoms/disorders to vary from 15% to 62% (Table 6.5). Only one study utilized standardized diagnostic criteria for depression (DSM-III). Unfortunately, the high rates of depression observed by Rabkin, Charles, and Kass (1983) may have been attributable to the use of psychiatric outpatients, whose blood pressure levels were obtained nonsystematically through chart review. Furthermore, although they presented the rates

TABLE 6.5. Prevalence of Depressive Disorders/Symptoms in Hypertension

Author(s)	n	Source of patients	Basis for depression diagnosis	Controls	Rate of depression	Significance
Bulpitt & Dollery (1973)	475	Outpatient	Middlesex Hospital Questionnaire	General-practice patients	37% depressive symptoms	$p < .05$
Bant (1974)	75	Clinic	British Hospital Progressive Test	Chronic chest patients	33% depressive symptoms	n.s.
Wheatley, Balter, & Levine (1975)	174	Outpatient	SCL-90	Other medical patients	36% depressive symptoms	n.s.
Mann (1977)	55	Clinic	SPI[a]	Normotensive family members	18% dysthymia	n.s.
Friedman & Bennett (1977)	183	Outpatient	SDS	Chronic medical patients	No elevation in depression	n.s.
Wood & Elias (1979)	27	Clinic	SDS	Normals	—	$p < .05$
Monk (1980)	488	Community	GWB[b]	Normotensive	—	n.s.
Goldberg, Comstock, & Graves (1980)	190	Community	CES-D	None	15% depressive symptoms	n.s.
Rabkin, Charles, & Kass (1983)	66	Psychiatric outpatient	Interview/DSM-III	Medical patients/normals	62% affective disorder; 36% major depressive disorder	—
Boutelle, Epstein, & Ruddy (1987)	60	Clinic	Anger/Fear/ Depression Scale	Relatives	—	n.s.
Goldstein et al. (1990)	690	Inpatient	SDS	None	23% depressive symptoms	—
Prisant et al. (1991)	466	Inpatient	SDS	None	35% depressive symptoms	—

[a]Standardized Psychiatric Interview.
[b]General Well-Being Questionnaire.

158

of depression in both their normotensives who were medically ill and their normotensives who were not medically ill, they did not provide any statistical evidence to discriminate between these groups. Thus it is not clear whether the hypertensives could be distinguished from the chronic medically ill.

Several studies examined depressive symptoms in patients with hypertension. Wood and Elias (1979), using the Zung SDS, found significantly increased levels of somatic symptoms in a hypertensive compared to a normotensive sample. Moreover, these hypertensive patients were essentially free of severe hypertension-related pathology (e.g., visual problems, kidney disease, cardiovascular disease); this suggested that depressive symptoms were common in a relatively homogeneous group of hypertensive patients. In a community sample where depression was assessed before the onset of hypertension, no association was found between the two conditions (Goldberg, Constock, & Graves, 1980).

Incidence.   No incidence studies have been reported examining the association between hypertension and depression.

Methodological Challenges.   Hypertension is both a cause and a symptom of disease. For example, in less than 10% of hypertension cases, it is a symptom of chronic kidney disease or (more rarely) of an adrenal disorder. Under other circumstances hypertension may precipitate more serious illnesses, such as MI, stroke, or ophthalmological disease. In this sense, it acts as a potential confounder of the association between disease and exposure. Many of the studies described in Table 6.5 that did not report an association between depression and hypertension suffered from this methodological flaw. This lack of association is augmented by the fact that hypertension is generally found in elderly individuals who have a myriad of other physical and emotional problems. For example, Friedman and Bennett (1977), using a sample of elderly patients, found that there was no association between depression and high blood pressure; the negative finding was largely explained by the high rates of chronic illness in this sample. Similarly, Wheatley et al. (1975) failed to find an association, because their normotensive subjects were not free from other concomitant medical problems.

The lack of consistent results described in Table 6.5 may partly be explained by varying measures of high blood pressure and the cutoff criterion for hypertension. For example, some studies used only systolic pressure, some used only diastolic, and others used a ratio between the two measures. An interesting but not widely accepted notion, posited by Wheatley et al. (1975), is that there may be a functional relationship between psychopathology and high systolic blood pressure, whereas the association between high blood pressure and diastolic pressure may be organic. Systolic blood pressure is reportedly affected by emotional factors, while the diastolic pressure tends to remain stable during times of stress. Further studies in which systematic criteria for hypertension are utilized are needed before any conclusions may be drawn regarding an association between psychopathology and hypertension.

Measurement of hypertension invokes a unique set of methodological problems in addition to those described above. There is considerable evidence to suggest that autonomic nervous system response patterns (including blood pressure) associated with emotional changes may be consistent within an individual; however, interindividual variation is enormous. Comparisons across subjects and certainly across studies may be problematic. Finally, the sampling of patients has often been problematic, because the subjects in the majority of studies were taking antihypertensive drugs, which often induce depression.

Putative Causal Mechanisms.   The association between hypertension and depression may be explained by a number of possible mechanisms. For example, the two disorders may share the same underlying factors; prolonged psychological stress may lead to increased blood pressure; knowledge of a chronic disease may lead to depression; the treatment regimen may lead to depression; or interactions may occur among any or all of these factors. None of these hypotheses has been examined systematically.

Several CNS mechanisms have been postulated. One general impression is that over time hypertension leads to changes in the CNS, particularly to functional changes of the hypothalamus and/or structural changes of the blood vessels leading to other cortical and subcortical areas involved in regulating emotional behaviors (Davies, 1971). Certain patterns of sensory stimuli provoke an increase in blood pressure. With prolonged or frequent elevation, the blood pressure fails to return to its original level, thus reaching hypertensive criteria for diagnosis and perhaps altering the structure of the arterial walls in these brain structures permanently. Heine (1969) examined 25 depressed patients and found a significant correlation between blood pressure level and both the duration and number of depressive episodes. A more specific association has been postulated with abnormal adrenergic activity, which has been implicated in both depression and hypertension (Portnoy & Engelman, 1969; Ghose & Turner, 1975).

Genetic factors have also been suggested as an important contribution to the association between hypertension and depression, particularly since a positive family history has been observed for both disorders independently. However, the role of familial factors has been examined in only one study: Heine (1969) compared the rates of depression and hypertension in the first-degree relatives of patients with depression with and without hypertension, and found no familial association.

Treatment of Depression and Hypertension. A very interesting relationship has been observed between drugs commonly used in the treatment of hypertension and of depression. A number of pharmacological agents specific for the treatment of hypertension have been shown to induce depression; conversely, some drugs specific for the treatment of depression have been shown to cause hypertension (Pottash, Black, & Gold, 1981; Paykel et al., 1982). For example, reserpine, propranolol, methyldopa, guanidinium compounds, and clonidine deplete the stores of noradrenaline and other amines, both cortically and at peripheral nerve endings theoretically producing depression. Daniels and Goodman (1983) reported that depressive syndromes occurred on average 5 months after their patients began antihypertensive treatment. It is generally recommended that patients who are at risk for depression (e.g., positive family history or prior depressive episodes) or have had a recent bereavement not be given these drugs. However, controlled trials have been unsuccessful in establishing the depressogenic properties of these drugs when compared with other treatments (Prichard & Johnston, 1968; Bulpitt & Dollery, 1973; Snaith & McCourie, 1974). The most conservative recommendation is that any antihypertensive agent should be monitored carefully for depression as a side effect.

In contrast, antidepressants such as those in the tricyclic category (Bryant, Reid, & Torosdag, 1963) have been shown to interfere with antihypertensive action by blocking the reuptake of adrenergic neurotransmitters. MAOIs such as pargyline, when used in the treatment of hypertension, have been shown to induce psychotic behaviors (McCurdy & Kane, 1964; Paykel, 1966; Sutnick, Weiss, Schindler, & Soloff, 1964). Finally, diuretics have been thought to produce psychiatric complications indirectly, through the creation of an electrolyte imbalance.

Neurological Disorders

Epilepsy

Prevalence. Epilepsy is a chronic, debilitating neurological condition affecting approximately 1% of the population. There have been several systematic investigations of the association between epilepsy and psychopathology, although they have largely focused on a subset of patients with temporal lobe epilepsy. Patients with temporal lobe epilepsy are characterized by psychotic symptoms, obsessionality, and mood swings, among other aberrant personality features—but, interestingly, not by depressive symptomatology (see review by Hermann & Whitman, 1984). The clinical association between epilepsy and depression was first noted by Hippocrates. Further evidence for an association has been based on survey studies (Pond & Bidwell,1960; Gunn, 1977), controlled studies using psychological tests, utilization of psychiatric services, and high suicide rates. Interestingly, the suicide rate in epilepsy is approximately 5% (Hawton & Marsack, 1980), compared to a population base rate of 1.4%. Betts and Pond (1976) reported that depression was the most salient clinical feature of epileptics presenting for psychiatric consultation.

The prevalence rate of depression in epilepsy ranges from 11% to 75% (Table 6.6). Despite the wide variation in methodology, the majority of studies support a high rate of depressive symptoms/disorders in patients with epilepsy. There is no evidence to suggest that depression is associated with either seizure type, severity, or duration of epilepsy. The only controlled investigation of community-based epileptics that used systematic diagnostic criteria for depression and epilepsy found the rate of depressive symptoms to be substantially higher in the epileptics than in a group of other chronically dis-

TABLE 6.6. Prevalence of Depressive Symptoms/Disorders in Epilepsy

Author(s)	n	Basis for depression diagnosis	Source of patients	Type of epilepsy	Controls	Results
Pond & Bidwell (1960)	150	Interview	Outpatient/inpatient	—	None	15% neurotic symptoms
Dominian (1963)	43	Interview	Inpatient	Mixed	None	44.2% depression
Meier & French (1965)	53	MMPI	Outpatient	TLE[a]	None	Elevated depression
Matthews & Klove (1968)	182	MMPI	Outpatient	Mixed	Non-neurological patients	Elevated depression
Mignone & Sadowsky (1970)	112	MMPI	Hospital	Mixed	None	Elevated depression
Currie & Henson (1971)	666	Interview	Outpatient	TLE	None	11% depression
Dalby (1971)	93	Interview	Inpatient	Mixed	None	19.4% depression
Betts (1974)	72	Interview	Inpatient	—	None	54.5% depression
Standage & Fenton (1975)	27	PSE	Outpatient	Mixed	Locomotor disorder patients	75% depressive symptoms
Rodin, Katz, & Lennox (1976)	78	MMPI	Outpatient	TLE	Other seizure patients	Elevated depression, paranoia
Roy (1979)	42	Interview/HDRS/GHQ	Inpatient/outpatient	Mixed	None	54.8% depressive symptoms
Trimble & Perez (1980)	281	PSE	Outpatient	—	None	Elevated depressive symptoms
Kogeorgos & Scott (1982)	66	GHQ/CCEI	Outpatient	Mixed	Neurological patients	45.5% depressive symptoms
Dikmen, Wilensky, Rainwater, & Hermann (1983)	165	MMPI	Outpatient	Mixed	None	Elevated depression
Mendez, Cummings, & Benson (1986)	175	DSM-III	Outpatient	Mixed	Nonepileptics	55% hopelessness (vs. in 30% controls)
Mendez et al. (1986)	20	DSM-III	Inpatient	Mixed	Depressed patients	67% major depressive disorder (vs. 21% in controls)
Robertson & Townsend (1987)	66	Interview/BDI/HDRS	Inpatient/outpatient	Mixed	None	42.4% depression
Edeh & Toone (1987)	88	Interview	Outpatient	Mixed	None	22% depressive neurosis
Victoroff & Engel (1990)	47	SCID-Epilepsy	—	Complex partial seizures	None	38% depression
Saccomani, Cordella, & Cirrincione (1991)	47	—	—	—	Locomotor disorder patients	74% depression (vs. 52% in controls)

[a]Temporal lobe epilepsy.

161

abled patients (Mendez, Cummings, & Benson, 1986). Furthermore, in a comparison of differences between a group of psychiatric inpatients with epilepsy and comorbid depression and a group of depressives without epilepsy, Mendez et al. found several factors that differentiated the two groups; the former were distinguished by a negative family history of depression, chronic dysthymia, lack of neurotic traits, and episodes of peri-ictal psychotic behavior. In the only other study to use standardized diagnostic criteria, Victoroff and Engel (1990) found that 38% of their patients with complex partial seizures had a history of interictal major depression. Interestingly, those with left-sided temporal lobe foci were more prone to depression.

Incidence.   There have been no incidence studies on the association between epilepsy and depression.

Methodological Challenges.   Depression in epilepsy may occur as either a peri-ictal or an interictal phenomenon. The postictal changes are transient mood changes, including depression, but are often short-lasting. Therefore, investigation of mood changes in epilepsy need to distinguish between these two states. The most salient criticism of studies on the association between depression and epilepsy are based on operational definitions of epilepsy. There is often heterogeneity with regard to electroencephalographic (EEG) confirmation of epileptiform abnormalities, which is not necessarily consistent with clinical impressions. Depression may also be a manifestation of treatment of epilepsy. For example, barbiturates have been shown to cause depression in epileptic adolescents (Ferrari, Barabas, & Matthews, 1983). In addition, some antidepressants have been shown to enhance epileptiform activity.

Putative Causal Associations.   There are a number of potential mechanisms for the pathogenesis of depression in epilepsy. First, although the evidence is limited, psychosocial factors (such as the stigma associated with having a seizure disorder) have been implicated in the development of depression. Second, the sedative effect of some antiepileptic medications may be mistaken for symptoms of depression. Third, other medical conditions may be the cause of symptomatic depression in epilepsy. Several pathophysiological mechanisms have been suggested by Mendez et al. (1986): focal

lesions within the limbic system; continuous subclinical EEG alterations that affect the limbic system; hypometabolism; or a combination of some or all of these factors.

The kindling model of epilepsy has been postulated as a mechanism by which depression may develop in epilepsy. In this model, repeated activation of limbic structures following repeated seizures leads to behavioral changes, including affective disorders, aggression, and psychosis. Adamec (1993) has extended this model to suggest that depression is an indirect effect of limbic system activation, based on an increased threshold to psychosocial stressors. Trimble (1991) has further hypothesized that the kindling process occurs within dopaminergic pathways, leading to dopaminergic "supersensitivity," which ultimately leads to psychopathology.

Although disturbances in several biochemical systems have been implicated in the pathogenesis of epilepsy and depression (i.e., noradrenaline, dopamine, gamma-aminobutyric acid, and folic acid), there have been no convincing studies of an association. For example, folic acid deficiencies have been noted in both disorders independently and in combination (for a review, see Robertson, 1989). Indeed, folic acid deficiency may be a consequence of antiepileptic medication.

Although imaging studies are sparse, one study found that patients with both epilepsy and depression had CT scan abnormalities than a nondepressed epileptic control group (Robertson & Townsend, 1987).

Treatment of Depression and Epilepsy.   The focus of treatment regimens in epilepsy is to minimize polytherapy. There is some evidence to suggest that several antiepileptic agents (e.g., carbamazepine, sodium valproate, clonazepam, lamotrigine) have psychotropic effects. However, it is not uncommon for these agents to fail in the management of depressed patients. Several studies have reported on the efficacy of tricyclics in the treatment of depression in epilepsy, although there have been few controlled clinical trials. Scott (1978) was one of the first to suggest tricyclics at low doses and ECT for severe depression that does not respond well to drug treatment. Ojemann and Trejo (1983) have advocated the use of doxepin, which, in addition to alleviating depression, was effective in reducing seizure frequency in a small sample of epileptics. Several years later, the same group (Ojemann, Baugh-

Bookman, & Dudley, 1987) conducted a retrospective case–control study of psychotropic medications prescribed to a heterogeneous seizure group with clinically diagnosed major depressive disorder ($n = 40$). In general, the epileptics responded well to a variety of psychotropic medications, regardless of the questionable epileptogenicity of this classification of drugs.

In contrast, based on a review of the literature, Trimble (1972) has questioned the use of all psychotropics with the exception of MAOIs. He argues that tricyclic antidepressants increase epileptogenic activity, contraindicating their use in an epileptic population. The only double-blind trial of a tricylic medication was with amitriptyline, which was found to be slightly more efficacious than placebo, with 6 of 13 patients improving after 12 weeks of therapy (Robertson & Trimble, 1985). Others report that imipramine, which is a first-line agent in the treatment of depression, has antiepileptic effects for some but not all seizure types (Fromm, Amores, & Thies, 1972; Fromm & Glass, 1978). Clomipramine has been suggested for absence seizures (Setiey & Courjon, 1978).

Medications that have been shown to be contraindicated include maprotiline, mianserin (Edwards, 1979, 1983; Blackwell, 1981), phenobarbitone, vigabatrin (which either can trigger seizures or can initiate or exacerbate a depressive episode), trazodone, chlorimipramine, buproprion, and drugs that lower the seizure threshold. Although the use of ECT seems counterintuitive, Betts (1981) reported that it is indicated in epileptic patients who are suicidal with severe depression. Carbamazepine may be the drug of choice in the treatment of comorbid depression and epilepsy, because of its simultaneous antiepileptic and mood-stabilizing properties. The serotonin reuptake inhibitors may also provide worthwhile results.

Stroke

Prevalence. Approximately half a million people each year in the United States suffer from the debilitating effects of thromboembolic or hemorrhagic stroke, with the outcome varying from substantial morbidity to high rates of mortality. Stroke is a cerebrovascular disorder characterized by physical and behavioral manifestations that include disfigurement, in the form of facial paralysis or hemiparesis; cognitive impairment, encompassing memory, attention, and problem-solving deficits; language problems, including dysarthria and aphasia; and emotional disorders, including depression and extreme lability of mood.

Kraepelin (1913/1921) was one of the first to note the association between depression and stroke. However, it was not until the early 1980s that systematic attempts to document the association were made. Studies by Robinson and colleagues (Robinson & Price, 1982; Robinson, Kubos, Starr, Rao, & Price, 1983; Robinson, Lipsey, Rao, & Price, 1986) demonstrated that although the onset of depression commonly occurs in the acute phase after stroke, it appears to be most prevalent between 3 months and 2 years after the initial brain insult, with the majority occurring within the first year. When data were collected cross-sectionally from time since stroke, 20% of patients were depressed in a 3- to 10-year period following stroke (Robinson & Price, 1982). Interestingly, a 10-year follow-up of Robinson et al.'s original sample (Morris, Robinson, Andrzejewski, Samuels, & Price, 1993) revealed that patients with poststroke depression were at much greater risk for mortality (3.4 times) than their nondepressed counterparts.

In the only community-based study, Wade, Legh-Smith, and Hewer (1987) found 30% of their stroke patients to be depressed, and 50% of these patients remained depressed at 1 year. Of the seven studies reported in the literature (Table 6.7), only one used systematic diagnostic criteria, and this study reported the rate of depression to be as high as 50% (Eastwood, Rifat, & Ruderman, 1989). Lipsey, Spencer, Ravins, and Robinson (1986) compared a group of patients with poststroke depression and a group of patients diagnosed with major depressive disorder, and found no differences in background characteristics or depressive symptom profiles. However, unlike the major depression group, the poststroke depression group did not have a positive family history of psychiatric disorder. In terms of functional impairment, the poststroke patients were as impaired as the patients with major depression.

Fedoroff et al. (1991) compared groups with poststroke depression, acute MI, and acute spinal injury on features of depression. The poststroke patients had more anxious depression, suggesting that the disorders may follow different etiological pathways.

Incidence. There have been no incidence studies on the association between stroke and depression.

TABLE 6.7. Prevalence of Depressive Disorders/Symptoms in Stroke

Author(s)	n	Basis for depression diagnosis	Source of patients	Controls	Results (baseline–2 weeks)	Results (follow-up)
Robinson & Price (1982)	103	GHQ	Clinic	None	30% depressed	68% (6 months still depressed)
Finklestein et al. (1982)	25	Interview	Inpatient	Hospital	48% depressed mood	—
Robinson, Kubos, Starr, Rao, & Price (1983)	103	PSE/HRSD/SDS	Inpatient	None	27% depressed	77% (6 months)
Wade, Legh-Smith, & Hewer (1987)	976	Wakefield[a]	Community	None	25–30% depressed	50% (1 year still depressed)
Ebrahim, Barer, & Nouri (1987)	149	GHQ	Inpatient	None	23% depressed	—
Sinyor, Jacques, & Kaloupek (1986)	35	SDS	Inpatient	None	32% depressed	—
Eastwood, Rifat, & Ruderman (1989)	87	SADS/HRSD/SDS	Inpatient	None	50% depressed	—

[a]Derived from SDS (Snaith, Ahmed, Mehta, & Hamilton, 1971).

Methodological Challenges. The diagnosis of thromboembolic stroke is based on evidence of arterial occlusion as shown by arteriography, or evidence of infarction as shown by CT scan or MRI. The pattern of behavior following stroke is typified by stages of denial and anxiety over the immediate event and depression later. It is hard to disentangle the contributions of physical disability and language problems to the development of depressive symptoms; however, many agree that these issues are secondary.

Putative Causal Mechanisms. Psychosocial factors have been implicated as causal factors in the development of depression following stroke. As noted above, stroke victims suffer substantial morbidity, including cognitive impairment, language impediments, disfigurement, low self-esteem, enforced dependency, and in many cases financial problems due to loss of working capacity. However, when stroke patients are compared with other patient groups, including orthopedic controls or controls with traumatic brain injuries who have similar degrees of disability, they tend to have significantly more depression; these findings minimize the role of psychogenic factors (Folstein, Maiberger, & McHugh, 1977; Robinson & Szetela, 1981).

The primary target organ for stroke is the brain. This offers the unique opportunity to investigate the association between psychopathology and identifiable structural lesions in the brain. Indeed, several investigators have independently reported laterality effects of depression following stroke (Gainotti, 1972; Lipsky et al., 1987; Robinson & Price, 1982; Robinson, Kubos, Starr, Rao, & Price, 1984): Significantly more depression is noted with left- versus right-hemispheric lesions. Furthermore, severity of depression is related to proximity of the lesion site to the anterior frontal lobes. Aphasia, a common sequela of stroke, is also associated with anterior left-sided lesions. What are not understood are the confounding effects of aphasia on the severity of depression. In contrast to the studies mentioned above, other studies have not found a laterality effect for depression (Folstein et al., 1977; Finklestein et al., 1982; Sinyor, Jacques, & Kaloupek, 1986; Ebrahim, Barer, & Neuri, 1987). Starkstein, Robinson, Berthier, and Price (1988) found that patients with infarcts disrupting the area of the middle cerebral artery had more severe depressive episodes, compared to those with brainstem/cerebellar infarcts. Thus it is not well established that there are interhemispheric differences between poststroke patients with and without depression. One explanation for these discrepant findings may be the different methodologies employed in measuring lesion sites. For example, CT scan results may not be as definitive as MRI, single photon emission computed tomography (SPECT), or positron emission tomography (PET) in detecting the extent of cerebral infarctions. In fact, only with PET or SPECT can diaschisis (areas of hypometabolism distal from the primary lesion) be detected.

Although in general poststroke patients with depression do not differ from those without depression in socioeconomic status, age, or sex, there is some evidence to suggest that the depressed group has more cognitive impairment. Starkstein, Robinson, and Price (1987) assert that the cognitive differences may be explained by neuroanatomical abnormalities in poststroke depression patients, who as a group have larger ventricles and more subcortical atrophy as measured by CT scan. Evidence in favor of the subcortical degeneration's preceding the onset of stroke is that the time from stroke to CT scan is probably not sufficient for such extensive degeneration to occur.

In general, the evidence is in favor of multiple causal pathways in the association between depression and stroke. For example, the finding that 80% of patients with left-sided basal ganglia lesions and 60% of patients with anterior frontal lobe lesions have depression following stroke suggests at least two different pathways (Starkstein et al., 1987). In addition, family history of depression may be important, at least in those poststroke depression patients with right-sided lesions (Starkstein & Robinson, 1989), suggesting a genetic predisposition for the disorder. Eastwood et al. (1989) compared groups of stroke patients with and without depression, and found that a history of previous psychiatric disorder and a family history of cerebrovascular accident were both important risk factors.

Lipsey et al. (1986) present arguments in favor of a "biogenic amine hypothesis," supported by findings from animal and human studies. This model predicts that poststroke depression results from brain injury in which depletions of biogenic amine neurotransmitters such as serotonin or noradrenaline occur; these are thought to affect pathways innervating cortical and subcortical structures.

Treatment of Depression and Stroke. The correct management of hypertension has been shown to be effective in delaying mortality and recurrence in younger stroke survivors. However, antihypertensive agents as well as anticoagulants or antiplatelet agents have been implicated in causing depression, so potential side effects should be considered in patients at risk for depression (Carter, 1970).

In general, depression has been largely ignored as a major sequela of stroke; subsequently, many patients have not received adequate treatment. Only a few treatment trials have been undertaken. Lipsey and Robinson (1984) examined the effects of nortriptyline in a double-blind placebo-controlled trial of patients with poststroke depression and found it to be highly efficacious, with the only reported side effects being hypotension and sedation. Other tricyclic antidepressants were examined by Finklestein et al. (1987), who found that although there were no overall differences between treated and untreated patients with poststroke depression, a subgroup of patients did respond well with minimal side effects. In more severe cases of depression, ECT has been demonstrated to be effective (Murray, Shea, & Conn, 1987).

Huntington's Disease

Prevalence. Huntington's disease (HD) is a chronic, progressive, severely debilitating disease of the nervous system, first described by Huntington in 1872; it is characterized by choreiform movements, dementia, and behavioral abnormalities (Shoulson, 1990). The prevalence rate in the general population is approximately 10 per 100,000. The characteristic neuropathological changes in HD are neuronal loss in the caudate and putamen (Bruyn, 1968), with atrophy appearing in the cerebral cortex, particularly in the frontal lobes (Hedreen, Peyser, Folstein, & Ross, 1991; Sotrel & Paskevich, 1991). The gene for HD is inherited as an autosomal dominant gene with 100% penetrance (Conneally, 1984). HD is one of the most interesting diseases in neuropsychiatry because of its unique combination of high heritability, psychopathology, and identifiable structural lesions of the CNS.

Depression is the most common psychiatric disorder observed in HD, although other mood disorders, particularly mania and paranoia, exist (for a review, see Folstein, 1989). The prevalence rates of depression range from 4% to 53% (Table 6.8). Of the 11 studies that have observed the association between HD and depression, only 2 are particularly noteworthy. Both found similar rates of depression, using DSM-III criteria as the diagnostic criteria for depression (Folstein, Abbott, Chase, Jensen, & Folstein, 1983a; Folstein & Chase, 1987; Mindham, Steele, Folstein, & Lucas, 1985). Overall, Folstein and Chase (1987) found that 38% of their HD patients had affective disorders (this included 10% with bipolar disorder), and also found the distribution among blacks and whites to be different (i.e., blacks had significantly less depression at 10%). Thus far, there has been only one controlled study comparing HD patients to Alzheimer's patients (Mindham et al., 1985). The findings revealed that the former may have much greater rates of depression, suggesting that dementia may not be the cause of the affective disorder. Suicide in HD patients is at least six times more prevalent than in the general population (for a review, see Morris, 1991). This has led many to argue that the depression is a result of the psychological struggle of having a serious life-threatening disease and the inability to cope with this knowledge. However, the frequency with which depression precedes the onset of the abnormal movements by which the diagnosis is made would tend to negate this hypothesis.

Incidence. There have been no incidence studies on the association between HD and depression. However, in a follow-up study of intellectual and mood impairment in a cohort of 48 patients over several 6-month intervals, Mayeux, Stern, Herman, Greenbaum, and Fahn (1986) found that duration of illness, motor impairment, and age at onset had little association with functional capacity.

Methodological Challenges. Predictive testing for HD became available in 1986, soon after the HD gene was localized on the short arm of chromosome 4 (Gusella et al., 1983; Wasmuth & Hewitt, 1988). A diagnosis of HD has a significant impact on the affected individuals and their relatives. It is not surprising that the knowledge of a fatal disease before the onset of symptoms may lead to feelings of sadness, hopelessness, and fear. Although depression may appear for the first time at any stage of the disease process, it becomes more difficult to diagnose in the later stages of the disease. In the later stages of

TABLE 6.8. Prevalence of Depressive Symptoms/Disorders in Huntington's Disease

Author(s)	n	Basis for depression diagnosis	Source of patients	Severity of illness	Controls	Results
Rosenbaum (1941)	46	Chart review	Hospital	—	None	28.3% depression
Heathfield (1967)	66	Interview	Outpatient	—	None	15.2% depression
Oliver (1970)	60	—	—	—	None	4% depression
Dewhurst, Oliver, & McKnight (1970)	102	Interview	Hospital/ outpatient	—	None	6.9% depression
Bolt (1970)	334	Chart review	Hospital	Mixed	None	25% depression
Caine & Shoulson (1983)	17	SADS	Hospital	Mixed	None	40% depression
Folstein, Abbott, Chase, Jensen, & Folstein (1983)	88	DIS	Inpatient	Mixed	None	32% major depressive disorder
Mindham, Steele, Folstein, & Lucas (1985)	27	DIS	Clinic	—	Alzheimer's patients	44% depression
Webb & Trzepacz (1987)	10	SADS/DSM-III	Outpatient	—	None	10% major depressive disorder
Folstein & Chase (1987)	186	DIS	Clinic	—	—	38% depression
Pflanz, Besson, Ebmeier, & Simpson (1991)	86	PSE	Clinic	Mixed	None	53% depression

HD, it is not uncommon for speech to be severely affected, with mutism occurring in some cases. If recognized, the depression may be treated and resolved with antidepressants.

Putative Causal Mechanisms. Not all patients with HD experience depression, and there is evidence suggesting that depression may arise through multiple causal pathways. Although some may believe that any affective disorder in HD is an adjustment reaction to the disease, there is very little evidence for this notion. First, affective disorders may precede the onset of HD by an average of 5 years (Minski & Guttmann, 1938; Folstein, Folstein, & McHugh, 1979), and by as much as 20 years (Folstein et al., 1983a). Second, approximately 10% of HD patients experience other mood disorders, including mania, hypomania, delusions, and hallucinations (Folstein & Chase, 1987). Third, Folstein and Chase (1987) have found that affective disorders are more common in HD patients with a later age of onset. Fourth, neuropathological evidence suggests that distinct pathways for mood regulation are affected in HD.

There is evidence to suggest that affective disorders in HD are the result of genetic vulnerability. Folstein, Franz, Jensen, Chase, and Folstein (1983b) examined HD probands with and without affective disorders. Of the HD probands with affective disorders, 20 of 23 of their relatives with HD also had affective disorders; of the HD probands without affective disorders, only 5 of 23 of their HD relatives also

had affective disorders. These findings need to be replicated in other samples of HD patients.

In addition to their finding that depression precedes the onset of HD, Folstein and Chase (1987) also reported that patients with HD and affective disorders have a later age of onset of the disease. However, DiMaio et al. (1993) measured a number of physical and mental symptoms reported at the onset of disease and found no age-specific onset symptoms. Peyser and Folstein (1990) have suggested that the early onset of affective disorders in HD may be related to neuropathological changes in the striatum. These findings had been earlier described by VonSattel and Ferrante (1985), who have suggested that neuronal loss in the caudate may lead to disruption of a number of pathways thought to be involved in mood regulation.

Imaging studies of the association between HD and affective disorders have provided evidence for metabolic dysregulation. Mayberg et al. (1992) used regional cerebral glucose metabolism and PET to examine HD patients with and without affective disorders; they found altered metabolism in the expected target areas in both groups (i.e., caudate, putamen, and cingulate), but selective hypometabolism in the prefrontal cortex of the HD–affective disorder group. It is interesting that this same pattern of neuropathological changes occurs in Parkinson's disease. Neuropathological evidence implicates degeneration of cerebral cortical neurons, more specifically in the prefrontal region, as being responsible for depressive symptomatology (Hedreen et al., 1991). Only one study has examined neurochemical abnormalities in patients with HD and affective disorders. Kurlan and Caine (1988) examined 5-hydroxyindoleacetic acid (5-HIAA) levels in depressed and nondepressed HD patients, and found no differences between the two groups.

Treatment of Depression and Huntington's Disease. There have been no controlled treatment trials of depression in HD, although in the experience of Folstein and Folstein (1983), tricyclic antidepressants such as nortriptyline are efficacious in the treatment of HD and affective disorders. They have also found that low doses of fluoxetine are beneficial when tricyclics fail. They advocate the use of ECT in severe, intractable cases of depression, and report no counterindications. The treatment of bipolar disorder, however, requires departure from the norm. Carbamazepine is the treatment of choice because lithium toxicity often caused by dehydration, has occurred in their experience.

Migraine

Prevalence. Substantial evidence now corroborates early anecdotal clinical descriptions regarding the co-occurrence of migraine and depression. Clinicians involved in the treatment of migraine have often described a set of characteristic features of migraineurs, including anxiety, depression, and social fears. Wolff (1937) was so convinced of this constellation of attributes that he is often credited as being the initiator of the concept of the "migraine personality." However, more careful inspection of his description reveals that the characteristics of "extreme physical fatigue, apathy, and anxious anticipation" are more akin to psychiatric symptoms than to personality traits. Earlier descriptions of these characteristics can also be found throughout the clinical literature. The most common features of these descriptions are depression characterized by anergia and anxiety disorders, particularly panic disorder and phobia. The contemporary equivalent of these features is the "atypical features" subtype of depression.

Spurious associations between migraine and other disorders could be an artifact of sampling, in which clinically ascertained samples comprise persons with increased rates of secondary disorders (as mentioned earlier in the chapter, this is known as "Berkson's paradox"); population stratification, in which an erroneous association may result from sampling a particular stratum of the population in which there is an increased risk in the base rates of both of the conditions; or overlap in the symptoms of the two conditions, which may induce structural correlations. In the present review of studies of the association between migraine and depression, these possible sources of error are considered.

Studies of the association between migraine and depression that employed standardized diagnostic criteria are summarized in Table 6.9. In clinical samples, associations between the two disorders are consistently found, regardless of the index disorder for which the subjects sought treatment. The results of studies of community-based samples also demonstrate a strong association between depression and migraine. There is remarkable similarity in the magnitude of the association between depression and migraine across the five studies. The odds ratios in the latter three studies were nearly identical, despite the variation in the subjects' characteristics, geographic site, and specific assessments of migraine and depression. These findings exclude sampling as a source of bias in the co-occurrence of depression and migraine reported in previous clinical samples. The relationship between migraine and anxiety disorders has also been investigated, because of the well-known association between depression and anxiety (Merikangas, Merikangas, & Angst, 1993). Anxiety disorders alone are also associated with migraine in both clinical and community studies (Garvey, Tollefson, & Shaffer, 1984; Linet & Stewart, 1984; Merikangas, Angst, & Isler, 1990). However, the simultaneous association of all of these disorders needs to be examined systematically.

Incidence. The course and order of onset of comorbid conditions with respect to migraine were investigated, using data from a prospective longitudinal cohort study of young adults in Zurich, Switzerland (Merikangas et al., 1990). The prospective design of the study enabled investigation of the course and order of onset of the conditions without the bias inherent in retrospective recall of such phenomena. The findings revealed that the onset of anxiety disorders tended to *precede* that of migraine in about 80% of the cases of migraine with comorbid anxiety–depression, and that the onset of depression followed that of migraine in three-quarters of the comorbid cases.

TABLE 6.9. Prevalence of Depressive Symptoms/Disorders in Migraine

Author(s)	n	Basis for depression diagnosis	Source of patients	Controls	Results
Kashiwagi & McClure (1972)	38	RDC	Clinic	None	40% major depressive disorder
Couch & Ziegler (1975)	236	SDS	Clinic	None	Elevated depression
Crisp, Kalucy, McGuinness, Ralph, & Harris (1977)	126	MHQ[a]	Community	None	Elevated depression
Paulin & Waal-Manning (1985)	1,139	BDI	Community	None	Elevated neuroticism
Morrison & Price (1989)	46	SCID	Clinic	None	52% affective syndrome
Merikangas, Angst, & Isler (1990)	61	DSM-III	Community	Nonmigraineurs	14.7% major depressive disorder; 6.6% dysthymia
Jarman et al. (1990)	40	SADS-L	Clinic	None	37% major depressive disorder
Breslau, Davis, & Andreski (1991)	128	DIS	Community	Nonmigraineurs	53.9% major depressive disorder

[a]Middlesex Hospital Questionnaire.

Retrospective data from a community survey in Detroit, Michigan produced strikingly similar findings (Breslau, Davis, & Andreski, 1991). Not only were the associations among migraine, anxiety, and depression of the same magnitude; the order of onset of the three conditions was also the same (anxiety in childhood and adolescence, followed by migraine and then depression).

Methodological Challenges. Epidemiological studies have shown that migraine is a highly prevalent condition in the general population. Lifetime prevalence estimates range from 4% to 19% for men and from 8% to 29% for women (Crisp, Kalucy, McGuinness, Ralph, & Harris, 1977; Waters & O'Connor, 1975; Linet & Stewart, 1984). The severity of migraine ranges from mild to nearly total disability (Selby & Lance, 1960). Migraine is more common among women and persons between the ages of 20 and 45 years, and the incidence decreases after the fourth decade of life (Crisp et al., 1977).

Although specific diagnostic criteria for migraine are controversial, usual definitions of migraine include the presence of cyclic headaches associated with a variety of gastrointestinal and neurological symptoms (Anonymous, 1962). The International Headache Society (Anonymous, 1988) has recently developed a set of diagnostic criteria for migraine that should facilitate international standardization of the diagnoses of headache syndromes.

However, most studies to date have been based on data from symptom checklists administered to clinical samples, thereby limiting the specificity of the association. Systematic diagnostic interviews with established reliability and validity have rarely been employed. Moreover, few studies have been controlled or conducted with epidemiological samples from the community, to address the potential bias of increased treatment seeking among persons with both disorders. Despite these limitations in their methods and design, most studies confirm the clinical observation regarding an association between anxiety disorders and migraine.

Putative Causal Mechanisms. There are two possible explanations for the relationship between migraine and depression–anxiety: (1) Migraine and depression–anxiety share common underlying pathological mechanisms; or (2) migraine and depression–anxiety are causally related (either migraine causes depression–anxiety, or vice versa). Evidence for these explanations may be derived from follow-up studies, which can demonstrate the course and precursors of the conditions; neurobiological studies and challenge paradigms, which can identify common underlying susceptibility and etiological factors; and family studies, which can investigate the coaggregation of the two conditions.

Patterns of cosegregation of migraine and depression were investigated in two family studies conducted by our research group. The results of both studies indicated that migraine and depression share a syndromic relationship, representing manifestation of the same disease, as opposed to their representing distinct diseases resulting from the same underlying etiological factors (Merikangas et al., 1990).

When taken together, the prospective epidemiological and family study designs comprise a powerful method to investigate the mechanisms for comorbidity, including the source of the association as well as the temporal relationship between the two conditions. The application of this combined study design approach in our research has revealed that migraine and anxiety–affective disorders are strongly associated in the general community and in families of probands with these disorders; that this association is strongest for depression with atypical features and for phobic anxiety syndromes; and that the onset of anxiety disorders generally *precedes* the onset of migraine, thereby suggesting that these conditions may be early manifestations of a syndrome characterized by concomitant expression of anxiety, affective disorders, and migraine over the lifetime course (Merikangas et al., 1990, 1993).

The most likely explanation for these findings is that the combination of these disorders comprises a subtype of either migraine or depression–anxiety in which symptoms of all of these disorders are manifested at some point during the longitudinal course. Because disturbances in the same neurochemical systems have been implicated in migraine, depression, and anxiety disorders, perturbation of a particular system or systems may produce symptoms of all three conditions, thereby producing one syndrome rather than three discrete entities. Support for this interpretation comes from a large-scale epidemiological study in the United States, in which persons with a history of migraine who no longer suffered from episodic attacks of headache continued to have significantly more depression than those without a history of migraine (Breslau et al., 1991).

Treatment of Depression–Anxiety and Migraine. These findings underscore the importance of systematic assessment of depression and anxiety in persons with migraine. If there is a subtype of migraine associated with anxiety and depression, it is critical to treat the entire syndrome rather than limiting the treatment goal to headache cessation. The use of prophylactic medications with lassitude, fatigue, or depression as a side effect should be avoided, if possible; if not, careful clinical evaluation of the above-cited manifestations of depression, including anergia, hypersomnia, and irritability, should be monitored.

Because antidepressants are often used in migraine prophylaxis, they may be the treatment of choice in patients with simultaneous depression–anxiety and migraine. The MAOIs have been shown to have superior efficacy to the tricyclics in the treatment of anergic depression with concomitant anxiety (Merikangas & Merikangas, in press). Given reports of their efficacy in several uncontrolled studies, they should also be considered in treating patients with severe migraine with the above-cited psychiatric features. However, there is a clear need for controlled trials of traditional antimigraine agents that stratify patients by the presence of depression–anxiety.

The association between migraine and depression–anxiety, particularly in light of the findings from prospective data, warrants further study in other research endeavors as well. Studies that employ psychophysiology and brain imaging may help to differentiate pure migraine from migraine associated with affective and anxiety disorders.

Multiple Sclerosis

Prevalence. Multiple sclerosis (MS) is a chronic, recurring CNS disorder of uncertain etiology. It is characterized by progressive physical and mental deterioration. Demyelinating plaques in the cortex and subcortical structures are the principal neuropathological features. Charcot (1877), an eminent French physician, was the first to report on the neurological and psychiatric sequelae of MS. However, it was not until 1922 that clinicians began to take notice of the affective symptoms of irritability and depression (Wechsler, 1922). Although there have been several studies since then, there has been little unanimity of opinion as to the prevalence or severity of depressive disorders in MS (Table 6.10). In addition to depressive symptoms, euphoria and eutonia are often reported as predominant symptoms.

Many of the studies performed prior to 1950 (not reviewed here) did not comment on the

TABLE 6.10. Prevalence of Depressive Symptoms/Disorders in Multiple Sclerosis

Author(s)	n	Basis for depression diagnosis	Source of patients	Severity of illness	Controls	Results
Sugar & Nadell (1943)	28	Interview	Hospital	Severe	None	36% depression
Canter (1951)	47	MMPI	Clinic	Mixed	None	Elevated depressive symptoms
Surridge (1969)	108	Interview	Clinic	Mixed	Muscular dystrophy patients	26.8% depression (n.s.)
Whitlock & Siskind (1980)	30	Interview/BDI	Clinic	Mixed	Chronic neurological patients	53.3% depressive disorder
Schiffer, Caine, Bamford, & Levy (1983)	30	SADS-L/BDI	Clinic	Mixed	Normal controls	37% depressive disorder
Dalos, Rabins, Brooks, & O'Donnell (1983)	64	GHQ	Clinic	Mixed	Spinal cord injury patients	90% emotional symptoms
Schiffer & Babigan (1984)	368	Interview	Clinic	Mixed	Epileptics/amyotrophic lateral sclerosis patients	62% depression; MS > controls
Rabins et al. (1986)	87	GHQ	Clinic	Mixed	Spinal cord injury patients	MS = controls
Minden, Orav, & Reich (1987)	50	SADS-L	Clinic	Mild/moderate	None	54% depressive disorder
Joffe, Lippert, Gray, Sawa, & Horvath (1987a)	100	SADS-L/HRSD	Clinic	Mixed	None	42% major depression
Columbo, Aramani, Ferruzza, & Zuliaini (1988)	88	CES-D	Clinic	—	None	Elevated depression
Krupp, Alvarez, LaRocca, & Scheinberg (1988)	32	CES-D	Clinic	Mixed	Normal controls	47% depressive disorder
Good, Clark, Oger, Paty, & Klonoff (1992)	84	BDI/MMPI	Clinic	Early, mild	Normal controls	Depression vs. normal controls: n.s.

form of psychiatric assessment, and it was usually unclear whether a psychiatric interview, a review of hospital notes, or some other form of measurement was employed. Unfortunately, it was in these early studies with unclear methodology that the highest rates were reported. With the increasing use of the MMPI in the 1950s, a number of studies flourished. However, in several of these studies the MS patients were similar in affect to neurological and/or psychiatric controls. For example, Ross and Reitan (1955) administered the MMPI to an MS group, a brain-damaged group, and a psychiatric control group, and found no differences among the three groups. Surridge (1969), in a large well-controlled study, found that there was no significant difference in the severity of depression between an MS group and a control group consisting of muscular dystrophy patients (26.8% vs. 13.9%). He further commented that there was evidence to suggest that the psychiatric sequelae of MS increase in intensity as the disease progresses. The muscular dystrophy group was chosen as a neurologically impaired group

whose degree of disability was similar to that of the MS group, thus ruling out depression of exogenous origin. However, it was euphoria and not depression that was a key feature in the MS patients.

In contrast, Whitlock and Siskind (1980), using the BDI, found that depression was the predominant affective disturbance when MS patients were compared with a control group matched on severity of neurological impairment. In one of the largest studies thus far, Schiffer and Babigan (1984) compared the prevalence rates of depression in 368 MS patients, 402 temporal lobe epileptics, and 124 patients with amyotrophic lateral sclerosis, and found that the MS patients had a higher rate of affective disorders involving depression (62%) than patients suffering from the other two neurological disorders (0–23%). One of the most compelling studies to date (Joffe, Lippert, Gray, Sawa, & Horvath, 1987b), using a semistructured diagnostic interview and DSM-III criteria, found 14% of MS patients in a current episode of major depressive disorder, 47% with lifetime histories of depression, and no association between depression and severity of disease.

Although there have not been any systematic investigations of risk factors for the development of both conditions, Rabins et al. (1986) have speculated on three possible factors. First, a positive family history of depression may be associated with an increased likelihood of having both conditions. Second, a past history of depression prior to the onset of MS may be associated with future episodes of depression. Finally, although there have been too few MRI studies done, Rabins et al. suggest that the extent of CNS involvement in MS may be associated with risk of depression.

It is interesting to note that MS is one of the only medical disorders that has been shown to be highly associated with mania or bipolar disorder (Schiffer, Wineman, & Weitkamp, 1986; Joffe, Lippert, Gray, Sawa, & Horvath, 1987a).

Incidence. Thus far, no prospective studies have attempted to define the temporal relationship between MS and depression.

Methodological Challenges. MS generally presents in one of three forms: (1) The onset is slow and insidious, and the disease follows a progressive course without remissions and only minor fluctuations; (2) the onset is slow and insidious, followed by a period of well-being for months or years before a relapse occurs; and (3) the onset is abrupt, and the illness progresses rapidly to the point of incapacitating the patient. Accurate early diagnosis of MS is often difficult because of the paroxysmal nature of the early presentation of the disease. Often, even as the disease becomes established (i.e., several relapsing–remitting episodes), differential diagnosis is notoriously difficult. The most common clinical and laboratory findings include optic neuritis, abnormal oligoclonal banding in cerebrospinal fluid (CSF), abnormal visual or brain stem evoked potentials, ventriculomegaly on CT scan, areas of demyelination on MRI, and patchy areas of reduced activity on SPECT. Difficulties in establishing a diagnosis are the results of poor sensitivity and specificity of the laboratory procedures, as well as varied diagnostic criteria. Adding further to the complexity of establishing a diagnosis is the fact that several other disorders present with symptoms similar to that of MS (e.g., Lyme disease or systemic lupus erythematosus). Within the psychiatric domain, Briquet's syndrome (Guze, Woodruff,

& Clayton, 1972; Purtell, Robins, & Cohen, 1951) is a disorder in which patients present with polysymptomatic complaints, consistent with those of MS.

Chronic fatigue is one of the most prevalent symptoms reported in patients with MS. However, the type of fatigue present in MS may be readily distinguished from that typically observed in major depressive disorder. For example, in MS fatigue often occurs late in the day and is alleviated by rest, whereas in major depression it is often worse in the morning and persists despite rest.

MS as a demyelinating disease can affect both the brain and spinal cord, leading to various degrees of physical, cognitive, and emotional disability. Demyelinating plaques that present in the cerebral cortex can directly affect emotional lability and cognition. For example, Surridge (1969) reported that a common symptom in MS (25.9%) was euphoria, which in turn was associated with cognitive impairment. In addition, MS patients often exhibit abnormal emotional expressions, such as inappropriate laughter and crying with no provocative stimulus. Furthermore, Rabins et al. (1986) found higher rates of emotional disorder in MS patients with brain involvement than in patients with spinal cord involvement only. Using the Kurtzke disability scale as an index of severity for MS, Rabins et al. found a relationship with the severity of depressive disorder, but not with degree of functional impairment. However, Minden, Orav, and Reich (1987) reported that severity of depression was unrelated to severity of MS, type of disability, duration, age, sex, or clinical status. Similarly, Joffe et al. (1987a) found no relationship between Kurtzke disability rating and depression. Thus, it is methodologically important to match patients according to severity of disease. In general, there have been no systematic studies of the association between depression and MS that have used a combination of sophisticated laboratory techniques and clear operational criteria for disease (including multiple sources of validation).

Putative Causal Associations. There are several possible explanations for an association between MS and depression. First, depression may be an early manifestation of MS caused by similar mechanisms (i.e., brain lesions) (Whitlock & Siskind, 1980). Second, MS may trigger depression in persons already predisposed to depression (i.e., those with a positive family history) (Rabins, 1989). Third, an unknown factor, such as altered immune function or infectious agents, may be common to both diseases (Joffe et al., 1987a).

There is sparse evidence to support any of the claims above. Evidence that depression is an early manifestation of MS requires a prospective longitudinal study design, examples of which have been sparse to date. Minden et al. (1987) and Joffe et al. (1987b) ruled out a heritability factor by examining the rates of depression in first-degree relatives of patients with MS, and finding that depression was not increased in the relatives of MS patients with versus without major depression.

Several retrospective studies have speculated on an association between stressful life events and the development of MS; however, the results are controversial. For example, McAlpine, Lumsden, and Acheson (1965) suggested that stress precipitates the first episode and subsequent exacerbations of the disease, whereas several other studies have not supported a relationship between stress and MS (Pratt, 1951; Rabins et al., 1986; Foley et al., 1992; Warren, Greenhill, & Warren, 1982).

An intriguing MRI study (Honer, Hurwitz, Li, Palmer, & Paty, 1987) compared six MS patients with depression to eight matched nonpsychiatric control subjects, and found that the depression group had more plaques within temporal lobe structures. This would tend to support the notion that depression is a secondary response to demyelinating plaques appearing in subcortical structures. This finding needs to be substantiated in a larger sample with more control groups.

Treatment of Depression and Multiple Sclerosis. There have been no controlled treatment studies of depression and MS. Indeed, steroids (e.g., baclofen), which are the first-line agents for treatment of MS, are known to cause depression (Pinto, Palikar, & Debono, 1972; Korsgaard, 1976). Two studies have found that tricyclic antidepressants (imipramine, amitriptyline, or nortriptyline) may be efficacious in the treatment of depression in patients with MS (Schiffer, 1987; Rudick, Goodkin, & Ransohoff, 1992). In a recent study, Foley et al. (1992) compared a group of chronic progressing MS patients treated with cyclosporine to a placebo control group. They used self-report scales to examine psychological distress and immune function, and found at a 2-year follow-up that stress was strongly associated with immune dysregulation.

Parkinson's Disease

Prevalence. Parkinson's disease (PD) is a progressive, disabling disease of the CNS, affecting approximately 1% of the elderly population. The pathological hallmarks of PD are degeneration of the substantia nigra and occurrence of Lewy bodies. The first recorded clinical descriptions of PD were provided by James Parkinson in 1817, who noted tremor, rigidity, bradykinesia, and postural instability as the predominant motor symptoms, and melancholia (but not dementia) as a cognitive symptom pervasive in this disease. Although differential diagnosis of PD is often straightforward, there are many pathways to the development of the disease. For example, secondary parkinsonism may be caused by drugs (neuroleptics or metoclopramide), infectious agents (as in Creutzfeldt–Jakob disease or postencephalitic syndrome), ingested toxins (e.g., carbon monoxide), metabolic dysfunction (as in Wilson's disease or hypoparathyroidism), brain abnormalities, or other neurodegenerative disorders (e.g., Alzheimer's disease, spinocerebellar–nigral degeneration, Shy–Drager syndrome). Diagnosis is often based on the presence of tremor during the clinical exam, and substantia nigra involvement is verified by imaging (CT, MRI, or PET).

The most common psychiatric disorder in PD is depression (Table 6.11). Although not studied as extensively, anxiety disorders occur with a high frequency in PD patients with depression (Schiffer, Kurlan, Rubin, & Boer, 1988). Other mood disturbances (e.g., mania, hypomania) are usually seen in PD when there is concomitant dementia. Cross-sectional studies of the association between PD and depression show rates of depression ranging from 25% to 90%, depending on the methodology employed. Other less extensive reviews of the literature have suggested that approximately 20% of patients have had episodes of major depressive disorder and a further 20% have had dysthymia, although the estimates presented here are much higher. The prevalence rate of 90% found by Mindham (1970) is probably an overestimate, given that the study included patients with PD who were referred for psychiatric consultation. Several studies used DSM-III or DSM-III-R criteria, but lacked appropriate control groups. The most notable study was that by Mayeux, Stern, Cote, and Williams (1984), who used DSM-III criteria and comparison groups of neuromuscular and stroke patients with no evidence of depression.

TABLE 6.11. Prevalence of Depressive Symptoms/Disorders in Parkinson's Disease

Author(s)	n	Basis for depression diagnosis	Source of patients	Severity of illness	Controls	Results
Patrick & Levy (1922)	140	Interview		—	None	34% depression
Mjones (1949)	238	Interview		—	None	40% depressive symptoms
Warburton (1967)	140	Maudsley Personality Inventory	Inpatient	Mixed	Medical patients	56% depression
Mindham (1970)	89	Interview	Inpatient	Mixed	Psychiatric patients	90% depression
Brown & Wilson (1972)	111	Interview/HRSD	Inpatient	Mixed	None	52% depression
Celesia & Wannamaker (1972)	153	Interview	Outpatient	Mixed	None	37% depressive symptoms
Marsh & Markham (1973)	27	MMPI	Outpatient	Mixed	Normal controls	Elevated depressive symptoms
Horn (1974)	24	MMPI	Outpatients	—	Paraplegics/normal controls	Elevated depressive symptoms
Mindham, Marsden, & Parkes (1976)	50	Interview	—	—	None	48% depression
Lieberman et al. (1979)	520	Interview	—	—	None	29% depression
Mayeux, Stern, Rosen, & Leventhal (1981)	55	BDI/DSM-III	Clinic	Mixed	Normal controls (spouses)	47.2% depressed (symptoms vs. 12.9% in spouse controls)
Mayeux, Stern, Cote, & Williams (1984)	43	DIS/HRSD	Inpatient	Mixed	Neuromuscular/stroke patients	39% depression
Gotham, Brown, & Marsden (1986)	187	BDI	Outpatient	Mixed	Arthritis patients and normal controls	Depression: 29% PD, 30% arthritis, 6% controls
Santamaria, Tolosa, & Valles (1986)	34	DSM-III/BDI	Clinic	Mild/moderate	Normal	32.3% depressive symptoms
Sano et al. (1989)	339	DSM-III	Inpatient	Mixed	None	51% depression
Starkstein, Berthier, Bolduc, Preziosi, & Robinson (1989)	105	PSE/HRSD	Outpatient	Mixed	None	61% depression (early-onset), 27% depression (late-onset)
Starkstein & Preziosi (1990)	85	PSE/DSM-III	Outpatient	Mild/moderate	None	41% depression
Brown & MacCarthy (1990)	40	PSE	Clinic	Moderate/severe	None	25% depressive symptoms
Dooneief et al. (1992)	258	DSM-III-R	Clinic	Mixed	None	47% depression

Several studies have ruled out a relationship between depression and age, duration, or severity of PD (Warburton, 1967; Horn, 1974; Robins, 1976). The latter two studies examined the association between depression and severity of disease by using control groups consisting of paraplegics (Horn, 1974) or chronically disabled patients (Robins, 1976).

There is evidence to suggest that depression may begin before the onset of the motor symptoms of PD. Santamaria, Tolosa, and Valles (1986), in a small sample of 34 PD patients, noted that symptoms of depression began before PD in 10 of the 11 patients who were depressed. Starkstein, Berthier, Bolduc, Preziosi, and Robinson (1989) were able to differentiate between early-onset (<55) and late-onset (>55) PD with comorbid depression, and found that depression in those with early onset was more prevalent and more closely correlated with degree of cognitive impairment and duration of disease. In contrast, the depression in those with late-onset disease was correlated with activities-of-daily-living scores. This study was instrumental in defining several possible differential pathways.

Incidence.   Several longitudinal studies have suggested that over 40% of PD patients will develop depression over the course of their illness (Patrick & Levy, 1922; Mindham, 1970). Brown, MacCarthy, Gotham, Der, and Marsden (1988) followed a group of 132 PD patients previously administered the BDI (Gotham, Brown, & Marsden, 1986). One year later, 61.4% of the subjects remained nondepressed; 15.9% were depressed on both occasions; 11.3% were depressed at Time 1 but not Time 2; and a further 11.3% who were not depressed at Time 1 became depressed at Time 2. Starkstein, Mayberg, Leiguarda, Preziosi, and Robinson (1992) completed a 1-year follow-up of their 21 PD patients with major depressive disorder at initial evaluation. Of these, 56% still had major depression, 33% were dysthymic, and 11% were nondepressed. Dooneief et al. (1992) completed a retrospective chart review of a series of PD patients and found the incidence of depression to be 1.86% per year. This value falls within the expected range of 0.13–7.8% for depression in the general population (Boyd & Weissman, 1981).

Methodological Challenges.   There is considerable overlap between the presentation of depression in PD and that of other chronic,

debiliating diseases of the CNS. As in MS, patients may present with depression as the first symptom of the disease (Goullard & Fenelon, 1983). In addition, PD patients commonly suffer from psychomotor retardation, fatigue, anorexia, concentration problems, and insomnia, all of which occur in primary depression. Indeed, some patients with severe depression and psychomotor retardation may resemble the akinesia of PD. Starkstein and Preziosi (1990) differentiated depressive symptoms in a depressed and a nondepressed PD group, and found that what distinguished the former from the latter was the absence of early morning awakenings, anergia, and motor retardation. Otherwise, they exhibited elevations in all vegetative and affective symptoms.

Several studies suggest that depression is not of psychogenic origin. Starkstein and Preziosi (1990) compared early- and late-onset PD patients with and without concomitant depression, using activities-of-daily-living measurements, and found that depression was not related to these measurements. However, Fletcher, Maguire, and MacMahon (1990), using the Hospital Anxiety and Depression Scale, found similar rates of depressive symptoms in PD and their spouses; the rates of anxiety were more specific to PD.

Significant mood changes are known to occur when PD patients go from an "on" phase (levodopa-responsive) to an "off" phase (levodopa-nonresponsive) during treatment of the illness (Friedenberg & Cummings, 1989). Physicians need to be aware of this phenomenon and to alter medications accordingly. In addition to this poorly understood pharmacological paradox, there is evidence that long-term levodopa treatment may result in behaviors resembling schizophreniform psychosis (e.g., paranoid delusions, hallucinations, hypomania, toxic delirium). Sweet, McDowell, and Feigenson (1976) reported that at least 60% of patients developed psychosis on levodopa therapy by the end of 6 years. Finally, depression was reported as a side effect of levodopa treatment in a series of 908 patients (Goodwin, 1971).

Dementia is a commonly occurring symptom of CNS dysfunction and may confound any association with depression unless it is carefully ruled out. The prevalence of dementia is 2.3% in the general population, and in PD inpatients it has been reported to be 10.9% (Sano et al., 1989). However, much higher rates of dementia have been reported, ranging from 20% to 68%

(Brown & Wilson, 1972; Celesia & Wanna-maker, 1972; Mindham, 1970; Pollock & Hornabrook, 1966). Sano et al. (1989) also reported the comorbidity between depression and dementia to be 5.4%, suggesting that a subsample of demented PD patients have comorbid depression. In addition, they linked their findings to altered serotonin metabolism, because 5-HIAA was reduced in this group. Starkstein and Preziosi (1990), in a comparison of PD patients with and without depression, found PD patients with depression to have poorer performance on tasks involving frontal lobe function.

Putative Causal Mechanisms. Although some effort has been directed towards elucidating the mechanisms underlying the association between PD and depression, the search has not been fruitful. Competing hypotheses involve genetic vulnerability, psychosocial risk factors, perturbations in biogenic amine metabolism, and neuropathological lesions. Evidence against a psychogenic origin for the association comes from observations that the prevalence of depression is similar in early and later stages of the disease (Starkstein & Preziosi, 1990). Family studies of PD patients have shown that the prevalence of mood disorders is not elevated in their first-degree relatives (Winokur, Dugan, Mendels, & Hurtig, 1978). More systematic studies of genetic vulnerability need to be undertaken in order to determine the exact role that genes play in these two conditions.

There have been several brain laterality studies, although the results have been controversial with respect to hemispheric localization. For example, Starkstein and Preziosi (1990) found that patients with right-sided PD symptoms had increased rates of depression, implicating left-hemispheric dysfunction. In contrast, Fleminger (1991) implicated the right hemisphere because he found that the prevalence of depression and of anxiety disorders was significantly increased in patients whose symptoms were worse on the left. However, Barber, Tomer, Sroka, and Myslobodsky (1985) found no differences between left- and right-hemispheric function in PD patients with depression. All three of these studies were based on small numbers of subjects and may have included PD patients with different types of depression (e.g., Fleminger's [1991] subjects were atypical depressives).

Biochemical challenge studies and imaging studies have proven to be more promising than other studies of the association between depression and PD. Regional cerebral glucose metabolism results comparing PD patients with and without depression show that those with depression have areas of hypometabolism localized to the head of the caudate nucleus and orbito-frontal cortex (Starkstein et al., 1988; Mayberg et al., 1990). Both these areas are richly innervated by dopaminergic axons, implicating biogenic amine pathways (i.e., dopamine, noradrenaline, adrenaline) in the pathogenesis of depression in PD. Interestingly, CSF concentrations of the dopamine metabolite homovanillic acid are lower in PD patients with depression (Mayeux et al., 1986). However, in addition to dopamine metabolites, serotonergic metabolism has also been implicated. Mayeux et al. (1986) found lower levels of 5-HIAA in the CSF of PD patients with comorbid depression, compared to their nondepressed PD counterparts. Taken together, these findings suggest that abnormal biogenic amine metabolism, including both dopaminergic and serotonergic systems, may be affected in PD comorbid with depression.

Paulus and Jellinger (1991), in a neuropathological investigation based on autopsy information of PD patients, found that those with comorbid depression had more extensive cell loss in the dorsal raphe nucleus than did PD patients with dementia, who showed neuronal loss in the medial substantia nigra and more cortical Alzheimer's lesions. Starkstein and Preziosi (1990) more specifically suggest that degeneration of mesocortical and mesolimbic dopamine connnections to the frontal lobe may lead to "metabolic dysfunction of the orbitofrontal region, which may secondarily affect serotonergic cell bodies in the dorsal raphe."

Treatment of Depression and Parkinson's Disease. Several randomized, double-blind, placebo-controlled trials have demonstrated the efficacy of tricyclic antidepresssants in the treatment of parkinsonian patients with depression who do not have a history of heart disease (Denmark, David, & McComb, 1961; Laitinen, 1969, Strang, 1965; Andersen, Aabro, Gulmann, Hjelemsted, & Pedersen, 1980), with nortriptyline as the first-line agent of choice. A serious side effect of the combination of tricyclics and levodopa is orthostatic hypotension, although the effects appear to be minimized with nortriptyline (Andersen et al., 1980). The use of MAOIs is contraindicated, given the concern that the combination of levodopa and an MAOI may cause a hypertensive crisis. However, selegiline, a selective MAO_B inhibitor that does not induce hypertensive episodes, has been shown to be promising in reducing the rate of progression of PD. There are currently several clinical trials investigating this promising new therapy. In severe cases of depression in PD, ECT has been shown to be efficacious, with few side effects (Burke, Peterson, & Rubin, 1988; Lebensohn & Jenkins, 1975; Douyon, Serby, Klutchko, & Rotrosen, 1989).

Endocrine Disorders

Diabetes

Prevalence. Insulin-dependent diabetes mellitus (IDDM) and its more benign non-insulin-dependent counterpart (NIDDM) comprise one of the leading causes of morbidity and mortality in the world today. The incidence rate of IDDM in the United States is 15 of every 100,000, and it is currently the third leading cause of death. IDDM is the more severe form, which begins in childhood and follows an insidious course and outcome. Over the longitudinal course of the disease, complications such as progressive blindness, renal failure, MI, stroke, and eventually death ensue, generally within four decades of onset. NIDDM, on the other hand, typically begins in middle adulthood, with the prevalence increasing with age (approximately 18% of those over 65 years old have the disease); moreover, it is not associated with severe morbidity. Diabetes mellitus was first described in the 17th century by Thomas Willis, who commented on the sweet urine and the prolonged sadness and grief experienced by the patient as the most notable physical and psychological manifestations of the disease (Major, 1965). As yet the cause of the disease is unknown, but there is much speculation as to whether the disease is of viral or autoimmune origin (Cahill & McDevitt, 1981).

An extensive literature exists on the psychosocial aspects of diabetes mellitus. Menninger (1935) was the first to tout the concept of a "diabetic personality," consisting of memory and concentration problems, depression, apathy, anxiety, hypochondrias, and sexual impulses. This concept has yet to be substantiated in other studies. Studies examining the rates of psychopathology conducted before 1963 yielded conflicting results. Whereas Menninger (1935), in a review of the literature, found elevations in depression and anxiety, Treuting (1962) found no particular psychiatric condition to be more prevalent in patients with diabetes. Studies since then have consistently demonstrated high rates of psychopathology, particularly the affective and anxiety disorders. Of the 17 studies described in the literature using different methodologies, the prevalence rate of depression in IDDM/NIDDM ranges from 11% to 74% (Table 6.12). Three controlled studies of NIDDM patients using the BDI showed the prevalence rates of depressive symptomatology to range from 24% to 74%. This broad range may be a function of more disabled patients' being included in the sample obtained from the outpatient clinic, as opposed to those recruited through advertisement. Only two studies employed standardized diagnostic instruments and DSM-III-R criteria for major depression. The results of these two studies were comparable, yielding prevalence rates of depression of 24% (Popkin & Lentz, 1988) and 26% (Lustman & Clouse, 1986) in IDDM patients.

Incidence. IDDM's early age of onset and chronic course provide a unique opportunity to examine the association between depression and a chronic disease. Surprisingly, no longitudinal investigations have been conducted. However, depression is strongly associated with IDDM in children and adolescents. Although no systematic longitudinal studies have examined the association between depression and diabetes, Neimcryk and Travis (1990) measured glycosylated hemoglobin, which is an index of blood glucose control, in a cohort of 48 IDDM diabetic adolescents and evaluated them 6 months after their initial examination. They found no association between depression scores on the CES-D at baseline or follow-up; they did find an association with anxiety disorders and glycosylated hemoglobin at baseline, but not at the follow-up evaluation.

Methodological Challenges. The differential diagnosis of diabetes mellitus is often straightforward, with the definitive test being abnormally high fasting glucose levels. The most consistent problem in the literature has been the inclusion of a mixture of IDDM and NIDDM patients in study samples, when it is well established that the two types of diabetes have different risk factors, pathophysiological mechanisms, and treatments. Over the longitudinal

TABLE 6.12. Prevalence of Depressive Symptoms/Disorders in Diabetes

Author(s)	n	Basis for depression diagnosis	Source of patients	Type of diabetes	Controls	Results
Slawson, Flynn, & Kollar (1963)	25	MMPI/interview	Inpatient/outpatient	—	None	33% depression
Murawski, Chazan, Balodimos, & Ryan (1970)		MMPI	—	—	None	Elevated depression
Bagadia & Gada (1975)	147	Interview/HRSD	Clinic	IDDM (mixed severity)	None	70% depression
Surridge & Lawson (1984)	50	Interview/HRSD	Clinic	IDDM	None	Depression n.s.
Friis & Nanjundappa (1986)	56	CES-D	—	IDDM/NIDDM	Normal controls	60% depression
Lustman & Clouse (1986)	114	DIS	Clinic	50% IDDM/50% NIDDM	None	33% major depressive disorder (26% IDDM); 17.5% dysthymia
Geringer, Perlmuter, Stern, & Nathan (1988)	64	SDS	—	IDDM	None	18.8% depression
Popkin & Lentz (1988)	75	DIS	Inpatient	IDDM	Medical/surgical patients	24% major depressive disorder; 10.7% dysthymia
Robinson, Fuller, & Edmeades (1988)	130	PSE	Clinic	IDDM/NIDDM	Normal controls	17.7% depression
Bradley (1990)	219	GWB	Outpatient	NIDDM	None	Lower well-being
Winocour & Medlicott (1990)	130	SDS	Outpatient	IDDM	None	Depression: 19.1% female, 12% male
Niemcryk & Travis (1990)	48	CES-D	Clinic	IDDM (mild to moderate)	None	Depression n.s.; anxiety common
Littlefield & Murray (1990)	158	BDI	Outpatient	IDDM (mixed severity)	None	Depression n.s.
Wing & Blair (1990)	32	BDI	Community	NIDDM	Spouses	24% depressive symptoms; NIDDM > spouses
Palinkas & Wingard (1991)	1586	BDI	Community	NIDDM	Normal controls	NIDDM > depression
Mayou & Davies (1991)	113	PSE	Community	IDDM	None	11% depression
Leedom & Procci (1991)	113	BDI/SDS	Clinic	NIDDM	Normal controls	74% depressive symptoms

course, both types may have similar endpoints; however, there is a broad range of severity in the NIDDM group and earlier onset of complications in the IDDM group. Therefore, it is important in studies to note duration and severity of disease.

In studies of depression and diabetes, a possible source of confusion is the fact that when patients are depressed they may be malnourished, which may lead to false-positive testing for hyperglycemia. In addition, there is some degree of symptom overlap between depression and hyperglycemia. For example, weakness, fatigue, and weight loss are common manifestations of both conditions. Lustman and Carney (1992) compared depressed diabetic patients to depressed psychiatric patients and found that both groups differed from a nondepressed diabetic control group on the BDI, with the exception of weight loss. Otherwise, the two depressed groups shared similar symptom profiles.

Putative Causal Associations. A number of mechanisms have been postulated in the pathogenesis of depression and diabetes, including psychosocial factors, vulnerability factors, and biological factors. Psychosocial factors that have been systematically investigated include loneliness and low levels of social support (Mazze & Shamoon,1984; Turkat, 1982) and stress and anxiety (Thiots, 1984; Arnetz, 1984). Hinkle and Wolf (1952) demonstrated an association between stressful life events and glucose metabolism by measuring blood sugar volume changes in response to stress; they suggested that emotional deprivation leads to a metabolic response similar to starvation.

If diabetes mellitus is causally associated with depression, then in addition to observing high rates of depression in diabetic patients, one would also expect to observe high rates of diabetes in depressed patients. Abnormally high blood glucose volume is a reliable indicator of diabetes mellitus but is not necessarily pathognomonic. Kymissis and Brown (1979) studied the distribution of psychiatric disorders, using DSM-II criteria in a random sample of psychiatric patients with abnormally high fasting blood sugar levels (>145 mg%), and found no evidence that depression was elevated in these patients.

Only a few studies have examined the role of genetic factors in depression and diabetes. A positive family history for psychosomatic illness was reported by Bagadia and Gada (1975) in 24% of a diabetic sample. Furthermore, Lustman and Harper (1987) examined the lifetime rates of major depression in first-degree relatives of depressed diabetic patients and found a rate of 27%, compared to 3% in their nondepressed diabetic counterparts; this finding suggests the importance of genetic vulnerabilty factors in the association between depression and diabetes.

There is some evidence that the presence of depressive symptomatology is strongly associated with severity of diabetes, as measured by the number of disease complications (e.g., retinopathy, macrovascular disease, neuropathy, nephropathy) (Lloyd & Wing, 1992). This suggests the importance of pathophysiological mechanisms in the association between these two conditions and is supported by neuropathological investigations. For example, there is some evidence that depression in diabetes may be a function of changes in CNS vasculature (Popkin & Lentz, 1988); this is supported by postmortem studies (Alex & Goldberg, 1962; Kannel & McGee, 1979). It is important that these findings be replicated in larger samples of depressed and nondepressed diabetic patients.

Several studies have implicated hypothalamic–pituitary–adrenal axis dysregulation in diabetic patients (Roy & Rick, 1989; Hudson et al., 1984; Cameron & Kronfol, 1984). The dysregulation is manifested as an elevation in plasma cortisol and adrenocorticotropic hormone (ACTH) both before and after dexamethasone administration. Similar findings have been observed in psychiatrically depressed patients; however, the exact nature of this association remains to be determined.

Treatment of Depression and Diabetes. Few systematic treatment trials have been conducted in this area; hence, no one treatment regimen has been shown to be effective. There is some evidence to suggest the efficacy of tricyclic antidepressants in the treatment of depressed diabetics, although the results are controversial. Turkington (1980) reported the efficacy of imipramine or amitriptyline in 59 patients with painful diabetic neuropathy who had elevated depression scores. However, Max and Culnane (1987), in a double-blind crossover placebo-controlled trial, found amitriptyline to have no effect on mood but considerable effect in reducing pain levels in diabetic neuropathy. Kaplan and Pixley (1960) were able to reduce high blood sugar levels in depressed diabetics using imipramine. Others have reported on the efficacy of MAOIs in the treatment of depressed diabetics, but the studies were not particularly well designed (Van Praag, Van Praagh, & Vlad, 1965; Wickstrom & Petterson, 1964). Although relaxation therapy has been shown to reduce blood glucose levels (Fowler & Vandenbergh, 1976; Seeberg & DeBoer, 1980; Surwit & Scovern, 1983), there have been no studies of how this may affect mood in depressed diabetic patients.

The role of serotonin uptake blockers, including fluvoxamine, fluoxetine, and citalopram, has thus far only been examined in animal models of diabetes, although their efficacy has been demonstrated in numerous clinical trials of major depressive disorder in general (Rosenberg, Damsbo, Fuglum, Jacobsen, & Horsgard, 1994; Milne & Goa, 1991). Massol and Pueck (1989) examined the efficacy of these three agents, using an animal model of diabetes and a learned helplessness paradigm; they were not able to demonstrate a reversal of the performance deficit, suggesting that the serotonergic system is not involved in the pathogenesis of diabetes and depression.

Cushing's Syndrome

Prevalence. Cushing's syndrome is a disorder of the endocrine system first noted by Cushing (1912), who described a case history of a 23-year-old patient with a "syndrome of painful obesity, hypertrichosis and amenorrhoea" (p. 25). In 1932, he published a monograph based on his observations of 12 patients with similar features (predominantly weight gain and centripetal obesity). Cushing's syndrome arises as the result of high corticosteroid levels, regardless of etiology (i.e., pituitary hypersecretion of ACTH, Cushing's disease, adrenal gland tumors, iatrogenic administration of ACTH or corticosteroids, cortisol hypersecretion by tumors) (Howlett & Besser, 1985). A diagnosis of Cushing's syndrome is based on high cortisol secretion (based on the dexamethasone suppression test, which yields few false-negative diagnoses), circadian rhythm analysis of cortisol and ACTH, and abnormal glucose tolerance. The disorder is 10 times more common in females (Howlett & Besser, 1985). Paradoxically, patients with severe depression may also secrete high levels of cortisol (Butler & Besser, 1968) in the absence of Cushing's syndrome. It has been reported that approximately 40–50% of patients with depression have high cortisol levels

and abnormal suppression of plasma cortisol after administration of dexamethasone (Carroll et al., 1980).

Table 6.13 presents several studies completed since 1950 on the association between depression and Cushing's syndrome. In general, previous studies suggest that approximately one-third of patients present with psychiatric problems; of these, approximately two-thirds exhibit depression and at least 10% attempt suicide (for a review, see Murphy, 1991). However, no controlled studies using systematic criteria have been completed.

There is some evidence to suggest that the severity of psychiatric disorders may be related to the type of Cushing's syndrome (e.g., adrenoma vs. hyperplasia of the adrenal glands) (Trethowan & Cobb, 1952). The psychiatric symptoms most commonly associated with Cushing's syndrome are depression, psychomotor retardation, sleep disturbances, and irritability, as well as impairment in cognitive function (Starkman & Schteingart, 1981).

Incidence. There have been no incidence studies of Cushing's syndrome and depression.

Methodological Challenges. Differential diagnosis of Cushing's syndrome is often straightforward because of the overt physical manifestations of the disease. There is considerable symptom overlap between depression and Cushing's syndrome, but the telltale signs of the latter are the centripetal obesity and disruption of the circadian rhythm (Schlechte & Pfohl, 1986). In addition to depression, high cortisol levels have also been reported in bulimia and anorexia nervosa; however, diagnostically, the eating disorders are very distinct. One source of confusion in these studies may be the lack of distinction between Cushing's syndrome and Cushing's disease and the different subtypes thereof (e.g., adrenal vs. pituitary hypersecretion of cortisol).

Putative Causal Mechanisms. Very little is known about the association between Cushing's syndrome and depression. Gifford and Gunderson (1970), in a review of the literature, made note of many anectodal descriptions suggesting that Cushing's disease may be the end result of a barrage of significant psychosocial stressors. Their argument was based on the observation that development of the disease was often preceded by traumatic life events, such as divorce,

TABLE 6.13. Prevalence of Depressive Symptoms/Disorders in Cushing's Syndrome

Author(s)	n	Basis for depression diagnosis	Source of patients	Type of illness	Controls	Results
Trethowan & Cobb (1952)	25	Chart review	Hospital	Mixed	None	33.3% depressive symptoms
Gifford & Gunderson (1970)	10	Interview	Hospital	—	None	100% depressive symptoms
Carroll & Mendels (1976)	78	—	—	Disease	Patients with adrenal tumors	66% depressive symptoms (compared to 25% in adrenal tumor controls)
Jeffcoate & Silverstone (1979)	38	—	—	Syndrome	None	57.9% depressive symptoms
Cohen (1980)	29	Interview	Inpatient	Syndrome	None	86% depressive symptoms
Kelly & Bender (1980)	15	PSE	Inpatient	Syndrome	Patients with pituitary tumors	53.3% depressive symptoms
Starkman & Schork (1981)	35	Interview/ HRSD	Inpatient	Mixed	None	74% depressed mood

death in the family, poor family relationships in childhood, and a heightened vulnerability toward depression. However, their findings were based on a small number of patients and have yet to be substantiated in larger samples.

There is some evidence to suggest that the depression accompanying Cushing's syndrome may be secondary to neuropathological changes in the CNS (Trethowan & Cobb, 1952). For example, Heinbecker and Pfeiffenberger (1950) described cases with hydrocephaly and subsequent atrophy of the paraventricular nuclei as dominant features, although later studies revealed that these changes were more likely to occur in patients with adrenal hyperplasia as opposed to adrenocortical tumors. More recently, a neurochemical lesion has been isolated in suicide victims; this is expressed as a hypersecretion of corticotropin-releasing hormone localized to the frontal cortex, and measured as a reduction in the number of binding sites for this hormone (Nemeroff & Golden, 1984). Although it was initially believed that surgical removal or irradiation of adrenocortical tumor would alleviate depressive symptoms and the physical signs of disease, depression may still occur in adrenalectomized patients who are maintained on steroid medication; this interesting finding suggests that the adrenal glands themselves are not necessary for the expression of depression (Crisp & Roberts, 1963).

Treatment of Depression and Cushing's Syndrome. There have been no systematic investigations of the efficacy of antidepressants in the treatment of Cushing's syndrome. Sonino and Boscaro (1986) administered metyrapone and aminoglutethimide, with favorable results, to six patients who had previously failed to respond to antidepressant therapy (Sonino & Boscaro, 1985). An additional study has demonstrated the efficacy of metyrapone (which acts on cortisol metabolism) in alleviating depression, although the exact mechanism is unknown (Jeffcoate & Silverstone, 1979).

Other Metabolic Conditions Associated with Depression

Whereas Cushing's disease leads to excess cortisol secretion, Addison's disease reflects the converse, a low cortisol output. Psychiatric and mental symptoms include apathy, irritability, depression, memory problems, suspiciousness, and agitation (Cleghorn, 1951; Lishman, 1983).

Immunological Disorders

Rheumatoid Arthritis

Prevalence. Rheumatoid arthritis (RA) is a chronic, painful inflammatory disease that can occur throughout the lifespan. A number of earlier studies report the prevalence rate of RA to be anywhere in the range from 0.7% to 7.5%, depending on the criteria employed and sampling technique utilized. Like depression, it is more common in women, increases with age, and can be found all over the world. Although the cause of this disease is unknown, a number of theories have been advanced, including infection, allergic reaction, mechanical trauma, avitaminoses, abnormal immune response, insufficient blood circulation, and metabolic dysregulation. Diagnosis of RA is based on evidence of joint dysfunction on physical examination, positive rheumatoid factor, and elevated erythrocyte sedimentation rate in the blood.

The association between RA and depression has been noted for centuries and was well documented by Paulus Aegine, who wrote, "Sorrow, care and watchfulness, and the other passions of the mind not only excite an attack of the disorder but also generate a cacochymy either primarily or incidentally" (quoted in Thomas, 1936, p. 27). A review of the literature on the prevalence rate of depressive symptoms/disorders in RA (Table 6.14) suggests that it ranges from 17% to 74%. To date, no systematic studies have been done using standardized diagnostic criteria and sound methodology, including control groups. In the only study to use systematic diagnostic criteria elicited by the DIS, R. G. Frank et al. (1988a) found the prevalence rate of major depression to be 17%. In general, it appears that depression may not be as debilitating or as common in RA as in other chronic medical illnesses.

Incidence.   Thus far, no prospective longitudinal studies have been initiated in which a cohort of patients with RA is followed longitudinally and depression status is measured at baseline as well as during follow-up. However, one study followed a cohort of RA patients (*n* = 74) for over 15 years, and found that approximately 46% developed psychiatric symptoms severe enough to warrant treatment. Approximately 50% of these patients also had psychopathology at baseline, most notably depression (Rimon & Laakso, 1984). Of the 13 patients identified at baseline as having depression, 8 were depressed at the follow-up interview. However, this finding needs to be replicated in larger samples, using systematic diagnostic criteria for depression, before definitive conclusions regarding an association between depression and RA can be made.

Bishop, Green, Cantor, and Torresin (1987) measured depression (BDI) and anxiety levels (Spielberger Anxiety Scale) in 39 RA patients during hospitalization and then monthly for 6 months. Over the period of follow-up, an interesting positive association emerged between the occurrence of depressive episodes and RA exacerbation.

Methodological Challenges.   Fibrositis is a form of rheumatoid disease similar to rheumatoid arthritis in symptomatology but of questionable validity due to the reliance on patients description and localization of pain rather than on the ability to detect and confirm clinical signs. Interestingly, Goldenberg (1986), using the DIS, found an association between depression and fibrositis but not RA. This was also substantiated by Hudson (1985), using the same instrument, and by Payne et al. (1982), using the MMPI. Several other studies have confirmed the elevated rates of depression in fibrositis, using symptom checklists (Payne et al., 1982; Ahles & Yunus, 1984; Wolfe & Cathey, 1984). However, despite these findings, many investigators still question the utility of diagnoses based on subjective reporting of pain and prefer to believe that fibrositis is a disorder of personality.

Two features of RA—the presence of rheumatoid factor and swelling of synovial joints—may also be present in other diseases, including arthralgia induced by oral contraceptives and osteoarthritis.

Putative Causal Mechanisms.   Although RA is most commonly regarded as a disease affecting the synovial joints in the periphery, it is also known to affect the CNS (Hausmanova & Herman, 1957), creating various psychopathological phenomena.

Hawley and Wolfe (1988) studied a group of RA patients prospectively and found that depression was strongly associated with various socioecononomic factors, including educational level, marital status, and income. Over time, worsening of depression was associated with socioeconomic but not with clinical variables.

Treatment of Depression and Rheumatoid Arthritis.   Few studies exist on the efficacy of drugs in the treatment of RA and depressive illness. One of the cytotoxic agents commonly used in the treatment of RA is 6-azauridine triacetate, which has reported side effects at doses

TABLE 6.14. Prevalence of Depressive Disorders/Symptoms in Rheumatoid Arthritis

Author(s)	n	Basis for depression diagnosis	Source	Severity of illness	Controls	Results
Pottenger (1938)	50	—	—	—	None	74% depression
Thomas (1936)	3½	—	—	—	None	9/31 depression
Cohen (1949)	75	MMPI	Hospital	—	Normal controls/patients with other medical disorders	Increased depression, hypochondriasis, hysteria
Wiener (1952)	50	MMPI	Hospital	—	Nondisabled controls	Increased depression, hypochondriasis, hysteria
Nalven & O'Brien (1964)	45	MMPI	Outpatient	—	None	Increased depression, hypochondriasis, hysteria
Moos & Solomon (1964)	49	MMPI/interview	Outpatient	Mixed	Unaffected family members	Increased depression, hypochondriasis, hysteria
Rimon (1969)	100	Interview	Outpatients	—	None	29% depression
Polley, Swensen, & Steinhelber (1970)	726	MMPI	Inpatient	Mixed	Mayo Clinic norms	Increased depression, hypochondriasis, hysteria
Zaphiropoulos & Burry (1974)	50	BDI	Inpatient	Moderate/severe	Patients with painful locomotor disorders	46% depression (compared to 18.7% in controls)
Robinson, Hernandez, Dick, & Buchanan (1977)	144	Interview	Outpatient	Mixed	None	50% depressive symptoms
Pancheri, Teodori, & Aparo (1978)	35	Interview/MMPI	Inpatient	Moderate/severe	Patients with asteorthrosis/normals	Depression: RA > controls
Spergel, Erlich, & Glass (1978)	46	MMPI	Inpatient	—	None	Increased depression, hypochondriasis, hysteria
Rimon & Laakso (1984)	74	Interview	Outpatient	—	None	44% depression
Wolfe & Cathey (1984)		MMPI	—	—	None	Increased depression, hypochondriasis, hysteria
Liang et al. (1984)	23	MMPI	Outpatient	Mild/moderate	Lupus patients	Increased depression, hypochondriasis, hysteria
Pincus, Callahan, Bradley, Vaughan, & Wolfe (1986)	70	MMPI	Outpatient	Mild/moderate	Normal controls	Increased depression, hypochondriasis, hysteria
R. G. Frank et al. (1988a)	137	DIS	Outpatient	Mild/moderate	None	17% major depression; 40.7% dysthymia
Hawley & Wolfe (1988)	400	AIMS[a]	Outpatient	Mixed	Patients with fibrositis/back pain	Elevated depression in all groups
Parker et al. (1990)	84	SCL-90	Outpatient	Mixed	None	Elevated depression
Eberhardt, Larsen, & Nivied (1993)	89	SCL-90	Outpatient	Mild	None	Depression n.s.

[a]Arthritis Impact Measurement Scales (depression and anxiety sections from the RAND health instrument).

exceeding 100 mg/kg; these side effects include depressive symptoms (Elis, Slavik, & Raskova, 1971). Although the mechanisms are unknown, Elis et al. (1971) suggest a leakage in the blood–brain barrier, which is normally impermeable to this drug.

Rimon (1974) examined the efficacy of psychotropic drugs (sulpiride and chlorimipramine) in the treatment of a sample of 37 depressed female patients with RA. Overall, the treatment was beneficial in 57% of the women, and joint recovery was more marked in those whose depression also disappeared.

Although the findings have been controversial, several studies have explored the effects of patient education on improving the overall well-being and health status of RA patients. In a prospective randomized trial of 22 arthritic men assigned to either a patient education group or a control group with standard medical care, the majority of patients in the former group showed significant improvement in health, knowledge, dexterity, and depression (as measured by the BDI) (Parker et al., 1984).

There are some who believe that effective treatment of the depressive disorder with antidepressants will ameliorate/diminish the painful tortuous course of RA (Scherbel & Harrison, 1958; Shochet & Lisansky, 1969). Indeed, there is some evidence to suggest that antidepressants may have an analgesic effect in RA patients. R. G. Frank et al. (1988b), in a double-blind crossover trial of a number of psychotropic agents (including amitriptyline, desipramine, and trazodone) and placebo, found amitriptyline to be beneficial in reducing pain sensitivity as well as depression, as measured by the DIS at both baseline and termination.

Systemic Lupus Erythematosus

Prevalence. Systemic lupus erythematosus (SLE) is a rare inflammatory disease of unknown cause that affects all organ systems and is characterized by exacerbations and remissions. Common features of this disorder include fever, acute migratory arthritis, dermatitis, vasculitic lesions, alopecia, and cardiac lesions. A review of the literature on the association between depression and SLE prior to 1960 revealed few if any systematic studies. The majority of these anecdotal case reports and unselected case series yielded few consistent results (Shearn & Pirofsky, 1952; Clark & Bailey, 1956; O'Connor, 1959; Stern & Robbins, 1960).

For example, Shearn and Pirofsky reported a prevalence rate of endogenous depression to be approximately 50%. Guze (1967) classified the psychopathology observed in SLE into three distinct categories, based on a retrospective series of 101 patients: (1) organic brain syndrome (9%); (2) affective disorders (10%); (3) schizophreniform disorders (5%). In another case review series, Heine (1969) reported the incidence of depressive illness to be 18%, and described it as a "functional illness"; he also defined an additional category of patients based on "organic toxicity," which was evident in 24% of his series.

Although the prevalence rate of depression is lower in SLE than in other chronic medical diseases, among the immunological disorders it may present with a higher frequency. For example, Ganz, Gurland, Deming, and Fisher (1972) using a structured clinical interview found higher rates of depression in SLE than in RA patients, particulary in those over 45 years of age, although in general the two groups were remarkably similar.

Previous studies of the association between depression and SLE have not been informative, largely because of methodological problems. Although a recent study by Krupp, LaRocca, Muir, and Steinberg (1990) that utilized the CES-D found the prevalence of depressive symptoms to be approximately 42%, the results must be considered preliminary, given that only patients with mild to moderate symptoms participated and an inappropriate control group was chosen.

Incidence. There have been no incidence studies of the association between SLE and depression.

Methodological Challenges. Fatigue is a common complaint in SLE, as it is in many other chronic, debilitating diseases. Krupp et al. (1990) examined depression and symptoms of fatigue in 59 patients with SLE, and found that fatigue correlated significantly with depression and accounted for at least part of the variability in fatigue scores.

Putative Causal Mechanisms. SLE is known to affect all organ systems, including the brain; however, few pathological studies of the brain have been undertaken. In a clinical case series, Glaser (1952) described the pathology reports of three SLE patients who all showed marked vascular lesions of the CNS. Given the available evidence, Waring (1972) postulated at least three neuropsychiatric scenarios to account for the association between depression and SLE. First, depression may be the result of an organic brain syndrome secondary to neurodegenerative changes in cerebral vasculature. Second, it may be a response to brain toxicity (e.g., due to drug treatment of SLE or uremia). Third, depression may be a functional disorder with little or no CNS involvement. With the advent of more sophisticated neuroimaging techniques, future studies will undoubtedly lead to more definitive descriptions of the association between depression and SLE.

Treatment of Depression and Systemic Lupus Erythematosus. There have been no systematic treatment studies of the efficacy of psychotropic medications on depression in SLE. Indeed, only case reports of toxic responses to SLE therapy have been reported in the literature, as well as indirect reports of antidepressant therapy causing SLE-like phenomena. There is one case report linking SLE development to the toxic reaction of phenelzine, an MAOI (Swartz, 1978). It has also been suggested that lithium toxicity may cause SLE symptoms (Shukla & Borison, 1982).

Corticosteroid and antimalarial agents, which are the first-line agents in the treatment of SLE, may produce side effects that affect personality. Long-term steroid therapy may produce Cushing-like symptoms that include depressive features.

DISCUSSION

Summary

A summary of the findings regarding comorbidity of depression and medical illnesses from controlled or epidemiological studies is presented in Table 6.15. The disorders for which there is consistent evidence for comorbidity with depression are cancer, migraine, and stroke. Prospective studies of the latter two disorders have confirmed the results of cross-sectional studies and have shown that depression tends to follow the onset of both stroke and migraine (Robinson & Price, 1982; Merikangas et al., 1990). Although the evidence is compelling for an association between depression and MI, epilepsy, HD, MS, and PD, further studies employing prospective designs and standard-

TABLE 6.15. Diseases Associated with Depression

Disease	Predominant system affected	Assoc. with depression
Cancer	CNS, PNS[a]	° ° °
Myocardial infarction	Cardiovascular	° °
Hypertension	Cardiovascular	°
Stroke	CNS	° °
Epilepsy	CNS	° °
Huntington's disease	CNS	° °
Migraine	CNS	° ° °
Multiple sclerosis	CNS, PNS	° °
Parkinson's disease	CNS	° °
Cushing's syndrome	Endocrine	°
Diabetes mellitus	Endocrine	°
Rheumatoid arthritis	Immunological	°
Systemic lupus erythematosus	Immunological	°

Note. ° ° ° consistent evidence; ° ° suggestive evidence; ° minimal evidence/inconsistent.

[a]Peripheral nervous system.

ized operational criteria for depression are necessary. Less convincing evidence for an association with depression exists for the immunological and endocrine diseases examined here.

Implications of Findings

Implications for Clinical Psychiatry

The results of this review have important implications for clinical psychiatry. The importance of considering possible underlying causes of or contributory factors to clinical depression is particularly emphasized. Even without comprehensive evaluation of somatic disorders in large series of depressed patients, the data suggest that between 10% and 15% of inpatient depressives suffer from a medical illness that contributes to or may even cause symptoms of clinical depression (Hall, Popkin, Devaul, Faillau, & Stickney, 1978). This suggests that somatic symptoms should not be automatically explained as manifestations of depression, without adequate attempts to identify possible comorbid conditions that could be equally likely to produce a particular constellation of symptoms. Aside from specific medical disorders, numerous other known biological factors may contribute to the expression of depression: effects of both prescribed and nonprescribed drugs; hormonal, nutritional, electrolyte, or endocrine abnormalities; intracerebral disease; and manifestations of autoimmune or other systemic conditions (Hall, 1980).

The magnitude of the association between medical illnesses and clinically significant depression, which is approximately 25% when aggregated across medical disorders (including stroke, cancer, MI, and diabetes), suggests the importance of classification and treatment of comorbidity. As described above, several approaches have been employed to represent the co-occurrence of disorders, both within the realm of psychiatry and between psychiatry and other medical specialties (Cohen-Cole & Stoudemire, 1987). The first method, known as the "inclusive approach," is phenomenological and DSM-based, and utilizes symptom counts (Rifkin & Siris, 1985). This approach tends to yield high sensitivity but low specificity. The second method, the "etiological approach," is also DSM-based, but symptoms are only counted if the disease was not responsible for the presentation of it (Spitzer et al., 1992). This method results in poor reliability, because in most cases it is unclear which disease has caused which symptoms. The third method is known as the "substitutive method," and uses a different set of diagnostic criteria when referring to depression in the medically ill. This was first discussed by Cavanaugh (1983), who used latent trait analysis to select symptom clusters of depression in the medically ill. However, his method was based on results from a symptom checklist inventory that lacks specificity. Rice, Rochberg, Endicott, Lavori, and Miller (1992) have proposed a more sensitive method for the measurement of depression in patients with medical illness, based on modifications to the DSM criteria for major depressive disorder. The fourth method, the "exclusive approach," has been utilized extensively by Holland's group (Massie & Holland, 1984). This method requires the elimination of anorexia and fatigue, two symptoms common in medically ill patients. A diagnosis of major depression is based on four of the remaining six symptoms. This method has the advantage of increased specificity, but at the cost of reduced sensitivity.

The lack of evidence for the associations and mechanisms thereof precludes selection of one method over the others. However, for clinical practice, the inclusive method appears to be the most appropriate method, since this method makes no assumptions about causal relationships and implies that the disorders should both be considered in treatment decisions. In the recently established clinical practice guidelines for the treatment of depression in primary care, it is recommended that the medical disorder be treated first, and that depression be re-evaluated and treated as an independent disorder if it persists (Depression Guideline Panel, 1993).

Research Implications

One of the major goals of the investigation of comorbidity is to elucidate the mechanisms for nonrandom associations between diseases. Documentation of an association between depression and other conditions is only the first step in this process. The two major classes of explanations for associations between disorders include "etiological models," in which an index disease causes or precipitates the manifestation of the comorbid condition, and "shared-pathophysiology models," in which risk factors common to the two diseases may exhibit disparate manifestations.

The two key study designs in discriminating between these alternatives are family/genetic studies and longitudinal studies. In family studies, evidence for shared pathophysiology would be derived from an increase in rates of the comorbid disorder (and *not* the index disorder) in the relatives of probands with only the index disorder, as compared to the relatives of controls. Similarly, in twin studies, increased rates of the comorbid disorder in the cotwins of probands with only the index disorder would support shared pathophysiology. Alternatively, if the comorbid disorder is elevated among the relatives of probands with the "pure" index disorder, but only when coupled with the index disorder, an etiological model would be more likely to explain the association (Merikangas, Risch, Merikangas, Weissman, & Kidd, 1988). Application of the family study paradigm to elucidate mechanisms for comorbidity requires a group of unaffected controls and direct interviews with relatives.

Longitudinal studies may also be employed to identify mechanisms of comorbidity. The prospective design enables elucidation of the causal relationship between the index disorder and the comorbid disorder, as well as of common risk factors and the sequelae thereof. Homogeneous subtypes of these conditions may also be identified according to the stability of patterns of expression across the longitudinal course.

Aside from identification of bias, the investigation of patterns of comorbidity between medical disorders and depression is important for several reasons. First, identification of differential patterns of comorbidity may lead to the elucidation of subtypes of a particular index disorder for which the comorbid condition may indicate a different form or subtype, thereby enhancing the validity of their distinction in the classification system. For instance, the finding that left-sided stroke is more strongly associated with depression as a sequela provides clues regarding possible brain mechanisms of depression. Second, differential associations between particular pairs of diseases may yield clues regarding the pathogenesis of the index disease. For example, if depression precedes the onset of several nonspecific autoimmune disorders, research could be directed toward the investigation of possible mechanisms through which depression may lead to changes in immune function. Alternatively, if two conditions emanate from the same underlying etiological factors, investigations of their etiology can be targeted to risk factors that are common to both conditions.

Implications for Future Studies

Future research is necessary to investigate these findings in controlled studies and from systematically selected samples of persons with specific index diseases. Aggregation of the findings of previous studies was precluded by differences in methodology and by the use of symptom checklists of depression, with attendant lack of specificity in identifying persons with clinically significant depression requiring intervention. Other salient methodological factors included a lack of standardized diagnostic definitions of the comorbid disorder; sampling from a single treatment setting; failure to include controls; lack of comparability of the treated samples with respect to gender, age, and clinical severity; lack of statistical power to detect associations with rare conditions; and wide variability in the inclusion of confounders in the analyses of the associations. Therefore, future studies need to focus on the application of standardized diagnostic definitions, with reliable methods of assessing both the depressive disorders and comorbid conditions. It is particularly critical to formulate the hypotheses regarding the associa-

tions in advance, in order to avoid the possibility of false-positive errors due to multiple testing, particularly in large samples. Moreover, specific risk factors for each of the conditions need to be identified carefully, and their effects on the association need to be investigated systematically. Indeed, the identification of purported "confounding" risk factors may be the most important finding with respect to the nature of nonrandom associations between comorbid disorders. Such extrinsic mechanisms can provide targets for prevention of the development of both conditions or of the secondary disorder as a consequence of the index disease.

Acknowledgments. Preparation of this chapter was supported by a Research Scientist Development Award from the Alcohol, Drug Abuse and Mental Health Administration of the U.S. Public Health Service (No. MH00499) and by a grant from the MacArthur Foundation Task Force on the Psychobiology of Depression and Other Affective Disorders to Kathleen Ries Merikangas, as well as by a predoctoral fellowship from a National Institute of Mental Health training grant award to Denise E. Stevens (No. MH14235).

REFERENCES

Adamec, R. E. (1993). Partial limbic kindling: Brain, behavior, and the benzodiazepine receptor. *Physiology and Behavior, 54*, 531–545.

Ahles, F. A., & Ruckdeschel, A. (1984). Cancer related pain: II. Assessment of usual analogue scales. *Journal of Psychometric Research, 28*, 121–129.

Ahles, T. A., & Yunus, S. A. (1984). Psychological factors associated with primary fibromyalgia syndromes. *Arthritis and Rheumatism, 27*, 1101–1105.

Alex, M., & Goldberg, E. K. (1962). An autopsy study of cerebrovascular accident in diabetes mellitus. *Circulation, 25*, 663–673.

Alexander, H. (1902). A few observations on the blood pressure in mental disease. *Lancet, ii*, 18–20.

Altschule, M. D. (1953). *Bodily physiology in mental and emotional disorders.* New York: Grune & Stratton.

American Psychiatric Association. (1980). *Diagnositic and statistical manual of mental disorders* (3rd ed.). Washington, DC: Author.

American Psychiatric Association. (1987). *Diagnostic and statistical manual of mental disorders* (3rd ed., rev.). Washington, DC: Author.

American Psychiatric Association. (1994). *Diagnostic and statistical manual of mental disorders* (4th ed.). Washington, DC: Author.

Amkraut, A., & Solomon, G. F. (1975). From the symbolic stimulus from the pathophysiologic response: Immune mechanisms. *International Journal of Psychiatry and Medicine, 5*, 541–563.

Andersen, J., Aabro, E., Gulmann, N., Hjelemsted, A., & Pedersen, H. E. (1980). Anti-depressive treatment in Parkinson's disease: A controlled trial of the effect of nortriptyline in patients with Parkinson's disease treated with L-dopa. *Acta Neurologica Scandinavica, 62,* 210–219.

Anonymous. (1962), Ad hoc committee on classification of headache. *Archives of Neurology, 6,* 173–176.

Anonymous. (1988). Headache classification committee of the International Headache Society: Classification and diagnostic criteria for headache disorders, cranial neuralgias and facial pain. *Cephalalgia, 8*(Suppl. 7), 9–96.

Arnetz, B. B. (1984). The potential role of psychosocial stress on levels of hemoglobin HbAlc and fasting plasma glucose in elderly people. *Journal of Gerontology, 39,* 424–429.

Bagadia, V. N., & Gada, P. (1975). Diabetes mellitus: A psychosomatic study of 147 cases. *Journal of Postgraduate Medicine, 21,* 17–29.

Bant, W. (1974). Do antihypertensive drugs really cause depression? *Proceedings of the Royal Society of Medicine, 67,* 919–921.

Barber, J., Tomer, R., Sroka, H., & Myslobodsky, M. S. (1985). Does unilateral dopamine deficit contribute to depression? *Psychiatry Research, 15,* 17–24.

Beck, A. T., Ward, C. H., Mendelson, M., Mock, J. E., & Erbaugh, J. K. (1961). An inventory for measuring depression. *Archives of General Psychiatry, 4,* 561–571.

Berkson, J. (1946). Limitation of the application of the 4-fold table analysis to hospital data. *Biometrics, 2,* 47–53.

Betts, T. A. (1974). A follow up study of a cohort of patients with epilepsy admitted to psychiatric care in an English city. In *Epilepsy: Proceedings of the Hans Berger Centenary Symposium* (pp. 326–338).

Betts, T. A. (1981). Depression, anxiety, and epilepsy. In E. H. Reynolds & M. Trimble (Eds.), *Epilepsy and psychiatry* (pp. 60–71). Edinburgh: Churchill Livingstone.

Betts, T. A., & Pond, H. (1976). A textbook of epilepsy. Edinburgh: Churchill Livingstone.

Bishop, D., Green, A., Cantor, S., & Torresin, W. (1987). Depression, anxiety and rheumatoid arthritis activity. *Clinical and Experimental Rheumatology, 5,* 147–150.

Blackwell, B. (1981). Adverse effects of antidepressant drugs: II. "Second generation" antidepressants and rational decision making in antidepressant therapy. *Drugs, 21,* 273–282.

Bolt, J M. W. (1970). Huntington's chorea in the west of Scotland. *British Journal of Psychiatry, 116,* 259–270.

Boutelle, R. C., Epstein, S., & Ruddy, M. C. (1987). The relation of essential hypertension to feelings of anxiety, depression and anger. *Psychiatry, 50,* 206–217.

Boyd, J. H., & Weissman, M. M. (1981). Epidemiology of affective disorders: A re-examination and future directions. *Archives of General Psychiatry, 38,* 1039–1046.

Bradley, C. (1990). Measures of psychological well-being and treatment satisfaction developed from the responses of people with tablet-treated diabetes. *Diabetic Medicine, 7,* 445–451.

Breslau, N., Davis, G. C., & Andreski, P. (1991). Migraine, psychiatric disorders, and suicide attempts: An epidemiologic study of young adults. *Psychiatry Research, 37,* 11–23.

Brown, G. L., & Wilson, A. (1972). Parkinsonism and depression. *Southern Medical Journal, 65,* 540–545.

Brown, H. J. (1982). Cancer and depression: Cancer presenting with depressive illness. An autoimmune disease. *British Journal of Psychiatry, 141,* 227–232.

Brown, R. G., & MacCarthy, B. (1990). Psychiatric morbidity in patients with Parkinson's disease. *Psychological Medicine, 20,* 77–87.

Brown, R. G., MacCarthy, B., Gotham, A. M., Der, G. J., & Marsden, C. D. (1988). Depression and disability in Parkinson's disease: A follow-up of 132 cases. *Psychological Medicine, 18,* 49–55.

Bruce, L. C., & Alexander, A. (1901). The treatment of melancholia. *Lancet, ii,* 516–518.

Bruhn, J. G., Chandler, B., & Wolf, S. (1969). A psychological study of survivors and nonsurvivors of myocardial infarction. *Psychosomatic Medicine, 31*(1), 8–19.

Bruhn, J. G., & Wolf, S. (1971). A psycho-social study of surviving male coronary patients and controls followed over nine years. *Journal of Psychosomatic Research, 15,* 305–313.

Bruyn, G. W. (1968). Huntington's chorea: Historical, clinical, and laboratory synopsis. In P. J. Vinken & G. W. Bruyn (Eds.), *Handbook of clinical neurology* (pp. 298–378).

Bryant, R. H., Reid, J. L., & Torosdag, S. (1963). Long-term antihypertensive effect of pargyline HCl with and without diuretic sulfonaminde. *Annals of the New York Academy of Sciences, 107,* 1023–1032.

Bukberg, J., Penman, D., & Holland, J.C. (1984). Depression in hospitalized cancer patients. *Psychosomatic Medicine, 45,* 199–212.

Bulpitt, C. J. & Dollery, C. T. (1973). Side effects of hypotensive agents evaluated by a self-administered questionnaire. *British Medical Journal, iii,* 485–490.

Burke, W. J., Peterson, J., & Rubin, E. H. (1988). Electroconvulsive therapy in the treatment of combined depression and Parkinson's disease. *Psychosomatics, 29,* 341–346.

Butler, P. W., & Besser, G. M. (1968). Pituitary–adrenal function in severe depressive illness. *Lancet, i,* 1234–1236.

Cahill, G. F., & McDevitt, H. O. (1981). Insulin-dependent diabetes mellitus: The initial lesion. *New England Journal of Medicine, 304,* 1454–1465.

Cain, E. N., Kohorn, E. I., Quinlan, D. M., Schwartz, P. E., Latimer, K., & Rogers, L. (1983). Psychosocial reactions to the diagnosis of gynecologic cancer. *Obstetrics and Gynecology, 62*(5), 635–641.

Caine, E. D., & Shoulson, I. (1983). Psychiatric syndromes in Huntington's disease. *American Journal of Psychiatry, 140*(6), 728–733.

Cameron, O., & Kronfol, N. (1984). Hypothalamic–pituitary adrenocorticol activity in patients with diabetes mellitus. *Archives of General Psychiatry, 41,* 1090–1095.

Canter, A. H. (1951). MMPI profiles in multiple sclerosis. *Journal of Consulting Psychology, 15,* 253–256.

Carney, R. M., Rich, M. W., Tevelde, A., Saini, J., Clark, K., & Jaffe, A. S. (1987). Major depressive disorder in coronary artery disease. *American Journal of Cardiology, 60,* 1273–1275.

Carroll, B. J., Greden, J. F., Haskett, R., Feinberg, M., Albala, A. A., Martin, F. I., Rubin, R. T., Heath, B., Sharp, P. T., McLeod, W. L., & McLeod, M. F. (1980). Neurotransmitter studies of neuroendocrine pathology in depression. *Acta Psychiatrica Scandinavica,* Suppl. 280, 183–199.

Carroll, B. J., & Mendels, G. (1976). Neuroendocrine regulation in depression. *Archives of General Psychiatry, 33,* 1051–1058.

Carter, A. B. (1970). Hypotensive therapy in stroke survivors. *Lancet, i,* 485–489.

Cassem, E. H. (1990). Depression and anxiety secondary to medical illness. *Psychiatric Clinics of North America*, *13*(4), 597–612.

Cassem, E. H., & Hackett, T. P. (1977). Psychological aspects of myocardial infarction. *Medical Clinics of North America*, *61*(4), 711–721.

Cassileth, B. R., & Strouse, E. J. (1984). Psychosocial status in chronic illness: A comparative analysis of six diagnostic groups. *New England Journal of Medicine*, *311*(8), 506–511.

Cavanaugh, S. V. (1983). The prevalence of emotional and cognitive dysfunction in a general medical population using the MMSE, GHQ, and BDI. *General Hospital Psychiatry*, *5*, 15–24.

Cavanaugh, S. V., & Gibbons, D. C. (1983). Diagnosing depression in the hospitalized medically ill. *Psychosomatics*, *24*, 809–815.

Cay, E. L., Vetter, N., Philip, A. E., & Dugard, P. (1972). Psychological status during recovery from an acute heart attack. *Journal of Psychosomatic Research*, *16*, 425–435.

Celesia, G. G., & Wannamaker, W. M. (1972). Psychiatric disturbances in Parkinson's disease. *Diseases of the Nervous System*, *33*, 577–583.

Charcot, J. M. (1877). *Lectures on the diseases of the nervous system delivered at La Salpêtrière*. London: New Sydenham Society.

Clark, D., & Gibbons, S. (1983). Core symptoms of depression in medical and psychiatric patients. *Journal of Nervous and Mental Disease*, *171*, 705–713.

Clark, E. C., & Bailey, C. (1956). Neurologic and psychiatric signs associated with systemic lupus erythematosus. *Journal of the American Medical Association*, *160*, 455–457.

Cleghorn, R. A. (1951). Adrenal corticol insufficiency: Psychological and neurological observations. *Canadian Medical Association Journal*, *65*, 449–454.

Cochrane, R. (1973). Hostility and neuroticism among unselected essential hypertensives. *Journal of Psychosomatic Research*, *17*, 215–218.

Cohen, D. (1949). *Psychological concomitants of chronic illness: A study of emotional correlates of pulmonary tuberculosis, peptic ulcer, the arthritides, and cardiac disease*. Unpublished doctoral dissertation, University of Pittsburgh.

Cohen, S. I. (1980). Cushing's syndrome: A psychiatric study of 29 patients. *British Journal of Psychiatry*, *136*, 120–124.

Cohen-Cole, S. A., & Stoudemire, A. (1987). Major depression and physical illness: Special considerations in diagnosis and biological treatment. *Psychiatric Clinics of North America*, *10*, 1–17.

Columbo, G., Aramani, M., Ferruzza, E., & Zuliaini, C. (1988). Depression and neuroticism in multiple sclerosis. *Italian Journal of Neuroscience*, *9*(6), 551–557.

Conneally, P. M. (1984). Huntington's disease: Genetics and epidemiology. *American Journal of Human Genetics*, *36*, 506–526.

Cooper, A. F., & Russell, C. S. (1979). Psychiatric morbidity associated with adjuvant chemotherapy following mastectomy for breast cancer. *British Journal of Surgery*, *66*, 362.

Corsellis, J. A. N. (1969). Subacute encephalitis and malignancy. In C. W. M. Whitty & W. Hughes (Eds.), *Virus disease of the nervous system* (pp. 31–50). Oxford: Blackwell Scientific.

Costa, D., Mosos, I., & Toma, T. (1985). Efficacy and symptoms of mianserin in the treatment of depression of women. *Acta Psychiatrica Scandinavica*, Suppl. 120, 85–92.

Couch, J. R., & Ziegler, E. (1975). Evaluation of the relationship between migraine headache and depression. *Headache*, *15*, 41–50.

Craig, M. (1898). Blood pressure in the insane. *Lancet*, *i*, 1742–1747.

Craig, T. J. (1974). Psychiatric symptomatology among hospitalized cancer patients. *American Journal of Psychiatry*, *131*, 1323–1327.

Crisp, A. H., Kalucy, R. S., McGuinness, B., Ralph, P. C., & Harris, G. (1977). Some clinical, social and psychological characteristics of migraine subjects in the general population. *Postgraduate Medical Journal*, *53*, 691–697.

Crisp, A. H., & Roberts, F. J. (1963). The response of an adrenalectomized patient to ECT. *American Journal of Psychiatry*, *119*, 784–785.

Currie, S., & Henson, W. G. (1971). Clinical course and prognosis of temporal lobe epilepsy. *Brain*, *94*, 173–190.

Cushing, H. (1912). *The pituitary body and its disorders: Clinical states produced by disorders of the hypophysis cerebri*. Philadelphia.

Cushing, H. (1932). Basophil adenomas of the pituitary body and their clinical manifestations. *Johns Hopkins Hospital Bulletin*, *50*, 137.

Dalack, G. W., Roose, S. P., & Glassman, A. H. (1991). Tricyclics and heart failure. *American Journal of Psychiatry*, *148*(11), 1601.

Dalby, M. (1971). Antiepileptic and psychotropic effects of carbamazepine (Tegratol) in the treatment of psychomotor epilepsy. *Epilepsia*, *12*, 325–334.

Dalos, N. P., Rabins, P. V., Brooks, B. R., & O'Donnell, P. (1983). Disease activity and emotional state in multiple sclerosis. *Annals of Neurology*, *13*, 573–577.

Daniels, J., & Goodman, A. D. (1983). Hypertension and hyperparathyroidism: Inverse relation of serum phosphate level and blood pressure. *American Journal of Medicine*, *75*(1), 17–23.

Dattore, P. J., & Coyne, F. C. (1980). Premorbid personality differentiation of cancer and non-cancer groups: A test of the hypothesis of cancer proneness. *Journal of Consulting and Clinical Psychology*, *48*(3), 388–394.

Davies, M. H. (1971). Is high blood pressure a psychosomatic disorder? *Journal of Chronic Diseases*, *24*, 239–258.

Denmark, J. C., David, J. D., & McComb, S. G. (1961). Imipramine hydrochloride (Tofranil) in parkinsonism. *British Journal of Clinical Practice*, *15*, 523–524.

Depression Guideline Panel, U.S. Department of Health and Human Services. (1993). Treatment of major depression. *Depression in Primary Care*, *2*. (Abstract)

Derogatis, L. R. (1977a). Confirmation of the dimensional structure of the SCL-90: A study in construct validation. *Journal of Clinical Psychology*, *33*, 981–989.

Derogatis, L. R. (1977b). *Symptom Checklist 90, revised version, manual I: Scoring, administration and procedures for the SCL-90*. Baltimore: Johns Hopkins University Press.

Derogatis, L. R., & McBeth, M. D. (1976). Cancer patients and their physicians in the perception of psychological symptoms. *Psychosomatics*, *17*, 197–201.

Derogatis, L. R., & Melisaratos, M. D. (1979). Psychological coping mechanisms and survival time in metastatic breast cancer. *Journal of the American Medical Association*, *242*, 1504–1508.

Derogatis, L. R., Morrow, G. R., Fetting, J., Penman, D., Piasetsky, S., Schmale, A. M., Henrichs, M., & Carnicke, C. L. J. (1983). The prevalence of psychiatric disorders among cancer patients. *Journal of the American Medical Association, 249*(6), 751–757.

Dewhurst, K., Oliver, J. E., & McKnight, A. L. (1970). Socio-psychiatric consequences of Huntington's disease. *British Journal of Psychiatry, 116,* 255–258.

Dikmen, S., Wilensky, A., Rainwater, G., & Hermann, B. (1983). The validity of the MMPI to psychopathology in epilepsy. *Journal of Nervous and Mental Disease, 171,* 114–122.

DiMaio, L., Squitieri, F., Napolitano, G., Campanella, G., Trofatter, J. A., & Conneally, P. M. (1993). Onset symptoms in 510 patients with Huntington's disease. *Journal of Medical Genetics, 30,* 289–292.

Dominian, J. (1963). A follow-up study of late-onset epilepsy: Psychiatric and social findings. *British Medical Journal, 52,* 431–435.

Dooneief, G., Mirabello, E., Bell, K., Marder, K., Stern, Y., & Mayeux, R. (1992). An estimate of the incidence of depression in idiopathic Parkinson's disease. *Archives of Neurology, 49,* 305–307.

Douyon, R., Serby, M., Klutchko, B., & Rotrosen, J. (1989). ECT and Parkinson's disease revisited: A "naturalistic" study. *American Journal of Psychiatry, 146,* 1451–1455.

Drummond, P. D. (1982). Personality traits in young males at risk for hypertension. *Journal of Psychosomatic Research, 26,* 585–589.

Eastwood, M. R., Rifat, S. L., & Ruderman, J. (1989). Mood disorder following cerebrovascular accident. *British Journal of Psychiatry, 154,* 195–200.

Eberhardt, K., Larsson, B., & Nived, K. (1993). Psychological reactions in patients with early rheumatoid arthritis. *Patient Education and Counseling, 20,* 93–100.

Ebrahim, S., Barer, D., & Nouri, F. (1987). Affective illness after stroke. *British Journal of Psychiatry, 151,* 52–56.

Edeh, J., & Toone, B. (1987). Relationship between interictal psychopathology and the type of epilepsy: Results of a survey in general practice. *British Journal of Psychiatry, 151,* 95–101.

Editorial. (1979). Psychiatric illness among medical patients. *Lancet, i,* 478–479.

Edwards, J. G. (1979). Antidepressants and convulsions. *Lancet, ii,* 1368–1369.

Edwards, J. G. (1983). Mianserin and convulsive siezures. *British Journal of Clinical Psychiatry, 15,* 299–311.

Elis, J., Slavik, M., & Raskova, H. (1971). Side effects of 6–azauridine triacetate in rheumatoid arthritis. *Clinical Pharmacology and Therapeutics, 11*(3), 404–407.

Ellison, J. M., Milofsky, J. E., & Ely, E. (1990). Fluoxetine-induced bradycardia and syncope in two patients. *Journal of Clinical Psychiatry, 51*(9), 385–386.

Endicott, J., & Spitzer, R. L. (1978). A diagnostic interview: The Schedule for Affective Disorders and Schizophrenia—Lifetime Version (modified for the study of anxiety disorders). *Archives of General Psychiatry, 35,* 837–844.

Evans, D. L., McCartney, C. F., Nemeroff, C. B., Raft, D., Quade, D., Golden, R. N., Haggerty, J. J. J., Holmes, V., Simon, J. S., & Droba, M. (1986). Depression in women treated for gynecological cancer: Clinical and neuroendocrine assessment. *American Journal of Psychiatry, 143*(4), 447–452.

Fava, G. A., Pilowsky, I., Pierfederici, A., Bernardi, M., &

Pathak, D. (1982). Depression and illness behavior in a general hospital: A prevalence study. *Psychotherapy and Psychosomatics, 38*(1), 141–153.

Fedoroff, J. P., Lipsey, J. R., Starkstein, S. E., Forrester, A., Price, T. R., & Robinson, R. G. (1991). Phenomenological comparisons of major depression following stroke, myocardial infarction or spinal cord lesions. *Journal of Affective Disorders, 22,* 83–89.

Feighner, J. P., Robins, E., Guze, S. B., Woodruff, R. A., Winokur, G., & Munoz, R. (1972). Diagnostic criteria for use in psychiatric research. *Archives of General Psychiatry, 26,* 56–73.

Feinstein, A. R. (1970). The pre-therapeutic classification of co-morbidity in chronic disease. *Journal of Chronic Diseases, 23,* 455–468.

Ferrari, M., Barabas, G., & Matthews, W. S. (1983). Psychological and behavioral disturbance among epileptic children treated with barbiturate anticonvulsants. *American Journal of Psychiatry, 140*(1), 112–113.

Finklestein, S., Benowitz, L. I., Baldessarini, R. J., Arana, G. W., Levine, D., Woo, E., Bear, D., Moya, K., & Stoll, A. (1982). Mood, vegetative disturbance, and dexamethasone suppression test after stroke. *Annals of Neurology, 12,* 463–468.

Finklestein, S. P., Weintraub, R. J., Karmouz, N., Askinazi, C., Davar, G., & Baldessarini, R. J. (1987). Antidepressant drug treatment for poststroke depression: Retrospective study. *Archives of Physical Medicine and Rehabilitation, 68*(11), 772–776.

Fleminger, S. (1991). Left-sided Parkinson's disease is associated with greater anxiety and depression. *Psychological Medicine, 21,* 629–638.

Fletcher, P., Maguire, R., & MacMahon, D. G. (1990). The prevalence of anxiety and depression in elderly Parkinson's disease patients and their carers. *Movement Disorders, 5*(Suppl. 1), 70–71.

Foley, F. W., Traugott, U., LaRocca, N. G., Smith, C. R., Perlman, K. R., Caruso, L. S., & Scheinberg, L. C. (1992). A prospective study of depression and immune dysregulation in multiple sclerosis. *Archives of Neurology, 49,* 238–244.

Folstein, M. F., Maiberger, R., & McHugh, P. R. (1977). Mood disorder as a specific complication of stroke. *Journal of Neurology, Neurosurgery and Psychiatry, 40,* 1018–1020.

Folstein, S. E. (1989). *Huntington's disease: A disorder of families.* Baltimore: Johns Hopkins University Press.

Folstein, S. E., Abbott, M. H., Chase, G. A., Jensen, B. A., & Folstein, M. F. (1983a). The association of affective disorder with Huntington's disease in a case series and in families. *Psychological Medicine, 13,* 537–542.

Folstein, S. E., & Chase, M. (1987). Huntington's disease: Clinical aspects of racial variation. *American Journal of Human Genetics, 24933,* 17576–29545.

Folstein, S. E., & Folstein, M. F. (1983). Psychiatric features of Huntington's disease: Recent approaches and findings. *Psychiatric Developments, 1*(2), 193–205.

Folstein, S. E., Folstein, M. F., & McHugh, P. R. (1979). Psychiatric syndromes in Huntington's disease. In T. N. Chase, N. S. Wexler, & A. Barbeau (Eds.), *Advances in neurology* (pp. 281–289). New York: Raven Press.

Folstein, S. E., Franz, M. L., Jensen, B. A., Chase, G. A., & Folstein, M. F. (1983b). Conduct disorder and affective disorder among the offspring of patients with Huntington's disease. *Psychological Medicine, 13*(1), 45–52.

Fowler, J. E., & Vandenbergh, T. H. (1976). Effects of an EMG biofeedback relaxation program on the control of diabetes. *Biofeedback and Self-Regulation, 1,* 105–112.

Frank, R. G., Beck, N. C., Parker, J. C., Kashani, J. H., Elliot, T. R., Haut, A. E., Smith, E., Atwood, C., Brownlee-Duffeck, M., & Kay, D. R. (1988a). Depression in rheumatoid arthritis. *Journal of Rheumatology, 15*(6), 920–925.

Frank, R. G., Kashani, J. H., Parker, J. C., Beck, N. C., Brownlee-Duffeck, M., Elliot, T. R., Haut, A. E., Atwood, C., Smith, E., & Kay, D. R. (1988b). Antidepressant analgesia in rheumatoid arthritis. *Journal of Rheumatology, 15*(11), 1632–1638.

Fras, I., & Pearson, E. M. (1967). Comparison of psychiatric symptoms in cancer of the pancreas with those in some other intra-abdominal neoplasms. *American Journal of Psychiatry, 123,* 1553–1562.

Friedenberg, D. L., & Cummings, J. L. (1989). Parkinson's disease, depression, and the on–off phenomenon. *Psychosomatics, 30,* 94–99.

Friedman, M. J., & Bennett, P. (1977). Depression and hypertension. *Psychosomatic Medicine, 39,* 134–142.

Friis, R., & Nanjundappa, G. (1986). Diabetes, depression, and employment status. *Social Science and Medicine, 23,* 471–475.

Fromm, G. H., Amores, C. Y., & Thies, W. (1972). Imipramine in epilepsy. *Archives of Neurology, 27*(3), 198–204.

Fromm, G. H., & Glass, H. B. (1978). Imipramine in absence and myoclonic–astastic seizures. *Neurology, 28,* 953–957.

Gainotti, G. (1972). Emotional behavior and hemispheric side of the lesion. *Cortex, 8*(1), 41–55.

Ganz, V. H., Gurland, B. J., Deming, W. E., & Fisher, B. (1972). The study of the psychiatric symptoms of systemic lupus erythematosus. *Psychosomatic Medicine, 34,* 207–220.

Garvey, M. J., Tollefson, G. D., & Shaffer, C. B. (1984). Migraine headaches and depression. *American Journal of Psychiatry, 141,* 986–988.

Gelasko, D., & Thal, P. F. (1988). Intracranial mass lesions associated with late-onset psychosis and depression. *Psychiatric Clinics of North America, 11,* 151–166.

Geringer, E. S., Perlmuter, L. C., Stern, T. A., & Nathan, D. M. (1988). Depression and diabetic neuropathy: A complex relationship. *Journal of Geriatric Psychiatry and Neurology, 1*(1), 11–15.

Ghose, K., & Turner, P. (1975). Intravenous tyramine pressor response in depression. *Lancet, i,* 1317–1318.

Gifford, S., & Gunderson, J. (1970). Cushing's disease as a psychosomatic disorder: A selective review of the clinical and experimental literature and a report of ten cases. In W. Gorman (Ed.), *Perspectives in biology and medicine* (pp. 169–221). Chicago: University of Chicago Press.

Glaser, G. H. (1952). Lesions of the C.N.S. in disseminated lupus erythematosus. *Archives of Neurology and Psychiatry, 67,* 745.

Glassman, A. H., & Johnson, A. (1983). The use of imipramine in depressed patients with congestive heart failure. *Journal of the American Medical Association, 250,* 1977–2001.

Goldberg, D. P. (1972). *The detection of psychiatric illness by questionnaire,* London: Oxford University Press.

Goldberg, D. P., & Blackwell, B. (1970). Psychiatric illness in general practice: A detailed study using a new method of case identification. *British Medical Journal, i,* 439–443.

Goldberg, E. L., Comstock, G. W., & Graves, C. G. (1980). Psychosocial factors and blood pressure. *Psychological Medicine, 10,* 243–255.

Goldenberg, D. L. (1986). Psychologic studies in fibrositis. *American Journal of Medicine, 81,* 67–70.

Goldstein, G., Materson, B. J., Cushman, W. C., Reda, D. J., Freis, E. D., Ramirez, E. A., Talmers, F. N., White, T. J., Nunn, S., Chapman, R. H., Khatri, I., Schnaper, H., Thomas, J. R., Henderson, W. G., & Fye, C. (1990). Treatment of hypertension in the elderly: II. Cognitive and behavioral function. *Hypertension, 15*(4), 361–369.

Good, K., Clark, C. M., Oger, J., Paty, D., & Klonoff, H. (1992). Cognitive impairment and depression in mild multiple sclerosis. *Journal of Nervous and Mental Disease, 180*(11), 730–732.

Goodwin, F. K. (1971). Psychiatric side effects of levodopa in man. *Journal of the American Medical Association, 218,* 1915–1919.

Gordon, G. S. (1974). Hyper- and hypocalcaemia: Pathogenesis and treatment. *Annals of the New York Academy of Sciences, 230,* 181–186.

Gotham, A. M., Brown, R. G., & Marsden, C. D. (1986). Depression in Parkinson's disease: A quantitative and qualitative analysis. *Journal of Neurology, Neurosurgery and Psychiatry, 49,* 381–389.

Goullard, A., & Fenelon, M. (1983). Maladie de Parkinson et syndromes parkinsoniens. *Encyclopédie Med. Chir. Paris Neurology, 170,* 62.

Greer, S., & Morris, T. (1975). Psychological attributes of women who develop breast cancer: A controlled study. *Journal of Psychosomatic Research, 19,* 147–153.

Guirdham, A. (1950). Some new concepts of blood pressure. *Medical Press, 223,* 344–345.

Gunn, J. (1977). Criminal behaviour and mental disorder. *British Journal of Psychiatry, 130,* 317–329.

Gusella, J. F., Wexler, N. S., Conneally, P. M., Naylor, S. L., Anderson, M. A., Tanzi, R. E., Watkins, P. C., Ottina, K., Wallace, M. R., Sakaguchi, A. Y., Young, A. B., Shoulson, I., Bonilla, E., & Martin, J. B. (1983). A polymorphic DNA marker genetically linked to Huntington's disease. *Nature, 306,* 234–238.

Guze, S. B. (1967). The occurrence of psychiatric illness in systemic lupus erythematosus. *American Journal of Psychiatry, 123,* 1562–1570.

Guze, S. B., Woodruff, R. A. J., & Clayton, P. J. (1972). Sex, age, and the diagnosis of hysteria (Briquet's syndrome). *American Journal of Psychiatry, 129*(6), 745–748.

Hahn, R. C., & Petitti, D. B. (1988). Minnesota Multiphasic Personality Inventory-rated depression and the incidence of breast cancer. *Cancer, 61*(4), 845–848.

Hall, R. C. W. (1980). *Depression in psychiatric presentations of medical illness: Psychosomatic disorders.* New York: SP Medical and Scientific Books.

Hall, R. C. W., Popkin, M. K., Devaul, R. A., Faillau, L. A., & Stickney, S. K. (1978). Physical illness presenting as psychiatric disease. *Archives of General Psychiatry, 35,* 1315.

Hamilton, M. (1960). A rating scale for depression. *Journal of Neurology, Neurosurgery and Psychiatry, 23,* 56–62.

Harburg, F., Erfurt, J. C., Hauenstein, L. S., Chape, C., Schull, W. J., & Shork, M. A. (1973). Socio-ecological stress, suppressed hostility, skin color, and black–white male blood pressure. *Psychosomatic Medicine, 35,* 276.

Hardman, A., Maguire, P., & Crowther, D. (1989). The recognition of psychiatric morbidity on a medical oncology ward. *Journal of Psychosomatic Research*, 33(2), 235–239.

Hathaway, S. R., & McKinley, J. C. (1951). *Minnesota Multiphasic Personality Inventory manual* (rev. ed.). Minneapolis: University of Minnesota Press.

Hausmanova, I., & Herman, H. (1957). Effects of ACTH on experimental diseases of the nervous system in laboratory animals. *Neurologica*, 6(6), 747–759.

Hawley, D. J., & Wolfe, F. (1988). Anxiety and depression in patients with rheumatoid arthritis: A prospective study of 400 patients. *Journal of Rheumatology*, 15(6), 932–941.

Hawton, K., & Marsack, J. (1980). Association between epilepsy and attempted suicide. *Journal of Neurology, Neurosurgery and Psychiatry*, 43, 168–170.

Heathfield, K. W. G. (1967). Huntington's chorea: Investigation into the prevalence of this disease in the area covered by the North East Metropolitan Regional Hospital Board. *Brain*, 90, 203–232.

Hedreen, J. C., Peyser, C. E., Folstein, S. E., & Ross, C. A. (1991). Neuronal loss in layers V and VI of cerebral cortex in Huntington's disease. *Neuroscience Letters*, 133, 257–261.

Heinbecker, P., & Pfeiffenberger, A. (1950). Further clinical and experimental studies on the pathogenesis of Cushing's syndrome. *American Journal of Medicine*, 9, 3–5.

Heine, B. E. (1969). Psychiatric aspects of systemic lupus erythematosus. *Acta Psychiatrica Scandinavica*, 45, 307–326.

Hellerstein, H. K., & Friedman, E. H. (1970). Sexual activity and the postcoronary patient. *Archives of Internal Medicine*, 125, 987–999.

Hermann, B., & Whitman, S. (1984). Behavioral and personality correlates of epilepsy: A review, methodological critique and conceptual model. *Psychological Bulletin*, 95(3), 451–497.

Hinkle, L. E., & Wolf, H. (1952). Importance of life stresses in course management of diabetes mellitus. *Archives of Medicine*, 98, 110.

Hinton, J. M. (1963). The physical and mental distress of the dying. *Quarterly Journal of Medicine*, 32, 1.

Holland, J. C., & Tross, A. L. L. (1986). Comparative psychological disturbance in patients with pancreatic and gastric cancer. *American Journal of Psychiatry*, 143, 982–986.

Honer, W. G., Hurwitz, T., Li, D. K. B., Palmer, M., & Paty, D. W. (1987). Temporal lobe involvement in multiple sclerosis patients with psychiatric disorders. *Archives of Neurology*, 44, 187–190.

Hopwood, P., & Maguire, A. (1984). A pilot study to evaluate the psychiatric morbidity in patients with advanced breast cancer. *British Journal of Cancer*, 50, 260.

Horn, S. (1974). Some psychological factors in parkinsonism. *Journal of Neurology, Neurosurgery and Psychiatry*, 37, 27–31.

Howlett, T. A., & Besser, L. H. (1985). Cushing's syndrome. *Clinics in Endocrinology and Metabolism*, 14, 911–944.

Hudson, J. I. (1985). Fibromyalgia and major affective disorders: A controlled phenomenology and family history study. *American Journal of Psychiatry*, 142, 441–446.

Hudson, J. I., Hudson, M. S., Rothschild, A. J., Vignati, L., Schatzberg, A. F., & Melby, J. C. (1984). Abnormal results of dexamethasone suppression tests in nondepressed patients with diabetes mellitus. *Archives of General Psychiatry*, 44(6), 1086–1089.

Huntington, G. (1872). On chorea. *Medical and Surgical Reporter*, 26, 317.

Jacobson, L., & Ottosson, A. (1971). Initial mental disorders in carcinoma of the pancreas and stomach. *Acta Psychiatrica Scandinavica*, Suppl. 22, 120.

Jarman, J., Fernandez, M., Davies, P. T., Glover, V., Steiner, T. J., Thompson, C., Rose, F. C., & Sandler, M. (1990). High incidence of endogenous depression in migraine: Confirmation by tyramine test. *Journal of Neurology, Neurosurgery and Psychiatry*, 53(7), 573–575.

Jeffcoate, W. J., & Silverstone, P. H. (1979). Psychiatric manifestations of Cushing's syndrome: Response to lowering of plasma cortisol. *Quarterly Journal of Medicine*, 48, 465–472.

Joffe, R. T., & Denicoff, D. R. (1986). Depression and carcinoma of the pancreas. *General Hospital Psychiatry*, 8, 241–245.

Joffe, R. T., Lippert, G. P., Gray, T. A., Sawa, G., & Horvath, Z. (1987a). Mood disorder and multiple sclerosis. *Archives of Neurology*, 44, 376–378.

Joffe, R. T., Lippert, G. P., Gray, T. A., Sawa, G., & Horvath, Z. (1987b). Personal and family history of affective illness in patients with multiple sclerosis. *Journal of Affective Disorders*, 12, 63–65.

Kannel, W. B., & McGee, D. L. (1979). Diabetes and cardiovascular disease. *Journal of the American Medical Association*, 241, 2035–2038.

Kaplan, G. A., & Reynolds, P. (1988). Depression and cancer mortality and morbidity: Prospective evidence from the Alameda County study. *Journal of Behavioral Medicine*, 11(1), 1–13.

Kaplan, M. H., & Feinstein, A. R. (1974). The importance of classifying initial co-morbidity in evaluating the outcome of diabetes mellitus. *Journal of Chronic Diseases*, 27, 387–404.

Kaplan, S. M., & Pixley, J. W. (1960). Use of imipramine in diabetics: Effects on glycosuria and blood sugar levels. *Journal of the American Medical Association*, 174, 511–517.

Kashiwagi, T., & McClure, A. (1972). Headache and psychiatric disorders. *Diseases of the Nervous System*, 33, 659–663.

Kathol, R. G., & Petty, C. (1981). Relationship of depression to medical illness: A critical review. *Journal of Affective Disorders*, 3, 111–121.

Kathol, R. G., & Williams, A. (1990). Diagnosis of major depression in cancer patients according to four sets of criteria. *American Journal of Psychiatry*, 147(8), 1021–1024.

Kavanagh, T., Shepard, R. J., & Tuck, J. A. (1975). Depression after myocardial infarction. *Canadian Medical Association Journal*, 113, 23–27.

Kelly, W. F., & Bender, S. A. (1980). Cushing's syndrome, tryptophan and depression. *British Journal of Psychiatry*, 136, 125–132.

Klerman, G. L. (1987). Depression associated with medical and neurological diseases, drugs, and alcohol. In A. J. Marsella, R. M. A. Hirschfeld, & M. M. Katz (Eds.), *The measurement of depression* (pp. 20–29). New York: Guilford Press.

Koenig, R., Levin, S. M., & Brennan, M. J. (1967). The emotioinal status of cancer patients as measured by a psychological test. *Journal of Chronic Diseases*, 20(11), 923–930.

Kogeorgos, J., & Scott, P. (1982). Psychiatric symptom patterns of chronic epileptics attending a neurologic clinic: A controlled investigation. *British Journal of Psychiatry*, 140, 236–243.

Korsgaard, S. (1976). Baclofen (Lioresal) in the treatment

of neuroleptic-induced tardive dyskinesia. *Acta Psychiatrica Scandinavica*, 54, 17–24.

Kraepelin, E. (1921). *Textbook of psychiatry* (8th ed.): *Vol. 3. Manic–depressive insanity and paranoia* (R. M. Barclay, Trans.; G. M. Robertson, Ed.). Edinburgh: E. & S. Livingstone. (Original work published 1913).

Krupp, L. B., Alvarez, L. A., LaRocca, N. G., & Scheinberg, L. C. (1988). Fatigue in multiple sclerosis. *Archives of Neurology*, 45, 435–437.

Krupp, L. B., LaRocca, N. G., Muir, J., & Steinberg, A. D. (1990). A study of fatigue in systemic lupus erythematosus. *Journal of Rheumatology*, 17, 1450–1452.

Kurlan, R., & Caine, K. (1988). Cerebrospinal fluid correlates of depression in Huntington's disease. *Archives of Neurology*, 45, 881–883.

Kymissis, P., & Brown, L. (1979). Relationships between high fasting blood sugar and depression in a mental hygiene clinic population. *Canadian Journal of Psychiatry*, 24, 133–138.

Ladwig, K. H., Roll, G., Breithardt, G., Budde, T., & Borggrefe, M. (1994). Post-infarction depression and incomplete recovery 6 months after acute myocardial infarction. *Lancet*, 343, 20–23.

Laitinen, L. (1969). Desipramine in treatment of Parkinson's disease. *Acta Neurologica Scandinavica*, 45, 109–113.

Lansky, S. B., List, M. A., Herrmann, C. A., Ets-Hokin, E. G., DasGupta, T. K., Wilbanks, G. D., & Hendrickson, F. R. (1985). Absence of major depressive disorder in female cancer patients. *Journal of Clinical Oncology*, 3(11), 1553–1560.

Lebensohn, Z. M., & Jenkins, R. B. (1975). Improvement of Parkinsonism in depressed patients treated with ECT. *American Journal of Psychiatry*, 132(3), 283–285. (Abstract)

Leedom, L., & Procci, W. P. (1991). Symptoms of depression in patients with type II diabetes mellitus. *Psychosomatics*, 32, 280–286.

Lesko, L. M., & Holland, J. C. (1988). Psychological issues in patients with hematological malignancies. *Recent Results in Cancer Research*, 108, 243–270.

Levine, P. M., Silberfarb, P. M., & Lipowski, Z. J. (1978). Mental disorders in cancer patients: A study of 100 psychiatric referrals. *Cancer*, 42(3), 1385–1391.

Lewis, S. (1994). ICD-10: A neuropsychiatrist's nightmare? *British Journal of Psychiatry*, 164, 157–158.

Liang, M. H., Rogers, M., Larson, M., Eaton, H. M., Murawski, B. J., Taylor, J. E., Swafford, J., & Schur, P. H. (1984). The psychosocial impact of systemic lupus erythematosus and rheumatoid arthritis. *Arthritis and Rheumatism*, 27, 13–19.

Lieberman, A., Dziatolowski, M., Kupersmith, M., Serby, M., Goodgold, A., Korein, J., & Goldstein, M. (1979). Dementia in Parkinson disease. *Annals of Neurology*, 6(4), 355–359.

Linet, M., & Stewart, W. (1984). Migraine headache: Epidemiologic perspectives. *Epidemiologic Reviews*, 6, 107–139.

Linkins, R. W., & Comstock, G. W. (1990). Depressed mood and development of cancer. *American Journal of Epidemiology*, 132(5), 962–972.

Lipsey, J. R., & Robinson, R. G. (1984). Nortriptyline treatment of post-stroke depression: A double-blind treatment trial. *Lancet*, i, 297–300.

Lipsey, J. R., Spencer, W. C., Rabins, P. V., & Robinson, R. G. (1986). Phenomenological comparison of post-stroke depression and functional depression. *American Journal of Psychiatry*, 143, 527–529.

Lishman, W. A. (1983). The apparatus of mind: Brain structure and function in mental disorder. *Psychosomatics*, 24, 699–703.

Littlefield, C. H., & Murray, G. M. (1990). Influence of functional impairment and social support on depressive symptoms in persons with diabetes. *Health Psychology*, 9(6), 737–749.

Lloyd, C. E., & Wing, K. A. (1992). The Pittsburgh Epidemiology of Diabetes Complications Study: VIII. Psychosocial factors and complications of IDDM. *Diabetes Care*, 15(2), 166–172.

Lloyd, G. G., & Cawley, R. H. (1982). Psychiatric morbidity after myocardial infarction. *Quarterly Journal of Medicine*, 51, 33–42.

Lloyd, G. G., & Cawley, R. H. (1983). Distress or illness? A study of psychological symptoms after myocardial infarction. *British Journal of Psychiatry*, 142, 120–125.

Lohr, J. B. (1987). Neuropsychiatric aspects of brain tumors. In R. E. Hales (Ed.), *Textbook of neuropsychiatry* (pp. 351–364). Washington DC: American Psychiatric Press.

Lustman, P. J., & Carney, K. E. (1992). Similarity of depression in diabetic and psychiatric patients. *Psychosomatic Medicine*, 54, 602–611.

Lustman, P. J., & Clouse, L. S. (1986). Psychiatric illness in diabetes mellitus: Relationship to symptoms and glucose control. *Journal of Nervous and Mental Disease*, 174, 736–742.

Lustman, P. J., & Harper, G. W. (1987). Nonpsychiatric physicians' identification and treatment of depression in patients with diabetes. *Comprehensive Psychiatry*, 28, 22–27.

Maguire, G. P., & Brook, A. (1980). Psychiatric morbidity and physical toxicity associated with adjuvant chemotherapy after mastectomy. *British Medical Journal*, 281, 1179–1180.

Major, R. H. (1965). Therapeutics 16 BC–1965 AD: Ageless remedies, a historical reminder. *Journal of the Kansas Medical Society*, 66, 174–176.

Mann, A. H. (1977). Psychiatric morbidity and hostility in hypertension. *Psychological Medicine*, 7, 653–659.

Marsh, G. G., & Markham, C. H. (1973). Does levodopa alter depression and psychopathology in parkinsonism patients? *Journal of Neurology, Neurosurgery and Psychiatry*, 36, 925–935.

Massie, M. J., & Holland, J. C. (1984). Diagnosis and treatment of depression in the cancer patient. *Journal of Clinical Psychiatry*, 45, 25–29.

Massie, M. J., & Holland, J. C. (1990). Depression and the cancer patient. *Journal of Clinical Psychiatry*, 51(Suppl.), 12–19.

Massie, M. J., & Mastrovito, G. (1979). The diagnosis of depression in hospitalized patients with cancer. *Proceedings of the American Association for Cancer Research*, 20, 432.

Massol, J., & Pueck, P. (1989). Antidepressant effects of tricyclic antidepressants and selective serotonin-uptake blockers in diabetic rats. *Diabetes*, 38, 1161–1164.

Matthews, C. G., & Klove, H. (1968). MMPI performances in major motor, psychomotor, and mixed seizure classifications of known and unknown etiology. *Epilepsia*, 9, 43–53.

Max, M. B., & Culnane, M. (1987). Amitriptyline relieves diabetic neuropathy pain in patients with normal or depressed mood. *Neurology*, 37, 589–596.

Mayberg, H. S., Starkstein, S. E., Peyser, C., Brandt, J., Dannals, R. F., & Folstein, S. (1992). Paralimbic frontal lobe hypometabolism in depression associated with Huntington's disease. *Neurology*, *42*(9), 1791–1797.

Mayberg, H. S., Starkstein, S. E., Sadzot, B., Preziosi, T., Andrezejewski, P. L., Dannals, R. F., Wagner, H. N., & Robinson, R. G. (1990). Selective hypometabolism in the inferior frontal lobe in depressed patients with Parkinson's disease. *Annals of Neurology*, *28*, 57–64.

Mayeux, R., Stern, Y., Cote, L., & Williams, J. B. W. (1984). Altered serotonin metabolism in depressed patients with Parkinson's disease. *Neurology*, *34*, 642–646.

Mayeux, R., Stern, Y., Herman, A., Greenbaum, L., & Fahn, S. (1986). Correlates of early disability in Huntington's disease. *Annals of Neurology*, *20*(6), 727–731.

Mayeux, R., Stern, Y., Rosen, J., & Levanthal, J. (1981). Depression, intellectual impairment, and Parkinson's disease. *Neurology*, *31*, 645–650.

Mayou, R., & Davies, R. (1991). Psychiatric morbidity in young adults with insulin-dependent diabetes mellitus. *Psychological Medicine*, *21*, 639–645.

Mazze, R. S., & Shamoon, D. (1984). Psychological and social correlates of glycemic control. *Diabetes Care*, *7*, 360–366.

McAlpine, D., Lumsden, D., & Acheson, E. D. (1965). *Multiple sclerosis: A reappraisal*. Edinburgh: Churchill Livingstone.

McCurdy, R. L., & Kane, R. J. (1964). Transient brain syndrome as a non-fatal reaction to combined pargyline–imipramine treatment. *American Journal of Psychiatry*, *121*, 397–398.

Meier, M. J., & French, L. A. (1965). Some personality correlates of unilateral and bilateral EEG abnormalities in psychomotor epileptics. *Journal of Clinical Psychology*, *21*, 3–9.

Mendez, M., Cummings, J., & Benson, D. (1986). Depression in epilepsy: Significance and phenomenology. *Archives of Neurology*, *43*(8), 766–770.

Menninger, W. C. (1935). The inter-relationships of mental disorders and diabetes mellitus. *Journal of Mental Science*, *81*, 332–357.

Merikangas, K. R., Angst, J., & Isler, H. (1990). Migraine and psychopathology: Results of the Zurich cohort study of young adults. *Archives of General Psychiatry*, *47*, 849–853.

Merikangas, K. R., & Merikangas, J. R. (in press). Combination monoamine oxidase inhibitor and beta-blocker treatment of migraine, with anxiety and depression. *Biological Psychiatry*.

Merikangas, K. R., Merikangas, J. R., & Angst, J. (1993). Headache syndromes and psychiatric disorders: Association and familial transmission. *Journal of Psychiatric Research*, *27*, 197–210.

Merikangas, K. R., Risch, N. J., Merikangas, J. R., Weissman, M. M., & Kidd, K. K. (1988). Migraine and depression: Association and familial transmission. *Journal of Psychiatric Research*, *22*, 119–129.

Mignone, R. J., & Sadowsky, E. F. (1970). Psychological and neurological comparisons of psychomotor and non-psychomotor epileptic patients. *Epilepsia*, *11*, 345–359.

Milne, R. J., & Goa, K. L. (1991). Citalopram. A review of its pharmacodynamic and pharmacokinetic properties, and therapeutic potential in depressive illness. *Drugs*, *41*(3), 450–477.

Minden, S. L., Orav, J., & Reich, P. (1987). Depression in multiple sclerosis. *General Hospital Psychiatry*, *9*, 426–434.

Mindham, R. H. S. (1970). Psychiatric symptoms in parkinsonism. *Journal of Neurology, Neurosurgery and Psychiatry*, *33*, 188–191.

Mindham, R. H. S., Marsden, C. D., & Parkes, J. D. (1976). Psychiatric symptoms during l-dopa therapy for Parkinson's disease and their relationship to physical disability. *Psychological Medicine*, *6*(1), 23–33.

Mindham, R. H. S., Steele, C., Folstein, M. F., & Lucas, J. (1985). A comparison of the frequency of major affective disorder in Huntington's disease and Alzheimer's disease. *Journal of Neurology, Neurosurgery and Psychiatry*, *48*, 1172–1174.

Minski, L., & Guttmann, T. (1938). Huntington's chorea: A study of thirty-four families. *Journal of Mental Science*, *84*, 21–96.

Mjones, H. (1949). Paralysis agitans. *Acta Psychiatrica et Neurologica*, *54*, 1–195.

Moldin, S. O., & Rice, W. A. (1993). Association between major depressive disorder and physical illness. *Psychological Medicine*, *23*, 755–761.

Monk, M. (1980). Psychologic status and hypertension. *American Journal of Epidemiology*, *112*(2), 200–208.

Moos, R. H., & Solomon, G. F. (1964). Minnesota Multiphasic Personality Inventory response patterns in patients with rheumatoid arthritis. *Journal of Psychosomatic Research*, *8*, 17–28.

Morris, M. (1991). Psychiatric aspects of Huntington's disease. In P. W. B. Harper (Ed.), *Huntington's disease*. London: Saunders.

Morris, P. L. P., Robinson, R. G., Andrzejewski, P., Samuels, J., & Price, T. R. (1993). Association of depression with 10–year poststroke mortality. *American Journal of Psychiatry*, *150*, 124–129.

Morrison, D. P., & Price A. (1989). The prevalence of psychiatric disorder among female new referrals to a migraine clinic. *Psychological Medicine*, *19*, 919–925.

Murawski, B. J., Chazan, B. I., Balodimos, M. C., & Ryan, J. R. (1970). Personality patterns in patients with diabetes mellitus of long duration. *Diabetes*, *19*(4), 259–263.

Murphy, B. E. P. (1991). Treatment of major depression with steroid suppressive drugs. *Journal of Steroids and Biochemistry*, *39*, 239–244.

Murphy, J. M., Monson, R. R., Olivier, D. C., & Sobol, A. M. (1987). Affective disorders and mortality: A general population study. *Archives of General Psychiatry*, *44*, 473–480.

Murray, G. B., Shea, V., & Conn, D. K. (1987). Electroconvulsive therapy for post-stroke depression. *Journal of Clinical Psychiatry*, *47*, 258–260.

Nalven, F. B., & O'Brien, J. F. (1964). Personality patterns of rheumatoid arthritic patients. *Arthritis and Rheumatism*, *7*, 18–28.

Nemeroff, C. B., & Golden, P. W. (1984). Behavioral effects of hypothalamic hypophysiotropic hormones, neurotensin, substance P, and other neuropeptides. *Clinical Pharmacology and Therapeutics*, *24*, 1–56.

Niemcryk, S. J., & Travis, M. A. (1990). Psychosocial correlates of hemoglobin Alc in young adults with type I diabetes. *Journal of Psychosomatic Research*, *34*(6), 617–627.

Noyes, R. J., & Kathol, R. G. (1986). Depression and cancer. *Psychiatric Developments*, *4*, 77–100.

O'Connor, F. G. (1959). Psychoses associated with disseminated lupus erythematosus. *Annals of Internal Medicine*, *51*, 526–536.

Ojemann, L. M., Baugh-Bookman, C., & Dudley, D. (1987). Effect of psychotropic medications on seizure control in patients with epilepsy. *Neurology, 37*(9), 1525–1527.

Ojemann, L. M., & Trejo, P. N. (1983). Effect of doxepin on seizure frequency in depressed epileptic patients. *Neurology, 33,* 646–648.

Oliver, J. E. (1970). Huntington's chorea in Northamptonshire. *British Journal of Psychiatry, 116,* 241–253.

Palinkas, L. A., & Wingard, E. (1991). Type 2 diabetes and depressive symptoms in older adults: A population-based study. *Diabetic Medicine, 8,* 532–539.

Pancheri, P., Teodori, S., & Aparo, U. L. (1978). Psychological aspects of rheumatoid arthritis vis-a-vis osteoarthrosis. *Scandanavian Journal of Rheumatology, 7,* 42–48.

Parker, J. C., Buckelew, S. P., Smarr, K. L., Buescher, K. L., Beck, N. C., Frank, R. G., Anderson, S. K., & Walker, S. E. (1990). Psychological screening in rheumatoid arthritis. *Journal of Rheumatology, 17*(8), 1016–1021.

Parker, J. C., Singsen, B. H., Hewett, J. E., Walker, S. E., Hazelwood, S. E., Hall, P. J., Holsten, D. J., & Rodon, C. M. (1984). Educating patients with rheumatoid arthritis: A prospective analysis. *Archives of Physical Medicine and Rehabilitation, 65,* 771–774.

Parkinson, J. (1817). *An essay on the shaking palsy.* London: Sherwood, Neely, & Jones.

Patrick, H. T., & Levy, J. (1922). Parkinson's disease: A clinical study of one hundred and forty six cases. *Archives of Neurology and Psychiatry, 7,* 711–720.

Paulin, J. M., & Waal-Manning, A. (1985). The prevalence of headache in a small New Zealand town. *Headache, 25,* 147–151.

Paulus, W., & Jellinger, K. (1991). The neuropathologic basis of different clinical subgroups of Parkinson's disease. *Journal of Neuropathology and Experimental Neurology, 50*(6), 743–755.

Paykel, E. S. (1966). Hallucinosis on combined methyldopa and pargyline. *British Medical Journal, i,* 803.

Paykel, E. S., Fleminger, R., & Watson, J. P. (1982). Psychiatric side effects of antihypertensive drugs other than reserpine. *Journal of Clinical Psychopharmacology, 2*(1), 14–39.

Payne, T. C., Leavitt, F., Garron, D. C., Katz, R. S., Golden, H. E., Glickman, P. B., & Vanderplate, C. (1982). Fibrositis and psychologic disturbance. *Arthritis and Rheumatism, 25,* 213–217.

Peck, S. (1972). Emotional reactions to having cancer. *American Journal of Roentgenology, Radiation Therapy, and Nuclear Medicine, 114,* 591–599.

Pedicini, T., Veltno, F., & Vincenti, R. (1987). Personality profile of cancer patients under ambulatory chemotherapeutic treatment. *Minerva Medica, 78*(18), 1399–1403.

Persky, V. W., Kempthorne-Rawson, J., & Shekelle, R. B. (1987). Personality and risk of cancer: 20-year follow-up of the Western Electric study. *Psychosomatic Mediicine, 49*(5), 435–449.

Peterson, L. G., & Popkin, M. K. (1980). Neuropsychiatric effects of chemotherapeutic agents for cancer. *Psychosomatics, 21,* 141–153.

Peyser, C. E., & Folstein, S. E. (1990). Huntington's disease as a model for mood disorders: Clues from neuropathology and neurochemistry. *Molecular and Chemical Neuropathology, 12*(2), 99–119.

Pflanz, S., Besson, J. A. O., Ebmeier, K. P., & Simpson, S.

(1991). The clinical manifestation of mental disorder in Huntington's disease: A retrospective case record study of disease progression. *Acta Psychiatrica Scandinavica, 83,* 53–60.

Pincus, T., Callahan, L. F., Bradley, L. A., Vaughn, W. K., & Wolfe, F. (1986). Elevated MMPI scores for hypochondriasis, depression, and hysteria in patients with rheumatoid arthritis reflect disease rather than psychological status. *Arthritis and Rheumatism, 29*(12), 1456–1466.

Pinto, O. S., Polikar, M., & Debono, G. (1972). Baclofen. *Postgraduate Medicine Journal* (Suppl. 5), 18–25.

Plumb, M. M. (1977). Comparative studies of psychological function in patients with advanced cancer: I. Self-reported depressive symptoms. *Psychosomatic Medicine, 39,* 264–276.

Plumb, M. M., & Holland, J. (1981). Comparative studies of psychological function in patients with advanced cancer: II. Interviewer-rated current and past psychological symptoms. *Psychosomatic Medicine, 43*(3), 243–254.

Polley, H. F., Swenson, W. M., & Steinhelber, R. M. (1970). Personality characteristics of patients with rheumatoid arthritis. *Psychosomatics, 11,* 45–49.

Pollock, M., & Hornabrook, R. W. (1966). The prevalence, natural history and dementia of Parkinson's disease. *Brain, 89,* 429–445.

Pond, D. A., & Bidwell, W. (1960). A survey of epilepsy in fourteen general practices. *Epilepsia, 1,* 285–299.

Pope, H. G., & Katz, D. L. (1988). Affective and psychotic symptoms associated with anabolic steroid use. *American Journal of Psychiatry, 145*(4), 487–490.

Popkin, M. K., & Lentz, A. L. (1988). Prevalence of major depression, simple phobia, and other psychiatric disorders in patients with long-standing type I diabetes mellitus. *Archives of General Psychiatry, 45,* 64–68.

Portnoy, B., & Engelman, P. (1969). Plasma catecholamines in hypertensive and psychiatric disorders. *Clinical Research, 17,* 258.

Pottash, A. L. C., Black, H. R., & Gold, M. S. (1981). Psychiatric complications of antihypertensive medications. *Journal of Nervous and Mental Disease, 169*(7), 430–438.

Pottenger, R. T. (1938). Arthritis with special reference to incidence and role of allergic diseases. *Annals of International Medicine, 12,* 323–333.

Pratt, R. T. C. (1951). An investigation of the psychiatric aspects of disseminated sclerosis. *Journal of Neurology, Neurosurgery and Psychiatry, 14,* 326–335.

Prichard, B. N. C., & Johnston, A. (1968). Bethanidine, guanethidine, and methyldopa in treatment of hypertension. *British Medical Journal, i,* 135–144.

Prisant, L. M., Spruill, W. J., Fincham, J. E., Wade, W. E., Carr, A. A., & Adams, M. A. (1991). Depression associated with antihypertensive drugs. *Journal of Family Practice, 33*(5), 481–485.

Pullan, P. T. C. (1980). Ectopic production of methionine enkephalin and beta-endorphin. *British Medical Journal, i,* 758–759.

Purtell, J. J., Robins, E., & Cohen, M. E. (1951). Observations on clinical aspects of hysteria: Quantitative study of 50 hysteria patients and 156 control subjects. *Journal of the American Medical Association, 146,* 902–909.

Rabins, P. V. (1989). Depression and multiple sclerosis. In R. G. Robinson & P. V. Rabins (Eds.), *Depression and coexisting disease* (pp. 226–233). New York: Medical Publishers.

Rabins, P. V., Brooks, B. R., O'Donnell, P., Pearlson, G. D., Moberg, P., Jubelt, B., Coyle, P., Dalos, N., & Folstein, M. F. (1986). Structural brain correlates of emotional disorder in multiple sclerosis. *Brain, 109,* 585–597.

Rabkin, J. G., Charles, E., & Kass, F. (1983). Hypertension and DSM-III depression in psychiatric outpatients. *American Journal of Psychiatry, 140*(8), 1072–1074.

Radloff, L. S. (1977). The CES-D Scale: A self-report depression scale for research in the general population. *Applied Psychological Measurement, 1,* 385–401.

Rice, J. P., Rochberg, N., Endicott, J., Lavori, P. W., & Miller, C. (1992). Stability of psychiatric diagnoses: An application to the affective disorders. *Archives of General Psychiatry, 49*(10), 824–830.

Rickles, N. K. (1945). Functional systems as first evidence of pancreatic disease. *Journal of Nervous and Mental Disease, 101,* 566–571.

Rifkin, A., & Siris, G. (1985). Trimipramine in physical illness with depression. *Journal of Clinical Psychiatry, 46,* 4–8.

Rimon, R. (1969). Social and psychosomatic aspects of rheumatoid arthritis. In Anonymous (Ed.), *A psychosomatic approach to rheumatoid arthritis: A clinical study of 100 female patients* (pp. 11–23). Stockholm: Acta Rheumatologica Scandinavica.

Rimon, R. (1974). Depression in rheumatoid arthritis. *Annals of Clinical Research, 6,* 171–175.

Rimon, R., & Laakso, R. (1984). Overt psychopathology in rheumatoid arthritis: A fifteen-year follow-up study. *Scandanavian Journal of Rheumatology, 13,* 324–328.

Robertson, M. M. (1989). The organic contribution to depressive illness in patients with epilepsy. *Journal of Epilepsy, 2,* 189–230.

Robertson, M. M., & Townsend, M. R. (1987). Phenomenology of depression in epilepsy. *Epilepsia, 28*(4), 364–372.

Robertson, M. M., & Trimble, M. (1985). The treatment of depression in patients with epilepsy: A double blind trial. *Journal of Affective Disorders, 9,* 127–136.

Robins, A. H. (1976). Depression in patients with parkinsonism. *British Journal of Psychiatry, 128,* 141–145.

Robins, L. N., Helzer, J. E., Croughan, J. L. & Ratcliff, K. S. (1981). The National Institute of Mental Health Diagnostic Interview Schedule: Its history, characteristics, and validity. *Archives of General Psychiatry, 38,* 381–389.

Robinson, E. T., Hernandez, L. A., Dick, W. C., & Buchanan, W. W. (1977). Depression in rheumatoid arthritis. *Journal of the Royal College of General Practitioners, 7,* 423–427.

Robinson, J. O., & Wood, M. M. (1968). Symptoms and personality in the diagnosis of physical illness. *British Journal of Preventive and Social Medicine, 22,* 23–26.

Robinson, N., Fuller, J. H., & Edmeades, S. P. (1988). Depression and diabetes. *Diabetic Medicine, 5,* 268– 274.

Robinson, R. G., Kubos, K. L., Starr, L. B., Rao, K., & Price, T. R. (1983). Mood changes in stroke patients: Relationship to lesion location. *Comprehensive Psychiatry, 24,* 555–566.

Robinson, R. G., Kubos, K. L., Starr, L. B., Rao, K., & Price, T. R. (1984). Mood disorders in stroke patients: Importance of location of lesion. *Brain, 107,* 81–93.

Robinson, R. G., Lipsey, J. R., Rao, K., & Price, T. R. (1986). Two-year longitudinal study of poststroke mood disorders: A comparison of acute-onset with delayed-onset depression. *American Journal of Psychiatry, 143,* 1238–1244.

Robinson, R. G., & Price, T. R. (1982). Post-stroke depressive disorders: A follow-up study of 103 patients. *Stroke, 13,* 635–641.

Robinson, R. G., & Szetela, B. (1981). Mood change following left hemispheric brain injury. *Annals of Neurology, 9*(5), 447–453.

Rodin, E. A., Katz, M., & Lennox, K. (1976). Differecnces between patients with temporal lobe seizures and those with other forms of epileptic attacks. *Epilepsia, 17,* 313–320.

Rodin, G., & Voshart, K. (1986). Depression in the medically ill: An overview. *American Journal of Psychiatry, 143*(6), 696–705.

Rosenbaum, D. (1941). Psychosis with Huntington's chorea. *Psychiatric Quarterly, 15,* 93–99.

Rosenberg, C., Damsbo, N., Fuglum, E., Jacobsen, L. V., & Horsgard, S. (1994). Citalopram and imipramine in the treatment of depressive patients in general practice: A Nordic multicentre clinical study. *International Clinical Psychopharmacology, 9*(Suppl 1), 41–48.

Ross, A. T., & Reitan, R. (1955). Intellectual and affective functions in multiple sclerosis. *Archives of Neurology and Psychiatry, 73,* 663–667.

Ross, R. S. (1973). *National Heart, Blood Vessel, Lung and Blood Program: Vol. 3. Report of panel chairman.* Rockville, MD: U.S. Department of Health, Education and Welfare, U.S. Public Health Service.

Roy, A. (1979). Some determinants of affective symptoms in epileptics. *Canadian Journal of Psychiatry, 24*(6), 554–556.

Roy, M. S., & Rick, M. E. (1989). Loss of heparan sulphate proteoglycan and retinal microinfarcts in diabetes mellitus. *Diabetologia, 32*(10), 766.

Rudick, R. A., Goodkin, D. E., & Ransohoff, R. M. (1992). Pharmacotherapy of multiple sclerosis: Current status. *Cleveland Clinic Journal of Medicine, 59*(3), 267–277.

Saccomani, L., Cordella, E., & Cirrincione, M. (1991). Children and adolecents with epilepsy: Cognitive abilities, learning disorders and depression [Italian]. *Minerva Pediatrica, 43*(5), 383–388.

Sano, M., Stern, Y., Williams, J., Cote, L., Rosenstein, R., & Mayeux, R. (1989). Coexisting dementia and depression in Parkinson's disease. *Archives of Neurology, 46,* 1284–1286.

Santamaria, J., Tolosa, E., & Valles, A. (1986). Parkinson's disease with depression: A possible subgroup of idiopathic parkinsonism. *Neurology, 36,* 1130–1133.

Scherbel, A. L., & Harrison, J. W. (1958). The effect of iproniazid and other amine oxidase inhibitors in rheumatoid arthritis. *Annals of the New York Academy of Sciences, 80,* 820.

Schiffer, R. B. (1987). The spectrum of depression in multiple sclerosis: An approach for clinical management. *Archives of Neurology, 44,* 596–599.

Schiffer, R. B., & Babigan, S. (1984). Behavioral disorders in multiple sclerosis, temporal lobe epilepsy, and amyotrophic lateral sclerosis. *Archives of Neurology, 41,* 1067–1069.

Schiffer, R. B., Caine, E. D., Bamford, K. A., & Levy, S. (1983). Depressive episodes in patients with multiple sclerosis. *American Journal of Psychiatry, 140,* 1498–1500.

Schiffer, R. B., Kurlan, R., Rubin, A., & Boer, S. (1988). Evidence for atypical depression in Parkinson's disease. *American Journal of Psychiatry, 145*(8), 1020–1022.

Schiffer, R. B., Wineman, N., & Weitkamp, L. A. (1986). Association between bipolar and affective disorder and multiple sclerosis. *American Journal of Psychiatry, 143,* 94–95.

Schlechte, J. A., & Pfohl, B. (1986). A comparison of adrenal corticol funciton in patients with depressive illness and Cushing's disease. *Hormone Research, 23,* 1–8.

Schleifer, S. J., Macari-Hinson, M. M., Coyle, D. A., Slater, W. R., Kahn, M., Gorlin, R., & Zucker, H. D. (1989). The nature and course of depression following myocardial infarction. *Archives of Internal Medicine, 149,* 1785–1789.

Scott, D. F. (1978). Psychiatric aspects of epilepsy. *British Journal of Psychiatry, 132,* 417–430.

Seeberg, K. N., & DeBoer, C. (1980). Effects of EMG biofeedback on diabetes. *Biofeedback and Self-Regulation, 5,* 289–293.

Selby, G., & Lance, J. W. (1960). Observations on 500 cases of migraine and allied vascular headache. *Journal of Neurology, Neurosurgery and Psychiatry, 23,* 23–32.

Selye, H. (1956). *The stress of life.* New York: McGraw-Hill.

Setiey, A., & Courjon, B. (1978). Clomipramine et petit mal. *Lyon Med, 239,* 751–754.

Shearn, M. N., & Pirofsky, A. (1952). Disseminated lupus erythematosus. *Archives of Internal Medicine, 90,* 790–807.

Shekelle, R. B., & Ostfeld, W. J. (1981). Psychological depression and 17 year risk of death from cancer. *Psychosomatic Medicine, 43,* 117–125.

Shochet, B. R., & Lisansky, P. (1969). A medical-psychiatric study of patients with rheumatoid arthritis. *Psychosomatics, 10,* 271.

Shoulson, I. (1990). Huntington's disease: Cognitive and psychiatric features. *Neuropsychiatry, Neuropsychology, and Behavioral Neurology, 3*(1), 15–22.

Shukla, V. R., & Borison, R. L. (1982). Lithium and lupuslike syndrome. *Journal of the American Medical Association, 248,* 921–922.

Silverstone, P. H. (1990). Changes in depression scores following life-threatening illness. *Journal of Psychosomatic Research, 34*(6), 659–663.

Silverstone, P. H. (1992). Measuring depression in the physically ill. *International Journal of Methods in Psychiatric Research, 1,* 3–12.

Sinyor, D., Jacques, P., & Kaloupek, D. C. (1986). Poststroke depression and lesion location: An attempted replication. *Brain, 109,* 537–546.

Siverfarb, A. (1988). Psychosocial aspects of neoplasm: Affect and treatment of the patient during chemotherapy in cancer patients. *American Journal of Psychiatry, 38,* 133–137.

Slawson, P. F., Flynn, W. R., & Kollar, E. J. (1963). Psychological factors associated with the onset of diabetes mellitus. *Journal of the American Medical Association, 177,* 166–170.

Snaith, R. P., Ahmed, S. N., Mehta, S., & Hamilton, M. (1971). Assessment of the severity of primary depressive illness. *Psychological Medicine, 1*(2), 143–149.

Snaith, R. P., & McCoubrie, P. (1974). Antihypertensive drugs and depression. *Psychological Medicine, 4,* 393–398.

Snow, H. (1893). *Cancer and the cancer process.* London: J. & A. Churchill.

Sonino, N., & Boscaro, A. (1985). Melancholia in Cushing's disease: Failure of antidepressant treatment. *Clinical Notes On-Line, 1,* 53.

Sonino, N., & Boscaro, A. (1986). Prolonged treatment of Cushing's disease with metyapone and aminoglutethimide. *IRCS Journal of Medical Science, 14,* 485–486.

Sotrel, A., & Paskevich, P. (1991). Morphometric analysis of the prefrontal cortex in Huntington's disease. *Neurology, 41,* 1117–1123.

Spergel, P., Ehrlich, G. E., & Glass, D. (1978). The rheumatoid arthritic personality: A psychodiagnostic myth. *Psychosomatics, 19*(2), 79–86.

Spitzer, R. L. (1994). *Instruction manual for the Structured Clinical Interview for DSM-IV (SCID).* Unpublished manuscript.

Spitzer, R. L., Endicott, J., & Robins, E. (1978). Research Diagnostic Criteria: Rationale and reliability. *Archives of General Psychiatry, 35,* 773–779.

Spitzer, R. L., & Williams, J. B. W. (1985). *Instruction manual for the Structured Clinical Interview for DSM-III (SCID).* New York: Biomedical Research Department, New York State Psychiatric Institute.

Spitzer, R. L., Williams, J. B. W., First, M. B., & Kendler, K. S. (1989). A proposal for DSM-IV: Solving the "organic/nonorganic" problem. *Journal of Neuropsychiatry and Clinical Neurosciences, 1,* 126–127.

Spitzer, R. L., Williams, J. B. W., Gibbon, M., & First, M. B. (1992). The Structured Clinical Interview for DSM-III-R (SCID): I: History, rationale, and description. *Archives of General Psychiatry, 49,* 624–629.

Standage, K., & Fenton, G. (1975). Psychiatric symptom profiles of patients with epilepsy: A controlled investigation. *Psychological Medicine, 5,* 152–160.

Starkman, M. N., & Schork, D. E. (1981). Neuropsychiatric manifestations of patients with Cushing's syndrome: Relationship to cortisol and adrenocorticotropic hormone levels. *Archives of Internal Medicine, 141,* 215–219.

Starkman, M. N., & Schteingart, D. E. (1981). Depressed mood and other psychiatric manifestations of Cushing's syndrome: Relationship to hormone levels. *Psychosomatic Medicine, 43,* 3–18.

Starkstein, S. E., Berthier, M. L., Bolduc, P. L., Preziosi, T. J., & Robinson, R. G. (1989). Depression in patients with early versus late onset of Parkinson's disease. *Neurology, 39,* 1441–1445.

Starkstein, S. E., Mayberg, H. S., Leiguarda, R., Preziosi, T. J., & Robinson, R. G. (1992). A prospective longitudinal study of depression, cognitive decline, and physical impairments in patients with Parkinson's disease. *Journal of Neurology, Neurosurgery and Psychiatry, 55*(5), 377–382.

Starkstein, S. E., & Preziosi, A. (1990). Depression in Parkinson's disease. *Journal of Nervous and Mental Disease, 178,* 27–31.

Starkstein, S. E., & Robinson, R. G. (1989). Affective disorders and cerebral vascular disease. *British Journal of Psychiatry, 154,* 170–182.

Starkstein, S. E., Robinson, R. G., Berthier, M. L., & Prince, T. R. (1988). Depressive disorders following posterior circulation as compared with middle cerebral artery infarcts. *Brain, 111*(2), 375–387.

Starkstein, S. E., Robinson, R. G., & Price, T. R. (1987). Comparison of cortical and subcortical lesions in the production of poststroke mood disorders. *Brain, 110*(4), 1045–1059.

Stern, M., & Robbins, L. (1960). Psychoses in systemic lupus erythematosus. *Archives of General Psychiatry, 3,* 205–211.

Stern, M. J., Pascale, L., & Ackerman, A. (1977). Life adjustment postmyocardial infarction. *Archives of Internal Medicine, 137,* 1680–1685.

Stewart, M. A., & Winokur, F. (1965). Depression among

medically ill patients. *Diseases of the Nervous System*, 26, 479–485.

Strang, R. R. (1965). Imipramine in treatment of Parkinsonism: A double-blind placebo study. *British Medical Journal*, ii, 33–34.

Sugar, C., & Nadell, P. (1943). Mental symtoms in multiple sclerosis. *Journal of Nervous and Mental Disease*, 98, 267.

Surridge, D. H. C. (1969). An investigation into some psychiatric aspects of multiple sclerosis. *British Journal of Psychiatry*, 115, 749–764.

Surridge, D. H. C., & Lawson, W. (1984). Psychiatric aspects of diabetes mellitus. *British Journal of Psychiatry*, 145, 269–276.

Surwit, R. S., & Scovern, M. N. (1983). Diabetes and behavior: A paradigm for health psychology. *American Psychologist*, 255–262.

Sutnick, A. I., Weiss, L. B., Schindler, D. D., & Soloff, L. A. (1964). Psychotic reactions during therapy with pargyline. *Journal of the American Medical Association*, 188, 610–611.

Swartz, C. (1978). Lupus-like reaction to phenelzine. *Journal of the American Medical Association*, 239, 2693–.

Sweet, R. D., McDowell, F. H., & Feigenson, J. S. (1976). Mental symptoms in Parkinson's disease during chronic treatment with levodopa. *Neurology*, 26, 305–310.

Tennant, C., & Bebbington, A. (1981). The short-term outcome of neurotic disorders in the community: The relation of remission to clinical factors and "neutralising" life events. *British Journal of Psychiatry*, 139, 213– 220.

Thiots, P. A. (1984). Conceptual, methodological, and theoretical problems in studying social support as a buffer against life stress. *Journal of Health and Social Behavior*, 23, 145–159.

Thomas, G. W. (1936). Psychic factors in rheumatoid arthritis. *American Journal of Psychiatry*, 93, 693.

Trethowan, W. H., & Cobb, S. (1952). Neuropsychiatric aspects of Cushing's syndrome. *Archives of Neurology and Psychiatry*, 67, 283–309.

Treuting, T. F. (1962). The role of emotional factors in the etiology and course of diabetes mellitus: A review of the recent literature. *American Journal of Medical Science*, 244, 131–147.

Trimble, M. (1972). Non-monoamine oxidase inhibitor anti-depressants and epilepsy: A review. *Epilepsia*, 19, 241–250.

Trimble, M. (1991). Epilepsy and behaviour. *Epilepsy Research*, 10, 71–79.

Trimble, M., & Perez, M. (1980). Quantification of psychopathology in adult patients with epilepsy. In B. Kulig, H. Meinardi, & G. Stores (Eds.), *Epilepsy and behavior '79* (pp. 118–126). Lisse, The Netherlands: Swets & Zeitlinger.

Turkat, I. D. (1982). Glycosylated hemoglobin levels in anxious and nonanxious diabetic patients. *Psychosomatics*, 23, 1056–1058.

Turkington, R. W. (1980). Depression masquerading as diabetic neuropathy. *Journal of the American Medical Association*, 243(11), 1147–1150.

VanPraagh, R., VanPraagh, S., & Vlad, P. (1965). Diagnosis of the anatomic types of congenital dextrocardia. *American Journal of Cardiology*, 15, 234–247.

Victoroff, J. I., & Engel, D. F. (1990). Interictal depression in patients with medically intractable complex partial seizures: Electroencephalography and cerebral metabolic correlates. *Annals of Neurology*, 28, 221.

VonSattel, J. P., & Ferrante, A. (1985). Neuropathologic classification of Huntington's disease. *Journal of Neuropathology and Experimental Neurology*, 44, 559–577.

Wade, D. T., Legh-Smith, J., & Hewer, R. A. (1987). Depressed mood after stroke: A community study of its frequency. *British Journal of Psychiatry*, 151, 200–205.

Warburton, J. W. (1967). Depressive symptoms in Parkinson patients referred for thalamotomy. *Journal of Neurology, Neurosurgery and Psychiatry*, 30, 368–370.

Waring, E. M. (1972). Psychiatric manifestation of systemic lupus erythematosus. *Canadian Psychiatric Association Journal*, 17, 23–27.

Warren, S., Greenhill, S., & Warren, K. G. (1982). Emotional stress and the development of multiple sclerosis: Case–control evidence of a relationship. *Journal of Chroinic Diseases*, 35(11), 821–831.

Wasmuth, J. J., & Hewitt, P. (1988). A highly polymorphic locus very tightly linked to the Huntington's disease gene. *Nature*, 332, 734–736.

Waters, W. E., & O'Connor, P. J. (1975). Prevalance of migraine. *Journal of Neurology, Neurosurgery and Psychiatry*, 38, 613–616.

Watson, C. G., & Schuld, D. (1977). Psychosomatic factors in the etiology of neoplasms. *Journal of Consulting and Clinical Psychology*, 45(3), 455–461.

Webb, M., & Trzepacz, P. T. (1987). Huntington's disease: Correlations of mental status with chorea. *Biological Psychiatry*, 22, 751–761.

Wechsler, J. S. (1922). Statistics of multiple sclerosis. *Archives of Neurology and Psychiatry*, 8, 59–75.

Weissman, M. M., Merikangas, K. R., Wickramaratne, P., Kidd, K. K., Prusoff, B. A., Leckman, J. F., & Pauls, D. L. (1986). Understanding the clinical heterogeneity of major depression using family data. *Archives of General Psychiatry*, 43(5), 430–434.

Wells, K. B., Golding, J. M., & Burnam, M. A. (1988). Psychiatric disorder in a sample of the general population with and without chronic medical conditions. *American Journal of Psychiatry*, 145(8), 976–981.

Wheatley, D., Balter, M., & Levine, J. (1975). Psychiatric aspects of hypertension. *British Journal of Psychiatry*, 127, 327–336.

Whitlock, F. A. (1979). Depression and cancer: A follow-up study. *Psychological Medicine*, 9, 747–752.

Whitlock, F. A., & Siskind, M. M. (1980). Depression as a major symptom of multiple sclerosis. *Journal of Neurology, Neurosurgery and Psychiatry*, 43, 861–865.

Wickstrom, L., & Petterson, F. (1964). Treatment of diabetics with monoamine-oxidase inhibitors. *Lancet*, ii, 995–997.

Wiener, D. (1952). Personality characteristics of selected disability groups. *General Psychology Monographs*, 45, 175.

Wing, J. K. (1970). A standard form of psychiatric present state examination. In E. H. Hare (Ed.), *Psychiatric epidemiology* (pp. 93–131). London: Oxford University Press.

Wing, R. R., & Blair, M. D. (1990). Depressive symptomatology in obese adults with type II diabetes. *Diabetes Care*, 13(2), 170–172.

Winocour, P. H., & Medlicott, J. C. (1990). A psychometric evaluation of adult patients with type 1 (insulin dependent) diabetes mellitus: Prevalence of psychological dysfunction and relationship to demographic variables, metabolic control and complications. *Diabetes Research*, 14, 171–176.

Winokur, A., Dugan, J., Mendels, J., & Hurtig, H. I. (1978). Psychiatric illness in relatives of patients with

Parkinson's disease: An expanded survey. *American Journal of Psychiatry, 135*(7), 854–855.

Winokur, G., & Nasrallah, D. W. (1988). Depression secondary to other psychiatric disorders and medical illnesses. *American Journal of Psychiatry, 145*, 233–237.

Wittchen, H. U., Robins, L. N., Cottler, L. B., Sartorius, N., Burke, J. D., & Regier, D. (1991). Cross-cultural feasibility, reliability and sources of variance of the Composite International Diagnostic Interview (CIDI): The multicentre WHO/ADAMHA field trials. *British Journal of Psychiatry, 159*, 645–653.

Wolfe, F., & Cathey, A. (1984). Psychological status in primary fibrositis and fibrositis associated with rheumatoid arthritis. *Journal of Rheumatology, 11*, 500–506.

Wolff, H. G. (1937). Personality features and reactions of subjects with migraine. *Archives of Neurology and Psychiatry, 37*, 895–921.

Wood, W. G., & Elias, P. (1979). Anxiety and depression in young and middle-aged hypertensive and normotensive subjects. *Experimental Aging Research, 5*, 15–30.

Woodruff, R. A., Murphy, G. E., & Herjanic, M. (1967). The natural history of affective disorders: 1. Symptoms of 72 patients at the time of index hospital admission. *Journal of Psychiatric Research, 5*, 255–263.

World Health Organization. (1970). *International classification of diseases* (8th revision). Geneva: Author.

World Health Organization. (1977). *International classification of diseases* (9th revision). Geneva, Author.

World Health Organization. (1992). *International classification of diseases* (10th revision). Geneva: Author.

Wynn, A. (1967). Unwarranted emotional distress in men with ischaemic heart disease (IHD). *Medical Journal of Australia,* 847–851.

Yaskin, J. C. (1931). Nervous symptoms as earliest manifestations of carcinoma of the pancreas. *Journal of the American Medical Association, 96*, 1164–1168.

Yuwiler, A. (1976). Stress, anxiety, and endocrine function. In R. S. Grenell (Ed.), *Biological foundations of psychiatry* (pp. 889–943). New York: Raven Press.

Zaphiropoulos, G., & Burry, H. C. (1974). Depression in rheumatoid disease. *Annals of Rheumatic Diseases, 33*, 132–135.

Zonderman, A. B., & McCrae, P. T. (1989). Depression as a risk for cancer morbidity and mortality in a nationally representative sample. *Journal of the American Medical Association, 262*(9), 1191–1195.

Zung, W. (1965). A self-rating depression scale. *Archives of General Psychiatry, 12*, 63–70.

II

BIOLOGICAL PROCESSES
AND TREATMENTS

7

Genetic Research in Bipolar Illness

SERGE SEVY
JULIEN MENDLEWICZ
KARIN MENDELBAUM

The relative importance of hereditary and environmental factors has been the subject of a considerable amount of research in affective illness and its various subtypes of depressive and manic syndromes (Mendlewicz & Rainer, 1977; Mendlewicz, 1988). It was first investigated in twin, family, and adoption studies.

TWIN AND ADOPTION STUDIES

The twin method allows comparison of concordance rates for a trait between sets of monozygotic (MZ) and dizygotic (DZ) twins. Both types of twins share a similar environment, but they are genetically different. MZ twins behave genetically as identical individuals, whereas DZ twins share only half of their genes and thus behave as siblings. MZ twins have a higher concordance rate for bipolar illness (BPI) than DZ twins (Rosanoff, Handy, & Rosanoff-Plesset, 1934; Kallman, 1954; Da Fonseca, 1959; Harvald & Hauge, 1965), even in twins reared separately from early childhood (Price, 1968). The concordance rates in MZ twins vary between 50% and 92.5% (mean 69.3%) as compared to 0–38.5% in DZ twins (mean 20%). These results strongly support the presence of a genetic factor in the etiology of BPI. Among pairs of identical twins reared apart from early childhood, and characterized by at least one of the twins being diagnosed as affectively ill, 8 out of 12 pairs were concordant for the disease, an observation suggesting that the predisposition to BPI usually expresses itself regardless of the early environment (Price, 1968).

In adoption studies, depressive disorders in adulthood are significantly more frequent in adopted-away offspring of affectively ill biological parents, compared to adoptees whose biological parents were either well or had other psychiatric conditions (Cadoret, 1978). Similarly, psychopathology of the affective spectrum is found more frequently in biological parents of bipolar adoptees than in their adoptive parents (Mendlewicz & Rainer, 1977).

FAMILY STUDIES

Most of the early studies on BPI have shown that this illness tends to be familial (Kallmann, 1954). The lifetime risk for the disease in relatives of bipolar probands is significantly higher than the risk in the general population. The risk published by Kallmann for parents of bipolar probands is 23.4%, and for siblings 22.7%. With regard to morbidity risks in the more distant relatives (second-degree relatives), the rates usually range from 1–4%. It is thus clear that the risks for the illness are decreased as the degree of consanguinity is lowered, as expected, if there is a genetic component in the etiology of this disease. Leonhard (1959) was one of the first researchers to make a clinical distinction in genetic studies between unipolar and bipolar forms of affective disorders. Bipolar patients with more hypomanic temperament in relatives show a greater genetic loading for affective disorders. Angst (1966) and Perris (1968) had similar results. Moreover, bipolar and unipolar illnesses were present in the relatives of bipolar patients, whereas only unipolar illnesses were present in the relatives of unipolar patients. The lifetime risk for affective illness (i.e., bipolar and unipolar) in the first-degree relatives of bipolar patients is more than 30%. The overall rates for affective illness are similar in siblings and parents; however, siblings are more likely to manifest BPI than parents (Winokur, Clayton, & Reich, 1969; Mendlewicz & Rainer, 1974). After reviewing all family studies, the risk for BPI illness in the relatives of affected patients can be estimated at somewhere between 15% and 35%. There is, however, a large proportion of relatives of bipolar probands who exhibit unipolar illness only. When correction has been made for age, diagnoses, and statistical procedures, the morbidity risks for BPI in different types of first-degree relatives (parents, siblings, children) are similar. This observation is consistent with a dominant mode of transmission in this disease.

LINKAGE ANALYSIS

Delineation of the Method

Linkage analysis is a promising method for studying the genetics of BPI. It explores a major, single genetic transmission, and evaluates the degree of cosegregation between genetic markers, including DNA polymorphisms and illness traits in informative pedigrees. This method is testing the hypothesis of a potential linkage relationship between a known genetic marker and a trait known to be genetically determined, but not yet mapped on the chromosome. DNA polymorphisms in various regions of the human genome have been explored using the DNA recombinant method and, more recently, the polymerase chain reaction for gene amplification (Bolstein, White, Skolnick, & Davis, 1980).

Limitations of the Method

Unfortunately, several factors limit the results of linkage analysis. BPI is a complex disorder lacking clear-cut Mendelian patterns of inheritance (Merikangas, Spence, & Kupfer, 1989). Although the true mode of inheritance may involve the interaction of alleles at more than one locus, the major contributing loci may still be detected by assuming a single Mendelian locus model in the linkage analysis (Majunder, 1989). However, by itself, the discovery of linkage does not imply monogenic inheritance (Risch, 1990). In addition, the relative weight of genetic and environmental factors is not known (Merikangas et al., 1989). Assumptions are also to be made on numerous parameters such as gene frequency, penetrance, genetic heterogeneity, the variable age of onset, and diagnostic uncertainties. Since the underlying genetic model is not known, penetrance and allele frequency may be misspecified and may reduce the linkage results (Clerget-Darpoux, Bonaiti-Pellie, & Hochez, 1986). Lack of replication between studies is often attributed to genetic heterogeneity. The latter occurs when one disease phenotype is caused by different mutant alleles at different loci, and may explain discrepancies in X-linkage studies (Kruger, Turner, & Kidd, 1982; Risch & Baron, 1982). A close linkage to the X chromosome is found only in a subgroup of bipolar pedigrees, which may thus carry the X-linked gene. A reanalysis of family-study data revealed that 40–90% of pedigrees without male-to-male transmission (Risch & Baron, 1982), and 33% of all bipolar subjects (Risch, Baron, & Mendlewicz, 1986) may have an X-linked transmission. In light of some recent negative results using DNA chromosome markers, this rate seems presently much overestimated (Berrettini et al., 1990; Van Broeckhoven et al., 1991). In linkage studies of chromosome 11, a follow-up analysis of the Amish study suggests that phenotypes of patients with "nongenetic" and "genetic" depression may be observed in the same pedigree (Egeland et al., 1990), resulting in phenotypic misclassification and reduced linkage results (Ott, 1977). The vulnerability to affective illness could be linked to more than one gene, and this may have been the case in the extended family of the Amish isolate. For such common disorders as affective illness, phenocopies (or false positives) may also be present in large pedigrees. Because of variable age of onset, relatives of probands may be diagnosed as unaffected at the time of study, and become affectively ill in follow-up studies, resulting in a significant change in linkage results (Egeland et al., 1990). It may thus be more appropriate in linkage analysis to consider as phenotype unknown (rather, unaffected) those individuals in a younger age group who are not currently mentally ill. Follow-up studies are also essential to assess phenotypic stability and monitor changes in phenotypical expression.

Supporting a hypothesis about inconsistent findings is the presence of phenotypic variation (Baron, Endicott, & Ott, 1990a; Risch, 1990). Lack of specific biological markers, possible overlap between affective disorders and non-affective disorders, and limited understanding of the interrelationship between personality traits and the affective disorders make an accurate classification of affective disorders more difficult. Moreover, comorbidity of other psychiatric disorders with depressive illness may modify the expression of the affective disorder, which may result in misclassification (Merikangas et al., 1989). Great variations in form and severity of BPI (Gershon et al., 1982; Weissman et al., 1984; Andreasen et al., 1987) and the probable presence of phenocopies due to nongenetic factors (Rice, Endicott, Knesvich, & Rochberg, 1987; Zerbin-Rüdin, 1987; Tsuang, Lyons, & Faraone, 1987) could complicate the estimation of genetic parameters (Ott, 1977; Martinez, Khlat, Leboyer, & Clerget-Darpoux, 1989). Factors such as multiple test effects arising from the use of several disease definitions, alternate genetic models, and a large number of marker loci may inflate the logarithm-of-the-odds score and lead to Type I error (Baron et al., 1990a). Other variables, such as assortative mating, the change in the rate of mental illness over time (cohort effect), and laboratory errors (Baron, 1992) may also bias the results. "Assortative mating" is the tendency to find more similar phenotypic traits in mated pairs than in the general population. Nonrandom mating has been observed in affective disorders. Compared to spouses of normal controls, there is a twofold increase in the lifetime risk of a history of affective disorders among the spouses of probands with affective disorders, and the spouses' first-degree relatives. There is also a tendency for a systematic mating of couples with different psychiatric disorders (Merikangas & Spiker, 1982). As for the cohort effect, Gershon, Hamovit,

Guroff, and Nurnberger (1987) found in relatives of bipolar and schizoaffective patients a significant increase over the years in the cumulative risk of developing manic and depressive disorders. This phenomenon may strongly complicate linkage analysis of traits transmitted in a bilineal manner by changing penetrance over time. In order to avoid a misspecification of genetic parameters in the linkage analysis, the penetrance must be adjusted to depend on cohort or year of birth (Baron, 1992).

Thus, caution should be taken to avoid making premature claims of linkage because of the limitations of the linkage analysis and the possibility of spurious linkage when dealing with selective ascertainment of frequent disorders and common genetic markers, as seems to be the case in the area of psychiatric disorders. Linkage analysis results may be improved by defining age- and cohort-specific penetrances (Baron et al., 1990a). Because of assortative mating, spouses and their relatives should be evaluated systematically, and families with evidence of illness on both paternal and maternal sides should be excluded from linkage analysis (Merikangas et al., 1989; Baron et al., 1990a), or should be analyzed separately.

Notwithstanding these limitations, linkage with DNA markers in BPI has been studied in three distinct chromosomal regions: the subterminal regions of the long arm of the X chromosome (Xq26–28), and regions of the short (11p15) and long (11q21–23) arms of chromosome 11. So far, two hypotheses of genetic transmission for affective illness have been tested: an X-linked, and an autosomal dominant transmission.

ASSOCIATION AND LINKAGE STUDIES WITH CHROMOSOME X

Rosanoff et al. (1934) first postulated a chromosome X transmission for BPI, which was also suggested by studies reporting a sex ratio of two females to one male in the distribution of BPI (Helgasson, 1964), and an observed excess of females over males among the relatives of bipolar probands (Table 7.1).

According to an X-linked hypothesis, the X chromosome of a male can only be transmitted through the mother's side of the kindred, therefore permitting no male-to-male transmission of the trait. Although male-to-male transmission

TABLE 7.1. Percentage of Affectively Ill by Sex in First-Degree Relatives of Bipolar Patients

Study	Year	Total	Male (%)	Female (%)
Angst et al.	1980	38	15 (39)	23 (61)
Gershon et al.	1975	36	20 (55)	16 (45)
Gerson et al.	1982	79	38 (48)	41 (52)
Goetzl et al.	1974	35	13 (37)	22 (63)
James & Chapman	1975	52	13 (25)	39 (75)
Kadrmas et al.	1979	102	54 (53)	48 (47)
Mendlewicz & Rainer	1974	229	93 (40)	136 (60)
Mendlewicz & Rainer	1977	29	9 (31)	20 (69)
Stenstedt	1952	41	19 (47)	22 (53)
Taylor & Abrams	1981	36	11 (31)	25 (69)
Winokur et al.	1969	76	20 (26)	56 (74)
Winokur et al.	1982	40	15 (38)	25 (63)
Total		793	320 (40)	473 (60)

Note. From Winokur & Crowe (1983). Copyright 1983 by the American Medical Association. Reprinted by permission.

was observed in family studies by some investigators (Perris, 1968; Brown, Ellston, Pollitzer, Prange, & Wilson, 1973; Goetzl, Green, Whybrow, & Jackson, 1974; Mendlewicz & Rainer, 1974), this is nevertheless a rare event among the kindred of bipolar probands (Mendlewicz, 1986).

Linkage studies have tested the X-linked transmission hypothesis by using several markers on chromosome X: Xg blood group, color blindness, glucose-6-phosphate dehydrogenase (G6PD), and factor IX (hemophilia B).

Winokur and Tanna (1969) described a dependent assortment for BPI and the Xg blood group (a dominant X-linked marker) in three families. In two large families (Reich, Clayton, & Winokur, 1969) and in seven other families (Mendlewicz, Fleiss, & Fieve, 1972), a dependent assortment has been found for color blindness (an X-linked recessive marker) and BPI. There occurred no independent assortment between the marker and the illness in either study. Mendlewicz and Fleiss (1974) were able to demonstrate in 17 informative pedigrees close linkage between BPI and both deutan and protan color blindness, as well as loose linkage with the Xg blood group, but the absence of such linkage in 11 unipolar pedigrees. (Deutan colour blindness is a deficiency of perception of the color green; protan is deficiency of perception of the color red. The chromosomal loci of

these two conditions are closely linked, but not identical.) In several studies, there was a linkage relationship between color blindness and BPI (Belmaker & Wyatt, 1976; Baron, 1977; Mendlewicz, Linkowski, Guroff, & van Praag, 1979; Reading, 1979; Del Zompo, Bocchetta, Goldin, & Corsini, 1984; Baron et al., 1987), although one study did not find such a linkage (Gershon, Targum, Matthyse, & Bunney, 1979). In a more comprehensive study—part of the Biological Psychiatry Collaborative Program of the World Health Organization—conducted in four collaborative centers (Bethesda, Basel, Brussels, and Copenhagen) on 16 informative families, the overall results are consistent with the presence of linkage between BPI and color blindness. However, an X-linked pattern of inheritance was not observed in all families, suggesting a genetic heterogeneity in BPI (Mendlewicz, 1974; Gershon et al., 1980).

Despite the presence of genetic heterogeneity, a comprehensive analysis of linkage data from the available literature shows that X-linkage between color blindness and BPI is indeed demonstrated in a large sample of families described in different geographic areas (Risch & Baron, 1982; Risch, 1989; Van Eerdewegh, 1989). Figure 7.1 illustrates the cosegregation of deuteranopia and bipolar–unipolar disorders in successive generations of a family, informative for the analysis of linkage between color blindness and affective illness.

Several authors reported a positive linkage between bipolar illness and G6PD deficiency, a genetic marker on the region Xq28 (Mendlewicz, Linkowski, & Wilmott, 1980; Baron et al., 1987). In two pedigrees studied for linkage between BPI, color blindness, and G6PD deficiency, which is closely linked with color blindness on the X chromosome (Siniscalco, Filippi, & Latte, 1964), results were also consistent with X-linkage in BPI (Del Zompo et al., 1984). Baron et al. (1990b) recently reanalyzed their data by including in the analysis phenotypic diversity and diagnostic uncertainties. Their results confirm X-linkage in BPI, suggesting that the X-linked phenotype may be a severe form of BPI characterized by early onset, high familial prevalence of the bipolar form, and a high recurrence rate of major depression.

In 10 Belgian pedigrees (Mendlewicz et al., 1987) and in one French pedigree (Lucotte et al., 1992), a positive linkage between BPI and factor IX in region Xq27 was found. However, in the Belgian study, linkage results were not

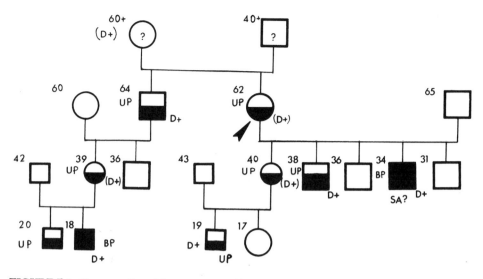

FIGURE 7.1. Cosegregation of deuteranopia and bipolar–unipolar disorders in successive generations of a family. UP, unipolar illness; BP, bipolar illness; filled or half-filled symbol, subject with BP (filled) or UP (half-filled); arrow, proband; D+, deuteranopia homozygous; (D+), deuteranopia heterozygous; +, deceased; (?), status unknown; SA, schizoaffective disorder.

very robust for a penetrance of 1, and even fell with 0.9 penetrance, and 0.8 penetrance (Mendlewicz, Sevy, Charon, & Legros, 1991a). In a subsequent study, linkage could not be statistically confirmed using five additional pedigrees (Van Broeckhoven et al., 1991). Negative linkage results were reported in seven pedigrees (Gejman et al., 1990). In a very recent study, an apparent cosegregation between F9 and affective disorder was reported (Gill, Castle, & Duggan, 1992; Craddock & Owen, 1992).

Berretini et al. (1990) could not demonstrate a linkage between BPI and DNA markers (DXS15, DXS52, and F8C) located in the color blindness and G6PD region (Xq28). However, there are several limitations in their study. They investigated a limited sample of small or moderate-size families with polymorphic psychiatric disturbances and few bipolar cases. Moreover, the presence of affective illness on both the paternal and maternal sides, apparent transmission of illness from father to son in some families, and positive linkage scores for the ST14 probes (Xq28 region) in two families renders these negative results difficult to interpret.

Following the observation of a possible association between the fragile-X syndrome and affective illness (Pascalis, Teyssier, & Carre-Pigeon, 1985; Reiss et al., 1986), an apparent cosegregation between BPI and the Taq I polymorphism at factor IX locus (Xq27) near the

fragile-X site was reported in fragile-X individuals of a Belgian family (Mendlewicz & Hirsch, 1991). This observation was recently confirmed in a linkage analysis of a pedigree assorting for fragile-X syndrome and affective illness (Jeffries et al., 1993).

In the Xq28 region, the gene of the α_3 subunit of the gamma-aminobutyric acid (GABA) receptor (GABRA 3; Buckle et al., 1989) is another interesting candidate gene for the genetic study of BPI. However, in a preliminary study, no evidence of linkage was found between BPI and the GABRA 3 gene (Van Broeckhoven et al., in press).

ASSOCIATION AND LINKAGE STUDIES WITH AUTOSOMAL CHROMOSOMES

Besides X-linked transmission, a major autosomal dominant gene with reduced penetrance for BPI has also been postulated (Strömgren, 1938; Stenstedt, 1952; Kallman, 1954). Indeed, in first-degree relatives, a preponderance of affected females, as compared to males, has not been found in some studies, and a male-to-male transmission of the disease is present in some families (Perris, 1968; Brown et al., 1973; Goetzl et al., 1974). Although it is nevertheless a rare event in the kindred of bipolar probands

(Mendlewicz, 1985), the male-to-male transmission of the disease has been observed by Mendlewicz and Rainer (1974) in about 10% of their overall sample. The hypothesis of an autosomal transmission has been investigated in association studies with the type O blood group, located on chromosome 9, as well as linkage studies on chromosome 6 with the human leukocyte antigen (HLA) haplotypes, and on chromosome 11, with DNA markers for the following genes: D_2 dopamine receptor, tyrosinase, C-Harvey-Ras-A (HRAS) oncogene, insulin (INS), and tyrosine hydroxylase (TH).

The type O blood group has been found to occur more frequently in BPI patients (Barker, Theillie, & Spielberger, 1961; Mendlewicz, Massart-Guiot, Wilmotte, & Fleiss, 1974). Although poorly understood, the association between a blood-group factor and a major psychosis indicates that the ABO genotype located on 9q34 may play a role in the predisposition to BPI.

Although a linkage to HLA genes located on the short arm of chromosome 6 has been proposed for affective illness (Wirtkamp, Stancer, Persad, Flood, & Guttorsmen, 1981; Stancer et al., 1988), it has not been confirmed in other studies (Targum, Gerson, Van Gerdewegh, & Rogenline, 1979; Goldin, Clerget-Darpoux, & Gerson, 1982; Clerget-Darpoux, Golding, & Gerson, 1982; Suarez, Rice, Crouse, & Reich, 1983). Further work will be needed to clarify these conflicting results.

On the long arm of chromosome 11, a balanced translocation from 11q23.3 to chromosome 9p22 was described in five bipolar patients in an American pedigree (Smith et al., 1989). In patients of a Scottish family having schizophrenia, schizoaffective illness and other psychiatric disorders, a translocation from region 11q21–22 to region q43 of chromosome 1 was reported (Saint-Clair et al., 1990). In both families, a linkage between psychiatric illness and genes at the site of the translocation was suggested. The human D_2 dopamine receptor gene, located on 11q22–23, and the tyrosinase gene, also located on the long arm of chromosome 11 (Grandy et al., 1989), may be close to the translocation point observed in the American pedigree (Smith et al., 1989). Consequently, a linkage analysis between these markers and BPI was performed in five Icelandic (Holmes et al., 1991), and four American pedigrees (Byerley et al., 1990). However, no evidence of linkage was found in either study. Concerning the short arm of chromosome 11, a positive linkage between BPI and the HRAS oncogene, as well as the INS marker on the short arm of chromosome 11 (11p15), was reported in studying a large pedigree of the Old Order Amish community (Egeland et al., 1987). However, linkage analysis in American bipolar pedigrees of non-Amish origin (Detera-Wadleigh et al., 1987), in other European pedigrees of bipolar disorders (Hodgkinson et al., 1987; Gill, McKeon, & Humphries, 1988; Mitchell et al., 1991; Mendlewicz et al., 1991b), and in pedigrees of unipolar disorders (Neiswanger et al., 1990; Wesner et al., 1990), could not confirm these results. Additionally, the probability of linkage of affective illness to the 11p15 region of chromosome 11 was almost excluded by a reanalysis of the original Amish pedigree with two lateral extensions (Kelsoe et al., 1989). Because of a close link between the genes coding for TH, INS, and HRAS loci on chromosome 11, linkage between BPI and the TH locus has also been investigated in BPI, but with negative results so far (Mendlewicz et al., 1991b). In association studies, positive results between the TH gene and affective illness have been achieved in one investigation (Leboyer et al., 1990), but have not been confirmed in other studies (Todd & O'Malley, 1989; Körner, Fritze, & Propping, 1990).

DISCUSSION

The presence of a major locus of transmission of BPI in the Xq27–28 region on the long arm of the X chromosome seems to be confirmed by linkage studies, which are summarized in Table 7.2. On a total of 61 pedigrees collected in eight centers located in various countries—the United States ($n = 3$), Israel ($n = 2$), Belgium ($n = 1$), Italy ($n = 1$), Australia ($n = 1$), and the United Kingdom ($n = 1$)—positive X-linkage results have been confirmed in 15 different samples.

Nevertheless, the prevalence rate and clinical phenotypical characteristics of the X-linked form of BPI remain to be defined in the general population. According to some authors, X-linked BPI may be characterized by an early onset (before age 30; Mendlewicz & Simon, 1987; Baron et al., 1990b), and a greater psychiatric morbidity as suggested by an increase relapse rate and a greater loading of bipolar disorders in relatives (Baron et al., 1990b).

The hypothesis of a locus for unipolar illness on chromosome X and chromosome 11 has so

TABLE 7.2. X-Linkage Studies of Bipolar Illness

	Pedigrees	Studies	Centers	Countries
Positive	61	15	8	United States Israel Belgium Italy Australia United Kingdom France
Negative	24	4	2	United States Belgium

far been rejected by linkage studies (Mendlewicz & Fleiss, 1974; Neiswanger et al., 1990; Wesner et al., 1990).

Although non-X-linked forms of the illness are most likely to be present, a major susceptibility gene for BPI on the short arm of chromosome 11 is at present not confirmed. Results of linkage studies so far have been inconclusive in the search for a single-transmission model (Mendlewicz & Fleiss, 1974; Hill, Wison, Felston, & Winokur, 1988; Neiswanger et al., 1990; Wesner et al., 1990), but heterogeneity and phenocopies are probably more common in the unipolar forms of affective illness than in BPI.

In conclusion, a better clinical, biochemical, and therapeutic approach to BPI may be achieved by identifying and separating genetic subgroups of affective disorders with the use of genetic markers and candidate genes. However, a major challenge for research strategies in BPI is the study of the interaction between genetic and nongenetic vulnerability factors. The collection of a large number of pedigrees and the investigation of different chromosome locations with highly polymorphic and informative markers, including relevant candidate genes, can only be accomplished through collaborative efforts by groups such as the European Science Foundation or the NIMH in the United States. It is hoped that a major susceptibility locus for BPI will be detected through a systematic screen covering the whole human genome, together with nonparametric tests (sibling-pair method, affected pedigree-member method), and population-based association studies.

REFERENCES

Andreasen, N. C., Rice, J., Endicott, J., Coryell, W., Grove, W. M., & Reich, T. (1987). Familial rates of affective disorder. *Archives of General Psychiatry, 44,* 461–469.

Angst, J., (1966). *Zur Atiologie und Nosologie endogene depressiver Psychosen* (Monographien aus dem Gesamtgebiete der Neurologie und Psychiatrie). Berlin: Springer.

Angst, J., Frey, R., Lohmeyer, B., & Zerbin-Rudin, E. (1980). Bipolar manic–depressive psychosis: Results of a genetic investigation. *Human Genetics, 55,* 237–254.

Barker, J. B., Theillie, A., & Spielberger, C. D. (1961). Frequency of blood types in an homogenous group of manic–depressive patients. *Journal of Mental Sciences, 107,* 936–942.

Baron, M. (1977). Linkage between an X-chromosome marker (deutan color blindness) and bipolar affective illness. *Archives of General Psychiatry, 34,* 721–725.

Baron, M. (1992). Molecular genetics of affective psychoses. In J. Mendlewicz & H. Hippius (Eds.), *Genetic research in psychiatry* (pp. 1–25). Berlin: Springer-Verlag.

Baron, M., Endicott, J., & Ott, J. (1990a). Genetic linkage in mental illness: Limitations and prospects. *British Journal of Psychiatry, 157,* 645–655.

Baron, M., Hamburger, R., Sandkuyl, L. A., Risch, N., Mandel, B., Endicott, J., Belmaker, R. H., & Ott, J. (1990b). The impact of phenotypic variation on genetic analysis: Application to X-linkage in manic–depressive illness. *Acta Psychiatrica Scandinavica, 82,* 196–203.

Baron, M., Rich, N., Hamburger, R., Mandel, B., Kushner, S., Newman, M., & Belmaker, R. H. (1987). Genetic linkage between X-chromosome markers and bipolar affective illness. *Nature, 326,* 289–292.

Belmaker, R. H., & Wyatt, R. J. (1976). Possible X-linkage in a family with varied psychosis. *Israel Annals of Psychiatry, 14,* 345–353.

Berrettini, W. H., Goldin, L. R., Gelernter, J., Gesman, P. V., Gershon, E. S., & Detera-Wadleigh, S. D. (1990). X-chromosome markers and manic–depressive illness: Rejection of linkage to Xq28 in nine bipolar pedigrees. *Archives of General Psychiatry, 47,* 366–373.

Bolstein, D., White, R. L., Skolnick, M., & Davis, R. W. (1980). Construction of a genetic linkage map in man using restriction fragment length polyporphism. *American Journal of Human Genetics, 32,* 314–331.

Brown, R. J., Elston, R. C., Pollitzer, W. S., Prange, A., & Wilson, E. (1973). Sex-ratio in relatives of patients with affective disorder. *Biological Psychiatry, 6,* 307–309.

Buckle, V. J., Fujita, N., Ryder-Cook, A. S., Derrz, J., Barnard, P. J., Lebo, R. V., Schofield, P. R., Seeburg, P. H., Bateson, A. N., Darlison, M. G., & Barnard, E. A. (1989). Chromosomal localisation of GABRA receptor subunit genes, relationship to human genetic disease. *Neuron, 3,* 647–654.

Byerley, W., Leppert, M., O'Connell, P., Mellon, C., Holik, J., Lubbers, A., Reimherr, F., Jenson, S., Hill, K., Wender, P., Grandy, D., Litt, M., Lalouel, J.-M., Civelli, O., & White, R. (1990). D2 dopamine receptor gene not linked to manic–depression in three families. *Psychiatric Genetics, 1,* 55–62.

Cadoret, R. J. (1978). Evidence for genetic inheritance of primary affective disorders in adoptees. *American Journal of Psychiatry, 134,* 463–466.

Clerget-Darpoux, F., Bonaiti-Pellie, C., & Hochez, J. (1986). Effects of mis-specifying genetic parameters in LOD score analysis. *Biometrics, 42,* 393–399.

Clerget-Darpoux, F., Golding, L. R., & Gershon, E. S. (1982). A new method for analysis of HLA-associated diseases. *American Journal of Human Genetics, 35,* 127–130.

Craddock, N., & Owen, M. (1992). Christmas disease and

major affective disorder. *British Journal of Psychiatry*, *160*, 715.

Da Fonseca, A. F. (1959). *Analise heredo-clinica das perturbacoes affectivas*. Dissertation, University of Porto, Oporto, Portugal.

Del Zompo, M., Bocchetta, A., Goldin, L. R., & Corsini, G. U. (1984). Linkage between X-chromosome markers and manic–depressive illness, two sardinian pedigrees. *Acta Psychiatrica Scandinavica*, *70*, 282–287.

Detera-Wadleigh, S. D., Berrettini, W. H., Goldin, L. R., Boorman D., Anderson, S., & Gershon, E. S. (1987). Close linkage of C-Harvey-Ras-1 and the insulin gene to affective disorder is ruled out in three North American pedigrees. *Nature*, *325*, 806–807.

Egeland, J. A., Gerhard, D. S., Paul, D. C., Sussex, J. N., Kidd, K. K., Allen, C. R., Hostetter, A. M., & Housman, D. E. (1987). Bipolar affective disorder linked to DNA markers on chromosome 11. *Nature*, *325*, 783–787.

Egeland, J. A., Sussex, J. N., Endicott, J., Hostetter, A. A., Offord, D. R., Schwab, J. J., Allen, C. R., & Pauls, D. L. (1990). The impact of diagnoses on genetic linkage study for bipolar affective disorders among the Amish. *Psychiatric Genetics*, *1*, 5–18.

Gejman, P. V., Detera-Wadleigh, S., Martinez, M. M., Berrettini, W. H., Goldin, L. R., Gelernter, J., Hsieh, W.-T., & Gershon, E. S. (1990). Manic depressive illness not linked to factor IX region in an independent series of pedigrees. *Genomics*, *8*, 648–655.

Gershon, E. S., Hamovit, J., Guroff, J. J., Dibble, E., Leckman, J. F., Sceery, W., Targum, S. D., Nurnberger, J. I., Jr., Goldin, L. R., Bunney, W. E., Jr. (1982). A family study of schizoaffective, bipolar I, bipolar II, unipolar, and normal control probands. *Archives of General Psychiatry*, *39*, 1157–1167.

Gershon, E. S., Hamovit, J. H., Guroff, J. J., & Nurnberger, J. I., (1987). Birth cohort changes in manic and depressive disorders in relatives of bipolar and schizoaffective patients. *Archives of General Psychiatry*, *44*, 314–319.

Gershon, E. S., Mark, A., Cohen, N., Belizon, N., Baron, M., & Knobe, K. E. (1975). Transmitted factors in the morbid risk of affective disorders: A controlled study. *Journal of Psychiatry Research*, *12*, 283–299.

Gershon, E. S., Mendlewicz, J., Gastpar, M., Bech, P., Goldin, L. R., Kielhols, P., Rafaelsen, O. J., Vartanian, F., & Bunney, W. E., Jr. (1980). WHO collaborative study of genetic linkage of bipolar manic–depressive illness and red/green color blindness. *Acta Psychiatrica Scandinavica*, *61*, 319–338.

Gershon, E. S., Targum, S. D., Matthyse, S., Bunney, & W. E., Jr. (1979). Color blindness not closely linked to bipolar illness. *Archives of General Psychiatry*, *36*, 1423–1431.

Gill, M., Castle, D., & Duggan, C. (1992). Cosegregation of Christmas disease and major affective disorder in a pedigree. *British Journal of Psychiatry*, *160*, 112–114.

Gill, M., McKeon, P., Humphries, P. (1988). Linkage analysis of manic depression in an Irish family using H-Ras 1 and INS DNA markers. *Journal of Medical Genetics*, *25*, 634–637.

Goetzl, V., Green, R., Whybrow, P., & Jackson, R. (1974). X-linkage revisited: A further family study of manic–depressive illnesss. *Archives of General Psychiatry*, *31*, 665–672.

Goldin, L. R., Clerget-Darpoux, F., & Gershon, E. S. (1982). Relationship of HLA to major affective disorders not supported. *Psychiatry Research*, *7*, 28–45.

Grandy, D. K., Litt, M., Allen, L., Bunzow, J. R., Marchionni, M., Makam, H., Reed, L., Magenis, R. E., & Civelli, O. (1989). The human dopamine D2 receptor gene is located on chromosome 11 at q22–23 and identifies a Taq I RFLP. *American Journal of Human Genetics*, *45*, 778–785.

Harvald, B., & Hauge, M. (1965). Hereditary factors elucidated by twin studies. In J. V. Neel, M. W. Shaw, & W. J. Schull (Eds.), *Genetics and the epidemiology of chronic diseases* (pp. 61–76). Washington, DC: U.S. Department of Health, Education and Welfare.

Helgasson, T. (1964). Epidemiology of mental disorders in Iceland. *Acta Psychiatrica Scandinavica*, *173*, 1–258.

Hill, E,, Wison, A. F., Felston, R. C., & Winokur, G. (1988). Evidence for possible linkage between genetic markers and affective disorders. *Biological Psychiatry*, *24*, 903–917.

Hodgkinson, S., Sherrington, R., Gurling, H., Marchbanks, M., Reeders. S., Mallet, J., McInnis, M., Peturson, H., & Brynjolsfson, J. (1987). Molecular genetic evidence of heterogeneity in manic–depression. *Nature*, *325*, 805–806.

Holmes, D., Brynjolfsson, J., Brett, P., Curtis, D., Petursson, H., Sherrington, R., & Gurling, H. (1991). No evidence for a susceptibility locus predisposing to manic depression in the region of the dopamine (D2) receptor gene. *British Journal of Psychiatry*, *158*, 635–641.

James, N., & Chapman, C. (1975). A genetic study of bipolar affective disorder. *British Journal of Psychiatry*, *126*, 449–456.

Jeffries, F. M., Reiss, A. L., Brown, W. T., Meyers, D. A., Glicksman, A. C., & Bandyopadhyay, S. (1993). The association of bipolar spectrum disorder and fragile X syndrome: A family study. *Biological Psychiatry*, *33*, 213–216.

Kadrmas, A., Winokur, G., & Crowe; R. (1979). Postpartum mania. *British Journal of Psychiatry*, *135*, 551–554.

Kallman, F. J. (1954). Genetic principles in manic–depressive psychoses. In P. Hoch & J. Zubin (Eds.), *Depression* (pp. 1–24). New York: Grune & Stratton.

Kelsoe, J. R., Ginns, E. I., Egeland, J. A., Gerhard, D. S., Gostein, A. M., Bale, S. J., Pauls, D. L., Long, R. J., Kidd, K. K., Conte, G., Housman, D. E., & Paul, S. M. (1989). Re-evaluation of the linkage relationship between chromosome 11p loci and the gene for bipolar affective disorder in the Old Order Amish. *Nature*, *342*, 238–243.

Körner, J., Fritze, J., & Propping, P. (1990). RFLP alleles at the tyrosine hydroxylase locus: No association found to affective disorders. *Psychiatry Research*, *32*, 275–280.

Kruger, S. D., Turner, J. W., & Kidd, K. K. (1982). The effects of requisite assumptions on linkage analyses of manic–depressive illness with HLA. *Biological Psychiatry*, *17*, 1081–1099.

Leboyer, M., Malafosse, A., Boularand, S., Campion, D., Gheysen, F., Samolyk, D., Henriksson, B., Denise, E., Des Lauriers, A., Lepine, J. P., Zarifian, E., Clerget-Darpoux, F., & Mallet, J. (1990). Tyrosine hydroxylase polymorphisms associated with manic–depressive illness. *Lancet*, *335*, 1219.

Leonhard, K. (1959). *Aufteilung der Endogenen Psychosen*. Berlin: Akademie-Verlag.

Lucotte, G., Landoulsi, A., Berriche, S., David, F., & Babron, M. C. (1992). Manic depressive illness is linked to factor IX in a French pedigree. *Annales de Génétique*, *35*(2), 93–95.

Majunder, P. P. (1989). Strategies and sample size considerations for mapping a two-locus autosomal recessive disorder. *American Journal of Human Genetics, 45,* 412–423.

Martinez, M., Khlat, M., Leboyer, M., & Clerget-Darpoux, F. (1989). Performance of linkage analysis under misclassification error when the genetic model is unknown. *Genetic Epidemiology, 6,* 253–258.

Mendlewicz, J. (1974). Le concept d'hétérogénéité dans la psychose maniaco–depressive. *L'évolution Psychiatrique, 2,* 411–416.

Mendlewicz, J. (1985). X-linked inheritance in affective disorders. In P. Pichot, P. Berner, R. Wolf, & K. Thau (Eds.), *Psychiatry* (Vol. 2, pp. 95–99). New York: Plenum Press.

Mendlewicz, J. (1986). X-linked inheritance in affective disorders. In P. Berner (Ed.), *VII World Congress of Psychiatry, Vienna.*

Mendlewicz, J. (1988). Population and family studies in depression and mania. *British Journal of Psychiatry, 153*(Suppl. 3), 16–25.

Mendlewicz, J., & Fleiss, J. L. (1974). Linkage studies with X-chromosome markers in bipolar (manic–depressive) and unipolar depressive illness. *Biological Psychiatry, 9,* 261–294.

Mendlewicz, J., Fleiss, J., & Fieve, R. R. (1972). Evidence for X-linkage in the transmission of manic–depressive illness. *Journal of the American Medical Association, 222, 13,* 1624–1627.

Mendlewicz, J., & Hirsch, D. (1991). Fragile X syndrome and manic–depression. *Biological Psychiatry, 29,* 295–308.

Mendlewicz, J., & Rainer, J. (1974). Morbidity risk and genetic transmission in manic–depressive illness. *American Journal of Human Genetics, 26,* 692–701.

Mendlewicz, J., & Rainer, J. D. (1977). Adoption study supporting genetic transmission in manic–depression illness. *Nature, 268,* 327–329.

Mendlewicz, J., & Simon, P. (1987). Linkage analysis in manic–depressive illness. *Lancet, 2,* 345.

Mendlewicz, J., Leboyer, M., Malafosse, A., Sevy, S., Hirsch, D., Babron, M. C., Van Broeckhoven, C., & Mallet, J. (1991b). No linkage between chromosome 11p15 markers and manic–depressive illness in a Belgian pedigree. *American Journal of Psychiatry, 148,* 1683–1687.

Mendlewicz, J., Linkowski, P., Guroff, J. J., & van Praag, H. M. (1979). Color blindness linkage to bipolar manic–depressive illness: New evidence. *Archives of General Psychiatry, 36,* 1442–1447.

Mendlewicz, J., Linkowski, P., & Wilmotte, J. (1980). Linkage between glucose-6-phosphate dehydrogenase deficiency and manic–depressive psychosis. *British Journal of Psychiatry, 137,* 337–342.

Mendlewicz, J., Massart-Guiot, T., Wilmotte, J., & Fleiss, J. L. (1974). Blood groups in manic–depressive illness and schizophrenia. *Diseases of the Nervous System, 35,* 39–41.

Mendlewicz, J., Sevy, S., Charon, F., & Legros, S. (1991a). Manic–depressive illness and X chromosome (letter). *Lancet, 338,* 1213.

Mendlewicz, J., Simon, P., Sevy, S., Charon, F., Brocas, H., Legros, S., & Vassart, G. P. (1987). Polymorphic DNA marker on X-chromosome and manic–depression. *Lancet, 1,* 1230–1232.

Merikangas, K. R., Spence, A., & Kupfer, D. J. (1989). Linkage studies of bipolar disorder: Methodologic and analytic issues. Report of MacArthur Foundation workshop on linkage and clinical features in affective disorders. *Archives of General Psychiatry, 46,* 1137–1141.

Merikangas, K. R., & Spiker, D. G. (1982). Assortative mating among inpatients with primary affective disorder. *Psychological Medicine, 12,* 753–764.

Mitchell, P., Waters, B., Morrison, N., Shine, J., Donald, J., & Eisman, J. (1991). Close linkage of bipolar disorder to chromosome 11 markers is excluded in two large Australian pedigrees. *Journal of Affective Disorders, 21,* 23–32.

Neiswanger, K., Slaugenhaulst, S. A., Hughes, H. B., Frank, E., Frankel, D. R., McCarthy, M. I., Chakravarti, A., Zubenko, G. S., Kupfer, D. J., & Kaplan, B. B. (1990). Evidence against close linkage of unipolar affective illness to human chromosome 11p markers HRAS 1 and INS and chromosome Xq marker DX552. *Biological Psychiatry, 28,* 63–72.

Ott, J. (1977). Linkage analysis with misclassification at one locus. *Clinical Genetics, 12,* 119–124.

Pascalis, G., Teyssier, J. R., & Carre-Pigeon, F. (1985). Presence d'un Xq-Fra chez un maniaque, situation du gène de la P.M.D. sur le bras long du chromosome X. *Annales Médicales Psychologiques, 146,* 594–595.

Perris, C. (1968). Genetic transmission of depressive psychoses. *Acta Psychiatrica Scandinavica,* Suppl. 203, 45–52.

Price, J. (1968). The genetics of depressive behavior. In A. Coppen & A. Walk (Eds.), Recent developments in affective disorders. *British Journal of Psychiatry,* Spec. Publ. 2.

Reading, C. M. (1979). X-linked dominant manic–depressive illness: Linkage with Xg blood group, red–green color blindness, and vitamin B12 deficiency. *Orthomolecular Psychiatry, 8,* 68–77.

Reich, T., Clayton, P. J., & Winokur, G. (1969). Family history study in the genetics of mania. *American Journal of Psychiatry, 125,* 1358–1359.

Reiss, A. L., Feinstein, C., Toomey, K. E., Goldsmith, B., Rosenbaum, K., & Caruso, M.A. (1986). Psychiatric disability associated with the fragile X-chromosome. *American Journal of Medical Genetics, 23,* 394–401.

Rice, J., Endicott, J., Knesvich, M. A., & Rochberg, N. J. (1987). The estimation of diagnostic sensitivity using stability data: An application to major depressive disorder. *Journal of Psychiatry Research, 21,* 337–346.

Risch, N. (1989). Description of X-linkage pedigrees. *Genetic Epidemiology, 6,* 187–189.

Risch, N. (1990). Genetic linkage and complex diseases, with special reference to psychiatric disorders. *Genetic Epidemiology, 7,* 3–16.

Risch, N., & Baron, M. (1982). X-linkage and genetic heterogeneity in bipolar related major affective illness: Reanalysis of linkage data. *Annals of Human Genetics, 46,* 153–166.

Risch, N., Baron, M., & Mendlewicz, J. (1986). Assessing X-linked inheritance in bipolar-related major affective disorder. *Journal of Psychiatry Research, 20,* 275–288.

Rosanoff, A. H., Handy, L. M., & Rosanoff-Plesset, I. B. A. (1934). The etiology of manic–depressive syndromes with special reference to their occurrence in twins. *American Journal of Psychiatry, 91,* 725–762.

Saint-Clair, D., Blackwood, D., Muir, W., Carothers, A., Walkers, M., Spowart, G., Gosden, C., & Evans, H. J. (1990). Association within a family of a balanced autosomal translocation with mental illness. *Lancet, 336,* 13–16.

Siniscalco, M., Filippi, G., & Latte, B. (1964). Recombination between protan and deutan genes: Data on their relative positions in respect of the G6PD locus. *Nature, 204,* 1061–1064.

Smith, M., Wasmuth, J., McPherson, J. D., Wagner, C., Grandy, D., Civelli, O., Potkin, S., & Litt, M. (1989). Cosegregation of an 11q22.3–9p22 translocation with affective disorder: Proximity of the D-2 receptor gene relative to translocation breakpoint. *American Journal of Human Genetics, 45,* 864.

Stancer, H. C., Weitkamp, L. R., Persad, E., Flood, C., Jorna, T., Guttormsen, S. A., & Yagnow, R. L. (1988). Confirmation of the relationship of HLA (chromosome 6) genes to depression and manic–depression. *Annals of Human Genetics, 52,* 279–298.

Stenstedt, A. (1952). A study in manic–depressive psychosis. *Acta Psychiatrica Scandinavica, 79,* 1–111.

Strömgren, E. (1938). *Beitrage zur psychiatrischen erblehre.* Copenhagen: Munskgaard.

Suarez, B. K., Rice, J. P., Crouse, J., Reich, T. (1983). HLA and disease: Haplotype sharing in multiflex families. *Clinical Genetics, 23,* 267–275.

Targum, S. D., Gershon, E. J., Van Eerdewegh, M., & Rogenline, N. (1979). Human leucocytes antigen (HLA) system not closely linked to or associated with bipolar manic–depressive illness. *Biological Psychiatry, 14,* 615–636.

Taylor, M., & Abrams, R. (1981). Gender difference in bipolar affective disorder. *Journal of Affective Disorders, 3,* 261–277.

Todd, R., & O'Malley, K. (1989). Population frequencies of tyrosine hydroxylase RFLP in bipolar affective disorders. *Biological Psychiatry, 25,* 626–630.

Tsuang, M. T., Lyons, M. J., & Faraone, S. V. (1987). Problems of diagnoses in family studies. *Journal of Psychiatry Research, 21,* 391–400.

Van Broeckhoven, C., De Bruyn, A., Raeymaekers, P., Sandkuijl, L., Hicks, A. A., Barnard, E. A., Darlison, M. G., Mendelbaum, K., & Mendlewicz, J. (in press). Exclusion of manic–depressive illness from the chormosomal regions Xq27–Xq28 and 11p15. *Cytogenetic Cell Genetics.*

Van Broeckhoven, C., De Bruyn, A., Raeymaekers, P., Sandkuyl, L., Mendelbaum, K., Delvenne, V., & Mendlewicz, J. (1991). Molecular genetic analysis in bipolar illness. *Biological Psychiatry, 29,* 452–454.

Van Eerdewegh, P. (1989). Linkage analysis with cohort effects: An application to X-linkage. *Genetic Epidemiology, 6,* 271–276.

Weissman, M. M., Gershon, E. S., Kidd, K. K., Prusoff, B. A., Leckman, J. F., Dibble, E., Hamovit, J., Thompson, W. D., Pauls, D. L., & Guroff, J. J. (1984). Psychiatric disorders in the relatives of probands with affective disorders. *Archives of General Psychiatry, 41,* 13–21.

Wesner, R. B., Tanna, V. L., Palmer, P. J., Goedken, R. J, Crowe, R. R., & Winokur, G. (1990). Linkage of C-Harvey-Ras-1 and INS DNA markers to unipolar depression and alcoholism is ruled out in 18 families. *European Archives of Psychiatric and Neurological Sciences, 239,* 356–360.

Winokur, G., & Crowe, R. R. (1983). Bipolar illness: The sex-polarity effects in affectively ill family members. *Archives of General Psychiatry, 40,* 57–58.

Winokur, G., Clayton, P., & Reich, T. (1969). *Manic depressive illness.* St Louis: Mosby.

Winokur, G., & Tanna, V. L. (1969). Possible role of X-linked dominant factor in manic–depressive disease. *Diseases of the Nervous System, 30,* 89–93.

Winokur, G., Tsuang, M., & Crowe, R. (1982). The Iowa 500: Affective disorder in relatives of manic and depressed patients. *American Journal of Psychiatry, 139,* 209–212.

Wirtkamp, L. R., Stancer, H. C., Persad, E., Flood, C., & Guttorsmen, S. (1981). Depressive disorders and HLA: A gene on chromosome 6 that can affect behavior. *New England of Journal of Medicine, 305,* 1301–1306.

Zerbin-Rüdin, E. J. (1987). Psychiatric genetics and psychiatric nosology. *Journal of Psychiatry Research, 21,* 377–384.

8

Biological Processes in Depression: An Updated Review and Integration

MICHAEL E. THASE
ROBERT H. HOWLAND

Considerable attention has been devoted to the investigation of the biological aspects of depression, and over the past three decades a number of significant advances have been made. Our group has reviewed these developments on several occasions (Howland & Thase, 1991; Kupfer & Thase, 1987, 1989; Thase, Frank, & Kupfer, 1985) and, in this chapter, we present an updated review and integration of the research literature. We begin by discussing background, conceptual, and methodological issues pertinent to the study of biological processes in depression. Next, the empirical status of the role neurochemical, neurophysiological, and neuroendocrine processes play in clinical depression is examined. The heterogeneity within the DSM-IV category of major depressive disorder is emphasized, and potential implications for treatment are also considered. Finally, a psychobiological model of depression is presented, based on disturbances of key neurobiological response systems, including behavioral facilitation and stress response systems.

BACKGROUND

The role of biological processes in mood disorders has been contemplated since antiquity. For example, Hippocrates proposed that melancholia (i.e., a black mood) was due to a systemic excess of black bile (see Jackson, 1986). In modern times, several lines of evidence emerged that pointed to the role of some form of biological abnormality in severe depressive states, long before the technology was available to study those processes directly (see Table 8.1). First, clinical studies of the phenomenology and illness course were instrumental in differentiating depression from other forms of psychopathology. The natural history of depression was noted to be typically characterized by a cyclical course, with periods of remission alternating with episodes of depression and/or mania (Kraepelin, 1921; Lundquist, 1945). This suggested a phasic underlying process, which unlike grief or normal sadness, appeared to cycle autonomously, independent of losses or other types of life stress. Furthermore, the severity and intensity of such periods of elation and depression exceeded the "boundaries" of normal reactions to such an extent that clinicians postulated the existence of an endogenous (i.e., arising from within) illness process (e.g., Gillespie, 1929).

Second, a relatively distinctive pattern of signs and symptoms was described in severe depression, including disturbances of sleep,

TABLE 8.1. Historical Evidence of Biological Factors in Depression

1. Longitudinal course marked by apparently autonomous episodes of depression and/or mania is suggestive of an episodic or phasic illness.
2. Discontinuity of selected symptoms from normal reactive mood disturbances (i.e., suicidal ideation, delusions, psychomotor retardation, and anhedonia).
3. Constellation of somatic symptoms is suggestive of disruption (i.e., sleep and appetite disturbances, and decreased libido, hypothalamic, and limbic processes).
4. Evidence of familial or genetic transmission.
5. Response to somatic treatments such as ECT and antidepressants, as well as observations of drug-induced hypomania.

Note. Adapted from Thase, Frank, & Kupfer (1985).

psychomotor behavior (i.e., agitation and retardation), appetite, libido, and hedonic capacity, as well as abnormal patterns of mood diurnality (Gillespie, 1929; Kraepelin, 1921). Increasing knowledge about the normal function of the brain indicated that such neurovegetative symptoms might point to disturbances of function in the prefrontal cortex, forebrain, and limbic system (see, e.g., Whybrow, Akiskal, & McKinney, 1985). These characteristic signs and symptoms formed the basis of what was subsequently called "endogenomorphic" (Klein, 1974), "endogenous" (Spitzer, Endicott, & Robins, 1978), "vital" (van Praag, 1982), or "melancholic" (American Psychiatric Association, 1987, 1994) depression.

Third, a number of family history studies (see, e.g., the review by Tsuang & Faraone, 1990) documented consistently higher concordance rates for affective illness in monozygotic twins when compared to dizygotic twins, siblings or other first-degree relatives. Demonstration of such associations indicated a very high likelihood that some type of inherited biological dysfunction was associated with vulnerability to severe depression or manic–depression.

Fourth, by the early 1960s, several distinctly different forms of "somatic" therapy were shown to be effective treatments of severe depressive states. Electroconvulsive therapy (ECT) (Huston & Locher, 1948), the tricyclic antidepressant (TCA) imipramine hydrochloride (Kuhn, 1958), and the monoamine oxidase inhibitor (MAOI) iproniazid (Loomer, Saunders, & Kline, 1958) were found to be relatively specific treatments of depression. Here, the term "specific" refers to the

treatments conveying therapeutic benefit beyond sedative or anxiolytic actions *and* helping depressed patients significantly more than those patients with schizophrenia or organic brain syndromes. The issue of treatment specificity was illustrated by the discovery that salts of a simple metallic ion, lithium, could be used to treat the most severe affective disorder, manic–depressive illness (Cade, 1949; Schou, Juel-Neilson, Stromgren, & Voldby, 1954).

The efficacy of ECT and the TCAs appeared to be particularly robust in patients manifesting prominent neurovegetative symptoms of depression (e.g., Bielski & Friedel, 1976), further pointing to the involvement of central nervous system (CNS) dysfunction in at least a subset of affective disorders. Moreover, these treatments often helped depressed patients who had not responded to psychodynamically oriented psychotherapies (Jackson, 1986). On occasion, these antidepressant treatments also appeared to cause a "switch" into manic or hypomanic episodes in vulnerable individuals. The discontinuity between severe depression and more transient mood states was underscored by the consistent observation that lithium salts and the other major somatic treatment strategies did not exert pronounced psychoactive properties in healthy individuals.

And fifth, recognition of the *in vitro* neurochemical actions of antidepressant treatments stimulated considerable interest in potential biological mechanisms of treatment effects. For example, antidepressant agents such as imipramine and iproniazid were found to enhance acutely the concentration of monoamines available at the neuronal synapse (Bunney & Davis, 1965; Schildkraut, 1965). Conversely, reserpine, an antihypertensive medication with a pronounced tendency to cause depression, was found to deplete monoamines in the CNS (Bunney & Davis, 1965). These observations set the stage for future investigations of possible neurotransmitter abnormalities in depression.

CAVEATS REGARDING THE RESEARCH ON BIOLOGICAL PROCESSES

Conceptual Issues

Clinical Heterogeneity

The DSM-IV diagnosis of major depression (American Psychiatric Associatioin, 1994) is a syndromal classification rather than a specific disease entity. The syndrome of major depression encompasses substantial clinical heterogeneity. For example, whereas most depressed persons report insomnia and/or decreased appetite and weight loss, substantial minorities overeat, gain weight, and/or oversleep (e.g., Casper et al., 1985; Davidson, Miller, Turnbull, & Sullivan, 1982; Thase, Carpenter, Kupfer, & Frank, 1991). Some depressed patients experience panic attacks, phobias, and/or obsessions, whereas most do not (Davidson et al., 1982). These so-called atypical or reversed neurovegetative symptoms are more common in younger individuals and, perhaps, are more prevalent in younger women (Casper et al., 1985; Davidson et al., 1982; Thase et al., 1991). Yet, other depressed persons experience hallucinations and delusions, have a history of episodes of hypomania and mania, and/or report a distinctly seasonal pattern of episodes. Reviews of clinical, biological, genetic, and pharmacological studies support the validity of at least several distinct subtypes of depression (e.g., Blehar & Rosenthal, 1989; Kupfer, Pickar, Himmelhoch, & Detre, 1975; Perris, 1966; Quitkin et al., 1993; Schatzberg & Rothschild, 1992; Thase et al., 1991). It is essentially implausible that a single set of biological disturbances could be found to account for these diverse clinical presentations. Even within a relatively homogeneous diagnostic condition, such as bipolar depression, it seems likely that different biological subforms may exist (Goodwin & Jamison, 1990). Moreover, if a particular type of biological abnormality was present in only a small number of cases, its identification might be overlooked in analyses of grouped data (Buchsbaum & Rieder, 1979).

Recent epidemiological studies demonstrate the relative preponderance of the less severe, ambulatory forms of affective disorder (e.g., Weissman et al., 1988). For example, although lifetime prevalence rates for all mood disorders may be as high as 5–8% for men and 10–16% for women, only 1–2% prevalence rates are observed for bipolar disorder (Goodwin & Jamison, 1990). Similarly, extrapolation from outpatient clinical studies (e.g., Thase, Hersen, Bellack, Himmelhoch, & Kupfer, 1983) would suggest that lifetime prevalence rates of melancholia would be expected to be on the order of 1–2% for men and 2–4% for women. Thus, it would appear that the majority of cases of clinical depression would be considered nonbipolar

and nonmelancholic, a residual grouping suggested by some to have a largely "nonbiological" basis (e.g., Feinberg & Carroll, 1984; Kocsis, 1993).

The search for biological correlates of milder depressions, including subsyndromal cases of intermittent depression, cyclothymia, and dysthymia, presents a daunting challenge for investigators (Howland & Thase, 1991, 1993; Kupfer & Thase, 1989). Indeed, we proposed in the earlier edition of this volume that, for a majority of persons experiencing a major depressive episode, specifically those with nonpsychotic, nonbipolar, and nonmelancholic presentations, there may be no discernable evidence of biological disturbance, at least, within the limits of assessment methods currently available (Thase et al., 1985). The relatively high placebo response rate observed in such patients, coupled with comparable outpatient responses to psychotherapy and pharmacotherapy (e.g., Elkin et al., 1989), further underscore the likelihood that many people meeting criteria for a DSM-IV mood disorder do not suffer from an autonomous dysfunction of CNS processes. For such individuals, research concerning CNS mechanisms in more reactive mood states may be worthwhile, including studies of cognition and information processing, psychobiologic responses to stress, and their interaction (e.g., Pardo, Pardo, & Raichle, 1993; Monroe, Thase, & Simons, 1992; Simons, Angell, Monroe, & Thase, 1993).

The Question of Causality

It is important to keep in mind that identification of a replicable biological abnormality does not necessarily prove that the disturbance is causally related to depression. The abnormality may simply reflect a process that can be measured objectively, such as quantification of a change in psychomotor activity, (e.g., Greden, Genero, Price, Feinberg, & Levine, 1986; Teicher et al., 1988) or an epiphenomenon resulting from some other disturbance, such as sleep deprivation or weight loss (e.g., Thase et al., 1985). For example, in an innovative study of 28 normal controls, changes in electroencephalographic (EEG) sleep patterns and hormonal profiles characteristic of severe depression were induced by an experimental program consisting of repeated nocturnal awakenings and caloric restriction (Mullen, Linsell, & Parker, 1986). Although epiphenomenal disturbances still may be of value in the assessment of the severity of depression, there is no guarantee that useful information will be gained regarding underlying mechanism(s) of the illness's pathophysiology (Thase et al., 1985). Definitive conclusions about the etiopathological significance of biological abnormalities are predicated upon the development of a more complete knowledge of neuronal and neurophysiological regulatory mechanisms in both health and various disease states. The CNS mechanisms involved in regulating the neurobehavioral response systems typically are multidetermined and, at best, are only partly understood at this time (i.e., Cartwright, 1993; Depue & Spoont, 1986; Thayer, 1989). Therefore, few conclusions can yet be reached with certainty, even after 30 years of research.

State versus Trait Abnormalities

In considering the role of biological processes in depression, it is useful to distinguish between state-dependent abnormalities and more persistent, traitlike disturbances (see Figure 8.1; Kupfer & Thase, 1989). A fully state-dependent disturbance, such as a fever or an elevated white blood cell count resulting from a bacterial infection, is present only during the active illness state (i.e., it is not detectable either beforehand or afterward). State-dependent disturbances thus may reflect pathophysiological correlates of an acute episode of illness. State-dependent abnormalities may be used to help confirm a clinical diagnosis (i.e., a biological marker) or elucidate underlying pathophysiology. State-dependent abnormalities also may point to potential treatment mechanisms (e.g., Vogel, 1983).

Conversely, traitlike correlates are detectable in cases at risk for development of a particular illness. Traitlike or state-independent abnormalities may be detected before, during, or after the acute illness state. State-independent disturbances may be inherited (i.e., a true trait, which may serve as a genetic marker) or acquired, like a scar. In the latter case, the acquired abnormality may shortly precede development of the illness (e.g., an asymptomatic prodromal viral infection) or follow as a consequence of the illness (e.g., an antibody titer, in response to a virus, or radiographic evidence of a healed bone fracture). Traitlike correlates may prove particularly useful as markers in family studies or as predictors of depressive vulnerability in recovered individuals, or their never-ill relatives.

Longitudinal studies are an important method for differentiation of state-dependent and state-independent abnormalities (e.g., Greden et al., 1983; Kupfer et al., 1993; Thase & Simons, 1992). Unfortunately, one cannot be certain if an apparent trait observed in a recently remitted individual was actually present prior to development of the first episode of depression, or if it is a residual "scar" of the index episode (Kupfer & Thase, 1989). Either early adversity (e.g., Insel, 1991) or repeated episodes of illness (e.g., Post, 1992) also may increase the likelihood of such scarring. Thus, studies of traitlike processes require concomitant family history studies in order to differentiate among true familial traits, acquired vulnerabilities, and residual scars.

A summary of selected conceptual issues is provided in Table 8.2.

Methodological Issues

Diagnosis

The poor reliability of psychiatric diagnoses posed significant problems for early investigators studying biological parameters in depression. Major progress in the reliability of diagnoses has been made over the past 20 years, following adoption of classification systems based on historical and symptomatic (syndromal) criteria. Diagnostic approaches such as the Washington University (St. Louis) criteria (Feighner et al., 1972) and the Research Diagnostic Criteria (Spitzer et al., 1978) were the first to achieve acceptably high levels of reliability by characterizing syndromes in terms of history and symptom clusters, rather than presumed etiology. These operationalized diagnostic systems reduced variability within the depression grouping considerably by joining several less reliable diagnoses from DSM-II (e.g., involutional melancholia, acute depressive reaction, and depressive neurosis) and separating those syndromes in which affective symptoms developed after the onset of another well-validated psychiatric disorder, such as schizophrenia or alcoholism. Diagnostic variance was further reduced by use of semistructured interviews to ensure uniform collection data, such as the Schedule for Affective Disorders and Schizophrenia (Endicott & Spitzer, 1978) and, more recently, the Structured Clinical Interview for Diagnosis (Spitzer, Williams, Gibbon, & First, 1992). These efforts

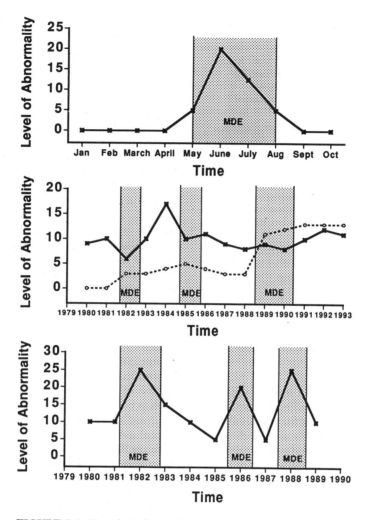

FIGURE 8.1. Hypothetical examples demonstrating (1) a state-dependent abnormality (top panel); (2) state-independent abnormalities, including trait (middle panel, ×—×) and acquired (scarlike) (o—o) disturbances; and (3) mixed abnormalities (state and trait; lower panel). Shaded areas represent major depressive episodes (MDE).

led to DSM-IV, the most recent refinement of descriptive psychiatric nosology. Improvements in diagnostic reliability have enabled investigators to turn to issues of enhancing the validity of affective disorder diagnoses (Kupfer & Thase, 1989; Howland & Thase, 1991). Nevertheless, it must be kept in mind that even with a highly reliable diagnosis (i.e., 90% interrater agreement), some error variance still remains. Moreover, some investigators have argued that the DSM concept of major depression remains too broad and overinclusive to be optimally useful (e.g., Kocsis, 1993; van Praag, 1982).

Confounding Variables

A number of factors are recognized as potentially confounding variables. The effects of factors such as age, nutritional status, sex, menstrual phase, and/or time of day, and/or season of year may influence biological systems (e.g., Thase et al., 1985). The existence of so many potential confounds mandates the use of carefully specified research protocols, as well as the selection of appropriately matched control groups to ensure that an apparent biological abnormality is not due to a sampling artifact.

TABLE 8.2. Conceptual Issues Important to the Study of the Biology of Major Depression

1. More meaningful results may come from studies focused on biological correlates of clinically distinct subtypes (i.e, bipolar, delusional, recurrent, melancholic, familial, or seasonal subtypes) of major depression.

2. Biological heterogeneity may exist even within a clinically distinct subgroup of major depression (e.g., familial and nonfamilial forms of melancholic depression).

3. The largest clinical subgroup of major depression is the residual category of nondelusional, nonbipolar, nonmelancholic depression, a group with the lowest likelihood of finding biological abnormalities.

4. Identification of a biological abnormality may represent an epiphenomenon rather than a finding with etiopathogenetic significance.

5. A biological abnormality may be present only during an episode (state marker), persist during recovery (trait marker), or occur in never-ill relatives (genetic marker).

Note. Adapted from Thase, Frank, & Kupfer (1985).

Similarly, it is important to study comparison groups of patients with nonaffective psychiatric disorders in order to control for potentially confounding nonspecific effects, such as diet, psychic distress, or factors related to hospitalization. The importance of careful screening of apparently normal controls requires more careful attention than was previously appreciated, because an unfortunately high proportion of purportedly normal controls may have concealed or dissimulated important information in order to be accepted into studies (e.g., Butler, Jenkins, & Braff, 1993).

Medication "Washout"

The effects of alcohol and various drugs (both prescribed and illicit) on biological parameters also must be recognized. To minimize the impact of such potential experimental pitfalls, biological studies often limit enrollment to subjects who may be evaluated in an unmedicated state for 1 week (Lauer & Pollmächer, 1992), 2 weeks (Kupfer & Thase, 1983), or even longer. For those patients receiving compounds with a long elimination half-lives, such as injectable "depot" neuroleptics or the antidepressant fluoxetine hydrochloride, protracted washout periods up to several months may be necessary. A prolonged delay prior to beginning definitive treatment in order to conduct research has significant ethical implications that must be balanced against methodological benefits. Furthermore, in an era characterized by intense concern about cost-containment, it typically is not feasible to conduct drug-free "washouts" of appropriate duration for hospitalized patients, unless the costs of inpatient care are subsidized by the research program. These problems bias enrollment of subjects into contemporary research by excluding large numbers of otherwise appropriate cases. Inpatient research on biological processes is now generally limited to programs such as those found in state hospitals, Department of Veterans Affairs hospitals, or well-funded, university-based clinical research centers. In such settings, it is almost certain that there are sampling biases in the direction of chronicity, complexity, severity, and/or treatment resistance.

Method Variance

A final significant source of variability in research relates to the actual procedures used to assess the process in question. Standardization and confirmation of the reliability of research methods, such as neurochemical, neurophysiological, and neuroradiological measurements, are of critical importance. Determination of inter- and intra-assay coefficients of variation, comparisons across laboratories, and development of quality control standards are essential. Furthermore, when several measurement techniques are available for the same biological parameter, as is now the case with single photon emission computed tomography (SPECT) and positron emission tomography (PET) studies of cerebral metabolism, consensual agreement regarding the most accurate technique is ultimately necessary. The comparison of SPECT and PET illustrates the complexity of research methods: PET has advantages with respect to clarity and resolution of images, whereas SPECT is substantially less expensive, more widely available, and better suited for repeated study (Reba, 1993).

A summary of sources of methodological variance and suggested solutions is provided in Table 8.3.

NEUROCHEMICAL AND RECEPTOR ABNORMALITIES

Most biological theories of depression hypothesize disturbances of one or more neurochemi-

TABLE 8.3. Methodological Problems in Depression Research

Problem	Suggested solution
1. Diagnostic reliability	Use of operationalized diagnostic criteria
	Use of standardized interviews and collateral sources of information
2. Heterogeneous diagnostic entities	Stratification of samples according to relevant clinical characteristics
3. Epiphenomenal variables (e.g., age, sex, nutritional status, menstrual status, time of day, and season)	Use of matched patient and control groups
	Methodological or, if necessary, statistical control for relevant variables
4. Nonspecific effects of stress, illness, and hospitalization	Use of hospitalized (nonaffective) patient controls
5. Acute or withdrawal effects of medication, alcohol, or other illicit drugs	Use of medication-free washout periods prior to study
	Screening of samples with urine drug screens
6. Confounding effects of intercurrent medical illness	
	Evaluation of controls and patients to exclude those with potentially confounding medical conditions
7. Accuracy and reliability of biological measurements	Determination of intra- and interassay variability
	Determination of norms for both patient and control groups
	Assessment of interlaboratory variability
8. Choice of best method of measurement	Consensual validation for selection of the most appropriate method to assess the variable in question

Note. Adapted from Thase, Frank, & Kupfer (1985).

cal systems within the brain. Considerable research has addressed the role of various CNS neurotransmitters, including the catecholamines norepinephrine (NE) and dopamine (DA), the indoleamine serotonin (5-HT), and acetylcholine (ACh; see Figure 8.2). Each of these substances has been localized in the brain tracts and nuclei involved in regulation of sleep, reward, appetite, and emotional expression (e.g., Cooper, Bloom, & Roth, 1991; Depue & Spoont, 1986; Kandel, Schwartz, & Jessell, 1991). The precursors, metabolites, and enzymes involved in synthesis and degradation, and important receptors of these neurotransmitters, are summarized in Table 8.4.

The Neuronal Synapse

Before we turn to the function of neurochemical systems, a brief review of the characteristics of a more basic functional unit, the neuronal synapse, is in order. The synapse represents the essential junction of neural transmission and signal transduction between neurons. The synapse is where the electrophysiological signal is passed on from the axon terminal of an activated cell to the next cell, via release of neurotrans-

mitters into the synaptic cleft (see Figure 8.3). Neurotransmitters are stored as granules in membrane-bound vesicles in the axon terminals. When the cell is stimulated, the storage vesicle migrates and joins with the cell membrane in order to release neurotransmitter into the synaptic cleft. Once released, neurotransmitters may do the following:

1. Attach to membrane-bound receptors on the postsynaptic cell.
2. Be reabsorbed back into the presynaptic cell's axonal terminal (a process called "reuptake").
3. Attach to so-called autoreceptors on the presynaptic cell.

The principal function of autoreceptors is to provide feedback inhibition to help "turn down," or down-regulate, the sending potential of the presynaptic cell.

The reuptake of neurotransmitters has an important homeostatic role, in that the reabsorbed molecules may be "recycled" and, thus, do not have to be replaced by biosynthesis. Reabsorption of small molecules or ions back into cells may occur by passive diffusion but, for

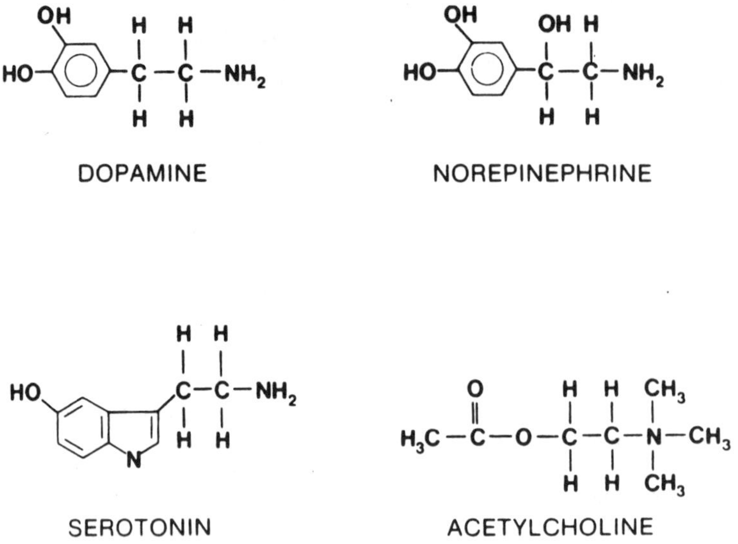

FIGURE 8.2. Structural depictions of dopamine, norepinephrine, serotonin, and acetylcholine. From Thase, Frank, & Kupfer (1985).

the most part, neurotransmitters are taken back in by energy-dependent, membrane-bound complexes that include reuptake transporter sites.

Neurotransmitters and their receptors interact like so many keys and locks. The receptors (i.e., the "locks") are polypeptide structures embedded in the cell membrane. The lock and key metaphor has its limitations (e.g., Cooper et al., 1991), but captures the specificity of receptor–neurotransmitter interactions. For example, 5-HT will not attach to receptors for NE or DA.

Many receptors are linked to intracellular "second messenger" systems by a protein complex referred to as a "G-protein," so named because of its dependence on the nucleic acid guanine. Second messengers, such as the cyclic nucleotides adenosine monosphosphate (cAMP) and guanine monophosphate (cGMP), trigger at least three major biological "cascades": protein phosphorylation, phosphoinositide hydrolysis, and metabolism of arachidonic acids, such as prostaglandins (Cooper et al., 1991). These processes result in changes in cell membrane conformation or permeability that alter the activity of the ion channels for Na^+, K^+, Ca^{++}, and Cl^-. As a result, neurotransmission is modified in terms of the amount of transmitter released (presynaptic), the firing rate of the cell (postsynaptic), and the number of receptors available (pre- and postsynaptic; Cooper et al., 1991).

Specific genes code for receptors and, as a result, variations in the exact sequence of each receptor's amino acid chains are under genetic control. Advances in molecular genetics have permitted the cloning of a number of neurotransmitter receptors. There are distinct families of receptors that share affinities for different types of neurotransmitters (i.e., receptors that are noradrenergic, dopaminergic, serotonergic, etc.). Within families of receptors, differences in chemical structure and ligand binding characteristics are categorized by assigning Greek letters and numerical and/or letter subscripts. For example, the family of serotonin (5-HT) receptors includes 5-HT_{1A}, 5-HT_{1B}, 5-HT_2, and 5-HT_3 receptors, as well as others. Likewise, noradrenergic receptors may be divided into α and β types, with at least two subtypes of each (i.e., α_1 and α_2 and β_1 and β_2).

Neurotransmitter receptors are dynamically responsive to changes in the cellular milieu, which also helps to ensure homeostasis. For example, a prolonged excess in neural activation may result in an increased number, or up-regulation, in presynaptic inhibitory sites and/or a decreased number (down-regulation) of postsynaptic sites. Conversely, chronic treatment with agents that block postsynaptic sites may result in an increased number and/or affinity of receptors. As will subsequently be discussed,

TABLE 8.4. Summary of Neurotransmitter Synthesis and Metabolism

Neurotransmitter	Precursors	Metabolites	Synthetic enzyme(s)	Degradative enzyme(s)	Selected receptor subtypes	Selected agonists (+) or antagonists (−)
Norepinephrine	Phenylalanine Tyrosine Dopa Dopamine	Normetanephrine 3-Methoxy-4-hydroxyphenyl glycol (MHPG)	Dopamine β-hydroxylase (DBH)	Monoamine oxidase (MAO) Catechol-O-methyl transferase (COMT)	α_1 α_2 β_1 β_2	Prazosin (−) Clonidine (+) Yohimbine (−) Isoproterenol (+) Epinephrine (+)
Serotonin (5-HT)	L-Tryptophan 5-Hydroxytryptophan (5-HTP)	5-Hydroxyindoleacetic acid (5-HIAA)	Tryptophan hydroxylase	MAO	5-HT_{1A} 5-HT_2 5-HT_3	Ipsapirone (+) Ketanserin (−) Ondanserton (+)
Dopamine (DA)	Phenylalanine Tyrosine Dopa	Homovanillic acid (HVA) Norepinephrine	Tyrosine hydroxylase Dopa decarboxylase	MAO COMT DBH	D_1 D_2 D_3 D_4	Raclopride (−) Apomorphine (+) Quinpirol (−) Clozapine (−)
Acetylcholine (ACh)	Choline Phosphatidylcholine	None	Choline acetyltransferase	Cholinesterase	Muscarinic Nicotinic	Atropine (−) Nicotine (+)

Note. Adapted from Thase, Frank, & Kupfer (1985), and Cooper, Bloth, & Roth (1991).

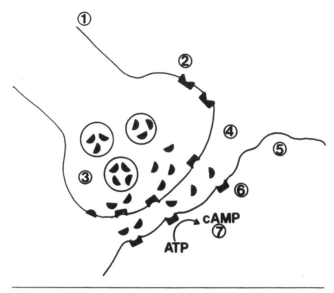

Key:
1. Representing the efferent terminal.
2. Presynaptic receptor sites.
3. Intracellular monoamine storage vesicles.
4. The synaptic cleft.
5. The afferent terminal.
6. Postsynaptic receptor sites.
7. Membrane-bound adenylate cyclase for conversion of the "second messenger" cAMP.

FIGURE 8.3. Schematic illustration of a monoamine synapse. From Thase, Frank, & Kupfer (1985).

these various receptor "behaviors" have been increasingly implicated in both the pathophysiology of depression and the mechanism of action in various antidepressant compounds.

Neurobiology of Emotional and Vegetative Function

Noradrenergic Systems

The principal nuclei (i.e., clusters of cell bodies) containing noradrenergic neurons are located in two areas of the pons in the brain stem: (1) the locus ceruleus and (2) the ventral lateral tegmentum (see Figure 8.4; Cooper et al., 1991; Kandel et al., 1991). Neurons from the ventral lateral tegmentum project their axons primarily to other brain stem nuclei and the spinal cord, where they contribute mainly to the control and integration of the autonomic nervous system. The axons of noradrenergic neurons from the locus ceruleus travel upward, through the medial forebrain bundle, and project their axons diffusely throughout the brain. Noradrenergic axons project to the cerebral cortex, cerebellum,

hypothalamus, thalamus, basal ganglia, septum, and hippocampus. Such diffuse projection within the CNS is consistent with the noradrenergic system's primary role in initiating and maintaining arousal (Thayer, 1989), as well as its modulation of the function of other neurotransmitters (Cooper et al., 1991). Projections to the adrenal medulla via the sympathetic nervous system control the release of NE within peripheral circulation, a key component in activating the "fight or flight" response. Cognitive processes, such as expectancy or contextual sets, serve to amplify or dampen sympathoadrenal responses to internal or external stimuli (Thayer, 1989). Thus, the perception of stress is relayed through the locus ceruleus, ventral lateral tegmentum, and sympathoadrenal components.

Increased firing of neurons in the locus ceruleus occurs following presentation of novel stimuli, whereas decreased firing occurs during vegetative functions, such as feeding or sleeping (Cooper et al., 1991). Electrical stimulation of the locus ceruleus also causes heightened physiological arousal (e.g., Kaitin et al., 1986).

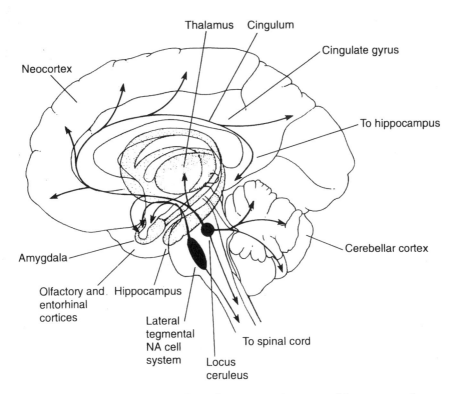

FIGURE 8.4. A lateral view of the brain demonstrates the course of the major noradrenergic pathways emanating from the locus ceruleus and from the lateral brain stem tegmentum. From Kandel, Schwartz, & Jessell (1991). Copyright 1991 by Appleton & Lange. Reprinted by permission.

Noradrenergic projections from the locus ceruleus to the hippocampus have recently been implicated in behavioral sensitization to various stressors, as illustrated by studies utilizing the learned helplessness paradigm (Petty, Chae, Kramer, Jordan, & Wilson, 1994). With respect to severe depression, pathologically increased noradrenergic activity appears to contribute to dysphoric arousal (including both sadness and anxiety), agitation, disturbances of cognition (i.e., poor concentration), and altered neurovegetative processes (e.g., diminished appetite and insomnia; e.g., Thase et al., 1985).

Stimulation of other noradrenergic pathways, such as the medial forebrain bundle, can produce increased levels of goal-directed behavior (Cooper et al., 1991). Such enhanced noradrenergic neurotransmission has been implicated in the pathophysiology of hypomanic and manic states (Bunney & Davis, 1965; Carroll, 1991). Conversely, an abnormal reduction of noradrenergic activity may result in depressive symptoms such as anergia and anhedonia (e.g.,

Bunney & Davis, 1965). Sustained stress may eventually result in decreased NE activity via depletion of storage granules, resulting in a behavioral state that may be analogous to some forms of depression (Weiss, 1991).

Serotonergic Systems

The principal serotonergic neurons in the CNS are found in the raphe nuclei of the midbrain and upper pons of the brain stem (Cooper et al., 1991). These serotonergic nuclei project their axons extensively to the cerebral cortex, hypothalamus, thalamus, basal ganglia, septum, and hippocampus (see Figure 8.5). Serotonergic neurotransmission is proposed to have both inhibitory and facilitatory functions (e.g., Carroll, 1991; Depue & Spoont, 1986). For example, much evidence suggests that the serotonin system is an important tonic regulator of sleep, appetite, and libido (Depue & Spoont, 1986). Serotonergic neurons also influence sleep architecture by tonically inhibiting rapid eye move-

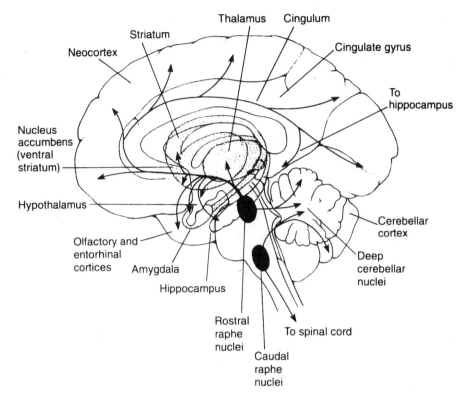

FIGURE 8.5. A lateral view of the brain demonstrates the course of the major serotonergic pathways. Although the raphe nuclei form a fairly continuous collection of cell groups throughout the brain stem, they are graphically illustrated here as two groups, one rostral and one caudal. From Kandel, Schwartz, & Jessell (1991). Copyright 1991 by Appleton & Lange. Reprinted by permission.

ment (REM) activity; these cells are active during deep, slow-wave sleep (SWS) and become electrically "silent" during REM sleep periods (Horne, 1993; McCarley, 1982).

Serotonergic neurons project axons to the suprachiasmatic nucleus of the hypothalamus and, therefore, are presumed to contribute to regulation of circadian rhythms of neurovegetative processes (e.g., the sleep–wake cycles, body temperature, and hypothalamic–pituitary–hormonal function; Depue & Spoont, 1986). Serotonin also is implicated in the regulation of goal-directed motor behavior (Jacobs, 1991) and consummatory behaviors (Amit, Smith, & Gill, 1991), as well as inhibition of aggression in both primates (Higley et al., 1992a) and human beings (Brown & Linnoila, 1990). Thus, pathological reductions of serotonergic neurotransmission are implicated in disturbances of appetite, sleep, and sexual behavior, as well as aggressivity and violent suicidal behavior (e.g.,

Golden & Gilmore, 1990; Malone & Mann, 1993).

Some evidence suggests that basal levels of 5-HT and its metabolites are partly under genetic control (Higley et al., 1992a). Abnormally low basal metabolite levels may be the result of an allele of the gene coding for the enzyme tryptophan hydroxylase (Nielsen et al., 1994). By contrast, acute stress mobilizes 5-HT release, resulting in a transient increase in 5-HT activity (Depue & Spoont, 1986). Chronic stress may result in a level of utilization of 5-HT that surpasses synthesis, producing a depletion of intracellular serotonin stores (Weiss, 1991).

Similar to the noradrenergic system, serotonin modulates the activity of other neurotransmitter systems throughout the brain. For example, experimentally induced lesions dampening 5-HT activity also diminish responsivity to NE and DA (Cooper et al., 1991). The terms "behavioral quieting" (Whybrow et al., 1985) and "behavioral facilitation" (Depue & Spoont, 1986) have been coined to describe the functional roles of 5-HT in the CNS.

Dopaminergic Systems

The dopaminergic system involves four relatively discrete neuronal pathways: (1) tuberoinfundibular, (2) nigrostriatal, (3) mesolimbic, and (4) mesocortical (see Figure 8.6; Cooper et al., 1991; Kandel et al., 1991). The tuberoinfundibular system originates in the hypothalamus and projects to the pituitary stalk, where it has an inhibitory effect on prolactin secretion. The nigrostriatal system originates in the substantia nigra and projects to the basal ganglia, where it helps to regulate involuntary extrapyramidal motor activity. The mesolimbic system originates in the ventral tegmental area and projects axons throughout the limbic system, including the nucleus accumbens, amygdala, hippocampus, septum, and cingulate cortex. The mesolimbic system is involved in emotional regulation, learning and memory, positive reinforcement mechanisms, and hedonic capacity. Finally, the mesocortical system, which also originates in the ventral tegmental area, projects axons to the cerebral cortex, particularly the prefrontal region. This system may be involved in motivation, initiation of goal-directed activity, attention, "executive" cognitive tasks, and social behavior (Spoont, 1992). Thus, increased mesocortical and mesolimbic dopaminergic activity may be related to such symptoms as euphoria, psychomotor activation, increased sexual activity, or the reckless, adventurous behavior that characterizes manic states (Carroll, 1991). Conversely, decreased dopaminergic neurotransmission may contribute to poor concentration, anhedonia, volitional inhibition, psychomotor retardation, and anergia (van Praag, 1980; Wilner, 1993).

Monoamine Disturbances in Affective States

Interest in the potential involvement of the CNS monoamine neurotransmitters (e.g., NE, DA, and 5-HT) in depression was stimulated in the early 1960s, when it was discovered that antidepressant medications increase levels of NE, DA, and/or 5-HT within the synaptic cleft. The TCAs subsequently were shown to block neuronal uptake of NE and/or 5-HT, whereas the MAOI antidepressants were found to increase neurotransmitter availability by inhibit-

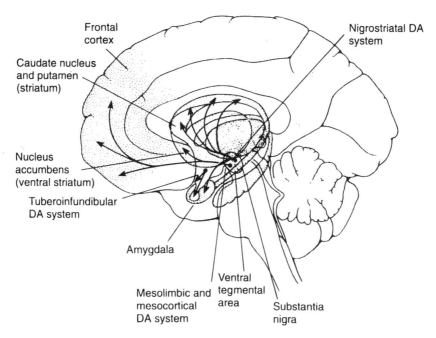

FIGURE 8.6. A lateral view of the brain demonstrates the course of the four major dopaminergic tracts. From Kandel, Schwartz, & Jessell (1991). Copyright 1991 by Appleton & Lange. Reprinted by permission.

ing enzymatic degradation of NE, DA, and 5-HT (Bunney & Davis, 1965; Schildkraut, 1965). Conversely, the depressogenic effect of the antihypertensive agent reserpine was linked to depletion of monoamines in neuronal storage granules. These observations led to hypotheses about catecholamine (Bunney & Davis, 1965; Schildkraut, 1965) and indoleamine (Glassman, 1969) deficiencies in depression. Heuristically, a functional deficiency of neurotransmitter may arise through diverse mechanisms, including decreased synthesis, increased degradation, impaired release, decreased reuptake, or altered receptor binding. In fact, since the early 1980s, these hypotheses have broadened to emphasize the likelihood of altered pre- or postsynaptic monoamine receptor function. The central tenets of the monoamine hypotheses are summarized in Table 8.5. A substantial body of empirical data addressing these points has been collected, and evidence for and against the monoamine hypotheses has been reviewed extensively (e.g., Coppen & Doogan, 1988; Delgado, Price, Heninger, & Charney, 1992; Meltzer & Lowy, 1987; Potter, Grossman, & Rudorfer, 1993; Siever, 1987).

Norepinephrine

To briefly summarize, an NE deficiency state has not been demonstrated in the majority of depressed patients in studies of their plasma, urine, and cerebrospinal fluid (CSF) samples,

TABLE 8.5. Tenets of the Contemporary Monoamine Hypotheses of Depression

1. Decreased functional activity of monoamine (i.e., NE, DA, and/or 5-HT) causes depression.

2. Increased functional activity of catecholamines (i.e., NE and/or DA) causes mania.

3. Alterations of functional activity of monoamines may result from impaired synthesis or storage, increased degradation, or altered receptor function.

4. Agents that deplete monoamines or impair synthesis cause depression.

5. Administration of monoamine precursors should produce or enhance antidepressant effects.

6. Antidepressant agents induce increased functional monoamine activity.

7. Agents that increase functional monoamine activity increase the risk of hypomania or mania.

Note. Adapted from Thase, Frank, & Kupfer (1985).

as well as postmortem assays of brain tissue of suicide victims, (see, e.g., Coppen & Doogan, 1988; Delgado et al., 1992; Potter et al., 1993). However, paradigms relying on measurement of NE metabolites in body fluids leave much to be desired with respect to their power to yield definitive information about noradrenergic function in the CNS.

Perhaps the best-studied neurochemical indicator of CNS noradrenergic activity is the metabolite 3-methoxy-4-hydroxyphenyl glycol (MHPG; Schildkraut, 1982; Siever, 1987). Several early studies found that a subgroup of major depression cases was characterized by low 24–hour levels of urinary excretion of MHPG, suggesting a deficiency of brain NE (see, e.g., Maas, 1975; Schildkraut, 1982). Significantly lower levels of urinary MHPG have been reported in bipolar and schizoaffective depressions relative to patients with nonbipolar or nonendogenous syndromes (e.g., Goodwin & Post, 1975; Schatzberg et al., 1989; Schildkraut, 1982). Moreover, longitudinal studies of bipolar patients have demonstrated increased urinary MHPG levels following shifts from depression into mania (Schildkraut, 1982). Similarly, high CSF levels of MHPG in mania have been reported (Post et al., 1989; Swann et al., 1983).

Several groups have found that depressed persons with low urinary MHPG levels respond more favorably to "adrenergic" antidepressants, such as desipramine or maprotiline, than to "serotonergic" antidepressants like amitriptyline or clomipramine (e.g., Maas et al., 1984; Schatzberg et al., 1989; Schildkraut, 1982). Moreover, available evidence suggests that abnormally reduced urinary MHPG at least partially normalizes with effective treatment (see Potter et al., 1993). Several other studies have yielded contradictory results, however, clouding inferences about the role of decreased NE in major depression (see the reviews of Delgado et al., 1992, or Potter et al., 1993). For example, some studies have not confirmed the existence of a distinct, "low"-MHPG subgroup (e.g., Davis et al., 1988), and as few as 25% of nonbipolar depressives have urinary MHPG concentrations that fall below the normal range (DeLisi, Karoum, Targum, Byrnes, & Wyatt, 1983). Part of the problem rests with the limited reliability and validity of MHPG measurement. For example, urinary MHPG levels may vary greatly from day to day and levels are affected by factors such as diet, activity, drug use, and anxiety. Perhaps most important, only a fraction of MHPG measured in peripheral specimens is derived from the brain (Potter et al., 1993).

Inferences about biochemical "types" of depression on the basis of antidepressant response are similarly flawed (Siever, 1987). For example, studies conducted in the 1970s and early 1980s utilized older antidepressant agents that are now known to be relatively unselective for adrenergic or serotonergic effects (Potter et al., 1993; Siever, 1987). Furthermore, recent studies employing selective serotonin reuptake inhibitors (SSRIs) have failed to show the predicted relationship between NE metabolites and antidepressant response (e.g., DeBellis, Geracioti, Altemus, & King, 1993a; Potter et al., 1985). It is possible that low urinary MHPG may have predictive value for antidepressant treatment response per se (Potter & Linnoila, 1989), perhaps because of a relationship between low urinary MHPG levels and psychomotor retardation (Thase et al., 1985).

A number of studies over the past decade have documented that a subgroup of more severely depressed persons manifested *increased* peripheral adrenergic activity (e.g., Davis et al., 1988; Redmond et al., 1986; Roy, Pickar, DeJong, Karoum, & Linnoila, 1988a). For example, in a large study of 132 severely depressed inpatients, 45% were found to have elevated levels of epinephrine and metanephrine, compared to only 5% of 80 controls (Davis et al., 1988). Increased peripheral levels of NE and its metabolites suggest an aberrant and sustained increase in the sympathomedullary component of the stress response system (Veith et al., 1994). As discussed previously, such increased peripheral NE is likely to be triggered by over-activation of the locus ceruleus. It therefore is of interest that a variety of antidepressant compounds decrease the firing rate of the locus ceruleus and reduce CSF MHPG levels (e.g., Potter et al., 1993).

Some evidence suggests that the high-output noradrenergic state is more common in unipolar depression or bipolar "mixed" states than in bipolar depressions (e.g., Maas et al., 1987; Swann et al., 1994). This is consistent with past findings of studies utilizing urinary MHPG levels as the indicator of NE function (Schildkraut, 1982). Increased NE output is particularly characteristic of unipolar patients with more severe, melancholic features (Roy, Pickar, Linnoila, & Potter, 1985). Sustained adrenergic "drive" also may be inferred from studies of completed suicides, in which decreased postsynaptic α_1 bind-

ing most likely reflects down-regulation of receptor function in response to chronic over-stimulation (Gross-Isseroff, Dillon, Fieldust, & Biegon, 1990).

There is also evidence of abnormal postsynaptic β-adrenergic receptor function in depression (Halper et al., 1988; Mann, Stanley, McBride, & McEwen, 1986; Mazzola-Pomietto, Azorin, Tramoni, & Jenningros, 1994). For example, in research studying the lymphocytes of depressed patients (Halper et al., 1988; Mazzola-Pomietto et al., 1994), blunted β-adrenergic sensitivity has been demonstrated, which, again, is likely to be the result of a sustained increase in sympathoadrenal activity. Abnormal β-adrenergic function in depression has additional implications because of its association with the cAMP second-messenger system (Cooper et al., 1991). Such β-adrenergic dysregulation has been reported to be corrected by both antidepressant pharmacotherapy (see Elliott, 1991) and electroconvulsive therapy (Mann et al., 1990).

Existing data regarding presynaptic α_2-receptors also suggest that their sensitivity is reduced in depression (Elliott, 1991; Potter et al., 1993). Yet again, blunted presynaptic α_2-receptor function most likely results from sustained overstimulation. Unlike β-adrenergic dysfunction, however, some evidence suggests that blunted α_2 responsivity may persist during periods of remission (Katona, Theorodou, & Horton, 1987; Elliott, 1991). The issue of reversibility remains in doubt: In a study using a more selective ligand to measure platelet α_2-receptor binding, treatment with desipramine resulted in significantly reduced receptor binding (Piletz, Halaris, Saran, & Marler, 1991).

Increased noradrenergic neurotransmission is not specific to severe depression. Sympathoadrenal hyperactivity has been reported in mania (Post et al., 1989; Swann et al., 1983; Swann et al., 1991), panic disorder (Charney & Heninger, 1986), and acute exacerbations of schizophrenia (van Kammen et al., 1990). Such nonspecificity suggests that increased sympathoadrenal activity is present in many forms of psychopathology characterized by sustained hyperarousal.

Additional studies have examined levels of the degradative enzyme monoamine oxidase (MAO) in blood platelets. Despite fairly extensive research, conflicting results are the rule rather than the exception (see, e.g., a review of earlier studies by Rotman, 1983). Both elevated and decreased platelet MAO levels have been reported in studies of major depression and other psychiatric disorders, including schizophrenia, dementia, and anxiety disorders (Georgotas et al., 1986; Rotman, 1983). It is likely that such inconsistencies in platelet MAO levels reflect state-dependent variabilities in circulating levels of monamines and their metabolites (Thase et al., 1985). It is also now clear that the type of MAO found in the platelet (referred to as Type B) is much more specific for degradation of DA and the trace amine phenylethylamine than either NE or 5-HT. Moreover, platelet MAO activity levels have almost no correlation with enzymatic activity, which is predominantly Type A, in the CNS (Young, Laws, Sharbrough, & Weinshilboum, 1986). It is therefore not surprising that studies of platelet MAO activity may vary as a function of the patient's level of arousal and/or observable psychomotor state, such that higher levels are found in persons with more severe, agitated, or anxious depression, and lower levels in cases characterized by psychomotor retardation (Georgotas et al., 1986; Samson et al., 1985; Schatzberg et al., 1987).

Recent research has indicated that the hypothalamic–pituitary–adrenocortical (HPA) axis acts in tandem with sympathoadrenal function as part of systemic adaptation to sustained stress (e.g., Gold, Goodwin, & Chrousos, 1988; Nemeroff, 1992). For example, corticotropin-releasing hormone (CRH) increases both HPA activity and the firing rate of the locus ceruleus, and increased locus ceruleus firing "turns on" HPA activity (Nemeroff, 1992; Plotsky, Cunningham, & Widmaier, 1989). This line of research suggests that otherwise appropriate neurohormonal responses to acute stress may be amplified or distorted by selected psychopathological processes, consequently producing a destabilizing positive-feedback loop. The use of more sophisticated functional neuroimaging techniques, such as PET or functional magnetic resonance imaging (fMRI), should help to differentiate the four disorders characterized by increased noradrenergic tone: agitated melancholic depression, mania, acute schizophrenia, and panic disorder.

Serotonin

Although the role of 5-HT in major depression has been an area of intensive research for over 25 years (e.g., Glassman, 1969), interest has been further stimulated by the recent introduction of a class of antidepressant drugs that are essentially specific for blocking the reuptake of 5-HT back into the presynaptic neuron (Malone & Mann, 1993). This ever-growing family of SSRIs now includes fluoxetine, sertraline, paroxetine, fluvoxamine, and citalopram.

The most consistently reported finding in support of serotonergic dysfunction in depression is reduced levels of CSF 5-hydroxyindoleacetic acid (5-HIAA) in at least a subset of patients (e.g., Coppen & Doogan, 1988; Gibbons & Davis, 1986; Malone & Mann, 1993; Meltzer & Lowy, 1987). Similarly, low levels of 5-HIAA have been reported in postmortem brain specimens of bipolar patients (Young, Warsh, Kish, Shannak, & Hornykeiwicz, 1994b) and suicide victims (Beskow, Gottfries, Roos, & Winbald, 1976). However, not all studies have documented the existence of a subgroup with abnormally low 5-HIAA (e.g., Åsberg & Wägner, 1986; Cheetham, Katona, & Horton, 1991).

Attempts to correlate CSF 5-HIAA levels with clinical subtypes of depression or treatment response have yielded largely disappointing results. The only widely replicated clinical correlate of low CSF 5-HIAA is a history of violent or impulsive suicidal behavior (e.g., Brown & Linnoila, 1990; Linnoila & Virkkunen, 1992). Of note, low 5-HIAA levels also have been found in individuals with other psychiatric conditions characterized by impulsive or aggressive behavior, such as alcoholism and antisocial personality disorder (see, e.g., Linnoila & Virkkunen, 1992; Virkkunen et al., 1994). Recently, these findings have been partially extended to less invasive measurements, such as measurement of 5-HT in whole blood or platelets and neuroendocrine responses to serotonergic probes (e.g., Mann, McBride, Anderson, & Mieczkowski, 1992a; Coccaro et al., 1989). It is more likely that low 5-HT "tone" is a marker of a broader dimension of impulsivity (more closely linked to temperament or personality traits) than a specific correlate of affective illness (Coccaro, Silverman, Klar, Horvath & Seiver, 1994; Linnoila and Virkkunen, 1992; Siever & Davis, 1991). From this perspective, among the total population of depressed persons, those who manifest a traitlike disturbance of reduced serotonergic neurotransmission are more likely to express their suicidal ideations in terms of violent behaviors.

Consistent with the notion of a traitlike disturbance, various antidepressant treatments have not been shown to incease CSF 5-HIAA levels (e.g., Kelwala, Jones, & Sitaram, 1983; Linnoila, Miller, Bartko, & Potter, 1984). Nevertheless, the SSRIs have been shown to be useful in a broad range of disorders of impulse regulation in addition to depression (e.g., Dominguez, 1992; Golden & Gilmore, 1990; Stein et al., 1992).

Some research suggests that a 5-HT deficiency state in depression may be either caused or exacerbated by reduced plasma levels and/or altered metabolism of selected dietary precursors, such as L-tryptophan and 5-hydroxytryptophan (e.g., Coppen & Doogan, 1988; Cowen, Parry-Billings, & Newsholme, 1989). The former hypothesis is strengthened by reports of decreased 5-HT concentrations in the platelets of depressed patients (e.g., Guicheney et al., 1988; Mann et al., 1992; Quintana, 1992). Such findings could suggest alterations in the competitive balance of the serotonin precursor 5-hydroxytryptophan in relation to neutral amino acids (i.e., valine, leucine, and isoleucine) diffusing across the blood–brain barrier. The existence of such an abnormality is supported by results of one study utilizing PET measurement of uptake of radioactively labeled 5-hydroxytryptophan (Agren et al., 1991).

Although CSF 5-HIAA levels are not increased by antidepressant treatments, functional potentiation of 5-HT neurotransmission has been shown in studies using serotonergic agonists in combination with standard antidepressant agents (e.g., Blier, DeMontigny, & Chaput, 1987; Shapira, Lerer, & Kindler, 1992b; Shapira, Cohen, Newman, & Lerer, 1993; Upadhayaya, Pennell, Cowan, & Deakin, 1991) or lithium/antidepressant combinations (Price, Charney, Delgado, & Heninger, 1990; Shapira, Yagmur, Gropp, Mewman, & Lerer, 1992b). Furthermore, effective antidepressant treatment may result in significant alterations in platelet 5–HT levels and/or changes in platelet membrane kinetics (Kuhs, Schlake, Rolf, & Rudolf, 1992; Quintana, 1992). Conversely, experimentally induced dietary depletion of 5-HT has been reported to precipitate rapid exacerbation of depressive symptoms in recently remitted patients receiving antidepressant medications (Delgado et al., 1990). Some evidence suggests that patients who have responded to treatment with SSRI antidepressants are particularly vulnerable to the depressogenic effect of dietary 5-HT depletion (Miller et al., 1992).

Several interesting findings have emerged from studies of membrane-bound 5-HT transporter sites in depression. One strategy involves measurement of radioactively labeled imipramine ([3H]IMI) or [3H] paroxetine binding sites (Maguire, Tuckwell, Pereira, Dean, & Singh, 1993; Mellerup & Plenge, 1986, 1988), which are adjacent to 5-HT transporters on cell membranes. Most studies of [3H]IMI binding have found reduced levels in depression (see Mellerup & Plenge, 1988), although this finding has not been uniformly replicated (e.g., Bech et al., 1988). Such a discrepancy may be due to methodological issues (e.g., Halbreich, Rojansky, Zander, & Barkai, 1991). For example, [3H]IMI binding sites include both low- and high-affinity subtypes, and only the latter appears relevant to reuptake phenomena (Hrdina, 1989). By contrast, [3H]paroxetine binding sites are exclusively of the high-affinity subtype (Maguire et al., 1993). It may also be true that the ligand binding characteristics of the platelet reuptake site, the most common cell type studied, are not highly correlated with 5-HT function within the CNS. Only a small number of studies have examined [3H]IMI or [3H]paroxetine binding in the brain, and, to date, results have not been conclusive (e.g., Gross-Isseroff, Israeli, & Biegon, 1989; Malone & Mann, 1993).

Another source of potential variation may stem from depressive subgroups with different [3H]IMI and/or [3H]paroxetine binding characteristics (Arora & Meltzer, 1988; Åsberg & Wägner, 1986; Mellerup & Plenge, 1988). For example, associations have been reported between decreased platelet [3H]IMI binding and hypercortisolemia (Roy, Everett, Pickar, & Paul, 1987), older age (Nemeroff et al., 1988), and/or familial depressions (Baron et al., 1987; Lewis & McChesney, 1985). Of note is an increased level of a stress-related glycoprotein that inhibits [3H]IMI binding, which was reported in a study of hospitalized older depressed patients (Nemeroff, Krishnan, Blazer, Knight, Benjamin, & Meyerson, 1990).

The nature of diminished [3H]IMI or [3H] paroxetine binding as a trait or state marker of depression is unresolved (Berretini, Nurnberger, Post, & Gershon, 1982; Marazziti et al., 1988; Wägner et al., 1987). This line of investigation may be complicated by the observation that reduced [3H]IMI binding may be associated with poorer antidepressant response (Åsberg & Wägner, 1986; Malone et al., 1993; Wägner et al., 1987). Such an association would increase the likelihood that the abnormality will appear traitlike. One long-term study of a small number of remitted patients successfully treated with ECT did document eventual normalization (Langer, Sechter, Loo, Raisman, & Zarifian, 1986). In any event, the induction of reduced [³H]IMI binding in rats exposed to the learned helplessness paradigm (Sherman & Petty, 1984) indicates that a state-dependent abnormality can be induced under stressful circumstances without a genetic or familial diathesis.

In contrast to the presynaptic 5-HT transporter sites, whose function may be reduced in depression, an increase in postsynaptic 5-HT$_2$ receptors have been found in the blood platelets of high-lethality suicide attempters (McBride et al., 1994) and in the brains of depressed persons who have committed suicide (Arango et al., 1990; Mann et al., 1986; McKeith et al., 1987). Although not confirmed in all studies (e.g., Cheetham, Crompton, Katona, & Horton, 1988), these findings are significant, in that reduced presynaptic 5-HT function would be expected to induce a compensatory increase in the number of postsynaptic receptor sites (Malone & Mann, 1993).

Consistent with the up-regulation hypothesis of the illness state, chronic antidepressant treatment down-regulates, or decreases, the number of 5-HT$_2$ receptors (e.g., Garattini & Samanin, 1988). Antidepressant treatment similarly sensitizes postsynaptic CNS neurons to the effects of 5-HT or its agonists (e.g., Blier et al., 1987). These observations illustrate possible pharmacologic mechanisms by which antidepressants counteract the diathesis of diminished 5-HT neurotransmission in depression. Development of methods to test other types of post-synaptic serotonin receptors that are implicated in depression (i.e., 5-HT$_{1A}$ and 5-HT$_3$ receptors) is a topic of considerable current interest.

Until the past decade, studies of state-dependent changes in 5-HT function were hampered by problems in measurement of metabolites in plasma or urine. Other measures of central 5-HT activity include challenge studies utilizing either 5-hydroxytryptophan (Cowen & Charig, 1987; Heninger, Charney, & Sternberg, 1984; Meltzer, Perline, Tricou, Lowy, & Robertson, 1984a; Meltzer et al., 1984b) or d-fenfluramine, a drug with both releasing and reuptake-inhibiting effects on 5-HT at presynaptic sites (e.g., Coccaro et al., 1989; Malone et al., 1993; Myers et al., 1993; O'Keane & Dinan, 1991). Both lines of research reveal blunted release of prolactin

from the anterior pituitary following provocative challenge, providing further evidence of decreased functional 5-HT activity in depression. Abnormal fenfluramine responses also have been reported in nondepressed personality disorder patients with a history of impulsive aggression (e.g., Coccaro et al., 1989). Mann et al., (1992b) have reported a significant correlation between prolactin response to fenfluramine challenge and CSF levels of 5-HIAA in a diverse group of suicidal patients. These findings bring this line of research back, full circle, to the fundamental significance of decreased 5-HT in both depression and other states of pathological impulsivity. Preliminary evidence suggests that the blunted prolactin response to d-fenfluramine normalizes with effective treatment (Shapira et al., 1993).

In addition to the importance of 5-HT in isolation, research has examined the interactive nature of 5-HT, NE, and DA. For example, 5-HT and DA are significantly correlated in the CSF (e.g., Agren, Mefford, Rudorfer, Linnoila, & Potter, 1986; Hsiao et al., 1987), indicating that patients with low levels of one transmitter also tend to have low levels of the other. In fact, effective antidepressant treatment tends to increase the ratio of homovanillic acid (HVA) to 5-HIAA in the CSF (e.g., Linnoila et al., 1983). Patients who show "unlinked" CSF HVA and 5-HIAA levels may be less responsive to antidepressant treatment (Hsiao et al., 1987). Conversely, 5-HT may have an inhibitory or modulatory effect on NE neurotransmission, so that abnormally low 5-HT levels may "permit" noradrenergic dyscontrol at times of stress (Depue & Spoont, 1986).

Dopamine

Research concerning the role of DA in depression has yielded findings that largely complement those from studies of NE and 5-HT (Jimerson, 1987; Kapur & Mann, 1992). As noted previously, levels of DA and 5-HT are correlated in the CNS, so that low levels of one transmitter are associated with low levels of the other (Agren et al., 1986; Hsiao et al., 1987). Reduced CSF levels of HVA have been found in some cases of depression (e.g., Reddy, Khanna, Subhash, Channabasavanna, & Rao, 1992; van Praag, 1980), as has increased postsynaptic D$_2$ receptor binding (D'haenen & Bossuyt, 1994). Low levels of HVA in CSF and urine also have been linked to both recent and subsequent suicidal behavior (Jones et al., 1990; Roy et al., 1986a; Roy, DeJong, & Linnoila, 1989; Roy, Karoum, & Pollack, 1992). As noted earlier, antidepressant medication may increase the ratio of HVA to 5-HIAA in the CSF of depressed patients.

By contrast, increased DA and/or HVA levels have been reported in both psychotic depression and mania (Bowers, 1991; Bowers, Swigar, Hoffman, & Goicoechea, 1988; Gjerris, Werdelin, Rafaelsen, Alling, & Christensen, 1987; Mazure, Bowers, Hoffman, Miller, & Nelson, 1987). Similarly, development of agitation or psychosis during antidepressant treatment has been correlated with increased levels of HVA in the CSF (Golden, Markey, Risby, Rudorfer, Cowdry, & Potter, 1988b). Some evidence suggests that patients with low levels of the degradative enzyme dopamine β-hydroxylase may be particularly likely to develop psychotic depression (Matuzas, Meltzer, Uhlenhuth, Glass, & Tong, 1982; Meltzer, Cho, Carroll, & Russo 1976; Mod et al., 1986), perhaps especially in combination with hypercortisolemia (Schatzburg & Rothschild, 1992). Therefore, it is plausible that an inherited abnormality or polymorphism of the gene coding for dopamine β-hydroxylase predisposes some individuals to become psychotic when depressed. A family study of enzyme activity levels in first-degree relatives of psychotically depressed probands would be necessary to test this hypothesis.

The effects of chronic antidepressant treatment on presynaptic DA receptor sensitivity and mesolimbic DA activity also suggest a role for DA in depression (Garattini & Samanin, 1988; Muscat, Sampson, & Wilner, 1990). Recently, the more acute antidepressant effect of sleep deprivation also has been linked to enhancing effects on postsynaptic DA receptors (Ebert, Feistel, Kaschlea, Barocka, & Pirner, 1994). The utility of treatment with antipsychotic agents (i.e., compounds that block postsynaptic DA receptors) in psychotic depression (Spiker et al., 1985), the apparent antidepressant effects of several DA receptor agonists (Garattini & Samanin, 1988; Jimerson, 1987), and possible correlations between reversed neurovegetative symptom profiles and responses to antidepressants that increase dopaminergic neurotransmission (e.g., Goodnick & Extein, 1989; Himmelhoch, Thase, Mallinger, & Houck, 1991; Rampello, Nicoletti, & Raffaele, 1991; Thase, Mallinger, McKnight, & Himmelhoch, 1992a) provide further indirect support for such a relationship.

Further evidence of dopaminergic involvement in the pathophysiology of depression comes from animal studies utilizing the learned helplessness paradigm. One missing "link" in understanding how sustained, unresolvable stress might relate to clinical depression has been the elucidation of the mechanism causing anhedonia and decreased instrumental activity. Wilner, Golembiowski, Klimer, and Muscat (1991) found that experimentally induced helplessness in rodents decreases levels of mesolimbic DA, with a resultant reduction of operant performance and reinforcer salience. Thus, the helplessness state appears to be associated with a deficit in the behavioral facilitation system.

Studies utilizing contemporary neuroimaging methods to investigate severe depression similarly document decreased cerebral metabolism in DA-innervated regions of the prefrontal cortex responsible for complex, "executive" cognitive processes (Baxter et al., 1989; Cohen et al., 1992; Drevets et al., 1992; Martinot et al., 1990a).

From an ethological perspective, anhedonia and inhibition of more complex cognitive operation may be a compensatory response to conserve energy expenditure until the stressful circumstance is resolved (e.g., Peterson, Maier, & Seligman, 1993). Unfortunately, in depressed people, such an ancient adaptational response may contribute to a downward spiral through the interactive effects of loss of positive reinforcement, reduction of coping behaviors, and/ or diminution of the cognitive skills needed for higher-order problem solving.

Antidepressant Modulation of Monamine Systems

Studies of the effects of antidepressant treatment continue to provide some support for the role of monoamines in depression, while simultaneously illustrating the complexity of CNS phenomena in depression (e.g., Charney, Menkes, & Heninger, 1981; Elliott, 1991; Hsiao et al., 1987). Most clinically effective antidepressants have a variety of direct and indirect effects on both pre- and postsynaptic CNS receptors (Elliott, 1991; Garattini & Samanin, 1988; Potter et al., 1993). For example, significant effects are observed on both measures of dopaminergic and noradrenergic neurotransmission after several weeks of antidepressant treatment with apparently selective serotonergic compounds

(O'Flynn, O'Keane, Lucey, & Dinan, 1991; Potter et al., 1985). Indeed, most forms of antidepressant treatment produce a down-regulation of $5\text{-}HT_2$, β-adrenergic, and a_2-adrenergic receptors (Charney et al., 1981; Elliott, 1991). The interactive relationship of these neurotransmitter systems probably explains the nonselective effects of otherwise specific antidepressant compounds (Potter et al., 1993).

One possible common pathway of diverse yet effective antidepressant treatments is increased efficiency of adrenergic neurotransmission. Enhanced noradrenergic efficiency in response to effective treatment is reflected by increased excretion of melatonin metabolites (Golden et al., 1988a), decreased whole body norepinephrine turnover (Golden et al., 1988b), normalization of exaggerated norepinephrine responsivity to postural changes (Rudorfer, Ross, Linnoila, Sherer, & Potter, 1985), alteration of sympathetic nervous system function (Veith et al., 1994), and restoration of lymphocyte β-adrenergic sensitivity (Mann et al., 1990). As noted earlier, enhanced NE function may be achieved by treatments with no acute synaptic effects of this neurotransmitter, including SSRIs and bupropion (Potter et al., 1993). Studies similarly document that the effects of diverse antidepressants include enhancement of 5-HT neurotransmission (Malone & Mann, 1993). We wonder if effective psychotherapeutic treatment of depression similarly enhances NE and 5-HT neurotransmission.

Results from investigations testing various aspects of the monoamine hypotheses are summarized in Table 8.6.

ACETYLCHOLINE

ACh was included in contemporary models of depression at a somewhat later date than the monoamines, partly as a result of a delayed appreciation of its neuroregulatory role within the CNS (e.g., Janowsky, Risch, & Gillin, 1983). Cholinergic neurons are distributed diffusely throughout the cerebral cortex and brain stem (Cooper et al., 1991). In the latter case, ACh plays an important role via the descending parasympathetic tracts that modulate basic vegetative functions, such as heart rate and peristalsis. In the cortex, ACh's relationship vis-à-vis the monoamines may be described in terms of a reciprocal balance or ratio, such that *increased*

TABLE 8.6. Summary of Investigations of the Monoamine Hypothesis

1. There is no consistent evidence of decreased monoamine synthesis or increased degradation in depression.

2. There is well-replicated evidence of low urinary MHPG, low CSF 5-HIAA, and high plasma and CSF levels of catecholamines in certain subgroups of depressed patients.

3. Monoamine precursors do not have consistent antidepressant effects.

4. Reserpine and other amine-depleting agents induce depression in vulnerable individuals

5. Clinical benefits of antidepressant agents develop much more slowly that their acute synaptic effects on monoamines.

6. Alterations of α_2-adrenergic, β-adrenergic, and $5\text{-}HT_2$ receptors occur with chronic use of most clinically effective antidepressants.

7. The time course of antidepressant effects on receptor sensitivity more closely parallels their clinical effects.

8. Treatment-related effects on one transmitter system typically have indirect effects on other systems.

Note. Adapted from Thase, Frank, & Kupfer (1985).

central cholinergic tone is associated with relatively *decreased* monoaminergic activity (Dilsaver, 1986; McCarley, 1982). Conversely, enhanced monoaminergic function may be viewed as inducing a state of relatively *decreased* central cholinergic tone. Data from neuroendocrine and sleep research paradigms support the likelihood of interactive disturbances of ACh in depression, as described later.

Agents that enhance cholinergic activity often produce lethargy, anergia, and psychomotor slowing in normal subjects (e.g., Janowsky et al., 1983). Administration of cholinergic agonists to depressed patients also may cause symptomatic exacerbations; in the case of mania, a reduction of symptoms is sometimes noted (Janowsky et al, 1983; Leong & Brown, 1987). Experimental administration of cholinergic agonists to normal subjects also transiently induces neuroendocrine abnormalities similar to those seen in depression, such as elevations of CRH, β-endorphin, adrenocorticotropic hormone (ACTH), and hypercortisolemia (see Dubé, 1993, or Thase et al., 1985). Similarly, the cholinergic agonists arecoline and physostigmine reliably reduce the latency to onset of

REM sleep and increase nocturnal awakenings in normal controls, thus mimicking several of the neurophysiological features of severe depression (e.g., Dubé et al., 1985; Gillin et al., 1991). Such responses are enhanced in depressed persons relative to healthy controls (Dubé et al., 1985; Gillin et al., 1991). Moreover, cholinergic supersensitivity may be most marked in depressed patients with a family history of mood disorder (Kupfer, Targ, & Stack, 1982). Remitted individuals with a history of bipolar disorder and never-ill subjects with family histories of mood disorder also show supersensitive EEG sleep responses to cholinergic agonists (Sitaram, Dubé, Keshavan, Davies, & Reynal, 1987; Sitaram, Nurnberger, Gershon, & Gillin, 1982). Finally, sleep deprivation, which has transient antidepressant effects in some depressions, may induce a brief decrease in ACh tone (Dilsaver, 1986).

Not all efforts to link ACh with depression have yielded positive results. For example, research assessing postmortem brain tissue for changes in muscarinic receptor function or number has yielded inconclusive results in suicide victims (see Dilsaver, 1986; Dubé, 1993). There also is essentially no evidence that would indicate that purely anticholinergic agents are useful as antidepressant agents (Leong & Brown, 1987). Finally, a report suggesting normalization of cholinergic supersensitivity in remitted, yet unmedicated depressed patients (Berger, Riemann, Hochi, & Spiegel, 1989) raises significant doubts concerning the traitlike behavior of this measure, at least for some nonbipolar patients. In summary, while there appears to be some evidence for increased cholinergic activity in depression, it may be that cholinergic disturbances have a secondary role in the pathophysiology of affective disorders.

OTHER NEUROCHEMICAL STUDIES

Numerous other investigations have examined the role in depression of trace amines, neuropeptides, intracellular electrolyte and mineral regulation, membrane composition and transport mechanisms, cyclic nucleotides, and prostaglandin. Although such studies have not yet yielded conclusive evidence of specific biological disturbance, they do present interesting leads for future research.

Phenylethylamine

The trace biogenic amine 2–phenylethylamine (PEA), which is structurally similar to amphetamine, has been suggested as playing a role in some forms of depression (Sabelli & Mosnaim, 1974). Several studies have found low levels of PEA and its metabolite in depression, and drugs that enhance levels of PEA have been purported to have treatment efficacy (see Sabelli & Mosnaim, 1974). However, this line of research has not been widely replicated. Moreover, the Type B selective MAOI selegiline, which enhances PEA levels by preventing enzymatic degradation, is not an effective antidepressant until the dosage is increased to nonselective dosages (Mann et al. 1989).

Gamma-Aminobutyric Acid

The amino acid gamma-aminobutyric acid (GABA) also has been found to be reduced in the plasma and CSF of depressives (e.g., Lloyd, Morselli, & Bartholini, 1987; Petty, Kramer, & Hendrickse, 1993; Roy, DeJong, & Ferraro, 1991). These findings have potential conceptual importance because of the role of GABA in the CNS as an inhibitory neurotransmitter (Cooper et al., 1991). Roy et al. (1991) found that reductions of GABA were limited to more severely depressed patients characterized by melancholic features; less severely depressed patients did not differ from normal controls.

The role for disturbance of GABA neurotransmission in severe unipolar depression and bipolar disorder is further supported by studies demonstrating a functional link between GABAergic and nonadrenergic systems (Garattini & Samanin, 1988; Lloyd et al., 1987). For example, low GABA levels are significantly correlated with high CSF NE concentrations (Roy et al., 1991). Thus, reduced GABA levels may either be a cause or a consequence of increased sympathoadrenal function in mania or severe depression. Petty et al. (1993) proposed that a persistent reduction of GABA levels in remitted bipolar patients suggests traitlike involvement in some forms of affective illness. However, experimental studies of animals utilizing the learned helplessness paradigm document that reduced GABA levels also can be induced by sustained, uncontrollable stress (Weiss, 1991).

Several studies indicate that the GABA agonist alprazolam, a benzodiazepine anxiolytic agent, has significant antidepressant activity in milder cases presenting with a mixture of anxiety and depression (Rickels, Feighner, & Smith, 1985; Warner, Peabody, Whiteford, & Hollister, 1988). However, the apparent inefficacy of potent benzodiazepine agents as treatments of severe depressions characterized by neurobiologic disturbances, such as reduced REM latency (Ansseau et al., 1991; Rush et al., 1985), suggests that treatments that principally strengthen GABA systems are not sufficient to reverse severe depression.

Tyramine

The amino acid tyramine, which is metabolized following oral ingestion by MAO in the gut and liver, has been studied by several groups using an oral loading dose paradigm (Hale, Sandler, Hannah, Glover, & Bridges, 1991; Harrison et al., 1984; Sandler, Ruthven, Goodwin, & Coppen, 1979). Although this strategy has not been studied extensively, research published to date has found decreased urinary tyramine excretion (in the form of conjugated tyramine-*o*-sulfate) in severe or melancholic cases of depression. Low tyramine-*o*-sulfate levels also have been associated with favorable response to antidepressants (e.g., Hale, Sandler, Hannah, & Bridges, 1989). The etiology of this abnormality is obscure, and, beyond tyramine's importance in precipitating hypertensive crises in patients taking nonselective MAO inhibitors, it has little known significance. We suspect that reduced tyramine excretion may be the result of increased competition for MAO enzymatic sites associated with high circulating levels of NE in severe unipolar depression (e.g., Hale et al., 1991; Roy et al., 1991).

Membrane–Second-Messenger Interactions

A number of investigators have studied possible abnormalities of intracellular sodium and calcium concentrations in depression (e.g., Bowden et al., 1988; Dubovsky, Murphy, Thomas, & Rademacher, 1992). Such findings most likely are the result of changes in ion transport channels in cellular membranes. Altered calcium disposition in depression could be important because this element's role in modulation of the cAMP second-messenger systems (Jesberger & Richardson, 1985; MacDonald, Rubinow, & Linnoila, 1984; Risby et al., 1991). As noted ear-

lier, blunted cAMP responses to β-adrenergic stimulation have been noted in depressed patients (Halper et al., 1988; Mazzola-Polietto et al., 1994).

Membrane phospholipid composition and prostaglandin levels are important functions modulated by second-messenger systems involving guanine monophosphate (GMP; Cooper et al., 1991; Kandel et al., 1991). Several studies have found prostaglandin levels to be abnormal in depression (e.g., Linnoila et al., 1983; Ohishi, Ueno, Nishino, Sakai, & Hayaishi, 1988). Recently, more direct evidence has emerged suggesting increased levels of stimulatory guanine nucleotide binding G-proteins in the peripheral blood cells (Schreiber, Avissar, Danon, & Belmaker, 1991; Young, Li, Kamble, Siu, & Warsh, 1994a) and brain tissue (Young et al., 1993) of bipolar patients. Of significance are the mood-stabilizing effects of lithium salts, which may be mediated through action on the phospholipid composition of cell membranes and/or membrane-bound G-proteins (Jesberger & Richardson, 1985; Kofman & Belmaker, 1993).

NEUROPHYSIOLOGICAL ABNORMALITIES

Electroencephalographic Sleep Studies

A great majority of depressed persons experience some form of sleep difficulty. Clinically, these difficulties may be characterized as disorders of initiating and maintaining sleep (DIMS) or disorders of excessive sleepiness (DOES; Nofzinger, Buysse, Reynolds & Kupfer, 1993a). Depressive sleep difficulties may be further subdivided into primary disorders (i.e., classical sleep disorders that antedate development of depression, such as sleep apnea or narcolepsy) and secondary disorders (i.e., sleep disturbances accompanying depression). Individuals suffering from primary sleep disorders are at significantly increased risk for development of depression. For example, in Ford and Kamerow's (1990) epidemiological survey, a significant number of patients complaining of insomnia subsequently developed a major depression during a 1-year follow-up.

The subjective sleep disturbances of depression include various forms of insomnia (i.e., prolonged sleep latency, multiple awakenings, frequent sleep-stage shifts, and decreased sleep efficiency) in a majority of cases (Mendlewicz

& Kerkhofs, 1991; Thase & Kupfer, 1987). Nevertheless, a large minority of cases experience hypersomnia, particularly younger and/or bipolar patients (e.g., Casper et al., 1985; Davidson et al., 1982; Thase et al., 1991). Some depressed individuals also report an increase in dreaming, whereas others have decreased dream recall. In either case, dream content in depression is consonant with waking cognitive and affective experience, as reflected by themes of loss, rejection, frustration, and disappointment (Cartwright, 1993; Kramer, 1993).

The sleep changes in depression have been objectified by all-night EEG sleep recordings (see Table 8.7). Extensive study over the past 30 years has documented four basic types of EEG sleep disturbances in major depression: (1) poor sleep maintenance, (2) reduced levels of SWS, (3) altered distribution and increased phasic activity of REM sleep, and (4) reduced REM latency (Benca, Obermeyer, Thisted, & Gillin, 1992; Buysse & Kupfer, 1993; Mendlewicz & Kerkhofs, 1991). Prototypical EEG sleep profiles for a normal individual and a severely depressed person are illustrated in Figure 8.7.

Studies utilizing computer-scored counts of individual REMs and slow waves have also yielded potentially important new findings (Reynolds & Kupfer, 1987). For example, results of a study of recurrent depression suggest that a decrease in delta wave counts in the first non-REM period relative to the second non-REM period (i.e., reduced delta sleep ratio) may indicate the need for ongoing prophylaxis with antidepressant medications (e.g., Kupfer, Frank, McEachran, & Grochocinski, 1990). Although these automated methods have not yet been extensively studied by other groups, preliminary

TABLE 8.7. Characteristic EEG Sleep Disturbances in Depression

1. Sleep continuity disturbances, including difficulty falling asleep, frequent awakenings, and early morning awakening

2. Decreased SWS for the whole night and reduced number of computer-scored delta waves in the first non-REM period (relative to the second non-REM period; decreased delta sleep ratio)

3. Increased phasic REM sleep activity and shift of REM activity into the first hours of sleep

4. Earlier time of onset of the first REM period (reduced REM latency)

Note. Adapted from Thase, Frank, & Kupfer (1985).

work by investigators at the University of Pittsburgh suggests that the selective decrease of slow waves in the first non-REM period may be more specific to endogenous depression than other disturbances of SWS (e.g., Buysse & Kupfer, 1993).

Sleep Continuity and Sleep Maintainence

Sleep-continuity disturbances include prolongation of sleep latency, an increased number of nocturnal awakenings, and early morning awakening; such changes characterize at least 80% of hospitalized depressed persons and about one-half of depressed outpatients (Thase & Kupfer, 1987). However, EEG-verified sleep continuity disturbances are seen in many medical and psychiatric conditions, as well as during normal aging (Benca et al., 1992; Thase & Kupfer, 1987). Although sleep continuity disturbances are not specific to depression, they do illustrate the impact of pathophysiologic arousal on the sleep–wake cycle. Furthermore, the cumulative effects of sleep deprivation resulting from persistent sleep continuity disturbances may contribute to the attentional and concentration disturbances of severe depression (Horne, 1993; McCann et al., 1992). Antidepressant treatments typically correct or normalize sleep continuity disturbances associated with depression (e.g., Thase & Kupfer, 1987). Recently, this observation has been extended to treatment with psychotherapy (Thase et al., 1994a). Nevertheless, the antidepressant efficacy of specific compounds is not correlated with improvements in sleep continuity disturbances (Thase & Kupfer, 1987), and some agents, such as fluoxetine, are effective antidepressants without producing changes in sleep continuity (e.g., Hendrickse et al., 1994; Nofzinger et al., 1995).

Depressed persons' complaints of hypersomnia, which are more difficult to confirm in the sleep laboratory, are characterized by long recording periods, extended total sleep time, increased REM time, and/or reduced sleep latency (e.g., Hawkins, Taub, & Van de Castle, 1985; Nofzinger et al., 1991; Thase, Himmelhoch, Mallinger, Jarrett, & Kupfer, 1989). In contradistinction to the primary DOES, such as narcolepsy and sleep apnea, hypersomnic depressed patients do not show objective evidence of excessive daytime sleepiness (Nofzinger et al., 1991), sleep onset REM periods during daytime naps (Nofzinger et al., 1991), or

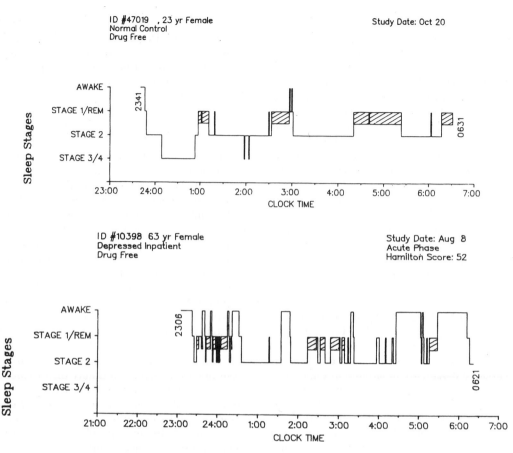

FIGURE 8.7. Electroencephalographic recordings of sleep from a healthy control subject and a patient suffering from severe major depression. From Thase, Frank, & Kupfer (1985).

fragmentation of night-time sleep (Reynolds, Christiansen, Taska, Coble, & Kupfer, 1983; Thase et al., 1989).

Slow-Wave Sleep

Decreased SWS (i.e., reduced percentage of sleep Stages III and IV) is another common but nonspecific correlate of major depression. SWS is characterized by slow, high-amplitude delta waves. Measures of SWS are associated with perceptions of the restful or restorative quality of sleep (Horne, 1993). Moreover, the density of slow waves during sleep is highest in areas of the prefrontal cortex associated with executive cortical functions (Horne, 1993). Decreased SWS is seen in advanced age and in chronic medical and psychiatric conditions other than depression (Benca et al., 1992; Thase & Kupfer, 1987). In some cases, the early onset of REM sleep characteristic of depression may be the

"passive" consequence of a deficit of SWS during the first non-REM period (Kupfer & Ehlers, 1989). It thus has been proposed that a deficiency in a process triggering the onset of SWS might underlie vulnerability to some forms of depression (e.g., Borbely & Wirz-Justice, 1982; Horne, 1993).

The deficit in SWS observed in depression is consistent with reduced serotonergic neurotransmission (see Thase & Kupfer, 1987). Consistent with this hypothesis, reduced levels of CSF 5-HIAA have been correlated with decreased SWS in both depression and schizophrenia (Benson, Faull, & Zarcone, 1993). Similarly, a recent study by our group demonstrated that reduced SWS can be induced experimentally by acute depletion of intraneuronal 5-HT stores via d-fenfluramine (Myers et al., 1993).

Reduced SWS and poor sleep continuity in some depressions also may be the result of excessive arousal caused by pathologically increased noradrenergic or dopaminergic activity (Thase & Kupfer, 1987). This process is best exemplified in psychotic depression (Thase, Kupfer, & Ulrich 1986). The proposal that decreased SWS in depression is due to an excess of arousing neurotransmission (rather than a deficit of inhibitory or restraining tonic control) is also indirectly supported by our group's observation of essentially normal SWS in hypersomnolent bipolar depressions (Nofzinger et al., 1991; Thase et al., 1989). This alternate hypothesis is not, however, consistent with the observation that SWS is essentially intact in mania (Hudson et al., 1992; Linkowski, Kerkhofs, Rielaert, & Mendlewicz, 1986). Thus, at least one psychopathological state of CNS hyperarousal, mania, is not associated with reduced SWS. It therefore seems likely that at least two pathophysiological processes account for SWS disturbances in mood disorders.

Some evidence suggests that SWS deficits in depression are relatively traitlike (Kupfer & Ehlers, 1989; Thase & Simons, 1992). Furthermore, SWS appears to be partly under genetic control (Linkowski, Kerkhofs, Hauspie, & Mendlewicz, 1991). Consistent with traitlike behavior, successful treatment with most antidepressant medications does not increase visually scored SWS (Thase & Kupfer, 1987). Exceptions to this rule include lithium (e.g., Friston, Sharpley, Solomon, & Cowen, 1989; Kupfer, Reynolds, Weiss, & Foster, 1974) and the 5-HT$_2$ antagonist ritanserin (Sharpley et al., 1990). Although one might speculate that these agents' effects on 5-HT neurotransmission account for this finding, treatment with the serotonin-selective antidepressants (e.g., zimelidine, fluoxetine, fluvoxamine, and paroxetine) generally do not increase visually scored SWS (Hendrickse et al., 1994; Kupfer et al., 1991b; Nofzinger et al., 1995; Saletu et al., 1991). Interestingly, our group has found that hypersomnolent patients characterized by high pretreatment levels of SWS often show a decrease following successful treatment with either antidepressants or psychotherapy (Thase & Howland, unpublished observations). SWS thus appears to be differentially affected by treatment in depressions of varying phenomenology.

Computer-scored delta wave counts have recently been shown to be increased by successful antidepressant treatment, with an increase in delta ratio values (Kupfer et al., 1994; Reynolds et al., 1991). Such antidepressant-mediated "normalization" of reduced delta-

sleep ratios may be intimately related to prophylactic efficacy in recurrent depressions (Thase, 1992). Further studies of the effect of various forms of treatment on automated measures of SWS are underway in our laboratory, and we recently found a significant increase in delta sleep ratio values of unmedicated depressed patients after treatment with cognitive–behavioral therapy (see Figure 8.8). Thus, psychotherapeutic interventions also may alter a neurophysiological correlate of vulnerability to recurrent depression.

REM Sleep Dysfunction

Disturbances of REM sleep are common in major depression. In healthy adults, the first REM period normally begins about 70–90 minutes after sleep onset, with subsequent REM periods of increasing length and activity occurring at approximately 90-minute intervals throughout the night. About 20–25% of the night is spent in REM sleep and the ratio of REM activity to REM time (i.e., REM density) ranges from 1.0 to 1.7 units/minute. In depression, REM latency is typically reduced to less than 60 minutes, with a corresponding shift of REM time and activity into the first 90 minutes of sleep (see Benca et al., 1992; Mendlewicz & Kerkhofs, 1991; Thase & Kupfer, 1987). The increased activity of REM sleep is often disproportionate to the increase in REM time, such that REM density values range from 1.5 to 2.5, or even higher. REM sleep disturbances are most marked in acute depressions, particularly among recurrent cases (e.g., Kupfer, Ehlers, Frank, Grochocinski, & McEachran, 1991a; Kupfer, Frank, Grochocinski, Gregor, & McEachran, 1988; Thase et al., in press). Even greater reductions of REM latency (i.e., < 40 minutes) are seen in elderly depressives (e.g., Buysse et al., 1988; Reynolds et al., 1988) and in psychotic depression (Thase et al., 1986). Some of the most severely ill patients may exhibit sleep-onset REM periods (e.g., Kumar et al., 1987; Thase et al., 1986), an abnormality usually only seen in narcolepsy and drug-withdrawal REM rebound states (Thase & Kupfer, 1987).

Reduced REM latency in depression is, to some extent, an age-dependent process (Kupfer & Thase, 1983; Lauer, Riemann, Wiegand, & Berger, 1991). However, unlike normal aging, reduced REM latency in nonpsychotic depression is typically associated with increased pha-

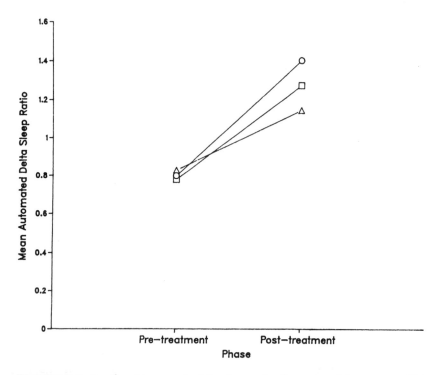

FIGURE 8.8. Significant increase in delta sleep ratio after successful treatment of 18 depressed outpatients with cognitive–behavioral therapy. The study group all had abnormal values prior to treatment (i.e., ratio values ≥ 1.1) and, at posttreatment, is divided into fully remitted (circles), partially remitted (squares), and unremitted (triangles) subgroups (Thase, unpublished data).

sic REM sleep, as exemplified by increased REM activity and density (Benca et al., 1992; Thase & Kupfer, 1987). Moreover, the combination of reduced REM latency *and* increased phasic REM sleep are not characteristic of other acutely dysphoric states unless accompanied by significant depressive symptomatology (Cartwright, 1993; Cohen, 1979; Reynolds et al., 1992). The psychopathologic significance of increased phasic REM sleep in depression is illustrated by the correlation of higher levels of affective disturbance or negative cognitions with increased REM activity (Nofzinger et al., 1994).

Reduced REM latency and increased REM density have been reported in most subtypes of major depression (Benca et al., 1992; Mendlewicz & Kerkhofs, 1991; Thase & Kupfer, 1987), as well as a significant subgroup of dysthymics (Arriaga, Rosado, & Paiva, 1990; Howland & Thase, 1991). Such prevalence has led to the suggestion that REM sleep disturbances may be used as laboratory "marker" of depression (e.g.,

Kupfer & Thase, 1983; Mendlewicz & Kerkhofs, 1991). When examined as a laboratory test, reduced REM latency performs with a sensitivity ranging from 40–90%, and a specificity of 80–96% in comparisons with healthy controls (see Mendlewicz & Kerkhofs, 1991; Thase & Kupfer, 1987). With an average test sensitivity of only about 60%, an unacceptably large number of false negatives (i.e, clinically depressed patients with normal REM sleep) results, compromising reduced REM latency for routine diagnostic use (Buysse & Kupfer, 1990). Moreover, test specificity plummets when patients with schizophrenia, alcoholism, or obsessive–compulsive disorder are studied as the comparison group (e.g., Benca et al., 1992; Ganguli, Reynolds, & Kupfer, 1987; Gillin et al., 1990; Hudson et al., 1993; Insel et al., 1982; Neylan, van Kammen, Keley, & Peters, 1992; Tandon et al., 1992; Zarcone, Benson, & Berger, 1987). Thus, the mechanism(s) underlying reduced REM latency also appear to be involved in a number of forms of severe psychopathology (Benca et al., 1992; Linkowski & Mendlewicz, 1993).

Reduced REM latency values recently have been shown to be associated with higher rates of relapse during longitudinal follow-up of depressed patients (Giles, Jarrett, Roffwarg, & Rush, 1987a; Kupfer & Frank, 1989; Reynolds, Perel, Frank, Imber, & Kupfer, 1989). This finding may have important practical implications, because reduced REM latency values typically do not fully "normalize" in recently recovered, unmedicated cases (Buysse et al., 1992a; Giles, Jarrett, Rush, Biggs, & Roffwarg, 1993; Lee et al., 1993; Rush et al., 1986; Steiger, von Bardeleben, Herth, & Holsboer, 1989; Thase et al., 1994a; Thase & Simons, 1992).

In studies of acutely depressed children or adolescents, fewer EEG sleep abnormalities are typically observed (Dahl et al., 1991; Goetz et al., 1987; Puig-Antich et al., 1982). Nevertheless, severely depressed, hospitalized children appear to manifest greater EEG sleep abnormality than do milder cases (e.g., Dahl et al., 1991; Emslie, Rush, Weinberg, Rintelman, & Roffwarg, 1990). One longitudinal study found that children with relatively normal REM latency values during hospitalization exhibited reduced REM latency following recovery from depression (Puig-Antich et al., 1983). Our group also has observed this phenomenon in younger adults, following recovery from depression (Thase & Simons, 1992). It is unclear if these findings are illustrative of neurobiological scarring or, more simply, reflect a greater degree of instability of REM latency values in younger persons. We have not found evidence of such "scarring" in a recent study comparing carefully matched cases of first-episode and highly recurrent depressions, in which REM latency value did not differ significantly between groups (Thase et al., in press).

Antidepressant Effects on REM Sleep. Sleep EEG studies provide a useful window to neurochemical and/or receptor disturbances in the CNS. As discussed in earlier sections, investigations of sleep in normal individuals and animals indicate that either decreased 5-HT or an increase of DA, NE, and/or CRH are implicated in disturbances of induction and maintenance of non-REM sleep. As noted earlier, a reduction of 5-HT is implicated in SWS deficits in depression (Benson et al., 1993). By contrast, the

early onset of REM sleep may either be actively "triggered" by hyperactive cholinergic processes (Dilsaver, 1986; Gillin & Borbely, 1985) or passively "released" as a result of a 5-HT-mediated deficit of SWS (Kupfer & Ehlers, 1989). In a study utilizing the α_2 agonist clonidine, depressed patients showed significantly less drug-induced REM suppression than either healthy controls or patients with generalized anxiety disorder, suggesting that the early onset of REM sleep in depression results from an active process that is resistant to inhibitory adrenergic control (Schittecat et al., 1992). Thus, perturbations of multiple neurotransmitter systems are implicated in the genesis of depressive sleep disturbances.

Studies of the effects of various classes of antidepressant treatment on EEG sleep provide a useful vantage point. Most effective somatic treatments produce rapid and marked suppression of REM sleep, an effect that is largely unrelated to anticholinergic activity (Thase & Kupfer, 1987). Antidepressant effects on REM sleep may persist for years during maintenance treatment (Kupfer et al., 1994). Vogel (1983) proposed that REM suppression may represent a common action of effective antidepressant treatments. Rebound of REM sleep following either sleep deprivation (see Wu & Bunney, 1990) or withdrawal of antidepressant pharmacotherapy (see Thase & Kupfer, 1987) also has been correlated with the degree of antidepressant response. By contrast, patients who do not respond to pharmacotherapy generally do not evidence as pronounced a degree of REM suppression during treatment, or as marked an REM rebound upon drug discontinuation (Thase & Kupfer, 1987).

Not all evidence supports the role of REM suppression in treatment of depression. For example, REM suppression does not always accompany successful treatment with ECT, nor does complete suppression of REM sleep guarantee response to antidepressant treatment (Thase & Kupfer, 1987). Successful treatment of depression with nonpharmacological modalities, such as interpersonal psychotherapy (Buysse et al., 1992b) or cognitive therapy (Thase et al., 1994a; Thase & Simons, 1992), also does not result in a pronounced suppression of REM sleep. Comparative studies of patients randomly assigned to treatment with pharmacotherapy or to either ECT (inpatients) or psychotherapy (outpatients) are needed to determine if such apparent differences are due to sampling artifacts (i.e., patients with milder REM sleep disturbances were enrolled in the psychotherapy studies) or to distinctly different psychobiological mechanisms of action across treatment modalities.

Perhaps most damaging to the REM-suppression hypothesis is the observation that at least two newer antidepressants, nefazodone (Armitage, Rush, Trivedi, Cain, & Roffwarg, 1994; Sharpley, Walsh, & Cowen, 1992) and bupropion (Nofzinger et al., 1995) do not suppress REM sleep indices. In fact, bupropion treatment may result in an increase in REM measures (Nofzinger et al., 1995). At the least, these findings suggest that REM suppression is not an *essential* concomitant of antidepressant response.

State versus Trait Issues

The apparent heterogeneity of effects of treatment on EEG sleep has led to a hypothesized differentiation between reversible (i.e., potentially state-dependent) and persistent (i.e., purportedly traitlike or state-independent) sets of abnormalities (Kupfer & Ehlers, 1989; Thase & Simons, 1992). In severe depression, a constellation of multiple sleep abnormalities are frequently observed during the acute illness state (Kupfer & Ehlers, 1989; Thase & Kupfer, 1987), whereas residual disturbances are apparent in studies of remitted patients (e.g., Buysse et al., 1992b; Cartwright & Wood, 1991; Giles et al., 1993; Lee et al., 1993; Rieman & Berger, 1989; Rush et al., 1986; Steiger et al., 1989; Thase et al., 1994a; Thase & Simons, 1992). Specifically, features such as sleep continuity disturbances and increased REM density are proposed to be associated with (1) higher levels of clinical severity, and (2) normalization after resolution of the depressive episode. Accordingly, these features are best viewed as state-dependent (Kupfer & Ehlers, 1989). By contrast, reduced REM latency and diminished SWS typically remain abnormal despite clinical recovery; they are considered traitlike (Kupfer & Ehlers, 1989). Further long-term studies are needed to establish the persistence of reduced REM latency and diminished SWS across years of remission. Consistent with the notion of traitlike behavior, Giles et al. (1989) and Krieg et al. (1990) have reported reduced REM latency in never-ill first-degree relatives of affected probands. Similarly, Battaglia et al. (1993) observed reduced REM latency in bor-

derline personality disorder patients who have never suffered an episode of major depression.

Waking Electroencephalographic Studies

Waking EEG Rhythms

In recent years, waking EEG rhythms have been studied by sophisticated computerized methods of quantitative and topographical analysis. Interpretation of research in this area is compromised because the studies suffer from numerous methodological problems (see Pollock & Schneider, 1990; Thase et al., 1985). Nevertheless, abnormal lateralization of waking EEG rhythms (i.e., increased nondominant cerebral hemispheric activity) generally have been reported in studies of major depression (Coffey, 1987; Pollock & Schneider, 1990; Zahn, 1986). This finding is consistent with other lines of evidence implicating nondominant cerebral hemispheric function in the processing of negative affect (Coffey, 1987; Otto, Yeo, & Dougher, 1987). Hemispheric EEG asymmetry in clinical depression may be the consequence of normal neurobiological processes mediating sadness (Banich, Stolar, Heller, & Goldman, 1992), expression of affectively charged material (Sackheim, Putz, Vingiano, Coleman, & McElhiney, 1988), and/or dysphoric arousal (Thayer, 1989), rather than depressive disorder per se.

Studies comparing depression with states of normal sadness are needed to distinguish pathologic mechanisms associated with an illness state from normal emotion. Recent research suggests that some aspects of cerebral asymmetry may be a correlate of the illness state. First, depressed patients characterized by marked perceptual asymmetry were found to show preferential response to TCAs (compared to MAOIs and placebo), whereas patients with no asymmetry did not (Bruder et al., 1990). Second, Otto, Fava, Rosenbaum, and Murphy (1991) found perceptual asymmetry to be associated with poorer response to placebo pharmacotherapy. These studies suggest that abnormal lateralization in clinical depression may be different in quality and/or magnitude from the changes observed in normal dysphoric states.

Research examining mean frequency and amplitude of EEG rhythms in depression has yielded conflicting results. Some research suggests a lower level of EEG activation in depression, when compared to normal controls or individuals with schizophrenia or mania (see

Pollock & Schneider, 1990; Zahn, 1986). Other research indicates complex changes in the organization of the EEG rhythms in depression, including variability of frequency bands and/or alterations of topographical distribution (Pockberger, Petsche, Rappelsberger, Zidek, & Zapotoczky, 1985; Pollock & Schneider, 1990; Zahn, 1986).

Evoked Potentials

Evoked EEG potentials have been studied in major depression for several decades. Evoked potential studies utilize various visual, auditory, and somatosensory stimuli to elicit characteristic EEG waveform responses, including waves known as P100, N120, P200, and P300. In depression, the latencies to these responses are typically normal, but much variability has been reported with respect to their amplitudes (see Zahn, 1986). Patients with bipolar depression tend to show an augmented P100 amplitude in response to stimuli of increasing intensity, whereas amplitude reductions are more characteristic of nonbipolar depressions (e.g., Buchsbaum, 1975). We suspect that this "augmenter–reducer" dichotomy may be perceptual correlates of psychomotor retardation or, conversely, anxious arousal. Specifically, the neurophysiological state accompanying agitated depression (i.e., melancholia) is proposed to be characterized by heightened cortical arousal, resulting in compensatory inhibition or "gating" of responses to sensory input (Thase et al., 1985). Depressed individuals also typically exhibit a reduction in P300 amplitude (when compared to controls), a finding comparable to that observed in schizophrenia (Zahn, 1986). However, unlike schizophrenia, depressed patients generally have normal P300 latency values (Blackwood et al., 1987; Zahn, 1986).

Abnormalities of Smooth Pursuit Eye Movements

Smooth pursuit eye movements have been studied for some time as an indicator of the integrity of frontal lobe function (Zahn, 1986). A significant minority of bipolar, schizoaffective, and psychotic depressions manifest this dysfunction, although the proportions of abnormal cases are lower than in schizophrenia (reviewed by Thase et al., 1985). Smooth pursuit eye movement dysfunction has not yet been documented convincingly in milder cases of nonbipolar, nonpyschotic depressions. These findings thus suggest that the presence of psychosis, rather than depression, may be the operative variable (Zahn, 1986).

Neuroradiological Abnormalities

Structural/Anatomical Studies

The computed tomography (CT) scan provided the first sensitive, noninvasive method for visualizing brain structures. CT scans have proved quite valuable in the assessment of neurological abnormalities, such as strokes or tumors, which may occasionally cause atypical affective symptoms. Brain imaging technology has been advanced further by introduction of progressively more sensitive MRI scans, which provide greater visualization of subcortical tracts and white matter lesions (Garber, Weilburg, Buonanno, Manschreck, & New, 1988; Keshavan, Kapur, & Pettegrew, 1991). With respect to the prevalence of subcortical lesions in affective disorders, a number of groups have documented an increased frequency of small, punctate hyperintensities in the paraventricular regions of patients with unipolar or bipolar disorders (Coffey, Figiel, Djang, & Weiner, 1990; Dupont et al., 1990; McDonald, Krishnan, Doraiswamy, & Blazer, 1991; Swayze, Andreasen, Alliger, Ehrhardt, & Yuh, 1990). These puzzling "unidentified bright objects" (UBOs), which are similar to the plaques seen in diffuse atherosclerotic disease or multiple sclerosis, provide further evidence of neurobiological sequelae of severe affective illnesses (Nasrallah, Coffman, & Olson, 1989).

There has been considerable interest in the use of CT and MRI scans to compare structural corelates of CNS dysfunction in various psychiatric disorders. Numerous studies have documented atrophy of the cerebral cortex and cerebellum in schizophrenia (e.g., Nasrallah et al., 1989). Investigations also have documented cortical atrophy in severe unipolar and bipolar affective syndromes, as reflected by increased ventricle-to-brain ratios (e.g., Andreasen, Swayze, Flaum, Alliger, & Cohen, 1990). There is no evidence that cortical atrophy in affective disorder is an effect of previous treatment with either ECT or medication; rather, such changes have been related to age, illness severity, chronicity, and elevated plasma cortisol levels (Andreasen et al., 1990; Coffey, Wilkinson, Weiner, Ritchie, & Aque, 1993; Kellner, Rubinow, & Post, 1986). More recently, depressed patients were found to have a bilateral reduction in the volume of the caudate nucleus, a key "relay" juncture for dopaminergic tracts extending from the prefrontal cortex and limbic system to the basal ganglia (Krishnan et al., 1992). Although the long-term implications of brain atrophy and UBOs in the affective disorders are not known, such changes are probably most characteristic of patients suffering from more chronic or refractory affective states (e.g., Coffey et al., 1993; Kellner et al., 1986).

Studies of Cerebral Metabolism

A number of methods for measurement of cerebral metabolism have been applied to study the neurobiology of affective disorders. These types of studies provide a useful counterpart to neurophysiological studies with respect to question of abnormal hemispheric lateralization. Results from investigations measuring regional cerebral blood flow (rCBF) do not consistently support the hypothesis of abnormal hemispheric lateralization in depression, although methodological inconsistencies may account for some of the differences in the early studies (see Thase et al., 1985). When present, abnormalities generally are characterized by global or bifrontal reductions of blood flow (e.g., Sackheim et al., 1990; Silfverskiöld & Risberg, 1989). Moreover, differences may exist between diagnostic subgroups, with the most abnormal findings occurring in psychotic depression (Silfverskiöld & Risberg, 1989).

Studies of lateralization employing SPECT also have yielded somewhat inclusive results (see Devous, 1989). Failure to control medication status and use of [133]xenon (i.e., a tracer that yields technically less satisfactory images) in earlier studies may, in part, account for these discrepancies. A recent study utilizing a more technically satisfactory tracer, Tc-99m-hexamethylpropylenamineoxine (HMPAO), documented hypoperfusion in the left prefrontal cortex in 10 unmedicated depressed patients, with relative increase in perfusion observed in 5 patients following sleep deprivation (Wu et al., 1992). Philpot, Banerjee, Needham-Bennett, Costa, and Ell (1993) similarly found reduced rCBF in a study of 10 patients utilizing HMPAO. However, a study by Maes and associates (1993) did not. Within-subject changes in rCBF was also documented in two small SPECT studies of patients successfully treated with various types of antidepressant therapies (Dubé, Dobkin, Bowler, Thase, & Kupfer, 1993; Kumar

et al., 1991). Of note, the Dubé et al. (1993) study included unmedicated patients treated with cognitive–behavioral therapy, as well as those receiving somatic therapies.

PET scanning has emerged as the most powerful method for visualizing in vivo brain metabolism. This technique uses radioactively labeled substances, such as [18F]deoxyglucose, to visualize areas of cerebral metabolic activity. A number of studies have now examined PET scans in bipolar and nonbipolar depressions. The most widely replicated finding in depression has been decreased anterior cerebral metabolism (Baxter et al., 1985; Baxter et al., 1989; Berman, Doran, Pickar & Weinberger, 1993; Buchsbaum, DeLisi, Holcomb, Cappelletti, King, Johnson, et al., 1984; Buchsbaum et al., 1986; Cohen et al., 1992; Drevets et al., 1992; Martinot et al., 1990a; see Figure 8.9). Generally, this abnormality is more pronounced on the left (dominant) side, and it may be more pronounced in bipolar patients relative to unipolar patients. Such anterior hypofrontality is similar to that observed in schizophrenia (e.g., Buchsbaum et al., 1984), although depressed and schizophrenic patients may differ in responses to cortical activation procedures such as a card sorting task (Berman et al., 1993). Other abnormalities reported in unipolar depression include reduced metabolic activity in the caudate nucleus (Drevets et al., 1992; Schwartz, Baxter, Mazziotta, Gerner, & Phelps, 1987) and, among familial cases, increased metabolism in the amygdala (Drevets et al., 1992). The former abnormality appears to correlate with neuroradiological findings (Krishnan et al., 1992), whereas the latter may be linked to the severity of depressive ruminations (Drevets et al., 1992). It seems likely that increased metabolism in the amygdala will be correlated with increased levels of phasic REM activity during sleep.

Longitudinal studies of PET scans in patients across the recovery process are underway by several groups of investigators. Preliminary findings suggest that successful treatment normalizes indices of cerebral metabolism (Baxter et al., 1985; Cohen et al., 1992; Drevets et al., 1992; Schwartz et al., 1987). Moreover, serial studies of patients with bipolar depression demonstrate reversal of hypofrontality following shifts from depression into hypomania (Baxter et al., 1985; see Figure 8.10).

An interesting application of PET technology involves measurement of cerebral metabolism during various types of mental activity (e.g.,

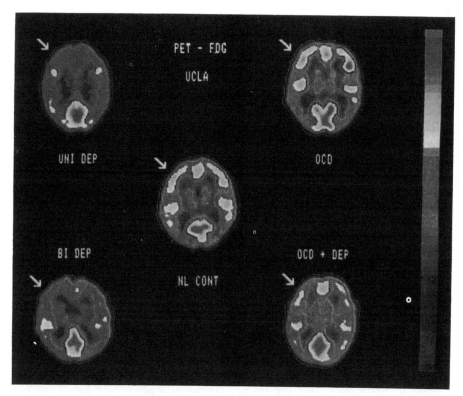

FIGURE 8.9. Positron emission tomography (PET) scans illustrating decreased frontal cerebral metabolism in severe depression. In the upper- and lower-left and lower-right scans, the abnormality is evident in patients with primary unipolar, primary bipolar, and secondary major depressive syndromes, respectively. Metabolic rates are computed for each area of the brain, divided by that of the whole brain. Normal brain metabolism is illustrated in the center scans of a healthy control and a nondepressed patient with obsessive–compulsive disorder. From Baxter et al. (1989). Copyright 1989 by the American Medical Association. Reprinted by permission.

Berman et al., 1993; Volkow & Tancredi, 1991). This method has been used recently in studies of anxiety disorder, documenting significantly increased metabolism during panic attacks (Reiman et al., 1989) and obsessions (Rausch et al., 1994), but not during exposure to phobia stimuli (Mountz et al., 1989). The relationship between changes in PET scans during experimentally induced changes in mood and psychopathology is a fertile area of investigation that is just underway (e.g., Pardo et al., 1993).

Functional Receptor Imaging

Another rapidly evolving area of research involving SPECT, PET, and functional MRI scanning techniques utilizes radioactively labeled neurotransmitters or neurotransmitterlike substances. This research technique holds immense promise for the study of neurotransmitters and neuro-

receptors in the living brain and, ultimately, should provide much information about brain function in depression and other psychopathological states (Gur, Erwin, & Gur, 1990; Sedvall, Farde, Persson, & Wiesel, 1986). To date, studies using these methods have concentrated on investigation of DA receptors in schizophrenia (e.g., Farde et al., 1992; Martinot et al., 1990b) and cocaine abuse disorders (e.g., London et al., 1990; Volkow et al., 1990). In the first study of 5-HT receptors (Mayberg et al., 1988), no abnormality was found in patients with poststroke depressive syndromes. More recently, Agren and associates (1991) reported decreased uptake of radioactively labeled 5-hydroxytryptophan in a study of six depressed patients. Of note is a repeated study of two patients after remission, which suggested that the presumed abnormality of the blood–brain barrier persists into early remission (Agren et al., 1991). Abnor-

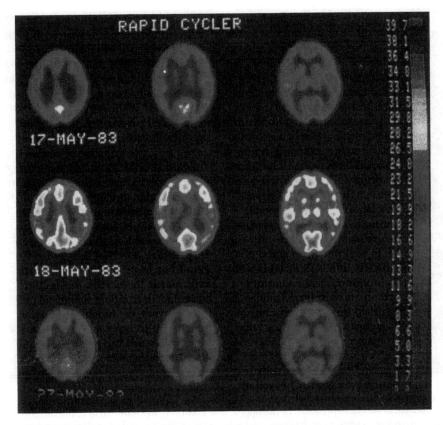

FIGURE 8.10. The state dependence of cerebral metabolism is illustrated in the sequential PET scans of a patient with rapid-cycling bipolar affective disorder. The whole-brain metabolic rate is 36% greater on the hypomanic day (middle row of scans) than on the depressed day (upper and lower rows of scans). From Baxter et al. (1985). Copyright 1985 by the American Medical Association. Reprinted by permission.

malities of postsynaptic DA binding also have been demonstrated in a study utilizing SPECT (D'haenen & Bossuyt, 1994). Although highly preliminary, these observations are consistent with results of neurochemical studies reviewed earlier.

Autonomic Activity Studies

The somatic symptomatology experienced by many severely depressed persons might suggest a state of autonomic nervous system (ANS) dysfunction of central origin. Abnormalities of NE and ACh would be the obvious candidates as potential causative factors. A number of investigators have studied ANS functions in depression, including research on cardiovascular reactivity, salivary flow, colonic motility, and electrodermal activity. In general, most investigations have suggested decreased or blunted

autonomic responses in depression, as compared to normal controls (see Thase et al., 1985; Zahn, 1986). Recent reports of diminished nocturnal penile tumescence (NPT) in depressed men (Thase et al., 1992b; Thase et al., 1988) similarly suggest blunted autonomic function. Available evidence from studies of recently remitted depressed patients suggests traitlike persistence of both blunted electrodermal reactivity (Ward & Doerr, 1986) and diminished NPT (Nofzinger et al., 1993b).

Efforts to relate diminished autonomic activity with clinical correlates of depression have produced conflicting results. Several investigations suggest that suicidal behavior may be associated with reduced electrodermal reactivity (see Thorell, 1987; Zahn, 1986). Specifically, patients with a history of violent suicidal behavior have been characterized by a more rapid pattern of habituation (Edman, Asberg, Levander, & Schalling, 1986; Keller, Wolfersdorf, Straub, & Hole, 1991).

With respect to neurochemical correlates, one study found no relationship between rapid habituation and low levels of CSF 5-HIAA (Edman et al., 1986), even though such a relationship might logically be expected. Abnormal electrodermal activity may, however, be related to blunted thyroid axis responsivity and/or hypercortisolemia (Thorell, Kjellman, & d'Elia, 1993). It will be useful in future studies to examine the relationship between correlates of autonomic dysfunction and measures of psychomotor activity (i.e., musculoskeletal disturbances of CNS origin), as well as alternate measures of serotonergic function. In our group's research on NPT in depression, for example, decreased tumescence was correlated with EEG sleep measures indicative of nocturnal hyperarousal (e.g., multiple nocturnal awakenings and poor sleep maintenance; Thase et al., 1988).

Blunted autonomic activity in depression suggests a *deficit* in peripheral cholinergic tone, a conclusion at odds with the observations of hyperactive cholinergic function in the CNS (Bernstein et al., 1988; Thase et al., 1985). It may be that a sustained increase in cortical "drive" or input to brain stem nuclei of sympathetic and parasympathetic tracts results in a compensatory down-regulation of autonomic and peripheral tone. Simultaneous study of central (e.g., the arecoline–REM induction test) and peripheral (e.g., electrodermal activity, NPT, or colonic motility) assessments of cholinergic activity is needed.

NEUROENDOCRINE ABNORMALITIES

It has been recognized for nearly a century that mood disorders may be caused by diseases of the endocrine glands, including hypo- and hyperthyroidism, Cushing's disease, and hyperparathyroidism. Consequently, identification of neural mechanisms regulating secretory activity of the hypothalamus and the pituitary gland has proved especially important to depression research. The hypothalamus and pituitary are contiguous and richly interconnected with the limbic and thalamic regions involved in regulation of sleep, appetite, reward, and libido (see Figure 8.11). Moreover, control of many of the hypothalamic neuroendocrine releasing and in-

hibiting hormones is regulated, in part, by monoaminergic and/or ACh neurons. Most recently, the hypothalamic peptide hormones, including CRH, vasopressin, and thyrotropin-releasing hormone (TRH), have been shown to function as neurotransmitters in other brain regions as well (e.g., Cooper et al., 1991; Nemeroff, 1992). Thus, both clinical and theoretical contexts provide the background for hypotheses linking endocrine function and depression. In the next subsections, we summarize research concerning abnormalities of endocrine regulation in depression, including the hypothalamic–pituitary–adrenocortical (HPA) axis, the hypothalamic–pituitary–thyroid (HPT) axis, and regulation of growth hormone.

HPA Axis Abnormalities

The relationship between stress and increased HPA axis activity has been known for most of the 20th century. Because hypercortisolemia has long been recognized as an essential part of a normal adaptational process to stress, early studies demonstrating elevated cortisol levels in depression were often viewed as simply a nonspecific finding. Nevertheless, some investigators suggested that such elevations actually might be the result of a more specific form of CNS dysfunction in depression (e.g., Carroll, Curtis, & Mendels, 1976; Rubin & Mandell, 1966). Extensive research over the past two decades has partially confirmed this hypothesis.

Approximately one-half to three-fourths of hospitalized depressed patients exhibit elevated concentrations of glucocorticoids in CSF, plasma, saliva, and/or urine (Haskett, 1993; Holsboer, 1992; Stokes & Sikes, 1988). The degree of hypercortisolemia seen in such severe depressions may on occasion approach the level observed in Cushing's disease, although depressed patients typically do not exhibit the physical stigmata of this disease (Haskett, 1993; Holsboer, 1992; Stokes & Sikes, 1988). A slightly lower percentage of severely depressed patients show failure or dysfunction of feedback inhibition (the mechanism that normally shuts down the HPA axis after resolution of a transient stressor), as measured by the dexamethethasone suppression test (DST; Arana, Baldessarini, & Ornsteen, 1985; Stokes & Sikes, 1988). In addition to hypercortisolemia and impaired feedback inhibition, some depressed persons show abnormalities of circadian regulation of the HPA axis, as illustrated by a blunting of the daily cortisol

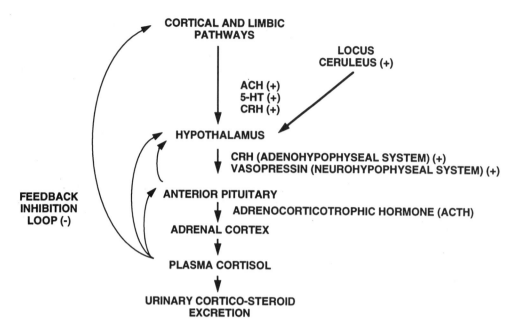

FIGURE 8.11. Schematic illustration of the hypothalamic–pituitary–adrenocortical axis, highlighting sites for feedback inhibition and potential sources of dysregulation. Adapted from Thase, Frank, & Kupfer (1985).

rhythm and an early rise in nocturnal secretion of cortisol (e.g., Jarrett et al., 1987; Sachar et al., 1973; Sherman, Pfohl, & Winokur, 1984).

Inhibitory Control of HPA Function

The overall integrity of the HPA axis is controlled by an intricate feedback inhibition system, which receives input from both the limbic system and the cerebral cortex (see Figure 8.11).

The pulsatile secretion of cortisol by the adrenal cortex is directly controlled by the anterior pituitary hormone ACTH, which is normally released in short-lived bursts, particularly at times of stress. ACTH release, in turn, is triggered by the neuropeptide CRH, which is secreted by adenohypophyseal cells of the hypothalamus (Holsboer, 1992; Stokes & Sikes, 1988). Recent research has established that CRH is also released by other specialized cells distributed diffusely throughout the cortex (Nemeroff, 1992). Studies evaluating ACTH response in depression generally indicate an attenuated or blunted response to CRH injections (e.g., Amsterdam, Maislin, Winokur, Kling, & Gold, 1987; Roy, Gallucci, Avgerinos, Linnoila, & Gold, 1988b). Blunted pituitary ACTH responsivity, in the context of increased adrenocorti-

cal function, is a prime example of a homeostatic down-regulatory response to sustained overactivation. Moreover, this finding indicates that the origin of the abnormal stimulation driving the HPA axis is located above the pituitary (Holsboer, 1992).

The principal sites for feedback inhibition of the HPA axis include adrenocorticoid receptors in the pituitary, hypothalamus, and hippocampus (see Figure 8.11). Fast feedback inhibition of the HPA axis, the process by which ACTH release is inhibited or "turned off" after a sudden increase in plasma cortisol levels, has recently been shown to be diminished in depression (Young, Haskett, Murphy-Weinberg, Watson, & Akil, 1991). Fast feedback inhibition depends on glucocorticoid receptors in the hippocampus (Holsboer, 1992). The number of hippocampal glucocorticoid receptors appears somewhat age-dependent, decreasing in number with older age (e.g., Eldridge, Brodish, Kute, & Landfield, 1989; Sapolsky & Altmann, 1991). This finding most likely accounts for greater incidence of hypercortisolemia in older depressed persons (Holsboer, 1992). Moreover, the learned helplessness procedure can induce a similar abnormality in rats (Greenberg, Edwards, & Henn, 1989). Recent research suggests that sustained stress-related elevations of corticosteriods may have toxic effects on the hippocampal cells regulating fast feedback inhibition, particularly during critical developmental periods (McEwen et al., 1992). Thus, hypercortisolism associated with childhood traumas may induce a state of persistent HPA axis dysregulation throughout adult life (Gold et al., 1988; Insel, 1991). This may explain the high incidence of DST nonsuppression in patients with borderline personality disorder, which may be independent of severity of depressive symptoms (e.g., Carroll et al., 1981; Soloff, George, & Nathan, 1982).

The Dexamethasone Suppression Test

The integrity of feedback inhibition of the HPA axis has been widely studied by measuring plasma or urinary cortisol levels for up to 24 hours after ingestion of a test dose of the potent synthetic glucocorticoid dexamethasone (DEX; e.g., Carroll, 1982). Measurement of cortisol nonsuppression has been standardized using a 1- or 2-mg overnight DST, with post-DEX cortisol blood levels assessed at 8 A.M., 4 P.M., and/or 11 P.M. the following day. Post-DEX plasma cortisol levels of > 4 or 5 µg/dl are generally considered abnormal (Carroll, 1982). Post-DEX plasma cortisol levels are significantly, but imperfectly, correlated with others measures of increased HPA activity (e.g., explaining 16–25% of the common variance; Carroll, 1982; Holsboer, 1992; Thase et al., 1985). This indicates overlapping but complementary methods of assessment of HPA function.

The DST received extensive study in the early 1980s as a possible diagnostic test for depression. However, neither the test's sensitivity (i.e., the proportion of depressed cases correctly identified) nor its specificity (i.e., one minus the proportion of nondepressed cases manifesting false-positive cases) showed adequate test performance for routine clinical practice (Arana et al., 1985; Stokes & Sikes, 1988). The test performance of the DST is affected by a number of factors that alter the metabolism of DEX, including drugs such as phenobarbital and carbamazepine, significant weight loss, and severe physical illnesses, including malignancies and endocrinopathies. Of note among the conditions that affect DEX metabolism, severe depression has been documented to have a significant effect, resulting in significant reductions of plasma DEX levels during severe episodes of illness (e.g., Devanand et al., 1991).

Rates of DST abnormality are highest (i.e., 60–90% abnormality) in more severely ill cases, such as those manifesting melancholic features and/or delusional depressions (Arana et al., 1985; Holsboer, 1992). The rates of hypercortisolemia and DST nonsuppression in milder depressions are typically lower (i.e., 20–40%). In some samples of depressed outpatients, rates of test abnormality do not differ significantly from normal control groups (see, e.g., the review of Arana et al., 1985). Similarly, lower rates of hypercortisolemia and DST nonsuppression have been reported in studies of depressed children and adolescents (e.g., Dahl et al., 1992; Goodyer, Herbert, Moor, & Altham 1991; Pfeffer et al., 1989). As is the case with EEG sleep abnormalities, the interaction of aging and illness severity is important in the genesis of HPA abnormalities.

State versus Trait Issues

A number of groups have documented that the HPA disturbances of depression are usually state-dependent, typically resolving with clinical remission (e.g., Greden et al., 1983; Ribeiro, Tandon, Grunhaus, & Greden, 1993; Young et al., 1984). Of note are recent studies measuring CSF neuropeptide levels that document significant reductions of CRH levels following treatment with desipramine (Veith et al., 1992), fluoxetine (DeBellis et al., 1993b), and ECT (Nemeroff, Bissette, Akil, & Fink, 1991). Persistent abnormalities are observed on occasion, however, and these disturbances often forbode a stormy subsequent clinical course (Greden et al., 1983; Ribeiro et al., 1993). In the simplest terms, increased HPA activity despite clinical improvement almost certainly indicates that an illness process involving the hypothalamus, limbic system, and/or cerebral cortex remains active, rendering the individual markedly vulnerable to depressive relapse.

Research concerning the treatment responsivity of depressed patients in relation to pretreatment HPA disturbances has yield mixed findings (see Ribeiro et al., 1993). As a state-dependent and severity-linked correlate of depression, it is not surprising that patients with HPA disturbances are generally less responsive to attention–placebo interventions (Ribeiro et al., 1993). Evidence recently collected by our group (Thase, Simons, & Reynolds, 1993) and others (see p. 261) suggests that patients with increased HPA activity may also be significantly less responsive to psychotherapy (see Figure 8.12).

HPA–Sleep Interactions

The relationship between hypercortisolemia and EEG sleep abnormalities in depression has been studied by a number of researchers (Asnis et al., 1983; Giles et al., 1987b; Feinberg & Carroll, 1984a; Jarrett, Greenhouse, Coble, & Kupfer, 1986; Kerkhofs, Missa, & Mendlewicz, 1986; Poland, McCracken, Lutchmansingh, & Tondo, 1992; Rush, Giles, Roffwarg, & Parker, 1982; Thase et al., 1989). Results consistently indicate that nearly all hypercortisolemic depressed patients manifest EEG sleep disturbances, whereas approximately one-half of depressed persons with normal HPA profiles show EEG sleep disturbances (see Thase & Kupfer, 1987). As might be expected, depressed patients manifesting both hypercortisolemia and EEG sleep abnormalities are typically older and show more severe clinical symptomatology (e.g., Giles, Roffwarg, Schlesser, & Rush, 1986; Staner, Maes, Bouillon, & Linkowski, 1992). This suggests a common mechanism of neurobiological dysfunction in depression. Corticosteroids have an inherently disruptive effect on sleep, causing increased awakenings and decreased SWS (Born, DeKloet, Wenz, Kern, & Fehm, 1991; Feinberg, Carroll, King, & Greden, 1984b), and patients with Cushing's disease have markedly abnormal sleep profiles (Shipley et al., 1992). Unlike depressed patients, however, patients with Cushing's disease do not typically show increased phasic REM sleep (Shipley et al., 1992), and exogenous corticosteroids reduce REM sleep time in normal controls (Feinberg et al., 1984b). The sleep disturbances of depression thus cannot be fully explained by HPA hyperactivity.

Neurochemical Correlates of HPA Dysfunction

Efforts to identify the neurochemical disturbance(s) underlying HPA hyperactivity have been relatively fruitful. Much of the research indicates that a disinhibition of hypothalamic function results from the combination of impaired feedback control and/or abnormally increased CRH secretion (Holsboer, 1992; Nemeroff, 1992; Stokes & Sikes, 1988). Evidence concerning the former vulnerability was discussed previously. The latter possibility is supported by the findings of elevated CRH concentrations in the CSF of depressed patients (see Nemeroff, 1992), as well as evidence of decreased (down-regulated) CRH receptors in the brains of suicide victims (Nemeroff, Owens, Bissette, Andorn, & Stanley, 1988b).

Direct infusions of CRH produce a variety of behavioral and physiological effects that mimic some of the symptoms of depression (see, e.g.,

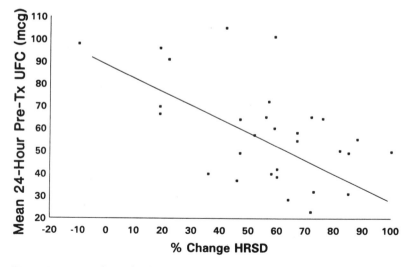

FIGURE 8.12. Relationship between 24-hour mean urinary free cortisol (UFC) excretion and response to cognitive–behavioral therapy in 30 hospitalized depressed patients (Thase, unpublished data).

Gold et al., 1988; Lesch et al., 1988; Nemeroff, 1992). Studies of blunted ACTH response to CRH stimulation suggest that the HPA axis abnormality of depression begins at a level "above" the pituitary (Holsboer, 1992). Nevertheless, a predisposing inherited decrease of feedback inhibition sites has not been ruled out (Gold et al., 1988). This possibility is supported by the observation of increased rates of HPA abnormality in familial depressive disorders (e.g., Coryell, Gaffney, & Burkhardt, 1982; Zimmerman, Coryell, & Pfohl, 1985). Preliminary evidence suggests that antidepressants may bind directly to intracellular structures to modulate synthesis of corticosteroid receptors (Pepin, Beaulieu, & Barden, 1989).

The relationship between HPA function and catecholamines has received considerable attention (see, e.g., Plotsky et al., 1989). Pharmacological challenge studies have been used to explore the relationship between HPA activity and nonadrenergic receptor activity. Nonspecific noradrenergic agonists, such as amphetamine, tend to increase cortisol levels in normals, yet decrease them in depressed patients (e.g., Checkley, 1979; Sachar et al., 1981). Clonidine, a drug with more specific effects on the inhibitory presynaptic α_2-adrenergic receptors, has minimal effects on cortisol levels in normal controls, but produces a significant reduction in hypercortisolemia in depressed patients (see Checkley, 1992). Depressed patients with elevated cortisol levels also fail to show the expected reduction in peripheral adrenergic activity in response to clonidine, as inferred from serial plasma MHPG measurements (see Siever, 1987). Finally, the adrenergic agonist yohimbine has been found to elicit an exaggerated cortisol response in depressed patients (Price, Charney, Rubin, & Heninger, 1986). Taken together, these findings suggest that hypercortisolemia in depression is associated with *hypo*responsive postsynaptic adrenergic receptors and/or upregulated presynaptic receptors, pointing to the role of sustained sympathomedullary activation (Katona et al., 1987; Siever, 1987). These abnormalities appear to be state-dependent (e.g., Trestman et al., 1993).

Consistent with receptor studies, a large body of work documents a positive correlation between measures of increased levels of peripheral adrenergic metabolites and HPA hyperactivity (e.g., Jimerson, Insel, Reyus, & Kopin, 1983; Roy, Guthrie, Karoum, Pickar, & Linnoila, 1988c). At a more basic level, both CRH and glucocorticoids have important agonistlike effects on noradrenergic systems in the brain (Gold et al., 1988; Holsboer, 1992). For example, direct application of CRH increases the responsivity of the locus ceruleus (e.g., Valentino, Foote, & Aston-Jones, 1983). Thus, at times of stress, both noradrenergic and HPA responses act in tandem until removal of the stressor and/or negative feedback inhibition permit homeostatic restabilization. The combination of sustained, unresolvable stress and impaired feedback inhibition thus may cause a deteriorative positive feedback loop, with prolonged pathologic elevations of both norepinephrine and cortisol. As we discuss later, such sustained, coupled activation of these neurobiological response systems undoubtedly serves as one final common pathway to severe depression, regardless of specific etiologies.

Most research with normal individuals suggests that increased serotonergic activity stimulates the HPA axis and, in turn, glucocorticoids may transiently facilitate 5-HT systems in the brain (Holsboer, 1988). Acute stress induces a transient increase in both cortisol and 5-HT (Higley, Suomi, & Linnoila, 1992b). By contrast, persistent stress may induce an uncoupling of this relationship, with sustained hypercortisolemia, despite decreased 5-HT neurotransmission (Weiss, 1991). These findings suggest that 5-HT's role in stimulation of cortisol responses is more pertinent to acute or normal stress than to depression (Weiss, 1991). From an ethological perspective, a sustained increase in HPA activity may be viewed as a partial compensation for low basal levels of 5-HT (Meltzer & Lowy, 1987).

Corticosteroids also have an interactive relationship with DA and its metabolite HVA. For example, DST nonsuppression and hypercortisolemia have been associated with purportedly dopaminergically mediated features such as delusions and agitation (Schatzburg & Rothschild, 1992). Experimentally administered doses of corticosteroid tend to increase levels of HVA (Wolkowitz, Doran, Breier, Roy, & Pickar, 1989). As noted earlier, experimentally administered doses of DEX induce significant reductions of sleep maintenance and REM sleep (e.g., Feinberg et al., 1984), suggestive of increased CNS arousal secondary to increased DA activity (Schatzberg & Rothchild, 1992). We again view these relationships as consistent with a broader neurobiological mobilization in response to stress. Of note, the HPA axis is relatively quiescent in anergic bipolar depression

(Thase et al., 1989) and may be overactive in psychotic manic states (e.g., Stokes et al., 1984), that is, conditions presumed to be related to hypo- and hyperactive dopaminergic function, respectively.

Not all HPA pathology in depression is found within the CNS. For example, hyperresponsivity of the adrenal cortex is suggested by studies documenting an exaggerated cortisol release in response to infusion of ACTH, CRH, or vasopressin (see Stokes & Sikes, 1988). Furthermore, adrenocortical hypertrophy was recently documented in some depressed patients (Nemeroff et al., 1992). Such changes are most likely secondary to chronic overstimulation of the HPA axis in depression. Several investigators have also reported increased adrenal sensitivity to ACTH (Amsterdam, Maislin, Berwish, Phillips, & Winokur, 1989; Jaeckle, Kathol, Lopez, Meller, & Krummel, 1987). Thus, HPA abnormalities in depressed cases may be sustained by both central and peripheral sources. One practical implication of these observations is the development of a modified HPA challenge test, in which plasma cortisol levels are measured in response to CRH after pretreatment with DEX, which may result in a better differentiation of depressed cases from controls (see Holsboer, 1992).

Thyroid Axis Disturbances

Initial interest in the role of thyroid disturbance in depression was prompted by clinical observations of mood disorders in patients with thyroid disease. For example, hypothyroidism, which commonly causes fatigue, anergia, and weight gain, may sometimes present as a full depressive syndrome (Gold & Pottash, 1983). Conversely, behavioral symptoms of hyperthyroidism include anxiety, agitation, weight loss, and insomnia. Hypo- and hyperthyroid states therefore "model" anergic and agitated depressions, respectively. Surveys of thyroid function conducted in large, unselected series, however, reveal hypothyroidism in only a small number of depressed patients (e.g., 2–5%). Furthermore, depression and mania secondary to hyperthyroidism are quite rare (see Gold & Pottash, 1983).

Studies of basal levels of thyroid-stimulating hormone (TSH), the pituitary neuropeptide "driving" the axis, have suggested a trend toward lower levels and blunted circadian rhythms in depressives, and some recent evidence suggests increased CSF levels of the hypothalamic peptide TRH in depression (see Loosen, 1988; Winokur, 1993). Interestingly, high levels of reverse T_3, a physiologically inactive form of thyroid hormone, have been reported in depression (e.g., Baumgartner, Graf, Kurten, & Meinhold, 1988c). These findings suggest metabolic dysregulation of the thyroid axis in depression, rather than a more generalized trend of hypoactivity or hyperfunction.

Stimulation tests using the hypothalamic neuropeptide TRH have enabled investigators to study the integrity of the HPT axis regulation. This axis is normally controlled by inhibitory feedback loops such that, in cases of thyroid failure, increased TSH is secreted in order to increase production of thyroid hormone. Several large surveys suggest that approximately 5–10% of newly diagnosed depressed patients may have an exaggerated TSH response following TRH infusion (e.g., Gold & Pottash, 1983). Such patients are considered to have a covert or subclinical form of hypothyroidism and often require treatment with thyroid hormone, in addition to antidepressant medication (Loosen, 1988). A more tenuous finding is the possible association between thyroid hypofunction and unstable or rapid cycling forms of bipolar affective disorder (e.g., Bauer, Whybrow, & Winokur, 1990). It is not yet clear if this abnormality represents a major or minor risk factor for development of rapid cycling.

TRH Stimulation Test

Systematic application of the TRH stimulation test in major depression has consistently demonstrated a blunted TSH response in 25–40% of patients (Loosen, 1988; Winokur, 1993). Such a prevalence is higher than the rates observed in controls or nonaffective psychiatric patients, although false-negative cases outnumber true positives. With respect to test specificity, a significant minority of schizophrenics and alcoholics also manifest a blunted TSH response to TRH (e.g., Loosen & Prange, 1982). As was the case with the DST, a number of medical illnesses and medications affect TRH stimulation test results (Loosen & Prange, 1982; Winokur, 1993). The TRH stimulation test thus is not suitable for routine application as a diagnostic test for depression (Loosen, 1988; Winokur, 1993).

Most evidence suggests that TSH blunting,

in contrast to the DST nonsuppression, is not related to severity of depression (Loosen, 1988). TSH responses to TRH stimulation also do not typically differentiate between euthyroid bipolar and nonbipolar cases (Loosen, 1988). A blunted TSH response has been associated in several studies with suicidal behavior and a family history of affective disorder (see Loosen, 1988). It is not clear if TSH blunting is a trait- or state-dependent dysfunction (Winokur, 1993). Nevertheless, persistent TSH blunting after treatment may predict a poor prognosis or a high risk of relapse (e.g., Langer, Aschauer, Koing, Resch, & Schonbeck, 1983).

Neurochemical Correlates

Several investigations have attempted to relate TSH blunting to neurochemical abnormalities in depression. Basic research suggests that TSH release is stimulated by NE and inhibited by both 5-HT and DA (Loosen, 1988; Winokur, 1993). From this vantage point, a blunted TSH response could be attributed to either deficient noradrenergic tone or excessive inhibition from tonic serotonergic and/or dopaminergic stimulation at the level of the pituitary. Because the latter possibilities seem implausible in depression, deficient noradrenergic modulation seems to be a more viable hypothesis. Chronically elevated CSF levels of the neuropeptide TRH (e.g., Banki, Bissette, Arato, & Nemeroff, 1988) may be another etiological candidate. Specifically, sustained hypothalamic or cortical release of TRH may cause the apparently down-regulated pituitary response. Finally, because TRH also may stimulate other pituitary hormones, its role in triggering a cascade of abnormal neuroendocrine responses in depression warrants further investigation (Loosen, 1988; Winokur, 1993).

Growth Hormone Regulation

Interest in growth hormone (GH) secretion in depressives has been stimulated for several reasons. Perhaps most important, GH secretion is regulated by processes both temporally and proximally related to other pathophysiological disturbances associated with depression. Cells secreting GH are located in the anterior pituitary. The control of GH secretion involves both a hypothalamic inhibiting factor, somatostatin, and a hypothalamic releasing factor, growth-hormone-releasing hormone (GHRH). The release of GH also is under the partial control of excitatory noradrenergic and dopaminergic stimulation. Furthermore, a predictable peak of GH secretion occurs during the first few hours of sleep (i.e., temporally contiguous with reduced REM latency and decreased delta sleep ratio values). Study of GH regulation in depression thus provides the opportunity to investigate the role of a variety of neurochemical and neurophysiological disturbances. Unfortunately, GH is a difficult hormone to study, partly because factors such as stress, physical activity, food intake, and estrogen levels affect its regulation (Checkley, 1992).

Most investigations of GH regulation have utilized challenge paradigms, measuring response of GH following administration of various drugs and hormones (see Checkley, 1992). Conflicting results have been reported in studies using dopaminergic agents, including amphetamine, L-dopa, and apomorphine (e.g., Ansseau et al., 1988; Checkley, 1992). More consistent evidence indicates that depressed patients have a diminished GH response to clonidine, once again suggesting dysfunctional α_2-adrenergic receptors in depression (e.g., Katona et al., 1987; Schittecatte et al., 1994). The abnormally blunted GH response to clonidine is most pronounced in depressed men and postmenopausal women (Schittecatte et al., 1994). Because premenopausal depressed women may have relatively normal GH responses to clonidine, one must wonder what role estrogen may have in minimizing down-regulation of α_2 receptors in depression.

GH responses to both desipramine and its parent drug, imipramine, are blunted in depressives as well (Checkley, 1992). These abnormal responses appear to persist despite effective treatment (Delgado et al., 1992; Siever, Trestman, & Coccaro, 1992), including studies of recovered patients withdrawn from antidepressants (Jarrett, Miewald, & Kupfer, 1990). Therefore, it appears that blunted GH responses are more likely to reflect either a traitlike abnormality of α_2 autoreceptors or an enduring "scar" of the illness.

Depressed patients also are likely to evidence a diminished GH response to insulin-induced hypoglycemia when compared to normal controls (Checkley, 1992). This abnormality may reflect a state of relative insulin-resistance due to hypercortisolemia (Thase et al., 1985). Consistent with this hypothesis, CRH elicits an abnormally increased GH response in major depression (Lesch, Laux, Schulte, Pfüller, & Beckmann, 1988a). However, this response also could be mediated by either an acute mobilization of catecholamines or a CRH-mediated increase in GHRH. Studies directly examining GHRH stimulation have produced conflicting results (e.g., Krishnan et al., 1988; Lesch, Laux, Erb, Pfüller, & Beckmann, 1987). With respect to the role of 5-HT, GH response to tryptophan may be reduced in major depression (Cowen & Charig, 1987). Other studies have examined the circadian pattern of GH secretion. This work has demonstrated that GH secretion in major depression may be relatively increased during the daytime, while reduced at night (Jarrett et al., 1986; Mendlewicz et al., 1985).

Somatostatin, a hypothalamic neuropeptide inhibiting GH release, also has been found to be decreased in the CSF of depressed individuals (see Gold & Rubinow, 1987). Low levels of an inhibitory hypothalamic releasing hormone, in concert with blunted pituitary responsiveness, would, again, be consistent with a suprahypothalamic drive. As reviewed above, increased NE activity and/or increased CRH levels are likely candidates.

There is much evidence to suggest that somatostatin also functions as a neuromodulator or neurotransmitter elsewhere in the CNS, with promising implications for the study of depression (Gold & Rubinow, 1987). For example, somatostatin administration results in reductions of the amounts of total sleep time, delta sleep, and REM sleep (i.e., a profile indicative of CNS arousal; Gold & Rubinow, 1987). The constellation of low levels of somatostatin, reduced nocturnal GH secretion, and decreased SWS in the first non-REM period would thus appear to be an important area for future research.

Prolactin Secretion

Regulation of prolactin secretion in depression is of interest in part because of its secretion by cells in the anterior pituitary. Moreover, 5-HT neurotransmission has been implicated in prolactin release and DA has a well-established role in the tonic inhibition of prolactin secretion (Checkley, 1992).

Most studies of basal prolactin secretion have not demonstrated significant differences between depressed persons and controls (Check-

ley, 1992), although one group has reported within-subject increases in prolactin levels in patients restudied following clinical recovery (Baumgartner, Graf, & Kurten, 1988a, 1988b). Early reports of abnormal circadian secretion of prolactin also have not been replicated consistently (e.g., Baumgartner et al., 1988a; Jarrett et al., 1987). However, in a recent study of seasonally depressed patients, prolactin levels were found to be *reduced* (relative to controls) in both winter and summer (Depue et al., 1990). This finding suggests a traitlike abnormality of low DA activity throughout the year in seasonal depressions.

In contrast to basal studies, blunted prolactin responses following administration of opiates, tryptophan, and fenfluramine have been reported in patients with major depression (see Meltzer & Lowy, 1987; Thase et al., 1985). Blunted prolactin response to L-5-hydroxytryptophan has also recently been documented in depressed prepubertal children (Ryan et al., 1992). These findings are consistent with a deficit of serotonergic neurotransmission in depressives (Malone & Mann, 1993; Meltzer & Lowy, 1987). Prolactin responses to tryptophan also may vary as a function of diagnostic subtype, with more abnormal results observed in endogenous depressions (e.g., Price, Charney, Delgado, & Heninger, 1991). The paired association of 5-HT and DA levels within the CNS is consistent with studies suggesting that low levels of both neurotransmitters may be implicated in prolactin dysregulation.

Several studies have noted an association between hypercortisolemia and blunted prolactin responses (Baumgartner et al., 1988a; Cowen & Charig, 1987), although the effects of CRH have not been ruled out. It is conceivable that elevated cortisol levels may contribute to the blunted prolactin response in depressives (Lisansky, Fava, Zielezny, Morphy, & Kellner, 1987), perhaps through a secondary action mediated by dopaminergic activation (Thase et al., 1985). Numerous investigations of the prolactin response following TRH stimulation have not yielded consistent results, although one study found within-subject increases in prolactin response to TRH following clinical recovery (Baumgartner et al., 1988b).

Endorphins

The identification of endogenous opiatelike substances (endorphins) and localization of opiate receptors in the CNS have several potential implications for the study of the affective disorders. For example, the transient euphoria induced by narcotic use, the agitated dysphoria accompanying opiate withdrawal, and changes in pain tolerance observed in some depressed persons might suggest that mania and depression are associated with fluctuations in levels of endorphins (Davis, 1983; Adler & Gattaz, 1993). Attempts to test these possibilities by administration of β-endorphin and other endorphinlike substances to depressed patients have not yielded conclusive results, although interpretation of such studies is limited by the short-term administration of these agents (Berger & Nemeroff, 1987).

A number of investigators have studied β-endorphin levels in depression (see, e.g., Berger & Nemeroff, 1987; Maes, Vandervorst, Suy, Minner, & Raus, 1991). β-Endorphin is secreted from the pituitary as a subunit of the large neuropeptide precursor, or prohormone, pro-opiomelanocortin (Berger & Nemeroff, 1987). When fragmented, this prohormone also yields ACTH. As might be expected, elevated levels of β-endorphin have been linked to measures of hyperactive HPA function (Berger & Nemeroff, 1987; Young et al., 1990), and may be partially suppressed by dexamethasone (Maes et al., 1991). Published studies have yielded conflicting findings, with reports of both normal and elevated β-endorphin levels in depressives (see Berger & Nemeroff, 1987; Maes et al., 1991; Young et al., 1990). Observation of such mixed results would be anticipated: Only a subset of depressed patients have increased ACTH levels, and most of the reports concerning β-endorphin levels have not studied large enough samples to detect the existence of an abnormal subgroup. As was the case with studies measuring HPA activity, exaggerated β-endorphin response to the cholinergic agonist physostigmine has been reported, providing further evidence of cholinergic supersensitivity in depression (Berger & Nemeroff, 1987).

In summary, it appears that elevated β-endorphin levels in depression are the result of either a cholinergically mediated abnormality and/or a more generalized, aberrant HPA response. Although purely conjectural, there is an elegant simplicity revealed in the pairing of release of an endogenous analgesic in tandem with a stress-related activation of the HPA stress response system.

CHRONOBIOLOGY AND DEPRESSION

Chronobiological Patterns

Many neurophysiological and neuroendocrine processes are characterized by regular, periodic patterns throughout the day, referred to as "circadian rhythms." Cortisol secretion, the sleep–wake cycle, body temperature, and propensity to REM sleep all show such a 24-hour pattern (Monk, 1993; Anderson & Wirz-Justice, 1991). Other biological rhythms, such as the 90-minute REM sleep cycle, occur with a periodicity of less than 24 hours, and are referred to as "ultradian rhythms." Rhythms that have a seasonal or yearly ("circannual") pattern also have been described for selected biochemical and neuroendocrine parameters (Oren & Rosenthal, 1992; Wehr & Goodwin, 1981; Wirz-Justice & Richter, 1979). Researchers have expended considerable effort trying to understand how the neurobiological abnormalities associated with depression fit within a broader pattern of disturbed biological rhythms.

Circadian rhythms are maintained by internal generators or biological "clocks" within the CNS (Monk, 1993). Circadian rhythms will run "freely" on about a 25-hour cycle when environmental stimuli are removed. The extent of possible entrainment in human beings may range from 21-hour to 27-hour "days" using experimental manipulations of the light–dark cycle. In daily life, circadian rhythms are guided or influenced by external cues (zeitgebers). The "generator" for the sleep–wake circadian cycle is located in the suprachiasmatic nuclei (SCN) of the hypothalamus, with neural connections to the retina, pineal gland, and limbic system (Hallonquist, Goldberg, & Brandes, 1986; Monk, 1993). These connections provide an anatomical pathway between the environment (i.e., perceptions of light and dark, or zeitgebers) and the brain regions that modulate the sleep–wake cycle.

During isolation experiments, the sleep–wake cycle typically becomes uncoupled from circadian rhythms for body temperature, REM propensity, plasma MHPG levels, and cortisol secretion (Monk, 1993). Such uncoupling indicates that a second circadian generator may exist in addition to the SCN (Hallonquist et al., 1986; Monk, 1993). Experimental dissociation of these rhythms produces a variety of behavioral effects suggestive of depression, including fatigue, cognitive dulling, and impaired quality of sleep

(Anderson & Wirz-Justice, 1991). Conversely, blunting of the diurnal rhythm of cortisol (Holsboer, 1992) and selected clinical symptoms (i.e., early morning awakening and diurnal mood disturbances) also suggest that circadian rhythm disturbances are implicated in depression (Wehr & Wirz-Justice, 1982).

Hypothesized Abnormalities in Depression

Hypotheses concerning circadian abnormalities have emphasized several possible disturbances in depression:

1. Chaos or disorganization of daily rhythms resulting from disruption of social zeitgebers (Ehlers, Frank, & Kupfer, 1988).
2. A blunted amplitude of circadian rhythms (Czeisler, Kronauer, Mooney, Anderson, & Allan, 1987).
3. Pathological desynchronization of circadian rhythms (Wehr & Wirz-Justice, 1982).

The latter hypothesis is best characterized by a proposed phase advance of body temperature, REM propensity, and cortisol secretion circadian rhythms in relation to the sleep–wake rhythm in endogenous depression (Anderson & Wirz-Justice, 1991). Such a dissociation could explain the phenomena of reduced REM latency, increased activity of the first REM period, and early morning awakening. This is because the propensity for both REM sleep and nocturnal arousal normally reach their maximum near dawn (Wehr & Wirz-Justice, 1982). Phase advancement of the circadian MHPG rhythm in depressives also has been reported (Piletz et al., 1994). High levels of nocturnal psychomotor activity seen in some depressives similarly suggest phase advancement of noradrenergic activity from its normal daytime peak (Wehr & Goodwin, 1981). Likewise, nocturnal hypercortisolemia and early onset of cortisol secretion during sleep are consistent with phase advancement (see Sack, Rosenthal, Parry, & Wehr, 1987). The transient antidepressant effect of sleep deprivation has been suggested to result from a temporary resetting of an abnormally phase-advanced circadian rhythm (Wu & Bunney, 1990). However, it has not yet been established that sleep deprivation's mood-altering effects are directly mediated by effects on dissociated circadian rhythms (Anderson & Wirz-Justice, 1991; Hallonquist et al., 1986).

Body temperature is another circadian rhythm that has been extensively studied for evidence of phase advancement in depression. Abnormalities of body temperature are of interest; this rhythm is thought to be linked to the same circadian generator as REM propensity and cortisol secretion. It has been proposed that one physiological function of REM sleep is to increase temperature in a small homeothermic core, including the CNS (Monk, 1993).

A number of investigators have examined body temperature in depression, either by studying a small number of patients longitudinally or by cross-sectional comparison of larger groups of depressed patients and normal controls (see Anderson & Wirz-Justice, 1991). Results of several longitudinal studies tend to support a phase advance of body temperature in depression (e.g., Avery, Wildschiodtz, & Rafaelson, 1982; Beersma, van den Hoofdakker, & van Berkestijn, 1983). By contrast, most cross-sectional comparisons of patients and controls have failed to find any differences (e.g., Pollak, Alexopoulos, Moline, & Wagner, 1989; Von Zerssen et al., 1985; Wehr et al., 1986). Despite this apparent discrepancy, many of the studies have noted more consistent alterations in the amplitude of the temperature curve, indicating a blunting of the circadian temperature rhythm rather than phase advancement (Anderson & Wirz-Justice, 1991). Other groups have emphasized a phase delay of circadian rhythms in hypersomnic depressions, particularly those associated with a seasonal pattern of illness characterized by winter depressions and/or spring–summer hypomanias (e.g., Lewy, Sack, Miller, & Toban, 1987; Sack et al., 1990). Clinical aspects of winter depression are discussed in the next section.

In summary, evidence from studies of EEG sleep, body temperature, and HPA axis function are generally not fully consistent with the existence of phase advancement of circadian rhythms in most depressed patients. Available data are more suggestive of blunted or disorganized circadian rhythms in depression, which may be attributable to disruption of social zeitgebers (Ehlers et al., 1988). Evidence of phase delay appears limited to cases of winter depression. Future studies will need simultaneously to measure multiple circadian rhythms in order to explore their inter-relationships in depression.

Seasonal Affective Disorder

It has been suggested that seasonal changes in the amount of sunlight may unmask faulty entrainment of circadian rhythms. Fall and spring are the seasons with the most dramatic changes in sunlight in temperate climates, and the higher prevalence of depression and mania during these periods provides some support for the hypothesis of increased vulnerability to changes in sunlight (Oren & Rosenthal, 1992; Wehr & Rosenthal, 1989). Patients with seasonal depression often are characterized by reversed vegetative symptoms (i.e., increased appetite and hypersomnia) and they often do not manifest the biological abnormalities characteristic of melancholia, such as DST nonsuppression, TRH blunting, or reduced REM latency (Oren & Rosenthal, 1992; Thase, 1989). Wehr, Sack, and Rosenthal (1987) also have described an opposite or reverse form of seasonal affective disorder (SAD), in which more clinically and neurobiologically severe summer depressions alternate with winter hypomanias.

The hormone melatonin has been implicated in SAD. Melatonin is secreted by the pineal gland in response to darkness, and its release is suppressed by bright light via input from the retina and the SCN. Furthermore, in order for phototherapy to be an effective treatment for seasonal depression, a level of bright light sufficient to suppress melatonin levels must be administered (Blehar & Rosenthal, 1989; Oren & Rosenthal, 1992). However, most empirical studies have not confirmed that melatonin plays a central role in the pathophysiology of seasonal depressions (Grasby & Cowen, 1987; Rosenthal, Jacobsen, Sack, Arendt, & James, 1988; Rosenthal et al., 1986; Rubin, Heist, McGeoy, Hananda, & Lesser, 1992; Sack et al., 1987).

Patients with winter depression have been shown to have significantly increased basal metabolic rates (Gaist et al., 1990). Basal metabolism may be influenced by multiple factors, including dysregulation of 5-HT. As noted earlier, decreased basal prolactin levels in winter depression might implicate decreased 5-HT and/or decreased DA neurotransmission. Parallel findings have been observed using an elevated spontaneous blink rate as the "marker" of DA activity (Depue, Iacono, Muir, & Arbisi, 1988). Some investigators have suggested that carbohydrate craving and hypersomnia in winter depression represent compensatory homeostatic processes intended to enhance 5-HT neurotransmission within the CNS (Oren & Rosenthal, 1992; O'Rourke, Wurtman, Wurtman, Chebli, & Gleason, 1989). Consistent with this model, the 5-HT agonist *d*-fenfluramine may be an effective treatment of SAD (O'Rourke et al., 1989). Like nonseasonal forms of anergic or atypical depression, winter depression also appears responsive to nonsedating antidepressants that affect 5-HT and/or DA (Dilsaver & Jaeckle, 1990; Dilsaver, Qamar, & DelMedico, 1990). However, phototherapy is not an effective treatment of nonseasonal atypical depressions (Stewart, Quitkin, Terman, & Terman, 1990).

IMMUNOLOGICAL DISTURBANCES

Although it has long been suspected that depression may have an adverse effect on an individual's "hardiness" or resistance to disease (Jackson, 1986), the methology necessary to assess immunological function has only been available for the past 20 years. In a comprehensive review of the literature on depression and immune function, covering 22 studies of depressed patients and healthy controls, Stein, Miller, and Trestman (1991) concluded that (1) there is no evidence of increased mortality in depression attributable to immune-related diseases (i.e., infection, autoimmune disease, etc.); and (2) no study has demonstrated depression-related abnormalities in natural-killer (NK) cell activity, abnormal responses of lymphocytes to mitogens, *and* changes in health in the same patients. Stein et al. (1991) noted numerous inconsistencies across studies and identified a number of methodological problems with early research. Among pertinent negative studies is one conducted by Stein's group: No differences were found between a group of 91 depressed patients and an equal number of age- and sex-related healthy controls on a variety of measures of immune function (Schleifer, Keller, Bond, Cohen, & Stein, 1989). However, in the midst of such a conflicted literature, tantalizing findings do emerge. For example, Schleifer et al. (1989) observed a significant correlation between clinical severity and suppression of mitogen proliferation among depressed patients, as well as blunting of the normal age-related increase in mitogen-induced lymphocyte responses. These findings suggest that a subgroup of older and more severely depressed patients may show at least subtle evidence of immune dysfunction.

The association between older age, higher levels of symptom severity, and immune dysfunction in depressives points to a probable mechanistic link to HPA hyperactivity and/or increased sympathomedullary activity (e.g., Maes et al., 1994; Stein et al., 1991). This suggestion is particularly salient in view of these systems' effects on immune function in conditions other than depression (Felten et al., 1987; Parillo & Fauci, 1979). A number of groups have directly studied HPA and sympathoadrenal parameters in depressed patients and the literature is relatively evenly divided between negative reports (e.g., Kronfol, House, Silva, Greden & Carroll, 1986; Syvalahti, Eskola, Ruuskanen, & Laine, 1985) and those suggesting altered immune function in hypercortisolemic patients (e.g., Kronfol, Nasrallah, Chapman & House, 1985; Maes, Bosmans & Suy, 1990; Maes, Meltzer, Stevens, Cosyns & Blockx, 1994). The results of studies by Hickie, Hickie, Lloyd, Silove, and Wakefield (1993) and Maes, Bosman, and Suy (1990) also specifically implicate the melancholic subtype of major depression as a risk factor for impaired cell-mediated immune responses, further reinforcing the importance of both older age and clinical severity in the genesis of this abnormality.

Lymphocytes activated by mitogens produce a number of neuromodulators capable of intensifying the CNS stress response, including CRH and a family of cytokine peptides known as the interleukins (Berkenbosch, van Oers, Del Rey, Tilders, & Besedovsky, 1987; Dunn, 1988; Heinrich, Castell, & Andus, 1990). Furthermore, the cytokine interleukin-1 may induce expression of the gene coding for glucocorticoid synthesis (Brown, Smith, & Blalock, 1987). Thus, although we share the reservations of Stein et al. (1991) about the research findings on immunological dysfunction in major depressive disorder, available evidence does suggest that abnormalities are associated with the most serious forms of mood disorder and, in fact, may play a role in maintaining dysregulated CNS stress responses.

SEX DIFFERENCES IN BIOLOGICAL PROCESSES IN DEPRESSION

The 2:1 sex difference in the incidence and prevalence of major depression is a robust and well-replicated finding, begging the question of whether the increased risk of depression in women is at least partly attributable to sex differences in neurobiology. Research has not established, however, that such differences exist, beyond the several potential contributory factors to be discussed. First, women undoubtedly have at least some increased risk of depression associated with childbirth (Cox, 1992). However, studies of psychosocial and/or biological risk factors in relation to childbirth suggest that factors such as a past history of depression, level of residual depressive symptoms, low levels of social support, and increased life stress may be more strongly associated with such increased risk than neurohormonal factors (e.g., Cox, Connor, & Kendell, 1982; O'Hara, Neunaber, & Zekoski, 1984; O'Hara, Schlecht, Lewis, & Wright, 1991; Paykel, Emms, Fletcher, & Rassaby, 1980; Watson, Elliot, Rugg, & Brough, 1984). Second, women may also have a higher risk of mood disorder because of oral contraceptive use (Parry & Rush, 1979). Third, women have higher rates of subclinical hypothyroidism (Gold & Pottash, 1983), which poses a modest increase in risk of depression. Fourth, monthly shifts in mood and associated symptomatology during the menstrual cycle may predispose some women to more severe episodes of major depression (Rivera-Tovar & Frank, 1990). Fifth, women may be more likely to have experienced the types of abuse and trauma early in life that may alter CNS stress response systems (e.g., DeBellis, Lefter, Trickett & Putnam, 1994; Finkelhor, Hotaling, Lewis, & Smith, 1990). And sixth, neuroticism, a heritable correlate of more generalized vulnerability to psychopathology, may interact with life stress and/or level of social supports to yield higher rates of depression in women (Kendler, Kessler, Neale, Heath, & Eaves, 1993).

Evidence for the magnitude of risk associated with several of these factors is tenuous, however. For example, late luteal phase disorder may be more likely to be a consequence of prior depression than a risk factor for future episodes of illness (Hurt et al., 1992). Similarly, although girls may indeed be more likely to suffer sexual traumas than boys, there is little evidence from studies of depression that adult women show greater evidence of disturbances of EEG sleep (Reynolds et al., 1990) or HPA function (Akil et al., 1993) than their male counterparts before age 45. Nevertheless, the relatively greater proportion of HPA abnormalities observed in older, postmenopausal females (Akil et al., 1993) warrants further study. As discussed earlier, neuroendocrine dysregulation attributable to early trauma may be more pertinent to understanding state-independent neurobiological disturbances in severe personality disorders.

Epidemiological studies of bipolar disorder provide a striking counterpoint for understanding sex differences in depression. Specifically, incidence and prevalence rates in bipolar depression more closely approximate a 1:1 sex ratio (Goodwin & Jamison, 1990). In Pennsylvania's Old Order Amish, rates of unipolar depression are not only comparable in men and women, they are only about one-fourth as prevalent as those observed in other American community samples (Egeland & Hostetter, 1983). It has been suggested that in an agrarian community such as the Old Order Amish, in which substance abuse, spousal infidelity, poverty, and divorce are minimized and social support is maximized, there is no "gender gap" in rates of depression (Thase & Himmelhoch, 1983). It thus seems likely that sex differences in rates of depression have more to do with culturally defined gender differences in symptom reporting, help seeking, social support, coping styles, treatment utilization, and/or life stress than differences in neurobiology. (e.g., Kessler, Brown, & Broman, 1981; Nolen-Hoeksema, 1987; Silverstein & Perlick, 1991; Thase et al., 1994b; Wilhelm & Parker, 1994).

SUMMARY OF RESEARCH ON THE BIOLOGY OF MAJOR DEPRESSION

Despite voluminous research conducted over the past several decades, explicit understandings about the role of biological factors in the etiology and pathogenesis of major depression are still surprisingly limited. Investigation in this area is a dynamic and evolving process, however, and, despite many complicating methodological issues, progress is being made. In particular, improvements and refinements in experimental methodology provide the necessary foundation for continued research. Furthermore, recognition and appropriate control of the effects of selected nondiagnostic variables, such as age, sex, menstrual status, and time of day, improve replicability and increase confidence in the validity of research findings. A summary "box score" of evidence concerning a selected set of

neurobiological disturbances is provided in Table 8.8.

Conclusions

Our first conclusion is that the evidence does not support the classical monoamine hypotheses of depression. The complex regulatory and compensatory relationships of the monoamines and ACh mitigate against demonstration of isolated deficits for a given neurotransmitter system. Similarly, the clinical and, in all probability, genetic heterogeneity of major depression make it extremely unlikely that a single abnormality would be found in all depressed patients. Nevertheless, further study of presynaptic and postsynaptic receptor activity, membrane physiology (e.g., Pettegrew et al., 1993), and second-messenger systems will prove especially informative in the investigation of depression. Moreover, research using the techniques of PET scanning and functional MRI will provide immensely valuable *in vivo* data in this area, as will the continued use of various pharmacological probes.

Second, we conclude that consistent documentation of abnormalities of a number of neurotransmitter, neuroendocrine, and neurophysiological parameters provides compelling evidence that severe depressive states are associated with underlying neurobiological regulatory disturbances. The strategy of simultaneously studying neurochemical, neuroendocrine, and neurophysiological variables is increasingly employed in affective disorders research to capture the interactive and additive nature of such disturbances. For example, available data suggest that recurrent melancholia may be a manifestation of the dysregulation of multiple biological systems, comprising a sustained, maladaptive stress response (Gold et al., 1988; Siever & Davis, 1985; Nemeroff, 1992; Post, 1992).

Third, we propose that the problem of clinical heterogeneity is best addressed by "splitting" major depression into validated subgroups, rather than "lumping" diverse cases into a broad, common grouping. The relationships between selected biological abnormalities in specific subgroups of major depression are summarized in Table 8.8. On the whole, there is far greater evidence of neurobiological dysregulation in more severe depressive syndromes, particularly bipolar disorder and syndromes characterized by melancholic and delusional symptoms. Patients with nonbipolar, nondelusional, nonmel-

TABLE 8.8. Summary of Selected Biological Abnormalities in Depressive Subgroups

Subgroup	Reduced urinary MHPG	Increased peripheral catechols	Reduced CSF 5-HIAA	Reduced REM latency	Hypercortisolism	Blunted TSH response to TRH	Decreased frontal glucose metabolism
Melancholia	+	++	++	+++	+++	++	+++
Bipolar depression	+++	+	+	++	++	++	+++
Delusional	+	++	+	+++	+++	++	++
Nonmelancholic, nonbipolar, nonpsychotic	0	0	0	++	+	+	+
Seasonal	?	0	?	++	0	+	++
Dysthymia	?	0	?	++	0	+	?

Note. +++, present in a majority of patients; ++, consistently present in a subgroup of patients; +, possibly present in a subgroup of patients; 0, not associated with subgroups.

ancholic major depressions or dysthymia are the least likely to show evidence of biological dysfunction, although even in these less biologically disturbed subgroups, reduced REM latency may be found in 40–50% of cases (Kupfer & Thase, 1983; Howland & Thase, 1991). We again wish to emphasize that the broad nonbipolar/nonmelancholic residual grouping of major depression and dysthymia account for, in aggregate, at least three-fourths of all current cases of depression detected in community surveys!

Fourth, neurobiological disturbances of depression may be divided into subsets of state-dependent and state-independent (or traitlike) abnormalities (see Table 8.9). State-dependent disturbances, which tend to be correlated with clinical measures of severity, include various measures of hypercortisolism, increased NE activity, alterations of β-adrenergic receptors,

poor sleep efficiency, increased REM density, sleep-onset REM latency, and hypofrontality on PET scans. Not surprisingly, these state-dependent abnormalities have been most consistently documented in samples of melancholic and/or delusional depressions. State-independent or traitlike abnormalities include reduced REM latency, diminished SWS, decreased CSF 5-HIAA levels, blunted TRH response, diminished GH responses, blunted α_2-receptor function, and supersensitive response to cholinergic agonists. Family history studies suggest that at least several of these abnormalities are, indeed, likely to be true traits (Giles et al., 1989; Krieg et al., 1990; Sitaram et al., 1987).

Fifth, it is heuristically useful to categorize biological disturbances on the basis of relationships with functional neurobehavioral systems. In this regard, the following functional systems

TABLE 8.9. Characterization of the Reversibility of Biological Abnormalities Associated with Depression

Type of abnormality	State-dependent	State-independent
Neurochemical	Reduced urinary MHPG Increased peripheral catechols Increased 5-HT$_2$ receptor sensitivity Blunted β-adrenergic receptor sensitivity Decreased [^{3}H]imipramine binding	Reduced CSF 5-HIAA Increased α_2-adrenergic sensitivity (?)
Neurophysiological	Increased phasic REM activity Markedly reduced REM latency Sleep continuity disturbances Nondominant hemispheric activation (?)	Reduced SWS Reduced delta sleep ratio (?) Modestly reduced REM latency Blunted autonomic responsivity ?)
Neuroendocrine	Increased HPA activity Increased CRH levels Increased TRH levels (?) Blunted insulin response	Blunted TSH response to TRH (?) Blunted GH responses
Neuroradiological	Frontal hypometabolism	Cortical atrophy (?) Increased metabolism in amygdala (?)

are relevant to clinical depression: (1) behavioral facilitation, (2) behavioral quieting, (3) acute stress response, (4) biological rhythms, (5) executive cortical function, and (6) central pain regulation. Behavioral facilitation (Depue & Spoont, 1986) is impaired in depression, as reflected by anhedonia, loss of interest, decreased appetite, and diminished goal-seeking behavior. Abnormal behavioral facilitation may be induced by prolonged, uncontrollable stress (Weiss, 1991) and is best understood as a state of diminished functional activity of NE and DA, perhaps superimposed upon a background of reduced 5-HT "tone" (Depue & Spoont, 1986; Wilner, 1993). In depressed human beings, this functional presentation is best reflected by a "pure" retarded depression (i.e., retardation without concomitant agitation).

Impaired behavioral quieting (Gray, 1991) is best illustrated by decreased SWS, reduced REM latency, early morning awakening, and blunted autonomic function. Clinical features such as insomnia, generalized anxiety or apprehension, increased irritability, and/or violent suicidal behavior also may reflect a failure of behavioral inhibition (DePue & Spoont, 1986). Both traitlike (Kagan, Reznick, & Snidman, 1987) and acquired (Rosenblum et al., 1994) deficits of 5-HT are implicated in impaired behavioral quieting; cholinergic supersensitivity also may be involved. Impaired behavioral quieting is evident in many cases of mild to moderately severe depression, particularly in mid- or late life. Moreover, an impaired behavioral quieting system, while possibly quiescent in remitted states, may be an enduring vulnerability factor in patients at risk for recurrent depression. The illness transduction or kindling model of Post (1992) further suggests that progressively greater abnormalities of behavioral quieting may result from each recurrent episode of depression.

The overactivation of stress response systems is perhaps the best-established disturbance in severe depression. Sustained activation of stress response systems, as manifested by the paired increase of HPA and sympathoadrenal activity, appears to induce compensatory changes in behavioral facilitation. Increased stress responsivity may also reflect an overtaxed behavioral quieting system. An abnormal stress response system is most evident in severe episodes of illness, such as melancholia and delusional depressions. Age-dependent trends increase the likelihood of this abnormality in older depressed patients.

Biological rhythm disturbances represent the fourth dysfunctional neurobiological process associated with depression. Abnormalities may include seasonal vulnerabilities (i.e., circannual rhythms), circadian phase shifts (i.e., phase delay or phase advance), blunting of rhythmic processes (e.g., core body temperature), and/or disorganization of rhythms following a breakdown of social zeitgebers.

Diminished executive cortical function is the fifth, more recently recognized systemic function. Impaired exective cortical function is reflected in depressed patients' poor problem-solving abilities (Spoont, 1992), difficulties in utilizing abstraction, and problems in mastering more effortful cognitive tasks (Rubinow, Post, Savard, & Gold, 1984; Reus, 1985). Studies utilizing PET scans have consistently documented hypofrontality of cerebral metabolism, including regions of the prefrontal cortex responsible for abstraction and executive functions (e.g., Buchsbaum et al., 1984; Martinot et al., 1990a). Some evidence implicates decreased DA in disturbances of executive cortical function. Conversely, increased NE activity may fractionate concentration and attentional processes (Spoont, 1992). Hypercortisolemia (Reus, 1985; Rubinow et al., 1984) and neurotransmitter deficits secondary to sleep deprivation (McCann et al., 1992) also probably contribute to cognitive impairments in severe depression. Thus, disturbances of executive cortical function would be expected to follow impairments of behavioral facilitation and sustained activation of stress response systems. Unfortunately, such deficits may help to maintain the depressed patient in a hopeless/helpless state.

The sixth and most speculative CNS system implicated in depression was proposed by Carroll (1991) to account for the persistent and intense dysphoria experienced by depressed people. It should be recognized that none of the other neurobehavioral systems considered previously account for this essential aspect of the depressive experience. Dysregulation of mechanisms regulating central pain perception may be inferred from studies documenting increased pain tolerance and elevated β-endorphin levels. Perhaps more important, the association of increased REM density or increased metabolism in the amygdala with the intensity of depressive cognitions and ruminations suggests a bidirectional circuit between cortical, limbic, and brain stem regions (Drevets et al., 1992).

Directions for Future Research

Integration of biological and psychosocial research in depression is an especially promising area of study. Unfortunately, a disproportionate amount of the psychosocial research conducted to date has studied less severely impaired outpatient or volunteer samples; it is difficult to generalize findings to the groups of major depressives that are typically examined in biological studies. For example, although a vast literature has addressed the role of stressful life events in depression, it is unclear if individuals with underlying biological abnormalities are differentially sensitive to life stress and, therefore, may convey an important degree of vulnerability to stress-related depressions. In this regard, depressions associated with reduced REM latency (Monroe et al., 1992) or DST nonsuppression (Roy, Pickar, Linnoila, & Paul, 1986b) have been reported to have significantly lower rates of associated life stress than "nonbiological" cases.

Several groups have proposed hypotheses that link life stress with circadian rhythm disturbances and other biological abnormalities in depression (Ehlers et al., 1988; Healy, 1987; Healy & Williams, 1988; Gold et al., 1988). Although these theories integrate much of the existing data, they await prospective empirical validation. Such integrative research also will be important for studies of the vulnerability to relapse in depression (Belsher & Costello, 1988; Thase, 1992), as well as studies of the variability of response to antidepressant treatments (Thase & Howland, 1994).

One interesting area of research addresses the relationship between biological correlates and cognitive changes in depression. For example, one line of research links deficits on neuropsychological performance with various EEG abnormalities (Sackeim, 1991; Coffey, 1987) and increased HPA axis activity (Rubinow et al., 1984; Reus, 1985). Another line of research focuses on the role of cognitive distortions (i.e., ruminations, negative thoughts, dysfunctional attitudes) in depression. Recent studies have associated increased levels of negative cognitions with increased REM density (Nofzinger et al., 1993a), high levels of hopelessness with increased CRH levels (DeJong & Roy, 1990), and self-rated helplessness with increased peripheral catecholamine levels (Samson et al., 1992). Drevets et al. (1992) similarly reported an association between increased glucose metabolism in the amygdala and severity of depressive ruminations. Although much of the available data would indicate that such distorted attitudes and beliefs are symptoms rather than causes of depression, there also is evidence to suggest that activation of right (nondominant) cerebral hemispheric processing of cognitive–emotional information has a critical role in the etiopathogenesis of depression (Coffey, 1987; Otto et al., 1987).

Another promising research direction explores biological correlates of animal models of depression, using psychosocially relevant paradigms such as learned helplessness (e.g., Maier, 1991; Weiss, 1991) or primate separation (Suomi, 1991; McKinney, 1992). Although such animal models are lacking in terms of the psychological/self-representational aspects of the depressive experience, they do offer experimental control over the stressful experience, the social milieu, and treatment interventions. Moreover, lifelong follow-up and direct assessment of neurochemical changes are possible. Various neurochemical, neuroendocrine, and circadian rhythm abnormalities have been described using these experimental paradigms (Insel, 1991; Weiss, 1991; McKinney, 1992; Wilner et al., 1991). Furthermore, chronic treatment with antidepressants has been found to reverse animal models of depression (Garattini & Samanin, 1988). Naturalistic studies of the neurobiological effects of stress on primates living in the wild or in controlled colonies also are of considerable interest (Higley et al., 1992b; Sapolsky, 1990). These animal models provide the unique opportunity to examine various experiential factors implicated in depressive vulnerability, such as traumatic early experience (Insel, 1991), disruption of attachment relationships (Reite & Short, 1978), or decline in social status (Raleigh, Brammer, & McGuire, 1988).

Finally, several research groups have employed various forms of psychotherapy to study the neurobiology of unmedicated patients across the recovery process. An increasing body of evidence indicates that interpersonal, cognitive, and behavioral therapies may be as effective as antidepressant medication in the treatment of ambulatory, nonbipolar, major depression patients (Dobson, 1989; Jarrett, 1990; Thase, 1995). Nevertheless, traditional clinical wisdom suggests that more neurobiologically disturbed depressives are less responsive to psychotherapy (e.g., Free & Oei, 1989; Rush, 1984; Thase et al., 1984). Several investigations have studied reduced REM latency as the marker of biological disturbance and found that "affected" cases respond as well to outpatient psychotherapy as those cases with more normal values (Buysse et al., 1992b; Corbishley et al., 1990; Jarrett, Eaves, Grannenmann, & Rush, 1991; Simons & Thase, 1992; Thase et al., 1993). Interpretation of these studies is limited by the fact that reduced REM latency is now probably better understood as a trait-like correlate of depression and, hence, actually may provide little information about state-dependent dysfunction.

More recent work by our group indicates that when reduced REM latency is coupled with two more state-dependent EEG sleep abnormalities (i.e., poor sleep efficiency and increased REM density), the abnormal profile is associated with significantly poorer response to cognitive–behavioral therapy (Thase et al., 1993). Similarly, poorer response to psychotherapy has been reported in both uncontrolled (Robbins, Alessi, & Colfer, 1989; Rush, 1984; Thase et al., 1993) and controlled (Corbishley et al., 1990; McKnight, Nelson-Gray, & Barnhill, 1992) studies of depressed hypercortisolemic patients. Future research strategies will need to address the manifold potential interactions of biological variables, psychosocial variables, and treatment response in depression. If the findings pertaining to poor response to psychotherapy in patients with state-dependent neurobiological disturbance are more widely replicated, there may be a threshold of depressive neurobiological disturbance beyond which somatic therapy is required.

In conclusion, research on the biology of major depression has confirmed the existence of multiple overlapping disturbances, as well as suggesting the existence of numerous other abnormalities. The significance of these findings with respect to the etiology and pathogenesis of depression is only now beginning to be understood. Future research focusing on the interrelationships of multiple biological disturbances, and integrating these findings within the broader body of knowledge about the natural history, psychosocial aspects, and treatment, will lead to an even richer understanding of the etiopathogenesis of the depressive disorders.

Acknowledgements. Preparation of this chapter was supported in part by Grant Nos. MH-41884, MH-40023, and MH-30915 (Mental Health Clinical Research Center) from the National Institute of Mental Health, and by Grant Nos. DA-07673 and DA-08541 from the National Institute on Drug Abuse to Michael E. Thase, as well as by a Young Investigator's Award from NARSAD to Robert H. Howland. The secretarial assistance of Ms. Lisa Stupar and Ms. Janice Jozefov is gratefully appreciated.

REFERENCES

Adler, G., & Gattaz, W. F. (1993). Pain perception threshold in major depression. *Biological Psychiatry, 34,* 687–689.

Agren, H., Mefford, I. N., Rudorfer, M. V., Linnoila, M., & Potter, W. Z. (1986). Interacting neurotransmitter systems:, A. nonexperimental approach to the, 5HIAA–HVA correlation in human CSF. *Journal of Psychiatric Research, 20,* 175–193.

Agren, H., Reibring, L., Hartvig, P., Tedroff, J., Bjurling, P., Hornfeldt, K., Andersson, Y., Lundqvist, H., & Langstrom, B. (1991). Low brain uptake of L-[^{11}C]5-hydroxytryptophan in major depression: A positron emission tomography study on patients and healthy volunteers. *Acta Psychiatrica Scandinavica, 83,* 449–455.

Akil, H., Haskett, R. F., Young, E. A., Grunhaus, L., Kotun, J., Weinberg, V., Greden, J., & Watson S. J. (1993). Multiple HPA profiles in endogenous depression: Effect of age and sex on cortisol and beta-endorphin. *Biological Psychiatry, 33,* 73–85.

American Psychiatric Association. (1987). *Diagnostic and statistical manual of mental disorders* (3rd ed., rev.). Washington, DC: Author.

American Psychiatric Association. (1994). *Diagnostic and statistical manual of mental disorders* (4th ed.). Washington, DC: Author.

Amit, Z., Smith, B. R., & Gill, K. (1991). Serotonin uptake inhibitors: Effects on motivated consummatory behaviors. *Journal of Clinical Psychiatry, 52,* 55–60.

Amsterdam, J. D., Maislin, G., Berwish, N., Phillips, J., & Winokur, A. (1989). Enhanced adrenocortical sensitivity to submaximal doses of cosyntropin (a$^{1-24}$-corticotropin) in depressed patients. *Archives of General Psychiatry, 46,* 550–554.

Amsterdam, J. D., Maislin, G., Winokur, A., Kling, M., & Gold, P. (1987). Pituitary and adrenocortical responses to the ovine corticotropin releasing hormone in depressed patients and healthy volunteers. *Archives of General Psychiatry, 44,* 775–781.

Anderson, J. L., & Wirz-Justice, A. (1991). Biological rhythms in the pathophysiology and treatment of affective disorders. In R. W. Horton, & C. L. E. Katona (Eds.), *Biological aspects of affective disorders* (pp. 224–260). San Diego: Academic Press.

Andreasen, N. C., Swayze, V., Flaum, M., Alliger, R., & Cohen, G. (1990). Ventricular abnormalities in affective disorder: clinical and demographic correlates. *American Journal of Psychiatry, 147,* 893–900.

Ansseau, M., Devoitille, J.-M., Papart, P., Vanbrabant, E., Mantanus, H., & Timsit-Berthier, M. (1991). Comparison of adinazolam amitriptyline and diazepam in endogenous depressive inpatients exhibiting DST nonsuppression or abnormal contingent negative variation. *Journal of Clinical Psychopharmacology, 11,* 160–165.

Ansseau, M., Von Frenckell, R., Cerfontaine, J. L., Papart, P., Franck, G., Timsit-Berthier, M., Geenen, V., & Legros,

J. J. (1988). Blunted response of growth hormone to clonidine and apomorphine in endogenous depression. *British Journal of Psychiatry*, 153, 65–71.

Arana, G. W., Baldessarini, R. J., & Ornsteen, M. (1985). The dexamethasone suppression test for diagnosis and prognosis in psychiatry: Commentary and review. *Archives of General Psychiatry*, 42, 1193–1204.

Arango, V., Ernsberger, P., Marzuk, P. M., Chen J.-S., Tierney, H., Stanley, M., Reis, D. J., & Mann, J. J. (1990). Autoradiographic demonstration of increased serotonin, 5-HT$_2$ and β-adrenergic receptor binding sites in the brain of suicide victims. *Archives of General Psychiatry*, 47, 1038–1047.

Armitage, R., Rush, A. J., Trivedi, M., Cain, J., & Roffwarg, H. P. (1994). The effects of nefazodone on sleep architecture in depression. *Neuropsychopharmacology*, 10, 123–127.

Arora, R. C., & Meltzer, H. Y. (1988). Seasonal variation of imipramine binding in the blood platelets of normal controls and depressed patients. *Biological Psychiatry*, 23, 217–226.

Arriaga, F., Rosado, P., & Paiva, T. (1990). The sleep of dysthymic patients: A comparison with normal controls. *Biological Psychiatry*, 27, 649–656.

Åsberg, M., & Wägner, A. (1986). Biochemical effects of antidepressant treatment-studies of monoamine metabolites in cerebrospinal fluid and platelet ^{3}H-imipramine binding. *Ciba Foundation Symposium*, 123, 57–83.

Asnis, G. M., Hasbreich, U., Sachar, E. J., Nathan, R. S., Ostrow, L., Novacenko, H., Davis, M., Endicott, J., & Puig-Antich, J. (1983). Plasma cortisol secretion and REM period latency in adult endogenous depression. *American Journal of Psychiatry*, 140, 750–753.

Avery, D. H., Wildschiodtz, G., & Rafaelsen O, J. (1982). Nocturnal temperature in affective disorder. *Journal of Affective Disorders*, 4, 61–71.

Banich, M. T., Stolar, N., Heller, W., & Goldman, R. B. (1992). A deficit in right-hemisphere performance after induction of a depressed mood. *Neuropsychiatry, Neuropsychology and Behavioral Neurology*, 5, 20–27.

Banki, C. M., Bissette, G., Arato, M., & Nemeroff, C. B. (1988). Elevation of immunoreactive CSF TRH in depressed patients. *American Journal of Psychiatry*, 145, 1526–1531.

Baron, M., Barkai, A., Gruen, R., Peselow, E., Fieve, R. R., & Quitkin, F. (1987). Platelet ^{3}H-imipramine binding and familial transmission of affective disorders. *Neuropsychobiology*, 17, 182–186.

Battaglia, M., Ferini-Strambi, L., Smirne, S., Bernardeschi, L., & Bellodi, L. (1993). Ambulatory polysomnography of never-depressed borderline subjects: A high-risk approach to rapid eye movement latency. *Biological Psychiatry*, 33, 326–334.

Bauer, M. S., Whybrow, P. C., & Winokur, A. (1990). Rapid cycling bipolar affective disorder: I. Association with grade I. hypothyroidism. *Archives of General Psychiatry*, 47, 427–432.

Baumgartner, A., Graf, K.-J., & Kurten, I. (1988a). Prolactin in patients with major depressive disorder and in healthy subjects: I. Cross-sectional study of basal and post-TRH and postdexamethasone prolactin levels. *Biological Psychiatry*, 24, 249–267.

Baumgartner, A., Graf, K.-J., & Kurten, I. (1988b). Prolactin in patients with major depressive disorder and in healthy subjects: II. Longitudinal study of basal prolactin and post-TRH-stimulated prolactin levels. *Biological Psychiatry*, 24, 268–285.

Baumgartner, A., Graf, K.-J., Kurten, I., & Meinhold, H. (1988c). The hypothalamic–pituitary–thyroid axis in psychiatric patients and healthy subjects: Parts 1–4. *Psychiatry Research*, 24, 271–332.

Baxter, L. R., Phelps, M. E., Mazziotta, J. C., Schwartz, J. M., Gerner, R. H., Selin, C. E., & Sumida, R. M. (1985). Cerebral metabolic rates for glucose in mood disorders: Studies with positron emission tomography and fluorodeoxygulcose F18. *Archives of General Psychiatry*, 42, 441–447.

Baxter, L. R., Schwartz, J. M., Phelps, M. E., Mazziotta, J. C., Guze, B. H., Selin, C. E., Gerner, R. H., & Sumida, R. M. (1989). Reduction of prefrontal cortex glucose metabolism common to three types of depression. *Archives of General Psychiatry*, 46, 243–250.

Bech, P., Eplov, L., Gastpar, M., Gentsch, C., Mendlewicz, J., Plenge, P., Rielaert, C., & Mellerup, E. T. (1988). WHO pilot study on the validity of imipramine platelet receptor binding sites as a biological marker of endogenous depression. *Psycharmacopsychiatry*, 21, 147–150.

Beersma, D. G. M., van den Hoofdakker, R. H., & van Berkestijn, H. W. B. M. (1983). Circadian rhythms in affective disorders: Body temperature and sleep physiology in endogenous depressives. *Advances in Biological Psychiatry*, 11, 114–127.

Belsher, G., & Costello, C. G. (1988). Relapse after recovery from unipolar depression: A critical review. *Psychological Bulletin*, 104, 84–96.

Benca, R. M., Obermeyer, W. H., Thisted, R. A., & Gillin, J. C. (1992). Sleep and psychiatric disorders. A meta-analysis. *Archives of General Psychiatry*, 49, 651–668.

Benson, K. L., Faull, K. F., Zarcone, V. P., Jr. (1993). The effects of age and serotonergic activity on slow-wave sleep in depressive illness. *Biological Psychiatry*, 33, 842–844.

Berger, M., Riemann, D., Höchi, D., & Spiegel, R. (1989). The cholinergic rapid eye movement sleep induction test with RS-86. *Archives of General Psychiatry*, 46, 421–428.

Berger, P. A., & Nemeroff, C. B. (1987). Opioid peptides in affective disorders. In H. Y. Meltzer (Ed.), *Psychopharmacology: The third generation of progress* (pp. 637–646). New York: Raven Press.

Berkenbosch, F., van Oers, J., Del Rey, A., Tildes, F., & Besedovsky, H. (1987). Corticotropin releasing factor-producing neurons in the rat activated by interleukin-1. *Science*, 238, 524–526.

Berman, K. F., Doran, A. R., Pickar, D., & Weinberger D. R. (1993). Is the mechanism of prefrontal hypofunction in depression the same as in schizophrenia? Regional cerebral blood flow during cognitive activation. *British Journal of Psychiatry*, 162, 183–192.

Bernstein, A. S., Riedel, J. A., Graae, F., Seidman, D., Steele, H., Connolly, J., & Lubowsdy, J. (1988). Schizophrenia is associated with altered orienting activity: Depression with electrodermal (cholinergic?) deficit and normal orienting response. *Journal of Abnormal Psychology*, 97, 3–12.

Berrettini, W. H., Nurnberger, J. I., Post, R. M., & Gershon, E. S. (1982). Platelet ^{3}Himipramine binding in euthymic bipolar patients. *Psychiatry Research*, 7, 215–219.

Beskow, J., Gottfries, C. G., Roos, B. E., & Winbald, B. (1976). Determination of monoamine and monoamine metabolites in the human brain: Postmortem studies in a group of suicides and in a control group. *Acta Psychiatrica Scandinavica*, 53, 7–20.

Bielski, R. J., & Friedel, R. O. (1976). Prediction of tricyclic antidepressant response. *Archives of General Psychiatry, 33*, 1479–1489.

Blackwood, D. H. R., Whalley, L. J., Christie, J. E., Blackburn, I. M., St. Clair, D. M., & McInnes, A. (1987). Changes in auditory P300 event-related potential in schizophrenia and depression. *British Journal of Psychiatry, 150*, 154–160.

Blehar, M. C., & Rosenthal, N. E. (1989). Seasonal affective disorders and phototherapy. Report of a National Institute of Mental Health-sponsored workshop. *Archives of General Psychiatry, 46*, 469–474.

Blier, P., De Montigny, C., Chaput, Y. (1987). Modifications of the serotonin system by antidepressant treatments: Implications for the therapeutic response in major depression. *Journal of Clinical Psychopharmacology, 7* (Suppl. 6), 245–355.

Borbely, A. A., & Wirz-Justice, A. (1982). Sleep deprivation and depression: A hypothesis derived from a model of sleep regulation. *Human Neurobiology, 1*, 205–215.

Born, J., DeKloet, E. R., Wenz, H., Kern, W., & Fehm, H. L. (1991). Gluco- and antimineralocorticoid effects on human sleep: A role of central corticosteroid receptors. *American Journal of Physiology, 22*, E183–E188.

Bowden, C. L., Huang, L. G., Javors, M. A., Johnson, J. M., Seleshi, E., McIntyre, K., Contreras, S., & Maas, J. W. (1988). Calcium function in affective disorders and healthy controls. *Biological Psychiatry, 23*, 367–376.

Bowers, M. B. J. (1991). Characteristics of psychotic inpatients with high or low HVA levels at admission. *American Journal of Psychiatry, 148*, 240–243.

Bowers, M. B. J., Swigar, M. E., Hoffman, F. J., & Goicoechea, N. (1988). Characteristics of patients with the highest plasma catecholamine metabolite levels. *American Journal of Psychiatry, 145*, 246–248.

Brown, G. L., & Linnoila, M. I. (1990). CSF serotonin metabolite (5-HIAA) studies in depression impulsivity and violence. *Journal of Clinical Psychiatry, 51*(Suppl. 4), 31–41.

Brown, S. L., Smith, L. R., & Blalock, J. E. (1987). Interleukin-1 and interleukin-2 enhance proopiomelanocortin gene expression in pituitary cells. *Journal of Immunology, 139*, 3181–3183.

Bruder, G. E., Stewart, J. W., Voglmaier, M. M., Harrison, W. M., McGrath, P., Tricamo, E., & Quitkin, F. M. (1990). Cerebral laterality and depression: Relations of perceptual asymmetry to outcome of treatment with tricyclic antidepressants. *Neuropsychopharmacology, 3*, 1–10.

Buchsbaum, M. S. (1975). Average evoked response augmenting/reducing in schizophrenia and affective disorders. In D. X. Freedman (Ed.), *The biology of major psychoses: A comparative analysis* (pp. 129–142). New York: Raven Press.

Buchsbaum, M. S., De Lisi, L. E., Holcomb, H. H., Cappelletti, J., King, A. C., Johnson, J., Hazlett, E., Dowling-Zimmerman, S., Post, R. M., Morihisa, J., Carpenter, W., Cohen, R., Pickar, D., Weinberger, D. R., Margolin, R., & Kessler, R. H. (1984). Anteroposterior gradients in cerebral glucose use in schizophrenia and affective disorders. *Archives of General Psychiatry, 41*, 1159–1161.

Buchsbaum, M. S., & Rieder, R. O. (1979). Biological heterogeneity and psychiatric research. *Archives of General Psychiatry, 36*, 1163–1169.

Buchsbaum, M. S., Wu, J., De Lisi, L. E., Holcomb, H., Kessler, R., Johnson, J., King, A. C., Hazlett, K.,

Langston, K., & Post, R. M. (1986). Frontal cortex and basal ganglia metabolic rates assessed by positron emission tomography with, ^{18}F-2-deoxyglucose in affective illness. *Journal of Affective Disorders, 10*, 137–152.

Bunney, W, E., Jr., & Davis, J. M, (1965). Norepinephrine in depressive reactions: A review. *Archives of General Psychiatry, 13A*, 483–494.

Butler, R. W., Jenkins, M. A., & Braff, D. L. (1993). The abnormality of normal comparison groups: The identification of psychosis proneness and substance abuse in putatively normal research subjects. *American Journal of Psychiatry, 150*, 1386–1391.

Buysse, D. J., & Kupfer, D. J. (1990). Diagnostic and research applications of electroencephalographic sleep studies in depression. *Journal of Nervous and Mental Disease, 178*(7), 405–414.

Buysse, D. J., & Kupfer, D. J. (1993). Sleep disorders in depressive disorders. In J. J. Mann, & D. J. Kupfer (Eds.), *Biology of depressive disorders: Part A. A systems perspective* (pp. 123–154). New York: Plenum Press.

Buysse, D. J., Kupfer, D. J., Frank, E., Monk, T., Rittenour, A., & Ehlers, C. L, (1992a). Electroencephalographic sleep studies in depressed patients treated with interpersonal psychotherapy: Part I. Baseline studies in responders and nonresponders. *Psychiatry Research, 40*, 13–26.

Buysse, D. J., Kupfer, D. J., Frank, E., Monk, T., Rittenour, A., & Ehlers, C. L, (1992b). Electroencephalographic sleep studies in depressed outpatients treated with interpersonal psychotherapy: Part II. Longitudinal studies at baseline and recovery. *Psychiatry Research, 40*, 27–40.

Buysse, D. J., Reynolds, C. F., Kupfer, D. J., Houck, P. R., Hoch, C. C., Stack, J. A., & Berman, S. R. (1988). Electroencephalographic sleep in depressive pseudodementia. *Archives of General Psychiatry, 45*, 568–575.

Cade, J. F. J. (1949). Lithium salts in the treatment of psychotic excitement. *Medical Journal of Australia, 2*, 349–352.

Carroll, B. J. (1982). The dexamethasone suppression test for melancholia. *British Journal of Psychiatry, 140*, 292–304.

Carroll, B. J. (1991). Psychopathology and neurobiology of manic–depressive disorders. In B. J. Carroll, & J. E. Barrett (Eds.), *Psychopathology and the brain* (pp. 265–285). New York: Raven Press.

Carroll, B. J., Curtis, G. C., & Mendels, J. (1976). Neuroendocrine regulation in depression. I: Limbic system-adrenocortical dysfunction. *Archives of General Psychiatry, 33*, 1039–1044.

Carroll, B. J., Greden, J. F., Feinberg, M., Lohr, N., James, N. M., Steiner, M., Haskett, R. F., Albala, A. A., DeVigne, J. P., & Tarika, J. (1981). Neuroendocrine evaluation of depression in borderline patients. *Psychiatric Clinics of North America, 4*, 89–99.

Cartwright, R. D. (1993). Sleeping problems. In C. G. Costello (Ed.), *Symptoms of depression* (pp. 243–257). New York: Wiley.

Cartwright, R. D., & Wood, E. (1991). Adjustment disorders of sleep: The sleep effects of a major stressful event and its resolution. *Psychiatry Research, 39*, 199–209.

Casper, R. C., Redmond, E. Jr., Katz, M. M., Schaffer, C. B., Davis, J. M., & Koslow, S. H. (1985). Somatic symptoms in primary affective disorder presence and relationship to the classification of depression. *Archives of General Psychiatry, 42*, 1098–1104.

Charney, D. S., & Heninger, G. R. (1986). Abnormal regulation of noradrenergic function in panic disorders. *Archives of General Psychiatry*, 43, 1042–1054.

Charney, D. S., Menkes, D. B., & Heninger, G. R. (1981). Receptor sensitivity and the mechanism of action of antidepressant treatment: Implications for the etiology and therapy of depression. *Archives of General Psychiatry*, 38, 1160–1180.

Checkley, S. A. (1979). Corticosteroid and growth hormone responses to methylamphetamine in depressive illness. *Psychological Medicine*, 9, 107–116.

Checkley, S. A. (1992). Neuroendocrinology. In E. S. Paykel (Ed.), *Handbook of affective disorders* (2nd ed., pp. 255–266). New York: Guilford Press.

Cheetham, S. C., Crompton, M. R., Katona, C. L. E., & Horton, R. W. (1988). Brain 5-HT$_2$ receptor binding sites in depressed suicide victims. *Brain Research*, 443, 272–280.

Cheetham, S. C., Katona, C. L. E., & Horton, R. W. (1991). Postmortem studies in neutrotransmitter biochemistry in depression and suicide. In R. Horton & C. L. E. Katona (Eds.), *Biological aspects of affective disorders* (pp. 191–222). London: Academic Press.

Coccaro, E. F., Silverman, J. M., Klar, H. M., Horwath, T. B., & Siever, L. J. (1994). Familial correlates of reduced central serotonergic system function in patients with personality disorders. *Archives of General Psychiatry*, 51, 318–324.

Coccaro, E. F., Siever, L. J., Klar, H. M., Maurer, G., Cochrane, K., Cooper, T. B., Mohs, R. C., & Davis, K. L. (1989). Serotonergic studies in patients with affective and personality disorders. *Archives of General Psychiatry*, 46, 587–599.

Coffey, C. E. (1987). Cerebral laterality and emotion: The neurology of depression. *Comprehensive Psychiatry*, 28, 197–219.

Coffey, C. E., Figiel, G. S., Djang, W. T., & Weiner, R. D. (1990). Subcortical hyperintensity on magnetic resonance imaging: A comparison of normal and depressed elderly subjects. *American Journal of Psychiatry*, 147 (2), 187–189.

Coffey, C. E., Wilkinson, W. E., Weiner, R. D., Ritchie, J. C., & Aque, M. (1993). The dexamethasone suppression test and quantitative cerebral anatomy in depression. *Biological Psychiatry*, 33, 442–449.

Cohen, D. B. (1979). Dysphoric effect and REM sleep. *Journal of Abnormal Psychology*, 88, 73–77.

Cohen, R. M., Gross, M., Nordahl, T. E., Semple, W. E., Oren, D. A., & Rosenthal, N. (1992). Preliminary data on the metabolic brain pattern of patients with winter seasonal affective disorder. *Archives of General Psychiatry*, 49, 545–552.

Cooper, J. R., Bloom, F. E., & Roth, R. H. (1991). *The biochemical basis of neuropharmacology* (6th ed.). New York: Oxford University Press.

Coppen, A. J., & Doogan, D. P. (1988). Serotonin and its place in the pathogenesis of depression. *Journal of Clinical Psychiatry*, 49, 4–11.

Corbishley, M., Beutler, L., Quan, S., Bamford, C., Meredith, K., & Scogin, F. (1990). Rapid eye movement density and latency and dexamethasone suppression as predictors of treatment response in depressed older adults. *Current Therapeutic Research*, 47, 846–859.

Coryell, W., Gaffney, G., & Burkhardt, P. E. (1982). The dexamethasone suppression test and familial subtypes of depression: A naturalistic replication. *Biological Psychiatry*, 17, 33–40.

Cowen, P. J., & Charig, E. M. (1987). Neuroendocrine responses to intravenous tryptophan in major depression. *Archives of General Psychiatry*, 44, 958–966.

Cowen, P. J., Parry-Billings, M., Newsholme, E. A. (1989). Decreased plasma tryptophan levels in major depression. *Journal of Affective Disorders*, 16, 27–31.

Cox, J. L. (1992). Depression after childbirth. In E. S. Paykel (Ed.), *Handbook of affective disorders* (2nd ed., pp. 569–583). New York: Guilford Press.

Cox, J. L., Connor, Y., & Kendell, R. E. (1982). Prospective study of the psychiatric disorders of childbirth. *British Journal of Psychiatry*, 140, 111–117.

Czeisler, C. A., Kronauer, R. E., Mooney, J. J., Anderson, J. L., & Allan, J. S. (1987). Biologic rhythm disorders depression and phototherapy: A new hypothesis. *Psychiatric Clinics of North America*, 10, 687–709.

D'Haenen, H. A., & Bossuyt, A. (1994). Dopamine D$_2$ receptors in depression measured with single photon emission computed tomography. *Biological Psychiatry*, 35, 128–132.

Dahl, R. E., Kaufman, J., Ryan, N. D., Perel, J., Al-Shabbout, M., Birmaher, B., Nelson, B., & Puig-Antich, J. (1992). The dexamethasone suppression test in children and adolescents: A review and a controlled study. *Biological Psychiatry*, 32, 109–126.

Dahl, R. E., Ryan, N. D., Birmaher, B., Al-Shabbout, M., Williamson, D. E., Neidig, M., Nelson, B., & Puig-Antich, J. (1991). Electroencephalographic sleep measures in prepubertal depression. *Psychiatry Research*, 38, 201–214.

Davidson, J. R. T., Miller, R. D., Turnbull, C. D., & Sullivan, J. L. (1982). Atypical depression. *Archives of General Psychiatry*, 39, 527–534.

Davis, G. C. (1983). Endorphins and pain. *Psychiatric Clinics of North America*, 6, 473–487.

Davis, J. M., Koslow, S. H., Gibbons, R. D., Maas, J. W., Bowden, C. L., Casper, R., Hanin, I., Javaid, J. I., Chang, S. S., & Stokes, P. E. (1988). Cerebrospinal fluid and urinary biogenic amines in depressed patients with healthy controls. *Archives of General Psychiatry*, 45, 705–717.

De Bellis, M. D., Geracioti, T. D., Jr., Altemus, A., & Kling, M. A. (1993a). Cerebrospinal fluid monoamine metabolites in fluoxetine-treated patients with major depression and in healthy volunteers. *Biological Psychiatry*, 33, 636–641.

De Bellis, M. D., Gold, P. W., Geracioti, T. D., Jr., Listwak, S. J., & Kling, M. A. (1993b). Association of fluoxetine treatment with reductions in CSF concentrations of corticotropin-releasing hormone and arginine vasopressin in patients with major depression. *American Journal of Psychiatry*, 150, 656–657.

De Bellis, M. D., Lefter, L., Trickett, P. K., & Putnam, F. W. (1994). Urinary catecholamine excretion in sexually abused girls. *Journal of the American Academy of Child and Adolescent Psychiatry*, 33, 320–327.

Delgado, P. L., Charney, D. S., Price, L. H., Aghajanian, G. K., Landis, H., & Heninger, G. R. (1990). Serotonin function and the mechanism of antidepressant action reversal of antidepressant-induced remission by rapid depletion of plasma tryptophan. *Archives of General Psychiatry*, 47, 411–418.

Delgado, P. L., Price, L. H., Heninger, G. R., & Charney, D. S. (1992). Neurochemistry. In E. S. Paykel (Ed.), *Handbook of affective disorders* (2nd ed., pp. 219–253). New York: Guilford Press.

DeLisi, L. E., Karoum, F., Targum, S., Byrnes, S., Wyatt,

R. J. (1983). The determination of urinary 3-methoxy-4-hydroxy-phenylglycol excretion in acute schizophreniform and depressed patients. *Biological Psychiatry*, *18*, 1189–1196.

Depue, R. A., Arbisi, P., Krauss, S., Iacono, W. G., Leon, A., Muir, R., & Allen, J. (1990). Seasonal independence of low prolactin concentration and high spontaneous eye blink rates in unipolar and bipolar II seasonal affective disorder. *Archives of General Psychiatry*, *47*, 356–364.

Depue, R. A., Iacono, W. G., Muir, R., & Arbisi, P. (1988). Effect of phototherapy on spontaneous eye blink rate in subjects with seasonal affective disorder. *American Journal of Psychiatry*, *145*(11), 1457–1459.

Depue, R. A., & Spoont, M. R. (1986). Conceptualizing a serotonin trait as a behavioral dimension of constraint. In J. J. Mann & M. Stanley (Eds.), *Psychobiology of suicidal behavior* (pp. 47–62). New York: New York Academy of Sciences.

Devanand, D. P., Sackeim, H. A., Lo, E.-S., Cooper, T., Huttinot, G., Prudic, J., & Ross, F. (1991). Serial dexamethasone suppression tests and plasma dexamethasone levels. *Biological Psychiatry*, *48*, 525–533.

Devous, M. D. (1989). Imaging brain function by single-photon emission computer tomography. In N. C. Andreasen (Ed.), *Brain imaging: Applications in psychiatry* (pp. 147–234). Washington, DC: American Psychiatric Press.

Dilsaver, S. C. (1986). Cholinergic mechanisms in depression. *Brain Research Reviews*, *11*, 285–316.

Dilsaver, S. C., & Jaeckle, R. S. (1990). Winter depression responds to an open trial of tranylcypromine. *Journal of Clinical Psychiatry*, *51*, 326–329.

Dilsaver, S. C., Qamar, A. B., & DelMedico, V. J. (1990). The efficacy of bupropion in winter depression: Results of an open trial. *Journal of Clinical Psychiatry*, *53*, 252–255.

Dobson, K. S, (1989). A meta-analysis of the efficacy of cognitive therapy for depression. *Journal of Consulting Clinical Psychology*, *57*, 414–419.

Dominguez, R. A. (1992). Serotonergic antidepressants and their efficacy in obsessive compulsive disorder. *Journal of Clinical Psychiatry*, *53*, 56–59.

Drevets, W. C., Videen, T. O., Price, J. L., Preskorn, S. H., Carmichael, S. T., & Raichle, M, E. (1992). A functional anatomical study of unipolar depression. *Journal of Neuroscience*, *12*, 3628–3641.

Dubé, S. (1993). Cholinergic supersensitivity in affective disorders. In J. J. Mann & D. J. Kupfer (Eds.), *Biology of depressive disorders: Part A. A systems perspective* (pp. 51–78). New York: Plenum Press.

Dubé, S., Dobkin, J. A., Bowler, K. A., Thase, M. E., & Kupfer, D. J. (1993). Cerebral perfusion changes with antidepressant treatment in depression. *Biological Psychiatry*, *33*, 6A–47A.

Dubé, S., Kumar, N., Ettedugi, E., Pohl, R., Jones, D., & Sitaram, N. (1985). Cholinergic REM-induction response separation of anxiety and depression. *Biological Psychiatry*, *20*(4), 408–418.

Dubovsky, S. L., Murphy, J., Thomas, M., & Rademacher, J. (1992). Abnormal intracellular calcium ion concentration in platelets and lymphocytes of bipolar patients. *American Journal of Psychiatry*, *149*, 118–120.

Dunn, A. J. (1988). Systemic interleukin-1 administration stimulates hyothalamic norepinephrine metabolism paralleling the increased plasma corticosterone. *Life Sciences*, *43*, 429–435.

Dupont, R. M., Jernigan, T. L., Butters, N., Delis, D.,

Hesselink, J. R., Heindel, W., & Gillin, J. C. (1990). Subcortical abnormalities detected in bipolar affective disorder using magnetic resonance imaging. *Archives of General Psychiatry*, *47*, 55–59.

Ebert, D., Feistel, H., Kaschka, W., Barocka, A., & Pirner, A. (1994). Single photon emission computerized tomography assessment of cerebral dopamine D2 receptor blockade in depression before and after sleep deprivation—preliminary results. *Biological Psychiatry*, *35*, 880–885.

Edman, G., Asberg, M., Levander, S., & Schalling, D. (1986). Skin conductance habituation and cerebrospinal fluid, 5-hydroxyindoleacetic acid in suicidal patients. *Archives of General Psychiatry*, *43*, 586–592.

Egeland, J. A., & Hostetter, A. M. (1983). Amish study: I. Affective disorders among the Amish. *American Journal of Psychiatry*, *140*, 56–61.

Ehlers, C. L., Frank, E., & Kupfer, D. J. (1988). Social zeitgebers and biological rhythms. *Archives of General Psychiatry*, *45*, 948–952.

Eldridge, J. C., Brodish, A., Kute, T. E., & Landfield, P. W. (1989). Apparent age-related resistance of Type II hippocampal corticosteroid receptors to down-regulation during chronic escape training. *Journal of Neuroscience*, *9*, 3237–3242.

Elkin, I., Shea, M. T., Watkins, J. T., Imber, S. D., Sotsky, S. M., Collins, J. F., Glass, D. R., Pilkonis, P. A., Leber, W. R., Docherty, J. P., Fiester, S. J., & Parloff, M. B. (1989). National Institute of Medical Health Treatment of Depression Collaborative Research Program: General effectiveness treatments. *Archives of General Psychiatry*, *46*, 971–982.

Elliott, J. M. (1991). Peripheral markers in affective disorders. In R. W. Horton & C. L. E. Katona (Eds.), *Biological aspects of affective disorders* (pp. 96–144). San Diego: Academic Press.

Emslie, G. J., Rush, A. J., Weinberg, W. A., Rintelmann, J. W., & Roffwarg, H. P. (1990). Children with major depression show reduced rapid eye movement latencies. *Archives of General Psychiatry*, *47*, 119–124.

Endicott, J., & Spitzer, R. L. (1978). A diagnostic interview: The schedule for affective disorders and schizophrenia. *Archives of General Psychiatry*, *35*, 837–848.

Farde, L., Nordström, A.-L., Wiesel, F.-A., Pauli, S., Halldin, C., & Sedvall, G. (1992). Positron emission tomographic analysis of central D_1 and D_2 dopamine receptor occupancy in patients treated with classical neuroleptics and clozapine. *Archives of General Psychiatry*, *49*, 538–544.

Feighner, J. P., Robins, E., Guze, S. B., Woodruff, R. A., Winokur, G., & Munoz, R. (1972). Diagnostic criteria for use in psychiatric research. *Archives of General Psychiatry*, *26*, 57–63.

Feinberg, M., & Carroll, B. J. (1984). Biological "markers" for endogenous depression: Effect of age severity illness weight loss and polarity. *Archives of General Psychiatry*, *41*, 1080–1085.

Feinberg, M., Carroll, B. J., King, D., & Greden, J. F. (1984). The effect of dexamethasone on sleep: Preliminary results in eleven patients. *Biological Psychiatry*, *19*, 771–775.

Felten, D. L., Felten, S. Y., Bellinger, D. L., Carlson, S. L., Ackerman, K. D., Madden, K. S., Olschowki, J. A., & Livnat, S. (1987). Noradrenergic sympathetic neural interactions with the immune system: Structure and function. *Immunology Review*, *100*, 255–260.

Finkelhor, D., Hotaling, G., Lewis, I. A., & Smith, C.

(1990). Sexual abuse in a national survey of adult men and women: Prevalence characteristics and risk factors. *Child Abuse and Neglect*, *14*, 19–28.

Ford, D. E., & Kamerow, D, B. (1990). Epidemiologic study of sleep disturbances and psychiatric disorders: An opportunity for prevention? *Journal of the American Medical Association*, *262*, 1479–1484.

Free, M. L., & Oei, T. P. S. (1989). Biological and psychological processes in the treatment and maintenance of depression. *Clinical Psychology Review*, *9*, 653–688.

Friston, K. J., Sharpley, A. L., Solomon, R. A., & Cowen, P. J. (1989). Lithium increases slow wave sleep: Possible mediation by brain 5-HT$_2$ receptors? *Psychopharmacology*, *98*, 139–140.

Gaist, P. A., Obarzanek, E., Skwerer, R. G., Duncan, C. C., Shultz, P. M., & Rosenthal, N. E. (1990). Effects of bright light on resting metabolic rate in patients with seasonal affective disorder and control subjects. *Biological Psychiatry*, *28*, 989–996.

Ganguli, R., Reynolds, C. F., & Kupfer, D. J. (1987). Electroencephalographic sleep in young never-medicated schizophrenics. *Archives of General Psychiatry*, *44*, 36–44.

Garattini, S., & Samanin, R. (1988). Biochemical hypotheses on antidepressant drugs: A guide for clinicians or a toy for pharmacologists? *Psychological Medicine*, *18*, 287–304.

Garber, H. J., Weilburg, J. B., Buonanno, F. S., Manschreck, T. C., & New, P. F. J. (1988). Use of magnetic resonance imaging in psychiatry. *American Journal of Psychiatry*, *145*, 164–171.

Georgotas, A., McCue, R. E., Friedman, E., Hapworth, W. E., Kim, O. M., Cooper, T. B., Chang, I., & Stokes, P. E. (1986). Relationship of platelet MAO activity to characteristics of major depressive illness. *Psychiatry Research*, *19*, 247–256.

Gibbons, R. D., & Davis, J. M. (1986). Consistent evidence for a biological subtype of depression characterized by low CSF monoamine levels. *Acta Psychiatrica Scandinavica*, *74*, 8–12.

Giles, D. E., Jarrett, R. B., Roffwarg, H. P., & Rush, A. J. (1987). Reduced REM latency: A predictor of recurrence in depression. *Neuropsychopharmacology*, *1*, 33–39.

Giles, D. E., Jarrett, R. B., Rush, A. J., Biggs, M. M., & Roffwarg, H. P. (1993). Prospective assessment of electroencephalographic sleep in remitted major depression. *Psychiatry Research*, *46*, 269–284.

Giles, D. E., Roffwarg, H. P., Kupfer, D. J., Rush, A. J., Biggs, M. M., & Etzel, B. A. (1989). Secular trend in unipolar depression: A hypothesis. *Journal of Affective Disorders*, *16*, 71–75.

Giles, D. E., Roffwarg, H. P., Schlesser, M. A., & Rush, A. J. (1986). Which endogenous depressive symptoms relate to REM latency reduction? *Biological Psychiatry*, *21*, 473–482.

Giles, D. E., Schlesser, M. A., Rush, A. J., Orsulak, P. J., Fulton, C. L., & Roffwarg, H. P. (1987b). Polysomnographic findings and dexamethasone nonsuppression in depression: A replication and extension. *Biological Psychiatry*, *22*, 872–882.

Gillespie, R. D. (1929). The clinical differentiation of types of depression. *Guy's Hospital Reports*, *79*, 306–344.

Gillin, J. C., & Borbely, A. A. (1985). Sleep: A neurobiological window on affective disorders. *Trends in Neuroscience*, *8*, 537–542.

Gillin, J. C., Smith, T. L., Irwin, M., Kripke, D. F., Brown, S., & Schuckit, M. (1990). Short REM latency in primary alcoholic patients with secondary depression. *American Journal of Psychiatry*, *147*, 106–109.

Gillin, J. C., Sutton, L., Ruiz, C., Kelsoe, J., Dupont, R. M., Darko, D., Risch, S. C., Golshan, S., & Janowsky, D. (1991). The cholinergic rapid eye movement induction tests with arecoline in depression. *Archives of General Psychiatry*, *48*, 264–270.

Gjerris, A., Werdelin, L., Rafaelsen, O. J., Alling, C., & Christensen, N. J. (1987). CSF dopamine increased in depression: CSF dopamine noradrenaline and their metabolites in depressed patients and in controls. *Journal of Affective Disorders*, *13*, 279–286.

Glassman, A. H. (1969). Indoleamines and affective disorders. *Psychomatic Medicine*, *31*, 107–114.

Goetz, R. R., Puig-Antich, J., Ryan, N., Rabinovich, H., Ambrosini, P. J., Nelson, B., & Krawiec, V. (1987). Electroencephalographic sleep of adolescents with major depression and normal controls. *Archives of General Psychiatry*, *44*, 61–68.

Gold, M. S., & Pottash, A. L. C. (1983). Thyroid dysfunction or depression? In F. J. Ayd, I. J. Taylor, & B. T. Taylor (Eds.), *Affective disorders reassessed* (pp. 179–191). Baltimore: Ayd Medical Communications.

Gold, P. W., Goodwin, F. K., & Chrousos, G. P. (1988). Clinical and biochemical manifestations of depression: Part 2. Relation to the neurobiology of stress. *New England Journal of Medicine*, *319*, 413–420.

Gold, P. W., & Rubinow, D. R. (1987). Neuropeptide function in affective illness: Corticotropin-releasing hormone and somatostatin as model systems. In: H. Y. Meltzer (Ed.), *Psychopharmacology: The third generation of progress* (pp. 617–627). New York: Raven Press.

Golden, R. N., De Vane, C. L., Laizure, S. C., Rudorfer, M. V., Sherer, M. A., & Potter, W. Z. (1988a). Bupropion in depression. II. Role of metabolites in clinical outcome. *Archives of General Psychiatry*, *45*, 145–149.

Golden, R. N., Gilmore, J. H. (1990). Serotonin and mood disorders. *Psychiatric Annals*, *20*, 580–586.

Golden, R. N., Markey, S. P., Risby, E. D., Rudorfer, M. V., Cowdry, R. W., & Potter, W. Z. (1988b). Antidepressants reduce whole-body norepinephrine turnover while enhancing, 6-hydroxymelatonin output. *Archives of General Psychiatry*, *45*, 150–154.

Goodnick, P. J., & Extein, I. L. (1989). Bupropion and fluoxetine in depressive subtypes. *Annals of Clinical Psychiatry*, *1*, 119–122.

Goodwin, F. K., & Jamison, K. R. (1990). *Manic–depressive illness*. New York: Oxford University Press.

Goodwin, F. K., & Post, R. M. (1975). Studies of amine metabolites in affective illness and in schizophrenia. In D. X. Freedman (Ed.), *Biology of the major psychoses* (pp. 299–332). New York: Raven Press.

Goodyer, I., Herbert, J., Moor, S., & Altham, P. (1991). Cortisol hypersecretion in depressed school-aged children and adolescents. *Psychiatry Research*, *37*, 237–244.

Grasby, P. M., & Cowen P, J. (1987). The pineal and psychiatry: Still fumbling in the dark? *Psychological Medicine*, *17*, 817–820.

Gray, J. A. (1991). Neural systems emotion and personality. In J. Madden IV (Ed.), *Neurobiology of learning, emotion, and affect* (pp. 273–306). New York: Raven Press.

Greden, J. F., Gardner, R., King, D., Grunhaus, L., Carroll, B. J., & Kronfol, Z. (1983). Dexamethasone suppression test in antidepressant treatment of melancholia. *Archives of General Psychiatry*, *40*, 493–500.

Greden, J. F., Genero, N., Price, L., Feinberg, M., & Levine, S. (1986). Facial electromyography in depression. *Archives of General Psychiatry, 43,* 269–274.

Greenberg, L., Edwards, E., & Henn, F. A. (1989). Dexamethasone suppression test in helpless rats. *Biological Psychiatry, 26,* 530–532.

Gross-Isseroff, R., Dillon, K. A., Fieldust, S. J., & Biegon, A. (1990). Autoradiographic analysis of α₁-noradrenergic receptors in the human brain postmortem: Effect of suicide. *Archives of General Psychiatry, 47,* 1049–1053.

Gross-Isseroff, R., Israeli, M., & Biegon, A. (1989). Autoradiographic analysis of tritiated imipramine binding in the human brain postmortem: Effects of suicide. *Archives of General Psychiatry, 46,* 237–241.

Guicheney, P., Leger, D., Barrat, J., Treveux, R., De Lignieres, B., Roques, P., Garnier, J. P., Boyer, P., Grenier, J., & Dreux, C. (1988). Platelet serotonin content and plasma tryptophan in peri- and postmenopausal women: Variations with plasma oestrogen levels and depressive symptoms. *European Journal of Clinical Investigations, 18,* 294–304.

Gur, R. C., Erwin, R. J., & Gur, R. E. (1990). Neurobehavioral probes for physiologic neuroimaging studies. *Archives of General Psychiatry, 49,* 409–414.

Halbreich, U., Rojansky, N., Zander, K. J., & Barkai, A. (1991). Influence of age, sex, and diurnal variability on imipramine receptor binding and serotonin uptake in platelets of normal subjects. *Journal of Psychiatric Research, 25,* 7–18.

Hale, A. S., Sandler, M., Hannah, P., & Bridges, P. K. (1989). Tyramine conjugation test for prediction of treatment response in depressed patients. *Lancet, 1,* 234–236.

Hale, A. S., Sandler, M., Hannah, P., Glover, V., & Bridges, P. K. (1991). Tyramine conjugation test distinguishes unipolar from bipolar depressed patients and controls. *Journal of Psychiatric Research, 25*(4), 185–190.

Hallonquist, J. D., Goldberg, M. A., & Brandes, J. S. (1986). Affective disorders and circadian rhythms. *Canadian Journal of Psychiatry, 31,* 259–272.

Halper, J. P., Brown, R. P., Sweeney, J. A., Kocsis, J. H., Peters, A., & Mann, J. J. (1988). Blunted β-adrenergic responsivity of peripheral blood mononuclear cells in endogenous depression: Isoproterenol dose–response studies. *Archives of General Psychiatry, 45,* 241–244.

Harrison, W. M., Cooper, T. B., Stewart, J. W., Quitkin, F. M., McGrath, P. J., Liebowitz, M. R., Rabkin, J. R., Markowitz, J. S., & Klein, D. F. (1984). The tyramine challenge test as a marker for melancholia. *Archives of General Psychiatry, 41,* 681–685.

Haskett, R. F. (1993). The HPA axis and depressive disorders. In J. J. Mann & D. J. Kupfer (Eds.), *Biology of depressive disorders: Part A. A systems perspective* (pp. 171–188). New York: Plenum Press.

Hawkins, D. R., Taub, J. M., & Van de Castle, R. L. (1985). Extended sleep (hypersomnia) in young depressed patients. *American Journal of Psychiatry, 142,* 905–910.

Healy, D. (1987). Rhythms and blues: Neurochemical neuropharmacological and neuropsychological implications of a hypothesis of circadian rhythm dysfunction in the affective disorders. *Psychopharmacology, 93,* 271–285.

Healy, D., & Williams, J. M. G. (1988). Dysrhythmia dysphoria and depression: The interaction of learned helplessness and circadian dysrhythmia in the pathogenesis of depression. *Psychological Bulletin, 103,* 163–178.

Heinrich, P. C., Castell, J. V., & Andus, T. (1990). Review article: Interleukin-6 and the acute phase response. *Biochemical Journal, 265,* 621–636.

Hendrickse, W. A., Roffwarg, H. P., Grannemann, B. D., Orsulak, P. J., Armitage, R., Cain, J. W., Battaglia, J., Debus, J. R., & Rush, A. J. (1994). The effects of fluoxetine on the polysomnogram of depressed outpatients: A pilot study. *Neuropsychopharmacology, 10,* 85–91.

Heninger, G. R., Charney, D. S., & Sternberg, D. E. (1984). Serotonergic function in depression. *Archives of General Psychiatry, 41,* 398–402.

Hickie, I., Hickie, C., Lloyd, A., Silove, D., & Wakefield, D. (1993). Impaired *in vivo* immune responses in patients with melancholia. *British Journal of Psychiatry, 162,* 651–657.

Higley, J. D., Mehlman, P. T., Taub, D. M., Higley, S. B., Suomi, S. J., Linnoila, M., & Vickers J, H. (1992a). Cerebrospinal fluid monoamine and adrenal correlates of aggression in free-ranging rhesus monkeys. *Archives of General Psychiatry, 49,* 436–441.

Higley, J. D., Suomi, S. J., & Linnoila, M. (1992b). A longitudinal assessment of CSF monoamine metabolite and plasma cortisol concentrations in young rhesus monkeys. *Biological Psychiatry, 32,* 127–145.

Himmelhoch, J. M., Thase, M. E., Mallinger, A. G., & Houck, P. (1991). Tranylcypromine versus imipramine in anergic bipolar depression. *American Journal of Psychiatry, 148,* 910–916.

Holsboer, F. (1992). The hypothalamic–pituitary–adrenocortical system. In E. S. Paykel (Ed.), *Handbook of affective disorders* (2nd ed., pp. 267–287). New York: Guilford Press.

Holsboer, F. (1988). Implications of altered limbic–hypothalamic–pituitary–adrenocortical (LHPA)-function for neurobiology of depression. *Acta Psychiatrica Scandinavica* (Supp. 341), 72–111.

Horne, J. A. (1993). Human sleep loss and behavior implications for the prefrontal cortex and psychiatric disorder. *British Journal of Psychiatry, 162,* 413–419.

Howland, R. H., & Thase, M. E. (1991). Biological studies of dysthymia. *Biological Psychiatry, 30,* 283–304.

Howland, R. H., & Thase, M. E. (1993). A comprehensive review of cyclothymic disorder. *Journal of Nervous and Mental Disease, 181,* 485–493.

Hrdina, P. D. (1989). Differences between sodium-dependent and desipramine defined, 3H-imipramine binding in intact human platelets. *Biological Psychiatry, 25,* 576–584.

Hsiao, J. K., Agren, H., Bartko, J. J., Rudorfer, M. V., Linnoila, M., & Potter, W. Z. (1987). Monoamine neurotransmitter interactions and the prediction of antidepressant response. *Archives of General Psychiatry, 44,* 1078–1083.

Hudson, J. I., Lipinski, J. F., Keck, P. E., Jr., Aizley, H. G., Lukas, S. E., Rothschild, A. J., Waternaux, C. M., & Kupfer, D. J. (1992). Polysomnographic characteristics of young manic patients: Comparison with unipolar depressed patients and normal control subjects. *Archives of General Psychiatry, 49,* 378–383.

Hudson, J. I., Lipinski, J. F., Keck, P. E., Aizley, H. G., Vuckovic, A., Zierk, K. C., & Pope, H. G. (1993). Polysomnographic characteristics of schizophrenia in comparison with mania and depression. *Biological Psychiatry, 34,* 191–193.

Hurt, S. W., Schnurr, P. P., Severino, S. K., Freeman, E. W., Gise, L. H., Rivera-Tovar, A., & Steege, J. F. (1992). Late luteal phase dysphoric disorder in 670 women evaluated for premenstrual complaints. *American Journal of Psychiatry*, 149, 525–530.

Huston, P. E., & Locher, L. M. (1948). Manic–depressive psychosis: Course when treated and untreated with electric shock. *Archives of Neurology and Psychiatry*, 50, 37–48.

Insel, T, R. (1991). Long-term neural consequences of stress during development: Is early experience a form of chemical imprinting? In B. J. Carroll & J. E. Barrett (Eds.), *Psychopathology and the brain* (pp. 133–152). New York: Raven Press.

Insel, T. R., Gillin, J. C., Moore, A., Mendelson, W. B., Loewenstein, R. J., & Murphy, D. L. (1982). The sleep of patients with obsessive–compulsive disorder. *Archives of General Psychiatry*, 39:1372–1377.

Jackson, S. W. (1986). *Melancholia and depression from Hippocratic times to modern times*. New Haven: Yale University Press.

Jacobs, B. L. (1991). Serotonin and behavior: Emphasis on motor control. *Journal of Clinical Psychiatry*, 52(12), 17–23.

Jaeckle, R. S., Kathol, R. G., Lopez, J. F., Meller, M. H., & Krummel, S. J. (1987). Enhanced adrenal sensitivity to exogenous cosyntropin (ACTH α^{1-24}) stimulation in major depression: Relationship to dexamethasone suppression test results. *Archives of General Psychiatry*, 44, 233–240.

Janowsky, D. S., Risch, S. C., & Gillin, J. C. (1983). Adrenergic–cholinergic balance and the treatment of affective disorders. *Progress in Neuropsychopharmacology* and *Biological Psychiatry*, 7, 297–307.

Jarrett, D. B., Greenhouse, J. B., Coble, P., & Kupfer, D. J. (1986). Sleep-EEG and neuroendocrine secretion in depression. In C. Shagass, R. C. Josiassen, W. H. Bridger, K. J. Weiss, D. Stoff, & G. M. Simpson (Eds.), *Biological psychiatry 1985* (pp. 966–968): *Proceedings of the IVth World Congress of Biological Psychiatry*. New York: Elsevier.

Jarrett, D. B., Miewald, J. M., Fedorka, I. B., Coble, P., Kupfer, D. J., & Greenhouse, J. B. (1987). Prolactin secretion during sleep: A comparison between depressed patients and healthy control subjects. *Biological Psychiatry*, 22, 1216–1226.

Jarrett, D. B., Miewald, J. M., & Kupfer, D. J. (1990). Recurrent depression is associated with a persistent reduction in sleep-related growth hormone secretion. *Archives of General Psychiatry*, 47, 113–118.

Jarrett, R. B. (1990). Psychosocial aspects of depression and the role of psychotherapy. *Journal of Clinical Psychiatry*, 51, 26–35.

Jarrett, R. B., Eaves, G. G., Grannenmann, B. D., & Rush, A. J. (1991). Clinical, cognitive, and demographic predictors of response to congitive therapy for depression: A preliminary report. *Psychiatry Research*, 37, 245–260.

Jesberger, J. A., & Richardson, J. S. (1985). Neurochemical aspects of depression: The past and the future? *International Journal of Neuroscience*, 27, 19–47.

Jimerson, D. C. (1987). Role of dopamine mechanisms in the affective disorders. In H. Y. Meltzer (Ed.), *Psychopharmacology: The third generation of progress* (pp. 505–511). New York: Raven Press.

Jimerson, D. C., Insel, T. R., Reyus, V. I., & Kopin, I. J. (1983). Increased plasma MHPG in dexamethasone-resistant depressed patients. *Archives of General Psychiatry*, 40, 173–176.

Jones, J. S., Stanley, B., Mann, J. J., Frances, A. J., Guido, J. R., Traskman-Bendz, L., Winchel, R., Brown, R. P., & Stanley, M. (1990). CSF 5-HIAA and HVA concentrations in elderly depressed patients who attempted suicide. *American Journal of Psychiatry*, 147(9), 1225–1227.

Kagan, J., Reznick, J. S., & Snidman, N. (1987). The physiology and psychology of behavioral inhibition in children. *Child Development*, 58, 1459–1473.

Kaitin, K. I., Bliwise, D. L., Gleason, C., Nino-Murcia, G., Dement, W. C., & Libet, B. (1986). Sleep disturbance produced by electrical stimulation of the locus coeruleus in a human subject. *Biological Psychiatry*, 21, 710–716.

Kandel, E. R., Schwarz, J. H., & Jessell, T. M. (Eds.). (1991). *Principles of neural science* (3rd ed.). New York: Elsevier.

Kapur, S., & Mann, J. J. (1992). Role of the dopaminergic system in depression. *Biological Psychiatry*, 32, 1–17.

Katona, C. L. E., Theodorou, A. E., & Horton, R. W. (1987). Alpha-2-adrenoceptors in depression. *Psychiatric Developments*, 2, 129–149.

Keller, F., Wolfersdorf, M., Straub, R., & Hole, G. (1991). Suicidal behaviour and electrodermal activity in depressive inpatients. *Acta Psychiatrica Scandinavica*, 83, 324–328.

Kellner, C. H., Rubinow, D. R., & Post, R. M. (1986). Cerebral ventricular size and cognitive impairment in depression. *Journal of Affective Disorders*, 10, 215–219.

Kelwala, S., Jones, D., & Sitaram, N. (1983). Monoamine metabolites as predictors of antidepressant response: A critique. *Progress in Neuropsychopharmacology* and *Biological Psychiatry*, 7, 229–240.

Kendler, K. S., Kessler, R. C., Neale, M. C., Heath, A. C., & Eaves, L. J. (1993). The prediction of major depression in women: Toward an integrated etiologic model. *American Journal of Psychiatry*, 150, 1139–1148.

Kerkhofs, M., Missa, J.-N., & Mendlewicz, J. (1986). Sleep electroencephalographic measures in primary major depressive disorders: Distinction between DST suppressor and nonsuppressor patients. *Biological Psychiatry*, 21, 228–232.

Keshavan, M. S., Kapur, S., & Pettegrew, J. W. (1991). Magnetic resonance spectroscopy in psychiatry: Potential pitfalls and promise. *American Journal of Psychiatry*, 148, 976–985.

Kessler, R. C., Brown, R. L., & Broman, C. L. (1981). Sex differences in psychiatric help-seeking: Evidence from four large-scale surveys. *Journal of Health and Social Behavior*, 22, 49–64.

Klein, D. F. (1974). Endogenomorphic depression—A conceptual and terminological revision. *Archives of General Psychiatry*, 31, 447–454.

Kocsis, J. H. (1993). DSM-IV "major depression": Are more stringent criteria needed? *Depression*, 1, 24–28.

Kofman, O., & Belmaker, R. H. (1993). Biochemical, behavioral, and clinical studies of the role of inositol in lithium treatment and depression. *Biological Psychiatry*, 34, 839–852.

Kraepelin, E. (1921). Manic depressive insanity and paranoia. Edinburgh: Livingstone.

Kramer, M. (1993). The selective mood regulatory function of dreaming: An update and revision. In A. R. Moffitt, M. Kramer, & R. F. Hoffman (Eds.), *The function of dreaming* (pp. 139–195). Albany: State University of New York Press.

Krieg, J. C., Lauer, C., Hermle, L., von Bardeleben, U.,

Pollmächer, T., & Holsboer, F. (1990). Psychometric polysomnographic and neuroendocrine measures in subjects at high risk for psychiatric disorders: Preliminary results. *Neuropsychobiology, 23,* 57–67.

Krishnan, K. R. R., Manepalli, A. N., Ritchie, J. C., Rayasam, K., Melville, M. L., Daughtry, G., Thorner, M. O., Rivier, J. E., Vale, W. W., Nemeroff, C. B., & Carroll, B. J. (1988). Growth hormone-releasing factor stimulation test in depression. *American Journal of Psychiatry, 145,* 90–92.

Krishnan, K. R. R., McDonald, W. M., Escalona, P. R., Doraiswamy, P. M., Na, C., Husain, M. M., Figiel, G. S., Boyko, O. B., Ellinwood, E. H., & Nemeroff, C. B. (1992). Magnetic resonance of the caudate nuclei in depression. *Archives of General Psychiatry, 49,* 553–557.

Kronfol, Z., House, J. D., Silva, J., Greden, J., & Carroll, B. J. (1986). Depression, urinary free cortisol secretion and lymphocyte function. *British Journal of Psychiatry, 148,* 70–73.

Kronfol, Z., Nasrallah, H. A., Chapman, S., & House, J. D. (1985). Depression, cortisol metabolism and lymphocytopenia. *Journal of Affective Disorders, 9,* 169–173.

Kuhn, R. (1958). The treatment of depressive states with G-22355 (imipramine hydrochloride). *American Journal of Psychiatry, 115,* 459–464.

Kuhs, H., Schlake, H.-P., Rolf, L. H., & Rudolf, G. A. E. (1992). Relationship between parameters of serotonin transport and antidepressant plasma levels or therapeutic response in depressive patients treated with paroxetine and amitriptyline. *Acta Psychiatrica Scandinavica, 85,* 364–369.

Kumar, A., Mozley, D., Dunham, C., Velchik, M., Reilley, J., & Gottlieb, G. (1991). Semiquantitative I-123 IMP SPECT studies in late onset depression before and after treatment. *International Journal of Geriatric Psychiatry, 6,* 775–777.

Kumar, A., Shipley, J. E., Eiser, A. S., Feinberg, M., Flegel, P., Grunhaus, L., & Haskett, R. F. (1987). Clinical correlates of sleep onset REM periods in depression. *Biological Psychiatry, 22,* 1473–1477.

Kupfer, D. J., & Ehlers, C. L. (1989). Two roads to REM latency. *Archives of General Psychiatry, 46,* 945–948.

Kupfer, D. J., Ehlers, C. L., Frank, E., Grochocinski, V. J., & McEachran, A. B. (1991). EEG sleep profiles and recurrent depression. *Biological Psychiatry, 30,* 641–655.

Kupfer, D. J., Ehlers, C. L., Frank, E., Grochocinski, V. J., McEachran, A. B., & Buhari, A. (1993). EEG sleep studies in depressed patients during long-term recovery. *Psychiatry Research, 49,* 121–138.

Kupfer, D. J., Ehlers, C. L., Frank, E., Grochocinski, V. J., McEachran, A. B., & Buhari, A. (1994). Persistent effects of antidepressants: EEG sleep studies in depressed patients during maintenance treatment. *Biological Psychiatry, 35,* 781–793.

Kupfer, D. J., & Frank, E. (1989). EEG sleep changes in recurrent depression. In B. Lerer & S. Gershon (Eds.), *New directions in affective disorders* (pp. 225–228). New York: Springer-Verlag.

Kupfer, D. J., Frank, E., Grochocinski, V. J., Gregor, M., & McEachran, A. B. (1988). Electroencephalographic sleep profiles in recurrent depression: A logitudinal investigation. *Archives of General Psychiatry, 45,* 678–681.

Kupfer, D. J., Frank, E., McEachran, A. B., & Grochocinski. V. J. (1990). Delta sleep ratio: A biological correlate of early recurrence in unipolar affective disorder. *Archives of General Psychiatry, 47,* 1100–1105.

Kupfer, D. J., Perel, J. M., Pollock, B. G., Nathan, R. S., Grochocinski, V. J., Wilson, M. J., & McEachran, A. B. (1991). Fluvoxamine versus desipramine: Comparative polysomnographic effects. *Biological Psychiatry, 29,* 23–40.

Kupfer, D. J., Pickar, D., Himmelhoch, J. M., & Detre, T. P. (1975). Are there two types of unipolar depression? *Archives of General Psychiatry, 32,* 866–871.

Kupfer, D. J., Reynolds, C. F., III, Weiss, B. L., & Foster, F. G. (1974). Lithium carbonate and sleep in affective disorders. *Archives of General Psychiatry, 30,* 79–84.

Kupfer, D. J., Targ, E., & Stack, J. (1982). Electroencephalographic sleep in unipolar depressive subtypes: Support for a biological and familial classification. *Journal of Nervous and Mental Disease, 170,* 494–498.

Kupfer, D. J., & Thase, M. E. (1983). The use of the sleep laboratory in the diagnosis of affective disorders. *Psychiatric Clinics of North America, 5,* 3–25.

Kupfer, D. J., & Thase, M. E. (1987). Validity of major depression: A psychobiological perspective. In G. L. Tischler (Ed.), *Diagnostic and classification in psychiatry: A critical appraisal of DSM-III* (pp. 32–60). New York: Cambridge University Press.

Kupfer, D. J., & Thase M, E. (1989). Laboratory studies and validity of psychiatric diagnosis: Has there been progress? In L. N. Robins & J. E. Barrett (Eds.), *Validity of psychiatric diagnosis* (pp. 177–201). New York: Raven Press.

Langer, G., Aschauer, H., Koing, G., Resch, F., & Schonbeck, G. (1983). The TSH response to TRH: A possible predictor of outcome to antidepressant and neuroleptic treatment. *Progress in Neuropsychopharmacology and Biological Psychiatry, 7,* 335–352.

Langer, S. Z., Sechter, D., Loo, H., Raisman, R., & Zarifian, E. (1986). Electroconvulsive shock therapy and maximum binding of platelet titrated imipramine binding in depression. *Archives of General Psychiatry, 43,* 949–952.

Lauer, C. J., & Pollmächer, T. (1992). On the issue of drug washout prior to polysomnographic studies in depressed patients. *Neuropsychopharmacology, 6*(1), 11–16.

Lauer, C. J., Riemann, D., Wiegand, M., & Berger, M. (1991). From early to late adulthood changes in EEG sleep of depressed patients and healthy volunteers. *Biological Psychiatry, 29,* 979–993.

Lee, J. H., Reynolds, C. F., III, Hoch, C. C., Buysse, D. J., Mazumdar, S., George, C. J., & Kupfer, D. J. (1993). Electroencephalographic sleep in recently remitted elderly depressed patients in double-blind placebo-maintenance therapy. *Neuropsychopharmacology, 8,* 143–150.

Leong, S. S., & Brown, W. A. (1987). Acetylcholine and affective disorder. *Journal of Neural Transmission, 70,* 295–312.

Lesch, K.-P., Laux, G., Erb, A., Pfüller, H., & Beckmann, H. (1987). Attenuated growth hormone response to growth hormone-releasing hormone in major depressive disorder. *Biological Psychiatry, 22,* 1491–1495.

Lesch, K.-P., Laux, G., Schulte, H. M., Pfüller, H., & Beckmann, H. (1988a). Abnormal responsiveness of growth hormone to human corticotropin-releasing hormone in major depressive disorder. *Journal of Affective Disorders, 14,* 245–250.

Lesch, K.-P., Widerlöv, E., Ekman, R., Laux, G., Schulte, H. M., Pfüller, H., & Beckmann, H. (1988b). Delta sleep-inducing peptide response to human corticotropin-releasing hormone (CRH) in major depressive disorder: Comparison with CRH-induced corticotropin and cortisol secretion. *Biological Psychiatry, 24*, 162–172.

Lewy, A. J., Sack, R. L., Miller, L. S., & Toban, T. M. (1987). Antidepressant and circadian phase-shifting effects of light. *Science, 235*, 352–354.

Lewis, D. A., McChesney, C. (1985). Tritiated imipramine binding distinguishes among subtypes of depression. *Archives of General Psychiatry, 42*, 485–488.

Linkowski, P., & Mendlewicz, J. (1993). Sleep electroencephalogram and rhythm disturbances in mood disorders. *Current Opinion in Psychiatry, 6*, 35–37.

Linkowski, P., Kerkhofs, M., Hauspie, R., & Mendlewicz, J. (1991). Genetic determinants of EEG sleep: A study in twins living apart. *Electroencephalography and Clinical Neurophysiology, 79*, 114–118.

Linkowski, P., Kerhofs, M., Rielaert, C., & Mendlewicz, J. (1986). Sleep during mania in manic–depressive males. *European Archives of Psychiatry and Neurological Sciences, 6*, 339–341.

Linnoila, M., Miller, T. L., Bartko, J., & Potter, W. Z. (1984). Five antidepressant treatments in depressed patients. *Archives of General Psychiatry, 41*, 688–692.

Linnoila, V. M., & Virkkunen, M. (1992). Aggression suicidality and serotonin. *Journal of Clinical Psychiatry, 53*, 46–51.

Linnoila, V. M., Whorton, A. R., Rubinow, D. R., Cowdry, R., Ninan, P. T., & Waters, R. N. (1983). CSF prostaglandin levels in depressed and schizophrenic patients. *Archives of General Psychiatry, 40*, 405–406.

Lisansky, J., Fava, G. A., Zielezny, M. A., Morphy, M. A., Kellner, R. (1987). Nocturnal prolactin and cortisol secretion and recovery from melancholia. *Psychoneuroendocrinology, 12*, 303–311.

Lloyd, K. G., Morselli, P. L., & Bartholini, G. (1987). GABA and affective disorders. *Medical Biology, 65*, 159–165.

London, E. D., Cascella, N. G., Wong, D. F., Phillips, R. L., Dannals, R. F., Links, J. M., Herning, R., Grayson, R., Jaffe, J. H., & Wagner, H. N. (1990). Cocaine-induced reduction of glucose utilization in human brain. *Archives of General Psychiatry, 47*, 567–574.

Loomer, H. P., Saunders, J. C., & Kline, N. S. (1958). A clinical and pharmacodynamic evaluation of iproniazid as a psychic energizer. *American Psychiatric Association Research Reports, 8*, 329.

Loosen, P. T. (1988). Thyroid function in affective disorders and alcoholism. *Endocrinology and Metabolism Clinics of North America, 17*, 55–82.

Loosen, P. T., & Prange, A. J. (1982). The serum thyrotropin response to thyrotropin-releasing hormone in psychiatric patients: A review. *American Journal of Psychiatry, 139*, 405–416.

Lundquist, G. (1945). Prognosis and course in manic–depressive psychoses: A follow-up study of 319 first admissions. *Acta Psychiatrica et Neurologica, 35* (Suppl. 1), 1–96.

Maas, J. W. (1975). Biogenic amines and depression: Biochemical and pharmacological separation on two types of depression. *Archives of General Psychiatry, 32*, 1357–1361.

Maas, J. W., Koslow, S. H., Davis, J., Katz, M., Frazer, A., Bowden, C. L., Berman, N., Gibbons, R., Stokes, P., &

Landis, D. H. (1987). Catecholamine metabolism and disposition in healthy and depressed subjects. *Archives of General Psychiatry, 44*, 337–344.

Maas, J. W., Koslow, S. H., Katz, M. M., Gibbons, R. L., Bowden, C. L., Robins, E., & Davis, J. M. (1984). Pretreatment neurotransmitter metabolites and tricyclic antidepressant drug response. *American Journal of Psychiatry, 141*, 1159–1171.

MacDonald, E., Rubinow, D., & Linnoila, M. (1984). Sensitivity of RBC membrane Ca^{2+}-adenosine triphosphatase to calmodulin stimulation. *Archives of General Psychiatry, 41*, 487–493.

Maes, M., Bosmans, E., & Suy, E. (1990). Impaired lymphocyte stimulation by mitogens in severely depressed patients: A complex interface with HPA-axis hyperfunction, noradrenergic activity and the ageing process. *British Journal of Psychiatry, 155*, 793–798.

Maes, M., Dierckx, R., Meltzer, H. Y., Ingels, M., Schotte, C., Vandewoude, M., Calabrese, J., & Cosyns, P. (1993). Regional cerebral blood flow in unipolar depression measured with Tc-99m-HMPAO single photon emission computed tomography: negative findings. *Psychiatry Research: Neuroimaging, 50*, 77–88.

Maes, M., Meltzer, H. Y., Stevens, W., Cosyns, P., Blockx, P. (1994). Multiple reciprocal relationships between *in vivo* cellular immunity and hypothalamic–pituitary–adrenal axis in depression. *Psychological Medicine, 24*, 167–177.

Maes, M., Vandervorst, C., Suy, E., Minner, B., & Raus, J. (1991). A multivariate study of simultaneous escape from suppression by dexamethasone of urinary free cortisol, plasma cortisol, adrenocorticotropic hormone and β-endorphin in melancholic patients. *Acta Psychiatrica Scandinavica, 83*, 480–491.

Maguire, K., Tuckwell, V., Pereira, A., Dean, B., Singh, B. (1993). Significant correlation between, 14C-5-HT uptake by and 3H-paroxetine binding to platelets from healthy volunteers. *Biological Psychiatry, 34*, 356–360.

Maier S, F. (1991). Stressor controllability cognition and fear. In J. Madden IV (Ed.), *Neurobiology of learning, emotion, and affect* (pp. 155–193). New York: Raven Press.

Malone, K., & Mann, J. J. (1993). Serotonin and major depression. In J. J. Mann & D. J. Kupfer (Eds.), *Biology of depressive disorders: Part A. A systems perspective* (pp. 29–49). New York: Plenum Press.

Malone, K. M., Thase, M. E., Mieczkowski, T., Myers, J. E., Stull, S. D., Cooper, T. B., & Mann, J. J. (1993). Fenfluramine challenge test as a predictor of outcome in major depression. *Psychopharmacology Bulletin, 29*, 155–161.

Mann, J. J., Aarons, S. F., Wilner, P. J., Keilp, J. G., Sweeney, J. A., Pearlstein, T., Frances, A. J., Kocsis, J. H., & Brown, R. P. (1989). A controlled study of the antidepressant efficacy and side effects of (−)-deprenyl: A selective monoamine oxidase inhibitor. *Archives of General Psychiatry, 46*, 45–50.

Mann, J. J., Mahler, J. C., Wilner, P. J., Halper, J. P., Brown, R. P., Johnson, K. S., Kocsis, J. H., & Chen, J.-S. (1990). Normalization of blunted lymphocyte β-adrenergic responsivity in melancholic inpatients by a course of electroconvulsive therapy. *Archives of General Psychiatry, 47*, 461–464.

Mann, J. J., McBride, A., Anderson, G. M., & Mieczkowski, T. A. (1992a). Platelet and whole blood serotonin content in depressed inpatients: Correlations with acute and life-time psychopathology. *Biological Psychiatry, 32*, 243–257.

Mann, J. J., McBride, A., Brown, R. P., Linnoila, M., Leon, A. C., DeMeo, M., Mieczowski, T., Myers, J. E., & Stanley, M. (1992b). Relationship between central and peripheral serotonin indexes in depressed and suicidal psychiatric inpatients. *Archives of General Psychiatry*, 49, 442–446.

Mann, J. J., Stanley, M., McBride, A., & McEwen, B. S. (1986). Increased serotonin$_2$ and β-adrenergic receptor binding in the frontal cortices of suicide victims. *Archives of General Psychiatry*, 43, 954–959.

Marazziti, D., Perugi, G., Deltito, J., Lenzi, A., Maremmani, I., Placidi, G. F., & Cassano, G. B. (1988). High-affinity ^{3}H-imipramine binding sites: A possible state-dependent marker for major depression. *Psychiatry Research*, 23, 229–237.

Martinot, J.-L., Hardy, P., Feline, A., Huret, J.-D., Mazoyer, B., Attar-Levy, D., Pappata, S., & Syrota, A. (1990a). Left prefrontal glucose hypometabolism in the depressed state: A confirmation. *American Journal of Psychiatry*, 147(10), 1313–1317.

Martinot, J.-L., Peron-Magnan, P., Huren, J.-D., Mazoyer, B., Baron, J.-C., Boulenger, J.-P., Loc'h, C., Maziere, B., Caillard, V., Loo, H., & Syrota, A. (1990b). Striatal D$_2$ dopaminergic receptors assessed with positron emission tomography and [^{76}Br]bromospiperone in untreated schizophrenic patients. *American Journal of Psychiatry*, 147, 44–50.

Matuzas, W., Meltzer, H. Y., Uhlenhuth, E. H., Glass, R. M., & Tong, C. (1982). Plasma dopamine-β-hydroxylase in depressed patients. *Biological Psychiatry*, 17, 1415–1424.

Mayberg, H. S., Robinson, R. G., Wong, D. F., Parikh, R., Bolduc, P., Starkstein, S. E., Price, T., Dannals, R. F., Links, J. M., Wilson, A. A., Ravert, H. T., & Wagner, H. N. (1988). PET imaging of cortical S$_2$ serotonin receptors after stroke: Lateralized changes and relationship to depression. *American Journal of Psychiatry*, 145, 937–943.

Mazure, C. M., Bowers, M. B., Hoffman, F., Miller, K. B., & Nelson, J. C. (1987). Plasma catecholamine metabolites in subtypes of major depression. *Biological Psychiatry*, 22, 1469–1472.

Mazzola-Pomietto, P., Azorin, J. M., Tramoni, V., & Jeanningros, R. (1994). Relation between lymphocyte β-adrenergic responsivity and the severity of depressive disorders. *Biological Psychiatry*, 35, 920–925.

McBride, P. A., Brown, R. P., DeMeo, M., Keilp, J., Mieczkowski, T., & Mann, J. J. (1994). The relationship of platelet 5-HT$_2$ receptor indices to major depressive disorder, personality traits, and suicidal behavior. *Biological Psychiatry*, 35, 295–308.

McCann, U. D., Penetar, D. M., Shaham, Y., Thorne, D. R., Gillin, J. C., Sing, H. C., Thomas, M. A., & Belenky, G. (1992). Sleep deprivation and impaired cognition. Possible role of brain catecholamines. *Biological Psychiatry*, 31, 1082–1097.

McCarley, R. W. (1982). REM sleep and depression: Common neurobiological control mechanisms. *American Journal of Psychiatry*, 139, 565–570.

McDonald, W. M., Krishnan, K. R. R., Doraiswamy, P. M., & Blazer, D. G. (1991). Occurrence of subcortical hyperintensities in elderly subjects with mania. *Psychiatry Research: Neuroimaging*, 40, 211–220.

McEwen, B. S., Angulo, J., Cameron, H., Chao, H. M., Daniels, D., Gannon, M. N., Gould, E., Mendelson, S., Sakai, R., Spencer, R., & Woolley, C. (1992). Paradoxical effects of adrenal steroids on the brain: Protection versus degeneration. *Biological Psychiatry*, 31, 177–199.

McKeith, I. G., Marshall, E. F., Ferrier, I. N., Armstrong, M. M., Kennedy, W. N., Perry, R. H., Perry, E. K., & Eccleston, D. (1987). 5-HT receptor binding in postmortem brain from patients with affective disorder. *Journal of Affective Disorders*, 13, 67–74.

McKinney, W. T. (1992). Animal models. In E. S. Paykel (Ed.), *Handbook of affective disorders* (2nd ed., pp. 209–217). New York: Guilford Press.

McKnight, D. L., Nelson-Gray, R. O., & Barnhill, J. (1992). Dexamethasone suppression test and response to cognitive therapy and antidepressant medication. *Behavior Therapy*, 1, 99–111.

Mellerup, E. T., & Plenge, P. (1986). High affinity binding of 3H-imipramine and 3H-paroxetine to rat neuronal membranes. *Psychopharmacology*, 89, 436–439.

Mellerup, E. T., & Plenge, P. (1988). Imipramine binding in depression and other psychiatric conditions. *Acta Psychiatrica Scandinavica*, Suppl. 345, 61–68.

Meltzer, H. Y., Cho, H. W., Carroll, B. J., & Russo, P. (1976). Serum dopamine-β-hydroxylase activity in the affective psychoses and schizophrenia. *Archives of General Psychiatry*, 33, 585–591.

Meltzer, H. Y., & Lowy, M. T. (1987). The serotonin hypothesis of depression. In H. Y. Meltzer (Ed.), *Psychopharmacology: the third generation of progress* (pp. 513–526). New York: Raven Press.

Meltzer, H. Y., Perline, R., Tricou, B. J., Lowy, M., & Robertson, A. (1984a). Effect of 5-hydroxytryptophan on serum cortisol levels in major affective disorders. II. Relation to suicide, psychosis, and depressive symptoms. *Archives of General Psychiatry*, 41, 379–387.

Meltzer, H. Y., Umberkoman-Wiita, B., Robertson, A., Tricou, B. J., Lowy, M., & Perline, R. (1984). Effect of 5-hydroxytryptophan on serum cortisol levels in major affective disorders: I. Enhanced response in depression and mania. *Archives of General Psychiatry*, 41, 366–374.

Mendlewicz, J., & Kerkhofs, M. (1991). Sleep electroencephalography in depressive illness: A collaborative study by the World Health Organization. *British Journal of Psychiatry*, 159, 505–509.

Mendlewicz, J., Linkowski, P., Kerkhofs, M., Desmedt, D., Goldstein, J., Copinschi, G., & Van Cauter, E. (1985). Diurnal hypersecretion of growth hormone in depression. *Journal of Clinical Endocrinology and Metabolism*, 60, 505–512.

Miller, H. L., Delgado, P. L., Salomon, R. M., Licinio, J., Barr, L. C., & Charney, D. S. (1992). Acute tryptophan depletion: A method of studying antidepressant action. *Journal of Clinical Psychiatry*, 53, 28–35.

Mod, L., Rihmer, Z., Magyar, I., Arato, M., Alfoldi, A., & Bagdy, G. (1986). Serum DBH activity in psychotic vs. nonpsychotic unipolar and bipolar depression. *Psychiatry Research*, 19, 331–333.

Monk, T. H. (1993). Biological rhythms and depressive disorders. In J. J. Mann & D. J. Kupfer (Eds.), *Biology of depressive disorders: Part A. A systems perspective* (pp. 109–122). New York: Plenum Press.

Monroe, S. M., Thase, M. E., & Simons, A. D. (1992). Social factors and the psychobiology of depression: Individual differences in life stress and the rapid eye movement sleep latency. *Journal of Abnormal Psychology*, 101, 528–537.

Mountz, J. M., Modell, J. G., Wilson, M. W., Curtis, G. C., Lee, M. A., Schmaltz, S., & Kuhl, D. E. (1989). Positron emission tomographic evaluation of cerebral blood flow during state anxiety in simple phobia. *Archives in General Psychiatry, 46*, 501–504.

Mullen, P. E., Linsell, C. R., & Parker, D. (1986). Influence of sleep disruption and calorie restriction on biological markers for depression. *Lancet, ii*, 1051–1055.

Muscat, R., Sampson, D., & Wilner, P. (1990). Dopaminergic mechanism of imipramine action in an animal model of depression. *Biological Psychiatry, 28*, 223–230.

Myers, J. E., Buysse, D. J., Thase, M. E., Perel, J., Miewald, J. M., Cooper, T. B., Kupfer, D. J., & Mann, J. J. (1993). The effects of fenfluramine on sleep and prolactin in depressed inpatients: A comparison of potential indices of brain serotonergic responsivity. *Biological Psychiatry, 34*, 753–758.

Nasrallah, H. A., Coffman, J. A., & Olson S, C. (1989). Structural brain-imaging findings in affective disorders: An overview. *Journal of Neuropsychiatry: Clinical Neuroscience, 1*, 21–26.

Nemeroff, C. B. (1992). New vistas in neuropeptide research in neuropsychiatry: Focus on corticotropin-releasing factor. *Neuropsychopharmacology, 6*, 69–75.

Nemeroff, C. B., Bissette, G., Akil, H., Fink, M. (1991). Cerebrospinal fluid neuropeptides in depressed patients treated with ECT: Corticotropin-releasing factor, β-endorphin and somatostatin. *British Journal of Psychiatry, 158*, 59–63.

Nemeroff, C. B., Knight, D. L., Krishnan, K. R. R., Slotkin, T. A., Bissette, G., Melville, M. L., & Blazer, D. G. (1988a). Marked reduction in the number of platelet-tritiated imipramine binding sites in geriatric depression. *Archives of General Psychiatry, 45*, 919–923.

Nemeroff, C. B., Krishnan, K. R. R., Blazer, D. G., Knight, D. L., Benjamin, D., & Meyerson, L. R. (1990). Elevated plasma concentrations of α_1-acid glycoprotein a putative endogenous inhibitor of the tritiated imipramine binding site in depressed patients. *Archives of General Psychiatry, 47*, 337–340.

Nemeroff, C. B., Krishnan, K. R. R., Reed, D., Leder, R., Beam, C., & Dunnick, R. (1992). Adrenal gland enlargement in major depression. *Archives of General Psychiatry, 49*, 384–387.

Nemeroff, C. B., Owens, M. J., Bissette, G., Andorn, A. C., & Stanley, M. (1988b). Reduced corticotropin releasing factor binding sites in the frontal cortex of suicide victims. *Archives of General Psychiatry, 45*, 577–579.

Neylan, T. C., van Kammen, D. P., Keley, M. E., & Peters, J. L. (1992). Sleep in schizophrenic patients on and off haloperidol therapy: Clinically stable vs. relapsed patients. *Archives of General Psychiatry, 49*, 643–649.

Nielsen, D. A., Goldman, D., Virkunen, M., Tokola, R., Rawlings, R., & Linnoila, M. (1994). Suicidality and 5-hydroxyindoleacetic acid concentration associated with a tryptophan hydroxylase polymorphism. *Archives of General Psychiatry, 51*, 34–38.

Nofzinger, E. A., Buysse, D. J., Reynolds, C. F., III, & Kupfer, D. J. (1993a). Sleep disorders related to another mental disorder (nonsubstance/primary): A DSM-IV literature review. *Journal of Clinical Psychiatry, 54*, 244–255.

Nofzinger, E. A., Reynolds, C. F., III, Thase, M. E., Frank, E., Jennings, J. R., Fasiczka, A. L., Sullivan, L. R., & Kupfer, D. J. (1995). REM sleep enhancement by bupropion in depressed men. *American Journal of Psychiatry, 152*, 274–276.

Nofzinger, E. A., Schwartz, R. M., Reynolds, C. F., III,

Thase, M. E., Jennings, R. J., Frank, E., Fasiczka, A. L., Garamoni, G. L., & Kupfer, D. J. (1994). Affect intensity and phasic REM sleep in men before and after treatment with cognitive behavior therapy. *Journal of Consulting and Clinical Psychology, 62*, 83–91.

Nofzinger, E. A., Thase, M. E., Reynolds, C. F., III, Himmelhoch, J. M., Mallinger, A., Houck, P., & Kupfer, D. J. (1991). Hypersomnia in bipolar depression: A comparison with narcolepsy using the multiple sleep latency test. *American Journal of Psychiatry, 148*, 1177–1181.

Nofzinger, E. A., Thase, M. E., Reynolds, C. F., III, Frank, E., Jennings, J. R., Garamoni, G. L., Fasiczka, A., & Kupfer, D. J. (1993b). Sexual function in depressed men: Assessment using self-report, behavioral and nocturnal penile tumescence measures before and after treatment with cognitive behavior therapy. *Archives of General Psychiatry, 50*, 24–30.

Nolen-Hoeksema, S. (1987). Sex differences in unipolar depression: Evidence and theory. *Psychological Bulletin, 101*(2), 259–282.

O'Flynn, K., O'Keane, V., Lucey, J. V., & Dinan T. G. (1991). Effect of fluoxetine on noradrenergic mediated growth hormone release: A double blind placebo-controlled study. *Biological Psychiatry, 30*, 377–382.

O'Hara, M. W., Neunaber, D. J., & Zekoski, E. M, (1984). A prospective study of postpartum depression: Prevalence cause and predictive factors. *Journal of Abnormal Psychology, 93*, 158–171.

O'Hara, M. W., Schlecht, E. J. A., Lewis, D. A., & Wright, E. J. (1991). Prospective study of postpartum blues: Biological and psychosocial factors. *Archives of General Psychiatry, 48*, 801–806.

O'Keane, V., & Dinan T, G. (1991). Prolactin and cortisol responses to *d*-fenfluramine in major depression: Evidence for diminished responsivity of central serotonergic function. *American Journal of Psychiatry, 148*(8), 1009–1015.

O'Rourke, D., Wurtman, J. J., Wurtman, R. J., Chebli, R., Gleason, R. (1989). Treatment of seasonal depression with d-fenfluramine. *Journal of Clinical Psychiatry, 50*, 343–347.

Ohishi, K., Ueno, R., Nishino, S., Sakai, T., Hayaishi, O. (1988). Increased level of salivary prostaglandins in patients with major depression. *Biological Psychiatry, 23*, 326–334.

Oren, D. A., & Rosenthal, N. E. (1992). Seasonal affective disorders. In E. S. Paykel (Ed.), *Handbook of affective disorders* (2nd ed., pp. 551–567). New York: Guilford Press.

Otto, M. W., Fava, M., Rosenbaum, J. F., Murphy, & C. F. (1991). Perceptual asymmetry plasma cortisol and response to treatment in depressed outpatients. *Biological Psychiatry, 30*, 703–710.

Otto, M. W., Yeo, R. A., & Dougher, M, J. (1987). Right hemisphere involvement in depression: Toward a neuropsychological theory of negative affective experiences. *Biological Psychiatry, 22*, 1201–1215.

Pardo, J. V., Pardo, P. J., & Raichle, M. E. (1993). Neural correlates of self-induced dysphoria. *American Journal of Psychiatry, 150*, 713–719.

Parillo, J. E., & Fauci, A. S. (1979). Mechanisms of glucocorticoid action on immune processes. *Annual Review of Pharmacology and Toxicology, 19*, 179–201.

Parry, B. L., & Rush, A. J. (1979). Oral contraceptives and depressive symptomatology: Biologic mechanisms. *Comprehensive Psychiatry, 20*, 347–358.

Paykel, E. S., Emms, E. M., Fletcher, J., & Rassaby, E. S. (1980). Life events and social support in puerperal depression. *British Journal of Psychiatry*, *136*, 339–346.

Pepin, M. C., Beaulieu, S., & Barden, N. (1989). Antidepressants regulate glucocorticoid receptor messenger RNA concentrations in primary neuronal cultures. *Molecular Brain Research*, *6*, 77–83.

Perris, C. 1966, A. study of bipolar and unipolar recurrent depressive psychoses. *Acta Psychiatrica Scandinavica*, *42*(Suppl. 194), 1–183.

Peterson, C., Maier, S. F., & Seligman, M. E. P. (Eds.). (1993). *Learned helplessness: A theory for the age of personal control*. New York: Oxford University Press.

Pettegrew, J. W., Minshew, N. J., Spiker, D., Tretta, M., Strychor, S., McKeag, D., Muenz, L. R., Miller, G. M., Carbone, D., & McClure, R. J. (1993). Alterations in membrane molecular dynamics in erythrocytes of patients with affective illness. *Depression*, *1*, 88–100.

Petty, F., Chae, Y., Kramer, G., Jordan, S., Wilson, L. (1994). Learned helplessness sensitizes hippocampal norephrine to mild restress. *Biological Psychiatry*, *35*, 901–902.

Petty, F., Kramer, G. L., & Hendrickse, W. (1993). GABA and depression. In J. J. Mann & D. J. Kupfer (Eds.), *Biology of depressive disorders: Part A. A systems perspective* (pp. 79–108). New York: Plenum Press.

Pfeffer, C., Stokes, P., Weiner, A., Shindledecker, R., Faughnan, L., Mintz, M., Stoll, P. M., & Heiligenstein, E. (1989). Psychopathology and plasma cortisol responses to dexamethasone in prepubertal psychiatric inpatients. *Biological Psychiatry*, *26*, 677–689.

Philpot, M. P., Banerjee, S., Needham-Bennett, H., Costa, D. C., & Ell, P. J. (1993). ^{99m}Tc-HMPAO single photon emission tomography in late life depression: A pilot study of regional cerebral blood flow at rest and during a verbal fluency task. *Journal of Affective Disorders*, *28*, 233–240.

Piletz, J. E., DeMet, E., Gwirtsman, H. E., & Halaris, A. (1994). Disruption of circadian MHPG rhythmicity in major depression. *Biological Psychiatry*, *35*, 830–842.

Plotsky, P. M., Cunningham, E. T., & Widmaier, E. P. (1989). Catecholaminergic modulation of corticotropin-releasing factor and adrenocorticotropin secretion. *Endocrine Reviews*, *10*, 437–458.

Pockberger, H., Petsche, H., Rappelsberger, P., Zidek, B., & Zapotoczky, H. G. (1985). Ongoing EEG in depression: A topographic spectral analytical pilot study. *Electroencephalography and Clinical Neurophysiology*, *61*, 349–358.

Poland, R. E., McCracken, J. T., Lutchmansingh, P., & Tondo, L. (1992). Relationship between REM sleep latency and nocturnal cortisol concentrations in depressed patients. *Journal of Sleep Research*, *1*, 54–57.

Pollak, C. P., Alexopoulos, G. S., Moline, M. L., & Wagner, D. R. (1989). Circadian period and phase of body temperature and plasma cortisol rhythms of depressives living in isolation from all temporal cues. *Sleep Research*, 18, 438.

Pollock, V. E., & Schneider, L. S. (1990). Quantitative, waking EEG research on depression. *Biological Psychiatry*, *27*, 757–780.

Post, R. M. (1992). Transduction of psychosocial stress into the neurobiology of recurrent affective disorder. *American Journal of Psychiatry*, *149*, 999–1010.

Post, R. M., Rubinow, D. R., Uhde, T. W., Roy-Byrne, P. P., Linnoila, M., Rosoff, M., & Cowdry, R. (1989).

Dysphoric mania: Clinical and biological correlates. *Archives of General Psychiatry*, *46*, 353–358.

Potter, W. Z., & Linnoila, M. (1989). Biochemical classifications of diagnostic subgroups and D-type scores. *Archives of General Psychiatry*, *46*, 269–271.

Potter, W. Z., Grossman, F., & Rudorfer, M. V. (1993). Noradrenergic function in depressive disorders. In J. J. Mann & D. J. Kupfer (Eds.), *Biology of depressive disorders: Part A. A systems perspective* (pp. 1–27). New York: Plenum Press.

Potter, W. Z., Scheinin, M., Gold, R. N., Rudorfer, M. V., Cowdry, R. W., Calil, H. M., Ross, R. J., & Linnoila, M. (1985). Selective antidepressants and cerebrospinal fluid. *Archives of General Psychiatry*, *42*, 1171–1177.

Price, L. H., Charney, D. S., Delgado, P. L., & Heninger, G. R. (1990). Lithium and serotonin function: Implications for the serotonin hypothesis of depression. *Psychopharmacology*, *100*, 3–12.

Price, L. H., Charney, D. S., Delgado, P. L., & Heninger, G. R. (1991). Serotonin function and depression: Neuroendocrine and mood responses to intravenous L-tryptophan in depressed patients and healthy comparison subjects. *American Journal of Psychiatry*, *148*, 1518–1525.

Price, L. H., Charney, D. S., Rubin, A. L., & Heninger, G. R. (1986). α-adrenergic receptor function in depression. *Archives of General Psychiatry*, *43*, 849–858.

Puig-Antich, J., Goetz, R., Hanlon, C., Davies, M., Thompson, J., Chambers, W. J., Tabrizi, M. A., & Weitzman, E. D. (1982). Sleep architecture and REM sleep measures in prepubertal children with major depression. *Archives of General Psychiatry*, *39*, 932–939.

Puig-Antich, J., Goetz, R., Hanlon, C., Tabrizi, M. A., Davies, M. A., & Weitzman, E. D. (1983). Sleep architecture and REM sleep measures in prepubertal major depressives: Studies during recovery from the depressive episode in a drug-free state. *Archives of General Psychiatry*, *40*, 187–192.

Quintana, J. (1992). Platelet serotonin and plasma tryptophan decreases in endogenous depression: Clinical, therapeutic and biological correlations. *Journal of Affective Disorders*, *24*, 55–62.

Quitkin, F. M., Stewart, J. W., McGrath, P. J., Tricamo, E., Rabkin, J. G., Ocepek-Welikson, K., Nunes, E., Harrison, W., & Klein, D. F. (1993). Columbia atypical depression: A subgroup of depressives with better response to MAOI than to tricyclic antidepressants or placebo. *British Journal of Psychiatry*, *163*, 30–34.

Raleigh, M. J., Brammer, G. L., & McGuire, M. T. (1988). CSF 5-HIAA male dominance and aggression in vervet monkeys. *American Journal of Primatology*, *14*, 437.

Rampello, L., Nicoletti, G., & Raffaele, R. (1991). Dopaminergic hypothesis for retarded depression: A symptom profile for predicting therapeutical responses. *Acta Psychiatrica Scandinavica*, *84*, 552–554.

Rauch, S. L., Jenike, M. A., Alpert, N. M., Baer, L., Breiter, H. C. R., Savage, C. R., & Fischman, A. J. (1994). Regional cerebral blood flow measured during symptom provocation in obsessive–compulsive disorder using oxygen 15-labeled carbon dioxide and positron emission tomography. *Archives of General Psychiatry*, *51*, 62–70.

Reba, R. C. (1993). PET and SPECT: Opportunities and challenges for psychiatry. *Journal of Clinical Psychiatry*, *54*, 26–32.

Redmond, D. E., Katz, M. M., Maas, J. W., Swann, A., Casper, R., & Davis, J. M. (1986). Cerebrospinal fluid amine metabolites. *Archives of General Psychiatry, 43,* 938–947.

Reddy, P. L., Khanna, S., Subhash, M. N., Channabasavanna, S. M., & Sridhara Rama Rao, B. S. (1992). CSF metabolites in depression. *Biological Psychiatry, 31,* 112–118.

Reiman, E. M., Raichle, M. E., Robins, E., Mintun, M. A., Fusselman, M. J., Fox, P. T., Price, J. L., & Hackman, K. A. (1989). Neuroanatomical correlates of a lactate-induced anxiety attack. *Archives of General Psychiatry, 46,* 493–500.

Reite, M., & Short, R. A. (1978). Nocturnal sleep in separated monkey infants. *Archives of General Psychiatry, 35,* 1247–1253.

Reus, V. I. (1985). Hormonal mediation of the memory disorder in depression. *Drug Development Research, 4,* 489–500.

Reynolds, C. F., Christiansen, C. L., Taska, L. S., Coble, P. A., & Kupfer, D. J. (1983). Sleep in narcolepsy and depression: Does it all look alike? *Journal of Nervous and Mental Disease, 171,* 290–295.

Reynolds, C. F., Hoch, C. C., Buysse, D. J., George, C. J., Houck, P. R., Mazumdar, S., Miller, M., Pollock, B. G., Rifai, H., Frank, E., Cornes, C., Morycz, R. K., & Kupfer, D. J. (1991). Sleep in late-life recurrent depression: Changes during early continuation therapy with nortriptyline. *Neuropsychopharmacology, 5,* 85–96.

Reynolds, C. F., Hoch, C. C., Buysse, D. J., Houck, P. R., Schlernitzauer, M., Frank, E., Mazumdar, S., Kupfer, D. J. (1992). Electroencephalographic sleep in spousal bereavement and bereavement-related depression of late life. *Biological Psychiatry, 31,* 69–82.

Reynolds, C. F., & Kupfer, D. J. (1987). Sleep research in affective illness: State of the art circa 1987. *Sleep, 10,* 199–215.

Reynolds, C. F., Kupfer, D. J., Houck, P. R., Hoch, C. C., Stack, J. A., Berman, S. R., & Zimmer, B. (1988). Reliable discrimination of elderly depressed and demented patients by electroencephalographic sleep data. *Archives of General Psychiatry, 45,* 258–264.

Reynolds, C. F., Kupfer, D. J., Thase, M. E., Frank, E., Jarrett, D. B., Coble, P. A., Hoch, C. C., Buysse, D. J., Simons, A. D., & Houck, P. R. (1990). Sleep gender and depression: An analysis of gender effects on the electroencephalographic sleep of 302 depressed outpatients. *Biological Psychiatry, 28,* 673–684.

Reynolds, C. F., Perel, J. M., Frank, E., Imber, S., & Kupfer, D. J. (1989). Open-trial maintenance nortriptyline in late-life depression: Survival analysis and preliminary data on the use of REM latency as a predictor of recurrence. *Psychopharmacology Bulletin, 25,* 129–132.

Ribeiro, S. C. M., Tandon, R., Grunhaus, L., & Greden. J. F. (1993). The DST as a predictor of outcome in depression: A meta-analysis. *American Journal of Psychiatry, 150,* 1618–1629.

Rickels, K., Feighner, J. P., & Smith, W. T. (1985). Alprazolam, amitriptyline, doxepin, and placebo in the treatment of depression. *Archives of General Psychiatry, 42,* 134–141.

Riemann, D., & Berger, M. (1989). EEG sleep in depression and in remission and the REM sleep response to the cholinergic agonist RS 86. *Neuropsychopharmacology, 2(2),* 145–152.

Risby, E. D., Hsiao, J. K., Manji, H. K., Bitran, J., Moses, F., Zhou, D. F., & Potter, W. Z. (1991). The mechanisms of action of lithium. II. Effects on adenylate cyclase ac-

tivity and β-adrenergic receptor binding in normal subjects. *Archives of General Psychiatry, 48,* 513–524.

Rivera-Tovar, A. D., & Frank, E. (1990). Late luteal phase dysphoric disorder in young women. *American Journal of Psychiatry, 147,* 1634–1636.

Robbins, D. R., Alessi, N. E., & Colfer, M. V. (1989). Treatment of adolescents with major depression: Implications of the DST and the melancholic clinical subtype. *Journal of Affective Disorders, 17,* 99–104.

Rosenthal, N. E., Jacobsen, F. M., Sack, F. M., Arendt, J., & James, S. P. (1988). Atenolol in seasonal affective disorder: A test of the melatonin hypothesis. *American Journal of Psychiatry, 145,* 52–56.

Rosenthal, N. E., Sack, D. A., Jacobsen, F. M., James, S. P., Parry, B. L., Arendt, J., Tamarkin, L., & Wehr, T. A. (1986). Melatonin in seasonal affective disorder and phototherapy. *Journal of Neural Transmission, 21,* 257–567.

Rosenblum, L. A., Coplan, J. D., Friedman, S., Bassoff, T., Gorman, J. M., & Andrews, M. W. (1994). Adverse early experiences affect noradrenergic and serotonergic functioning in adult primates. *Biological Psychiatry, 35,* 221–227.

Rotman, A. (1983). Blood platelets in psychopharmacological research. *Progress in Neuropsychopharmacology and Biological Psychiatry, 7,* 135–151.

Roy, A., Agren, H., Pickar, D., Linnoila, M., Doran, A., Cutler, N., & Paul, S. (1986a). Reduced CSF concentration of homovanillic acid and homovanillic acid to 5-hydroxyindoleacetic acid ratios in depressed patients: Relationship to suicidal behavior and dexamethasone nonsuppression. *American Journal of Psychiatry, 143,* 1539–1545.

Roy, A., DeJong, J., & Ferraro, T. (1991). CSF GABA in depressed patients and normal controls. *Psychological Medicine, 21,* 613–618.

Roy, A., DeJong, J., & Linnoila, M. (1989). Cerebrospinal fluid monoamine metabolites and suicidal behavior in depressed patients. *Archives of General Psychiatry, 46,* 609–612.

Roy, A., Everett, D., Pickar, D., & Paul, S. M. (1987). Platelet tritiated imipramine binding and serotonin uptake in depressed patients and controls: Relationship to plasma cortisol levels before and after dexamethasone administration. *Archives of General Psychiatry, 44,* 320–327.

Roy, A., Gallucci, W., Avgerinos, P., Linnoila, M., & Gold, P. (1988b). The CRH stimulation test in bereaved subjects with and without accompanying depression. *Psychiatry Research, 25,* 145–156.

Roy, A., Guthrie, S., Karoum, F., Pickar, D., & Linnoila, M. (1988). High intercorrelations among urinary outputs of norepinephrine and its major metabolites: A replication in depressed patients and controls. *Archives of General Psychiatry, 45,* 158–161.

Roy, A., Karoum, F., & Pollack, S. (1992). Marked reduction in indexes of dopamine metabolism among patients with depression who attempt suicide. *Archives of General Psychiatry, 49,* 447–450.

Roy, A., Pickar, D., DeJong, J., Karoum, F., & Linnoila, M. (1988a). Norepinephrine and its metabolites in cerebrospinal fluid plasma and urine. *Archives of General Psychiatry, 45,* 849–857.

Roy, A., Pickar, D., Linnoila, M., & Paul, S. M. (1986b). Cerebrospinal fluid monoamine and monamine metabolite levels and the dexamethasone suppression test in depression: Relationship to life events. *Archives of General Psychiatry, 43,* 356–360.

Roy, A., Pickar, D., Linnoila, M., & Potter, W. K. (1985). Plasma norepinephrine in affective disorders: Relationship to melancholia. *Archives of General Psychiatry, 42,* 1181–1185.

Rubin, R. T., Heist, E. K., McGeoy, S. S., Hanada, K., & Lesser, I. M. (1992). Neuroendocrine aspects of primary endogenous depression: XI. Serum melatonin measures in patients and matched control subjects. *Archives of General Psychiatry, 49,* 558–567.

Rubin, R. T., & Mandell, A. J. (1966). Adrenal cortical activity in pathological emotional states: A review. *American Journal of Psychiatry, 123,* 387–400.

Rubinow, D. R., Post, R. M., Savard, R., & Gold, P. W. (1984). Cortisol hypersecretion and cognitive impairment in depression. *Archives of General Psychiatry, 41,* 279–283.

Rudorfer, M. V., Ross, R. J., Linnoila, M., Sherer, M. A., & Potter, W. Z. (1985). Exaggerated orthostatic responsivity of plasma norepinephrine in depression. *Archives of General Psychiatry, 42,* 1186–1192.

Rush, A. J, (1984). A phase III study of cognitive therapy of depression. In J. B. W. Williams & R. L. Spitzer (Eds.), *Psychotherapy research: Where are we and where should we go?* (pp. 216–233). New York: Guilford Press.

Rush, A. J., Erman, M. K., Giles, D. E., Schlesser, M. A., Carpenter, G., Vasavada, N., & Roffwarg, H. P. (1986). Polysomnographic findings in recently drug-free and clinically remitted depressed patients. *Archives of General Psychiatry, 43,* 878–884.

Rush, A. J., Erman, M. K., Schlesser, M. A., Roffwarg, H. P., Vasavada, N., Khatami, M., Fairchild, C., & Giles, D. E. (1985). Alprazolam vs. amitriptyline in depressions with reduced REM latencies. *Archives of General Psychiatry, 42,* 1154–1159.

Rush, A. J., Giles, D. E., Roffwarg, H. P., & Parker, C. R. (1982). Sleep EEG and dexamethasone suppression test findings in outpatients with unipolar major depressive disorders. *Biological Psychiatry, 17,* 327–342.

Ryan, N. D., Birmaher, B., Perel, J. M., Dahl, R. E., Meyer, V., Al-Shabbout, M., Iyenger, S., & Puig-Antich, J. (1992). Neuroendocrine reponse to l-5-hydroxytryptophan challenge in prepubertal major depression depressed vs. normal children. *Archives of General Psychiatry, 49,* 843–851.

Sabelli, H. C., & Mosnaim, A. D. (1974). Phenylethylamine hypothesis of affective behavior. *American Journal of Psychiatry, 131,* 695–699.

Sachar, E. J., Halbreich, U., Asnis, G. M., Nathan, R. S., Halpern, F. S., & Ostrow, L. (1981). Paradoxical cortisol responses to dextroamphetamine in endogenous depression. *Archives of General Psychiatry, 38,* 1113–1117.

Sachar, E. J., Hellman, L., Roffwarg, H., Halpern, F. S., Fukushima, D. K., & Gallaher, T. F. (1973). Disrupted, 24-hour patterns of cortisol secretion in psychotic depression. *Archives of General Psychiatry, 28,* 19–24.

Sack, D. A., Rosenthal, N. E., Parry, B. L., & Wehr, T. A. (1987). Biological rhythms in psychiatry. In H. Y. Meltzer (Ed.), *Psychopharmacology: The third generation of progress* (pp. 669–685). New York: Raven Press.

Sack, R. L., Lewy, A. J., White, D. M., Singer, C. M., Fireman, M. J., & Van Diver, R. (1990). Morning versus evening light treatment for winter depression: Evidence that the therapeutic effects of light are mediated by circadian phase shifting. *Archives of General Psychiatry, 47,* 343–351.

Sackeim, H. A. (1991). Emotion, disorders of mood, and hemispheric functional specialization. In B. J. Carroll & J. E. Barrett (Eds.), *Psychopathology and the brain* (pp. 209–242). New York: Raven Press.

Sackeim, H. A., Prohovnik, I., Moeller, J. R., Brown, R. P., Apter, S., Prudic, J., Devanand, D. P., & Mukherjee, S. (1990). Regional cerebral blood flow in mood disorders. *Archives of General Psychiatry, 47,* 60–70.

Sackeim, H. A., Putz, E., Vingiano, W., Coleman, E., & McElhiney, M. (1988). Lateralization in the processing of emotionally laden information: I. Normal functioning. *Neuropsychiatry, Neuropsychology and Behavioral Neurology, 1,* 97–110.

Saletu, B., Frey, R., Krupka, M., Anderer, P., Grunberger, J., & See, W. R. (1991). Sleep laboratory studies on the single-dose effects of serotonin reuptake inhibitors paroxetine and fluoxetine on human sleep and awakening qualities. *Sleep, 14,* 439–447.

Samson, J. A., Mirin, S. M., Hauser, S. T., Fenton, B. T., & Schildkraut, J. J. (1992). Learned helplessness and urinary MHPG levels in unipolar depression. *American Journal of Psychiatry, 149,* 806–809.

Sandler, M., Ruthven, C. R. J., Goodwin, B. L., & Coppen, A. (1979). Decreased cerebrospinal fluid concentration of free phenylacetic acid in depressive illness. *Clinica Chimica Acta, 93,* 169–171.

Sapolsky, R. M. (1990). Adrenocortical function social rank and personality among wild baboons. *Biological Psychiatry, 28,* 862–878.

Sapolsky, R. M., & Altmann, J. (1991). Incidence of hypercortisolism and dexamethasone resistance increases with age among wild baboons. *Biological Psychiatry, 30,* 1008–1016.

Schatzberg, A. F., & Rothschild, A. J. (1992). Psychotic (delusional) major depression: Should it be included as a distinct syndrome in DSM-IV? *American Journal of Psychiatry, 149,* 733–745.

Schatzberg, A. F., Rothschild, A. J., Langlais, P. J., Lerbinger, J. E., Schildkraut, J. J., & Cole, J. O. (1987). Psychotic and nonpsychotic depressions: II. Platelet MAO activity plasma catecholamines, cortisol and specific symptoms. *Psychiatry Research, 20,* 155–164.

Schatzberg, A. F., Samson, J. A., Bloomingdale, K. L., Orsulak, P. J., Gerson, B., Kizuka, P. P., Cole, J. O., & Schildkraut, J. J. (1989). Toward a biochemical classification of depressive disorders. *Archives of General Psychiatry, 46,* 260–268.

Schildkraut, J. J. (1965). The catecholamine hypothesis of affective disorder a review of supporting evidence. *American Journal of Psychiatry, 122,* 509–522.

Schildkraut, J. J. (1982). The biochemical discrimination of subtypes of depressive disorders: An outline of our studies on norepinephrine metabolism and psychoactive drugs in the endogenous depression since 1967. *Pharmacopsychiatry, 15,* 121–127.

Schittecatte, M., Charles, G., Machowski, R., Dumont, F., Garcia-Valentin, J., Wilmotte, J., Papart, P., Pitchot, W., Wauthy, J., Ansseau, M., Hoffmann, G., & Pelc, I. (1994). Effects of gender and diagnosis on growth hormone response to clonidine for major depression: A large-scale multicenter study. *American Journal of Psychiatry, 151,* 216–220.

Schittecatte, M., Charles, G., Machowski, R., Garcia-Valentin, J., Mendlewicz, J., & Wilmotte, J. (1992). Reduced clonidine rapid eye movement sleep suppression in patients with primary major affective illness. *Archives of General Psychiatry, 49,* 637–642.

Schleifer, S. J., Keller, S. E., Bond, R. N., Cohen, J., &

Stein, M. (1989). Major depressive disorder: Role of age, sex, severity and hospitalization. *Archives of General Psychiatry, 46*, 81–87.

Schou, M., Juel-Neilson, N., Stromgren, E., & Voldby, H. (1954). The treatment of manic psychoses by the administration of lithium salts. *Journal of Neurology, Neurosurgery and Psychiatry, 17*, 250–260.

Schreiber, G., Avissar, S., Danon, A., & Belmaker, R. H. (1991). Hyperfunctional G proteins in mononuclear leukocytes of patients with mania. *Biological Psychiatry, 29*, 273–280.

Schwartz, J. M., Baxter, L. R., Mazziotta, J. C., Gerner, R. H., & Phelps M, E. (1987). The differential diagnosis of depression: Relevance of positron emission tomography studies of cerebral glucose metabolism to the bipolar–unipolar dichotomy. *Journal of the American Medical Association, 258*, 1368–1374.

Sedvall, G., Farde, L., Persson, A., & Wiesel, F.-A. (1986). Imaging of neurotransmitter receptors in the living human brain. *Archives of General Psychiatry, 43*, 995–1005.

Shapira, B., Cohen, J., Newman, M. E., & Lerer, B. (1993). Prolactin response to fenfluramine and placebo challenge following maintenence pharmacotherapy withdrawal in remitted depressed patients. *Biological Psychiatry, 33*, 531–535.

Shapira, B., Lerer, B., & Kindler, S. (1992a). Enhanced serotonergic responsivity following electroconvulsive therapy in patients with major depression. *British Journal of Psychiatry, 160*, 223–229.

Shapira, B., Yagmur, M. J., Gropp, C., Mewman, M. E., & Lerer, B. (1992b). Effect of clomipramine and lithium on fenfluramine-induced hormone release in major depression. *Biological Psychiatry, 31*, 975–983.

Sharpley, A. L., Solomon, R. A., Fernando, A. I., da Roza Davis, J. M., & Cowen P, J. (1990). Dose-related effects of selective 5-HT$_2$ receptor antagonists on slow-wave sleep in humans. Psychopharmacology, 101, 568–569.

Sharpley, A. L., Walsh, A. E. S., & Cowen P, J. (1992). Nefazodone—a novel antidepressant—may increase REM sleep. *Biological Psychiatry, 31*, 1070–1073.

Sherman, A. D., & Petty, F. (1984). Learned helplessness decreases [³H]imipramine binding in rat cortex. *Journal of Affective Disorders, 6*, 25–32.

Sherman, B., Pfohl, B., & Winokur, G. (1984). Circadian analysis of plasma cortisol levels before and after dexamethasone administration in depressed patients. *Archives of General Psychiatry, 41*, 271–275.

Shipley, J. E., Schteingart, D. E., Tandon, R., Pande, A. C., Grunhaus, L., Haskett, R. F., & Starkman, M. N. (1992). EEG sleep in Cushing's disease and Cushing's syndrome: Comparison with patients with major depressive disorder. *Biological Psychiatry, 32*, 146–155.

Siever, L. J. (1987). Role of nonadrenergic mechanisms in the etiology of the affective disorders. In H. Y. Meltzer (Ed.), *Psychopharmacology: The third generation of progress* (pp. 493–504). New York: Raven Press.

Siever, L. J., & Davis, K. L. (1991). A psychobiological perspective on the personality disorders. *American Journal of Psychiatry, 148*(12), 1647–1658.

Siever, L. J., Trestman, R. L., & Coccaro, E. F. (1992). The growth hormone response to clonidine in acute and remitted depressed male patients. *Neuropsychopharmacology, 6*, 165–177.

Silfverskiöld, P., & Risberg, J. (1989). Regional cerebral blood flow in depression and mania. *Archives of General Psychiatry, 46*, 253–259.

Silverstein, B., & Perlick, D. (1991). Gender differences in depression: Historical changes. *Acta Psychiatrica Scandinavica, 84*, 327–331.

Simons, A. D., Angell, K. L., Monroe, S. M., & Thase, M. E. (1993). Cognition and life stress in depression: Cognitive factor and the definition rating and generation of negative life events. *Journal of Abnormal Psychology, 102*, 584–591.

Simons, A. D., & Thase, M. E. (1992). Biological markers, treatment outcome, and 1-year follow-up of endogenous depression: Electroencephalographic sleep studies and response to cognitive therapy. *Journal of Consulting and Clinical Psychiatry, 60*, 392–401.

Sitaram, N., Dubé, S., Keshavan, M., Davies, A., & Reynal, P. (1987). The association of super-sensitive cholinergic REM-induction and affective illness within pedigrees. *Journal of Psychiatric Research, 21*, 487–497.

Sitaram, N., Nurnberger, J. I., Jr., Gershon, E. S., & Gillin, J. C. (1982). Cholinergic regulation of mood and REM sleep: A potential model and marker of vulnerability to affective disorder. *American Journal of Psychiatry, 139*, 571–576.

Soloff, P. H., George, A., & Nathan, R. S. (1982). The dexamethasone suppression test in patients with borderline personality disorders. *American Journal of Psychiatry, 139*, 1621–1623.

Spiker, D. G., Weiss, J. C., Dealy, R. S., Griffin, S. J., Hanin, I., Neil, J. F., Perel, J. M., Rossi, A. J., & Soloff, P. H. (1985). The pharmacological treatment of delusional depression. *American Journal of Psychiatry, 142*, 430–436.

Spitzer, R. L., Endicott, J., & Robins, E. (1978). Research diagnostic criteria. *Archives of General Psychiatry, 34*, 773–782.

Spitzer, R. L., Williams, J. B. W., Gibbon, M., First, M. (1992). The Structured Clinical Interview for DSM-III-R (SCID). *Archives of General Psychiatry, 49*, 624–629.

Spoont, M. R. (1992). Modulatory role of serotonin in neural information processing: Implications for human psychopathology. *Psychological Bulletin, 112*(2), 330–350.

Staner, L., Maes, M., Bouillon, E., & Linkowski, P. (1992). Biological correlates of the Newcastle scale in depressive illness: A multivariate approach. *Acta Psychiatrica Scandinavica, 85*, 345–350.

Steiger, A., Von Bardeleben, U., Herth, T., & Holsboer, F. (1989). Sleep EEG and nocturnal secretion of cortisol and growth hormone in male patients with endogenous depression before treatment and after recovery. *Journal of Affective Disorders, 16*, 189–195.

Stein, D. J., Hollander, E., Anthony, D. T., Schneier, F. R., Fallon, B. A., Liebowitz, M. R., & Klein, D. F. (1992). Serotonergic medications for sexual obsessions sexual addictions and paraphilias. *Journal of Clinical Psychiatry, 53*, 267–271.

Stein, M., Miller, A. H., & Trestman, R. L. (1991). Depression, the immune system, and health and illness: Findings in search of meaning. *Archives of General Psychiatry, 48*, 171–177.

Stewart, J. W., Quitkin, F. M., Terman, M., & Terman, J. S. (1990). Is seasonal affective disorder a variant of atypical depression? Differential response to light therapy. *Psychiatry Research, 33*, 121–128.

Stokes, P. E., & Sikes, C. R. (1988). The hypothalamic–pituitary–adrenocortical axis in major depression. *Endocrinology and Metabolism Clinics of North America, 17*, 1–19.

Stokes, P. E., Stoll, P. M., Koslow, S. H., Maas, J. W., Davis, J. M., Swann, A. C., & Robins, E. (1984). Pretreatment DST and hypothalamic–pituitary–adrenocortical function in depressed patients and comparison groups. *Archives of General Psychiatry, 41*, 257–267.

Suomi, S. J. (1991). Primate separation models of affective disorders. In J. Madden IV (Ed.), *Neurobiology of learning, emotion, and affect* (pp. 195–214). New York: Raven Press.

Swann, A. C., Secunda, S., Davis, J. M., Robins, E., Hanin, I., Koslow, S. H., & Maas, J. W. (1983). CSF monoamine metabolites in mania. *American Journal of Psychiatry, 140*, 396–400.

Swann, A. C., Secunda, S. K., Koslow, S. H., Katz, M. M., Bowden, C. L., Maas, J. W., Davis, J. M., & Robins, E. (1991). Mania: Sympathoadrenal function and clinical state. *Psychiatry Research, 37*, 195–205.

Swann, A. C., Stokes, P. E., Secunda, S. K., Maas, J. W., Bowden, C. L., Berman, N., & Koslow, S. H. (1994). Depressive mania versus agitated depression: Biogenic amine and hypothalamic–pituitary–adrenocortical function. *Biological Psychiatry, 35*, 803–813.

Swayze, V. W., Andreasen, N. C., Alliger, R. J., Ehrhardt, J. C., & Yuh, W. T. (1990). Structural brain abnormalities in bipolar affective disorder. *Archives of General Psychiatry, 47*, 1054–1059.

Syvalahti, E., Eskola, J., Ruuskanen, O., & Laine, T. (1985). Nonsuppression of cortisol in depression and immune function. *Progress in Neuropsychopharmacology and Biological Psychiatry, 9*, 413–422.

Tandon, R., Shipley, J. E., Taylor, S., Greden, J. F., Eiser, A., DeQuardo, J., & Goodson, J. (1992). Electroencephalographic sleep abnormalities in schizophrenia. *Archives of General Psychiatry, 49*, 185–194.

Teicher, M. H., Lawrence, J. M., Barber, N. I., Finklestein, S. P., Lieberman, H. R., & Baldessarini, R. J. (1988). Increased activity and phase delay in circadian motility rhythms in geriatric depression preliminary observations. *Archives of General Psychiatry, 45*, 913–917.

Thase, M. E. (1989). Comparison of seasonal affective disorder with other forms of recurrent depression. In N. E. Rosenthal & M. Blehar (Eds.), *Seasonal affective disorders and phototherapy* (pp. 64–78). New York: Guilford Press.

Thase, M. E. (1992). Long-term treatments of recurrent depressive disorders. *Journal of Clinical Psychiatry, 53*(Suppl. 8), 33–44.

Thase, M. E. (1995). Reeducative psychotherapy. In G. O. Gabbard (Ed.), *Treatments of psychiatric disorders: DSM-IV edition* (pp. 1169–1204). Washington, DC: American Psychiatric Press.

Thase, M. E., Carpenter, L., Kupfer, D. J., & Frank, E. (1991). Clinical significance of reversed vegetative subtypes of recurrent major depression. *Psychopharmacology Bulletin, 27*, 17–22.

Thase, M. E., Frank, E., & Kupfer, D. J. (1985). Biological processes in major depression. In E. E. Beckham & W. R. Leber (Eds.), *Handbook of depression: Treatment, assessment, and research* (pp. 816–913). Homewood, IL: Dorsey Press.

Thase, M. E., Hersen, M., Bellack, A. S., Himmelhoch, J. M., Kornblith, S. J., & Greenwald, D. (1984). Social skills training and endogenous depression. *Journal of Behavior Therapy and Experimental Psychiatry, 15*, 101–108.

Thase, M. E., Hersen, M., Bellack, A. S., Himmelhoch, J. M., & Kupfer, D. J. (1983). Validation of a Hamilton

subscale for endogenomorphic depression. *Journal of Affective Disorders, 5*, 267–278.

Thase, M. E., & Himmelhoch, J. M. (1983). On the Amish study. *American Journal of Psychiatry, 140*, 1263–1264.

Thase, M. E., Himmelhoch, J. M., Mallinger, A. G., Jarrett, D. B., & Kupfer, D. J. (1989). Sleep EEG and DST findings in anergic bipolar depression. *American Journal of Psychiatry, 146*, 329–333.

Thase, M. E., & Howland, R. (1994). Refractory depression: Relevance of psychosocial factors and therapies. *Psychiatric Annals, 24*, 232–240.

Thase, M. E., & Kupfer, D. J. (1987). Current status of EEG sleep in the assessment and treatment of depression. In G. D. Burrows & J. S. Werry (Eds.), *Advances in human psychopharmacology* (Volume, 4, pp. 93–148). Greenwich, CT: JAI Press.

Thase, M. E., Kupfer, D. J., Frank, E., Buysse, D. J., Simons, A. D., McEachran, A. B., Rashid, K. F., & Grochocinski, V. J. (in press). Electroencephalographic sleep profiles in single and multiple episode forms of major depression: I. Comparison during acute depressive states. *Biological Psychiatry*.

Thase, M. E., Kupfer, D. J., & Ulrich, R. F. (1986). Electroencephalographic sleep in psychotic depression: A valid subtype? *Archives of General Psychiatry, 43*, 886–893.

Thase, M. E., Mallinger, A. G., McKnight, D., & Himmelhoch, J. M. (1992). Treatment of imipramine resistant recurrent depression: IV. A double-blind crossover study of tranylcypromine in anergic bipolar depression. *American Journal of Psychiatry, 149*, 195–198.

Thase, M. E., Reynolds, C. F., III, Frank, E., Jennings, J. R., Nofzinger, E., Fasiczka, A., Garamoni, G., & Kupfer, D. J. (1994a). Polysomnographic studies of unmedicated depressed men before and after cognitive behavior therapy. *American Journal of Psychiatry, 151*, 1615–1622.

Thase, M. E., Reynolds, C. F., III, Frank, E., Simons, A. D., McGeary, J., Fasiczka, A. L., Garamoni, G. G., Jennings, J. R., & Kupfer, D. J. (1994b). Do depressed men and women respond similarly to cognitive behavior therapy? *American Journal of Psychiatry, 151*, 500–505.

Thase, M. E., Reynolds, C. F., III, Jennings, J. R., Frank, E., Garamoni, G. L., Nofzinger, E. A., Fasiczka, A. L., & Kupfer, D. J. (1992). Diminished nocturnal penile tumescence in depression: A replication study. *Biological Psychiatry, 31*, 1136–1142.

Thase, M. E., Reynolds, C. F., III, Jennings, J. R., Frank, E., Howell, J. R., Houck, P. R., Berman, S., & Kupfer, D. J. (1988). Nocturnal penile tumescence is diminished in depressed men. *Biological Psychiatry, 24*, 33–46.

Thase, M. E., & Simons, A. D. (1992). The applied use of psychotherapy in the study of the psychobiology of depression. *Journal of Psychotherapy Practice and Research, 1*, 72–80.

Thase, M. E., Simons, A. D., & Reynolds, C. F., III. (1993). Psychobiological correlates of poor response to cognitive behavior therapy: Potential indications for antidepressant pharmacotherapy. *Psychopharmacology Bulletin, 29*, 293–301.

Thayer, R. E. (1989). *The biopsychology of mood and arousal*. New York: Oxford University Press.

Thorell, L.-H. (1987). Electrodermal activity in suicidal and nonsuicidal depressive patients and in matched healthy subjects. *Acta Psychiatrica Scandinavica, 76*, 420–430.

Thorell L.-H., Kjellman, B. F., & d'Elia, G. (1993). Electrodermal activity in relation to basal and postdexamethasone levels of thyroid stimulating hormone and basal levels of thyroid hormones in major depressive patients and healthy subjects. *Psychiatry Research, 47*, 23–36.

Trestman, R. L., Coccaro, E. F., Mitropoulou, V., Gabriel, S. M., Horvath, T., & Siever, L. J. (1993). The cortisol response to clonidine in acute and remitted depressed men. *Biological Psychiatry, 34*, 373–379.

Tsuang, M. T., & Faraone, S. V. (1990). *The genetics of mood disorders.* Baltimore: Johns Hopkins University Press.

Upadhayaya, A. K., Pennell, I., Cowan, P. J., & Deakin, J, F. W. (1991). Blunted growth hormone and prolactin response to L-tryptophan in depression: A state dependent abormality. *Journal of Affective Disorders, 21*, 213–218.

Valentino, R. J., Foote, S. L., & Aston-Jones, G. (1983). Corticotropin releasing factor activates noradrenergic neurons of the locus coeruleus. *Brain Research, 270*, 363–367.

van Kammen, D. P., Peters, J., Yao, J., van Kammen, W. B., Neylan, T., Shaw, D., & Linnoila, M. (1990). Norepinephrine in acute exacerbations of chronic schizophrenia: Negative symptoms revisited. *Archives of General Psychiatry, 47*, 161–168.

van Praag, H. M. (1980). Central monoamine metabolism in depressions: II. Catecholamines and related compounds. *Comprehensive Psychiatry, 21*, 44–54.

van Praag, H. M, (1982). A transatlantic view of the diagnosis of depression according to the DSM-III: I. Controversies and misunderstandings in depression diagnosis. *Comprehensive Psychiatry, 23*, 315–329.

Veith, R. C., Lewis, N., Langohr, J. I., Murburg, M. M., Ashleigh, E. A., Castillo, S., Peskind, E. R., Pascualy, M., Bissette, G., Nemeroff, C. B., & Raskind, M. A. (1992). Effect of desipramine on cerebrospinal fluid concentrations of corticotropin-releasing factor in human subjects. *Psychiatry Research, 46*, 1–8.

Veith, R. C., Lewis, N., Linares, O. A., Barnes, R. F., Raskind, M. A., Villacres, E. C., Murburg, M. M., Ashleigh, E. A., Castillo, S., Peskind, E. R., Pascualy, M., & Halter, J. B. (1994). Sympathetic nervous system activity in major depression. Basal and desipramine-induced alterations in plasma norepinephrine kinetics. *Archives of General Psychiatry, 51*, 411–422.

Virkkunen, M., Kallio, E., Rawlings, R., Tokola, R., Poland, R. E., Guidotti, A., Nemeroff, C., Bissette, G., Kalogeras, K., Karonen, S.-L., & Linnoila, M. (1994). Personality profiles and state aggressiveness in Finnish alcoholic, violent offenders, fire setters, and healthy volunteers. *Archives of General Psychiatry, 51*, 28–33.

Vogel, G. W. (1983). Evidence for REM sleep deprivation as the mechanism of action of antidepressant drugs. *Progress in Neuropsychopharmacology and Biological Psychiatry, 7*, 343–349.

Volkow, N. D., & Tancredi, L. R. (1991). Biological correlates of mental activity studies with PET. *American Journal of Psychiatry, 148*(4), 439–443.

Volkow, N. D., Fowler, J. S., Wolf, A. P., Schlyer, D., Shive, C.-Y., Alpert, R., Dewey, S. L., Logan, J., Bendriem, B., Christman, D., Hitzemann, R., & Henn, F. (1990). Effects of chronic cocaine abuse on postsynaptic dopamine receptors. *American Journal of Psychiatry, 147*(6), 719–724.

von Zerssen, D., Kirlich, G., Doerr, P., Emrich, H. M.,

Lund, R., & Ploog, D. (1985). Are biological rhythms disturbed in depression? *Acta Psychiatrica Belgica, 85*, 624–635.

Wägner, A., Åberg-Wistedt, A., Åsberg, M., Bertilsson, L., Mårtensson, B., & Montero, D. (1987). Effects of antidepressant treatments on platelet tritiated imipramine binding in major depressive disorder. *Archives of General Psychiatry, 44*, 870–877.

Ward, N. G., & Doerr, H. O. (1986). Skin conductance: A potentially sensitive and specific marker for depression. *Journal of Nervous and Mental Disease, 174*, 553–559.

Warner, M. D., Peabody, C. A., Whiteford, H. A., & Hollister, L. E. (1988). Alprazolam as an antidepressant. *Journal of Clinical Psychiatry, 49*, 148–150.

Watson, J. P., Elliot, S. A. M., Rugg, A. J., & Brough, D. I. (1984). Psychiatric disorder in pregnancy and the first postnatal year. *British Journal of Psychiatry, 144*, 453–462.

Wehr, T. A., & Goodwin, F. K. (1981). Biological rhythms and psychiatry. In S. Arieti & H. K. H. Brodie (Eds.), *American handbook of psychiatry* (Vol. 7, pp. 46–74). New York: Basic Books.

Wehr, T. A., Jacobsen, F. M., Sack, D. A., Arendt, J., Tamarkin, L., & Rosenthal, N. E. (1986). Phototherapy of seasonal affective disorder: Time of day and suppression of melatonin are not critical for antidepressant effects. *Archives of General Psychiatry, 43*, 870–875.

Wehr, T. A., & Rosenthal, N. E. (1989). Seasonality and affective illness. *American Journal of Psychiatry, 146*, 829–839.

Wehr, T. A., Sack, D. A., & Rosenthal, N. E. (1987). Seasonal affective disorder with summer depression and winter hypomania. *American Journal of Psychiatry, 144*, 1602–1603.

Wehr, T. A., & Wirz-Justice, A. (1982). Circadian rhythm mechanisms in affective illness and in antidepressant drug action. *Pharmacopsychiatry, 15*, 31–39.

Weiss, J. M. (1991). Stress-induced depression: Critical neurochemical and electrophysiological changes. In J. IV Madden (Ed.), *Neurobiology of learning emotion and affect* (pp. 123–154). New York: Raven Press.

Weissman, M. M., Leaf, P. J., Tischler, G. L., Blazer, D. B., Karno, M., Bruce, M. L., & Florio, L. P. (1988). Affective disorders in five United States communities. *Psychological Medicine, 18*, 141–153.

Whybrow, P. C., Akiskal, H. S., & McKinney, W. T. (1985). *Mood disorders: Toward a new psychobiology.* New York: Plenum Press.

Wilhelm, K., & Parker, G. (1994). Sex differences in lifetime depression rates: Fact or artifact? *Psychological Medicine, 24*, 97–111.

Wilner, P. (1993). Anhedonia. In C. G. Costello (Ed.), *Symptoms of depression* (pp. 63–84). New York: Wiley.

Wilner, P., Golembiowski, K., Klimer, V., & Muscat, R. (1991). Changes in mesolimbic dopamine may explain stress-induced anhedonia. *Psychobiology, 19*, 79–84.

Winokur, A. (1993). Thyroid axis and depressive disorders. In J. J. Mann & D. J. Kupfer (Eds.), *Biology of depressive disorders: Part A. A systems perspective* (pp. 155–170). New York: Plenum Press.

Wirz-Justice, A., & Richter, R. (1979). Seasonality in biochemical determinations: A source of variance and clue to the temporal incidence of affective illness. *Psychiatry Research, 1*, 53–60.

Wolkowitz, O. M., Doran, A., Breier, A., Roy, A., & Pickar,

D. (1989). Specificity of HVA response to dexamethasone in psychotic depression. *Psychiatry Research, 29*, 177–186.

Wu, J. C., & Bunney, W. E. (1990). The biological basis of an antidepressant response to sleep deprivation and relapse: Review and hypothesis. *American Journal of Psychiatry, 147*(1), 14–21.

Wu, J. C., Gillin, J. C., Buchsbaum, M. S., Hershey, T., Johnson, J. C., & Bunney, W. E. (1992). Effect of sleep deprivation on brain metabolism of depressed patients. *American Journal of Psychiatry, 149*, 538–543.

Young, E. A., Haskett, R. F., Murphy-Weinberg, V., Watson, S. J., & Akil, H. (1991). Loss of glucocorticoid fast feedback in depression. *Archives of General Psychiatry, 48*, 693–699.

Young, E. A., Watson, S. J., Kotun, J., Haskett, R. F., Grunhaus, L., Murphy-Weinberg, V., Vale, W., Rivier, J., & Akil, H. (1990). β-Lipotropin β-endorphin response to low-dose ovine corticotropin releasing factor in endogenous depression. *Archives of General Psychiatry, 47*, 449–457.

Young, L. T., Li, P. P., Kamble, A., Siu, K. P., & Warsh, J. J. (1994). Mononuclear leukocyte levels of G proteins in depressed patients with bipolar disorder or major depressive disorder. *American Journal of Psychiatry, 151*, 594–596.

Young, L. T., Li, P. P., Kish, S. J., Siu, K. P., Kamble, A., Hornykiewicz, O., & Warsh, J. J. (1993). Cerebral cortex Gs-α protein levels and forskolin stimulated cAMP formation are increased in bipolar affective disorder. *Journal of Neurochemistry, 61*, 890–898.

Young, L. T., Warsh, J. J., Kish, S. J., Shannak, K., & Hornykeiwicz, O. (1994b). Reduced brain 5-HT and elevated NE turnover and metabolites in bipolar affective disorder. *Biological Psychiatry, 35*, 121–127.

Young, R. C., Alexopoulos, G. S., Manley, M. W., Shamoian, C. A., Dhar, A. K., & Kutt, H. (1984). Treatment outcome in elderly depressives: Plasma nortriptyline concentration and pretreatment dexamethasone suppression test. In E. Usdin, M. Asberg, L. Bertilsson, & F. Sjoqvist (Eds.), *Frontiers in biochemical and pharmacological research in depression* (pp. 207–211). New York: Raven Press.

Young, W. F., Laws, E. R., Sharbrough, F. W., & Weinshilboum, R. M. (1986). Human monoamine oxidase. *Archives of General Psychiatry, 43*, 604–609.

Zahn, T. P. (1986). Psychophysiological approaches to psychopathology. In M. G. H. Coles, E. Donchin, & S. W. Porges (Eds.), *Psychophysiology: Systems, processes, and applications* (pp. 545–558). New York: Guilford Press.

Zarcone, V. P., Benson, K. L., & Berger, P. A. (1987). Abnormal rapid eye movement latencies in schizophrenia. *Archives of General Psychiatry, 44*, 45–48.

Zimmerman, M., Coryell, W., & Pfohl, B. M. (1985). The importance of diagnostic thresholds in familial classification: The dexamethasone suppression test and familial subtypes of depression. *Archives of General Psychiatry, 42*, 300–304.

9

Pharmacotherapy and Somatic Therapies

MAURIZIO FAVA

JERROLD F. ROSENBAUM

Although depression features marked neuro-vegetative and somatic symptoms, the use of medications and somatic therapies is a relatively recent development in the history of psychiatry. Electroconvulsive treatment, the first somatic treatment of depression, was widely used in the 1950s and 1960s, but its acceptability declined with the discovery of tricyclic antidepressants and monoamine oxidase inhibitors. The antidepressant efficacy of these two classes of psychotropic drugs was serendipitously observed and later proven by several dozen controlled studies, most employing a double-blind, parallel design. In the typical study, patients suffering from depressive syndromes of various types (e.g., endogenous, reactive, atypical) would be randomly assigned to two or more treatments for several weeks, and the improvement in their depressive symptoms would be assessed by clinicians blind to the assignment to treatment. The efficacy of antidepressants would then be examined by comparison with a placebo, an inactive substance used to control for the tendency of depressed patients to respond to many different, nonspecific factors. The use of tricyclic antidepressants and monoamine oxidase inhibitors expanded in the 1970s and 1980s, even though these medications continued to be underutilized in the treatment of depression (Keller et al., 1982). Over the past few years, the introduction of newer agents, chemically distinct from the old ones and with improved side effect profiles, has facilitated the use of medications in the treatment of depressed patients. In addition, innovative techniques, such as light therapy, have become additional effective options for the treatment of certain forms of depression. Medication and somatic therapies are now considered a standard and well-accepted form of treatment of depression. In this chapter, we review the various antidepressant drugs currently available, and, briefly, the use of electroconvulsive treatment and light therapy. Finally, we discuss medication strategies employed with "treatment-resistant" patients, as well as issues that arise in continuation and long-term treatments of depression.

PHARMACOTHERAPY

The modern era of psychopharmacological treatment of depression began in the late 1950s with the almost simultaneous introduction of imipramine and iproniazid—the prototypical tricyclic antidepressant and monoamine oxidase (MAO) inhibitor, respectively—following serendipitous discoveries (Klerman, 1989). The success of these drugs generated enthusiasm for the development of compounds similar in structure or in pharmacological action *in vitro*. The monoamine theories—which followed the introduction of the first antidepressants and proposed that depression was caused by a depletion of the central nervous system (CNS) monoamines norepinephrine, serotonin, and dopamine—offered a rationale for the use of these agents on the basis of their ability to either facilitate monoaminergic neurotransmission or prevent the metabolic breakdown of these amines. In reviewing the literature on drug treatments of depression, one important methodological issue is that depressions are likely to be a heterogeneous group of disorders and that, over the years, the populations included in research studies have varied depending on the operational criteria used to define depression and on the exclusion criteria employed to select more or less "pure" samples of depressed patients. This, for example, led to the earlier conclusion that MAO inhibitors were less effective than tricyclic antidepressants (Klerman, 1989), when, in fact, they may be more effective in outpatient samples enriched with depressed patients of the atypical or anergic type (Leibowitz et al., 1984; Thase, 1992). In fact, the great majority of depressed outpatients referred to us in our current studies meet criteria for either probable or definite atypical depression. Although depressed patients in U.S. studies were commonly found to be undertreated or treated without antidepressant drugs (Keller et al., 1982), this problem may be even greater in Europe, where low-dose tricyclic antidepressants are frequently the only treatment offered to those depressed patients referred for pharmacological treatment. When the efficacy of various antidepressants is compared in North American and European studies, these different treatment standards lead to very different results because of substantial differences in sampling and dosing.

Tricyclic Antidepressants

Tricyclic antidepressants are characterized by a chemical structure with two benzene rings joined through a central seven-member ring. Imipramine was the first compound to be developed as part of Geigy Laboratories' program that was originally developed for the investigation of the iminodibenzyl derivatives as potential sedative and antihistaminic agents. The observation of efficacy of this drug in the treatment of depression over the years has stimulated the search for chemically related compounds with antidepressant properties (Klerman, 1972). Of the several dozen of tricyclic drugs, only nine are marketed

in the United States. These agents are structurally related to each other and share anticholinergic, antihistaminic, and anti-α_1-adrenergic side effects. Tricyclic antidepressants are dealkylated and oxidized by hepatic microsomal enzymes, followed by conjugation with glucuronic acid. The traditional view among researchers has been that possible mechanisms of tricyclic antidepressant action are (1) increased monoaminergic activity through a block of monoamine uptake, (2) enhancement of norepinephrine neurotransmission via desensitization of presynaptic α_2-receptors, or (3) the induction of subsensitivity of the β-adrenoceptor system (Baldessarini, 1985). However, many researchers now believe that CNS intracellular changes involving second-messenger systems and gene regulation most likely account for the mechanism of action of antidepressants.

The tricyclic class of antidepressants is often viewed as a fairly homogeneous one, so that failure of a depressed patient to respond to one agent is considered by many clinicians as an indication for a switch to a different class of antidepressants. There is no clear evidence to support this approach. Although the efficacy of most tricyclic antidepressants has been tested through comparisons with other agents of the same class (usually amitriptyline or imipramine), almost all these studies have used a parallel double-blind design and not a crossover one. Given the marked heterogeneity of depressive disorders, comparable efficacy without a stratification for depressive subtypes does not rule out the possibility of a selective specificity of certain agents versus others in the treatment of certain types of depression. For example, in the treatment of obsessive–compulsive patients, clomipramine is clearly the most effective tricyclic antidepressant available (Thoren, Asberg, Cronholm, Jornestedt, & Traskman, 1980). Nonetheless, for the treatment of depression, there is no evidence arguing for superior efficacy of one tricyclic antidepressant over another.

Tricyclic antidepressants have side effects that are closely related to their chemical structure and their affinity to postsynaptic receptors; during treatment they often cause anticholinergic side effects (dry mouth, constipation, blurred vision), orthostatic hypotension, sedation, and weight gain. Carbohydrate craving and increased appetite are commonly associated with treatment with tricyclic antidepressants and are thought to be related to the histamine

H_1 receptor blockade. In fact, a study comparing the incidence of these symptoms with different tricyclic antidepressants found that desipramine, which has only mild affinity for H_1 receptors, was the least likely to induce these symptoms when compared to imipramine, amitriptyline, and doxepin (Yeragani et al., 1988). Tricyclic antidepressants can cause sexual dysfunction, may have significant effects on cardiac conduction, and are contraindicated in the treatment of patients with narrow-angle glaucoma and prostatic hypertrophy; rare adverse events also reported with tricyclic antidepressants are an allergic–obstructive type of jaundice and grand mal seizures (Baldessarini, 1985). Most of the typical side effects tend to subside after a few weeks for those patients who continue treatment, particularly if dosage escalation has been slow and gradual. In general, the tertiary amine tricyclic antidepressants, those with three methyl groups on the amine side chain (e.g., amitriptyline and imipramine), have greater side effect burdens than the secondary amine tricyclic antidepressants, those with two methyl groups on the side chain (e.g., nortriptyline and desipramine). Persistence of bothersome anticholinergic side effects is usually handled by decreasing the dose or by adding cholinergic smooth-muscle stimulants, such as bethanechol (Pollack & Rosenbaum, 1987). An important caution in the use of tricyclic antidepressants with depressed patients is their lethality in overdose.

While many patients are administered tricyclic antidepressants for the management of depression, few receive adequate antidepressant treatment, which requires a dose equal to or greater than 150 mg/day of imipramine or its tricyclic equivalent for at least 4–8 weeks. The reason for assuming that less than 4 weeks of treatment are insufficient is that few patients respond before 2–4 weeks of treatment with a therapeutic dose of tricyclic antidepressants, and many require treatment of 4–8 weeks to show significant improvement (Quitkin, Rabkin, Stewart, McGrath, & Harrison, 1986). All antidepressants have this obligatory latency to efficacy. Plasma levels of tricyclic antidepressants are a rough guide to dosing adequacy and appear more specifically useful for guiding dosage for imipramine, desipramine, amitriptyline, and nortriptyline.

Amitriptyline is a tertiary amine tricyclic antidepressant with mild affinity for dopamine D_2 receptors, moderate affinity for 5-HT_2 receptors, and strong affinity for α_1-adrenoceptors, muscarinic cholinergic receptors, and histamine H_1 receptors (Wander, Nelson, Okazaki, & Richelson, 1986; Richelson & Nelson, 1984). This antidepressant is a moderate norepinephrine uptake blocker and a moderate inhibitor of serotonin uptake *in vitro* (Richelson & Pfenning, 1984). The average half-life of this antidepressant is 21 hours (Richelson, 1989). Relatively frequent side effects are dryness of mouth, drowsiness, increased appetite, dizziness, constipation, blurred vision, and tachycardia (Weissman, Lieb, Prusoff, & Bothwell, 1975). Most cases of lethal overdose have been reported following the ingestion of more than 1.3 g of amitriptyline (American Medical Association, 1992).

Amitriptyline is available in tablets of 10, 25, 50, 75, 100, and 150 mg. The customary initial dose is 25–50 mg/day at bedtime, with gradual upward titration to 150–300 mg/day as tolerated. In a review of the literature (Morris & Beck, 1974), amitriptyline was found to be superior to placebo in 14 out of 20 comparisons. Because of its widespread use since its introduction in the market, it has often been used in comparative trials of newer antidepressants. Nevertheless, given its relatively high side effect burden, most experts do not consider it as a first-line agent among tricyclic antidepressants, except for patients with marked psychomotor agitation and severe insomnia.

Amoxapine is a secondary amine tricyclic antidepressant dibenzoxazepine, with weak affinity for muscarinic cholinergic receptors, moderate affinity for dopamine D_2 and histamine H_1 receptors, and strong affinity for α_1-adrenoceptors (Richelson & Nelson, 1984) and 5-HT_2 receptors (Wander et al., 1986). This antidepressant has been found to be a relatively strong norepinephrine uptake blocker and a mild inhibitor of serotonin uptake *in vitro* (Richelson & Pfenning, 1984), but it also possesses potential neuroleptic activity similar to that reported with loxapine, of which amoxapine is the demethylated metabolite (Greenblatt, Lippa, & Ostenberg, 1978). The average half-life of amoxapine is 8 hours (Richelson, 1989). The most commonly observed side effects are dryness of mouth, constipation, blurred vision, stimulation, and sedation (Jue, Dawson, & Brogden, 1982). Acute dystonic reactions and signs of parkinsonism have been observed in patients taking amoxapine at high doses (Charalampous, 1972). Because amoxapine carries possible short- and long-term neuroleptic-like side effects, including a risk of tardive dyskinesia (Huang, 1986) and particular lethality in overdose (Litovitz & Troutman, 1983), amoxapine is not considered a first-line antidepressant option.

Amoxapine is available in tablets of 50, 100, and 150 mg. The typical initial dose is 50 mg three times/day, with gradual dosage escalation up to 200–400 mg/day over 3–4 weeks, if necessary. A review of the literature (Jue et al., 1982) pointed out the relative paucity of controlled studies showing the superiority of amoxapine compared to placebo.

Clomipramine is a tertiary amine tricyclic antidepressant with moderate affinity for dopamine D_2, histamine H_1, and 5-HT_2 receptors, and strong affinity for muscarinic cholinergic receptors and α_1-adrenoceptors (Richelson & Nelson, 1984; Wander et al., 1986). *In vitro*, it is a very potent serotonin uptake inhibitor and a moderate norepinephrine uptake blocker (Richelson & Pfenning, 1984). Clomipramine in plasma is 98% bound to protein and undergoes significant first-pass metabolism in the liver, with its main metabolite being desmethyl-clomipramine; its half-life ranges from 20 to 40 hours (Trimble, 1990). Its most common side effects are anticholinergic symptoms (particularly dry mouth), somnolence, tremor, dizziness, constipation, gastrointestinal problems, and sexual disturbances (Trimble, 1990). The seizure incidence tends to be mildly higher than with other tricyclic antidepressants, being 0.7% among patients receiving doses up to 300 mg/day for up to 6 years (Trimble, 1990). Deaths due to clomipramine overdose have also been reported (Cassidy & Henry, 1987; Crome, 1993).

Clomipramine is available in tablets of 25, 50, and 75 mg. The recommended initial dose is 25 mg at bedtime, with upward titration to usual doses in the range of 150–200 mg/day. A large study found clomipramine significantly more effective than placebo (Pecknold, Gratton, Ban, & Klinger, 1976) and, in at least five comparison trials, clomipramine showed either a trend toward greater efficacy or actual greater efficacy than other antidepressants (Trimble, 1990). Clomipramine is the tricyclic antidepressant of choice for the treatment of depression with comorbid obsessive–compulsive disorder, and is also considered to be very effective for depressed patients with panic attacks.

Desipramine is a secondary amine tricyclic antidepressant with weak affinity for 5-HT_2 re-

ceptors (Wander et al., 1986), mild affinity for dopamine D_2, muscarinic cholinergic, and histamine H_1 receptors, and moderate affinity for α_1-adrenoceptors (Richelson & Nelson, 1984). *In vitro* studies have found desipramine to be a potent norepinephrine uptake blocker and a fairly mild inhibitor of serotonin uptake (Richelson & Pfenning, 1984). The average half-life of this antidepressant is 21 hours (Richelson, 1989). With minimal sedation and milder anticholinergic side effects, desipramine is one of the tricyclic antidepressants of choice for the treatment of depression. Occasionally patients experience "activating" effects, including transient jitteriness. Other side effects include palpitations, tachycardia, and orthostatic hypotension (Stewart et al., 1983). Desipramine overdoses have been reported to be fatal (Cassidy & Henry, 1987; Crome, 1993).

Desipramine is available in tablets of 10, 25, 50, 75, 100, and 150 mg. The initial dose is usually 30–50 mg/day in divided doses, with gradual dose escalation up to 150–300 mg/day. Plasma levels are a fairly reliable guide to dosing adequacy for desipramine, and nonresponders should have doses increased to ensure plasma levels greater than 125 ng/ml. A large study in patients meeting Research Diagnostic Criteria for major depression found desipramine significantly more effective than placebo (Stewart et al., 1983). An earlier review of the literature (Morris & Beck, 1974) found four of six double-blind studies reporting a superiority of desipramine in comparison with placebo.

Doxepin is a tertiary amine tricyclic antidepressant with mild affinity for dopamine receptors, moderate affinity for muscarinic cholinergic and 5-HT_2 receptors, and strong affinity for α_1-adrenoceptors and histamine H_1 receptors (Richelson & Nelson, 1984; Wander et al., 1986). This antidepressant is a moderate norepinephrine uptake blocker, and a mild inhibitor of serotonin uptake *in vitro* (Richelson & Pfenning, 1984), with an average half-life of 17 hours (Richelson, 1989). Its most common side effects are dry mouth, blurred vision, difficulty in urination, tachycardia, drowsiness, constipation, and orthostatic hypotension (Hollister, 1974). There have been reports of lethal overdoses with doxepin (American Medical Association, 1992).

Doxepin is available in tablets of 10, 25, 50, 75, 100, and 150 mg. The initial dose is usually 25–50 mg/day at bedtime, with gradual dose escalation to 150–300 mg/day if tolerated. There have not been many double-blind, placebo-controlled studies involving doxepin. However, doxepin has been found to be significantly more effective than placebo in one large study (Kiev, 1974) and in a study with sequential design (Burrows, Mowbray, & Davies, 1972).

Imipramine is a tertiary amine tricyclic antidepressant with mild affinity for dopamine D_2 and 5-HT_2 receptors, moderate affinity for muscarinic cholinergic and histamine H_1 receptors, and strong affinity for α_1-adrenoceptors (Richelson & Nelson, 1984; Wander et al., 1986). This drug appears to be a moderate norepinephrine and serotonin uptake blocker *in vitro* (Richelson & Pfenning, 1984), and it has an average half-life of 28 hours (Richelson, 1989). Common side effects are orthostatic hypotension, dryness of mouth, constipation, tachycardia, and blurred vision (Singh, Saxena, Gent, & Nelson, 1976). Deaths occurring from imipramine overdose have also been reported (Cassidy & Henry, 1987; Crome, 1993).

Imipramine is available in tablets of 10, 25, 50, 75, 100, 125, and 150 mg. The initial dose is typically 30–50 mg/day in divided doses, with gradual upward titration to 150–300 mg/day as tolerated. Morris and Beck (1974) reviewed the literature on placebo-controlled studies and found that only 30 out of 50 investigations showed imipramine to be significantly more effective than placebo. Some of the negative studies may have had populations enriched with patients with atypical depression, a subtype with relatively low response rate to imipramine (Liebowitz et al., 1984). A more likely reason for these negative results is that early studies lacked adequacy in dose and duration of treatment, because a target dose of 150 mg/day of imipramine is, for many, too low (Quitkin, 1985) and a 4- to 6-week period is often too short to establish efficacy (Quitkin et al., 1986). Combined plasma levels of imipramine and its demethylated metabolite, desipramine, greater than 225 ng/ml are associated with greatest efficacy. Given its well-established efficacy in the treatment of panic disorder, this tricyclic antidepressant is often prescribed to patients with depression and panic attacks.

Nortriptyline is a secondary amine tricyclic antidepressant with mild affinity for dopamine D_2 and muscarinic cholinergic receptors, moderate affinity for histamine H_1 and 5-HT_2 receptors, and strong affinity for α_1-adrenoceptors (Richelson and Nelson, 1984; Wander et al., 1986). This antidepressant has been found to be

in vitro a strong norepinephrine uptake inhibitor and a mild serotonin uptake blocker (Richelson & Pfenning, 1984). Its average half-life is 36 hours (Richelson, 1989). This antidepressant's most common side effects are dryness of mouth, sweating, blurred vision, tremor, headache, and tiredness (Ziegler, Taylor, Wetzel, & Biggs, 1978). Like desipramine, nortriptyline has a relatively favorable side effect profile when compared to other tricyclic antidepressants, and is associated with a decreased risk of postural hypotension. Thus, it is also a first-line agent, especially for the elderly, who are more vulnerable to falls. Death due to nortriptyline overdose has been documented (Rudorfer & Robins, 1981).

Nortriptyline is available in tablets of 10, 25, 50, and 75 mg. The recommended initial dose is 10–25 mg/day at bedtime, with gradual upward titration to 50–150 mg/day. As pointed out by Morris and Beck (1974), five of eight double-blind studies showed that nortriptyline was more effective than placebo in treating depression. Nortriptyline is considered by many experts to be most likely to be effective when doses used achieve plasma levels greater than 50 ng ml and less than 150 ng/ml. However, the apparent diminished efficacy of higher doses and blood levels may be due to increased side effects and reduced compliance with treatment, rather than to a hypothetical "therapeutic window." Lack of response to nortriptyline in doses associated with therapeutic blood levels should therefore suggest a trial with higher doses of this drug.

Protriptyline is a secondary amine tricyclic antidepressant with mild affinity for dopamine D_2 receptors, moderate affinity for α_1-adrenoceptors, 5-HT_2, and histamine H_1 receptors, and strong affinity for muscarinic cholinergic receptors (Richelson & Nelson, 1984; Wander et al., 1986). This antidepressant is a potent norepinephrine uptake blocker and a fairly mild inhibitor of serotonin uptake *in vitro* (Richelson & Pfenning, 1984). The average half-life of this drug is 78 hours (Richelson, 1989). Its most common side effects are dryness of mouth, somnolence, restlessness, dizziness, constipation, difficulties urinating, and blurred vision (Isaksson, Larkander, Morsing, Ottoson, & Rapp, 1968). Lethality following protriptyline overdose has been observed (Cassidy & Henry, 1987).

Protriptyline is available in tablets of 5 and 10 mg. The typical initial dose is 10–15 mg/day in single or divided doses in the morning, with gradual upward titration to 30–60 mg/day. All three studies comparing this antidepressant with placebo found protriptyline to be more effective than the inactive compound (Morris & Beck, 1974). This antidepressant is rarely considered to be a first-line agent for the treatment of depression, mostly because of concerns about its long half-life.

Trimipramine is a tricyclic antidepressant with moderate affinity for muscarinic cholinergic, 5-HT_2, and dopamine D_2 receptors, and strong affinity for α_1-adrenoceptors and histamine H_1 receptors (Richelson & Nelson, 1984; Wander et al., 1986). *In vitro* studies showed this antidepressant to be a weak serotonin uptake inhibitor and a weak norepinephrine uptake blocker (Richelson & Pfenning, 1984). This drug's average half-life is 13 hours (Richelson, 1989). Its most common side effects are dry mouth, blurred vision, drowsiness, dizziness, and constipation (Hussain & Chaudhry, 1973). Death from overdose has been reported as well (Crome & Newman, 1979).

Trimipramine is available in tablets of 25, 50, and 100 mg. The recommended initial dose is 25–50 mg at bedtime, with gradual dose increases up to 150–200 mg/day over 7 to 14 days. A fairly large study found this antidepressant significantly more effective than placebo (Rickels et al., 1970).

Tetracyclic Antidepressants

The only tetracyclic (comprised of four benzene rings) antidepressant available is maprotiline, which is a derivative of dibenzo(b,e,)bicyclo-(2.2.2.)octadiene, and is distinguished from tricyclic antidepressants only by the rigidity of its molecular structure due to its ethylene bridge. Maprotiline has mild affinity for dopamine D_2 and 5-HT_2 receptors, weak affinity for muscarinic cholinergic receptors, and strong affinity for α_1-adrenoceptors and histamine H_1 receptors (Richelson & Nelson, 1984; Wander et al., 1986). *In vitro* studies have shown that maprotiline is a strong norepinephrine uptake inhibitor and weak serotonin uptake blocker (Richelson & Pfenning, 1984). Its average half-life is 43 hours (Richelson, 1989). The side effects that are reported most frequently are dryness of mouth, tremor, constipation, blurred vision, dizziness, and drowsiness (Pinder, Brogden, Speight, & Avery, 1977). Although the overall incidence of seizures is low, grand mal seizures

have been reported more frequently at normal therapeutic dosages of maprotiline than at such dosages of tricyclic antidepressants (Pinder et al., 1977). Fatal overdoses with maprotiline have also been reported (Pinder et al., 1977).

Maprotiline is available in tablets of 25, 50, and 75 mg. The usual initial dose is 50–75 mg/day in divided doses, with gradual upward titration to 150–200 mg/day. Doses over 225 mg/day are not recommended because of the risk of grand mal seizures. Of 29 double-blind but not placebo-controlled trials (using the Hamilton Rating Scale for Depression as outcome measure) reviewed by Pinder et al. (1977), all but two trials showed no difference between maprotiline and a comparison drug, and in two cases a significant superiority was observed for maprotiline. On the other hand, the only two placebo-controlled trials failed to show a statistically significant difference between maprotiline and placebo (Pinder et al., 1977).

Monoamine Oxidase Inhibitors

MAO inhibitors are an important class of antidepressants that over the past few years have been used primarily in the treatment of certain depressive subtypes, or as a second, but robust, line of treatment of depression. These antidepressants inhibit the MAO enzymes located in monoamine-containing nerve terminals, as well as in the liver and other tissues that metabolize such monoamines as norepinephrine, serotonin, and dopamine. There are two types of MAO isozymes: MAO-A and MAO-B. As Mann, Aarons, Frances, and Brown (1984) point out, human brain MAO-A preferentially denatures norepinephrine, serotonin and, in the cortex, dopamine, whereas MAO-B denatures dopamine and phenylethylamine. Although the mechanism of action of MAO inhibitors is usually thought to be their potentiation of aminergic activity by inhibition of these isozymes, many researchers now believe that CNS intracellular changes involving second-messenger systems and gene regulation most likely account for the mechanism of action of this class of antidepressants.

These antidepressants are relatively devoid of any postsynaptic receptor affinity. MAO enzymes are also crucial in inactivating exogenous monoamines arising from foods or the action of bacteria in the gut, including the sympathomimetic pressor amine tyramine (Baldessarini, 1985). The use of MAO inhibitors is therefore associated with a risk of lethal hypertensive crisis related to interactions with foods containing tyramine or sympathomimetic drugs (McGilchrist, 1975; Larsen & Rafaelsen, 1980; McGrath et al., 1989). Other rare, but severe, adverse events such as heat stroke, vascular collapse, or death may follow interactions with potent serotonergic agents (Beasley, Masica, Heiligenstein, Wheadon, & Zerbe, 1993).

MAO inhibitors have been found to be particularly effective in treating both anergic and atypical depression, as well as the subtypes of anxious and hostile depression (Davidson, Giller, Zisook, & Overall, 1988; Liebowitz et al., 1984; Thase, 1992).

Three of the four currently marketed MAO inhibitors (phenelzine, isocarboxazid, and tranylcypromine) are nonselective and inhibit both isozymes. The fourth marketed MAO inhibitor, L-deprenyl, preferentially inactivates MAO-B, whereas it has little effect on MAO-A within a dose range of 5–10 mg/day (Knoll, 1983). All of the aforementioned drugs have a prolonged biological half-life, and are considered relatively irreversible MAO inhibitors, in that they exert a persistent inhibitory effect on these isozymes. The normal function of these enzymes is restored only after several drug-free days to allow regeneration of new stores of enzymes. More recently, moclobemide, a newer antidepressant with reversible effects of inhibition of MAO and greatly diminished risk of dietary or other interactions, has become available in Europe and Canada.

It is a safe and common practice to wait 2 weeks after discontinuing non-MAO-inhibitor antidepressants and 5 weeks after discontinuing protriptyline or fluoxetine before starting treatment with nonselective, irreversible MAO inhibitors. It is also recommended to wait 2 weeks before starting another antidepressant following discontinuation of an irreversible MAO inhibitor. Hepatotoxicity is a rare but possible event during the use of MAO inhibitors (Baldessarini, 1985). Because insomnia is a potential side effect of this class of antidepressants, it is best to administer the last daily dose in the early afternoon.

Phenelzine is a hydrazine derivative MAO inhibitor that has an average half-life of 2.8 hours (Richelson, 1989) and exerts a persistent inhibition of MAO-A and MAO-B activity, which lasts long after the drug is no longer detectable in plasma. Common side effects are insomnia or sedation, orthostatic hypotension (Ravaris, Robinson, Ives, Nies, & Bartlett, 1980),

and sexual dysfunction (Baldessarini, 1985). Despite the apparent lack of affinity for muscarinic cholinergic receptors, such anticholinergic side effects as dry mouth, constipation, and urinary retention may also be observed. The incidence of hypertensive crisis related to a food or drug interaction is relatively low (McGilchrist, 1975), and there have been reports of several cases of lethal overdoses with this drug (American Medical Association, 1992).

Phenelzine is available in 15-mg tablets. The customary initial dose is commonly 15 mg twice or three times daily, with gradual upward titration to 45–90 mg/day in divided doses after 3 weeks if no significant response is observed. A review by Quitkin, Rifkin, and Klein (1979) concluded that phenelzine was superior to placebo in most outpatient studies, but commented on the lack of good evidence pertaining to its effectiveness for inpatients with endogenous depression. In addition, phenelzine has been found to be more effective than imipramine in treating atypical depression (Liebowitz et al., 1984).

Isocarboxazid is another hydrazine derivative MAO inhibitor with a persistent inhibition of MAO-A and MAO-B activity lasting long after the drug is administered. Relatively frequent side effects of this drug are insomnia or sleepiness, orthostatic hypotension, constipation, restlessness, weight gain, and sexual dysfunction (Larsen & Rafaelsen, 1980). Deaths from overdose have also been reported (Cassidy & Henry, 1987). The production of this drug has been recently discontinued.

Isocarboxazid is available in 10-mg tablets and its usual initial dosage is 20–30 mg/day in divided doses, with gradual increases up to 50 mg/day after 3–4 weeks if no significant response is noted. Hypertensive crisis related to either food or drug interactions have also been reported with this antidepressant (Larsen & Rafaelsen, 1980). The results of a large multicenter study (Davidson et al., 1988) showed that isocarboxazid was superior to placebo in patients with major depression, as well as in patients with atypical depression with reversed vegetative symptoms (e.g., hypersomnia and hyperphagia), and in the subtypes of anxious and hostile depression.

Tranylcypromine is a nonhydrazine MAO inhibitor that is formed from cyclization of the side chain of amphetamine. This drug's half-life is very short (1.5–3 hours; Richelson, 1989) with a persistent inhibition of MAO-A and MAO-B activity lasting long after the drug is no longer detectable in the blood. The most common side effects of this antidepressant are dry mouth, insomnia, tremor, dizziness, constipation, blurred vision, sedation, and overexcitement (White et al., 1984). The incidence of intracranial hemorrhage (sometimes fatal) associated with paradoxical hypertension and severe occipital headache appears to be greater than with phenelzine or isocarboxazid (American Medical Association, 1992). Death due to tranylcypromine overdose has been reported (Boniface, 1991).

Tranylcypromine is available in 10-mg tablets and its typical initial dose is 20-30 mg/day in divided doses. After 3 weeks of treatment, the dosage can be gradually increased up to 60 mg/day if no significant response is observed. Five of six double-blind, placebo-controlled studies (Bartholomew, 1962; Khanna, Pratt, Bordizk, & Chaddha, 1963; Glick, 1964; Gottfries, 1963; Himmelhoch, Fuchs, & Symons, 1982; White et al., 1984) found this drug to be more effective than placebo in the treatment of depression.

A relatively selective MAO-B inhibitor, L-deprenyl, is marketed for the treatment of Parkinson's disease. This drug's most common side effects are dry mouth, drowsiness, tremor, insomnia, sexual dysfunction, and orthostatic symptoms (Mann et al., 1989). There have been reports of hypertensive crisis with this antidepressant when higher doses have been used (McGrath et al., 1989). Meeker and Reynolds (1990) reported one case of death in a 72-year-old woman on L-deprenyl, following overdose with methyprylon, nortriptyline, and trazodone. No fatal overdoses of L-deprenyl alone have been reported to date (data on file at Somerset Pharmaceuticals).

This medication is available in 10-mg tablets, with a customary initial dose of 20 mg/day in divided doses and gradual upward titration to 30–40 mg/day if necessary. In a double-blind study, L-deprenyl at doses of 10 mg/day was not more effective than placebo during the first 3 weeks, but at higher doses (averaging about 30 mg/day for the second 3 weeks of the study), it was superior to placebo (Mann et al., 1989). These findings suggest that the antidepressant efficacy of this drug may be present only at dosages where it begins to have other effects, such as inhibition of dopamine uptake (Lader, Sakalis, & Tansella, 1972) and inhibition of MAO-A.

Moclobemide is a benzamide derivative that is available only in Europe and Canada. It is a short-acting, reversible MAO inhibitor, preferentially inhibiting MAO-A (Da Prada, Kettler, Keller, & Haefely, 1983). In preclinical experiments, moclobemide showed neither a toxic effect on the liver nor a significant potentiation of tyramine (Da Prada, Kettler, Burkard, & Haefely, 1984). Its most frequently observed side effects are dry mouth, somnolence, headache, dizziness, and psychomotor agitation (Ucha Udabe, Marquez, Traballi, & Portes, 1990). Although several reports suggest that moclobemide is relatively nontoxic in overdose (Heinze & Sanchez, 1986; Moll & Hetzel, 1990; Myrenfors, Eriksson, Sandstedt, & Sjöberg, 1993), fatal interactions of moclobemide with citalopram and clomipramine, leading to a serotonergic syndrome, have been observed (Neuvonen, Pohjola-Sintonen, Tacke, & Vuori, 1993).

Typically, the initial dose is 300 mg/day with gradual upward titration to 600–1,200 mg/day if no response is observed within 3 weeks. Several multicenter studies found moclobemide more effective than placebo in the treatment of depression (Ucha Udabe et al., 1990; Versiani, Nardi, Mundim, Alves, & Schmid-Burgk, 1990; Bakish et al., 1992).

Selective Serotonin Reuptake Inhibitors

The development of selective serotonin reuptake inhibitors (SSRIs) offered a new class of psychotropic compounds with antidepressant activity, an improved side effect profile, and potentially unique therapeutic effects. There is some evidence that SSRIs have selective efficacy in the treatment of bulimia nervosa (Fluoxetine Bulimia Nervosa Collaborative Study Group, 1992), obsessive–compulsive disorder (Jenike et al., 1990), and, possibly, atypical depression (Pande, Haskett, & Greden, 1992). These agents are structurally unrelated to tricyclic or tetracyclic antidepressants and lack associated anticholinergic, antihistaminic and anti-α_1-adrenergic effects. The postulated mechanism of SSRIs' antidepressant action has been traditionally that of enhancement of serotonergic neurotransmission through a desensitization of somatodendritic autoreceptors, allowing serotonergic neurons to recover a normal rate of firing despite sustained serotonin reuptake blockade (de Montigny, Chaput, & Blier, 1990). The induction of subsensitivity of the β-adrenoceptor system also occurs and has also been hypothesized as an alternative mechanism of action for these antidepressants (Koe, Koch, Lebel, Minor, & Page, 1987). As mentioned before, however, many researchers now believe that CNS intracellular changes involving second-messenger systems and gene regulation are most likely to account for the mechanism of action of this class of antidepressants.

SSRIs have fewer side effects than tricyclic antidepressants; they do not have significant effects on cardiac conduction and do not tend to cause either weight gain or orthostatic hypotension (Rickels & Schweizer, 1990). They also are far safer in overdose. These characteristics make these drugs particularly suitable for the treatment of both mildly to moderately depressed outpatients and depression in the elderly.

Five drugs of this class (fluoxetine, sertraline, paroxetine, fluvoxamine, and venlafaxine) are available in the United States. As shown in Table 9.1, when the ability to inhibit uptake of serotonin in vitro is compared with the inhibition of norepinephrine uptake, fluvoxamine and sertraline are the most selective, and fluoxetine and venlafaxine, the least selective. Similarly, when the ability to inhibit uptake of serotonin in vitro is compared with the inhibition of dopamine uptake, fluvoxamine and paroxetine are the most selective, whereas sertraline is the least selective. It is unclear whether relative selectivity is truly an advantage for drugs of this particular class; for example, it has been argued that a greater efficacy of SSRIs in the treatment of obsessive–compulsive disorder is associated with less serotonergic specificity (Jenike et al., 1990). In addition, in vitro uptake inhibition studies do not necessarily reflect in vivo potency; for example, Shank et al. (1988) found that sertraline was 10 times more potent

than fluoxetine in vitro, but almost half as potent in vivo, using as an animal model the potentiation of L-5-hydroxytryptophan-induced head twitches in mice.

Fluoxetine, $(\pm)$-N-methyl-3-phenyl-3-[$(\alpha, \alpha, \alpha$-trifluoro-p-tolyl)oxy]propylamine, was the first SSRI released in the United States and has been available since 1988. Both fluoxetine and its metabolite norfluoxetine are potent and selective inhibitors of serotonin uptake in vitro (Schmidt, Fuller, & Wong, 1988; Bolden-Watson & Richelson, 1993). Fluoxetine has mild affinity for 5-HT$_2$ receptors and very low affinity for α_1-adrenoceptors, histamine H$_1$ receptors, muscarinic cholinergic receptors (Lemberger, Farid, Bergstrom, & Wolen, 1987), and dopamine D$_2$ receptors (Cusack, Nelson, & Richelson, 1994). Fluoxetine's chemical structure lacks the three-fused ring system contained in tricyclic antidepressants, with the p-trifluoromethyl substituent on the phenoxy ring being an important determinant of its specificity as a serotonin uptake inhibitor (Schmidt et al., 1988). Fluoxetine and norfluoxetine demonstrate long plasma half-lives (approximately 2 and 7 days, respectively) and are highly bound to plasma proteins (94%; Bergstrom, Lemberger, Farid, & Wolen, 1988). Since these two drugs are metabolized in the liver and excreted primarily in the urine, their pharmacokinetics are not affected by renal impairment, but there is a clear prolongation of their half-lives in patients with hepatic dysfunction (Bergstrom et al., 1988). Although Teicher, Glod, and Cole (1990) described six depressed patients who developed "intense, violent suicidal preoccupation" after 2 to 7 weeks of treatment, two studies, one retrospective (Fava & Rosenbaum, 1991) and one prospective (Beasley et al., 1991), failed to find evidence of a relationship between fluoxetine and suicidal ideation or acts.

A review by Lader (1988) of studies comparing fluoxetine with tricyclic and tetracyclic antidepressants concluded that fluoxetine's efficacy was comparable to that of other antidepressants, although fluoxetine has fewer and less severe side effects. Hall (1988) reviewed the placebo-controlled studies and concluded that fluoxetine, in doses of 5, 20, and 40 mg/day, although not in doses of 60 mg/day, was significantly more effective than placebo in patients with moderate to severe major depressive disorder. The relatively higher dropout rate among patients treated with 60 mg/day of fluoxetine because of a dose relationship for adverse events seems to

TABLE 9.1. Selectivity for Inhibition of Serotonin (5-HT) Uptake versus Either Norepinephrine (NE) or Dopamine (DA) Uptake in Rat Brain Synaptosomes *In Vitro*

Antidepressant	5-HT/NE K_i ratio	5-HT/DA K_i ratio
SSRIs		
Paroxetine	0.02	0.0004
Fluvoxamine	0.006	0.0006
Sertraline	0.015	0.01
Desmethylsertraline	0.18	0.17
Fluoxetine	0.10	0.005
Norfluoxetine	0.06	0.02
Venlafaxine	0.19	0.007
Tricyclic antidepressant		
Amitriptyline	6.0	0.01

Note. Data from Tulloch & Johnson (1992) and Bolden-Watson & Richelson (1993).

be the main reason for the relative lack of efficacy of this dosage (Beasley, Bosomworth, & Wernicke, 1990). The possibility remains that for some patients gradual dose escalation to 60 mg/day might result in greater efficacy compared to 20 mg/day, although one study failed to demonstrate this hypothesis (Schweizer et al., 1990). However, we have observed that patients who had failed to respond to an 8-week trial with fluoxetine 20 mg/day subsequently responded to a 4-week trial of fluoxetine increased up to 40–60 mg/day (Fava et al., 1992). In terms of safety and tolerability, fluoxetine's more common side effects are nausea, headache, nervousness, and insomnia; overdose appears to be relatively safe, without evidence of cardiotoxicity (Cooper, 1988). Rash, rarely associated with joint pain and swelling, appears to be the most common potentially serious adverse event (Cooper, 1988).

Sertraline, 1S,4S,-N-methyl-4-(3,4-dichlorophenyl)-1,2,3,4-tetrahydro-1-naphthylamine, is a fairly potent competitive inhibitor of synaptosomal serotonin uptake (Koe, Weissman, Welch, & Browne, 1983; Bolden-Watson & Richelson, 1993). Sertraline has mild affinity for α_1-adrenoceptors and low affinity for dopamine D_2, histamine H_1, 5-HT_2, and muscarinic cholinergic receptors (Koe, 1990; Cusack et al., 1994). Sertraline's metabolism occurs in the liver, with N-demethylation to desmethylsertraline and deamination to desmethylsertraline ketone; its half-life is roughly 26 hours (Fouda, Ronfeld, & Weidler, 1987). Its longer lived major metabolite, desmethylsertraline, is felt to be clinically inactive, because it is virtually inactive in the behavioral despair paradigm of the mouse Porsolt swim test (Reimherr et al., 1990). However, this metabolite is fairly active in vitro (Bolden-Watson & Richelson, 1993). Sertraline's most common side effects are nausea, diarrhea, dryness of mouth, somnolence, insomnia, male sexual dysfunction, and headache (Reimherr et al., 1990). Not enough information is available about the safety of sertraline in overdose, although three reported overdoses were uneventful (International Drug Therapy Newsletter, 1992).

Sertraline was introduced in the U.S. market early in 1992 and is available in tablets of 50 and 100 mg. It is usually administered with a meal to increase plasma levels otherwise reduced by first-pass hepatic extraction. The recommended initial dose is 50 mg, with upward titration to 100 mg after 2 weeks, and to 150 mg and 200 mg

thereafter if no significant response is observed. A large multicenter U.S. study found sertraline (at a mean dose of 145 mg/day) significantly more effective than placebo and as effective as amitriptyline (Reimherr et al., 1990). There are no reports to date that sertraline worsens suicidality (International Drug Therapy Newsletter, 1992).

Paroxetine is a phenyl-piperidine derivative with the most potent inhibition of serotonin reuptake in vitro (Tulloch & Johnson, 1992; Bolden-Watson & Richelson, 1993). Paroxetine has low affinity for α_1-adrenoceptors and dopamine D_2, histamine H_1, and 5-HT_2 receptors, and has mild/moderate affinity for the muscarinic cholinergic receptor (Thomas, Nelson, & Johnson, 1987; Tulloch & Johnson, 1992; Cusack et al., 1994). Paroxetine undergoes extensive first-pass metabolism in the liver (Lund et al., 1982), and its metabolites are pharmacologically inactive in vivo (Haddock et al., 1989); this antidepressant does not induce significant changes in electrocardiographic parameters (Edwards, Goldie, & Papayanni-Parasthatis, 1989). The terminal elimination half-life of paroxetine, with 85% of the drug bound to plasma proteins, exhibits wide variability, with a mean of 24 hours (Kaye et al., 1989). Paroxetine is available in tablets of 20 and 30 mg. Because of its half-life, once-daily morning dosing between 20 and 50 mg is usually recommended, with 20 mg/day being the minimum effective dosage. In clinical practice, patients initially receive 20 mg/day of paroxetine, with an upward titration in 10-mg increments after 3 weeks if adequate response is not observed (Dunner & Dunbar, 1992).

The most common side effects of this medication are nausea, headache, somnolence, dryness of mouth, and insomnia, and overdose appears to be relatively safe (Boyer & Blumhardt, 1992). Given the issue of whether SSRIs may cause or aggravate suicidal ideation among depressed patients, Dunner and Dunbar (1991) analyzed data from the U.S. database and found that paroxetine and active control were significantly better than placebo at both reducing suicidality present at baseline and, among patients with no suicidal thoughts at baseline, protecting against the emergence of suicidality. Paroxetine was found to be significantly more effective than placebo (Claghorn, 1992; Cohn & Wilcox, 1992; Fabre, 1992; Feighner & Boyer, 1992; Kiev, 1992; Rickels et al., 1992; R. K. Shrivastava, Shrivastava, Overweg, &

Blumhardt, 1992) and to have an effect comparable (Cohn & Wilcox, 1992; Dunner et al., 1992; Fabre, 1992) or even superior (Feighner & Boyer, 1992; Shrivastava et al., 1992) to that of tricyclic antidepressants.

Fluvoxamine is a 2-aminoethyloxime aralkylketone with strong inhibition of serotonin uptake in vitro (Richelson & Pfenning, 1984). Apart from a moderate affinity for $5\text{-}HT_2$ and α_1-adrenergic receptors, fluvoxamine has low affinity for dopamine D_2, histamine H_1, and muscarinic cholinergic receptors (Tulp, Mol, Rademaker, & Schipper, 1988). Its most common side effects are nausea, vomiting, headache, dryness of the mouth, and sedation (Benfield & Ward, 1986). Over 90% of a dose of fluvoxamine is recovered in urine in the form of at least 11 metabolites; the initial elimination half-life of fluvoxamine is about 2 hours, but a second elimination phase with a half-life of nearly 15 hours occurs, with 77% of the drug being bound to plasma proteins (Benfield & Ward, 1986). Most of the metabolites are produced by oxidative demethylation of the aliphatic methoxyl group of the parent compound and by degradation of the primary amino group (Overmars, Scherpenisse, & Post, 1983).

Fluvoxamine is available in tablets of 50 and 100 mg. In single or divided daily dosages of between 50 and 300 mg it has been found to have antidepressant activity in placebo-controlled studies (Amin, Anath, Coleman, Darcourt, & Farkas, 1984; Benfield & Ward, 1986) and to possess efficacy comparable to that of tricyclic antidepressants (De Wilde, Mertens, & Wakelin, 1983; Benfield & Ward, 1986). Fluvoxamine does not seem to cause any cardiovascular side effects except for a clinically nonsignificant slight reduction of heart rate (Roos & Sharp, 1984). Overdose seems to be relatively safe (Benfield & Ward, 1986). Because of the possibility of sedation, fluvoxamine is usually administered as a single evening dose of 50–300 mg.

Venlafaxine, (R/S)-1-[2-(dimethylamino)-1-(4-methoxyphenyl)ethyl]cyclohexanol, is an SSRI with moderate/strong inhibition of serotonin uptake in vitro (Bolden-Watson & Richelson, 1993). Its mild ability to inhibit norepinephrine uptake is comparable to that of fluoxetine (Bolden-Watson & Richelson, 1993). It has low or absent affinity for muscarinic cholinergic, α_1-adrenergic, histamine H_1, dopamine D_2, and $5\text{-}HT_2$ receptors (Cusack et al., 1994). The most common side effects of venlafaxine are nausea, insomnia, sedation, dizziness, constipation,

sweating, nervousness, and sexual dysfunction (Rosenbaum, Fava, & Nierenberg, 1994). The clinical efficacy of venlafaxine in the treatment of depression has been established in six placebo-controlled trials involving more than 700 patients (Feighner, 1992).

Venlafaxine is available in tablets of 25, 37.5, 50, 75, and 100 mg. The recommended starting dose is 75 mg/day, administered in two or three divided doses with meals. The dosage may be increased in increments of up to 75 mg/day to a maximum dosage of 350 mg/day. Of the 14 reported cases of overdose with venlafaxine to date, none were fatal (data on file at Wyeth Laboratories, Inc.).

At this point, there are no efficacy data to recommend one SSRI over another for the treatment of depression. Fluoxetine has the advantage of years of use and millions of patients treated. As with other classes of antidepressants, however, there are expectations for differential responses of individual patients. In particular, variations in side effect intensity may occur across patients treated with different types of SSRIs. For example, some patients who experience agitation on fluoxetine may have less distress on sertraline or paroxetine; others who suffer from marked gastrointestinal distress on sertraline or venlafaxine may better tolerate fluoxetine or paroxetine; and, finally, others who complain of severe symptoms of sexual dysfunction on sertraline or paroxetine, may experience a lessening of this side effect on fluoxetine. It is therefore possible that in the next few years clinicians will select the SSRI based on subtle differences in side effect profile.

Atypical Antidepressants

A number of agents used in the treatment of depression have chemical structures different from those of tricyclic antidepressants, MAO inhibitors, and SSRIs. These include the antidepressants trazodone, nefazodone, and bupropion, as well as other agents such as alprazolam, s-adenosyl-L-methionine, and the stimulants dextroamphetamine and methylphenidate.

Bupropion (2-ter-butylamino-3'-chlorophenone hydrochloride) is an aminoketone with almost no affinity for dopamine D_2, muscarinic cholinergic, and $5\text{-}HT_2$ receptors and very weak affinity for α_1-adrenoceptors and histamine H_1 receptors (Hall, Sallemark, & Wedel, 1984; Richelson & Nelson, 1984; Wander et al., 1986). In vivo studies have shown that this antidepressant is a relatively selective dopamine uptake blocker *in vivo* (Cooper, Hester, & Maxwell, 1980). Bupropion in plasma is 80% bound to protein and undergoes extensive first-pass metabolism in the liver: four metabolites have been identified, two of which are active (Schroeder, 1983; Laizure, Devane, Stewart, Dommisse, & Lai, 1985). The half-life of this drug is biphasic, and its beta phase ranges from 8 to 24 hours (Lai & Schroeder, 1983). Its most common side effects are agitation, dry mouth, insomnia, headache, nausea, vomiting, constipation, and tremor (Van Wyck Fleet et al., 1983). Bupropion was approved by the FDA in 1985. Just before being marketed, seizures were observed in 4 of 30 patients in a study of bulimia (Horne et al., 1988). Marketing was then delayed and further studies on the incidence of seizures have since established the risk as 0.4% at doses up to 450 mg/day (Weisler, 1991). The incidence increases almost tenfold at higher doses, so that 450 mg is the maximum recommended daily dose, with 150 mg being the maximum single dose to avoid high peak concentrations of the drug and its metabolites. Only two lethal overdoses with bupropion have been reported, suggesting a relative safety in overdose compared to tricyclic antidepressants (Weisler, 1991).

Bupropion is available in tablets of 75 and 100 mg. The customary initial dose is 75 or 100 mg twice daily, with upward titration to 100 mg three times daily after 4–7 days, and to 100 mg four times daily or 150 mg three times daily after 2–3 weeks if no significant response is observed. A large multicenter study found bupropion (at a dose of 300 mg/day) significantly more effective than placebo by day 21 (Lineberry et al., 1990).

Trazodone is a triazolopyridine antidepressant with low affinity for dopamine D_2 and histamine H_1 receptors, strong affinity for α_1-adrenoceptors and 5-HT_2 receptors, and essentially no affinity for muscarinic cholinergic receptors (Cusack et al., 1994). This antidepressant is a relatively weak norepinephrine uptake blocker and a mild inhibitor of serotonin uptake *in vitro* (Bolden-Watson & Richelson, 1993). The average half-life of this antidepressant is 7 hours (Richelson, 1989). Common side effects are drowsiness, dizziness, headache, nausea, and hypotension, with priapism being an extremely rare but potentially serious side effect in men (Feighner & Boyer, 1988). In a series of 88 reported cases of trazodone overdose, there were no deaths when trazodone was the only substance ingested (Gamble & Peterson, 1986).

Trazodone is available in tablets of 50, 100, 150, and 300 mg. The initial dose is 50–100 mg/day at bedtime, with upward titration to 200–400 mg/day. In their review of the literature, Feighner and Boyer (1988) pointed out that in two large multicenter studies, a greater efficacy of trazodone compared to placebo was observed. Nonetheless, there is an impression among experts that trazodone is less effective than other antidepressants.

Nefazodone is a phenylpiperazine compound chemically related to trazodone, but has less α_1-adrenergic blocking properties and is expected to cause less sedation and priapism. *In vivo*, it strongly inhibits serotonin uptake and is a strong blocker of 5-HT_2 receptors (Fontaine, 1993; Cusack et al., 1994), with essentially no affinity for muscarinic cholinergic and histamine H_1 receptors, strong affinity for α_1-adrenoceptors, and low affinity for D_2 receptors (Cusack et al., 1994). The half-life of nefazodone, which increases both with dose and with time, is about 5 hours. Its most common side effects are headache, dry mouth, and nausea (Rosenbaum et al., 1994). A meta-analysis of several placebo-controlled trials suggests that the therapeutic dose range of nefazodone is 300–500 mg/day (Archibald, Copp, Anton, Gammans, & Kensler, 1993). This antidepressant has been recently introduced in the United States and is available in tablets of 100 and 150 mg. The recommended starting dose is 100 mg twice daily.

Alprazolam is a triazolobenzodiazepine with known anxiolytic and hypnotic properties. It is marketed for the treatment of anxiety disorders. As Eriksson, Nagy, and Starmark (1987) pointed out, this drug is devoid of anticholinergic properties and has a low order of toxicity in animal systems. Although it does not seem to affect the uptake of neurotransmitters, it does reduce total body norepinephrine turnover (Charney & Heninger, 1985). The half-life of this medication ranges from 12 to 15 hours, with its major metabolite, α-hydroxyalprazolam, being conjugated and excreted in the urine (American Medical Association, 1992). Alprazolam is available in 0.25-, 0.5-, 1-, and 2-mg tablets. The usual initial dosage is 0.5 mg three times daily, with gradual increase every 3–4 days up to 1–2 mg three times daily if no improvement is noted. The most common side effects observed with this medication are drowsiness, ataxia, headache, and lightheadedness. Physical or psychological dependence is commonly observed when the treatment is protracted and withdrawal re-

292 BIOLOGICAL PROCESSES AND TREATMENTS

actions, including seizures, have been reported when the dosage was changed, or if the drug was discontinued abruptly. Overdose of alprazolam with markedly elevated serum concentrations has been reported to cause only mild toxicity (McCormick, Nielsen, & Jatlow, 1985).

In two separate multicenter studies (Feighner, Aden, Fabre, Rickels, & Smith, 1983; Rickels, Feighner, & Smith, 1985), alprazolam was found to be more effective than placebo in treating depression. Despite these reports, alprazolam has not found acceptance as an antidepressant of comparable efficacy to others. Many feel its putative antidepressant efficacy reflects anxiolytic effects common to the benzodiazepine class. As a short-acting, high-potency agent requiring careful tapering to discontinue treatment, it is rarely used as a first-line agent for major depressive disorder in the absence of a concomitant anxiety disorder, such as panic disorder.

S-adenosyl-L-methionine (SAMe) is a physiological substance available in Europe as an antidepressant in both parenteral and oral forms. SAMe is naturally produced in mammals from L-methionine and adenosine triphosphate, and takes part in numerous metabolic pathways, being the major source of methyl groups in the brain (Baldessarini, 1987).

The most common side effects of SAMe, which tend to be mild and transient, are anxiety, increased salivation, and dry mouth (Rosenbaum et al., 1990). A meta-analysis of the controlled studies comparing parenteral and oral SAMe with placebo found a greater efficacy for SAMe over placebo (Bressa, 1994). There may not be enough evidence yet to support the efficacy of the oral preparation of SAMe (up to 1,600 mg/day) in depression, in spite of a positive, preliminary placebo-controlled study (Kagan, Sultzer, Rosenlicht, & Gerner, 1990). An interaction of SAMe and clomipramine has been linked to the development of serotonin syndrome (Iruela, Minguez, Merino, & Monedero, 1993).

Dextroamphetamine is a noncatecholamine, sympathomimetic amine with CNS stimulant activity, and methylphenidate (methyl-α-phenyl-2-piperidineacetate hydrochloride) is a CNS stimulant whose mode of action is still poorly understood. While the average half-life of dextroamphetamine is roughly 10 hours, methylphenidate's half-life is much shorter, with only the sustained-release form having a duration of effect comparable to that of dextroamphetamine. The usual dosage is 10–40 mg/day in divided doses for dextroamphetamine (available in 5-, 10-, and 15-mg capsules) and 30–90 mg/day in divided doses for methylphenidate (available in 5-, 10-, and 20-mg tablets).

The most common side effects of these two stimulants are insomnia, nausea, tremor, appetite change, palpitations, blurred vision, dry mouth, constipation, and dizziness (Satel & Nelson, 1989). Other reported side effects are blood pressure changes in either direction, dysrhythmias, tachycardia, tremor, and exacerbation of pre-existing anxiety (Satel & Nelson, 1989). As Satel and Nelson point out, the 10 placebo-controlled studies of these two stimulant drugs in primary depression, with one exception, indicated little advantage of the drug over placebo. For these reasons, stimulants have been primarily used as adjuncts to other treatments in patients with depression.

CONTINUATION PHARMACOTHERAPY IN DEPRESSION

Prien and Kupfer (1986) classified the treatment of depressive disorders with antidepressant drugs into three phases: (1) acute therapy, (2) continuation therapy, and (3) long-term preventive therapy. While "continuation therapy" is usually defined as the continued administration of the drug for 5–6 months following the disappearance of acute symptoms in order to maintain control over the episode, "long-term therapy" refers to pharmacological treatment extending beyond the continuation phase and being administered for long periods of time (months or years) to prevent recurrences. While the acute efficacy of antidepressants has been extensively documented, very few studies have been conducted to assess their efficacy during continuation and long-term therapy (Fava & Kaji, 1994). Prien and Kupfer (1986) reviewed a number of early investigations on the efficacy of long-term antidepressant drug treatment in depressed patients and concluded that the risk of relapse was approximately 50% when recently improved patients were switched to placebo, as opposed to 20% in patients receiving ongoing treatment with lithium or tricyclic antidepressants. A more recent meta-analysis (Loonen, Peer, & Zwanikken, 1991) of studies on the efficacy of long-term antidepressant drug treatment in patients with recurrent major depression found that continuation therapy with antidepressants (amitriptyline and imipramine) was effective. Prien and Kupfer (1986) also re-analyzed data from a multicenter clinical trial and found that the risk of relapse after antide-pressant withdrawal only abated after at least 4 months of sustained response, underscoring the importance of continuation therapy.

LONG-TERM PHARMACOTHERAPY IN DEPRESSION

Maintenance treatment strategies are extremely important in depression, because most of the patients who have had an episode of a major af-fective disorder are likely to suffer a recurrence (Angst, Dobler-Mikola, & Hagnell, 1985). Both the literature review by Kleinman and Schach-ter (1988) and the meta-analysis by Loonen et al. (1991) of the studies published between 1974 and 1987 on the efficacy of maintenance antidepressant drug treatment in patients with recurrent major depression found that there were insufficient data to allow any conclusions about the efficacy of maintenance therapy with antidepressants. Even when a protective effect of pharmacotherapy had been found (Prien et al., 1984; Glen, Johnson, & Shepherd, 1984), the magnitude of such effect was only that of a 30–40% reduction compared to placebo in re-currence rates over a 2- to 3-year period, suggest-ing that pharmacotherapy alone may not be a sufficient maintenance treatment strategy, or that maintenance treatments under study employed suboptimal dosages. More recent studies, how-ever, have shown a greater-than-placebo prophy-lactic effect for several types of antidepressants, with the combination of pharmacotherapy with psychotherapies being perhaps even more prom-ising (Fava & Kaji, 1994).

ELECTROCONVULSIVE THERAPY

Cerletti and Bini first introduced in 1938 a tech-nique that would safely apply electrical current to the skull and induce generalized seizure. Electroconvulsive therapy (ECT) quickly proved to be effective in certain depressive and psy-chotic disorders and became widely used in the 1950s and 1960s.

As Welch (1989) pointed out in his review of the literature, all but 1 of 11 controlled studies found ECT to be superior to sham ECT, that is, administering anesthesia without the seizure. Greenblatt, Grosser, and Wechsler (1964) com-pared ECT in depressed patients with a tricy-clic antidepressant and a MAO inhibitor and found that 76% of patients receiving ECT, 49% of patients receiving imipramine, and 50% of patients receiving phenelzine showed marked improvement in their symptoms. The general consensus is that ECT should primarily be used only after adequate antidepressant trials have failed, or with patients whose depression is marked by delusions, even though ECT has consistently been reported to yield a higher re-sponse rate and prompter remission than anti-depressants (Welch, 1989).

The mechanism of action of ECT is not yet known. However, one hypothesis is that this treatment may induce a down-regulation of β receptors (Pandey, Heinze, Brown, & Davis, 1979). ECT is usually administered by placing on the head either bilateral or unilateral non-dominant electrodes and by delivering either sine wave or brief pulse current in order to in-duce seizures of adequate intensity and dura-tion in patients under anesthesia. Heart arrhyth-mias or hypertension can occur during the course of ECT. Although there are no absolute contraindications to ECT, relative contraindica-tions are represented by the presence of coro-nary artery disease, digitalis toxicity, increased intracranial pressure, and intracranial lesions (e.g., arteriovenous malformation, arterial aneu-rysm, hemorrhagic stroke) (Welch, 1989). Spe-cific modifications in anesthetic technique are necessary in order to safely treat patients with recent myocardial infarction, congestive heart failure, conduction abnormalities, coronary artery disease, hypertension, and impaired pul-monary function (Gaines & Rees, 1986).

The most common side effect of ECT is ret-rograde and anterograde amnesia; difficulty re-taining new information is very frequently ex-perienced by patients during the course of ECT and up to several months after the last treat-ment, followed by a gradual normalization of memory functions (Squire, 1986). Unilateral nondominant ECT appears to have a less marked effect on cognition than bilateral ECT, and transient changes in nonmemory cognitive functions such as discrimination, synthesis, and abstraction have also been described (Welch, 1989). Death, mostly due to cardiovascular complications, is an extremely rare complication of ECT, with a mortality rate of 4.5 deaths per 100,000 treatments (Welch, 1989).

LIGHT THERAPY

Over the past few years, numerous studies have investigated the clinical usefulness of light therapy (phototherapy) in the treatment of depression. This treatment involves exposure of the eyes to light containing very little ultraviolet light. The primary indication for the use of phototherapy has been seasonal affective disorder, a condition characterized by recurrent fall and winter depressions alternating with nondepressed periods in spring and summer (Rosenthal et al., 1984).

Rosenthal (1989) pointed out in his review of the literature that all 14 studies using a crossover design had found phototherapy to be more effective than an alternate (control) treatment condition, and that, while there was a consensus that bright light (2,500 lux) was superior to dimmer light ($\leq$ 400 lux), optimal timing of light treatment was somewhat more controversial. Even though Kripke (1985) and Yerevanian, Anderson, Grota, and Bray (1986) have also studied the use of this treatment modality in nonseasonal depressives, there is no clear evidence yet for the efficacy of light therapy in this population.

Full-spectrum fluorescent light has been the most commonly used source of light, with the light box placed at eye level and a light intensity of about 2,500 lux. The most frequent side effects observed during the course of phototherapy are insomnia, headaches, eyestrain, and irritability (Rosenthal, 1989). Although the mechanism of action of phototherapy is still poorly understood, one hypothesis is that its antidepressant effect may be due to the circadian phase-shifting properties of bright light (Lewy, Sack, Miller, & Hoban, 1987).

PHARMACOLOGICAL TREATMENT OF RESISTANT DEPRESSION

The "treatment-resistant" patient is one who has failed to respond to adequate therapeutic interventions. Since a substantial proportion (20–40%) of patients consistently fail to respond to treatment, there is a clear need to develop effective strategies in the treatment of these patients. As Rosenbaum and Gelenberg (1989) point out, the first step in the evaluation of the nonresponder is to ensure that patient's previous treatments were of adequate dose and duration, that the diagnosis was correct, that the patient complied with treatment, and that there were no other biological causes for refractoriness. Following this, clinicians have to decide what to try next. One approach is that of changing to a agent of a different class (e.g., a patient who has failed a trial with imipramine is switched to fluoxetine). Another approach, which has become extremely common in clinical practice, is that of adding another agent (i.e. lithium, thyroid hormone, psychostimulant, buspirone, neuroleptic). The extreme paucity of controlled clinical trials comparing the efficacy of these different strategies, which may be explained by the great difficulty to obtain large samples of treatment-refractory patients, does not allow definition of a clear algorithm. Since very little is known about the efficacy of the switch to another class of antidepressants, we focus our analysis on some of the most commonly prescribed adjunctive strategies.

Lithium Augmentation

In the early 1970s, it was observed that the addition of lithium to standard antidepressant therapies would lead to dramatic improvement in previously intractable depression (Himmelhoch, Detre, & Kupfer, 1972). Only in the early 1980s, beginning with a report by de Montigny, Grunberg, Mayer, and Deschenes (1981), the strategy of adding "low-dose lithium" to antidepressants became increasingly employed. Schopf (1989) reviewed the 26 open studies and the 6 controlled studies that had been published so far in the literature on this topic; a therapeutic effect of lithium addition was described in all open studies, although there was considerable variation with respect to the proportion of patients who improved and the degree of improvement. Four out of six controlled investigations reported a positive effect of combined therapy administered in the indicated sequence (Schopf, 1989). Although it is premature to regard the efficacy of lithium addition as definitely established, it is roughly estimated on the basis of the existing data that about every fourth to fifth patient will markedly improve within 48 hours, and every second to third, within 2 weeks of lithium addition (Schopf, 1989). Interestingly, successful lithium addition has been reported also with SSRIs such as fluvoxamine (Price, Charney, & Heninger, 1986) and fluoxetine (Pope, McElroy, & Nixon, 1988). In addition, one study found the addition of lithium more effective than placebo in potentiating the effects of the anticonvulsant carbamazepine in treatment-resistant depression (Kramlinger & Post, 1989), and another reported no significant difference in improvement rates for treatment-resistant depressed patients between a lithium/tricyclic combination and ECT, with the former inducing a more rapid response (Dinan & Barry, 1989).

Combined Antidepressant Treatment

Although, in the 1960s, combined antidepressant therapy with MAO inhibitors and tricyclic antidepressants was common, concern over the safety of this combination led to recommendations that these drugs should not be used together (Sheperd, Lader, & Rodnight, 1968). This combination, however, appears safe if both treatments are initiated in low doses simultaneously and gradually increased together (White & Simpson, 1981).

Some uncontrolled reports and studies have found combined MAO inhibitor and tricyclic antidepressant treatment to be effective in treatment-refractory depression (Goldberg & Thornton, 1978; Manshadi & Lippmann, 1984; Schmauss, Kapfhammer, Mayr, & Hoff, 1988; Tyrer & Murphy, 1990). The only controlled study on the efficacy of this combination in treatment refractory patients found ECT to be more effective than amitriptyline and phenelzine together in a sample of 17 patients (Davidson, McLeod, Law-Yone, & Linnoila, 1978); however, the average dosage of amitriptyline (71 mg/day) and phenelzine (34 mg/day) used in this study was fairly low and might account for the poor results of the combination.

The strategy of combining an SSRI with a non-MAO-inhibitor antidepressant in the treatment of refractory patients has become increasingly popular; in 30 depressed nonresponders, 87% reported a significant improvement when a non-MAO-inhibitor antidepressant was combined with fluoxetine (Weilburg et al., 1989).

Stimulants have also been used as adjuncts to tricyclic antidepressants, and they were found to potentiate antidepressant treatment in patients with inadequate initial response (Wharton, Perel, Dayton, & Malitz, 1971). Even with MAO inhibitors, the use of stimulants as adjuncts has been reported to be safe and effective when the dose is initiated and titrated with small increments (Feighner, Herbstein, & Damlouji, 1985).

Adjunctive Thyroid Hormone

Anecdotal observations of the usefulness of augmenting antidepressant response with thyroid hormone have led to reports suggesting that both triiodothyronine (T_3) (Goodwin, Prange, Post, Muscettola, & Lipton, 1982) and thyroxine (T_4) (Targum et al., 1984) may be successful adjuncts. The data and experience, however, are greater for the use of T_3 in doses of 10–75 µg/day. Potential side effects include flushing, tachycardia, increased blood pressure, and anxiety.

Antipsychotics

Although the treatment of choice for delusional depression is considered to be the combined use of a tricyclic antidepressant and a neuroleptic, a combination superior to either drug individually (Spiker et al., 1985), there is no evidence that the combination of an antidepressant with an antipsychotic medication offers any advantage in treating refractory nondelusional patients.

Amino Acid Precursors

Most of the evidence for the efficacy of amino acid precursors (L-tryptophan, phenylalanine, and tyrosine) as adjuncts is derived from uncontrolled studies or case series, and their usefulness seems to be confined to particular patients or depressive subtypes (Rosenbaum & Gelenberg, 1989).

CONCLUSION

In summary, pharmacotherapy is a very effective treatment of depression during both the acute and the continuation phase. Several classes of antidepressants are available, with significant differences in side effect profiles and, in some cases, spectrum of efficacy. Electroconvulsive therapy also remains a valid and effective treatment for depression, even though its use is most accepted for certain subtypes of depression, or for refractory patients. Phototherapy represents a very useful tool in the treatment of seasonal affective disorder, but its efficacy in nonseasonal depression has not been established. In spite of the fact that most patients with depression respond to trials of adequate dose and duration, a substantial minority do not. For these patients, numerous adjunctive strategies have been developed over the past few years, but their efficacy has not been studied in a systematic fashion. Over the next few years, the field of pharmacotherapy and somatic therapy of depression needs to concentrate more on assessing the efficacy of combining these treatments with psychotherapy, and on defining consistent predictors of response.

REFERENCES

American Medical Association. (1992). *Drug evaluations annual*. Washington, DC: Author.

Amin, M. M., Anath, J. V., Coleman, B. S., Darcourt, G., & Farkas, T. (1984). Fluvoxamine: Antidepressant effects confirmed in a placebo-controlled international study. *Clinical Neuropharmacology*, 7(Suppl. 1), 580– 581.

Angst, J., Dobler-Mikola, A., & Hagnell, O. (1985). How many, and which patients with affective disorders need long-term maintenance therapy? *Advances in Biochemical Psychopharmacology*, 40, 169–172.

Archibald, D., Copp, J., Anton, S., Gammans, R., & Kensler, T. (1993, June 1–4). *Determination of the therapeutic dose range of nefazodone from clinical trial data*. Paper presented at the New Clinical Drug Evaluation Unit, Boca Raton, FL.

Bakish, D., Bradwejn, J., Nair, N., McClure, J., Remick, R., & Bulger, L. (1992). A comparison of moclobemide, amitriptyline and placebo in depressed patients: A Canadian multicentre study. *Psychopharmacology*, 106, S98– S101.

Baldessarini, R. J. (1985). *Chemotherapy in psychiatry*. Cambridge, MA: Harvard University Press.

Baldessarini, R. J. (1987). The neuropharmacology of S-adenosyl-l-methionine. *American Journal of Medicine*, 83, 95–103.

Bartholomew, A. A. (1962). An evaluation of tranylcypromine in the treatment of depression. *Medical Journal of Australia*, 49, 655–662.

Beasley, C. M., Jr., Bosomworth, J. C., & Wernicke, J. F. (1990). Fluoxetine: Relationships among dose, response, adverse events, and plasma concentrations in the treatment of depression. *Psychopharmacology Bulletin*, 26, 18–24.

Beasley, C. M., Jr., Dornseif, B. E., Bosomworth, J. C., Sayler, M. E., Rampey, A. H., Jr., Heiligenstein, J. H., Thompson, V. L., Murphy, D. J., & Masica, D. N. (1991). Fluoxetine and suicide: A meta-analysis of controlled trials of treatment for depression. *British Medical Journal*, 303, 685–692.

Beasley, C. M., Jr., Masica, D. N., Heiligenstein, J. H., Wheadon, D. E., & Zerbe, R. L. (1993). Possible monoamine oxidase inhibitor–serotonin uptake inhibitor interaction: Fluoxetine clinical data and preclinical findings. *Journal of Clinical Psychopharmacology*, 13, 312–320.

Benfield, P., & Ward, A. (1986). Fluvoxamine: A review of its pharmacodynamic and pharmacokinetic properties, and therapeutic efficacy in depressive illness. *Drugs*, 32, 313–334.

Bergstrom, R. F., Lemberger, L., Farid, N. A., & Wolen, R. L. (1988). Clinical pharmacology and pharmacokinetics of fluoxetine: A review. *British Journal of Psychiatry*, 153(Suppl. 3), 47–50.

Bolden-Watson, C., & Richelson, E. (1993). Blockade by newly developed antidepressants of bigenic amine uptake into rat brain synaptosomes. *Life Sciences*, 52, 1023–1029.

Boniface, P. J. (1991). Two cases of fatal intoxication due to tranylcypromine overdose. *Journal of Analytical Toxicology*, 15, 38–40.

Boyer, W. F., & Blumhardt, C. L. (1992). The safety profile of paroxetine. *Journal of Clinical Psychiatry*, 53(Suppl. 2), 61–66.

Bressa, G. M. (1994). S-adenosyl-l-methionine (SAMe) as antidepressant: Meta-analysis of clinical studies. *Acta Neurologica Scandinavica* (Suppl. 154), 7–14.

Burrows, G. D., Mowbray, R. M., & Davies, B. (1972). A sequential comparison of doxepin (Sinequan) and placebo in depressed patients. *Medical Journal of Australia*, 1, 364–366.

Cassidy, S., & Henry, J. (1987). Fatal toxicity of antidepressant drugs in overdose. *British Medical Journal*, 295, 1021–1024.

Cerletti, U., & Bini, L. (1938). Un nuevo metodo di shock-terapie "L'elettro-shock." *Bollettino dell'Academia di Medicina, Roma*, 64, 136–138.

Charalampous, K. D. (1972). Amoxapine: A clinical evaluation in depressive syndromes. *Current Therapeutic Research*, 14, 657–663.

Charney, D. S., & Heninger, G. R. (1985). Noradrenergic function and the mechanism of action of antianxiety treatment: I. The effect of long-term alprazolam treatment. *Archives of General Psychiatry*, 42, 458–467.

Claghorn, J. L. (1992). The safety and efficacy of paroxetine compared with placebo in a double-blind trial of depressed outpatients. *Journal of Clinical Psychiatry*, 53(Suppl. 2), 33–35.

Cohn, J. B., & Wilcox, C. S. (1992). Paroxetine in major depression: A double-blind trial with imipramine and placebo. *Journal of Clinical Psychiatry*, 53(Suppl. 2), 52–56.

Cooper, B. R., Hester, T. J., & Maxwell, R. A. (1980). Behavioral and biochemical effects of the antidepressant bupropion (Wellbutrin): evidence for selective blockade of dopamine uptake *in vivo*. *Journal of Pharmacology and Experimental Therapeutics*, 215, 127–134.

Cooper, G. L. (1988). The safety of fluoxetine—An update. *British Journal of Psychiatry*, 153(Suppl. 3), 77–86.

Crome, P. (1993). The toxicity of drugs used for suicide. *Acta Psychiatrica Scandinavica*, Suppl. 371, 33–37.

Crome, P., & Newman, B. (1979). Fatal tricyclic antidepressant poisoning. *Journal of the Royal Society of Medicine*, 72, 649–653.

Cusack, B., Nelson, A., & Richelson, E. (1994). Binding of antidepressants to human brain receptors: Focus on newer generation compounds. *Psychopharmacology*, 114, 559–565.

Da Prada, M., Kettler, R., Burkard, W. P., & Haefely, W. E. (1984). Moclobemide, an antidepressant with short-lasting MAO-A inhibition: Brain catecholamines and tyramine pressor effects in rats. In P. Dostert, M. S. Benedetti, & K. F. Tipton (Eds.), *Monoamine oxidase and disease—Prospects for therapy with reversible inhibitors* (p. 137). London: Academic Press.

Da Prada, M., Kettler, R., Keller, H. H., & Haefely, W. E. (1983). Neurochemical effects *in vitro* and *in vivo* of the antidepressant Ro 11-1163, a specific and short-acting MAO-A inhibitor. *Modern Problems of Pharmacopsychiatry*, 19, 231–245.

Davidson, J., McLeod, M., Law-Yone, B., & Linnoila, M.

(1978). A comparison of electroconvulsive therapy and combined phenelzine–amitriptyline in refractory depression. *Archives of General Psychiatry, 35,* 639–642.

Davidson, J. R. T., Giller, E. L., Zisook, S., & Overall, J. E. (1988). An efficacy study of isocarboxazid and placebo in depression, and its relationship to depressive nosology. *Archives of General Psychiatry, 45,* 120–127.

de Montigny, C., Chaput, Y., & Blier, P. (1990). Modification of serotonergic neuron properties by long-term treatment with serotonin reuptake blockers. *Journal of Clinical Psychiatry, 51*(Suppl. 12B), 4–8.

de Montigny, C., Grunberg, F., Mayer, A., & Deschenes, J. P. (1981). Lithium induces rapid relief of depression in tricyclic antidepressant drug non-responders. *British Journal of Psychiatry, 138,* 252–256.

De Wilde, J. E., Mertens, C., & Wakelin, J. S. (1983). Clinical trials of fluvoxamine vs. chlorimipramine with single and three times daily dosing. *British Journal of Clinical Pharmacology, 15*(Suppl. 3), 427S–431S.

Dinan, T. G., & Barry, S. (1989). A comparison of electroconvulsive therapy with a combined lithium and tricyclic combination among depressed tricyclic non-responders. *Acta Psychiatrica Scandinavica, 80,* 97–100.

Dunner, D. L., & Dunbar, G. C. (1991, December). *Reduced suicidal thoughts and behavior (suicidality) with paroxetine.* Paper presented at the American College of Neuropsychopharmacology meeting. San Juan, Puerto Rico.

Dunner, D. L., & Dunbar, G. C. (1992). Optimal dose regimen for paroxetine. *Journal of Clinical Psychiatry, 53*(Suppl. 2), 21–26.

Dunner, D. L., Cohn, J. B., Walshe, T., Cohn, C. K., Feighner, J. P., Fieve, R. R., Halikas, J. P., Hartford, J. T., Hearst, E. D., Settle, E. C., Menolascino, F. J., & Muller, D. J. (1992). Two combined, multicenter double-blind studies of paroxetine and doxepin in geriatric patients with major depression. *Journal of Clinical Psychiatry, 53*(Suppl. 2), 57–60.

Edwards, J. G., Goldie, A., & Papayanni-Parasthatis S. (1989). Effect of paroxetine on the electrocardiogram. *Psychopharmacology, 97,* 96–98.

Eriksson, B., Nagy, A., & Starmark, J. E. (1987). Alprazolam compared to amitriptyline in the treatment of major depression. *Acta Psychiatrica Scandinavica, 75,* 656–663.

Fabre, L. F. (1992). A 6-week, double-blind trial of paroxetine, imipramine, and placebo in depressed outpatients. *Journal of Clinical Psychiatry, 53*(Suppl. 2), 40–43.

Fava, M., & Kaji, J. (1994). Continuation and maintenance treatments of major depressive disorder. *Psychiatric Annals, 24,* 281–290.

Fava, M., & Rosenbaum J. F. (1991). Suicidality and fluoxetine: Is there a relationship? *Journal of Clinical Psychiatry, 52,* 108–111.

Fava, M., Rosenbaum, J. F., Cohen, L., Reiter, S., McCarthy, M., Steingard, R., & Clancy, K. (1992). High-dose fluoxetine in the treatment of depressed patients not responsive to a standard dose of fluoxetine. *Journal of Affective Disorders, 25,* 229–234.

Feighner, J. P. (1992, June). *The efficacy of venlafaxine in major depression and preliminary findings in the treatment of refractory depression.* Paper presented at the 17th Collegium Internationale Neuro-Psychopharmacologicum Congress, Nice, France.

Feighner, J. P., Aden, G. C., Fabre, L. F., Rickels, K., &

Smith, W. T. (1983). Comparison of alprazolam, imipramine, and placebo in the treatment of depression. *Journal of the American Medical Association, 249,* 3057–3064.

Feighner. J. P., & Boyer, W. F. (1988). Overview of USA controlled trials of trazodone in clinical depression. *Psychopharmacology, 95,* S50–S53.

Feighner, J. P., & Boyer, W. F. (1992). Paroxetine in the treatment of depression: A comparison with imipramine and placebo. *Journal of Clinical Psychiatry, 53*(Suppl. 2), 44–47.

Feighner, J. P., Herbstein, J., & Damlouji, N. (1985). Combined MAOI, TCA., and direct stimulant therapy of treatment-resistant depression. *Journal of Clinical Psychiatry, 46,* 206–209.

Fluoxetine Bulimia Nervosa Collaborative Study Group. (1992). Fluoxetine in the treatment of bulimia nervosa: A multicenter, placebo-controlled, double-blind trial. *Archives of General Psychiatry, 49,* 139–147.

Fontaine, R. (1993). Novel serotonergic mechanisms and clinical experience with nefazodone. *Clinical Neuropharmacology, 16*(Suppl. 3), S45–S50.

Fouda, H. G., Ronfeld, R. A., & Weidler, D. J. (1987). Gas chromatographic mass spectrometric analysis and preliminary human pharmacokinetics of sertraline, a new antidepressant drug. *Journal of Chromatography—Biomedical Applications, 417,* 197–202.

Gaines, G. Y., & Rees, I. (1986). Electroconvulsive therapy and anesthetic considerations. *Anesthesia and Analgesia, 65,* 1345–1356.

Gamble, D. E., & Peterson, L. G. (1986). Trazodone overdose: Four years of experience from voluntary reports. *Journal of Clinical Psychiatry, 47,* 544–546.

Glen, A. I. M., Johnson, A. L., & Shepherd, M. (1984). Continuation therapy with lithium and amitriptyline in unipolar depressive illness: A randomized double-blind, controlled trial. *Psychological Medicine, 14,* 37–50.

Glick, B. S. (1964). Double-blind study of tranylcypromine and phenelzine in depression. *Diseases of the Nervous System, 25,* 617–619.

Goldberg, R. S., & Thornton, W. E. (1978). Combined tricyclic–MAOI therapy for refractory depression: A review, with guidelines for appropriate usage. *Journal of Clinical Psychopharmacology, 18,* 143–147.

Goodwin, F. K., Prange, A. J., Jr., Post, R. M., Muscettola, G., & Lipton, M. A. (1982). Potentiation of antidepressant effects by l-triiodothyronine in tricyclic nonresponders. *American Journal of Psychiatry, 139,* 34–38.

Gottfries, C. G. (1963). Clinical trial with the monoamine oxidase inhibitors tranylcypromine on a psychiatric clientele. *Acta Psychiatrica Scandinavica, 39,* 463–472.

Greenblatt, M., Grosser, G. H., & Wechsler, H. (1964). Differential response of hospitalized depressed patients to somatic therapy. *American Journal of Psychiatry, 120,* 935–943.

Greenblatt, E. N., Lippa, A. S., & Ostenberg, A. C. (1978). The neuropharmacological actions of amoxapine. *Archives Internationales de Pharmacodynamic, 233,* 107–135.

Haddock, R. E., Johnson, A. M., Langley, P. F., Nelson, D. R., Pope, J. A., Thomas, D. R., & Woods, F. R. (1989). Metabolic pathway of paroxetine in animals and man and the comparative pharmacological properties of its metabolites. *Acta Psychiatrica Scandinavica, 80*(Suppl. 350), 24–26.

Hall, J. (1988). Fluoxetine: Efficacy against placebo and by dose—An overview. *British Journal of Psychiatry, 153*(Suppl. 3), 59–63.

Hall, H., Sallemark, M., & Wedel, I. (1984). Acute effects of atypical antidepressants on various receptors in the rat brain. *Acta Pharmacologica et Toxicologica, 54,* 379–384.

Heinze, G., & Sanchez, A. (1986). Overdose with moclobemide. *Journal of Clinical Psychiatry, 47,* 438.

Himmelhoch, J. M., Detre, T., & Kupfer, D. J. (1972). Treatment of previously intractable depression with tranylcypromine and lithium. *Journal of Nervous and Mental Disease, 155,* 216–220.

Himmelhoch, J. M., Fuchs, C. Z., & Symons, B. J. (1980). A double-blind study of tranylcypromine treatment of major anergic depression. *Journal of Nervous and Mental Disease, 170,* 628–634.

Hollister, L. E. (1974). Doxepin hydrochloride. *Annals of Internal Medicine, 81,* 360–363.

Horne, R. L., Ferguson, J. M., Pope, H. G., Hudson, J. I., Lineberry, C. G., Ascher, J., & Cato, A. E. (1988). Treatment of bulimia with bupropion: A multicenter controlled trial. *Journal of Clinical Psychiatry, 49,* 262–266.

Huang, C. C. (1986). Persistent tardive dyskinesia associated with amoxapine therapy—Two case reports. *Hillside Journal of Clinical Psychiatry, 8,* 209–213.

Hussain, M. Z., & Chaudhry, Z. A. (1973). Single versus divided daily doses of trimipramine in the treatment of depressive illness. *American Journal of Psychiatry, 130,* 1142–1144.

International Drug Therapy Newsletter. (1992). Sertraline: The latest FDA-approved serotonin uptake inhibitor antidepressant. *International Drug Therapy Newsletter, 27*(3), 9–12.

Iruela, L. M., Minguez, L., Merino, J., & Monedero, G. (1993). Toxic interaction of s-adenosylmethionine and clomipramine. *American Journal of Psychiatry, 150,* 522.

Isaksson, A., Larkander, O., Morsing, C., Ottoson, J. O., & Rapp, W. (1968). A comparison between imipramine and protriptyline in the treatment of depressed outpatients. *Acta Psychiatrica Scandinavica, 44,* 205–223.

Janicak, P. G., Lipinski, J., Davis, J. M., Comaty, J. E., Waternaux, C., Cohen, B., Altman, E., & Sharma, R. P. (1988). S-adenosylmethionine in depression: A literature review and preliminary report. *Alabama Journal of Medical Sciences, 25,* 306–313.

Jenike, M. A., Hyman, S., Baer, L., Holland, A., Minichiello, W. E., Buttolph, L., Summergrad, P., Seymour, R., & Ricciardi, J. (1990). A controlled trial of fluvoxamine in obsessive–compulsive disorder: Implications for a sertonergic theory. *American Journal of Psychiatry, 147,* 1209–1215.

Jue, S. G., Dawson, G. W., & Brogden, R. N. (1982). Amoxapine: A review of its pharmacology and efficacy in depressed states. *Drugs, 24,* 1–23.

Kagan, B. L., Sultzer, D. L., Rosenlicht, N., & Gerner, R. H. (1990). Oral s-adenosylmethionine in depression: A randomized, double-blind, placebo-controlled trial. *American Journal of Psychiatry, 147,* 591–595.

Kaye, C.M., Haddock, R. E., Langley, P. F., Mellows, G., Tasker, T. C., Zussman, B. D., & Greb, W. H. (1989). A review of the metabolism and pharmacokinetics of paroxetine in man. *Acta Psychiatrica Scandinavica, 80*(Suppl. 350), 60–75.

Keller, M. B., Klerman, G. L., Lavori, P. W., Fawcett, J. A., Coryell, W., & Endicott, J. (1982). Treatment received by depressed patients. *Journal of the American Medical Association, 248,* 1848–1855.

Khanna, J. L., Pratt, S., Burdizk, E. G., & Chaddha, R. L. (1963). A study of certain effects of tranylcypromine, a new antidepressant. *Journal of New Drugs, 3,* 227–232.

Kiev, A. (1974). The role of chemotherapy in managing potentially suicidal patients. *Diseases of the Nervous System, 35,* 108–111.

Kiev, A. (1992). A double-blind, placebo-controlled study of paroxetine in depressed outpatients. *Journal of Clinical Psychiatry, 53*(Suppl. 2), 27–29.

Kleinman, I., & Schachter, D. (1988). Tricyclic maintenance therapy in unipolar depression. *Canadian Journal of Psychiatry, 33*(1), 7–10.

Klerman, G. L. (1989). Introduction. In T. B. Karasu (Ed.), *Treatment of psychiatric disorders: A task force report of the American Psychiatric Association* (Vol. 3, pp. 1727–1745). Washington, DC: American Psychiatric Association Press.

Klerman, G. L. (1972). Drug therapy of clinical depressions—Current status and implications for research on neuropharmacology of the affective disorders. *Journal of Psychiatric Research, 9,* 253–270.

Knoll, J. (1983). Deprenyl (selegiline): The history of its development and pharmacological action. *Acta Neurologica Scandinavica, 95,* 57–80.

Koe, B. K. (1990). Preclinical pharmacology of sertraline: A potent and specific inhibitor of serotonin reuptake. *Journal of Clinical Psychiatry, 51*(Suppl. 12B), 13–17.

Koe, B. K., Koch, S. W., Lebel, L. A., Minor, K. W., & Page, M. G. (1987). Sertraline, a selective inhibitor of serotonin uptake, induces subsensitivity of beta-adrenoceptor system of rat brain. *European Journal of Pharmacology, 141,* 187–194.

Koe, B. K., Weissman, A., Welch, W. M., & Browne, R. G. (1983). Sertraline, 1S-, 4S-N-methyl-4-(3,4-dichlorophenyl)-1,2,3,4-tetrahydro-l-naphthylamine, a new uptake inhibitor with selectivity for serotonin. *Journal of Pharmacology and Experimental Therapeutics, 226,* 686–700.

Kramlinger, K. G., & Post, R. M. (1989). The addition of lithium to carbamazepine. *Archives of General Psychiatry, 46,* 794–800.

Kripke, D. F. (1985). Therapeutic effects of bright light in depression. In R. J. Wurtman, M. J. Baum, & J. T. Potts (Eds.), *The medical and biological effects of light. Annals of the New York Academy of Sciences, 453,* 270–281.

Lader, M. (1988). Fluoxetine efficacy vs. comparative drugs: An overview. *British Journal of Psychiatry, 153*(Suppl. 3), 51–58.

Lader, M. H., Sakalis, G., & Tansella, M. (1972). Interaction between sympathetic amines and a new monoamine oxidase inhibitor. *Psychopharmacologia, 18,* 118–123.

Lai, A. A., & Schroeder, D. H. (1983). Clinical pharmacokinetics of bupropion: A review. *Journal of Clinical Psychiatry, 44*(5, sec. 2), 82–84.

Laizure, S. C., Devane, C. L., Stewart, J. T., Dommisse, C. S., & Lai A. A. (1985). Pharmacokinetics of bupropion and its major basic metabolites in normal subjects after a single dose. *Clinical Pharmacology and Therapeutics, 38,* 586–589.

Larsen, J. K., & Rafaelsen, O. J. (1980). Long-term treatment of depression with isocarboxazide. *Acta Psychiatrica Scandinavica, 62,* 456–463.

Lemberger, L., Farid, N. A., Bergstrom, R. F., & Wolen, R. L. (1987). Fluoxetine, pharmacology and physiologic disposition. *International Journal of Obesity, 11*(Suppl. 3), 157–161.

Lewy, A. J., Sack, R. L., Miller, L. S., & Hoban, T. M. (1987). Antidepressant and circadian phase-shifting effects of light. *Science, 235,* 352–354.

Liebowitz, M. R., Quitkin, F. M., Stewart, J. W., McGrath, P. J., Harrison, W., Rabkin, J., Tricamo, E., Markowitz, J. S., & Klein, D. F. (1984). Phenelzine vs. imipramine in atypical depression. *Archives of General Psychiatry, 41,* 669–677.

Lineberry, G. C., Johnston, J. A., Raymond, R. N., Samara, B., Feighner, J. P., Harto, N. E., Granacher, R. P., Jr., Weisler, R. H., Carman, J. S., & Boyer, W. F. (1990). A fixed-dose (300 mg) efficacy study of bupropion and placebo in depressed outpatients. *Journal of Clinical Psychiatry, 51,* 194–199.

Litovitz, T. L., & Troutman, W. J. (1983). Amoxapine overdose: Seizures and fatalities. *Journal of the American Medical Association, 250,* 1069–1071.

Loonen, A. J., Peer, P. G., & Zwanikken, G. J. (1991). Continuation and maintenance therapy with antidepressive agents. Meta-analysis of research. *Pharmaceutisch Weekblad—Scientific Edition, 13*(4), 167–175.

Lund, J., Thayssen, P., Mengel, H., Pedersen, O. L., Kristensen, C. B., & Gram, L. F. (1982). Paroxetine: Pharmacokinetics and cardiovascular effects after oral and intravenous single doses in man. *Acta Pharmacologica et Toxicologica (Copenhagen), 51,* 351–357.

Mann, J. J., Aarons, S. F., Frances, A. J., & Brown, R. D. (1984). Studies of selective and reversible monoamine oxidase inhibitors. *Journal of Clinical Psychiatry, 45*(7, Sec. 2), 62–66.

Mann, J. J., Aarons, S. F., Wilner, P. J., Keilp, J. G., Sweeney, J. A., Pearlstein, T., Frances, A. J., Kocsis, J. H., & Brown, R. P. (1989). A controlled study of the antidepressant efficacy and side effects of (–)-deprenyl. *Archives of General Psychiatry, 46,* 45–50.

Manshadi, M. S., & Lippmann, S. B. (1984). Combined treatment of refractory depression with an MAO inhibitor and a tricyclic. *Psychosomatics, 25,* 929–931.

McCormick, S. R., Nielsen, J., & Jatlow, P. I. (1985). Alprazolam overdose: Clinical findings and serum concentrations in two cases. *Journal of Clinical Psychiatry, 46,* 247–248.

McGilchrist, J. M. (1975). Interactions with monoamine oxidase inhibitors. *British Medical Journal, iii,* 591–592.

McGrath, P. J., Stewart, J. W., Harrison, W., Wager, S., Nunes, E. N., & Quitkin, F. M. (1989). A placebo-controlled trial of l-deprenyl in atypical depression. *Psychopharmacology Bulletin, 25,* 63–67.

Meeker, J. E., & Reynolds, P. C. (1990). Postmortem tissue methamphetamine concentrations following selegiline administration. *Journal of Analytical Toxicology, 14,* 330–331.

Moll, E., & Hetzel, W. (1990). Moclobemide (Ro 11-1163) safety in depressed patients. *Acta Psychiatrica Scandinavica,* Suppl. 360, 69–70.

Morris, J. B., & Beck, A. T. (1974). The efficacy of antidepressant drugs. *Archives of General Psychiatry, 30,* 667–674.

Myrenfors, P. G., Eriksson, T., Sandstedt, C. S., & Sjöberg, G. (1993). Moclobemide overdose. *Journal of Internal Medicine, 233,* 113–115.

Neuvonen, P. J., Pohjola-Sintonen, S., Tacke, U., & Vuori, E. (1993). Five fatal cases of serotonin syndrome after moclobemide-citalopram or moclobemide-clomipramine overdoses. *Lancet, 342,* 1419.

Overmars, H., Scherpenisse, P. M., & Post, L. C. (1983). Fluvoxamine maleate: Metabolism in man. *European Journal of Drug Metabolism and Pharmacokinetics, 8,* 269–280.

Pande, A. C., Haskett, R. F., & Greden, J. F. (1992, May). *Fluoxetine treatment of atypical depression.* CME Syllabus and Proceedings Summary of the 145th annual meeting of the American Psychiatric Association, Washington, DC.

Pandey, G. H., Heinze, W., Brown, B., & Davis, J. M. (1979). Electroconvulsive shock treatment decreases beta adrenergic receptor sensitivity in rat brain. *Nature, 280,* 234–235.

Pecknold, J. C., Gratton, L., Ban, T. A., & Klinger, A. (1976). Systematic clinical studies with clomipramine in depressed psychiatric patients—III: Standard controlled clinical trial. *Psychopharmacology Bulletin, 12,* 26–27.

Pinder, R. M., Brogden, R. N., Speight, T. M., & Avery, G. S. (1977). Maprotiline: A review of its pharmacological properties and therapeutic efficacy in mental depressive states. *Drugs, 13,* 321–352.

Pollack, M. H., & Rosenbaum, J. F. (1987). Management of antidepressant-induced side effects: A practical guide for the clinician. *Journal of Clinical Psychiatry, 48,* 3–8.

Pope, H. G., Jr., McElroy, S. L., & Nixon, R. A. (1988). Possible synergism between fluoxetine and lithium in refractory depression. *American Journal of Psychiatry, 145,* 1292–1294.

Price, L. H., Charney, D. S., & Heninger, G. R. (1986). Variability of response to lithium augmentation in refractory depression. *American Journal of Psychiatry, 143,* 1387–1392.

Prien, R. F., & Kupfer D. J. (1986). Continuation drug therapy for major depression episodes: How long should it be maintained? *American Journal of Psychiatry, 143,* 18–23.

Prien, R. F., Kupfer, D. J., Mansky, P. A., Small, J. G., Tuason, V. B., Voss, C. B., & Johnson, W. E. (1984). Drug therapy in the prevention of recurrences in unipolar and bipolar affective disorders: A report of the NIMH Collaborative Study Group comparing lithium carbonate, imipramine, and a lithium carbonate–imipramine combination. *Archives of General Psychiatry, 41,* 1096–1104.

Quitkin, F. M. (1985). The importance of dosage in prescribing antidepressants. *British Journal of Psychiatry, 147,* 593–597.

Quitkin, F. M., Rabkin, J. G., Stewart, J. W., McGrath, P. J., & Harrison, W. (1986). Study duration in antidepressant research: Advantages of a 12-week trial. *Journal of Psychiatric Research, 20*(3), 211–216.

Quitkin, F., Rifkin, A., & Klein, D. F. (1979). Monoamine oxidase inhibitors. *Archives of General Psychiatry, 36,* 749–764.

Ravaris, C. L., Robinson, D. S., Ives, J. O., Nies, A., & Bartlett, D. (1980). Phenelzine and amitriptyline in the treatment of depression: A comparison of present and past studies. *Archives of General Psychiatry, 37,* 1075–1080.

Reimherr, F. W., Chouinard, G., Cohn, C. K., Cole, J. O., Itil, T. M., LaPierre, Y. D., Masco, H. L., & Mendels, J. (1990). Antidepressant efficacy of sertraline: A double-blind, placebo- and amitriptyline-controlled, multicenter comparison study in outpatients with major depression. *Journal of Clinical Psychiatry, 51*(Suppl. 12B), 18–27.

Richelson, E. (1989). Antidepressants: Pharmacology and clinical use. In T. B. Karasu (Ed.), *Treatment of psy-*

chiatric disorders: A task force report of the American Psychiatric Association (Vol. 3, pp. 1773–1787). Washington, DC: American Psychiatric Association Press.

Richelson, E., & Nelson A. (1984). Antagonism by antidepressants of neurotransmitter receptors of normal human brain in vitro. Journal of Pharmacology and Experimental Therapeutics, 230, 94–102.

Richelson, E., & Pfenning, M. (1984). Blockade by antidepressants and related compounds of biogenic amine uptake into rat brain synaptosomes: Most antidepressants selectively block norepinephrine uptake. European Journal of Pharmacology, 104, 277–286.

Rickels, K., Amsterdam, J., Clary, C., Fox, I., Schweizer, E., & Weise C. (1992). The efficacy and safety of paroxetine compared with placebo in outpatients with major depression. Journal of Clinical Psychiatry, 53(Suppl. 2), 30–32.

Rickels, K., Feighner, J. P., & Smith, W. T. (1985). Alprazolam, amitriptyline, doxepine and placebo in the treatment of depression. Archives of General Psychiatry, 42, 134–141.

Rickels, K., Gordon, P. E., Weise, C. C., Bazilian, S. E., Feldman, H. S., & Wilson, D. A. (1970). Amitriptyline and trimipramine in neurotic depressed outpatients: A collaborative study. American Journal of Psychiatry, 127, 208–218.

Rickels, K., & Schweizer E. (1990). Clinical overview of serotonin reuptake inhibitors. Journal of Clinical Psychiatry, 51(Suppl. 12B), 9–12.

Roos, J. C., & Sharp, D. J. (1984). Antidepressant drugs and cardiovascular side effects. A comparison of fluvoxamine and the tricyclic antidepressant drugs. In G. D. Burrows, T. R. Norman, & K. P. Maguire (Eds.), Biological psychiatry: Recent studies. London: John Libbey.

Rosenbaum, J. F., Fava, M., Falk, W. E., Pollack, M. H., Cohen, L. S., Cohen, B. M., & Zubenko, G. S. (1990). The antidepressant potential of oral S-adenosyl-l-methionine. Acta Psychiatrica Scandinavica, 81, 432–436.

Rosenbaum, J. F., Fava, M., & Nierenberg, A. A. (1994). The pharmacologic treatment of mood disorders. In D. L. Dunner (Ed.), Psychiatric clinics of North America (Vol. 1, pp. 17–49). Philadelphia: Saunders.

Rosenbaum, J. F., & Gelenberg, A. J. (1989). Drug treatment of resistant depression. In T. B. Karasu (Ed.), Treatment of psychiatric disorders. A task force report of the American Psychiatric Association (Vol. 3, pp. 1787–1802). Washington, DC: American Psychiatric Association Press.

Rosenthal, N. E. (1989). Light therapy. In T. B. Karasu (Ed.), Treatment of psychiatric disorders. A task force report of the American Psychiatric Association (Vol. 3, pp. 1890–1896). Washington, DC: American Psychiatric Association Press.

Rosenthal, N. E., Sack, D. A., Gillin, J. C., Lewy, A. J., Goodwin, F. K., Davenport, Y., Mueller, P. S., Newsome, D. A., & Wehr, T. A. (1984). Seasonal affective disorder: a description of the syndrome and preliminary findings with light therapy. Archives of General Psychiatry, 41, 72–80.

Rudorfer, M. V., & Robins, E. (1981). Fatal nortriptyline overdose, plasma levels and in vivo methylation of tricyclic antidepressants. American Journal of Psychiatry, 138, 982–983.

Satel, S. L., & Nelson, J. C. (1989). Stimulants in the treatment of depression: A critical overview. Journal of Clinical Psychiatry, 50, 241–249.

Schmauss, M., Kapfhammer, H. P., Mayr, P., & Hoff, P. (1988). Combined MAO-Inhibitor and tri-(tetra) cyclic antidepressant treatment in therapy resistant depression. Progress in Neuropsychopharmacology and Biological Psychiatry, 12, 523–532.

Schmidt, M. J., Fuller, R. W., & Wong, D. T. (1988). Fluoxetine, a highly selective serotonin reuptake inhibitor: A review of preclinical studies. British Journal of Psychiatry, 153(Suppl. 3), 40–46.

Schopf, J. (1989). Treatment of depressions resistant to tricyclic antidepressants, related drugs or MAO-inhibitors by lithium addition: Review of the literature. Pharmacopsychiatrica, 22, 174–182.

Schroeder, D. H. (1983). Metabolism and kinetics of bupropion. Journal of Clinical Psychiatry, 44(5, sec. 2), 79–81.

Schweizer, E., Rickels, K., Amsterdam, J. D., Fox, I., Puzzuoli, G., & Weise, C. (1990). What constitutes and adequate antidepressant trial for fluoxetine? Journal of Clinical Psychiatry, 51, 8–11.

Shank, R. P., Vaught, J. L., Pelley, K. A., Setler, P. E., McComsey, D. F., & Maryanoff, B. E. (1988). McN-5652: A highly potent inhibitor of serotonin uptake. Journal or Pharmacology and Experimental Therapeutics, 247, 1032–1038.

Sheperd, M., Lader, M., & Rodnight R. (1968). Clinical psychopharmacology. London: English Universities Press.

Shrivastava, R. K., Shrivastava, S. H. P., Overweg, N., & Blumhardt, C. L. (1992). A double-blind comparison of paroxetine, imipramine, and placebo in major depression. Journal of Clinical Psychiatry, 53(Suppl. 2), 48–51.

Singh, A. N., Saxena, B., Gent, M., & Nelson, H. L. (1976). Maprotiline (ludiomil, CIBA 34, 276-BA) and imipramine in depressed outpatients: A double-blind clinical study. Current Therapeutic Research, 19, 451–462.

Spiker, D. G., Weiss, J. C., Dealy, R. S., Griffin, S. J., Hanin, I., Neil, J. F., Perel, J. M., Rossi, A. J., & Soloff, P. H. (1985). The pharmacological treatment of delusional depression. American Journal of Psychiatry, 142, 430–436.

Squire, L. R. (1986). Memory functions as affected by electroconvulsive therapy. Annals of the New York Academy of Sciences, 462, 307–314.

Stewart, J. W., Quitkin F. M., Liebowitz, M. R., McGrath, P. J., Harrison, W. M., & Klein, D. F. (1983). Efficacy of desipramine in depressed outpatients: Response according to Research Diagnostic Criteria diagnoses and severity of illness. Archives of General Psychiatry, 40, 202–207.

Targum, S. D., Greenberg, R. D., Harmon, R. L., Kessler, K., Salerian, A. J., & Fram, D. H. (1984). The TRH test and thyroid hormone in refractory depression. American Journal of Psychiatry, 141, 463.

Teicher, M. H., Glod, C., & Cole, J. O. (1990). Emergence of intense suicidal preoccupation during fluoxetine treatment. American Journal of Psychiatry, 147, 207–210.

Thase, M. E. (1992, May). Anergic major depressive syndromes. CME Syllabus and Proceedings Summary of the 145th annual meeting of the American Psychiatric Association, Washington, DC.

Thomas, D. R., Nelson, D. R., & Johnson, A. M. (1987). Biochemical effects of the antidepressant paroxetine, a specific 5-hydroxytryptamine uptake inhibitor. Psychopharmacology, 93, 193–200.

Thoren, P., Asberg, M., Cronholm, B., Jornestedt, L., & Traskman, L. (1980). Clomipramine treatment of obsessive–compulsive disorder: I. A controlled clinical trial. *Archives of General Psychiatry, 37,* 1281–1285.

Trimble, M. R. (1990). Worldwide use of clomipramine. *Journal of Clinical Psychiatry, 51*(Suppl. 8), 51–54.

Tulloch, I. F., & Johnson, A. M. (1992). The pharmacologic profile of paroxetine, a new selective serotonin reuptake inhibitor. *Journal of Clinical Psychiatry, 53*(Suppl. 2), 7–12.

Tulp, M. T. M., Mol, F., Rademaker, B., & Schipper, J. (1988). *In vitro* pharmacology of fluvoxamine: Inhibition of monoamine uptake, receptor binding profile and functional receptor antagonism. Comparison with tricyclics and mianserin. In B. Olivier & J. Mos (Eds.), *Depression, anxiety and aggression: Preclinical and clinical interfaces* (pp. 9–19). Houten, The Netherlands: Medidact.

Tyrer, P., & Murphy, S. (1990). Efficacy of combined antidepressant therapy in resistant neurotic disorder. *British Journal of Psychiatry, 156,* 115–118.

Ucha Udabe, R., Marquez, C. A., Traballi, C. A., & Portes, N. (1990). Double-blind comparison of moclobemide, imipramine and placebo in depressive patients. *Acta Psychiatrica Scandinavica,* Suppl. 360, 54–56.

Van Wyck Fleet, J., Manberg, P. J., Miller, L. L., Harto-Truax, N., Sato, T., Fleck, R. J., Stern, W. C., & Cato, A. E. (1983). Overview of clinically significant adverse reactions to buproprion. *Journal of Clinical Psychiatry, 44*(5, sec. 2), 191–196.

Versiani, M., Nardi, A. E., Mundim, F. D., Alves, A., & Schmid-Burgk, W. (1990). Moclobemide, imipramine and placebo in the treatment of major depression. *Acta Psychiatrica Scandinavica,* Suppl. 360, 57–58.

Wander, T. J., Nelson, A., Okazaki, H., & Richelson, E. (1986). Antagonism by antidepressants of serotonin S-1 and S-2 receptors of normal human brain *in vitro. Europan Journal of Pharmacology, 132,* 115–121.

Weilburg, J. B., Rosenbaum, J. F., Biederman, J., Sachs, G. S., Pollack, M. H., & Kelly K. Fluoxetine added to non-MAOI antidepressants converts nonresponders to responders: A preliminary report. *Journal of Clinical Psychiatry, 50,* 447–449.

Weisler, R. H. (1991). A profile of bupropion: A non-serotonergic alternative. *Journal of Clinical Psychiatry Monograph, 9*(1), 29–35.

Weissman, M. M., Lieb, J., Prusoff, B., & Bothwell, S. (1975). A double-blind trial of maprotiline (Ludiomil) and amitriptyline in depressed outpatients. *Acta Psychiatrica Scandinavica, 52,* 225–236.

Welch, C. A. (1989). Electroconvulsive therapy. In T. B. Karasu (Ed.), *Treatment of psychitaric disorders: A task force report of the American Psychiatric Association* (Vol. 3, pp. 1803–1813). Washington, DC: American Psychiatric Association Press.

Wharton, R. N., Perel, J. M., Dayton, P. G., & Malitz, S. (1971). A potential clinical use for methylphenidate with tricyclic antidepressants. *American Journal of Psychiatry, 127,* 1619–1625.

White, K., Razani, J., Cadow, B., Gelfand, R., Palmer, R., Simpson, G., & Sloane, R. B. (1984). Tranylcypromine vs. nortriptyline vs. placebo in depressed outpatients: A controlled trial. *Psychopharmacology, 82,* 258–262.

White, K., & Simpson G. (1981). Combined MAOI–tricyclic antidepressant treatment: A re-evaluation. *Journal of Clinical Psychopharmacology, 1,* 264–282.

Yeragani, V. K., Pohl, R., Aleem, A., Balon, R., Sherwood, P., & Lycaki, H. (1988). Carbohydrate craving and increased appetite associated with antidepressant therapy. *Canadian Journal of Psychiatry, 33,* 606–610.

Yerevanian, B. J., Anderson, J. L., Grota, L. J., & Bray, M. (1986). Effects of bright incandescent light on seasonal and nonseasonal major depressive disorder. *Psychiatry Research, 18,* 355–364.

Ziegler, V. E., Taylor, J. R., Wetzel, R. D., & Biggs, J. T. (1978). Nortriptyline plasma levels and subjective side effects. *British Journal of Psychiatry, 132,* 55–60.

10

Medical Diagnostic Procedures for Depression: An Update from a Decade of Promise

HOWARD M. KRAVITZ
ALAN J. NEWMAN

The surprising thing is not how well the bear dances, but rather that the bear dances at all. (Andreasen, 1993, p. 688)

In the first edition of this book, we enthusiastically and optimistically described the new medical techniques that would assist the clinician in diagnosing depression and predicting treatment outcome (Fawcett & Kravitz, 1985). In particular, we highlighted disturbances in monoamine metabolism, hormonal dysregulation, and electrophysiological manifestations of altered sleep structure. A pharmacological probe, the stimulant challenge test, also was reviewed. We ended with hints of new information about brain structure and functioning that brain imaging techniques might reveal.

In this, the "Decade of the Brain" (U.S. Congress, 1992), the search for the biological correlates underlying and defining depression continues. All antidepressants affect monoaminergic systems, directly or indirectly. Newer antidepressant medications have been introduced that are more specific in their monoamine reuptake and receptor blocking effects (e.g.,

selective serotonin reuptake inhibitors). However, virtually all of these drugs interact with more than one amine system. The evidence is rather clear that a simple decrement in the biogenic amines serotonin, norepinephrine, or dopamine is not the cause of depression.

Accordingly, the focus has shifted from measurements of static levels of biogenic amines to more dynamic assessments of neurophysiological activity and responses to pharmacological challenges in order to understand better these functional interrelationships. The study of monoamines has expanded to the study of their receptors and postreceptor events, such as those mediated by second messenger systems. Now, a cascade of events must be considered (Sulser, 1986).

Similarly, changes in hormonal levels, including cortisol, thyroid, and, in women, various reproductive hormones, often are associated with vegetative symptoms such as sleep, appetite, and libido disturbances. However, these hormonal changes may be epiphenomena of psychobiological dysfunctions rather than causally related.

Recently, Bauer and Whybrow (1993) stated broadly that

> there are no laboratory studies by which one can validly and reliably identify rapid cycling, at least not with sufficient predictive validity for clinical or research use. This is currently true for all other forms of affective disorder as well. (p. 13)

Any dismay engendered by their statement should be tempered by Andreasen's quote (1993) in our epigraph, from her commentary on a study showing regional cerebral blood flow (rCBF) changes during self-induced dysphoria. Despite there being few, if any, useful laboratory aids for diagnosing, monitoring the treatment of, or determining prognosis for depression (Risch & Gillin, 1988), we remain optimistic about the future for developing these biological markers.

Yes, the goal is to find sensitive and specific biological markers that have high predictive validity and can guide diagnosis and treatment (how well the bear can dance). But first, markers must be reliably identified and the potential advantages and limitations of these tests must be understood (finding a bear that can dance).

There is another objective: How (and why) does the bear dance? Identifying biological correlates should not be equated with understanding pathophysiological mechanisms. Epiphenomena must be identified and accounted for in the explanatory equation. Any identified laboratory abnormality must be examined in the context of clinical, genetic, and other risk factors. Studying clinical and biological aspects together should facilitate understanding their interrelationships.

However, neither discovering a biological abnormality nor demonstrating its association with specific clinical features is sufficient to demonstrate an etiopathogenetic relationship. Furthermore, biological heterogeneity may exist within a clinically "pure" subgroup, whereas clinically distinct subgroups may share a common pathobiological finding. Including measurements of outcome may help distinguish state and trait markers. Thus, interpreting the results of trials claiming specific neurophysiological and neurochemical alterations for as broadly defined an entity as depression requires circumspection. The clinical criteria used for diagnosing depression should be comparable across studies.

Also, with any technological procedure, issues such as reliability, sensitivity, and specificity of the test must be considered. If a screening test is used for risk stratification, the prevalence of the disease in question in the cohort studied affects the determination of the predictive value of a positive test (Applegate, 1993). The prevalence of depression on an inpatient psychiatric unit is presumably higher than on a medical-surgical unit or in the general population. Because the sensitivity and specificity of a test vary from population to population, which population is sampled becomes an important factor; the results may apply only to that sample (Kraemer, 1987).

In this update, we examine the potential clinical utility and practical significance of diagnostic procedures for depression that have been investigated during the past decade. Promising (and not so promising) clinical and research data are surveyed and highlighted. The interested reader is referred to our previous review (Fawcett & Kravitz, 1985) for details of earlier research.

MONOAMINES AND RECEPTORS

An important fact to remember is that neurotransmitter systems do not exist in isolation. In the mid-1970s, Sabelli and associates (1976) observed that a single neuron can produce and release more than one family of transmitters, extending Dale's law (Dale, 1935). These coexisting, metabolically related cotransmitters, including peptides as well as monoamines, may affect each other's levels and metabolism, allowing for complex interactions (O'Donohue, Millington, Handelmann, Contreras, & Chronwall, 1985; Sabelli et al., 1976). Meltzer and Lowy (1987, p. 516) suggested that "multiple neurotransmitter metabolites and neuromodulators will have to be accounted for to reliably ascertain the significance of any one neurotransmitter system." Thus, depression is biochemically heterogeneous.

A thorough examination of synaptic events requires study of both monoamines and receptors. Neurotransmitters provide information about presynaptic and synaptic events, and receptors provide information about presynaptic and postsynaptic events. The complexity of these neurotransmitter–receptor interactions may at least partly explain the discrepancies observed in biochemical and physiological measurements among apparently clinically homogeneous depressive subgroups.

Receptor numbers can be evaluated directly in peripheral tissues using techniques such as measuring the amount of binding of a radiolabeled ligand to platelets or white blood cells. Alternatively, *in vitro* physiological responsiveness of peripheral tissue receptors to an exogenous pharmacological "challenge" tests the receptor's actual functional responsiveness. However, receptor number and responsiveness results are not necessarily linked to one another. Diminished responsiveness may suggest a postreceptor abnormality or desensitized high-affinity site due to elevated levels of neuroamines (Siever, 1987). A caveat to interpreting the data is that receptor regulation may differ in brain and peripheral tissue.

Catecholamines

Blackwell (1979) designated the biological marker 3-methoxy-4-hydroxyphenyl glycol (MHPG) as the "Myth of Heterogeneous Psychiatric Groups." Early research suggested that MHPG was the major central nervous system (CNS) metabolite of norepinephrine (NE) measurable peripherally, and that its levels could distinguish subtypes of depression, as well as predict treatment responsiveness. Thus, it became the focus of research on the catecholamine (CA) hypothesis of affective disorders. Depression, this hypothesis posits, is associated with an absolute or relative deficiency of CAs, particularly NE (and, to a lesser extent, dopamine [DA]), at functionally important central adrenergic receptor sites (Bunney & Davis, 1965; Schildkraut, 1965). Because the principal organ of interest, the brain, is otherwise inaccessible, urine, plasma, and cerebrospinal fluid (CSF) MHPG levels alternatively have served as indirect indicators of central NE activity, despite variability in the estimates of NE activity actually represented by MHPG (Filser, Muller, & Beckmann, 1986).

However, early promising findings that argued for low MHPG as a clinically useful indicator of a particular depressive subtype and a predictor of specific antidepressant responsiveness have not been confirmed. In a large multicenter National Institute of Mental Health-funded study of the psychobiology of affective disorders, Maas et al. (1982) found no significant difference in therapeutic effectiveness between amitriptyline (AMI) and imipramine (IMI). Among 87 subjects studied pretreatment and during treatment, IMI responders had both low urinary MHPG and CSF 5-hydroxyindoleacetic acid (5-HIAA), while AMI response was not related to pretreatment monoamine levels. Extein, Gold, and Goggans (1986) claimed that the assessment of antidepressant efficacy can be confounded by clinically and biologically heterogeneous depressive subtypes, variation in antidepressant response rates among depressed subgroups, and high rates of spontaneous remission and placebo response.

A meta-analysis by Davis and Bresnahan (1987) indicated that urinary MHPG in depressives is about the same as in normals and that differences between unipolar and bipolar subtypes were modest at best. Garvey, Hollon, DeRubeis, Evans, and Tuason (1990), summarizing the literature on MHPG and treatment response, observed that depressives with low urinary MHPG respond better to imipramine than do those with high MHPG. A consensus summary from these reviews indicates that, except for special situations, measurement of this CA metabolite is not recommended for clinical use, neither for selecting antidepressant treatment nor subtyping depression (Davis & Bresnahan, 1987; Garvey et al., 1990). Low MHPG may predict IMI outcome, but an initial drug-free evaluation period is needed to maximize identifying true pharmacological responders. Furthermore, this prediction may be specific for IMI, and not predict response to other drugs (Garvey et al., 1990). Although a subgroup of depressives with low homovanillic acid (HVA), the primary metabolite of DA, has been identified (Davis & Bresnahan, 1987), HVA also has not consistently defined clinical subgroups of depression or predicted treatment response (Jimerson, 1987; Nair & Sharma, 1989).

Extending earlier work (Koslow et al., 1983), Maas et al. (1987) further analyzed differences in CA metabolic excretion patterns and proportional changes in the excretion of CAs and their metabolites in depressed and healthy subjects. These data suggest that depressives may differ from control subjects in releasing more NE and epinephrine from adrenergic tissues, as well as synthesizing more CAs, consequently demonstrating disproportionate excretion rates of these CAs and their metabolites. Therefore, it may be more meaningful to examine patterns of metabolite excretion rather than the absolute excretion of a single metabolite. Schatzberg et al. (1989) applied the D-type score, a mathematically generated equation they derived a decade earlier from 24-hour collections of CAs and their metabolites (Schildkraut et al., 1978), to a new validation sample of 114 subjects. Research Diagnostic Criteria-diagnosed bipolar I subjects had D-type scores that were significantly lower than all other depressive subtypes, including bipolar II.

Gold, Goodwin, and Chrousos (1988a) suggested that increases in MHPG are not inconsistent with depression. This indication of a hyperactive peripheral sympathetic nervous system likely reflects similar activity in the central NE system, since the two work in parallel (Nair & Sharma, 1989). Anxiety, or stress, can activate the locus ceruleus–NE system, producing this increase. Antidepressants both decrease locus ceruleus firing rate and down-regulate β-adrenoceptors. Thus, the clinical state must be considered in interpreting metabolite levels.

These observations suggest that the function and activity of the receptors where neurotransmitters act also must be considered. As reviewed by Nair and Sharma (1989), factors such as the time lag to clinical response and the effectiveness of antidepressants that do not block NE or serotonin neuronal uptake were not accounted for by monoamine hypotheses, but could be understood by receptor theories of depression. In short, chronic antidepressant treatment decreases the number of postsynaptic β-adrenoceptors and reduces NE-stimulated adenylate cyclase activity in rat brain slices in a time frame consistent with the observed delay in effectiveness. This delayed action is not dependent on the acute presynaptic neuronal monoamine reuptake blockade that occurs minutes after acute tricyclic or monoamine oxidase inhibitor administration (Pryor & Sulser, 1991; Sulser, 1982).

While down-regulation of postsynaptic β-adrenoceptors has been a rather consistent antidepressant effect (but not with selective 5-HT reuptake inhibitors; Marsden, 1991), this response is not specific and may only be a secondary effect (Elliott, 1991). It does not assist diagnostically or predict treatment outcome. Reduced α_2-adrenoceptor responsiveness has been found in a subgroup of depressives. More consistent evidence of functional abnormalities of postsynaptic α_2-adrenoceptors (i.e., lowered sensitivity) in depression is found in the blunted (i.e., reduced) growth hormone response to clonidine, a selective receptor agonist (Nair & Sharma,

1989; Siever, 1987). Also, chronic antidepressant treatment appears to reduce postsynaptic α_2-adrenoceptor activity (Elliott, 1991). While some studies suggested that presynaptic α_2-adrenoceptor responsiveness may be reduced in some depressives, other data suggest no marked abnormalities in the noradrenergic inhibitory function of this autoreceptor (Heninger, Charney, & Price, 1988a).

Study of the major enzymes involved in biogenic amine metabolism, monoamine oxidase (MAO) and catechol-O-methyltransferase, are no longer recommended as a diagnostic test for depression, because earlier reported deficiencies have not been replicated (Pryor & Sulser, 1991; Risch & Gillin, 1988). However, Rothschild (1988) reported higher platelet MAO levels in persons with endogenous depression and lower levels in bipolar compared with unipolar depressives.

Indoleamines

So too, serotonin (5-hydroxytryptamine; 5-HT) and its principal metabolite, 5-HIAA, have been studied extensively in relation to their potential role in depression. Analogous to the CA hypothesis, the 5-HT hypothesis of depression (Meltzer & Lowy, 1987) posits that reduced functional levels of central 5-HT contribute or predispose to depression. Meltzer and Lowy (1987, p. 516) summarized the CSF 5-HIAA research with a statement that "no finding is robust enough to achieve widespread replication." Assay differences, spontaneous fluctuations in the levels, diagnostic methods, and severity of illness did not appear to account for the discrepancies (Meltzer & Lowy, 1987; Nair & Sharma, 1989). Although there is some evidence that there may be a subgroup of depressives with low CSF 5-HIAA, other data suggest that this metabolite may be a better predictor of suicide, violent, or impulsive behavior (Asberg, Schalling, Traskman-Bendz, & Wagner, 1987; Brown & Linnoila, 1990; Roy, DeJong, & Linnoila, 1989; van Praag et al., 1987). However, performing spinal taps for CSF 5-HIAA has not yet been established as part of a standard diagnostic protocol for evaluating depression or aggressive behaviors in clinical practice.

Maas et al.'s (1982) results also suggest an interaction between the NE and 5-HT systems. Furthermore, Agren, Mefford, Rudorfer, Linnoila, and Potter (1986) suggested that the 5-HTergic system regulates the DAergic system by facilitating dopamine turnover in the brain. Using gaussian mixture distributions, Davis et al. (1988) found no evidence for a depressive subgroup with low urinary MHPG and normal CSF 5-HIAA, or the converse. However, they found a subgroup with increased peripheral CA excretion, and one with low CSF HVA. MHPG, 5-HIAA, and HVA levels were highly intercorrelated; the former two were slightly elevated and the latter was moderately decreased.

Hsaio et al. (1987) studied the interrelationships among measurements of the CSF metabolites MHPG, 5-HIAA, and HVA to characterize antidepressant responders and nonresponders. Absolute pretreatment levels of the three metabolites did not distinguish treatment responders from nonresponders, but pre- and posttreatment levels of these metabolites, as well as treatment-induced differences, were correlated in the responders. Monoamine metabolite absolute levels and changes in these concentrations occurred independently of one another in the nonresponders. However, they cautioned that the observed interactions cannot be used as a biochemical test for predicting treatment responsiveness in individual patients, because these correlations represent a group phenomenon.

Delgado et al. (1994) demonstrated that change in depressive symptoms the day following acute tryptophan depletion via dietary manipulation in untreated outpatients during a major depressive episode correlated with eventual treatment response. Patients whose symptoms improved were more likely to respond, and those whose symptoms worsened were more likely not to respond to treatment. In an earlier report, Delgado et al. (1990) observed that two-thirds of remitted depressives experienced the reappearance of significant depressive symptoms during repeat tryptophan depletion testing performed while they continued to receive successful antidepressant therapy. Remission ensued after the patients resumed their regular food intake. These results suggest that the process(es) involved in 5-HT dysfunction, to the extent that 5-HT is related to the depressive behaviors, can be complex and may include presynaptic and/or postsynaptic dysregulation (Delgado et al., 1994).

The complexity of the 5-HT system in the CNS has been a formidable obstacle to developing simple models for explaining 5-HT's role and function in depression. Currently, about nine 5-HT receptors have been identified, and

a number of antidepressants with relative specificity for one or more of these receptor subtypes has been developed (Marsden, 1991). Possible roles for regulating central 5-HTergic function have been identified for specific receptors, but the lack of appropriate methods for studying CNS mechanisms has limited our ability to understand physiological function in the brain (Marsden, 1991).

Because the platelet demonstrates high-affinity active uptake and storage of 5-HT, and its receptors closely mimic human central neuronal receptors, it has been used widely as a model for the central 5-HT nerve terminal (Elliott, 1984). Of the 5-HT receptors, only the 5-HT$_2$ subtype has been demonstrated to be dysfunctional (increased number of binding sites and reduced responsiveness) in depression and normalized after effective treatment (Leonard, 1992). However, down-regulation of 5-HT$_2$ receptors is not necessary for an antidepressant effect (Marsden, 1991).

Reduced platelet 5-HT uptake and low imipramine binding (IB), which reflect a defect in the 5-HT transport mechanism and fewer neuronal presynaptic 5-HT reuptake sites, had shown promise as laboratory markers of central 5-HTergic function. However, Elliott (1991) suggested that neither test may be specific for depression or distinguish depressive subtypes.

The World Health Organization (WHO) multicenter study of platelet IB was conducted to examine the validity of IB as a biological marker of endogenous depression and to investigate the role of transcultural factors (Mellerup & Langer, 1990). No significant differences were found in IB capacity or affinity between depressed patients and matched controls from any individual center or for the combined sample. Although nonendogenous depressed patients had a significantly higher number of IB sites compared to the endogenous subgroup, the former subgroup was represented at only four of nine centers. Thus, the transcultural question remains speculative. While conceding that the data did not support the validity of IB as a biological marker of endogenous depression, the possibility that differences in the number of IB sites may distinguish among subgroups of depressives was left open for consideration.

Owens and Nemeroff (1994) found decreased platelet binding to the 5-HT transporter (which is involved in the presynaptic uptake of 5-HT) both with [3H]imipramine and the more selective ligand, [3H]paroxetine. Low numbers of platelet 5-HT transporter binding sites predicted treatment response in never-medicated patients, suggesting that the decreased density of platelet 5-HT transporters may be a state-dependent marker of depression (Owens & Nemeroff, 1994; Nemeroff, Knight, Franks, Craighead, & Krishnan, 1994).

Therefore, research must address a number of issues before these tests can be applied to the clinical diagnosis and management of depression. Methodological problems continue to confound the interpretation of the results. For example, antidepressant medication (particularly serotonin reuptake inhibitors) can inhibit 5-HT uptake, and the medication effect on IB varies with the specific drug used (Elliott, 1991). In the WHO study, subjects were free of antidepressants, neuroleptics, lithium, and barbiturates for at least 4 weeks. Also, geographical, seasonal, and diurnal variation may influence the interpretation (Elliott, 1991; Mellerup & Langer, 1990). These factors also can affect the interpretation of IB as a predictor of treatment response, or the use of serial IB levels for monitoring clinical state. The question of state versus trait has not been resolved. More recently, paroxetine binding studies have been conducted using this highly selective 5-HT uptake inhibitor to try to better characterize the 5-HT transport protein.

That 5-HT modulates NE neurotransmission in the CNS has been demonstrated by changes in ß-adrenergic receptor number (increase) and function (decreased [^{3}H]5-HT uptake) following 5-HTergic system lesions in rats (Stockmeier, Martino, & Kellar, 1985). Down-regulation of supersensitive β-adrenoceptors was prevented by disruption of central 5-HT neurons. Thus, β-adrenoceptor down-regulation in response to antidepressant treatment is dependent upon an intact 5-HTergic system. 5-HT receptors also appear to be involved (Pryor & Sulser, 1991). Likewise, changes induced in the 5-HTergic system by antidepressants require noradrenergic input (Siever, 1987). Hsiao et al. (1987) suggested that in nonresponders the normal adaptive synaptic changes induced by antidepressants are prevented by uncoupling of monoamine systems, analogous to the effect of 5-HTergic system lesions in rats.

Sulser (1986; Pryor & Sulser, 1991) hypothesized a role for glucocorticoid modulation of this linked 5-HT–NE adrenoceptor system. This suggests a role for steroid regulation of central monoaminergic function (Beigon, 1990;

McEwen, 1988) and is consistent with Roy, Everett, Pickar, and Paul's (1987) data, which suggest that the decreased number of IB sites found among depressed patients may be an epiphenomenon associated with hypercortisolism. Significant negative correlations were found between platelet IB and plasma cortisol levels both before and after dexamethasone administration (Roy et al., 1987).

Other Neurotransmitters

Other neurotransmitters have been implicated in the pathophysiology of depression, including phenylethylamine (PEA), acetylcholine (ACh), and gamma-aminobutyric acid (GABA), but have attracted less attention. These must be considered as potentially interacting with the NE and 5-HT systems.

Phenylethylamine

Sabelli and associates (1986) continued to study the role of PEA in modulating affective behavior, using urinary and plasma phenylacetic acid (PAA) as a peripheral marker of PEA metabolism. Sabelli et al. found reduced 24-hour urinary PAA excretion and total plasma PAA concentrations in subjects with DSM-III major depression (unipolar and bipolar) compared with healthy controls. A sensitivity of 52–71% and a specificity of 85% was reported. A similar range of sensitivity (51–69%) and specificity (69–100%) was reported for 24-hour urinary PAA levels by Gonzales-Sastre et al. (1988), depending on the cutoff points used. They also found lower excretion rates among subjects with DSM-III major depression compared with healthy controls.

Sabelli et al. (1986) claimed that factors such as sex, race, diet (others claimed that gut flora may increase PAA excretion [Gonzales-Sastre et al., 1988]), and motor activity do not seem to interfere with the test results. Although concluding that PAA may be a simple, reliable, and rapid state marker of depression, Sabelli et al. (1986) cautioned that this measurement alone is not sufficient for evaluating mood. Greenshaw (1989) hypothesized that PEA, as a metabolite of the monoamine oxidase inhibitor phenelzine, partially mediates the down-regulation of the β-adrenoceptors, thereby suggesting a possible PEA–CAergic interaction mediating the antidepressant action.

Acetylcholine

ACh activity appears to counter CAergic and 5-HTergic neurotransmitter activity. Studies showing activation of the hypothalamic–pituitary–adrenal (HPA) axis, dysregulation of the hypothalamic–pituitary–thyroid (HPT) axis, and shortened latency to rapid eye movement (REM) sleep suggest that supersensitive central muscarinic mechanisms may be present in at least some forms of depression (Dilsaver & Coffman, 1989; Janowsky & Overstreet, 1990). These physiological changes, as well as clinical symptoms of depression, can be elicited by administering anticholinesterase and cholinomimetic drugs systemically and centrally. These pharmacological agents act at central muscarinic ACh receptors.

Dilsaver (1986a, 1986b) described cholinergic–monoaminergic interactions involving regulation of receptor binding density; synthesis of enzymes involved in neurotransmitter synthesis; and in neurotransmitter synthesis, turnover, and release. This description extended earlier observations on a hypothesis of cholinergic–adrenergic balance (Janowsky, El-Yousef, Davis, & Sekerke, 1972). The described events involve neurochemical and molecular processes acting on membrane and receptor dynamics. Ionic (e.g., sodium and calcium) flux is one regulator. Second messengers (see below) also may mediate the interactive effects between cholinergic and monoaminergic neuronal systems. This system may be amenable to study with neuroimaging techniques, such as positron emission tomography (PET). Presently, however, these procedures are for research rather than practical and readily available diagnostic and assessment tools.

Unfortunately, a finding of increased functional muscarinic receptors on cultures of adult human skin fibroblasts, providing direct biochemical evidence of possible muscarinic cholinergic abnormalities in patients with major affective disorder and in their relatives (Nadi, Nurnberger, & Gershon, 1984), could not be replicated (Gershon, Nadi, Nurnberger, & Berrettini, 1985; Kelsoe et al., 1985, 1986; Lenox, Hitzemann, Richelson, & Kelsoe, 1985; Lin & Richelson, 1986).

Gamma-Aminobutyric Acid

GABA, an important inhibitory neurotransmitter in the CNS, also may play a role in the pathogenesis of depression (Emrich, von Zerssen, Kissling, Moller, & Windorfer, 1980). Its plasma levels reportedly parallel brain GABA activity (Petty, Kramer, Gullion, & Rush, 1992). Lloyd, Zivkovic, Scatton, Morselli, and Bartholini (1989) reviewed the GABAergic hypothesis of depression and presented findings indicating a correlation between behavioral and biochemical changes following antidepressant treatment. They suggested that antidepressant-induced down-regulation of β-adrenoceptors and up-regulation of $GABA_B$ receptors may be linked in terms of controlling cyclic adenosine monophosphate (cAMP) production. More important, only these two receptor interactions appear to be consistent with an antidepressant action (Lloyd et al., 1989). Increased GABA tone may have an antidepressant effect.

Petty et al. (1992) found low plasma GABA levels in a subset of males with major depression with shorter duration of illness and higher endogenous symptom severity score. Because GABA can facilitate NE and possibly 5-HT neurotransmission in cortical areas, the authors suggested that GABA influences can complement the biogenic amine theories of depression.

Second Messengers

Second messengers (e.g., cAMP) mediate postreceptor events. cAMP formation is stimulated by the enzyme adenylate cyclase (AC), which is activated by the postsynaptic receptor. AC and cAMP activity have been measured peripherally in platelets, leukocytes, plasma, and CSF. In recent reviews, Thilo and Burnet (1992) and Elliott (1991) concluded that functioning of the AC complex tends to be decreased in depression. But these changes are nonspecific, and it is difficult to distinguish primary from secondary changes in AC activity. Though suspected to be secondary, further studies are recommended in which AC changes can be correlated with other neurochemical and pathological changes (Thilo & Burnet, 1992). Elliott (1991) suggests that the extent of change in AC activity during treatment may be an indicator of therapeutic response. (The phosphoinositide system, the other major class of second messengers will not be reviewed here.)

Neurotransmitter–Hormone Interactions

Monoamines and their receptors can affect neuroendocrine activity. Exploring the relationship between the HPA axis and adrenomedullary function, Stokes et al. (1987) demonstrated a relationship between cortisol hypersecretion and high urinary epinephrine excretion (lower CSF 5-HIAA and MHPG levels also were found). The direction of the causal arrow is unclear, because either event could induce the other. This noradrenergic–HPA axis relationship may depend on basal HPA axis activity, the relative responsiveness of different adrenoceptor subtypes, or direct adrenal sympathetic innervation (Siever, 1987).

These factors may be state-dependent, varying with the clinical condition. Increased corticotropin-releasing hormone (CRH) release, which has been observed in depression, also can cause cortisol hypersecretion and increase epinephrine excretion via its effect on noradrenergic neuronal firing and receptor responsiveness (Siever, 1987). Wolkowitz et al. (1987) found that dexamethasone administration significantly increased plasma MHPG and nonsignificantly decreased plasma HVA levels in depressives relative to normal controls. These changes were not related to differences in plasma dexamethasone levels. Larger increases in MHPG were associated with smaller postdexamethasone reductions in cortisol levels. Thus, hypercortisolemia may stimulate NE turnover.

Summary and Conclusions

The weight of the evidence supports the contention that there are disturbances in monoamine systems in depression. However, both the heterogeneity of depression and inconsistent findings in monoamine metabolite research confound attempts to draw valid and meaningful conclusions. Potter and Linnoila (1989) suggest that the D-type score, in relating multiple biochemical parameters, may have utility for distinguishing phenotypes of depression. However, the generalizability of this multifactorially derived algorithm requires study in other settings.

No single monoaminergic theory of depression can be supported in its entirety by the data. An explanatory mechanism that can account for the inconsistencies in the data remains an elusive challenge. That these systems do not work in isolation from each other likely accounts for at least part of the variance. Also, these are indirect measurements. Therefore, due consideration must be given to simultaneously monitoring multiple neurotransmitter systems.

Overall, measurements of NE and 5-HT metabolites may have modest clinical utility, perhaps distinguishing among depressive subtypes. However, monoamine metabolite measurements alone presently do not seem to offer any benefits to the clinician as tests for either diagnosing depression or predicting treatment response. There seem to be no uniform monoamine increments or decrements measured in biological fluids. Gjerris (1988, p. 18) stated that "no unambiguous conclusion can be drawn from studies on changes in CSF amine, amine metabolite or peptide change after recovery from depression induced by antidepressant treatment." Sources of variance in these levels and factors that may influence and limit their specificity are many (Fawcett, Kravitz, & Sabelli, 1984). Methodological issues with regard to CSF studies have been reviewed by Gjerris (1988).

Siever and Davis (1985) suggested that the variance reflects the development of noradrenergic system dysregulation. Exposure to a stressful stimulus may unmask pre-existing abnormalities in regulatory control mechanisms, such as receptor function, and repeated episodes may lead to impaired noradrenergic responsiveness. Consistent with this idea, the time lag from initiation of antidepressant treatment to clinical benefits, often at least 2 weeks, suggests that compensatory receptor modifications must precede therapeutic effects. These modifications occur in response to increased monoamine availability, which may be rapid but, in accordance with Siever and Davis (1985), may occur more slowly in chronically depressed persons.

Changes in monoamine concentrations may be reflected in modified receptor responsiveness and response to pharmacological challenges (Siever and Davis, 1985). However, it remains unsettled whether the adaptation of receptors to different levels of neurotransmitters, as well as to the effects of pharmacological agents, is a primary or secondary response. Also, whether the observed monoamine or receptor changes are state- or trait-dependent remains unresolved (e.g., low MHPG in bipolar depression, and high MHPG in bipolar mania).

Receptor sensitivity hypotheses have been proposed to explain antidepressant action. Reviews of the studies examining the usefulness of β- and α$_2$-adrenoceptors, as well as 5-HT receptors, find shortcomings with the current methods (Leonard, 1982; Meltzer & Lowy, 1987; Nair & Sharma, 1989; Siever, 1987). Elliott

(1991) concludes that none of the peripheral models reviewed is reliable enough to serve as a biochemical marker for affective disorder. The evidence linking abnormal activity of precise 5-HT receptor subtypes in the brain to depression, or to antidepressant action, remains unclear (Leonard, 1992).

Furthermore, a practical means to investigate central receptor function is not available. Siever (1987) concluded that studies of adrenoceptor responsiveness have yet to provide results indicating their clinical usefulness as a diagnostic test. Heninger, Charney, and Price (1988b) found that pharmacological challenge tests of both noradrenergic receptor function (using clonidine and yohimbine to measure MHPG, cortisol, blood pressure, sedation, nervousness, and growth hormone) and 5-HTergic receptor function (using fenfluramine, 5-hydroxytryptophan, and intravenous tryptophan to measure prolactin, cortisol, and growth hormone) produced only small differences and much overlap between depressives and controls. They concluded that these tests were not clinically useful diagnostically or prognostically.

The 5-HT–NE–glucocorticoid link hypothesis (Pryor & Sulser, 1991) emphasizes the integration of multiple intracellular signals regulating neuronal responses. Clearly, the complexity of this cascade of events, derived from studies of antidepressant action, bespeaks the need to move beyond simple monoaminergic theories, perhaps even beyond receptors (Pryor & Sulser, 1991).

PSYCHONEUROENDOCRINE STRATEGIES

Psychoneuroendocrine assessments, in addition to providing clinical information about a person's medical status, may permit inferences regarding neurotransmitter activity. Because neuroendocrine abnormalities are presumed to reflect neural regulatory defects in the CNS, and are associated with neurotransmitter activity, these techniques potentially offer a "window on the brain." Psychoendocrine studies of a variety of neuropeptides and hormones suggest that many patients with major depression have evidence of dysfunctional HPA and HPT axes. However, because the regulatory mechanisms that affect pituitary function are multiple and often redundant, the results of these studies often are inconclusive (Gold, Goodwin, & Chrousos, 1988b).

In the previous edition of this chapter (Fawcett & Kravitz, 1985), psychoendocrine studies of depression were reviewed extensively. Herein we review the clinically relevant advances in our knowledge and understanding of dynamic tests of psychoneuroendocrine function as aids to diagnosis and treatment. In particular, the focus will be on the HPA and HPT axes. Because the psychoneuroendocrine challenge strategies remain predominantly research techniques for assessing the role of CA and indoleamine neurotransmission and the mechanism of antidepressant action, they will not be detailed here. Instead, the reader is referred to the relevant chapters in Psychopharmacology: The Third Generation of Progress (Meltzer, 1987) and to Delgado and Charney (1991). (See also Thase & Howland, Chapter 8, this volume.)

Tests of the Hypothalamic–Pituitary–Adrenal Axis

In depression, a dysfunctional HPA axis is characterized by increased basal cortisol secretion and high circulating glucocorticoid levels, reduced cortisol release following adrenocorticotropic hormone (ACTH) administration, nonsuppression of glucocorticoids postdexamethasone, a discrepancy between the cortisol secretory and diurnal rhythms, and flattening of cortisol circadian periodicity (Gold et al., 1988b; McEwen, 1988; Risch & Gillin, 1988; Thilo & Burnet, 1992). Abnormalities of this axis have been among the most studied putative biological markers in depression, and hypercortisolism is probably the most consistent finding in persons with major depression.

While it continues to be one of the most replicated tests for depression, the dexamethasone suppression test (DST) has failed to live up to its early promise as a diagnostic test, a state-dependent monitor of the course of illness, and/or a predictor of treatment responsiveness, although persistent nonsuppression may herald relapse if treatment is withdrawn (APA Task Force, 1987; Brown, 1989; Carroll, 1982; Carroll et al., 1981). Arana, Baldessarini, and Ornsteen (1985), in an extensive literature review of the use of the DST, emphasizing its role in diagnosis, prediction of treatment outcome, and clinical course, observed that it has not proved to reflect pathophysiological changes at the CNS or pituitary levels, and dexamethasone tissue availability may contribute to test outcome. They concluded that the DST has a limited ability to help predict either initial responses to treatment once a diagnosis has been made or later outcome, and is not associated with responses to a specific type of antidepressant. A WHO study involving nine centers and 293 patients examining the relationship of psychopathology and psychiatric history to cortisol levels and suppression/nonsuppression status did not find a typical symptom profile characterizing a depressive cortisol suppressor or nonsuppressor (Gastpar, Gilsdorf, Abou-Saleh, & Ngo-Khac, 1992).

A meta-analysis of the DST as a predictor of suicide showed that nonsuppression was associated with subsequent completed suicide but not with earlier attempts (Lester, 1992). However, depression, which is correlated with suicidal behavior, was not controlled for in comparing suicidal versus nonsuicidal patients in the studies of completed suicides (Lester, 1992). While Roy (1992) found no significant differences between depressives who had or had never attempted suicide, and between depressives who did or did not reattempt suicide during a 5-year follow-up and those who had never attempted suicide, significantly more of the violent suicide attempters were nonsuppressors. Thus, evidence of HPA axis dysregulation may indicate a potential for violent suicidal behavior, similar to its possible usefulness as an indicator of more severe depressive illness.

Risch and Gillin (1988, p. 307) pointed out that the DST is "subject to many conditions that may produce false-positive and false-negative results [see APA Task Force, 1987, Appendix 1; Kraus, Grof, & Brown, 1988] and make the test contraindicated and uninterpretable." A part of the problem, as delineated by Kraemer (1987), may be attributed to methodological flaws in study design and data analysis that are crucial to the development, implementation, and interpretation of diagnostic tests. Using a signal detection method, the receiver operating characteristic curve, Mossman and Somoza (1989) showed that to optimize the test's performance, the criterion cutoff for DST nonsuppression must vary with the estimated prevalence of depression in the study population.

Among diverse subject populations and including less-well-controlled conditions, sensitivity is 50–60% in severely ill inpatient melancholic depressives and 40% or less in less severely ill outpatient depressives, and specificity is only about 80% (APA Task Force, 1987). Thus, DST nonsuppression may indicate sever-

ity of depressive illness but, because of reduced specificity, it may not be a good screening test for it. Only tentative predictive validity has been established (Delgado & Charney, 1991; Gastpar et al., 1992). A normal test neither excludes a diagnosis of major depression nor militates against antidepressant therapy.

A meta-analysis of the role of the DST as a predictor of the course and outcome in major depression indicated that the pretreatment DST has no clinical utility as a predictor of short-term response to antidepressant treatment or of longer-term outcome (Ribeiro, Tandon, Grunhaus, & Greden, 1993). However, persistent posttreatment cortisol nonsuppression was associated with a higher risk for early relapse and poor outcome on short-term follow-up. These investigators also found that pretreatment nonsuppressors responded more poorly to placebo (Ribeiro et al., 1993).

Thus, the DST currently serves primarily as a research tool, with the principal focus on attempting to understand the pathophysiological basis for nonsuppression in depressed patients. There is probably no single unique cause for DST nonsuppression, although common or shared mechanisms may include stress. Risch and Gillin (1988) concluded more optimistically that with refinements it may yet prove to be a useful laboratory test.

Along these lines, Arana, Reichlin, Workman, Haaser, and Shader (1988) demonstrated improved performance in diagnosing depression using a modification of the DST, the dexamethasone suppression index (DSI). The DSI, calculated as the product of cortisol and dexamethasone blood levels, expresses cortisol concentration as an inverse curvilinear function of dexamethasone concentration. This relationship suggests that both an abnormality in dexamethasone kinetics and resistance to dexamethasone suppression centrally may occur in depression.

Hypersecretion of CRH has been proposed as the basis for hypercortisolism. Depressives, compared with controls, have blunted pituitary ACTH and exaggerated cortisol release in response to CRH stimulation (Gold et al., 1984); increased cortisol levels are thought to inhibit ACTH release. Excessive HPA activation in depression can result from altered regulatory mechanisms between various sites within this axis, particularly in higher brain centers (hypothalamus and hippocampus; Young, Haskett, Murphy-Weinberg, Watson, & Akil, 1991), and CRH hypersecretion ("overdrive") due to limbic–

hypothalamic dysfunction (Amsterdam, Maislin, Gold, & Winokur, 1989). The sensitivity, specificity, and clinical utility of these findings remain uncertain (Risch & Gillin, 1988).

Tests of the Hypothalamic–Pituitary–Thyroid Axis

While thyroid function tests usually are within the normal range in depressed patients, evidence of subclinical dysfunction has been observed. Because a number of the signs and symptoms of overt thyroid disease overlap with vegetative and cognitive phenomena of depression, the availability of laboratory tests that can distinguish the two is important. Bauer and Whybrow (1988) reviewed the evidence indicating that affective psychopathology is associated with changes in thyroid status.

The thyroid's response to hypothalamic thyrotropin-releasing hormone (TRH [protirelin] stimulation test) appears to be disturbed in depression, and a persistently blunted response after clinical improvement may herald a relapse. The TRH stimulation test has been used both as an indicator of subclinical hypothyroidism in depressed patients and as a potential biological marker of major depression in euthyroid patients (Rosse, Giese, Deutsch, & Morihisa, 1989a). However, the reason for, and meaning, of this diminished maximal response in depressives, in the absence of abnormal peripheral thyroid function indices, remains unanswered (Arana, Zarzar, & Baker, 1990; Langer et al., 1986; Loosen & Prange, 1982).

Approximately 20–40% of patients with major depression demonstrate a blunted thyroid-stimulating hormone (TSH) response to intravenous TRH, and Kronig and Gold (1986) reported a 40% sensitivity and 85% specificity for this blunting in unipolar major depression. This reduced sensitivity and specificity limit its usefulness as a routine diagnostic test for depression. Also, age, gender, and various medications, including psychotropics, can affect the results and the interpretation of the test (Arana et al., 1990; Langer et al., 1986; Loosen & Prange, 1982).

Arana et al. (1990) demonstrated that the sensitivity of the TRH stimulation test depends upon which diagnostic criteria for depression are used. They reviewed the literature for studies involving unipolar depressed patients who were diagnosed using either the Research Diagnostic Criteria (RDC) or the DSM-III criteria.

Information indicating that the accepted procedure for the test was performed and sufficient data to allow assessment of individual responses rather than group means were both required. Six studies involving 249 RDC-diagnosed patients had a sensitivity of 51%, and four studies involving 161 DSM-III-diagnosed patients had a sensitivity of only 34.8%, a statistically significant difference (Arana et al., 1990). Thus, the blunting criteria alone (i.e., < 5 μU/ml vs. < 7 μU/ml) are not the sole reason for sensitivity differences.

Langer et al. (1986), using the TSH-blunting criteria of < 5 μU/ml, examined the usefulness of the TRH stimulation test as a predictor of recovery and relapse for patients with major ($n = 73$) and minor ($n = 10$) depression, as well as for patients with various functional psychoses ($n = 31$) who were treated with either antidepressants or neuroleptics. All patients were receiving psychotropics, which could have influenced the results, prior to test administration. Blunted TSH responses were reported in 39% of depressives, and in 35% of the group of schizophrenics, schizoaffectives, and manics, and 7% of normal controls. There was no association between baseline and follow-up responses. Of all 114 patients who were tested at admission, 25% converted to a normal response after 2 months of treatment, while 15% converted from a normal to a blunted response; the remainder had similar responses before and after treatment.

Langer et al. (1986) concluded that the test is a useful state marker and predictor of outcome. During the symptomatic phase, a blunted response predicted a greater likelihood of recovery with treatment, and blunted response at clinical recovery indicated a risk for early relapse, despite maintenance antidepressant therapy. In contrast, Loosen (1985) and Loosen, Garbutt, and Prange (1987) indicated that sometimes TSH blunting can be a state marker and sometimes a trait marker. In the latter case, the abnormality persisted into remission in over half the patients retested. Vanelle et al. (1990) could not demonstrate the usefulness of the TRH test for selecting antidepressants according to their predominant monoaminergic action.

Maes, Schotte, Vandewoude, Martin, and Blockx (1992) suggested that an improved and ultrasensitive immunoradiometric assay for basal TSH determinations could replace the TRH test. Studying 84 depressed women, they found that the TRH-induced TSH responses were linearly and positively correlated with basal TSH levels, and concluded that peak stimulated TSH responses were "a magnified but biased signal" of the basal level. Free thyroxine and basal TSH levels were negatively correlated. They also observed that the basal TSH levels were inversely related to the severity of the depression, with the lowest levels (still within the euthyroid range) occurring in melancholics. Only when the basal TSH level is blunted or increased do they advise additional thyroid function tests.

Analogous to the situation with the HPA axis, the biological basis for the HPT axis dysfunction may be hypersecretion of TRH from the hypothalamus. But, because the bulk of brain TRH is extrahypothalamic and its receptors exist in significant quantities outside of the pituitary, Bauer and Whybrow (1988) questioned whether basal or TRH-stimulated serum TSH reflects CNS thyroid function. Further study is required to elucidate the pathophysiological mechanism(s) of the TRH stimulation test and to understand the clinical significance and consequences of the results.

Also as in the case of the DST, the primary utility for the TRH stimulation test as a neuroendocrine marker presently appears to be for research rather than as a clinical tool for identifying or confirming an existing psychiatric diagnosis, owing to its low sensitivity and specificity (Loosen et al., 1987). The blunted TSH response is not specific for depression. Also, it may coexist with, or occur independently of DST nonsuppression. This is of some interest, because glucocorticosteroids can suppress the TSH response to TRH (Maes, Vandewoude, Schotte, Martin, & Blockx, 1990) and therefore, if the TRH test and DST are performed sequentially, the former should be done first.

Data showing that TSH blunting and DST nonsuppression can occur independently in depressed patients suggest that there is no direct relationship between the two phenomena (Loosen & Marciniak, 1988). Thus, one abnormality is not an endocrine epiphenomenon of the other. Loosen and Marciniak presented data suggesting that patients with a positive DST have a reduced binding capacity for thyroid hormones.

The test's clinical value requires further study, including its role as a predictor of acute treatment response, long-term outcome, and risk for relapse and violent suicide attempts.

Other Psychoneuroendocrine Tests

Growth hormone, prolactin, and gonadotropins, which were reviewed in the first edition, as well as melatonin and endorphins, also have been studied. Growth hormone has probably been the most studied in this regard. However, use of these tests remains research-oriented rather than for clinically practical applications. Although growth hormone secretion appears to be normal in depression, variations in its responsiveness to a variety of stimuli, including mood state, have yielded conflicting results and confused interpretation of these changes (Pearsall & Gold, 1986). For example, glucocorticoid excess can suppress growth hormone secretion. This susceptibility to change has limited its clinical use (Brown, 1989). Despite these limitations, there have been multiple abnormalities indicating dysregulation of growth hormone secretion in depressed patients (Brown, 1989; Matussek, 1994; Musselman & Nemeroff, 1993). The observation of reduced responsiveness to insulin-induced hypoglycemia during depression has been one major application in depression. The response to apomorphine, a DA receptor agonist, may be reduced in depression (Matussek, 1984; Musselman & Nemeroff, 1993). (The response to clonidine was described earlier.)

The prolactin circadian secretory pattern may be abnormal in depression (Halbreich, Grunhaus, & Ben-David, 1979). Overall, higher fluctuations in prolactin secretion, and earlier elevations in evening levels before sleep, have been observed in depressives. However, prolactin assays have not been demonstrated as clinically useful for diagnosing depression or assessing its treatment.

Evidence indicates that melatonin secretion, which is mediated by noradrenergic activity, is low in depression (Nair & Sharma, 1989). Melatonin, found in the pineal gland, is related to circadian rhythms, too. Its secretion is related to the light–dark cycle. A reduced nocturnal peak level may be associated with depression. Considerable interindividual and intergroup variation may limit its clinical utility, although increased nocturnal levels in treatment-responsive depression suggests that it may be a useful state marker. Bright light, which has been used for treating seasonal affective disorder, suppresses melatonin and has been effective for treating this depressive disorder. Thus, longitudinal study is needed. The data suggest an abnormality in the system between the retina and pineal gland (Brown, 1989).

THE STIMULANT CHALLENGE TEST

Prediction of antidepressant response continues to be an unsolved objective in biological psychiatry and psychopharmacotherapy. Little (1988) and Goff (1986) both reviewed the use of stimulant challenges to predict antidepressant efficacy. Positive stimulant responses have been described as improvements in mood (e.g., mood elevation) and in other behavioral manifestations of depression (Fawcett & Kravitz, 1985). Goff (1986) found that 5 of 10 studies showed a positive association between stimulant and antidepressant responses. Four of 6 studies, including 2 with a placebo control, showed that tricyclic response was related to stimulant response. Generally, extended stimulant challenges had greater predictive value. Little (1988) found that the acute response to amphetamine better distinguished antidepressant responders (85%) from nonresponders (43%), as compared with methylphenidate, which did not predict differential antidepressant improvement rates (66% vs. 68% for stimulant responders and nonresponders, respectively). Kravitz, Edwards, Fawcett, and Fogg (1990) reported that the response to a 1-day dextroamphetamine challenge (20 mg) was linearly related to the level of improvement in depression following 6 weeks of antidepressant treatment. Absolute response rates were not provided, and the stimulant response did not preferentially distinguish responsiveness to a particular treatment.

The clinical utility of the test is not clear, nor is the mechanism for the response (Goff, 1986; Little, 1988). The method remains nonstandardized, which limits the reliability, and questions regarding the test's validity as a predictor of antidepressant treatment outcome remain (Kravitz et al., 1990; Little, 1988). Sensitivity and specificity vary among studies (Little, 1988). The measurement and interpretation of the stimulant response require standardization and clarification before it can be recommended routinely for clinical practice (Kravitz et al., 1990).

SLEEP MARKERS: A BEDTIME STORY

The most characteristic polysomnographic findings in depressed patients involve changes in REM (dream) sleep—REM is too early, too long, and too active. Thus, the first REM latency is short (≤ 60 minutes; the time from sleep onset to onset of the first REM period); REM density is increased (more active eye movements), most evident in the first REM period, which also is lengthened; and REM is temporally redistributed to the first half of the sleep period. Other changes include reduced slow-wave sleep (delta, or Stages 3 and 4), and disrupted sleep continuity (increased awakenings, arousals, and stage shifts; a longer sleep latency; early morning wakening; less sleep time and less sleep efficiency).

About 10–20% of patients with major depression, often bipolar, report spending more time in bed, and their polysomnograms show high sleep efficiencies (Garvey, Mungas, & Tollefson, 1984; Reynolds, Coble, Kupfer, & Shaw, 1982; Reynolds & Kupfer, 1987). Generally, the sleep measurement changes observed in depression are in the direction of age-related changes in sleep parameters. Computerization of polysomnographic data now permits more refined descriptions of sleep electrophysiological activity.

The REM latency distribution in major depression appears to be unimodal, after the effects of age and psychosis are controlled (Ansseau, Kupfer, Reynolds, & McEachran, 1984; Reynolds & Kupfer, 1987). Night-to-night variability may correlate with clinical features of the depression (Ansseau, Kupfer, & Reynolds, 1985a; Ansseau, Kupfer, Reynolds, & Coble, 1985b; Reynolds & Kupfer, 1987). Thus, clinical characteristics, including depression subtype and symptom severity, should be considered in interpreting REM latency data. Although age can be a confounder, Reynolds et al. (1988) reliably discriminated depressed (depressive pseudodementia) from demented (primary dementia with depressive features) elderly persons using REM latency (shorter in depressives), together with REM and indeterminant non-REM sleep, and early morning wakening.

Reynolds et al. (1990) explored the effects of gender in outpatients with major depression (RDC diagnosis). Depressed men had less delta sleep and lower delta wave counts both during the whole night and during the first non-REM period than depressed women, but the temporal distribution of delta wave density between the first two non-REM periods was similar between genders. Age effects, but no significant gender or gender × age interaction effects, were found for REM latency, duration of the first REM period, and sleep efficiency. An age × gender interaction was evident for REM density.

Reynolds and Kupfer (1987) estimated that approximately 90% of depressed inpatients show some form of electroencephalogram (EEG)-verified sleep disturbance. Sensitivity for REM latency depends on the definition used and on depression subtype and severity, and ranges from 62.5–70.8% (Reynolds & Kupfer, 1987). Specificity for sleep EEG markers is equivocal. Sleep continuity disturbances are common, but less specific for depression. Decreased delta sleep is seen in other psychiatric disorders. Medical illness can reduce REM sleep.

While the polysomnographic findings have relative specificity for depression compared with normal controls, further comparative data involving other psychiatric disorders are needed. To try to address the paucity of comparative data, Benca, Obermeyer, Thisted, and Gillin (1992) performed a comprehensive meta-analysis on sleep in psychiatric disorders. These analyses included cross-sectional data from 7,151 patients and control subjects from 177 studies. Affective disorders differed most frequently and significantly from normal controls. However, no clear-cut differences between affective disorders and other diagnostic categories emerged.

No single sleep variable has been shown to have absolute specificity for any particular psychiatric disorder, or has reliably distinguished affective from other disorders (Benca et al., 1992). Although a short REM latency is not unique to affective disorders, it is quantitatively shorter most significantly in affective disorders. It has also distinguished some diagnostic affective disorder subtypes from others. However, Hudson, Lipinski, Frankenburg, Grochocinski, and Kupfer (1988) and Hudson et al. (1992a) found a shortened REM latency and increased REM density in unmedicated bipolar manic inpatients, not different from the findings in major depression.

Increased REM density also was not found consistently in depressives compared with other diagnostic categories or controls (Benca et al., 1992). In fact, this marker was greater in anxiety disorders, borderline personality, and schizophrenia, compared with affective disorders. Benson and Zarcone (1993) reported no differences in eye movement density among schizophrenics, depressives, and healthy nonpsychiatric volunteers within and across nights. However, within nights the depressives displayed a flatter temporal distribution of REM density, consistent with the altered REM distribution in depression. Thus, caution was suggested in using REM density as a biological marker for depression (Benson & Zarcone, 1993).

Reynolds and Kupfer (1987) also observed a redistribution of delta activity from the first to the second non-REM period. More recent data from Kupfer, Frank, McEachran, and Grochocinski (1990) suggest that the delta sleep ratio between non-REM periods 1 and 2 may be a more robust predictor of recurrent depressive episodes than REM latency. Those with a high ratio remained clinically remitted five times longer than those with a low ratio.

Hudson et al. (1992b) constructed a sleep disturbance index from wakefulness after sleep onset, percentage of Stage 1, percentage of delta sleep, REM latency, and REM density, and demonstrated that insomnia, depression, and narcolepsy represented a continuum of progressively more disturbed sleep. This meta-analytical attempt to parsimoniously explain polysomnographic findings did not include other psychiatric disorders to assess the value of their index for distinguishing these disorders on the basis of a set of sleep EEG features.

The WHO conducted a cross-cultural multicenter study of patients with major depression (RDC diagnosis; $n = 67$) and age- and sex-matched controls ($n = 66$) to assess the reliability of the sleep EEG measures (Mendlewicz & Kerkhofs, 1991). A shortening of REM latency and increased REM density were consistently observed among depressives. Further analysis controlling for study site (eight centers on three continents) revealed that REM density, as well as total sleep time, sleep efficiency, and sleep architecture variables, were influenced by cultural effects, whereas a diagnosis of depression remained the principal determinant of REM latency. Decreased REM latency and Stage 4 sleep were not related to endogenicity (subtype/severity factor) after adjusting for the effects of age and site.

The extent to which sleep disturbances are state- versus trait-dependent in depression is unresolved (Risch & Gillin, 1988). Longitudinal follow-up studies with polysomnography performed during, after, and just before recurrent depressive episodes are needed to investigate this question, and are ongoing (Reynolds, 1989; Reynolds & Kupfer, 1987). An examination of changes in sleep in relation to clinical data would contribute to understanding mechanisms of response to treatment. Acutely, REM

suppression following antidepressant administration appears to predict clinical improvement,
but whether this extends to predicting outcome
to medications with specific neuropharmacological profiles requires further study (Reynolds,
1989). Mouret and associates (Mouret, Lemoine,
& Minuit, 1987; Mouret, Lemoine, Minuit, &
Robelin, 1988) identified a "dopamine-depen-
dent depression" in patients who displayed
polysomnographic features of parkinsonism, but
lacked clinical features of this dopamine-defi-
ciency disease. These treatment-resistant patients were successfully treated with piribedil,
a dopamine agonist (Mouret et al., 1987), and
subsequently with the CA precursor tyrosine
(Mouret et al., 1988).

However, it is not clear whether persisting
REM suppression is a pharmacological effect or
an indicator of remission/recovery. Also, it is
uncertain whether maintaining/reverting to a
short first REM latency predicts risk for relapse.
Rush et al. (1986) found that 8 of 11 major
depressives (RDC diagnosis) who had a short
first REM latency (≤ 65 minutes) pretreatment
maintained this abnormality while in remission
6 months later, suggesting that it may be a trait
marker. Alternatively, this finding may indicate
that physiological disturbances are slower to
normalize than clinical symptoms and/or are a
risk for relapse. This marker also may serve as
an antecedent to the onset of a new episode.
Kupfer, Frank, Grochocinski, Gregor, and
McEachran (1988) found that a consistent profile of shortened REM latency, increased REM
activity, decreased delta sleep, and abnormalities in sleep continuity was repeated early
(within the first month) in the course of a recurrent depressive episode.

Cartwright, Kravitz, Eastman, and Wood
(1991) evaluated community volunteers undergoing divorce at baseline and at follow-up 1 year
later. Fifteen subjects (38%) had a short first
REM latency at baseline, and seven subjects
showed it again at follow-up, despite no longer
meeting criteria for depression. These seven
had higher recovery rates and better life adjustment than depressed subjects with normal
REM latencies, suggesting that a short REM
latency may be a traitlike vulnerability marker
for an affective response to a major stressor, as
well as an indicator of a greater capacity for recovery. A tendency for subjects in the short
REM latency group to have a stronger family
history of depression (five of seven subjects) did
not help to explain their better outcome.

These findings suggest that this biological
correlate may be useful for monitoring for
depressive relapse/recurrence. However, the
potential confounding effect of medication on
sleep parameters must be considered. A 2-week
drug-free period before baseline sleep studies
are performed has been recommended (Reynolds & Kupfer, 1987). Longitudinal polysomnographic studies undertaken while patients
receive nonpharmacological long-term interventions, such as cognitive–behavioral therapy,
may more clearly address the state–trait question (Reynolds & Kupfer, 1987).

Another important question raised is whether
sleep changes are epiphenomena of or related
to changes in other biological systems which
are pathophysiologically related to depression rather than direct biological manifestations
(Reynolds & Kupfer, 1987). Reynolds and Kupfer suggest that both the persistence of polysomnographic indicators into remission and
their association with treatment response point
toward a direct relationship. Kupfer and Ehlers
(1989) further broaden our perspective on
REM latency as a sleep marker by proposing
that this measurement is modified by (at least)
two factors: one related to slow-wave sleep and
one related to REM sleep. Thus, as a research
as well as a clinical instrument, sleep EEG may
increase our understanding of the neurobiology
of depression.

OTHER ELECTROPHYSIOLOGICAL MARKERS

Although EEG asymmetries have been observed in depression, this finding is nonspecific;
the EEG has no clinical utility for diagnosing
this disorder (Rosse, Giese, Deutsch, & Morihisa, 1989b). Evoked potentials (EP), an extension of EEG, measure brain EEG responses to
repeated exposure to specific sensory stimuli.
Computer averaging of multiple evoked brain
electrical responses produces the characteristic
EP waveform, absent the background, non-
stimulus-related activity. The usefulness of EP
in diagnosing specific psychiatric disorders is
uncertain (Rosse et al., 1989b).

Advances in computer technology have led to
the development of an EEG topographic two-
dimensional imaging procedure, brain electrical activity mapping (BEAM). While large quantities of EEG and EP data can be represented

in pretty, color-coded pictures, the problem remains that the electrical activity recorded is from the scalp surface (Morihisa, 1989).

The primary focus of EEG mapping in psychiatry has been in schizophrenia; there are few data on the clinical application of this technique in affective disorders. Williamson and Kaye (1989), summarizing EEG studies in affective disorders, concluded that although depressives seem to differ from normals, variations in techniques make it difficult to compare the findings. Therefore, further investigation is needed to evaluate the specificity of these changes before it can be recommended as a clinical tool and guide to diagnosis or treatment.

BRAIN IMAGING: IMAGES, ANATOMY, AND ACTIVITY— JUST ANOTHER PRETTY PICTURE OR A CLEARER WINDOW ON THE BRAIN?

Many technological advances have occurred in this area since the first edition of this chapter. There is some suggestion that depression may be associated with structural brain abnormalities. Abnormalities in large areas of the brain, particularly the frontal and temporal lobes, as well as alterations in the usual left-versus-right hemispheric activity differences, have been found. Nevertheless, because these early results have been variable, the data regarding anatomical defects and altered cerebral activity in depressed persons are equivocal.

Computed Tomography

Computed tomography (CT) images present cross-sectional views of the brain from multiple levels. By detecting differences in tissue density, it provides a detailed view of structural abnormalities of brain tissue. Contrast enhancement improves the identification of certain defects. CT scanning is used widely in clinical psychiatric practice, and Hapworth (1986) has reviewed indications for its use.

The use of CT for examining the brains of depressed patients has not been well researched (Hapworth, 1986). Ventricular enlargement and an increased ventricle-to-brain ratio, similar to what have been found in schizophrenia, have been reported in major depressives, especially in bipolar patients, and have been associated with a greater number of hospitalizations, per-

sistent unemployment, and psychotic symptoms (Coffman, 1989; Hapworth, 1986; Pearlson et al., 1984; Risch & Gillin, 1988). Decreased cortical volume, particularly in bipolar disorder, has been correlated with psychotic symptoms and a poor treatment response. Firm associations between structural abnormalities on CT and clinical outcome or response patterns have not been established (Coffman, 1989).

Until we have a better understanding of the sensitivity, specificity, and overall clinical utility of assessments of subtle structural changes in the brain, Coffman (1989) suggests that CT's major use in general clinical settings is for detecting gross neuropathological conditions. Following Weinberger's (1984) recommendation, cost–benefit analysis shows that CT in affective disorder should be guided by the clinical situation, and considered if the first episode of a major depression or personality change begins after age 50.

Magnetic Resonance Imaging

Magnetic resonance imaging (MRI) offers the advantage over CT of improved resolution for detecting discrete brain lesions. Its clinical uses, indications, and contraindications have been described by Garber, Weilburg, Buonanno, Manschreck, and New (1988). The small number of controlled studies of MRI in affective-disorder patients suggests that structural abnormalities are evident in the frontal and temporal lobes of bipolar patients (Coffey et al., 1993; Jeste, Lohr, & Goodwin, 1988; Nasrallah, Coffman, & Olson, 1989), but the findings have been inconsistent (Coffey et al., 1993). Areas of subcortical hyperintensity (unidentified bright objects, or "UBOs") have more commonly been found, but their cause and significance are unknown (Andreasen, 1989; Coffey et al., 1993).

Functional Brain Imaging: Overview

Functional brain imaging methods have been used to quantify brain activity. These functional studies offer advantages over the structural images obtained with CT and MRI because brain structure is largely normal in depression (George, Ketter, & Post, 1993). Included among these dynamic imaging techniques are cerebral blood flow (CBF), positron emission tomography (PET), single photon emission computed tomography (SPECT), and now magnetic resonance spectroscopy (MRS). Kety and Schmidt

(1948), using the nitrous oxide technique to measure CBF, pioneered this study of brain functional activity. Methods for measuring regional CBF (rCBF) were developed almost two decades later. However, studies of rCBF in depression are few and the results have been inconsistent (Sackheim et al., 1990).

Positron Emission Tomography

PET was developed as a safe, noninvasive technique that provides quantitative measurements *in vivo* of neuroanatomically localized (i.e., regional) cerebral biochemical processes in living humans in three dimensions. Cerebral glucose use, which can be studied with PET, is a sensitive indicator of cerebral function (Phelps, Mazziotta, & Schelbert, 1986). Resting state determinations have shown that persons with major depression and bipolar disorder have decreased activity in the whole cortex and the left frontal lobe.

Cerebral glucose hypometabolism has been found in the anterolateral prefrontal cortex of patients with major depression (Baxter et al., 1989; Martintot et al., 1990). Baxter et al. (1985) obtained measurements of cerebral glucose metabolic rates with PET scanning in order to identify biologically distinct depressive subgroups (DSM-III diagnosis). Supratentorial whole-brain glucose metabolic rates were significantly lower among a group of bipolar depressed and mixed mood disorder patients, compared with the healthy control and unipolar depressive groups, which were not significantly different from each other. Bipolar patients exhibited increasing whole-brain metabolic rates as they went from a depressed or mixed state to a euthymic or manic state, suggesting that global hypometabolism is a state marker of depressed mood. A subgroup of unipolar depressives exhibited left frontal cortex hypometabolism.

Buchsbaum et al. (1986) found that both unipolar and bipolar depressives had significantly higher global cerebral metabolism compared with normal controls. These different results may be attributed to their subjects' psychological state or to the pain stimulation task in which subjects were engaged during the tracer injection. Both Baxter et al. (1985) and Buchsbaum et al. (1986) found that bipolar depressives had a lower anterior–posterior (A–P) gradient (relative hypofrontality), and unipolar depressives had a higher (A–P gradient (relative hyper-

frontality) compared with normal controls. Subcortically, both groups of investigators observed basal ganglia glucose hypometabolism (Baxter et al., 1985; Buchsbaum et al., 1986).

Extending their work, Baxter et al. (1989) demonstrated a single discrete abnormality, cerebral glucose hypometabolism in the anterolateral prefrontal cortex, that was common to major depression in bipolars, unipolars, and obsessive–compulsives with depression (DSM-III diagnosis). While the finding was consistent for the left side only, there were no statistically significant left–right differences. Successful treatment reduced this hypometabolism.

Martintot et al. (1990) also found left prefrontal glucose hypometabolism in unipolar and bipolar depressed patients (DSM-III diagnosis). Asymmetry was not found after successful treatment, but the hypofrontality persisted, suggesting that hypofrontality may not be state-dependent. The left–right differences may be related to the clinical state, disappearing with improvement, or may be medication-induced, independent of treatment outcome.

Post et al. (1987) found reduced rates of glucose utilization in the temporal lobe of moderately to severely depressed patients compared with normal controls. Left–right comparisons indicated greater reduction in glucose utilization rates in the left temporal cortex of these depressed subjects.

Drevets et al. (1992) studied a relatively homogeneous subgroup of depressives who met criteria for familial pure depressive disease, and reported increased blood flow (which correlates with glucose metabolism) in the left prefrontal cortex and left amygdala. They found no dorsal anterolateral–prefrontal difference. The increased activity in the left prefrontal cortex was not found in a remitted group of depressives, while both depressed and remitted groups had increased activity in the left amygdala.

These changes may not be specific for depression; cerebral glucose hypometabolism has been observed in schizophrenics. It remains to be determined whether these changes are the cause or the result of the mood change, or an epiphenomenon of another pathophysiological process. Horne (1993) has speculated that hypofrontality and diminished slow-wave sleep in depression may be related. Also, contrary to these PET and blood flow study findings, neuropsychological testing and brain electrical activity studies during task performance indicate a deficit in the right (nondominant) cerebral hemisphere rather than in the left (dominant) hemisphere (Goodwin & Jamison, 1990). Imaging studies during activation might reconcile this discrepancy, although Guze, Baxter, Schwartz, and Szuba (1990) suggested that the activation of different brain areas is subject-rather than task-specific.

Presently, there is no immediate clinical application for PET in depression, but research continues (Hapworth, 1986). Much of the background has been presented elsewhere and is beyond the scope of this review (Hapworth, 1986; Holcomb, Links, Smith, & Wong, 1989). Other studies and methodological concerns have been reviewed by Guze et al. (1990). Ultimately, its uses may include the ability to study regional brain activity in order to clarify the pathophysiological basis for depression, and potentially to understand receptor physiology and the mechanism of action of antidepressants.

Single Photon Emission Computed Tomography

SPECT has been described as the "poor man's PET scan." Because a cyclotron is not necessary, it is more readily available and is cheaper to perform than PET. Three-dimensional measurement of rCBF is obtained, providing information about physiological and neurochemical function of the brain. Normal rCBF images are very symmetrical, and asymmetry often can be detected visually with SPECT (Devous, 1989), but regional glucose metabolic rate determinations are not obtained, and methods that would allow quanititative interpretations of the blood flow data are limited and still being developed. Thus, this technique may not satisfy those who find pictures less informative than the actual numbers.

An important technical fact is that cerebral SPECT images are representations of the physiology at the time of the injection, not the time of the scanning (Van Heertum, 1992). This is because the radiotracer compounds in use are stable and remain relatively constant in the brain rather than moving back across the blood–brain barrier. Thus, the resulting "snapshot" image reflects the presence of the stimulus and the rCBF at the time of the injection.

Like PET, SPECT still is mainly a research tool. Too few data on affective disorders are available (Devous, 1989, 1992), so it is premature to offer comments on its clinical utility. Published clinical trials demonstrating the exact sensitivity and specificity of SPECT and PET in diagnosing depression in individual patients are not available (George et al., 1993).

However, SPECT studies in primary and secondary depression have generally confirmed the PET findings (George et al., 1993). Frontal lobe hypometabolism is found regardless of the original cause of the depression, and the degree of hypometabolism often correlates with the severity of the depression. Also, abnormal blood flow, observed in the temporal and parietal regions, is higher in bipolar depressives than normal controls, and lower in unipolar endogenous depressives than normal controls (Devous, 1989). Bipolars also had increased blood flow relative to unipolar endogenous depressives. Right–left asymmetries were observed in the parietal lobe in unipolars and in the temporal and parietal lobes of bipolars.

The hypometabolism may normalize following successful somatic or psychotherapeutic treatment for depression (George et al., 1993). One study detected detected no difference in temporal lobe asymmetries between treatment-responsive and treatment-nonresponsive depressed patients (Amsterdam & Mozley 1992). Further study is needed to determine whether changes in blood flow and symmetry patterns with clinical recovery could provide a basis for using SPECT for monitoring clinical state (George et al., 1993; Mozley, 1992).

SPECT activation studies (i.e., imaging performed while the brain is stimulated by performing a task) are being conducted to assess its role as a diagnostic, management, and prognostic tool (Devous, 1992; George et al., 1993). One example of its use may be to map an induced mood response to an amphetamine challenge. Thus, SPECT may be used as an objective measure to validate the stimulant challenge test.

Magnetic Resonance Spectroscopy

The latest advance beyond MRI, MRS (or functional MRI), allows noninvasive *in vivo* investigation of brain function and physiology, in addition to anatomy. Thus, structure and function can be correlated directly. Guze (1991) and Keshavan, Kapur, and Pettegrew (1991) have reviewed the benefits as well as the limitations of MRS, compared with PET, SPECT, and MRI. Metabolic substances in the brain can be studied. No radioactivity is required, and spatial and temporal resolution is improved—two advantages over PET and SPECT. Also, there are no known side effects. Thus, it may be useful for longitudinal studies. However, the activity of *in situ* living tissues, such as receptors, can still be better studied with radionuclide imaging.

Compared with MRI, it takes several minutes to obtain a single magnetic resonance spectrum from the weaker MRS signals. This prolonged signal acquisition time and requirement for a larger volume of interest, compared with MRI, limit the ability to detect transient biochemical changes with MRS. Therefore, MRS is not yet applicable to cognitive or neurophysiological challenge paradigms (Keshavan et al., 1991).

Application of MRS to the study of depression is now being explored. Kato, Takahashi, Shioiri, and Inubushi (1992) measured brain phosphorus metabolism (a measure of energy metabolism) with MRS, but could not find definite evidence for abnormal high-energy phosphate concentrations in depressed patients.

CONCLUSIONS

Depression is a phenomenologically and biologically heterogeneous disorder. This heterogeneity complicates attempts to reconcile the clinical and biological components of depression. Confounding and nonspecificity have been the two main obstacles confronted by researchers investigating the clinical applications of these putative biological markers of depression.

In this chapter, we have focused on assessing the clinical utility of laboratory tests that have been used for the diagnosis and management of depression. There is yet no objective "gold standard" laboratory test for depression, against which clinicians' impressions can be gauged, or which assists in selecting or predicting treatment response, or which prognosticates outcome. Rothschild (1988) suggested that simultaneous or sequential use of more than one of these biological tests may better define subgroups of depressive disorders. More progress is needed in finding sensitive and specific biological markers of depressive disorders.

It is clear that monoamines interact with one another, so study of single monoaminergic systems is unlikely to be a fruitful endeavor. At the level of the receptor, there is no evidence for the consistent disruption of the activity of any one monoamine in particular, although the postsynaptic β- and α₂-adrenoceptors do seem to be involved with some regularity. Whether any specific 5-HT receptor subtype(s) is/are involved in the pathophysiological process is even more uncertain.

Because hormonal regulation is under the control of the same brain neurotransmitters that are thought to be dysfunctional in depression, one might expect more than just a proportion of these individuals to demonstrate neuroendocrine abnormalities. Why only a proportion of depressives have positive responses to dynamic psychoendocrine tests, such as the DST and TRH stimulation test, is yet another unanswered question; presently, these tests remain unreliable markers for depression. Interindividual differences, including hereditability factors and vulnerability to stress, may play a role.

Sleep markers still have appeal, but methodologically they are more cumbersome than a simple blood test (though drug washout periods apply to both). In the past decade, we have learned that REM markers are more complex and less unique for depression, and new areas for research have developed. The relationship between REM and delta sleep, described by Kupfer and Ehlers (1989), as well as how these may relate to circadian rhythm disturbances in depression (also common to psychoneuroendocrine studies; not reviewed here) are other exciting areas for study. Thus, although there may be some clinical utility for sleep studies, especially for predicting treatment response and monitoring outcome, other applications remain to be explored through research.

Neuroimaging is an evolving area that promises to offer glimpses of the brain not otherwise available. How diagnostically sensitive and specific are these techniques for depressive disorders, and can functional measures such as SPECT and PET serve as screening tools for predicting treatment response? Brain imaging may help make differential diagnoses in cases in which illnesses that can masquerade as depression or other psychiatric disorders must be excluded, but psychiatric diagnoses cannot be made solely on the basis of brain imaging (Weinberger, 1993). Although neuroimaging techniques are in widespread clinical use, more research is needed to determine the cost-effectiveness of these high-tech, high-priced instruments. Perhaps one day we may even be able to record consciousness (Skolnick, 1992)!

In our zeal to medicalize psychiatry, *caveat emptor* is the watchword against premature and uncritical acceptance of unproven diagnostic and therapeutic monitoring methods and techniques. Not uncommonly, diagnostic tests are introduced into clinical practice before procedural standards are established and the predictive value can be examined among patients with a full spectrum of conditions, with and without comorbid conditions (Nierenberg & Feinstein, 1988). Unfortunately, innovative research advances and technology do not always lend themselves to rational clinical utility. To minimize the risks and costs resulting from the use of inadequately studied diagnostic marker tests, Nierenberg and Feinstein (1988) describe a five-phase evaluation process that developing tests should undergo.

Also important, while an appropriately applied laboratory test can enhance the quality of patient care and management, Davis and Bresnahan (1987) remind us that the clinician should treat the patient, not the laboratory test result. The information overload generated in the past decade is formidable, and we need to be wary consumers as we try to sort it all out. The study of biological markers in psychiatry remains an area of hope and promise. We should, as recommended by Arana et al. (1985), continue to search for biological measures to help validate clinical diagnosis and to objectify the categorization of patients and assist in predicting treatment response and long-term outcome.

Acknowledgment. This work was supported in part by U.S. Public Health Service Grant No. MH46450 to Dr. Howard M. Kravitz from the National Institute of Mental Health.

REFERENCES

Agren, H., Mefford, I. N., Rudorfer, M. V., Linnoila, M., & Potter, W. Z. (1986). Interacting neurotransmitter systems: A nonexperimental approach to the 5HIAA–HVA correlation in human CSF. *Journal of Psychiatric Research, 20,* 175–193.

APA Task Force on Laboratory Tests in Psychiatry. (1987). The dexamethasone suppression test: An overview of its current status in psychiatry. *American Journal of Psychiatry, 144*(10), 1253–1262.

Amsterdam, J. D., Maislin, G., Gold, P., & Winokur, A. (1989). The assessment of abnormalities in hormonal responsiveness at multiple levels of the hypothalamic–pituitary–adrenocortical axis in depressive illness. *Psychoneuroendocrinology, 14*(1&2), 43–62.

Amsterdam, J. D., & Mozley, P. D. (1992). Temporal lobe asymmetry with iofetamine SPECT imaging in patients with major depression. *Journal of Affective Disorders, 24,* 43–53.

Andreasen, N. C. (1989). Nuclear magnetic resonance imaging. In N. C. Andreasen (Ed.), *Brain imaging: Appli-*

cations in psychiatry (pp. 67–121). Washington, DC: American Psychiatric Press.

Andreasen, N. C. (1993). Neural correlates of mental phenomena. *American Journal of Psychiatry, 150*(5), 687–688.

Ansseau, M., Kupfer, D. J., & Reynolds, C. F. (1985a). Internight variability of REM latency in major depression: Implications for the use of REM latency as a biological correlate. *Biological Psychiatry, 20,* 489–505.

Ansseau, M., Kupfer, D. J., Reynolds, C. F., & Coble, P. A. (1985b). "Paradoxical" shortening of REM latency during first recording night in major depressive disorder: Clinical and polysomnographic correlates. *Biological Psychiatry, 20,* 135–145.

Ansseau, M., Kupfer, D. J., Reynolds, C. F., & McEachran, A. B. (1984). REM latency distribution in major depression: Clinical characteristics associated with sleep onset REM periods. *Biological Psychiatry, 19*(12), 1651–1666.

Applegate, W. B. (1993). Ankle/arm blood pressure index. A useful test for clinical practice? *Journal of the American Medical Association, 270*(4), 497–498.

Arana, G. W., Baldessarini, R. J., & Ornsteen, M. (1985). The dexamethasone suppression test for diagnosis and prognosis in psychiatry. *Archives of General Psychiatry, 42*(12), 1193–1204.

Arana, G. W., Reichlin, S., Workman, R., Haaser, R., & Shader, R. I. (1988). The dexamethasone suppression index: Enhancement of DST diagnostic utility for depression by expressing serum cortisol as a function of serum dexamethasone. *American Journal of Psychiatry, 145*(6), 707–711.

Arana, G. W., Zarzar, M. N., & Baker, E. (1990). The effect of diagnostic methodology on the sensitivity of the TRH stimulation test for depression: A literature review. *Biological Psychiatry, 28,* 733–737.

Asberg, M., Schalling, D., Traskman-Bendz, L., & Wagner, A. (1987). Psychobiology of suicide, impulsivity, and related phenomena. In H. Y. Meltzer (Ed.), *Psychopharmacology: The third generation of progress* (pp. 655–668). New York: Raven Press.

Bauer, M. S., & Whybrow, P. C. (1988). Thyroid hormones and the central nervous system in affective illness: Interactions that may have clinical significance. *Integrative Psychiatry, 6,* 75–85.

Bauer, M. S., & Whybrow, P. C. (1993). Validity of rapid cycling as a modifier for bipolar disorder in DSM-IV. *Depression, 1*(1), 11–19.

Baxter, L. R., Phelps, M. E., Mazziotta, J. C., Schwartz, J. M., Gerner, R. H., Selin, C. E., & Sumida, R. M. (1985). Cerebral metabolic rates for glucose in mood disorders. Studies with positron emission tomography and fluorodeoxyglucose F 18. *Archives of General Psychiatry, 42*(5), 441–447.

Baxter, L. R., Schwartz, J. M., Phelps, M. E., Mazziotta, J. C., Guze, B. H., Selin, C. E., Gerner, R. H., & Sumida, R. M. (1989). Reduction of prefrontal cortex glucose metabolism common to three types of depression. *Archives of General Psychiatry, 46*(3), 243–250.

Benca, R. M., Obermeyer, W. H., Thisted, R. A., & Gillin, J. C. (1992). Sleep and psychiatric disorders. A meta-analysis. *Archives of General Psychiatry, 49*(8), 651–668.

Benson, K. L., & Zarcone, V. P. (1993). Rapid eye movement sleep eye movements in schizophrenia and depression. *Archives of General Psychiatry, 50*(6), 474–482.

Biegon, A. (1990). Effects of steroid hormones on the serotonergic system. In P. M. Whitaker-Azmitia & S. J.

Peroutka (Eds.), The neuropharmacology of serotonin. *Annals of the New York Academy of Sciences, 600,* 427–434.

Blackwell, B. (1979). Current psychiatric research: MHPG in depression. *Psychiatric Opinion, 16*(7), 2, 47.

Brown, G. L., & Linnoila, M. I. (1990). CSF serotonin metabolite (5-HIAA) studies in depression, impulsivity, and violence. *Journal of Clinical Psychiatry, 51*(4, Suppl.), 31–41.

Brown, G. M. (1989). Psychoneuroendocrinology of depression. *Psychiatric Journal of the University of Ottawa, 14*(2), 344–348.

Buchsbaum, M. S., Wu, J., DeLisi, L. E., Holcomb, H., Kessler, R., Johnson, J., King, A. C., Hazlett, K., Langston, K., & Post, R. M. (1986). Frontal cortex and basal ganglia metabolic rates assessed by positron emission tomography with [^{18}F]2–deoxyglucose in affective illness. *Journal of Affective Disorders, 10,* 137–152.

Bunney, W. E., & Davis, J. M. (1965). Norepinephrine in depressive reactions: A review. *Archives of General Psychiatry, 13,* 483–494.

Carroll, B. J. (1982). The dexamethasone suppression test for melancholia. *British Journal of Psychiatry, 140,* 292–304.

Carroll, B. J., Feinberg, M., Greden, J. F., Tarika, J., Albala, A. A., Haskett, R. F., James, N. M., Kronfol, Z., Lohr, N., Steiner, M., de Vigne, J. P., & Young, E. (1981). A specific laboratory test for the diagnosis of melancholia: Standardization, validation, and clinical utility. *Archives of General Psychiatry, 38*(1), 15–22.

Cartwright, R. D., Kravitz, H. M., Eastman, C. I., & Wood, E. (1991). REM latency and the recovery from depression: Getting over divorce. *American Journal of Psychiatry, 148*(11), 1530–1535.

Coffey, C. E., Wilkinson, W. E., Weiner, R. D., Parashos, I. A., Djang, W. T., Webb, M. C., Figiel, G. S., & Spritzer, C. E. (1993). Quantitative cerebral anatomy in depression: A controlled magnetic resonance imaging study. *Archives of General Psychiatry, 50*(1), 7–16.

Coffman, J. A. (1989). Computed tomography in psychiatry. In N. C. Andreasen (Ed.), *Brain imaging: Applications in psychiatry* (pp. 1–65). Washington, DC: American Psychiatric Press.

Dale, H. H. (1935). Pharmacology and nerve endings. *Proceedings of the Royal Society of Medicine, 28,* 319–332.

Davis, J. M., & Bresnahan, D. B. (1987). Psychopharmacology in clinical psychiatry. In R. E. Hales & A. J. Frances (Eds.), *Psychiatry update: American Psychiatric Association annual review* (Vol. 6, pp. 159–187). Washington, DC: American Psychiatric Press.

Davis, J. M., Koslow, S. H., Gibbons, R. D., Maas, J. W., Bowden, C. L., Casper, R., Hanin, I., Javaid, J. I., Chang, S. S., & Stokes, P. E. (1988). Cerebrospinal fluid and urinary biogenic amines in depressed patients and healthy controls. *Archives of General Psychiatry, 45*(8), 705–717.

Delgado, P. L., & Charney, D. S. (1991). Neuroendocrine challenge tests in affective disorders: Implications for future pathophysiological investigations. In R. W. Horton & C. L. E. Katona (Eds.), *Biological aspects of affective disorders* (pp. 145–190). London: Academic Press.

Delgado, P. L., Charney, D. S., Price, L. H., Aghajanian, G. K., Landis, H., & Heninger, G. R. (1990). Serotonin function and the mechanism of antidepressant action: Reversal of antidepresant-induced remission by rapid depletion of plasma tryptophan. *Archives of General Psychiatry, 47*(5), 411–418.

Delgado, P. L., Price, L. H., Miller, H. L., Salomon, R. M., Aghajanian, G. K., Heninger, G. R., & Charney, D. S. (1994). Serotonin and the neurobiology of depression: Effects of tryptophan depletion in drug-free depressed patients. *Archives of General Psychiatry, 51*(11), 865–874.

Devous, M. D. (1989). Imaging brain function by single-photon emission computer tomography. In N. C. Andreasen (Ed.), *Brain imaging: Applications in psychiatry* (pp. 147–234). Washington, DC: American Psychiatric Press.

Devous, M. D. (1992). Comparison of SPECT applications in neurology and psychiatry. *Journal of Clinical Psychiatry, 53*(11, Suppl.), 13–19.

Dilsaver, S. C. (1986a). Cholinergic mechanisms in affective disorders. Future directions for investigation. *Acta Psychiatrica Scandinavica, 74,* 312–334.

Dilsaver, S. C. (1986b). Cholinergic–monoaminergic interaction in the pathophysiology of the affective disorders? *International Clinical Psychopharmacology, 1,* 181–198.

Dilsaver, S. C., & Coffman, J. A. (1989). Cholinergic hypothesis of depression: A reappraisal. *Journal of Clinical Psychopharmacology, 9*(3), 173–179.

Drevets, W. C., Videen, T. O., Price, J. L., Preskorn, S. H., Carmichael, S. T., & Raichle, M. E. (1992). A functional anatomical study of unipolar depression. *The Journal of Neuroscience, 12*(9), 3628–3641.

Elliott, J. M. (1984). Platelet receptor binding studies in affective disorders. *Journal of Affective Disorders, 6,* 219–239.

Elliott, J. M. (1991). Peripheral markers in affective disorders. In R. W. Horton & C. L. E. Katona (Eds.), *Biological aspects of affective disorders* (pp. 95–144). London: Academic Press.

Emrich, H. M., von Zerssen, D., Kissling, W., Moller, H.-J., & Windorfer, A. (1980). Effects of sodium valproate on mania. The GABA-hypothesis of affective disorders. *Archiv für Psychiatrie und Nervenkrankheiten, 229,* 1–16.

Extein, I., Gold, M. S., & Goggans, F. C. (1986). Evaluation of affective syndromes. In M. S. Gold & A. L.C. Pottash (Eds.), *Diagnostic and laboratory testing in psychiatry* (pp. 179–190). New York: Plenum Medical.

Fawcett, J., & Kravitz, H. M. (1985). New medical diagnostic procedures for depression. In E. E. Beckham & W. R. Leber (Eds.), *Handbook of depression: Treatment, assessment, and research* (pp. 445–513). Homewood, IL: Dorsey Press.

Fawcett, J., Kravitz, H. M., & Sabelli, H. C. (1984). CNS amine metabolites. In R. C. W. Hall & T. P. Beresford (Eds.), *Handbook of psychiatric diagnostic procedures* (Vol. 1, pp. 49–108). New York: Spectrum.

Filser, J. G., Muller, W. E., & Beckmann, H. (1986). Should plasma or urinary MHPG be measured in psychiatric research? A critical comment. *British Journal of Psychiatry, 148,* 95–97.

Garber, H. J., Weilburg, J. B., Buonanno, F. S., Manschreck, T. C., & New, P. F. J. (1988). Use of magnetic resonance imaging in psychiatry. *American Journal of Psychiatry, 145*(2), 164–171.

Garvey, M., Hollon, S. D., DeRubeis, R. J., Evans, M. D., & Tuason, V. B. (1990). Does 24–h urinary MHPG predict treatment response to antidepressants? I. A review. *Journal of Affective Disorders, 20,* 173–179.

Garvey, M. J., Mungas, D., & Tollefson, G. D. (1984). Hypersomnia in major depressive disorders. *Journal of Affective Disorders, 6,* 283–286.

Gastpar, M., Gilsdorf, U., Abou-Saleh, M. T., & Ngo-Khac, T. (1992). Clinical correlates of response to DST. The dexamethasone suppression test in depression: A World Health Organisation collaborative study. *Journal of Affective Disorders, 26,* 17–24.

George, M. S., Ketter, T. A., & Post, R. M. (1993). SPECT and PET imaging in mood disorders. *Journal of Clinical Psychiatry, 54*(11), Suppl.), 6–13.

Gershon, E. S., Nadi, N. S., Nurnberger, J. I., & Berrettini, W. H. (1985). Failure to confirm muscarinic receptors on skin fibroblasts [letter]. *New England Journal of Medicine, 312*(13), 862.

Gjerris, A. (1988). Baseline studies on transmitter substances in cerebrospinal fluid. *Acta Psychiatrica Scandinavica, 78*(Suppl. 346), 5–35.

Goff, D. C. (1986). The stimulant challenge test in depression. *Journal of Clinical Psychiatry, 47*(11), 438–543.

Gold, P. W., Chrousos, G., Kellner, C., Post, R., Roy, A., Augerinos, P., Schulte, H., Oldfield, E., & Loriaux, D. L. (1984). Psychiatric implications of basic and clinical studies with corticotropin-releasing factor. *American Journal of Psychiatry, 141*(5), 619–627.

Gold, P. W., Goodwin, F. K., & Chrousos, G. P. (1988a). Clinical and biochemical manifestations of depression: Relation to the neurobiology of stress (First of two parts). *New England Journal of Medicine, 319*(6), 348–353.

Gold, P. W., Goodwin, F. K., & Chrousos, G. P. (1988b). Clinical and biochemical manifestations of depression: Relation to the neurobiology of stress (Second of two parts). *New England Journal of Medicine, 319*(7), 413–420.

Gonzales-Sastre, F., Mra, J., Guillamat, R., Queralto, J. M., Alvarez, E., Udina, C., & Massana, J. (1988). Urinary phenylacetic acid excretion in depressive patients. *Acta Psychiatrica Scandinavica, 78,* 208–210.

Goodwin, F. K., & Jamison, K. R. (1990). Anatomical, physiological, and medical studies. In *Manic–depressive illness* (pp. 503–540). New York: Oxford University Press.

Greenshaw, A. J. (1989). Functional interactions of 2-phenylethylamine and of tryptamine with brain catecholamines: Implications for psychotherapeutic drug action. *Progress in Neuro-Psychopharmacology and Biological Psychiatry, 13,* 431–443.

Guze, B. H. (1991). Magnetic resonance spectroscopy. A technique for functional brain imaging. *Archives of General Psychiatry, 48*(6), 572–574.

Guze, B. H., Baxter, L. R., Schwartz, J. M., & Szuba, M. P. (1990). PET offers insights into the physiology of mood disorders. *Journal of Clinical Brain Imaging, 1*(2), 13–22.

Halbreich, U., Grunhaus, L., & Ben-David, M. (1979). Twenty-four hour rhythm of prolactin in depressive patients. *Archives of General Psychiatry, 36,* 1183–1186.

Hapworth, W. (1986). Central nervous system diagnostic devices. In M. S. Gold & A. L. C. Pottash (Eds.), *Diagnostic and laboratory testing in psychiatry* (pp. 107–130). New York: Plenum Medical.

Heninger, G. R., Charney, D. S., & Price, L. H. (1988a). α_2-Adrenergic receptor sensitivity in depression. The plasma MHPG, behavioral, and cardiovascular responses to yohimbine. *Archives of General Psychiatry, 45*(8), 718–726.

Heninger, G. R., Charney, D. S., & Price, L. H. (1988b). Noradrenergic and serotonergic receptor system function in panic disorder and depression. *Acta Psychiatrica Scandinavica, 77*(Suppl. 341), 138–150.

Holcomb, H. H., Links, J., Smith, C., & Wong, D. (1989). Positron emission tomography: Measuring the metabolic and neurochemical characteristics of the living human nervous system. In N. C. Andreasen (Ed.), *Brain imaging: Applications in psychiatry* (pp. 235–370). Washington, DC: American Psychiatric Press.

Horne, J. A. (1993). Human sleep, sleep loss and behavior: Implications for the prefrontal cortex and psychiatric disorder. *British Journal of Psychiatry, 162,* 413–419.

Hsiao, J. K., Agren, H., Bartko, J. J., Rudorfer, M. V., Linnoila, M., & Potter, W. Z. (1987). Monoamine neurotransmitter interactions and the prediction of antidepressant response. *Archives of General Psychiatry, 44*(12), 1078–1083.

Hudson, J. I., Lipinski, J. F., Frankenburg, F. R., Grochocinski, V. J., & Kupfer, D. J. (1988). Electroencephalographic sleep in mania. *Archives of General Psychiatry, 45*(3), 267–273.

Hudson, J. I., Lipinski, J. F., Keck, P. E., Aizley, H. G., Lucas, S. F., Rothschild, A. J., Waternaux, C. M., & Kupfer, D. J. (1992a). Polysomnographic characteristics of young manic patients: Comparison with unipolar depressed patients and normal control subjects. *Archives of General Psychiatry, 49*(5), 378–383.

Hudson, J. I., Pope, H. G., Sullivan, L. E., Waternaux, C. M., Keck, P. E., & Broughton, R. J. (1992b). Good sleep, bad sleep: A meta-analysis of polysomnographic measures in insomnia, depression, and narcolepsy. *Biological Psychiatry, 32,* 958–975.

Janowsky, D. S., El-Yousef, M. K., Davis, J. M., & Sekerke, H. J. (1972). A cholinergic–adrenergic hypothesis of mania and depression. *Lancet, 2,* 632–635.

Janowsky, D. S., & Overstreet, D. H. (1990). Cholinergic dysfunction in depression. *Pharmacology and Toxicology, 66*(Suppl. 3), 100–111.

Jeste, D. V., Lohr, J. B., & Goodwin, F. K. (1988). Neuroanatomical studies of major affective disorders: A review and suggestions for further research. *British Journal of Psychiatry, 153,* 444–459.

Jimerson, D. C. (1987). Role of dopamine mechanisms in the affective disorders. In H. Y. Meltzer (Ed.), *Psychopharmacology: The third generation of progress* (pp. 505–511). New York: Raven Press.

Kato, T., Takahashi, S., Shioiri, T., & Inubushi, T. (1992). Brain phosphorus metabolism in depressive disorders detected by phosphorus-31 magnetic resonance spectroscopy. *Journal of Affective Disorders, 26,* 223–230.

Kelsoe, J. R., Gillin, J. C., Janowsky, D. S., Brown, J. H., Risch, S. C., & Lumpkin, B. (1985). Failure to confirm muscarinic receptors on skin fibroblasts [letter]. *New England Journal of Medicine, 312*(13), 861–862.

Kelsoe, J. R., Gillin, J. C., Janowsky, D. S., Brown, J. H., Risch, S. C., & Lumpkin, B. (1986). Specific ^{3}H-N-methylscopolamine binding without cholinergic function in cultured skin fibroblasts. *Life Sciences, 38,* 1399–1408.

Keshavan, M. S., Kapur, S., & Pettegrew, J. W. (1991). Magnetic resonance spectroscopy in psychiatry: Potential, pitfalls, and promise. *American Journal of Psychiatry, 148*(8), 976–985.

Kety, S. S., & Schmidt, C. E. (1948). The nitrous oxide method for the quantitative determination of cerebral blood flow in man: Theory, procedure and normal values. *Journal of Clinical Investigation, 27,* 476–483.

Koslow, S. H., Maas, J. W., Bowden, C. L., Davis, J. M., Hanin, I., & Javaid, J. (1983). CSF and urinary biogenic amines and metabolites in depression and mania: A controlled, univariate analysis. *Archives of General Psychiatry, 40*(9), 999–1010.

Kraemer, H. C. (1987). The methodological and statistical evaluation of medical tests: The dexamethasone suppression test in psychiatry. *Psychoneuroendocrinology, 12*(6), 411–427.

Kraus, R. P., Grof, P., & Brown, G. M. (1988). Drugs and the DST: Need for a reappraisal. *American Journal of Psychiatry, 141*(2), 247–249.

Kravitz, H. M., Edwards, J. H., Fawcett, J., & Fogg, L. (1990). Challenging the amphetamine challenge test: Report of an antidepressant treatment study. *Journal of Affective Disorders, 20*, 121–128.

Kronig, M. H., & Gold, M. S. (1986). Thyroid testing in psychiatric patients. In M. S. Gold & A. L. C. Pottash (Eds.), *Diagnostic and laboratory testing in psychiatry* (pp. 47–58). New York: Plenum Medical.

Kupfer, D. J., & Ehlers, C. L. (1989). Two roads to rapid eye movement latency. *Archives of General Psychiatry, 46*(10), 945–948.

Kupfer, D. J., Frank, E., Grochocinski, V. J., Gregor, M., & McEachran, A. B. (1988). Electroencephalographic sleep profiles in recurrent depression: A longitudinal investigation. *Archives of General Psychiatry, 45*(7), 678– 681.

Kupfer, D. J., Frank, E., McEachran, A. B., & Grochocinski, V. J. (1990). Delta sleep ratio: A biological correlate of early recurrence in unipolar affective disorder. *Archives of General Psychiatry, 47*(12), 1100–1105.

Langer, G., Koinig, G., Hatzinger, R., Schonbeck, G., Resch, F., Aschauer, H., Keshavan, M. S., & Sieghart, W. (1986). Response of thyrotropin to thyrotropin-releasing hormone as predictor of treatment outcome: Prediction of recovery and relapse in treatment with antidepressants and neuroleptics. *Archives of General Psychiatry, 43*(9), 861–868.

Lenox, R. H., Hitzemann, R. J., Richelson, E., & Kelsoe, J. R. (1985). Failure to confirm muscarinic receptors on skin fibroblasts [Letter]. *New England Journal of Medicine, 312*(13), 861.

Leonard, B. E. (1992). Subtypes of serotonin receptors: Biochemical changes and pharmacological consequences. *International Clinical Psychopharmacology, 7*, 13–21.

Lester, D. (1992). The dexamethasone suppression test as an indicator of suicide: A meta-analysis. *Pharmacopsychiatry, 25*, 265–270.

Lin, S.-C., & Richelson, E. (1986). Low levels and lack of function of muscarinic binding sites in human skin fibroblasts from five affectively ill patients and two control subjects. *American Journal of Psychiatry, 143*(5), 658–660.

Little, K. Y. (1988). Amphetamine, but not methylphenidate, predicts antidepressant efficacy. *Journal of Clinical Psychopharmacology, 8*(3), 177–183.

Lloyd, K. G., Zivkovic, B., Scatton, B., Morselli, P. L., & Bartholini, G. (1989). The GABAergic hypothesis of depression. *Progress in Neuro-Psychopharmacology and Biological Psychiatry, 13*, 341–351.

Loosen, P. T. (1985). The TRH-induced TSH response in psychiatric patients: A possible neuroendocrine marker. *Psychoneuroendocrinology, 10*(3), 237–260.

Loosen, P. T., Garbutt, J. C., & Prange, A. J. (1987). Evaluation of the diagnostic utility of the TRH-induced TSH response in psychiatric disorders. *Pharmacopsychiatry, 20*, 90–95.

Loosen, P. T., & Marciniak, R. (1988). Platelet MAO activity, TRH test, and dexamethasone suppression test

in depressed patients. *Pharmacopsychiatry, 21*, 131–135.

Loosen, P. T., & Prange, A. J. (1982). Serum thyrotropin response to thyrotropin-releasing hormone in psychiatric patients: A review. *American Journal of Psychiatry, 139*(4), 405–416.

Maas, J. W., Kocsis, J. H., Bowden, C. L., Davis, J. M., Redmond, D. E., Hanin, I., & Robins, E. (1982). Pretreatment neurotransmitter metabolites and response to imipramine or amitriptyline treatment. *Psychological Medicine, 12*, 37–43.

Maas, J. W., Koslow, S. H., Davis, J., Katz, M., Frazer, A., Bowden, C. L., Berman, N., Gibbons, R., Stokes, P., & Landis, H. (1987). Catecholamine metabolism and disposition in healthy and depressed subjects. *Archives of General Psychiatry, 44*(4), 337–344.

Maes, M., Schotte, C., Vandewoude, M., Martin, M., & Blockx, P. (1992). TSH responses to TRH as a function of basal serum TSH: Relevance for unipolar depression in females—a multivariate study. *Pharmacopsychiatry, 25*, 136–144.

Maes, M., Vandewoude, M., Schotte, C., Martin, M., & Blockx, P. (1990). Suppressive effects of dexamethasone on hypothalamic–pituitary–thyroid axis function in depressed patients. *Journal of Affective Disorders, 20*, 55–61.

Marsden, C. A. (1991). The neuropharmacology of serotonin in the central nervous system. In J. P. Feighner & W. F. Boyer (Eds.), *Selective serotonin re-uptake inhibitors* (pp. 11–35). Chichester, England: Wiley.

Martintot, J.-L., Hardy, P., Feline, A., Huret, J.-D., Mazoyer, B., Attar-Levy, D., Pappata, S., & Syrota, A. (1990). Left prefrontal glucose hypometabolism in the depressed state: A confirmation. *American Journal of Psychiatry, 147*(10), 1313–1317.

Matussek, N. (1994). Neuroendocrinology and depression. In H. Hippuis, C. Stefanis, & F. Muller-Spahn (Eds.), *Research in mood disorders: An update* (pp. 61–72). Seattle, WA: Hogrefe & Huber.

McEwen, B. S. (1988). Glucocorticoid receptors in the brain. *Hospital Practice, 23*(8), 107–121.

Mellerup, E. T., & Langer, S. Z. (1990). Validity of imipramine platelet binding sites as a biological marker of endogenous depression: A World Health Organization collaborative study. *Pharmacopsychiatry, 23*, 113–117.

Meltzer, H. Y. (Ed.). (1987). *Psychopharmacology: The third generation of progress*. New York: Raven Press.

Meltzer, H. Y., & Lowy, M. T. (1987). The serotonin hypothesis of depression. In H. Y. Meltzer (Ed.), *Psychopharmacology: The third generation of progress* (pp. 513–526). New York: Raven Press.

Mendlewicz, J., & Kerkhofs, M. (1991). Sleep electroencephalography in depressive illness. A collaborative study by the World Health Organization. *British Journal of Psychiatry, 159*, 505–509.

Morihisa, J. M. (1989). Computerized EEG and evoked potential mapping. In N. C. Andreasen (Ed.), *Brain imaging: Applications in psychiatry* (pp. 123–145). Washington, DC: American Psychiatric Press.

Mossman, D., & Somoza, E. (1989). Maximizing diagnostic information from the dexamethasone suppression test. An approach to criterion selection using receiver operating characteristic analysis. *Archives of General Psychiatry, 46*(7), 653–660.

Mouret, J., Lemoine, P., & Minuit, M.-P. (1987). Marqueurs polygraphiques, cliniques et thérapeutiques des dépressions dopamino-dépendantes (DDD). *Comptes Rendus de l'Académie des Sciences. Ser. III, Sciences de la Vie (Paris) (Medicine and Therapeutics/Neurophysiology), 305*(Ser. III), 301–306.

Mouret, J., Lemoine, P., Minuit, M.-P., & Robelin, N. (1988). La L-tyrosine guérit, immédiatement et à long terme, les dépressions dopamino-dépendantes (DDD): Étude clinique et polygraphique. *Comptes Rendus de l'Académie des Sciences. Ser. III, Sciences de la Vie (Paris) (Medicine and Therapeutics/Neurophysiology), 306*(Ser. III), 93–98.

Mozley, P. D. (1992). SPECT brain imaging in patients with depression. In *Functional brain imaging with SPECT in psychiatry: Nuclear medicine at the frontier of psychiatric illness* (pp. 6–8). New York: St. Vincent's Hospital and Medical Center.

Musselman, D. L., & Nemeroff, C. B. (1993). Neuroendocrinology of depression. *Clinical Neuroscience, 1,* 115–121.

Nadi, N. S., Nurnberger, J. I., & Gershon, E. S. (1984). Muscarinic cholinergic receptors on skin fibroblasts in familial affective disorder. *New England Journal of Medicine, 311*(4), 225–230.

Nair, N. P. V., & Sharma, M. (1989). Neurochemical and receptor theories of depression. *Psychiatric Journal of the University of Ottawa, 14*(2), 328–341.

Nasrallah, H. A., Coffman, J. A., & Olson, S. C. (1989). Structural brain-imaging findings in affective disorders: An overview. *The Journal of Neuropsychiatry and Clinical Neurosciences, 1*(1), 21–26.

Nemeroff, C. B., Knight, D. L., Franks, J., Craighead, W. E., & Krishnan, K. R. R. (1994). Further studies on platelet serotonin transporter binding in depression. *American Journal of Psychiatry, 151*(11), 1623–1625.

Nierenberg, A. A., & Feinstein, A. R. (1988). How to evaluate a diagnostic marker test. Lessons from the rise and fall of dexamethasone suppression test. *Journal of the American Medical Association, 259*(11), 1699–1702.

O'Donohue, T. L., Millington, W. R., Handelmann, G. E., Contreras, P. C., & Chronwall, B. M. (1985). On the 50th anniversary of Dale's law: Multiple neurotransmitter neurons. *Trends in Pharmacological Sciences* (Ref. Ed.), *6*(1), 305–308.

Owens, M. J., & Nemeroff, C. B. (1994). Role of serotonin in the pathophysiology of depression: Focus on the serotonin transporter. *Clinical Chemistry, 40*(2), 288–295.

Pearlson, G. D., Garbacz, D. J., Tompkins, R. H., Ahn, H. S., Getterman, D. F., Veroff, A. E., & DePaulo, J. R. (1984). Clinical correlates of lateral ventricular enlargement in bipolar affective disorder. *American Journal of Psychiatry, 141*(2), 253–256.

Pearsall, H. R., & Gold, M. S. (1986). Other neuroendocrine tests. In M. S. Gold & A. L. C. Pottash (Eds.), *Diagnostic and laboratory testing in psychiatry* (pp. 59–75). New York: Plenum Medical.

Petty, F., Kramer, G. L., Gullion, C. M., & Rush, A. J. (1992). Low plasma γ-aminobutyric acid levels in male patients with depression. *Biological Psychiatry, 32,* 354–363.

Phelps, M. E., Mazziotta, J. C., & Schelbert, H. R. (1986). *Positron emission tomography and autoradiography.* New York: Raven Press.

Post, R. M., DeLisi, L. E., Holcomb, H. H., Uhde, T. W., Cohen, R., & Buchsbaum, M. S. (1987). Glucose utilization in the temporal cortex of affectively ill patients: Positron emission tomography. *Biological Psychiatry, 22,* 545–553.

Potter, W. Z., & Linnoila, M. (1989). Biochemical classifications of diagnostic subgroups and D-type scores. *Archives of General Psychiatry, 46*(3), 269–271.

Pryor, J. C., & Sulser, F. (1991). Evolution of the monoamine hypotheses of depression. In R. W. Horton & C. L. E. Katona (Eds.), *Biological aspects of affective disorders* (pp. 77–94). London: Academic Press.

Reynolds, C. F. (1989). Sleep in affective disorders. In M. H. Kryger, T. Roth, & W. C. Dement (Eds.), *Principles and practice of sleep medicine* (pp. 413–415). Philadelphia, PA: Saunders.

Reynolds, C. F., Coble, P. A., Kupfer, D. J., & Shaw, D. H. (1982). Depressive patients and the sleep laboratory. In C. Guilleminault (Ed.), *Sleeping and waking disorders: Indications and techniques* (pp. 245–263). Menlo Park, CA: Addison-Wesley.

Reynolds, C. F., & Kupfer, D. J. (1987). Sleep research in affective illness: State of the art circa 1987. *Sleep, 10*(3), 199–215.

Reynolds, C. F., Kupfer, D. J., Houck, P. R., Hoch, C. C., Stack, J. A., Berman, S. R., & Zimmer, B. (1988). Reliable discrimination of elderly depressed and demented patients by electroencephalographic sleep data. *Archives of General Psychiatry, 45*(3), 258–264.

Reynolds, C. F., Kupfer, D. J., Thase, M. E., Frank, E., Jarrett, D. B., Coble, P. A., Hoch, C. C., Buysse, D. J., Simons, A. D., & Houck, P. R. (1990). Sleep, gender, and depression: An analysis of gender effects on the electroencephalographic sleep of 302 depressed outpatients. *Biological Psychiatry, 28,* 673–684.

Ribeiro, S. C. M., Tandon, R., Grunhaus, L., & Greden, J. F. (1993). The DST as a predictor of outcome in depression: A meta-analysis. *American Journal of Psychiatry, 150*(11), 1618–1629.

Risch, S. C., & Gillin, J. C. (1988). Biological markers in affective disorders. In A. Georgotas & R. Cancro (Eds.), *Depression and mania* (pp. 305–311). New York: Elsevier.

Rosse, R. B., Giese, A. A., Deutsch, S. I., & Morihisa, J. M. (1989a). Endocrine evaluations of potential relevance to psychiatrists. In R. B. Rosse, A. A. Giese, S. I. Deutsch, & J. M. Morihisa (Eds.), *Concise guide to laboratory and diagnostic testing in psychiatry* (pp. 4–30). Washington, DC: American Psychiatric Press.

Rosse, R. B., Giese, A. A., Deutsch, S. I., & Morihisa, J. M. (1989b). Additional diagnostic tests commonly used in psychiatry. In R. B. Rosse, A. A. Giese, S. I. Deutsch, & J. M. Morihisa (Eds.), *Concise guide to laboratory and diagnostic testing in psychiatry* (pp. 83–101). Washington, DC: American Psychiatric Press.

Rothschild, A. J. (1988). Biology of depression. *Medical Clinics of North America, 72*(4), 765–790.

Roy, A. (1992). Hypothalamic–pituitary–adrenal axis function and suicidal behavior in depression. *Biological Psychiatry, 32,* 812–816.

Roy, A., DeJong, J., & Linnoila, M. (1989). Cerebrospinal fluid monoamine metabolites and suicidal behavior in depressed patients: A 5-year follow-up study. *Archives of General Psychiatry, 46*(7), 609–612.

Roy, A., Everett, D., Pickar, D., & Paul, S. M. (1987). Platelet tritiated imipramine binding and serotonin uptake in depressed patients and controls: Relationship to plasma cortisol before and after dexamethasone administration. *Archives of General Psychiatry, 44*(4), 320–327.

Rush, A. J., Erman, M. K., Giles, D. E., Schlesser, M. A., Carpenter, G., Vasavada, N., & Roffwarg, H. P. (1986).

Polysomnographic findings in recently drug-free and clinically remitted depressed patients. *Archives of General Psychiatry*, *43*(9), 878–884.

Sabelli, H. C., Fawcett, J., Gusovsky, F., Javaid, J. I., Wynn, P., Edwards, J., Jeffriess, H., Kravitz, H. (1986). Clinical studies of the phenylethylamine hypothesis of affective disorder: Urine and blood phenylacetic acid and phenylalanine dietary supplements. *Journal of Clinical Psychiatry*, *47*(2), 66–70.

Sabelli, H. C., Mosnaim, A. D., Vazquez, A. J., Giardina, W. J., Borison, R. L., & Pedemonte, W. A. (1976). Biochemical plasticity of synaptic transmission: A critical review of Dale's principle. *Biological Psychiatry*, *11*(4), 481–524.

Sackheim, H. A., Prohovnik, I., Moeller, J. R., Brown, R. P., Apter, S., Prudic, J., Devanand, D. P., & Mukherjee, S. (1990). Regional cerebral blood flow in mood disorders: I. Comparison of major depressives and normal controls at rest. *Archives of General Psychiatry*, *47*(1), 60–70.

Schatzberg, A. F., Samson, J. A., Bloomingdale, K. L., Orsulak, P. J., Gerson, B., Kizuka, P. P., Cole, J. O., & Schildkraut, J. J. (1989). Toward a biochemical classification of depressive disorders: X. Urinary catecholamines, their metabolites, and D-type scores in subgroups of depressive disorders. *Archives of General Psychiatry*, *46*(3), 260–268.

Schildkraut, J. J. (1965). The catecholamine hypothesis of affective disorders: A review of supporting evidence. *American Journal of Psychiatry*, *122*, 509–522.

Schildkraut, J. J., Orsulak, P. J., LaBrie, R. A., Schatzberg, A. F., Gudeman, J. E., Cole, J. O., & Rohde, W. A. (1978). Toward a biochemical classification of depressive disorders: II. Application of multivariate discriminant function analysis to data on urinary catecholamines and metabolites. *Archives of General Psychiatry*, *35*(12), 1436–1439.

Siever, L. J. (1987). Role of noradrenergic mechanisms in the etiology of the affective disorders. In H. Y. Meltzer (Ed.), *Psychopharmacology: The third generation of progress* (pp. 493–504). New York: Raven Press.

Siever, L. J., & Davis, K. L. (1985). Overview: Toward a dysregulation hypothesis of depression. *American Journal of Psychiatry*, *142*(9), 1017–1031.

Skolnick, A. A. (1992). New MRI techniques allow noninvasive peek inside the thinking human brain. *Journal of the American Medical Association*, *268*(11), 1387–1388.

Stockmeier, C. A., Martino, A. M., & Kellar, K. J. (1985). A strong influence of serotonin axons on β-adrenergic receptors in rat brain. *Science*, *230*, 323–325.

Stokes, P. E., Mass, J. W., Davis, J. M., Koslow, S. H., Casper, R. C., & Stoll, P. M. (1987). Biogenic amine and metabolite levels in depressed patients with high versus normal hypothalamic–pituitary–adrenocortical activity. *American Journal of Psychiatry*, *144*(7), 868–872.

Sulser, F. (1982). Antidepressant drug research: Its impact on neurobiology and psychobiology. In E. Costa & G. Racagni (Eds.), *Typical and atypical antidepressants: Molecular mechanisms* (pp. 1–20). New York, Raven Press.

Sulser, F. (1986). Update on neuroreceptor mechanisms and their implication for the pharmacotherapy of affective disorders. *Journal of Clinical Psychiatry*, *47*(10, Suppl.), 13–18.

Thilo, J. B., & Burnet, P. W.J. (1992). The role of adenylate cyclase in neuropsychiatric disease. *Psychopharmacology Bulletin*, *28*(4), 477–500.

U.S. Congress, Office of Technology Assessment. (1992). Appendix A. Decade of the brain. In *The biology of mental disorders—New developments in neuroscience, OTA-BA-538* (pp. 169–170). Washington, DC: U. S. Government Printing Office.

Van Heertum, R. L. (1992). Brain SPECT imaging and psychiatry. *Journal of Clinical Psychiatry*, *53*(11, Suppl.), 7–12.

van Praag, H. M., Kahn, R. S., Asnis, G. M., Wetzler, S., Brown, S. L., Bleich, A., & Korn, M. L. (1987). Denosology of biological psychiatry or the specificity of 5-HT disturbances in psychiatric disorders. *Journal of Affective Disorders*, *13*, 1–8.

Vanelle, J. M., Poirier, M. F., Benkelfat, C., Galinowski, A., Sechter, D., Suzini de Luca, H., & Loo, H. (1990). Diagnostic and therapeutic value of testing stimulation of thyroid-stimulating hormone by thyrotropin-releasing hormone in 100 depressed patients. *Acta Psychiatrica Scandinavica*, *81*, 156–161.

Weinberger, D. R. (1984). Brain disease and psychiatric illness: When should a psychiatrist order a CAT scan? *American Journal of Psychiatry*, *141*(12), 1521–1527.

Weinberger, D. R. (1993). SPECT imaging in psychiatry: Introduction and overview. *Journal of Clinical Psychiatry*, *54*(11, Suppl), 3–5.

Williamson, P. C., & Kaye, H. (1989). EEG mapping applications in psychiatric disorders. *Canadian Journal of Psychiatry*, *34*(7), 680–686.

Wolkowitz, O. M., Doran, A. R., Breier, A., Roy, A., Jimerson, D. C., Sutton, M. E., Golden, R. N., Paul, S. M., & Pickar, D. (1987). The effects of dexamethasone on plasma homovanillic acid and 3-methoxy-4-hydroxyphenylglycol: Evidence for abnormal corticosteroid–catecholamine interactions in major depression. *Archives of General Psychiatry*, *44*(9), 782–789.

Young, E. A., Haskett, R. F., Murphy-Weinberg, V., Watson, S. J., & Akil, H. (1991). Loss of glucocorticoid fast feedback in depression. *Archives of General Psychiatry*, *48*(8), 693–699.

III

PSYCHOLOGICAL THERAPIES AND COMBINED TREATMENTS

11

Cognitive Theory and Therapy

WILLIAM P. SACCO
AARON T. BECK

The cognitive theory of depression (Beck, 1967, 1976) and the psychotherapeutic strategies that have grown from the theory (Beck, Rush, Shaw, & Emery, 1979) are now based upon a history of over 30 years of theory and research (Beck, 1991). In a very early study, Beck (1961) first reported on the dream content of depressed clients. The study's purpose was to evaluate the psychoanalytic view that depression results from inverted hostility; thus, it was hypothesized that depressed clients would show more hostility in their dreams than would nondepressed clients. The psychoanalytic hypothesis was not supported. Rather, depressed clients reported a greater than normal incidence of dreams with content that centered around being deprived, thwarted, depreciated, excluded, or punished in some way. This serendipitous finding has been replicated on several occasions (e.g., Beck & Ward, 1961; Hauri, 1976). Extending these observations, Beck (1963) described the free associations and verbal reports of depressed clients. The idiosyncratic cognitive content and cognitive distortions observed (Beck, 1963) led to a clinically based theory that depressed persons view the self, the world, and the future negatively, and that a theme of loss permeates their cognitive distortions. Furthermore, it was theorized that these cognitive propensities play a central role in the development and maintenance of depression.

Since then, tremendous energy and enthusiasm have been directed toward empirical examination of the cognitive theory; development of a treatment program based on this theory for depressed clients (Beck et al., 1979); and empirical examination of the efficacy of the cognitive therapy of depression (e.g., Beck, 1991; Hollon & Najavits, 1988; Hollon, Shelton, & Davis, 1993). Today, many aspects of the cognitive theory of depression have received substantial support (Haaga, Dyck, & Ernst, 1991). In addition, there is now abundant evidence that cognitive therapy for depression is effective with respect to short-term symptom reduction of symptoms (e.g., Dobson, 1989; Robinson, Berman, & Neimeyer, 1990), and recent studies suggest the superiority of cognitive therapy over other psychological and pharmacological therapies in the prevention of relapse (Hollon & Najavits, 1988; Hollon, Shelton, & Loosen, 1991; Hollon et al., 1993; Shea et al., 1992).

In this chapter, we first describe the cognitive theory of depression. Next, the stages of cognitive therapy of depression are outlined. In our description of the therapy, we attempt to communicate the underlying structure that guides the cognitive therapist. As will be seen, cognitive therapy of depression is designed to be "transportable." A treatment manual has been designed so that with adequate training and supervision, cognitive therapy (and its apparent effectiveness) can be replicated by therapists at large. We then provide a summary of the large body of empirical evidence bearing on the validity of the cognitive theory and the efficacy of cognitive therapy for depression. Finally, we consider the variables related to the effectiveness of cognitive therapy.

THE COGNITIVE THEORY OF DEPRESSION

Simply stated, the cognitive theory of depression proposes that the essential component of a depressive disorder is a negative cognitive set—that is, the tendency to view the self, the future, and the world in a dysfunctional, negative manner. This dysfunctional view of self, future, and world, which often reflects an underlying theme of loss, is termed the "negative triad" (Beck, 1967). Depressed persons regard themselves as unworthy, incapable, and undesirable. They expect failure, rejection, and dissatisfaction, and perceive most experiences as confirming these negative expectations. Their thoughts are automatic, repetitive, unintended, and not readily controllable; hence they are termed "negative automatic thoughts." Depressed people experience these negative automatic thoughts as valid, and in severely depressed individuals they dominate consciousness. All depressive disorders, regardless of subtype, are said to manifest the negative cognitive triad, and the major symptoms of a depressive disorder (affective, behavioral, somatic, and motivational) are viewed as a direct consequence of the negative thinking pattern. Thus, "intervention at the cognitive level may reduce the other symptoms, whereas persistence or exacerbation of the cognitive processes may maintain or increase the other symptoms" (Beck, 1991, p. 371).

A central feature of the theory is that the depressed individual's negative thinking is systematically biased in a negative direction. Idiosyncratic cognitive schemas are proposed as hypothetical structures that maintain the negatively biased view despite contradictory evidence. "Schemas" are viewed as cognitive structures through which events are processed; they vary from person to person with respect to their content, valence, permeability, density, and flexibility. Functioning like templates, schemas actively screen, code, categorize, and evaluate stimuli. In depression, these schemas or response categories, especially those related to the self-concept and personal expectations, tend to be global, rigid, and negatively toned (Hollon & Beck, 1979). Once activated, these depressive schemas influence how external stimuli are interpreted, resulting in the cognitive distortions commonly observed in the thinking of depressed persons.

Beck (1967) has described several common systematic errors in the depressed individual's information processing, which reflect the activity of dysfunctional cognitive schemas. These systematic errors in logic are listed below:

1. Arbitrary inference—drawing a conclusion in the absence of evidence or when the evidence is contrary to the conclusion.
2. Selective abstraction—the tendency to focus on a negative detail in a situation and to conceptualize the entire experience on the basis of this negative fragment.
3. Overgeneralization—the tendency to draw a general rule or conclusion on the basis of one isolated incident, and to apply the concept indiscriminately to both related and unrelated situations.
4. Magnification and minimization—the tendency to overestimate the significance or magnitude of undesirable events, and to underestimate the significance or magnitude of desirable events.
5. Personalization—the tendency to relate external events to oneself without evidence.
6. All-or-none thinking—the tendency to think in absolute, black-or-white, all-or-none terms.

The dysfunctional cognitive schemas are said to take the form of basic beliefs or "silent assumptions" (Beck et al., 1979). Examples of these beliefs are found operationalized in the Dysfunctional Attitude Scale (Weissman & Beck, 1978), which includes items such as these: "I cannot be happy unless most people I know admire me," I am nothing if a person I love doesn't love me," and "If I fail at my work, then I am a failure as a person."

It is important to recognize that the cognitive theory of depression proposes a "diathesis–stress" model of reactive depression, although many writers and researchers have failed to acknowledge this critical feature. Specifically, it is hypothesized that a psychological predisposition toward depression proneness is acquired through early experiences that shape the development of cognitive schemas in a negative, self-referential manner. The dysfunctional cognitive schemas will remain latent until activated by stressors (precipitating factors) to which the individual is sensitized.

Recent extensions of the cognitive theory elaborate on the notion of "specific vulnerability." It is proposed that two "types" of belief systems (types of schema content) may interact with two classes of stressors to provoke a depressive reaction (Beck, 1983, 1991). "Sociotropy" refers to the tendency to value closeness, acceptance, dependency, and sharing. Individuals whose cognitive schemas are highly developed around sociotropic themes should be more likely to become depressed when confronted with sociotropic trauma, such as social deprivation or rejection. "Autonomy" refers to the tendency to value independent functioning, mobility, choice, and achievement. Individuals whose cognitive schemas are highly developed around autonomous themes are expected to be vulnerable to depression if exposed to stressors such as failure or immobilization. For example, some individuals who lose a parent in childhood may develop a schema centering around loss (i.e., become sociotropic), which predisposes them to develop a depressive disorder upon the termination of a love relationship in adult life. These same individuals may not develop a depressive disorder in response to loss of employment—a stressor that might precipitate a depression in an individual who has been sensitized to failing to live up to excessively high standards imposed by parents in early childhood (i.e., an individual of the autonomous type).

The concept of specific vulnerability may help explain why the relationship between life stressors and depression is not as strong as many have expected (e.g., Paykel, 1979). This account suggests that individuals who are predisposed to depressive disorders will avoid depression if experiences to which they are sensitized are absent from their environment. In such cases, the negative cognitive schemas will remain latent and inactive; consequently, fewer negative thoughts will occur (see Eaves & Rush, 1984).

Although the cognitive theory of depression focuses on an intrapsychic mechanism to describe the development and maintenance of depression, the role of interpersonal factors in the development and maintenance of depressive disorders is acknowledged (Beck et al., 1979; Beck, 1988, 1991). As noted above, real or symbolic interpersonal loss and/or (interpersonal) threats to autonomy can precipitate a reactive depression. Beck (1988) has also described how dysfunctional thinking styles in married couples can result in pathological outcomes.

A host of evidence indicates that depressed persons have a powerful impact on their social environment, which in turn can create additional interpersonal stressors for the depressed individual (e.g., Coyne, 1976). For example, others typically react to the depressed person's failures with greater negative affect (e.g., upset, anger, shame); others are more likely to socially reject a depressed person; and marital dissatisfaction is commonly found when one spouse is depressed (e.g., Sacco, Milana, & Dunn, 1985, 1988; Sacco & Dunn, 1990; Sacco & Macleod, 1990; Sacco, Dumont, & Dow, 1993).

Evidence also indicates that these interpersonal reactions may be mediated by cognitive processes. Both acquaintances and spouses of depressed persons are more likely to attribute the failures of depressed (relative to nondepressed) persons/spouses to internal, stable, global, and controllable factors (Sacco & Dunn, 1990; Sacco et al., 1993). In addition, recent evidence suggests that marital dissatisfaction in marriages with a depressed partner may be reflecting, in part, an underlying negative cognitive bias in perceptions of the depressed person (Sacco et al., 1993). This bias is also found among mental health professionals (Jenkins-Hall & Sacco, 1991). Cognitive theory and therapy thus recognize the role of interpersonal processes in depression, but underscore the importance of cognitive processes in determining interpersonal reactions (see Beck, 1988).

COGNITIVE THERAPY OF DEPRESSION: BASIC TREATMENT STRATEGIES

Cognitive therapy of depression is an active, directive, structured, psychoeducational approach based upon Beck's cognitive theory of depression (Beck et al., 1979). Three theoretical assumptions underlie cognitive therapy interventions. The principal underlying assumption is that a depressed individual's affect and behavior are largely determined by the way in which he/she views the world. A second assumption is that cognitions (thoughts, beliefs, fantasies, images, etc.) can be self-monitored by the client and communicated. Identification and self-monitoring of cognitions may require training, but these cognitions are not unconscious, and the concept of unconscious processes is largely irrelevant to cognitive therapy. Finally, it is assumed that the modification of cognitions will lead to changes in affect and behavior. Research bearing on the validity of these assumptions is reviewed in a later section.

The cognitive therapist employs a variety of cognitive and behavioral techniques to alter the depressed client's dysfunctional style of thinking. A series of highly specific learning experiences is incorporated into treatment. The basic steps of this treatment program are outlined below. However, a few preliminary points must first be made.

Prior to the beginning of treatment, it is recommended that all clients receive a thorough diagnostic evaluation and case formulation. Making sure that a client is suitable for cognitive treatment is of utmost importance (Beck et al., 1979). Generally speaking, nonbipolar, nonpsychotic depressed clients are well suited for cognitive therapy (see also outcome study results in a later section of this chapter). Suicidal clients and severely depressed clients may require hospitalization and/or "somatic" therapy, though these approaches may be used in conjunction with cognitive therapy.

Cognitive therapists are also encouraged to assess the potential benefits of involving significant others in the therapy process (Beck et al., 1979; Bedrosian, 1981). For example, significant others are often useful for helping depressed clients test the validity of their thinking (Rush, Shaw, & Khatami, 1980). However, severe marital discord may require marital therapy in addition to cognitive therapy (e.g., O'Leary & Beach, 1990), though in many cases cognitive therapy appears to provide additional benefits even after interpersonal difficulties have been resolved.

In recent years, there has been increasing interest in the role of cognitive therapy with individuals who exhibit a personality disorder along with other Axis I mental disorders, such as depression (Beck, Freeman, & Associates, 1990). Evidence suggests that short-term cognitive therapy for depression is less successful with individuals who also manifest characteristics of a personality disorder (Burns & Nolen-Hoeksema, 1992; Persons, Burns, & Perloff, 1988; Rush & Shaw, 1983). In cases with coexisting personality disorders, standard cognitive therapy techniques are recommended for the treatment of the depressive (or anxious) symptoms; however, special efforts and a longer

duration of treatment must be expected for modification of the more stable and elaborate underlying cognitive processes that are believed to maintain personality disorders (Beck et al., 1990).

Cognitive therapy is designed to be a time-limited, short-term treatment. General guidelines suggest 15 to 25 (50-minute) sessions at weekly intervals, with more seriously depressed clients usually requiring twice-weekly meetings for the initial 4–5 weeks. To avoid an abrupt termination, a "tapering-off" process is recommended, with the last few sessions occurring once every 2 weeks. After termination, some clients may also need a few "booster sessions" (four or five are common).

It is recommended that the client's level of depression be assessed throughout treatment. The Beck Depression Inventory (BDI; Beck, 1967) is useful for this purpose, as it has demonstrated reliability and validity and can be completed by clients prior to each session in approximately 10 minutes. The BDI thus provides a useful method for monitoring clients' progress. It also includes items relevant to assessing suicidal ideation and intent. Obviously, substantial increases or decreases in depression level provide important information and suggest that a therapist and client try to determine possible causes for the changes.

Before every session, the client and therapist should establish an agenda of issues that each would like to deal with during the session. It is the therapist's responsibility to control the use of time during a therapy session, so that, to the extent possible, the high-priority agenda items are covered. Those items not discussed should be brought up in the following session. The agenda achieves a variety of goals, including enhancing the efficiency of each session, providing a structure for the session (which seems in itself to be therapeutic for depressed clients), and actively involving the client in the direction of each session. Clients should begin to take on more responsibility for agenda setting as therapy progresses; this underscores one of the principal goals of any psychoeducational therapy, greater self-reliance.

Although cognitive therapy adopts a psychoeducational approach, utilizing structure and a variety of techniques designed to modify cognitive–behavioral patterns, the therapeutic process itself is also considered important. Effective cognitive therapy requires, first of all, the development of a strong therapeutic relationship—for example, development of trust, genuine concern for and acceptance of the client, and accurate empathy. Thus, the cognitive therapist must possess the basic characteristics of an effective psychotherapist. Moreover, although cognitive therapy is described below as a very structured therapy, when it is properly conducted the implicit structure is melded into the therapy process, such that the goals of each session are accomplished within a therapeutic context involving a natural and effective flow of communication between the therapist and client. Similarly, although it is accurate to infer that therapy proceeds in a relatively stepwise fashion, the boundaries between the steps described below are typically blurred during the actual therapeutic process.

Indeed, it is important to stress that cognitive therapy does not involve simply teaching the client a predetermined series of cognitive and behavioral techniques. To help promote the adoption of a flexible and coherent approach to the management of each client's idiosyncratic difficulties, the therapist should develop a case formulation or conceptualization during the evaluation or during the first few interviews (see Beck et al., 1990). This conceptualization should serve as an organized framework to guide the therapy process. Specifically, the therapist attempts to develop a broad picture of the various factors relevant to the patient's depression. This formulation involves, first of all, a cross-sectional analysis that takes into account the individual's automatic thoughts, how these are shaped by the person's underlying beliefs, and how the beliefs and automatic thoughts ultimately generate symptoms during the depression. Case conceptualization thus provides a kind of road map. The particular techniques are analogous to vehicles that one might use in moving from the beginning to the end of the trip. In other words, the nature of the terrain and the available routes will determine what techniques are used. This approach seems to produce better results than proceeding with a predetermined sequence of techniques. Consequently, in any one session, the therapist may employ a variety of strategies and techniques. The case formulation can be shared with the client and may be modified as new data emerge. It therefore serves as a "working model" for both the therapist and the client as therapy proceeds within the underlying structure of cognitive therapy, as described below.

The pace at which the therapist and client proceed through the steps of cognitive therapy is also likely to vary, primarily because of individual client characteristics such as severity of depression, motivation, and suitability for cognitively oriented interventions. However, guidelines can be extrapolated from the research protocol for outcome studies conducted at the Center for Cognitive Therapy (see Beck et al., 1979). These guidelines are presented here simply to provide the reader with an approximate time frame for the steps outlined below. Note that these guidelines were developed for an outcome study that limited treatment to a maximum of 20 sessions. Thus, in nonresearch settings, the pace and duration of treatment are likely to vary to a much greater extent.

With these caveats in mind, the research protocol suggests that Steps 1 and 2 should occur during Sessions 1–4; Steps 3 and 4 should occur during Sessions 6–8; and Step 5 should occur during Sessions 8–12. The remaining sessions (up to 20 for the outcome study) are designed to prepare the client for termination. During these sessions the principles and strategies learned previously are practiced, with the client taking on a greater responsibility for enacting self-help strategies, so that he/she is prepared for the termination of treatment.

Step 1: Identify and Monitor Dysfunctional Automatic Thoughts

One of the most important goals of cognitive therapy is to teach the client to identify and monitor dysfunctional automatic thoughts. As noted earlier, automatic thoughts are specific subvocalizations or self-statements that occur automatically and without conscious effort. Clients are often unaware of having these thoughts unless they are taught to recognize them. When their automatic thoughts are brought to their attention, depressed persons usually see them as accurate representations of reality, even though they are often unreasonably negative. Clinical experience and data also indicate that the degree to which an individual believes a negative dysfunctional ideation is related to the strength of the negative emotional response (Rogers & Craighead, 1977).

Various interventions are designed to teach clients to identify and monitor dysfunctional ideation. Clients are first taught the basic concepts of cognitive theory and cognitive therapy. Automatic thoughts are described to clients in a didactic manner, and clients are provided relevant reading material to increase their intellectual understanding of cognitive therapy, such as a booklet titled *Coping with Depression* (Beck & Greenberg, 1974). The therapist then attempts to engage the client as a collaborator, or fellow scientist, to work together to discover whether the client does indeed tend to experience a great number of these negative thoughts.

Beck et al. (1979) consider the application of "collaborative empiricism" to be essential for effective cognitive therapy with depressed individuals. By joining in the collaborative empirical venture, clients learn under nonthreatening conditions to evaluate their thinking more objectively. Thus, the idea that a client may be thinking in an unrealistically negative manner should be raised as a tentative hypothesis, to be decided by various data-gathering techniques. No attempt is made to argue the veracity or reasonableness of the client's thoughts in this beginning stage of therapy. The therapist simply encourages the client to identify and monitor his/her negative automatic thoughts.

Several techniques are useful in helping the therapist and client identify dysfunctional thoughts within the therapy session. The therapist may make direct inquiries about cognitive reactions to past events that led to strong emotional responses. For example, during the first session, a client may be asked about thoughts he/she had prior to meeting the therapist. This type of questioning often elicits a variety of automatic thoughts about expectations of therapy outcome, the therapist's characteristics, how the therapist will view the client, and so on. Past events associated with negative mood can also be examined by asking the client to imagine the chain of events occurring just prior to a particular negative reaction, and then to focus on specific thoughts occurring at that time. Role playing may promote accurate recall of past events and associated cognitions. Mood shifts during the session (e.g., tearful eyes) are also very effective cues for the therapist to inquire about the client's thoughts.

Homework assignments are used to promote recognition of automatic thoughts between sessions. For instance, the Daily Record of Dysfunctional Thoughts (Beck et al., 1979; see Figure 11.1 and Table 11.1) is especially helpful in teaching clients to dissect an emotion-producing situation into three components: the objective situation, the emotion, and the automatic thoughts that led to the emotion. Another homework assignment, "thought counting," is de-

signed to help clients monitor the frequency of certain automatic thoughts. Clients may use either a wrist counter or an index card simply to count thoughts with a specific theme (e.g., guilt-inducing thoughts).

Weekly homework is an integral feature of cognitive therapy. Cognitive therapy is designed to be a short-term treatment, and work done by a client between therapy sessions serves to accelerate progress. The idea of weekly homework is presented to the client at the beginning of treatment. Most clients are quite receptive to working on their problems outside of the therapy session, and some experience increased optimism simply because they themselves can do something that may alleviate their depressed condition. Only in the very early sessions does the therapist take full responsibility for suggesting a homework assignment. In keeping with the spirit of "collaborative empiricism," the therapist should soon begin to involve the client more and more in planning the weekly homework, until finally the client is taking a major role in determining what work will be done between therapy sessions.

Step 2: Recognize the Connection among Thoughts, Emotions, and Behaviors

The next step of cognitive therapy involves teaching clients to recognize the connection among thoughts, emotions, and behaviors. Frequently a client will discover this connection while learning to identify automatic thoughts. It is again important to point out that a hypothesis-testing attitude is recommended when trying to establish this connection. Thus the therapist should ask, "How did you feel [or what did you do] when you had those thoughts?" Most clients readily see the connection among their thoughts, emotions, and behaviors. Clients may also be told at this point that most people experiencing the same thoughts would probably have similar behavioral and emotional reactions. Thus, the connection among thoughts, emotions, and behaviors is presented as a general principle, applicable to all people and situations.

Step 3: Evaluate the Reasonableness of the Automatic Thoughts

After the therapist and client have demonstrated the client's tendency to experience negative automatic thoughts (negative view of self,

DATE	SITUATION Describe: 1. Actual event leading to unpleasant emotion, or 2. Stream of thoughts, daydream, or recollection, leading to unpleasant emotion.	EMOTION(S) 1. Specify sad/ anxious/ angry, etc. 2. Rate degree of emotion, 1-100.	AUTOMATIC THOUGHT(S) 1. Write automatic thought(s) that preceded emotion(s). 2. Rate belief in automatic thought(s), 0-100%.	RATIONAL RESPONSE 1. Write rational response to automatic thought(s). 2. Rate belief in rational response, 0-100%.	OUTCOME 1. Rerate belief in automatic thought(s). 0-100%. 2. Specify and rate subsequent emotions, 0-100.

Explanation: When you experience an unpleasant emotion, note the situation that seemed to stimulate the emotion. (If the emotion occurred while you were thinking, daydreaming, etc., please note this.) Then note the automatic thought associated with the emotion. Record the degree to which you believe this thought: 0% = not at all; 100% = completely. In rating degree of emotion: 1 = a trace; 100 = the most intense possible.

FIGURE 11.1.   The Daily Record of Dysfunctional Thoughts.

TABLE 11.1. Instructions for Completing the Daily Record of Dysfunctional Thoughts

---

The Daily Record of Dysfunctional Thoughts is designed to help you analyze and resolve situations that cause you to feel or act in a way that is not in your best interest.

Column 1: Situation. In this column you describe the actual event(s) that led to the unpleasant emotion. In filling out this column, you must be objective. That is, briefly describe what happened, just as a videotape would have recorded it. Sometimes there is no specific event that led to the unpleasant emotion. Rather, unpleasant emotions often result from just daydreaming about something. In that case, briefly describe the daydream or stream of thought leading to the unpleasant emotion.

Column 2: Emotion(s). Indicate how you felt (feel) at the time. Emotions are feelings such as sad, angry, depressed, lonely, afraid, and anxious. These are your emotions, *not your thoughts*. Remember that thoughts are really words, phrases, or sentences that we say to ourselves. It may take some practice to be able to distinguish between thoughts and emotions, but you will be able to do so. Also, indicate the degree to which you felt these emotions, using the 0–100 scale described on the bottom of the form.

Column 3: Automatic Thought(s). Most people assume that it is the situation that causes the feeling. In actuality, our thoughts about the situation are what lead to our feelings. For this column you are to write down the automatic thoughts that preceded the emotion. Sometimes it is easy for you to identify your automatic thoughts. Sometimes they are harder to identify because they are so automatic. For these cases, you must concentrate on what happened and your reaction to the event. Then write down all your thoughts, exactly as they came to you, verbatim. Then rate how strongly you believe the automatic thoughts to be true, using the 0–100 scale described on the bottom of the form.

Column 4: Rational Response. After you have written down your automatic thoughts, examine the reasonableness of each thought. Is the thought accurate? What is the evidence to support it? Is there another, less depression-producing interpretation of the event? Is there another way of looking at the situation that would not make you feel so bad? Work hard at these rational responses. It may help to pose these questions to someone who can be more objective and rational about the event. Also, rate the degree to which you believe the rational response to be true, using the 0–100 scale described on the bottom of the form.

Column 5: Outcome. After you have completed columns 1–4, rerate how strongly you believe the automatic thoughts to be true and how you now feel.

Practice this technique often.

---

world, and future), and have established that these thoughts appear causally related to negative affect and dysfunctional behavior, the empirical approach is extended to examining the reasonableness of the client's thoughts. In essence, therapist and client test the hypothesis that the automatic thoughts are either illogical, inconsistent with the facts of the situation, or self-defeating because there is little or no advantage to thinking them. The goal of this step is to teach the client to think as a scientist—that is, to view his/her thoughts and conclusions more tentatively, as hypotheses that should be examined in light of the available evidence. This goal is to be contrasted with directly attacking the irrationality of the client's thoughts.

This third stage represents the quintessential element of Beck's cognitive therapy. Hence, the majority of therapist–client interactions center around achieving this psychoeducational goal. Negative automatic thoughts are scrutinized to evaluate their accuracy and logic. Various cog-

nitive cues are taught to facilitate the search for possible cognitive distortions and erroneous conclusions. It is helpful to teach clients to ask themselves four questions regarding their automatic thoughts.

First, clients should be taught to ask themselves, "What is the evidence to support this thought?" The therapist may use Socratic questioning to examine the logic or the premises upon which conclusions are based. This type of questioning helps clarify a client's thinking in response to the particular situation. In addition, perhaps a greater value comes from the therapist's modeling of rational thinking processes. Another very effective, if not essential, mechanism to help the client critically examine the evidence regarding a thought is to conduct "miniexperiments," designed to gather data bearing on the validity of a client's thoughts (Hollon & Beck, 1979).

For example, a new grandmother reported feeling very depressed after being irritated with her new grandchild. Examining her automatic thoughts revealed the following ideation: "Other grandmothers never have negative reactions to their grandchildren; therefore, because I felt irritation with my grandchild, I am a bad grandmother." Rather than trying to attack verbally the logic or reasonableness of these ideas, the therapist asked the client how she could test her cognitions and her basic premise. Together, they devised a plan to ask several grandmothers whether they ever felt annoyed or irritated with their grandchildren. By doing so, the client discovered that her peers frequently had similar feelings and at times felt relief when their grandchildren left at the end of a visit.

A second important question for clients to learn to ask themselves is this: "Are there any alternative interpretations of this event?" Depressed clients are notorious for reaching singular and negative interpretations of ambiguous situations, when in actuality a host of alternative, less depression-inducing views are quite possible and often accurate. The therapist encourages the client to "brainstorm" about other interpretations in hopes of teaching the client to maintain an open mind until more data are obtained.

A third question is designed to help depressed clients recognize their tendency to attribute the cause of negative events erroneously to internal, stable (unchanging), global factors, rather than to external factors or causes that can be altered (see Abramson, Seligman, & Teasdale, 1978). Thus, clients are taught reattribution techniques that induce them to ask themselves: "Is my explanation of the causes of this event completely accurate?" For example, depressed persons often attribute any response even remotely resembling a symptom of depression to a stable defect within them. This tendency was exemplified by a client who felt depressed for several days because she had decided against attending a social gathering with her teammates following a tennis match. Rather than attributing the decision to the fact that she was hot and sweaty, and wanted to go home to relax and cool down, she perceived it as evidence of her hopelessly depressed condition. This tendency to make depression-inducing attributions can often be demonstrated to clients by having them make attributions for hypothetical others in the same situation. Depressed individuals often have a "double standard," making more tolerant attributions for others. Evidence indicates that reattribution techniques can be

effective in modifying attributional tendencies (e.g., Forsterling, 1985), and that altering the tendency to attribute negative events to stable factors will result in greater persistence and hopefulness (e.g., Wilson & Linville, 1982).

Finally, clients are taught to ask themselves a fourth question: "So what if my worst fear (i.e., my negative conclusion) is true? Why would that outcome be so terrible?" This strategy is designed to help clients realize that they can cope with negative events that sometimes occur to all people. For example, a client may be asked: "Even if it is true that your girlfriend is going to leave you, why is that so terrible?" By confronting the worst possibility, clients often gain a more realistic perspective. The therapist and client acknowledge that losing a girlfriend is a negative event and is likely to be disruptive and to lead to unpleasant emotions; however, it is also something that people live through.

Step 4: Substitute More Reasonable Interpretations for the Dysfunctional Automatic Inferences

Learning to substitute more reasonable interpretations for dysfunctional automatic conclusions typically occurs as a direct result of Step 3. Clients are taught to change their evaluations to be more in accord with available evidence and logic. The Daily Record of Dysfunctional Thoughts (see Figure 11.1 and Table 11.1, above) is frequently used to attain this goal. Initially, clients are strongly encouraged to *write down* their dysfunctional thoughts and then their rational counterresponses, rather than simply processing them in their minds. Written dissection of emotion-producing situations may be essential in the beginning stages of this learning process. Later, clients can learn to answer their dysfunctional automatic thoughts without writing them down.

It is important that a client truly believe his/her rational counterresponse. Simple parroting of rational responses provided by the therapist is usually ineffective; thus, the therapist must involve the client in the process of developing rational responses. The therapist should be sensitive to unstated reservations about the accuracy of the rational response. These reservations often take the form of additional negative automatic thoughts in reaction to proposed rational responses. These automatic thoughts must then be examined until the client genuinely believes the rational responses. Figure 11.2 provides a

Date	Situation	Emotion(s)	Automatic Thought(s)	REASONABLE/ADAPTIVE RESPONSE(S)			
				Questioning the Evidence	Alternative Therapy	Re-attribution	De-catastrophizing
5/23	At home, reading—waiting for Bob to call—it's now 10 P.M.—he hasn't called.	Sad Miserable Abandoned Lonely	Why didn't he call? Why is he rejecting me? I feel so miserable, I don't know what to do—why can't I hold on to a guy? Why does this always happen to me—I just can't go on like this—what did I do wrong?	Just because he didn't call doesn't mean he is rejecting me—I have no real proof of that—I already saw him twice this week—if he didn't like me he would not have spent that much time with me—I shouldn't jump to crazy conclusions like that—and it's not true that "this" always happens to me. With John, I was the one who didn't want to keep the relationship!	There could be many reasons why he didn't call—besides rejection? He could be tied up with his clients, he could be trying to set bail for someone—it may have skipped his mind—he could be with friends—he may have had something to do! But even if he is having second thoughts about me—we could talk about it—it doesn't automatically mean that I can't hold on to him.	Why should I assume that his not calling has to do with me? He may have a lot of reasons for doing what he does—things that have nothing to do with me. It doesn't make sense to think that everything happens because of me—that I did something wrong! He must have his own feelings, ideas and fears—just like I. If things don't work out the way I'd like then, it could be because of his own things—it doesn't make sense to believe that I am solely responsible for what happens between the TWO OF US!	Here I go again? thinking that I am rejected? – but even if I am (which I don't know for sure)—even if he doesn't want to see me it's not true that I can't go on. It's just a feeling that I have—I have survived before even if this doesn't work—the worst that can happen is that I'll be sad, unhappy but it's not the end of the world—there are other men out there, and I have my friends, my job—I can go on.

FIGURE 11.2. Example of a filled-out form similar to the Daily Record of Dysfunctional Thoughts, illustrating various types of rational responses to negative automatic thoughts. Adapted from Kovacs (1977). Used by permission of the author.

sample of various types of rational responses that might result from evaluating automatic thoughts in light of the four questions discussed in Step 3 (adapted from Kovacs, 1977).

Step 5: Identify and Alter Dysfunctional Silent Assumptions

Toward the latter part of treatment, when symptoms have lessened, the therapist should begin to focus on identifying and modifying the basic underlying beliefs that predispose the client toward depressogenic thinking. Depressed individuals harbor dysfunctional premises or "silent assumptions" that cause them to bias their interpretations of life events. These assumptions are "silent" in that an individual is typically unaware of their existence and of their impact on the way he/she perceives the world. Although each individual's silent assumptions or rules are idiosyncratic, common themes are found in the belief systems of depressed clients (e.g., the systems of sociotropy and autonomy described earlier), which tend to be rigid and excessive.

For example, a common belief is that one must be loved or life is meaningless. Such a belief is likely to result in hyperdependency, with hypervigilance and anxiety regarding possible rejection by loved ones. If an important relationship ends, depression is likely to ensue. Examples of other dysfunctional assumptions that predispose individuals to excessive depression or sadness have been described by Beck (1976):

1. In order to be happy, I have to be successful in whatever I undertake.
2. To be happy, I must be accepted by all people at all times.
3. If I make a mistake, it means that I am inept.
4. I can't live without you.
5. If somebody disagrees with me, it means that person doesn't like me.
6. My value as a person depends on what others think of me.

Identification of these underlying beliefs usually occurs as a product of the examination of automatic thoughts. An individual's automatic thoughts typically center around one or two themes that reflect dysfunctional premises. For example, a client who believes it is necessary to be approved of by all people will usually have dysfunctional automatic thoughts in response to social interactions that the client has perceived

as evidence of rejection or disapproval. The Dysfunctional Attitude Scale (Weissman & Beck, 1978), which has been developed to measure these silent assumptions, can also aid the therapist and client in identifying and conceptualizing the client's underlying dysfunctional beliefs.

The "downward arrow" technique has also been described as an effective means of identifying underlying beliefs (Beck & Emery with Greenberg, 1985; Burns, 1980). The client is asked: "Why would this (negative) event be so upsetting to you?" or "What is the meaning of this (negative) event to you?" The therapist repeats the same question in response to each answer, in an attempt to ascertain the underlying belief that creates the event's importance. The sequence generally progresses to a more fundamental conviction held by the client.

Modification of silent assumptions involves basically the same process as modification of dysfunctional automatic thoughts, and various strategies are described by Beck et al. (1979) and Burns (1980). For example, clients may be asked to list the advantages and disadvantages of holding the beliefs. Or "response prevention" may be effectively used. This technique involves having clients perform an experiment in which they behave in a manner opposite to that which their dysfunctional silent assumptions would dictate. For example, clients driven by perfectionistic tendencies may be urged to perform tasks in an "only satisfactory" manner, in order to learn that excessively high standards are unnecessary for happiness and may even disrupt performance and reduce satisfaction.

Recent evidence indicates that "silent assumptions" are far less accessible when the client is no longer experiencing the depressive disorder (e.g., Barnett & Gotlib, 1988); thus, it is important to begin the process of identifying these underlying beliefs while symptoms are present. After symptoms have remitted, latent dysfunctional beliefs may only be apparent to the client during acute episodes of dysphoric mood (e.g., Miranda, Persons, & Byers, 1990). To continue the process of modifying dysfunctional assumptions after symptoms have remitted, it may be necessary to artificially activate the belief system by invoking imagery of situations that typically create negative emotional responses (Hollon & Garber, 1990).

Recent extensions of cognitive theory and therapy propose that strongly held dysfunctional beliefs underlie the presence of personality disorders, which, as noted earlier, often coexist with a depressive disorder (Beck et al., 1990). The dysfunctional beliefs of individuals with personality disorders are said to be strongly integrated into their "normal" cognitive processes; thus, they will continue to influence perceptions, affect, and behavior after the depressive episode wanes, to a greater extent than occurs in clients without an accompanying personality disorder. Many of the same basic diagnostic and treatment techniques mentioned above are employed in dealing with clients with personality disorders; however, it is recognized that success will be slower, may be more limited, and will require special efforts. In particular, greater concentration on building a positive therapist–client relationship is recommended, including increased emphasis on developing a spirit of collaboration, and expansion of the role that transference reactions play in the therapy process (Beck et al., 1990). Other specialized techniques for modification of dysfunctional schemas (belief systems) in personality-disordered clients include increased attention to the role of early childhood experiences in the development of the schemas; the use of imagery to re-experience prior traumatic events; and the use of daily diaries to record events that run counter to strongly held dysfunctional beliefs.

BEHAVIORAL TECHNIQUES IN COGNITIVE THERAPY

Various behavioral techniques are employed in cognitive therapy (Beck et al., 1979). Behavioral techniques are used primarily in the early stages of treatment; they are particularly helpful with more severely depressed clients who are less able to view their thoughts objectively. Although one immediate purpose of the behavioral techniques is to alter various behavioral symptoms (e.g., avoidance, reduced activity levels), the ultimate goal is cognitive change. That is, the cognitive therapist uses behavioral change primarily as a method to identify and alter dysfunctional expectations.

For example, "mastery experiments" are designed to identify and modify the tendency of depressed persons to expect little success from engaging in various tasks. A client and therapist plan activities for the client to engage in during the week. The activity scheduling is presented in part as a data-gathering exercise, to test whether the client's negative expectations are

accurate. Thus, prior to scheduling an activity, the client is asked to make a prediction about how much success he/she expects to attain. After completing the task, the client records the degree of success actually obtained. Because depressed clients often underestimate their actual performance, this "miniexperiment" helps to demonstrate and alter the tendency to make unrealistically negative expectations about future events. In addition, clients begin to see the role that negative expectations play in affecting their motivation.

Sometimes, however, a depressed person's negative expectation will be accurate. That is, activities will result in total failure and no change in mood (or, in some cases, more negative mood). In this situation, it is necessary for the therapist to help the client identify the various dysfunctional cognitions that are associated with the activity and that are responsible for induction of the negative mood.

Other behavioral techniques utilized in cognitive therapy are listed below:

1. *Weekly activity schedule.* This technique involves having clients monitor their daily activities on an hour-by-hour basis. Such monitoring helps depressed clients test their beliefs that they "never accomplish anything." Ratings of mastery and pleasure are used in conjunction with the activity schedule. These ratings force a client to attend to any degree of reward experienced. If the client does indeed remain inactive throughout the week, the therapist and client collaboratively schedule activities on an hour-by-hour basis for each day of the week. This technique is especially useful for suicidal clients and serves to counter a loss of motivation, inactivity, and rumination or worrying. Engaging in activities is often therapeutic simply because it distracts a depressed person from depressogenic thinking (Morrow & Nolen-Hoeksema, 1990; Teasdale & Rezin, 1978).

2. *Graded task assignments.* This behavioral technique involves three steps. First, the client and therapist identify a goal that the client wishes to attain but believes to be impossible. Second, the goal is broken down into simple component tasks. Third, the client is assigned one of these tasks that is highly likely to provide immediate and unambiguous successful feedback. This technique is designed to counter negative expectations and to alter the way in which the client conceptualizes future tasks, so that they no longer seem insurmountable.

RESEARCH BEARING ON THE VALIDITY OF THE COGNITIVE THEORY OF DEPRESSION AND THE EFFICACY OF COGNITIVE THERAPY

The cognitive theory of depression and the treatment developed from the theory have received considerable attention from researchers (see reviews by Dobson, 1989; Haaga et al., 1991; Hollon & Najavits, 1988; Hollon et al., 1993; Whisman, 1993). In 1979, Beck et al. noted that recent reviews (Beck & Rush, 1978; Hollon & Beck, 1979) had cited over 35 correlational and experimental studies supporting hypotheses derived from cognitive theory. In 1985, Ernst reported 200 supportive studies. Since then, many more studies relevant to the cognitive theory have been published. This large body of data can be conveniently broken down into three general areas: studies correlating depression level with relevant cognitive variables; studies providing evidence that the symptoms of depression occur primarily as a consequence of a negative thinking; and, finally, studies reporting on the efficacy of cognitive therapy interventions. The present review is not intended to be entirely comprehensive or to serve as a critical review of this area. Rather, the purpose here is to provide the reader with an overview of the empirical literature related to the cognitive theory and therapy of depression.

Correlational Studies

Correlational studies are clearly the most prolific of those published in support of the cognitive model. Numerous studies have reported significant covariation between level of depression and a variety of response categories reflective of the cognitive processes described by the cognitive theory. For convenience of presentation, the correlational studies are categorized according to the particular aspects of the cognitive theory upon which they reflect: the negative view of the self; the negative view of the future; the negative view of the world/experience; and general cognitive processes and content. It is important to note, however, that often the focus of a particular study or a particular measure does not fit unequivocally into one of the categories used here. Thus, in some instances, the categorization of a study has been somewhat arbitrarily determined.

Negative View of the Self

Numerous studies provide evidence that depressed persons view themselves more negatively than do nondepressed persons. Measurement of self-esteem provides a direct assessment of this aspect of the cognitive triad. As predicted, depressed persons score significantly lower than nondepressed individuals on a variety of measures of self-esteem (e.g., Beck, 1974; Feather & Barber, 1983; Karoly & Ruehlman, 1983; Lewinsohn, Larson, & Munoz, 1982; Sacco & Hokanson, 1978). A similar relationship has been found between self-esteem and childhood and adolescent depression (Kazdin, French, Unis, Esveldt-Dawson, & Sherick, 1983; McCauley, Mitchell, Burke, & Moss, 1988). Other studies have found that depression level is significantly related to feelings of guilt, helplessness, and lower confidence (Cofer & Wittenborn, 1980; Peterson, 1979); less perceived ability to deal with sources of stress (Hammen & DeMayo, 1982); less perceived control and fewer perceived accomplishments (Warren & McEachren, 1983); more negative and fewer positive and self-descriptive adjectives (e.g., Dobson & Shaw, 1987); judgments of being less self-efficacious in interpersonal functioning (Kanfer & Zeiss, 1983); and the tendency to generalize a single failure to a more generally negative view of other aspects of the self (Carver & Ganellen, 1983). The last-mentioned finding also provides direct support for Beck's (1976) assertion that depressives are likely to commit the cognitive distortion of overgeneralization. Finally, studies by Davis and Unruh (1981) and Derry and Kuiper (1981) provide evidence of an organized negative self-schema in long-term depressed clients.

Negative View of the Future

According to the cognitive model, the depressed person expects failure, dissatisfaction, and indefinite continuation of current difficulties. A number of studies have provided evidence in support of this aspect of the theory. Several studies have found depression scores to be significantly related to self-report measures of hopelessness (Beck, 1974; Beck, Kovacs, & Weissman, 1975; Dohr, Rush & Bernstein, 1989; Fibel & Hale, 1978; Karoly & Ruehlman, 1983; Layne, Lefton, Walters, & Merry, 1983). Kazdin et al. (1983) also found childhood depression to be related to scores on a modification of the adult Hopelessness Scale (Beck, Weissman, Lester, & Trexler, 1974). Depressed persons have been found to have more negative expectancies for self-relevant future events, but not for future events pertaining to the world (Lewinsohn et al., 1982). Depression level has also been related to lower expectancies for achievement and affection (Gurtman, 1981); lower expectations of satisfaction from planned pleasant activities (Sacco, 1985); and lower expectations for success on a skill task (Lobitz & Post, 1979).

Negative View of the World/Experience

The third component of the negative cognitive triad postulated by Beck (1974) is that depressed individuals tend to view their experiences in the world negatively. Various studies of cognitions about experience have indeed found depression level to be significantly correlated with more negative perceptions. Depressed persons view significant others in a more negative manner than do nondepressed persons. Specifically, more negative ratings of parents (Blatt, Wein, Chevron, & Quinlan, 1979) and of friends and family (Karoly & Ruehlman, 1983) have been related to depression level. Rogers and Forehand (1983) found that the depression level of mothers of clinic-referred children was related to perceptions of greater child maladjustment, despite the fact that objective raters were unable to distinguish the children of depressed mothers from those of nondepressed mothers on levels of compliance and deviant behavior.

Depressed individuals cognitively process their task performance in a more negative manner. Depressed subjects underestimate the amount of reinforcement they have received (DeMonbreun & Craighead, 1977; Dobson & Shaw, 1981; Nelson & Craighead, 1977; Wener & Rehm, 1975); recall fewer self-rewards and more self-punishments than are objectively the case (Gotlib, 1981); and recall more uncompleted tasks than completed tasks (Johnson, Petzel, Hartney, & Morgan, 1983). Sacco and Graves (1984) found that depression level in children was related to lower satisfaction with interpersonal problem-solving performance.

Finally, depressed individuals recall experiences with negatively toned content more easily and readily than material of a more positive nature (Lishman, 1972; Lloyd & Lishman, 1975), and attribute negative events in their lives to more internal, stable, and global causes (see Sweeney, Anderson, & Bailey, 1986, for a review). Taken together, these studies provide strong evidence that depression is related to more negative perceptions of experiences in the world.

Other Cognitive Processes and Content

Cognitive distortions and biases are considered central mechanisms explaining the development and maintenance of negative cognitions despite contradictory evidence. Several studies have provided evidence that depressed persons exhibit evidence of negative cognitive distortions (Blaney, Behar, & Head, 1980; Krantz & Hammen, 1979; Lefebvre, 1981; Norman, Miller, & Klee, 1983). In their review, Haaga et al. (1991) report various studies indicating that depressed persons engage in negatively biased information processing, including biased recognition memory, biased recall of events, and biased manipulation of information (e.g., reaching unwarranted negative conclusions).

Along these lines, it should be noted that much discussion has been made of the hypothesis that depressed people, though more negative than nondepressed people, are in fact more realistic in their appraisals of reality (see reviews by Ackerman & DeRubeis, 1991; Dobson & Franche, 1989). Data in support of this conjecture are inconsistent (e.g., Dunning & Story, 1991), with some studies suggesting that greater "realism" by depressed people occurs only when the "correct" answer happens to match the preexisting beliefs of the depressed group (Dykman, Abramson, Alloy, & Hartlage, 1989). The notion that the depressed are more realistic can also be questioned on conceptual grounds. This account appears to imply that the greater the depression, the more realistic the perception—a proposition that, on the basis of clinical observation, seems implausible. Rather, it seems more reasonable to argue that the positivity or negativity of cognitive schemas varies with level of depression–elation; extreme examples may be seen in the expansiveness and grandiosity of individuals in a manic state and the extremely negatively biased views of clinically depressed individuals (Beck, 1991; Sacco, 1985).

The Automatic Thoughts Questionnaire was designed to measure the extent to which people experience negative cognitions (Hollon & Kendall, 1980). Cross-validation studies show that depressed persons report experiencing more negative cognitions than nondepressed persons (Dobson & Breiter, 1983; Hollon & Kendall, 1980). Moreover, recent studies also support the contention that negative thinking in depressed people is indeed automatic, as predicted by the cognitive theory (e.g., Bargh & Tota, 1988).

Several studies have demonstrated that depressed persons possess more dysfunctional attitudes, which directly correspond to what the cognitive model terms "silent assumptions" (Hamilton & Abramson, 1983; Lapointe & Crandell, 1980; Nelson, 1977; O'Hara, Rehm, & Campbell, 1982; Weissman & Beck, 1978).

Finally, recent work has also demonstrated support for two additional features of the theory—universality and cognitive specificity. Evidence of the negative cognitive triad has been found among all clinical types and subtypes of depression (e.g., endogenous and exogenous, unipolar and bipolar), supporting the universality hypothesis (e.g., Hollon, Kendall, & Lumry, 1986). The cognitive specificity hypothesis posits that although negative thinking may occur in all emotional disorders, the cognitions of the depressed are distinct in form and content. In support of this hypothesis, several studies provide evidence that the thought content of individuals who exhibit primarily depressed symptoms, as opposed to nondepressive psychiatric problems (e.g., anxiety disorders), is centered around themes such as loss and hopelessness (e.g., Beck, Brown, Steer, Eidelson, & Riskind, 1987; Clark, Beck, & Stewart, 1990; Greenberg & Beck, 1989).

Causal Evidence

The large number of studies reported above provide convincing evidence that depressed persons engage in the negative cognitive processes described by the cognitive theory. According to the cognitive theory, the negative processing of information is the factor primarily responsible for the *immediate* onset, maintenance, and exacerbation of the affective, motivational, somatic, and behavioral symptoms associated with depression. The more distal (predisposing) causal factor (for reactive depression only) is the early development of negative cognitive schemas and of a corresponding maladaptive belief system; these make individuals vulnerable to depression, particularly if certain stressors to which they are sensitized occur.

Although the correlational evidence above is consistent with these contentions, it is still plausible that negative cognitions and maladaptive beliefs occur simply as a result of the other symptoms of depression. This following section thus describes studies providing support for the notion that negative cognitive processes are causally related to the development, maintenance, and worsening of depression.

The use of experimental designs in which subjects are induced to alter cognitive content is a common methodology employed to test the role of cognition as a causal agent in the development and maintenance of depressive symptoms. The Velten Mood Induction Procedure (VMIP; Velten, 1968) has been by far the most popular procedure in this area. Velten (1968) reported that when subjects were asked to read and "try to feel the mood suggested by" statements with depressed, elated, or neutral content, mood-relevant responses were altered in the expected directions. Since then, the effects of this experimental manipulation have been replicated and extended.

Numerous studies utilizing the VMIP, or variations thereof, have related the experimental induction of negative versus positive thought content to a variety of dependent variables relevant to the cognitive theory. These include self-reported level of dysphoric mood (e.g., Natale, 1977a, 1977b; Riskind, Rholes, & Eggers, 1982; Rush, Weissenburger, & Eaves, 1986; Teasdale & Bancroft, 1977); physiological responses such as heart rate and galvanic skin response (e.g., Rogers & Craighead, 1977; Russell & Brandsma, 1974; Schuele & Wiesenfeld, 1983; Teasdale & Bancroft, 1977); and behaviors such as speech rate (Natale, 1977a; Teasdale & Fogerty, 1979), gaze behavior (Natale, 1977b), writing speed (Alloy & Abramson, 1981), and anagram performance (Raps, Reinhard, & Seligman, 1980; Miller & Norman, 1981). Inductions of negative thought content have also been related to various other dependent variables that reflect depressive responding, including more rapid retrieval of unpleasant memories relative to pleasant memories (Teasdale & Fogerty, 1979), decreased ratings of the enjoyability of pleasant events (Carson & Adams, 1980), self-reports of increased desire for social withdrawal (Wilson & Krane, 1980), decreased perceptions of control (Alloy & Abramson, 1981), and lower expectancies for success (Miller & Norman, 1981). Thus, these studies examining the experimental manipulation of thought content support the notion that the negative cognitive "shift" said to occur in depression can lead to other symptoms of depression.

The role of cognitions as causally related to the dysphoria found in depression is also supported by two novel studies employing interactions between therapist and client. In a case report of a single subject, Peterson, Luborsky, and Seligman (1983) found that attributions in therapy sessions predicted mood swings as measured by the symptom context method. Teasdale and Fennell (1982) used a within-subjects design and systematically varied whether the therapist attempted to change depressive thoughts or simply explored the depressive thought of chronically depressed clients. Consistent with cognitive theory, modification of depressive thinking was consistently accompanied by reductions in self-reported depressed mood, while thought exploration produced minimal reduction. These data are consistent with the work of Teasdale and his colleagues, who have shown that the mood of depressed clients deteriorates when they are instructed to think thoughts with a negative content (Teasdale & Bancroft, 1977) and improves when they are sufficiently distracted to reduce the frequency of their negative thoughts (Teasdale & Rezin, 1978).

A second group of studies attempting to evaluate the causal relationship between cognitive content and depression has utilized designs in which cognitive content at one point in time is correlated with future depression level. These studies still utilize correlational data, and therefore are weaker than those that employ experimental manipulations. However, they do provide further evidence bearing on the validity of the cognitive theory of depression. Hammen, Krantz, and Cochran (1981) found support for the notion that cognitive appraisals of stressful events mediate the development of depression. Perceptions of low controllability (the belief that the event would affect other areas of a person's life) were predictive of later depression. Similarly, Golin, Sweeney, and Shaeffer (1981) used a cross-lagged panel correlational analysis to assess the possible causal role of attributional style in depression. Their results indicated that global and stable attributions for failure were causally related to subsequent depression level.

The cognitive theory considers that dysfunctional attitudes best reflect the negative cognitive schemas that predispose a person to reac-

tive depression. The theory does state, however, that these schemas may remain latent until activated by stressors to which the individual is sensitive. Thus, it is perhaps not surprising to find a number of studies indicating that, when assessed during symptom-free periods, depression-prone persons do not show evidence of more dysfunctional attitudes (e.g., Barnett & Gotlib, 1988). On the other hand, several studies have shown that asymptomatic depression-prone individuals exhibit more dysfunctional beliefs if they are experiencing a depressed mood (not a depressive disorder) at the time of measurement or if the measurement follows a stressful life event (Miranda & Persons, 1988, 1991; Miranda et al., 1990). These studies thus can be interpreted as supporting the cognitive theory's proposition that dysfunctional attitudes constitute a diathesis for a depressive disorder that will remain latent until activated by stressful events.

Several studies have also attempted to demonstrate that depression-prone persons differ with respect to the types of stressful events that will induce a depressive reaction (i.e., sociotropic and autonomous subtypes). These studies have provided mixed support (see Haaga et al., 1991). In two separate studies, congruence between specific vulnerability and stressful events has been found to predict later depression only for those high in autonomy (Hammen, Ellicott, & Gitlin, 1989) or only for those high in sociotropy (Segal, Shaw, & Vella, 1989). Beck (1991) has suggested that future tests of the specific-vulnerability hypothesis assess sociotropic and autonomous dysfunctional beliefs, using priming techniques such as those described by Miranda and Persons (1988).

Efficacy of Cognitive Therapy for Depression

Our prior review of controlled outcome studies yielded substantial support for the effectiveness of cognitive therapy as a treatment for unipolar depression (Sacco & Beck, 1985). Since then, considerable advances in the evaluation of treatments for depression have occurred. Numerous additional controlled outcome studies have been conducted, prompting additional critical reviews, including meta-analyses to compare effect size differences among various psychological and pharmacological treatments for depression (Dobson, 1989; Robinson et al., 1990; Svartberg & Torac, 1991). Meta-analyses provide a quantitative summary of a large number of outcome studies and thus allow a more objective and precise analysis of treatment effects. In addition, the National Institute of Mental Health (NIMH) has supported a large-scale, multisite evaluation of both the short-term and long-term effectiveness of cognitive, interpersonal (Klerman, Weissman, Rounsaville, & Chevron, 1984), and pharmacological therapies for depression (Elkin et al., 1989; Shea et al., 1992).

It must be noted, however, that although most of the cognitive interventions evaluated in these reviews were based upon Beck's (1967, 1976) cognitive theory of depression, the actual cognitive therapeutic strategies employed in "cognitive" treatments may differ in many ways from one another and from those explicitly prescribed by Beck et al. (1979) in their manual for cognitive therapy of depression. Thus, the reader should be aware that common use of the term "cognitive therapy" does not necessarily imply uniformity in procedures. Also lending confusion to this area is use of the terms "cognitive therapy" and "cognitive–behavioral therapy." The therapy described by Beck et al. (1979) involves the use of both cognitive and behavioral techniques, and thus could be accurately labeled "cognitive–behavioral"; however, in the literature both terms have been applied in describing the Beck et al. (1979) procedures, with more recent articles utilizing the term "cognitive therapy."

A summary of the literature can be presented in terms of two critical questions: (1) Is cognitive therapy an effective treatment for depression? (2) Is cognitive therapy more effective than other forms of psychotherapy or pharmacological therapies? Because depression is often a recurring problem (Keller et al., 1984), any therapy should be evaluated with respect to short-term reduction in symptoms, as well as its effectiveness in reducing relapse rates.

There is overwhelming evidence that cognitive therapy is an effective treatment for depression. Numerous reviews, including several meta-analyses, indicate that cognitive therapy reduces the level of depressive symptoms substantially faster than would occur without treatment (e.g., Dobson, 1989; Hollon & Najavits, 1988; Hollon et al., 1993; Robinson et al., 1990). In general, the reduction in symptoms is substantial. Typically, depression scores fall by about 65–70% from an average pretest level of moderate to severe depression (e.g., BDI score

of 30) (e.g., Beck, Hollon, Young, Bedrosian, & Budenz, 1985).

Meta-analytic reviews of evidence bearing on the relative superiority of cognitive therapy over other treatment modalities also tend to be supportive. Dobson's (1989) meta-analysis (based upon 28 studies from 1976 to 1987) indicated that on the basis of self-reported symptoms of depression, cognitive therapy was superior to behavior therapy, a heterogeneous group of other forms of psychotherapy, and pharmacotherapy. Robinson et al.'s (1990) meta-analysis of treatments for depression revealed that cognitive therapy was superior to general verbal therapies, and that cognitive–behavioral therapy was superior to behavioral therapy alone. A meta-analysis designed to evaluate the effectiveness of short-term psychodynamic psychotherapies concluded that for major depression, short-term psychodynamic psychotherapies were particularly *inferior* to cognitive–behavioral therapy (Svartberg & Torac, 1991).

Other data bearing on the issue of relative superiority come from a qualitative review by Hollon et al. (1991) and from the NIMH multisite outcome study (Elkin et al., 1989; Shea et al., 1992). Hollon et al. (1991) reviewed the literature bearing on the relative effectiveness of cognitive therapy versus pharmacotherapy for depression. They concluded (1) that cognitive therapy is neither more nor less effective than antidepressant medication in the short-term reduction of depressive symptoms; (2) that the available evidence does not yet indicate that combining antidepressant medication with cognitive therapy improves the efficacy of either treatment, though sufficient evidence warrants further evaluation of this question; and (3) that cognitive therapy appears to have a relative advantage over pharmacotherapy in protecting clients from subsequent relapse.

The NIMH multisite evaluation of the effectiveness of cognitive, interpersonal, and pharmacological therapies for depression indicated that for short-term reduction of symptoms, cognitive therapy is roughly equivalent to the other treatments (Elkin et al., 1989). However, follow-up data suggest that cognitive therapy has an advantage over the other treatments with respect to the need for further treatment and greater number of symptom-free weeks (Shea et al., 1992). In summary, evidence of the relative superiority of cognitive therapy for the short-term reduction of symptoms tends to be supportive (though not uniformly so), and evidence that cognitive therapy is more effective than other therapies with respect to long-term outcome is beginning to accumulate (see also Hollon et al., 1993; Munoz, Hollon, McGrath, Rehm, & VandenBos, 1994).

VARIABLES RELATED TO EFFECTIVENESS OF COGNITIVE THERAPY

A growing number of studies have investigated which therapy conditions, therapist behaviors, and client characteristics predict optimal effectiveness of cognitive therapy for depression (Whisman, 1993).

Group versus Individual Therapy

Early (albeit methodologically flawed) studies indicated that group cognitive therapy was more effective than no treatment, but somewhat less effective than individual therapy (e.g., Rush & Watkins, 1981; Shaw & Hollon, 1978). However, recent studies provide mixed findings. Two studies reported by Scott and Stradling (1990) found that group cognitive therapy was *not* less effective than individual cognitive therapy. In contrast, two other studies have suggested that group therapy produces attenuated effects relative to individual therapy (Wierzbicki & Bartlett, 1987). Clearly, more research is needed to determine whether, and under what conditions, group therapy will be as effective as individual therapy (cf. Robinson et al., 1990).

Inpatient Treatment

Few studies have examined cognitive therapy with inpatients. Two studies compared the addition of cognitive therapy versus other psychological treatments to standard pharmacological therapy (Bowers, 1990; Miller, Norman, & Keitner, 1989). Both studies indicated that all treatments were equally effective in the short-term reduction of symptoms, although Miller et al. (1989) also found that the addition of cognitive therapy (or social skills training) to drug therapy resulted in lower relapse rates than occurred with drug therapy alone. Consistent with this finding, Whisman, Miller, Norman, and Keitner (1991) found that, compared with standard drug and milieu therapy, the addition of cognitive therapy led to less hopelessness and fewer cognitive biases at 6- and 12-month

follow-up and to fewer dysfunctional attitudes at 6-month follow-up. Thase, Bowler, and Harden (1991) administered "intensive" cognitive–behavioral therapy (five sessions per week; average of 13 total sessions) to 16 *unmedicated* endogenous depressive inpatients. Thirteen patients (81%) showed definite improvement, defined as at least a 50% reduction in Hamilton Rating Scale for Depression (Hamilton, 1960) scores, *and* a final score of 10 or less on the this scale. Their evidence also indicated that continued cognitive–behavioral therapy after discharge may be necessary to maintain the reduction of symptoms.

Homework

As noted above, between-session homework assignments are an integral part of cognitive therapy. A recent study demonstrated improved response to treatment (i.e., greater reduction in symptoms) when homework was included as part of cognitive therapy (Neimeyer & Feixas, 1990). In addition, clients who respond favorably to initial homework assignments (Fennell & Teasdale, 1987), and who actually comply with homework assignments (Burns & Nolen-Hoeksema, 1991; Persons et al., 1988), show greater treatment gains.

Therapist Behaviors

DeRubeis and Feeley (1990) examined the relative contribution of the patient–therapist relationship, facilitative conditions (warmth, empathy, etc.), and therapist adherence to cognitive therapy methods to the success of cognitive therapy. Cognitive therapy methods were identified in the study as either "concrete," symptom-focused methods or "abstract" discussions. Only adherence to "concrete" methods (e.g., therapist asked clients to report and record thoughts, reviewed homework, examined evidence concerning beliefs) predicted subsequent symptom reduction when assessed early in treatment. This result is consistent with the finding that skill acquisition in completing core cognitive restructuring techniques predicted self-rated maintenance of treatment gains at follow-up (Neimeyer & Feixas, 1990). Therapist adherence to cognitive therapy methods has also been found to predict the degree to which clients' dysfunctional thinking was reduced in therapy, which in turn predicted degree of improvement in depressive symptoms (Evans,

Hollon, & DeRubeis, 1985). Degree of adherence was not, however, directly related to symptom reduction.

Client Variables

Although one might expect pharmacological therapy to be more effective than cognitive therapy with endogenous depression (relative to reactive depression), that has not proven to be the case. Cognitive therapy has generally been found to be equally effective for both endogenous and reactive depression (Hollon & Najavits, 1988; Thase et al., 1991; Whisman, 1993). Endogenous symptoms and having a personality disorder have, however, both been found to predict premature termination of cognitive therapy (Persons et al., 1988). Willingness to learn new coping strategies (Burns & Nolen-Hoeksema, 1991), high self-control (Simons, Lustman, Wetzel, & Murphy, 1985), endorsement of the cognitive conceptualization of depression, and feeling depressed about having depressive symptoms (Fennell & Teasdale, 1987) have also been found to predict improved response to cognitive treatments. Simons et al. (1985) also found that high-self-control subjects responded better than low-self-control subjects to cognitive therapy, and that the opposite pattern occurred for drug treatment.

CONCLUSION

In the last 30 years, the cognitive theory of depression has met numerous criteria by which any scientific theory should be evaluated. The theory explains in a parsimonious manner the development and maintenance of depression—a significant and pervasive problem in our society. The theory has heuristic value and is testable, as is evidenced by the very large number of studies conducted to test hypotheses derived from the cognitive theory and by the extent to which the theory continues to generate research. Moreover, the cognitive theory has an excellent "batting average" with respect to the number of studies providing evidence consistent with its postulates, thus providing support for the empirical validity of the theory. Finally, the cognitive theory has utility. The theory has led to a clearly articulated set of operations, which, based upon the results of a relatively large number of outcome studies, appears to constitute a very effective treatment for unipolar depression.

REFERENCES

Abramson, L. Y., Seligman, M. E. P., & Teasdale, J. D. (1978). Learned helplessness in humans: Critique and reformulation. *Journal of Abnormal Psychology, 87,* 102–109.

Ackerman, R., & DeRubeis, R. (1991). Is depressive realism real? *Clinical Psychology Review, 11,* 565–584.

Alloy, L. B., & Abramson, L. Y. (1981). Induced mood and the illusion of control. *Journal of Personality and Social Psychology, 41,* 1129–1140.

Bargh, J. A., & Tota, M. E. (1988). Context-dependent automatic processing in depression: Accessibility of negative constructs with regard to self but not others. *Journal of Personality and Social Psychology, 54,* 925–939.

Barnett, P. A., & Gotlib, I. H. (1988). Psychosocial functioning and depression: Distinguishing among antecedents, concomitants, and consequences. *Psychological Bulletin, 104,* 97–126.

Beck, A. T. (1961). A systematic investigation of depression. *Comprehensive Psychiatry, 2,* 163–170.

Beck, A. T. (1963). Thinking and depression: 1. Idiosyncratic content and cognitive distortions. *Archives of General Psychiatry, 9,* 324–333.

Beck, A. T. (1967). *Depression: Clinical, experimental, and theoretical aspects.* New York: Harper & Row.

Beck, A. T. (1974). The development of depression: A cognitive model. In R. Friedman & M. Katz (Eds.), *Psychology of depression: Contemporary theory and research* (pp. 3–28). Washington, DC: Winston/Wiley.

Beck, A. T. (1976). *Cognitive theory and the emotional disorders.* New York: International Universities Press.

Beck, A. T. (1983). Cognitive therapy of depression: New perspectives. In P. J. Clayton & J. E. Barrett (Eds.), *Treatment of depression: Old controversies and new approaches* (pp. 265–284). New York: Raven Press.

Beck, A. T. (1988). *Love is never enough.* New York: Harper & Row.

Beck, A. T. (1991). Cognitive therapy: A 30-year retrospective. *American Psychologist, 46,* 368–375.

Beck, A. T., Brown, G., Steer, R. A., Eidelson, J. K., & Riskind, J. H. (1987). Differentiating anxiety and depression: A test of the cognitive content-specificity hypothesis. *Journal of Abnormal Psychology, 96,* 179–183.

Beck, A. T., & Emery, G., with Greenberg, R. L. (1985). *Anxiety disorders and phobias: A cognitive perspective.* New York: Basic Books.

Beck, A. T., Freeman, A., & Associates. (1990). *Cognitive therapy of personality disorders.* New York: Guilford Press.

Beck, A. T., & Greenberg, R. I. (1974). *Coping with depression.* New York: Institute for Rational Living.

Beck, A. T., Hollon, S. D., Young, J. E., Bedrosian, R. C., & Budenz, D. (1985). Treatment of depression with cognitive therapy and amitriptyline. *Archives of General Psychiatry, 42,* 142–148.

Beck, A. T., Kovacs, M., & Weissman, A. (1975). Hopelessness and suicidal behavior: An overview. *Journal of the American Medical Association, 234,* 1146–1149.

Beck, A. T., & Rush, A. J. (1978). Cognitive approaches to depression and suicide. In G. Serban (Ed.), *Cognitive defects in the development of mental illness* (pp. 235–257). New York: Brunner/Mazel.

Beck, A. T., Rush, A. J., Shaw, B. F., & Emery, G. (1979). *Cognitive therapy of depression.* New York: Guilford Press.

Beck, A. T., & Ward, C. H. (1961). Dreams of depressed patients: Characteristic themes in manifest content. *Archives of General Psychiatry, 5,* 462–571.

Beck, A. T., Weissman, A., Lester, D., & Trexler, L. (1974). The measurement of pessimism: The Hopelessness Scale. *Journal of Consulting and Clinical Psychology, 42,* 861–865.

Bedrosian, R. C. (1981). The application of cognitive therapy techniques with adolescents. In G. Emery, S. D. Hollon, & R. C. Bedrosian (Eds.), *New directions in cognitive therapy* (pp. 63–83). New York: Guilford Press.

Blaney, P. H., Behar, V., & Head, R. (1980). Two measures of depressive cognitions: Their association with depression and with each other. *Journal of Abnormal Psychology, 89,* 678–682.

Blatt, S. J., Wein, S. J., Chevron, E., & Quinlan, D. M. (1979). Parental representations and depression in normal young adults. *Journal of Abnormal Psychology, 88,* 388–397.

Bowers, W. A. (1990). Treatment of depressed in-patients: Cognitive therapy plus medication, relaxatioin plus medication, and medication alone. *British Journal of Psychiatry, 156,* 73–78.

Burns, D. D. (1980). *Feeling good: The new mood therapy.* New York: Signet.

Burns, D. D., & Nolen-Hoeksema, S. (1991). Coping styles, homework compliance, and the effectiveness of cognitive–behavioral therapy. *Journal of Consulting and Clinical Psychology, 59,* 305–311.

Burns, D. D., & Nolen-Hoeksema, S. (1992). Therapeutic empathy and recovery from depression in cognitive-behavioral therapy: A structural equation model. *Journal of Consulting and Clinical Psychology, 60,* 441–449.

Carson, T. P., & Adams, H. E. (1980). Activity valence as a function of mood change. *Journal of Abnormal Psychology, 89,* 368–377.

Carver, C. S., & Ganellen, R. J. (1983). Depression and components of self-punitiveness: High standards, self-criticism, and overgeneralization. *Journal of Consulting and Clinical Psychology, 92,* 330–337.

Clark, D. A., Beck, A. T., & Stewart, B. (1990). Cognitive specificity and positive–negative affectivity: Complimentary or contradictory views on anxiety and depression? *Journal of Abnormal Psychology, 99,* 148–155.

Cofer, D. H., & Wittenborn, J. R. (1980). Personality characteristics of formerly depressed women. *Journal of Abnormal Psychology, 89,* 309–314.

Coyne, J. C. (1976). Depression and the response of others. *Journal of Abnormal Psychology, 85,* 186–193.

Davis, H., & Unruh, W. R. (1981). The development of the self-schema in adult depression. *Journal of Abnormal Psychology, 90,* 125–133.

DeMonbreun, B. G., & Craighead, W. E. (1977). Distortion of perception and recall of positive and neutral feedback in depression. *Cognitive Therapy and Research, 1,* 311–330.

Derry, P. A., & Kuiper, N. A. (1981). Schematic processing and self-reference in clinical depression. *Journal of Abnormal Psychology, 90,* 286–297.

DeRubeis, R. J., & Feeley, M. (1990). Determinants of change in cognitive therapy for depression. *Cognitive Therapy and Research, 14,* 469–482.

Dobson, K. S. (1989). A meta-analysis of the efficacy of cognitive therapy for depression. *Journal of Consulting and Clinical Psychology, 57,* 414–419.

Dobson, K. S., & Breiter, H. J. (1983). Cognitive assessment of depression: Reliability and validity of three measures. *Journal of Abnormal Psychology, 92,* 107–109.

Dobson, K. S., & Franche, R. (1989). A conceptual and empirical review of the depressive realism hypothesis. *Canadian Journal of Behavioural Science, 21,* 419–433.

Dobson, K. S., & Shaw, B. F. (1981). The effects of self-correction on cognitive distortions in depression. *Cognitive Therapy and Research, 5,* 391–404.

Dobson, K. S., & Shaw, B. F. (1987). Specificity and stability of self-referent encoding in clinical depression. *Journal of Abnormal Psychology, 96,* 34–40.

Dohr, K. B., Rush, A. J., & Bernstein, I. H. (1989). Cognitive biases and depression. *Journal of Abnormal Psychology, 98,* 263–267.

Dunning, D., & Story, A. L. (1991). Depression, realism, and the overconfidence effect: Are the sadder wiser when predicting future actions and events? *Journal of Personality and Social Psychology, 61,* 521–532.

Dykman, B. M., Abramson, L. Y., Alloy, L. B., & Hartlage, S. (1989). Processing of ambiguous and unambiguous feedback by depressed and nondepressed college students: Schematic biases and their implications for depressive realism. *Journal of Personality and Social Psychology, 56,* 431–445.

Eaves, G., & Rush, A. J. (1984). Cognitive patterns in symptomatic and remitted unipolar major depression. *Journal of Abnormal Psychology, 93,* 31–40.

Elkin, I., Shea, T., Watkins, J., Imber, S. D., Sotsky, S. M., Collins, J. F., Glass, D. R., Pilkonis, P. A., Leber, W. R., Docherty, J. P., Fiester, S. J., & Parloff, M. B. (1989). NIMH Treatment of Depression Collaborative Research Program: 1. General effectiveness of treatments. *Archives of General Psychiatry, 46,* 971–982.

Ernst, D. (1985). *Beck's cognitive theory of depression: A status report.* Unpublished manuscript, University of Pennsylvania.

Evans, M. D., Hollon, S. D., & DeRubeis, R. D. (1985, November). *Accounting for relapse in a treatment outcome study of depression.* Paper presented at the annual meeting of the Association for Advancement of Behavior Therapy, Houston.

Feather, N. T., & Barber, J. G. (1983). Depressive reactions and unemployment. *Journal of Abnormal Psychology, 92,* 185–195.

Fennell, M. J. V., Teasdale, J. D. (1987). Cognitive therapy for depression: Individual differences and the process of change. *Cognitive Therapy and Research, 11,* 253–271.

Forsterling, F. (1985). Attributional retraining: A review. *Psychological Bulletin, 98,* 495–512.

Fibel, B., & Hale, W. D. (1978). The Generalized Expectancy for Success Scale: A new measure. *Journal of Consulting and Clinical Psychology, 46,* 924–931.

Golin, S., Sweeney, P. D., & Shaeffer, D. E. (1981). The causality of causal attributions in depression: A cross-lagged panel correlational analysis. *Journal of Abnormal Psychology, 90,* 14–22.

Gotlib, I. H. (1981). Self-reinforcement and recall: Differential deficits in depressed and nondepressed psychiatric inpatients. *Journal of Abnormal Psychology, 90,* 521–530.

Greenberg, M. S., & Beck, A. T. (1989). Depression versus anxiety: A test of the content-specificity hypothesis. *Journal of Abnormal Psychology, 98,* 9–13.

Gurtman, M. B. (1981). The relationship of expectancies for need attainment to depression and hopelessness in college students. *Cognitive Therapy and Research, 5*, 313–316.

Haaga, D. A. F., Dyck, M. J., & Ernst, D. (1991). Empirical status of cognitive theory of depression. *Psychological Bulletin, 110*, 215–236.

Hamilton, E. W., & Abramson, L. Y. (1983). Cognitive patterns and major depressive disorder: A longitudinal study in a hospital setting. *Journal of Abnormal Psychology, 92*, 173–184.

Hamilton, M. (1960). A rating scale for depression. *Journal of Neurology, Neurosurgery and Psychiatry, 23*, 56–62.

Hammen, C., & DeMayo, R. (1982). Cognitive correlates of teacher stress and depressive symptoms: Implications for attributional models of depression. *Journal of Abnormal Psychology, 91*, 96–101.

Hammen, C., Ellicott, A., & Gitlin, M. (1989). Vulnerability to specific life events and prediction of course of disorder in unipolar depressed patients. *Canadian Journal of Behavioural Science, 21*, 377–388.

Hammen, C., Krantz, S. E., & Cochran, S. D. (1981). Relationships between depression and causal attributions about stressful life events. *Cognitive Therapy and Research, 5*, 351–358.

Hauri, P. (1976). Dreams in patients remitted from reactive depression. *Journal of Abnormal Psychology, 85*, 1–10.

Hollon, S. D., & Beck, A. T. (1979). Cognitive therapy of depression. In P. C. Kendall & S. D. Hollon (Eds.), *Cognitive–behavioral interventions: Theory, research, and procedures* (pp. 153–204). New York: Academic Press.

Hollon, S. D., & Garber, J. (1990). Cognitive therapy for depression: A social cognitive perspective. *Personality and Social Psychology Bulletin, 16*, 58–73.

Hollon, S. D., & Kendall, P. C. (1980). Cognitive self-statements in depression: Development of an Automatic Thoughts Questionnaire. *Cognitive Therapy and Research, 3*, 383–396.

Hollon, S. D., Kendall, P. C., & Lumry, A. (1986). Specificity of depressotypic cognitions in clinical depression. *Journal of Abnormal Psychology, 95*, 52–59.

Hollon, S. D., & Najavits, L. (1988). Review of empirical studies of cognitive therapy: In A. J. Frances & R. E. Hales (Eds.), *American Psychiatric Press review of psychiatry* (Vol. 7, pp. 643–666). Washington, DC: American Psychiatric Press.

Hollon, S. D., Shelton, R. C., & Loosen, P. T. (1991). Cognitive therapy and pharmacotherapy for depression. *Journal of Consulting and Clinical Psychology, 59*, 88–99.

Hollon, S. D., Shelton, R. C., & Davis, D. D. (1993). Cognitive therapy for depression: Conceptual issues and clinical efficacy. *Journal of Consulting and Clinical Psychology, 61*, 270–275.

Jenkins-Hall, K., & Sacco, W. P. (1991). Effect of client race and depression on evaluations by white therapists. *Journal of Social and Clinical Psychology, 10*, 322–333.

Johnson, J. E., Petzel, T. P., Hartney, L. M., & Morgan, R. A. (1983). Recall of importance ratings of completed and uncompleted tasks as a function of depression. *Cognitive Therapy and Research, 7*, 51–56.

Kanfer, R., & Zeiss, A. M. (1983). Depression, interpersonal standard setting, and judgments of self-efficacy. *Journal of Abnormal Psychology, 92*, 319–329.

Karoly, P., & Ruehlman, L. (1983). Affective meaning and depression: A semantic differential analysis. *Cognitive Therapy and Research, 7*, 41–50.

Kazdin, A. E., French, N. H., Unis, A. S., Esveldt-Dawson, K., & Sherick, R. B. (1983). Hopelessness, depression, and suicidal intent among psychiatrically disturbed inpatient children. *Journal of Consulting and Clinical Psychology, 51*, 504–510.

Keller, M. B., Klerman, G. L., Lavori, P. W., Coryell, W., Endicott, J., & Taylor, J. (1984). Long-term outcome of episodes of major depression. *Journal of the American Medical Association, 252*, 788–792.

Klerman, G. L., Weissman, M. M., Rounsaville, B. J., & Chevron, E. S. (1984). *Interpersonal psychotherapy of depression*. New York: Basic Books.

Kovacs, M. (1977, August). *Cognitive therapy of depression: Rationale and basic strategies*. Paper presented at the annual meeting of the American Psychological Association, San Francisco.

Krantz, S., & Hammen, C. (1979). Assessment of cognitive bias in depression. *Journal of Abnormal Psychology, 88*, 611–619.

Lapointe, K. A., & Crandell, C. J. (1980). Relationship of irrational beliefs to self-reported depression. *Cognitive Therapy and Research, 4*, 247–250.

Layne, C., Lefton, W., Walters,, D., & Merry, J. (1983). Depression: Motivational deficits versus social manipulation. *Cognitive Therapy and Research, 7*, 125–132.

Lefebvre, M. F. (1981). Cognitive distortion and cognitive errors in depressed psychiatric and low back pain patients. *Journal of Consulting and Clinical Psychology, 49*, 517–525.

Lewinsohn, P. M., Larson, D. W., & Munoz, R. F. (1982). The measurement of expectancies and other cognitions in depressed individuals. *Cognitive Therapy and Research, 6*, 437–446.

Lishman, W. A. (1972). Selective factors in memory: II. Affective disorders. *Psychological Medicine, 2*, 248–253.

Lloyd, G. G., & Lishman, W. A. (1975). Effect of depression on the speed of recall of pleasant and unpleasant experiences. *Psychological Medicine, 5*, 173–180.

Lobitz, C., & Post, D. (1979). Parameters of self-reinforcement and depression. *Journal of Abnormal Psychology, 88*, 33–41.

McCauley, E., Mitchell, J. R., Burke, P., & Moss, S. (1988). Cognitive attributes of depression in children and adolescents. *Journal of Consulting and Clinical Psychology, 56*, 903–908.

Miller, I. W., & Norman, W. H. (1981). Affects of attributions of success of alleviation of learned helplessness and depression. *Journal of Abnormal Psychology, 90*, 113–124.

Miller, I. W., Norman, W. H., & Keitner, G. I. (1989). Cognitive–bBehavioral treatment of depressed inpatients: Six- and twelve-month follow-up. *American Journal of Psychiatry, 146*, 1274–1279.

Miranda, J., & Persons, J. B. (1988). Dysfunctional attitudes are mood-state dependent. *Journal of Abnormal Psychology, 97*, 76–79.

Miranda, J., & Persons, J. B. (1991). *Implications of the mood-state hypothesis for studies of the process of cognitive therapy*. Paper presented at the annual meeting of the American Psychological Association, San Francisco.

Miranda, J., Persons, J. B., & Byers, C. N. (1990). Endorsement of dysfunctional beliefs depends on current mood state. *Journal of Abnormal Psychology, 99*, 237– 241.

Morrow, J., & Nolen-Hoeksema, S. (1990). Effects of responses to depression on the remediation of depressive affect. *Journal of Personality and Social Psychology, 58,* 519–527.

Munoz, R. F., Hollon, S. D., McGrath, E., Rehm, L. P., & VandenBos, G. R. (1994). On the AHCPR *Depression in Primary Care* guidelines: Further considerations for practitioners. *American Psychologist, 49,* 42–61.

Natale, M. (1977a). Effects of induced elation-depression on speech in the initial interview. *Journal of Consulting and Clinical Psychology, 45,* 45–52.

Natale, M. (1977b). Induction of mood states and their effect on gaze behavior. *Journal of Consulting and Clinical Psychology, 45,* 717–723.

Neimeyer, R. A., & Feixas, G. (1990). The role of homework and skill acquisition in the outcome of group cognitive therapy for depression. *Behavior Therapy, 21,* 281–292.

Nelson, R. E. (1977). Irrational beliefs in depression. *Journal of Consulting and Clinical Psychology, 45,* 1190–1191.

Nelson, R. E., & Craighead, W. E. (1977). Selective recall of positive and negative feedback, self-control behaviors, and depression. *Journal of Abnormal Psychology, 86,* 379–388.

Norman, W. H., Miller, I. W., & Klee, S. H. (1983). Assessment of cognitive distortion in a clinically depressed population. *Cognitive Therapy and Research, 7,* 133–140.

O'Hara, M. W., Rehm, L. P., & Campbell, S. B. (1982). Predicting depressive symptomatology: Cognitive-behavioral models and postpartum depression. *Journal of Abnormal Psychology, 91,* 457–461.

O'Leary, K. D., & Beach, S. R. H. (1990). Marital therapy: A viable treatment for depression and marital discord. *American Journal of Psychiatry, 147,* 183–186.

Paykel, E. S. (1979). Recent life events in the development of depressive disorders. In R. A. Depue (Ed.), *The psychobiology of the depressive disorders* (pp. 245–262). New York: Academic Press.

Persons, J. B., Burns, D. D., & Perloff, J. M. (1988). Predictors of dropout and outcome in cognitive therapy for depression in a private practice setting. *Cognitive Therapy and Research, 12,* 557–575.

Peterson, C. (1979). Uncontrollability and self-blame in depression: Investigation of the paradox in a college population. *Journal of Abnormal Psychology, 88,* 620–624.

Peterson, C., Luborsky, L., & Seligman, M. E. P. (1983). Attributions and depressive mood shifts: Case study using the symptom-context method. *Journal of Abnormal Psychology, 92,* 96–103.

Raps, C. S., Reinhard, K. E., & Seligman, M. E. P. (1980). Reversal of cognitive and affective deficits associated with depression and learned helplessness by mood elevation in patients. *Journal of Abnormal Psychology, 89,* 342–349.

Riskind, J. H., Rholes, W. S., & Eggers, J. (1982). The Velten Mood Induction Procedure: Effects on mood and memory. *Journal of Consulting and Clinical Psychology, 50,* 3–13.

Robinson, L. A., Berman, J. S., & Neimeyer, R. A. (1990). Psychotherapy for the treatment of depression: A comprehensive review of controlled outcome research. *Psychological Bulletin, 108,* 30–49.

Rogers, T., & Craighead, W. E. (1977). Physiological responses to self-statements: The effects of statement valence and discrepancy. *Cognitive Therapy and Research, 1,* 99–120.

Rogers, T. R., & Forehand, R. (1983). The role of parent depression in interactions between mothers and their clinic-referred children. *Cognitive Therapy and Research, 7,* 315–324.

Rush, A. J., & Shaw, B. F. (1983). Failure in treating depression by cognitive therapy. In E. B. Foa & P. G. M. Emmelkamp (Eds.), *Failures in behavior therapy* (pp. 217–228). New York: Wiley.

Rush, A. J., Shaw, B., & Khatami, M. (1980). Cognitive therapy of depression: Utilizing the couples' system. *Cognitive Therapy and Research, 4,* 103–114.

Rush, A. J., & Watkins, J. T. (1981). Group versus individual cognitive therapy: A pilot study. *Cognitive Therapy and Research, 5,* 95–104.

Rush, A. J., Weisenburger, J., & Eaves, G. (1986). Do thinking patterns predict depressive symptoms? *Cognitive Therapy and Research, 10,* 225–236.

Russell, P. L., & Brandsma, J. M. (1974). A theoretical and empirical investigation of the rational–emotive and classical conditioning theories. *Journal of Consulting and Clinical Psychology, 42,* 389–397.

Sacco, W. P. (1985). Depression and expectations of satisfaction. *Psychological Reports, 57,* 99–102.

Sacco, W. P., & Beck, A. T. (1985). Cognitive therapy for depression. In E. E. Beckham & W. R. Leber (Eds.), *Handbook of depression: Treatment, assessment, and research* (pp. 3–38). Homewood, IL: Dorsey Press.

Sacco, W. P., Dumont, C. D., & Dow, M. G. (1993). Attributional, perceptual, and affective responses to depressed and nondepressed marital partners. *Journal of Consulting and Clinical Psychology, 61,* 1076–1082.

Sacco, W. P., & Dunn, V. (1990). Effect of actor depression on observer attributions: Existence and impact of negative attributions toward the depressed. *Journal of Personality and Social Psychology, 59,* 517–524.

Sacco, W. P., & Graves, D. J. (1984). Childhood depression, interpersonal problem solving, and self-ratings of performance. *Journal of Clinical Child Psychology, 13,* 10–15.

Sacco, W. P., & Hokanson, J. E. (1978). Expectations of success and anagram performance of depressives in a public and private setting. *Journal of Abnormal Psychology, 87,* 122–130.

Sacco, W. P., & Macleod, V. A. (1990). Interpersonal responses of primary caregivers of adolescents differing on depression level. *Journal of Clinical Child Psychology, 19,* 265–270.

Sacco, W. P., Milana, S. A., & Dunn, V. (1985). Effect of depression level and length of acquaintance on reactions of others to a request for help. *Journal of Personality and Social Psychology, 49,* 1728–1737.

Sacco, W. P., Milana, S., & Dunn, V. K. (1988). The effect of duration of depressive episode on the response of others. *Journal of Social and Clinical Psychology, 7,* 297–311.

Schuele, J. G., & Wiesenfeld, A. R. (1983). Automatic response to self-critical thoughts. *Cognitive Therapy and Research, 7,* 189–194.

Scott, M. J., & Stradling, S. G. (1990). Group cognitive therapy for depression produces clinically significant reliable change in community-based settings. *Behavioural Psychotherapy, 18,* 1–19.

Segal, Z. V., Shaw, B. F., & Vella, D. D. (1989). Life stress and depression: A test of the congruency hypothesis for life event content and depressive subtype. *Canadian Journal of Behavioural Science, 21,* 389–400.

Shaw, B. F., & Hollon, S. D. (1978). *Cognitive therapy in*

a group format with depressed outpatients. Unpublished manuscript, University of Western Ontario.

Shea, M. T., Elkin, I., Imber, S. D., Sotsky, S. M., Watkins, J. T., Collins, J. F., Pilkonis, P. A., Beckham, E., Glass, D., Dolan, R. T., & Parloff, M. B. (1992). Course of depressive symptoms over follow-up: Findings from the National Institute of Mental Health Treatment of Depression Collaborative Research Program. *Archives of General Psychiatry*, 49, 782–787.

Simons, A. D., Lustman, P. J., Wetzel, R. D., & Murphy, G. E. (1985). Predicting response to cognitive therapy of depression: The role of learned resourcefulness. *Cognitive Therapy and Research*, 9, 79–89.

Svartberg, M., & Stiles, T. C. (1991). Comparative effects of short-term psychodynamic psychotherapy: A meta-analysis. *Journal of Consulting and Clinical Psychology*, 57, 704–714.

Sweeney, P. D., Anderson, K., & Bailey, S. (1986). Attributional style in depression: A meta-analytic review. *Journal of Personality and Social Psychology*, 50, 974–991.

Teasdale, J. D., & Bancroft, J. (1977). Manipulation of thought content as a determinant of mood and corrugator electromyographic activity in depressed patients. *Journal of Abnormal Psychology*, 86, 235–241.

Teasdale, J. D., & Fennell, M. J.V. (1982). Immediate effects on depression of cognitive therapy interventions. *Cognitive Therapy and Research*, 6, 343–352.

Teasdale, J. D., & Fogerty, S. J. (1979). Differential effects of induced mood on retrieval of pleasant and unpleasant events from episodic memory. *Journal of Abnormal Psychology*, 88, 248–257.

Teasdale, J. D., & Rezin, V. (1978). The effects of reducing frequency of negative thoughts on the mood of depressed patients: Tests of a cognitive model of depression. *British Journal of Social and Clinical Psychology*, 17, 65–74.

Thase, M. E., Bowler, K., & Harden, T. (1991). Cognitive behavior therapy of endogenous depression: Part 2. Preliminary findings in 16 unmedicated inpatients. *Behavior Therapy*, 22, 469–477.

Velten, E. (1968). A laboratory task for induction of mood states. *Behaviour Research and Therapy*, 6, 473–482.

Warren, L. W., & McEachren, L. (1983). Psychosocial correlates of depressive symptomatology in adult women. *Journal of Abnormal Psychology*, 92, 151–160.

Weissman, A., & Beck, A. T. (1978, November). *Development and validation of the Dysfunctional Attitude Scale*. Paper presented at the annual meeting of the Association for Advancement of Behavior Therapy, Chicago.

Wener, A. E., & Rehm, L. P. (1975). Depressive affect: A test of behavioral hypotheses. *Journal of Abnormal Psychology*, 84, 221–227.

Whisman, M. A. (1993). Mediators and moderators of change in cognitive therapy of depression. *Psychological Bulletin*, 114, 248–265.

Whisman, M. A., Miller, I. W., Norman, W. H., & Keitner, G. I. (1991). Cognitive therapy with depressed inpatients: Specific effects on dysfunctional cognitions. *Journal of Consulting and Clinical Psychology*, 59, 282–288.

Wierzbicki, M., & Bartlett, T. S. (1987). The efficacy of group and individual cognitive therapy for mild depression. *Cognitive Therapy and Research*, 11, 337–342.

Wilson, A. R., & Krane, R. V. (1980). Change in self-esteem and its effects on symptoms of depression. *Cognitive Therapy and Research*, 4, 419–422.

Wilson, T. D., & Linville, P. W. (1982). Improving the academic performance of college freshmen: Attribution therapy revisited. *Journal of Personality and Social Psychology*, 42, 367–376.

12

Behavioral Theory and Treatment of Depression

PETER M. LEWINSOHN
IAN H. GOTLIB

Over the past two decades, researchers have devoted considerable effort both to elucidating behavioral theories of unipolar depression and to developing and evaluating interventions based on these formulations. Spurred by conclusions offered in the mid-1970s that raised serious questions concerning the viability of behavioral approaches to the conceptualization and treatment of depression (e.g., Becker, 1974; Lieberman, 1975), investigators have since engaged in a flurry of research, the results of which indicate that these early conclusions may not be warranted. Indeed, there are now well over 50 outcome studies attesting to the efficacy of behavioral interventions in the treatment of depression.

We have three goals in writing this chapter. First, in order to place current behavioral approaches to the conceptualization and treatment of depression in an appropriate context, we briefly describe the history and development of early behavioral theories of depression. We then outline more recent behavioral formulations of depression. Second, we present behavioral approaches to the assessment of various aspects of unipolar depression, and describe several behavioral treatments for depression. In this section, we focus particularly on two treatment packages for unipolar depression developed at the Depression Research Unit of the University of Oregon: an individual therapy approach and a psychoeducational group intervention. We also discuss recent extensions of this group intervention to different populations (such as de-

pressed adolescents and the elderly), as well as adaptations for preventive purposes. Finally, we outline what we believe are important directions for future investigations in this field.

BEHAVIORAL THEORIES OF DEPRESSION

Historical Perspective

Skinner and Ferster

Over four decades ago, Skinner (1953) postulated that depression was the result of a weakening of behavior due to the interruption of established sequences of behavior that had been positively reinforced by the social environment. This conceptualization of depression as an extinction-related phenomenon and as a reduction in the frequency of emission of behavior has been central to all behavioral positions. Ferster (1966) provided more detail by suggesting that such diverse factors as sudden environmental changes, punishment and aversive control, and shifts in reinforcement contingencies can give rise to depression (i.e., to a reduced rate of behavior). He suggested that the depressive's failure to produce adaptive behaviors may be due to a number of factors, including (1) sudden environmental changes that require the establishment of new sources of reinforcement; (2) engaging in aversive or punishable behavior, which pre-empts the opportunity for positive reinforcement; and (3) inaccurate observation of the environment, resulting in socially inappropriate behavior and a low frequency of positive reinforcement. Ferster invoked the concept of "chaining" to explain the generalizability of the response to what is often a circumscribed loss of reinforcement (e.g., loss of a job). Ferster argued that the loss of a central source of reinforcement leads to a reduction in all behaviors "chained to," or organized around, the lost reinforcer. For example, retirement may lead to a reduction in all of the behaviors that are chained to working. Thus an individual who has retired may have difficulty getting up in the morning, grooming himself/herself, and seeing friends or colleagues if all of these behaviors were formerly organized around work, which in turn was a central source of reinforcement.

Costello

In a variant of this position, Costello (1972) distinguished between a reduction in the number of reinforcers available to the individual and a reduction in the effectiveness of available reinforcers. Costello proposed that depression results from a disruption in a chain of behavior, which in turn is probably caused by the loss of one of the reinforcers in the chain. Costello argued that the reinforcer effectiveness of all the components of the chain of behavior is contingent upon the completion of the chain. Thus, when a behavior chain is disrupted, there is a loss of reinforcer effectiveness associated with all of the components in the chain. Costello contended that the depressive's general loss of interest in the environment is a manifestation of this reduction of reinforcer effectiveness.

Lewinsohn

Lewinsohn and his colleagues (e.g., Lewinsohn & Shaw, 1969; Lewinsohn, 1974; Lewinsohn, Youngren, & Grosscup, 1979) refined and elaborated these positions. Lewinsohn maintained that a low rate of response-contingent positive reinforcement constitutes a sufficient explanation for aspects of the depressive syndrome, especially the low rate of behavior. Lewinsohn and his colleagues amplified the behavioral position through three additional hypotheses:

1. There is a causal relationship between the low rate of response-contingent positive reinforcement and the feeling of dysphoria.

2. Depressive behaviors are maintained by the social environment through the provision of contingencies in the form of sympathy, interest, and concern.
3. Deficiencies in social skills function as an important antecedent to the low rate of positive reinforcement.

Lewinsohn hypothesized that a low rate of response-contingent positive reinforcement in major life areas, *and/or* a high rate of aversive experiences, can lead to a reduction in behavior and to the experience of dysphoria. Lewinsohn suggested that three major factors may lead to a low rate of reinforcement. The first involves deficits in the individual's behavioral repertoire or skills, which prevent the attainment of reinforcers or diminish the individual's ability to cope with aversive experiences. The second factor that may lead to a low rate of reinforcement is a lack of potential reinforcers in the individual's environment due to impoverishment or loss, or a surplus of aversive experiences. For example, a person who is confined to home while recuperating from a long illness may engage in few activities that are followed by reinforcement. Or the death or social exit of an individual who has formerly provided social reinforcement may result in a loss of reinforcement. Finally, depression may result from a decrease in the person's capacity to enjoy positive experiences, or an increase in the individual's sensitivity to negative events (Lewinsohn, Lobitz, & Wilson, 1973).

Lewinsohn's formulation thus focused on the reduction of social reinforcement obtained by the depressed individual from significant others in his/her environment. Lewinsohn posited that depressed individuals may lack adequate social skills and may therefore find it difficult to obtain reinforcement from their social environment, leading them to experience a reduced rate of positive reinforcement. Libet and Lewinsohn (1973, p. 304) defined social skill as "the complex ability both to emit behaviors which are positively or negatively reinforced, and not to emit behaviors which are punished or extinguished by others." An individual is considered to be socially skillful, therefore, to the extent that he/she elicits positive (and avoids negative) consequences from the social environment. Because of insufficient positive reinforcement, depressed persons find it difficult to initiate or maintain instrumental behavior. The formulation also focused on the *maintenance* of depressive behavior (e.g., suicidal thoughts) by suggesting that the social environment often reinforces such behaviors through the provision of sympathy, interest, and concern.

Coyne

Complementing this formulation, Coyne (1976) contended that depression is a response to disruptions in the social field of the individual. Specifically, Coyne suggested that depression is maintained by the negative responses of significant others to the depressive's symptomatic behavior. Coyne maintained that depressed individuals create a negative social environment by engaging others in such a manner that support is lost, or at best becomes ambiguous. Both supportive and hostile reactions are elicited. Coyne postulated a sequence of behavior that begins with the depressed person's initial demonstration of depressive symptoms, typically in response to stress. Individuals in the depressed person's social environment respond immediately to these depressive symptoms with genuine concern and support. The depressive's behavior gradually becomes more demanding (i.e., is expressed with increasing frequency). Consequently, the depressive's behavior becomes aversive to others and elicits feelings of resentment and anger. At the same time, the depressed person's obvious distress also elicits feelings of guilt, which serve to inhibit the open expression of this hostility. In an attempt to reduce both their guilt and anger, other people respond to the depressed person with veiled hostility and with false reassurance and support. Being aware of, and feeling rejected by, these discrepant or incongruous messages, the depressed person becomes more symptomatic in an attempt to gain support, thus making it even more aversive for others to interact with him/her. This "deviation-amplifying" process continues to the point where other people either withdraw from interactions with the depressive, or have the person withdrawn through hospitalization.

Coates and Wortman

Coates and Wortman (1980) offered a similar formulation of the etiology of depression, but placed greater emphasis on the social comparison processes of depressed persons and the attempts made by others in the social environment to control directly the depressive's display of aversive symptoms. As in Coyne's (1976) model, Coates and Wortman suggested that others initially react sympathetically to the depressed person and try to ameliorate the negative feelings through encouragement and distraction. These initial attempts at controlling the depressed person, however, may leave the individual feeling worse, because he/she now begins to doubt the appropriateness of his/her feelings and reactions. Over time, others in the depressive's social environment become increasingly annoyed and frustrated with the depressive displays, and their initially supportive responses become more disjointed and ambiguous. The depressed person begins to emit more symptoms in order to regain the lost support, and as others' attempts to control the depressive's behavior become more overt and insistent, the depressed person is left feeling inadequate, isolated, and rejected. Thus Coates and Wortman, like Coyne, implicated the negative reactions of others in the maintenance of depression.

Rehm

Rehm (1977) proposed a self-control model of depression that attempts to integrate behavioral and cognitive aspects of the disorder. According to this model, specific deficits in self-monitoring, self-evaluation, and self-reinforcement may explain the various symptoms of depression. Specifically, Rehm postulated that the behavior of depressed persons may be characterized by one or more deficits in self-control behavior. First, with respect to self-monitoring, depressed individuals selectively attend to negative events that follow their behavior, to the relative exclusion of positive events—a cognitive style that might account for the pessimism and gloomy outlook of depressed individuals. Second, depressed persons selectively attend to immediate consequences of their behavior, to the relative exclusion of delayed outcomes; therefore, they cannot look beyond present demands when making behavioral choices.

The third deficit in the self-control behavior of depressed persons involves self-evaluation— essentially, a comparison between an estimate of performance (which derives from self-monitoring) and an internal criterion or standard. Rehm posited that depressed individuals set unrealistic, perfectionistic, global standards for themselves, making goal attainment improbable. As a consequence, they often do not succeed in reaching their goals, and therefore evaluate themselves negatively and in a global, overgeneralized manner. Depressed persons may also manifest a self-evaluation deficit with respect to their style of attribution. Rehm hypothesized that depressed persons may distort their perception of causality in order to denigrate themselves. If their performance is successful, for example, depressed persons may attribute their success to external factors such as luck and the simplicity of the task, thereby refusing to take credit for their success. Similarly, depressed persons may attribute the cause of an unsuccessful performance to internal factors such as lack of skill and effort, thus taking excessive responsibility for failure.

Finally, Rehm (1977) postulated that depressed persons fail to administer sufficient contingent rewards to themselves to maintain their adaptive behaviors. This low rate of self-reward may account in part for the slowed rates of overt behavior, the lower general activity level, and the lack of persistence that typify depression. In addition, depressed persons are hypothesized to administer excessive self-punishment, which suppresses potentially productive behavior early in a response chain, resulting in excessive inhibition.

More Recent Approaches

Nezu

Nezu and his colleagues (e.g., Nezu, 1987; Nezu, Nezu, & Perri, 1989) have articulated a formulation of depression that implicates ineffective problem-solving skills in the onset and maintenance of this disorder. Nezu notes that a number of investigations have demonstrated an association between problem-solving deficits and depressive symptomatology, both in adults (e.g., Gotlib & Asarnow, 1979) and in children (e.g., Sacco & Graves, 1984). Given this association, Nezu and Ronan (1985) have suggested that problem-solving skills may function to moderate the link between stress and depression. They hypothesize that effective problem-solving ability functions as a buffer against the potentially debilitating effects of negative life events. Moreover, Nezu has also postulated that problem solving may moderate the association between a negative attributional style and depression.

According to Nezu's (1987) formulation, individuals with ineffective problem-solving skills are at increased risk for the development of a depressive episode. More specifically, Nezu contends that depression can result from defi-

ciencies in any or all of five major components of problem solving: problem orientation, problem definition and formulation, generation of alternatives, decision making, and solution implementation and verification. For example, individuals who experience difficulty with problem orientation may appraise a situation as a "threat" rather than as a "challenge," or may attribute the cause of the problem to internal, stable, and/or global factors (cf. Abramson, Seligman, & Teasdale, 1978). Similarly, individuals who are deficient in generating alternatives may generate a restricted range of alternatives, or may generate less effective alternatives than do their more skillful counterparts.

Regardless of the specific problem-solving deficit, Nezu (1987) suggests that the onset of depression occurs when an individual is confronted with a difficult situation. Nezu argues that if these problematic situations are not resolved, negative consequences are likely to occur, which themselves result in a decrease in the individual's reinforcement. To the extent that the individual experiences deficits in problem-solving skills, the resulting depressive episode will be severe and long-lasting. Finally, Nezu also contends that deficits in problem-solving ability will increase relapse rates, because of the high probability of problems occurring in the future and remaining unresolved.

Pyszczynski and Greenberg

Pyszczynski and Greenberg (1987) have proposed a self-regulatory theory of reactive depression that emphasizes the central role of self-awareness, or self-focused attention, in the onset and maintenance of this disorder. This theory integrates aspects of psychoanalytic, cognitive, and behavioral theories of depression with Carver and Scheier's (1981) cybernetic model of self-regulation. Pyszczynski and Greenberg postulate a sequence of events that begins with the loss of a central source of self-esteem, such as the breakup of an important interpersonal relationship or the loss of a job. The loss must represent a central source of emotional security, identity, and self-worth (cf. Oatley & Bolton, 1985). Because of its importance, the loss not only undermines the stability of the individual's self-image, but leads to an increase in self-focus. This increased self-focus makes the significance of the loss even more salient.

Pyszczynski and Greenberg (1987) posit that the increase in self-focus leads to an increase in the internality of the attributions concerning the loss. This escalation of self-blame further increases the intensity of the negative affect experienced by the individual, and pushes the individual's self-image in a negative direction. This mounting negative affect and self-criticism may also interfere with the individual's social functioning, which exacerbates the negative cycle. Pyszczynski and Greenberg suggest that prolonged elevated self-focus following negative events represents a "depressive self-focusing style," which maintains and exacerbates the depressive symptomatology by magnifying the consequences of negative events. (See Ingram, 1990, for an elaborated but similar self-absorption model of psychopathology, and Pyszczynski, Greenberg, Hamilton, & Nix, 1991, for a response to this elaboration.)

Lewinsohn, Hoberman, Teri, and Hautzinger.

Lewinsohn, Hoberman, Teri, and Hautzinger (1985a) have argued that both cognitive and reinforcement theories of depression have been too narrow and simplistic. They have proposed an integrative, multifactorial model of the etiology and maintenance of depression that attempts to capture the complexity of this disorder. In this model, which is presented in Figure 12.1, the occurrence of depression is viewed as a product of both environmental and dispositional factors. More specifically, depression is conceptualized as the end result of environmentally initiated changes in behavior, affect, and cognitions. Whereas situational factors are important as "triggers" of the depressogenic process, cognitive factors are critical as "moderators" of the effects of the environment.

Briefly, in this model the chain of events leading to the occurrence of depression is postulated to begin with antecedent risk factors (A), which initiate the depressogenic process by disrupting important adaptive behavior patterns (B). Stressors at the macro level (e.g., negative life events) and the micro level (e.g., daily hassles) are probably the best examples of such antecedents. These stressors disrupt behavior patterns that are necessary for the individual's day-to-day interactions with the environment. Thus, for example, stressful life events are postulated to lead to depression to the extent that they disrupt important personal relationships or job responsibilities (C). This disruption itself

can result in a negative emotional reaction, which, combined with an inability to reverse the impact of the stressors, leads to a heightened state of self-awareness (D). This increased self-awareness makes salient the individual's sense of failure to meet internal standards, and therefore leads to increased dysphoria and to many of the other cognitive, behavioral, and emotional symptoms of depression (E). Finally, these increased symptoms of depression serve to maintain and exacerbate the depressive state (F), in part by making negative information about the self more accessible (cf. Gotlib & McCabe, 1992), and by reducing the depressed individual's confidence in his/her ability to cope with the environment (e.g., Jacobson & Anderson, 1982).

It is important to note that Lewinsohn et al.'s (1985a) model recognizes that stable individual differences, such as personality characteristics, may moderate the impact of the antecedent events both in initiating the cycle leading to depression, and in maintaining the depression once it begins. These person characteristics can be classified as "vulnerabilities," which increase the probability of depression, and "immunities," which decrease the probability of depression (G). Lewinsohn et al. suggest that vulnerability factors may include being female, having a history of prior depressions, and having low self-esteem. In contrast, examples of immunities include high self-perceived social competence, the availability of a confidant, and effective coping skills. Finally, it is important to note that Lewinsohn et al.'s model emphasizes the operation of "feedback loops" among the various factors. The feedback loops allow for either a "vicious cycle" or a "benign cycle." If any of the components of the model can be reversed, the depression will be progressively ameliorated.

It is apparent from this overview that behavioral theories of depression have evolved from relatively simple and constricted stimulus–response formulations emphasizing response-contingent reinforcement and the behavioral dampening effects of punishment, to more complex conceptualizations placing greater emphasis on the individual's characteristics and his/her interactions with the environment. There is a greater awareness that depressed individuals often function in demanding and stressful environments. Moreover, some investigators contend that depressed persons themselves may be instrumental in engendering much of this stress

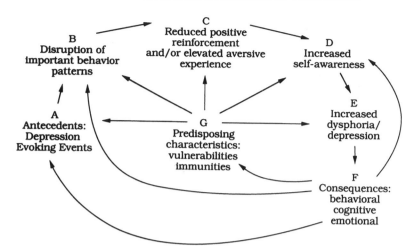

FIGURE 12.1. An integrative model of the etiology and maintenance of depression. From Lewinsohn, Hoberman, Teri, & Hautzinger (1985a). Copyright 1985 by Academic Press, Inc. Reprinted by permission.

(cf. Gotlib & Hammen, 1992). Given this changing perspective, it is clear that behavioral researchers and clinicians must examine depressed individuals in the context of their environment. As we indicate in the following section, behavioral assessment procedures are now characterized by a broader focus not only on depressed persons, but on their social environments as well.

BEHAVIORAL ASSESSMENT OF DEPRESSION

Behavioral approaches to the assessment of depression typically focus on overt features of the disorder, such as psychomotor and verbal behavior. In addition, however, given the focus of behavioral theories of depression on environmental contingencies, behaviorally oriented clinicians and researchers also attempt to assess aspects of the environment, and of the person–environment interaction, that may be related to the onset or maintenance of the depression. Thus, behavioral assessment may include an examination of such factors as the social skills of the depressed individual, the behaviors of others with whom the depressed patient interacts, and the activities and reinforcers available to the depressed person. Moreover, as we note below, information may be gathered through interviews, self-report, and direct observations.

Interviews

In regard to assessing the social skills of depressed persons, Becker and Heimberg (1985) recommend that a clinical interview be conducted in which the interviewer and the depressed patient role-play problematic target situations identified by the patient. During this role playing, the interviewer should carefully observe the patient's performance, in terms of speech content, volume, tone, eye contact, posture, and so forth (see also Lewinsohn, Biglan, & Zeiss, 1976). In addition, standardized role-play tests such as the Behavioral Assertiveness Test (Eisler, Hersen, Miller, & Blanchard, 1975) can serve to augment the situations provided by the patient.

Becker and Heimberg (1985) also suggest that a clinical interview be devoted to an examination of the depressed patient's life circumstances. More specifically, patients should be asked about interpersonal difficulties they may be experiencing in different settings, such as work, school, marital and/or family relationships, and social encounters with friends or strangers. The purpose of this interview is to identify behavior settings and individuals that appear to be associated with changes in the patient's mood. The patient's perception of this link between environmental characteristics and mood is critical to the success of therapy, which is aimed at altering the functional relation between the patient and the environment. Thus, Becker and Heimberg emphasize the importance of obtaining detailed descriptions of these settings and individuals, often using role-playing procedures to gather this information.

Self-Reports

A number of well-known and frequently used self-report measures of depressive symptomatology exist; these include the Beck Depression Inventory (BDI; Beck, Ward, Mendelson, Mock, & Erbaugh, 1961), the Center for Epidemiologic Studies Depression Scale (Radloff, 1977), and the Depression Adjective Check List (Lubin, 1967). Indeed, there have recently been several detailed reviews of these measures (e.g., Gotlib & Cane, 1989; Lewinsohn & Rohde, 1987). In addition to these measures of symptomatology, however, several self-report questionnaires have been developed to assess other aspects of the phenomena of depression. In particular, self-report measures are available to assess the social functioning of depressed persons. Youngren, Zeiss, and Lewinsohn (1977), for example, developed the Interpersonal Events Schedule (IES), a self-report measure for assessing social interaction in depressed persons. The IES consists of 160 items involving interpersonal activities or cognitions regarding these activities. Subjects rate both the frequency and impact of each item for the past month. The IES incorporates eight rationally derived subscales: Social Activity, Assertion, Cognition, Conflict, Give Positive, Receive Positive, Give Negative, and Receive Negative. Youngren and Lewinsohn (1980) reported that the IES significantly discriminated depressed subjects from both psychiatric and normal control groups. Specifically, depressed subjects reported experiencing lower activity levels, feeling less comfort in activities, giving and receiving less positive reinforcement for their interactions, and being less comfortable in assertive behavior. A set of the most discriminating IES items has been generated, based on one-way analyses of covariants controlling for age and sex.

Another self-report measure of social interaction is the Social Interaction Self-Statement Test (SISST; Glass, Merluzzi, Bierer, & Larsen, 1982). This measure consists of 30 statements that make up four subscales: Self-Depreciation, Positive Anticipation, Fear of Negative Evalu-

ation, and Coping. Glass et al. report acceptable psychometric properties for the SISST. Finally, Weissman, Prusoff, and Thompson (1978) developed the Social Adjustment Scale—Self-Report (SAS-SR). This measure is a self-report version of the interviewer-rated Social Adjustment Scale (SAS; Weissman & Paykel, 1974). The SAS-SR contains 42 questions that measure affective and instrumental performance in various roles; subscales include Occupational Role, Social and Leisure Activities, Relationship with Extended Family, Marital Role, Parental Role, Family Unit, and Economic Independence. The SAS-SR takes 15–20 minutes to complete, and assesses performance over the past 2 weeks. This measure has been found to have good agreement with the interviewer-rated SAS, as well as high internal consistency and test retest stability (cf. Edwards, Yarvis, Mueller, Zingale, & Wagman, 1978; see John & Weissman, 1987, for detailed reviews of these measures).

Behavioral Logs

As a somewhat different perspective on self-report measurement, many behavioral therapists require depressed patients to maintain daily event logs. These logs or diaries can be useful in assessing the response consequences of a depressed patient's social behaviors and in providing information about the patient's social environment and the available social reinforcers. For example, MacPhillamy and Lewinsohn (1982) developed the Pleasant Events Schedule (PES) to facilitate behavioral programs designed to increase the amount of positive reinforcement received by depressed persons. The PES is an inventory designed for use in assessing, tracking, and modifying positive activity levels in depressed persons. The PES consists of 320 items describing interactions with the environment that many people find to be pleasant (e.g., "being with friends," "being told I am loved," "seeing beautiful scenery," "going to a restaurant"). The patient first rates each item on a 3-point scale indicating the frequency of each event's occurrence during the past month. Each item is then rated a second time with respect to the subjective enjoyability of the event. The frequency ratings are assumed to measure the individual's rate of engagement in person–environment interactions, whereas the subjective enjoyability ratings are assumed to reflect the individual's potential for positive reinforcement. The cross-products of the frequency and impact ratings provide a measure of the total amount of positive reinforcement the patient has experienced over the past month. Several rational, factorial, and empirical scales, including brief scales, have been developed.

Similarly, the Unpleasant Events Schedule (UES) was developed to assess the frequency and the subjective impact of a wide range of stressful life events (Lewinsohn, Mermelstein, Alexander, & MacPhillamy, 1985b). The UES has been used to develop individualized lists of unpleasant activities for patients to use in daily monitoring. The UES includes both relatively minor daily hassles and major life events. This measure consists of 320 items assessing the rate of occurrence and the experienced aversiveness of stressful life events. The UES calls for the respondent to rate each of the 320 items twice, first on a 3-point scale of frequency, and again on a 3-point scale of subjective aversiveness. In addition to the frequency and aversiveness scores, cross-product scores are computed and summed across items. The cross-product score is assumed to be a measure of the level of experienced aversiveness. Several rational, empirical, and factor-analytic scales have been developed for the UES. The rationally derived scales can be used in treatment to identify specific actual or potential areas of distress and discomfort.

The UES and the PES may be used as "pre- and post-" measures in treatments aimed at reducing the frequency and experienced aversiveness of unpleasant events, and at increasing the frequency and enjoyability of pleasant ones. Shortened versions of the PES have been developed for use with the elderly (Teri & Lewinsohn, 1985) and with adolescents (Carey, Kelley, & Buss, 1986; Cole, Kelley, & Carey, 1988; Lewinsohn & Clarke, 1986). The PES and UES can also be used to generate individualized activity schedules for monitoring daily pleasant activities and for identifying potential target pleasant activities for change (Lewinsohn, 1976). Finally, Teri and Logsdon (1991) recently modified the PES into a 53-item PES-AD for use with Alzheimer's patients and family caregivers.

It is clear, therefore, that clinicians can choose from a number of self-report measures of behavioral aspects of depressive functioning. Although these measures provide important information, it is likely that they are strongly influenced by the general negative response set

characteristic of many depressed individuals. Consequently, some investigators have turned to observational measurement procedures, contending that measures based on objective data are more likely to represent "real" skill deficits, which can then become the targets for treatment intervention.

Observational Procedures

Numerous investigators have observed the overt behavior of depressed persons. In an early study, Williams, Barlow, and Agras (1972) developed an observer-rated scale to assess the behaviors of severely depressed inpatients on a hospital ward. Essentially, this scale assesses depressed patients' verbal behavior, social interactions, smiling, and motor activity (reading, sewing, grooming, etc.). This measure yields a longitudinal record of the patients' depressed behaviors, and correlates highly with clinician ratings of depression severity. Interestingly, Williams et al. reported that scores on this instrument were more predictive of relapse of depression 1 year later than were scores on the BDI or the Hamilton Rating Scale for Depression (Hamilton, 1960, 1967).

Subsequent investigations have examined the behaviors of depressed persons in interactions with strangers. The results of these studies indicate that, compared with nondepressed controls, depressed individuals demonstrate a variety of deficits in their social skills. Specifically, depressed individuals have been observed to smile less frequently (Gotlib, 1982; Gotlib & Robinson, 1982), to make less eye contact with those with whom they are interacting (Gotlib, 1982), to speak more slowly and more monotonously (Gotlib & Robinson, 1982; Libet & Lewinsohn, 1973; Youngren & Lewinsohn, 1980), to take longer to respond to others in a conversation (Libet & Lewinsohn, 1973), and to make more self-focused and negatively toned comments (Blumberg & Hokanson, 1983; Gotlib & Robinson, 1982; Jacobson & Anderson, 1982). Given these differences in both conversation behavior and content, with few exceptions (e.g., Gotlib & Meltzer, 1987; Youngren & Lewinsohn, 1980), the interpersonal behaviors of depressed persons have been found to be rated by observers as less socially competent than are those of nondepressed individuals (e.g., Dykman, Horowitz, Abramson, & Usher, 1991; Lewinsohn, Mischel, Chaplin, & Barton, 1980a;

see Feldman & Gotlib, 1993, for a more detailed review of these studies).

It is clear, therefore, that depressed persons demonstrate social skills deficits in their interactions with strangers. Gotlib and Hooley (1988) have argued, however, that the social skills difficulties of depressed individuals are even more pronounced in their marital and family interactions. In this context, several investigators have discussed the use of home observations of depressed persons, in order to delineate behavioral and environmental targets for intervention. Home visits (lasting about an hour), are ideally scheduled around mealtimes, when all members of the family are present. Detailed case descriptions illustrating the use of home visits as part of the initial assessment of depression are available elsewhere (e.g., Lewinsohn & Schaffer, 1971). Although costly in terms of the therapist's time, home observations can be valuable by identifying interpersonal behavior patterns in the family that the therapist may hypothesize to be causally related to the depression (cf. Hops et al., 1987). If, for practical purposes, the therapist is unable to conduct home observations, it is advisable at a minimum to schedule an interview with the spouse (cf. Gotlib & Colby, 1987).

Other researchers, though not explicitly conducting home observations, have described the results of laboratory-based observations of depressed persons interacting with their spouses and other family members. The results of these studies are consistent in reporting that the interactions of depressed persons and their spouses are associated with more negative verbal and nonverbal behaviors. For example, marital interactions of couples in which one partner is depressed have been found to be characterized by high levels of disruption, negative emotional outbursts, and incongruity between verbal messages and nonverbal behaviors (Hinchliffe, Hooper, & Roberts, 1978), such that depressed individuals emit a greater number of behaviors in which the nonverbal communication is more negative than is the accompanying verbal message (Ruscher & Gotlib, 1988). When interacting with their spouses, depressed individuals have been found to emit a lower proportion of positive verbal behaviors and a greater proportion of negative verbal behaviors than do nondepressed individuals (Hautzinger, Linden, & Hoffman, 1982; Ruscher & Gotlib, 1988). Moreover, Kowalik and Gotlib (1987) reported that this pattern of negative behavior on the part

of depressed individuals may be deliberate: Depressed persons in this study intentionally coded their communications to their spouses more negatively and less positively than did nondepressed persons. In addition, other findings suggest that depressed individuals are often openly aggressive when interacting with their spouses (Biglan et al., 1985; see Rehm, 1987).

Finally, there is evidence from observational assessment studies that depressed persons also experience problematic interactions with their children. A number of investigators have found that depressed women are withdrawn and/or overtly negative in interactions with their children. Livingood, Daen, and Smith (1983), for example, found that depressed mothers gazed less often at their infants than did nondepressed women, and seemed to be less ready to interact with them. Studies conducted by Field and her colleagues (e.g., Field, 1984; Field, Healy, Goldstein, & Guthertz, 1990) similarly indicate that depressed mothers are less active, less playful, and less contingently responsive in face-to-face interactions with their 3- to 6-month-old infants than are nondepressed mothers. In fact, Field et al. (1990) reported that depressed mothers displayed angry, negative, and intrusive behaviors toward their babies. Bettes (1988) reported that symptomatic mothers were delayed in speech directed toward their infants, and Fleming, Ruble, Flett, and Shaul (1988) found that, compared to nondepressed mothers, women with postpartum depression showed less reciprocal vocalization and affectionate contact with their infants. Finally, results indicating similarly negative behavioral interactions between depressed parents and their children have been obtained in studies with older children as well (e.g., Goodman & Brumley, 1990; Gordon et al., 1989; Mills, Puckering, Pound, & Cox, 1985; see Gotlib & Lee, 1990, in press, and Hammen, 1991, for more detailed reviews of this literature).

It is clear from the results of these studies, therefore, that the overt behaviors of depressed persons are problematic not only on hospital wards and in their interactions with strangers, but in their interactions with their spouses and children. A primary contribution of behavioral approaches to the assessment of the social functioning of depressed persons has been to identify and clarify the precise behaviors that appear to be particularly troublesome. We turn now to an examination of behavioral approaches to the treatment of depressed persons.

BEHAVIORAL TREATMENT OF DEPRESSION

Given the focus of behavioral theories of depression on environmental contingencies and reinforcers, a major goal of behaviorally oriented therapies for depression is to increase the positive reinforcement received by the depressed individual. In this context, a number of different behavioral treatment approaches have been described, all of which share this common goal (cf. Antonuccio, Ward, & Tearnan, 1991). Moreover, as Hoberman and Lewinsohn (1985) note, behavioral approaches to the treatment of depression have a number of other commonalities. For example, patients are usually required to monitor activities, mood, and thoughts. Patients are encouraged to set achievable goals in order to ensure early success experiences, and to give themselves rewards for reaching their goals. Finally, most behavioral approaches involve training designed to remedy the various performance and skill deficits of depressed patients (e.g., social skills training, assertiveness training) and are time-limited, typically designed to run between 4 and 12 weeks.

Increasing Pleasant Activities and Decreasing Unpleasant Events

Lewinsohn and his colleagues (e.g., Lewinsohn, Sullivan, & Grosscup, 1980b; Libet & Lewinsohn, 1973) have underscored the significant relationship of depression with low rates of positive reinforcement and with high rates of aversive experience. As noted earlier, these investigators posited that depression may be due in part to a low rate of response-contingent positive reinforcement. On the basis of this formulation, Lewinsohn et al. (1980b) developed a 12-session, highly structured behavioral program aimed at changing the quality and quantity of depressed patients' interactions with their environments. Specifically, through the use of overlapping behavioral and cognitive intervention strategies—including training in assertiveness, relaxation, self-control, decision making, problem solving, communication, and time management—depressed patients are taught to manage and reduce the intensity and frequency of aversive events and to increase their rate of engagement in pleasant activities. Lewinsohn et al. reported that this program of decreasing unpleasant activities and increasing engagement in pleasant activities was effective in reducing

levels of depression (see also Hammen & Glass, 1975; Zeiss, Lewinsohn, & Muñoz, 1979).

Social Skills Therapy

Given the consistent finding that depressed persons have poor social skills (e.g., Gotlib, 1982; Libet & Lewinsohn, 1973; Youngren & Lewinsohn, 1980), a number of investigators (e.g., Sanchez, Lewinsohn, & Larsen, 1980) have described behaviorally oriented treatment programs for depression that focus explicitly on the training of social skills. One such treatment program for depression has been described by Becker, Heimberg, and Bellack (e.g., Becker & Heimberg, 1985; Becker, Heimberg, & Bellack, 1987; Bellack, Hersen, & Himmelhoch, 1981). This program is based on the following assumptions:

1. Depression is a result of an inadequate schedule of positive reinforcement contingent on the person's nondepressed behavior.
2. A substantial portion of the most salient positive reinforcers in the adult world are interpersonal in nature.
3. A meaningful portion of the rewards in adult life may be received or denied, contingent on the person's interpersonal behavior.
4. Therefore, a treatment that helps the depressed patient to increase the quality of his or her interpersonal behavior should act to increase the amount of response-contingent positive reinforcement, and thereby decrease depressive affect and increase the rate of "nondepressed behavior." (Becker & Heimberg, 1985, p. 205)

Becker and Heimberg suggest that inadequate interpersonal behavior may be the result of a number of factors, such as insufficient exposure to interpersonally skilled models, learning of maladaptive interpersonal behaviors, insufficient opportunity to practice important interpersonal routines, decaying of specific behavioral skills because of disuse, and failure to recognize environmental cues for specific interpersonal behaviors.

Given this context, Becker et al. (1987) describe assessment and treatment procedures that focus jointly on decreasing depressive symptoms and enhancing expressive and receptive interpersonal communication skills. With respect to assessment, as we have noted earlier, Becker et al. recommend the use of a clinical interview to assess the patient's life circumstances and experience of interpersonal difficulties. Becker et al. then describe a social skills training program based on this assessment and composed of four general components: social skills training, social perception training, practice, and self-evaluation and self-reinforcement. The program utilizes strategies and techniques that include instruction, feedback, social reinforcement, modeling, behavioral rehearsal, and graded homework assignments in a highly structured format. Because social skills tend to be situation-specific, training is provided in each of four problem areas: interactions with strangers, with family members, with friends, and at work or school. Becker et al. suggest that treatment across these different social contexts maximizes the likelihood that the training will generalize across a variety of situations.

The training program focuses primarily on three specific behavioral repertoires that appear to be particularly relevant to depressed individuals: negative assertion, positive assertion, and conversational skills. Negative assertion involves behaviors that allow persons to stand up for their rights and to act in their own best interest. Positive assertion refers to the expression of positive feelings about others, such as affection, approval, praise, and appreciation, as well as offering appropriate apologies. Training in conversational skills involves initiating conversations, asking questions, making appropriate self-disclosures, and ending conversations gracefully. In all of these areas, depressed patients are given direct behavior training as well as training in social perception. Patients are encouraged to practice the skills and behaviors across different situations.

Treatment takes place over 12 weekly 1-hour sessions, in which patients receive training in the four problem areas described above. These treatment sessions are followed by six to eight maintenance sessions over a six-month period, in which the emphasis is on problem solving and review. Bellack and his colleagues (e.g., Bellack, Hersen, & Himmelhoch, 1983; Hersen, Bellack, Himmelhoch, & Thase, 1984) have demonstrated the efficacy of this approach in the treatment of depression. The results of these studies indicated that social skills training was more effective than psychotropic medication and insight-oriented psychotherapy in increasing patients' levels of social skills. Moreover, the gains made by patients in the social skills treatment groups were maintained at a 6-month follow-up assessment.

A similar approach to the treatment of depression that also focuses on the training of social skills has been described by McLean (1976, 1981). Because McLean views depression as resulting from individuals' perceived loss of control over their interpersonal environment, his treatment for depression is aimed at training in coping and social skills. McLean outlines a structured, time-limited treatment program aimed at improving social behaviors that are incompatible with depression. Graduated practice and modeling are used to effect improvements in the following six skills areas: communication, behavioral productivity, social interaction, assertiveness, decision making and problem solving, and cognitive self-control. Patients are required to engage in daily skill development activities and to use structured log sheets to monitor their achievements. Patients are also prepared for the experience of future depressive episodes, and contingency plans for coping are established and rehearsed with the patients.

McLean and Hakstian (1979) assessed the efficacy of this behavioral treatment with 178 unipolar depressed outpatients, randomly assigned to four treatment conditions: behavior therapy, "traditional" insight-oriented psychotherapy, relaxation training, and amitriptyline. Treatment was conducted over a period of 10 weeks. The results of this investigation indicated that behavior therapy was superior to the other treatments on 9 of the 10 outcome measures administered immediately following treatment, and on 7 of the 10 outcome measures at a 3-month follow-up assessment. Patients in the behavior therapy condition also had the lowest dropout rate. Data from a 2-year follow-up of these patients reported by McLean and Hakstian (1990) indicated that this pattern of results was stable: Over a 27-month follow-up period, behavior therapy patients were found to be significantly improved in mood, more socially active, and more personally productive than were patients in the other treatment conditions, particularly in the relaxation therapy condition.

Self-Control Therapy

Self-control therapy, developed from Rehm's (1977) self-control model of depression, emphasizes progressive goal attainment, self-reinforcement and contingency management strategies, and behavioral productivity (Antonuccio et al., 1991). As noted earlier, the self-control model posits that depression is associated with deficits in self-monitoring, self-evaluation, and self-reinforcement. Consequently, these areas of functioning constitute the focus of self-control therapy. This therapy is a structured, time-limited, group format treatment. It consists of 6 to 12 sessions divided into three parts, each focusing on one of the three deficit areas described above. With respect to self-monitoring, patients are required to maintain a daily record and graph of positive experiences and their associated mood. In the self-evaluation phase, patients are taught to develop specific, overt, and attainable goals in terms of positive activities and behavioral productivity. In addition, patients assign points to these goals and keep a tally of their points as they meet their goals. Finally, patients are taught to identify reinforcers and to administer these rewards to themselves as they accomplish their specific goals.

Rehm has demonstrated the efficacy of this self-control treatment for depression in a number of studies. In one of the first tests of this therapy, Fuchs and Rehm (1977) reported that self-control treatment was more effective than was nonspecific group therapy or a waiting-list control condition in reducing depression in a sample of clinically depressed women. Moreover, improvement was maintained at a 6-week follow-up assessment. Rehm, Fuchs, Roth, Kornblith, and Romano (1979) subsequently reported that self-control therapy was more effective in the treatment of depressed patients than was assertion skills training (see also Roth, Bielski, Jones, Parker, & Osborn, 1982). Interestingly, Rehm (1990) notes that the effectiveness of this treatment does not depend on the inclusion of all three components; outcomes do not seem to be affected by the omission of the self-evaluation or self-reinforcement portions of the program. Finally, Rehm also notes that this therapy appears to be equally effective in altering cognitive and behavioral aspects of depression, suggesting a nonspecificity of treatment effects (cf. Zeiss et al., 1979).

Problem-Solving Therapy

Earlier in this chapter, we have described a problem-solving model of depression formulated by Nezu (1987; Nezu et al., 1989). The model focuses on relations among major negative life events, current problems, problem-solving coping, and depressive symptomatology. Thus, the treatment strategies and procedures that have been developed from this model are designed to reduce depressive symptomatology through training in problem-solving skills. Nezu et al. outline four goals of problem-solving therapy for depressed individuals: (1) to help them identify previous and current life situations that may be antecedents of a depressive episode; (2) to minimize the negative impact of depressive symptoms on current and future coping attempts; (3) to increase the effectiveness of problem-solving efforts at coping with current life situations; and (4) to teach general skills to deal more effectively with future problems. Training in maintenance and generalization are also built into this program.

Nezu et al.'s (1989) problem-solving therapy is a structured 12-week intervention program in which such therapeutic techniques as instruction, prompting, modeling, behavioral rehearsal, homework assignments, shaping, reinforcement, and feedback are utilized to increase problem-solving ability and decrease depressive symptomatology. The results of several studies suggest that problem-solving therapy may be efficacious for the treatment of depression. For example, Caple and Blechman (1976), Shipley and Fazio (1973), and Nezu (1986) demonstrated that problem solving is an important component of an effective treatment program for depression. More recently, Nezu and Perri (1989) also demonstrated the efficacy of problem-solving therapy in reducing depression, both at the end of therapy and at a 6-month follow-up assessment. Finally, Arean et al. (1993) reported that problem-solving therapy was superior to reminiscence therapy and to a waiting-list control condition in the treatment of major depressive disorder in older adults.

Marital/Family Therapy

Given the consistent association described earlier between depression and difficulties in marital and family functioning, it is not surprising that a number of therapies have been developed aimed simultaneously at decreasing levels of depression and improving marital/family relationships. Because marital/family interventions for depression are the focus of other chapters in this volume and have also been reviewed in detail elsewhere (e.g., Gotlib, Wallace, & Colby, 1990; Gotlib & Beach, 1995), we simply point out here that several recent studies have documented the efficacy of behaviorally oriented marital or family therapy for depression.

For example, O'Leary and Beach (1990) randomly assigned married couples in which the wives were depressed to individual cognitive therapy, conjoint behavioral marital therapy, or a 15-week waiting-list condition. At both post-therapy and 1-year follow-up assessments, O'Leary and Beach found the two types of therapy to be equally effective in reducing depressive symptomatology. Only behavioral marital therapy, however, was found to be effective in improving the marital relationship. At post-therapy, only 25% of persons receiving cognitive therapy, compared with 83% of those receiving behavioral marital therapy, had at least 15-point increases in their scores on a measure of marital adjustment from pretest to posttest. The same general pattern of results was obtained at follow-up. The results of this study suggest that marital therapy can effectively reduce depressive symptomatology while simultaneously enhancing marital satisfaction, at least for those couples in which both depression and marital discord exist (cf. O'Leary, Risso, & Beach, 1990).

Similar results for the treatment of depressed, maritally discordant couples were reported by Jacobson, Dobson, Fruzzetti, Schmaling, and Salusky (1991). Again, although individual cognitive therapy and behavioral marital therapy were equally effective in reducing depression in these couples, only marital therapy was found to be successful in enhancing marital satisfaction. Finally, Foley, Rounsaville, Weissman, Sholomskas, and Chevron (1989) randomly assigned depressed outpatients to either individual interpersonal psychotherapy (IPT; Klerman, Weissman, Rounsaville, & Chevron, 1984), which was one of the two psychological therapies evaluated in the recent multisite National Institute of Mental Health (NIMH) Treatment of Depression Collaborative Research Program (Elkin, Parloff, Hadley, & Autry, 1985), or to a newly developed couples format version of IPT. These investigators found that the inclusion of spouses in cases in which there were ongoing marital disputes was well received by patients and resulted in greater improvement in the marital relationships than did the standard individual format of IPT. Both formats produced significant and comparable reductions in symptoms of depression. The results of these studies, therefore, are consistent in suggesting that behaviorally oriented marital therapy enhances marital functioning while reducing depression to levels comparable to those obtained with standard individual treatments. At present, the

advantage of using marital interventions for depression rather than individual approaches appears to lie primarily in their greater efficacy in patients with co-occurring marital discord and depression.

The Coping With Depression Course

General Description

The Coping With Depression (CWD) course for adults (Lewinsohn, Antonuccio, Steinmetz, & Teri, 1984) grew out of a series of early investigations (e.g., Lewinsohn & Atwood, 1969; Lewinsohn & Schaffer, 1971; Lewinsohn & Shaw, 1969; Lewinsohn, Weinstein, & Alper, 1970; Lewinsohn, Weinstein, & Shaw, 1969), in which an early group behavioral treatment for depression was included. Most directly related to the development of the CWD course, however, were results reported by Zeiss et al. (1979), who compared the efficacy of three treatments for depression (cognitive therapy, increasing pleasant activities, and social skills training). The results of this study indicated that though all three treatments were equally effective in reducing levels of depression, changes in the intervening dependent variables were not specific to the type of treatment received. For example, the cognitions of the patients who received social skills training changed as much as the cognitions of patients who were in the cognitive therapy group. Similarly, the pleasant activities of the patients in the pleasant activities treatment increased as much as those of the patients in the cognitive treatment. Thus, it appeared both that none of the treatments was necessary for therapeutic change to occur, and that the effects of the treatments were nonspecific, affecting all of the assessed areas of psychosocial functioning that have been shown to be related to depression.

On the basis of these results, Zeiss et al. (1979) advanced the following hypotheses concerning what might be critical components for successful short-term, cognitive–behavioral therapy for depression:

1. Therapy should begin with an elaborated, well-planned rationale. This rationale should provide the initial structure that guides the patient to the belief that s/he can control his/her own behavior and thereby change his/her depression.
2. Therapy should provide training and skills which the patient can use to feel more effective in handling his/her daily life. The skills

must be of some significance to the patient, and must fit with the rationale that has been presented.

3. Therapy should emphasize the independent use of these skills by the patient outside of the therapy context, and must provide enough structure so that the attainment of independent skills is possible for the patient.

4. Therapy should encourage the patient's attribution that improvement in mood was caused by the patient's own increased skill from this, not by the therapist's skillfulness. (pp. 437–438)

The CWD course was designed to incorporate these hypotheses. The course (and each of its subsequent modifications for special populations; see below) was designed to be offered as an educational course or small seminar, teaching people techniques and strategies to cope with the problems assumed to be related to their depression. Specifically, the CWD course addresses several target behaviors (social skills, depressogenic thinking, pleasant activities, and relaxation), as well as more general components hypothesized to be critical to successful cognitive–behavioral therapy for depression (e.g., self-monitoring, baselining, self-change).

In its present configuration, the CWD course for adults consists of 12 sessions lasting 2 hours each, conducted over 8 weeks. Sessions are held twice weekly for the first 4 weeks. Groups typically consist of 6 to 10 adults (aged 18 and over), with a single group leader (although two therapists may be used). Follow-up sessions ("class reunions") are held at 1 and 6 months, to encourage maintenance of treatment gains and to collect information on improvement or relapse.

The first two CWD sessions are devoted to the presentation of the course rules, the rationale of the treatment and the social learning view of depression, and instruction in self-change skills. Participants are taught that being depressed does not mean that they are "crazy." Instead, their depression is conceptualized as a result of their difficulty in dealing with stresses in their lives. The CWD course is presented as a way to learn new skills to allow the participants to deal more effectively with the stressors that have contributed to their depression. Next, several self-change skills are taught, including monitoring specific behaviors targeted for change, establishing a baseline, setting realistic goals, and developing a plan and a contract to make changes in their behavior. The following eight sessions are devoted to teaching specific skills, including relaxation, increasing pleasant activities, gaining control of negative or irrational thinking, and social skills. Two sessions are devoted to each skill area.

The relaxation sessions focus primarily on the Jacobson (1929) method, which requires participants to tense and then relax major muscle groups throughout the body until they are fully relaxed. The rationale for teaching relaxation rests on the well-demonstrated co-occurrence of depression and anxiety (e.g., Maser & Cloninger, 1990). The relaxation sessions take place early in the CWD course because this form of relaxation is a relatively easy skill to learn, and thus provides participants with an initial success experience. Using the PES, described earlier, the pleasant activity sessions focus on identifying, baselining, and increasing pleasant activities. The cognitive therapy sessions incorporate elements of interventions developed by Beck, Rush, Shaw, and Emery (1979) and Ellis and Harper (1961) for identifying and challenging negative and irrational thoughts. Finally, the social skills sessions focus on assertion, the planning of more social activities, and strategies for making more friends.

The final two sessions of the CWD course focus on integrating the skills learned, on maintaining therapy gains, and on preventing relapse. Participants identify those skills that they have found to be most effective for overcoming their depressed mood. Aided by the group leader, all participants develop a written, personalized "emergency plan," detailing the steps they will take to counteract feelings of depression if they should ever experience them again.

All sessions are highly structured and make use of a text, *Control Your Depression* (Lewinsohn, Muñoz, Youngren, & Zeiss, 1986), as well as a participant workbook (Brown & Lewinsohn, 1979). In addition, an instructor's manual (Lewinsohn et al., 1984) provides scripts, exercises, and guidelines. Each session involves a lecture, a review of homework assignments, discussion, and role playing. A 10-minute break in the middle of each session permits participants to socialize and to practice the new skills they have learned. An important feature of the CWD course is that it is nonstigmatizing. Because it is presented and conducted as a class rather than as therapy, it avoids the usual client reluctance and resistance that may prevent many depressed individuals from seeking help. The course also represents a cost-effective, community-oriented approach to reach the great majority of depressives, who do not make use of the services of clinics and mental health professionals. For a more detailed description of the CWD course, the reader is referred to Lewinsohn et al. (1984).

The efficacy of the CWD course has been demonstrated in several outcome studies. For example, Brown and Lewinsohn (1984), Steinmetz, Lewinsohn, and Antonuccio (1983), and Hoberman, Lewinsohn, and Tilson (1988) all found that the CWD course was more effective in the treatment of depression than was a waiting-list control condition, and that it was as effective as individual behavior therapy. Interestingly, Hoberman et al. found that positive perceptions of group cohesiveness were a significant predictor of treatment outcome, attesting to the efficacy of the group format of this approach.

Extensions of the Course for Different Populations and Purposes

Adolescents. Modeled after the adult CWD course, the adolescent Coping With Depression (CWD-A) course (Clarke, Lewinsohn, & Hops, 1990) consists of 16 sessions lasting 2 hours each, conducted over 7 weeks. The content of the CWD-A course, though similar to the content of the adult CWD course, has been substantially simplified, with a greater emphasis on experiential learning and fewer homework assignments. Adolescents and their parents are provided with comprehensive participant workbooks consisting of homework assignments, forms, short handouts, and readings. These participant workbooks are closely integrated with the group sessions. In addition to the skill areas included in the adult CWD course, the CWD-A course has been expanded to incorporate the teaching of basic communications, negotiation, and conflict resolution skills. The addition of communication skills was based on the assumptions that adolescence is a period in which many parent–child conflicts arise as teenagers increasingly assert their independence from their families, and that unsuccessful resolution of the conflicts leads to reciprocally punishing parent–child transactions. The specific negotiation and communication techniques were adapted from materials developed by Robin (e.g., Robin, 1979; Robin, Kent, O'Leary, Foster, & Prinz, 1977; Robin & Weiss, 1980), Gottman (e.g., Gottman, Notarius, Gonso, & Markman, 1976), and Alexander (e.g., Alexander

& Parsons, 1973; Alexander, Barton, Schiavo, & Parsons, 1976).

Lewinsohn, Rohde, Hops, and Clarke (1991a) have recently developed an addition to the adolescent course—a simultaneous intervention for the parents of depressed teenagers. The parental intervention consists of nine 2-hour, weekly sessions that run concurrently with the CWD-A course. The teen and parent groups are led by separate leaders. The parent group was developed to provide parents with an overview of the skills and techniques that are taught in the adolescent group sessions, in order to promote parental acceptance and reinforcement of the expected positive changes for their teenagers. The parent group also provides parents with training in the same communication, negotiating, and problem-solving techniques that are taught to their teenagers, in order to equip parents and teens with the same techniques so that they may address family problems without resorting to arguments or fights. Detailed therapist manuals have been prepared for both the adolescent and parent groups (Clarke et al., 1990; Lewinsohn et al., 1991a).

Two studies have examined the efficacy of the CWD-A course. The initial study (Clarke, 1985) was conducted with a sample of 21 adolescents, 14 of whom met Research Diagnostic Criteria (Spitzer, Endicott, & Robins, 1978) at intake for either major depression or intermittent depression. The results of this initial study were promising. From intake to posttreatment, there was a significant decrease in reported depressive symptomatology, and only one adolescent met criteria for any affective disorder at the end of treatment. In the second study, Lewinsohn, Clarke, Hops, and Andrews (1990) randomly assigned clinically depressed adolescents to one of three conditions: (1) a cognitive–behavioral, psychoeducational group for adolescents only; (2) an identical group for adolescents, with their parents enrolled in a separate parent group; and (3) a waiting-list condition. Adolescents and their parents participated in extensive follow-up interviews at intake, at posttreatment, and at 1, 6, 12, and 24 months posttreatment. The results of this study demonstrated that, compared to the waiting-list subjects, treated subjects improved significantly on the depression measures. These gains were maintained at the 2-year follow-up. Although there was a trend for the results to favor the adolescent-and-parent condition over the adolescent-only condition, only one of numerous comparisons attained statistical significance.

The Elderly. Cognitive–behavioral interventions have been used in the treatment of older depressed adults for some time (e.g., Evans, Werkhoven, & Fox, 1982; Steuer & Hammen, 1983; Teri & Uomoto, 1991; Waller & Griffin, 1984; Yost, Beutler, Corbishley, & Allender, 1986). In a recent review of this literature, Teri, Curtis, Gallagher-Thompson, and Thompson (1994a) concluded that all variants of cognitive–behavioral interventions (cognitive only, behavioral only, and combined) appear to be effective in decreasing depression, not only in physically healthy older adults, but in less healthy subgroups (such as those with chronic disease and dementia). Moreover, treatment gains across all modalities appear to be maintained at follow-up.

The CWD course has been modified for use with the elderly (Steinmetz-Breckenridge, Thompson, Breckenridge, & Gallagher, 1985; Hedlund & Thompson, 1980). Thompson, Gallagher, Nies, and Epstein (1983) evaluated the modified course, the Life Satisfaction Course (LSC), in the treatment of depressed elderly persons. Six to eight participants per group met in 2-hour weekly sessions over 6 weeks. Sessions focused on monitoring and rating mood, as well as on identifying pleasant activities and unpleasant events in the participants' lives and helping them learn how to record and monitor them on a daily basis. Participants were provided with exercises to help them experience the association between activity level and mood, and to help them gain some control over their mood through engagement in pleasant activities. In the fourth session self-reward techniques were taught, and each participant was instructed to identify one specific personal problem that appeared to be amenable to change. In the fifth session, a second reachable goal was identified. The sixth class focused on how to maintain and generalize progress attained in the course. The findings indicated that the approach was effective in reducing distress in elderly individuals. The participants who completed the course reported fewer symptoms of depression, less frequent negative thoughts about themselves and the future, and increased enjoyability and frequency of pleasant events in daily living.

Lovett (1984; Lovett & Gallagher, 1988) developed a variation of the LSC for use with caregivers of frail elderly persons. This application is potentially important because such caregivers are at elevated risk of depression. Indeed, several investigators have reported depression prevalence rates of 50% or higher among caregivers (e.g., Coppell, Burton, Becker, & Fiore, 1985; Gallagher, Wrabetz, Lovett, DeMaestro, & Rose, 1988). Other researchers have noted additional difficulties among caregivers, such as guilt and resentment (York & Calsyn, 1977), low morale (Fengler & Goodrich, 1979), and perceived burden and stress (e.g., Zarit, Reever, & Bach-Peterson, 1980; see Gallagher, Lovett, & Zeiss, 1989, for a more detailed review of these studies).

The LSC for caregivers includes 10 weekly 2-hour sessions during which caregivers are taught to monitor their mood and pleasant activities; to identify pleasant activities in which they wish to engage more frequently; to set realistic, step-by-step goals for increasing their rate of these pleasant events; and to use the techniques of self-monitoring and self-reward to achieve these goals. Maximum enrollment in each group is limited to 10 caregivers, with two coinstructors. Preliminary results of this program indicate that the depression levels of both caregivers and nonclinically depressed elderly were reduced from pre- to posttreatment, whereas the waiting-list control groups did not report any significant changes (Lovett & Gallagher, 1988).

Patients with Alzheimer's Disease and Other Medical Conditions. Depression is a serious concern in patients with Alzheimer's Disease (AD) (Reifler, Larson, Teri, & Poulsen, 1986); in fact, between one-third and one-half of AD patients meet criteria for a diagnosis of depressive disorder. Teri (Teri & Uomoto, 1986; Teri & Gallagher-Thompson, 1991) recently described a modification of the CWD course as a behavioral intervention in the treatment of depression in AD. In this program, the Seattle Protocol for Behavioral Treatment of Depressed Dementia Patients, therapists meet with both patients and their caregivers for nine weekly sessions. The goal of the treatment is to offer caregivers behavioral strategies for improving the patients' depressed mood by increasing pleasant events and decreasing unpleasant events, using behavioral problem-solving strategies. Caregivers rate the patients' mood and monitor the frequency and duration of pleasant events each day throughout treatment. They also monitor changes in behavior problems that occur as they implement behavior management strategies (for a more detailed description of this program, see Teri, Logsdon, Wagner, & Uomoto, 1994b).

Depression is also a problem for many patients with other medical conditions, such as myocardial infarction and bypass surgery (Mayou, Williamson, & Foster, 1978), diabetes (Lustman, Griffeth, & Clouse, 1988; Robinson, Fuller, & Edmeades, 1988), arthritis, and other diseases (Hall, 1980); moreover, depression can occur as a consequence of certain medications (Maricle, Kinzie, & Lewinsohn, 1988). As a matter of fact, in a substantial proportion of elderly depressed individuals, the depression may be secondary to a concurrent medical condition (Kinzie, Lewinsohn, Maricle, & Teri, 1986). It is encouraging, therefore, that recent attempts to adapt behavioral interventions for the treatment of depression in the management of such patients have had very promising results (e.g., Appelbaum, Blanchard, Hickling, & Alfonso, 1988; Brown, Munford, & Munford, 1992).

Prevention of Depression. Finally, the CWD course has also been adapted and examined as a means of preventing episodes of depression among individuals at elevated risk of developing such episodes. Muñoz, Ying, Armas, Chan, and Guzza (1987) modified the CWD course and employed it with a group known to be at high risk for future depressive disorders: low-income, minority medical outpatients. Persons already experiencing an episode of depression were screened out of the study. Members of the experimental group were compared to two control groups: a no-intervention group and an information-only group who received a 40-minute videotaped presentation of the ideas in the CWD course. The results of this study indicated that participants receiving the CWD course showed a significantly greater decrease in the level of depressive symptoms, as measured by the BDI (Muñoz et al., 1988).

Manson and his colleagues (Manson, Mosely, & Brenneman, 1988; Manson, 1988) have similarly modified the CWD course for use as a preventive intervention with Native Americans, aged 45 and older. The course was modified to be culturally relevant to tribes from three Northwest reservations, and was simplified to accommodate the limitations imposed by the physical illnesses of the participants. Finally, Clarke (1990) has modified the CWD course to be offered to mildly depressed adolescents, to help them avoid becoming more seriously depressed. The mildly depressed are an especially relevant target population for prevention, because such individuals are known to be at

elevated risk for developing a more serious episode of depression (Lewinsohn, Hoberman, & Rosenbaum, 1988). A study designed to evaluate the efficacy of this intervention has been published (Clarke et al., 1995).

FUTURE DIRECTIONS

In this chapter we have presented a historical overview of behavioral theories of depression, and have described a number of behavioral procedures for the assessment and treatment of this disorder. It is clear that there are a number of effective behavioral interventions for depression, virtually all of which attempt to alter the patient's interactions with the social environment in order to decrease the level of depression. Interestingly, these programs are diverse, focusing variously on helping depressed patients to engage more frequently in pleasant activities; to sharpen their social skills; to become more accurate in self-monitoring, less stringent in self-evaluation, and more liberal in self-reinforcement; and to learn more effective coping and social problem-solving skills. Despite this diversity, it is apparent that a primary goal of these programs is to increase the amount of positive reinforcement received by depressed patients; it is also evident that attainment of this goal typically leads to a significant reduction in depressive symptomatology.

We have noted earlier that significant progress has been made in the evolution of behavioral theories of depression. Similar advances are also apparent with respect to both assessment of depression and behavioral interventions for this disorder. Nevertheless, further work is clearly required in a number of areas. For example, although investigators have demonstrated the general efficacy of behavioral approaches to the treatment of depression, we know comparatively little about which components of these interventions are responsible for changes in levels of depression, or about what mechanisms are involved in the process of change. In this respect, the literature on behavioral therapies for depression lags behind its cognitive counterpart in regard to examining mechanisms and processes of change in therapy (e.g., DeRubeis & Feeley, 1990; Persons & Burns, 1985; cf. Barber & DeRubeis, 1989). Rehm et al. (1979), Turner, Ward, and Turner (1979), and Nezu (1986; Nezu & Perri, 1989) have conducted dismantling studies, but more work remains to be done to pinpoint the critical components of behavioral treatment programs.

As a related point, it is important to note that investigators have generally *not* found the outcomes of therapies for depression to be specific to the treatment under investigation. For example, Simons, Garfield, and Murphy (1984) and Zeiss et al. (1979) both found that cognitive changes were as likely to occur in noncognitive interventions as in cognitive therapy. Similarly, the recent NIMH Collaborative Research Program also failed to find mode-specific differences in outcome measures in patients treated with IPT, cognitive therapy, or antidepressant medication (Imber et al., 1990). It appears, therefore, that regardless of the presumed specific target area of intervention (e.g., cognitions, behavior, affect), all areas are affected by treatment, and probably also affect one another in a reciprocal manner. With respect to behavioral interventions, this nonspecificity raises important questions about the role that changes in the target areas (e.g., increase in pleasant activities, improvement in social skills, increase in self-reinforcement) actually play in the amelioration of depression. It will be imperative to examine this issue more explicitly in future research. In this context, investigators should consider using causal modeling analyses in order to provide greater clarity concerning mechanisms of change in psychotherapy (cf. Hollon, DeRubeis, & Evans, 1987).

Four final areas for future research warrant comment. First, although behavioral interventions have been demonstrated to be reasonably effective in alleviating depressive symptomatology by the end of treatment, it is now apparent that depression is a recurrent disorder (Belsher & Costello, 1988). Approximately 50% of patients who are recovered at the end of treatment will relapse within 1 year (Gonzales, Lewinsohn, & Clarke, 1985; Keller et al., 1984), and perhaps as many as 90% of patients with one major depressive episode will have at least one subsequent episode of depression in their lifetimes (Clayton, 1983). Indeed, Angst et al. (1973) reported that the mean number of lifetime episodes in patients with unipolar depression is five to six. Given this high rate of relapse, it will be important for investigators to develop behavioral interventions that not only decrease levels of depression immediately following treatment, but also focus on preventing the recurrence of future episodes of depression. Preventing relapse through the use of booster sessions

after the termination of treatment (e.g., Baker & Wilson, 1985) should become an area of active investigation. This additional focus on prevention (e.g., Muñoz, 1987) will be especially important in the treatment of depressed persons who are at increased risk for relapse: patients with a history of depressive episodes (Lewinsohn, Zeiss, & Duncan, 1989); patients with secondary, as opposed to primary, depression (Keller, Shapiro, Lavori, & Wolfe, 1982); and patients who live with hostile or critical relatives (Hooley & Teasdale, 1989).

Second, most investigators who have examined the efficacy of behavioral interventions with depression have selected patients with "pure depression" for inclusion in their studies. In particular, they have excluded depressed patients with other, comorbid disorders. The results of recent studies indicate, however, that a substantial proportion of depressed individuals do present with comorbid psychiatric disorders, such as anxiety disorders, substance abuse, and (in children and adolescents) conduct disorder (Maser & Cloninger, 1990; Lewinsohn, Rohde, Seeley, & Hops, 1991b; Rohde, Lewinsohn, & Seeley, 1991). It is critical, therefore, that investigators examine the impact of comorbid disorders on the efficacy of behavioral interventions for depression.

Third, studies are needed to identify the distinguishing characteristics of those who benefit most and least from behavioral interventions. For example, five variables have consistently emerged as predictors of improvement for depressed participants in the CWD course (Brown & Lewinsohn, 1979; Steinmetz et al., 1983; Teri & Lewinsohn, 1982): higher expectations of improvement, greater life satisfaction, lack of concurrent psychotherapy or antidepressive medication, higher levels of perceived social support, and younger age. A number of writers have discussed the potential value of matching treatment components to patient characteristics, in order to provide a problem-specific approach to the treatment of depression (e.g., Biglan & Dow, 1981; McLean, 1981). For example, McKnight, Nelson, Hayes, and Jarrett (1984) compared the relative efficacy of treatments that were directly related to initial target areas and found that depressed patients with social skills difficulties or irrational cognitions improved more after receiving specific interventions for those deficits than did patients who received interventions not related to their presenting problem areas. Some of the underlying theoretical issues in this area have been discussed recently by Rude and Rehm (1991), and we refer the interested reader to that article.

Finally, it is well documented in the depression literature that approximately twice as many women than men will experience this disorder (e.g., Nolen-Hoeksema, 1990; Weissman, Leaf, Holzer, Myers, & Tischler, 1984). Despite the consistency of this finding, little attention has been given to the possibilities that depressed males and females may manifest different psychosocial problems, and that they may respond differentially to behavioral interventions. In one of the few studies to address this issue, Wilson (1982) reported that depressed male and female patients demonstrated comparable responses to behavioral treatments. Nevertheless, it is possible that the mechanisms responsible for change are different in males and females. For example, McGrath, Keita, Strickland, and Russo (1990, p. 59) suggest that behavioral treatments may be effective with depressed women "because they teach women to confront and overcome the passive, dependent role they may have been taught since childhood and that may be feeding their depressions." It is not clear that this is in fact an active mechanism of behavioral interventions for depressed females, nor is it apparent that this process does not hold for males. Nevertheless, it is possible that behavioral treatment has a differential effect on depressed men and women. Certainly, this is an important area for further exploration. It is our hope that this chapter will serve as an impetus for such investigations.

REFERENCES

Abramson, L. Y., Seligman, M. E. P., & Teasdale, J. (1978). Learned helplessness in humans: Critique and reformulation. *Journal of Abnormal Psychology, 87*, 49–74.

Alexander, J. F., & Parsons, B. V. (1973). Short-term behavioral intervention with delinquent families: Impact on family process and recidivism. *Journal of Abnormal Psychology, 81*, 219–225.

Alexander, J. F., Barton, C., Schiavo, R. S., & Parsons, B. O. (1976). Systems–behavioral intervention with families of delinquents: Therapist characteristics, family behavior and outcome. *Journal of Consulting and Clinical Psychology, 44*, 656–664.

Angst, J., Baastrup, P. C., Grof, P., Hippius, H., Poeldinger, W., & Weiss, P. (1973). The course of monopolar depression and bipolar psychoses. *Psychiatrie, Neurologie et Neurochirurgie, 76*, 246–254.

Antonuccio, D. O., Ward, C. H., & Tearnan, B. H. (1991). The behavioral treatment of unipolar depression in adult outpatients. In M. Hersen, R. M. Eisler, & P. M. Miller (Eds.), *Progress in behavior modification* (Vol. 24, pp. 152–191. Newbury Park, CA: Sage.

Appelbaum, K. A., Blanchard, E. B. Hickling, E. J., & Alfonso, M. (1988). Cognitive–behavioral treatment of a veteran population with moderate to severe rheumatoid arthritis. *Behavior Therapy, 19*, 489–502.

Arean, P. A., Perri, M. G., Nezu, A. M., Schein, R. L., Christopher, F., & Joseph, T. X. (1993). Comparative effectiveness of social problem-solving therapy and reminiscence therapy as treatments for depression in older adults. *Journal of Consulting and Clinical Psychology, 61*, 1003–1010.

Baker, A. L., & Wilson, P. H. (1985). Cognitive-behavior therapy for depression: The effects of booster sessions on relapse. *Behavior Therapy, 16*, 335–344.

Barber, J. P., & DeRubeis, R. J. (1989). On second thought: Where the action is in cognitive therapy for depression. *Cognitive Therapy and Research, 13*, 441–457.

Beck, A. T., Rush, A. J., Shaw, B. F., & Emery, G. (1979). *Cognitive therapy of depression*. New York: Guilford Press.

Beck, A. T., Ward, C. H., Mendelson, M., Mock, J., & Erbaugh, J. (1961). An inventory for measuring depression. *Archives of General Psychiatry, 4*, 561–571.

Becker, J. (1974). *Depression: Theory and research*. New York: Holt, Rinehart & Winston.

Becker, R. E., & Heimberg, R. G. (1985). Social skills training approaches. In M. Hersen & A. S. Bellack (Eds.), *Handbook of clinical behavior therapy with adults* (pp. 201–226). New York: Plenum.

Becker, R. E., Heimberg, R. G., & Bellack, A. S. (1987). *Social skills training treatment for depression*. Elmsford, NY: Pergamon Press.

Bellack, A. S., Hersen, M., & Himmelhoch, J. (1981). Social skills training compared with pharmacotherapy and psychotherapy in the treatment of unipolar depression. *American Journal of Psychiatry, 138*, 1562–1567.

Bellack, A. S., Hersen, M., & Himmelhoch, J. (1983). A comparison of social skills training, pharmacotherapy, and psychotherapy for depression. *Behaviour Research and Therapy, 21*, 101–107.

Belsher, G., & Costello, C. G. (1988). Relapse after recovery from unipolar depression: A critical review. *Psychological Bulletin, 104*, 84–96.

Bettes, B. (1988). Maternal depression and motherese: Temporal and intonational features. *Child Development, 59*, 1089–1096.

Biglan, A., & Dow, M. G. (1981). Toward a "second generation" model of depression treatment: A problem specific approach. In L. P. Rehm (Ed.), *Behavior therapy for depression: Present status and future directions* (pp. 97–121). New York: Academic Press.

Biglan, A., Hops, H., Sherman, L., Friedman, L. S., Arthur, J., & Osteen, V. (1985). Problem-solving interactions of depressed women and their husbands. *Behavior Therapy, 16*, 431–451.

Blumberg, S. R., & Hokanson, J. E. (1983). The effects of another person's response style on interpersonal behavior in depression. *Journal of Abnormal Psychology, 92*, 196–209.

Brown, M., Munford, A. M., & Munford, P. R. (1992). *Comparison of behavior and supportive therapy of psychological distress in myocardial infarction/bypass patients*. Unpublished manuscript.

Brown, M. A., & Lewinsohn, P. M. (1979). *Coping With Depression workbook*. Eugene: University of Oregon.

Brown, R. A., & Lewinsohn, P. M. (1984). A psycho-educational approach to the treatment of depression: Comparison of group, individual, and minimal contact procedures. *Journal of Consulting and Clinical Psychology*, *52*, 774–783.

Caple, M. A., & Blechman, E. A. (1976, December). *Problem-solving and self-approval training with a depressed single mother: Case study*. Paper presented at the meeting of the Association for Advancement of Behavior Therapy, New York.

Carey, M. P., Kelley, M. L., & Buss, R. R. (1986). Relationship of activity of depression in adolescents: Development of the Adolescent Activities Checklist. *Journal of Consulting and Clinical Psychology*, *54*, 320–322.

Carver, C. S., & Scheier, M. F. (1981). *Attention and self-regulation: A control theory approach to human behavior*. New York: Springer-Verlag.

Clarke, G. N. (1985). *A psychoeducational approach to the treatment of depressed adolescents*. Unpublished manuscript, University of Oregon.

Clarke, G. N. (1990). *School-based prevention of adolescent depression*. Unpublished manuscript (supported by NIMH Research Grant No. MH48118).

Clarke, G. N., Hawkins, W., Murphy, M., Sheeber, L., Lewinsohn, P. M., & Seeley, J. R. (1995). Targeted prevention of unipolar depressive disorder in an at-risk sample of high school adolescents: A randomized trial of a group cognitive intervention. *Journal of the American Academy of Child and Adolescent Psychiatry*, *34*, 312–321.

Clarke, G. N., Lewinsohn, P. M., & Hops, H. (1990). *Adolescent Coping With Depression course*. Eugene, OR: Castalia.

Clayton, P. J. (1983). The prevalence and course of the affective disorders. In J. M. Davis & J. W. Maas (Eds.), *The affective disorders* (pp. 193–201). Washington, DC: American Psychiatric Press.

Coates, D., & Wortman, C. B. (1980). Depression maintenance and interpersonal control. In A. Baum & J. E. Singer (Eds.), *Advances in environmental psychology: Vol. 2. Applications of personal control* (pp. 149–182). Hillsdale, NJ: Erlbaum.

Cole, T. L., Kelley, M. L., & Carey, M. P. (1988). The Adolescent Activities Checklist: Reliability, standardization data and factorial validity. *Journal of Abnormal Child Psychology*, *16*, 475–484.

Coppell, D. B., Burton, C., Becker, J., & Fiore, J. (1985). Relationships of cognitions associated with coping reactions to depression in spousal caregivers of Alzheimer's disease patients. *Cognitive Therapy and Research*, *9*, 253–266.

Costello, C. G. (1972). Depression: Loss of reinforcers or loss of reinforcer effectiveness? *Behavior Therapy*, *3*, 240–247.

Coyne, J. C. (1976). Toward an interactional description of depression. *Psychiatry*, *39*, 28–40.

DeRubeis, R. J., & Feeley, M. (1990). Determinants of change in cognitive therapy for depression. *Cognitive Therapy and Research*, *14*, 469–482.

Dykman, B. M., Horowitz, L. M., Abramson, L. Y., & Usher, M. (1991). Schematic and situational determinants of depressed and nondepressed students' interpretation of feedback. *Journal of Abnormal Psychology*, *100*, 45–55.

Edwards, D. W., Yarvis, R. M., Mueller, D. P., Zingale, H. C., & Wagman, W. J. (1978). Test-taking and the stability of adjustment scales: Can we assess patient deterioration? *Evaluation Quarterly*, *2*, 275–291.

Eisler, R., Hersen, M., Miller, P., & Blanchard, E. (1975). Situational determinants of assertive behavior. *Journal of Consulting and Clinical Psychology*, *43*, 330–340.

Elkin, I., Parloff, M. B., Hadley, S. W., & Autry, J. H. (1985). NIMH Treatment of Depression Collaborative Research Program. *Archives of General Psychiatry*, *42*, 305–316.

Ellis, A., & Harper, R. A. (1961). *A guide to rational living*. Hollywood, CA: Wilshire Books.

Evans, R. L., Werkhoven, W., & Fox, H. R. (1982). Treatment of social isolation and loneliness in a sample of visually impaired elderly persons. *Psychological Reports*, *51*, 103–108.

Feldman, L., & Gotlib, I. H. (1993). Social dysfunction. In C. G. Costello (Ed.), *Symptoms of depression* (pp. 85–112). New York: Wiley.

Fengler, A. & Goodrich, N. (1979). Wives of elderly disabled men: The hidden patients. *The Gerontologist*, *19*, 175–183.

Ferster, C. B. (1966). Animal behavior and mental illness. *Psychological Record*, *16*, 345–356.

Field, T. (1984). Early interactions between infants and their postpartum depressed mothers. *Infant Behavior and Development*, *7*, 517–522.

Field, T., Healy, B., Goldstein, S., & Guthertz, M. (1990). Behavior–state matching and synchrony in mother–infant interactions of nondepressed versus depressed dyads. *Developmental Psychology*, *26*, 7–14.

Fleming, A., Ruble, D., Flett, G., & Shaul, D. (1988). Postpartum adjustment in first-time mothers: Relations between mood, maternal attitudes, and mother–infant interactions. *Developmental Psychology*, *24*, 71–81.

Foley, S. H., Rounsaville, B. J., Weissman, M. M., Sholomskas, D., & Chevron, E. (1989). Individual versus conjoint interpersonal psychotherapy for depressed patients with marital disputes. *International Journal of Family Psychiatry*, *10*, 29–42.

Fuchs, C. Z., & Rehm, L. P. (1977). A self-control behavior therapy program for depression. *Journal of Consulting and Clinical Psychology*, *45*, 206–215.

Gallagher, D., Lovett, S., & Zeiss, A. (1989). Interventions with caregivers of frail elderly persons. In M. G. Ory & K. Bond (Eds.), *Aging and health* (pp. 167–190). London: Routledge.

Gallagher, D., Wrabetz, A., Lovett, S., DeMaestro, S., & Rose, J. (1988). Depression and other negative affects in family caregivers. In E. Light & B. D. Lebowitz (Eds.), *Alzheimer's disease treatment and family stress: Directions for research* (DHHS Publication No. ADM 89-1569, pp. 218–244). Washington, DC: U.S. Government Printing Office.

Glass, C. R., Merluzzi, T. V., Bierer, J. L., & Larsen, K. H. (1982). Cognitive assessment of social anxiety: Development and validation of a self-statement questionnaire. *Cognitive Therapy and Research*, *6*, 37–55.

Gonzales, L. R., Lewinsohn, P. M., & Clarke, G. N. (1985). Longitudinal follow-up of unipolar depressives: An investigation of predictors of relapse. *Journal of Consulting and Clinical Psychology*, *33*, 461–469.

Goodman, S. H., & Brumley, H. E. (1990). Schizophrenic and depressed mothers: Relational deficits in parenting. *Developmental Psychology*, *26*, 31–39.

Gordon, D., Burge, D., Hammen, C., Adrian, C., Jaenicke, C., & Hiroto, D. (1989). Observations of interactions of depressed women with their children. *American Journal of Psychiatry*, *146*, 50–55.

Gotlib, I. H. (1982). Self-reinforcement and depression in

interpersonal interaction: The role of performance level. *Journal of Abnormal Psychology, 91*, 3–13.

Gotlib, I. H., & Asarnow, R. F. (1979). Interpersonal and impersonal problem-solving skills in mildly and clinically depressed university students. *Journal of Consulting and Clinical Psychology, 47*, 86–95.

Gotlib, I. H., & Beach, S. R. H. (1995). A marital/family discord model of depression: Implications for therapeutic intervention. In N. S. Jacobson & A. S. Gurman (Eds.), *Clinical handbook of couple therapy* (pp. 411–436). New York: Guilford Press.

Gotlib, I. H., & Cane, D. B. (1989). Self-report assessment of depression and anxiety. In P. C. Kendall & D. Watson (Eds.), *Anxiety and depression: Distinctive and overlapping features* (pp. 131–169). Orlando, FL: Academic Press.

Gotlib, I. H., & Colby, C. A. (1987). *Treatment of depression: An interpersonal systems approach*. Elmsford, NY: Pergamon Press.

Gotlib, I. H., & Hammen, C. L. (1992). *Psychological aspects of depression: Toward a cognitive–interpersonal integration*. Chichester, England: Wiley.

Gotlib, I. H., & Hooley, J. M. (1988). Depression and marital distress: Current status and future directions. In S. Duck (Ed.), *Handbook of personal relationships* (pp. 543–570). Chichester, England: Wiley.

Gotlib, I. H., & Lee, C. M. (1990). Children of depressed mothers: A review and directions for future research. In C. D. McCann & N. S. Endler (Eds.), *Depression: New directions in theory, research, and practice* (pp. 187–208). Toronto: Wall & Thompson.

Gotlib, I. H., & Lee, C. M. (in press). The impact of parental depression on young children and infants. In H. Freeman (Ed.), *Interpersonal factors in the origin and course of affective disorders*. London: Royal College of Psychiatry.

Gotlib, I. H., & McCabe, S. B. (1992). An information-processing approach to the study of cognitive functioning in depression. In E. F. Walker, B. A. Cornblatt, & R. H. Dworkin (Eds.), *Progress in experimental personality and psychopathology research* (Vol. 15, pp. 131–161). New York: Springer.

Gotlib, I. H., & Meltzer, S. J. (1987). Depression and the perception of social skill in dyadic interaction. *Cognitive Therapy and Research, 11*, 41–53.

Gotlib, I. H., & Robinson, L. A. (1982). Responses to depressed individuals: Discrepancies between self-report and observer-rated behavior. *Journal of Abnormal Psychology, 91*, 231–240.

Gotlib, I. H., Wallace, P. M., & Colby, C. A. (1990). Marital and family therapy for depression. In B. B. Wolman & G. Stricker (Eds.), *Depressive disorders: Facts, theories, and treatment methods* (pp. 396–424). New York: Wiley.

Gottman, J., Notarius, C., Gonso, J., & Markman, H. (1976). *A couple's guide to communication*. Champaign, IL: Research Press.

Hall, R. C. W. (Ed.). (1980). *Psychiatric presentations of medical illness: Somatopsychic disease*. New York: Spectrum.

Hamilton, M. (1960). A rating scale for depression. *Journal of Neurology, Neurosurgery and Psychiatry, 23*, 56–61.

Hamilton, M. (1967). Development of a rating scale for primary depressive illness. *British Journal of Social and Clinical Psychology, 6*, 278–296.

Hammen, C. (1991). *Depression runs in families: The social context of risk and resilience in children of depressed mothers*. New York: Springer-Verlag.

Hammen, C. L., & Glass, D. R. (1975). Depression, activity, and evaluation of reinforcement. *Journal of Abnormal Psychology, 84*, 718–721.

Hautzinger, M., Linden, M., & Hoffman, N. (1982). Distressed couples with and without a depressed partner: An analysis of their verbal interaction. *Journal of Behavior Therapy and Experimental Psychology, 13*, 307–314.

Hedlund, B., & Thompson, L. W. (1980, August). *Teaching the elderly to control depression using an educational format*. Paper presented at the annual meeting of the American Psychological Association, Montreal.

Hersen, M., Bellack, A. S., Himmelhoch, J. M., & Thase, M. E. (1984). Effects of social skills training, amitriptyline, and psychotherapy in unipolar depressed women. *Behavior Therapy, 15*, 21–40.

Hinchliffe, M., Hooper, D., & Roberts, F. J. (1978). *The melancholy marriage*. New York: Wiley.

Hoberman, H. M., & Lewinsohn, P. M. (1985). The behavioral treatment of depression. In E. E. Beckham & W. R. Leber (Eds.), *Handbook of depression: Treatment, assessment, and research* (pp. 39–81). Homewood, IL: Dorsey Press.

Hoberman, H. M., Lewinsohn, P. M., & Tilson, M. (1988). Group treatment of depression: Individual predictors of outcome. *Journal of Consulting and Clinical Psychology, 56*, 393–398.

Hollon, S. D., DeRubeis, R. J., & Evans, M. D. (1987). Causal mediation of change in treatment for depression: Discriminating between nonspecificity and noncausality. *Psychological Bulletin, 102*, 139–149.

Hooley, J. N., & Teasdale, J. D. (1989). Predictors of relapse in unipolar depressives: Expressed emotion, marital distress, and perceived criticism. *Journal of Abnormal Psychology, 98*, 229–235.

Hops, H., Biglan, A., Sherman, L., Arthur, J., Friedman, L., & Osteen, V. (1987). Home observations of family interactions of depressed women. *Journal of Consulting and Clinical Psychology, 55*, 341–346.

Imber, S. D., Pilkonis, P. A., Sotsky, S. M., Elkin, I., Watkins, J. T., Collins, J. F., Shea, M. T., Leber, W. R., & Glass, D. R. (1990). Mode-specific effects among three treatments for depression. *Journal of Consulting and Clinical Psychology, 58*, 352–359.

Ingram, R. (1990). Self-focused attention in clinical disorders: Review and a conceptual model. *Psychological Bulletin, 107*, 156–176.

Jacobson, E. (1929). *Progressive relaxation*. Chicago: University of Chicago Press.

Jacobson, N. S., & Anderson, E. (1982). Interpersonal skills deficits and depression in college students: A sequential analysis of the timing of self-disclosures. *Behavior Therapy, 13*, 271–282.

Jacobson, N. S., Dobson, K., Fruzzetti, A. E., Schmaling, K. B., & Salusky, S. (1991). Marital therapy as a treatment for depression. *Journal of Consulting and Clinical Psychology, 59*, 547–557.

John, K., & Weissman, M. M. (1987). The familial and psychosocial measurement of depression. In A. J. Marsella, R. M. A. Hirschfeld, & M. M. Katz (Eds.), *The measurement of depression* (pp. 344–375). New York: Guilford Press.

Keller, M. B., Klerman, G. L., Lavori, P. W., Coryell, W., Endicott, J., & Taylor, J. (1984). Long-term outcome of episodes of major depression: Clinical and public health significance. *Journal of the American Medical Association, 252,* 788–792.

Keller, M. B., Shapiro, R. W., Lavori, P. W., & Wolfe, N. (1982). Recovery in major depressive disorder: Analysis with the life table and regression models. *Archives of General Psychiatry, 39,* 905–910.

Kinzie, J. D., Lewinsohn, P. M., & Maricle, R. (1986). The relationship of depression to medical illness in an older community population. *Comprehensive Psychiatry, 27,* 241–246.

Klerman, G. L., Weissman, M. M., Rounsaville, B. J., & Chevron, E. (1984). *Interpersonal psychotherapy of depression.* New York: Basic Books.

Kowalik, D. L., & Gotlib, I. H. (1987). Depression and marital interaction: Concordance between intent and perception of communication. *Journal of Abnormal Psychology, 96,* 127–134.

Lewinsohn, P. M. (1974). A behavioral approach to depression. In R. J. Friedman & M. M. Katz (Eds.), *The psychology of depression: Contemporary theory and research* (pp. 157–185). New York: Wiley.

Lewinsohn, P. M. (1976). Activity schedules in the treatments of depression. In J. D. Kruboltz & C. E. Thoreseu (Eds.), *Counseling methods* (pp. 74–83). New York: Holt, Rinehart & Winston.

Lewinsohn, P. M., Antonuccio, D. O., Steinmetz, J. L., & Teri, L. (1984). *The Coping With Depression course: A psychoeducational intervention for unipolar depression.* Eugene, OR: Castalia.

Lewinsohn, P. M., & Atwood, G. E. (1969). Depression: A clinical research approach. *Psychotherapy: Theory, Research, and Practice, 6,* 166–171.

Lewinsohn, P. M., Biglan, A., & Zeiss, A. M. (1976). Behavioral treatment of depression. In P. O. Davidson (Ed.), *The behavioral management of anxiety, depression and pain* (pp. 91–146). New York: Brunner/Mazel.

Lewinsohn P. M. & Clarke, G. N. (1986). *Pleasant Events Schedule for Adolescents.* Unpublished manuscript.

Lewinsohn, P. M., Clarke, G. N., Hops, H., & Andrews, J. (1990). Cognitive–behavioral treatment for depressed adolescents. *Behavior Therapy, 21,* 385–401.

Lewinsohn, P. M., Hoberman, H., & Rosenbaum, M. (1988). A prospective study of risk factors for unipolar depression. *Journal of Abnormal Psychology, 97,* 251– 264.

Lewinsohn, P. M., Hoberman, H., Teri, L., & Hautzinger, M. (1985a). An integrative theory of depression. In S. Reiss & R. Bootzin (Eds.), *Theoretical issues in behavior therapy* (pp. 331–359). New York: Academic Press.

Lewinsohn, P. M., Lobitz, W. C., & Wilson, S. (1973). "Sensitivity" of depressed individuals to aversive stimuli. *Journal of Abnormal Psychology, 81,* 259–263.

Lewinsohn, P. M., Mermelstein, R. M., Alexander, C., & MacPhillamy, D. J. (1985b). The Unpleasant Events Schedule: A scale for the measurement of aversive events. *Journal of Clinical Psychology, 41,* 483–498.

Lewinsohn, P. M., Mischel, W., Chaplin, C., & Barton, R. (1980a). Social competence and depression: The role of illusory self-perceptions. *Journal of Abnormal Psychology, 89,* 203–217.

Lewinsohn, P. M., Muñoz, R. F., Youngren, M. A., & Zeiss, A. M. (1986). *Control your depression* (2nd ed.). Englewood Cliffs, NJ: Prentice-Hall.

Lewinsohn, P. M., & Rohde, P. (1987). Psychological measurement of depression: Overview and conclusions. In A. J. Marsella, R. M. A. Hirschfeld, & M. M. Katz (Eds.), *The measurement of depression* (pp. 240–266). New York: Guilford Press.

Lewinsohn, P. M., Rohde, P., Hops, H., & Clarke, G. N. (1991a). *Leader's manual for parent groups: Adolescent Coping With Depression course.* Unpublished manuscript.

Lewinsohn, P. M., Rohde, P., Seeley, J. R., & Hops, H. (1991b). Comorbidity of unipolar depression: I. Major depression with dysthymia. *Journal of Abnormal Psychology, 100,* 205–213.

Lewinsohn, P. M., & Schaffer, M. (1971). The use of home observations as an integral part of the treatment of depression: Preliminary report of case studies. *Journal of Consulting and Clinical Psychology, 37,* 87–94.

Lewinsohn, P. M., & Shaw, D. A. (1969). Feedback about interpersonal behavior as an agent of behavior change: A case study in the treatment of depression. *Psychotherapy and Psychosomatics, 17,* 82–88.

Lewinsohn, P. M., Sullivan, J. M., & Grosscup, S. J. (1980b). Changing reinforcing events: An approach to the treatment of depression. *Psychotherapy: Theory, Research, and Practice, 47,* 322–334.

Lewinsohn, P. M., Weinstein, M., & Alper, T. (1970). A behavioral approach to the group treatment of depressed persons: A methodological contribution. *Journal of Clinical Psychology, 26,* 525–532.

Lewinsohn, P. M., Weinstein, M., & Shaw, D. (1969). Depression: A clinical–research approach. In R. D. Rubin & C. M. Frand (Eds.), *Advances in behavior therapy* (pp. 231–240). New York: Academic Press.

Lewinsohn, P. M., Youngren, M. A., & Grosscup, S. J. (1979). Reinforcement and depression. In R. A. Depue (Ed.), *The psychobiology of the depressive disorders: Implications for the effects of stress* (pp. 291–315). New York: Academic Press.

Lewinsohn, P. M., Zeiss, A. M., & Duncan, E. M. (1989). Probability of relapse after recovery from an episode of depression. *Journal of Abnormal Psychology, 98,* 107–116.

Libet, J., & Lewinsohn, P. M. (1973). The concept of social skill with special reference to the behavior of depressed persons. *Journal of Consulting and Clinical Psychology, 40,* 304–312.

Lieberman, M. A. (1975). *Survey and evaluation of the literature in verbal psychotherapy of depressive disorders.* Rockville, MD: Clinical Research Branch, National Institute of Mental Health.

Livingood, A. B., Daen, P., & Smith, B. D. (1983). The depressed mother as a source of stimulation for her infant. *Journal of Clinical Psychology, 39,* 369–375.

Lovett, S. (1984). *Caregiver research program: "Increasing life satisfaction" class for caregivers manual.* Unpublished manuscript.

Lovett, S. & Gallagher, D. (1988). Psychoeducational interventions for family caregivers: Preliminary efficacy data. *Behavior Therapy, 19,* 321–330.

Lubin, B. (1967). *Manual for Depression Adjective Check Lists.* San Diego: Educational and Industrial Testing Service.

Lustman, P. J., Griffith, L. S., & Clouse, R. E. (1988). Depression in adults with diabetes. *Diabetes Care, 11,* 605–612.

MacPhillamy, D. J., & Lewinsohn, P. M. (1982). The Pleasant Events Schedule: Studies on reliability, validity, and scale intercorrelations. *Journal of Consulting and Clinical Psychology, 50,* 363–380.

Manson, S. M. (1988). American Indian and Alaska Native

mental health research. *Journal of the National Center*, *1*, 1–64.

Manson, S. M., Mosely, R. M., & Brenneman, D. L. (1988). *Physical illness, depression, and older American Indians: A preventive intervention trial*. Unpublished manuscript, Oregon Health Sciences University.

Maricle, R. A., Kinzie, J. D., & Lewinsohn, P. M. (1988). Medication associated depression: A two and a half year follow-up of a community sample. *International Journal of Psychiatry in Medicine*, *8*, 283–292.

Maser, J. D., & Cloninger, C. R. (Eds.). (1990). *Comorbidity in anxiety and mood disorders*. Washington, DC: American Psychiatric Press.

Mayou, R., Williamson, B., & Foster, A. (1978). Outcome two months after myocardial infarction. *Journal of Psychosomatic Research*, *22*, 439–445.

McGrath, E., Keita, G. P., Strickland, B. R., & Russo, N. F. (Eds.). (1990). *Women and depression: Risk factors and treatment issues*. Washington, DC: American Psychological Association.

McKnight, D. L., Nelson, R. O., Hayes, S. C., & Jarrett, R. B. (1984). Importance of treating individually-assessed response classes in the amelioration of depression. *Behavior Therapy*, *15*, 315–335.

McLean, P. D. (1976). Therapeutic decision-making in the behavioral treatment of depression. In P. O. Davidson (Ed.), *The behavioral management of anxiety, depression, and pain* (pp. 54–89). New York: Brunner/Mazel.

McLean, P. D. (1981). Remediation of skills and performance deficits in depression: Clinical steps and research findings. In J. Clarkin & H. Glazer (Eds.), *Behavioral and directive strategies* (pp. 172–204). New York: Garland.

McLean, P. D., & Hakstian, A. R. (1979). Clinical depression: Comparative efficacy of outpatient treatments. *Journal of Consulting and Clinical Psychology*, *47*, 818–836.

McLean, P. D., & Hakstian, A. R. (1990). Relative endurance of unipolar depression treatment effects: Longitudinal follow-up. *Journal of Consulting and Clinical Psychology*, *58*, 482–488.

Mills, M., Puckering, C., Pound, A., & Cox, A. (1985). What is it about depressed mothers that influences their children's functioning? In J. E. Stevenson (Ed.), *Recent research in developmental psychopathology* (pp. 11–17). Oxford: Pergamon Press.

Muñoz, R. F. (Ed.). (1987). *Depression prevention: Research directions*. Washington, DC: Hemisphere.

Muñoz, R. F., Ying, Y. W., Armas, R., Chan, F., & Guzza, R. (1987). The San Francisco Depression Prevention Project: A randomized trial with medical outpatients. In R. F. Muñoz (Ed.), *Depression prevention: Research directions* (pp. 199–215). Washington, DC: Hemisphere.

Muñoz, R. F., Ying, Y. W., Bernal, G., Perez-Stable, E. J., Sorensen, J. L., & Hargreaves, W. A. (1988). *The prevention of clinical depression: A randomized controlled trial*. Unpublished manuscript, University of California at San Francisco.

Nezu, A. M. (1986). Efficacy of a social problem-solving therapy approach for unipolar depression. *Journal of Consulting and Clinical Psychology*, *54*, 196–202.

Nezu, A. M. (1987). A problem-solving formulation of depression: A literature review and proposal of a pluralistic model. *Clinical Psychology Review*, *7*, 121–144.

Nezu, A. M., Nezu, C. M., & Perri, M. G. (1989). *Problem-solving therapy for depression: Theory, research, and clinical guidelines*. New York: Wiley.

Nezu, A. M., & Perri, M. G. (1989). Social problem-solving therapy for unipolar depression: An initial dismantling investigation. *Journal of Consulting and Clinical Psychology*, *57*, 408–413.

Nezu, A. M., & Ronan, G. F. (1985). Life stress, current problems, problem solving, and depressive symptoms: An integrative model. *Journal of Consulting and Clinical Psychology*, *53*, 693–697.

Nolen-Hoeksema, S. (1990). *Sex differences in depression*. Stanford, CA: Stanford University Press.

Oatley, K., & Bolton, W. (1985). A social-cognitive theory of depression in reaction to life events. *Psychological Review*, *92*, 372–388.

O'Leary, K. D., & Beach, S. R. H. (1990). Marital therapy: A viable treatment for depression. *American Journal of Psychiatry*, *147*, 183–186.

O'Leary, K. D., Risso, L. P., & Beach, S. R. H. (1990). Attributions about the marital discord/depression link and therapy outcome. *Behavior Therapy*, *21*, 413–422.

Persons, J. B., & Burns, D. D. (1985). Mechanisms of action of cognitive therapy: The relative contributions of technical and interpersonal interventions. *Cognitive Therapy and Research*, *9*, 539–551.

Pyszczynski, T., & Greenberg, J. (1987). Self-regulatory perseveration and the depressive self-focusing style: A self-awareness theory of reactive depression. *Psychological Bulletin*, *102*, 122–138.

Pyszczynski, T., Greenberg, J., Hamilton, J., & Nix, G. (1991). On the relationship between self-focused attention and psychological disorder: A critical reappraisal. *Psychological Bulletin*, *110*, 538–543.

Radloff, L. S. (1977). The CES-D Scale: A new self-report depression scale for research in the general population. *Applied Psychological Measurement*, *1*, 385–401.

Rehm, L. P. (1977). A self-control model of depression. *Behavior Therapy*, *8*, 787–804.

Rehm, L. P. (1987). The measurement of behavioral aspects of depression. In A. J. Marsella, R. M. A. Hirschfeld, & M. M. Katz (Eds.), *The measurement of depression* (pp. 199–239). New York: Guilford Press.

Rehm, L. P. (1990). Cognitive and behavioral theories. In B. B. Wolman & G. Stricker (Eds.), *Depressive disorders: Facts, theories, and treatment methods* (pp. 64–91). New York: Wiley.

Rehm, L. P., Fuchs, C. Z., Roth, D. M., Kornblith, S. J., & Romano, J. M. (1979). A comparison of self-control and assertion skills treatments of depression. *Behavior Therapy*, *10*, 429–442.

Reifler, B. V., Larson, E., Teri, L., & Poulsen, M. (1986). Alzheimer's disease and depression. *Journal of the American Geriatrics Society*, *34*, 855–859.

Robin, A. L. (1979). Problem-solving communication training: A behavioral approach to the treatment of parent–adolescent conflict. *American Journal of Family Therapy*, *7*, 69–82.

Robin, A. L., Kent, R. N., O'Leary, K. D., Foster, S., & Prinz, R. J. (1977). An approach to teaching parents and adolescents problem solving skills: A preliminary report. *Behavior Therapy*, *8*, 639–643.

Robin, A. L., & Weiss, J. G. (1980). Criterion-related validity of behavioural and self-report measures of problem-solving communication skills in distressed and nondistressed parent–adolescent dyads. *Behavioural Assessment*, *2*, 339–352.

Robinson, N., Fuller, J. H., & Edmeades, S. P. (1988). Depression and diabetes. *Diabetic Medicine*, *5*, 268–274.

Rohde, P., Lewinsohn, P. M., & Seeley, J. R. (1991). Comorbidity of unipolar depression: Comorbidity with other mental disorders in adolescents and adults. *Journal of Abnormal Psychology, 100,* 214–222.

Roth, D., Bielski, R., Jones, J., Parker, W., & Osborn, G. (1982). A comparison of self-control therapy and combined self-control therapy and antidepressant medication in the treatment of depression. *Behavior Therapy, 13,* 133–144.

Rude, S. S., & Rehm, L. P. (1991). Response to treatments for depression: The role of initial status on targeted cognitive and behavioral skills. *Clinical Psychology Review, 11,* 493–514.

Ruscher, S. M., & Gotlib, I. H. (1988). Marital interaction patterns of couples with and without a depressed partner. *Behavior Therapy, 19,* 455–470.

Sacco, W. P., & Graves, D. J. (1984). Childhood depression, interpersonal problem-solving, and self-ratings of performance. *Journal of Clinical Child Psychology, 13,* 10–15.

Sanchez, V. C., Lewinsohn, P. M., & Larson, D. W. (1980). Assertion training: Effectiveness in the treatment of depression. *Journal of Clinical Psychology, 36,* 526–529.

Shipley, C. R., & Fazio, A. F. (1973). Pilot study of a treatment for psychological depression. *Journal of Abnormal Psychology, 82,* 372–376.

Simons, A. D., Garfield, S. L., & Murphy, G. E. (1984). The process of change in cognitive therapy and pharmacotherapy: Changes in mood and cognitions. *Archives of General Psychiatry, 41,* 45–51.

Skinner, B. F. (1953). *Science and human behavior.* New York: Free Press.

Spitzer, R. S., Endicott, J., & Robins, E. (1978). Research Diagnostic Criteria: Rationale and reliability. *Archives of General Psychiatry, 35,* 773–782.

Steinmetz, J. L., Lewinsohn, P. M., & Antonuccio, D. O. (1983). Prediction of individual outcome in a group intervention for depression. *Journal of Consulting and Clinical Psychology, 51,* 331–337.

Steinmetz-Breckenridge, J., Thompson, L. W., Breckenridge, J. N., & Gallagher, D. E. (1985). Behavioral group therapy with the elderly: A psychoeducational approach. In D. Upper & S. Ross (Eds.), *Handbook of behavioral group therapy* (pp. 275–302). New York: Plenum.

Steuer, J. L., & Hammen, C. L. (1983). Cognitive–behavioral group therapy for the depressed elderly: Issues and adaptations. *Cognitive Therapy and Research, 7,* 285– 296.

Teri, L., Curtis, J., Gallagher-Thompson, D., & Thompson, L. W. (1994a). Cognitive-behavior therapy with depressed older adults. In L. S. Scheider, C. S. Reynolds, B. Lebowitz, & A. Friedhoff (Eds.), *Diagnosis and treatment of depression in the elderly: Proceedings of the NIH consensus development conference* (pp. 279–291). Washington, DC: American Psychiatric Press.

Teri, L., & Gallagher-Thompson, D. (1991). Cognitive–behavioral interventions for treatment of depression in Alzheimer's patients. *Gerontologist, 31,* 413–416.

Teri, L., & Lewinsohn, P. M. (1982). Modification of the Pleasant and Unpleasant Events Schedules for use with the elderly. *Journal of Consulting and Clinical Psychology, 50,* 444–445.

Teri, L., & Lewinsohn, P. M. (1985). *Depression and age: The relationship of age, gender, and method of assessment on the symptom pattern of depression.* Unpublished manuscript.

Teri, L., & Logsdon, R. G. (1991). *Identifying pleasant activities for individuals with Alzheimer's disease: The Pleasant Events Schedule-AD.* Unpublished manuscript.

Teri, L., Logsdon, R. G., Wagner, A., & Uomoto, J. (1994b). The caregiver role in behavioral treatment of depression in dementia patients. In E. Light, B. Lebowitz, & G. Niederehe (Eds.), *New directions in Alzheimer's disease and family stress* (pp. 185–204). New York: Springer.

Teri, L., & Uomoto, J. (1986). *Alzheimer's disease: Teaching the caregiver behavioral strategies.* Paper presented at the annual meeting of the American Psychological Association, Washington, DC.

Teri, L., & Uomoto, J. (1991). Reducing excess disability in dementia patients: Training caregivers to manage patient depression. *Clinical Gerontologist, 10,* 49–63.

Thompson, L. W., Gallagher, D., Nies, G., & Epstein, D. (1983, November). *Cognitive–behavioral vs. other treatments of depressed alcoholics and inpatients.* Paper presented at the 17th Annual Convention of the Association for Advancement of Behavior Therapy, Washington, DC.

Turner, R. W., Ward, M. F., & Turner, J. D. (1979). Behavior therapy for depression: An evaluation of the therapeutic components. *Journal of Clinical Psychology, 55,* 166–175.

Waller, M., & Griffin, M. (1984). Group therapy for depressed elders. *Geriatric Nursing,* 309–311.

Weissman, M. M., Leaf, P. J., Holzer, C. E., Myers, J. K., & Tischler, G. L. (1984). The epidemiology of depression: An update on sex differences in rates. *Journal of Affective Disorders, 7,* 179–188.

Weissman, M. M., & Paykel, E. S. (1974). *The depressed woman: A study of social relationships.* Chicago: University of Chicago Press.

Weissman, M. M., Prusoff, B. A., & Thompson, W. E. (1978). Social adjustment by self-report in a community sample and in psychiatric outpatients. *Journal of Nervous and Mental Disease, 166,* 317–326.

Williams, J. G., Barlow, D. H., & Agras, W. S. (1972). Behavioral measurement of severe depression. *Archives of General Psychiatry, 27,* 330–333.

Wilson, P. H. (1982). Combined pharmacological and behavioural treatment of depression. *Behaviour Research and Therapy, 20,* 173–184.

York, J. L., & Calsyn, R. J. (1977). Family involvement in nursing homes. *The Gerontologist, 17,* 500–505.

Youngren, M. A., & Lewinsohn, P. M. (1980). The functional relationship between depression and problematic behavior. *Journal of Abnormal Psychology, 89,* 333–341.

Youngren, M. A., Zeiss, A. M., & Lewinsohn, P. M. (1977). *Interpersonal Events Schedule.* Unpublished manuscript, University of Oregon.

Yost, E., Beutler, L., Corbishley, M. A., & Allender, J. (1986). *Group cognitive therapy: A treatment approach for depressed older adults.* Elmsford, NY: Pergamon Press.

Zarit, A. M., Reever, K., & Bach-Peterson, J. (1980). Relatives of the impaired elderly: Correlates of feelings of burden. *The Gerontologist, 20,* 649–655.

Zeiss, A. M., Lewinsohn, P. M., & Muñoz, R. F. (1979). Nonspecific improvement effects in depression using interpersonal, cognitive, and pleasant events focused treatments. *Journal of Consulting and Clinical Psychology, 47,* 427–439.

13

Interpersonal Psychotherapy

JOHN C. MARKOWITZ
MYRNA M. WEISSMAN

Interpersonal therapy (IPT) was developed by Klerman and colleagues in the late 1960s and 1970s as part of a clinical trial to test the efficacy of maintenance psychotherapy for outpatients with major depression (Klerman, Weissman, Rounsaville, & Chevron, 1984). Its success with depressed patients in a series of controlled comparative treatment trials has led to its evolving use in treating a range of psychiatric diagnoses. Such expansion parallels the growth of cognitive–behavioral therapy (CBT; Beck, Rush, Shaw, & Emery, 1979) in moving from mood disorders to other psychiatric disorders. Despite its impressive research achievements, relatively few practitioners have been trained in IPT. This situation is now changing, however, as training programs are being developed, including one at Cornell University Medical College. The technique of IPT and its new adaptations, detailed elsewhere (Klerman et al., 1984; Klerman & Weissman, 1993), can be broadly outlined here.

IPT is a time-limited, manualized, antidepressant treatment. Its time frame permits comparison with pharmacological treatments. IPT as an acute treatment usually consists of 12–20 weeks of once-a-week outpatient treatment; as a monthly maintenance treatment, it may continue for years. The IPT manual (Klerman et al., 1984) specifies techniques and distinguishes IPT from alternative psychotherapeutic treatments. The IPT therapist explicitly targets the patient's Axis I mood disorder, as opposed to attempting character change.

Based on the interpersonal theories of Meyer (1957), Sullivan (1953), and others, IPT is fo-cused on the relationship between mood and interpersonal events. Disturbing events (Brown, Harris, & Copeland, 1978; Henderson et al., 1978; Weissman, 1987) and psychosocial stress (Pearlin & Lieberman, 1979) may precipitate depression, whereas having confidants and other intimate relationships may protect against depression (Brown et al., 1978). Once a depressive episode arises, it impairs interpersonal functioning. Depressed patients tend to withdraw socially. As depression compromises their mood, energy, enjoyment, cognitive functioning, and expectations of each encounter they have with others, the patients function less competently at work and in relationships. IPT theory avoids etiological statements about whether untoward psychosocial events cause depression or vice versa; indeed, for clinical purposes, causality may not matter. The salient therapeutic points are that patients learn to link mood with interpersonal contacts, and to recognize that by appropriately addressing interpersonal situations, they may simultaneously improve both their relationships and their depressed state.

Of the brief psychotherapies employed in clinical research trials, IPT may most closely approximate what many psychodynamic practitioners do in their offices, and hence may be the most generalizable of these treatments. Nonetheless, few practitioners focus their therapy in the fashion described below. Prerequisites for training in IPT include several years of clinical experience in psychotherapy, including exposure to patients with mood disorders. Psychiatrists, psychologists, and social workers have been trained in IPT. Training consists of reading the manual (Klerman et al., 1984) and relevant literature (Markowitz, 1995), supervision of videotaped sessions of at least three cases by a trained IPT clinician; and certification by an expert in IPT based on those tapes.

TECHNIQUE IN INTERPERSONAL PSYCHOTHERAPY

Time Frame

When IPT is used as an acute treatment, its brevity requires an adjustment for therapists used to long-term therapies. Sitting back is a luxury neither patients nor therapists can afford; nor are long silences helpful for depressed, ruminative patients. The time frame imposes both a structure and a pressure on treatment. At the same time, therapists must not feel so hurried that they sacrifice the therapeutic alliance or interrupt their patients' focus on affectively laden interpersonal experiences. Balancing these opposing pulls takes some experience.

Maintenance use of IPT assumes that depression has already remitted; hence time pressure is less of an issue.

Directive, Active Stance

Given the time limits of IPT and the goal of treating depression, IPT therapists do not avoid focusing the therapy for their patients, to indicate that certain topics are more important than others. Therapists engage patients on an affectively laden focus, stressing the interaction between depressive symptoms and events in the interpersonal area. Therapists actively provide encouragement, explore options, and offer direct suggestions when appropriate. Role playing is often helpful to help patients test out new interpersonal approaches. The active, brief approach of IPT appears effective even for a chronic disorder such as dysthymic disorder (Mason, Markowitz, & Klerman, 1993; Markowtiz, 1994).

Adjusting to IPT from Different Backgrounds

The more experience one has, and the better one's natural skills as a therapist, the better.

A background in psychodynamic training is a mixed blessing for IPT, offering good insights but sometimes bad instincts. On the one hand, it is crucial to be able to read a patient's character and to approach him/her accordingly. Psy-chodynamic understanding helps in formulating a sense of the key interpersonal problem areas. On the other hand, there is a danger in sitting back too passively. Technical differences include avoiding genetic interpretations, an intrapsychic conflict model, dream interpretation, and transferential focus in favor of interpersonal techniques. IPT stays mainly in the "here and now."

Some psychodynamic therapists feel uncomfortable "cheerleading" by overtly supporting patients. It is important to keep in mind that depressed patients are unlikely to view their own behavior objectively; rather, they will tend to underappreciate accomplishments and to emphasize negative prognostications. Until that outlook improves, it is reasonable for a therapist to freely praise steps taken by a patient that appear to be unalloyed accomplishments. This does not mean that the therapist inevitably "takes the patient's side." The therapist should not excuse the patient's role in situations the patient contributes to or sabotages; rather, the interpersonal situation should be carefully explored so that the patient can learn to alter maladaptive interpersonal behaviors.

A similar issue is that making direct suggestions may feel to some therapists like a violation of neutrality, putting words in the patient's mouth. Our sense is that most therapists in most therapies communicate their biases; in IPT, this is sometimes overt. The key question is this: *What does the patient want?* Asking a patient what he/she wants in a given situation, and *what options exist* to achieve those desires, can relieve the therapist of having to make direct suggestions in many instances. It is preferable and empowering when the patient, thus prompted, can resolve an issue unaided. At times, however, when a resolution to the patient's situation appears obvious and the patient fails to see it, direct suggestions can be useful. Depressed patients sometimes need a gentle push. Thus an IPT therapist is *not* neutral, at least in the sense that he/she is actively working to relieve patients of their psychiatric disorders.

A therapist trained in CBT who is learning IPT will have to readjust his/her approach to focus on feelings surrounding interpersonal situations, rather than on the automatic thoughts and underlying schemas such encounters may evoke. Cognitive training may bring the risk of minimizing affect, or of intervening too quickly, before a link between mood and interpersonal events clearly emerges or is fully experienced by the patient. There are also technical differences between IPT and CBT: IPT is on the whole less structured, and lacks an itemized agenda and formal homework, for example.

Learning any directed technique such as IPT increases therapists' awareness of how they handle patients, whether or not they are employing that technique at the moment. Just as psychodynamic understanding informs IPT, IPT adds to understanding of a patient in other psychotherapies. Put another way, we all tend to make interpersonal, cognitive, behavioral, psychodynamic, and other interventions in the blend we each think of, idiosyncratically, as generic psychotherapy. Learning a particular technique helps parse one aspect of psychotherapeutic work.

STRUCTURE OF INTERPERSONAL PSYCHOTHERAPY

IPT can be divided into three phases. An initial phase, usually lasting one to three sessions, permits anamnesis and diagnosis, and introduces the patient to his/her role in the therapy. In the middle phase, which occupies most of the therapeutic work, therapist and patient focus on one of four interpersonal problem areas: grief, role dispute, role transition, or interpersonal deficits. In the final sessions, the therapist helps the patient review and consolidate gains in preparation for termination.

Sessions are generally scheduled weekly (twice weekly at the start of therapy in some protocols), for 50–60 minutes each. The first session, in which the diagnosis is made and much of the basic history may emerge, sometimes runs a bit longer.

Initial Session

The first sessions set the tone and structure for all that follows. The therapist has multiple tasks to achieve in this relatively brief time: at once evaluating, educating, and preparing the patient for his/her role in the therapy. The goals are described below:

Diagnosing the Depression

The IPT therapist follows a "medical model," diagnosing major depression according to formal criteria (American Psychiatric Association, 1994).

Assessments such as the Hamilton Rating Scale for Depression (Hamilton, 1960) and the Beck Depression Inventory (Beck, 1978) may be useful both as change measures and as ways of demonstrating to the patient the constellation and severity of depressive symptomatology.

Eliciting the Interpersonal Inventory

At the same time, the therapist explores the important past and present relationships in the patient's life, constructing an "interpersonal inventory." Particularly important are the depth of intimacy the patient has been able to achieve, the presence of confidants, dysfunctional patterns that emerge across relationships, the reciprocal expectations surrounding relationships, and the degree to which these are fulfilled. What does the patient want from relationships, and upon whom can he/she rely? What changes have occurred in key relationships preceding and during the depressive interval?

Establishing the Interpersonal Problem Area

On the basis of the history of present illness and the interpersonal inventory, the therapist decides which of the four interpersonal problem areas best fits the patient's situation. Often the hardest decision comes in choosing among problem areas. From a practical viewpoint, too many foci tend to diffuse the treatment, and provide less of a comfortable framework for therapy. The area of interpersonal deficits should be reserved as a last resort, to be used only when none of the other three problem areas fit.

Developing a Treatment Plan

In concluding the evaluation, the sophisticated therapist will consider differential therapeutics (Frances, Clarkin, & Perry, 1984). Is a trial of medication indicated? The medically oriented approach of IPT, giving the patient a diagnosis and the sick role, facilitates combining psychotherapy and pharmacotherapy. Is IPT likely to be effective for a given patient? Our knowledge of the mode specificity of antidepressant psychotherapy is limited, but patients who have massive social dysfunction (Sotsky et al., 1991) or interpersonal deficits, or who lack definable interpersonal problem areas, are probably suboptimal candidates for IPT.

Having concluded these assessments, the therapist makes a series of linked interventions that frame the remainder of the therapeutic work.

Giving the Sick Role

As described by Parsons (1951), the sick role excuses patients from usual social roles and obligations that their illness renders impossible, but substitutes the requirement that the patients work to recover their health. IPT explicitly inducts patients into the sick role, with accompanying psychoeducation about the nature of depression. Since depressed patients and those around them may regard their symptoms as signs of willfulness and weakness (fatigue as laziness, inappropriate guilt as deserved, etc.), this matter-of-fact medical explanation often provides some relief.

Making the Interpersonal Formulation

The IPT therapist's key gambit is to combine information gleaned from diagnostic measures and the interpersonal inventory into a brief narrative explanation linking the patient's depressed mood to the interpersonal problem area.

> Your mood, sleep disturbance, fatigue, suicidal thoughts, and feelings of being helpless, hopeless, and worthless are all symptoms of depression, and this depression is related to what's been happening in your [interpersonal situation]. Your situation may feel hopeless and untreatable, but it isn't. That feeling is itself a symptom of depression, and depression is a highly treatable disorder. About 1 in 10 Americans become depressed in their lifetimes; with treatment, the great majority get better. Depression affects and is affected by interpersonal relationships . . . [here the therapist notes the patient's social withdrawal, losses, and altered relationships]. Interpersonal psychotherapy, a brief treatment based on this connection, has been proven to be highly effective for the kind of depression you have. We'll focus on stresses and relationships in your life that may be contributing to depression.

The patient must agree to this formulation before work moves into the middle phase of treatment.

Other Aspects

Other key aspects of the early stage of IPT include establishing a therapeutic alliance, with the therapist as a positive, supportive figure; beginning psychoeducation about depression; and instilling hope. The early sessions also provide the patient with instruction on how to be an IPT patient: the "here-and-now" focus on the link between mood and interpersonal events; the brief treatment framework; and the limited goals of treating depression and associated interpersonal issues (rather than character pathology per se). (See Table 13.1.)

Mobilizing the patient is important from the start. Depressed patients often sit home, feeling helpless and ruminating on their worthlessness. This should be identified as symptomatic of depression and dealt with. Without prescribing the patient homework, the therapist can encourage him/her to get out of the house, despite feelings of social avoidance and inadequacy. The therapist explains that activity is likely to make the patient feel better than inactivity, will provide some sense of accomplishment, and will leave less time for worry. Moreover, it will provide the opportunity for occurrence of interpersonal interactions to work on together in therapy.

Middle Sessions

The middle phase of IPT begins with agreement on the interpersonal formulation as a treatment contract. The therapist and patient thereafter focus on one or more of the four IPT problem areas in this, the heart of the treatment process.

Sessions begin with the therapist's question, "How have things been since we last met?" This query keeps the focus in the here and now, and elicits one of two responses: Patients typically reply with a description of their mood or of recent events. Either response allows the therapist to help a patient make the crucial connection between mood and interpersonal events. If the patient is feeling better or worse, what has happened—or what has the patient done—during the week that might account for the change? If the patient reports an event, what was his/her emotional response to it? Sessions focus explicitly on the interpersonal problem area (e.g., "So this is where you stand in your role dispute"), which provides a framework for understanding the depressive episode and thematic continuity across sessions. Summaries at the ends of sessions are helpful to reinforce key points. There are different strategies for handling each of the four interpersonal problem areas.

TABLE 13.1. Goals of Early IPT Sessions

A. Deal with the depression.

   1. Review depressive symptoms.
   2. Give the syndrome a name: formal diagnosis.
   3. Provide psychoeducation about depression and its treatment.
   4. Give the patient the "sick role."
   5. Evaluate the need for medication.

B. Relate depression to interpersonal context. Review current and past interpersonal relationships as they relate to current depressive symptoms. Determine with the patient the "interpersonal inventory":

   1. Nature of interaction with significant persons.
   2. Patient's and significant persons' expectations of each other, and whether these were fulfilled.
   3. Satisfying and unsatisfying aspects of the relationships.
   4. Changes the patient wants in the relationships.

C. Identify the major problem area.

   1. Determine the problem area related to current depression and set treatment goals.
   2. Determine which relationship or aspect of a relationship is related to the depression and what might change in it.

D. Explain the IPT concepts and contract.

   1. Outline your understanding of the problem.
   2. Agree on treatment goals (which problem area will be the focus)
      a. Emphasize *brief* treatment (element of time).
      b. Stress that target is depression (not character).
   3. Describe procedures of IPT: "here-and-now" focus, need for patient to discuss important concerns; review of current interpersonal relations; discussion of practical aspects of treatment (length, frequency, times, fees, policy for missed appointments).

Note. Adapted from Klerman, Weissman, Rounsaville, & Chevron (1984). Copyright 1984 by Basic Books. Adapted by permission of HarperCollins Publishers.

Grief

Uncomplicated bereavement is not a psychiatric disorder, despite its long-recognized symptomatic overlap with depression (e.g., Freud, 1917/1957). Only a minority of bereavements become complicated by depression. Yet loss of an important person is a severe interpersonal stress that clearly can precipitate depression. For the purposes of IPT, grief is narrowly defined as the reaction to the death of a significant other; other losses, such as those of jobs, ideals, and divorces, are categorized as role transitions. The therapist should determine whether the patient has lost significant people, and if so when, under what circumstances and with what reactions. If the patient has not been able to grieve, the therapist may suspect that a delayed or distorted grief reaction may be related to the presenting depression (Klerman et al., 1984).

The IPT therapist treating a patient with complicated bereavement strives to facilitate the grieving process—to encourage catharsis, as well as to explore what the lost person meant to the patient, the happy and unhappy aspects of their relationship, and the void that the death has left in the patient's life. (See Table 13.2.) Once patients have recognized grief as an appropriate connection to their depressed state, they frequently can mourn with little more than gentle encouragement from the therapist. The therapist thus often takes a quietly empathic role, occasionally intervening to reinforce the linkage between the loss and a patient's subsequent symptoms.

Still, the treatment of grief is not simply an encouragement of abreaction. As the mourning process continues, the therapist can help the patient look for alternative supports and relationships to fill the needs of the lost relationship. Although replacement can never fully substitute for a loss, the grieving patient can once again begin to pursue interests, develop other relationships, and re-establish a satisfying life in the aftermath of the loss.

TABLE 13.2. Outline of IPT Goals and Strategies for Middle Sessions: Grief

Goals:
1. Facilitate the mourning process.
2. Help the patient re-establish interest and relationships to substitute for what has been lost.

Strategies:
1. Review depressive symptoms.
2. Relate symptom onset or exacerbation to death of significant other.
3. Reconstruct the patient's relationship with the deceased.
4. Describe the sequence and consequences of events just prior to, during, and after the death.
5. Explore associated feelings (negative and positive).
6. Consider possible ways for the patient to become involved with others.

Note. Adapted from Klerman, Weissman, Rounsaville, & Chevron (1984). Copyright 1984 by Basic Books. Adapted by permission of HarperCollins Publishers.

Role Dispute

Depressed patients frequently present with an interpersonal dispute: a struggle with a sexual partner, family member, roommate, or coworker. The social withdrawal of depression may have isolated patients from important confidants; decreased libido may have exacerbated marital tensions; or cognitive inefficiency may have provoked difficulties at work. Conversely, dysfunctional relationships in any social setting may have contributed to the development of the depressive syndrome.

The therapist helps such a patient to understand his/her role in the dispute, and the link between friction in this relationship and the patient's depressive symptoms. Next, the therapist encourages the patient to explore potential options in changing the relationship, and the likely consequences of each option. Again, establishing what it is that the patient wants and how he/she can best achieve it are central issues. (See Table 13.3.)

A primary question is whether the relationship in question has truly reached an impasse. Sometimes clarification of communication patterns or simple compromise is sufficient to reestablish a generally positive relationship. It may sometimes be appropriate to see a couple jointly in the course of IPT, although the patient may feel more independent if able to handle the situation on his/her own. If the interpersonal situation proves truly impassable and impossible, the patient may come to realize that ending the relationship is preferable to its unhappy continuation.

One interesting theme we have explored in role disputes is that of transgression. Some interpersonal disputes arise in complex circumstances, with no party truly "wrong"; at other times, however, people clearly violate the implicit or explicit rules of societal conduct. Examples of such a broken trust would be knowingly practicing unprotected sexual intercourse with an unsuspecting partner while infected with the human immunodeficiency virus (HIV) (Markowitz, Klerman, Perry, Clougherty, & Josephs, 1993), or having an extramarital affair.

When a person has been wronged, he/she has a moral right to justice, retribution, or at least an apology. Depressed patients often describe situations in which they have been unjustly hurt yet have not defended themselves. This may be attributable to difficulties with self-assertion and guilt that constitute symptoms of the mood disorder. It is therapeutic to assist injured patients in seeing the justice of self-assertion, confronting their tormentors, and declaring their moral rights. Patients thereby mobilize themselves in a more constructive interpersonal role, end further damage within their role disputes, and build self-esteem.

Role Transition

The broad category of role transition encompasses any shift in interpersonal role. Such a transition may be the beginning or ending of any life situation: marriage or divorce; matriculation or graduation; hiring or firing; the diagnosis of medical disease or the prescription of its cure. Each situation represents a potentially disconcerting change in identity to a patient, who, particularly once depressed, may harp on the disadvantages of the change rather than the opportunities it presents.

The therapist's goals are to help the patient understand the role transition and its ramifications (both positive and negative), so as to facilitate better adjustment to the new interpersonal situation (see Table 13.4). The initial step is to acknowledge that the patient is indeed in a role transition, and to link this transition to mood symptoms. The patient can come to terms with the loss of the previous role, mourning its benefits and celebrating its achievements; can ex-

TABLE 13.3. Outline of IPT Goals and Strategies for Middle Sessions: Role Disputes

Goals:
1. Identify dispute.
2. Choose plan of action.
3. Modify expectations or faulty communication to bring about a satisfactory resolution.

Strategies:
1. Review depressive symptoms.
2. Relate symptom onset to overt or covert dispute with significant other with whom patient is currently involved; in particular, search for any transgressions in relationship.
3. Determine stage of dispute:
   a. Renegotiation (calm participants).
   b. Impasse (increase disharmony in order to reopen negotiation).
   c. Dissolution (assist mourning).
4. Explore how nonreciprocal role expectations contribute to dispute:
   a. What are the issues in the dispute?
   b. What are differences in expectations and values?
   c. What are the options?
   d. What is the likelihood of finding alternatives?
   e. What resources are available to bring about change in the relationship?
5. Are there parallels in other relationships?
   a. What is the patient gaining?
   b. What unspoken assumptions lie behind the patient's behavior?
6. How is the dispute perpetuated? (inability to express anger, excessive guilt, caretaking role, etc.)
7. How does depression affect the patient's behaviors and choices?

Note. Adapted from Klerman, Weissman, Rounsaville, & Chevron (1984). Copyright 1984 by Basic Books. Adapted by permission of HarperCollins Publishers.

plore current options to achieve what he/she wants; and can gradually come to see the advantages as well as the drawbacks of the change.

Interpersonal Deficits

Several factors make interpersonal deficits the most difficult of the IPT problem areas. Patients who fit into this category by default do not fit into the other three problem areas, all of which provide intuitively reasonable connections between depression and an interpersonal situation. As the rubric suggests, these patients have significant characterological problems and a paucity of intimate or supportive interpersonal relationships. The therapist thus faces the unenviable task of addressing character pathology in brief therapy with a patient who has few interpersonal resources.

This IPT problem area has been least used, least studied, and least conceptually developed. It is in effect a residual category for patients whose interpersonal difficulties may indicate comorbid personality disorders and a worse prognosis. Some may meet criteria for schizoid or schizotypal personality disorder, and may lack any history of intimate relationships. On the other hand, if a patient is dysthymic or chronically depressed, apparent interpersonal deficits may reflect the lingering state effect of chronic mood disorder rather than characterological traits (Markowitz, Moran, Kocsis, & Frances, 1992b; Markowitz, 1993). For many patients with such deficits, it is usually possible (and preferable), to find a role transition instead.

Despite these caveats, depressed patients with interpersonal deficits may respond to treatment and should not be dismissed as hopeless by therapists. Treatment encourages such a patient to reduce social isolation and experiment with new social relationships and behavior patterns, using IPT as a setting for reviewing progress and setbacks. (See Table 13.5.) Discussion may address dysfunctional patterns in which the patient has participated in relationships, with an emphasis on exploring alternative options in the present rather than seeking an explanation of the past. Many depressed patients with interpersonal deficits have problems with appropriate self-assertion, expression of anger,

TABLE 13.4. Outline of IPT Goals and Strategies for Middle Sessions: Role Transitions

Goals:
1. Help the patient mourn and accept the loss of the old role.
2. Help the patient regard the new role as more positive.
3. Build self-esteem by developing a sense of mastery over demands of new roles.

Strategies:
1. Review depressive symptoms.
2. Relate depressive symptoms to difficulty in coping with recent life change (e.g., diagnosis of dysthymia as role transition).
3. Review positive and negative aspects of old and new roles.
4. Explore feelings about what is lost.
5. Explore feelings about the change itself.
6. Explore opportunities in the new role.
7. Realistically evaluate what is lost.
8. Encourage appropriate release of affect.
9. Encourage development of social support system and of new skills necessary to the new role.

Note. Adapted from Klerman, Weissman, Rounsaville, & Chevron (1984). Copyright 1984 by Basic Books. Adapted by permission of HarperCollins Publishers.

and taking social risks. Given many such patients' poverty of intimate relationships, the therapist may be forced to rely more than with other IPT problem areas upon patterns arising in therapist–patient interactions.

Final Sessions

By the final few weeks of IPT, the patient's depressive symptoms should in most cases have resolved; patient and therapist can now review what has happened in therapy and look ahead beyond it. Assessing the patient's gains should stress the patient's role in having achieved them: the interpersonal steps taken in mourning, resolving a role dispute or transition, developing self-assertion, or the like. Although the therapist may have pointed out connections, the patient is the one who has put them to use and actually made important life changes.

This summary of therapy serves several purposes. It empowers once-depressed patients with an appreciation of their ability to influence their mood and relationships; this consolidates their gains, fosters independence, and eases the

threat of the impending termination. A second aim is to review patients' depressive symptoms and interpersonal problem areas, so that they can recognize potential recurrence or relapse and anticipate their points of vulnerability. Like the summaries at the ends of sessions, this recapitulation ending the course of treatment provides a sense of closure and reinforcement of important issues.

Sixteen weeks or thereabouts constitute a considerable period of time—a period that is usually ample to achieve the resolution of a mood episode. On the other hand, it would be unrealistic to expect all loose ends in the patient's life to be neatly knotted in this interval. Mourning, role disputes, role transitions, and interpersonal deficits may persist beyond the length of the therapy itself. The message for the patient is that therapy has at least permitted an understanding of and an initial attack on the problem, which the patient will be able to continue addressing after therapy ends.

Some therapists sometimes have difficulty ending brief therapy. They have just begun to really get to know the patient. The patient and therapist have just achieved a significant, gratifying result as a successful team. The patient, no longer symptomatic from depression, may be identifying other maladaptive interpersonal traits that invite further therapy. Both patient and therapist may regret the ending they face and be tempted to continue. The time pressure

TABLE 13.5. Outline of IPT Goals and Strategies for Middle Sessions: Interpersonal Deficits

Goals:
1. Reduce the patient's social isolation.
2. Encourage formation of new relationships.

Strategies:
1. Review depressive symptoms.
2. Relate depressive symptoms to problems of social isolation or unfulfillment.
3. Review past significant relationships, including both their negative and positive aspects.
4. Explore repetitive patterns in relationships.
5. Discuss patient's positive and negative feelings about therapist, and seek parallels in other relationships.

Note. Adapted from Klerman, Weissman, Rounsaville, & Chevron (1984). Copyright 1984 by Basic Books. Adapted by permission of HarperCollins Publishers.

that has been useful up to this point may now threaten to undo the therapy.

Yet it is crucial that the therapist not end a brief therapy with an ambivalent tone carrying an implicit message of melancholy or regret. To do so undermines the patient's sense of self-sufficiency and may leave him/her at greater risk for recurrence. Rather, the therapist should note that termination is sometimes a sad time, precisely *because* they've worked so well together as a team and accomplished so much. Reminding the patient that the initial goal of treating depression has been accomplished, the IPT therapist should make termination a sort of graduation from therapy—a natural and appropriate step forward, rather than a defeat. The patient has gained a knowledge of depression and of interpersonal interventions to forestall its return; thus, he/she should leave the therapy with the sense of a task completed and well done.

In the event that depression persists at the end of IPT, the therapist should credit the patient fully for his/her efforts in therapy, to minimize the possibility of depressed self-blame for treatment failure. Following the IPT model of exploring options, the therapist should point out that many treatment options remain that may still be successful, and should refer the patient to such alternatives.

Booster Sessions

In a series of publications, Frank and colleagues (Frank, Kupfer, & Perel, 1989; Frank et al., 1990; Frank, Kupfer, Wagner, McEachran, & Cornes, 1991) have demonstrated the prophylactic value of maintenance IPT sessions, even on a monthly basis, in averting recurrence among patients who had had three or more episodes of major depression. Since major depression is more often than not a recurrent disorder, some form of ongoing therapy may well be appropriate for remitted patients. The frequency of maintenance sessions may vary—for example, the inaugural trial of IPT consisted of 8 months of weekly sessions—but IPT remains in any case time-limited.

Even when maintenance IPT is contemplated, however, psychotherapists should frame the end of acute treatment as a type of termination. With the initial task accomplished, patients are now graduated to a less intensive, protective therapy in which they can maintain euthymia and continue to work on remaining interpersonal problems. Therapist and patient should agree on the duration and frequency of booster sessions prior to termination of acute IPT.

RESEARCH QUESTIONS FOR INTERPERSONAL PSYCHOTHERAPY

IPT was developed to meet the need for a standardized antidepressant psychotherapy of acute major depression. Its development took place over a 12-year span in the Boston–New Haven Collaborative Depression Project (Klerman, DiMascio, Weissman, Prusoff, & Paykel, 1974; DiMascio et al., 1979; Weissman et al., 1979; Weissman, Klerman, Prusoff, Sholomskas, & Padian, 1981). As with any efficacious treatment, success in that project naturally led to a search for new indications. Adapting IPT by modifying the techniques to specific settings and diagnoses, and detailing these changes in new manuals, researchers have expanded its use.

Questions to address in research on IPT are as follows.

1. What are the limits of expansion? Given that interpersonal issues are ubiquitous, are there mood or nonmood disorders for which an adaptation of IPT would not be helpful? To date, the treatment of patients with substance abuse is the only diagnostic area in which IPT has been tried without clear benefit.

2. What makes IPT effective? Process issues have received relatively little study; most research involving IPT has primarily considered outcome data. Studies have demonstrated that trained IPT therapists can capably adhere to a manualized treatment protocol (Hill, O'Grady, & Elkin, 1992), although "difficult" patients can interfere with therapists' performance (Foley, O'Malley, Rounsaville, Prusoff, & Weissman, 1987). Krupnick and colleagues (1992) found that treatment alliance significantly influenced acute treatment outcome for IPT but not for other brief interventions, while Frank et al. (1991) noted that the thematic purity of maintenance IPT sessions correlated with sustained remission. Yet little research to date has addressed the active elements of IPT—for example, how reliably therapists agree in choosing IPT problem areas; whether the choice of problem areas affects outcome; and which of the numerous psychoeducational and psychotherapeutic components of IPT are effective for which subgroups of patients.

EFFICACY STUDIES

This section summarizes the development and adaptation of IPT for various diagnostic groups and patient populations.

Efficacy in Acute Major Depression

The Boston–New Haven study was a four-cell, 16-week trial of 81 depressed outpatients (DiMascio et al., 1979; Weissman et al., 1979, 1981)). It compared IPT, the tricyclic antidepressant amitriptyline, their combination, and a nonscheduled psychotherapy treatment. Both active treatments were more effective than the control, and the combination of psychotherapy and psychopharmacology was superior to either alone. At a 1-year follow-up, many patients sustained their benefits from the 16-week IPT intervention, and patients who received IPT with or without medication demonstrated better psychosocial functioning than those who had received either amitriptyline alone or the control condition (Weissman et al., 1981). Some patients in each cell relapsed and required further treatment.

The most ambitious comparative psychotherapy study to date has been the National Institute of Mental Health Treatment of Depression Collaborative Research Program (Elkin et al., 1989), in which 250 depressed outpatients at four sites were randomly assigned to 16 weeks of IPT, CBT, imipramine, or placebo treatment. Most subjects completed at least 15 weeks or 12 treatment sessions. Less severely depressed patients improved in all cells. Imipramine produced the most rapid response and was most clearly superior to placebo. The IPT cell had the least attrition. IPT patients rivaled those receiving the medication on numerous outcome measures, and IPT had a mean outcome superior to placebo for more severely depressed patients, whereas CBT did not.

Efficacy in Depressed Subpopulations

Depressed Geriatric Patients

The elderly are socially marginalized, suffer physical difficulties in addition to other psychosocial stressors (such as the death of spouses and friends), and have a significant suicide risk. Their sensitivity to the adverse effects of medication suggests the potential benefit of antide-

pressant psychotherapies for this population. In a 6-week pilot study comparing IPT to nortriptyline in 30 depressed geriatric patients, IPT showed some advantages over the tricyclic antidepressant. This was largely attributable to medication side effects, which led to higher attrition in the nortriptyline group (Sloane, Stapes, & Schneider, 1985).

Depressed HIV-Positive Patients

IPT has also been modified to address the needs of depressed HIV-positive patients (IPT-HIV). Learning that one is infected with the virus that causes acquired immune deficiency syndrome (AIDS) is itself a role transition, and the infected individual faces a variety of additional psychosocial stressors. In an open trial of IPT, the depressed subjects were mostly gay men besieged by losses of lovers, friends, jobs, lifestyle, and health. Therapists had to choose from a surfeit of IPT problem areas. Patients were given the sick role with the statement that they had *two* medical conditions, depression and HIV infection. Of the 23 patients, 20 improved, despite worsening medical problems in some instances (Markowitz, Klerman, & Perry, 1992a). The time pressure of HIV seemed to synergize with that of the brief therapy format.

In a randomized treatment trial currently underway at Cornell University Medical College in New York (Markowitz et al., in press), HIV-positive patients are being randomly assigned to IPT, CBT, supportive therapy alone, and imipramine plus supportive therapy.

Depressed Adolescents

Adolescents have a high prevalence of mood disorder, carry a risk of suicide, and are also at risk for ongoing psychiatric and social dysfunction; moreover, the efficacy of antidepressant medication for this population has not been proven. Mufson and colleagues at Columbia University have modified IPT for depressed adolescents (IPT-A). Modifications include the consideration of adolescents' developmental issues and the addition of a fifth problem area— that of the single-parent family, an interpersonal situation that arose frequently in pilot cases (Moreau, Mufson, Weissman, & Klerman, 1991; Mufson, Moreau, Weissman, & Klerman, 1993). This pilot study of IPT-A is currently in progress.

Dysthymic Patients

Attempting to treat a chronic, often lifelong mood disorder in a brief 4-month therapy might seem foolhardy. Yet pilot data suggest that IPT may be as effective as antidepressant medication in treating dysthymia, whose hallmark is impaired interpersonal functioning (Mason et al., 1993). IPT-D modifies the concept of role transition to include the diagnosis and treatment of dysthymic disorder in IPT as itself a role transition out of dysthymic disorder and into a healthier mode of interpersonal functioning. The pressure of the brief treatment format on patient and therapist may counterbalance the tendency with a chronic psychiatric diagnosis to lower treatment expectations and settle for partial improvement.

Seventeen patients, including seven desipramine failures, have received IPT-D at the Payne Whitney Clinic to date. None have worsened, and 10 have reached remission (Hamilton Rating Scale for Depression scores < 6): Hamilton scores fell from 21.5 at baseline to 7.4 after 16 weeks (Markowitz, 1994). The several patients followed for as long as 2 years after acute treatment have maintained these gains.

Efficacy in Maintenance Treatment of Major Depression

The first use of IPT, in 1967, was in the Boston–New Haven study (Klerman et al., 1974; Paykel, DiMascio, Haskell, & Prusoff, 1975). This 8-month trial of weekly sessions would today be considered a study of continuation therapy (i.e., about 6 months) rather than a study of maintenance treatment (a year or longer). Klerman, Weissman, and colleagues compared the effects of IPT, amitriptyline, and their combination for 150 outpatients with acute depression who had already shown a response to the tricyclic medication. Maintenance pharmacotherapy averted relapse and symptom exacerbation (Klerman et al., 1974; Paykel et al., 1975), whereas IPT had the delayed effect of enhancing social functioning in the final months of treatment (Weissman, Klerman, Paykel, Prusoff, & Hanson, 1974). There were no negative interactions between the two treatments, and accordingly, combined psychotherapy and pharmacotherapy produced the best outcome (Klerman et al., 1974; Paykel et al., 1975).

The Pittsburgh group has completed a most impressive treatment study of 128 outpatients who had suffered at least three episodes of major depression (Frank et al., 1989, 1990, 1991). Patients were stabilized on combined high-dose imipramine pharmacotherapy and IPT, then randomly assigned to 3 years of maintenance treatment in one of five cells: a monthly maintenance form of IPT (IPT-M), either (1) alone, (2) combined with imipramine, or (3) combined with placebo; or medication clinic visits for either (4) continuing high-dose imipramine or (5) placebo, without additional psychotherapy. Patients received a host of psychosocial and biological assessments. Imipramine maintenance was associated with the lowest rate of recurrence. IPT-M, a relatively dilute dosage of psychotherapy, had an intermediate recurrence rate, significantly lower than that of the placebo conditions. IPT-M did not augment the prophylactic effect of medication alone (Frank et al., 1989, 1990). IPT-M treatments that maintained a strong interpersonal focus were associated with lower recurrence rates (Frank et al., 1991).

Another Pittsburgh study is currently comparing a separate modification of IPT for maintenance treatment of recurrent late-life depression (IPT-LLM) to antidepressant medication in a double-blind maintenance study of their efficacy (Reynolds et al., 1992). Geriatric patients with recurrent major depression are being treated with nortriptyline and IPT-LLM, and, if response persists through a continuation phase, are randomly assigned to one of four maintenance cells.

Efficacy for Nonaffective Diagnoses

The demonstration of the efficacy of IPT in treating depression has encouraged its expansion to other diagnostic areas.

Bulimia

Fairburn and colleagues (1991) treated 75 patients with bulimia nervosa, who were randomly assigned to 18 sessions of either CBT, a simplified behavioral therapy, or IPT. All three treatments effectively reduced psychopathology, including depressive symptoms and overeating. That CBT more effectively modified patients' disturbed attitudes toward shape and weight is not surprising, since IPT was not modified for the treatment of bulimia and hence not directed toward eating-related issues. These findings persisted at a 1-year follow-up (Fairburn, Jones, Peveler, Hope, & O'Connor, 1993). IPT also proved as effective as CBT for bulimic patients treated in a group format—the first use of IPT as a group therapy (Wifley et al., 1993). A research study at Columbia and Stanford Universities is attempting to replicate the results of the Fairburn study.

Substance Abuse

Rounsaville and colleagues have made two attempts to adapt IPT to the treatment of substance-related disorders. In the first, 72 opiate abusers maintained on methadone were treated either with weekly IPT or with a low-contact monthly clinic visit. Recruitment, attrition, and other methodological difficulties compromised this comparison, which found no added benefit for IPT (Rounsaville, Glazer, Wilber, Weissman, & Kleber, 1983). The authors noted both that IPT was added to an already intensive treatment program (which may have accounted for its lack of efficacy), and that the brief IPT framework may have been incompatible with the longer-range goals of the methadone maintenance program. A maintenance model of IPT might better fit such circumstances.

In a second study, 42 outpatient cocaine-abusing patients were assigned to 12 weeks of either IPT or behavioral treatment. The outcome goal was drug abstinence. Although most treatment differences did not achieve statistical significance, IPT generally appeared less effective than the alternative treatment, particularly in analyses that stratified patients for severity of initial substance abuse (Carroll, Rounsaville, & Gawin, 1991).

Efficacy in Other Formats

Some studies have altered the format of IPT.

Conjoint Treatment

Marital conflict, separation, and divorce have been strongly associated with the precipitation of depressive episodes (Rounsaville, Weissman, Prusoff, & Herceg-Baron, 1979), and individual psychotherapy for depressed patients who are in marital disputes may prematurely end some marriages (Locke & Wallace, 1976; Gurman & Kniskern, 1978). Because the interpersonal focus of IPT might be expected to work for couples, a manual and training procedure were developed for a conjoint therapy for depressed patients with marital disputes (IPT-CM).

Eighteen patients whose major depression was linked to the onset or worsening of marital disputes were treated in a pilot study in which they were randomly assigned to 16 weeks of IPT or IPT-CM. In the latter condition both spouses were required to attend therapy, whereas the standard IPT retained an individual treatment format. Both treatment cells reported improvement of depressive symptoms and social functioning in therapy. But though the two groups did not differ on these outcome measures, the IPT-CM patients showed better marital adjustment, greater demonstration of marital affection, and better sexual relations than did IPT patients (Foley, Rounsaville, Weissman, Sholomskas, & Chevron, 1989). These pilot findings require replication with a larger sample and a no-treatment control group.

Interpersonal Counseling for Primary Care Medical Patients

Patients in primary care medical settings have been shown to have high levels of anxiety, depression, and somatic complaints (Goldberg, 1972; Brodaty & Andrews, 1983). Not all of these patients have psychiatric disorders, but even depressive symptoms in the absence of a full clinical syndrome can be debilitating (Wells et al., 1989). Many patients present, and present repeatedly, to primary care physicians because of these psychological rather than medical symptoms.

Klerman and colleagues (1987) developed interpersonal counseling (IPC), a brief psychosocial intervention based on IPT, to treat this patient population. Nurse practitioners in the primary care setting were trained with a scripted treatment manual to administer a maximum of six 30-minute counseling sessions focusing on a patient's current functioning: recent life events, familial and occupational stress, and patterns and changes in interpersonal relationships. The IPC therapist considers the interpersonal environment the context in which anxious and depressive somatic and emotional symptoms arise.

A total of 128 patients scoring 6 or higher on the Goldberg General Health Questionnaire (GHQ; Goldberg, 1972) were matched for GHQ scores and assigned either to IPC or to a naturalistic follow-up group that received no psychological intervention. Over an average of 3 months (which often included only one or two IPC sessions), the treated subjects reported greater symptom relief than the control group, particularly an alleviation of depressed mood.

This preliminary study suggested that a brief intervention could benefit psychologically distressed medical patients. On the other hand, rather than reducing utilization of health care services, IPC was associated with greater use of mental health services by patients newly attuned to the psychological source of their symptoms. The use of psychological interventions such as IPC among primary care patients deserves further study.

Efficacy of Other Adaptations

Excitement over the potential benefits of IPT has encouraged the development of projects in a number of areas. Frank and colleagues in Pittsburgh have combined a form of IPT with a social zeitgeber model (Ehlers, Frank, & Kupfer, 1988) of minimizing disruptive life events, to create a maintenance treatment for bipolar patients pharmacologically stabilized on lithium. Prophylactic strategies focus on symptom management and the relation of symptoms to the frequency and intensity of social interactions, overstimulation, and the quotidian rhythms of social functioning (particularly sleep).

A group in Buffalo, New York is exploring forms of IPT to treat depressed caretakers of chronic patients with traumatic brain injuries. Investigators at Columbia University are exploring IPT for depressed peripartum women. Other projects are addressing IPT for borderline personality disorder, IPT for recovering alcohol-dependent patients, and IPT as an inpatient and as a group therapy. An adaptation of IPT usually involves the evolution of a manual to address the characteristic interpersonal issues of a given treatment population. Therapists trained according to the manual can then test the adaptation of IPT for efficacy in outcome studies.

CONCLUSION

IPT has proven its efficacy both as a form of acute treatment (particularly for outpatients with major depression) and also increasingly as a maintenance treatment. It shows promise in various adaptations to particular diagnostic populations, including geriatric, adolescent, HIV-positive, dysthymic, and bulimic patients, although the studies in many of these areas are preliminary. It also appears adaptable to treatment modes other than individual outpatient

psychotherapy. As a treatment for substance-related disorders, IPT has not been shown to be effective for either opiate or cocaine abusers. Continuing research may further specify indications for the use of IPT in contrast to other antidepressant psychotherapies, and in combination with pharmacotherapies.

REFERENCES

American Psychiatric Association. (1994). *Diagnostic and statistical manual of mental disorders* (4th ed.). Washington, DC: Author.

Beck, A. T. (1978). *Beck Depression Inventory*. Philadelphia: Center for Cognitive Therapy.

Beck, A. T., Rush, A. J., Shaw, B. F., & Emery, G. (1979). *Cognitive therapy of depression*. New York: Guilford Press.

Brodaty, H., Andrews, G. (1983). Brief psychotherapy in family practice: A controlled perspective intervention trial. *British Journal of Psychiatry, 143*, 11–19.

Brown, G. W., Harris, T., & Copeland, J. R. (1978). Depression and loss. *British Journal of Psychiatry, 130*, 1–18.

Carroll, K. M., Rounsaville, B. J., & Gawin, F. H. (1991). A comparative trial of psychotherapies for ambulatory cocaine abusers: Relapse prevention and interpersonal psychotherapy. *American Journal of Drug and Alcohol Abuse, 17(3)*, 229–247.

DiMascio, A., Weissman, M. M., Prusoff, B. A., Neu, C., Zwilling, M., & Klerman, G. L. (1979). Differential symptom reduction by drugs and psychotherapy in acute depression. *Archives of General Psychiatry, 36*, 1450–1456.

Ehlers, C. L., Frank, E., & Kupfer, D. J. (1988). Social zeitgebers and biological rhythms: A unified approach to understanding the etiology of depression. *Archives of General Psychiatry, 45*, 948–952.

Elkin, I., Shea, M. T., Watkins, J. T., Imber, S. D., Sotsky, S. M., Collins, J. F., Glass, D. R., Pilkonis, P. A., Leber, W. R., Docherty, J. P., Fiester, S. J., & Parloff, M. B. (1989). National Institute of Mental Health Treatment of Depression Collaborative Research Program: General effectiveness of treatments. *Archives of General Psychiatry, 46*, 971–982.

Fairburn, C. G., Jones, R., Peveler, R. C., Carr, S. J., Solomon, R. A., O'Connor, M. E., Burton, J., & Hope, R. A. (1991). Three psychological treatments for bulimia nervosa: A comparative trial. *Archives of General Psychiatry, 48*, 463–469.

Fairburn, C. G., Jones, R., Peveler, R. C., Hope, R. A., & O'Connor, M. (1993). Psychotherapy and bulimia nervosa: Longer-term effects of interpersonal psychotherapy, behavior therapy, and cognitive behavior therapy. *Archives of General Psychiatry, 50*, 419–428.

Foley, S. H., O'Malley, S., Rounsaville, B., Prusoff, B. A., & Weissman, M. M. (1987). The relationship of patient difficulty to therapist performance in interpersonal psychotherapy of depression. *Journal of Affective Disorders, 12*, 207–217.

Foley, S. H., Rounsaville, B. J., Weissman, M. M., Sholomskas, D., & Chevron, E. (1989). Individual versus conjoint interpersonal psychotherapy for depressed patients with marital disputes. *International Journal of Family Psychiatry*, *10*, 29–42.

Frances, A., Clarkin, J. F., & Perry, S. (1984). *Differential therapeutics in psychiatry: The art and science of treatment selection*. New York: Brunner/Mazel.

Frank, E., Kupfer, D. J., & Perel, J. M. (1989). Early recurrence in unipolar depression. *Archives of General Psychiatry*, *46*, 397–400.

Frank, E., Kupfer, D. J., Perel, J. M., Cornes, C., Jarrett, D. B., Mallinger, A. G., Thase, M. E., McEachran, A. B., & Grochocinski, V. J. (1990). Three-year outcomes for maintenance therapies in recurrent depression. *Archives of General Psychiatry*, *47*, 1093–1099.

Frank, E., Kupfer, D. J., Wagner, E. F., McEachran, A. B., & Cornes, C. (1991). Efficacy of interpersonal psychotherapy as a maintenance treatment of recurrent depression. *Archives of General Psychiatry*, *48*, 1053–1059.

Freud, S. (1957). Mourning and melancholia. In J. Strachey (Ed. and Trans.), *The standard edition of the complete psychological works of Sigmund Freud* (Vol. 14, pp. 237–260). London: Hogarth Press.

Goldberg, D. P. (1972). *The detection of psychiatric illness by questionnaire* (Maudsley Monograph No. 21). Oxford: Oxford University Press.

Gurman, A. S., & Kniskern, D. P. (1978). Research on marital and family therapy: Progress, perspective, and prospect. In S. B. Garfield & A. B. Bergin (Eds.), *Handbook of psychotherapy and behavior change* (pp. 817–902). New York: Wiley.

Hamilton, M. (1960). A rating scale for depression. *Journal of Neurology, Neurosurgery and Psychiatry*, *25*, 56–62.

Henderson, S., Byrne, D. G., Duncan-Jones, P., Adcock, S., Scott, R., & Steele, G. P. (1978). Social bonds in the epidemiology of neurosis. *British Journal of Psychiatry*, *132*, 463–466.

Hill, C. E., O'Grady, K. E., & Elkin, I. (1992). Applying the collaborative study psychotherapy rating scale to rate therapist adherence in cognitive-behavior therapy, interpersonal therapy, and clinical management. *Journal of Consulting and Clinical Psychology*, *60*, 73–79.

Klerman, G. L., Budman, S., Berwick, D., Weissman, M. M., Damico-White, J., Demby, A., & Feldstein, M. (1987). Efficacy of brief psychosocial intervention for symptoms of stress and distress among patients in primary care. *Medical Care*, *25*, 1078–1088.

Klerman, G. L., DiMascio, A., Weissman, M. M., Prusoff, B. A., & Paykel, E. S. (1974). Treatment of depression by drugs and psychotherapy. *American Journal of Psychiatry*, *131*, 186–191.

Klerman, G. L., & Weissman, M. M. (Eds.). (1993). *New applications of interpersonal therapy*. Washington, DC: American Psychiatric Press.

Klerman, G. L., Weissman, M. M., Rounsaville, B. J., & Chevron, E. (1984). *Interpersonal psychotherapy of depression*. New York: Basic Books.

Krupnick, J. L., Elkin, I., Collins, J., Sotsky, S. M., Imber, S., & Watkins, D. (1992, May). *Therapeutic alliances and treatment outcomes*. Paper presented at the 145th Annual Meeting of the American Psychiatric Association, Washington, DC.

Locke, H. J., & Wallace, K. M. (1976). Short-term marital adjustment and prediction tests: Their reliability and validity. *Marriage and Family Living*, *38*, 15–25.

Markowitz, J. C. (1993). Psychotherapy of the post-dysthymic patient. *Journal of Psychotherapy Practice and Research*, *2*(2), 157–163.

Markowitz, J. C. (1994). Psychotherapy of dysthymia. *American Journal of Psychiatry*, *151*, 1114–1121.

Markowitz, J. C. (1995). Interpersonal therapy. In M. H. Sacks & W. H. Sledge (Eds.), *Core readings in psychiatry: An annotated guide to the literature* (2nd ed., pp. 591–598). Washington, DC: American Psychiatric Press.

Markowitz, J. C., Klerman, G. L., Clougherty, K. F., Spielman, L. A., Jacobsberg, L. B., Fishman, B., Frances, A. J., Kocsis, J. H., & Perry, S. W. (in press). Individual psychotherapies for depressed HIV-positive patients. *Amercian Journal of Psychiatry*.

Markowitz, J. C., Klerman, G. L., & Perry, S. W. (1992a). Interpersonal psychotherapy of depressed HIV-seropositive patients. *Hospital and Community Psychiatry*, *43*, 885–890.

Markowitz, J. C., Moran, M. E., Kocsis, J. H., & Frances, A. J. (1992b). Prevalence and comorbidity of dysthymic disorder among psychiatric outpatients. *Journal of Affective Disorders*, *24*, 63–71.

Markowitz, J. C., Klerman, G. L., Perry, S. W., Clougherty, K. F., & Josephs, L. (1993). Interpersonal therapy for depressed HIV-seropositive patients. In G. L. Klerman & M. M. Weissman (Eds.), *New applications of interpersonal therapy*. Washington, DC: American Psychiatric Press.

Mason, B. J., Markowitz, J., & Klerman, G. L. (1993). IPT for dysthymic disorder. In G. L. Klerman, & M. M. Weissman (Eds.), *New applications of interpersonal therapy*. Washington, DC: American Psychiatric Press.

Meyer, A. (1957). *Psychobiology: A science of man*. Springfield, IL: Charles C Thomas.

Moreau, D., Mufson, L., Weissman, M. M., & Klerman, G. L. (1991). Interpersonal psychotherapy for adolescent depression: Description of modification and preliminary application. *Journal of the American Academy of Child and Adolescent Psychiatry*, *30*(4), 642–651.

Mufson, L., Moreau, D., Weissman, M. M., & Klerman, G. L. (1993). *Interpersonal psychotherapy for depressed adolescents*. New York: Guilford Press.

Parsons, T. (1951). Illness and the role of the physician: A sociological perspective. *American Journal of Orthopsychiatry*, *21*, 452–460.

Paykel, E. S., DiMascio, A., Haskell, D., & Prusoff, B. A. (1975). Effects of maintenance amitriptyline and psychotherapy on symptoms of depression. *Psychological Medicine*, *5*, 67–77.

Pearlin, L. I., & Lieberman, M. A. (1979). Social sources of emotional distress. In R. Simmons (Ed.), *Research in community and mental health* (Vol. 1, pp. 217–248). Greenwich, CT: JAI Press.

Reynolds, C. F., Frank, E., Perel, J. M., Imber, S. D., Cornes, C., Morycz, R. K., Mazumdar, S., Miller, M. D., Pollock, B. G., Rifai, A. H., Stack, J. A., George, C. J., Houck, P. R., & Kupfer, D. J. (1992). Combined pharmacotherapy and psychotherapy in the acute and continuation treatment of elderly patients with recurrent major depression: A preliminary report. *American Journal of Psychiatry*, *149*, 1687–1692.

Rounsaville, B. J., Glazer, W., Wilber, C. H., Weissman, M. M., & Kleber, H. D. (1983). Short-term interpersonal psychotherapy in methadone-maintained opiate addicts. *Archives of General Psychiatry*, *40*, 629–636.

Rounsaville, B. J., Weissman, M. M., Prusoff, B. A., & Herceg-Baron, R. L. (1979). Marital disputes and treatment outcome in depressed women. *Comprehensive Psychiatry*, *20*, 483–490.

Sloane, R. B., Stapes, F. R., & Schneider, L. S. (1985). Interpersonal therapy versus nortriptyline for depression in the elderly. In G. D. Burrow, T. R. Norman & L. Dennerstein (Eds.), *Clinical and pharmacological studies in psychiatric disorders* (pp. 344–346). London: John Libbey.

Sotsky, S. M., Glass, D. R., Shea, M. T., Pilkonis, P. A., Collins, J. F., Elkin, I., Watkins, J. T., Imber, S. D., Leber, W. R., Moyer, J., & Oliveri, M. E. (1991). Patient predictors of response to psychotherapy and pharmacotherapy: Findings in the NIMH Treatment of Depression Collaborative Research Program. *American Journal of Psychiatry, 148,* 997–1008.

Sullivan, H. S. (1953). *The interpersonal theory of psychiatry.* New York: Norton.

Weissman, M. M. (1987). Advances in psychiatric epidemiology: Rates and risks for major depression. *American Journal of Public Health, 77,* 445–451.

Weissman, M. M., Klerman, G. L., Paykel, E. S., Prusoff, B. A., & Hanson, B. (1974). Treatment effects on the social adjustment of depressed patients. *Archives of General Psychiatry, 30,* 771–778.

Weissman, M. M., Klerman, G. L., Prusoff, B. A., Sholomskas, D., & Padian, N. (1981). Depressed outpatients: Results one year after treatment with drugs and/or interpersonal psychotherapy. *Archives of General Psychiatry, 38,* 52–55.

Weissman, M. M., Prusoff, B. A., DiMascio, A., Neu, C., Goklaney, M., & Klerman, G. L. (1979). The efficacy of drugs and psychotherapy in the treatment of acute depressive episodes. *American Journal of Psychiatry, 136,* 555–558.

Wells, K. B., Stewart, A., Hays, R. D., Burnam, A., Rogers, W., Daniels, M., Berry, S., Greenfield, S., & Ware, J. (1989). The functioning and well-being of depressed patients: Results from the medical outcomes study. *Journal of the American Medical Association, 262,* 914–919.

Wifley, D. E., Agras, W. S., Telch, C. F., Rossiter, E., Schneider, J., Cole, A. C., Sifford, L., & Raeburn, S. (1993). Group cognitive–behavioral therapy and group interpersonal psychotherapy for the nonpurging bulimic individual: A controlled comparison. *Journal of Consulting and Clinical Psychology, 61,* 296–305.

14

Long-Term Analytic Treatment of Depression

JULES R. BEMPORAD

The analytic treatment of depression is based on the belief that this clinical disorder is the result of a particular personality structure and is so embedded in the everyday functioning of the individual that less radical forms of therapy will be ineffective. Although the clinical manifestations of a single episode may be alleviated with other forms of treatment, the individual will remain vulnerable to future recurrences. Therefore, analytic treatment aims at preventing future depressions and not simply at treating the presenting episode. At the same time, not all depressions warrant extensive treatment (as will be discussed below), and analytic therapy is usually restricted to those depressions that are termed "characterological"—meaning that this form of pathological response to frustration or loss is extreme and repetitive, and results from the atavistic retention of childhood modes of estimating oneself and significant others. Such an individual is believed to be predisposed to recurrent depressions as a result of specific childhood experiences, which have shaped the individual in such a way that he/she cannot withstand the everyday vicissitudes of adult life. Throughout the history of psychoanalytic theory, this predisposition to depression has been described in various ways, reflecting the more fundamental evolution of a general theory of psychopathology.

During the early years of the psychoanalytic movement, Freud's prime intent was to prove the existence of the unconscious by demonstrating its effect on conscious thought and manifest behavior. Therefore, disorders such as hysteria and obsessive–compulsive neurosis, which were believed to reveal blatantly the power of unconscious forces, were initially investigated. Depressive states, which lacked the dramatic presentations of other disorders, came late to the attention of psychoanalysts.

HISTORICAL REVIEW

The first truly psychoanalytic interpretation of depression was published by Abraham (1911/ 1960). In this pioneer paper, Abraham interpreted depressive symptoms as resulting from repression of libidinal drives, in a manner similar to the mechanisms underlying anxiety. However, in anxiety, gratification was thought to be still possible, whereas in melancholia any hope of gratification was thought to have been abandoned. Abraham was impressed by the similarity between obsessional and depressed individuals. In both, he perceived a profound ambivalence toward others, with positive and negative feelings alternating and blocking the expression of each other. In his later works, Abraham explained the occurrence of this ambivalent form of relating as due to a regression to a fixated mode of object relationships in childhood. The depressive is quick to feel hatred toward others over slights and frustration. This propensity for hatred blocks the individual's capacity to love or to express his/her libidinal urges. Abraham believed that the depressive cannot accept his/her hatred of others and projects this hatred onto others, so that "I hate them" becomes "They hate me." The depressive then invents some imagined personal fault or defect that justifies others' hating him/her. Simultaneously, the depressive feels alone and alienated from others, since he/she has, in effect severed both libidinal and aggressive ties with them.

Aside from its theoretical exposition, this early contribution contains a wealth of astute clinical observations. Abraham mentioned the ambivalence, the inability to love genuinely, the manipulative use of guilt, and the underlying hostility of the depressive. He also included valuable suggestions on treatment. There is no mention in this early work, however, of the role of object loss or morality, which were later to play a significant role in psychodynamic theories of depression. Finally, Abraham concluded that depression is ultimately caused by the individual's inability to fulfill the demands of adult life—ironically, a formulation that was later adopted by the culturalists, who had rejected much of Freudian psychoanalysis.

Abraham's later contributions on depression (1916/1960, 1924/1960) also reflected the current developments in psychoanalytic theory of the time. In these works, Abraham focused on aspects of depression that would indicate a regression to the oral psychosexual stage, and attempted to interpret depressive symptoms as expressions of oral and anal drives. In his last work on this subject, Abraham also centered on the role of childhood object loss, echoing Freud's later contributions on depression. In a summary statement given in this same monograph (1924/1960), Abraham listed the multiple variables that predispose an individual to depression: (1) a constitutional factor that results in an increased amount of oral eroticism; (2) a libidinal fixation at the oral stage, leading not only to "oral" symptoms but to an unconscious predilection to incorporate objects; (3) a disappointment in love before the Oedipal complex; (4) the occurrence of a childhood form of depression, called "primal parathymia"; and (5) the recurrence of this childhood experience following disappointments in later life.

Abraham's contributions to the application of psychoanalytic theory to depression may be summarized as (1) pointing out the role of ambivalence; (2) indicating the importance of significant others in the predisposition to depression; (3) viewing the clinical episode as a recurrence of a childhood experience that is inappropriate

to adult behavior; and (4) elaborating upon the role of early love relations in later psychopathology.

Although Abraham's contributions are regarded as the pioneer works in depression, the most influential psychoanalytic work on this disorder has been Freud's (1917/1957) "Mourning and Melancholia." (Although it was written in 1915, World War I delayed its publication until 1917.) This short paper was unique in many ways: It was the first psychoanalytic contribution that did not mention inhibition of erotic drives as a causative factor for illness, and it may be seen today as the harbinger of Freud's socalled "mature" works. This paper also presaged the entire object relations school by enlarging the contents of the unconscious to include introjected objects as well as drives. In it may also be found the conceptual forerunner of what later became the superego.

Freud began the paper with an investigation of the clinical differences between grief and depression. He noted that in grief the person's loss is clearly external and there is no effect on his/her self-esteem; by contrast, in depression there is often difficulty in determining what has been lost, and there also appears to have been an internal impoverishment, whatever the environmental deprivation may have been. In addition, in melancholia, unlike mourning, the individual is full of self-recriminations that are loudly proclaimed without shame and do not seem to apply to himself/herself. Rather, these recriminations seem to better describe the object whose loss precipitated the depressive episode.

On the basis of these astute observations, Freud formulated a view of depression that was to influence psychiatry for half a century. He postulated that the self-recriminations are actually directed at an introject of the lost object, which has become part of the melancholic's own ego. This introjection of the object also accounts for the internal sense of loss and inner emptiness of the melancholic, since when he/she has lost the external object, he/she has also, in essence, lost a part of himself/herself.

The predisposition to this reaction to object loss was said to derive from a particular childhood experience, which Freud described as the young child's suffering a loss of the mother or loss of love from the mother and not being able to find an appropriate substitute. In order to rectify this major loss, the child does not find a new love object but creates within himself/herself an effigy of the forsaken object, predisposing him/her to future depressive episodes following significant losses. From this time forward, the individual will tend to react to losses of love objects with a reactivation of the anger that accompanied the original loss. However, since the object has become part of the ego, the anger is directed inward toward the introjected object, rather than outward toward the real object. This retroflected anger results in the depressive manifestation of self-debasement and recriminations, which are really aimed at the internalized object.

This ingenious theory explained depression as a misdirection of anger, and influenced therapists to get their patients to redirect the anger outward. It also created a logical relationship between early object loss and depression, even though Freud stressed that the mother need not be physically absent and that a loss of her love is sufficient to create the pathological incorporation. Finally, the predisposition to depression was seen as the tendency to introject the love object, rather than as the cathexis of a new object.

This formulation exerted an enormous effect on the interpretation and treatment of depression for many years, although Freud cautioned that it should be applied only to a small segment of all melancholics. Of greater importance, he later rejected his own theory. In subsequent works, Freud (1923/1961), 1933/1964) stated that the tendency to internalize lost objects is a normal, ubiquitous way in which a child deals with losses, and therefore cannot be specific to future depressives. The punishing agency was also seen as no longer limited to melancholics; it became the familiar superego of Freud's later writings. In his *New Introductory Lectures on Psycho-Analysis* (1933/1964), written almost two decades after "Mourning and Melancholia," Freud suggested that depression is simply due to an excessive severity of the superego, possibly resulting from a constitutional excess of death instinct.

Despite these later alterations in theory, a good many psychoanalysts continued to utilize the original retroflected-anger formulation in their understanding of depression. One of the authors who attempted to integrate the changes brought about by the structural theory, with its familiar division of the psyche into id, ego, and superego, was Sandor Rado, who published a revised theory of depression (Rado, 1927/1956). In this paper, Rado also depicted the abnormal relationship of the depressive to his/her adult

love objects. He speculated that prior to the onset of depression, the individual will punish the love object and push this significant other to the limits of patience. When the other is driven away by the depressive's hostile behavior, the depressive will attempt to regain the object by suffering, self-negation, and all of the symptoms that define the early stages of a depressive episode. Rado mentions that the depressive is like a love addict who cannot do without the object, although once the depressive has the love of the object, he/she will test the other continually. This behavior is a recapitulation in adult life of a childhood pattern of relating to the mother, typified by an anger–guilt–atonement sequence in which the object is utilized to absorb the rage of the depressive, as well as being necessary for an adequate sense of self-esteem.

If the depressive is able to regain the love object via contrition, then his/her depression subsides and the episode is resolved. However, if the object cannot be regained, then the depressive regresses to a psychotic position and gives up the world of real objects, attempting to gain love from the internalized childhood object that has become part of the superego. Eventually, when the individual has suffered sufficiently, he/she gains the forgiveness of the superego and recovers from the melancholia.

The significant aspects of Rado's theory were that it described depression as a process of repair that allows the individual either to win back a lost object or to gain forgiveness from within the self. It also described the depressive's own participation in his/her illness, related the clinical episode to the everyday mode of life of the depressive, and attempted to describe the transition from neurotic to psychotic depression. Finally, in keeping with the structural theory, Rado emphasized the role of the superego in severe melancholia.

These papers were part of the classical literature on depression, written at a time when psychoanalysis was still evolving its basic concepts. Subsequent works have not continued to present new postulates of psychoanalysis, but rather reflect refinements in theory, using the fundamental structures and concepts that have become universally accepted. These later works on depression reveal a return to formulations that, though less imaginative, seem closer to manifest clinical data.

Fenichel summarized this ego-oriented view of depression in his encyclopedic text on psychoanalysis, which was published in 1945. In the section on melancholia, Fenichel focused on a fall in self-esteem secondary to frustration of narcissistic needs as a cardinal feature of depression. The depressive-prone individual was described as living in constant need of external narcissistic supplies in order to maintain a satisfactory sense of self. The significant role of the ego can be appreciated when it is understood that this psychic structure is responsible for self-esteem by indicating the degree of disparity between an ego ideal and the actual state of self. Therefore, when the individual fails significantly to achieve an ego ideal (or suffers an experience that shatters the belief that he/she has fulfilled an ego ideal), and has to confront an unsatisfying state of self, a failure in self-esteem and clinical depression ensue.

Bibring (1953) elaborated this position in his own innovative formulations of depression. Bibring argued that depression may result from a variety of life's circumstances that share one basic common pattern: a breakdown of the mechanisms establishing self-esteem. Different individuals may be susceptible to different negative life events, depending on the particular sources of esteem. For Bibring, the conscious experience of depression is representative of the ego's helplessness and powerlessness to fulfill urgent narcissistic needs. Therefore, Bibring did not view depression as a result of a complex intersystemic conflict between psychic agencies, but as the direct emotional correlate of a basic state of the ego when faced with a specific situation of deprivation.

Although Bibring's position may appear to be a common-sense observation, it has far-reaching ramifications. By viewing depression as a primary ego state, Bibring shifted the emphasis in the understanding of depression from its alleged intrapsychic mechanisms to external precipitants and antecedent personality characteristics. He took the experience of depression as a fundamental given, which arises whenever the ego finds itself helpless to satisfy narcissistic needs in the maintenance of self-esteem. Some individuals may be more susceptible to depressive episodes because they harbor unrealistic ambitions that can never be met, or because they have learned to capitulate in the face of adversity and too readily lapse into hopelessness and helplessness. Finally, if depression is seen as a basic ego state, it is possible that the individual may create defenses against this painful experience, or that in milder forms depression may

serve some sort of alerting function that can mobilize the individual to alter patterns of functioning. On the other hand, Bibring believed that the symptoms of clinical depression are not reparative and do not have special symbolic meanings as described in the classical literature.

Sandler and Joffee (1965) have furthered the view of depression as an experiential state by proposing that depression should be conceptualized as a fundamental affect, much like anxiety. Though acknowledging their debt to Bibring, Sandler and Joffee consider "loss of self-esteem" as too elaborate or intellectual a concept to indicate the primal nature of the depressive experience. Rather, they propose that depression results whenever the individual has lost a former state of well-being. When depression occurs following the loss of a love object, they postulate that what is lost is the sense of well-being that the object has supplied, rather than the loss of the object in and of itself.

Sandler and Joffee also differentiate between the initial dysphoric reaction that follows immediately upon the loss of a state of well-being and clinical depression. The former is seen as a "psychobiological" reaction that occurs in everyone, whereas the latter represents an individual's failure to work through the loss. The initial reaction is somewhat analogous to signal anxiety in alerting the individual to compensate somehow for his/her loss. If the person cannot do this for internal or environmental reasons, the depression escalates to clinical proportions and no longer serves any homeostatic purpose.

Arieti (1978) has also conceived of depression as a basic affect that is a psychological equivalent to physical pain, and has proposed that its evolutionary purpose is to alarm the individual to alter his/her psychological self, much as pain forces the individual to alter his/her behavior. Arieti believes that the individual overcomes depression by going through "sorrow work," during which the person realigns his/her expectations, views of himself/herself and of others, and modes of obtaining meaning to conform to a new environmental situation. If the individual cannot go through this process adequately, the depression remains, intensifies, and loses its original purpose by overwhelming the individual and preventing any fruitful action.

The foregoing review of theory reveals a lessening of interest in the possible meaning of depressive symptoms themselves, and an increasing appreciation of the character structure that underlies the clinical manifestations. Recent theorists have directed their inquiries to those factors that predispose an individual to frequent or severe bouts of depression in terms of the individual's inability to reconstitute satisfactory sources of meaning, gratification, and self-esteem following a narcissistic blow. Bowlby (1980), for example, has conceived of susceptibility to depressive episodes as resulting from irrational or dysfunctional modes of processing experience that have been crystallized by particular childhood relationships with significant others. When an event in adult life both reactivates and seems to prove the validity of these aberrant working models of the self and others, depression results as the consequence of the coming into awareness of these erroneous yet exquisitely painful beliefs. Beck (1967) also considers depression to result from dysfunctional cognitive patterns that produce a negative view of the self, the environment, and the future (the "negative triad"). Though not denying the effects of past experiences or relationships as responsible for these pessimistic evaluations, Beck does not attempt to trace the origins of these cognitive schemas to the patient's childhood or to his/her formative relationships. Therefore, Beck's approach to therapy, and to theoretical formulations, is more slanted toward a "here-and-now" exploration of thought processes and an active role in modifying these beliefs.

Episodes of depression are seen as a commonplace and often appropriate reaction to life's vicissitudes. Most individuals can in time recover from these painful experiences by themselves, and go on to live relatively satisfying lives. Others, however, appear vulnerable to repeated and/or chronic states of melancholia, which are so integrated into their everyday functioning that their very personality structure predisposes them to recurrent psychopathology. It is for these individuals that analytic treatment, which aims at modifying the underlying personality, is the treatment of choice.

THE DEPRESSIVE PERSONALITY

The two attributes that are cited repeatedly in the psychodynamic literature on depression are pathological dependency and self-inhibition. These qualities describe the character of the chronic depressive and are not limited to the clinical episode. This underlying personality configuration may be in surprising contrast to the notable achievements and superficial maturity manifested by many depressives. In fact, objectively, one could consider those who succumb to depression as paragons of psychological health. The depressive is often stable, reliable, and hard-working. He/she is the one who gets the job done and does not shirk from onerous or unglamorous tasks. Yet the depressive appears to derive little direct pleasure from such accomplishments or from his/her exemplary moral standards. Rather, the depressive's arduous efforts are aimed at wrenching praise from an idealized other, and his/her exemplary behavior is based not on altruism or high ethical principles, but on the fear of guilt or abandonment.

Over 30 years ago, Arieti (1962) noted the tendency of some depressives to idealize and to need a particular individual in order to function without severe dysphoria. He wrote that whereas schizophrenic decompensation appears to involve a detachment stemming from a negation of the whole interpersonal world, depressives become markedly symptomatic following the failure of just one highly prized relationship. This led him to propose the term "dominant other" to describe the highly influential other who holds such sway over the mental health of the depressive. This pathological relationship is utilized by the depressive to derive a sense of worth, but is not so overwhelmingly narcissistic as to supply a sense of identity or reality, as in borderline or psychotic conditions. Rather, the dominant other is the resurrection of the moral parent who rewards industry and self-sacrifice, and can punish laziness or frivolity. The depressive reinstates this child–parent relationship with work and self-denial. When the relationship is threatened, the depressive may work all the harder in an effort to win back the needed praise and nurturance from the dominant other. If these efforts fail, then a clinical episode may ensue. Some depressives need a flesh-and-blood dominant other to allow them to feel worthy and free from guilt and anxiety. For some, however, the dominant other is not a person but an organization (such as the army, a church, or a corporation), which is personified and provides structure, rewards, and meaning in life.

Another variant of this basic form of depressive personality is that which we (Arieti & Bemporad, 1980) have called the "dominant-goal" type. In this case the individual is obsessed with the pursuit of some fantastic achievement, deriving almost all his/her gratification from this quest, and shunning other avenues of pleasure or meaning because they may detract from the possibility of realizing his/her dream. The person so dangerously limits other means of obtaining worth or meaning that he/she is left painfully vulnerable to depression if or when he/she realizes that the magical goal is not attainable. The individual then perceives himself/herself as an abysmal failure and succumbs to a clinical depressive episode.

Personality types similar to the "dominant-other" and "dominant-goal" characterizations have been described by other theorists as frequently found in depressed individuals. Blatt (1974) has proposed two major forms of personality organization in depression: the "anaclitic" and the "introjective." The former is typified by an overly dependent individual who needs to maintain relationships at all costs and decompensates after a rejection or other interpersonal loss. The latter represents a perfectionistic individual with high ideals and demands on the self. This introjective type has internalized harsh parental objects that cause him/her to react to failure with self-loathing and a collapse in self-esteem. Blatt writes that each type of depression may require a different emphasis in therapy, since the anaclitic form responds better to support and interpersonal empathy, whereas the introjective type can better appreciate insight-oriented interpretations. Recently, Beck (1983) has proposed a similar subtyping of depressive individuals, with different loadings on an "individuality versus sociality" dimension. Sociality-oriented depressives are more dependent, more needful of intimacy and of positive interaction, and highly rejection-sensitive. Individuality-oriented depressives are more assertive, goal-directed, and autonomous; have a need to control or dominate; and are highly sensitive to failure.

A common finding among all these theories is that in Western culture the "dominant-other/anaclitic/sociality" type is predominantly female, whereas the "dominant-goal/introjective/individuality" type is predominantly male. However, both forms of depressive personalities share important features. The underlying similarity of the dominant-goal type to the dominant-other type of depressive is manifested in the inhibition over pleasurable activity, but more so in the meaning that the goal has for the individual. The pursuit of fantasied objectives brings the person no pleasure. The meaning of the goal resides in the changes the depressive believes will take place after it is attained: The individual believes

that he/she will now be loved and will be a worthy individual. This lack of enjoyment in activities per se may lead to depression even when the person achieves the all-important goal and finds that the expected nurturance or approval is not forthcoming from others. The individual may then feel that no matter what he/she does or accomplishes, the desired loving response cannot be obtained.

These aspects of the depressive personality also demonstrate the massive inhibitions that the individual imposes on himself/herself, as well as the fear inherent in obtaining gratification directly from activity. The depressive looks for justification for any indulgence, and experiences anxiety when faced with the prospect of pure enjoyment for its own sake. One depressed woman, for example, could only bring herself to spend money on attractive clothes if she could convince herself that she needed them for work. Another woman who traveled frequently on business became overwhelmed with morbid fears of her parents' dying or her apartment's being vandalized when she was rewarded for her excellent work performance with a company-paid vacation.

This obsessive anxiety over pleasure also pervades those depressive individuals who do not demonstrate a predominant pattern of striving toward either a dominant other or a dominant goal. These depressives overvalue the opinions of others, and also strive toward objectives that are not inherently meaningful, but they are not able to defend against depressive episodes through even these pathological processes. Their sense of worth derives from fending off a dreaded sense of self by constantly attempting to reassure themselves that they measure up to some lofty moral idea. Leff, Roatch, and Bunney (1970) give a penetrating description of such an individual in their study of precipitants in depression. After being hospitalized following a serious suicide attempt, their patient exhibited a severe depression with vegetative signs. A reconstruction of her history revealed the following significant factors. She was the product of an illegitimate pregnancy by a sexually promiscuous mother; the patient vowed to be a "pure person" and never to allow herself to follow in her mother's footsteps. She was intensely ashamed of her mother's way of life, and derived a sense of worth from her higher standards of virtue. Nevertheless, she consented to premarital intercourse with her future husband. When their first child was born prematurely and died, she believed she had caused the death of the child. At this time, she developed clinical symptoms of anxiety and phobias as her concept of self was challenged. There followed a period of further stresses in her relationship with relatives, her mother, and her husband; her final collapse came when her husband slapped her during an argument and said, "You're a whore, just like your mother." This accusation crystallized her greatest fear and her greatest shame. After hearing these words spoken by her husband, she took a massive overdose of drugs, which caused her to remain in a coma for 3 days and which she barely survived.

This case illustrates the depressive's labile sense of self and his/her need to ward off feelings of shame, unworthiness, and guilt. Some depressives accomplish this by exemplary behavior, others by pursuit of some magical goal, and yet others by a relationship with a transferentially overidealized other. All, however, demonstrate an excessive dependency on others for their view of their own worth, as well as extreme inhibition in terms of self-gratification. If such a person loses an external source of esteem and, because of his/her limited alternatives, cannot find new avenues of meaning, then the affect of depression automatically arises and in time escalates to clinical proportions. Ernest Becker (1964) has poetically and accurately described the plight of the depressive as being "left in the hopeless despair of the actor who knows only one set of lines, and loses the one audience who wants to hear it" (p. 127).

Alice Miller (1979) has presented her own formulation of depression, which is not greatly dissimilar from that presented above. Miller postulates that the future depressive is forced to create an overblown "false self" in order to please and obtain love from a narcissistic mother. This false self often works well in everyday society, because it brings the individual the public success demanded by the mother. However, a large portion of the basic personality, which Miller calls the "real self," is suppressed and split off. Therefore, the individual does not have access to his/her true desires and views the real self with dread and disdain. At the same time, the success of the false self must be reaffirmed constantly; when the individual encounters obstacles that prevent its efficient functioning, the real self reasserts itself into consciousness, causing a radical restructuring of the personality and bringing about the symptoms of depression. Therefore, Miller also stresses the distorted evaluations of the self and others, the overreliance on external supplies for narcissistic equilibrium, and the massive inhibition over experiences of gratification and meaning.

PSYCHOANALYTIC PSYCHOTHERAPY

The task of psychoanalytic psychotherapy is to alter these patterns of personality structure so as to prevent future recurrences of clinical depression, as well as to improve the everyday functioning and feeling of the individual. Although this form of therapy attempts to go beyond the immediate clinical manifestations to underlying maladaptive patterns of self-estimation, the symptoms of the illness cannot be ignored. In mild forms of depression, the painful dysphoria may be used at times to motivate the patient to persevere in the unpleasant process of change. In severe depression, however, the symptoms may so overwhelm the individual that they prevent productive analytic work. Therefore, symptom relief by any useful means is the first task of therapy with severely depressed individuals.

Pharmacological treatments are certainly indicated to ease the burden of melancholia and to allow the depressive a respite from torment. Experienced analysts such as Arieti (1977) and Jacobson (1975), who have spent decades treating severely depressed patients, recommend the usage of medication to allay those symptoms that block the engagement of the individual in psychoanalysis. A number of research studies indicate that drugs and psychotherapy affect different aspects of the depressive syndrome (APA Commission on Psychotherapies, 1982). Medication ameliorates the more biologically based symptoms (e.g., early morning insomnia, anorexia, or anergia), whereas psychotherapy exerts an effect on the individual's more psychological functions (e.g., social withdrawal, suicidality, or low self-esteem). The use of medication in depressions that include vegetative symptoms—and most severe depressions do—is recommended. These very symptoms may become the focus of the patient's concerns and justifiably cause him/her to resist engaging in a mutual search, with the analyst, for the causes of his/her unhappiness.

Whatever the severity of the depression, one of the major tasks of the initial sessions is to interrupt the depressive's litany of complaints and protestations. Spiegel (1965) has described how the depressive's monotonous repetition of his/her preoccupations can frustrate the therapist and may lead to a negative countertransference. Levine (1965) has labeled the depressive's continual reporting of misery the "broken-record response," which must be interrupted if therapy is ever to be initiated. The usual silent or detached analytic stance and the use of the couch are to be avoided, since, if left to his/her own devices, the patient will fill the entire session with repetitious complaints.

The process of the initial stages of therapy may be illustrated by the example of a middle-aged nurse who became increasingly depressed after her husband of many years told her that he no longer loved her and that she no longer gave any pleasure to his life. After this shattering pronouncement, this woman tried by a variety of measures—from indulging her husband's every whim to threatening him with divorce—to force him to love her once again. After some time, during which her efforts were unsuccessful and during which she became more and more desperate, she and her husband had an angry confrontation and she again threatened him with divorce. To her surprise, this time he agreed to a separation and said he would move out shortly. Later that evening, after her husband had retired, the patient emptied her medicine cabinet of all drugs, drove to a secluded area, and ingested an unknown mixture of the drugs in an effort to kill herself. She was found accidentally and taken to a hospital, where she remained in a coma for a few days, but eventually recovered sufficiently to be transferred to a psychiatric unit. As her medical condition improved, she repeatedly stated that she wanted to be dead, as she could not go on living without her husband. He visited her in the hospital and essentially told her that their marriage was over, causing her to voice further suicidal intentions openly. She was prescribed tricyclic antidepressants, later augmented by lithium carbonate, which decreased her agitation and dysphoria to some extent. After some weeks, the patient was discharged to the care of her young adult daughter. She was still dysphoric but no longer acutely suicidal, having somewhat accepted her situation.

When seen for outpatient therapy, this woman appeared bewildered by the course her life had taken. She believed that she had always "done the right things," so she should be protected from any misfortune. She also strongly held to the paradoxically contrary belief that she had somehow caused the end of her marriage, and that if she had only tried harder her husband would still love her. Finally, she was certain that she would never be happy again, and that the remainder of her life would be a lonely, barren existence at best. She fully demonstrated Beck's (1967) "negative triad" of negative evaluations of herself, her future, and her environment (including the therapeutic situation, which she held could not help her). Despite her protestations of being beyond hope, she admitted that she did feel better after sessions because she felt connected to another person and could speak openly about her distress, which she tried to hide from her children and her friends. During these initial sessions, therapy was directed toward allowing the patient to feel understood and to sense that she could express herself freely without fear of criticism or rejection. She saw her relating her unhappy state as a terrible burden on the therapist, who could not tolerate such a whining and self-centered individual.

At this point, no interpretations of these transferential beliefs were attempted. Rather, the patient's beliefs were challenged—in this case, by asking her whether she, as a nurse, felt so terribly burdened by the complaints of her charges. She readily admitted that she was not and that she saw her job as making others feel better. The therapist then suggested that listening to her and taking her complaints seriously were equally the tasks of a therapist and not a psychological burden. It is important to emphasize that at this early stage of therapy, the major task is to create an open, honest relationship in which a patient feels respected and considered, regardless of the patient's opinion of himself/herself. Although this particular patient's fear of burdening others was based on her similar fear of upsetting her parents as a child, the exploration of such material at this point would have been premature and would not have been integrated by the patient. However, these initial transferential reactions were noted and stored for later use.

The picture that emerged of this woman's premorbid life was characterized by her desire to obtain love and acceptance at any price. She had been the major source of financial support during her marriage, often taking on extra shifts to earn more money. She had done remarkably well in her career because of her hard work and her repeated efforts to please others. She was also the emotional mainstay in her family, being responsible for taking care of the children and for fulfilling the usual responsibilities of running a household. Her husband was described as relatively uninvolved and somewhat solitary. He held a middle-level bureaucratic position that gave him little pleasure; since childhood, he had dreamed of being an artist. Although at first the patient lauded him as a marvelous companion, a more objective view of this man would be that of a chronically depressed and misanthropic individual. He was eventually described as unemotional, fairly oblivious to his children's needs, and always preoccupied with his own thoughts, the content of which he did not share with others. As more history was obtained, it appeared that as the husband had reached middle age he himself had become depressed, and that with his children grown, he wished to lead a solitary life in which he would be free to pursue his interests without the distractions of a marital relationship. His psychological liabilities were seen as assets by the patient, however, who sensed that someone so needy and socially withdrawn would never abandon her or seek the company of another woman. Throughout the marriage the patient had been the vital element in the relationship, accepting the role of the lively and whimsical housewife, while her husband assumed the role of the stable and responsible head of the household.

Once a trusting relationship had evolved in therapy, attention was directed to the psychological nature of the loss that the rupture of her marriage actually represented to the patient. She began to understand that the loss of her husband's love entailed the frustration of a number of important emotional needs—some that were quite realistic, but also others that were unconscious, irrational, and transferential carryovers from her past. These remnants of her childhood were far from clearly delineated, as the patient had never attempted to assess her prior relationships or her early experiences. She did acknowledge that she had never felt truly loved or appreciated by others, even her parents, and that the behavior of others (particularly rejection or criticism) had a devastating effect on her. She needed to be certain that everyone liked her and thought well of her, going to extremes of self-sacrifice to ensure the high regard of others.

The tone of these initial sessions is crucial, for they set the course for the rest of the therapy. The therapist has to tread a difficult path between a reflective analytic posture and his/her

innate wish to reassure and help a fellow human being in distress. The therapist should be warm and encouraging, but should consistently make clear that the burden of therapy and cure is the patient's responsibility. New topics can be introduced to break the repetitive cycle of complaints and misery. Idealization should be detected early, and transference distortions should be corrected as these arise. The therapist must be honest about his/her own shortcomings and the limitations of analysis in producing miraculous or rapid cures. This openness, which has been recommended by Kolb (1956), is very important, since the depressive has all too often been raised in an atmosphere of deceit, manipulation, and secret obligations; he/she must be shown that it is possible to be honest and forthright without being criticized or abandoned.

Once analysis has begun on the proper course, the patient should be encouraged to look inward toward the causes of the dysphoria. This search involves the patient's relating the precipitating factor of the clinical episode to his/her particular personality organization. The environmental loss, frustration, or rejection that provokes a severe depression has a deeper meaning for the individual; it threatens his/her needed sense of self and sources of narcissism. Therefore, what appears to the casual observer as a trivial event may reverberate with a deep-seated fear and shame in the vulnerable individual. The precipitating event sets off a chain reaction, which alters the psychic equilibrium of the individual and revokes childhood modes of self-evaluation and adaptation.

The patient described above began to relate her fears of loss to her feeling that she was an unlovable and repulsive person. These self-depreciating self-evaluations had been present for as long as she could remember; as she dwelled on these thoughts, she recreated much of her early life, particularly her relationship to her mother. Her earliest memories were of being in a refugee camp in Europe after World War II, where her parents had been sent after escaping persecution at the hands of Nazi invaders. She recalled being repeatedly told to be "good" or they would all be in danger, so that from an early age she had suppressed any childhood willfulness or exuberance. She was encouraged to be ingratiating toward the officials who administered the camp, being told that the family's welfare depended on their favorable opinion of them. However, she was not allowed to play with other children; she spent most of her time with the family maid, who had followed them into hiding. Her parents were understandably distraught and preoccupied with their uncertain circumstances, yet there seemed to be a belittling of the patient beyond what their situation might warrant. For example, her mother, who spent very little time with the patient, said on the occasion of an epidemic in the camp that the patient need not worry, since only smart or pretty children got sick. The mother was remembered as primarily concerned with her husband and with her own appearance. The patient felt that throughout her life, even when the family found itself in better circumstances, she ceased to exist for her mother when her father appeared. The mother doted on him and made it clear that his comfort came before that of others. The father accepted his privileged role as his God-given right, paying attention to his daughter only when she was deferential or complimentary.

In summary, this woman grew up feeling that she was a burden to her parents and had little to offer others; she was greatly desirous of attention and affection, yet believed she was too inadequate ever to fulfill her aspirations. The best she could hope for was to be tolerated by others if she worked very hard, did not make trouble, exceeded the expectations of others, and suppressed her own strivings for pleasure or autonomy. Her vivacity and cheeriness, which she had learned endeared her to others, actually hid a chronic dissatisfaction with herself and a painful insecurity as to her acceptability.

As the patient recounted her story in therapy sessions, she was able to see parallels between her feelings toward her parents and her feelings toward her husband, as well as the development of similar feelings toward the therapist. In each, she saw a powerful other who would validate her self-worth if she behaved so as to gratify the other's narcissistic needs. This omnipotent other would magically protect her and save her from the agony of being alone and unloved. Her acceptance by this other proved to her that she was a worthy human being; nothing else held much meaning for her.

During these sessions the patient realized that a major initial attraction of her husband was that his family had been in the United States for generations, so that by marrying him she would take on a legitimate status in this country, no longer subject to the type of political upheavals she had experienced in childhood. She also came to see her choice of career as a nurse as a

way of gaining immediate acceptance by patients, who needed her and therefore could not reject her.

The setting of the proper course of therapy in terms of dependency and transference; the relating of the clinical episode to a particular premorbid personality organization; and the connecting of the precipitating events with particular maladaptive modes of gaining and maintaining a sense of worth constitute the major objectives of the first stage of therapy. The next stage involves the process of relinquishing these ingrained modes of behavior, which, though pathological, offer the patient a sense of security, gratification, and predictability. This is the time of "working through"—the real battleground of therapy, with frequent advances, regressions, and stalemates. The fundamental struggle involves the depressive's giving up his/her excessive reliance on external props for self-esteem and venturing into new modes of deriving pleasure and meaning. The patient has often evolved a facade that may succeed in obtaining social rewards, just as it succeeded in obtaining parental praise, but that restricts his/her life excessively and excludes experiencing the full range of his/her potential. The resistances that are usually encountered are a fear that the patient's life will be totally empty without the familiar (if stifling) structure that the former beliefs and adaptations provided, and a crippling anxiety that the patient will be abandoned or ridiculed if he/she dares to break the childhood taboos.

As an example of self-inhibitions over pleasure, the woman described above could not spend money on herself without a fear of being criticized or shamed by others, despite her having no difficulty buying expensive gifts for others. During one session, she revealed that she had recently bought herself some new clothes, and then expected to be criticized; she began to make excuses for her purchase, trying to obtain some sort of sanction for her behavior from the therapist. She was confronted with her need to attain justification or permission to spend her own money. She perceived the irrationality of her beliefs, and enlarged on her feelings of shame over simply being perceived as happy or content with herself. Her superficial gaiety was not an authentic state of contentment, but was aimed at making others feel good, often at her expense. In later discussions of her discomfort with deriving pleasure from her activity, she confessed another alleged indiscretion of which she also felt ashamed. A man she had met had flirted with her and intimated some possible romantic interest, causing her to feel flattered and attractive on the one hand, but terribly embarrassed and guilty on the other. She again attempted to rationalize her feelings as her being too old for "such nonsense," but responded to confrontations that she had always felt humiliated by serious masculine attention, even as a young woman. Again, a lifelong pattern of self-defeating beliefs was unveiled and traced to everyday consequences. As a result of her being able to discuss her heterosexual fears and desires openly, the patient found the courage to describe her feelings toward the therapist. She admitted an attraction as well as a sense of neediness toward the therapist, but felt that even the mention of her feelings would be received by the therapist as a heavy burden and obligation.

The patient's belief that her feelings would be a burden to others was at this time traced to her early relationship with her mother, who indeed appeared compromised by the responsibilities of parenthood, responding to the patient's normal requests for care and attention with resentment and humiliation. From this fundamental relationship, the patient had evolved an image of herself as unlovable and despicable. Her only other childhood relationships, with her nursemaid and her father, seemed to confirm this dreaded self-image. This image of the self was largely repressed, and she soon learned defensive manipulations to guard against its resurfacing into consciousness. However, this image of the self continued to guide much of her behavior, particularly in regard to intimate relationships. Much of her life had been a defensive avoidance of situations that would cause her to be rejected or criticized by needed others. She chose a safe profession, in which others constantly needed her, and she chose a man she believed to be a safe spouse, who would also be so needful that he would never reject or abandon her. She avoided testing the veracity of her beliefs about herself (which were never clearly demarcated and which were kept largely out of consciousness) by limiting contact with others to superficial friendships or by forcing a positive response, as she often did in her work. When others responded to her in a truly caring manner, as some did during her adolescence, she refused to believe in the sincerity of their intentions. The process of therapy allowed this patient to explore more fully archaic self-representations that had never been completely

conscious but continued to guide her behaviors. Her new adult awareness of this self-image permitted her to judge its accuracy more objectively, and, as a result, to become more resistant to the painful affects associated with this realization. Finally, the patient perceived that she had more options to fulfill her needs as a mature adult than she had had as a child.

Each individual presents personally idiosyncratic distortions, fears, and resistances that relate to the different past histories he/she has experienced. However, the basic theme is that of real assertion and gratification versus inhibition and guilt or fear. A dream of a depressed middle-aged woman accurately illustrates this core conflict. She dreamed of two women in a beautiful room. One woman was thin, sad, and unattractive, while the other was voluptuous and beautiful, with intricate tattoos all over her body. The voluptuous woman said, " Use my body and I'm happy," and went into a luxurious bathroom, exuding a great sexual aura. This woman then did something "disgusting," which could not be specified by the patient. Suddenly, the scene changed to a hospital room where the patient learned from a boy who had pursued her during her adolescence that her father was dying. The patient felt terribly guilty when the father died in the dream. The boyfriend consoled her and said, "I've always loved you," whereupon she woke up.

This dream expressed the conflict between this woman's pleasure-seeking, sensuous "bad" self and her ascetic, self-depriving "good" self. Daring to become the gratified self would result in abandonment by and death of needed authority figures. (It might be mentioned here that this woman's father had been dead for many years, but his dictates lived on.) The dream also indicated that she was beginning to realize it was possible to find love outside the family orbit. Such references to adolescent suitors or to adolescent aspirations are not uncommon in depressives when they are well along in the process of change. It would seem that the normal pressure for independence and individuation at adolescence stirred up a desire to break out of the familial bonds, but that this aspiration was routinely squelched by intimidation or guilt. These adolescent dreams for freedom are often revived years later as a patient re-experiences a new desire for personal liberation from internalized "shoulds."

The obstacles to healthy change are not all internal, but frequently derive from others who have become comfortable with the depressive's prior mode of living. Significant others will often react negatively to the new—and, for them, alarming or irritating—sense of self that emerges in the therapeutic process. This resistance to change may be found in parents, colleagues, or employers of depressives, but is most strongly manifested in the spouses of older patients. These marital partners truly want the patients to be cured and certainly do not wish them to suffer the terrible episodes of clinical depression. At the same time, they do not want to give up the type of relationship that has fostered recurrent episodes of melancholia. This interlocking reinforcement of depression between marital partners is seen so frequently that Forrest (1967) recommends starting couples therapy in addition to individual psychotherapy with married depressives at the time of initial referral for optimal results.

If therapy has proceeded well up to this point, the depressive will exhibit a new integrity in his/her relationships, and will show his/her feelings of anger as well as spontaneous enjoyment openly; the person will no longer resort to the devious manipulations that typified so many of his/her previous interpersonal transactions. Other characteristics that are indicative of more profound change include a sense of spontaneity and humor in behavior, as well as a more philosophical attitude toward the failures and rejections that are inevitable in everyday life. Another positive sign is the relinquishing of a hypermoral view of all events, so that everything that occurs has to be someone's fault. Most significant is the evolving ability to achieve genuine empathy with others and to cease viewing other people transferentially, as either bestowers of praise and rewards or dispensers of temptation and evil.

Finally, there should be a coming to terms with the ghosts of the past. Just as the patient begins to perceive others in his/her current life as necessarily imperfect beings who are struggling against their own difficulties to find a satisfactory mode of life, the patient should also come to understand events and forces of the past as factors that helped shape his/her personality, not as ammunition to cast at the important personages of childhood. Ideally, this understanding will correct past distortions and prevent the individual from repeating errors in everyday life that ultimately result in clinically significant illness.

EFFECTIVENESS OF LONG-TERM ANALYTIC TREATMENT

No large follow-up studies of depressed patients who received long-term analytic treatment have been reported in the literature, nor have there been controlled studies comparing this form of therapy against other types of treatment. Most psychoanalytic therapists, by the very nature of the intensity of their work, can see only a few patients at one time and so do not compile a sizable treatment sample. Also, these clinicians are usually not inclined to perform research studies. Finally, some psychoanalysts believe that each patient engaged in analysis is unique, with his/her own particular constellation of defenses, memories, fantasies, and life situation, so that any comparison between individuals will not be valid. Others may doubt that the true efficacy of therapy resulting in a different appreciation of one's inner self or the freeing of neurotic inhibitions can be measured accurately.

Nevertheless, two senior psychoanalysts with decades of experience in the therapy of severe depressives have reported their results, albeit not in a research design format. Jacobson (1971) reported the follow-up status of severely depressed patients in an anecdotal manner, without giving the size or method of selection of her sample. She found that severely depressed patients often did well for 20 or more years after analysis. They continued to experience episodes of dysphoria secondary to life stresses, but these instances were much milder than those experienced before treatment. She noted that almost all patients showed marked improvement in their social functioning and were able to initiate satisfying relationships, raise families, and perform rewarding and productive work. Some returned for more treatment after a major change in their lives, which she described as beneficial. The two types of depressives who did not do well at follow-up were those with chronic rather than episodic severe depression, and those who experienced depression with suicidal ideation in childhood.

Arieti (1977) presented a more systematic report of a 3-year (or longer) follow-up of his psychoanalytic therapy of 12 severely depressed patients, all of whom were treated on an ambulatory basis. Of the 12 patients, 9 were female and 3 were male; 10 had suicidal ideation. Arieti found that 7 showed full recovery with no relapses, 4 showed marked improvement, and 1 was classified as a treatment failure.

Although these two reports are neither sufficiently large nor scientific, they do suggest that long-term analytic therapy can be a most effective treatment modality in ameliorating the acute episodes, attenuating of future episodes, and improving social functioning. Obviously, appropriate patients for this type of treatment must be carefully selected. Although the cost of analysis may seem unconscionable when there are quicker, cheaper ways to reduce symptoms, this form of treatment may well be more cost-effective for certain patients in preventing a lifetime of repeated short-term treatments, loss of income due to illness, and extensive personal suffering.

REFERENCES

Abraham, K. (1960). Notes on the psychoanalytic treatment of manic depressive insanity and allied conditions. In K. Abraham, *Selected papers on psychoanalysis*. New York: Basic Books. (Original work published 1911)

Abraham, K. (1960). The first pregenital stage of libido. In K. Abraham, *Selected papers on psychoanalysis*. New York: Basic Books. (Original work published 1916)

Abraham, K. (1960). A short study of the development of libido. In K. Abraham, *Selected papers on psychoanalysis*. New York: Basic Books. (Original work published 1924)

APA Commission on Psychotherapies. (1982). *Psychotherapy research: Methodological and efficacy issues*. Washington, DC: American Psychiatric Association.

Arieti, S. (1962). The psychotherapeutic approach to depression. *American Journal of Psychiatry, 16*, 397–406.

Arieti, S. (1977). Psychotherapy of severe depression. *American Journal of Psychiatry, 134*, 864–868.

Arieti, S. (1978). Psychobiology of sadness. In S. Arieti & J. R. Bemporad (Eds.), *Severe and mild depression*. New York: Basic Books.

Arieti, S., & Bemporad, J. R. (1980). Psychological organization of depression. *American Journal of Psychiatry, 137*, 1360–1365.

Beck, A. T. (1967). *Depression: Causes and treatment*. Philadelphia: University of Pennsylvania Press.

Beck, A. T. (1983). Cognitive therapy of depression: New perspectives. In P. J. Clayton & J. E. Barrett (Eds.), *Treatment of depression: Old controversies and new approaches*. New York: Raven Press.

Becker, E. (1964). *The revolution in psychiatry*. New York: Free Press.

Bibring, E. (1953). The mechanism of depression. In P. Greenacre (Ed.), *Affective disorders*. New York: International Universities Press.

Blatt, S. J. (1974). Levels of object representation in anaclitic and introjective depression. *Psychoanalytic Study of the Child, 24*, 107–157.

Bowlby, J. (1980). *Attachment and loss: Vol. 3. Loss: Sadness and depression*. New York: Basic Books.

Fenichel, O. (1945). *The psychoanalytic theory of neurosis*. New York: Norton.

Forrest, T. (1967). The combined use of marital and individual therapy in depression. *Contemporary Psychoanalysis, 6*, 76–83.

Freud, S. (1957). Mourning and melancholia. In J. Strachey (Ed. and Trans.), *The standard edition of the complete psychological works of Sigmund Freud* (Vol. 14). London: Hogarth Press. (Original work published 1917)

Freud, S. (1961). The ego and the id. In J. Strachey (Ed. and Trans.), *The standard edition of the complete psychological works of Sigmund Freud* (Vol. 19). London: Hogarth Press. (Original work published 1923)

Freud, S. (1964). New introductory lectures on psychoanalysis. In J. Strachey (Ed. and Trans.), *The standard edition of the complete psychological works of Sigmund Freud* (Vol. 22). London: Hogarth Press. (Original work published 1933)

Jacobson, E. (1971). *Depression*. New York: International Universities Press.

Jacobson, E. (1975). The psychoanalytic treatment of depressed patients. In E. J. Anthony & T. Benedek (Eds.), *Depression and human existence*. Boston: Little, Brown.

Kolb, L. C. (1956). Psychotherapeutic evolution and its implications. *Psychiatric Quarterly, 30*, 1–19.

Leff, M. L., Roatch, J. F., & Bunney, W. E. (1970). Environmental factors preceding the onset of severe depression. *Psychiatry, 33*, 293–311.

Levine, S. (1965). Some suggestions for treating the depressed patient. *Psychoanalytic Quarterly, 34*, 37–65.

Miller, A. (1979). Depression and grandiosity as related forms of narcissistic disturbances. *International Review of Psychoanalysis, 6*, 61–76.

Rado, S. (1956). The problem of melancholia. In S. Rado, *Collected papers* (Vol. 1). New York: Grune & Stratton. (Original work published 1927)

Sandler, J., & Joffee, W. G. (1965). Notes on childhood depression. *International Journal of Psycho-Analysis, 46*, 80–96.

Spiegel, R. (1965). Communications with depressed patients. *Contemporary Psychoanalysis, 2*, 30–35.

15

Couple and Family Therapy for Depression

STACEY E. PRINCE

NEIL S. JACOBSON

Of all problems that are presented by patients at psychiatric and mental health clinics, some form of depression is most common. It is estimated that between 10% and 25% of women in the United States will experience at least one episode of major depressive disorder during their lives, while the range for males is 5% to 12% (American Psychiatric Association [APA], 1994). Research on the etiology and treatment of depression has focused on major (unipolar) depression, largely because the prevalence of major depression is much greater than that of bipolar disorders. In this chapter we also focus on the etiology and treatment of major depression as defined in DSM-IV (APA, 1994), since the treatment approaches we describe here were developed for individuals experiencing major depression.

Until recently, virtually all of the standard treatments for depression have been intrapersonal, with the depressed client seen alone. The focus on individual therapies is in keeping with most theoretical models of depression, which view intrapersonal variables (whether behavioral, cognitive, or biological) as key factors in the etiology and maintenance of depression. For many clients, an individual approach is relatively successful, at least in alleviating symptoms associated with the current episode of depression. The efficacy of several individual approaches, including both psychotherapy and pharmacotherapy, has been well documented in the treatment outcome literature (e.g.,

Hollon & Beck, 1978; Kovacs, 1980; Kovacs, Rush, Beck, & Hollon, 1981; Wilson, Goldin, & Charbonneau-Powls, 1983; see also Steinbrueck, Maxwell, & Howard, 1983).

However, not everyone responds to individual treatment. In many treatment outcome studies, despite evidence of statistically significant changes in symptomatology during the course of therapy, a substantial percentage of patients remain clinically depressed at the conclusion of therapy (e.g., Bellack, Hersen, & Himmelhoch, 1983; Murphy, Simons, Wetzel, & Lustman, 1984; Roth, Bielski, Jones, Parker, & Osborne, 1982; Wilson et al., 1983). The recent National Institute of Mental Health (NIMH) Treatment of Depression Collaborative Research Program reported the following recovery rates: 57% for pharmacotherapy plus clinical management; 55% for interpersonal psychotherapy; and 51% for cognitive-behavior therapy (Elkin et al., 1989). Although the rates of recovery for each of the treatment conditions exceeded the 29% recovery rate for the placebo/clinical management condition, nearly half of the treated outpatients remained at least somewhat clinically depressed at the conclusion of therapy.

Since depressive episodes tend to be self-limiting even in the absence of treatment, an intervention's ability to produce durable benefits and reduce the likelihood of depressive relapse is at least as important as its capacity to alleviate symptoms of the current episode. Yet there is no definitive evidence that any of the available treatments produce improved maintenance or reduce relapse rates. It is estimated that more than 50% of recovered depressed patients experience a recurrence of symptoms within 1 year, regardless of what type of therapy they received (e.g., Billings & Moos, 1982; Kovacs, 1980; Prien et al., 1984; Weissman & Kasl, 1976). In a follow-up to the NIMH Collaborative Research Program (Shea et al., 1992), relapse rates for recovered patients assessed at 18 months posttreatment ranged from 36% to 50%. Furthermore, the proportion of patients exhibiting an optimal course (i.e., patients who were recovered at the end of treatment and who maintained recovery for the entire 18-month follow-up period) ranged from 19% to 30%, and did not differ across treatments.

Given these rates of treatment response and relapse, it appears that we may be overlooking some critical factors in the acquisition, maintenance, and resolution of depression. In the last decade, many researchers have begun to focus on interpersonal aspects of depression. The importance of close relationships with friends, family members, and spouses has been increasingly recognized. As our review will demonstrate, an impressive body of research is accumulating, both on the role of close relationships in the etiology and maintenance of depression, and on the negative impact of depression on close relationships. Such research suggests that, for some depressed clients, current individual treatments may not be having an effect on critical interpersonal and relationship variables. As Klerman and Weissman (1982) note:

Depression—regardless of symptom patterns, severity, the presumed biological vulnerability, or personality traits—occurs in a psychosocial and interpersonal context, and understanding and renegotiating the interpersonal context associated with the onset of symptoms is important to the depressed person's recovery and possibly to the prevention of further episodes. (p. 88)

Until recently, few of the prevailing treatments of choice paid much attention to the social and interpersonal environment of the depressed person. Even if the client's relationships did receive attention in the course of therapy, the people with whom the client regularly interacted were usually not included in therapy. However, recent years have seen considerable change in this area. Researchers and clinicians have begun to examine the impact of involving spouses and family members in the actual therapy process with the depressed client (e.g., Clarkin et al., 1990; Foley, Rounsaville, Weissman, Sholomskas, & Chevron, 1987; Jacobson, Dobson, Fruzzetti, Schmaling, & Salusky, 1991; O'Leary & Beach, 1990). These approaches show some promise in alleviating depression and enhancing marital and family relationships, although the verdict is still out on whether these treatments will reduce the likelihood of recurrence.

This chapter focuses on current theory and practice of couple and family therapy for depression. We begin with a review of relevant empirical findings bearing on the relationship between interpersonal functioning and depression. Based on these empirical findings, a rationale for treating depression in the context of couple and family relations is discussed, and the goals, treatment strategies, and interventions of couple/family therapy for depression are described. Finally, a review of treatment outcome studies comparing individual with couple/family therapies is provided.

Several different models of couple/family treatment for depression have been described and researched (e.g., Beach, Sandeen, & O'Leary, 1990; Clarkin, Haas, & Glick, 1988; Coyne, 1988; Dobson, Jacobson, & Victor, 1988; Foley et al., 1987). Although we describe these various approaches, we focus primarily on a model called integrative behavioral couple therapy (Christensen & Jacobson, 1991; Christensen, Jacobson, & Babcock, 1995), and on its applicability to the treatment of depression.

GENDER ISSUES IN COUPLE/ FAMILY TREATMENT OF DEPRESSION

Before undertaking an examination of the links between depression and marital distress, we note that the primary focus of this chapter is on couple/family therapies for depressed women, for several reasons. At the most basic level, it has been widely noted that women are at higher risk for most types of depression, whether one looks at clinical case records or community surveys (Nolen-Hoeksema, 1987; Weissman & Klerman, 1977, 1985; Weissman, Leaf, Bruce, & Florio, 1988). This is one of the most consistent findings in the literature, and occurs throughout many different countries and ethnic groups

(Nolen-Hoeksema, 1987, 1990). In her extensive review of the research on unipolar depression, Nolen-Hoeksema (1987) found that female-to-male ratios for the prevalence of unipolar depression averaged close to 2:1. A second and related reason for limiting our focus to depressed women is that the vast majority of studies reviewed in this chapter, including both research on the marriages of couples with a depressed spouse and treatment outcome research, have used couples in which the wife was the depressed member of the dyad. Although we hope that the therapy presented in this chapter will prove to be applicable to a wide variety of dyads, including those in which the husband is the depressed client or in which both partners are the same sex, these questions must be answered through further clinical research. For the moment, the available research data necessitate our limiting clinical examples and conclusions about treatment efficacy to couples in which the wife is the depressed client.

In addition to these practical concerns, a growing body of research suggests that the quality of the marital relationship constitutes a particularly important risk factor for depression in women. Although a number of studies have found that depression is less common among married than among single people (e.g., Aneshensel, Frerich, & Clark, 1981; Gove, Hughes, & Style, 1983; Pearlin & Johnson, 1977), other studies have indicated that the "protective" function of marriage may apply only to men (Gove, 1975; Gove & Tudor, 1973; Radloff, 1975; Radloff & Rae, 1979; Rosenfield, 1980; Weissman, 1987). It appears that whereas men are more likely than women to become depressed during marital separation, women are more likely than men to become depressed during marriage (Radloff, 1975). Weissman (1987) noted that even in happy marriages, women are five times as likely as men to experience depression. Several researchers have suggested that these gender differences are due in part to the differential roles played by women and men in the couple and family. Specifically, women provide emotional support and nurturance to other family members, including their spouses, children, and elderly relatives, more frequently than do men (reviewed in McGrath, Keita, Strickland, & Russo, 1990). Women's role obligations to care for, support, and nurture others in the context of marriage and family may heighten their risk for stress and depression (Belle, 1982).

Finally, women in distressed marriages appear to be at particularly high risk for depression. Women seem to be more vulnerable than men to problems persisting within their marriages, and more likely to experience symptoms of depression and anxiety as a result (Pearlin & Lieberman, 1979, cited in McGrath et al., 1990). Aneshensel (1986) reported that unhappily married women experienced more depressive symptoms than either unmarried or happily married women. Weissman (1987) found that in unhappy marriages, women were three times as likely as men to be depressed; close to half of all the women in his sample who were in distressed marriages were also depressed. The development of a treatment approach that has an impact on both depression and distressed marriages is thus especially relevant for women.

THE RELATIONSHIP BETWEEN DEPRESSION AND MARITAL DISCORD

We begin by reviewing several converging lines of evidence that support the viability of spouse-involved treatment for depression. Four main areas of investigation are discussed: (1) the relationships among marital distress, loss of social support, and depression; (2) evidence pointing to marital distress as a precursor, concomitant, and consequence of depression; (3) patterns of communication and behavior in couples with a depressed spouse; and (4) marital functioning as a predictor of treatment response.

Marital Distress and Loss of Social Support

In general, the stress-buffering effects of intimacy and social support in the context of marriage, family, and other close relationships have been well documented (Costello, 1982; Dean, Lin, & Ensel, 1981). For many individuals, the marital relationship is a primary source of social support. In general, depression is less common among married than among single people (Aneshensel et al., 1981; Cochrane & Stopes-Role, 1981; Pearlin & Johnson, 1977; Warheit, 1979), suggesting to some that marriage may serve a protective function. For example, Kessler and Essex (1982) found that stressful events had a significantly less damaging emotional impact on married versus nonmarried subjects, and concluded that the greater intimacy afforded the married subjects offered resilience to stress. Yet other studies have indicated that it is the *quality* of the marital relationship, rather than married status in and of itself, that has an impact on one's ability to respond with resilience to stressful life events. Brown and Harris (1978) identified the lack of a close, confiding relationship with the spouse as a significant vulnerability factor for depression in women—one that was not compensated for by close relationships with other relatives or friends. Weissman (1987) determined that a spouse in a distressed marriage is 25 times more likely to be depressed than a spouse in a nondistressed marriage, and that this is true for both husbands and wives. These and other studies have suggested that the lack of a confiding, intimate relationship may leave individuals more vulnerable to depression in the wake of stressful life events (Costello, 1982; Roy, 1978). Clearly, the marital relationship is a crucial component in the social support network of the depressed individual.

Marital Distress as an Antecedent, Concomitant, and Consequence of Depression

The next line of evidence suggests that marital problems are a common *precipitant* of depressive episodes. It is well documented that depressive episodes are more likely to occur following stressful life events (e.g., Dohrenwend & Dohrenwend, 1974), especially those involving interpersonal loss or disruption in intimate relationships (Bloom, Asher, & White, 1978; Brown & Harris, 1978; Costello, 1982; Paykel, 1979). In particular, it has been noted that of all the stressful life events that precede the onset of depression, increases in marital conflict or disruption are the most common (Paykel et al., 1969).

Second, numerous cross-sectional studies have indicated that marital distress is a frequent *concomitant* of depression (e.g., Bothwell & Weissman, 1977; Coleman & Miller, 1975; Hinchcliffe, Hooper, & Roberts, 1978; Weiss & Aved, 1978; Weissman & Paykel, 1974). Given the prevalence of both depression and marital distress, one would expect to find a substantial population suffering from both, simply by chance occurrence. Yet the co-occurrence of marital distress and depression in clinical samples is greater than would be predicted by chance alone. In one study (Rounsaville, Weissman, Prusoff, & Herceg-Baron, 1979), 50% of individuals re-

questing treatment for depression also evidenced marital distress. Conversely, in a sample of couples seeking marital therapy, over 50% of the couples had at least one spouse scoring in the depressed range on the Beck Depression Inventory (BDI) (Beach, Jouriles, & O'Leary, 1985). It should be noted that elevated BDI scores may be a result of the marital distress itself, and are not necessarily indicative of a diagnosis of major depression as defined by DSM-IV. However, these studies indicate that depressive symptomatology and marital conflict can and frequently do occur simultaneously. Clearly, practicing clinicians regularly face the task of choosing an appropriate treatment for individuals experiencing both depression and marital discord.

Finally, several prospective studies have shown that interpersonal friction and conflict between couples with a depressed spouse is frequently a *consequence* of depression, lingering even after the depressive episode has subsided (Bothwell & Weissman, 1977; Hinchcliffe et al., 1978; Rounsaville et al., 1979; Weissman & Paykel, 1974). These studies suggest that the marital distress associated with depression is not merely a concomitant or consequence of the acute episode itself, but can be a lasting consequence even after depressive symptoms have remitted.

Patterns of Communication and Behavior in Couples with a Depressed Spouse

Many of the studies demonstrating a link between depression and marital distress have relied almost exclusively on the self-report data of depressed persons. A number of theorists have suggested that such data may be problematic. Depressed individuals demonstrate negatively distorted perceptions of their environments (e.g., Beck, Rush, Shaw, & Emery, 1979), and may be demonstrating this negative bias when asked to provide self-report data on the quality of their relationships. Several investigators have addressed this issue by conducting direct observations of marital interactions in couples with a depressed spouse, in order to identify what interaction patterns, if any, are unique to these couples. In one of the earliest of these studies, Hinchcliffe et al. (1978) compared a sample of female depressed inpatients and their spouses with a sample of female nondepressed surgical inpatients and their spouses. The investigators found that the conversations of couples with a depressed spouse were characterized by greater conflict, tension, and expression of negative affect, higher levels of disruption, and incongruity between verbal and nonverbal communication, compared with the interactions of the nondepressed controls. Hautzinger, Linden, and Hoffman (1982) examined verbal interactions in maritally distressed couples with and without a depressed spouse. They found that communication in depressed couples was more uneven, negative, and asymmetrical, and that it focused more on somatic and psychological complaints.

Other investigators have compared the problem-solving behavior of couples with and without a depressed spouse. Kahn, Coyne, and Margolin (1985) asked couples with and without a depressed wife to discuss a topic that both spouses selected as a relevant marital issue. They found that, compared to the nondepressed controls, couples in which one spouse was depressed engaged in less constructive problem solving and more destructive behavior, and experienced significantly more negative affect following the interaction. Biglan et al. (1985) coded direct observations of a problem-solving interaction to compare couples with a depressed spouse who were also maritally distressed, depressed couples who were happily married, and a control group of nondepressed, nondistressed couples. The investigators found that several interactional variables distinguished depressed from nondepressed couples. Depressed women exhibited higher rates of dysphoric affect and less problem-solving behavior than their husbands, while both husbands and wives in couples with a depressed wife exhibited less self-disclosure than normal couples. Furthermore, sequential analyses showed that wives' depressive behavior functioned as a suppressor of their spouses' negative, aversive behavior. These differences were also found during home observations with children and spouses, where the wives' depressive behavior appeared to suppress aggressive affect from other family members (Hops et al., 1987).

Depressive behavior appeared to serve a coercive function in the above-described studies, as it reduced the probability of negative responding on the part of other family members. This suggested to some that the distinct, dysfunctional interaction patterns in these marriages were actually functioning to maintain depressive behavior (e.g., Coyne, 1976; Hinch-

cliffe et al., 1978). However, an investigation in our laboratory contradicted these earlier findings and called into question the coercive theory of depressive behavior. Schmaling and Jacobson (1990) attempted to separate dysfunctional marital interactions that were unique to depression from those that were associated with marital distress by observing interactions in four groups of subject couples: distressed and nondistressed couples in which the wife was depressed, and distressed and nondistressed couples in which the wife was not depressed. In contrast to previous findings, results did not indicate any dysfunctional interaction patterns that were unique to depression. The investigators concluded that the observed dysfunctional marital interactions in couples with a depressed spouse in past studies were due to marital distress rather than to depression. Furthermore, this study failed to replicate previous findings that depressive behavior functioned to suppress negative responding on the part of spouses. Similarly, Nelson and Beach (1990) found that the suppressive effect of depressive behavior on spousal aggression was a function of level of marital distress rather than level of depression. Given the strong association between marital distress and depression, it is difficult to separate the effects of the two variables. Further research with nondepressed, maritally distressed control groups is needed to clarify which maladaptive interaction patterns are specific to depression.

Another area of investigation with important implications for the conjoint treatment of depression is, put simply, spouses' ability to please each other. Distressed couples exhibit proportionately fewer pleasing behaviors than nondistressed couples (e.g., Wills, Weiss, & Patterson, 1974). Furthermore, the frequency of pleasing behaviors has been correlated with both daily and global ratings of marital satisfaction (Barnett & Nietzel, 1979; Jacobson, Waldron, & Moore, 1980). It seems quite likely that there is also a relationship between spouse-emitted positive and negative behaviors and depression. Lewinsohn's (1974) behavioral theory of depression proposes that low rates of response-contingent positive reinforcement evoke depressive symptomatology. Since spouses typically function as primary sources of reinforcement for each other, and since individuals who are depressed usually emit and receive few reinforcing behaviors, it is likely that both the depressed and the nondepressed spouse are experiencing a paucity of positive events. The tendency for spouses in a long-term relationship to gradually lose their ability to please each other has been termed "reinforcement erosion" (Jacobson & Margolin, 1979). Couples who present with both depression and marital distress are at even greater risk for this erosion process to have occurred. Thus implementing strategies that are designed to increase the exchange of positive behaviors may be an important goal in the conjoint treatment of depression.

Marital Distress as a Predictor of Treatment Response

An important line of evidence supporting the viability of spouse-involved treatment for depression is the link between marital conflict and response to treatment. Rounsaville et al. (1979) found that marital distress was related to a poor response to interpersonal psychotherapy for depression (Rounsaville & Chevron, 1982), that resolving marital disputes during the course of therapy was associated with recovery from depressive symptoms, and that unresolved marital disputes were predictive of rapid relapse. Hooley, Orley, and Teasdale (1986) found that the single best predictor of relapse following inpatient treatment of depression was the frequency of criticisms from the nondepressed spouse. Frequency of the nondepressed spouse's criticism has been highly correlated with the depressed spouse's self-reported marital distress (Hooley, 1986; Hooley et al., 1986). It appears from these results that failure to address the interpersonal environment of the depressed individual, both during and after recovery from an acute episode, may in part be responsible for the high rates of treatment failure and relapse in individual treatment of depression.

An Empirical Dilemma: Which Comes First?

There continues to be some debate as to the temporal and causal sequencing of marital distress and depression. Marital problems may precipitate depression, but depression often precedes marital conflict and divorce (Briscoe & Smith, 1973). The question of "Which comes first?" remains to be empirically answered, and it seems to us that any linear explanation is oversimplifying the issue. The historical and causal relationship between depression and marital distress is an important question—one that should be assessed specifically *for each couple*

and should be considered when designing appropriate interventions. However, our model of behavioral couple therapy for depression does not presuppose an underlying causality—that is, that marital distress causes depression, or vice versa. This is in contrast to other models of conjoint treatment for depression, which are based on an assumption of causality between marital distress and depression (e.g., Beach et al., 1990). Rather, the approach we are suggesting is *idiographic*: Treatment goals and interventions should fit the presenting problems and the historical development of those problems for each couple. Rather than widely applying a model of causality that may not be accurate for a given couple, we recommend careful assessment and continuing functional analysis of the couple's behavior, in order to gain an understanding of the causal link (if any) between one spouse's depression and the state of the marriage. Treatment is undertaken with the understanding that both relationship and person variables may be influencing the depression. Furthermore, given the evidence of high concordance rates between marital distress and depression, and the link between unresolved marital disputes and recurrence of depressive symptoms, it seems prudent to pursue the clinical utility of couple therapy for depression even if the research question of "Which comes first?" has not yet been answered.

BEHAVIORAL COUPLE THERAPY FOR DEPRESSION

In this section, we describe the principles and strategies of treatment for couples or families in which one member (or more) is depressed. We focus on a behavioral/social learning model of couple therapy, and cite relevant research findings that have influenced the development of particular interventions and procedures. Although the reader is referred to other sources for more detailed descriptions of the interventions, here we stress the modification of procedures for the treatment of couples with a depressed spouse.

Our approach to the treatment of distressed and/or depressed couples has evolved considerably over nearly 20 years of clinical practice and research. Many of these changes have involved improvement in the technology of basic behavioral couple therapy (BCT; Holtzworth-Munroe & Jacobson, 1991; Jacobson & Holtzworth-Munroe, 1986; Jacobson & Margolin, 1979).

However, as we will document, clinical outcome studies have revealed the limitations of traditional BCT in effecting change for some couples. In response to these findings, our conceptualization and practice of BCT has recently undergone its most significant evolution to date. We make a distinction in the following sections between "traditional" behavioral couple therapy (which we refer to simply as BCT) and the more recent innovations in the behavioral treatment of couples, which we have termed "integrative" behavioral couple therapy (IBCT; Christensen & Jacobson, 1991; Christensen et al., 1995).

We are enthusiastic about the new approach and feel that it has important implications for the conjoint treatment of depression. However, we note that to date the two clinical trials comparing individual therapy with BCT have utilized what we are referring to as the "traditional" BCT approach (Jacobson et al., 1991; Jacobson, Fruzzetti, Dobson, Whisman, & Hops, 1993; O'Leary & Beach, 1990). IBCT, though showing great promise in our pilot work with distressed, nondepressed couples, has yet to be implemented with couples in which one spouse is depressed. In addition, IBCT builds on fundamental components of the traditional approach. Therefore, before going on to a description of IBCT and a consideration of why it may be especially suited to the conjoint treatment of depression, we begin with an explication of the traditional approach.

Traditional Behavioral Couple Therapy: General Principles

As a behavioral/social learning approach, the BCT model of relationship discord assumes that the behavior of individuals in a marital relationship is best understood by focusing on the social environment of each spouse. In particular, each spouse's behavior is viewed largely as a function of the consequences provided for that behavior by the partner. Each spouse continually provides consequences for the other, and therefore exerts a significant controlling influence on the other's behavior. The marital relationship can thus be viewed as an ongoing process of reciprocal sequences of behavior and consequences, in which each spouse's behavior is simultaneously a response to, and an influence on, the other's behavior.

In general, the treatment goals in traditional BCT for depression include (1) gaining the social support of the nondepressed spouse; (2)

increasing satisfaction with the relationship and exchange of positive behaviors for both spouses; (3) remedying specific skills deficits in one or both partners, including communication, problem-solving, and coping skills; (4) resolving marital problems that may have precipitated or been caused by the depression; and (5) identifying and modifying any marital interactions that appear to be maintaining depressive behavior.

Introducing Conjoint Treatment

Once BCT has been selected as an appropriate treatment modality for a couple with a depressed spouse, an initial and crucially important task is presenting therapy as a joint undertaking. Often the depressed client has sought therapy alone, or has been brought to therapy by the spouse or another family member. In either case, depression is usually the presenting complaint. Little or nothing is said about the effects of one spouse's depression on the marital relationship, or the possible contribution of the relationship in precipitating or maintaining the depression. Therefore, the first task the therapist faces is to provide a rationale for conjoint treatment that justifies inclusion of the nondepressed spouse (again, this is frequently the husband; see the discussion of gender issues above) and helps to ensure his participation.

The specific form of this rationale will vary somewhat from case to case, depending on the characteristics of the couple and their own understanding of the association between one spouse's depression and the marital relationship. In our work, we have identified four types of depressive marital constellations (Dobson et al., 1988). We use these typologies as a framework for our discussion.

"Classic" couples present with complaints of both depression and marital problems. In this case, when marital distress exists and is recognized by both spouses, it is usually not difficult to justify conjoint treatment. However, it is still important for the therapist to present treatment in a way that allows the nondepressed spouse to participate without feeling blamed for his partner's depression. To accomplish this, we may emphasize the family's preoccupation with the depression. We explain that frequently marital and family interactions are restructured around the depression in such a way that it becomes the center of family activity, which in turn can easily reinforce the depression. Classic couples often acknowledge that the depression has led them to pay less and less attention to the quality of their relationship. The dual focus of treatment on both alleviating the depression and enhancing the relationship may come as a relief to partners who have been preoccupied with one spouse's depression. At other times, it is helpful to acknowledge the difficulties that the nondepressed partner may have had in coping with the depressive behavior of the spouse. We may point out that depression can cause frustration, resentment, and marital conflict, which in turn can exacerbate the depression. We suggest that in addition to providing a valuable resource to the depressed partner, the nondepressed spouse can learn more effective ways of coping with the depression by coming to therapy.

Second, "denial" couples present with complaints of depression on the part of the wife, but both spouses deny marital problems. Yet a careful marital assessment identifies them as distressed. Such a couple can be most difficult to treat within the BCT framework, since one or both partners are likely to react negatively to the suggestion that conjoint therapy is called for. However, since the likelihood of relapse among recovered depressives in this group is quite high if no attention is paid to improving the marital relationship, we feel that conjoint treatment can be quite beneficial. For these couples, the dilemma involves engaging them in therapy without directly confronting their denial of marital conflict. The solution lies in presenting treatment in such a way that the emphasis stays with the depression; there is no attempt to redefine the problem as a marital problem. The spouse is asked to participate as a resource for the depressed partner, and he is given support and empathy for the frustration he may have experienced in living with a depressed person. Typically, even when marital distress is denied, the nondepressed spouse can admit to frustration at his inability to help. Thus the rationale may emphasize helping the husband learn more effective ways to cope with his wife's depression.

The third typology is relatively rare in a clinic specializing in the treatment of depression, but is quite common among clients presenting for couple and family therapy, and is worth noting here. "Systemic" couples present only with complaints of marital distress, but upon assessment it becomes clear that one or both spouses suffer from major depression. It may be that the depressive disorder triggered the marital distress, or perhaps it was caused by the marital dis-

tress. In either case, these couples, like the "classic" couples described earlier, are likely to be receptive to and well suited for a conjoint treatment approach. For a systemic couple, however, it is important to keep the rationale for treatment focused on the relationship issues the couple presented with, rather than shifting the focus too heavily to the depression. If the marital distress in fact triggered the depressive episode, then improvements in relationship quality over the course of treatment should also result in relief from depressive symptomatology. If, on the other hand, improvements in the marriage do not result in remission of depressive symptoms, the therapist can then reassess treatment needs for the depressed individual.

Finally, "social support" couples present with complaints of depression on the part of one spouse and deny marital distress, which is also found to be absent after a thorough marital assessment. Thus, in contrast to the three previous typologies, for a social support couple marital distress is not noted as a presenting problem (either by the couple or by the therapist). Clearly, for such a couple, relief from the depressive episode is the primary goal; there is no need to force a dyadic rationale on a couple whose marriage has remained strong despite the depression. Yet in this case at least some conjoint therapy can be helpful to enhance the social support potential of the relationship for both spouses. For example, even in a nondistressed couple, depression in one spouse almost always results in a reduction in the time and attention devoted to the relationship. The behavior exchange component of treatment described below can be useful in helping both spouses to concentrate again on their relationship and reduce their preoccupation with the depression. As another example, during a depressive episode there is often a tendency toward slippage in family-related tasks such as parenting, household and financial responsibilities, and the coordination of joint social activities. Communication and problem-solving training can provide a safe and effective format for dealing with these issues. The rationale presented to spouses in a social support couple will emphasize their existing strengths and the potential social support that the relationship has to offer, both to the depressed and to the nondepressed spouse. Often for such a couple, several sessions of conjoint therapy can be integrated effectively with the depressed client's individual treatment (e.g., Addis & Jacobson,

1991; Coffman & Jacobson, 1990; Dobson et al., 1988).

At times the need for a conjoint, relationship-focused treatment will become apparent to both spouses over the course of treatment, even when initially the couple presented as non-distressed or the depressed spouse sought therapy alone. For example, at times marital problems are masked by depression in the early phases of therapy. It has been our experience that as a wife's depression lifts and her self-blame diminishes, she may become angrier at her husband. Denial of marital distress becomes more difficult to sustain as the conflict becomes more overt. For many such couples, this pro-vokes a minor crisis in the marriage, allowing for a natural transition into a more relationship-focused therapy.

With the examples above, we do not mean to imply that we are merely providing a convenient rationale for treatment in order to enlist the cooperation of the nondepressed spouse. Rather, we present those justifications for doing con-joint therapy that we believe have empirical and clinical support. Furthermore, we are ac-curately representing our own thinking about conjoint treatment: Although we view involve-ment of the spouse as a useful adjunct, and improvement in the relationship as an impor-tant treatment goal, nonetheless our ultimate criterion for success is alleviation of the depres-sive episode.

Initial Sessions

The goals of the initial sessions are (1) to fur-ther the collaborative set between the couple and the therapist; (2) to provide a structure for increasing the quality and quantity of pleasant events that the couple experiences together and each spouse experiences individually; and (3) to help both spouses recognize their ability to in-fluence each other's mood and satisfaction. In the initial stages of therapy, we continue to em-phasize the many different factors that may play a role in depression, and to point out how the treatment is designed to influence those factors. For example, we may explain that some people become depressed when they are not experi-encing enough pleasurable or satisfying events in their lives. Others become depressed because they are not satisfied with the way they are re-lating to other people. Still others are depressed because they feel they are not getting what they want or need from people close to them. Since therapy will often focus on interaction issues, it naturally validates participation of the non-depressed spouse. At the same time, present-ing multiple influences on the depression helps reduce the threat and feelings of guilt both part-ners may be experiencing.

If it seems relevant for a particular case, we will also discuss common reactions to a de-pressed person that others are likely to experi-ence. For example, we may explain that in their efforts to help, family members may inadvert-ently reinforce the depression by not letting the client resume normal activities. Or we may note that people sometimes begin to find interacting with someone who is depressed to be aversive and may subsequently withdraw. We assure the nondepressed spouse that his reactions are understandable and legitimate, while also em-phasizing that changes in these patterns will benefit both spouses. It is usually very reassur-ing to spouses to learn that their experiences are not unique to their relationship.

Increasing Exchange of Positive Behaviors

Traditional BCT for depression generally begins with an emphasis on inducing positive changes in the couple's natural environment through a series of procedures known as "behavior exchange" interventions. In a general sense, "behavior ex-change" in couple therapy refers to procedures that are designed to help spouses gain an in-creased frequency of positive behaviors from each other. Since depressed individuals usually receive and emit few reinforcing behaviors, an increase in the exchange of positive behaviors is especially critical for couples in which one spouse is depressed. Furthermore, since spouses typi-cally function as a major source of reinforce-ment for each other, it is often the case that the nondepressed spouse is also experiencing low rates of positive reinforcement. Although there are many procedural variations among behav-ior exchange strategies, they share two basic steps. First, behaviors identified as desirable by one or both spouses are pinpointed; second, there is an attempt to increase the frequency of these behaviors. Behavior exchange procedures are therefore designed to have a short-term but rapid effect on relationship satisfaction for both spouses, by increasing the benefits they provide for one another.

Several modifications to the behavior ex-change procedures have been made over the years. These include encouraging unilateral, parallel change agreements rather than contingent, *quid pro quo* exchanges; giving each spouse a maximum amount of choice in how homework assignments will be implemented; and placing the initiative for change in the hands of the giver rather than having the receiver request changes. All of these modifications are intended to ensure that when changes do occur, they will be well received. Finally, a special consideration when working with couples in which one spouse is depressed is that pleasant activities should be implemented in gradual steps. If one of the depressed client's presenting problems is difficulty in accomplishing objectives, this will probably affect the client's ability to carry out behavior exchange assignments and other therapeutic tasks. In working with such a client, it is necessary to take this problem into consideration by assigning manageable tasks, and by recognizing that the completion of agreed-upon activities represents a significant accomplishment for the depressed individual.

Communication and Problem-Solving Training

Whereas the behavior exchange phase of therapy is primarily instigative, designed to produce rapid but short-term improvements in the relationship, the next phase in traditional BCT is devoted to the acquisition of new skills that are intended to have continued, long-term benefits for the couple. Most often, the primary focus in this phase of treatment is on communication skills, and in particular on problem-solving skills. Less frequently, other skills such as parenting or sexual enrichment will also be addressed. The strategies employed to foster the development of these skills are intended to promote generalization to the couple's natural environment and maintenance following termination.

This phase of treatment often begins with the teaching of expressive and receptive communication skills. During work with a couple in which one spouse is depressed, it is especially important to assess whether information is sent and received accurately within the dyad. Depressed individuals tend to perceive comments directed toward them as more negative than do non-depressed individuals (Gotlib, 1983). Furthermore, McClean, Ogston, and Grauer (1973) reported that nondepressed spouses were prone to offer "constructive criticism" that was perceived by independent observers as hostile.

Communication exercises can therefore be used as an opportunity to detect and modify negative distortions on the part of both spouses. Specifically, the speaker is encouraged to use positive, specific, and nonaccusatory statements in giving feedback regarding the spouse's behavior; the listener is then asked to paraphrase what was said before responding. The use of behavior-specific rather than global statements facilitates the nondepressed spouse's ability to give accurate feedback to the depressed spouse in a truly constructive way. For example, if the husband of a depressed wife is able to say, "I feel angry when I suggest we do something together and you answer 'Why would you want to spend time with me?' and then walk away," a great deal has been accomplished. First, the antecedents of the husband's negative affect are clearly specified; this acts against the depressed wife's tendency toward overgeneralization (e.g., "Nothing I ever do is good enough"). Second, the wife receives some validation for her perception that her husband is angry. If the wife distorts the message, the therapist is present to point out the distortion. On the other hand, if the husband communicates hostility or anger but is unaware of the impact of his communication, the therapist can legitimize the wife's reaction to the style of the comments. The husband can then rephrase his message so that its intent and impact are more congruent. Conjoint therapy provides the therapist with an opportunity that rarely exists when a depressed individual is involved in treatment alone: the opportunity to see whether clear communication in the dyad is hindered by distorted thinking on the part of the depressed spouse, or whether most interactions are in fact negative. In either case, the therapist is able to intervene, and spouses can clarify both the intent of their messages and the impact of their communications on each other. Training in expressive and receptive communication skills can also be used to shift spouses' interactions away from habitual patterns of asymmetry and dominance (Jacobson & Holtzworth-Munroe, 1986). Finally, when communication training emphasizes affective self-disclosure on the part of the speaker, and reflection and validation on the part of the listener, this should enhance emotional closeness and intimacy in the dyad as well as more instrumental communication skills.

As communication skills are learned and refined, the next step is for the couple to apply these skills to problem-solving tasks. Through instruction, modeling, practice, and feedback, the couple is taught a variety of skills that have been associated with effective conflict resolution, including defining problems specifically and in behavioral terms, expressing complaints within a context of caring and appreciation, and acknowledging one's own role in the development and maintenance of a problem. During problem-solving sessions there is also a continued emphasis on the communication skills learned earlier, including paraphrasing, the use of "I" statements, and the avoidance of sidetracking. Although during this stage of therapy the spouses will be working on resolving conflicts that are currently problematic in their marriage, the hope is that they will continue to use these skills after therapy is over to deal with future conflicts that may arise.

The problem-solving process is divided into two distinct phases: problem definition and resolution. First the partners are taught to define the problem, during which time they learn to refrain from considering or suggesting possible solutions. During problem definition, spouses learn to apply the following rules: (1) Discuss only one problem at a time; (2) precede identification of the problem by expressions of appreciation; (3) identify the problem specifically, in behavioral terms; and (4) include feeling statements when defining a problem. Spouses are asked to alternate the selection of problems for a particular session, in order to encourage their awareness that each has a legitimate right to request changes in the relationship.

Once a problem has been defined, a habitual response for many spouses is to defend themselves through denials, cross-complaints, excuses, or justifications. In the problem-solving format alternative, more collaborative responses are encouraged, including empathy, admission of responsibility, and recognition of the other's feelings. Paraphrasing skills learned earlier are also helpful here. In addition to letting the speaker know that he/she has been heard accurately, a paraphrase of the problem statement seems to "pace" the listener; this can help to avoid more habitual reactions to criticism. It is also important for the spouse who has identified a problem behavior in the partner to acknowledge whatever role he/she may have played in creating or maintaining the problem. This can be especially helpful for the depressed spouse, who may be all too willing to take the blame for everything that goes wrong in the relationship.

Mutual responsibility for the interpersonal problems the couple is experiencing and collaborative efforts at resolution are emphasized throughout the problem-solving phase of therapy.

After the problem has been adequately defined, the spouses move into the resolution phase of the discussion, where they are encouraged to focus exclusively on finding a mutually acceptable solution, and to avoid further elaboration of the problem. The partners proceed through three tasks: brainstorming, identifying the components of a solution, and forming a contract for implementing the solution. The final step in the problem-solving process is to synthesize and further specify the agreed-upon components. The specific behaviors involved in the solution are detailed, with each spouse taking responsibility for his/her part of the plan. A behaviorally specific agreement for implementation is outlined, including the behaviors each spouse has agreed to, when they will be implemented, and cues the couple will adopt to maximize the likelihood that the plan will be carried out. All plans are implemented on a trial basis, to be renegotiated if they are not effective or if either spouse becomes dissatisfied with them.

If problem-solving sessions work as they are intended to, the spouses not only have resolved current problems in their relationship, but have acquired skills they can continue to use to resolve problems that arise after therapy has ended. The goal of generalization is further achieved by gradually fading the influence of the therapist, having the couple practice skills at home, and having the spouses take increasing responsibility for evaluating the effectiveness of the solutions. As in the behavior exchange phase of therapy, the idea that the partners have a shared responsibility for maintaining a satisfying relationship continues to be underscored.

Generalization and Maintenance

In the final phase of traditional BCT, we emphasize generalization of the skills learned during therapy. Specific treatment goals during this phase of therapy include the following: individualizing the problem-solving format so that the couple is maximally likely to continue using it after therapy is over; fading contact with and input from the therapist, so that the couple gets used to functioning autonomously; and continuing to monitor change agreements that were established earlier in therapy. Much time is also spent helping the couple to recognize areas of improvement and accomplishment. In particular, the spouses are asked to review what they have learned about how their behaviors affect their mood and marital satisfaction. Finally, during this phase of therapy there is an attempt to anticipate and openly discuss the possibility of future problems (including recurrence of depression), and to describe how they might be handled using the skills acquired during therapy.

Empirical Status of Traditional Behavioral Couple Therapy: Successes and Limitations

If conjoint treatment of depression is to be viewed as a viable alternative to standard individual treatments, several empirical questions must be answered: (1) Is conjoint treatment more effective in alleviating symptoms of the current depressive episode? (2) Does conjoint treatment result in greater improvement in the marital relationship? (3) Can conjoint treatment produce lower rates of relapse for recovered depressives? and (4) What subset of married depressed clients is most likely to benefit from conjoint treatment? To date, two major treatment outcome studies have been conducted in an attempt to answer these questions. We note before reviewing these results that in both studies the conjoint approach represented what we have called "traditional" BCT.

In the first of these studies, O'Leary and Beach (1990) randomly assigned couples with a depressed wife to either conjoint BCT, cognitive therapy with the depressed spouse alone, or a waiting-list control group. All couples reported marital distress as well as depression in one spouse (i.e., according to the typologies outlined earlier, all couples were "classic"). Posttreatment results showed that BCT was just as effective as individual cognitive therapy in reducing depressive symptomatology, and was significantly more effective than cognitive therapy in increasing marital satisfaction. One year following treatment the two therapy groups did not differ on depression scores, and the BCT group maintained significantly higher marital satisfaction scores than the cognitive therapy group. Although this study supported the hypothesis that conjoint, relationship-focused therapy would be more effective in improving the marriage, BCT *did not* result in increased efficacy over individual treatment in terms of alleviation

of current symptoms or rates of recurrence at follow-up.

The O'Leary and Beach (1990) study evaluated individual versus conjoint therapy for a particular subset of depressed patients: those who also presented with marital distress. Yet this selective sample makes comparison difficult with other studies of treatment for depression, which usually require only that subjects meet criteria for major depression, regardless of marital satisfaction or marital status. A recent outcome study by Jacobson et al. (1991) attempted to complement the work of O'Leary and Beach by using a sample of couples who were heterogeneous with respect to marital satisfaction. Married depressed women were randomly assigned to individual cognitive-behavior therapy, conjoint BCT, or a treatment combining the two components. Posttreatment results revealed an interesting pattern of interaction between pretreatment marital quality and treatment outcome. Individual cognitive therapy, either alone or combined with conjoint BCT, was most effective in alleviating depression when the couple was nondistressed. However, when one or both spouses reported pretreatment marital distress, BCT and cognitive therapy were equally effective in alleviating depression, and BCT was the only treatment to produce significant pre- to posttest changes in marital satisfaction.

As we have already documented, there is reason to believe that response to treatment would improve and recurrence rates would be reduced if the quality of the marital relationship were to improve during the course of therapy. Empirical findings have clearly demonstrated an association between unresolved marital distress and posttreatment relapse (e.g., Hooley et al., 1986; Rounsaville et al., 1979). This has been one of the primary rationales for evaluating couple therapy as a treatment for depression. In a follow-up to the Jacobson et al. (1991) outcome study, Jacobson et al. (1993) compared the effects of individual cognitive therapy, conjoint BCT, and the combined treatment on relapse rates at 6- and 12-month follow-up. It was predicted that depressed subjects who received the conjoint treatment (either alone or in combination with cognitive therapy) would be less likely to relapse than those who received only individual cognitive therapy. However, results showed that neither of the treatments that included couple therapy produced reductions in relapse rates relative to the individual cognitive therapy. Although these results did not provide support for the hypothesis that a conjoint approach would produce lower relapse rates, the investigators noted that relapse rates were low across *all* the groups, and that longer follow-up intervals may be required in order to uncover differential treatment effects. However, the study did provide some support for the hypothesis that changes in marital interaction would predict improvement in depressive symptomatology. In particular, in couples where the husbands became less distressed and more supportive toward their wives during the course of therapy, the wives were more likely to be nondepressed at the end of therapy, and were more likely to stay nondepressed for at least 1 year. These findings were consistent with previous research (e.g., Brown & Harris, 1978) showing that a close, confiding relationship with the spouse moderated the effects of life stress and bore a direct inverse relationship to subsequent depression.

Taken together, these results may be used to evaluate the empirical status of traditional BCT as a treatment for depression:

1. *Is conjoint treatment more effective in alleviating symptoms of the current depressive episode?* BCT and individual cognitive therapy were equally effective for depressives who also complained of marital distress ("classic" couples), and BCT was actually less effective when the couples were nondistressed ("social support" couples).

2. *Does conjoint treatment result in greater improvement in the marital relationship?* In all cases, including couples who were nondistressed initially, BCT resulted in greater improvements in marital satisfaction than did individual therapy. These results are consistent with previous research showing that standard individual treatments have little effect on marital issues and residual marital distress, even following successful therapy (e.g., Beach & O'Leary, 1986; Gurman & Kniskern, 1978). However, although the improvements in marital satisfaction were statistically significant, the clinical significance of these improvements was less than optimal: In each study, fewer than half of the couples treated conjointly were nondistressed at posttest (an established cutoff on the Dyadic Adjustment Scale was used as the criterion for recovery).

3. *Can conjoint treatment produce lower rates of relapse for recovered depressives?* Relapse rates did not discriminate between individual therapy and BCT at follow-up in either

study. However, results at follow-up in the Jacobson et al. (1993) study did indicate that improvements in the supportiveness of the nondepressed spouse played an important role in the processes of relapse and recovery.

4. *What subset of married depressed clients is most likely to benefit from conjoint treatment?* For depressed subjects who were also in distressed marriages (i.e., "classic" couples), conjoint therapy was at least as effective as individual interventions in reducing depressive symptomatology, and had the additional benefit of improving the marital relationship. However, individual treatment was more effective for depressives who did not present with marital distress. These results indicate that when *both* the relationship and the depression are viewed as problematic, BCT is the treatment of choice.

RECENT CLINICAL INNOVATIONS: INTEGRATIVE BEHAVIORAL COUPLE THERAPY

Despite the relative efficacy and widespread popularity of traditional BCT, the results cited above, taken together with the results of clinical trials with distressed but nondepressed couples, have led us to recognize the limitations of the approach and the need for clinical innovation in our treatment of couples. In considering which couples were not being reached by traditional BCT, four variables were consistently revealed as predictors of treatment response: severity of marital distress, with, as would be expected, more severely distressed couples showing less favorable response; age, with younger couples more likely to respond favorably; emotional disengagement, with an inverse relationship between degree of disengagement and treatment response; and incompatibility, with a high degree of polarization on basic marital issues predicting less favorable response (Christensen et al., 1995). All of these factors relate in some way to a couple's amenability to accommodation and compromise. Spouses who are severely distressed, who are older and have been engaging in habitual interaction patterns for many years, who are highly disengaged, and who are incompatible on fundamental issues are the very spouses who would find it most difficult to accommodate to each other, to compromise, and to make collaborative efforts to change the relationship.

In terms of the conjoint treatment of depression, we have seen that BCT is not effective when the relationship is not viewed as a primary problem. It is not surprising to find that couples who view one spouse's depression as the primary problem (these may be either "denial" or "social support" couples) are not as responsive to the relationship change strategies promoted in traditional BCT. Yet traditional BCT is based largely on change-oriented interventions—techniques that are designed to foster collaboration, compromise, and accommodation on the part of each spouse to the partner's needs. Behavior exchange procedures, problem solving, and establishing and maintaining change agreements all require each partner to respond positively to the other's requests for change. As we have seen, this approach works well for some problems and with some couples. But for couples for whom accommodation and compromise are more difficult, the traditional approach seems to miss the mark.

Our response to these findings has been an attempt to expand the applicability and effectiveness of BCT. Our new integrative approach, IBCT (Christensen & Jacobson, 1991; Christensen et al., 1995) builds on the technology of traditional BCT but attempts to integrate the promotion of change with the fostering of emotional acceptance. "Emotional acceptance" in IBCT refers to situations in which behavior change (the hallmark of traditional BCT) does not occur, or does not occur to the degree that the requesting partner would prefer. However, what does occur is a change in the way the requesting partner experiences the spouse's behavior. Whereas it was previously experienced as intolerable, unacceptable, and blameworthy, when emotional acceptance has occurred the behavior will be experienced as at least understandable and tolerable, or at times will even be appreciated as a valuable aspect of the partner's behavior. Thus, whereas strategies oriented to "change" foster compromise and accommodation, "acceptance" refers to letting go of the struggle to change, and at times even embracing those differences that have been sources of conflict. Whereas "change" interventions attempt to solve couples' presenting problems, "acceptance" work implies that some problems may be unsolvable, and that areas of conflict may be turned into sources of increased intimacy and understanding. It should be noted that IBCT is adjunctive to, but in no way incompatible with, traditional BCT. IBCT includes virtually all of the procedures of traditional

BCT, but modifies those procedures and adds new ones in an effort to enhance both emotional acceptance and change.

We now briefly outline the procedures of IBCT, including both the alteration of treatment strategies from the traditional approach, and new strategies that are unique to the integrative approach. Before doing so, we note again that IBCT has been piloted with couples who are distressed, but not with couples in which one spouse is experiencing an episode of major depression. At this point we can only speculate as to how IBCT might represent an improvement in the conjoint treatment of depression; the comparative efficacy of the model remains to be determined empirically.

Modification of Change Strategies

Usually, traditional BCT places behavior exchange interventions at the beginning of therapy, in order to promote early and rapid improvements in marital satisfaction. Furthermore, in an effort to ensure the positive outcome of the interventions, a common characteristic of traditional behavior exchange is to focus only on nonconflictual behaviors. In traditional BCT, behaviors that are emotionally too "high-cost" for one or both partners are avoided. IBCT shares with traditional BCT the behavioral model of reinforcement exchange, and views behavior exchange as a valuable treatment component for many couples. However, behavior exchange is typically used in a different way by IBCT, often at different stages in therapy, and with somewhat different goals. Rather than a focus on only "low-cost," nonconflictual behaviors, IBCT does not exclude, and in fact explicitly includes, core conflict areas to be focused on in behavior exchange. Furthermore, since anger and resentment often interfere with positive changes early in therapy, in IBCT behavior exchange often occurs later in therapy, after a certain amount of emotional acceptance has occurred, or concurrently with emotional acceptance strategies. Most importantly, when behavior exchange is attempted within IBCT, less is riding on the success of the procedures. For example, if change in a particular area is agreed upon but does not occur, or occurs with considerable ambivalence, this may be an indication that work on emotional acceptance should be emphasized. Thus lack of success in implementing behavior exchange assignments is viewed not as a failure, but rather as a clue to areas where further exploration and emotional acceptance may be called for.

Communication and problem-solving strategies are also conceptualized and implemented differently in IBCT. The traditional BCT approach is to have spouses learn to express their feelings about a problem more constructively, and to have them solve the problem using rules for effective conflict resolution. Although IBCT does not rule out the possibility of change on core issues and indeed often promotes it, it suggests that acceptance of differences and a realization that partners will not be able to change completely in accordance with each other's wishes is both realistic and necessary. Therefore, IBCT attempts to integrate accommodation and change with an equal emphasis upon understanding and accepting the differences between the partners.

Communication and problem solving are integrated with emotional acceptance throughout the course of therapy. For example, acceptance work will often precede formal training in communication and conflict resolution skills, in an attempt to preempt difficulties and in fact to foster more constructive problem solving. Alternately, acceptance work can be focused on whenever the couple is having trouble with problem solving. When the partners have achieved increased acceptance and understanding of each other's position, problem solving can then be resumed. Finally, in IBCT acceptance is promoted by teaching a different method of discussing problems, which we describe in the next section.

Strategies to Promote Emotional Acceptance

IBCT employs three strategies to promote emotional acceptance: acceptance through talking about the problem as an "it"; acceptance through greater tolerance of the partner's aversive behaviors; and acceptance through increased self-care. First, in discussing core relationship problems, the therapist attempts to foster acceptance by reformulating both the problem and the partner's behavior in terms of common differences between people and understandable emotional reactions to those differences. This is what we mean by talking about the problem as an "it." Rather than placing blame for the problem on the undesirable behavior or flawed character of the partner, the spouses are encouraged to view the problem as a common adversary with which they are faced. If they can develop a repertoire for discussing the problem in a way that acknowledges its seeming unsolvability and unites them against it, intimacy can actually be enhanced as a result of the way they discuss it. To promote acceptance, IBCT therapists guide couples in a different way of talking about problems. Therapists encourage spouses to talk about their own feelings and thoughts, rather than focusing on what their partners did or what they think their partner are thinking or feeling. When clients talk about themselves, IBCT therapists encourage disclosure of "soft" feelings and thoughts (e.g., hurt, fear, disappointment, doubt) versus "hard" ones (e.g., anger, resentment, power, and control). The goal of these discussions is to develop compassion and understanding for each partner's position, an increased capacity for the partners to discuss their problems as an "it" that they share, and a way to talk about their problems that brings them closer rather than placing them as adversaries. One of the ironies of emotional acceptance work is that change is often facilitated by giving up on the struggle for change. Often when spouses stop trying to solve a problem using their habitual self-defeating strategies, and join in an effort to understand the problem and each other's position, the problem begins to seem more solvable.

The second strategy used to foster acceptance in IBCT is the promotion of tolerance for the spouse's behavior in a way that will reduce the pain caused by that behavior. Strategies to accomplish this include pointing out the positive features of a partner's behavior; role playing or behavior rehearsal of the negative behavior; and "faking" incidents of the negative behavior when there is really no inclination to engage in that behavior. The last two strategies are designed to provide a more neutral affective atmosphere in which the behaver can more clearly observe his/her impact on the partner, and the partner can desensitize himself/herself to the aversive behavior. We must clarify here that we are *not* asking spouses to tolerate oppressive, offensive, or abusive behavior from each other; "acceptance" should not be interpreted as "resignation." Acceptance means using relationship problems as a vehicle to enhance intimacy and understanding, so that the process of change leads to greater closeness rather than greater conflict.

The third strategy in IBCT is promoting emotional acceptance through greater self-care.

If partners are especially needy or vulnerable, they will have greater difficulty accepting each other when their needs go unfulfilled. Thus an avenue toward greater acceptance is to increase each partner's self-reliance, so that the spouse's undesirable behavior becomes less devastating. One way in which greater self-care is promoted is through helping each spouse to explore alternative means of need satisfaction. For example, a partner may be encouraged to seek support and intimacy from friends at times when his/her spouse is unable to be close. Exploration of alternative need satisfaction is conditional—for those times when the partner is unable to satisfy needs—rather than a way of releasing the partner from responsibility for need satisfaction. Although therapy continues to be aimed at promoting greater closeness, partners are likely to be more amenable to collaborative work if they are able to take care of themselves better in the face of inevitable lapses in closeness.

Increased self-care is also encouraged in the face of a partner's negative behavior. Partners' vulnerability to each other is often most apparent in the presence of provocative, negative behavior. IBCT therapists promote the idea that change strategies, however successful, will rarely be exhaustive. Therefore, spouses need some means of protecting and caring for themselves in the face of provocative behavior. These strategies may include leaving the situation, seeking solace from others, assertively altering the situation, or defining the situation differently (e.g., as a temporary slip or setback). With greater self-care, spouses may experience less pain and greater tolerance; moreover, by removing some of the pressure to change, these strategies may also remove one of the greatest barriers to change.

Again, we want to underscore that we are not asking partners to continue to tolerate intolerable behavior. What we are suggesting is that change efforts, no matter how successful, will not eliminate all future occurrences of the problem, that partners have a responsibility to take care of themselves in these situations, and that a recurrence of the problem behavior does not have to mean that the relationship is falling apart. Acceptance strategies in IBCT are integrated with and designed to enhance change strategies, while increasing the couple's feelings of closeness and intimacy. They are not a substitute for changing destructive relationship patterns.

Implications for the Conjoint Treatment of Depression

Our pilot data suggest that IBCT is a clinically powerful and flexible approach to the treatment of distressed marriages. The integration of emotional acceptance strategies may be one of the missing links in traditionally change-oriented BCT, although this remains to be clinically determined. We also feel enthusiastic about the potential for IBCT to improve the treatment of depression in the context of marriage, for several reasons. First, traditional BCT, perhaps more than any other approach to couple therapy, has developed an effective technology to foster change, accommodation, and compromise, whereas other treatment modalities have emphasized enhancing acceptance. Most approaches to couple therapy have tended to focus on one to the relative exclusion of the other. Our assertion is that a complete approach must integrate the two, and IBCT is an attempt to achieve that integration. It is hoped, then, that this approach will be more effective in alleviating depression, enhancing the marital relationship, and preventing relapse for those couples who were not reached by traditional BCT.

Second, the addition of emotional acceptance work may enhance treatment acceptability for certain couples. As we noted earlier, in our clinical outcome study comparing individual cognitive therapy with BCT (Jacobson et al., 1993), those couples who benefited most from conjoint treatment presented with complaints of both depression and marital distress. Couples who deny marital distress (i.e., "denial" couples) and those who are truly not distressed according to our assessment (i.e., "social support" couples) are likely to be less amenable to a treatment that explicitly targets relationship change, as traditional BCT does. Furthermore, even in a "classic" couple one or both spouses may still view the depression as the primary problem, although it is clear to the clinician that relationship-focused therapy is called for. IBCT may be a more palatable way of accessing relationship issues without either spouse feeling blamed for the depression or the marital conflict.

Finally, IBCT is designed to enhance partners' feelings of intimacy, mutual understanding, and compassion for each other, even during phases of therapy when "change" in the traditional sense is not occurring. Given the accumulation of data on the protective, stress-buffering effects of close, intimate relationships, it seems likely that anything that can enhance intimacy in the course of therapy can only be advantageous for both the depressed and the nondepressed spouse. This may be especially important in treating depressed women. In recent years, a great deal of writing on the psychology of women has emphasized the importance of relationships to women's sense of self and emotional well-being (e.g., Gilligan, 1982; Miller, 1987). Stiver (1991) suggests:

> Depression found in women who are married . . . cannot be seen solely as deprivation or loss of psychological supplies; it is also a result of the lack of an adequate relational context. Thus some women may experience a continuous sense of loss when they are in relationships in which there are limited opportunities for mutual empathy and mutual empowerment. (p. 264)

IBCT is designed to create opportunities both for empowerment (through behavior change) and empathy (through emotional acceptance) in the treatment of depression. It is hoped that IBCT will enhance feelings of "connectedness" and intimacy, even in a nondistressed marriage.

OTHER MODELS OF COUPLE/FAMILY THERAPY FOR DEPRESSION

Numerous other models for the treatment of depression in the context of marriage and family have been described and researched. Here we briefly describe several of the more prominent approaches, and provide clinical outcome data whenever it is available.

First, the couple therapy model that most clearly asserts a causal link between depression and marital discord is Coyne's (1988) strategic therapy, a brief, interactional therapy that conceptualizes depression in the context of ongoing interpersonal systems. Strategic therapy is based on the assumption that depression persists as the result of ineffective coping on the part of both spouses, and therapy is aimed at examining and modifying the way each spouse is coping with their problems. Although there is no explicit assumption of a directional, causal relationship between depression and marital conflict, it is assumed that the two are interwoven over time, and that marital interactions are relevant to the persistence of the depression. The therapist typically works individually with each spouse, as well as with the dyad together.

Interpersonal psychotherapy (IPT) for depression (Klerman, Weissman, Rounsaville, & Chevron, 1984; Rounsaville & Chevron, 1982) focuses on interpersonal issues and attachment in depression. Without assuming a specific causal pathway, the model assumes that the symptoms of depression may be interfering with interpersonal functioning, while interpersonal difficulties may also be associated with depression. Therapy may target one or more of four interpersonal problem areas: grief and mourning; interpersonal role disputes; role transitions; and interpersonal deficits. IPT has long been the individual treatment approach that has most explicitly addressed interpersonal issues. Yet until recently IPT did not include the spouse of the depressed client in the therapy process. Recently, Foley et al. (1987) compared IPT with and without involvement of the spouse. The spouse-involved treatment was as effective as individual IPT in alleviating depressive symptomatology, and was more effective at improving marital quality.

Although treatment involving family members has been widely used on inpatient psychiatric units, until recently very few controlled outcome data comparing its effectiveness to individual treatment approaches were available. This gap has been filled by a randomized clinical trial of inpatient family intervention (IFI) versus standard individual hospital treatment, for patients with both unipolar and bipolar depression (Haas et al., 1988). IFI is a brief, psychoeducational therapy, with an emphasis on acceptance and understanding of the patient's illness; identification of possible life stressors precipitating the current episode and likely future stressors; elucidation of family interactions that may produce stress for the patient; and planning strategies for managing future stresses. Results upon discharge showed a treatment effect favoring IFI for female patients with major affective disorder, whereas for male patients who received IFI, there was no effect or a relatively worse outcome at discharge. In a subsequent report, Clarkin et al. (1990) presented the results at 6- and 18-month follow-up for the patients with affective disorders, with separate analyses for unipolar versus bipolar patients. Interestingly, at both 6 and 18 months bipolar patients showed better outcome with IFI in addition to standard treatment, whereas unipolar patients did better without the addition of IFI. In speculating about these results, the authors noted that IFI emphasizes psycho-education and stress management, and that it was originally developed for use with schizophrenic patients (for whom family education about the illness has proven to be particularly helpful in preventing relapse). They suggested that the goals of IFI may be better suited to the needs of bipolar patients, and noted in support that achievement of the specified goals of IFI was not positively associated with outcome for unipolar patients.

Finally, problem-centered systems therapy is a family-based intervention that has been effectively combined with pharmacotherapy (Epstein, Keitner, Bishop, & Miller, 1988). This model assumes that family pathology may increase vulnerability to and perpetuate depression. The therapy includes as many of the depressed client's family members as possible, and stresses an active collaboration between family members and the therapist. Assessment and intervention are aimed at communication and problem solving, family roles, affective involvement and responsiveness, and behavioral control. In a small 1-year pilot project, Epstein et al. (1988) found that the addition of family therapy sessions resulted in improved recovery from depression.

SUMMARY AND CONCLUSIONS

In recent years, there has been a general trend toward considering the interpersonal context of individual psychopathology and actively including family members in treatment. This chapter has reviewed a similar trend in the treatment of depression. As our review of the outcome literature suggests, intervention in the context of the couple and family shows some promise as a means of simultaneously reducing depressive symptomatology and improving couple and family relationships. Yet we have also reviewed the limitations of couple and family approaches. We would like to suggest several directions for future research. First, in each of the clinical trials of couple and family interventions for depression, the beneficial effects of including the spouse and other family members appear to be limited to particular subsets of the original sample. Clearly, a crucial direction for future research is identifying those subpopulations of depressed individuals who will most benefit from couple and family approaches to treatment. Factors that should be considered include severity of depression, particular diagnosis (e.g.,

unipolar depression, bipolar disorders, dysthymia, double depression), level of marital or family conflict, inpatient versus outpatient treatment, and gender issues. Second, research on the course of recovery and relapse following individual versus couple or family treatment will help to identify the mechanisms of change in both depression and marital satisfaction. It is possible that there are many potential mediators of recovery from depression, and that different treatment approaches make use of different mediators. Perhaps a treatment approach that enhances both interpersonal and intrapersonal mediators of change will prove to be most effective. A related area deserving further investigation is the efficacy of treatments combining individual and couple/family sessions. Finally, further exploration of the functional relationship between couple and family discord and depression is warranted. It is possible that different typologies of depression in relation to couple and family discord may emerge; if so, they will certainly have important implications for effective intervention. Thus, although much has been accomplished in our understanding of the interpersonal context and treatment of depression, much remains to be learned. We hope that this chapter has served to stimulate interest in these directions.

REFERENCES

Addis, M. E., & Jacobson, N. S. (1991). Integration of cognitive therapy and behavioral marital therapy for depression. *Journal of Psychotherapy Integration, 1*, 249–264.

American Psychiatric Association (APA). (1994). *Diagnostic and statistical manual of mental disorders* (4th ed.). Washington, DC: Author.

Aneshensel, C. S. (1986). Marital and employment role-strain, social support, and depression among adult women. In S. Hobfall (Ed.), *Stress, social support, and women* (pp. 99–114). Washington, DC: Hemisphere.

Aneshensel, C. S., Frerich, R. R., & Clark, V. A. (1981). Family roles and sex differences in depression. *Journal of Health and Social Behavior, 22*, 379–393.

Barnett, L., & Nietzel, M. (1979). Relationship of instrumental and affectional behaviors and self-esteem to marital satisfaction in distressed and non-distressed couples. *Journal of Consulting and Clinical Psychology, 47*, 946–957.

Beach, S. R. H., Jouriles, E. N., & O'Leary, K. D. (1985). Extramarital sex: Impact on depression and commitment in couples seeking marital therapy. *Journal of Sex and Marital Therapy, 11*, 99–108.

Beach, S. R. H., & O'Leary, K. D. (1986). The treatment of depression occurring in the context of marital discord. *Behavior Therapy, 17*, 43–49.

Beach, S. R. H., Sandeen, E. E., & O'Leary, K. D. (1990).

Depression in marriage: A model for etiology and treatment. New York: Guilford Press.

Beck, A. T., Rush, A. J., Shaw, B., & Emery, G. (1979). *Cognitive therapy of depression.* New York: Guilford Press.

Bellack, A. S., Hersen, M., & Himmelhoch, J. M. (1983). A comparison of social skills training, pharmacotherapy, and psychotherapy for depression. *Behaviour Research and Therapy, 21,* 101–107.

Belle, D. (1982). *Lives in stress: Women and depression.* Beverly Hills, CA: Sage.

Biglan, A., Hops, H., Sherman, L., Friedman, L., Arthur, J., & Osteen, V. (1985). Problem solving interactions of depressed women and their husbands. *Behavior Therapy, 16,* 431–451.

Billings, A. G., & Moos, R. H. (1982). Psychosocial theory and research in depression: An integrative framework and review. *Clinical Psychology Review, 2,* 213–238.

Bloom, B., Asher, S. J., & White, S. W. (1978). Marital disruption as a stressor: A review and analysis. *Psychological Bulletin, 85,* 867–894.

Bothwell, S., & Weissman, M. M. (1977). Social impairments four years after an acute depressive episode. *American Journal of Orthopsychiatry, 47,* 231–237.

Briscoe, C. W., & Smith, J. B. (1973). Depression and marital turmoil. *Archives of General Psychiatry, 29,* 811–817.

Brown, G. W., & Harris, T. O. (1978). *Social origins of depression: A study of psychiatric disorder in women.* New York: Free Press.

Christensen, A., & Jacobson, N. S. (1991). *Integrative behavioral couple therapy: treatment manual.* Unpublished manuscript, University of Washington.

Christensen, A., Jacobson, N. S., & Babcock, J. C. (1995). Integrative behavioral couple therapy. N. S. Jacobson & A. S. Gurman (Eds.), *Clinical handbook of couple therapy* (pp. 31–64). New York: Guilford Press.

Clarkin, J. F., Glick, I. D., Haas, G. L., Spencer, J. H., Lewis, A. B., Peyser, J., DeMane, N., Good-Ellis, M., Harris, E., & Lestelle, V. (1990). A randomized clinical trial of inpatient family intervention: V. Results for affective disorders. *Journal of Affective Disorders, 18,* 17–28.

Clarkin, J. F., Haas, G. L., & Glick, I. D. (1988). Inpatient family intervention. In J. F. Clarkin, G. L. Haas, & I. D. Glick (Eds.), *Affective disorders and the family: Assessment and treatment* (pp. 134–152). New York: Guilford Press.

Cochrane, R., & Stropes-Role, M. (1981). Women, marriage, employment and mental health. *British Journal of Psychiatry, 139,* 373–381.

Coleman, R. E., & Miller, A. G. (1975). The relationship between depression and marital maladjustment in a clinic population: A multitrait–multimethod study. *Journal of Consulting and Clinical Psychology, 43,* 647–651.

Costello, C. G. (1982). Social factors associated with depression: A retrospective community study. *Psychological Medicine, 12,* 329–339.

Coyne, J. C. (1976). Toward an interactional description of depression. *Psychiatry, 39,* 28–40.

Coyne, J. C. (1988). Strategic therapy. In J. F. Clarkin, G. L. Haas, & I. D. Glick (Eds.), *Affective disorders and the family: Assessment and treatment* (pp. 89–113). New York: Guilford Press.

Dean, A., Lin, N., & Ensel, W. M. (1981). The epidemiological significance of social support systems in depression. *Research in Community Mental Health, 2,* 77–109.

Dobson, K. S., Jacobson, N. S., & Victor, J. (1988). Integration of cognitive therapy and behavioral marital therapy. In J. F. Clarkin, G. L. Haas, & I. D. Glick (Eds.), *Affective disorders and the family: Assessment and treatment* (pp. 53–88). New York: Guilford Press.

Dohrenwend, B. S., & Dohrenwend, B. P. (Eds.). (1974). *Stressful life events: Their nature and effects.* New York: Wiley.

Elkin, I., Shea, T., Watkins, J. T., Imber, S. C., Sotsky, S. M., Collins, J. F., Glass, D. R., Pilkonis, P. A., Leber, W. R., Fiester, S. J., Docherty, J., & Parloff, M. B. (1989). NIMH Treatment of Depression Collaborative Research Program. *Archives of General Psychiatry, 46,* 971–982.

Epstein, N. B., Keitner, G. I., Bishop, D. S., & Miller, I. W. (1988). Combined use of pharmacological and family therapy. In J. F. Clarkin, G. L. Haas, & I. D. Glick (Eds.), *Affective disorders and the family: Assessment and treatment* (pp. 153–172). New York: Guilford Press.

Foley, S. H., Rounsaville, B. J., Weissman, M. M., Sholomskas, D., & Chevron, E. (1987, May). *Individual versus conjoint interpersonal psychotherapy for depressed patients with marital disputes.* Paper presented at the annual meeting of the American Psychiatric Association, Chicago.

Gilligan, C. (1982). *In a different voice: Psychological theory and women's development.* Cambridge, MA: Harvard University Press.

Gotlib, I. H. (1983). Perceptions and recall of interpersonal feedback: Negative bias in depression. *Cognitive Therapy and Research, 7,* 399–412.

Gove, W. R. (1975). The relationship between sex roles, marital status, and mental illness. *Social Forces, 51,* 34–44.

Gove, W. R., Hughes, M., & Style, C. B. (1983). Does marriage have positive effects on the psychological well-being of the individual? *Journal of Health and Social Behavior, 24,* 122–131.

Gove, W. R., & Tudor, J. F. (1973). Adult sex roles and mental illness. *American Journal of Sociology, 78,* 812–835.

Gurman, A. S., & Kniskern, D. P. (1978). Research on marital and family therapy: Progress, perspective and prospect. In S. L. Garfield & A. E. Bergin (Eds.), *Handbook of psychotherapy and behavior change: An empirical analysis* (2nd ed., pp. 817–901). New York: Wiley.

Haas, G. L., Glick, I. D., Clarkin, J. F., Spencer, J. H., Lewis, A. B., Peyser, J., DeMane, N., Good-Ellis, M., Harris, E., & Lestelle, V. (1988). Inpatient family intervention: A randomized clinical trial. II. Results at hospital discharge. *Archives of General Psychiatry, 45,* 217–224.

Hautzinger, M., Linden, M., & Hoffman, N. (1982). Distressed couples with and without a depressed partner: An analysis of their verbal interaction. *Journal of Behavior Therapy and Experimental Psychiatry, 13,* 307–314.

Hinchcliffe, M. K., Hooper, D., & Roberts, F. J. (1978). *The melancholy marriage: Depression in marriage and psychosocial approaches to therapy.* New York: Wiley.

Hollon, S. D., & Beck, A. T. (1978). Psychotherapy and drug therapy: Comparisons and combinations. In S. L. Garfield & A. E. Bergin (Eds.), *Handbook of psychotherapy and behavior change: An empirical analysis* (2nd ed., pp. 437–490). New York: Wiley.

Holtzworth-Munroe, A., & Jacobson, N. S. (1991). Behavioral marital therapy. In A. S. Gurman & D. P. Kniskern

(Eds.), *Handbook of family therapy* (Vol. 2, pp. 96–133). New York: Brunner/Mazel.

Hooley, J. M. (1986). Expressed emotion and depression: Interactions between patients and high- vs. low-expressed-emotion spouses. *Journal of Abnormal Psychology, 95,* 237–246.

Hooley, J. M., Orley, J., & Teasdale, J. D. (1986). Levels of expressed emotion and relapse in depressed patients. *British Journal of Psychiatry, 148,* 642–647.

Hops, H., Biglan, A., Sherman, L., Arthur, J., Friedman, L., & Osteen, V. (1987). Home observations of family interactions of depressed women. *Journal of Consulting and Clinical Psychology, 55,* 341–346.

Jacobson, N. S., Dobson, K., Fruzzetti, A. E., Schmaling, K. B., & Salusky, S. (1991). Marital therapy as a treatment for depression. *Journal of Consulting and Clinical Psychology, 59*(4), 547–557.

Jacobson, N. S., Fruzzetti, A. E., Dobson, K., Whisman, M., & Hops, H. (1993). Couple therapy as a treatment for depression: II. The effects of marital relationship quality and therapy on depressive relapse. *Journal of Consulting and Clinical Psychology, 61,* 516–519.

Jacobson, N. S., & Holtzworth-Munroe, A. (1986). Marital therapy: A social learning–cognitive perspective. In N. S. Jacobson & A. S. Gurman (Eds.), *Clinical handbook of marital therapy* (pp. 29–70). New York: Guilford Press.

Jacobson, N. S., & Margolin, G. (1979). *Marital therapy: Strategies based on social learning and behavior exchange principles.* New York: Brunner/Mazel.

Jacobson, N. S., Waldron, H., & Moore, D. (1980). Toward a behavioral profile of marital distress. *Journal of Consulting and Clinical Psychology, 48,* 696–703.

Kahn, J., Coyne, J. C., & Margolin, G. (1985). Depression and marital disagreement: The social construction of despair. *Journal of Social and Personal Relationships, 2,* 447–461.

Kessler, R. C., & Essex, M. (1982). Marital status and depression: The importance of coping resources. *Social Forces, 61*(2), 484–507.

Klerman, G. L., & Weissman, M. M. (1982). Interpersonal psychotherapy: Theory and research. In A. J. Rush (Ed.), *Short-term psychotherapies for depression* (pp. 88–106). New York: Guilford Press.

Klerman, G. L., Weissman, M. M., Rounsaville, B. J., & Chevron, E. S. (1984). *Interpersonal psychotherapy of depression.* New York: Basic Books.

Kovacs, M. (1980). The efficacy of cognitive and behavioral therapies for depression. *American Journal of Psychiatry, 137*(12), 1495–1504.

Kovacs, M., Rush, A. J., Beck, A. T., & Hollon, S. (1981). Depressed outpatients treated with cognitive therapy or pharmacotherapy. *Archives of General Psychiatry, 38*(1), 33–39.

Lewinsohn, P. M. (1974). A behavioral approach to depression. In R. J. Friedman & M. M. Katz (Eds.), *The psychology of depression: Contemporary theory and research* (pp. 157–185). New York: Wiley.

McClean, P. D., Ogston, K., & Grauer, L. (1973). A behavioral approach to the treatment of depression. *Journal of Behavior Therapy and Experimental Psychiatry, 4,* 323–330.

McGrath, E., Keita, G. P., Strickland, B. R., & Russo, N. F. (Eds.). (1990). *Women and depression: Risk factors and treatment issues. Final report of the American Psychological Association Task Force on Women and*

Depression. Washington, DC: American Psychological Association.

Miller, J. B. (1987). *Toward a new psychology of women* (2nd ed.). Boston: Beacon Press.

Murphy, G. E., Simons, A. D., Wetzel, R. D., & Lustman, P. J. (1984). Cognitive therapy and pharmacotherapy: Singly and together in the treatment of depression. *Archives of General Psychiatry, 41,* 33–41.

Nelson, G. M., & Beach, S. R. H. (1990). Sequential interaction in depression: Effects of depressive behavior on spousal aggression. *Behavior Therapy, 21,* 167–182.

Nolen-Hoeksema, S. (1987). Sex differences in unipolar depression: Evidence and theory. *Psychological Bulletin, 101,* 259–282.

Nolen-Hoeksema, S. (1990). *Sex differences in depression.* Stanford, CA: Stanford University Press.

O'Leary, K. D., & Beach, S. R. H. (1990). Marital therapy: A viable treatment for depression and marital discord. *American Journal of Psychiatry, 147,* 183–186.

Paykel, E. S. (1979). Recent life events in the development of depressive disorders. In R.A. Depue (Ed.), *The psychobiology of depressive disorders: Implications for the effects of stress* (pp. 245–262). New York: Academic Press.

Paykel, E. S., Myers, J. D., Dienelt, M. N., Klerman, G. L., Lindenthal, J. J., & Pepper, M. P. (1969). Life events and depression: A controlled study. *Archives of General Psychiatry, 21,* 753–760.

Pearlin, L. I., & Johnson, J. (1977). Marital status, life strains, and depression. *American Sociological Review, 42,* 704–715.

Pearlin, L. I., & Lieberman, M. (1979). Social sources of emotional distress. In R. G. Simmons (Ed.), *Research in community and mental health* (pp. 217–248). Greenwich, CT: JAI Press.

Prien, R. F., Kupfer, D. J., Mansky, P. A., Small, J. G., Twason, V. B., Voss, C. B., & Johnson, W. E. (1984). Drug therapy in the prevention of recurrences in unipolar and bipolar affective disorders: Report of the NIMH collaborative study group comparing lithium carbonate, imipramine, and a lithium carbonate–imipramine combination. *Archives of General Psychiatry, 41,* 1096–1104.

Radloff, L. S. (1975). Sex differences in depression: The effects of occupation and marital status. *Sex Roles, 1,* 249–265.

Radloff, L. S., & Rae, D. S. (1979). Susceptibility and precipitating factors in depression: Sex differences and similarities. *Journal of Abnormal Psychology, 88,* 174–181.

Rosenfield, S. (1980). Sex differences in depression: Do women always have higher rates? *Journal of Health and Social Behavior, 21,* 33–42.

Roth, D., Bielski, R., Jones, M., Parker, W., & Osborne, G. (1982). A comparison of self-control therapy and combined self-control therapy and antidepressant medication in the treatment of depression. *Behavior Therapy, 13,* 133–144.

Rounsaville, B. J., & Chevron, E. (1982). Interpersonal psychotherapy: Clinical applications. In A. J. Rush (Ed.), *Short-term psychotherapies for depression* (pp. 107–142). New York: Guilford Press.

Rounsaville, B. J., Weissman, M. M., Prusoff, B. A., & Herceg-Baron, R. L. (1979). Marital disputes and treatment outcome in depressed women. *Comprehensive Psychiatry, 20,* 483–490.

Roy, A. (1978). Vulnerability factors and depression in women. *British Journal of Psychiatry, 133,* 106–110.

Schmaling, K. B., & Jacobson, N. S. (1990). Marital inter-action and depression. *Journal of Abnormal Psychology,* 99(3), 229–236.

Shea, M. T., Elkin, I., Imber, S. D., Sotsky, S. M., Watkins, J. T., Collins, J. F., Pilkonis, P. A., Beckham, E., Glass, D. R., Dolan, R. T., & Parloff, M. B. (1992). Course of depressive symptoms over follow-up: Findings from the National Institute of Mental Health Treatment of De-pression Collaborative Research Program. *Archives of General Psychiatry,* 49(10), 782–787.

Steinbrueck, S. M., Maxwell, S. E., & Howard, G. S. (1983). A meta-analysis of psychotherapy and drug therapy in the treatment of unipolar depression with adults. *Journal of Consulting and Clinical Psychology, 51,* 856–863.

Stiver, I. P. (1991). The meaning of care: Reframing treat-ment models. In J. V. Jordan, A. G. Kaplan, J. B. Miller, I. P. Stiver, & J. L. Surrey, *Women's growth in connec-tion: Writings from the Stone Center* (pp. 250–267). New York: Guilford Press.

Warheit, G. J. (1979). Life events, coping, stress, and de-pressive symptomology. *American Journal of Psychia-try, 136,* 502–507.

Weiss, R. L., & Aved, B. M. (1978). Marital satisfaction and depression as predictors of physical health status. *Journal of Consulting and Clinical Psychology, 46,* 1379–1384.

Weissman, M. M. (1987). Advances in psychiatric epide-miology: Rates and risks for major depression. *Ameri-can Journal of Public Health, 77,* 445–451.

Weissman, M. M., & Kasl, S. V. (1976). Help-seeking in depressed outpatients following maintenance therapy. *British Journal of Psychiatry, 129,* 252–260.

Weissman, M. M., & Klerman, G. L. (1977). Gender and depression. *Trends in Neurosciences, 8,* 416–420.

Weissman, M. M., & Klerman, G. L. (1985). Sex differ-ences in the epidemiology of depression. *Archives of General Psychiatry, 34,* 98–111.

Weissman, M. M., Leaf, P. J., Bruce, M. L., & Florio, L. (1988). The epidemiology of dysthymia in five commu-nities: Rates, risks, comorbidity, and treatment. *Ameri-can Journal of Psychiatry, 145,* 815–819.

Weissman, M. M., & Paykel, E. S. (1974). *The depressed woman: A study of social relationships.* Chicago: Uni-versity of Chicago Press.

Wills, T. A., Weiss, R. L., & Patterson, G. R. (1974). A behavioral analysis of the determinants of marital sat-isfaction. *Journal of Consulting and Clinical Psychol-ogy, 42,* 802–811.

Wilson, P. H., Goldin, J. C., & Charbonneau-Powls, N. (1983). Comparative efficacy of behavioral and cogni-tive treatments of depression. *Cognitive Therapy and Research, 7,* 111–124.

16

Psychotherapy Integration: Implications for the Treatment of Depression

JEREMY D. SAFRAN
THOMAS A. INCK

In this chapter we explore some of the issues that we consider relevant to the treatment of depression from an integrative perspective. Although, rightfully speaking, any in-depth exploration of this type should consider both psychosocial and biological treatment approaches, in the present context we limit the scope of our task by restricting our discussion to the topic of psychotherapeutic integration. Our focus is on general conceptual issues relevant to the enterprise of psychotherapy integration, rather than on the discussion of specific integrative approaches for the treatment of depression.

A variety of different therapeutic treatment modalities have been described in this volume, and there is empirical evidence to suggest that most, or all, of them can be effective treatments for depression. There was a time in the not too distant past when it was customary for proponents of different therapeutic approaches to argue for the superior efficacy of their own approaches on the basis of empirical evidence. While it would be premature to say that the sound of the battle drums has completely ceased, it is probably fair to say that the climate of self-congratulatory exuberance has given way to a more sanguine and tolerant period. Researchers and clinicians echo Luborsky, Singer, and Luborsky's (1975) quotation from Lewis Carroll's dodo bird: "All have won and all must have prizes," even if in their hearts they nurture

a secret belief that their particular treatment is more effective, more thorough, more profound, more moral, or more aesthetically pleasing.

Like it or not, the findings of therapeutic equivalence (Luborsky et al., 1975; Smith & Glass, 1977) force us to confront some tough issues, just as Eysenck's (1965) reviews of the psychotherapy research in the mid-1960s forced psychotherapists to question some fundamental beliefs about their enterprise, and galvanized a tremendous evolution in the sophistication of psychotherapy research methodology.

One response to the findings of therapeutic equivalence has been to attempt to identify the methodological factors that impede the demonstration of differences in the effectiveness of different treatments (Beutler, 1991; Stiles, Shapiro, & Elliott, 1986). The other response has taken the findings of therapeutic equivalence seriously and uses them as a springboard for a consideration of the issue from a more integrative perspective. This movement toward a more integrative perspective is consistent with a more general cultural zeitgeist of relativity in what has come to be known as the "postmodern era."

CONVERGING TRENDS

One of the results of postmodernism in the psychotherapy arena is that the boundaries between different traditional forms of psychotherapy are becoming less clear-cut. All forms of psychotherapy are modifying fundamental premises and assumptions in response to influences of the culture at large.

One example of this convergence is a movement in diverse orientations toward a grounding in a constructivist epistemology. In the psychoanalytic tradition, critics from a hermeneutic perspective (e.g., Spence, 1982; Schafer, 1983) argue that the classical psychoanalytic emphasis on the discovery of historical truth should be replaced by an emphasis on the construction of coherent narratives, because memory is, in the final analysis, always a constructive process. This grounding has also been affirmed by theorists such as Hoffman (1991), who emphasizes that psychotherapy is inevitably a social-constructivist process in which both therapist and patient work together in a mutually influencing process to construct a new, adaptive reality that is inevitably social in nature.

In the cognitive–behavioral tradition, theorists such as Guidano (1991), Mahoney (1991), and Safran and Segal (1990) argue that the traditional cognitive–behavioral emphasis on modifying distorted cognitions makes the mistaken assumption that there is an objective reality that can be more or less accurately represented. Instead, they emphasize the importance of helping clients to first conceptualize reality as having amorphous qualities and then to form adaptive, flexible, and creative understandings of themselves and their relationships.

Another general shift has been a movement toward increased flexibility in technique. In psychoanalytic practice, the traditional emphasis on maintaining a rigorous stance of therapeutic neutrality and abstinence has given way to fundamental questions regarding the meaning of therapeutic neutrality (Greenberg, 1991; Kohut, 1984; Wachtel, 1986), and an emphasis on responding flexibly to the needs of the individual patient, rather than being guided by overly restrictive technical guidelines.

In the cognitive–behavioral tradition, a host of different therapeutic conceptualizations and interventions are being incorporated from both psychoanalytic and experiential traditions as theorists come to recognize the value of constructs such as "unconscious" and "defensive processing" (Mahoney, 1991; Guidano, 1991; Meichenbaum & Gilmore, 1984), the centrality of affective processes in psychological functioning and in therapeutic intervention (Mahoney,

1991; Greenberg & Safran, 1987; Foa & Kozak, 1991), and the potential usefulness of developmental reconstruction (Guidano, 1987; Liotti, 1991; Young, 1987).

A final common theme in diverse orientations has been the movement toward a more interpersonal, or relational, perspective. In the psychoanalytic tradition, this movement has been well documented and catalyzed by important contributions, such as those of Greenberg and Mitchell (1983) and Eagle (1984). What appears to be emerging is what Greenberg and Mitchell (1983) have termed the "relational perspective," in which object relations and interpersonal theory are being synthesized in a creative fusion that challenges certain fundamental assumptions of classical psychoanalytic theory. Another example is the resurgence of interest in Ferenczi, with his emphasis on the therapeutic relationship and such novel technical experiments as "mutual analysis" (Dupont, 1988; Haynal, 1988).

Theorists in the cognitive–behavioral tradition have shifted from the traditional belief that an emphasis on the therapeutic relationship is of secondary importance (Ayllon & Michael, 1959; Eysenck, 1969) toward the perspective that the therapeutic relationship is an important vehicle for exploring and modifying dysfunctional schemas (e.g., Arnkoff, 1983; Goldfried & Davison, 1976; Jacobson, 1989; Reeve, Inck, & Safran, 1993). Moreover, a growing number of cognitive theorists, who have been influenced by attachment theory and related research in developmental psychology, have come to see the desire for interpersonal relatedness as a fundamental motivational principle (Guidano & Liotti, 1983; Liotti, 1991; Mahoney, 1991; Safran & Segal, 1990)

COMMON VERSUS SPECIFIC CHANGE FACTORS

The finding of therapeutic equivalence has generated new interest in an old question: What are the underlying mechanisms of change? How is it that forms of psychotherapy that appear dissimilar at a clinical level achieve comparable results? One possibility is that all forms of psychotherapy operate through common change mechanisms. For example, it may be that Frank's initial hypothesis about the role that faith and remoralization play in all forms of healing accounts at least in part for the failure to find consistent differences in therapeutic efficacy. The hypothesis harmonizes well with the empirical evidence that the quality of the therapeutic alliance is the best predictor of outcome in diverse forms of psychotherapy (Horvath & Symonds, 1991).

An alternative hypothesis is that different forms of treatment operate through different mechanisms. For example, cognitive therapy may operate through the modification of dysfunctional cognitive processes, whereas interpersonal therapy may operate through the acquisition of new interpersonal skills. This hypothesis is less readily supported by the empirical evidence. For example, the NIMH Collaborative Research Program on the Treatment of Depression (Elkin et al., 1989) reported that patients benefiting from either cognitive therapy, interpersonal psychotherapy, or antidepressant medication failed to show theory-consistent differences on measures tapping dimensions consistent with the theoretical premises underlying the different approaches. One factor preventing the discovery of therapy-specific change mechanisms may be that the level of analysis is too global in nature. It may be that therapeutic approaches that appear similar at one level of analysis may emerge as different approaches at other levels of analysis.

MECHANISMS OF CHANGE: THE MOLAR–MOLECULAR CONTINUUM

Theories about the mechanisms through which psychotherapy change takes place can be advanced at both molar and molecular levels. The more molar level of analysis consists of theories about the ultimate nature of the change that takes place in psychotherapy. For example, the hypothesis that change in the cognitive therapy of depression takes place through changes in dysfunctional attitudes is formulated at a relatively molar level of analysis. Hypotheses can also be advanced, however, regarding the more molecular subprocesses through which dysfunctional attitudes are changed. For example, one can postulate that in order to change his/her attitudes, a depressed patient in cognitive therapy must go through a sequence of (1) developing trust in the therapist, (2) cultivating an experimental attitude, (3) owning his/her beliefs as personal constructs, and (4) trying out alternative constructions.

Hypotheses and research regarding the nature of change at a molar level are necessary in order to establish empirically whether the basic assumptions regarding the nature of change in different psychotherapy schools are valid. In addition, once methodologies are developed for testing hypotheses at the more molar level of analysis, it is possible to apply the methodology developed to test a change process hypothesis developed for one therapy tradition within the framework of another therapy approach. For example, Weiss, Sampson, and the Mount Zion Psychotherapy Research Group (1986) hypothesized that a patient's psychopathology stems from pathogenic beliefs about relationships with others. They have demonstrated empirically that patients undergoing psychodynamic therapy improve when the therapist behaves in a manner that disconfirms these beliefs. This methodology can easily be adapted to test the hypothesis that the same change process operates in the cognitive therapy of depression.

Hypotheses and research regarding the nature of the change process at the more molecular level of analysis are necessary in order to provide us with information regarding the more subtle, molecular steps that ultimately lead to change at the more molar level of analysis. Rice and Greenberg's (1984) task analysis methodology, Horowitz's (1979) configurational analysis, and Elliott's (1984) comprehensive process analysis are all examples of process research methodologies that can be employed to clarify the nature of this more molecular type of change process. It may well be that important differences among approaches may emerge at this more molecular level of analysis, even if they fail to do so at the more molar level. For example, therapy-specific change mechanisms may be revealed through a molecular analysis that focuses on how an interpretation shifts a depressed patient's mood state in session, or through one that focuses on how a cognitive reattribution intervention reduces depressive affect within a session.

THE INTERDEPENDENCE OF SPECIFIC AND COMMON FACTORS

Another factor that may bedevil attempts to discover therapy-specific change mechanisms is that common and specific factors may be sufficiently interdependent to make it difficult to disentangle the two empirically (Butler & Strupp, 1986; Safran & Segal, 1990). Bordin's (1979) transtheoretical conceptualization of the therapeutic alliance provides a useful framework for clarifying the nature of this interdependence. He suggests that the therapeutic alliance can be seen as consisting of bond, goal, and task components, and that these three components, are interdependent in nature and mutually influencing. Different therapeutic approaches employ different therapeutic tasks in order to work toward goals that are specific to them. An example of a task in psychoanalysis would be to free-associate, whereas an example of a task in cognitive therapy would be to monitor and challenge automatic thoughts. Whereas the goals in more behaviorally oriented approaches have traditionally been circumscribed in nature, aiming at symptom remission, the goals in more analytic or humanistic approaches tend to be more open-ended.

Bordin asserts that the quality of the alliance consists of the degree to which patient and therapist agree about the goals and tasks of therapy, as well as the quality of the affective bond between them (e.g., the extent to which the patient feels valued and understood by the therapist). When therapist and patient agree about the goals and tasks of therapy, this tends to enhance the bond. Conversely, the quality of the bond mediates the agreement about tasks and goals. For example, a patient in psychoanalysis is more likely to free-associate if he/she trusts the therapist, and a patient in behavior therapy is more likely to engage in a threatening behavioral tasks if he/she has faith in the therapist's expert status.

To further illustrate the nature of this interdependence, consider the following example. There is a growing consensus among theorists from diverse orientations that the disconfirmation of dysfunctional beliefs is a central mechanism of change (Jacobson, 1989; Strupp & Binder, 1984; Weiss et al., 1986). Depending on the different dysfunctional beliefs or interpersonal schemas that may be characteristic of a particular patient, different therapeutic tasks are likely to either confirm or disconfirm their core dysfunctional schemas. For example, patients who fear that others will attempt to control or dominate them may experience a behavioral assignment as a confirmation of their dysfunctional interpersonal schema, and may experience the nondirective stance of the client-centered therapist as schema-disconfirming. On the

other hand, patients who fear that others will abandon them if they are dependent in any way may experience behavioral assignments as schema-disconfirming, and may in turn construe the client-centered therapist's nondirective stance as schema-confirming. Patients who fear that others will abandon them emotionally may experience the task of free association in the context of a less responsive analyst as schema-confirming, and may experience the affirmative stance of a self psychologist as schema-disconfirming. In all scenarios, participation in a therapeutic task that is schema-disconfirming will influence the quality of the therapeutic relationship in a positive direction. This type of interdependence has important implications for the treatment of depression. Rather than suggesting the selection of a therapeutic modality at a global level, such as cognitive or psychoanalytic therapy, this interdependence suggests the potential usefulness of selecting specific interventions from a range of different therapeutic schools on the basis of their potential for disconfirming a specific patient's dysfunctional schema.

PATIENT × TREATMENT INTERACTIONS

Another response to the discovery of therapeutic equivalence has been to suggest that different patients may benefit from different treatments. Relevant research findings, however, have been quite disappointing. One of the important factors obstructing the discovery of consistent interactions in this respect has been the general lack of a good a priori basis for predicting patient × treatment interactions, and the consequent tendency to conduct studies of this sort on a post hoc basis (Beutler, 1991).

A second and from our perspective even more fundamental problem is the mistaken tendency to conceptualize patients as static and unchanging over the course of many therapy sessions, or, for that matter, within the context of a single session. The problem deepens because treatment modalities also are often conceptualized as static, homogeneous, uniform packages, as is sometimes the tendency with manualized therapies. As Rice and Greenberg (1984) have argued, clinical decision making in the real world takes place on a much more molecular basis. Skilled therapists are constantly modifying their interventions in response to ongoing fluctuations in the patient's state. The most fruitful question to ask may thus not be "What treatment for what patient?", but rather "What specific intervention in what specific context?" For example, when a patient who complains of low self-esteem is self-critical within the context of a good therapeutic alliance, is it more useful to intervene with an interpretation, or with a hypothesis-testing intervention from cognitive therapy? Or, when a patient avoids a therapist's question by changing the subject, thus causing a slight rupture in the therapeutic alliance, is it more useful to intervene with an interpretation, or with an empathic intervention?

This move toward contextual specificity in psychotherapy research has been referred to as the "change events paradigm" (Gendlin, 1991; Elliott, 1984; Rice & Greenberg, 1984; Greenberg, 1984; Safran, Rice, & Greenberg, 1988). A "change event" is a pattern of therapeutic process leading to change, which occurs with sufficient regularity to make it worth investigating (Rice & Greenberg, 1984). It is a unit consisting of a particular client state, a therapeutic intervention that takes place in the context of that state, and a therapeutic process that is activated by that intervention. For example, the client has difficulty acknowledging a particular emotion, such as sadness; the therapist interprets the defense, and a warded off emotion emerges. These units are the building blocks of psychotherapy. From an integrative perspective, analyzing therapeutic process at this more molecular level allows one to explore what particular intervention will be most useful in what specific context, regardless of the particular therapeutic tradition from which the intervention is initially derived.

THERAPEUTIC CHOICE POINTS

This emphasis on contextual specificity brings to the foreground the question of what clinical cues therapists from different orientations employ to guide their interventions. An analyst working with a depressed patient will be more likely to intervene in response to a perceived allusion to the transference than will a cognitive therapist. A cognitive therapist will be more likely to intervene in response to a self-critical statement by a depressed patient than will an analyst. In these cases, specific choice points are favored by, or are unique to, therapists from

specific orientations. In other cases, therapists from different orientations may attend to the same choice point. Therapeutic choice points play important roles in shaping the course that the therapy takes. The comparative analysis of choice points guiding therapists from different orientations has the potential of providing a much more comprehensive map of the potential openings for therapeutic interventions than is provided by any individual psychotherapy theory. The possibility of empirically generating a taxonomy of therapeutic choice points by examining therapy transcripts is one potentially promising avenue for integrative efforts (Goldfried & Safran, 1986; Messer, 1986a; Rice & Greenberg, 1984).

A TAXONOMY
OF THERAPEUTIC TASKS

Bordin's formulation of the therapeutic alliance articulates the idea that different forms of psychotherapy operate through engaging patients in different therapeutic tasks, and that different patients will be characteristically predisposed to engage in and benefit from different therapeutic tasks. As Bordin (1994) and others (e.g., Rice & Greenberg, 1984; Goldfried & Safran, 1986) point out, a promising transtheoretical avenue for developing an understanding of the therapeutic change process would be to develop a taxonomy of tasks utilized by different forms of psychotherapy. Examples of tasks from the psychodynamic treatment of depression would include such activities as exploring disowned thoughts and feelings, and collaborating with the therapist to examine one's transferential reactions. Examples of tasks from the cognitive therapy of depression consist of such activities as self-monitoring automatic thoughts between sessions, and challenging one's perceptions (e.g., through testing hypotheses or examining alternative perspectives) both within and outside of sessions.

As the taxonomy of therapeutic tasks evolves, tasks from different theoretical orientations can be classed together into groups that bear family resemblances (Bordin, 1994). Members of the different families of tasks will be characterized by common substratal change processes. The notion of a family resemblance lends itself well to the exploration of how tasks from different therapeutic orientations share common underlying workings, just as the geneticist explores how individuals within a family share common genetic structures. The metaphor of a family also leaves room for exploring how the unique theoretical contexts, from which the individual tasks evolve, differentiate these tasks in both obvious and subtle ways. For example, Bordin (1994) has asserted that there is considerable overlap in patients' psychic processes when they are engaged in a client-centered experiencing task and when they are engaged in psychoanalytic free association. Moreover, both challenging a depressed client's automatic thoughts and analyzing the transference can work to modify cognitive distortions. Safran and Greenberg (1991) have suggested that there are a number of core affective change processes that can be activated through the use of different tasks. The particular task that is employed to activate the change process will ultimately color it in a specific way. For example, the use of transference interpretation to activate a corrective emotional experience will color the corrective emotional experience in one way; a corrective emotional experience activated through an evocative empathy will be colored in a different way. Further thought and research are needed to probe these hypotheses in order to further articulate both similarities and differences between tasks.

DECISION RULES FOR COMBINING TASKS AND GOALS FROM DIFFERENT APPROACHES

An important conceptual advance from the perspective of psychotherapy integration involves the recognition that different kinds of psychotherapy, or different kinds of tasks in psychotherapy, may require different kinds of bonds between the therapist and the client (Bordin, 1979). For example, it may be that the kind of bond that strategic therapists require with their clients is very different from the bond that analysts require with their clients. An important conceptual question to be resolved here is whether it is useful to think of qualitatively different types of bonds, or simply differences in the strength or intensity of the bond. If there are qualitative differences in the bonds appropriate to different psychotherapy tasks or different schools of pure-form psychotherapy, it would be important to begin describing the nature of these different bonds (Bordin, 1994).

It is important to recognize that certain tasks may be compatible with certain kinds of bonds, whereas other tasks may not. Thus, for example, it may be possible to combine the empathic reflection of client-centered therapy with the exploration of automatic thoughts in cognitive therapy, but not the paradoxical injunction of strategic therapy with the analysis of the transference in psychoanalysis. In addition, it may well be that the order of sequencing of different tasks in the context of the same bond is important. Thus, for example, it may be that it is possible for the same therapist to move from the paradoxical injunction of strategic therapy to the empathic reflection and exploration of client-centered therapy, but not vice versa (Greenberg & Pinsof, 1986).

Work is required at the conceptual level to establish preliminary hypotheses about the compatibility between different kinds of bonds and tasks, as well as sequencing rules. In addition, research strategies need to be developed to empirically evaluate hypotheses regarding the combination and sequencing of different tasks in the contexts of the same bond. A final potentially important topic for empirical investigation is the nature of the intervention that can be used for modifying bonds to allow the transition from one general type of task to another.

THEORETICAL INTEGRATIONISM VERSUS TECHNICAL ECLECTICISM

An important debate in the literature on psychotherapy integration centers on whether we should aspire to theoretical integration or to the pragmatic application of interventions derived from different approaches.

Those in the integrationist camp (Prochaska & DiClemente, 1992; Wachtel & McKinney, 1992) argue that true progress can only come at a higher level of abstraction, from a systematic and disciplined attempt to integrate concepts at an explanatory and overarching level of theory. They also argue that a more pragmatic technical approach is in danger of devolving into a type of undisciplined, muddleheaded eclecticism.

Proponents of technical eclecticism (Beutler & Consoli, 1992; Lazarus, 1992) argue that the bottom line is what "works." They stress that a misplaced emphasis on theory neglects the real concerns of the clinician, which center on a need for pragmatic, real-life guidelines regarding how to work with specific clients in specific situations.

We believe that both integrative perspectives are important, and argue for methodological pluralism in this respect. Moreover, we note that integration proceeds in different ways at different levels of abstraction.

Proponents of technical eclecticism focus on the lower levels of abstraction, where specific features of technique are employed. For example, we might compare the challenging of automatic thoughts used in the cognitive therapy of depression to the use of interpretation in psychodynamic therapy. At this level of analysis, it is possible to empirically compare the relative efficacy of the two techniques in a specific context.

At a somewhat higher level of analysis is the level of theory regarding the process or processes through which specific interventions operate. For example, what is the process through which the challenging of automatic thoughts operates? What is the process through which a transference interpretation operates? At this level of analysis, we are able to articulate process hypotheses, and develop and refine process models through a combination of conceptual and empirical means.

At a still higher level of analysis are metatheoretical models of human functioning—for example, information-processing metatheory versus psychoanalytic conflict theory. At this level, there is no simple empirical test of the relative usefulness of different metatheories. It is, however, possible to collect a wealth of empirical data relevant to selected aspects of different metatheories. Thus, empirical analysis can play some role in the refinement of metatheory and in the evaluation of the relative advantages and disadvantages of different metatheoretical approaches.

At the highest level of analysis are fundamental worldviews and beliefs about the meaning of life, healthy human functioning, and so on. At this level of analysis, empirical tests are impossible; rather, integration takes place through an ongoing dialogue between different philosophical positions.

These specific levels of analysis (which we have summarized in Table 16.1) are not intended as an exhaustive list, but are merely an illustration of the importance of analyzing change at vary-

TABLE 16.1. Integration at Different Levels of Analysis

Level IV: Worldview	Health = "scientific," empirically oriented, or logical thinking	Health = openness to internal experience
Level III: Metatheory	Information-processing theory	Psychoanalytic conflict theory
Level II: Change mechanism theory	Decentering	Acknowledging disowned experience
Level I: Intervention	Challenging of automatic thoughts	Interpretation

ing levels and of recognizing that different kinds of analysis are appropriate at different levels.

COMPLEMENTARITY OF DIFFERENT ORIENTATIONS

At a fundamental and conceptual level, any theoretical system is ultimately only a limited map of the territory it represents, and every such map has its own particular distortions and blind spots. Viewing reality through multiple theoretical systems, rather than through one system, increases the possibility of understanding aspects of reality that would otherwise remain elusive.

Within the realm of psychotherapy, different therapeutic orientations highlight different aspects of human functioning and therapeutic process (Safran & Segal, 1990). For example, psychoanalysts attend closely to the manner in which past relationships affect the present therapeutic relationship, and they thus have developed a body of wisdom and associated interventions elucidating this phenomenon. Behavior therapists focus on and clarify how therapeutic changes are integrated into out-of-session behavior. Experiential therapists have mapped out some of the complex workings of emotional experience, and have developed a range of interventions to arouse and deepen these experiences. The development of more integrative approaches will permit clinicians to avail themselves of expertise previously limited to practitioners of other theoretical orientations.

As in the parable about the four blind men touching different parts of the elephant, different therapeutic orientations are all somewhat correctly, though somewhat blindly, grasping different aspects of the ultimately ineffable experiences that constitute being human. Our greatest hope for deepening their understanding of the human condition comes from open dialogue with others who are touching different parts of the elephant.

THE INTEGRATIVE STANCE

The hope of many theorists and researchers with an integrative bent has been to develop a grand unifying theoretical paradigm. In contrast, we argue that the pursuit of a grand unifying paradigm stems from a misunderstanding of the way in which higher level theory works. Messer's (1986a, 1986b) use of Northrop Frye's (1957, 1965) taxonomy of different mythic forms eloquently illustrates how different therapeutic theories are fundamentally incommensurable. Messer states that major schools of psychotherapy, such as psychoanalysis, humanism, and behaviorism, stem from fundamentally different visions of what it means to be a human being and what constitutes a flourishing human life. An attempt to force the perspective of these schools into a superordinate integrative theory will only distort the unique and important insights of each theory. Just as quantum physics has not superseded Newtonian physics, in that each has its domain of applicability, it seems inconceivable that one therapeutic system will incorporate and supersede all others.

We argue that the proliferation of different approaches to therapy is a sign of our field's health and vitality. Different therapeutic systems focus on different aspects of human life and have their own respective strengths and weaknesses.

But then, how are we to understand integration? We believe that it is an ongoing process centered on dialogue. Adherents of different therapeutic worldviews engage in the process of integration by discussing their relative positions in an open-minded way. Attempting to view a therapeutic issue through a different worldview, interlocutors are forced to confront their most cherished and deepest beliefs. A metaphor for this process of viewing therapeutic issues through different worldviews is the perception of an ambiguous perceptual figure. In the same way that two competing perceptions cannot be apprehended simultaneously, it may be that integration at the more philosophical levels of discourse must take place through a type of serial consideration of events from competing perspectives.

We believe that this understanding of integration holds the greatest promise of growth for both individual therapists and for our field as a whole. A cognitive therapist who strives to perceive a therapeutic problem from within a psychoanalytic worldview, or a dynamically oriented therapist who strives to view things from within a cognitive worldview, has the opportunity to radically reconceptualize things in a way that opens up entirely new vistas for clients.

This understanding of integration harmonizes well with more modern understandings of what constitutes a healthy scientific process. Lakatos (1970), for example, shifts the focus away from the ability of a static theoretical framework to comprehensively explain a particular phenomenon. In his idea of a research program, he emphasizes the capacity of a theoretical system to evolve in an ongoing and creative fashion. Our understanding of integration focuses on the same process, the continual creation of new developments in theory, research, and practice. Long before the writings of more modern philosophers of science, John Stuart Mill (Cohen, 1961) argued the advantages of theoretical pluralism in science, because no single approach can ever comprehensively capture reality, and the existence of multiple approaches increases the possibility that the blind spots of each of the individual approaches will be highlighted.

There is an old tale that is relevant to our concluding point. It goes as follows:

> Three seekers of knowledge who had resolved to find the Truth arrived at the home of one of the great teachers. They asked him to help them; and for answers he took them into his garden. Picking up a stick of dead wood, he walked from one bed of flowers to another, striking off the blooms of the tallest plants.
>
> When they returned to the house, the sage seated himself among his students and asked, "What was the meaning of my actions? Whichever of you can interpret them right will be accepted for the Teaching."
>
> The first student said, "My interpretation of the lesson is 'people who imagine that they know more than others may have to suffer a leveling in the Teaching.'"
>
> The second student said, "My understanding of the actions is 'things which are beautiful in appearance may be unimportant in the totality.'"
>
> The third student said, "I would describe what you did as indicating 'a dead thing, even a stick of repetitious knowledge, can still harm what is alive.'"

The master said, "You are all enrolled, for between you meanings are shared. Not one of you
knows all; for what all of you have is not complete;
but what each of you says is correct." (Shah, 1972)

REFERENCES

Arnkoff, D. G. (1983). Common and specific factors in
cognitive therapy. In M. J. Lambert (Ed.), *Psychotherapy and patient relationships.* Homewood, IL:
Dorsey Press.

Ayllon, T., & Michael, J. (1959). The psychiatric nurse as
a behavioral engineer. *Journal of the Experimental
Analysis of Behavior, 2,* 323–334.

Beutler, L. E. (1991). Have all won and must all have
prizes? Revisiting Luborsky et al.'s verdict. *Journal of
Consulting and Clinical Psychology, 59*(2), 226–232.

Beutler, L. E., & Consoli, A. J. (1992). Systematic eclec-
tic psychotherapy. In J. C. Norcross & M. R. Goldfried,
(Eds.), *Handbook of psychotherapy integration.* New
York: Basic Books.

Bordin, E. (1979). The generalizability of the psychoanalytic concept of the working alliance. *Psychotherapy:
Theory, Research, and Practice, 16,* 252–260.

Bordin, E. (1994). Theory and research on the therapeutic working alliance: New directions. In A. Horvath &
L. S. Greenberg (Eds.), *The working alliance: Theory,
research, and practice.* New York: Wiley.

Butler, S. F., & Strupp, H. H. (1986). Specific and nonspecific factors in psychotherapy: A problematic paradigm for psychotherapy research. *Psychotherapy, 23,*
30–40.

Cohen, M. (Ed.). (1961). *The philosophy of John Stuart
Mill.* New York: Modern Library.

Dupont, J. (1988). Ferenczi's "madness." *Contemporary
Psychoanalysis, 24,* 250–261.

Eagle, M. N. (1984). *Recent developments in psychoanalysis.* New York: McGraw-Hill.

Elkin, I., Shea, M. T., Watkins, J. T., Imber, S. D., Sotsky,
S. M., Collins, J. F., Glass, D. R., Pilkonis, P. A., Leber,
W. R., Docherty, J. P., Feister, S. J., & Parloff, M. G.
(1989). National Institute of Mental Health Treatment
of Depression Collaborative Research Program. *Archives of General Psychiatry, 42,* 305–316.

Elliott, R. (1984). A discovery-oriented approach to significant change events in psychotherapy: Interpersonal
process recall and comprehensive process analysis. In
L. N. Rice & L. S. Greenberg (Eds.), *Patterns of change:
Intensive analysis of psychotherapy process* (pp. 249–
286). New York: Guilford Press.

Eysenck, H. (1965). The effects of psychotherapy. *Journal of Psychology, 1,* 97–118.

Eysenck, H. (1969). *The effects of psychotherapy.* New
York: Science House.

Foa, E. B., and Kozak, M. J. (1991). Emotional processing: Theory, research and clinical implications for anxiety disorders. In J. D. Safran & L. S. Greenberg (Eds.),
Emotion and the process of therapeutic change (pp. 21–
49). Orlando, FL: Academic Press.

Frye, N. (1957). *Anatomy of criticism.* Princeton, NJ:
Princeton University Press.

Frye, N. (1965). *A natural perspective: The development
of Shakespearean comedy and romance.* New York: Columbia University Press.

Gendlin, E. T. (1991). On emotion in therapy. In J. D.
Safran & L. S. Greenberg (Eds.), *Emotion, psycho-

therapy, and change* (pp. 255–279). New York: Guilford
Press.

Goldfried, M. R. & Davison, G. C. (1976). *Clinical behavior therapy.* New York: Holt, Rinehart & Winston.

Goldfried, M. R. & Safran, J. D. (1986). Future directions
in psychotherapy integration. In J. C. Norcross (Ed.),
Handbook of eclectic psychotherapy (pp. 463–483).
New York: Brunner/Mazel.

Greenberg, J. R. (1991). Countertransference and reality.
Psychoanalytic Dialogues, 1(1), 52–73.

Greenberg, J. R., & Mitchell, S. A. (1983). *Object relations
in psychoanalytic theory.* Cambridge, MA: Harvard
University Press.

Greenberg, L. S. (1984). A task analysis of intrapersonal
conflict resolution. In L. N. Rice & L. S. Greenberg
(Eds.), *Patterns of change: Intensive analysis of psychotherapy process* (pp. 67–123). New York: Guilford
Press.

Greenberg, L. S., & Pinsof, W. M. (Eds.). (1986). *The
psychotherapeutic process: A research handbook.* New
York: Guilford Press.

Greenberg, L. S., & Safran, J. D. (1987). *Emotion in psychotherapy.* New York: Guilford Press.

Guidano, V. F. (1987). *Complexity of the self: A developmental approach to psychopathology, and therapy.* New
York: Guilford Press.

Guidano, V. F. (1991). Affective change events in a cognitive therapy system approach. In J. D. Safran & L. S.
Greenberg (Eds.), *Emotion, psychotherapy, and change*
(pp. 50–78). New York: Guilford Press.

Guidano, V., & Liotti, G. (1983). *Cognitive processes and
the emotional disorders.* New York: Guilford Press.

Haynal, A. (1988). *Controversies in psychoanalytic method.*
New York: New York University Press.

Hoffman, I. Z. (1991). Discussion: Toward a social–
constructivist view of the psychoanalytic situation. *Psychoanalytic Dialogues, 1*(1), 74–105.

Horowitz, M. J. (1979). *States of mind.* New York: Plenum
Press.

Horvath, A. O., & Symonds, B. D. (1991). Relation between working alliance and outcome in psychotherapy:
A meta-analysis. *Journal of Counseling Psychology, 38,*
139–149.

Jacobson, N. S. (1989). The therapist–client relationship
in cognitive behavior therapy: Implications for treating
depression. *Journal of Cognitive Psychotherapy, 3,*
85–96.

Kohut, H. (1984). *How does analysis cure?* (A. Goldberg
& P. Stepansky, Eds.). Chicago: University of Chicago
Press.

Lakatos, I. (1970). Falsification and the methodology of scientific research programs. In I. Lakatos & A. Musgrave
(Eds.), *Criticism and the growth of knowledge.* Cambridge, England: Cambridge University Press.

Lazarus, A. A. (1992). Multimodal therapy: Technical
eclecticism with minimal integration. In J. C. Norcross
& M. R. Goldfried (Eds.), *Handbook of psychotherapy
integration* (pp. 231–263). New York: Basic Books.

Liotti, G. (1991). Attachment and cognition: A guideline
for the reconstruction of early pathogenic experiences
in cognitive psychotherapy. In C. Perris, I. Blackburn,
& H. Perris (Eds.), *Handbook of cognitive psychotherapy.* New York: Springer.

Luborsky, L., Singer, B., & Luborsky, L. (1975). Comparative studies of psychotherapies: Is it true that "Everyone has won and all must have prizes"? *Archives of
General Psychiatry, 32,* 995–1008.

Mahoney, M. J. (1991). *Human change processes*. New York: Basic Books.

Meichenbaum, D, & Gilmore, B. (1984). The nature of unconscious processes: A cognitive–behavioral perspective. In K. S. Bowers & D. Meichenbaum (Eds.), *The unconscious reconsidered*. New York: Wiley.

Messer, S. B. (1986a). Behavioral and psychoanalytic perspectives at therapeutic choice points. *American Psychologist*, *41*(11), 1261–1272.

Messer, S. B. (1986b). Eclecticism in psychotherapy: Underlying Assumptions, problems and trade-offs. In J. C. Norcross (Ed.), *Handbook of eclectic psychotherapy*. New York: Brunner/Mazel.

Prochaska, J. O., & DiClemente, C. C. (1992). The transtheoretical approach. In J. C. Norcross & M. R. Goldfried (Eds.), *Handbook of psychotherapy integration*. New York: Basic Books.

Reeve, J. A., Inck, T. A., & Safran, J. D. (1993). Cognitive–behavioral–humanistic approaches. In G. Stricker & J. Gold (Eds.), *A comprehensive handbook of psychotherapy integration*. New York: Plenum Press.

Rice, L. N. & Greenberg, L. S. (Eds.). (1984). *Patterns of change: Intensive analysis of psychotherapy process*. New York: Guilford Press.

Safran, J. D., & Greenberg, L. S. (1991). Hot cognition and psychotherapy process: An information processing/ecological perspective. In P. C. Kendall (Ed.), *Advances in cognitive–behavioral research and therapy* (Vol 5, pp. 143–177. Orlando, FL: Academic Press.

Safran, J. D., Rice, L. N., & Greenberg, L. S. (1988). Integrating psychotherapy research and practice: Modeling the change process. *Psychotherapy*, *25*(1), 1–17.

Safran, J. D., & Segal, L. S. (1990). *Interpersonal process in cognitive therapy*. New York: Basic Books.

Schafer, R. (1983). *The analytic attitude*. New York: Basic Books.

Shah, I. (1972). *Thinkers of the East*. New York: Penguin.

Smith, M. L., & Glass, G. V. (1977). Meta-analysis of psychotherapy outcome studies. *American Psychologist*, *32*, 752–760.

Spence, D. P. (1982). *Narrative truth and historical truth: Meaning and interpretation in psychoanalysis*. New York: Norton.

Stiles, W. B., Shapiro, D. A., & Elliott, R. (1986). Are all psychotherapies equivalent? *Psychotherapy*, *31*(2), 165–180.

Strupp, H. H., & Binder, J. L. (1984). *Psychotherapy in a new key: A guide to time-limited dynamic therapy*. New York: Basic Books.

Wachtel, P. L. (1986). You can't go far in neutral: On the limits of therapeutic neutrality. *Contemporary Psychoanalysis*.

Wachtel, P. L., & McKinney, M. K. (1992). Cyclical psychodynamics and integrative psychodynamic therapy. In J. C. Norcross & M. R. Goldfried (Eds.), *Handbook of psychotherapy integration* (pp. 335–372). New York: Basic Books.

Weiss, J., Sampson, H., & the Mount Zion Psychotherapy Research Group. (1986). *The psychoanalytic process: Theory, clinical observations, and empirical research*. New York: Guilford Press.

Young, J. E. (1987). *Schema-focused cognitive therapy for personality disorders*. Unpublished manuscript, Center for Cognitive Therapy, New York.

17

Comparing and Combining Short-Term Psychotherapy and Pharmacotherapy for Depression

ROBIN B. JARRETT

This chapter responds to the basic question clinicians answer routinely when treating adult patients who suffer from unipolar major depression: When is short-term psychotherapy, pharmacotherapy or the combination of short-term psychotherapy and pharmacotherapy used most effectively? This chapter (1) summarizes the results from clinical trials that focus on the effectiveness of short-term psychotherapy compared to pharmacotherapy, or the two modalities combined, in reducing depressive symptoms; (2) identifies important research challenges and areas in which the literature is silent; and (3) offers relevant hypotheses organized within a clinical model for deciding when to treat unipolar major depression with short-term psychotherapy, pharmacotherapy, or their combination, at a time when too few depressed people request professional help and the literature lags behind the clinical realities.

WHICH TREATMENT TO USE?: ONE DECISION IN MANY

A survey conducted by the National Mental Health Association (1991) revealed that 43% of respondents sampled from communities in Chicago, Dallas, Los Angeles, Miami, Minneapolis, New York, St. Louis, and San Francisco regarded depression as a "personal or emotional weakness." Two-thirds of the respondents who had suffered from depressive symptoms elected to handle their symptoms without professional treatment. Unfortunately, each year only one-third of all people who suffer from depression actually seek treatment (National Institute of Mental Health [NIMH], 1989).

Americans who do seek treatment for depressive symptoms must decide where to seek which treatment and from what type of practitioner. Subsequently, the chosen practitioner must decide what type of evaluation to perform, what (if any) consultation is required, and whether to refer, treat, or continue to evaluate the patient. Then, the clinician must select a somatic, psychological, or combination of treatment, at a given dose and/or schedule of appointments. The clinician must recommend a treatment setting (e.g., outpatient or inpatient, public or private), a modality (e.g., individual, group, couple, or family), and a duration of treatment. The clinician must decide on the method used to evaluate the extent to which the recommended treatment plan is followed and effective. Throughout this procedure, the patient decides to what extent he/she will comply with the recommendations, for how long, against recognized and unrecognized economic, practical, physical, and emotional costs.

Within this complex clinical reality, both patient and clinician make decisions and provide rationales for themselves and others. Sadly, the lack of information as well as the continued social stigma of psychiatric illness and treatment influence decision making. Simultaneously, the decisions occur in an environment filled with social, political, and economic debate, and tension among policy makers, third-party payers, and clinicians, as well as among different types of practitioner guilds.

WHICH TREATMENTS REDUCE DEPRESSIVE SYMPTOMS MOST?: A SUMMARY OF EXISTING DATA

Research Question

The following summary of the literature is an updated subset of a large review on short-term psychotherapy for depression, commissioned by the U.S. Public Health Service's Agency for Health Care Policy and Research (Jarrett & Maguire, 1991; see also Jarrett & Down, in press). The question addressed here is: "What is the relative effectiveness of short-term psychotherapy, pharmacotherapy, and the combination of short-term psychotherapy plus pharmacotherapy in treating adults with nonpsychotic, unipolar, major depressive disorder? This review highlights clinical trials that include comparisons of pharmacotherapy, but it focuses on (1) interpersonal psychotherapy, (2) cognitive therapy, (3) behavior therapy, (4) family therapy, (5) brief dynamic psychotherapy, or (6) one of these short-term psychotherapies combined with pharmacotherapy. These five short-term psychotherapies have been the subject of most studies completed to date. In this chapter, when the term "psychotherapy" is used, it refers to one of these five short-term psychotherapies. The relative effectiveness of the acute phase of each psychotherapy used alone or in combination with pharmacotherapy in reducing depressive symptoms of adult outpatients with major depressive disorder is stressed in this review. Follow-up studies and trials of continuation and/or maintenance phases of psychotherapy are infrequent, but are mentioned here in relation to maintaining reductions in depressive symptoms and reducing the likelihood of relapse or recurrence. Data from studies of depressed inpatient samples are summarized also.

Research Method

To identify clinical trials that compared short-term psychotherapy, pharmacotherapy, or their combination, computerized psychological and medical databases (PsychInfo and Medline) were searched. The searches were restricted to trials published in English between January 1, 1967, and November 30, 1993. Because computerized searches are estimated to be approximately 3 months behind in publication, the current psychiatric and psychological journals of the library at the University of Texas Southwestern Medical Center at Dallas were hand-searched also. The key words used in computer searches, as well as the journals that were hand-searched, are described in Jarrett and Maguire (1991) and Jarrett and Down (in press). Only the clinical trials that compared psychotherapy, pharmacotherapy, or their combination are reviewed here.

To select relevant clinical trials, the following inclusion–exclusion criteria were used. To be included, the clinical trial must have:

1. Been published in English between January 1, 1967, and November 30, 1993.
2. Included psychotherapy, pharmacotherapy, or combination treatment.
3. Included a sample of unipolar, nonpsychotic outpatients who were diagnosed with major depressive disorder using some criterion-based diagnostic system (e.g., Research Diagnostic Criteria [RDC]; *Diagnostic and Statistical Manuals* [DSM]; St. Louis criteria; *International Classification of Diseases* [ICD-6, -7,- 8, or -9]; etc.).
4. Included a sample diagnosed with major depression, but could have included more than one type of unipolar depression (e.g., dysthymia *and* major depression).
5. Included an adult sample aged 18–geriatric.
6. Included dependent measures of depressive symptoms.
7. Included a psychotherapy provided to individuals or groups that was described clearly enough to identify or label (i.e., the investigators must have referred to a manual or described procedures in such a way that replication would be possible).
8. Involved a therapy that was verbal.

To be excluded, the clinical trial must have met at least one of the following criteria:

1. Was published in a non-English language and/or published before January 1, 1967, or after December 31, 1991.
2. Was not published in a journal (e.g., was published in a book).
3. Did not use some criterion-based diagnostic system.
4. Included patients without a unipolar mood disorder.
5. Included pure samples of dysthymia or adjustment disorder with depressed mood, but excluded patients with major depression (i.e., mixed samples of unipolar depression were included if major depression was represented).
6. Involved studies of children and adolescents.
7. Lacked dependent measures of depressive symptoms.
8. Did not describe or reference the therapy in a manner that allowed reliable categorization or replication.
9. Focused on nonverbal intervention such as phototherapy, exercise, computerized psychotherapy, or bibliotherapy without a psychotherapy comparison group or pharmacotherapy (or pill placebo) comparison group with some documented efficacy.
10. Included patients with a concurrent, complicating medical illness (e.g., rheumatoid arthritis) or psychiatric illness that might require significant modification of the standard form of the treatment (e.g., substance abuse).
11. Did not include a pharmacotherapy or pharmacotherapy plus short-term psychotherapy comparison condition.

CLINICAL TRIALS IN OUTPATIENTS WITH UNIPOLAR MAJOR DEPRESSION

Acute Phase Effects of Short-Term Psychotherapy or Pharmacotherapy

Nine clinical trials (Rush, Beck, Kovacs, & Hollon, 1977; McLean & Hakstian, 1979; Weissman et al., 1979; Blackburn, Bishop, Glen, Whalley, & Christie, 1981; Murphy, Simons, Wetzel, & Lustman, 1984; Elkin et al., 1989; Scott & Stradling, 1990; Hollon et al., 1992; McKnight, Nelson-Gray, & Barnhill, 1992) with samples of depressed outpatients met the inclusion–exclusion criteria for review. Table 17.1 details each report, including the following information:

1. The name of the investigators and date of publication.
2. The sample, its source, the interview method and/or diagnostic system used, any specific characteristics of the sample (e.g., female only), as well as the number of patients completing treatment.
3. The treatment modality (e.g., individual or group), the treatment conditions, and the number of patients completing each treatment cell.
4. The number of weeks in the acute treatment phase and the number of months or years in the follow-up phase.
5. The primary results that were statistically significant ($p \geq .05$).

These studies are organized in Table 17.1 by the type of psychotherapy studied.

Table 17.2 summarizes major results from the nine studies comparing a short-term psychotherapy used alone to a pharmacotherapy used alone.

The majority of the findings ($n = 8$ findings, from 10 comparisons) revealed no statistically significant differences between antidepressant medication and short-term psychotherapy in reducing depressive symptoms. With respect to control conditions, Scott and Stradling (1990) showed that cognitive therapy (in which half the sample also received pharmacotherapy from their general practitioners) reduced depressive symptoms significantly more than the waiting-list control. Similarly, Weissman et al. (1979) showed that amitriptyline, interpersonal psychotherapy, and interpersonal psychotherapy plus amitriptyline reduced depressive symptoms significantly more than nonscheduled treatment. In contrast, the NIMH Treatment of Depression Collaborative Research Program (Elkin et al., 1989) revealed no statistically significant difference among pill placebo plus clinical management, cognitive therapy, interpersonal psychotherapy, and imipramine in reducing depressive symptoms for all outpatients who completed treatment. Similarly, McLean and Hakstian (1979) found no difference among behavior therapy, amitriptyline, and relaxation training in reducing depressive symptoms. Both of the studies producing null results included "control" conditions that can be conceptualized as active

TABLE 17.1. Effects of Short-Term Psychotherapy or Pharmacotherapy: Acute Phase

Study	Sample	Treatment	Weeks	Results
		Efficacy of interpersonal psychotherapy		
Weissman, Prusoff, DiMascio, Neu, Goklaney, & Klerman (1979)	81 acutely depressed outpatients diagnosed by SADS/RDC • Raskin Depression Scale ≥ 7 accepted treatment and were analyzed	Individual: 1. Amitriptyline 2. IPT 3. Amitriptyline + IPT 4. Nonscheduled supportive treatment	16	• All active treatments > nonscheduled • IPT = amitriptyline • Combination > IPT alone or amitriptyline alone ($p = .10$) • Combination patients least likely to refuse treatment or to drop out
Rounsaville, Klerman, & Weissman (1981)	81 depressed patients diagnosed by SADS/RDC • Raskin Depression Scale ≥ 7 [Same sample as Weissman et al. (1979)]	Individual: 1. Amitriptyline 2. IPT 3. Amitriptyline + IPT 4. Nonscheduled treatment	16	• No negative interactions found between psychotherapy and pharmacotherapy • No evidence for patients receiving combination to spend more time on interpersonal issues, hold "antipsychotherapeutic expectations," use psychotherapy less, terminate early, show symptom substitution, show greater symptom recurrence
DiMascio, Weissman, Prusoff, Neu, Zwilling, & Klerman (1979)	81 depressed outpatients diagnosed by SADS/RDC • Raskin Depression Scale ≥ 7 [Same sample as Weissman et al. (1979)]	Individual: 1. Amitriptyline 2. IPT 3. Amitriptyline + IPT 4. Nonscheduled treatment	16	• Amitriptyline affected vegetative symptoms (i.e., sleep and appetite disturbances) beginning at week 1 • Psychotherapy affected mood, suicidal ideation, work, and interests beginning at week 1–4
Elkin et al. (1989) [NIMH Treatment of Depression Collaborative Research Program; 3 sites: University of Pittsburgh ($n = 82$), George Washington University ($n = 84$), University of Oklahoma ($n = 84$)]	155 outpatients[a] referred from mental health facilities, outpatient research sites, or self-referred and diagnosed with MDD (2-week duration) by RDC and 17-item HRSD ≥ 14	Individual: 1. CBT ($n = 37$) 2. IPT ($n = 47$) 3. IMP-CM ($n = 37$) 4. PLA-CM ($n = 34$)	16 (16–20 sessions)	• IMP-CM = IPT = CBT = PLA-CM Null results between treatments All treatments produced significant reductions in symptoms • IMP-CM > PLA-CM on SCL-90 for completers • (IMP-CM > PLA-CM on GAS in intention-to-treat sample) • No difference between the psychotherapies: IPT = CBT *Rate of recovery* • IPT (43%) > PLA-CM (21%) on HRSD in intention-to-treat sample • IMI-CM (42%) > PLA-CM (21%) on HRSD in intention-to-treat sample • Same findings for recovery as above at trends level for completers and minimally exposed samples • CBT (36%) on HRSD in intention-to-treat sample • CBT (51%) in completers sample

(continued)

Efficacy of cognitive therapy

Influence of severity
GAS ≥ 50
- Less severe: all treatments equal
- More severe: IMP-CM > PLA-CM
- IPT = CBT and less severe > more severe

HRSD ≥ 20
- IMP-CM = IPT: more severe = less severe
- CBT = PLA-CM and less severe > more severe
- Less severe: all treatments =
- More severe: IPT > PLA-CM and IMP-CM > PLA-CM

Study	Sample	Efficacy of cognitive therapy	Sessions	Influence of severity
Rush, Beck, Kovacs, & Hollon (1977)	32 nonbipolar major depressives who sought treatment or were referred by professionals and diagnosed by interview and Feighner criteria and MMPI • 17-item BDI ≥ 20 • HRSD ≥ 14	Individual: 1. CT (Beck) (n = 18) 2. Imipramine (n = 14)	12 + 3-month follow-up (20 CT sessions; 12 pharma-cotherapy sessions)	• CT > imipramine in reducing depressive symptoms • 78.9% CT showed marked improvement or completely remitted • 22.7% pharmacotherapy showed marked improvement or completely remitted • Dropout rate higher with pharmacotherapy than with CT • CT = imipramine in reducing anxiety • Treatment gains maintained at 3-month follow-up
Rush, Kovacs, Beck, Weissenburger, & Hollon (1981)	35 depressed outpatients diagnosed by interview and Feighner criteria • BDI ≥ 20 • HRSD ≥ 14 [Partial sample from Rush et al. (1977)]	Individual: 1. CT (Beck) (n = 18) 2. Imipramine (n = 17)	12 (20 CT sessions; 12 pharma-cotherapy sessions)	• With CT, mood and views of self/future changed before vegetative and motivational systems • With drugs, no consistent pattern was revealed
Rush, Beck, Kovacs, Weissenburger, & Hollon (1982)	35 depressed outpatients diagnosed by Feighner criteria • BDI ≥ 20 • HRSD ≥ 14 [Partial sample from Rush et al. (1977)]	Individual: 1. CT (Beck) (n = 18) 2. Imipramine (n = 17)	Approx. 11 (weekly sessions)	• CT > imipramine in improving hopelessness and general self-concept • Hopelessness and overall depressive symptoms positively related, but self-concept on a different dimension • No difference at 3-month follow-up
Blackburn, Bishop, Glen, Whalley, & Christie (1981)	64 clinic-referred major depressed outpatients diagnosed by PSE/RDC • BDI ≥ 14 (British norm)	1. Group CT (Beck) (n = 22) 2. Group CT + medication (n = 22) 3. Medication (n = 20)	12–20 (12–23 sessions)	• General-practice patients: CT = CT + medication > medication alone • Psychiatric outpatients: CT + medication > CT = medication alone
Blackburn & Bishop (1983)	64 outpatients seen either in a hospital outpatient department or in a general practice and diagnosed as MDD by PSE/RDC	1. Group CT (n = 22) 2. Pharmacotherapy (n = 20) 3. Group CT + pharmacotherapy (n = 22)	12–15	• For hospital outpatient group, CT + pharmacotherapy = CT > pharmacotherapy alone in altering views of self, world, and future • For general-practice group, CT = CT +

TABLE 17.1 (Continued)

Study	Sample	Treatment	Weeks	Results
				• pharmacotherapy alone for improving views of self, views of world, and views of future • CT + drugs had quicker and greater rate of improvement than either treatment alone; CT alone has quicker response than drugs alone
Murphy, Simons, Wetzel, & Lustman (1984)	70 depressed clinic-referred outpatients diagnosed by DSM-III, Feighner criteria, or RDC • BDI ≥ 20 • HRSD ≥ 14	Individual: 1. CT (Beck) (n = 19) 2. Nortriptyline (n = 16) 3. CT + nortriptyline (n = 18) 4. CT + placebo (n = 17)	12 (approx. 20 sessions) + 1-month follow-up	• Treatments did not differ • Gains maintained at 1-month follow-up
Simons, Garfield, & Murphy (1984)	28 clinic-referred outpatients with primary affective disorder diagnosed by DIS/Feighner criteria • BDI ≥ 20 • HRSD ≥ 14 [Partial sample from Murphy et al. (1984)]	Individual: 1. CT (Beck) (n = 14) 2. Nortriptyline (n = 14)	12 (approx. 20 CT sessions and 12 pharmaco-therapy sessions)	• CT = nortriptyline • Both treatments effective in reducing depressive symptoms *and* cognitive variables (cognitive change part of clincial improvement) • Time course and magnitude of change similar in both groups • Nonresponders showed less cognitive change than responders
Simons, Levine, Lustman, & Murphy (1984)	70 depressed clinic-referred outpatients diagnosed by DSM-III, Feighner criteria, or RDC • BDI ≥ 20 • HRSD ≥ 14 [Same sample as Murphy et al. (1984)]	Individual: 1. CT (Beck) (n = 19) 2. Nortriptyline (n = 16) 3. CT + nortriptyline (n = 18) 4. CT + placebo (n = 17)	12 (approx. 20 sessions) + 1-month follow-up	• Combination therapies had lower dropout rates (18%) than either CT or pharmacotherapy alone, with pharmacotherapy alone having greater dropout rate (33%) than CT (21%)
Elkin et al. (1989)	See above			
Scott & Stradling (1990, Study 1)[b]	48 patients (completers) from a general-practice health center • PSE/RDC diagnosis of primary or probable MDD • BDI > 13	1. Group CT + treatment as usual[c] (n = 10) 2. Individual CT + treatment as usual (n = 19) 3. Waiting-list control + treatment as usual	12–15 (12 sessions) + 3-month follow-up	• Group CT + treatment as usual = individual CT + treatment as usual > waiting-list control • Note: In intention-to-treat analyses, group CT > individual CT = waiting-list control • Group CT and individual CT produced significant improvement in depressive symptoms
Scott & Stradling (1990, Study 2)[b]	33 patients from occupational health services • BDI > 19 • Duration of symptoms at least 1 month • RDC-diagnosed MDD	1. Group CT + treatment as usual[c] (n = 20) 2. Individual CT + treatment as usual (n = 13)	12–15 (12 sessions) + 1-, 2-, and 3-month follow-up	• Group CT + treatment as usual = individual CT + treatment as usual • Both treatments had significant effects in improving depressive symptoms (BDI) • Effect maintained at 1-, 2-, and 3-month follow-up

440

Study	Sample	Treatment	No. of sessions	Findings
Hollon et al. (1992)	64 depressed outpatients who requested treatment • SADS-L/RDC diagnosis of major affective disorder • BDI ≥ 20 • 17-item HRSD ≥ 14	Individual: 1. Imipramine ($n = 32$) 2. CT ($n = 16$) 3. CT) + imipramine ($n = 16$)	12 (CT = 16–20 sessions; pharmaco-therapy = 12 sessions)	• All treatments effective; no difference • No evidence that endogenous depressions were less responsive to CT or more responsive to medication • Patients with higher levels of symptom severity were more likely to terminate the combined treatment than were such patients in either of the two single modalities • Initial severity did *not* predict differential treatment response • Nonsignificant trends favored combination (produced highest rate of full response)
McKnight, Nelson-Gray, & Barnhill (1992)	43 depressed female volunteers diagnosed by SADS-L and DSM-III • MMPI-D raw score ≥ 29 • BDI ≥ 20 • DACL ≥ 18 • PBI mean score ≥ 3	1. Individual CT 2. Tricyclic antidepressant medication ($n = 21$; 3 dropouts; amitriptyline or desipramine)	8	• CT = medication in reducing MMPI-D, BDI, DACL
Efficacy of behavior therapy				
McLean & Hakstian (1979)	154 major depressives diagnosed by Feigner criteria[d] • Within or beyond moderate range on two out of three of the following measures: MMPI-D, BDI, DACL	Individual[e]: 1. BT ($n = 40$) 2. Brief dynamic psychotherapy (Marmor, 1975; Wolberg, 1967) ($n = 37$) 3. Amitriptyline ($n = 39$) 4. Relaxation training ($n = 38$)	10 + 3-month follow-up	• At posttreatment, BT = amitriptyline = relaxation training on BDI • At posttreatment, BT > brief dynamic psychotherapy on BDI and social variables • BT > brief dynamic psychotherapy = relaxation training on average satisfaction with treatment • At posttreatment, brief dynamic psychotherapy = amitriptyline = relaxation training • BT dropout rate < brief dynamic psychotherapy dropout rate = drug therapy dropout rate (5% vs. 30% vs. 36%, respectively) • At 3-month follow-up, there were no differences between treatments on BDI
Efficacy of brief dynamic psychotherapy				
McLean & Hakstian (1979)	See above			

Note. Explanation of abbreviations: BDI, Beck Depression Inventory; BT, behavior therapy; CBT, cognitive–behavioral therapy; CT, cognitive therapy; DACL, Lubin Depressive Adjective Checklist; DIS, Diagnostic Interview Schedule; DSM-III, *Diagnostic and Statistical Manual of Mental Disorders* (3rd ed.); GAS, Global Assessment Scale; HRSD, Hamilton Rating Scale for Depression; IMP-CM, imipramine + clinical management; IPT, interpersonal psychotherapy; MDD, major depressive disorder; MMPI, Minnesota Multiphasic Personality Inventory; MMPI-D, Minnesota Multiphasic Personality Inventory—Depression Scale; PBI, Personal Belief Inventory; PLA-CM, pill placebo + clinical management; PSE, Present State Examination; RDC, Research Diagnostic Criteria; SADS, Schedule for Affective Disorders and Schizophrenia; SADS-L, Schedule for Affective Disorders and Schizophrenia—Lifetime; SCL-90, Hopkins Symptom Checklist—90, total score.

[a] Completed treatment; 250 were randomized.

[b] There are two different studies described in Scott & Stradling (1990).

[c] Just under one-half of the subjects also received concurrent pharmacotherapy from their general practitioner (i.e., "treatment as usual").

[d] Fifty-five normals were evaluated but were excluded from analyses.

[e] Spouses were included in all treatments when available.

TABLE 17.2. Summary of Findings—Effects of Short-Term Psychotherapy or Pharmacotherapy: Acute Phase with Depressed Outpatients

Comparison Tx	Short-term psychotherapy > comparison Tx	Null	Comparison Tx > short-term psychotherapy
Pill placebo + clinical management	0	1 Elkin et al. (1989)[a]	0
Waiting-list control	1 Scott & Stradling (1990, Study 1)[b]	0	0
Nonspecific Tx	1 Weissman et al. (1979)	1 McLean & Hakstian (1979)[c]	0
Psychotherapy	2 McLean & Hakstian (1979)[c]; Covi & Lipman (1987)	1 Elkin et al. (1989)[a]	0
Antidepressants	2 Rush et al. (1977); Blackburn et al. (1981) (general practice)	8 McLean & Hakstian (1979)[c]; Weissman et al. (1979); Blackburn et al. (1981) (psychiatric clinic); Murphy et al. (1984); Elkin et al. (1989[a]; for both interpersonal therapy and cognitive therapy); Hollon et al. (1992); McKnight et al. (1992)	0

[a]This report and interpretation of the NIMH Treatment of Depression Collaborative is based on the analyses of the final sample of subjects *completing* treatment rather than on the total number of subjects who entered the study.

[b]In Scott & Stradling (1990, Study 1), when cognitive therapy plus treatment as usual was compared to waiting-list control plus treatment as usual, only half of the sample received *pharmacotherapy*.

[c]Posttreatment results; at 3-month follow-up behavior therapy = brief dynamic psychotherapy = relaxation training = amitriptyline.

treatments, unlike Scott and Stradling (1990), who used a waiting-list control, and Weissman et al. (1979), who used nonscheduled treatment as a control. Note that Rush et al. (1977), Murphy et al. (1984), Blackburn et al. (1981), Hollon et al. (1992), and McKnight et al. (1992) did not include a nonspecific or treatment control condition, relying instead on comparisons with standard treatment, pharmacotherapy.

No study conducted to date has produced main effects showing that antidepressants used alone reduce depressive symptoms in depressed outpatients significantly more than short-term psychotherapy. In contrast, Rush et al. (1977) reported that cognitive therapy reduced depressive symptoms significantly more than imipramine. Becker and Schuckit (1978), however, have argued that the imipramine dosing regimen used in this study was not optimal. Blackburn et al. (1981) also reported that when the general-practice patients were treated with cog-

nitive therapy alone, or with cognitive therapy plus pharmacotherapy, the treatments that included cognitive therapy reduced depressive symptoms more than medication alone.

Acute Phase Effects of Short-Term Psychotherapy, Pharmacotherapy, or Combination Therapy

Twelve trials (Weissman et al., 1979; Bellack, Hersen, & Himmelhoch, 1981; Blackburn et al., 1981; Rush & Watkins, 1981; Roth, Bielski, Jones, Parker, & Osborn, 1982; Murphy et al., 1984; Teasdale, Fennell, Hibbert, & Amies, 1984; Beck, Hollon, Young, Bedrosian, & Budenz, 1985; Beutler et al., 1987; Covi & Lipman, 1987; Hollon et al., 1990; Scott & Stradling, 1990) have compared a psychotherapy, a pharmacotherapy, or a short-term psychotherapy plus pharmacotherapy, which are detailed and/or listed in Table 17.3.

Table 17.4 summarizes these findings.

Three of these studies included conditions that attempted to control for nonspecific effects. Beutler et al. (1987) compared (1) pill placebo plus support, (2) alprazolam plus support, (3) cognitive therapy plus pill placebo, and (4) cognitive therapy plus alprazolam in treating depressed elderly outpatients. Beutler and colleagues found no statistically significant difference among the conditions in reducing depressive symptoms at the end of treatment and at the follow-up using the Hamilton Rating Scale for Depression (HRSD; Hamilton, 1960). However, according to the Beck Depression Inventory (BDI; Beck, Ward, Mendelson, Mock, & Erbaugh, 1961) < 7 at a 3-month follow-up, they found a greater response rate to cognitive therapy (29%) compared to a 12% response rate for alprazolam or pill placebo plus support. Weissman et al. (1979) revealed that amitriptyline plus interpersonal psychotherapy reduced depressive symptoms significantly more than nonscheduled treatment for depressed women. Scott and Stradling (1990, Study 1) showed that cognitive therapy plus treatment as usual (i.e., pharmacotherapy from a general practitioner) reduced depressive symptoms more than a waiting-list control. (Note that only half of the subjects received concurrent pharmacotherapy from their general practitioners.)

When a short-term psychotherapy plus pharmacotherapy (combination treatment) is compared to another short-term psychotherapy alone, the modal finding is that combination treatment does not significantly reduce depressive symptoms more than short-term psychotherapy alone in outpatients with unipolar major depressive disorder (Weissman et al., 1979; Blackburn et al., 1981, general-practice patients; Rush & Watkins, 1981; Roth et al., 1982; Murphy et al., 1984; Beck et al., 1985; Covi & Lipman, 1987; Hollon et al., 1992). The one exception to this modal finding is Blackburn et al. (1981), who revealed that cognitive therapy plus pharmacotherapy was more effective than cognitive therapy alone for patients who were referred from a psychiatric outpatient clinic. (Note that the rest of the sample was referred from the general-practice clinic, as noted above.)

Similarly, when a short-term psychotherapy plus pill placebo was compared to short-term psychotherapy plus pharmacotherapy, the modal finding has been no difference with respect to reducing depressive symptoms (Hersen, Bellack, Himmelhoch, & Thase, 1984; Murphy et al., 1984; Beutler et al., 1987). When combination therapy was compared to a pharmacotherapy alone, five null findings from eight studies resulted (Weissman et al., 1979; Hersen et al., 1984; Murphy et al., 1984; Beutler et al., 1987; Hollon et al., 1992 [at time of review cited in DeRubeis et al., 1990]).

It is noteworthy that Weissman et al. (1979) found that outpatients receiving amitriptyline plus interpersonal psychotherapy were the least likely to refuse treatment or to drop out. Likewise, Simons, Garfield, and Murphy (1984) found that cognitive therapy plus nortriptyline, or cognitive therapy plus pill placebo, evidenced lower dropout rates than either active treatment used alone. These results may reflect patients' general preference for combination therapy. Patients may be more likely to comply with the requirements of, and remain in, treatment they prefer (i.e., select). Such preferences and compliance may partially mediate treatment outcome. These effects may not be reflected in statistical analyses that focus only on the patients who completed treatment. These effects may be more evident in intention-to-treat analyses that include all the patients who meet the clinical trial's inclusion–exclusion criteria.

Although only one finding shows that combination therapy is more effective than a psychotherapy alone (Blackburn et al., 1981, with a subsample of psychiatric clinic patients), curiously, there are four findings from eight comparisons in which combination therapy is significantly more effective in reducing depressive symptoms than pharmacotherapy alone (Blackburn et al., 1981, with subsamples of general-practice and psychiatric clinic patients; Teasdale et al., 1984; Covi & Lipman, 1987).

Summary

Given how often practitioners must decide when to treat depressed outpatients with pharmacotherapy, psychotherapy, or their combination, it is surprising that there are not more relevant studies. In fact, using the preceding criteria, only nine controlled, randomized clinical trials comparing a short-term psychotherapy and pharmacotherapy were available when the review was conducted. Twelve randomized clinical trials comparing short-term psychotherapy plus pharmacotherapy and either treatment used alone (or in combination with a pill placebo) have been reported. If patients do in fact prefer combination treatment to either

TABLE 17.3. Effects of Short-Term Psychotherapy plus Pharmacotherapy: Acute Phase (Combination Studies)

Study	Sample	Treatment	Weeks	Results
		Interpersonal psychotherapy		
Weissman et al. (1979)	See Table 17.1	See Table 17.1		
		Cognitive therapy		
Blackburn, Bishop, Glen, Whalley, & Christie (1981)	See Table 17.1	See Table 17.1		
Rush & Watkins (1981)	44 depressed outpatients diagnosed by Feighner criteria • BDI ≥ 20 • 17-item HRSD ≥ 14	1. Group CT (Beck) (n = 28) 2. Individual CT (n = 9) 3. Individual CT (n = 7) + medication	10–12 (20 sessions)	• Individual CT = CT + medication, according to BDI • Individual CT > group CT, according to BDI • No difference on HRSD
Murphy, Simons, Wetzel, & Lustman (1984)	See Table 17.1			
Teasdale, Fennell, Hibbert, & Amies (1984)	34 depressed general-practice patients diagnosed by RDC • BDI ≥ 20 • HRSD ≥ 14	Individual: 1. Treatment as usual (typically antidepressants) (n = 17) 2. Treatment as usual + CT (Beck) (n = 17)	Not reported up to 20 sessions; mean = 15.2	• Combination > treatment as usual • No difference at 3-month follow-up (attributed improvement by treatment-as-usual group)
Beck, Hollon, Young, Bedrosian, & Budenz (1985)	25 major depressive outpatients self- or professionally referred and diagnosed by Feighner criteria • BDI ≥ 20 • 17-item HRSD ≥ 14	Individual: 1. CT (Beck) (n = 14) 2. CT + amitriptyline (n = 11)	12 (maximum of 20 sessions)	• Both treatments effective and did not differ in reducing depressive symptoms • Outcomes of two treatments did not differ with regard to overall magnitude of change, stability of change, or the acceptability of treatment
Beutler et al. (1987)	56 major unipolar depressives from various referrals and diagnosed by DSM-III (nonsuicidal, nonpsychotic) • 65 years or older • HRSD > 18 (21-item)	Group: 1. Pill placebo + support (n = 15) 2. Alprazolam + support placebo (n = 12) 3. CT + pill placebo (n = 16) 4. CT + alprazolam (n = 13)	20 (after 2-week washout) + 12-week follow-up	• Only time effect • All groups effective and did not differ in reducing depressive symptoms at posttreatment follow-up on HRSD • CT cells less dropout than medication cells • CT + placebo = CT + alprazolam > alprazolam alone = placebo on BDI at follow-up • According to the BDI < 7 at follow-up response to CT (29%) > response to alprazolam or pill placebo + support (12%)
Covi & Lipman (1987)	53 depressed volunteers recruited through media ads diagnosed by interview/RDC • BDI ≥ 20 • 17-item HRSD ≥ 14	Group[a]: 1. Traditional psychotherapy (interpersonal–psychodynamic) 2. CT (Beck) 3. CT + imipramine	14 + 3-month follow-up	• Group CT = group CT + imipramine > traditional psychotherapy • Effect maintained at 3-month follow-up

444

		Behavior therapy		
Hollon et al. (1990)	See Table 17.1			
Scott and Stradling (1990, Study 1)[b]	See Table 17.1			
Bellack, Hersen & Himmelhoch (1981) (preliminary report of Hersen et al., 1984)	50 depressed women referred for outpatient treatment or recruited by media ads • Feighner criteria for primary depression • ≥ 7 Raskin Depression Scale	Individual: 1. Amitriptyline (n = 8) 2. Social skills training + amitriptyline (n = 12) 3. Social skills training + placebo (n = 17) 4. Short-term dynamic psychotherapy + placebo (n = 13)	12	• Amitriptyline = social skills training + amitriptyline = social skills training + placebo + nonspecific treatment • Each treatment effective and produced substantial improvement in self-reported distress, symptoms, and social functioning • Social skills training + placebo only treatment with more than 50% of patients "substantially improved"
Bellack, Hersen, & Himmelhoch (1983)	82 depressed women referred for outpatient treatment or recruited through referrals or media ads[d] • Feighner criteria for primary depression • DSM-III criteria for MDD • ≥ 7 Raskin Depression Scale [Same sample as Hersen et al. (1984)]	Individual: 1. Social skills training + placebo (n = 25) 2. Social skills training + amitriptyline (n = 21) 3. Amitriptyline alone (n = 14) 4. Short-term dynamic psychotherapy + placebo (n = 22)	12	• No difference between treatments; all reduced depressive symptoms • Only social skills training was associated with social behavior similar to normals
Hersen, Bellack, Himmelhoch, & Thase (1984)	82 depressed women referred for outpatient treatment or recruited through media ads • Feighner criteria for primary depression • DSM-III criteria for MDD • No family history of bipolar illness • ≥ 7 Raskin Depression Scale	Individual: 1. Social skills training + placebo (n = 25) 2. Social skills training + amitriptyline (n = 21) 3. Amitriptyline alone (n = 14) 4. Short-term dynamic psychotherapy + placebo (n = 22)	12	• No difference between treatments in reducing depressive symptoms, extraversion, and neuroticism • Contrary to 1981 report, response rates across treatments did not differ • Greater proportion of treatment failures in the amitriptyline-alone condition
Roth, Bielski, Jones, Parker, & Osborn (1982)	26 volunteers with RDC MDD recruited through media ads • BDI ≥ 18 • HRSD ≥ 15	Group: 1. Self-control therapy (n = 13) 2. Self-control therapy + antidepressant medication (n = 13)	12 + 3-month follow-up (n = 24 for follow-up)	• Both treatments reduced symptoms, according to BDI and HRSD • Self-control therapy + antidepressant resulted in significantly more rapid improvement as measured by BDI • Gains maintained for both groups at 3-month follow-up

Note. For explanation of abbreviations, see Table 17.1.

[a]Prior to and after group treatment, some individual sessions held; cell sizes for subjects completing treating not available.
[b]There are two different studies described in Scott and Stradling (1990).
[c]Cell sizes derived from Hersen et al. (1984).
[d]Twenty-five nondepressed women were evaluated for normative data.

TABLE 17.4. Summary of Findings—Effects of Short-Term Psychotherapy plus Pharmacotherapy: Acute Phase with Depressed Outpatients

Comparison Tx	Psychotherapy + pharmacotherapy > comparison Tx	Null	Comparison Tx > psychotherapy + pharmacotherapy
Pill placebo	0	1 Beutler et al. (1987)	0
Nonscheduled Tx	1 Weissman et al. (1979)	0	0
Waiting-list control	1 Scott & Stradling (1990, Study 1)[a]	0	0
Nonspecific Tx	—	—	—
Another short-term psychotherapy (alone)	1 Blackburn et al. (1981; psychiatric clinic)	8 Weissman et al. (1979); Blackburn et al. (1981; general practice); Rush & Watkins (1981)[b] Roth et al. (1982); Murphy et al. (1984); Beck et al. (1985); Covi & Lipman (1987); Hollon et al. (1992)	0
Short-term psychotherapy + pill placebo	0	3 Hersen et al. (1984); Murphy et al. (1984); Beutler et al. (1987)	0
Pharmacotherapy (alone)	3 Blackburn et al. (1981; general practice); Blackburn et al. (1981; psychiatric clinic); Teasdale et al. (1984)	5 Weissman et al. (1979); Hersen et al. (1984); Murphy et al. (1984); Beutler et al. (1987); Hollon et al. (1992)	1 Covi & Lipman (1987)

[a]In Scott & Stradling (1990, Study 1), when cognitive therapy plus treatment as usual was compared to waiting-list control plus treatment as usual, only half of the sample received *pharmacotherapy*.
[b]Random assignment of subjects absent or incomplete.

psychotherapy or pharmacotherapy alone, combination treatment may be shown to be more effective when efficacy measures include treatment compliance, assess dropout rates, and involve intention-to-treat analyses. Alternatively, combination therapy may be shown to reduce depressive symptoms more than solitary treatment in some yet-to-be-identified subtypes of depression.

PROPHYLACTIC EFFECTS OF SHORT-TERM PSYCHOTHERAPY, PHARMACOTHERAPY, OR COMBINATION THERAPY

Definition of Prophylactic Effects

Since all of the short-term psychotherapies for depression purport to teach the patient some

adaptive skill or mode of reconceptualizing, questions concerning the prophylactic value of psychotherapy are reasonable.

The conceptual definition of relapse used in this review is the onset of a depressive syndrome followed by a brief period (e.g., lasting less than 2 months) of euthymia. In other words, here, a relapse represents a continuation of the index episode. The conceptual definition of recurrence is the onset of a *new* depressive episode, distinct from the index episode. Theoretically, learning acquired during the acute phase might reduce relapse/recurrence.

The continuation phase reduces the chance of relapse/recurrence, in theory. Logically, only patients who have remitted in the acute phase of treatment will be continued on that treatment. Here, "continuation therapy" is defined arbitrarily (rather than functionally) as treatment that lasts less than 6 months after the end of the acute phase of treatment. In theory, maintenance therapy reduces the chance that a new episode will develop. "Maintenance therapy" is defined here as lasting 6 or more months after the end of the acute phase of therapy. It is assumed that only the patients who have remitted during acute or continuation phases should be maintained on that treatment.

Finally, "prophylaxis" is defined here as treatment effects that endure after the acute, continuation, or maintenance phases of treatment have been discontinued (Frank et al., 1991).

Prophylactic Effects of the Acute Phase

Interestingly enough, at the time of the review only seven studies had been published that included pharmacotherapy as a comparison treatment in which the prophylactic effects of the acute phase could be estimated (Weissman et al., 1979; Beck et al., 1985; Simons, Murphy, Levine, & Wetzel, 1986; Covi & Lipman, 1987; Evans et al., 1990; McLean & Hakstian, 1990; Scott & Stradling, 1990). Of these seven studies, one focuses on interpersonal psychotherapy; five focus on cognitive therapy; and one focuses on behavior therapy. At a 1-year naturalistic follow-up, Weissman, Klerman, Prusoff, Sholomskas, and Padian (1981) found no difference among interpersonal psychotherapy, amitriptyline, amitriptyline plus interpersonal psychotherapy, and nonscheduled treatment in reducing relapse and recurrence. Most patients were asymptomatic at the 1-year follow-up and only exposure to interpersonal psychotherapy improved social adjustment significantly.

At a 1-year follow-up, Kovacs, Rush, Beck, and Hollon (1981) found that although patients treated with cognitive therapy had lower BDI scores than those treated with imipramine, there were no significant differences between the relapse/recurrence rates (defined as return to treatment). Beck et al. (1985) found no difference between the magnitude of change, stability of change, or acceptability of treatment for patients treated with cognitive therapy alone or cognitive therapy plus amitriptyline. Although both groups continued to experience fewer depressive symptoms (than before treatment) at 6- and 12-month follow-ups, most of the sample did return to treatment within a year. Simons et al. (1986) also found no difference in the re-

lapse/recurrence rates of patients receiving cognitive therapy, nortriptyline, cognitive therapy plus nortriptyline, and cognitive therapy plus pill placebo. Significant differences, however, emerged when the groups receiving cognitive therapy alone or cognitive therapy plus medication were combined. Specifically, the patients receiving cognitive therapy had a 28% relapse/recurrence rate (i.e., BDI ≥ 16 or return to treatment) 1 year after acute treatment, while those receiving nortriptyline had a 66% relapse/recurrence rate. Covi and Lipman (1987) showed that posttreatment reductions in depressive symptoms were maintained at a 9-month follow-up for patients treated in groups with cognitive therapy and cognitive therapy plus imipramine. Both cognitive therapy cells showed greater reductions in symptoms than did patients treated with traditional psychodynamic group psychotherapy.

McLean and Hakstian (1990) reported that 57% of their sample treated with either amitriptyline, behavior therapy, relaxation therapy, or brief dynamic psychotherapy returned to treatment. The rates did not differ among the groups.

At the time of the review, preliminary reports existed from two important follow-up studies that were later published. In the first report by Evans et al. (1990, later published as Evans et al., 1992), patients who showed a partial response were included in the 24-month follow-up. Treatment conditions included the following: (1) imipramine pharmacotherapy with a continuation phase; (2) imipramine pharmacotherapy without a continuation phase; (3) cognitive therapy without a continuation phase; (4) combined imipramine and cognitive therapy without a continuation phase.

The treatments involving cognitive therapy in the acute phase (3 and 4 above) showed approximately half the rate of relapse (i.e., two consecutive BDIs ≥ 16), as was found when imipramine pharmacotherapy was discontinued after 3 months (2 above). Furthermore, there were no significant differences between the relapse rates of imipramine continuation (1 above) and acute phase cognitive therapy used alone or combined with imipramine (3 and 4 above). These preliminary results are promising and suggest that the potential prophylactic value of cognitive therapy deserves further evaluation. Such evaluation is underway in our laboratory in Dallas through a clinical trial initiated in late 1993.

The second report by Shea et al. (1992) describes an 18-month naturalistic follow-up of depressed outpatients treated in the NIMH Treatment of Depression Collaborative Research Program study. No significant differences were found among the relapse rates (i.e., meeting RDC for major depressive disorder) of recovered patients treated with cognitive therapy (36% relapsed), interpersonal psychotherapy (33% relapsed), imipramine plus clinical management (50% relapsed), and pill placebo plus clinical management (33% relapsed). These results highlight the high risk for relapse after short-term antidepressant treatment of both modalities, as well as the potential importance of continuation/maintenance care for depressed outpatients.

Prophylactic Effects of the Continuation/Maintenance Phases

There are only four published short-term psychotherapy studies involving pharmacotherapy or combination therapy during continuation/maintenance phases (Klerman, DiMascio, Weissman, Prusoff, & Paykel, 1974; Frank et al., 1990; Blackburn, Eunson, & Bishop, 1986; Hersen et al., 1984). In each study, the treatment is continued for patients who show no or few depressive symptoms after the acute treatment phase. Two of these studies focus on interpersonal psychotherapy; one focuses on cognitive therapy; and one focuses on behavior therapy, combined with an active medication or pill placebo.

Klerman et al. (1974) randomized female depressed outpatients who had recovered after 6–8 weeks of amitriptyline to one of the following treatments: amitriptyline, pill placebo, and no pill placebo. Within each cell, randomization also included assignment to a condition of either high or low interpersonal contact. Only continuation/maintenance treatment with amitriptyline reduced the rate of relapse. Only continuation/maintenance treatment with high interpersonal contact improved social adjustment, which was not evident until the eighth month, and occurred only in patients who did not relapse (Weissman, Klerman, Paykel, Prusoff, & Hanson, 1974; Paykel, DiMascio, Haskell, & Prusoff, 1975). Weissman and Kasl (1976) reported that during the year following the continuation/maintenance phase, most patients received pharmacotherapy. Thirty percent sought no

additional treatment, 2% made minor suicide attempts, and the majority were asymptomatic at the 1-year follow-up. Weissman, Kasl, and Klerman (1976) reported no difference among treatments in relapse/recurrence rates at 1-year follow-up (after maintenance). Twenty-nine percent of the sample was remitted, 59% had recurred, and 12% were mildly and chronically symptomatic.

Frank and Kupfer (1986) treated remitted outpatients who had recurrent major depression with interpersonal psychotherapy plus imipramine during the acute and continuation phases, and reported that 8.5% to 15.3% of a preliminary sample experienced a recurrence (RDC major depressive disorder, HRSD $\geq$ 15, and Raskin [i.e., a clinical rating scale] $\geq$ 7) during the 20-week continuation phase. In their study, the maintenance phase consisted of interpersonal psychotherapy, interpersonal psychotherapy plus pill placebo, medication clinic plus pill placebo, interpersonal psychotherapy plus imipramine, or medication clinic with imipramine. Frank et al. (1990) reported that over 3 years, only the treatment cells containing imipramine reduced relapse/recurrence significantly more than medication clinic plus pill placebo. Treatment with interpersonal psychotherapy did, however, increase the survival time (i.e., until relapse/recurrence) significantly more than medication clinic plus pill placebo. Seventy-three percent of all recurrences occurred by the end of the first year of the maintenance phase.

To date, only Blackburn et al. (1986) have designed a study in which the prophylactic value of cognitive therapy with a continuation/maintenance phase can be estimated. Only patients deemed as responders to cognitive therapy alone, pharmacotherapy, or pharmacotherapy plus cognitive therapy were treated in a 6-month maintenance phase continuing the treatment to which the patient responded. Responders receiving cognitive therapy attended monthly "booster sessions." Responders to pharmacotherapy were maintained on the same medication, but sometimes at a reduced dose. At the end of the continuation/maintenance phase, the three groups did not differ in levels of symptom severity and were within normal limits. At 6 months, fewer patients in the cognitive therapy and combination groups had relapsed (i.e., BDI $\geq$ 9 and HRSD $\geq$ 8) compared to the pharmacotherapy group (i.e., 6% and 0% vs. 30%, respectively). When analyzed separately, no significant differences were found in recurrence rates at 12, 18, and 24 months. Over the entire 24 months of naturalistic follow-up, the cumulative proportion of relapse/recurrence in patients treated with cognitive therapy alone was 23%, compared to a rate of 21% for patients treated with cognitive therapy plus antidepressant medication, and a rate of 78% for patients treated with antidepressant medication alone.

Currently, only Bellack, Hersen, and Himmelhoch (1983) and Hersen et al. (1984) have reported data relevant to the effects of a continuation/maintenance phase in behavior therapy combined with medication or brief dynamic psychotherapy used alone. Their study included the following treatments: (1) social skills plus pill placebo, (2) social skills plus amitriptyline, (3) amitriptyline alone, and (4) short-term dynamic psychotherapy plus pill placebo. Note that no condition for behavior therapy alone existed. The continuation/maintenance phase involved six to eight sessions occurring over a 6-month period. At the end of the 6-month continuation/maintenance phase, all treatments resulted in significant improvement in depressive symptoms, extroversion, and neuroticism. No statistically significant differences emerged.

Summary

In conclusion, there have been too few studies conducted on the comparative prophylactic effects of short-term psychotherapy, pharmacotherapy, or their combination with or without continuation/maintenance phases. At present, conclusions about the comparable effects are premature, but are needed to foster the development of an empirically based decision tree in the treatment of unipolar depression. Most of the acute phase studies that included follow-ups of any type have methodological problems, because these studies were not originally designed to evaluate long-term effects. Too few well-designed follow-ups render conclusions premature. Operational definitions of relapse/recurrence vary across studies. It is important to determine the comparable effects of treatments and phases in reducing relapse/recurrence, as well as depressive symptoms. Future studies should include well-described samples (e.g., recurrent major depressive disorder), avoid including in the continuation and maintenance phases patients who showed a poor response to the acute treatment phase, and require controlled follow-ups that (1) are longitudinal rather than cross-sectional; (2) last between 1 and 3 years (depending on the research question asked); (3) include definitions of relapse/recurrence based on diagnostic criteria (e.g., DSM-IV), rather than relying exclusively on symptom severity measures; and (4) include measures of functional impairment.

DEPRESSED INPATIENTS

Although distinct models of inpatient psychotherapy exist (Brabender & Fallon, 1992), very few studies have been conducted to evaluate the efficacy of treating depressed inpatients with short-term psychotherapy used alone or combined with pharmacotherapy. To date, only cognitive therapy and family therapy for depression have been systematically evaluated with depressed inpatients. It is noteworthy that treatment manuals adapting these two therapies to depressed inpatients exist (Thase & Wright, 1991; Clarkin, Glick, Spencer, & Haas, 1984; Clarkin, Haas, & Glick, 1988).

Effects of Cognitive Therapy

The bulk of the research in cognitive therapy has been conducted on outpatients with major depressive disorder and moderate symptom severity. Interest is growing in determining the extent to which cognitive therapy may reduce the depressive symptoms of inpatients, particularly when cognitive therapy is used in the acute phase and combined with pharmacotherapy.

Miller, Norman, Keitner, Bishop, and Dow (1989) published the first controlled study of the efficacy of cognitive–behavioral therapy as an adjunctive treatment for depressed inpatients. (Their work was preceded by optimistic but uncontrolled reports [Shaw, 1981; Miller, Bishop, Norman, & Keitner, 1985]; studies that specifically excluded inpatients with melancholic or endogenous depression [de Jong, Henrich, & Ferstl, 1981]; and efficacy studies of inpatients with mixed psychiatric diagnoses [Brady, 1984; Monti et al. 1979].) Miller et al. (1989) showed that standard treatment (i.e., hospital milieu and pharmacotherapy), cognitive therapy plus standard treatment, and social skills treatment plus standard treatment did not differ with respect to reducing depressive symptoms at the end of a 3-week hospitalization. At the end of 20 weeks of outpatient treatment, however, both cognitive therapy (plus standard treatment) and social skills training (plus standard treatment) reduced scores on the BDI and the Hopkins Symptom Checklist—90 (SCL-90; Derogatis, Lipman, Rickles, Uhlenhuth, & Covi, 1974) more than standard treatment. This result may be conceptualized best as combination therapy with a continuation/maintenance phase, provided on an outpatient basis to former inpatients. Effects were maintained at 6- and 12-month follow-ups.

In contrast to the work by Miller and colleagues, Bowers (1990) found treatment differences at the end of a 29-day hospitalization. According to the HRSD, Bowers found that cognitive therapy plus nortriptyline reduced depressive symptoms more than either nortriptyline alone or nortriptyline plus relaxation therapy.

The work of de Jong and associates preceded Miller, Norman, and Keitner (1990) and involved depressed inpatients using multiple-baseline designs (across treatments) and waiting-list treatment controls (de Jong et al., 1981; de Jong, Treiber, & Henrich, 1986). However, the generalizability of these results is questionable because subtypes typical of depressed inpatients were excluded from the sample. The excluded subtypes were patients with endogenous or melancholic symptoms, positive family histories, or clearly episodic histories. The sample is described as chronic, neurotic inpatients with DSM-III (American Psychiatric Association, 1980) major depression and dysthymia. The sample size was small and the results suggest a nonsignificant trend ($p = .10$) for cognitive restructuring and cognitive–behavioral techniques to reduce depressive symptoms more than the low-contact waiting-list control conditions (de Jong et al., 1986).

Interestingly, Thase, Bowler, and Harden (1991) have reported that 13 of 16 (81%) unmedicated inpatients with RDC (Spitzer, Endicott, & Robins, 1978) probable or definite endogenous depression, who were treated with cognitive–behavioral therapy alone, responded. Furthermore, their preliminary results showed that 3 of 4 (75%) patients without continuation cognitive therapy (lasting at least 1 month) relapsed, compared to 1 of 7 (14%) patients receiving 1 month of continuation therapy. These initial results suggest that cognitive therapy (plus hospital milieu) reduces depressive symptoms not only for outpatients, but also for unmedicated inpatients. Again, the results also underscore the need for controlled studies of continuation/maintenance treatment.

Effects of Family Therapy

Haas et al. (1988) reported the results from their subsample, which included but was not limited to inpatients with major affective disorder. They found that depressed women benefited more from standard treatment plus family therapy than from standard multimodal hospital treatment (without family therapy). In contrast, for depressed men, effects for standard treatment with and without family therapy did not differ. Clarkin et al. (1990) add that at 18 months, unipolar patients, both men and women and their families, responded more to standard treatment alone than they did to standard treatment plus family therapy, while the converse was true for bipolar patients and their families.

WHICH TREATMENT FOR WHOM?: HYPOTHESES DERIVED FROM THE LITERATURE

Unfortunately, the current findings from controlled, randomized clinical trials offer the clinician little help in deciding when to treat a given depressed patient with short-term psychotherapy, pharmacotherapy, or the combination of the two. In order to assist the practitioner with this important decision, minimally, the trial needs to do the following:

1. Compare two or more treatments that previously have been demonstrated to be effective in reducing depressive symptoms.
2. Assess variables that may predict treatment response.
3. Assess variables that a clinician can assess with the aid of practical, cost-effective tools (rather than statistically derived constructs; e.g., residual scores).
4. Produce replicable effects (to increase the chance that a clinically important phenomenon has been documented).

Furthermore, to help the clinician choose between or among treatments, the trial must produce a significant interaction that is "prescriptive" (i.e., a between-subjects factor is crossed between two or more treatments) rather than simply "prognostic" (i.e., a between-subjects factor is used within a single treatment; terms used by Hollon & Najavits, 1988).

When these criteria are applied to results from the studies comparing psychotherapy, pharmacotherapy, or their combination, only a few findings emerge. Since the results highlighted next require replication, they represent hypotheses to stimulate further research rather than clinical directives or "practice guidelines." Until replication, the predictive results that have emerged should be associated with the particular "brand" of short-term psychotherapy tested, rather than generalized to the whole class of short-term psychotherapies for depression.

• *Does gender influence treatment effects?* Spencer et al. (1988) found that gender modified treatment effects. They showed that at 6- and 8-month follow-up, family intervention plus standard multimodal hospital treatment was more effective for previously hospitalized women than men with affective disorders, when compared against standard hospital treatment alone.

• *Does the presence or absence of endogenous depression and/or melancholic depression influence treatment effects?* The literature includes inconsistent results regarding the influence of nonendogenous symptoms and the effect of short-term psychotherapy for depression. Weissman et al. (1979) compared amitriptyline, interpersonal psychotherapy alone, interpersonal psychotherapy plus amitriptyline, and nonscheduled treatment. Klerman, Weissman, and Prusoff (1982) reported that patients diagnosed as having endogenous depression (according to the RDC) responded to combination treatment or amitriptyline alone and did not respond to interpersonal psychotherapy used alone. On the other hand, patients with situational depressions (a nonmutually exclusive diagnosis within the RDC) responded best to combination treatment, and also responded to either interpersonal psychotherapy or amitriptyline used alone, but did not respond to nonscheduled treatment.

The finding that endogenous depression is associated with poor response to interpersonal psychotherapy and a good response to imipramine was not replicated in the NIMH Treatment of Depression Collaborative Research Program (Sotsky et al., 1991). In fact, patients with endogenous depression who lacked double depression responded well to all four treatment conditions.

In predicting response to social skills train-

ing plus pill placebo, short-term psychodynamic psychotherapy plus pill placebo, amitriptyline, or social skills training plus amitriptyline, Last, Thase, Hersen, Bellack, and Himmelhoch (1985) reported that patients with RDC nonendogenous depression were more likely to complete the treatments containing psychosocial intervention than to complete treatment with amitriptyline used alone. In contrast, patients with RDC endogenous symptoms were more likely to complete amitriptyline treatment than the treatments containing psychosocial interventions. Similarly, patients with DSM-III melancholic symptoms were more likely to complete the treatments containing amitriptyline than the treatments without active medication. Nonmelancholic patients, on the other hand, were more likely to complete social skills training plus pill placebo and short-term psychotherapy plus pill placebo (i.e., the treatments without active medication).

To date, the predictive power of the endogenous depressive symptoms has not been reported in the cognitive therapy literature. Null results were reported by Kovacs et al. (1981) between high and low "endomorphs" at a 1-year follow-up, and between endogenous and nonendogenous depressed patients by Blackburn et al. (1981).

Similarly, the response rate that Thase and associates (Thase, Simons, Cahalane, & McGeary, 1991a; Thase, Bowler, & Harden 1991) reported for both inpatients and outpatients with major depressive disorder and endogenous features is comparable to the response rates reported throughout the literature on cognitive therapy.

• *Does pretreatment symptom severity influence treatment effects?* Initial reports from the NIMH Treatment of Depression Collaborative Research Program suggest that depressed outpatients with more severe symptoms (HRSD ≥ 20) responded best to imipramine plus clinical management or interpersonal psychotherapy. The response of severely depressed outpatients to cognitive therapy did not differ from the response to pill placebo plus clinical management. The response of patients with less severe depressive symptoms did not differ across the four treatments (Elkin et al., 1989). Because of the potential influence of site differences, and contradictory data from Thase, Simons, Cahalane, McGreary, and Harden (1991b) and McLean and Taylor (1992), additional analyses or studies are necessary in order to understand fully the effect that pretreatment severity of depressive symptoms has on treatment response. Although Sotsky et al. (1991) reported many interesting prognostic effects, they found no additional significant prescriptive effects (i.e., patient characteristics that predicted differential response among the four treatments).

• *Does the severity of dysfunctional cognition influence treatment effects?* Counterintuitively, based on the published literature to date, patients with high levels of dysfunctional cognition evidence a worse response rate and may be more difficult to treat with cognitive therapy than patients with fewer dysfunctional cognitions. DeRubeis et al. (1990) reported that outpatients who showed changes in the Attributional Style Questionnaire (ASQ; Peterson et al., 1982) and the Dysfunctional Attitudes Scale (DAS; Weissman, 1979) during the first half of a 12-week acute phase of cognitive therapy were more likely to respond than their counterparts without this pattern. These variables did not predict response to imipramine.

Last et al. (1985) reported that patients who completed medication treatment had higher DAS scores than patients who did not complete medication, compared to patients who did or did not complete social skills training, plus pill placebo or short-term psychotherapy plus pill placebo.

Miller et al. (1990) demonstrated that at the end of outpatient treatment, discharged inpatients with higher prehospitalization levels of cognitive distortion responded better to cognitive therapy plus standard inpatient treatment or social skills training plus standard inpatient treatment than they did to standard treatment alone. Conversely, patients with lower levels of cognitive distortion showed no preferential response. These data suggest testing the hypothesis that patients with high pretreatment levels of cognitive distortion are the best candidates for combination treatment (i.e., pharmacotherapy plus cognitive–behavioral therapy).

• *Does the extent of concurrent relationship discord influence treatment effects?* In addition to the preceding indications, studies of prognostic indication suggest that concurrent marital or relationship discord and/or personality disorder complicates most types of treatment for depressed patients. For example,

Shea et al. (1990) found that at the end of treatment (i.e., cognitive therapy, interpersonal psychotherapy, imipramine plus clinical management, or pill placebo plus clinical management), depressed outpatients with personality disorders had more depressive symptoms and worse social adjustment than depressed outpatients without personality disorders. Similarly, Thompson, Gallagher, and Czirr (1988) reported that depressed elders diagnosed with a personality disorder showed a poorer response to short-term psychotherapy (i.e., cognitive therapy, behavior therapy, brief psychodynamic psychotherapy) than elders without personality disorders.

O'Leary and Beach (1990) and Beach and O'Leary (1992) reported that although behavioral marital therapy or cognitive therapy reduced depressive symptoms significantly more than a waiting-list control, only marital therapy increased marital satisfaction. Rounsaville, Weissman, Prusoff, and Herceg-Baron (1979) found that depressed female outpatients with marital disputes (i.e., contradictory expectations between spouses) had more depressive symptoms and worse social adjustment after an 8-month maintenance phase of amitriptyline, placebo, or no placebo with either high or low interpersonal contact.

Controlled, randomized trials of short-term psychotherapy and pharmacotherapy alone and in combination, which include longitudinal follow-up methods, are needed to determine how to best treat depressed patients with concurrent and chronic relationship discord and personality disturbance.

WHAT IS A CLINICIAN TO DO?

Given the gaps and ambiguity in the current literature that compares short-term psychotherapy, pharmacotherapy, or their combination in treating depressed people, it is no wonder that the results of clinical research have little influence on the average practitioner. Practitioners are left to figure out how best to help their depressed patients, while controlled research, by design, is slow (thorough), indefinitive (in need of replication), and often inapplicable (has limited generalizability due to explicit inclusion–exclusion criteria) to the patient in the waiting room.

At the same time, the application of basic

research methods can help clinicians, be they psychotherapists or psychopharmacologists, decide which depressed patients to treat using what methods (i.e., short-term empirically driven psychotherapy, pharmacotherapy, or combination therapy) for how long. A model for empirical clinical practice is offered here for other clinicians to use, evaluate, and revise in treating depressed patients. The premise of this model is that when practitioners use basic research methods, they will help their patients more than when they do not. Its corollary is that practitioners who use these methods can not only contribute to the literature on depressive disorders but also can influence public policy decisions, because clinically relevant data are made public. The hallmark of such empirical clinical practice is using hypothesis testing and data to guide treatment decisions. This interplay among hypothesis generation, data collection, and treatment involves a "functional analysis," or identifying the variables that control or influence behavior (Ferster, 1965, 1973). The model is based on my colleagues' and my clinical experience with outpatients who present for evaluation and treatment of mood disorders at the University of Texas Southwestern Medical Center at Dallas, Department of Psychiatry and Mental Health Clinical Research Center. The model represents a set of initial clinical hypotheses to be revised as additional data, tools, and experience become available through randomized, controlled clinical trials, series of replicated single-case designs, and yet-to-be-created better methods. This working model is outlined to aid clinicians in determining which treatment(s) to use.

When applied to depressive illness, the empirical method useful to practitioners include the following:

1. Single-case research designs.
2. A thorough initial diagnostic evaluation.
3. The longitudinal assessment of syndromes and/or symptom severity.
4. The longitudinal assessment of the quality and adequacy of treatment.
5. The longitudinal assessment of relevant psychological problems and treatment goals.
6. The clinician's working knowledge of the treatment outcome literature on depression.
7. The clinician's previous empirical practice with depressed patients who are similar to the individual requesting help.

A MODEL FOR "EMPIRICAL CLINICAL PRACTICE": A SET OF HYPOTHESES REGARDING MOOD DISORDERS

Single-Case Research Designs

The classic text on single-case research designs, *Tactics of Scientific Research*, was written by Sidman (1960), who relied primarily on an operant paradigm. Srinika and Levy (1979) coined the term "empirical clinical practice," and along with Barlow and Hersen (1984) and Barlow, Hayes, and Nelson (1984), detailed how to apply single-case designs and employ functional analyses when treating psychiatrically ill and/or psychologically troubled patients.

The simplest and most practical single-case design is the A (baseline)–B (single treatment) design. Due to its lack of experimental controls, this design limits inference but is useful in making clinical decisions. In order to use this design, the empirical clinician must understand how to achieve the following:

1. Obtain baseline data and know how long to collect them.
2. Select and use practical, dependent measures that are sensitive to changes in depressive symptoms or to changes in the psychological problems that covary with depressive symptoms (e.g., relationship discord, dysfunctional cognition, vocational impairment).
3. Modify treatment(s) systematically.
4. Select and record uncontrolled but relevant events during assessment and treatment (e.g., new job, car accident, the flu, self-help group).
5. Monitor and record (i.e., graph) the relevant changes in treatment and in symptoms.

Examples of modifications in treatment include switching types of treatment (e.g., from psychotherapy to pharmacotherapy or vice versa), adding treatment strategies (e.g., adding psychotherapy to pharmacotherapy), altering technical aspects of therapy (e.g., increasing the medication dosage or changing the focus from behavioral to cognitive targets of change, or changing phases (e.g., initial diagnostic/baseline phase, acute treatment phase, continuation/maintenance phase, or treatment-free longitudinal follow-up phase). Every modification in treatment requires documentation of the type and date of the change, because the independent variable (i.e., treatment) has been changed and may change the dependent variable (i.e., symptom severity). In order to interpret a result, only one change in treatment can be made at a time. When the treatment has been changed, and a relevant but uncontrolled event occurs simultaneously, then symptoms may also change. The clinician is well served to delay additional changes in treatment until more data have been collected. Each change in treatment represents a change in the type of single-case design utilized (e.g., A_1 [baseline], B_1 [psychotherapy], and A_2 [treatment-free longitudinal follow-up]).

Initial Diagnostic Evaluation

The purpose of a thorough diagnostic evaluation is to determine what, if any, DSM-IV (American Psychiatric Association, 1994) psychiatric diagnoses best describe the patient's presenting and lifetime symptoms or disorders. Structured interviews, such as the Schedule for Affective Disorders and Schizophrenia (SADS; Endicott & Spitzer, 1978) and the Structured Clinical Interview for DSM-III-R (SCID; Spitzer, Williams, Gibbon, & First, 1989), can aid even the experienced diagnostician in obtaining data from interviews and in applying the criteria found in the RDC and DSM-III-R or DSM-IV.

Since diagnostic criteria for the major psychiatric illnesses (including the mood disorders) require the clinician to rule out organic factors, it is essential for the patient to undergo general medical laboratory screening and/or medical evaluation. Such diagnostic and laboratory screening is most informative when the patient is free of medications or substances that can influence mood. At times, such drug/medication washouts may require hospitalization or assistance from a treating primary care physician. Frequently, unscheduled toxicology screens can be useful in diagnosing substance abuse, which the patient may deny. All medications/drugs consumed should be listed in order to evaluate their potential for altering mood.

The nonmedical practitioner can consult with medical colleagues to review results from the medical laboratory and to obtain data addressing such questions as these: Could symptoms of a mood disorder result from, coexist with, or be influenced by (1) a nonpsychiatric, medical illness (e.g., thyroid disease), (2) using medications prescribed to treat or prevent another condition (e.g., blood pressure medication, birth control pills), or (3) abuse of substances (e.g., alcohol, cannabis, cocaine)? Are there comorbid nonpsychiatric illnesses or conditions present that should influence the type of treatment offered (e.g., heart disease, pregnancy)? Are there comorbid neurological (e.g., stroke, previous brain injury) problems that will complicate or restrict treatment options or influence the manner in which treatment is delivered best? To what extent will the patient's physical condition influence his/her compliance with what a potential treatment regimen requires (e.g., depressed patients with allergies who can be treated with a monoamine oxidase inhibitor only if they can substitute antihistamines for decongestants).

The diagnostic evaluation includes a review not only of past and present mood disorders and symptoms, but also of the onset, duration, and treatment of other primary, secondary, and comorbid psychiatric illnesses occurring throughout the patient's lifetime. With the exception of comorbid, organic mental disorders and substance use disorders, we typically focus initial treatment on the mood disorder. When comorbid, organic mental disorders or substance use disorders exist, we have referred such patients for specialty care first and have subsequently treated their mood disorder as necessary. Careful documentation of past response to adequate trials of psychiatric and psychological treatment will help the practitioner avoid initiating treatments that have previously proven ineffective. Similarly, documenting the somatic treatment histories of first-degree family members with mood disorders provides clues about what type of pharmacotherapy may be most likely to succeed with the patient. The diagnostic evaluation also includes a brief screen for the presence of psychiatric symptoms or syndromes in first-degree family members. When untreated but potentially symptomatic relatives are identified, educational material and a referral for further evaluation should be considered and discussed.

The diagnostic evaluation includes a brief social and personal history, with particular attention to past physical or psychological trauma, threat, and loss. Identifying deaths of significant others is particularly important in order to diagnose depression complicated by bereavement, or to distinguish a mood disorder from normal bereavement or adjustment disorders. It is helpful to identify current psychosocial events that the patient views as stressful, as well as significant environmental and/or social changes. Likewise, documenting apparent life-time strengths and current practical and inter-personal resources (e.g., the extent or presence of functional impairment) is helpful in overcom-ing obstacles to initiating treatment or achiev-ing treatment goals. In order to minimize the bias of the patient's depressed mood on the self-report or on the clinician's judgement in clini-cal practice, we have generally deferred the evaluation of personality and personality disor-ders until the patient has achieved a euthymic state.

During the initial evaluation, it is helpful to ask the patient to list the problems or symptoms he/she considers most distressing. After these problems are identified, the patient is asked to prioritize them (e.g., most to least distressing) and define what improvement represents in each problem area. This initial assessment al-lows the clinician and patient to identify a priori both the targets and goals of treatment.

Providing patients and third-party payers with the expectation that a thorough outpatient or inpatient evaluation takes a minimum of 2 or more visits (typically separated by 1 week) has the following advantages:

1. It allows the clinician to obtain baseline data on symptom severity over time (to be dis-cussed).
2. It allows medical laboratory tests to be com-pleted and reviewed.
3. It allows the possibility of a drug/medication washout during evaluation and prior to ini-tiating treatment.
4. It allows a family member or significant other to accompany the patient to the second (follow-up) evaluation, in order to provide additional diagnostic detail; to learn more about depressive illness, its recognition, and its treatment; and (potentially) to offer emo-tional support to the patient.

A thorough diagnostic evaluation allows the practitioner to determine (1) whether outpatient or inpatient treatment is necessary; (2) what type, if any, interdisciplinary or specialty con-sultation is necessary; (3) the extent to which the patient can obtain readily the emotional support of a significant other; (4) whether the patient prefers one type of treatment for depression over another; and (5) the extent to which the patient's treatment preference matches the clinician's treatment recommendation.

Clinical Hypotheses

The following treatment considerations (i.e., implicit hypotheses) have helped us evaluate and treat outpatients in Dallas who requested assistance for mood disturbances. When pa-tients consent, we have included a family mem-ber or significant other in the second session of diagnostic evaluation, which ends with a discus-sion of the patient's psychiatric disorders, treat-ment options, and their willingness or ability to comply with requirements of the recommended treatment. When given an opportunity to con-tribute, significant others often provide addi-tional data that is diagnostically important (e.g., the presence of manic and hypomanic symp-toms). Routinely, we detail the results of the diagnostic evaluation with the patient and sig-nificant other, recommend reading material (relevant to types, course, and treatment of mood disorders), consider the patient's prefer-ence when recommending a particular type of treatment, and recommend a treatment. Pa-tients are told that most depressions respond to treatment, and that failure to respond to the first (or subsequent) treatment initiated simply re-sults in changing the type of treatment offered.

We have hospitalized patients who (1) are psychotic; (2) are manic; (3) are judged to be at risk for acting upon suicidal or homicidal ide-ation; (4) require extended or complex evalua-tion from multiple medical personnel; (5) re-quire extensive or extended supervision or treatment in order to obtain a drug/medication-free state; or (6) have severe, often vegetative, depressive symptoms (e.g., a HRSD score ≥ 40). Note that most depressed inpatients receive a combination of pharmacotherapy and psycho-therapy, in addition to the local hospital milieu. The degree to which empirically validated, short-term psychotherapy for depression (i.e., cognitive therapy, behavior therapy or inter-personal psychotherapy) is available depends on the availability and accessibility of competent, trained therapists. On most inpatient units, such therapists are in short supply.

In treating patients who meet DSM-III, DSM-III-R, or DSM-IV criteria for major de-pressive disorder but are ineligible for research, we have hypothesized that meeting DSM-III or DSM-IV criteria for melancholia may be an in-dication for using pharmacotherapy alone as the first treatment initiated. It must be emphasized that there is no empirical justification for such a recommendation; however, clinical experience suggests that the pervasive anhedonia and unreactive mood always present, as well as the severe psychomotor retardation often present, make psychotherapy laborious and difficult. (Note that Nelson, Mazure, & Jatlow, 1990, have suggested that although melancholic and nonmelancholic patients may not differ in their response to antidepressant medication, melancholic patients may be particularly unresponsive to nonsomatic treatment. On the other hand, Thase et al., 1984, reported that three of four treatment resistant outpatients with RDC endogenous and DSM-III melancholic depression responded to social skills training plus pill placebo.)

In treating outpatients who meet criteria for DSM-IV bipolar I disorder (mixed, manic, or depressed), we have relied generally on pharmacotherapy to achieve remission and recovery. We have reported one case in which a pregnant outpatient with bipolar I disorder (most recent episode depressed) who presented off lithium treatment and with depressive symptoms, was treated with cognitive therapy while pregnant to reduce depressive symptoms, and was treated with lithium plus cognitive therapy following delivery (Jarrett, 1989a). Basco and Rush (in press) will provide an adjunctive treatment manual detailing how a cognitive–behavioral approach can be used in the continuation and maintenance phases of pharmacologically stabilized patients with bipolar I disorder. The existence of a well-specified manual offers a chance to improve clinical care and sets the stage for empirical evaluation. In clinical practice, we have found that cognitive therapy alone can be used successfully to reduce the depressive symptoms of depressed outpatients diagnosed with DSM-IV bipolar II disorder (recurrent major depressive episodes with hypomanic episodes).

We have encouraged patients to postpone making major life decisions (e.g., marital separation, divorce, changing jobs) until they are in a euthymic state and have recovered. If a patient is in a crisis situation (i.e., a decision must be made and action is required to avoid negative consequences) or insists upon making a decision prior to recovery, then we have encouraged the patient to consider short-term psychotherapy for depression to aid in the decision-making process. Similarly, depressed patients who are experiencing physical or psychological trauma or abuse in their current home or work environments have been encouraged to consider short-term psychotherapy for depression to determine how to best escape the abuse or trauma.

When asked about treatment preference, patients frequently request a combination of psychotherapy and pharmacotherapy, often reasoning that if one treatment is effective, two treatments are more effective. With the exceptions listed previously, we encourage the nonpsychotic outpatient with major depressive disorder to pursue one type of treatment at a time. Furthermore, we explain the basic rationale for and steps in empirical clinical practice, and overview the null results from the combination treatment literature. We describe "combination treatment" as a treatment option *after* it has been demonstrated empirically to be required. When the patient with unipolar major depressive disorder of moderate severity prefers pharmacotherapy over psychotherapy, or vice versa, we refer the patient to the preferred initial approach, unless treatment history or current symptom severity suggests otherwise.

Longitudinal Assessment of Symptom Severity

In both pharmacotherapy and psychotherapy, the overriding goals are to reduce the severity of depressive symptoms (compared to that of the patient's initial presentation) and to achieve recovery (i.e., a consistent, nondepressed state compared to that of people without depressive illness or to the patient's euthymic state). Establishing stable reductions in symptoms as the basic treatment goal enables both the patient and the therapist to determine the extent to which treatment works.

In our work in Dallas, clinicians have relied on the 17-, 21-, and 24-item HRSD to assess symptom severity, because it is widely used in clinical trials on psychotherapy and/or pharmacotherapy. These trials guide practitioners' expectations of treatment effectiveness. Because the original version of the HRSD does not allow the clinician to assess symptoms that are important in subtyping depressions (i.e., atypical, endogenous, and melancholic), we have supplemented the HRSD with the Inventory for Depressive Symptomatology (IDS; Rush et al., 1986) which includes clinician-rated (IDS-C) and patients' self-reported (IDS-SR) versions. Similarly, because clinician- and patient-rated measures produce correlated but distinct patterns of responding, patients have also completed the BDI and the IDS-SR. In general, when using these measures, we find that clinicians report reductions in depressive symptoms before patients do (Jarrett, Eaves, & Rush, 1990).

In order for symptom severity measures to help clinicians make decisions, baseline data must be gathered. To establish a baseline, we gather a HRSD for each week corresponding to the initial diagnostic evaluation and the follow-up diagnostic evaluation. If the evaluation phase takes more than 2 weeks, we collect a HRSD weekly. Typically a third baseline HRSD can be collected at the first treatment session, prior to the initiation of treatment. If the patient cancels an appointment, the weekly HRSD is collected by telephone when the appointment is rescheduled. Collecting a minimum of three baseline points allows the clinician to determine the extent to which symptoms are improving, worsening, or not changing.

During the evaluation phase, it is not uncommon to observe some reduction in depressive symptoms for patients with major depressive disorder. If this reduction is dramatic (i.e, 50% reduction and/or it places the patient in the normative range—17-item HRSD = 0–9), then the clinician and patient should consider continuing to evaluate the course and severity of the mood disorder, rather than initiating treatment for an episode that may be reaching its end. (Our experience suggests that approximately 15–20% of outpatients with unipolar major depressive disorder may evidence symptomatic reduction during the evaluation phase.) Weekly longitudinal assessment of depressive symptoms (e.g., completing a HRSD and reviewing diagnostic criteria) in the absence of active treatment allows the clinician to determine how long remission/recovery will last and whether active treatment is currently necessary or whether longitudinal evaluation of symptoms can be considered.

After the psychotherapist or pharmacotherapist decides to begin a trial of treatment, the next decision is how long to offer treatment and at what level (i.e., dose and/or schedule). Assuming adequate treatment is being provided and consumed, our experience suggests that depressed outpatients who eventually respond to pharmacotherapy or cognitive therapy typically show improvement during the first 4–6 weeks. (Note that this assumes cognitive therapy is offered for 60 minutes twice weekly by a highly competent therapist; Jarrett et al., 1990.) We collect the HRSD, IDS-C, IDS-SR, and BDI weekly. When the 17–item HRSD has not dropped at least 50% from baseline or is not approaching the normal range (0–9) by the end of the trial (4–6 weeks), then we consider changing treatment. A change from one modality to another assumes that the initial treatment trial was adequate. In pharmacotherapy, the dosage, duration, and metabolism must have been sufficient. Pharmacotherapy treatment manuals written by Bassuk, Schoonover, and Gelenburg (1991) and Schatzberg and Dole (1991) provide basic pharmacological protocols for clinical practice. In addition, there are now clinical practice guidelines (Depression Guideline Panel, 1993b) to foster adequacy in a pharmacotherapy trial. Similarly, in psychotherapy, the schedule of treatment (e.g., weekly or twice weekly and completed homework assignments) must have been sufficient. For both approaches, an adequate trial assumes that patient compliance with treatment requirements and therapist competence were good.

A change from psychotherapy to pharmacotherapy due to no change in, or worsening of, depressive symptoms after 4–6 weeks assumes that the patient has not been involved in some relevant psychosocial change (e.g., marital separation, loss of job) that could be expected to lower mood. If the patient has initiated psychological change relevant to the stated goals (see section on longitudinal assessment of psychological problems and treatment goals), and the depressive symptoms have not yet improved, then the length of psychological treatment might be extended in order to foster and maintain the ongoing psychosocial change. If, however, after 15–16 sessions of short-term psychotherapy, psychosocial change has occurred, yet depressive symptoms have not improved considerably, then pharmacotherapy is needed as an adjunctive or solitary treatment. Combination treatment, rather than pharmacotherapy alone, may be considered when psychosocial change is in process but the patient's depressive symptoms have not improved clearly.

Longitudinal Assessment of the Quality of Treatment

Our experience suggests that the clinical practice of experienced, well-trained psychotherapists and pharmacotherapists improves with weekly professional consultation and increases the chance that the trial is adequate and of high quality. This consultation provides an opportunity for both the treating and the consulting practitioner to review the patient's scores from symptom severity measures (e.g., HRSD, IDS-C, IDS-SR, and BDI), as well as any measures relevant to the adequacy of the trial (e.g., measures of patient compliance or therapist adherence and competence; see Meichenbaum and Turk, 1987, for methods designed to foster treatment adherence by the patient).

In pharmacotherapy, data relevant to the adequacy of the trial include dosage and (when available) data from periodic blood assays that assess the extent to which the antidepressant medication was both taken and metabolized. Even the experienced pharmacotherapist benefits from a pause and an opportunity to examine the data carefully. The treating practitioner "thinks out loud" while a colleague acting as devil's advocate listens and potentially raises alternative interpretations of the data that may suggest a change in the way treatment is provided.

In cognitive therapy, data relevant to the adequacy of the trial include weekly review of the symptom severity scores and weekly professional consultation from a group of trained cognitive therapists. In order to improve the quality of the trial, a videotaped session is reviewed and critiqued each week on-site. (We have found that four to five cognitive therapists per consultation group are ideal, giving each therapist a chance to present a session approximately monthly.) The Cognitive Therapy Scale (CTS; Young & Beck, 1980) can be used to assess the therapist's competence and provide a framework for the verbal critiques and case conceptualizations which follow. Additionally, CTS ratings of randomly selected sessions by an off-site expert protect the therapist from critiques that are influenced by a group process or other interpersonal factors inherent in ongoing multi-year, weekly consultation among the same professionals. Such weekly and longitudinal quality control helps therapists maintain a high-quality practice, even in difficult circumstances. The fact that the consultation is a routine part of the therapists' week provides a forum for readily available consultation when the clinical need exists. The fact that the consultation is longitudinal offers therapists an opportunity to identify the conditions (e.g., patient characteristics or therapist circumstances) that change or influence their practice of therapy compared to their baselines. When competence or adherence drifts, therapists know that individual supervision is indicated (Jarrett, 1989a).

Longitudinal Assessment of Psychological Problems and Treatment Goals

Longitudinal assessment of the patient's psychological problems and treatment goals is a complex enterprise that exploits the tools and principles of behavioral assessment. A thorough discussion of the underlying theory and associated techniques is beyond the scope of this chapter, but can be found in Nelson and Hayes (1986), Bellack and Hersen (1988), and Barlow (1981). (Similarly, Persons, 1989, outlines how assessment is essential while using a cognitive model to conceptualize the case during the practice of cognitive therapy.) Just as the non-medical practitioner benefits from consulting with medical colleagues to obtain data relevant to answering medication questions (see section on diagnostic evaluation and see also Depression Guideline Panel, 1993a), the practitioner without training in clinical psychology benefits from similar consultation with a behavioral assessor. Important guidelines include the following: Do the symptoms of a mood disorder result from or coexist with nonpsychiatric, psychological problem (e.g., marital disorder, vocational dissatisfaction)? Are there premorbid or comorbid psychological traits or disorders present that may influence the type or manner in which treatment can be provided (e.g., expectations regarding treatment efficacy)? How does the patient conceptualize his/her symptoms (e.g., "bad genes," "character defect")? What, if any, iatrogenic effects have help seeking and treatment had (e.g., "Now my spouse thinks I'm hard to live with and crazy")? What are the environmental, emotional, and interpersonal factors that will influence compliance with treatment?

The important principle in this context is that practitioners who treat depressed patients need to monitor a limited number of psychological problems (in addition to depressive symptoms) that the patient finds distressing (e.g., relationship discord, unemployment, dysfunctional cognitions). The principles of behavioral assessment, such as selecting a measure, setting an a priori standard for treatment success or failure, and obtaining baseline data, apply not only to assessing symptom severity but also to assessing other psychological problems and progress on the general goals of treatment.

If during the initial evaluation the depressed patient has identified the most distressing problems, then the clinician has a clue as to what psychological problems may require assessment. Texts such as *The Dictionary of Behavioral Assessment Techniques* (Hersen & Bellack, 1988) and *Tests in Print* (Buros, 1961; Buros Institute of Mental Measurements, 1983) provide helpful reference material. Application of the Visual Analog Scale (Folstein & Luria, 1973) is useful if or when a measure sensitive to treatment effects cannot be located readily (e.g., the measure is unavailable during the baseline phase).

Examples of psychological problems often associated with depression include deficits in social functioning, which can be assessed by the Social Adjustment Scale (SAS; Weissman & Bothwell, 1976); marital discord, which can be assessed by the Dyadic Adjustment Scale (DYS; Spanier, 1976); negative attributional style, which can be assessed by the ASQ (Peterson et al., 1982); and dysfunctional attitudes, which can be assessed by the DAS (Weissman, 1979).

Although most psychotherapists trained to provide short-term psychotherapy for depression include longitudinal assessment of psychological problems and treatment goals as a routine component of their psychotherapy, few pharmacotherapists routinely employ these procedures. The hypothesis here is that when pharmacotherapists do include behavioral assessment of psychological problems as a part of their routine practice, they will identify (1) those patients who may require additional therapy (probably psychotherapy) as an adjunct to, or as a solitary treatment which replaces pharmacotherapy in an effort toward true recovery, and/or (2) those patients who are at increased risk for early relapse/recurrence. The implicit hypothesis is that remitted or recovered depressed patients whose relationship discord, dysfunctional attitudes, cognitive style, or social adjustment remains untreated will relapse/recur more quickly and more often than similar patients without these (and other) psychological and interpersonal concomitants or sequelae.

When Is Continuation/Maintenance Therapy Necessary? How Long Should Treatment Last?

Continuation/maintenance therapy is necessary through the time of risk for patients who have recovered from the index episode and have recurrent major depressive disorder but have not received treatment having prophylactic value. The problem with such a clinical directive is that the clinician cannot know a priori which depressed patients with single episodes are likely to have other episodes, or how long remission or recovery from recurrent depression may last. Similarly, the actual prophylactic value of "antidepressant treatments" (either pharmacotherapy or psychotherapy, but especially psychotherapy) is not well studied.

Pharmacologists estimate the period of risk for relapse/recurrence for unipolar major depressive disorder to be 6–12 months after recovery from an index episode (Schatzberg & Dole, 1991) and tend to provide continuation/maintenance treatment for that period with beneficial results (Montgomery et al., 1988; Frank et al., 1990).

Even less is known about the prophylactic value of short-term psychotherapy for depression. In clinical practice of cognitive therapy, we have tended to gradually thin the schedule of appointments as the depressive symptoms decrease and the patient masters the requisite skills. The acute phase of treatment lasts until the patient no longer meets DSM-IV criteria for major depressive disorder.

After developing a treatment manual for the continuation/maintenance phase of cognitive therapy (Jarrett, 1989b), we began to offer a continuation/maintenance phase of cognitive therapy to depressed outpatients. Sessions follow the strategies originally outlined by Beck, Rush, Shaw, and Emery (1979). Continuation/maintenance treatment focuses on restructuring dysfunctional attitudes and "schemas" that may increase vulnerability for relapse/recurrence and generalizing the skills acquired during the acute phase. Anticipation of future stressors occurs, with discussion and role play of possible alternative solutions. The continuation/maintenance phase lasts 8 months (every other week for the first 2 months after acute treatment and monthly for the remaining 6 months). Preliminary data suggest that such a continuation/maintenance phase reduces the relapse/recurrence rate substantially (Jarrett et al., 1992; Jarrett, Ramanan, Basco, & Rush, 1995) and may promote improved clinical care for patients with recurrent major depressive disorder.

When treatment is discontinued, both psychotherapists and pharmacotherapists alike are well served to assess depressive symptoms monthly, after the diagnostic criteria for major depressive disorder have not been met for 2 or more months and the HRSD score consistently remains below 0–10. Patients and supportive significant others can be taught to monitor depressive symptoms and to recognize the difference between mood disturbance that represents isolated, transient symptoms and mood disturbance that is syndromal. The goal is to reinitiate treatment (or increase the dose or schedule of appointments during the continuation/maintenance phase) before transient depressive symptoms become syndromal.

CONCLUSIONS

Clinical trials conducted to date suggest that during the acute phase of pharmacotherapy, short-term psychotherapy, and the combination of pharmacotherapy plus short-term psychotherapy, reduce depressive symptoms significantly more than waiting-list control conditions. The modal finding among these three treatment conditions is that they do not differ significantly in reducing depressive symptoms. Results from studies that included conditions designed to control for the nonspecific aspects of treatment are few and remind investigators and clinicians of the contribution these factors make to the so-called "active" treatments. In treating adult outpatients who have nonpsychotic, unipolar major depressive disorder, the short-term psychotherapies with the best empirical support are interpersonal psychotherapy, cognitive therapy, and behavior therapy. Most trials involving brief psychodynamic psychotherapy have been conducted by investigators aligned with the "other" psychotherapy comparison condition. Thus, controlled, systematic research is needed on the efficacy of brief dynamic psychotherapy in order to state definitively that it is an equally viable treatment option for reducing depressive symptoms. Questions remain about which treatments are best to improve and normalize the typical psychosocial problems and sequelae associated with depressive illness (e.g., social adjustment, chronic personality disturbance, dysfunctional cognition). These efforts will document the extent to which clinically important differences (in psychosocial variables) will emerge among the various brands of treatment and short-term psychotherapy.

The literature has produced few prescriptive indicators to help clinicians decide when and for how long to use pharmacotherapy, short-term psychotherapy, or their combination. Clinical hypotheses based on the literature and clinical experience are organized here within a working model that exploits the methods used in single-subject designs and behavioral assessment. This model is offered to other practitioners for testing as they select treatment(s) and revision during their empirical clinical practice with depressed patients.

Ideally, future work will help answer the following practical questions: (1) Once depressive symptoms remit, which treatments both optimize recovery (using "normative" definitions that include social and psychological adjustment) and reduce the chance of, or time until, a psychiatric syndrome emerges or recurs? and (2) When are combination treatments best used as first-line treatments, and when are "sequences" of single treatments (e.g., 4 months of imipramine therapy during the acute phase, 8 months of cognitive therapy during the continuation/maintenance phase, and treatment-free follow-up until recurrence) better indicated? In order to be in a position to treat the large number of people suffering from depressive illness, we also must identify those treatments that the typical practicing clinician can apply most effectively. We must determine the extent to which the results of clinical trials generalize to clinical practice. Likewise, we must address which treatments' requirements are easiest for given types of depressed patients to comply with, learn initially, and continue to use over time. Patients' preferences and inclinations need to be studied as part of the research agenda if compliance and treatment effectiveness are to be understood fully. We must determine how to reduce the social stigma associated with depression and foster early detection and treatment for the initial onset of the illness, as well as for recurring episodes. Likewise, a major stride forward involves identifying the extent to which antecedent psychosocial and biological factors and treatment influence the course of illness in asymptomatic people who are at high risk for depression.

Additional promising frontiers for short-term psychotherapy used alone or combined with pharmacotherapy include (1) identifying the conditions under which continuation/maintenance phases of treatment are necessary; (2) improving the overall functioning of outpatients who suffer from chronic depression and may also have long-standing relationship and/or personality disturbance; (3) maximizing the best long-term prognosis for depressed inpatients; and (4) fostering meaningful recovery for pharmacologically stabilized bipolar patients.

Acknowledgements. The preparation of this chapter was supported in part by the Agency for Health Care Policy and Research and by grants from the National Institute of Mental Health to Robin B. Jarrett (No. MH-45043) and the Department of Psychiatry, University of Texas Southwestern Medical Center at Dallas, Mental Health Clinical Research Center (No. MH-41115). Appreciation is expressed to Melinda Down, BS, for her collaboration on a larger but related review commissioned by the U.S. Public Health Service's Agency for Health Care Policy and Research, and for her technical assistance in updating this review. Appreciation is expressed to Sheria Oswalt, BBA, and Judy Torres for their secretarial assistance. Thanks are due to Amy Neubauer, BA, and Joe Webster, BS, for their research support, and to Rodger D. Kobes, MD, PhD, for his comments on an earlier draft of this chapter. Special thanks are expressed to A. John Rush, MD, Betty Jo Hay Distinguished Chair in Mental Health, and to Kenneth Z. Altshuler, MD, Stanton Sharp Professor and Chairman, for administrative support.

REFERENCES

American Psychiatric Association. (1980). *Diagnostic and statistical manual of mental disorders* (3rd ed.). Washington, DC: Author.

American Psychiatric Association. (1987). *Diagnostic and statistical manual of mental disorders* (3rd ed., rev.). Washington, DC: Author.

American Psychiatric Association. (1994). *Diagnostic and statistical manual of mental disorders* (4th ed.). Washington, DC: Author.

Barlow, D. H. (Ed.). (1981). *Behavioral assessment of adult disorders*. New York: Guilford Press.

Barlow, D. H., Hayes, S. C., & Nelson, R. O. (1984). *The scientist practitioner: Research and accountability in clinical and educational settings*. New York: Pergamon Press.

Barlow, D. H., & Hersen, M. (1984). *Single case experimental designs: Strategies for studying behavior change* (2nd ed.). New York: Pergamon Press.

Basco, M. A., & Rush, A. J. (in press). *Cognitive–behavioral treatment of manic–depressive disorder*. New York: Guilford Press.

Bassuk, E. L., Schoonover, S. C., & Gelenberg, A. J. (Eds.). (1991). *The practitioner's guide to psychoactive drugs* (3rd ed.). New York: Plenum Press.

Beach, S. R., & O'Leary, K. D. (1992). Treating depression in the context of marital discord: Outcome and predictors of response of marital therapy versus cognitive therapy. *Behavior Therapy, 23*, 507–508.

Beck, A. T., Hollon, S. D., Young, J. E., Bedrosian, R. C., & Budenz, D. (1985). Treatment of depression with cognitive therapy and amitriptyline. *Archives of General Psychiatry, 42*, 142–145.

Beck, A. T., Rush, A. J., Shaw, B. F., & Emery, G. (1979). *Cognitive therapy of depression*. New York: Guilford Press.

Beck, A. T., Ward, C. E., Mendelson, M., Mock, J., & Erbaugh, J. (1961). An inventory for measuring depression. *Archives of General Psychiatry, 4*, 561–571.

Becker, J., & Schuckit, M. A. (1978). The comparative efficacy of cognitive therapy and pharmacotherapy in the treatment of depressions. *Cognitive Therapy and Research, 2*(2), 193–197.

Bellack, A. S., & Hersen, M. (Eds.). (1988). *Behavioral assessment: A practical handbook*. New York: Pergamon Press.

Bellack, A. S., Hersen, M., & Himmelhoch, J. (1981). Social skills training compared with pharmacotherapy and psychotherapy in the treatment of unipolar depression. *American Journal of Psychiatry, 138*(12), 1562–1567.

Bellack, A. S., Hersen, M., & Himmelhoch, J. (1983). A comparison of social-skills training, pharmacotherapy and psychotherapy for depression. *Behaviour Research and Therapy, 21*(2), 101–107.

Beutler, L. E., Scogin, F., Kirkish, P., Schretlen, D., Corbishley, A., Hamblin, D., Meredith, K., Potter, R., Bamford, C. R., & Levenson, A. I. (1987). Group cognitive therapy and alprazolam in the treatment of depression in older adults. *Journal of Consulting and Clinical Psychology, 55*, 550–556.

Blackburn, I. M., & Bishop, S. (1983). Changes in cognition with pharmacotherapy and cognitive therapy. *British Journal of Psychiatry, 143*, 609–617.

Blackburn, I. M., Bishop, S., Glen, A. I. M., Whalley, L. J., & Christie, J. E. (1981). The efficacy of cognitive therapy in depression: A treatment trial using cognitive and pharmacotherapy, each alone and in combination. *British Journal of Psychiatry, 139*(181), 181–189.

Blackburn, I. M., Eunson, K. M., & Bishop, S. (1986). A two-year naturalistic follow-up of depressed patients treated with cognitive therapy, pharmacotherapy and a combination of both. *Journal of Affective Disorders, 10*, 67–75.

Bowers, W. (1990). Treatment of depressed in-patients: Cognitive therapy plus medication, relaxation plus medication, and medication alone. *British Journal of Psychiatry, 156*, 73–78.

Brabender, V., & Fallon, A. E. (1992). *Models of inpatient group psychotherapy*. Hyattsville, MD: American Psychological Association.

Brady, J. P. (1984). Social skills training for psychiatric patients. I: Concepts, methods and clinical results. *American Journal of Psychiatry, 141*, 333–340.

Buros, O. K. (1961). *Tests in print: A comprehensive bibliography of tests for use in education, psychology, and industry*. Highland Park, NJ: Gryphon Press.

Buros Institute of Mental Measurements. (1983). *Tests in print 3: An index to tests, test reviews, and the literature on specific tests*. Lincoln: University of Nebraska Press.

Clarkin, J. F., Glick, I. D., Haas, G. L., Spencer, J. H., Lewis, A. B., Peyser, J., DeMane, N., Good-Ellis, M., Harris, E., & Lestelle, V. (1990). A randomized clinical trial of inpatient family intervention. *Journal of Affective Disorders, 18*, 17–28.

Clarkin, J. F., Glick, I. D., Spencer, J. H., & Haas, G. L. (1984). *IFI for Affective Disorders: A manual for inpatient family intervention*. Unpublished manuscript.

Clarkin, J. F., Haas, G. L., & Glick, I. D. (1988). Inpatient family intervention. In J. F. Clarkin, G. L. Haas, & I. D.

Glick (Eds.), *Affective disorders and the family* (pp. 134–152). New York: Guilford Press.

Covi, L., & Lipman, R. S. (1987). Cognitive behavioral group psychotherapy combined with imipramine in major depression. *Psychopharmacology Bulletin*, 23(1), 173–176.

de Jong, R., Henrich, G., & Ferstl, R. (1981). A behavioural treatment programme for neurotic depression. *Behaviour Analysis and Modification*, 4, 275–287.

de Jong, R., Trieber, R., & Henrich, G. (1986). Effectiveness of two psychological treatments for inpatients with severe and chronic depressions. *Cognitive Therapy and Research*, 10, 645–663.

Depression Guideline Panel. (Ed.). (1993a). *Depression in primary care: Vol. 1. Detection and diagnosis* (Clinical Practice Guideline No. 5, AHCPR Publication No. 93-0550). Rockville, MD: U.S. Department of Health and Human Services.

Depression Guideline Panel. (Ed.). (1993b). *Depression in primary care: Vol. 2. Treatment of major depression* (Clinical Practice Guideline No. 5, AHCPR Publication No. 93-0551). Rockville, MD: U.S. Department of Health and Human Services.

Derogatis, L. R., Lipman, R. S., Rickles, K., Uhlenhuth, E. H., & Covi, L. (1974). The Hopkins Symptom Checklist: A self-report symptom inventory. *Behavioral Science*, 19, 1–15.

DeRubeis, R. J., Evans, M. D., Hollon, S. D., Garvey, M. J., Grove, W. M., & Tuason, V. B. (1990). How does cognitive therapy work? Cognitive change and symptom change in cognitive therapy and pharmacotherapy for depression. *Journal of Consulting and Clinical Psychology*, 58(6), 862–869.

DiMascio, A., Weissman, M. M., Prusoff, B. A., Neu, C., Zwilling, M., & Klerman, G. L. (1979). Differential symptom reduction by drugs and psychotherapy in acute depression. *Archives of General Psychiatry*, 36, 1450–1456.

Elkin, I., Shea, M. T., Watkins, J. T., Imber, S. D., Sotsky, S. M., Collins, J. F., Glass, D. R., Pilkonis, P. A., Leber, W. R., Docherty, J. P., Fiester, S. J., & Parloff, M. B. (1989). National Institute of Mental Health Treatment of Depression Collaborative Research Program: General effectiveness of treatments. *Archives of General Psychiatry*, 46, 971–982.

Endicott, J., & Spitzer, R. L. (1978). A diagnostic interview: The schedule for affective disorders and schizophrenia. *Archives of General Psychiatry*, 35, 837–844.

Evans, M. D., Hollon, S. D., DeRubeis, R. J., Piasecki, J. M., Grove, W. M., Garvey, M. J., & Tuason, V. B. (1990). *Differential relapse following cognitive therapy, pharmacotherapy, and combined cognitive–pharmacotherapy for depression.* Unpublished manuscript.

Evans, M. D., Hollon, S. D., DeRubeis, R. J., Piasecki, J. M., Grove, W. M., Garvey, M. J. & Tuason, V. B. (1992). Differential relapse following cognitive therapy and pharmacotherapy for depression. *Archives of General Psychiatry*, 49(10), 802–808.

Ferster, C. B. (1965). Classification of behavioral pathology. In L. Krasner & L. P. Ullmann (Eds.), *Research in behavior modification* (pp. 6–26). New York: Holt, Rinehart & Winston.

Ferster, C. B. (1973). A functional analysis of depression. *American Psychologist*, 10, 857–870.

Folstein, M. F., & Luria, R. (1973). Reliability, validity and clinical application of the visual analogue mood scale. *Psychological Medicine*, 3, 479–486.

Frank, E., & Kupfer, D. J. (1986). Psychotherapeutic approaches to treatment of recurrent unipolar depression: Work in progress. *Psychopharmacology Bulletin*, 22(3), 558–563.

Frank, E., Kupfer, D. J., Perel, J. M., Cornes, C., Jarrett, D. B., Malinger, A. G., Thase, M. E., McEachran, A. B., & Grochocinski, V. J. (1990). Three-year outcomes for maintenance therapies in recurrent depression. *Archives of General Psychiatry*, 47, 1093–1099.

Frank, E., Prien, R., Jarrett, R. B., Keller, M. B., Kupfer, D. J., Lavori, P. W., Rush, A. J., & Weissman, M. M. (1991). Conceptualization and rationale for consensus definitions of terms in major depressive disorder. Remission, recovery, relapse, and recurrence. *Archives of General Psychiatry*, 48, 851–855.

Haas, G. L., Glick, I. D., Clarkin, J. F., Spencer, J. H., Lewis, A. B., Peyser, J., DeMane, N., Good-Ellis, M., Harris, E., & Lestelle, V. (1988). Inpatient family intervention: A randomized clinical trial. *Archives of General Psychiatry*, 45, 217–224.

Hamilton, M. (1960). A rating scale for depression. *Journal of Neurology, Neurosurgery and Psychiatry*, 12, 62–62.

Hersen, M., & Bellack, A. S. (1988). *Dictionary of behavioral assessment techniques*. New York: Pergamon Press.

Hersen, M., Bellack, A. S., Himmelhoch, J. M., & Thase, M. E. (1984). Effects of social skills training, amitriptyline, and psychotherapy in unipolar depressed women. *Behavior Therapy*, 15, 21–40.

Hollon, S. D., DeRubeis, R. J., Evans, M. D., Wiemer, M. J., Garvey, M. J., Grove, W. M., & Tuason, V. B. (1990). *Cognitive therapy, pharmacotherapy, and combined cognitive–pharmacotherapy in the treatment of depression.* Unpublished manuscript.

Hollon, S. D., DeRubeis, R. J., Evans, M. D., Wiemer, M. J., Garvey, M. J., Grove, W. M., & Tuason, V. B. (1992). Cognitive therapy and pharmacotherapy for depression: Singly and in combination. *Archives of General Psychiatry*, 49(10), 774–781.

Hollon, S. D., & Najavits, L. (1988). Review of empirical studies in cognitive therapy. In A. J. Frances & R. E. Hales (Eds.), *American Psychiatric Press review of psychiatry* (pp. 643–666). Washington, DC: American Psychiatric Press.

Jarrett, R. B. (1989a, June). Training a research cognitive therapist: Goals and methods. In R. D. Kobes (Chair), *Teaching cognitive therapy in a medical school—A case study*. Workshop presented at the World Congress of Cognitive Therapy, Oxford.

Jarrett, R. B. (1989b). *Cognitive therapy for recurrent unipolar major depressive disorder. The continuation/maintenance phase.* Unpublished treatment manual.

Jarrett, R. B. (1990). Psychosocial aspects of depression and the role of psychotherapy. *Journal of Clinical Psychiatry*, 51(Suppl., 6), 26–35.

Jarrett, R. B., & Down, M. (in press). Psychotherapy for adults with major depressive disorder. In *Detection, diagnosis and treatment of depression* (Clinical Practice Guideline No. 5, Agency for Health Care Policy and Research). Rockville, MD: National Technical Information Service.

Jarrett, R. B., Eaves, G. G., & Rush, A. J. (1990, November). *When do depressed outpatients respond during cognitive therapy?* Poster presented at the meeting of the Association for Advancement of Behavior Therapy, San Francisco.

Jarrett, R. B., & Maguire, M. A. (1991). *Short-term psychotherapy for depression* (Technical review commissioned by the Agency for Health Care Policy and Research Depression Guideline Panel). Unpublished manuscript.

Jarrett, R. B., Ramanan, J., Basco, M. R. & Rush, A. J. (1995). *Is there a role for continuation phase cognitive therapy for depressed outpatients?* Manuscript in preparation.

Jarrett, R. B., Ramanan, J., Eaves, G. G., Kobes, R., Basco, M. R., & Rush, A. J. (1992, June). *How prophylactic is cognitive therapy in treating depressed outpatients?* Paper presented at the World Congress of Cognitive Therapy, Toronto, Ontario, Canada.

Klerman, G. L., DiMascio, A., Weissman, M., Prusoff, B., & Paykel, E. (1974). Treatment of depression by drugs and psychotherapy. *American Journal of Psychiatry, 131*(2), 186–192.

Klerman, G. L., Weissman, M. M., & Prusoff, B. A. (1982). RDC endogenous depression as a predictor of response to antidepressant drugs and psychotherapy. *Advances in Biochemical Psychopharmacology, 32,* 165–174.

Kovacs, M., Rush, A. J., Beck, A. T., & Hollon, S. D. (1981). Depressed outpatients treated with cognitive therapy or pharmacotherapy: A one-year follow-up. *Archives of General Psychiatry, 38,* 33–41.

Last, C. G., Thase, M. E., Hersen, M., Bellack, A. S., & Himmelhoch, J. M. (1985). Patterns of attrition for psychosocial and pharmacologic treatments of depression. *Journal of Clinical Psychiatry, 46*(9), 361–366.

Marmor, J. (1975). Academic lecture: The nature of the psychotherapeutic process revisited. *Canadian Psychiatric Association Journal, 20,* 557–565.

McKnight, D. L., Nelson-Gray, R. O., & Barnhill, J. (1992). Dexamethasone suppression test and response to cognitive therapy and antidepressant medication. *Behavior Therapy, 23,* 99–111.

McLean, P. D., & Hakstian, A. R. (1979). Clinical depression: Comparative efficacy of outpatient treatments. *Journal of Consulting and Clinical Psychology, 47*(5), 818–836.

McLean, P. D., & Hakstian, A. R. (1990). Relative endurance of unipolar depression treatment effects: Longitudinal follow-up. *Journal of Consulting and Clinical Psychology, 58*(4), 482–488.

McLean, P., & Taylor, S. (1992). Severity of unipolar depression and choice of treatment. *Behaviour Research and Therapy, 30,* 443–451.

Meichenbaum, D., & Turk, D. C. (1987). *Facilitating treatment adherence. A practitioner's guidebook.* New York: Plenum Press.

Miller, I. W., Bishop, S. B., Norman, W. H., & Keitner, G. .I. (1985). Cognitive/behavioural therapy and pharmacotherapy with chronic, drug-refractory, depressed inpatients: A note of optimism. *Behavioural Psychotherapy, 13,* 320–327.

Miller, I. W., Norman, W. H., & Keitner, G. I. (1990). Treatment response of high cognitive dysfunction depressed inpatients. *Comprehensive Psychiatry, 30*(1), 62–71.

Miller, I. W., Norman, W. H., Keitner, G. I., Bishop, S. B., & Dow, M. G. (1989). Cognitive–behavioral treatment of depressed inpatients. *Behavior Therapy, 20,* 25–47.

Montgomery, S. A., Dufor, H., Brion, S., Gailledreau, J., Laqueille, X., Ferrey, G., Moron, P., Parant-Lucena, N., Singer, L., Danion, J. M., Beuzen, J. N., & Pierredon, M. A. (1988). The prophylactic efficacy of fluoxetine

in unipolar depression. *British Journal of Psychiatry, 153*(Suppl. 3), 69–76.

Monti, P. M., Fink, E., Norman, W. H., Curran, J., Hayes, S., & Caldwell, A. (1979). Effects of social skills training groups and social skills bibliotherapy with psychiatric patients. *Journal of Consulting and Clinical Psychology, 47,* 189–190.

Murphy, G. E., Simons, A. D., Wetzel, R. D., & Lustman, P. J. (1984). Cognitive therapy and pharmacotherapy: Singly and together in the treatment of depression. *Archives of General Psychiatry, 41,* 33–41.

National Institute of Mental Health. (1989). *Depressive illnesses: Treatments bring new hope* (DHHS Publication No. ADM 89–1491). Washington, DC: U.S. Government Printing Office.

National Mental Health Association. (1991). *Executive summary of findings from a survey of Americans on mental health and depression* (Peter D. Hart Research Associates, Inc.). Washington, DC: Author.

Nelson, R. O., & Hayes, S. C. (Eds.). (1986). *Conceptual foundations of behavioral assessment.* New York: Guilford Press.

Nelson, J. C., Mazure, C. M., & Jatlow, P. I. (1990). Does melancholia predict response in major depression? *Journal of Affective Disorders, 18,* 157–165.

O'Leary, K. D., & Beach, S. R. H. (1990). Marital therapy: A viable treatment for depression and marital discord. *American Journal of Psychiatry, 147*(2), 183–186.

Paykel, E. S., Dimascio, A., Haskell, D., & Prusoff, B. A. (1975). Effects of maintenance amitriptyline and psychotherapy on symptoms of depression. *Psychological Medicine, 5,* 67–77.

Persons, J. (1989). *Cognitive therapy in practice. A case formulation approach.* New York: Norton.

Peterson, C., Semmel, A., von Baeyer, C., Abramson, L. Y., Metalsky, G. I., & Seligman, M. E. P. (1982). The Attributional Style Questionnaire. *Cognitive Therapy and Research, 6,* 287–300.

Roth, D., Bielski, R., Jones, M., Parker, W., & Osborn, G. (1982). A comparison of self-control therapy and combined self-control therapy and anti-depressant medication in the treatment of depression. *Behavior Therapy, 13,* 133–144.

Rounsaville, B. J., Klerman, G. L., & Weissman, M. M. (1981). Do psychotherapy and pharmacotherapy for depression conflict? Empirical evidence from a clinical trial. *Archives of General Psychiatry, 38,* 24–29.

Rounsaville, B. J., Weissman, M. M., Prusoff, B. A., & Herceg-Baron, R. L. (1979). Marital disputes and treatment outcome in depressed women. *Comprehensive Psychiatry, 20*(5), 483–490.

Rush, A. J., Beck, A. T., Kovacs, M., & Hollon, S. D. (1977). Comparative efficacy of cognitive therapy and pharmacotherapy in the treatment of depressed outpatients. *Cognitive Therapy and Research, 1,* 17–37.

Rush, A. J., Beck, A. T., Kovacs, M., Weissenburger, J., & Hollon, S. D. (1982). Comparison of the effects of cognitive therapy and pharmacotherapy on hopelessness and self-concept. *American Journal of Psychiatry, 139*(7), 862–866.

Rush, A. J., Giles, D. E., Schlesser, M. A., Fulton, C. L., Weissenburger, J. E., & Burns, C. T. (1986). The Inventory for Depressive Symptomatology (IDS): Preliminary findings. *Psychiatry Research, 18,* 65–87.

Rush, A. J., Kovacs, M., Beck, A. T., Weissenburger, J., & Hollon, S. D. (1981). Differential effects of cognitive therapy and pharmacotherapy on depressive symptoms. *Journal of Affective Disorders*, 3, 221–229.

Rush, A. J., & Watkins, J. T. (1981). Group versus individual cognitive therapy: A pilot study. *Cognitive Therapy and Research*, 5(1), 95–103.

Schatzberg, A. F., & Dole, J. O. (1991). *Manual of clinical psychopharmacology* (2nd ed.). Washington, DC: American Psychiatric Press.

Scott, M. J., & Stradling, S. G. (1990). Group cognitive therapy for depression produces clinically significant reliable change in community-based settings. *Behavioural Psychotherapy*, 18, 1–19.

Shaw, B. F. (1981). Matching treatment to patient characteristics in an inpatient setting. In L. P. Rehm (Ed.), *Behavior therapy for depression* (pp. 209–227). New York: Academic Press.

Shea, M. T., Elkin, I., Imber, S. D., Sotsky, S. M., Watkins, J. T., Collins, J. F., Pilkonis, P. A., Beckham, E., Glass, D. R., Dolan, R. T., & Parloff, M. B. (1992). Course of depressive symptoms over follow-up: Findings from the National Institute of Mental Health Treatment of Depression Collaborative Research Program. *Archives of General Psychiatry*, 49(10), 782–787.

Shea, M. T., Pilkonis, P. A., Beckham, E., Collins, J. F., Elkin, I., Sotsky, S. M., & Docherty, J. P. (1990). Personality disorders and treatment outcome in the NIMH Treatment of Depression Collaborative Research Program. *American Journal of Psychiatry*, 147(6), 711–718.

Sidman, M. (1960). *Tactics of scientific research*. New York: Basic Books.

Simons, A. D., Garfield, S. L., & Murphy, G. E. (1984). The process of change in cognitive therapy and pharmacotherapy for depression. *Archives of General Psychiatry*, 41, 45–51.

Simons, A. D., Levine, J. L., Lustman, P. J., & Murphy, G. E. (1984). Patient attrition in a comparative outcome study of depression: A follow-up report. *Journal of Affective Disorders*, 6, 163–173.

Simons, A. D., Murphy, G. E., Levine, J. L., & Wetzel, R. D. (1986). Cognitive therapy and pharmacotherapy for depression. *Archives of General Psychiatry*, 43, 43–48.

Sotsky, S. M., Glass, D. R., Shea, T. M., Pilkonis, P. A., Collins, J. F., Elkin, I., Watkins, J. T., Imber, S. D., Leber, W. R., Moyer, J., & Oliveri, M. E. (1991). Patient predictors of response to psychotherapy and pharmacotherapy: Findings in the NIMH Treatment of Depression Collaborative Research Program. *American Journal of Psychiatry*, 148(8), 997–1008.

Spainer, G. B. (1976). Measuring dyadic adjustment: New scales for assessing the quality of marriage and similar dyads. *Journal of Marriage and the Family*, 38, 15–28.

Spencer, J. H., Glick, I. D., Haas, G. L., Clarkin, J. F., Lewis, A. B., Peyser, J., DeMane, N., Good-Ellis, M., Harris, E., & Lestelle, V. (1988). A randomized clinical trial of inpatient family intervention: III. Effects of 6-month and 18-month follow-ups. *American Journal of Psychiatry*, 145(9), 1115–1121.

Spitzer, R. L., Endicott, J., & Robins, E. (1978). Research Diagnostic Criteria: Rationale and reliability. *Archives of General Psychiatry*, 36, 773–782.

Spitzer, R. L., Williams, J. B. W., Gibbon, M., & First, M. B. (1989). *Structured Clinical Interview for DSM-III-R*

(SCID). New York: New York State Psychiatric Institute, Biometrics Research Department.

Srinika, S., & Levy, R. L. (1979). *Empirical clinical practice*. New York: Columbia University Press.

Teasdale, J. D., Fennell, M. J. V., Hibbert, G. A., & Amies, P. L. (1984). Cognitive therapy for major depressive disorder in primary care. *British Journal of Psychiatry*, 144, 400–406.

Thase, M. E., Bowler, K., & Harden, T. (1991). Cognitive–behavior therapy of endogenous depression: Part 2. Preliminary findings in 16 unmedicated inpatients. *Behavior Therapy*, 22, 469–477.

Thase, M. E., Hersen, M., Bellack, A. S., Himmelhoch, J. M., Kornblith, S. J., & Greenwald, D. P. (1984). Social skills training and endogenous depression. *Journal of Behavior Therapy and Experimental Psychiatry*, 15(2), 101–108.

Thase, M. E., Simons, A. D., Cahalane, J. F., & McGeary, J. (1991a). Cognitive behavior therapy of endogenous depression: Part 1: An outpatient clinical replication series. *Behavior Therapy*, 22, 457–467.

Thase, M. E., Simmons, A. D., Cahalane, J., McGeary, J., & Harden, T. (1991b). Severity of depression and response to cognitive behavior therapy. *American Journal of Psychiatry*, 148, 784–789.

Thase, M. E., & Wright, J. H. (1991). Cognitive behavior therapy manual for depressed inpatients: A treatment protocol outline. *Behavior Therapy*, 22, 579–595.

Thompson, L. W., Gallagher, D., & Czirr, R. (1988). Personality disorder and outcome in the treatment of late-life depression. *Journal of Geriatric Psychiatry*, 21(2), 133–146.

Weissman, A. N. (1979). The Dysfunctional Attitudes Scale: A validation study (Doctoral dissertation, University of Pennsylvania). *Dissertation Abstracts International*, 40, 1389B–1390B.

Weissman, A. W., & Bothwell, S. (1976). Assessment of social adjustment by patient self-report. *Archives of General Psychiatry*, 33, 1111–1115.

Weissman, M. M., & Kasl, S. V. (1976). Help-seeking in depressed out-patients following maintenance therapy. *British Journal of Psychiatry*, 129, 252–260.

Weissman, M. M., Kasl, S. V., & Klerman, G. L. (1976). Follow-up of depressed women after maintenance treatment. *American Journal of Psychiatry*, 133, 757–760.

Weissman, M. M., Klerman, G. L., Paykel, E. S., Prusoff, B. A., & Hanson, B. (1974). Treatment effects on the social adjustment of depressed patients. *Archives of General Psychiatry*, 30, 771–778.

Weissman, M. M., Klerman, G. L., Prusoff, B. A., Sholomskas, D., & Padian, N. (1981). Depressed out-patients: Results one year after treatment with drugs and/or interpersonal psychotherapy. *Archives of General Psychiatry*, 38, 51–55.

Weissman, M. M., Prusoff, B. A., DiMascio, A., Neu, C., Goklaney, M., & Klerman, G. L. (1979). The efficacy of drugs and psychotherapy in the treatment of acute depressive episodes. *American Journal of Psychiatry*, 136(4B), 555–558.

Wolberg, L. R. (1967). *Short-term psychotherapy*. New York: Grune & Stratton.

Young, J., & Beck, A. T. (1980). *Cognitive Therapy Scale: Rating manual*. Unpublished manuscript, Center for Cognitive Therapy, Philadelphia.

IV
SPECIFIC POPULATIONS

18

Depression in Children and Adolescents

PATRICIA L. SPEIER
DONALD L. SHERAK
SHARON HIRSCH
DENNIS P. CANTWELL

The study of depressive disorders in children and adolescents has a short history; only 30 years ago, the very existence of true depression as a disorder of children was hotly debated. Since then, much progress has been made in our understanding of depression. Research in childhood and adolescent depression has made significant gains over the past 30 years, with recent advances utilizing the studies of depression in adults as models for potential studies and inteventions with children.

In tracing historical trends of childhood depression, four significant viewpoints have evolved in overlapping periods. The earliest school of thought was that depression, as a clinical disorder similar to that seen in adults, did not exist in children. In the psychoanalytic thinking of the time, expressed by authors such as Rie (1966) and Mahler (1961), it was believed that depression could not emerge until adolescence, when the superego was more fully developed. The second and subsequent period of thought was that children could become depressed, but that in addition to adultlike symptomatology, there would be features unique to children with depression (Frommer, 1968; Ling, Oftedal, & Weinberg, 1970; Poznanski, Krahenbuhl, & Zrull, 1976; Kuhn & Kuhn, 1972). This viewpoint makes clinical sense, due to the differing

tasks children face at different developmental stages. No clinically consistent features could be delineated, however, and a wide variety of symptoms were ascribed to depression. The third viewpoint that emerged, similar in many ways to its predecessor, was that children with depression presented a picture very different from that of adults—a so-called "masked depression" (Toolan, 1962; Glaser, 1968; Cytryn & McKnew, 1972, 1980). According to this theory, symptoms as broad-based as enuresis, learning disabilities, and hyperactivity were all considered evidence of a masked depressive affect. Unfortunately, this tended to make any evidence of psychopathology evidence of a depressive disorder, and considerably muddied the water regarding the etiology and treatment of both depressive disorders and the whole spectrum of childhood psychopathology.

In the past 20 years, the fourth and prevailing viewpoint regarding childhood depression has gained acceptance. This is the view that childhood and adolescent depression can be diagnosed using the same basic criteria as those used for adults, such as DSM-III, DSM-III-R, DSM-IV, and the Research Diagnostic Criteria (Spitzer, Endicott, & Robins, 1977). This theoretical basis has been the springboard for leading research in the area of childhood and adolescent depression, such as that of Cantwell and Carlson (1983), Kovacs and Beck (1977), and Weller, Weller, Fristad, and Preskorn (1984). Although this last period has not been long, numerous studies using specific criteria and careful designs have greatly expanded our knowledge of childhood and adolescent depression.

This chapter gives an overview of current thinking and important issues facing researchers in the areas of etiology, natural history, epidemiology, diagnosis, assessment, and treatment of childhood and adolescent depression. Developmental issues are examined, especially in relation to diagnostic criteria; cognitive features of depression are overviewed; and suicide and its growing significance is discussed. Last, possible directions for future research in each of the foregoing areas are explored, as well as the problems and limitations that face both clinicians and researchers in this field.

ETIOLOGY

The etiology of depression is an elusive one, and research and clinical observation of children have been vital in this search. Several theories have been proposed, looking at psychodynamic, cognitive–behavioral, family/genetic, and biological models as the basis for depression. Although most of this work has focused on adults, each of these areas is discussed in light of current research with children and adolescents.

Three models of the etiology of depression have arisen from the psychodynamic perspective. In the first model, that of Abraham (1960) and Freud (1917/1957), depression is seen as anger turned inward. Although this is a widely held viewpoint, it does not seem adequate when researched in children. Studies of boys and girls using self-report measures find that children with high scores of depressive symptoms can outscore their peers in measures of outward-directed hostility (Akiskal & McKinney, 1975). In other words, they express their anger outwardly rather than inwardly. The theory of depression as anger turned on the self is pointed to only in the major depression of bereaved children (Weller et al., 1988), but it has not otherwise been a consistent finding.

In the second model, that of Bibring (1965), loss of self-esteem replaces anger as the central force creating depression. This viewpoint is closely correlated to the role of shame, as proposed by Lewis (1986). The third psychodynamic model proposed in the etiology of depression is that of object loss, or separation. Object loss is theorized to be the "final stress" that precipitates depression in a vulnerable individual, or to be a factor in the response to subsequent episodes of loss (Kraemer, 1986; Beardslee, Schultz, & Selman, 1987). Although it has been shown that these psychodynamic theories may prolong or exacerbate a depression in a vulnerable individual, research is not yet conclusive as to their unique ability to cause a depression.

Cognitive–behavioral models are based on clinical findings of abnormal ways of thinking that characterize depressed persons. In Beck's (1976) cognitive model of depression, negative thoughts of self, one's experiences, and the future (the "cognitive triad") cause and prolong depression, rather than simply being symptoms of depression. While Beck's theories have been studied extensively in adults, the literature on children and adolescents is limited. Self-reports of increased hopelessness in children correlate to increases in the severity of depressive symptoms and in the extent of suicidality (Keller et al., 1987). Depressed children evidence these cognitive abnormalities while in a depressed state, but return to normal when their depression lifts, thus weakening the argument that these abnormalities are the cause rather than the symptoms of depression.

Another cognitive model proposed in the etiology of depression is learned helplessness (Seligman & Peterson, 1986). McCracken (1992) describes learned helplessness as the behavioral state characterized by minimal attempts to adapt or respond to aversive stimuli, resulting from exposure to inescapable, overwhelming, or uncontrollable stressors. While the negative attributional style of the cognitive–behavioral model is consistent with depressive symptoms for the patient as both child and adult (Benfield, Palmer, Pfefferbaum, & Stowe, 1988; Jaenicke et al., 1987; Seligman & Peterson, 1986), its specificity and predictive value remain to be evaluated (McCracken, 1992).

In the behavioral model of depression, a vicious cycle occurs when the child or adolescent has a "loss of reinforcement" (Lazarus, 1968; Lewinsohn, 1974), and thus fails to use his/her adaptive resources appropriately. This results in a maintenance of the depressed state, because the patient fails to elicit more positive feedback from others. This is also consistent with the idea of reduced social competence. The resultant reduced positive feedback from peers also acts to maintain depression in these unfortunate youngsters. It is evident that there is much overlap in these cognitive–behavioral theories. There is also difficulty in sorting out whether these models represent causative factors of depression or are simply symptoms of depression.

The previous discussion has centered on the individual's abnormal response to the environment, which may contribute to or cause depression. It is also important to evaluate the role that family interaction may play in causing depression in children and adolescents. Psychopathology in a family can significantly contribute to depression. Parental depression, especially maternal depression, appears to be a nonspecific risk factor in the development of psychopathology in children (Mitchell, McCauley, Burke, Calderon, & Schloredt, 1989), and one can speculate about the role attachment may have in producing depression in children of depressed mothers. Other parental disorders are also correlated with an increased risk of major depressive disorder in children, as shown in the study of Merikangas, Weissman, Prusoff, and John (1988), in which 6- to 23-year-old children of mothers with a diagnosis of alcohol dependence were studied. This familial loading of affective disorders in the children of parents having psychopathology, especially affective disorders, has been studied by many investigators (Beardslee, Bemporad, Keller, & Klerman, 1983; Hammen et al., 1987; Weissman, et al., 1984; Welner, Welner, McCrary, & Leonard, 1977). These studies indicate a familial loading for psychopathology, specifically mood disorders, but researchers are not able to specify whether this is the result of biological–genetic factors or of family–environmental interactions. Family characteristics implicated as risk factors in the etiology of mood disorders include increased marital discord (Rae-Grant, Thomas, Offord, & Boyle, 1989) and high expressed emotion in the mother, especially when that emotion is related to criticism directed toward the child (Schwartz, Dorer, Beardslee, Lavori, & Keller, 1990).

The broader question arises as to whether the family's social or environmental interactions cause depression in these children, or whether genetic inheritance of depression causes these environmental problems. Genetic studies of depression show that the risk for affective disorder among first-degree relatives of bipolar and unipolar probands is increased (Strober &

Carlson, 1982). Adoption studies on monozygotic twins raised apart from their biological parents by adoptive parents without psychopathology also support a genetic theory of inheritance. A major gap in our understanding of genetic modes of transmission in mood disorders is the paucity of segregation analysis. Segregation analysis would help to determine the manner in which a gene is inherited in the population. Several studies, primarily in adults, have utilized modern genetic techniques of linkage analysis, but have failed to find a replicable gene transmitting depression. This continues to be an active area of research.

Genetic transmission of depression, unipolar or bipolar, may help in identifying potential biological mechanisms of depression. The biological hypotheses of depression in adults have focused on catecholamine or serotonin abnormalities, neuroendocrine changes, and cholinergic/aminergic balance. Research in children, however, has not always been consistent with the findings in the adult literature. Catecholamines, dopamine, and norepinephrine are involved in the regulation of such depressive symptoms as sleep, appetite, energy level, and mood, and are thought to be central to the mechanism of the etiology of depression (Siever & Davis, 1985). Catecholamine levels, however, have not been shown to differ between nondepressed children/adolescents and those with depression (Puig-Antich, 1987; DeVilliers et al., 1989). Catecholamines are known to regulate mood, activity, sleep, and appetite, all of which may be adversely affected in depression, and it is possible that the way in which they function in children and adolescents differs from that in adults. Indeed, catecholamine abnormalities may play a role in the neuroendocrine disturbances found in some depressed children and adolescents.

Neuroendocrine abnormalities in depressed children and adolescents include nonsuppression of cortisol with dexamethasone, blunted growth hormone release, and decreases in melatonin secretion. Some studies have shown nonsuppression of cortisol after a dexamethasone challenge as compared to controls, but others have not. Interestingly, growth hormone release is blunted after the administration of clonidine, growth hormone-releasing hormone, and insulin-induced hypoglycemia. Blunted growth hormone response in depressed adolescents to insulin-induced hypoglycemia, and hypersecretion of growth hormone at night, are found to persist even after resolution of the depression. Neuroendocrine regulation is a complicated system, and much research remains to be done.

Another possible biological theory proposed for depression in adults is that of an imbalance between the cholinergic and aminergic systems in the brain. Research with depressed adults has shown that dysphoria can be produced by acute increases in cholinergic activity. The decreased latency of the first episode of rapid-eye-movement (REM) sleep, a common finding in depressed adults, may at least in part be due to cholinergic mechanisms. These changes have not been consistently found in children or adolescents with depression. While some depressed children are found to have decreased REM latency, cholinergic stimulation has not induced changes in children. A study of adolescents and adults by McCracken, Poland, and Tondo (1991), however, did show a prolonged REM latency to the anticholinergic scopolamine. These biological theories of the etiology of depression (as well as many others studied in adults but not in children or adolescents) are inconclusive, although suggestive of a continuity between adults and juveniles.

The etiology of depression is most likely multifactorial, with some subsets of depression weighted toward a psychodynamic–cognitive–environmental etiology and others based more upon genetic–biological factors. This is strongly suggested by the different "paths" seen clinically from depressive symptomatology to depression as a diagnosable condition. Some children, under environmental stress, move slowly from dysthymia (neurotic depression) to a full-blown depressive disorder. Other children, without notable stressors, rapidly move from a well-functioning state into an acute depressive episode. What factors place these children at greater risk than other children from similar families or environmental backgrounds are still unclear. Continued research in all these areas is needed in order to further elucidate the causes contributing to depression and better understand their interrelationship.

EPIDEMIOLOGY

Prevalence

Epidemiological studies are vital to understanding the extent to which children experience depressive symptoms and disorders. Mood disorders have been shown to be among the most common psychiatric disorders of childhood and adolescence (Fleming & Offord, 1990). The child psychiatric literature on the epidemiology of these disorders, however, is sparse and contains numerous problems. Early studies were usually designed to assess symptoms or the patient's functional level (Gould, Wunsch-Hitzig, & Dohrenwend, 1980) rather than to assess subjects for clinically defined psychiatric diagnoses, including depressive disorder. Diagnosis can only be inferred retrospectively from the prevalence of listings of depressive symptoms evaluated. Varying methods of assessing depression and changing criteria for the diagnosis of depression are primary reasons for the marked differences in reported prevalence rates. For example, use of a lay-administered structured interview such as the Diagnostic Interview Schedule—Child (DISC) instead of a clinician's diagnostic assessment may inflate true prevalence rates by including a less symptomatic group of patients. Difference in the choice of weighing children's assessment of their symptoms and the parents' assessment may be another significant source of variance. In community surveys, use of self-report depression rating scales, without collateral evidence from parents and teachers, has led to reports of depressive disorders ranging from 2.6% to a high of 39% (in one adolescent sample; Albert & Beck, 1975). In large studies, where paper-and-pencil screenings are often given to parents or teachers to select subjects meeting criteria thresholds, there may be children (or adolescents) not adequately "discovered" by these screenings because of poor observational skills, a child's secretiveness, and so on. In spite of researchers' efforts to randomly screen below-threshold subsamples and use weighted estimates of prevalence to help reduce this potential for error, this, too, may cause significant variance. Other important sources of variance are outlined by Fleming and Offord (1990) and include sampling strategies (households, schools, etc.), sample representation, response rates, cultural factors, and measurement variability.

Community-based epidemiological studies have varied widely in their prevalence estimates of major depression in children and adolescents, from a low of 0.4% to a high of 8.8% (Fleming, Offord, & Boyle, 1989). The most significant variable accounting for this difference has been the age group examined. When children younger than 12 years old are sampled, prevalence rates range from 1.2% to 2.5% (Fleming et al., 1989). In the seminal Isle of Wight Study (Rutter, Cox, Tupling, Berger, & Yule, 1975), multiple informants were used to determine the frequency of depressed mood and associated symptoms in over one thousand 10-year-old children. Although it is likely that true prevalence rates were somewhat underestimated, because children who met criteria for conduct disorder were excluded from the group considered depressed, persistent sad mood was present in 12% of the sample, whereas criteria for depression were found in only 0.14% of the sample. When this cohort of children were reassessed at age 14 using similar methods, it is striking that Rutter (1989) found that the prevalence of depression had increased more than threefold within this 4-year span. Further data gathered from this study strongly suggested that pubertal development, rather than age, was associated with this marked increase in depression, because depressed 14-year-olds were significantly more likely to have reached puberty than nondepressed peers.

Numerous community-based studies since then have also reflected this large increase in rates of depression, as well as examining these groups for the presence of dysthymic disorder (minor depression). A study of 9-year-old New Zealand children (the Dunedin Study sample) found the rate of chronic minor depression was 1.5 times that of major depression (2.5% vs. 1.8), and that for past history of depressive diagnosis, rates of minor depression were much higher than rates of major depression (9.7% and 1.1%, respectively). When these children were reassessed at ages 11 and 15 (Anderson, Williams, McGee, & Silva, 1987), the prevalence figures of depression and dysthymic disorder decreased, probably reflecting the difference in diagnostic criteria and instruments used. Between ages 11 and 15, however, the prevalence estimates increased from 0.05% to 1.2% for major depressive disorder, but dropped from 1.6% to 1.1% for dysthymia.

Another study that corroborates the significant increase in rates of depressive disorder from childhood to adolescence is the Ontario Child Health Study (Boyle et al., 1987; Fleming, Offord, & Boyle, 1989), a screened sample of 2,674 children and adolescents. Using symptom data analysis to estimate "DSM-III-like" major depressive disorder, the investigators found a prevalence of 2.6% in both 6- to 11-year-old

girls and boys, but much higher and differing rates, 8.8% for girls and 6.9% for boys, in the adolescent group (12–16 years old).

Other studies have also borne out the difference in sex ratio between children and adolescents (Strober, Hanna, & McCracken, 1989; Garrison, Addy, Jackson, McKeown, & Walker, 1991), with prepubertal boys and girls equally at risk for depressive disorders, whereas there is a female predominance for depression in adolescence.

Few studies have looked at depression in preschool samples, though such studies may be important in the development of more accurate theories regarding etiology and risk factors. Kashani, Holcomb, and Orvaschel (1986), in studying a sample of 109 preschoolers (2–7 years old), found one 5-year-old child who met unmodified DSM-III criteria for major depression. In a survey utilizing mothers' reports, 8% of 100 children aged 3 were noted to have dysphoric mood (Earls, 1980).

Several studies have looked at how often depressive disorders present in pediatric settings. These studies indicate a need for pediatricians to be aware that children with depression may present primarily with somatic complaints or symptoms. In an early study examining this question, 10 out of 25 children referred to a children's neurology clinic because of headaches met Weinberg criteria (Velez, Johnson, & Cohen, 1989) for depression (Fleming et al., 1989). Kashani, Barbero, and Bolande (1981a) utilized DSM-III criteria to identify 7% of a hospitalized general pediatric sample of one hundred 7- to 12-year-old children as having major depression. Interestingly, the majority of these depressed patients were hospitalized for gastrointestinal problems. In another study by the same group, 13% of 100 consecutive 6-to 18-year-old children referred to a pediatric cardiology service met DSM-III criteria for major depression (Kashani, Lababibi, & Jones, 1982), but over 50% of the children reported dysphoric mood. A number of other studies of chronically ill children, including those with malignancies (Kashani & Hakami, 1982), diabetes (Kovacs et al., 1985), cystic fibrosis or inflammatory bowel disease (Burke et al., 1989) and those needing extensive orthopedic procedures (Kashani, Venzke, & Millar, 1981b) showed high rates of major depression. This contrasts vividly with children surveyed from primary care settings. For example, a study of nearly eight hundred 7- to 11-year-old children utilizing a U.S. health maintenance organization revealed a 1-year prevalence of major depression of 0.6%, with a dysthymic disorder prevalence of 1.3%. These results are similar to those of community samples, as noted earlier. Interpretation of these results needs to be made with caution. Physical illness can be a severe stressor, and these results suggest that physical illness can precipitate depressive disorders. Certain types of illness (i.e., those with more chronic courses, painful or debilitating symptoms, or disfigurement) probably are more depressogenic, although children often show emotional stability and good adaptation even in the face of daily medical procedures (Kovacs et al., 1985b) or life-threatening illness (Kashani & Hakami, 1982).

Depression is also a common disorder among child and adolescent psychiatric populations, although prevalence data vary widely depending on what population and what type of setting are examined. Twelve percent of 102 consecutive children seen in a university child psychiatry clinic met DSM-III criteria for major depression, as reported by Carlson and Cantwell (1979, 1980), based on parent and child interviews. Using modified Feighner criteria, a study (Kuperman & Stewart, 1979) of 175 consecutive psychiatric admissions of children and adolescents revealed a 7% prevalence of depressive disorder. Since these early reports, other studies examining diagnoses of children in psychiatry clinics or hospital units have reported even higher percentages of depression (Feinstein, Blouin, Egan, & Conners, 1984; Kashani, Cantwell, Shekim, & Reid, 1982; Kazdin, Esveldt-Dawson, Unis, & Rancurello, 1983) in their populations.

Comorbidity

Comorbid psychiatric disorders are very common in children and adolescents with depression; conduct disorders, anxiety, phobias, and somatic complaints are frequently seen. Hershberg, Carlson, Cantwell, and Strober (1982) found that 68% of 28 depressed children suffered from generalized anxiety, while 39% had situation-specific anxiety, and 61% had somatic complaints. In a study by Puig-Antich and Rabinovich (1986), 59% of a sample of 80 depressed prepubertal children had significant separation anxiety, and 48% had moderate to severe phobia. Epidemiological studies also show this high degree of associated diagnosis.

In the Dunedin Study mentioned earlier (Anderson et al., 1987), 80% of children (11 out of 14) diagnosed with major depression met criteria for another diagnostic category. Of all diagnostic categories, in fact, depression/dysthymia showed the greatest overlap with other diagnoses. Oppositional or conduct disorder was the most common comorbid diagnosis, noted in 78% of the subjects. Anxiety disorders were nearly as common, found in 71% of the children, whereas attention deficit was found in 57% of subjects. This high comorbidity rate was again borne out in the work of Bird et al. (1988). In their study, the majority of depressed children were diagnosed with conduct/oppositional disorder (45%), although attention deficit disorder (30%) and anxiety (18%) were also common. A study of adolescents (Kashani et al., 1987) yielded similar results to studies of younger children.

The comorbidity of alcohol or substance abuse has been documented in two studies (Kashani et al., 1987; Deykin, Levy, & Wells, 1987). Both studies demonstrated that 25% of those subjects meeting criteria for depression also met criteria for substance abuse. In the analysis of the study by Deykin et al. (1987), it is notable that those subjects diagnosed with substance abuse were not more likely to show depression than other forms of psychopathology.

It is difficult to determine what this high rate of comorbidity signifies. As Angold and Costello (1992) have shown, such high rates of comorbidity for depression with anxiety, and depression with conduct disorder, could not occur by chance alone. What this strong association between these disorders means, however, is unclear. Are the so-called internalizing disorders (depression, anxiety, etc.) pathogenetically related, representing different etiologies and outcomes from patients with externalizing (e.g., conduct) disorders? A study by Harrington, Fudge, Rutter, Pickles, and Hill (1991) supports the distinction between depressed children with conduct disorder and depressed children without conduct disorder. Upon reaching adulthood, there was a fourfold difference between these groups (nearly significant at the 5% level) in the probability of having major depression. Interestingly, both depressed and nondepressed children with conduct disorder had similar antisocial outcome as adults. These data strongly suggest a major subgrouping for depressed children and adolescents, between those with and without conduct disorder. This is reflected in the diagnostic controversy between DSM-IV criteria and ICD-10. It has yet to be determined what etiological links exist between these subgroups. The Harrington et al. (1991) work suggests that conduct symptoms may cause stressors that lead to depression, but this is only one possible explanation. Further work determining the etiology of these depressive subgroups and examining their diagnostic specificity will help in the understanding of these questions and may have important treatment implications.

NATURAL HISTORY

The natural history of mood disorders in children and adolescents has been studied rigorously only for the past 25 years. Follow-back (Zeitlin, 1986) and catch-up (Harrington et al., 1991) studies report the validity of the original diagnosis and find that previously depressed children and adolescents are prone to continuous or recurrent episodes of depression. Depression with onset closer to adulthood may have more severe consequences (Harrington et al., 1991). An 18-year retrospective–prospective study also found a greater than two times higher rate of adult depression in youths who had experienced postpubertal rather than prepubertal depression. Kashani et al. (1983) confirmed the diagnosis of depression within childhood by following two groups of depressed New Zealand children and matched controls from age 9 and re-evaluating them at ages 11 and 13. At the follow-ups, the depressed groups endorsed more depressive symptoms than the comparison groups. Kashani et al. also found that depression was somewhat more common and persistent in boys than girls and was associated with long-term antisocial behavior in boys.

Depression in children has been found to have affective specificity. That is, children who have been depressed were more likely to have subsequent affective disorders rather than other psychiatric disorders. On the other hand, nondepressed age-matched controls were at a relatively lower risk for future affective disorders compared to other psychiatric disorders (Harrington et al., 1991).

In a study of latency-age children, Kovacs et al. (1984b) found a cumulative 72% probability of children having a second episode of major depressive disorder within 5 years after the onset of the first episode. They were, however, at a low risk of developing other disorders, which suggests the specificity of affective disorder in this age group.

Garrison, Addy, Jackson, McKeown, and Walker (1991) conducted a 3-year longitudinal study on 550 children aged 11–12, using the Center for Epidemiologic Studies Depression Scale, in which the students rated their mood for the previous week. Current depression was a strong predictor of subsequent depression. Initially, girls endorsed higher scores than boys, and boys tended to endorse increasingly lower scores over time. These findings serve as a bridge between the higher rate of depression reported by adult females (Boyd & Weissman, 1981) and studies that show depression rates in younger children as equal for both sexes, or slightly higher for boys.

Preliminary findings from McCauley, Mitchell, Burke, and Moss (1988) shows that 61% of children and adolescents with a major depression experienced recurring episodes within 3 years. This recurrence was not associated with age, sex, family socioeconomic status, concurrent diagnosis, or dexamethasone suppression test status. However, it was associated with the severity of the initial depressive episode, endogenicity, and the patients' self-reports of depressive symptoms and hopelessness.

Zeitlin (1986) conducted a follow-back study and found 84% of the patients who had experienced a depressive disorder in childhood or adolescence developed similar episodes as adults. However, Weissman et al. (1984) noted that most depressed adults had not experienced an episode of depression in childhood. This suggests multiple etiologies and pathways to adult depressive disorders. Rutter (1986) has cautioned that the phenotypic similarities of adolescent and adult depression are no guarantee that these measurements represent intersects rather than parallel courses, and that the longitudinal courses may diverge. Therefore, symptoms may not be predictive of outcome across different age groups.

What factors are correlated with the duration, severity, and recurrence of depressive disorders? McCauley et al. (1988) used the Schedule of Affective Disorders and Schizophrenia for School-Aged Children on subjects first diagnosed at ages 8 to 16. They conducted follow-ups at 6 months and 1, 2, 3, and 6 years, and found that female sex, the severity of the index depressive episode, and family dysfunction were all positively correlated with the duration of the index episode. At the 3-year follow-up, 63% had experienced recurrence. Here, as in other adolescent studies, girls were more likely to have a recurrence and one of greater severity. The small subgroup that remained chronically depressed were all girls. As in studies conducted by Kovacs et al. (1984b), the depression diagnosis remained stable; those with the diagnosis tended to be subject only to affective disorders over time. The most common comorbid diagnoses were anxiety and conduct disorders. Bipolar outcomes were rare.

A first-episode depression in childhood is a significant risk factor for subsequent mood disorder episodes or chronic depression into adulthood (Harrington et al., 1991). Kovacs et al. (1984b) found that within 5 years of experiencing a first episode of dysthymic disorder, the cumulative probability of a child having a first episode of major depressive disorder was 69%, with 11% developing the disorder within the first year. Of children with dysthymic disorder, 38% had a major depression superimposed on it. Like adults, children with a pre-existing dysthymic disorder were at greater risk for relapse and shorter asymptomatic periods between major depressive episodes. Sex, age, duration of initial episode of depression, and presence of coexisting anxiety disorder all were not risk factors in recurrence. In comparison to the children with dysthymic disorder or major depressive disorder, children with adjustment disorder with depressed mood, as well as children in the Kovacs et al. (1984b) control group of children with nondepressed psychiatric disorders were all at minimal risk for developing major depression.

The most rigorous DSM-III based longitudinal studies to date on depressed school children (Kovacs et al., 1984a) have revealed much information in regard to the onset, duration, and recovery rate of depressive disorders. These studies found the age of onset for major depressive disorder to range from 8–14 years, and for adjustment disorder with depressed mood to range from 8–12 years. The age of onset for dysthymic disorder was wider and started younger, ranging from 6–13 years old. The average duration for the first episode for these disorders were, respectively, 25 weeks, 32 weeks, and approximately 3 years. In this group, the maximal recovery rate for adjustment disorder with depressed mood (90%) was attained at 9 months after the onset of the disorder. For major depression, the maximal recovery rate

(92%) was reached at 18 months after onset. This recovery is markedly robust, especially when contrasted to the recovery rate for adults of 64% at 2 years. The maximal recovery rate for dysthymic disorder (89%) was reached only at 6 years after onset. Earlier onset of the disorder is associated with a slower recovery from both major depression and dysthymia. It may also predict a poorer prognosis.

Depressed adolescents are fairly resilient, especially if environmental factors do not impinge. McCauley et al. (1988) showed that adolescents made significant academic and social gains between depressive episodes, suggesting that many of their impairments may be state-dependent. A more stressful family life was the strongest predictor of poorer psychological functioning at the 3-year and 6-year samplings, and of poorer school functioning at 3 years. Other predictors of later impaired functioning included later age of onset of depression, comorbid conduct disorder, and longer and more severe index depressive episode. At over 6 years from the initial episode, recurrence of depression was associated with difficulties in family and peer relationships, as well as poor self-esteem.

The extent to which environmental factors can influence long-term outcome in depression has long been understood empirically and is now being measured. Asarnow, Goldstein, Thompson, and Guthrie (1993) found a strong association in 1-year posthospitalization outcome for depressed children. Using a 5-minute speech sample to measure expressed emotion, they found that children returning to homes high in expressed emotion were likely to show persistent mood disorders. Possible mediating variables, such as clinical characteristics or treatment regimen, did not affect this predictive relationship.

Children hospitalized for depression were at significant risk for rehospitalization and to a lesser extent, placement outside the home. Asarnow et al. (1993) found that child psychiatric inpatients with diagnoses of major depressive disorder had rehospitalization rates of 35% and 45% in the first and second years after discharge. The most frequent reason for hospitalization was relapse of depressive symptoms or frank suicidal behavior. The onset of depression can have disruptive consequences in a child's life; 15% of the depressed cohort in this study were placed outside the home within the first year of discharge.

The presence of psychotic symptoms during a depressive episode has a significant effect on outcome. Strober et al. (1989) found that psychosis did not affect recovery rate from the index episode of depression. But 40% of their psychotically depressed sample (in comparison to 10% of their nonpsychotically depressed sample) become bipolar within 5 years. A more recent study (Strober, 1992) revealed that 28% of psychotically depressed adolescents switched into mania, while this was not the outcome in any of the sample who did not become psychotic.

Psychotically depressed youths who did not become bipolar were also different from the nonpsychotic cohort, in that they had a more severe disorder, a more protracted recovery, and a greater likelihood of recurrent episodes. Only those youths who were psychotic on initial presentation were psychotic on relapse. Strober et al. (1989) found that the course of adolescent depression began to approximate that of the adult disorder over time. Recovery of adolescents lagged behind adults at 8 weeks and 16 weeks, but at 28 weeks approached that of adults. Few differences were noted between psychotically depressed adolescents and adults at 6 months and 24 months. Studies by both Akiskal et al. (1983) and Strober and Carlson (1982) agreed on a trio of symptoms predicting a future outcome of bipolarity in depressives: (1) rapid onset of depressive symptoms, (2) psychomotor retardation, and (3) mood-congruent psychotic features. A family history of bipolar or other affective disorder in three successive generations was also found to be predictive of adolescent bipolarity. However, the strongest predictor of bipolarity was pharmacologically induced switching from depression into mania.

Adolescent bipolarity has a poorer long-term outcome (including higher rates of suicide) than unipolar depression. A 10-year follow-up study on 28 adolescents hospitalized for major depression (Welner, Welner, & Fishman, 1979) revealed eventual completed suicide in 3 of 12 bipolar patients, with the other bipolar patients making poor overall social and vocational adjustments. On the other hand, of 16 unipolar depressives, 5 had only a single episode and fully recovered, whereas 11 went on to have episodic courses. One retrospective study on the offspring of bipolar patients gives insight into the course in cyclothymia (Klein, Depue, & Slater, 1985). The average age of onset for cyclothymia is 12.4 years. The initial hypomanic and depressive episodes developed within 1 year of each other. Eight percent of the patients with cyclothymia had no more than 12 episodes per year; the rest had fewer than 6 episodes.

Conduct disorder is a factor in the natural history of childhood depression, being found in up to 37% of depressed youths (Kovacs et al., (1984b). The conduct disorder typically develops during the depressive episode and persists after the depressive symptoms remit. The presence of conduct disorder did not alter the presentation of depressive symptoms, but did affect long-term outcome. Harrington et al. (1991), in looking at adult outcomes, found that 21% of their sample with comorbid diagnoses of a depressive disorder and conduct disorder had a poorer short-term outcome and a higher rate of criminality as adults (when compared to those with depressive disorders alone). The additional finding that depressives with conduct disorder had a lower risk for adult depressive episodes than depressives without conduct disorder suggests that these patients represent a subgroup with conduct disorder and antisocial behavior as their primary diagnosis.

Kovacs et al. (1984b) found comorbid anxiety disorders in 41% of patients with index depressive episodes, and fewer in those patients with adjustment disorder with depressed mood rather than major depression or dysthymic disorder. The two most frequent comorbid diagnoses were separation anxiety and overanxious disorder of childhood, in that order. In two-thirds of the comorbid cases, the anxiety disorder preceded the depression and also often persisted after the depression remitted. Anxiety disorders did not appear to affect the risk of subsequent depressive disorders or the course of the index episode.

Childhood depression has long-range effects in all spheres of functioning. Puig-Antich et al. (1985a, 1985b) compared the psychological functioning of children with major depressive disorder, children with nondepressive psychiatric disorder, and children with no psychiatric diagnosis. He found impairments in academic performance, teacher–child relationship, and peer relationships for both major depressive and other psychiatric disorders, with the impairment being worse for children with major depressive disorders. A follow-up study (Garber, Kriss, Koch, & Lindholm, 1988) that tracked adolescents with a history of depressive disorder found that they retained greater impairment relative to nondepressed psychiatric controls, with the impairment extended to family, marital, and social relationships, but not to occupational and overall adjustment.

Suicidality, an important aspect of natural history of depression, is addressed fully in a separate section.

According to a recent study by Burke et al. (1989), depression as a clinical phenomenon is on the rise overall, and the age of onset of first depressive episode is lowering. This study confirmed the earlier findings of Klerman (1976) and Klerman and Weissman (1989), who found indications that depression was increasing in prevalence over different age groups, and predicted a forthcoming "Age of Melancholy" using data from the NIMH Epidemiologic Catchment Area Program. Burke, Burke, Rae, and Reiger (1991) identified a gradual, continuing shift to increased rates of major depression in the most recent 15- to 19-year-old cohort (born 1953–1966). They also found a shift to a younger age of onset of illness and a similar shift to increased drug abuse and dependence. For alcohol abuse and dependence, there was no parallel shift downward in peak age of onset; however, there was an increase in the measured magnitude and predominance of the hazard rate. No similar increase in onset was noted for bipolar disorder, panic disorder, or phobias, demonstrating that this trend pertains specifically to depressive disorders and drug abuse, not to overall psychopathology.

DIAGNOSIS

Children and adolescents are diagnosed according to the same DSM-IV criteria as adults, with minor concessions for age-adjusted symptom presentation. For example, children may appear irritable rather than depressed, and may fail to gain weight rather than lose weight (the reasoning here is that weight loss is unlikely unless a child is ill, deprived of food, or significantly overweight). DSM-IV is similar to DSM-III-R in philosophy and overall criteria, with no separate categories for mood disorders first presenting in childhood. One new emphasis is that diagnoses are now required to reflect clinical relevance and reflect discernible distress or impairment in one of the major realms of functioning. DSM-III was the first revision to include alternate developmental criteria for the depressive disorders, and this act of inclusion helped set the stage for research confirming that depression

similar to that found in adults was also affecting children and adolescents. However, the importance of developmentally different presentations has not been given the same emphasis as has been given to those conditions contained in the category "disorders usually first diagnosed in infancy, childhood, or adolescence."

The difficulty in using largely adult criteria to diagnose children and adolescents is exemplified by the problems in diagnosing mood disorders with seasonal pattern in these age groups. In children, autumnal patterns of depression are confounded by the recurring stressor of starting school each fall, as well as other environmental discontinuities such as relocating. Moreover, in DSM-IV, individuals with a seasonal pattern mood disorder must demonstrate the same timing of major depressive episode symptom presentation and remission in the last 2 years. This is harder to establish in children, in whom there is less basis for comparison; the diagnosis may be further complicated by concurrent pubertal developmental and hormonal growth spurt.

In DSM-IV, the subtyping of the diagnosis of dysthymic disorder into primary and secondary types has been eliminated, as the division, only instituted in DSM-III-R, has not been found to be a clinically useful distinction. The diagnosis of dysthymia in children and adolescents differs minimally from this diagnosis in adults. As with major depressive episode, irritability can replace depressed mood as one of the fundamental criteria, and this need be present for only 1 year in contrast to the 2 years for adults. Dysthymia commonly originates in childhood and in the past has been conceptualized as "depressive personality" or "neurotic depression." In children and adolescents with dysthymia, a major depressive disorder can develop subsequently (a "double depression"); it is therefore very important for clinicians to look carefully at the full history of symptom presentation to see whether this is the case. The prognosis is worse for children with both disorders.

To make a clear diagnosis of depression in children or adolescents, it is best to utilize patient history from a number of sources. Patients generally give the clearest account of their own internal state, but parents can generally give the best temporal account of depressive symptoms over time, and are more likely to be able to give a description of various behavioral changes over time. Teachers can be a good source of information about children's ability to function academically and about their relationship with peers. Depressive symptoms need to be considered from the viewpoint of children's daily activities. Oppositionality in a previously well-behaved child can be considered a symptom correlate of irritability; a sudden drop in grades may reflect a diminished interest in activities or a child's diminished ability to think clearly; and a tendency to stay home could be a child's expression of loss of energy or diminished interest in activities. The clinician must actively explore these behaviors with the child or adolescent in order to understand their meaning and to decide whether they fit as depressive criteria.

Since children (and, to a lesser extent, adolescents) have a smaller range of behaviors than adults, symptoms tend to overlap more for disorders presenting in these age groups. In making the diagnosis of childhood depression, it is essential that the contextual and interactive nature of the symptoms is appreciated. For example, a child with mental retardation or other developmental delay may show a marked disinterest in activities and a diminished ability to think or concentrate; these symptoms, however, may be part of a primary psychiatric disorder. Other symptomatic evidence would be needed for the additional diagnosis of a depressive disorder. Understanding individual symptoms can sometimes be quite difficult. For example, a child's picking fights with peers could be an indication of irritability, and could be seen as a depressive symptom, but this could as easily be a symptom of attention-deficit/hyperactivity disorder. Knowing the historical context may allow differentiation: It would be more likely that this fighting was symptomatic of depression if the child had gotten along well with others until recently, and had no previous history of fighting.

A number of disorders may predispose to the development of depression, presumably because of the psychological stress of the primary psychiatric disorder. These include posttraumatic stress disorder, learning disorders, mental retardation, attention-deficit/hyperactivity disorder, obsessive–compulsive disorder, and motor and vocal tics (Anderson et al., 1987). Other disorders may exist comorbidly with depression, such as anxiety disorders, in which the etiological interface may be secondary to similar biological underpinnings. In diagnosing children, it is vital not to dismiss comorbid diagnoses. Finding that a child fits one diagnostic category should suggest further inquiry into hidden symptoms of depression. For example, depression in youths with conduct disorder may go unattended because the patients are less likely to confide their symptoms truthfully to a clinician, and may be in denial as to the extent of their own depressive ideation.

Clinician threshold is an important problem to note in current diagnostic practice. Some clinicians, reluctant to "label" a child with depression, will diagnose an adjustment disorder with depressed mood, but then will not revise the diagnosis after 6 months. Alternately, children seen at community mental health centers are sometimes diagnosed as dysthymic, even though a full complement of criteria for a major depressive episode may be present. Behind this diagnosis may be a belief that the supposedly milder condition can be more comfortably treated, with less intensive services and less medical management. It is vital that clinicians diagnose children and adolescents as accurately as possible. Unless this occurs, children may be undertreated and their symptoms may only become more fixed over time, making treatment more palliative than curative.

Finally, symptoms' presentation needs to be placed in the developmental continuum. Carlson and Kashani (1988) have shown that for children meeting core DSM criteria for depression, some symptoms present with stable frequency across childhood and adolescence (suicidal ideation, depressed mood, decreased concentration, and insomnia). In contrast, some symptoms are more prevalent in younger depressed children (including low self-esteem, somatic complaints, and a depressed appearance). Symptoms that are more prevalent in older children and adolescents include anhedonia, diurnal variation, hopelessness, psychomotor retardation, and delusions. While this detailed breakdown of symptoms goes beyond current DSM categorization, it suggests that in the future, developmentally geared refinements of diagnosis will be possible, allowing for more accurate diagnosis of a greater spectrum of depressive disorders in childhood and adolescence.

DEVELOPMENTAL ASPECTS

Depressive disorders can occur at any point in the lifespan. The belief in continuity of depression across the lifespan is reflected in DSM-IV through the directive to apply a single set of criteria to children, adolescents, and adults. Developmental concerns are acknowledged, in that diagnosticians are permitted to make certain substitutions when establishing a diagnosis of depression. For example, in children, irritable mood is weighted as equivalent to an adult's depressed mood. Similarly, the failure of a child to attain an expected weight gain is considered equivalent to the adult symptom of weight loss.

While this approach answers some questions, it raises many others. When is a symptom an appropriate equivalent? Do equivalent symptoms cluster to form different developmentally based symptom profiles? What changes—neurological, hormonal, cognitive, and social—are associated with developmentally based criteria?

Shafii and Shafii (1992) have proposed a comprehensive examination of the developmental psychopathology of depression and its manifestations. Their analysis of depressive symptoms in children considers two kinds of pathological deviation from the norm. The first is "transformation," in which developmental progress can be seen as derailed and now proceeding on a deviated course; the symptoms seen in this case are clearly distortions and disruptions of normal development. The second deviation from normal development is "regression," in which the child no longer has access to previously acquired skills or functions; this response is similar to the depressive withdrawal seen in deprived or disappointed infants. Shafii and Shafii (1992) propose that this disengagement and down-modulation of responsiveness (a reversion to an earlier state) is a protective measure designed to "facilitate the conservation of energy and resources" (p. 4). The severity of the disorder can therefore be understood by gauging the depth of regression or delay, as well as the extent and speed of recovery.

Shafii and Shafii (1992) examined depression and depressivelike behavior in five age groups. They synthesized the findings of a range of clinicians to arrive at sets of developmental criteria.

First Year of Life

Spitz (1965) labeled as "anaclitic depression" the responses he saw in infants who were separated from their mothers between 6 and 8 months of age. He observed weepy and withdrawn behavior, which persisted for 2–3 months, and was then replaced by a frozen, rigid expression, weight loss instead of gain, increased incidence of colds and infection, insomnia, and in some cases, intellectual and psychological retardation.

Infants could sustain temporary maternal deprivation through a critical period of 3–5 months and, if then returned to a nurturing environment, could go on to overcome most of the delays and losses of function. However, if the deprivation persisted beyond 5 months, these children showed sustained deterioration in growth, development, expressiveness, and overall level of activity. This clinical picture was similar to a syndrome that Spitz observed in children who had been separated from their mothers at infancy and institutionalized, then subsequently deprived of adequate stimulation and nurturance. In this condition, which Spitz (1965) termed "hospitalism," these children showed motor retardation, poor eye contact, lack of facial expression, spasticity that persisted even after physical rehabilitation, and pervasive passivity. These children had a decreased resistance to disease, and developed wasting syndromes even in the face of adequate nutrition and medical attention. By the end of the first year, almost 30% had died; by the end of the second year, the survivors were functioning on average in the moderately to severely retarded range.

Failure to thrive can also be an example of an infant's response to severe environmental stressors. In about half of all diagnosed cases of failure to thrive, growth failure is secondary to a chronic infection, major-organ system dysfunction, or serious malnutrition. For the rest, however, the infants' failures are in response to a pathological environment of abuse and neglect. Weight is more affected than height, and the infants typically make significant gains once they are removed from the toxic environment.

"Failure to thrive" is defined by a failure to achieve specific developmental goals, including (1) visual tracking of eyes and a social smile by age 2 months; (2) orienting to verbal communication, spontaneous reaching to caretaker, and vocal reciprocity at 4 months; and (3) playing give-and-take games and exhibiting anticipatory response for being picked up at 5 months. These characteristics all involve active, self-motivated interactions with the environment and reflect a high degree of entrained awareness, as well as an increased expectation that is compatible with a consistent and nutritive environment. Children with failure to thrive are intellectually and motorically apathetic. They appear emotionally flat and lifeless, an advanced and deteriorated condition that is beyond dysphoria. As Shafii and Shafii (1992) note, "Evidence of sadness or depression, instead of overwhelming apathy, indicates that the infant is still experiencing and communicating internal feeling. This is a favorable sign" (p. 17).

Depressive symptoms in infants can be seen on a continuum. The less severe forms, such as brief anaclitic depression, can be seen as analogues to adjustment disorders. More pervasive or enduring conditions, such as hospitalism and failure to thrive, may have their corollary in life-threatening, adult major depression.

Ages 1–3

The age-specific clinical features seen in depressed 1- to 3-year-olds are on a continuum with the patterns observed in depressed newborns. All domains of function can show delays, regression, or deviance—including toileting, sleeping, eating, and intellectual growth. Problems can include delayed control of toileting, fecal smearing, loss of self-feeding skills, poor appetite or eating deviance (e.g., pica or coprophagy), excessive sleepiness (or, more rarely, insomnia), and increased nightmares and night terrors. The child may appear sad or expressionless, or avert his/her gaze. Injurious self-stimulating behavior can emerge, including head banging, self-biting, and excessive rocking.

The child may also be more clingy or may sink into chronic apathy. This falling progression from negativism to resignation parallels the protest–despair–detachment cycle observed with institutionalized toddlers (Bowlby, 1980) and is rarely observed in children less than 6 months or older than 4 years of age.

Psychoanalytic theory posits that the failure to accomplish specific integrative tasks leads to psychopathology. In a developmental context, a young child subject to a traumatic environment who is withdrawn and regressed will fail to fully internalize the maternal imago. From this failure, the child's capacity for empathy and object constancy is then impaired. The child reacts to these losses with a pathological mourning that bears a resemblance to the chronic, unresolved mourning of adults (Bibring, 1965; Bowlby, 1960; Freud, 1917/1957). Shafii and Shafii (1992) suggest that possible long-term outcome could include narcissistic and borderline personality disorders, alcohol and drug abuse, psychophysiological disorders, and psychosis, as well as major depression.

Ages 3–5

Shafii and Shafii (1992) identified symptoms that represent not only extensions upward of earlier phenomena but also the branching down of some adult symptoms. Motorically, there may be loss of interest in newly acquired skills, such as bike riding. Enuresis or encopresis may develop. The child may lose pleasure in eating or develop food refusal behavior, leading to anorexia or gorging. Nightmares with themes of annihilation are frequent, but dreams may also be of denial, such as a life without worries. There may be loss of intellectual and language skills, as well as social withdrawal. Often the child may believe that no one likes him/her. The child may show excessive anxiety and fear of separation from his/her mother, may complain of headaches or stomachaches, and may have thoughts or impulses to self-harm (such as jumping out a window or in front of a car).

Ages 6–12

The school-age child has more in common with the adult's symptom presentation. Poznanski (1982) found that depressed mood was the most prominent symptom in the clinical diagnosis of depression of the school-age child. Often, this is the only obvious sign and the depression is not reflected in the child's play or behavior.

Depressed school-age children may develop a number of academically related symptoms, including decline in performance, loss of motivation, fear of failure, and disruptive classroom behaviors (e.g., clowning, challenges to authority, and outright aggression). The disruptiveness can mimic the hyperactivity of attention-deficit/hyperactivity disorder. However, when these disorders are not comorbid, the hyperactivity of depression is accompanied by a dysphoric mood.

Consistent with the cognitive advances and the development of the open ego, depressed school-age children can also exhibit severe self-criticism and guilt.

As do younger children, depressed children in this age group also show eating and sleep disturbances, speech and language delays, suicidal ideation and plans. These children also spend less time with peers, but when they do play, their interactions are more negative and aggressive than those of younger children.

Adolescence

Depressed adolescents typically have school problems, including a falling off in academic performance, truancy, or dropping out. These adolescents can be increasingly argumentative and assaultive. The development of abstract thinking may also be slowed, and the onset of puberty may be delayed. Depressed adolescents may experience intense and precipitous mood swings. They can exhibit a wide range of risk-taking or antisocial behavior, including drug use, vandalism, frequent automobile accidents and traffic violations, and unsafe sexual practices. Self-esteem may be very low or fragile. Eating can be erratic; weight can fluctuate, and anorexia or bulimia may emerge.

The onset of puberty, rather than adolescence, may represent the significant developmental division in symptom presentation. Ryan et al. (1987) compared children and adolescents who met RDC criteria for major depressive disorder. There was a significant distribution in symptoms. Prepubertal children were more likely to exhibit agitation, somatic complaints, and hallucinations. On the other hand, postpubertal children were more likely to exhibit anhedonia, hopelessness, weight fluctuation, suicide attempts of greater lethality than those of prepubertal children, and hypersomnia. Kovacs and Gatsonis (1989) found that hypersomnia was the only symptom preferentially experienced by postpubertal adolescents, and at a prevalence seven times greater than that of the other mentioned symptoms.

Puberty has a strong impact on the prevalence of depression. A general survey of children aged 10–11 on the Isle of Wight showed depressed mood in 13% at the time of interviews (Rutter, Tizard, & Whitemore, 1970). When these same children were reassessed 4 years later, 40% reported depressive feelings (Rutter, 1979). Furthermore, within the 14- to 15-year-old group of this study, the prepubertal subgroup showed a 10% prevalence of depressive symptoms. By comparison, there was approximately a 20% prevalence of depression in the pubertal group. In the postpubertal group, this prevalence had risen to approximately 33% (Rutter, 1980).

There is also a sex ratio shift in prevalence of depression across puberty. Studies of clinical and nonclinical populations of children aged 6–12 have found the prevalence of depressive disorders in boys and girls to be equal (Lubovits & Handel,

1985). After puberty, girls are twice as likely as boys to exhibit depression (Reynolds, 1985).

Continuity over Course of Development

Carlson and Kashani (1988) compared four age group cohorts (preschoolers, prepubertal children, adolescents, and adults) in whom all the core features for depression were fulfilled. They evaluated the associated features and found that some symptoms (depressed mood, decreased concentration, insomnia, and suicidal ideation) presented with equal frequency in all four age groups. The following symptoms increased in frequency across all age groups: anhedonia, hopelessness, worsening of symptoms in the morning, psychomotor retardation, and delusions. However, they also found that some symptoms decreased in frequency across the four age groups (depressed appearance, low self-esteem, somatic complaints, and hallucinations). These intersecting trends raise the question of one diagnostic picture's fading out as the child progresses developmentally, and another, more adultlike presentation emerging simultaneously.

There is much evidence for the continuity of depressive disorders. Milder presentations in childhood may represent prodromes of major disorders. Kovacs and Gatsonis (1989) found that two-thirds of a sample of children with dysthymic states developed a major depressive disorder over the next 5 years. Other studies (e.g., Poznanski, 1982) have found that childhood depression is continuous with the adult disorder and that these children are at higher risk for hospitalization and psychotropic drug use, and are three times more likely to make suicide attempts (Harrington et al., 1991).

SUICIDE

Suicide of youths is now a nationally recognized concern. Pfeffer (1986) and Brent, Perper, and Allman (1983) have documented an alarming increase in suicide beginning in the 1960s. Suicide is now the second leading cause of death in adolescents in the United States (Centers for Disease Control, 1986; Shaffer & Fisher, 1981), accounting for 12% of adolescent and young adult mortality, with 1,372 deaths in adolescents aged 13–19 years in 1988 alone. Some researchers have speculated that the overall increase in suicide rate may simply be due to better awareness and reporting, as explained in the Hoberman and Garfinkel (1988) study showing that 26% of coroners' reports attributed suicides to other causes in 1975–1980, compared to only 5% in 1980–1985. However, other studies have shown a two- to threefold increase in adolescent suicide over the past 10 years (Brent et al., 1983; Pfeffer, 1986). It is estimated that approximately 9% of adolescents attempt suicide at least once, whereas only 1% of preadolescents attempt suicide (Pfeffer, Lipkins, Plutchik, & Mizruchi, 1988). Completed suicide is still very rare in prepubertal children—less than 1 per 100,000 for 5- to 14-year-olds (National Center for Health Statistics, 1988)—but it also has been increasing. While rates of suicide and suicide attempt differ between children and adolescents, several similarities exist. The first step in evaluating a potentially suicidal child or adolescent is to carefully identify the patient's history of suicide attempts and gestures, and fully delineate suicidal ideation, both past and present. Suicidal ideation, gestures, and attempts all play an important role in the evaluation of suicide risk. According to Pfeffer, Solomon, Plutchik, Mizruchi, and Weiner (1982), suicide is a continuum from nonsuicidal behavior to suicide. Cantwell and Carlson (1983), however, do not believe that there is such a continuum; they contend that many children and adolescents who are unlikely to attempt suicide have transient suicidal ideation.

Close attention must be paid to determine the child's intent. A child may not believe that taking a potentially lethal overdose of Tylenol is serious (because it is seen as a common and benign drug), but may believe that he/she will die from taking a few prescription pills. In this scenario, the child who overdoses on Tylenol may end up on a medical ward with severe liver injury but has only made a suicide gesture, whereas the child who believed he/she would die from the prescription medicine has made a serious suicide attempt for which psychiatric hospitalization should be considered. It is also important to explore previous accidents, since they may have been suicide attempts/gestures that were never uncovered. These suicide attempts must be taken seriously, because they can be important predictors of future attempts and completion. Seventy-five percent of completed adolescent suicides happened after previous attempts.

Suicidal behavior comes to medical attention only rarely—12% of the time, according to Smith and Crawford (1986). However, patients have frequently visited a health professional in the 6 months prior to their attempt. It would therefore be valuable for the clinician to be able to identify individuals at risk; knowing risk factors can be helpful in this identification. Males complete suicide attempts more frequently than females, but females attempt suicide more often than males. In the United States, a general picture of a patient at risk for suicide is an older adolescent white male, with a past history of suicide attempts, a family history of suicide or suicide attempts, affective disorder, and/or antisocial personality disorder, who is currently depressed and hopeless. While whites have greater suicide rates than blacks, and males have greater rates than females, sex differences are less marked in Hispanic teens and somewhat less marked in blacks. In other countries, such as India and Southeast Asia, the majority of those who commit suicide are female.

Factors that consistently have been found to increase risk of suicide are psychopathology (especially depressive symptomatology), perceived family stress, lack of family support, and age. The age of the youth is important, because children and adolescents are undergoing not only physical maturation, but also cognitive maturation. Their ability to understand and communicate is not as well developed, and therefore their ability to understand death and their ability to complete suicide are affected by their level of cognitive development. Suicide attempts tend to be more impulsive in adolescents, more of a "cry for help," whereas the elderly have more clear and sustained attempts. However, children may be more at risk for suicide because their social supports are often defined in terms of their family, and they may have little ability to change their environment to improve their support system, whereas adults may have a wider support system that is more amenable to change. Because symptoms of depression may present in children much differently than in adults, children's depression may go unrecognized or may be attributed to other difficulties until it is too late. Relatives, family members, and even professionals frequently discount a child's talk of death, whereas suicidality in adults is rarely questioned. Substance abuse and conduct disorder are diagnoses closely linked to suicide as well (Brent et al., 1987, 1988). The presence of firearms in the home is a significant factor in suicide completion versus attempt (Brent et al., 1991).

General risk factors and immediate precipitants to suicide, and their relation to disease (especially depression and other psychiatric disorders), are essential to understand in order to decrease the morbidity and mortality from suicide in children and adolescents. Several studies have looked at psychiatric diagnoses in relation to suicidality. Not surprisingly, depressive symptomatology is closely correlated to suicidal ideation (Brent et al., 1988; Pfeffer et al., 1991; Shafii, Steltz-Lenarsky, Derrick, Beckner, & Whittinghill, 1988). Asarnow (1992) and Asarnow and Carlson (1985) found more depressive symptoms in child psychiatric inpatients who had made suicide attempts than in nonattempters, although criteria for depressive disorder were not always met. Suicide attempts occur more frequently when antisocial symptomatology is present as well (Brent et al., 1988; Shaffer, 1974, 1988). Of particular significance is the poor outcome of bipolar patients or those with symptoms of psychosis, as described by Welner et al. (1979). Rosenthal, Rosenthal, Doherty, and Santora (1986) studied nine psychiatrically hospitalized suicidal children, ages 2½ to 5 years old. Their diagnoses were either anxiety or conduct disorder, but these children did not meet diagnosis of depression. Interestingly, the only physical illness that has been clearly associated with suicidal behavior is epilepsy. This may be due in part to the use of phenobarbital as an anticonvulsant (Brent, Crumrine, Varma, Allan, & Allman, 1987).

In a study of 55 children aged 6–13 years who were hospitalized on a psychiatric ward, Asarnow and Guthrie (1989) found suicidal ideation significantly associated with hopelessness but not depression, whereas suicide attempts were significantly associated with both helplessness and a diagnosis of depression. They also found the highest rates of depressive disorder in children who had made multiple suicide attempts. Asarnow (1992) found that children who attempt suicide describe their families as less cohesive and expressing higher degrees of conflict. Gispert, Davis, Marsh, and Wheeler (1987) found that knowledge of the internal state of adolescents, as evidenced by intent, anger, and dysphoria, was more predictive of future attempts than the more easily measurable external factors of school, life stress, demographics, or nature of attempt. Whereas negative cognitive styles (e.g., hopelessness, worthlessness) are associated with depression in children who are psychiatric inpatients, preadolescent child psychiatric inpatient attempters

versus nonattempters can be predicted with an 88% accuracy rate by perception of low family support alone. Measures of depression/hopelessness provide no further increments in clinical accuracy. Patients should be identified as to internal state as evidenced by hopelessness, as well as their external supports. It should be noted that both these aspects may be closely associated with children who are not accepted by peers at school. These children are typically more angry and may have comorbid depression and conduct disorder. Other factors that can alert the clinician to suicide risk are poor social adjustment, including school failure or dropout (analogous to loss of work in adults), legal problems, and social isolation.

Factors that may mediate when a patient attempts suicide, or that are indicators of an impending suicide, include (1) media/exposure events; (2) insults to the person; and (3) isolative behavior, especially in the presence of alcohol. "Cluster" suicides have been researched over the past 10 years. A study of risk factors in two teenage suicide clusters by Davidson, Rosenberg, Mercy, Franklin, and Simmons (1989) found that identification of long-term problems, such as violence (antisocial personality disorder) or a deterioration of schoolwork or social activities, did not differentiate cases from controls in cluster events. They did find that when teens say last good-byes, are involved in interpersonal violence, and have experience with previous suicide attempts or self-destructive activities, they may be at greater risk for imitating an earlier suicide in the cluster. Research by Ostroff and Boyd (1987) showed an increase in overdose attempts after a television show that highlighted a teenager's death by overdose, with a total of 14 cases in a 2-week period, compared to the normal number of 1.9 per month for that population. Phillips and Carstensen (1987) summarized a series of studies showing that suicide in single-car crashes increased after publicized suicide stories. Interestingly, this increase was proportional to the amount of publicity given a story, and the increases occurred primarily in the geographic area in which each story was publicized. A driver in a single-car crash often bore unusual similarity to the person depicted in a suicide story. Fights with friends (especially girlfriend/boyfriend) and/or family members have been shown to correlate significantly with overdose attempts. A situation unique to females is that there is an increase in suicide attempts with the discovery of pregnancy (Appleby, 1991). Gould, Shaffer, and Kleinman

(1988) suggested that acute disciplinary action, rejection, or humiliation may result in a brief "stress–suicide interval" in which many teenagers commit suicide.

Suicide completers are more likely to use means that have a higher probability of lethality (e.g., hanging or firearms) than suicide attempters, but the seriousness of an attempt must be determined from the psychological view of patients at their cognitive level, as discussed earlier. Another ominous sign that cannot be overemphasized is the last good-bye. Many completers make such statements 24 hours to 7 days prior to suicide. Since most suicides occur in isolation and are often at home (Brent et al., 1983), any attempts by persons to avoid contact should raise suspicions. Firearms, either locked away or accessible, are more readily available in the home of completers as compared to attempters. Of completers, 20% to 30% are intoxicated with either alcohol, drugs, or both. Illicit substance abuse should be carefully monitored and stopped when possible, because these substances lead to disinhibition and may be a significant contributing factor to completed suicide. Particular attention needs to be given to attempters who have the potentially lethal triad of psychopathology, impulsivity, and easily obtained lethal instruments, because these are the children/adolescents more likely to eventually complete suicide (Otto, 1972).

Many questions remain unanswered in the study of suicide by youths. Few studies have looked carefully at preadolescents, since the population of suicides in this group is small, and suicidal ideation and gestures often go undetected. The role that suicidal ideation may play in school violence today has only begun to be explored. Careful studies examining issues of ethnicity and socioeconomic differences may help in the understanding of their role in the loss of so many adolescents to suicide.

TREATMENT

There are many different treatment approaches used for children and adolescents with depressive disorders, based on a combination of anecdotal evidence, clinical observation, and extrapolation from the adult literature. Despite a significant growth in research in this area, particularly in the past 10 years, the literature on children and adolescents is still sparse, especially regarding psychotherapeutic and psychosocial treatment approaches. Most authors in

the field, however, stress the need for multimodal interventional strategies, based on information from a careful and comprehensive evaluation (Cantwell, 1982; Kashani et al., 1981a).

Psychosocial and Psychodynamic Therapies

Among the psychosocial and psychotherapeutic approaches to treatment, individual dynamic therapy is probably the most frequently used approach. Psychodynamic theorists have emphasized the importance of object loss, loss of self-esteem, and deficient, critical internal self-representations in the etiology of depression (Bemporad, 1988; Cohen, 1980). Clinical experience supports the importance of these issues in understanding childhood depression (McCracken, 1992). The psychodynamic model of treatment, while attempting to provide symptom relief, also seeks to rectify underlying deficits in personality organization, reducing more primitive defense mechanisms and allowing a resumption of normative emotional development. Implicit in this model is the expectation that these gains should serve as a buffer against relapse of depressive symptoms. There is considerable treatment variation, because treatment goals are not generally explicit and length of treatment is seldom predetermined. Method of treatment also varies according to the child's age and maturity. With latency-age or younger children, psychotherapy is usually play-focused, with fantasy play used by imaginative, bright, or insightful children, and more structured games used by children who want or need a more structured situation in which to work. Therapy gradually may shift to more discussion as the child becomes older or more cognitively mature, and talk usually subsumes play by midadolescence. Because of the wide variety of methods used and the less directive technique utilized in psychotherapy, there has been little research into the efficacy of psychodynamic therapy in the treatment of child and adolescent depression outside of case reports (Bemporad, 1982, 1988; Kestenbaum & Kron, 1987).

In cognitive therapy (e.g., as outlined by Beck, Rush, Shaw, & Emery, 1979) for adults, depression is considered to be a consequence of irrational or error-prone cognition. Therapy is aimed at systematic exploration and correction of these patterns. The form of cognitive therapy most utilized with depressed adults is the cognitive–behavioral therapy (CBT) of Beck, Hollon, Young, Bedrosian, and Budenz

(1985)—a short-term (15–20 sessions) didactic treatment modality that examines typical cognitive errors seen in depression, with a goal toward reduction in dysfunctional attitudes and negative views about oneself and the world. Modifications of CBT have been suggested (Wilkes & Rush, 1988) for use with adolescents, stressing greater attention on the maintenance of the therapeutic alliance, awareness of nonverbal communication, and appreciation of dichotomous thinking. The need for conjoint therapy with parents and family members, and the importance of their ideas and beliefs in maintaining the patient's attitudes, is also stressed. Lewinsohn, Clarke, Hops, and Andrews (1990) used an adaptation of CBT (the Coping with Depression Course), originally designed for adults in a research study involving depressed adolescents. Results were encouraging, with significant improvement on depression measures, and maintenance of gains at 2 years posttreatment. Lack of an adequate control group, however, limits the extent of conclusions that can be drawn from this study, as does the initial exclusion of patients having comorbid disorders.

Another cognitive therapy approach, the self-control method of therapy for depression (Rehm, 1977), has been modified for children (Stark, Reynolds, & Kaslow, 1987). This therapy is based on the theory that the depressed person preferentially attends to negative events, possesses unattained expectations, and is more likely to be self-punishing than self-rewarding. Therefore, the therapy focuses on the areas of cognitive retraining, aiming toward improvements in patients' ability to monitor, evaluate, and provide positive reinforcement for themselves. Stark, Reynolds, and Kaslow (1987) have studied the efficacy of this model in a 12-session group course combining cognitive and behavioral elements, and found clear evidence of improvement for both self-control and behavioral problem-solving treatment groups on measures of depressive symptoms, when compared to waiting-listed controls.

A third general approach in the treatment of depression utilizes behavioral techniques to help the patients change their relationship to the environment. Two methods of behavioral therapy have been used in treating adult depression: social learning and operant conditioning. The first of these has also been used with depressed children. Operant conditioning has not been formally studied as a way to reduce depressive symptomatology, but often is used in conjunction with other methods to alter certain prob-

lematic behaviors. In treatment of depressive symptomatology, the social learning approach focuses on improving social skills in order to increase positive reinforcement from the environment, and includes role playing, social problem solving, mutual storytelling, and social behavior reshaping. In the study by Stark et al. (1987), previously discussed, behavior problem solving (BPS) was noted to be the most efficacious of the treatments utilized (vs. self-control and waiting list). This, however, may have more to do with the utility of increased interaction between clinician and subject in the BPS therapeutic approach versus the self-control treatment, rather than the validity of the underlying theoretical concepts driving each treatment approach.

Other important forms of treatment generally serve as adjuncts to individual therapy with the child or adolescent. Foremost among these are parent therapy (or training) and family therapy. A good therapeutic alliance with the family is essential to create a firm alliance with the patient, assure compliance with treatment, and extend the scope of therapy into the home situation. Successful treatment of childhood and adolescent depression can seldom work with individual therapy alone; the patient is part of a complex social system that has adapted to, and may be actively contributing to, his/her depressive symptoms. This is especially true for children and adolescents, who are dependent upon adult caretakers and are often placed in stressful roles in which they see themselves as powerless to change.

Parent training utilizes cognitive and behavioral techniques in order to help parents work with their child in a way that allows them to see their child in a more positive light. It aids in their more effective problem solving when confronted with problematic behavior, using positive reinforcement and other techniques. For example, Lewinsohn et al. (1990), in the earlier-cited study of CBT, noted a strong trend favoring treatment that included a form of parent education in conjunction with the adolescent's treatment, over adolescent-only treatment.

Family therapy is often a necessary adjunct to individual therapy, both because of impairments in parent–child relationships in children with major depression (McCracken, 1992) and the higher incidence of psychopathology (especially depression) and nonspecific family problems (high expressed emotion, etc.) that may be found in these families (Schwartz et al., 1990). In spite of the importance of the role of the family in the treatment of the depressed child or adolescent, there has been little mentioned in the research literature explaining this.

Pharmacotherapy

Antidepressant medications are the mainstay of treatment of depression in adults, with approximately 65–75% of adult depressives responsive to antidepressant medication. In the treatment of children, however, the response rate is significantly lower, with an average rate of 51% for children and adolescents treated with active medication versus 38% receiving placebo (Alessi, 1991; Ambrosini, 1987; Geller, Cooper, McCombs, Graham, & Wells, 1989; Puig-Antich et al., 1987). Many reasons for this lower response rate have been suggested: that children with major depression may differ from adults in the underlying pathophysiology of depression; that earlier-onset depression may be a more severe, treatment-resistant form of depression; that higher rates of comorbidity may interfere with compliance or responsivity; or that environmental or dynamic factors may diminish the effectiveness of medications. The high rates of bipolar outcome in children and adolescents with depressive disorders, particularly those with psychotic symptoms, may also be a factor reflected in the pharmacological resistance of this group.

Despite these lower response rates, a number of studies have consistently shown that treatment with imipramine or amitriptyline is effective in decreasing depressive symptoms in prepubertal children (Weller & Weller, 1986), although few of these studies have been placebo-controlled and double-blind. In such a study by Puig-Antich et al. (1987), imipramine and placebo control groups showed similar response rates. When the medication group was separated into two groups, however, based on their median plasma level of imipramine plus desipramine, children with higher combined levels (> 150 ng/ml) had a 100% responsiveness to treatment, whereas children with lower levels showed only a 33% responsiveness. These results strongly suggest that a minimum steady-state plasma medication level is necessary in order for pharmacotherapy with tricyclics to be effective. It has not been ascertained if there is an optimum therapeutic blood level for imipramine, but a combined imipramine plus desipramine steady-state level should fall approximately between 150–300 ng/ml, because toxic confusional states have been associated with blood level above 450 ng/ml (Preskorn, Weller, Hughes, & Weller, 1988). Frequent blood level monitoring of children treated with imipramine or desipramine is advisable, especially in the initial course of treatment, since steady-state plasma levels can vary greatly between children receiving the same dosage of imipramine.

Similar studies with adolescents, however, do not show the same above-threshold plasma level responsiveness to treatment with imipramine that was shown in prepubertal children. Ryan et al. (1986) treated 34 depressed adolescents with imipramine for a 6-week period. Only 44% showed a medication response, and, importantly, patients having higher medication plasma levels did not show any greater symptom reduction. In explaining this difference in adolescent response from both depressed prepubertal and adult subjects, Ryan et al. (1986) suggested that sex hormone changes during adolescence may interfere with imipramine's antidepressant effects.

Possible predictors of positive or negative response to imipramine have been examined in a number of studies. One possible predictor of a positive response may be an abnormal dexamethasone suppression test (Preskorn, Weller, Hughes, Weller, & Bolte, 1987; Robbins, Alessi, & Colfer, 1989). Psychosis was noted to be a significant negative predictor of response in a study of prepubertal depressives (Puig-Antich et al., 1987). In another study with adolescents, comorbid separation anxiety and being female were both correlated with poor response to imipramine (Ryan et al., 1986).

Research utilizing other tricyclics, such as nortriptyline, has shown promising results (Geller, Cooper, Chestnut, Anker, & Schluchter, 1986), but in a placebo-controlled study, it was not significantly more effective than placebo for children with major depression. Geller has documented the need for more frequent dosing of nortriptyline in children and adolescents because their metabolism of these compounds is more rapid than that of adults.

In studies of depressed children and adolescents receiving tricyclic trials, side effects are common, similar to those seen in adults, and are fairly well tolerated. Researchers have been especially careful in the monitoring of cardiovascular effects (Puig-Antich et al., 1987; Schroeder et al., 1989). Generally, blood pressure is mildly increased, although orthostatic hypotension and increased resting heart rate have been reported. EKG changes include lengthening of PR and QRS or Q-Tc intervals. Regular EKG monitoring is recommended.

Four cases of sudden death occurred between 1986 and 1992 in children aged 12 years or younger who were being treated with desipramine, leading psychiatrists to use caution when considering tricyclic trials in children. Biederman, Thisted, Greenhill, and Ryan (1995) reviewed data from the National Center for Health Statistics and the National Disease and Therapeutic Index to examine the exposure risk of children treated with desipramine. Although the association between desipramine and sudden death appears weak, they state that the small possibility of this association underlines the importance of careful assessment of risks and benefits when using desipramine in the pediatric population.

Atypical depressive features, such as anxiety, mood lability, hyperphagia, and hypersomnia, are commonly seen in adolescent depressive disorders (Ryan et al., 1987). These symptoms are known to respond preferentially to monoamine oxidase inhibitors (MAOIs) in adult populations (Quitkin et al., 1990; Stewart et al., 1990; Stewart et al., 1989), but there are few studies that have used MAOIs to treat children and adolescents. In an open-label trial, Ryan et al. (1986) treated 23 adolescents, most of whom had been unresponsive or only partially responsive to tricyclic antidepressants (TCAs). Those subjects with a partial response to TCAs had MAOIs added to their medication regimen; nonresponders had MAOIs substituted for their TCAs. A 74% fair-to-good response rate was achieved in this trial, with the best responses noted in combined TCA–MAOI treatment. In 20% of the patients in the study, however, the MAOI was discontinued because of problems with dietary compliance. The authors therefore recommend caution in the use of MAOIs, especially in adolescents known to be impulsive or unreliable, or to have a history of drug abuse.

Clinical trials have begun on children using newer antidepressant medications such as fluoxetine, clomipramine, and bupropion, but few data regarding these are available. Some researchers believe that child and adolescent depressive disorders may be particularly responsive to medications that act to enhance serotonergic neurotransmission, such as MAOIs, clomipramine, fluoxetine, and mianserin. In an uncontrolled study of mianserin, a tetracyclic antidepressant only used experimentally in the United States because of significant side effects, depressive symptoms decreased notably after the first week of treatment. Interestingly, both children and adolescents showed similar good

response (Dugas, Mouren, Halfon, & Moron, 1985). The most promising of these new antidepressants are clearly the serotonergic agents. In a double-blind placebo-controlled study just reported by Emslie (1995), children and adolescents aged 8–17 with major depressive disorder showed significantly greater improvement with fluoxetine than with placebo. In general, child psychopharmacologists (e.g., Hazell, O'Connell, Heathcote, Robertson, & Henry, 1995) are recommending serotonergic agents as the first-line medication for pediatric patients because of their greater potential efficacy with a greater margin of safety than the tricyclics.

Augmentation of antidepressant medication with lithium or thyroid hormone is frequently employed in adults refractory to antidepressant treatment (Heninger, Charney, & Sternberg, 1983), but this has not been studied in clinical trials with depressed children. A retrospective review of 14 adolescents who were given lithium to augment their tricyclic regimen (Ryan, Meyer, Dachille, Mazzie, & Puig-Antich, 1988) noted that 6 of these patients showed a good clinical response on this combination. Lithium augmentation might be considered, therefore, when a child or adolescent is refractory to treatment, particularly when the possibility that the patient is bipolar is in question.

Other Treatment Modalities

Social skill groups and therapeutic support groups can also be important elements of a multimodal treatment, and are an intrinsic element of some behavioral and cognitive–behavioral models. These groups are particularly helpful when children have fallen behind in their social development because of problems such as poor self-esteem, or when they lack motivation to have friends due to anhedonia or excessive rumination.

Selection of the types of psychosocial and psychodynamic treatment utilized should consider multiple factors, such as age, cognitive ability and maturity, type of symptoms and their severity, and probable etiological factors. A combination of psychosocial and psychotherapeutic modalities should be used, based on whether the patient's symptomatology is most present at home, at school, or in other social situations. The child with severe problems in peer-related interactions, and with avoidant personality traits, would profit most from a combination of cognitive–behavioral and peer group therapies, whereas a child with a chaotic family would more likely benefit from family therapy in addition to individual therapy. In a more severe depressive disorder, these modalities may be combined with pharmacotherapy. Psychoanalytic theorists have raised concerns about the possible negative effects medication may have on the transference between therapist and patient, and also about the patient's possible expectation that the "magic pill" will obviate the need for introspection or change in behavior. If these problems are openly addressed, however, they seldom create major problems, and are not usually significant enough to keep a patient from a warranted medication trial. There is even evidence that pharmacotherapy (DiMascio et al., 1979) may enhance the psychotherapeutic process, because it may improve patients' cognitive functioning, allowing them to be more alert, clear-thinking, and cooperative.

Maintenance Treatment

There is a high risk of recurrence of child and adolescent depressive disorders. Because of this, treatment must be ongoing, even after recovery of function. Patients and their parents must be informed about the possibility of recurrence, and the need for some type of long-term maintenance treatment (dynamic, cognitive, or pharmacological) to help prevent relapse. The patient may continue to be seen, on a less frequent basis, for a period of a year or more. If medication has been of benefit in decreasing depressive symptoms, it should be continued for at least 5 months after symptom improvement has plateaued at the same level as was effective during the acute episode (Preskorn et al., 1988). Longer maintenance should be continued in children and adolescents with more severe depressive symptomatology, when a child has a recurrent depressive episode, or when there is strong genetic loading in the patient's family.

DIRECTIONS FOR FUTURE RESEARCH

The next decade will be an important period in the research of depression, and research in childhood and adolescent mood disorders should be at the forefront of increasing this vital knowledge base. Research needs to be globally directed toward the areas of diagnosis, etiology, epidemiology, and treatment. One of the difficulties faced in working in any of these areas, however, is the fact that each area is influenced by the others. For example, diagnostic criteria attempt to have etiological bases, but research in the etiology of depression relies on stable and valid diagnostic criteria.

The recent rapid changes in diagnostic systems have made etiological studies more difficult, since assessment instruments are tied to specific diagnostic criteria, and therefore must frequently be revised. Because of this, increased understanding of childhood and adolescent depression will have to occur in a stepwise manner, with each area of research modifying and in turn being modified by data from other areas.

At the beginning of this progress, careful examination of the utility of DSM criteria is necessary. Currently, the criteria for depression in children and adolescents are highly dependent on criteria based primarily on research with adults. Carlson's work has suggested the use of core criteria with age-specific symptomatology, or differing criteria for different developmental stages, in order to create a more accurate diagnostic system for children. Research needs to focus upon whether age or developmentally specific criteria for depression are necessary, or whether symptoms seen in children are just age-appropriate equivalents to symptoms seen in adults. Is social withdrawal, for example, the childhood equivalent of anhedonia in adults? Research might also examine whether gender-specific criteria would be helpful diagnostically. In looking at criteria for depression, it is also important to examine the significance of the high comorbidity rate in children and adolescents diagnosed as depressed. Does this overlap indicate that DSM criteria are too broad, or does this indicate that significant subgroups of depression exist, with different etiologies and outcomes?

In evaluation and diagnosis, the importance of multiple sources of information has been stressed. Research still needs to be directed, however, toward understanding how to weigh information from different sources, and how to optimize the use of different measurements. For example, is a self-rating scale by an adolescent more important or less important than an interview with a parent?

Researchers looking at the etiology of depression need to use models developed from the study of children, rather than using adult models to understand depression in youths, because studying a younger population gives a broader array of data with fewer complicating factors. It also allows for the greater possibility of tying studies of etiology and natural history together. Genetic studies searching for markers for depression in specific clinical populations could be invaluable, especially in combination with longitudinal follow-up studies, in finding possible answers to such questions as why there are differences between prepubertal and postpubertal depression. Biological correlates of depression, such as sleep pattern and endocrinological changes, might also be used to elucidate such questions. Familial studies might provide insight into whether subgroups of depressives exist, by examining such questions as whether families with anxious depressed children segregate independently from those with oppositional depressed children.

In the natural history of depression, prospective studies examining nonselected subject groups (such as all children born at a specific place or time) are vital to understanding the development of depression over time. This is the clearest way to establish whether childhood, adolescent, and adult disorders are continuous over time, what changes of symptomatology occur over time, and how treatment might affect the course of illness. Unfortunately, the cost of screening the large samples needed for such a study is high; the protocol is time-intensive, and thus rarely used. Longitudinal outcome studies should be used to investigate the significance of comorbid disorders, and whether these represent subgroups requiring different treatment strategies. Catch-up prospective studies such as Lee Robins's study of antisocial children (Cantwell & Carlson, 1983) allow selection of a childhood cohort that has already grown to adulthood, and are ideal for looking at outcome. This study design is becoming increasingly feasible, because there are a growing number of earlier-studied childhood and adolescent populations now grown to adulthood. This type of study should be used to further investigate the significance of comorbid subgroups and could potentially suggest differential treatment strategies for these groups. Retrospective studies can still broaden our information base by examining symptom patterns that existed in the childhood of adult depressives.

The management of depression in childhood and adolescence, in comparison to the treatment of adults, has been little researched. We need to know why children and adolescents respond less robustly to antidepressants than do adults, and whether there might be subgroups that respond preferentially to medication. The effect of serotonergic antidepressants on both prepubertal and postpubertal depressives needs

careful examination, because it is hypothesized that these agents may be more effective than tricyclic antidepressants on these populations. Research of psychosocial treatments, however, must not lag behind psychopharmacological research, since both interpersonal therapy and cognitive therapy have proven as effective as medication with adults, and may be more effective in children than pharmacotherapy. Ways of examining efficacy of psychotherapies that do not use protocols need to be developed, and the rationale for using one psychosocial intervention over another needs to be supported by empirical evidence. Greater emphasis also needs to be placed on integrating treatment modalities into the home and school environments, using parents and teachers to solidify changes in affect, cognition, and behavior that have been brought about through therapy.

Acknowledgment. We wish to acknowledge the help of Randi Abrams in the preparation of this chapter.

REFERENCES

Abraham, K. (1960). Notes on psychoanalytic investigation and treatment of manic–depressive insanity and allied conditions. In D. Bryan & A. Strachey (Eds. and Trans.), *Selected papers on psychoanalysis.* New York: Basic Books.

Akiskal, H. S., & Mckinney, W. T., Jr. (1975). Overview of recent research in depression: Integration of ten conceptual models into a comprehensive clinical frame. *Archives of General Psychiatry, 32,* 285–305.

Akiskal, H. S., Walker, P., Puzantian, V. R., King, D., Rosenthal, T. L., & Drannon, M. (1983). Bipolar outcome in the course of depressive illness: Phenomenologic, familial, and pharmacologic predictors. *Journal of Affective Disorders, 5,* 115–128.

Albert, N., & Beck, A. T. (1975). The incidence of depression in early adolescence: A preliminary study. *Journal of Youth and Adolescence, 4,* 301–307.

Alessi, N. (1991). Refractory childhood depressive disorders from a pharmacotherapeutic perspective. In J. Amsterdam (Ed.), *Advances in neuropsychiatry and psychopharmacology: Vol. 2. Refractory depression.* New York: Raven Press.

Ambrosini, P. J. (1987). Pharmacotherapy in child and adolescent major depressive disorder. In H. Y. Meltzer (Ed.), *Psychopharmacology: The third generation of progress.* New York: Raven Press.

Anderson, J. C., Williams, S., McGee, R., & Silva, P. A. (1987). DSM-III disorders in preadolescent children: Prevalence in a large sample from the general population. *Archives of General Psychiatry, 44,* 69–76.

Angold, A., & Costello, E. (1992). Comorbidity in children and adolescents with depression. *Child and Adolescent Psychiatric Clinics of North America, 1*(1), 31–52.

Appleby, L. (1991). Suicide during pregnancy and in the

first postnatal year [see comments]. *British Medical Journal, 302,* 67–69.

Asarnow, J. R. (1992). Suicidal ideation and attempts during middle childhood: Associations with perceived family stress and depression among child psychiatric inpatients. *Journal of Clinical Child Psychology, 21*(1), 35–40.

Asarnow, J. R., & Carlson, G. A. (1985). Depression self-rating scale: Utility with child psychiatric inpatients. *Journal of Consulting and Clinical Psychology, 53,* 491–499.

Asarnow, J. R., Goldstein, M. J., Thompson, M., & Guthrie, D. (1993). One-year outcomes of depressive disorders in child psychiatric inpatients: Evaluation of the prognostic power of a brief measure of emotion. *Journal of Child Psychology and Psychiatry, 34,* 129–137.

Asarnow, J. R., & Guthrie, D. (1989). Suicidal behavior, depression, and hopelessness in child psychiatric inpatients: A replication and extension. *Journal of Clinical Child Psychology, 18*(2), 129–136.

Beardslee, W. R., Bemporad, J., Keller, M., & Klerman, G. L. (1983). Children of parents with affective disorder: A review. *American Journal of Psychiatry, 140*(2), 825–832.

Beardslee, W. R., Schultz, L. H., & Selman, R. L. (1987). Level of social cognitive development, adaptive functioning, and DSM-III diagnoses in adolescent offspring of parents with affective disorders. *Developmental Psychology, 23,* 807–815.

Beck, A. T. (1976). *Cognitive therapy and the emotional disorders.* New York: International Universities Press.

Beck, A. T., Hollon, S. D., Young, J. E., Bedrosian, R. C., & Budenz, D. (1985). Treatment of depression with cognitive therapy and amitriptyline. *Archives of General Psychiatry, 42*(1), 142–148.

Beck, A. T., Rush, A. J., Shaw, B. F., & Emery, G. (1979). *Cognitive therapy of depression.* New York: Guilford Press.

Bemporad, J. R. (1982). Management of childhood depression: Developmental considerations. *Psychosomatics, 23,* 272–279.

Bemporad, J. R. (1988). Psychodynamic treatment of depressed adolescents. *Journal of Clinical Psychiatry, 49,* 26–31.

Benfield, C. Y., Palmer, D. J., Pfefferbaum, B., & Stowe, M. L. (1988). A comparison of depressed and nondepressed disturbed children on measures of attributional style, hopelessness, life stress and temperament. *Journal of Abnormal Child Psychology, 16,* 397–410.

Bibring, E. (1965). The mechanism of depression. In P. Greenacre (Ed.), *Affective disorders.* New York: International Universities Press.

Biederman, J., Thisted, R., Greenhill, L., & Ryan, N. (1995). Estimation of the association between desipramine and the risk of sudden death in 5- to 14-year old children. *Journal of Clinical Psychiatry, 56,* 87–93.

Bird, H. R., Canino, G., Rubio-Stipec, M., Gould, M. S., Ribera, J., Sesman, M., Woodburg, M., Huertas-Goldman, S., Pagan, A., Sanchez-Lacay, A., & Moscoso, M. (1988). Estimates of prevalence of childhood maladjustment in a community survey in Puerto Rico. *Archives of General Psychiatry, 45*(12), 1120–1126.

Bowlby, J. (1960). Grief and mourning in infancy and early childhood. *Psychoanalytic Study of the Child, 15,* 9–52.

Bowlby, J. (1980). *Attachment and loss: Vol. 3. Loss: Sadness and depression.* New York: Basic Books.

Boyd, J. H., & Weissman, M. M. (1981). Epidemiology of affective disorders: A re-examination and future directions. *Archives of General Psychiatry, 38,* 1039–1051.

Boyle, M. H., Offord, D., Hofmann, H. G., Catlin, G. P., Byles, J. A., Cadman, D. T., Crawford, J. W., Links, P. S., Rae-Grant, N I., & Szatmari, P. (1987). Ontario Child Health Study: I. Methodology. *Archives of General Psychiatry, 44,* 826–831.

Brent, D. A., Crumrine, P. K., Varma, R. R., Allan, M., & Allman, C. (1987). Phenobarbital treatment and major depressive disorder in children with epilepsy. *Pediatrics, 80*(6), 909–917.

Brent, D. A, Perper, J. A., & Allman, C. J. (1983). Alcohol, firearms, and suicide among youth: Temporal trends in Allegheny County, PA. *Journal of the American Medical Association, 257*(54), 3369-3372.

Brent, D. A., Perper, J. A., Allman, C. J., Moritz, G. M., Wartella, M. E., & Zelenak, J. P. (1991). The presence and accessibility of firearms in the homes of adolescent suicides: A case–control study. *Journal of the American Medical Association, 266*(21), 2989–2995.

Brent, D. A., Perper, J. A., Goldstein, C. E., Kolko, D. J., Allan, M. J., Allman, C. J., & Zelenak, J. P. (1988). Risk factors for adolescent suicide victims with suicidal inpatients. *Archives of General Psychiatry, 45,* 581–588.

Burke, K. C., Burke, J. D., Rae, D., & Reiger, D. A. (1991). Comparing age of onset of major depression and other psychiatric disorders by birth cohorts in five U.S. community populations. *Archives of General Psychiatry, 48,* 789–795.

Burke, P., Meyer, V., Kocoshis, S., Orenstein, D. M., Chandra, R., Nord, D. J., Sauer, J., & Cohen, E. (1989). Depression and anxiety in pediatric inflammatory bowel disease and cystic fibrosis. *Journal of the American Academy of Child and Adolescent Psychiatry, 28*(6), 948–951.

Cantwell, D. P. (1982). Childhood depression: A review of current research. In B. B. Lahey & A. E. Kazdin (Eds.), *Advances in clinical child psychology* (Vol. 1). New York: Plenum Press.

Cantwell, D. P., & Carlson, G. A. (1983). *Affective disorders in childhood and adolescence.* Jamaica, NY: Spectrum.

Carlson, G. A., & Cantwell, D. P. (1979). A survey of depressive symptoms in a child and adolescent psychiatric population. *Journal of the American Academy of Child and Adolescent Psychiatry, 18*(4), 587–599.

Carlson, G. A., & Cantwell, D. P. (1980). Unmasking masked depression. *American Journal of Psychiatry, 137,* 445–449.

Carlson, G. A., & Kashani, J. H. (1988). Phenomenology of major depression from childhood through adulthood: Analysis of three studies. *American Journal of Psychiatry, 145,* 1222–1225.

Centers for Disease Control. (1986). *Suicide surveillance, 1970–1980.* Atlanta, GA: U.S. Department of Health and Human Services.

Cohen, D. J. (1980). Constructive and reconstructive activities in the analysis of a depressed child. *Psychoanalytic Study of the Child, 35,* 237–266

Cytryn, L., & McKnew, D. H. (1972). Proposed classification of childhood depression. *American Journal of Psychiatry, 129,* 149–155.

Cytryn, L., & McKnew, D. H. (1980). Diagnosis of depression in children: A reassessment. *American Journal of Psychiatry, 137,* 22–25.

Davidson, L. E., Rosenberg, M. L., Mercy, J. A., Franklin,

J., & Simmons, J. T. (1989). An epidemiologic study of risk factors in two teenage suicide clusters. *Journal of the American Medical Association*, 262(19), 2687–2692.

de Villiers, A. S., Russell, V. A., Carstens, M. E., Searson, J. A., van Zyl, A. M., Lombard, C. J., & Taljaard, J. J. (1989). Noradrenergic function and hypothalamic-pituitary–adrenal axis activity in adolescents with major depression disorder. *Psychiatry Research*, 27, 101–109.

Deykin, E. Y., Levy, J. C., & Wells, V. (1987). Adolescent depression, alcohol and drug abuse. *American Journal of Public Health*, 76, 178–182.

DiMascio, A., Weissman, M. M., Prusoff, B. A., Carlos, N., Zwilling, M., & Klerman, G. L. (1979). Differential symptom reduction by drugs and psychotherapy in acute depression. *Archives of General Psychiatry*, 36(13), 1450–1456.

Dugas, M., Mouren, M. C., Halfon, O., & Moron, P. (1985). Treatment of childhood and adolescent depression with mianserin. *Acta Psychiatrica Scandinavica*, 72(Suppl. 320), 48–53.

Earls, F. (1980). Prevalence of behavior problems in 3-year-old children: A cross-national replication. *Archives of General Psychiatry*, 37, 1153–1157.

Emslie, G. (1995). *Double-blind placebo controlled study of fluoxetine in depressed children and adolescents*. Paper presented at the 35th Annual Meeting of the NCDEV New Clinical Drug Evaluation Unit, NIMH, Orlando, FL.

Feinstein, C., Blouin, A. G., Egan, J., & Conners, C. K. (1984). Depressive symptomatology in a child psychiatric outpatient population: Correlations with diagnosis. *Comprehensive Psychiatry*, 25, 379–391.

Fleming, J. E., & Offord, D. R. (1990). Epidemiology of childhood depressive disorders: A critical review. *Journal of the American Academy of Child and Adolescent Psychiatry*, 29, 571–580.

Fleming, J. E., Offord, D. R., & Boyle, M. H. (1989). Prevalence of childhood and adolescent depression in the community: Ontario Child Health Study. *British Journal of Psychiatry*, 155, 647–654.

Freud, S. (1957). Mourning and melancholia. In J. Strachey (Ed. and Trans.), *The standard edition of the complete psychological works of Sigmund Freud* (Vol. 14). London: Hogarth Press. (Original work published 1917)

Frommer, E. A. (1968). Depressive illness in childhood: Recent developments in affective disorders. *British Journal of Psychiatry* (Spec. Publ.), 2, 117–136.

Garber, J., Kriss, M. R., Koch, M., & Lindholm, L. (1988). Recurrent depression in adolescents: A follow-up study. *Journal of the American Academy of Child and Adolescent Psychiatry*, 27, 49–54.

Garrison, C. Z., Addy, C. L., Jackson, K. L., McKeown, R. E., & Walker, J. L. (1991). The CES-D as a screen for depression and other psychiatric disorders in adolescents. *Journal of the American Academy of Child and Adolescent Psychiatry*, 30(4), 636–641.

Geller, B., Cooper, T. B., Chestnut, E. C., Anker, J. A., & Schluchter, M. D. (1986). Preliminary data on the relationship between nortriptyline plasma level and response in depressed children. *American Journal of Psychiatry*, 143(10), 1283–1286.

Geller, B., Cooper, T. B., McCombs, H. G., Graham, D., & Wells, J. (1989). Double-blind placebo-controlled study of nortriptyline in depressed children using a "fixed plasma level" design. *Psychopharmacology Bulletin*, 25(1), 101–108.

Gispert, M., Davis, M. S., Marsh, L., & Wheeler, K. (1987).

Predictive factors in repeated suicide attempts by adolescents. *Hospital and Community Psychiatry*, 38(4), 390–393.

Glaser, K. (1968). Masked depression in children and adolescents. *Annual Progress in Child Psychiatry and Child Development*, 1, 345–355.

Gould, M. S., Shaffer, D., & Kleinman, M. (1988). The impact of suicide in television movies: Replication and commentary. *Suicide and Life-Threatening Behavior*, 18(1), 90–99.

Gould, M. S., Wunsch-Hitzig, R., Dohrenwend, B. P. (1980). Formulation of hypotheses about the prevalence, treatment and prognostic significance of psychiatric disorders in children in the United States. In B. P. Dohrenwend, B. S. Dohrenwend, M. S. Gould, B. Link, R. Neuebaruer, & R. Wunsch-Hitzig (Eds.), *Mental illness in the United States*. New York: Praeger.

Hammen, C., Gordon, D., Burge, D., Adrian, C., Jaenicke, C., & Hiroto, D. (1987). Maternal affective disorders, illness and stress: Risk for children's psychopathology. *American Journal of Psychiatry*, 144, 736–741.

Harrington, R., Fudge, H., Rutter, M., Pickles, A., & Hill, J. (1991). Adult outcomes of childhood and adolescent depression: II. Links with antisocial disorders. *Journal of the American Academy of Child and Adolescent Psychiatry*, 30(3), 434–439.

Hazell, P., O'Connell, D., Heathcote, D., Robertson, J., & Henry, D. (1995). The efficacy of tricyclic drugs in treating child and adolescent depression: A metaanalysis. *British Medical Journal*, 310(8), 897–901.

Heninger, G. R., Charney, D. S., & Sternberg, D. E. (1983). Lithium carbonate augmentation of antidepressant treatment. *Archives of General Psychiatry*, 40, 1336–1342.

Hershberg, S. G., Carlson, G., Cantwell, D. P., & Strober, M. (1982). Anxiety and depressive disorders in psychiatrically disturbed children. *Journal of Clinical Psychiatry*, 43, 358–361.

Hoberman, H. M., & Garfinkel, B. D. (1988). Completed suicide in children and adolescents. *Journal of American Academy of Child and Adolescent Psychiatry*, 27(6), 689–695.

Jaenicke, C., Hammen, C., Zupan, B., Hiroto, D., Gordon, D., Adrian, C., & Burge, D. (1987). Cognitive vulnerability in children at risk for depression. *Journal of Abnormal Psychology*, 15(4), 559–572.

Kashani, J. H., Barbero, G. J., & Bolande, F. D. (1981a). Depression in hospitalized pediatric patients. *Journal of the American Academy of Child and Adolescent Psychiatry*, 20, 123–134.

Kashani, J. H., Beck, N. C., Hoeper, E. W., Fallahi, C., Corcoran, C. M., McAllister, J. A., Rosenberg, T. K., & Reid, J. C. (1987). Psychiatric disorders in a community sample of adolescents. *American Journal of Psychiatry*, 144(5), 584–589.

Kashani, J. H., Cantwell, D. P., Shekim, W. O., & Reid, J. C. (1982). Major depressive disorder in children admitted to an inpatient community mental health center. *American Journal of Psychiatry*, 139(5), 671–672.

Kashani, J. H., & Hakami, N. (1982). Depression in children and adolescent with malignancy. *Canadian Journal of Psychiatry*, 27, 474–477.

Kashani, J. H., Holcomb, W. R., & Orvaschel, H. (1986). Depression and depressive symptoms in preschool children from the general population. *American Journal of Psychiatry*, 143, 1138–1143.

Kashani, J. H., Lababidi, Z., & Jones, R. S. (1982). Depression in children and adolescents with cardiovascular symptomatology: The significance of chest pain. *Journal of the American Academy of Child and Adolescent Psychiatry, 21*, 187–189.

Kashani, J. H., McGee, R. O., Clarkson, S. E., Anderson, J. C., Walton, L. A., Williams, S., Silva, P. A., Robins, A. J., Cytryn, L., & McKnew, D. H. (1983). Depression in a sample of 9-year-old children: Prevalence and associated characteristics. *Archives of General Psychiatry, 40*(7), 1217–1223.

Kashani, J. H., Venzke, R., & Millar, E. A. (1981b). Depression in children admitted to hospital for orthopaedic procedures. *British Journal of Psychiatry, 138*, 21–25.

Kazdin, A. E., Esveldt-Dawson, K., Unis, A. S., & Rancurello, M. D. (1983). Child and parent evaluations of depression and aggression in psychiatric inpatient children. *Journal of Abnormal Child Psychology, 11*(3), 401–413.

Keller, M. B., Beardslee, W. R., Dorer, D. J., Lavori, P. W., Samuelson, M. A., & Klerman, G. R. (1987). Impact of severity and chronicity of parental affective illness on adaptive functioning and psychopathology in children. *Archives of General Psychiatry, 43*(2), 930–937.

Kestenbaum, C. J., & Kron, L. (1987). Psychoanalytic intervention with children and adolescents with affective disorders: A combined treatment approach. *Journal of the American Academy of Psychoanalysis, 15*, 153–174.

Klein, D. N., Depue, R. A., & Slater, J. F. (1985). Cyclothymia in the adolescent offspring of parents with bipolar affective disorder. *Journal of Abnormal Psychology, 94*, 115–127.

Klerman, G. L. (1976). Age and clinical depression: Today's youth in the twenty-first century. *Journal of Gerontology, 31*, 318–323.

Klerman, G. L., & Weissman, M. M. (1989). Increasing rates of depression. *Journal of the American Medical Association, 261*, 2229–2235.

Kovacs, M., & Beck, A. T. (1977). An empirical approach toward definition of childhood depression. In J. G. Schulterbrandt (Ed.), *Depression in childhood: Diagnosis, treatment and conceptual models* New York: Raven Press.

Kovacs, M., Feinberg, T. L., Crouse-Novak, M., Paulauskas, S. L., & Finkelstein, R. (1984a). Depressive disorders in childhood: I. A longitudinal perspective study of characteristics and recovery. *Archives of General Psychiatry, 41*(1), 229–237.

Kovacs, M., Feinberg, T. L., Crouse-Novak, M., Paulauskas, S. L., Pollock, M., & Finkelstein, R. (1984b). Depressive disorders in childhood: II. A longitudinal study of the risk for a subsequent major depression. *Archives of General Psychiatry, 41*, 643–649.

Kovacs, M., Feinberg, T. L., Paulauskas, S., Finkelstein, R., Pollock, M., & Crouse-Novak, M. (1985). Initial coping responses and psychosocial characteristics of children with insulin-dependent diabetes mellitus. *Journal of Pediatrics, 106*, 827–834.

Kovacs, M., & Gatsonis, C. (1989). Stability and change in childhood-onset depressive disorders: Longitudinal course as a diagnostic validator. In L. N. Robins & J. E. Barrett (Eds.), *The validity of psychiatric diagnosis*. New York: Raven Press.

Kraemer, G. W. (1986). Developmental theories of depression in non-human primates. *Psychopharmacology Bulletin, 22*, 587–592.

Kuhn, V., & Kuhn, R. (1972). Drug therapy for depression in children. In A. L. Annell (Ed.), *Depressive states in childhood and adolescence*. New York: Halsted Press.

Kuperman, S., & Stewart, M. A. (1979). The diagnosis of depression in children. *Journal of Affective Disorders, 1*, 213–217.

Lazarus, A. (1968). Learning theory and the treatment of depression. *Behaviour Research and Therapy, 6*, 83–89.

Lewinsohn, P. M. (1974). A behavioral approach to depression. In R. Friedman & M. Katz (Eds.), *The psychology of depression: Contemporary theory and research*. Washington, DC: U.S. Government Printing Office.

Lewinsohn, P. M., Clarke, G. N., Hops, H., & Andrew, J. (1990). Cognitive–behavioral treatment for depressed adolescents. *Behavior Therapy, 21*(4), 385–401.

Lewis, H. B. (1986). The role of shame in depression. In M. Rutter, C. E. Izard, & P. B. Read (Eds.), *Depression in young people*. New York: Guilford Press.

Ling, W., Oftedal, G., & Weinberg, W. (1970). Depressive illness in childhood presenting as severe headache. *American Journal of Diseases of Children, 120*, 122–124.

Lubovits, D. A., & Handel, P. J. (1985). Childhood depression: Prevalence using DSM-III criteria and validity of parent and child depression scales. *Journal of Pediatric Psychology, 10*, 45–54.

Mahler, M. S. (1961). On sadness and grief in infancy and childhood. *Psychoanalytic Study of the Child, 16*, 332–354.

McCauley, E., Mitchell, J., Burke, P., & Moss, S. (1988). Cognitive attributes of depression in children and adolescents. *Journal of Consulting and Clinical Psychology, 14*, 903–908.

McCracken, J. T. (1992). Etiologic aspects of child and adolescent mood disorders. *Child and Adolescent Psychiatric Clinics of North America, 1*, 89–109.

McCracken, J. T., Poland, R. E., & Tondo, L. (1991). Cholinergic dysregulation in adolescent depression: Preliminary comparison with adult depression. *Proceedings of the 144th Annual Meeting of the American Psychiatric Association*, New Orleans, LA.

Merikangas, K. R., Weissman, M. M., Prusoff, B. A., & John, K. (1988). Assortative mating and affective disorders: Psychopathology in offspring. *Psychiatry, 51*, 48–57.

Mitchell, J., McCauley, E., Burke, P., Calderon, R., & Schloredt, B. S. (1989). Psychopathology in parents of depressed children and adolescents. *Journal of the American Academy of Child and Adolescent Psychiatry, 28*(3), 352–357.

National Center for Health Statistics. (1988). Advance report of final mortality statistics. *Monthly Vital Statistics*, Report 37.

Ostroff, R. B., & Boyd, J. H. (1987). Television and suicide: A letter to the editor. *New England Journal of Medicine, 316*(4), 876–878.

Otto, U. (1972). Suicidal acts by children and adolescents: A follow-up study. *Acta Psychiatrica Scandinavica, Suppl. 233*, 7–123.

Pfeffer, C. R. (1986). Suicidal behavior among children and adolescents: Risk identification and intervention. In A. J. Frances & R. E. Hales (Eds.), *Review of psychiatry* (Vol. 7). Washington, DC: American Psychiatric Press.

Pfeffer, C. R., Klerman, G. L., Hurt, S. W., Lesser, M., Peskin, J. R., & Siefker, C. A. (1991). Suicidal children grown up: Demographic and clinical risk factors for adolescent suicide attempts. *Journal of the American Academy of Child and Adolescent Psychiatry, 30*(4), 609–616.

Pfeffer, C. R., Lipkins, R., Plutchik, R., & Mizruchi, M. S. (1988). Normal children at risk for suicidal behavior: A two-year follow-up study. *Journal of the American Academy of Child and Adolescent Psychiatry, 27*, 34–41.

Pfeffer, C. D., Solomon, G., Plutchik, R., Mizruchi, M. S., & Weiner, A. (1982). Suicidal behavior in latency-age psychiatry inpatients: A replication and cross validation. *Journal of the American Academy of Child and Adolescent Psychiatry, 21*, 564–569.

Phillips, D. P., & Carstensen, L. L. (1987). Clustering of teenage suicides after television news stories about suicide. *New England Journal of Medicine, 315*(11), 685–689.

Poznanski, E. O. (1982). The clinical phenomenology of childhood depression. *American Journal of Orthopsychiatry, 52*(2), 308–313.

Poznanski, E. O., Krahenbuhl, V., & Zrull, J. (1976). Childhood depression. *Journal of the American Academy of Child and Adolescent Psychiatry, 15*, 491–501.

Preskorn, S. H., Weller, E. B., Hughes, C. W., & Weller, R. A. (1988). Relationship of plasma imipramine levels to CNS toxicity in children. *American Journal of Psychiatry, 145*, 897.

Preskorn, S. H., Weller, E. B., Hughes, C. W., Weller, R. A., & Bolte, K. (1987). Depression in prepubertal children: Dexamethasone nonsuppression predicts differential response to imipramine vs. placebo. *Psychopharmacology Bulletin, 23*(1), 128–133.

Puig-Antich, J. (1987). Affective disorders in children and adolescents: Diagnostic validity and psychobiology. In H. Y. Meltzer (Ed.), *Psychopharmacology: The third generation of progress.* New York: Raven Press.

Puig-Antich, J., Lukens, E., Davies, M., Goetz, D., Brennan-Quattrock, J., & Todak, G. (1985a). Psychosocial functioning in prepubertal major depressive disorders: I. Interpersonal relationships during the depressive episode. *Archives of General Psychiatry, 42*(5), 500–507.

Puig-Antich, J., Lukens, E., Davies, M., Goetz, D., Brennan-Quattrock, J., & Todak, G. (1985b). Psychosocial functioning in prepubertal major depressive disorders: II. Interpersonal relationships after sustained recovery from affective episode. *Archives of General Psychiatry, 42*(5), 511–517.

Puig-Antich, J., Perel, J. M., Lupatkin, W., Chambers, W. J., Tabrizi, M. A., King, J., Goetz, R., Davies, M., & Stiller, R. L. (1987). Imipramine in prepubertal major depressive disorder. *Archives of General Psychiatry, 44*(1), 81–89.

Puig-Antich, J., & Rabinovich, H. (1986). Relationship between affective and anxiety disorders in childhood. In R. Gittelman (Ed.) *Anxiety disorders of childhood.* New York: Guilford Press.

Quitkin, F. M., McGrath, P. F., Stewart, J. W., Harrison, W., Tricamo, E., Wager, S. G., Ocepek-Welikson, K., Nunes, E., Rabkin, J. G., & Klein, D. F. (1990). Atypical depression, panic attacks, and response to imipramine and phenelzine: A replication. *Archives of General Psychiatry, 47*(7), 935–941.

Rae-Grant, N., Thomas, B. H., Offord, D. R., & Boyle, M. H. (1989). Risk, protective factors, and the prevalence of behavioral and emotional disorders in children and adolescents. *Journal of American Academy of Child and Adolescent Psychiatry, 28*(2), 262–268.

Rehm, L. P. (1977). A self-control model of depression. *Behavior Therapy, 8*, 787–804.

Reynolds, W. M. (1985). Depression in childhood and adolescence: Diagnosis, assessment, intervention strategies and research. In T. R. Kratochwill (Ed.), *Advances in school psychology* (Vol. 4). Hillsdale, NJ: Erlbaum.

Rie, H. E. (1966). Depression in childhood: A survey of some pertinent contributors. *Journal of the American Academy of Child and Adolescent Psychiatry, 5*, 653–685.

Robbins, D. R., Alessi, N. E., & Colfer, M. V. (1989). Treatment of adolescents with major depression: Implications of the DST and the melancholic clinical subtype. *Journal of Affective Disorders, 17*, 99–104.

Rosenthal, P. A., Rosenthal, S., Doherty, M. B., & Santora, D. (1986). Suicidal thoughts and behaviors in depressed hospitalized preschoolers. *American Journal of Psychotherapy, 40*(2), 201–202.

Rutter, M. (1979). *Changing youth in a changing society: Patterns of adolescent development and disorder.* London: Nuffield Provincial Trust. (U.S. edition, 1980, Cambridge, MA: Harvard University Press.)

Rutter, M. (1980). Attachment and the development of social relationships. In M. Rutter (Ed.), *Scientific foundations of developmental psychiatry.* London: Heinemann Medical.

Rutter, M. (1986). The developmental psychopathology of depression: Issues and perspectives. In M. Rutter, C. E. Izard, & P. B. Read (Eds.), *Depression in young people: Developmental and clinical perspectives.* New York: Guilford Press.

Rutter, M. (1989). Isle of Wight Revisited: Twenty-five years of child psychiatric epidemiology. *Journal of the American Academy of Child and Adolescent Psychiatry, 28*, 633–653.

Rutter, M., Cox, A., Tupling, C., Berger, M., & Yule, W. (1975). Attainment and adjustment in two geographical areas: I. The prevalence of psychiatric disorder. *British Journal of Psychiatry, 126*, 493–509.

Rutter, M., Tizard, J., & Whitmore, K. (1970). *Education, health and behavior.* Huntington, NY: Krieger.

Ryan, N. D., Meyer, V., Dachille, S., Mazzie, D., & Puig-Antich, J. (1988). Lithium augmentation in TCA-refractory depression in adolescents. *Journal American Academy of Child and Adolescent Psychiatry, 27*(3), 371–371.

Ryan, N. D., Puig-Antich, J., Ambrosini, B., Rabinovich, H., Robinson, D., Nelson, B., Iyengan, S., & Twomey, J. (1987). The clinical picture of major depression in children and adolescents. *Archives of General Psychiatry, 44*, 854–861.

Ryan, N. D., Puig-Antich, J., Cooper, T., Rabinovich, H., Ambrosini, P., Davies, M., King, J., Torres, D., & Fried, J. (1986). Imipramine in adolescent major depression: Plasma levels and clinical response. *Acta Psychiatrica Scandinavica, 73*(3), 275–288.

Schroeder, J. S., Mullin, A. V., Elliott, G. R., Steiner, H., Nichols, M., Gordon, A., & Paulos, M. (1989). Cardiovascular effects of desipramine in children. *Journal of the American Academy of Child and Adolescent Psychiatry, 28*(3), 376–379.

Schwartz, C. E., Dorer, D. J., Beardslee, W. R., Lavori, P. W., & Keller, M. D. (1990). Maternal expressed emotion and parental affective disorder: Risk for childhood depressive disorder, substance abuse, or conduct disorder. *Journal of Psychiatry Research, 24*, 231–250.

Seligman, M. E. P., & Peterson, C. (1986). A learned helplessness perspective on childhood depression: Theory and research. In M. Rutter, C. E. Izard, & P. B. Read (Eds.), *Depression in young people*. New York: Guilford Press.

Shaffer, D. (1974). Suicide in childhood and early adolescence. *Journal of Clinical Psychology, 15*, 275–291.

Shaffer, D. (1988). The epidemiology of teen suicide: An examination of risk factors. *Journal of Clinical Psychiatry, 49*, 36–41.

Shaffer, D., & Fisher, P. (1981). The epidemiology of suicide in children and young adolescents. *Journal of the American Academy of Child and Adolescent Psychiatry, 20*, 545–565.

Shafii, M., & Shafii, S. L. (1992). Clinical manifestations and developmental psychopathology of depression. In M. Shafii & S. L. Shafii (Eds.), *Clinical guide to depression in children and adolescents*. Washington, DC: American Psychiatric Press.

Shafii, M., Steltz-Lenarsky, J., Derrick, A. M., Beckner, C., & Whittinghill, J. R. (1988). Commorbity of mental disorders in the post-mortem diagnosis of completed suicide in children and adolescents. *Journal of Affective Disorders, 15*, 227–233.

Siever, L. J., & Davis, K. L. (1985). Toward a dysregulation hypothesis of depression. *American Journal of Psychiatry, 142*, 1017–1031.

Smith, K., & Crawford, S. (1986). Suicidal behavior among "normal" high school students. *Suicide and Life-Threatening Behavior, 163*, 313–325.

Spitz, R. A. (1965). *The first year of life*. New York: International Universities Press.

Spitzer, R., Endicott, J., & Robins, E. (1977). *Research diagnostic criteria for a selected group of functional disorders* (3rd ed.). New York: New York State Psychiatric Institute.

Stark, K. D., Reynolds, W. M., & Kaslow, N. J. (1987). A comparison of the relative efficacy of self-control therapy and a behavioral problem-solving therapy for depression in children. *Journal of Abnormal Child Psychology, 15*, 91–113.

Stewart, J. W., McGrath, P. J., Quitkin, F. M., Harrison, W., Markowitz, J., Wagner, S., & Leibowitz, M. R. (1989). Relevance of DSM-III depressive subtype and chronicity of antidepressant efficacy in atypical depression: Differential response to phenelzine, imipramine, and placebo. *Archives of General Psychiatry, 46*(7), 1080–1087.

Strober, M. (July, 1992). Relevance of early age-of-onset in genetic studies of bipolar affective disorder. *Journal of the American Academy of Child and Adolescent Psychiatry, 31*(4), 606–610.

Strober, M., & Carlson, G. (1982). Bipolar illness in adolescents with major depression: Clinical, genetic, and psychopharmacologic predictors in a three- to four-year prospective follow-up investigation. *Archives of General Psychiatry, 39*, 549–555.

Strober, M., Hanna, G. L., & McCracken, J. T. (1989). Bipolar disorder. In C. G. Last & M. Hersen (Eds.), *Handbook of child psychiatric diagnosis*. New York: Wiley.

Toolan, J. H. (1962). Depression in children and adolescents. *American Journal of Orthopsychiatry, 32*, 404–414.

Velez, C. N., Johnson, J., & Cohen, P. (1989). A longitudinal analysis of selected risk factors for childhood psychopathology. *Journal of the American Academy of Child and Adolescent Psychiatry, 28*, 861–864.

Weissman, M. M., Gershon, E. S., Kidd, K. K., Prusoff, B. A., Leckman, J. F., Dibble, E., Hamovit, J., Thompson, W. B., Pauls, D. L., & Guroff, J. J. (1984). Psychiatric Disorders in the relatives of probands with affective disorders. *Archives of General Psychiatry, 41*, 13–21.

Weller, E. B. & Weller, R. A. (1986). Clinical aspects of childhood depression. *Pediatric Annals, 15*, 843–847.

Weller, E. B., Weller, R. A., Fristad, M. A., & Preskorn, S. H. (1984). The dexamethasone suppression test in hospitalized prepubertal depressed children. *American Journal of Psychiatry, 141*, 290–291.

Weller, E. B., Weller, R. A., Fristad, M. A., & Preskorn, S. H. (1988). *Depressive symptoms in acutely bereaved children*. Paper presented at the 41st Annual Meeting of the American Psychiatric Association, Montreal, Quebec, Canada.

Welner, A., Welner, Z., & Fishman, R. (1979). Psychiatric adolescent inpatients: A 10-year follow-up. *Archives of General Psychiatry, 36*, 698–700.

Welner, Z., Welner, A., McCrary, M. D., & Leonard, M. A. (1977). Psychopathology in children of inpatients with depression: A controlled study. *Journal of Nervous and Mental Disease, 164*(6), 408–413.

Wilkes, T. C. R., & Rush, A. J. (1988). Adaptations of cognitive therapy for depressed adolescents. *Journal of the American Academy of Child and Adolescent Psychiatry, 27*, 381–386.

Zeitlin, H. (1986). *The natural history of psychiatric disorder in children*. New York: Oxford University Press.

19

Depression in Later Life: Epidemiology, Assessment, Etiology, and Treatment

ANDREW FUTTERMAN
LARRY THOMPSON
DOLORES GALLAGHER-THOMPSON
ROBERT FERRIS

Depression is probably the most well-researched mental health problem of later life. From 1980 to 1991 alone, more than 900 articles appeared in the major research journals in the United States and abroad (National Library of Medicine, 1991). Although much progress has been made in understanding the diagnosis, etiology, and treatment of late-life depression in the past decade, many questions remain regarding the prevalence of depression in older adults, the differences between late-life depression and the depressions of youth and middle age, factors associated with the onset and impact of late-life depression, and the nature of safe and effective treatment for depression in older adults. In this chapter, we examine recent research relating to each of these issues and attempt to define important areas for future research.

In addition, we hope to challenge common misperceptions about aging and depression. For example, we find it disturbing that mental health professionals more frequently attribute depression in older clients than younger clients to organic illness or dementia (Gatz & Pearson, 1988; Perlick & Atkins, 1984; Rapp & Davis, 1989), and ascribe a poorer prognosis to older clients

than to younger clients (Dye, 1978; Ray, McKinney, & Ford, 1987; Settin, 1982). We hope that a closer look at recent research may help to dispel such stereotypically negative views regarding aging and depression.

CONCEPTUAL ISSUES

In a symposium on common late-life problems at the 1992 annual meeting of the Gerontological Society of America, Powell Lawton, the former editor of *Psychology and Aging* and the symposium discussant, commented that "if memory problems in later life are a muddy area of research then late-life depression is muddy-cubed." We would agree. At present, the term "geriatric depression" frequently signifies different things to different people in different situations.

According to the DSM-IV (American Psychiatric Association, 1994), diagnoses of depression refer to specific subsets of the following symptoms: depressed mood; loss of interest or pleasure in normal activities; feelings of worthlessness; self-reproach or excessive guilt; a pessimistic outlook or sense of hopelessness about the future; suicidal thoughts or acts; and other signs of impaired bodily functioning, such as sleep, appetite, or motor disturbance.

Researchers have noted that there is substantial heterogeneity among older adults receiving diagnoses of depression (see Blazer, 1991). We believe at least two reasons account for this heterogeneity. First, geriatric depression is defined and assessed differently depending on the particular goals of researchers or clinicians (e.g., in terms of severity of depressive symptoms or specific depression diagnoses). Second, each depressive symptom itself may represent a heterogeneous class of features in older adults (e.g., loss of pleasure may signify difficulties in experiencing pleasure or in recalling recent pleasurable experiences; Futterman, Hanser, Hanley-Peterson, Thompson, & Gallagher-Thompson, 1993). The point is that no two older adults identified as depressed *necessarily* demonstrate the same symptoms in the same way.

In light of the diversity of what passes for "geriatric depression" in the literature, we avoid conceptualizing geriatric depression a priori according to any particular definition or assessment strategy (e.g., DSM-IV criteria for major depressive disorder [MDD] or high scores on standard depression screening measures). Instead, we assume that geriatric depression represents a class of symptom pictures (generally defined by the symptoms listed previously) that demonstrate a "family resemblance" (Wittgenstein, 1953). Just as members of the same family demonstrate many similarities in features, eye color, gait, temperment, and so on, we assume that instances of geriatric depression demonstrate many similarities as well in the course of illness, functional disturbances, cognitive distortions, affective experiences, sleep disturbance, risk factors, treatment response, and so on. Resemblances among family members overlap and crisscross; we assume that resemblances among cases of geriatric depression also overlap and crisscross.

EPIDEMIOLOGY OF LATE-LIFE DEPRESSION

Prevalence: How Big a Problem Is Late-Life Depression?

By all accounts, America is getting older. According to the U.S. Bureau of the Census (1991), in 1970 the median age of the U.S. population was 28 years; by 1986, the median age had increased to 31.8 years. In keeping with the increase in median age, the number of people over 65 years of age has also increased: from 20 million people in 1970 to 29.4 million people in 1986. Proportionally, elders comprised 9% of the population in 1960; today, they comprise almost 13% of the population, and projections indicate that by 2010, elders will comprise over 15% of the population.

Among this growing elder population, it is generally agreed that depression is the most common psychiatric disorder (e.g., see Blazer, 1982, or Blazer, Hughes, & George, 1987). The NIMH/NIH Epidemiologic Catchment Area (ECA) study (Myers et al., 1984; Regier et al., 1988) estimated the prevalence of depression in community-dwelling elderly to be approximately 3–4%. In the ECA study, depression diagnoses were made according to DSM-III (American Psychiatric Association, 1980) criteria for MDD, based upon data obtained using the Diagnostic Interview Schedule (DIS; Robins, Helzer, Croughan, & Ratliff, 1981).

Prevalence estimates vary broadly, however, depending on the definition, method of assessment, and particular sample utilized. For example, in the ECA study, if one included as depression diagnoses for any disorder in which clinically significant depressive symptoms figure prominently (e.g., MDD, bereavement, and dysthymia), prevalence rates double to 6% using the same sample (Myers et al., 1984). Self-reported, questionnaire-based ratings of depressive symptoms suggest higher prevalence rates, as high as 15–20% in community samples.

In addition, prevalence estimates for subgroups of older adults may be different from those obtained from aggregate community samples. For example, throughout adulthood and old age, unipolar depression appears to be more prevalent in women than men (Nolen-Hoeksema, 1987; Weissman & Klerman, 1978). In addition, data from two large and growing groups of older adults—physically ill older outpatients and elders who live in residential care facilities due to chronic disease or extreme disability—suggest that prevalence estimates double or triple those typically obtained in the community. For example, prevalence of depression among elders receiving outpatient care for medical illness has been estimated at 6 to 9% (using Research Diagnostic Criteria [RDC; Spitzer, Endicott, & Robins, 1978] or DSM-III criteria for MDD [Katon & Sullivan, 1990; Rapp, Parisi, & Walsh, 1988; Von Korff et al., 1987]).

Among older adults living in residential care facilities, Parmelee, Katz, and Lawton (1989a, 1992a) estimated the prevalence of MDD to be approximately 15% and for incidence rates to increase over the course of a year. If one includes as cases of depression clinically significant depressive symptoms that do not meet the diagnosis of MDD, then prevalence estimates of depression are typically above 20% (Blazer, 1991). As Figure 19.1 shows, there is a "linear increase" in the prevalence of depression when comparing community-dwelling, outpatient, and residential care samples (Katon & Sullivan, 1990).

Since the numbers of institutionalized and physically ill elders are growing rapidly, the numbers of depressed elders in these subgroups will likely grow rapidly as well. More than 1.5 million elderly patients currently reside in nursing homes (94% of all such residents; U.S. Bureau of the Census, 1991). According to recent projections, this number will double by 2020, and triple soon after 2030. There is a pressing need for research to examine depression in this subgroup of older adults.

In summary, there is little question that depression in later life is a significant and growing problem. Is depression more of a problem for older adults than it is for younger adults? As will be seen in the next section, methodological differences among studies (definition of depression used, means of assessment, and sample selected) make answering this question difficult.

Depression across the Lifespan: Are Older People More Depressed Than Younger People?

Early studies that assessed the relationship between age and depression suggested that persons over age 65 suffer higher rates of depression than do younger adults (e.g., Gurland, 1976). More recent studies have come to precisely the opposite conclusion: Increased age is associated with lower rates of depression (e.g., Myers et al., 1984). The form of the relationship between age and depression, like prevalence estimates of late-life depression, differ substantially depending on the way in which depression is assessed.

Newmann (1989) divided 20 cross-sectional studies of age and depression based on different assessment strategies and observed different relations depending on the strategy used. One group of studies used standard self-report questionnaires designed to measure the severity of various components of depressive syndrome, and a second group of studies used a standard clinical interview approach emphasizing diagnosis of depressive disorders. Measuring the severity of depression using self-report questionnaires reflects a "test" approach to assessment, whereas diagnosing depressive disorder reflects a "classification" approach (Blashfield & Livesley, 1991; Loevinger, 1957). The test approach assumes that individuals vary along a single continuum of depressive severity

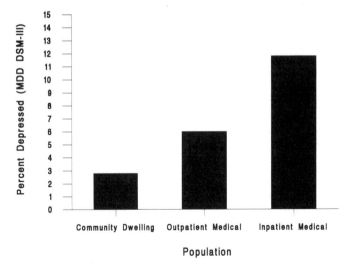

FIGURE 19.1. Prevalence of major depressive disorder in three samples (Katon & Sullivan, 1990).

or intensity—that is, every member of the population demonstrates depression to some extent. Individuals rate their depressive symptoms using standard screening measures, such as the Beck Depression Inventory (BDI; Beck, Ward, Mendelson, Mock, & Erbaugh, 1961) or the Center for Epidemiologic Studies Depression (CES-D) Scale (Radloff, 1977). Ratings are typically summed to get a single index of depression severity, and these summed scores are compared to cutoff scores reflecting severity of depression demonstrated by individuals receiving a diagnosis of depression (e.g., see Gallagher, Breckenridge, Steinmetz, & Thompson, 1983).

In contrast to the test approach to rating depression severity, the classification approach assumes that depression cannot be described in terms of a single quantitative dimension of severity or intensity, but must be understood in terms of qualitative differences among individuals (i.e., some individuals are diagnosed as depressed and some are not). The DSM-III, DSM-III-R, and DSM-IV (American Psychiatric Association, 1980, 1987, 1994) define specific configurations of symptoms as MDD and other depressive diagnoses (e.g., dysthymia). Probing of the symptoms required for diagnostic classification typically is conducted using standard clinical interviews such as the Diagnostic Interview Schedule (DIS; Robins et al., 1981), a structured clinical interview tied to DSM-III, or the Schedule for Affective Disorders and Schizophrenia (SADS; Spitzer & Endicott, 1978). Individuals who demonstrate the particular symptom configurations of each of the depressive diagnoses are classified accordingly.

The two approaches to assessing depression reflect different purposes. Proponents of the clinical diagnostic perspective have been primarily interested in assessing community needs for specific mental health services and determining factors related to service utilization (Regier et al., 1988). By contrast, the proponents of the test approach have been primarily concerned with identifying psychosocial risk factors for depression among different age groups (Murrell, Himmelfarb, & Wright, 1983; Phifer & Murrell, 1986). Their research is more closely tied to a prevention of depression than to determination of specific treatment needs and thus, broad assessment of the "family" of depressive disorders is important.

Figures 19.2 and 19.3 show the pattern of results demonstrated by test and classification studies, respectively. As Figure 19.2 shows, the pattern of results for studies using test measures is U-shaped: a decreasing percentage of individuals scoring above conventional cutoffs with increasing age until approximately age 55, after which rates of depression either increase (Murrell et al., 1983) or remain the same (e.g., Frerichs, Aneshensel, & Clark, 1981). Using a classification or diagnostic approach, an opposite, inverted U-shaped pattern typically appears (Figure 19.3): Prevalence of depression peaks in the middle-adulthood followed by gradual drop in rates of depression in age cohorts 55–75 years of age (see Newmann, 1989).

Several caveats should be noted in summarizing these epidemiological studies. First, most studies provide rates of depression for only two age intervals in later life—for 65–75 years and for 75–85 years—and actually include few "oldest-old" subjects over 85 years. The few classification or test studies with more than two age groups within older adulthood (e.g., 55–60 years, 65–70 years, etc.) including subjects over age 85 (e.g., Lewinsohn, Duncan, Stanton, & Hautzinger, 1986; Murrell et al., 1983) suggest that rates of depression may decrease over some intervals but increase in others, and that depression rates may increase markedly among the oldest-old. Clearly, more studies should examine the prevalence of depression in the oldest-old and address the possibility of a "nonlinear" relationship between age and depression in later life.

All epidemiological studies reviewed here are cross-sectional and thus confound age and cohort effects (Schaie, 1965), as well as effects of other factors correlated with age. The impact of ethnicity, gender, cohort (see next section), and other correlated factors (e.g., illness and spousal loss) on the rates of depression in later life can be substantial. Himmelfarb (1984) and Blazer, Burchett, Service, and George (1991) demonstrated that when factors associated with age (e.g. illness, marital status, socioeconomic status, functional disabilities, cognitive impairment, chronic illness, and social support) were statistically controlled, observed relationships between age and depression (on the CES-D) can change dramatically. Himmelfarb reported that age was no longer predictive of depression in men; in women, age demonstrated a "negative" linear relationship with depression. Similarly, Blazer et al. (1991) reported that the effects of age on depression were no longer significant once factors associated with age were statistically controlled.

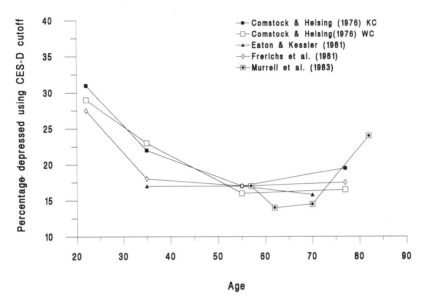

FIGURE 19.2. Percentage of age cohort with depression scores above CES-D cutoff. Adapted from Newmann (1989).

PROBLEMS IN ASSESSMENT OF GERIATRIC DEPRESSION

What is one to make of these different age–depression relationships? Test and classification assessment strategies appear to identify different late-life depressive "constructs" with differ-ent age distributions. Whereas increased age appears to be associated with an increase in "test" depression; risk for "classification" depres-sion decreases or remains the same in later life. Which age–depression relationship is accurate? Which assessment strategy best represents de-pression in later life?

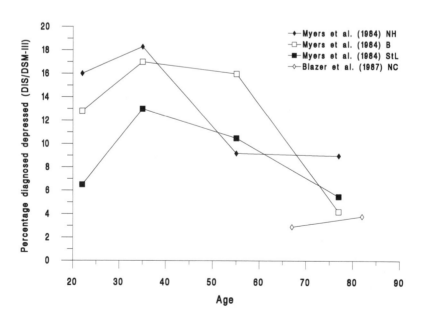

FIGURE 19.3. Percentage of age cohort with diagnosis of depressive disorder using DIS/DSM-III. Adapted from Newmann (1989).

These questions highlight difficulties relating to defining and assessing depression in later life. Although both standard screening measures and diagnostic criteria have demonstrated excellent reliability (see Thompson, Futterman, & Gallagher, 1988, for discussion), the validity of both approaches for assessing depression has been questioned (see National Institutes of Health Consensus Development Conference Consensus Statement, 1991). In this section, we examine criticisms directed at each type of assessment strategy and propose a strategy of assessment that capitalizes on the strengths of both approaches.

Criticism of the Test Approaches

Critics of the screening measures suggest that summing symptom ratings with little attention to the very different forms of underlying distress measured by the scale items may inflate estimates of late-life depression. That is, composite or mean scores on such screening measures do not differentiate the full array of symptoms in a depressive syndrome from more delimited and less severe forms of distress (Newmann, 1989).

For example, Zemore and Eames (1979) and Berry, Storandt, and Coyne (1984) have suggested that self-report measures of depression may be elevated in the elderly because of the effects of physical illness, the side effects of medications, and other physical complications. In keeping with this view, older adults would be expected to rate somatic symptoms, those that relate to impaired bodily functions (e.g., difficulties getting up in the morning, eating, talking, and moving about) as more highly distressing than mood disturbance and interpersonal difficulties items.

A series of studies have examined the extent to which somatic complaints inflate CES-D scores in community-dwelling older adults. Herzog, Van Alstine, Usala, Hultsch, and Dixon (1990) confirmed the four-factor structure of the CES-D originally proposed by Radloff (1977)—depressive affect, lack of well-being, somatic complaint, and interpersonal distress—and then examined factor age differences in several community samples. Contrary to expectation, age differences were not observed in level of somatic complaints or in the other three factors. This finding was corroborated by Gatz and Hurwicz (1990), who demonstrated higher levels of the lack of well-being factor among

older age-cohorts, but also reported no age differences in somatic complaints. Such studies suggest that somatic symptom complaints on standard screening measures do not inflate depression prevalence estimates on screening measures in older adults more than in younger adults.

Baldwin (1991) and others have further argued, however, that screening measures, such as the CES-D or the BDI, do not adequately differentiate depressive disorders in later life (e.g., MDD) from distress associated with other common late-life problems, such as physical illness, diminished activity levels, uncomplicated bereavement, and anxiety disorders. Several studies have examined the extent to which different types of distress are distinguishable on standard screening measures. For example, Rapp, Parisi, Walsh, and Wallace (1988), using standard screening measures, demonstrated that depression rates were overestimated among medically ill elders—large numbers of medically ill elders scored above conventional cutoffs, were identified as depressed, but did not meet RDC depression criteria. Among this group of "false positives," symptoms of depression were perhaps more appropriately attributed to effects of physical illness rather than to mood disorder.

In a series of studies, Newmann and colleagues also demonstrated that qualitatively different clusters of symptoms may produce high screening scores in young and old. Newmann, Engel, and Jensen (1990) factor analyzed self-reported depressive symptoms of community-dwelling older women between ages 51 and 92. Two depressive factors accounted for the variability in depressive symptoms. Newmann et al. described the first factor as the classic "depressive syndrome" (characterized by most of the emotional and cognitive features of depression, e.g., sad mood and self-blame), and the second as the "depletion syndrome" (characterized by loss of appetite, lack of interest, hopelessness, and thoughts of death). In subsequent studies, Newmann, Engel, and Jensen (1991a, 1991b) demonstrated longitudinally and cross-sectionally different relationships for each factor with age: The depression syndrome is more common among younger adults and diminishes with age; by contrast, the depletion syndrome appears to be more common among older adults and increases with age.

Finally, several studies have differentiated self-reported symptom patterns of unipolar depression from patterns characteristic of nor-

mal bereavement and anxiety disorders. Breckenridge, Gallagher, Thompson, and Peterson
(1986) demonstrated that elevated scores on the
BDI following the loss of one's spouse late in
life may indicate depression if the symptoms
reported suggest negative future and self-ap-
praisals (i.e., hopelessness, worthlessness), as
opposed to symptoms characteristic of acute
grief (e.g., appetite and sleep disturbance, difficulty concentrating; Breckenridge et al., 1986).
Similarly, Alexopoulos (1991a) demonstrated
distinctive and overlapping symptoms of anxiety and depression in late life .

Taken together, the studies cited previously
suggest that careful analysis of the symptoms reported on standard screening measures may distinguish different types of distress in later life.
It should be noted however, that studies have
yet to cross-validate the different types of distress in diverse elder samples or in samples of
elders diagnosed with a depressive disorder.
Until such cross-validation studies have been
completed, self-report measures are of questionable utility to differentiate distress types.

Criticism of Classification Approach

The validity of diagnostic criteria for late-life
depression has also been questioned. For example, Salzman and Shader (1978) and the
National Institutes of Health Consensus Development Conference Consensus Statement *Diagnosis and Treatment of Depression in Late
Life* (1991) argued that the diagnostic criteria
for "presence of dysphoric mood" may be more
appropriate for depression in younger adults
than for older adults. Depression in later life
may be expressed differently than earlier in
life: Depressive affect may be "masked" or de-
emphasized by depressed older adults when
other other vegetative and physical symptoms
are also prominent.

J. E. Barrett, J. A. Barrett, Oxman, and Gerber
(1988), in one of the few studies that specifically
assess the relationship between age and "masked
depression," provided support for this view.
Older adults (over 65 years), in their sample of
1,000 primary-care medical patients, were no
more likely to be diagnosed with depressive disorders than younger adults (under 45 years)
using the SADS and the RDC criteria (17% vs.
18%). However, substantially more older adults
(nearly 8%) than younger adults (1%) met their
"masked depression" diagnosis, defined as "patients who showed evidence of depression at the

interview, such as depressed faces or depressive
symptoms other than mood disturbance, but
who denied experiencing a depressive mood or
who gave a symptom picture not consistent with
any of the specific RDC categories" (p. 1102).

In several important studies, Blazer and colleagues (Blazer et al., 1988, 1989; Davidson,
Woodbury, Zisook, & Giller, 1989) provided
data suggesting that a substantial number of
older adults demonstrate patterns of depressive
symptoms not in keeping with standard diagnostic criteria for depressive disorders. Using a statistical modeling technique similar to cluster
analysis, these researchers examined the fit
between naturally occurring clusters of symptoms on the DIS and ratings of diagnostic criteria for depressive disorders in 3,900 community-dwelling younger and older adults.

The following five "pure types" of depression
or symptom clusters emerged from the Blazer
et al. (1988, 1989) analysis of DIS symptoms:

1. A relatively asymptomatic, mild dysphoric
   pure type.
2. A mildly dysphoric but cognitively impaired
   pure type.
3. A classic major depressive disorder with or
   without melancholic or manic symptoms
   pure type.
4. A pure type associated with being female and
   premenstrual symptomatology.
5. A moderate to severe depression mixed with
   anxiety pure type.

Of these five types, only pure type 3 (MDD with
or without melancholia or mania) fit DSM-III
or DSM-III-R criteria for depressive disorders;
other pure types represent merged diagnostic
pictures that are not readily classified using existing criteria. For example, neither DSM-III,
DSM-III-R, nor DSM-IV include criteria for a
merged depression–anxiety diagnosis (pure type
5), or for a diagnosis that includes depressive
symptoms mixed with cognitive impairment.

In addition, different pure types were associated with different age groups. Pure types 2
(mildly dysphoric/cognitively impaired) and 3
(classical MDD) typically occurred in late life,
whereas pure type 5 (mixed depression/anxiety)
was more common early in adulthood. These
findings (together with those of Newmann et al.,
1990, 1991a, 1991b, described previously) suggest
that the set of symptoms that characterize depressive disorders in younger adults may not characterize depressive disorders in older adults.

Bias may also be introduced into standard diagnostic systems, such as those in DSM-III, DSM-III-R, and DSM-IV, because of the "rules" for symptom inclusion and exclusion (Gallagher, 1986; Newmann, 1989). For example, according to DSM III-R, only those symptoms that interfere with everyday functioning (those causing impairments in occupational and other role performance) are included in a diagnosis. Since elders may experience fewer dramatic changes in role functioning in response to depressive symptoms than do younger adults (Newmann, 1989), this inclusionary rule would make it less likely for an older adult to be diagnosed as depressed. Exclusionary rules require ruling out physical illness or medication as a cause for the depressive symptom. For example, sleep disturbance and appetite loss are excluded as symptoms of depression if there is reason to believe prescribed medication impairs sleep and appetite. In such cases, the application of exclusionary rules may lead to not diagnosing depression in individuals who respond to physical illness or medication effects with depression (Gallagher, 1986; Newmann, 1989).

Taken together, there are clearly many potential problems with both test and classification approaches. In light of these problems, how can the clinician or researcher identify depression when it occurs in later life? In the next section, we attempt to provide some guidelines for clinicians and researchers who must do so.

Assessing Geriatric Depression in Clinical Research and Practice

We recommend a three-stage procedure for assessing geriatric depression. First, and perhaps the most important, older adults who demonstrate physical or emotional distress should be screened for depression. Unfortunately, many elders are not screened and their depression is consequently not identified or treated (Rapp et al., 1988). Thompson, Futterman, and Gallagher (1988) demonstrated that standard self-report measures of depression, which are reliable and valid measures of depression in younger adults, are also reliable and valid in older adults. For example, they identify nearly 100% of older adults who meet other standard criteria for depressive disorders (e.g., RDC, DSM-III, DSM-III-R) when used with appropriate cutoffs.

Two measures, in particular—the CES-D and BDI—are frequently used and either measure is recommended. The reliability and validity of the CES-D has been thoroughly examined in younger and older adults, in both clinical and community samples (e.g. Herzog et al., 1990). The BDI has been used extensively in treatment-outcome studies to assess change in both young and old depressives (e.g., Thompson, Gallagher, & Breckenridge, 1987).

The Geriatric Depression Scale (GDS; Yesavage et al., 1983) was developed specifically for use with older adults. The GDS has a simpler "yes"–"no" format as opposed to the multi-response format of the BDI and CES-D and de-emphasizes somatic symptomatology. Whereas the GDS demonstrates sound psychometrics in many different older samples and provides perhaps slightly improved sensitivity to DSM-III (and perhaps by extension, to DSM-IV) depression over standard screening measures (Norris, Gallagher, Wilson, & Winograd, 1987; Parmelee, Lawton, & Katz, 1989b; Rapp et al., 1988), the GDS has rarely been used with younger samples. Therefore, it is not useful to examine depression in different age groups.

Although most self-report measures of depression identify most individuals who meet standard criteria for depression diagnoses, they also falsely identify other older adults, whose distress may be more appropriately attributed to other causes (physical illness, or to psychiatric disorder other than depression; see Rapp et al., 1988). In order to provide convergent evidence that depression is present and not some other form of distress, positive screening should be followed by interview-based assessment. Two structured interviews, the DIS and SADS, have been used extensively in both research and clinical practice to diagnose late-life depression according to the RDC and DSM-III criteria. Newer instruments, such as the Structured Clinical Interview for DSM-III-R (SCID; Spitzer, Williams, Gibbon, & First, 1992), the Comprehensive Assessment of Symptoms and History (CASH; Andreasen, Flaum, & Arndt, 1992), and the Diagnostic Interview for Genetic Studies (DIGS; Nurnberger et al., 1994), have been used less frequently with older adults but provide information necessary for diagnosing depression and related disorders in later life according to DSM-III-R and other standard criteria. Although comprehensive structured interviews such as the SADS or the SCID are time-consuming and require training to administer properly, at present they are the most reliable and valid interview-based methods of identifying depression in keeping with the RDC, DSM-III, DSM-III-R, and DSM-IV criteria.

Shorter interview-based measures such as Hamilton Rating Scale for Depression (HRSD; Hamilton, 1967) supposedly improve accuracy of symptom rating over that of self-report screening measures, such as the BDI, yet require less time than longer interviews, such as the SADS. The HRSD has been used extensively in treatment studies with older adults, primarily as an index of residual symptomatology following treatment (Reynolds et al., 1992). Symptom ratings on the HRSD are obtained via interview (e.g., ratings may be extracted from the SADS; see Williams, 1988), but are summed together as in screening measures to obtain a severity measure.

Only recently has the hypothesis of improved accuracy of symptom rating using the HRSD in older adults been evaluated. Stukenberg, Dura, and Kiecolt-Glaser (1990) assessed the sensitivity and specificity of the HRSD for diagnosing depression in community-dwelling elders relative to other standard screening measures (e.g., the BDI). They demonstrated comparable sensitivity and specificity for RDC MDD and dysthymia for the HRSD and standard pen and paper measures, suggesting that the interview-based HRSD yields little incremental validity over standard screening measures. By contrast, Rapp, Smith, and Britt (1990) reported improved sensitivity and specificity for diagnosing RDC MDD in elderly medical patients, using the HRSD over standard screening measures. Based on these two studies, we cautiously recommend the HRSD for use with elderly medical patients, particularly in circumstances in which both screening and interview steps cannot both be completed due to cost or time constraints.

Regardless of the particular screening and interview measures used to make diagnoses, a third stage of assessment is usually necessary. This stage is oriented toward establishing specific treatment goals and baselines against which one might assess treatment efficacy, and involves systematical assessment of particular medical, psychological, and social problems. In situations in which diagnosis is unimportant or unnecessary (e.g., cases in which the patient seeks treatment for particular functional problems), this stage is usually of most interest to both practitioner and patient.

In our clinical trials of psychotherapy and pharmacotherapy for late-life depression, we have found it useful for both patient and therapist to monitor change in mood, engagement in pleasant activities, coping styles, and dysfunc-

tional attitudes during the course of treatment (Thompson et al., 1987). A host of geropsychiatric measures have been developed for use in monitoring treatment progress. Evaluating the reliability and validity of such measures is beyond the scope of this chapter. The interested reader is referred to an excellent issue of *Psychopharmacological Bulletin* (National Institute of Mental Health, 1988), which provides comprehensive, expert reviews of measures useful in geropsychiatric practice.

FACTORS ASSOCIATED WITH ONSET AND IMPACT OF GERIATRIC DEPRESSION

In this section, we review recent research on factors implicated in the development of late-life depression. We conceptualize depression in later life as both the outcome of biological, behavioral, cognitive, and social changes and the cause of such changes (Lewinsohn, 1974; Murrell & Meeks, 1992). In keeping with this viewpoint, we have divided the studies into two groups: (1) studies focusing on depression as a dependent variable or outcome of changes in other biological or psychosocial factors ("onset studies") and (2) a much smaller group of studies that conceptualize depression as an independent variable influencing quality-of-life variables, such as health, cognition, and social functioning ("impact studies"). Factors associated with onset can be further classified into two groups: (1) "internal" factors, such as genetics, age-related biological changes, comorbid- acute and chronic diseases, other psychiatric disorders, and personality characteristics; and (2) factors that are primarily "external," such as psychosocial stressors, social support, and cultural influences. It should be noted that most studies cited in this review are cross-sectional in nature and do not provide unambiguous descriptions of causal relationships (i.e., it is relatively arbitrary whether depression is an independent or dependent variable in many studies). In fact, there are few longitudinal studies that assess direct and indirect causes and effects of late-life depression.

Onset of Late-Life Depression

Internal Factors

Genetic Factors. Twin, adoption, and family studies assess the role of genetic factors in human behavioral phenotypes (e.g., temperament, locus of control, depression). Data from twin, adoption, and family studies suggest that unipolar depression with early age onset (earlier than age 30) is associated with genetic factors (Blehar, Weissman, Gershon, & Hirschfeld, 1988). Until recently, however, few studies have assessed genetic influences on depression late in life. The ongoing Swedish Adoption/Twin Study of Aging (SATSA; cited in Plomin & McClearn, 1990) examines genetic influences on behavioral traits and psychopathology in older adult twins (monozygotic and dizogotic), reared apart and together, using path-analytic modeling techniques. Based on SATSA data, Gatz, Pedersen, Plomin, Nesselroade, and McClearn (1992) reported that approximately 30% of the variance in depression severity (on the CES-D) was attributable to genetic factors, suggesting that a large portion of the variance in geriatric depression (70%) is associated, at least in part, with environmental factors. Methodologies used to estimate genetic and environmental influences on the development of human behavioral phenotypes both earlier and later in life have been sharply criticized both by molecular and population geneticists (e.g., Lewontin, 1974) and by biostatisticians (e.g., Kempthorne, 1978). These criticisms mainly focus on difficulties in defining heterogeneous and subjective behavioral traits (such as depression) and take issue with the assumptions underlying the statistical procedures used to derive heritabilty estimates with observational (as opposed to experimental) human behavioral data.

Age-Related Changes in Neurochemistry and Geriatric Depression. Substantial research has been completed in the past 10 years on brain chemistry changes associated with normal aging and depression. Excellent summaries of this large body of research may be found in various sources (e.g., Veith & Raskind, 1988).

Normal aging is associated with diminished brain concentrations of neurotransmitters— chemicals that provide the communication links between neurons. Changes in concentrations of norepinephrine, dopamine, serotonin, and their metabolites have been demonstrated (Alexopoulous, 1991b). Researchers postulate that late-life depression (particularly classic symptoms of MDD such as loss of pleasure, sad mood, psychomotor retardation) are due in part to such biochemical changes. However, studies of neurotransmitter and metabolite levels in blood plasma, cerebrospinal fluid, and urine of depressed older adults do not provide unequivocal support for the use of neurotransmitter levels as markers of geriatric depression. For example, no study has demonstrated that recovery from depression is directly related to changes in neurotransmitters in younger or older adults (Greenberg & Fisher, 1989).

Normal aging has also been associated with the increased brain, plasma, and urine levels of monoamine oxidase (MAO) (Alexopoulos, 1991b), an enzyme that is involved in the catabolism of neurotransmitters. Increased MAO levels have been associated with various characteristics of depression in later life: depression with anxiety and physical illness (Georgotas et al., 1986a); depression with late onset (Alexopoulos, Young, Lieberman, & Shamoian, 1984); and depression with "reversible" cognitive impairments (Alexopoulous, Lieberman, Young, & Shamoian, 1987). The utility of plasma levels of MAO as predictors of differential response to pharmacological treatment has also received attention (Georgotas, McCue, Friedman, & Cooper, 1987). As with neurotransmitter levels, consistent relations between MAO levels and the onset and lifting of late-life depression have not been demonstrated (Schneider, 1990).

Hyperactivity of the hypothalamic–pituitary–adrenal (HPA) axis has also been associated with the occurrence of depression in both young and old (Sapolsky, 1992; Stokes & Sikes, 1991). Studies have demonstrated that subgroups of mixed-age depressives have higher plasma levels of cortisol, and early escape of cortisol suppression following a challenge dose of dexamethasone (constituting an abnormal result on the dexamethasone suppression test [DST]; see Sapolsky, 1992, for discussion). In geriatric depression, abnormal results on the DST occur in 70–80% of patients (Alexopoulos et al., 1984). Since a number of medical conditions other than depression (e.g., hypertension), as well as drug use (e.g., corticosteroids), significantly influence HPA activity and DST results, the validity of DST results as a sensitive and specific marker for depression has been called into question (Arana & Baldessarini, 1987). For example, DST results are also abnormal in 30–50% of patients suffering from Alzheimer's disease, and DST results do not distinguish depressed individuals with dementialike symptoms (e.g., memory complaints) from those who have depression coexisting with Alzheimer's disease (Alexopolous et al., 1984).

Recent experiments with both laboratory animals and human beings have also examined changes in serotonin-based neurotransmission that occurs in depression. For example, Nemeroff et al. (1988) and Schneider, Severson, and Sloane (1985) demonstrated a marked reduction in the numbers of platelet binding sites for the radioactive isotope [^{3}H]imipramine in geriatric depressives versus nondepressives. Platelet binding sites for [^{3}H]imipramine are thought to be an index of serotonin-based synaptic-transport capacity (Meltzer & Lowy, 1987). Reductions in [^{3}H]imipramine binding sites were not observed in Alzheimer's patients (Nemeroff et al., 1988; Schneider et al., 1985), suggesting that this laboratory marker may be useful in differentiating depression-related cognitive impairment (e.g., memory complaints) from Alzheimer's disease. At present, however, reduction in [^{3}H]imipramine binding sites, like other biochemical markers for geriatric depression, lacks sufficient sensitivity and specificity and thus is not generally useful as a basis for diagnosis (Schneider, 1990).

While research on biochemical markers of geriatric depression is generally viewed by members of the psychiatric community as holding promise, other neuroscientists believe the whole enterprise of using brain chemistry changes to construct causal explanations of depression is flawed. Rose (1987), for example, argued that "biological determinist" theories of depression based on changes in neurotransmitters or their metabolites are akin to explanations "of the voting habits of a household based on examination of the groceries the household buys and the garbage thrown out " (p. 105). According to Rose, such neurochemical changes do not cause depression "in the same way . . . as the firing of a frog's motor nerve causes its muscle to twitch." Rose concluded that neurochemical accounts of depression are "at best . . . a translation of the problem from one language to another" (p. 105) rather than an adequate causal theory.

Neuroanatomical and Neurochemical Changes Associated with Late-Life Depression and Dementia. The overlap between depressive disorders and dementia is well documented. Studies show that on average, 30% of patients diagnosed with Alzheimer's disease also meet criteria for clinical depression (Teri & Wagner, 1992), and approximately 20% of depressed patients exhibit cognitive impairment severe

enough to be diagnosed as dementia (LaRue et al., 1986).

Historically, depression and dementia have been differentiated into distinct disorders, based primarily on differences in course and extent of organic etiology: Deficits in depression are reversible and functional in nature; deficits in dementia are irreversible, degenerative, and organically based (cf. Caine, 1981). Teri and Wagner (1992) and Emery and Oxman (1992) provide an alternative conceptualization of depression and dementia in terms of different types of causal relationships (e.g., depression may cause dementia; dementia may cause depression; depression and dementia may occur or co-occur independently of one another, and each may occur alone). Both reviews emphasize that although these different types of depression–dementia relationships are conceptually distinct, little data currently exists to differentiate the patterns of causation.

These researchers argue for prospective studies of demented and depressed elders using measures useful to identify depression in dementia, depression alone, and dementia alone. For example, measures have been developed specifically to assess depression in dementia patients; preliminary psychometric data exist for both the Cornell Scale for Depression in Dementia (CSDD; Alexopoulos, Abrams, Young, & Shamoian, 1988) and the NIMH Dementia Mood Assessment Scale (DMAS; Sunderland et al., 1988). In addition, patterns of response on existing biological and psychosocial measures have been shown to be differentially associated with the two disorders and thus may be useful to identify each disorder (e.g., sleep electroencephalograms [Reynolds et al., 1985, 1988] and memory complaints [Kahn, Zarit, Hilbert, & Niederehe, 1975; O'Connor, Pollit, Roth, Brook, & Reiss, 1990]). Neuroimaging procedures (e.g., magnetic resonance imaging [MRI] and single photon emission computed tomography [SPECT]) offer the hope of visually identifying brain characteristics of depressed versus nondepressed elders (e.g., subcortical hyperintensities; see Coffey et al., 1993), but as yet, consistent structural differences between depressed and demented elders have not been demonstrated (Devous, 1992; Emery & Oxman, 1992).

Depression may also cause other functional deficits in dementia patients that can not be attributed to the dementing process. For example, Alzheimer's patients with depression demonstrate greater behavioral disturbance

(Reifler, Larson, & Teri, 1987) and functional deficits (Pearson, Teri, Reifler, & Raskind, 1989; Rovner, Broadhead, Spencer, Carson, & Folstein, 1989) than Alzheimer's patients without depression. Interestingly, depressed Alzheimer patients also tend to have less cognitive impairment (see Teri & Wagner, 1992, for discussion). This pattern of relationships in demented elders—more severe depression, greater functional disturbance, yet less cognitive impairment—strongly suggests that depression is a source of excess (and treatable) disability in dementia (see Reifler & Larson, 1989 for discussion).

Physical Illness and Pain.   Research clearly demonstrates an association between physical illness, pain, and depression in young and old (Katon & Sullivan, 1990), outpatient and institutionalized samples (Berkman et al., 1986; Moss, Lawton, & Glicksman, 1991; Parmelee, Katz, & Lawton, 1991; Williamson & Schulz, 1992a, 1992b). In general, increased severity of illness and increased pain are both directly related to increased severity of depression (cf. Parmelee et al., 1991).

Although physical illness and pain are more common in older than younger adults (Katon & Sullivan, 1990), it is not necessarily true that older adults become depressed more often in the face of illness than do young adults. Koenig et al. (1991) examined depressive disorders using the DIS in young (20–39 years) and old (70–102 years) medically ill, hospitalized men. Major depressive disorder was diagnosed in 22% of the young and only 13% of old patients; minor depression was diagnosed in 18% of the young, and 29% of the old patients. While MDD was also associated with more severe symptomatology in the younger men, in general, both age groups report similar patterns of symptoms of prolonged duration. These findings suggest that illness and pain may have similar effects on depression in both young and old, and that medically ill older adults may be no more vulnerable to depression. Clearly, additional studies that include direct age comparisons would shed light on this hypothesis.

The reasons for the relationship between physical illness, pain, and depression are not entirely clear. Several studies have examined the importance of activity restriction and functional impairments (i.e., the inability to do everyday tasks) associated with illness and pain as a mediating variable in geriatric depression. William-

son and Schultz (1992a), for example, reported that in a sample of community-dwelling older adults, those who reported greater functional impairment associated with pain or illness were more likely to be depressed than those who reported pain or illness but did not suffer functional impairment.

Interestingly, Parmelee, Katz, and Lawton (1989b) reported quite different results for institutionalized elders. Increased levels of pain, illness, and functional impairment were all associated with greater severity of depression, but changes in functioning did not account for the relationship between illness and pain, and depression. Parmelee et al. (1989b) suggested that in their institutionalized sample all three factors may "signify" one another, that is, "pain complaints may . . . be parallel expressions of our frail elder's poor health and disability" (p. M27). Indeed, such a view is in keeping with studies suggesting that physical and emotional distress are confounded in older adults (Rapp, Parisi, Walsh, & Wallace, 1988; Salzman & Shader, 1978).

Sleep Disturbance and Geriatric Depression. Subjective complaints of sleep disturbance (e.g., initial, middle, and terminal insomnia) are included in most standard diagnostic criteria for depression (e.g., RDC, DSM-IV) and in most self-report depression-screening measures (e.g., BDI, CES-D). Specific physiological changes have been associated with these subjective sleep complaints. Reynolds et al. (1985) reported that alterations in electroencephalographic (EEG) sleep markers, such as increased percentage of rapid eye movement (REM) sleep, longer initial REM periods, increased length of first non-REM sleep (NREM), and diminished REM latency, are consistently found in depressed relative to healthy and demented older adults. In a recent comprehensive meta-analytic review, Benca, Obermeyer, Thisted, and Gillen (1992) corroborated these differences between individuals diagnosed with depression and both healthy elders and those with other psychiatric disorders.

Reynolds et al. (1988) argued for using a combination of sleep physiological measures over single sleep measures in comparing depressed, demented, and healthy elders. For example, linear combinations of the following set of four measures—REM sleep latency, REM sleep percentage, percentage "indeterminant" NREM sleep (NREM sleep without characteristic EEG markers), and early morning awakenings or sleep maintenance—correctly identified 80% of elder patients diagnosed with depression versus dementia. These results strengthen the impression that older adults diagnosed with depression differ from those diagnosed with dementia in terms of both sleep continuity (greater sleep fragmentation in depressed than demented elders) and sleep architecture (diminished REM latency and greater proportion of REM sleep in depressed than demented elders).

Results such as these are in keeping with the view that a single physiological process may be related to both sleep and mood regulation (e.g., Borbely, 1982). On the other hand, some studies with younger depressives suggest that sleep disturbance continues after symptom remission during nondepressed intervals (Rush et al., 1986) and is thus related to some extent to processes independent of mood regulation. In order to examine the extent to which disturbances in sleep and mood reflect common versus distinct physiological processes and the extent to which sleep disturbance is state-dependent or more traitlike, longitudinal studies that examine sleep physiology and mood disturbance during both depressed and remitted states need to be completed.

Personality Factors. Three issues have been discussed regarding the relationship between personality factors and depression. First, depression itself may represent a chronic or enduring characterological feature that remains largely unchanged across the life span. Second, personality disorders may influence older adults' vulnerability for initial onset and recurrence of depression. Third, long-term personality disturbances may be a consequence of recurrent depressive episodes (see Akiskal, Hirschfield, & Yerevanian, 1983, for complete discussion). The first two issues are discussed here, the third in a later section (see section on impact of depression).

Blazer et al. (1987) reported that approximately 2% of their random sample of 1,300 community-dwelling elders demonstrated symptoms in keeping with DSM-III criteria for dysthymia or "chronic disturbance of mood" with "impairment in social and occupational functioning" (p. 231). These findings suggest that a sizable group of older adults suffer from depressive symptoms for long periods of their adult lives. Moreover, Alexopolous, Young, & Abrams (1989) demonstrated that elders who are diagnosed as dysthymic are also at risk for more severe depression (e.g., MDD), and following initial remission of symptoms, for frequent relapse.

In light of such findings, Costa (1991) has argued that chronic forms of geriatric depression, such as dysthymia, may be meaningfully conceptualized in terms of personality traits such as "neuroticism"—defined as an individual's tendency to experience dysphoric affects (sadness, hopelessness, dejection, etc.). Similar to the test measures of depression described previously, neuroticism is conceived of as a continuously distributed trait in normal populations and is indicated by high scores on standardized measures of anxiety, hostility, self-consciousness, depression, impulsiveness, and vulnerability (such as the Guilford–Zimmerman Personality Inventory; see Costa & McCrae, 1980). Data in favor of this viewpoint derive from longitudinal studies of personality indicating that an individual's level of neuroticism remains remarkably stable over long periods of time (Costa & McCrae, 1988) and has been predictive of depression following common late-life stressors (e.g., spousal bereavement; Quintilliani, Anguillo, Futterman, Thompson, & Gallagher-Thompson, 1992).

Data pertaining to the second issue, that personality disorders are associated with onset and recurrence of geriatric depression, are derived mostly from studies that demonstrate comorbidity between depression and other personality disorders in clinical samples of younger and older adults (cf. Shea, Widiger, & Klein, 1992). Estimates of comorbid personality disorder vary in older depressed samples, from 10% (Abrams, Alexopoulos, & Young, 1987) to over 50% (Thompson, Gallagher, & Czirr, 1988). By contrast, in younger samples, approximately 30–40% of depressed patients on average are diagnosed as also having a DSM-III or DSM-III-R Axis II personality disorder (Shea et al., 1992). Clearly, there is potential bias in comorbidity estimates obtained from clinically depressed patients. Assessment of personality disorder in patients who are currently depressed or remitted may influence personality presentation and description (Shea et al., 1992). Given the elevated rates of personality disturbance in depressed elders, and the influence of personality factors on both treatment process and outcome in depressed older adults (e.g., in terms of compliance with treatment regimen; see Thompson et al., 1991a, for discussion), it is reasonable to assume that personality factors or disturbance may play a significant role in the development of depression in at least some older adults. Thus, we feel it is appropriate to screen for personality disturbance and modify treatment for depression accordingly.

External Factors

Psychosocial Stress and Coping. There are two conceptual models of psychosocial stress and coping: "coping styles" (e.g., Billings & Moos, 1984) and "coping processes" (e.g., Lazarus & Folkman, 1984). Proponents of the coping styles model argue that an individual demonstrates a relatively consistent approach to a variety of stressful situations. Moos, Brennan, Fondacaro, & Moos (1990), for example, described two basic coping styles: (1) avoidance coping, which emphasizes ignoring and distraction from stressful situations, and (2) approach coping, which emphasizes methods of emotional expression and problem solving. Stressful situations are defined as major life events (e.g., marriage, death in the family) in the individual's life.

In contrast, proponents of the coping process model argue that the way an individual copes with stress constantly changes, depending on the individual's appraisal of the situation (Lazarus & Folkman, 1984). Stressors are not necessarily major life events, but rather are a combination of daily hassles and uplifts that tax the individual's resources. As with the coping styles approach, the functions of coping tend to be emotional regulation (emotion-focused coping) or task management (problem-focused coping). The extent to which either of these functions is fulfilled is determined by the individual's appraisal of the nature of the stressor and the resources available to them.

Age-related differences have been demonstrated in types of stressors, in the appraisal of particular stressful situations, and in the types of coping strategies employed (Aldwin, 1991; Lazarus & Delongis, 1983). For example, older adults tend to see stressful situations as more out of their control than do younger adults (Aldwin, 1991), and in some instances, older adults have demonstrated an emphasis on emotion regulation, less active behavioral discharge, and less use of social support than younger adults dealing with similar situations (Keyes, Bisno, Richardson, & Marston, 1987; Pearlin & Schooler, 1978). However, in other instances, older and younger adults both appear to maintain similar coping styles (e.g., planful problem solving; Aldwin, 1991).

Parallels exist between age-related and depression-related differences in coping. For example, among depressed adults, stressful situations are also more frequently appraised as uncontrollable (Aldwin, 1991). In addition, Keyes et al. (1987) found that depressed individuals employ significantly more avoidance behavior than nondepressed individuals; and Billings and Moos (1984) revealed that depressed patients employ coping strategies that are passive and focused more on regulating emotions than on managing the problem. Clearly, more research is needed to determine the extent and significance of this similarity.

Researchers have investigated aspects of coping that are of particular importance to older adults. According to survey data (Princeton Religion Research Center, 1982) and sociological studies of aging and religiosity (Ainlay & Smith, 1984), informal organizational activity (e.g., prayer, watching religious programs on television, etc.) is especially important among older as opposed to younger adults. Moreover, older adults spontaneously reported using faith and prayer more than any other coping behavior by a wide margin (Koenig, George, & Siegler, 1988). Although studies have yet to clearly demonstrate the impact on mental health of formal or informal religious participation relative to other coping strategies (e.g., emotion- and problem-focused coping), initial studies suggest that these aspects of religion help older adults cope with late-life stress (Koenig et al., 1992; Krause & Tran, 1989).

Bereavement and Depression in Later Life. Elders are much more likely than younger adults to suffer the loss of a significant relationship due to death. For example, 85% of all widows and widowers are over the age of 55 (U.S. Bureau of Census, 1991). Historically, bereavement and depression have been closely linked, both theoretically (e.g., Freud, 1917) and empirically (e.g., Lindemann, 1944). Although it is still unclear where normal grieving ends and depression begins (i.e., DSM-III-R and DSM-IV provide little help in differentiating "uncomplicated bereavement" from MDD), recent studies have begun to converge regarding the impact of late-life loss on health and mental health (see M. S. Stroebe, W. Stroebe, & Hansson, 1993, for a thorough overview). In general, most elders are remarkably resilient following loss, perhaps more resilient than younger adults (Perkins & Harris, 1990). For example, fewer than one-fourth of older widows and widowers demonstrate clinical depression during the first year following the loss of a spouse of many years (Lund, Caserta, & Dimond, 1988; Thompson, Gallagher, Futterman, Gilewski, & Peterson, 1991c; Zisook & Schucter, 1991). In fact, by most "clinical" indicators, bereaved elders as a group are virtually indistinguishable from nonbereaved elders at one year following loss (Norris & Murrell, 1987; Thompson, Gallagher-Thompson, Futterman, Gilewski, & Peterson, 1991b). However, this finding should not be interpreted to mean that bereavement has few effects on functioning in later life. For one thing, a small number of older adults (15–20% by most studies) demonstrate moderate to severe depressive symptomatology initially following loss and tend to show some persistent emotional distress for years after loss (Gilewski, Farberow, Gallagher, & Thompson, 1991). Moreover, on measures that assess the impact of the loss directly (e.g., "Do you still cry over the loss?" "Do you still miss the lost person?"), most elders do not appear to "return to normal" after 30 months or more, even if they demonstrate few other symptoms of emotional and physical distress (Thompson et al., 1991c). Indeed, Wortman and Silver (1989) have questioned whether complete resolution is a reasonable standard for anyone to achieve following significant loss. Given the regularity of late-life bereavement and the long periods an elder may live as a widow or widower, studies need to establish what constitutes "grief resolution" and to better describe the relationship between grief and depression in the years following significant loss.

Social Support and Geriatric Depression. Much recent research has focused on social support among older adults (see Antonucci, 1990, for an excellent overview) and its positive impact on both physical and mental health among elders encountering a wide range of common acute and chronic stressors, such as heart attack (Berkman, Leo-Summers, & Horwitz, 1992) or caring for a frail elder (Rivera, Rose, Futterman, Lovett, & Gallagher-Thompson, 1991). In general, social support has been defined in various ways by different gerontological researchers: as a unitary and multidimensional construct (e.g., Lin, Dean, & Ensel, 1986), as perceived available and actually utilized social resources (e.g., Dunkel-Schetter & Bennett, 1990), as positive and negative social interactions (e.g., Rook, 1984), and finally in terms of specific types of received support (Thompson, Futterman, Gallgher-Thompson, Rose, & Lovett, 1993).

Although it is clear that in a general sense, social support helps older adults cope with late-life stress, not all types of social support are equally helpful in buffering *specific* late-life stressors, nor is it true that the same social support buffers *all* types of late-life stressors (see Thompson et al., 1993, for example). Several theoretical perspectives have described the process of social support stress-buffering in terms of the "transaction" or "match" between specific stressors and supports utilized in the coping process (Cutrona & Russell, 1990; Moos, 1987). Although research has begun to focus on the dynamic links between dimensions of stress, support, coping, and mental health (e.g. Thompson et al., 1993), clearly much empirical research remains to be done in this area.

Ethnic Background and Birth-Cohort Effects. A growing body of research demonstrates that sociocultural factors such as ethnic background, gender, social class, family relationships, and birth cohort influence the expression of distress and the prevalence of depression. Excellent reviews of this research may be found in Jenkins, Kleinman, & Good (1987) and Kleinman (1988). In this section, we focus on cultural influences and birth-cohort effects as they relate specifically to late-life depression.

Ethnic background appears to influence the way depression is expressed in several ways. In general, individuals reflecting "noncontemporary Western" cultural backgrounds tend to express distress in terms of bodily or somatic symptoms—"Only in the contemporary West is depression articulated as an intrapsychic experience, e.g., 'I feel blue'" (Jenkins, Kleinman, & Good, 1987, p. 74). This general tendency to somaticize distress may be particularly salient in older Americans, who frequently come from noncontemporary Western backgrounds and who, despite assimilating into mainstream American society, retain many traditions from their culture of origin. Data for Mexican elders from the ECA study tend to support this view: Individuals who retain cultural traditions are much more likely to somaticize depression than individuals who reflect mainstream Western values, and this difference in somatization is most marked in older adults (Escobar, Burnham, Karno, Forsythe, & Golding, 1987).

In addition to cultural influences, there is a growing body of evidence that cohort or period may influence the frequency and nature of late-life depression. A series of studies by Klerman and colleagues (Klerman et al., 1985; Lavori, Klerman, Keller, & Reich, 1987; Lewinsohn, Rohde, Seeley, & Fischer, 1993; Warshaw, Klerman, & Lavori, 1991) demonstrated an increased risk and earlier onset of MDD among individuals born after 1930 in the five samples of the ECA study. Furthermore, during the 1960s and 1970s, MDD prevalence rates were double pre-1930 levels for individuals between 17 and 50 years of age. This pattern of findings, demonstrated in Figure 19.4, has been replicated cross-nationally. Individuals born after 1930 in nine countries reported higher rates of depression at younger ages than individuals born before 1930 (Cross-National Collaborative Group, 1992). Taken together, these findings strongly suggest that cohort or period effects may account at least in part for the different rates of depression observed in cross-sectional studies (e.g., Murrell et al., 1983).

Summary of Onset Research

A study by Lewinsohn, Rohde, Seeley, and Fisher (1991) provides an apt summary of research on factors associated with onset of geriatric depression. In a large sample of community-dwelling subjects aged 50–88 years, age and depression demonstrated largely "independent" effects on a wide array of demographic, health, and psychosocial measures. Depression was associated with increased severity of life stress and daily hassles, diminished self-esteem, decreased frequency of social contacts, diminished comfort in interpersonal events, and diminished enjoyment of pleasant activities, regardless of age, whereas increased age was associated with impaired auditory and visual acuity, slower performance on speeded tasks, and reduced memory and respiratory capacity, regardless of depression severity. Such findings, coupled with those from studies that provide direct age comparisons of the effects of illness and loss on mental health (e.g., Koenig et al., 1991), suggest that older adults may be no less successful in coping and no more vulnerable to depression than younger adults who are faced with similar stressors. Older adults, as a group, however, may cope with different types of common stressors and use different coping styles than younger adults.

Finally, the prevalence and expression of depression is clearly influenced by cultural and cohort factors. Depression is more apt to be reported as bodily complaints in less acculturated and older adults, and is less prevalent in individuals born prior to 1930 than in those born after 1950.

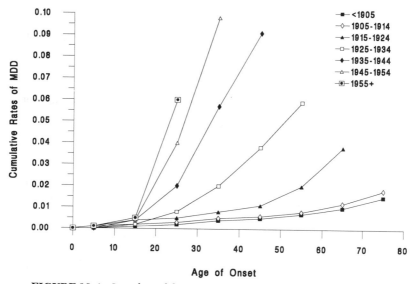

FIGURE 19.4. Cumulative lifetime rates of major depression by birth cohort and age of onset at five ECA sites (Cross-National Collaborative Group, 1993).

Impact of Depression on Quality of Later Life

A second smaller group of studies focuses on the "impact" or consequences of depression on health and functioning in older adults. These studies conceptualize depression as an independent variable with influences on health, cognition, behavior, and social relations, and typically use prospective or longitudinal designs.

Among the most well-documented consequences of depression across the life span is the increased risk of continued or recurrent episodes of depression and other negative health consequences (Keller, Shapiro, Lavori, & Wolfe, 1982; Lewinsohn, Zeiss, & Duncan, 1989; Phifer & Murrell, 1986). Rohde, Lewinsohn, and Seeley (1990) suggested as an explanation for this increased risk—the "scar hypothesis"—that depression leaves relatively permanent changes in the psychological and physiological state that increase vulnerability to subsequent depression. In order to assess the psychological side of this "scar hypothesis," Rohde et al. (1990) assessed by diagnostic interview and self-report questionnaire a community sample of 742 individuals aged 50 years or older at two time points on average 2½ years apart. Among these subjects, 73 were identified at the first assessment as MDD according to the RDC criteria, but were not depressed at the second assessment, and 351 subjects were identified as never having been depressed, according to the RDC. At each time of assessment, all subjects completed a battery of both self-report and interview measures focusing on health, stress, social support and social skills, interpersonal dependency, engagement and enjoyment of pleasurable activities, coping style, mood and life satisfaction, and cognitive functioning. Surprisingly, the formerly depressed subjects did not differ from the never depressed subjects at the second assessment on psychosocial variables, such as severity of stress, extent of social support, and coping style, suggesting that depression in later life leaves few if any psychosocial "scars."

In contrast, recent studies regarding the impact of depression on subsequent health suggest at least some physiological "scarring" due to depression. In general, depressed older adults are more vulnerable to illness and functional impairments following stress than are nondepressed older adults (see Gurland, 1991, for review). For example, depression predicted 6- and 18-month mortality and decreased functioning following a heart attack (Frasure-Smith, Lesperance, & Talajic, 1993, 1995); higher illness rates, functional impairments, and mortality among nursing home residents over a 1-year period (Parmelee, Katz, & Lawton, 1992b; Rovner et al., 1991); poorer health and functioning among bereaved elders over a 2½-year period following loss (Gilewski et al., 1991); and diminished immune functioning and social interaction among caregivers of Alzheimer's patients (Kiecolt-Glaser & Glaser, 1989). A wide variety of both animal and human studies suggest that stress and depression in later life cause changes directly in the central nervous system, including "neuron death," which might account for increased vulnerability to illness and subsequent depression (see Sapolsky, 1992, for an excellent review).

It is important to note, however, that negative health influences of depression are not consistently demonstrated among otherwise healthy, community-dwelling older adults. In two large surveys of community elders, for example, 2-year mortality rates were not associated with diagnoses of depression or severity of depressive symptoms (Fredman et al., 1989; Thomas, Kelman, Kennedy, Ahn, & Yang, 1992). Taken together, these studies and those cited previously suggest that depression may physiologically "scar" some older adults, but not others. Clearly, much remains to be demonstrated regarding the nature, mechanism, and generalizability of the negative effects of depression on physiological functioning and health in later life.

In the next section, we examine recent studies relating age and treatment outcome. How effective are existing treatments for late-life depression? Are existing treatment modalities more, or less effective in older adults? What modifications need to be made in working with older clients? Are there specific treatments that are effective for treating special groups of older adult depressives, such as those elders with coexisting medical illness or cognitive impairment?

EFFECTIVENESS OF TREATMENT FOR LATE-LIFE DEPRESSION

Treatment modalities are typically divided into two groups: psychosocial and somatic. Since most controlled-treatment studies of geriatric depression have focused on psychotherapy and pharmacotherapy, we focus our review on these studies. The interested reader is referred to

Salzman's (1992) excellent text, *Clinical Geriatric Psychopharmacology*, for a comprehensive overview of general issues pertaining to geriatric psychopharmacology. In addition, due to limitations of space, we have not reviewed controlled clinical outcome studies of electroconvulsive therapy (ECT). ECT is often used in the treatment of severe geriatric depression, and is not recommended as initial treatment for the majority of less severe forms of geriatric depression (Blazer, 1989). It remains a controversial form of treatment. The interested reader is referred to Sackheim (1989) and to Fisher and Greenberg (1989) for both positive and critical appraisals of the efficacy of ECT in treating geriatric depression.

Psychotherapy

A variety of forms of psychotherapy have been used to treat depressive disorder and depressive symptoms in older adults. These include psychodynamic psychotherapy, life review or reminiscent approaches, family therapy, psychoeducational approaches, and various cognitive–behavioral therapies. Most of the controlled empirical research on this topic has been conducted with cognitive–behavioral therapy (CBT) or its variants; thus we devote considerable space to that form of treatment. Excellent reviews of types of therapy used with older adults (including efficacy data) can be found in Bliwise (1987) and Smyer, Zarit and Qualls (1990). One review, specifically focusing on CBT, by Teri, Curtis, Gallagher-Thompson, and Thompson (1994) may be of particular interest to the reader.

Psychodynamic psychotherapies include insight-oriented, interpersonal, and supportive approaches (Smyer et al., 1990). In general, this form of treatment focuses on restitution of ego functioning and resolution of social and physical losses that occur with increasing frequency in later life. According to some researchers, long-term psychodynamic psychotherapy may be less appropriate for older adults than for persons of a younger age; thus short-term, time-limited adaptations of psychodynamic approaches have been developed. One example is the work of Horowitz, Marmar, Weiss, DeWitt, and Rosenbaum (1984), who assessed the efficacy of time-limited psychodynamic therapy for acutely bereaved persons, many of whom were depressed and elderly. They found that regardless of the age of the patient, those with higher motivation and better ego functioning benefited

most from this brief psychodynamic psychotherapy, whereas patients with lower motivation or poorer self-organization benefited most from supportive interventions.

In some of our own recent research done in collaboration with Marmar and Horowitz (e.g., Thompson et al., 1987; Marmar, Gaston, Gallagher, & Thompson, 1989), we compared the efficacy of brief psychodynamic psychotherapy with both cognitive and behavioral modalities. Ninety-one outpatient depressed elders were randomized to one of the three treatment conditions in which they received between 16 and 20 sessions of one type of therapy. Figure 19.5 shows that, overall, the three modalities were effective in reducing the severity of depression during the initial phase of treatment: 52% (47 of 91) subjects received no RDC diagnosis of depression at the posttreatment evaluation, and 70% showed significant improvement in depressive symptomatology at posttreatment (i.e., reduction in severity of distress on HDRS to levels of a "functional" elderly population). As can be seen in Figure 14.5, all three treatment modalities produced similar rates of improvement.

Additional data on the efficacy of psychotherapy for late-life depression can be derived from the 25–30 published studies in which various modalities, in both individual and group format, have been applied to various samples of depressed elders (e.g., dying patients, bereaved elders, depressed family caregivers, medically ill older adults). Of these Teri et al. (1994) reviewed 13 randomized or open clinical trials that utilized a waiting-list or control condition. In most of these 13 controlled studies, elements of cognitive and behavioral therapy were combined (as is frequently done in clinical practice) into a single form of treatment, CBT. Most controlled studies use CBT in an individual format. In general, these studies demonstrate that various forms of cognitive and behavioral psychotherapy can be as effective in treating geriatric depression as depressions occuring earlier in life, and that as in Thompson et al. (1987), one form of psychotherapy does not appear to be superior to other forms.

Reviews of psychotherapy outcome studies suggest that psychotherapy modalities effective for treatment of depression in younger adults may be equally effective for treatment of depression in older adults (Garfield, 1986). Meta-analyses of psychotherapy outcome studies provide additional support for this view. Smith, Glass, and Miller (1980) reported a .00 correla-

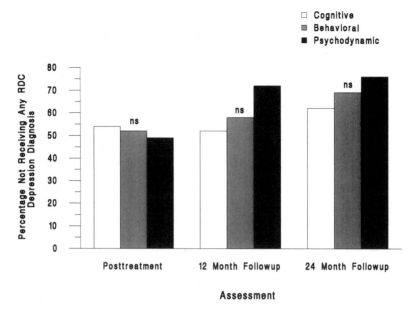

FIGURE 19.5. Success rates at posttreatment and follow-up for three psychotherapies (Thompson et al., 1987; Gallagher-Thompson et al., 1990).

tion between age and outcome. After matching studies with young and old subjects for duration of treatment and initial levels of symptom severity, Dobson (1987) also reported nonsignificant correlations between age and amount of symptom improvement following cognitive therapy. Moreover, the efficacy of psychotherapy for depression in older adults appears to be roughly comparable to efficacy of psychotherapy for depression in younger adults according to effect-size estimates derived from various meta-analyses (e.g., Scogin & McElreath, 1994, reported a .78 effect size for psychotherapy with older adults vs. Robinson, Berman, & Neimeyer, 1990, who reported a .73 effect size for psychotherapy with adults of all ages).

Other nontraditional forms of psychotherapy have also been used to treat depression in older adults, including bibliotherapy, marital and family therapies, life review approaches, psychoeducational group treatments (e.g., classes that teach psychological skills like problem solving and anger management), and self-help groups emphasizing growth and adaptation rather than symptom remission. Smyer et al. (1990) and Niederehe (1991) provide excellent reviews of many of these approaches. They note that few controlled studies have been conducted to assess their efficacy, and that unlike CBT, these alternative treatments of late-life depression are relatively diverse and

have been used primarily with normal community-dwelling older adults experiencing little psychological distress, or with nursing home residents experiencing adjustment problems, but rarely with clinically depressed older adults. In order to assess the efficacy of such treatments, more controlled outcome studies of well-defined versions of these treatments need to be completed. Good examples of such studies are Scogin, Jamison, and Gochneaur (1989) and Lovett and Gallagher (1988), who report generally positive findings for bibliotherapy with elder depressives, and for psychoeducational approaches to treating depression in caregivers, respectively.

Pharmacotherapy

In a review of 23 controlled clinical trials that assessed the efficacy of pharmacological treatment for late-life depression, Plotkin, Gerson, and Jarvik (1987) noted that "drugs are clearly superior to placebo; about 50% improvement [in symptom severity] versus 20–25% improvement on placebo; and all have undesirable side effects" (p. 311). More recent reviews of the pharmacological treatment of late-life depression literature (e.g., Reynolds, 1992) report somewhat greater differences in rates of response to medication and placebo: 50–70% with antidepressants versus approximately 10% with placebo. There is general consensus among geriatric psychiatrists that, given the effectiveness of different drugs in treating late-life depression, selection of particular antidepressant medication for particular patients is typically based on the extent to which side effects are noted and the medication is tolerated. Pharmacological agents most frequently evaluated in randomized, controlled treatment studies with elder depressives are tricyclic antidepressants (TCAs; e.g., nortriptyline, desipramine, imipramine, or doxepin), MAO inhibitors (e.g., phenelzine), or serotonin reuptake inhibitors (e.g., fluoxetine). Of these, the most detailed information about treatment efficacy and duration, and medication dosage and tolerance is available for TCAs, particularly nortriptyline.

Different response rates obtained in different pharmacotherapy trials reflect the manner in which response is assessed, the way drugs are administered and monitored, the duration of treatment, as well as the variability in efficacy of different medications. For example, response may be defined in terms of reduction in symptom severity (e.g., a drop in symptom severity of at least 50% on the HRSD or as remission of symptoms (e.g., a maintained HRSD < 10). In earlier studies, medication dosage for treatment of geriatric depression was often fixed at predetermined levels thought to be clinically effective. In light of the heterogeneity of drug response in older adults, more recent studies (particularly those using TCAs) have used "pharmacokinetic challenge" procedures to obtain optimal effective dosages for individual patients (e.g., Perel, 1991; Perel, Reynolds, & Pollack, 1989). In such procedures, a small dose of medication is administered prior to treatment and blood plasma levels are ascertained 48 hours later. Based on the individual's particular rate of drug metabolism, medication dosages are planned so that plasma levels reach the "therapeutic window" (i.e., range of steady-state plasma levels at which particular drugs are thought to be effective) more quickly and with a minimum of adverse effects. Medication dosages are then maintained by close monitoring of blood plasma levels and adverse effects.

Finally, pharmacological treatment studies of late-life depression vary in the duration and monitoring of treatment. Recent studies have extended treatment longer than earlier studies and monitor blood plasma levels closely in order to maximize initial response.

In a particularly well-designed placebo-controlled clinical trial, Georgotas et al. (1986b) described the safety and efficacy of two types of medication for the treatment of late-life depression—a TCA (nortriptyline), and an MAO inhibitor (phenelzine). After 7 weeks of treatment, both nortriptyline and phenelzine demonstrated significantly higher response rates than placebo: Approximately 60% of patients receiving either drug scored < 10 on the HRSD, indicating remission of symptoms, versus only 10% of placebo. Although side effects were noted, both drugs were reported to be well tolerated.

In several studies based on data from this clinical trial, Georgotas and colleagues demonstrated methods of maximizing and predicting initial response to antidepressant medication. For example, Georgotas and McCue (1989) demonstrated that by simply extending treatment from 7 weeks to 9 weeks, overall response rate for the older patients receiving either phenelzine or nortriptyline increased significantly (to 70% of patients). This finding suggests that the ameliorating effects of antidepressant medication may be delayed for some elder depressives. Moreover, certain groups of elder depressives predictably demonstrate longer response latencies. Lower plasma levels in the initial weeks of nortriptyline treatment and more severe depression were both associated with longer time to positive response (Georgotas, McCue, Cooper, Nagachandran, & Friedhoff, 1989).

Several randomized, placebo-controlled treatment studies have demonstrated that efficacy of pharmacological treatments for depression in elders with coexisting medical or psychological problems. Encouraging results have been demonstrated in pharmacological treatment of depression in elderly patients with Parkinson's disease (using a variety of antidepressants, including imipramine, nortriptyline, desipramine, and buproprion; see Cummings 1992), and in bereavement (using nortriptyline; Pasternak et al., 1991). In addition, Katz, Simpson, Curlik, Parmelee, and Muhly (1990) reported positive outcomes for nortriptyline in depressed, medically ill, nursing home residents. However, other studies have not been as encouraging with medically ill elders: Koenig et al. (1989) attempted a placebo-controlled treatment study using nortriptyline in depressed, older medical inpatients, but due to insufficient subject recruitment and dropout, the study had to be discontinued. In addition, although large numbers of elderly patients demonstrate coexisting Alzheimer's disease and depression (see Teri & Wagner, 1992, and the previous discussion), as yet only one controlled study has evaluated pharmacological treatment of depression in dementia patients (using imipramine), with mixed results (Reifler et al., 1989; Teri et al., 1991).

Comparative Effectiveness of Psychotherapy and Pharmacotherapy

Only a handful of studies have directly compared psychotherapy with pharmacotherapy for late-life depression. Sloane, Staples and Schneider (1985), used a variant of psychodynamic treatment for depression, interpersonal therapy (IPT; Klerman, Weissman, Rounsaville, & Chevron, 1984), to treat elderly depressives. In a randomized clinical trial, they found that IPT was as effective as nortriptyline at 6 and 16 weeks in obtaining initial remission of depressive symptoms, and was also associated with lower dropout rates.

Thompson and Gallagher-Thompson (1991) reported more favorable results for psychotherapy versus pharmacotherapy when CBT was compared with desipramine in the treatment of geriatric depression. In their study, older outpatient depressives with current episodes of greater than 2 years on average, were assigned to receive either CBT, desipramine, or a combination of both treatments. All patients were seen for 16–20 sessions over a 3- to 4-month period in the initial phase of treatment. By the end of the initial phase, approximately 60% of subjects receiving CBT were no longer exhibiting MDD using the SADS/RDC criteria; by contrast, only 35% of subjects receiving desipramine no longer had MDD.

Other studies that have directly compared CBT (both in individual and group formats) with pharmacotherapy (e.g., Jarvik, Mintz, Steuer, & Gerner, 1982; Beutler et al., 1987; Thompson & Gallagher-Thompson, 1991) have also demonstrated that CBT is at least as effective as pharmacological treatments of late-life depression, and more effective than a waiting-list control condition. As demonstrated in Thompson et al. (1987), however, when various forms of psychotherapy are directly compared to each other for treatment of late-life depression, in general, there are few advantages for one or the other type in the initial or acute phase of treatment.

Maintaining Gains Following Psychotherapy and Pharmacotherapy

Obtaining initial remission of depressive symptoms is one goal of treatment, but not the only goal. As Reynolds (1992) noted, "getting well is not enough, it is staying well that counts." In the early 1980s, it was assumed that prognosis for older adults following treatment for late-life depression was generally poor. As many as two-thirds of all treated older adult depressives had recurrent episodes of depression within 1–3 years of treatment (Murphy, 1983). Recent studies that have followed patients after successful treatment suggest that better long-term outcomes may now be expected.

For example, Gallagher-Thompson, Hanley-Peterson, and Thompson (1990) reported that initial gains made by patients receiving three types of psychotherapy (reported in Thompson, Gallagher, & Breckenridge, 1987) generally appear to be "durable." Using the RDC criteria, 52%, 58%, and 72% of depressed elders receiving brief cognitive, behavioral, and psychodynamic therapy, respectively, remained depression-free (i.e., received no RDC diagnosis of depression) at the 12-month follow-up assessment, and over 70% remained depression-free for all treatment modalities at the 24-month follow-up without additional treatment. These rates compare favorably with published reports of sustained remission rates of 56–70% over a 1-year period for younger depressed patients who received psychotherapy (e.g., Simons, Murphy, Levine, & Wetzel, 1986).

With respect to pharmacotherapy, Georgotas, McCue, Cooper, Nagachandran, and Chang (1988) were the first to demonstrate the safety and efficacy of continued, adequate antidepressant medication beyond initial remission of symptoms in order to prevent relapse (return of symptoms) and recurrence (appearance of a new episode). Of the subjects who participated in the initial comparative trial (Georgotas et al., 1986b), 72% (43 of 60 subjects) completed an additional 4- 8-month period of treatment, during which time they recieved either phenelzine or nortriptyline (depending on which medication they received in the trial). Of these responders, more than 68% remained in remission at the conclusion of the continuation phase of treatment (see Figure 19.6). Although side effects were reported by subjects receiving both drugs, the authors conclude that "both drugs

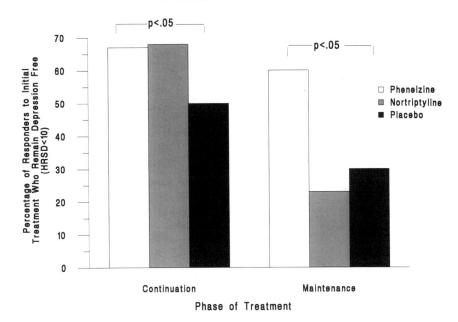

FIGURE 19.6. Success rates following continuation and maintenance phases of phenelzine and nortriptyline pharmacotherapy (Georgotas et al., 1986b; Georgotas, McCue, & Cooper, 1989).

were safe and effective in continuation therapy with a low risk of relapse" (p. 929).

Georgotas, McCue, and Cooper (1989) then completed a randomized clinical trial of the efficacy of "maintenance therapy" of phenelzine or nortriptyline using the 43 subjects who had remained well during the continuation phase of treatment (see Figure 19.6). Individuals who demonstrated positive outcome following initial and continuation treatment with either phenelzine or nortriptyline were randomized to a continued medication group (the "maintenance therapy condition") or to placebo. After 1 year of maintenance therapy, 44% (19 of 43 subjects) remained well, while 56% (24 of 43 subjects) had recurrences of depression. As Figure 19.6 demonstrates, patients receiving phenelzine had a significantly higher success rate (60% demonstrated HRSD < 10) and lower recurrence rate (13% demonstrated HRSD > 15) at 1 year than either nortriptyline (23% success; 54% recurrence) or placebo (30% success; 65% recurrence). Based upon these findings, the authors concluded that although both medications appear to be equally effective in the initial and stabilization phases of treatment, phenelzine may be more effective in maintaining gains over longer periods of time.

In a study of more severely depressed, inpatient older adults, Reynolds et al. (1989) reported somewhat better success with nortripyline maintenance therapy in elder inpatient depressives: a 58% success rate for continued medication with nortriptyline at 12–18 months (using HRSD < 10 criteria).

Combining Psychotherapy with Pharmacotherapy

The National Institute of Health Consensus Development Conference Consensus Statement (1991), *Diagnosis and Treatment of Depression in Late Life*, pointed to the special effectiveness of combination psychotherapy and pharmacotherapy in both acute and maintenance phases of treatment of late-life depression. Unfortunately, only two studies of treatment for late-life depression utilized a combination condition of both psychotherapy and pharmacotherapy.

Reynolds et al. (1992) examined the efficacy of nortriptyline and weekly sessions of IPT in combination during initial and continuation phases of treatment for geriatric depression. Seventy-three outpatient elderly depressives (mean age of 67.5 years) were randomized to the combined treatment condition or placebo.

Sixty-one patients (84% of those entering) completed the initial phase of treatment (9 weeks on average; range 2.7–37.3 weeks), and of these, 48 patients (79% of completers; 66% of those who entered) responded fully (achieved HRSD < 10 for 3 consecutive weeks) and 3 patients had a partial response (HRSD > 11 but < 14). These 51 patients who had full or partial response were then continued in combined treatment and stabilized (HRSD <10) for an additional 16 weeks. Five of these 51 patients (10%) relapsed during this period, but were then restabilized for 16 weeks. At the conclusion of continuation therapy, the 51 responders or partial responders were then randomized double-blind to a maintenance condition of nortriptyline alone or to placebo. Of the 25 subjects assigned to placebo, 6 relapsed in the first 4–6 weeks of maintenance therapy: by contrast, none of those assigned to the nortriptyline-alone condition relapsed.

Thompson and Gallagher-Thompson (1991) also examined the efficacy of combined treatment in a randomized, placebo-controlled, clinical trial comparing another TCA, desipramine (DMI), and CBT, each alone and in combination. Entering the study were 102 elderly outpatient depressives; 67 (68%) completed the initial phase of treatment, receiving 16–20 weeks of CBT, DMI, or combination treatment. Of these completers, approximately 60% of those receiving CBT alone or in combination with DMI were no longer depressed according to the RDC criteria, whereas only 34% of the completers in the DMI condition alone no longer met RDC criteria for MDD at end of 4–6 months of treatment. Almost 35% of those who entered the study dropped out, a figure much higher than that in Reynolds et al. (1992).

Thompson and Gallagher-Thompson (1991) also reported preliminary findings for their continuation phase of treatment. Patients who had not remitted after initial treatment were continued on CBT or combination treatment (depending on what they received in the initial phase of treatment). It is noteworthy that after approximately 4 months of continuation therapy, more than 90% of the combination condition had remitted (an increase of nearly 30% from the initial phase); a smaller increase (60–66%) was noted in the CBT continuation condition.

Although differences in study design, treatment modality, and assessment strategy make comparing some findings of Reynolds et al.

(1992) to Thompson and Gallagher-Thompson (1991) difficult, both studies clearly point to the effectiveness of combination treatment in both initial and continuation phases of treatment. Thompson and Gallagher-Thompson (1991) also suggest that CBT psychotherapy alone is effective in obtaining initial remission of symptoms for patients unable or unwilling to take antidepressant medication.

Depression Subtypes, Treatment Selection, and Treatment Modification

Are there types of depression for which particular types of psychotherapies and pharmacotherapies are most useful? Are there any modifications needed to the "standard" methods of treatment to increase treatment efficacy in elders? We next address each of these questions in turn.

Although a number of studies have been conducted on psychotherapy for late-life depression (as described previously), there is still a great deal to be learned regarding the best "match" between type of depression and type of treatment. Clinical lore has long held that more severe forms of depression (e.g., the endogenous or melancholic subtype, in particular) required psychotropic medication to be treated effectively, with probably only a small added benefit if psychotherapy were also included in the regimen (see Prusoff, Weissman, Klerman, & Rounsaville, 1980, for further discussion of this issue). However, our own work suggests that there are real problems in the validity of existing definitions of endogenous depression in the elderly and considerable confusion about how best to treat it. For example, different criteria identify different elders as endogenous, but regardless of the criteria used in older adults, greater severity of depression is not strongly associated with the endogenous diagnosis as it is in younger samples (Gallagher-Thompson et al., 1992). Subsets of endogenous older adults can be treated successfully with psychotherapy alone (Gallagher & Thompson, 1983; Thompson et al., 1991a), and at present there is no compelling evidence that pharmacotherapy is more effective in the treatment of late-life endogenous depression (however defined) than psychotherapy.

These studies suggest that much remains to be learned and empirically demonstrated regarding treatment for endogenous or melancholic late-life depression. Nevertheless, most researchers in the field today would argue a conservative position, and would prefer to treat severe late-life depression, and/or endogenous depression, with a treatment regimen that combined both psychotropic medication and one of the more efficacious methods of psychotherapy (Alexopoulos, 1991b). Other forms of depression, such as depression associated with chronic medical conditions or late-life bereavement, may be amenable to treatment with either psychotherapy or pharmacotherapy, as indicated previously.

Regarding the second question—how to modify "standard" therapies for older adults— the literature appears somewhat mixed. Many writers emphasize that modification should involve structural features (such as setting, length of session, or when and how to involve family members), rather than content or process features (Garfield, 1986). We have found that an awareness of changes in acuity of vision and hearing, as well as a knowledge of any changes in cognition, are obviously important in establishing an adequate context for treatment. Also, since all forms of psychotherapy involve learning of some kind, we have found that multimodal presentation of information can be very helpful. Suggestions for increasing the involvement of older adults in behavioral therapy, cognitive therapy, and CBT are discussed more fully in Zeiss and Lewinsohn (1986), Glantz (1989), and Thompson et al. (1991a), respectively.

In summary, treatment studies strongly indicate that certain forms of both psychosocial and pharmacological therapy, alone and in combination, can be very effective in treating geriatric depression. At the same time, much remains to be learned regarding which factors account for the efficacy of psychotherapy, the efficacy of combination therapy in initial, continuation, and maintenance phases of treatment, and the best "match" between types of depression and types of treatment. As with other areas of research, little or no data describe the efficacy of treatment for depression in the oldest-old.

CONCLUSIONS

The goal of this chapter was twofold: (1) to examine important research on the epidemiology, etiology, and, treatment of late-life depression published since Stoudemire and Blazer (1985),

and (2) to dispel certain prominent myths about aging and depression. We believe that the data (as of 1994) support the following conclusions:

1. Recent studies suggest that older adults do not necessarily demonstrate depression more frequently than younger adults. Depending on the assessment approach and definition used (e.g., classification vs. test approaches), and sample assessed (e.g., community vs. institutionalized), different relationships between depression and aging are described.

2. Few studies provide any data regarding depression for the oldest-old (those over 85 years of age). For example, in a review of the literature from 1986–1992, we were able to find fewer than a dozen studies providing any data on depression in this rapidly growing age group.

3. The validity of existing criteria for geriatric depressive disorders (e.g., DSM-III-R and DSM-IV MDD) continues to be questioned. Existing data suggest that there are differences in the clinical presentation of depression in younger and older adults.

4. Although many avenues of research on the genetics, biochemistry, and neuroanatomy of depression in later life appear to hold promise, *sensitive* and *specific* biological indicators for geriatric depression are currently lacking.

5. Stressors, such as illness and loss, associated with the onset of depression in young adulthood also tend to be associated with the onset of depression in later life. While older adults may cope differently with such stressors, in general, they appear to be *as successful as* younger adults in coping with similar stressors.

6. Ethnicity and birth cohort influence the presentation and prevalence of depression. Distress is more frequently expressed as somatic concerns in older and less acculturated adults. In addition, cross-national studies demonstrate that depression is diagnosed more frequently in younger age cohorts (e.g., those born after 1950) than in older cohorts (e.g., those born before 1930), suggesting that cohort effects may account at least in part for age differences in depression prevalence noted in other epidemiological studies.

7. Fewer studies address the *consequences* of late-life depression than address its *antecedents*. Having a depressive episode predicts the occurrence of subsequent depressive episodes in both community-dwelling and medically ill elders. Depression increases illness and mortality rates among elders experiencing physical illness, but

not generally in otherwise healthy community samples.

8. Finally, different forms of psychotherapy and pharmacotherapy, alone and in combination, can be effective in obtaining initial remission of depressive symptoms in later life, in maintaining gains, and in reducing the risk of relapse and recurrence. As in treatment-outcome research involving younger depressed patients, no single treatment (psychotherapy or pharmacotherapy or a specific type of either) emerges as the most efficacious for all depressed patients. Although results from the two studies that combine psychotherapy and pharmacotherapy suggest that combination treatment may yield high success rates, more comparative, controlled studies using different drugs and psychotherapy combinations in initial, continuation, and maintenance phases of treatment need to be conducted.

Acknowledgments. Portions of this chapter were presented as part of the symposium "Modifiability of Aging Effects: Clinical and Cognitive Changes" at the annual meeting of the Gerontological Society of America, Washington, DC, November 1992. Preparation of this chapter was partially supported by Grant Nos. AG11438 from the National Institute of Aging to Andrew Futterman and Grant Nos. MH47196 and MH19104 from the National Institute of Mental Health to Larry Thompson and Dolores Gallagher-Thompson.

Many thanks to Amy Gorin and Teresa Sanfelippo for their critical comments and work on several sections of the chapter, to Amy Wolfson for her clarification of points throughout the chapter, and to Tony Stankus for his extensive help in searching pertinent databases.

REFERENCES

Abrams, R. C., Alexopoulos, G., & Young, R. C. (1987). Geriatric depression and DSM-III-R personality disorder criteria. *Journal of the American Geriatrics Society, 35,* 383–386.

Ainlay, S. C., & Smith, D. R. (1984). Aging and religious participation. *Journal of Gerontology, 39,* 357–363.

Akiskal, H. S., Hirschfeld, R. M., & Yervanian, B. I. (1983). The relationship of personality to affective disorders: A critical review. *Archives of General Psychiatry, 40,* 801–810.

Aldwin, C. M. (1991). Does age effect the stress and coping process: Implications of age differences in perceived control. *Journals of Gerontology: Psychological Sciences, 46,* P174–P180.

Alexopoulos, G. (1991a). Anxiety and depression in the elderly. In C. Salzman & B. D. Lebowitz (Eds.), *Anxiety in the elderly* (pp. 63–74). New York: Springer.

Alexopoulos, G. (1991b). Biological correlates of late life depression. In *Abstracts of consensus development conference on the diagnosis and treatment of depression in late life* (pp. 34–36). Washington, DC: National Institutes of Health.

Alexopoulos, G., Abrams, R. C., Young, R. C., & Shamoian, C. A. (1988). Cornell scale for depression in dementia. *Biological Psychiatry, 23,* 271–284.

Alexopoulos, G., Young, R. C., & Abrams, R. C. (1989). Chronicity and relapse in geriatric depression. *Biological Psychiatry, 26,* 551–564.

Alexopoulos, G., Young, R. C., Kocsis, J. H., Brockner, N., Butler, T. A., & Stokes, P. E. (1984). Dexamethasone suppression test in geriatric depression. *Biological Psychiatry, 19,* 1567–1571.

Alexopoulos, G., Young, R. C., Lieberman, K. W., & Shamoian, C. A. (1984). Platelet MAO activity and age at onset of depression in elderly depressed women. *American Journal of Psychiatry, 141,* 1276–1278.

Alexopoulos, G., Lieberman, K. W., Young, R. C., & Shamoian, C. A. (1987). Platelet MAO activity in geriatric patients with depression and dementia. *American Journal of Psychiatry, 144,* 1480–1483.

American Psychiatric Association. (1980). *Diagnostic and statistical manual of mental disorders* (3rd ed.). Washington, DC: Author.

American Psychiatric Association. (1987). *Diagnostic and statistical manual of mental disorders* (3rd ed., rev.). Washington, DC: Author.

American Psychiatric Association. (1994). *Diagnostic and statistical manual of mental disorders* (4th ed.). Washington, DC: Author.

Andreasen, N. C., Flaum, M., & Arndt, S. (1992). The Comprehensive Assessment of Symptoms and History (CASH): An instrument for assessing diagnosis and psychopathology. *Archives of General Psychiatry, 49,* 615–623.

Antonucci, T. (1990). Social supports and social relationships. In R. H. Binstock & L. K. George (Eds.), *Handbook of aging and the social sciences* (3rd ed., pp. 205–227). New York: Wiley.

Arana, G. W., & Baldessarini, R. J. (1987). Clinical use of the dexamethasone suppression test in psychiatry. In H. Y. Meltzer (Ed.), *Psychopharmacology: The third generation of progress* (pp. 609–616). New York: Raven Press.

Baldwin, R. C. (1991). Depressive illness. In R. Jacoby & C. Oppenheimer (Eds.), *Psychiatry in the elderly* (pp. 676–719). Oxford: Oxford University Press.

Barrett, J. E., Barrett, J. A, Oxman, T. E., & Gerber, P. D. (1988). The prevalence of psychiatric disorders in a primary care practice. *Archives of General Psychiatry, 45,* 1100–1106.

Beck, A. T., Ward, C., Mendelson, M., Mock, J., & Erbaugh, J. (1961). An inventory for measuring depression. *Archives of General Psychiatry, 4,* 561–571.

Benca, R. M., Obermeyer, W. H., Thisted, R. A., & Gillin, J. C. (1992). Sleep and psychiatric disorders: A meta-analysis. *Archives of General Psychiatry, 49,* 651–668.

Berkman, L. F., Berkman, C. S., Kasl, S., Freeman, D. H., Leo, L. Ostfeld, A. M., Cornonih, J., & Brody, J. A. (1986). Depressive symptoms in relation to physical health and functioning in the elderly. *American Journal of Epidemiology, 124,* 372–388.

Berkman, L. F., Leo-Summers, L., & Horwitz, R. (1992). Emotional support and survival after myocardial infarction: A prospective, population-based study of the elderly. *Annals of Internal Medicine, 117,* 1003–1009.

Berry, J. M., Storandt, M., & Coyne, A. (1984). Age and sex differences in somatic complaints associated with depression. *Journal of Gerontology, 39,* 465–467.

Beutler, L. E., Scogin, F., Kirkish, P., Schretlen, D., Corbishley, A., Hamblin, D., Meredith, K. Potter, R., Bamford, C. R., & Levenson, A. I. (1987). Group cognitive therapy and alprazolam in the treatment of depression in older adults. *Journal of Consulting and Clinical Psychology, 55,* 450–556.

Billings, A. G., & Moos, R. H. (1984). Coping, stress, and social resources among adults with unipolar depression. *Journal of Personality and Social Psychology, 46,* 877–891.

Blashfield, R. K., & Livesley, W. J. (1991). Metaphorical analysis of psychiatric classification as a psychological test. *Journal of Abnormal Psychology, 100,* 262–270.

Blazer, D. G. (1982). *Depression in late life.* St. Louis, MO: Mosby.

Blazer, D. G. (1989). Affective disorders in late life. In E. Busse & D. G. Blazer (Eds.), *Geriatric psychiatry* (pp. 369–402). Washington, DC: American Psychiatric Press.

Blazer, D. G. (1991). Epidemiology of depressive disorders in late life. In *Abstracts of consensus development conference on the diagnosis and treatment of depression in late life* (p. 18). Washington, DC: National Institutes of Health.

Blazer, D. G., Burchett, B., Service, C., & George, L. K. (1991). The association of age and depression among the elderly. An epidemiological exploration. *Journals of Gerontology: Medical Sciences, 46,* M210–M215.

Blazer, D. G., Hughes, D. C., & George, L. K. (1987). The epidemiology of depression in an elderly community population. *Gerontologist, 27,* 281–287.

Blazer, D. G., Swartz, M., Woodbury, M., Manton, K. G., Hughes, D., & George, L. K. (1988). Depressive symptoms and depressive diagnoses in a community population: Use of a new procedure for analysis of psychiatric classification. *Archives of General Psychiatry, 45,* 1078–1084.

Blazer, D. G., Woodbury, M., Hughes, D. C., George, L. K., Manton, K. G., Bachar, J. R., & Fowler, N. (1989). A statistical analysis of the classification of depression in a mixed community and clinical sample. *Journal of Affective Disorders, 16,* 11–20.

Blehar, M. C., Weissman, M. M., Gershon, E. S., & Hirschfeld, R. M. (1988). Family and genetic studies of affective disorders. *Archives of General Psychiatry, 45,* 289–292.

Bliwise, N. G. (1987). The psychotherapeutic effectiveness of treatments for psychiatric illness in late-life. In E. Lurie & J. Swan (Eds.), *Serving the mentally ill elderly* (pp. 62–109). Lexington, MA: Lexington Books.

Borbely, A. A. (1982). A process model of sleep regulation. *Human Neurobiology, 1,* 195–204.

Breckenridge, J. N., Gallagher, D., Thompson, L. W., & Peterson, J. A. (1986). Characteristic depressive symptoms of bereaved elders. *Journal of Gerontology, 41,* 163–168.

Caine, E. (1981). Pseudodementia: Current concepts and future directions. *Archives of General Psychiatry, 38,* 1359–1364.

Coffey, C. E., Wilkinson, W. E., Weiner, R. D., Parashos, I. A., Djang, W. T., Webb, M. C., Figiel, G. S., & Spritzer, C. E. (1993). Quantitative cerebral anatomy in depression: A controlled magnetic resonance imaging study. *Archives of General Psychiatry, 50,* 7–16.

Comstock, G. W., & Helsing, K. J. (1976). Symptoms of depression in two communities. *Psychological Medicine, 6,* 551–563.

Costa, P. T. (1991). Depression as an enduring disposition. In *Abstracts of consensus development conference on the diagnosis and treatment of depression in late life* (p. 45). Washington, DC: National Institutes of Health.

Costa, P. T., & McCrae, R. R. (1980). Still stable after all these years: Personality as a key to some issues in adulthood and old age. In P. B. Baltes & O. G. Brim (Eds.), *Life-span development and behavior* (Vol. 3, pp. 65–102). New York: Academic Press.

Costa, P. T., & McCrae, R. R. (1988). Personality in adulthood: A six year longitudinal study of self-reports and spouse ratings on the NEO Personality Inventory. *Journal of Personality and Social Psychology, 54,* 853–863.

Cross-National Collaborative Group. (1992). The changing rate of major depression: Cross-national comparisons. *Journal of the American Medical Association, 268,* 3098–3105.

Cummings, J. L. (1992). Depression and Parkinson's disease: A review. *American Journal of Psychiatry, 149,* 443–454.

Cutrona, C., & Russell, D. (1990). Type of social support and specific stress: Toward a theory of optimal matching. In B. Sarason, I. Sarason, & G. Pierce (Eds.), *Social support: An interactional view* (pp. 319–366). New York: Wiley.

Davidson, J. R., Woodbury, M. A., Zisook, S., & Giller, E. L. (1989). Classification of depression by grade of membership analysis: A confirmation study. *Psychological Medicine, 19,* 987–989.

Devous, M. D. (1992). Comparison of SPECT applications in neurology and psychiatry. *Journal of Clinical Psychiatry, 53*(Suppl.), 13–19.

Dobson, K. S. (1987). A meta-analysis of the efficacy of cognitive therapy for depression. *Journal of Consulting and Clinical Psychology, 57,* 414–419.

Dunkel-Schetter, C., & Bennett, T. (1990). Differentiating the cognitive and behavioral aspects of social support. In B. Sarason, I. Sarason, & G. Price (Eds.), *Social support: An interactional view* (pp. 267–297). New York: Wiley.

Dye, C. J. (1978). Psychologists' role in the provision of mental health care for the elderly. *Professional Psychology, 9,* 38–49.

Eaton, W. E., & Kessler, L. G. (1981). Rates of symptoms of depression in a national sample. *American Journal of Epidemiology, 114,* 528–538.

Emery, V. O., & Oxman, T. E. (1992). Update on the dementia spectrum of depression. *American Journal of Psychiatry, 149,* 305–317.

Escobar, J. I., Burnam, M. A., Karno, M., Forsythe, A., & Golding, J. M. (1987). Somatization in the community. *Archives of General Psychiatry, 44,* 713–718.

Fisher, S., & Greenberg, R. P. (1989). A second opinion: Rethinking the claims of biological psychiatry. In S. Fisher & R. P. Greenberg (Eds.), *The limits of biological treatments for psychological distress* (pp. 309–336). Hillsdale, NJ: Erlbaum.

Frasure-Smith, N., Lesperance, F., Talajic, M. (1993). Depression following myocardial infarction: Impact on six-month survival. *Journal of the American Medical Association, 270,* 819–825.

Frasure-Smith, N., Lesperance, F., & Talajic, M. (1995). Depression and 18-month prognosis after myocardial infarction. *Circulation, 4*, 999–1005.

Fredman, L., Schoenback, V. J., Kaplan, B. H., Blazer, D. G., James, S. A., Kleinbau, D. G., & Yankaska, B. (1989). The association between depressive symptoms and mortality among older participants in the Epidemiological Catchment Area-Piedmont Health Survey. *Journals of Gerontology: Social Sciences, 44*, S141–S144.

Frerichs, R. R., Aneshensel, C. S., & Clark, V. A. (1981). Prevalence of depression in Los Angeles County. *American Journal of Epidemiology, 113*, 691–699.

Freud, S. (1917). Mourning and melancholia. In J. Strachey (Ed.), *The standard edition of the complete psychological works of Sigmund Freud* (Vol. 14, pp. 239–256). London: Hogarth Press.

Futterman, A., Hanser, S., Hanley-Peterson, P., Thompson, L. W., & Gallagher-Thompson, D. (1993). *Endogenous depression and pleasurable activity in older adults*. Unpublished manuscript.

Gallagher, D. (1986). Assessment of depression by interview methods and psychiatric rating scales. In L. Poon (Ed.), *Handbook for clinical memory assessment of older adults* (pp. 202–212). Washington, DC: American Psychological Association.

Gallagher, D., Breckenridge, J., Steinmetz, J., & Thompson, L. W. (1983). The Beck Depression Inventory and Research Diagnostic Criteria: Congruence in an older population. *Journal of Consulting and Clinical Psychology, 51*, 945–946.

Gallagher, D., & Thompson, L. W. (1983). Effectiveness of psychotherapy for both endogenous and nonendogenous depression in older adult outpatients. *Journal of Gerontology, 38*, 707–712.

Gallagher-Thompson, D., Futterman, A., Hanley-Peterson, P., Zeiss, A., Ironson, G., & Thompson, L. W. (1992). Endogenous depression in the elderly: Prevalence and agreement among measures. *Journal of Consulting and Clinical Psychology, 60*, 300–303.

Gallagher-Thompson, D., Hanley-Peterson, P. & Thompson, L. W. (1990). Maintenance of gains versus relapse following brief psychotherapy for depression. *Journal of Consulting and Clinical Psychology, 58*, 371–374.

Garfield, S. L. (1986). Research on client variables in psychotherapy. In S. L. Garfield & A. E. Bergin (Eds.), *Handbook of psychotherapy and behavior change* (3rd ed., pp. 213–257). New York: Wiley.

Gatz, M., & Hurwicz M. L., (1990). Are old people more depressed? Cross-sectional data on Center for Epidemiological Studies Depression Scale factors. *Psychology and Aging, 5*, 284–290.

Gatz, M., & Pearson, C. G. (1988). Ageism revised and the provision of psychological services. *American Psychologist, 43*, 184–188.

Gatz, M., Pedersen, N. L., Plomin, R., Nesselroade, J. R., & McClearn, G. E. (1992). Importance of shared genes and shared environments for symptoms of depression in older adults. *Journal of Abnormal Psychology, 101*, 701–708.

Georgotas, A., & McCue, R. E. (1989). The additional benefit of extending an antidepressant trial past seven weeks in depressed elderly. *International Journal of Geriatric Psychiatry, 4*, 191–195.

Georgotas, A., McCue, R. E., & Cooper, T. B. (1989). A placebo-controlled comparison of nortriptyline and phenelzine in maintenance therapy depressed patients. *Archives of General Psychiatry, 46*, 783–786.

Georgotas, A., McCue, R. E., Cooper, T. B., Nagachandran, N., & Chang, I. (1988). How effective and safe is continuation therapy in elderly depressed patients? *Archives of General Psychiatry, 45*, 929–932.

Georgotas, A., McCue, R. E., Cooper, T. B., Nagachandran, N., & Friedhoff, A. (1989). Factors affecting the delay of antidepressant response to nortriptyline and phenelzine. *Psychiatry Research, 28*, 1–9.

Georgotas, A., McCue, R. E., Friedman, E., & Cooper, T. B. (1987). Prediction of response to nortriptyline and phenelzine by platelet MAO activity. *American Journal of Psychiatry, 144*, 338–340.

Georgotas, A., McCue, R. E., Friedman, E, Hapworth, W., Kim, O. M., Cooper, T. B., Chang, I., & Stokes, P. E. (1986a). Relationship of platelet MAO activity to characteristics of major depressive illness. *Psychiatric Research, 19*, 247–256.

Georgotas, A., McCue, R. E., Hapworth, W., Friedman, E., Kim, O. M., Welkowitz, J., Chang, I., & Cooper, T. B. (1986b). Comparative efficacy and safety of MAOIs versus TCAs in treating depression in the elderly. *Biological Psychiatry, 21*, 1155–1166.

Gilewski, M., Farberow, N., Gallagher, D., & Thompson, L. W. (1991). Interaction of depression and bereavement on mental health in the elderly. *Psychology and Aging, 6*, 67–75.

Glantz, M. D. (1989). Cognitive therapy with the elderly. In A. Freeman, K. M. Simon, L. E. Beutler, & H. Arkowitz (Eds.), *Comprehensive handbook of cognitive therapy* (pp. 467–490). New York: Plenum Press.

Greenberg, R. P., & Fisher, S. (1989). Examining antidepressant effectiveness: Findings, ambiguities, and some vexing problems. In S. Fisher & R. P. Greenberg (Eds.), *The limits of biological treatments for psychological distress* (pp. 1–38). Hillsdale, NJ: Erlbaum.

Gurland, B. J. (1976). The comparative frequency of depression in various adult age groups. *Journal of Gerontology, 31*, 283–292.

Gurland, B. J. (1991). The impact of depression on the quality of life of the elderly. In *Abstracts of consensus development conference on the diagnosis and treatment of depression in late life* (pp. 25–30). Washington, DC: National Institutes of Health.

Hamilton, M. (1967). Development of a rating scale for primary depressive illness. *British Journal of Social and Clinical Psychology*, 278–296.

Herzog, C., Van Alstine, J., Usala, P. D., Hultsch, D. F., & Dixon, R. (1990). Measurement properties of the Center for Epidemiological Studies Depression Scale (CES-D) in older populations. *Psychological Assessment: A Journal of Consulting and Clinical Psychology, 2*, 64–72.

Himmelfarb, S. (1984). Age and sex differences in the mental health of older persons. *Journal of Consulting and Clinical Psychology, 52*, 844–856.

Horowitz, M. J., Marmar, C., Weiss, D., DeWitt, K., & Rosenbaum, R. (1984). Brief psychotherapy of grief reactions. *Archives of General Psychiatry, 41*, 439–448.

Jarvik, L. F., Mintz, J. M., Steur, J., & Gerner, R. (1982). Treating geriatric depression: A 26-week interim analysis. *Journal of the American Geriatrics Society, 30*, 713–717.

Jenkins, J. H., Kleinman, A., & Good, B. J. (1989). Cross-cultural aspects of depression. In J. Becker & A. Kleinman (Eds.), *Psychosocial aspects of depression* (pp. 67–99). Hillsdale, NJ: Earlbaum.

Kahn, R. L., Zarit, S. L., Hilbert, N. M., & Niederehe, G.

(1975). Memory complaint and impairment in the aged: The effect of depression and altereds brain function. *Archives of General Psychiatry, 32,* 1569–1573.

Katon, W., & Sullivan, M. D. (1990). Depression and chronic medical illness. *Journal of Clinical Psychiatry, 51,* 3–11.

Katz, I. R., Simpson, G. M., Curlik, S. M., Parmelee, P. A., Muhly, C. (1990). Pharmacolgic treatment of major depression for elderly patients in residential care settings. *Journal of Clinical Psychiatry, 51*(Suppl.), 41–47.

Keller, M. B., Shapiro, R. W., Lavori, P. W., & Wolfe, N. (1982). Recovery in major depressive disorder. *Archives of General Psychiatry, 39,* 905–910.

Kiecolt-Glaser, J. K., & Glaser, R. (1989). Caregiving, mental health, and immune function. In E. Light & B. Lebowitz (Eds.), *Alzheimer's disease, treatment, and family stress: Directions for research* (pp. 245–266). Washington, DC: Department of Health and Human Services.

Kempthorne, O. (1978). Logical, epistemological, and statistical aspects of nature–nurture data interpretation. *Biometrics, 34,* 1–23.

Keyes, K., Bisno, B., Richardson, J., & Marston, A. (1987). Age differences in coping, behavioral dysfunction and depression following colostomy surgery. *Gerontologist, 27,* 182–184.

Kleinman, A. (1988). *Rethinking psychiatry: From cultural category to personal experience.* New York: Free Press.

Klerman, G. L., Weissman, M. M, Rounsaville, B. J., & Chevron, E. S. (1984). *Interpersonal psychotherapy of depression.* New York: Basic Books.

Klerman, G. L., Lavori, P. W., Rice, J., Reich, T., Endicott, J., Ambrose, N. C., Keller, M. B., & Hirschfeld, R. M. (1985). Birth cohort trends in rates of major depressive disorder among relatives of patients with affective disorder. *Archives of General Psychiatry, 42,* 689–693.

Koenig, H. G., Cohen, H. J., Blazer, D. G., Pieper, C., Meador, K. G., Shelp, F., Goli, V. & DiPasquale, B. (1992). Religious coping and depression among elderly, hospitalized medically-ill men. *American Journal of Psychiatry, 149,* 1693–1700.

Koenig, H. G., George, L. W., & Siegler, I. C. (1988). The use of religion and other emotion-regulating coping strategies among older adults. *Gerontologist, 28,* 303–310.

Koenig, H. G., Meador, K. G., Shelp, F., Goli, V., Cohen, H. T., & Blazer, D. G. (1989). Antidepressant use in elderly medical inpatients: Lessons from an attempted clinical trial. *Journal of General Internal Medicine, 4,* 498–505.

Koenig, H. G., Meador, K. G., Shelp, F., Goli, V., Cohen, H. T., & Blazer, D. G. (1991). Major depressive disorder in hospitalized medically ill patients: An examination of young and elderly male veterans. *Journal of American Geriatrics Society, 39,* 881–890.

Krause, N., & Tran, T. V. (1989). Stress and religious involvement among older blacks. *Journals of Gerontology: Social Sciences, 44,* S4–S13.

LaRue, A., D'Elia, L. F., Clark, E. O., Spar, J. E., & Jarvik, L. F. (1986). Clinical tests of memory in dementia, depression, and healthy aging. *Psychology and Aging, 1,* 69–77.

Lavori, P. W., Klerman, G. L., Keller, M. B., & Reich, T. (1987). Age-period-cohort analysis of secular trends in onset of major depression: Findings in siblings of patients with major affective disorder. *Journal of Psychiatric Research, 21,* 23–35.

Lazarus, R. S., & DeLongis, A. (1983). Psychological stress and coping in aging. *American Psychologist, 38,* 245–254.

Lazarus, R. S., & Folkman, S. (1984). *Stress, appraisal, and coping.* New York: Springer.

Lewinsohn, P. M. (1974). A behavioral approach to depression. In R. J. Friedman & M. M. Katz (Eds.), *The psychology of depression: Contemporary theory and research.* Washington, DC: Winston.

Lewinsohn, P. M., Duncan, E. M., Stanton, A. K., & Hautzinger, M. (1986). Age at first onset for nonbipolar depression. *Journal of Abnormal Psychology, 95,* 378–383.

Lewinsohn, P. M., Rohde, P., Seeley, J. R., & Fischer, S. A. (1991). Age and depression: Unique and shared effects. *Psychology and Aging, 6,* 247–260.

Lewinsohn, P. M., Rohde, P., Seeley, J. R., & Fischer, S. A. (1993). Age-cohort changes in the lifetime occurrence of depression and other mental disorders. *Journal of Abnormal Psychology, 102,* 110–120.

Lewinsohn, P. M., Zeiss, A. M., & Duncan, E. M. (1989). Probability of relapse after recovery from an episode of depression. *Journal of Abnormal Psychology, 98,* 107–116.

Lewontin, R. (1974). The analysis of variance and analysis of causes. *American Journal of Human Genetics, 26,* 400–411.

Lin, N., Dean, A., & Ensel, W. (1986). Social support, life events, and depression. New York: Academic Press.

Lindemann, E. (1944). Symptomatology and management of acute grief. *American Journal of Psychiatry, 101,* 141–148.

Loevinger, J. (1957). Objective tests as instruments of psychological theory. *Psychological Reports, 3,* 635–694.

Lovett, S., & Gallagher, D., (1988). Psychoeducational interventions for family caregivers: Preliminary efficacy data. *Behavior Therapy, 19,* 321–330.

Lund, D. A., Caserta, M. S., & Dimond, M. F. (1989). Impact of spousal bereavement on the subjective well-being of older adults. In D.A. Lund (Ed.), *Older bereaved spouses: Research with practical applications* (pp. 3–15). New York: Taylor & Francis/Hemisphere.

Marmar, C., Gaston, L., Gallagher, D., & Thompson, L. W. (1989). Alliance and outcome in late-life depression. *Journal of Nervous and Mental Disease, 177* (8), 464–472.

Meltzer, H. Y., & Lowy, M. T. (1987). The serotonin hypothesis of depression. In H. Y. Meltzer (Ed.), *Psychopharmacology: The third generation of progress* (pp. 513–524). New York: Raven Press.

Moos, R. H. (1987). Life stressors, social resources, and the treatment of depression. In J. Becker & A. Kleinman (Eds.), *Psychosocial aspects of depression* (pp. 187–214). Hillsdale, NJ: Earlbaum.

Moos, R. H., Brennan, P. L., Fondacaro, M. R., & Moos, B. S. (1990). Approach and avoidance coping responses among older problem and nonproblem drinkers. *Psychology and Aging, 5,* 31–40

Moss, M. S., Lawton, M. P., & Glicksman, A. (1991). The role of pain in the last year of life of older persons. *Journals of Gerontology: Psychological Sciences, 46,* P51–P57.

Murphy, E. (1983). The prognosis of depression in old age. *British Journal of Psychiatry, 142,* 111–119.

Murrell, S. A., Himmelfarb, S., & Wright, K. (1983). Prevalence of depression and its correlates in older adults. *American Journal of Epidemiology, 117,* 173–185.

Murrell, S. A., & Meeks, S. (1992). Depressive symptoms in older adults: Predispositions, resources, and life experiences. In K. W. Schaie & M. P. Lawton (Eds.), *Annual Review of Gerontology and Geriatrics* (Vol. 11, pp. 261–286). New York: Springer.

Myers, J. K., Weissman, M. M., Tischler, G. L., Holzer III, C. E., Leaf, P. J., Orvaschel, H., Anthony, J. C., Boyd, J. H., Burke, J. D., Kramer, M., & Stoltzman, R. (1984). Six-month prevalence of psychiatric disorders in three communities. *Archives of General Psychiatry, 41,* 959–967.

National Institutes of Health Consensus Development Conference Consensus Statement. (1991). *Diagnosis and treatment of depression in late life* (Vol. 9, No. 3, pp. 1–27). Washington, DC: Author.

National Institute of Mental Health. (1988). Assessment in diagnosis and treatment of geropsychiatric patients. *Psychopharmacological Bulletin, 24,* 501–828.

National Library of Medicine. (1991). *Current bibliographies in medicine: Diagnosis and treatment of depression in late-life* (Document 91-10). Washington, DC: U.S. Government Printing Office.

Nemeroff, C. B., Knight, D. L., Krishnan, R. R., Slotkin, T. A., Bissette, G., Melville, M. L., & Blazer, D. G. (1988). Marked reduction in number of platelet-tritiated imipramine binding sites in geriatric depression. *Archives of General Psychiatry, 45,* 919–923.

Newmann, J. P. (1989). Aging and depression. *Psychology and Aging, 4,* 150–165.

Newmann, J. P., Engel, R. J., & Jensen, J. (1990). Depressive symptoms among older women. *Psychology and Aging, 5,* 101–118.

Newmann, J. P., Engel, R. J., & Jensen, J. (1991a). Age differences in depressive symptom experiences. *Journals of Gerontology: Psychological Sciences, 46,* 224–235.

Newmann, J. P., Engel, R. J., & Jensen, J. (1991b). Changes in depressive symptom experiences among older women. *Psychology and Aging, 6,* 212–222.

Niederehe, G. (1991). Psychosocial therapies with depressed elders. In *Abstracts of consensus development conference on the diagnosis and treatment of depression in late life* (pp 72–74). Washington, DC: National Institutes of Health.

Nolen-Hoeksema, S. (1987). Sex differences in unipolar depression. *Psychological Bulletin, 101,* 259–282.

Norris, F. N., & Murrell, S. A. (1987). Older adult family stress and adaptation before and after bereavement. *Journal of Gerontology, 42,* 609–616.

Norris, J. T., Gallagher, D., Wilson, A., & Winograd, C. H. (1987). Assessment of depression in geriatric medical outpatients: The validity of two screening measures. *Journal of the American Geriatrics Society, 35,* 989–995.

Nurnberger, J. I., Blehar, M. C., Kaufmann, C. A., York-Cooler, C., et al. (1994). Diagnostic Interview for Genetic Studies: Rationale, unique features, and training. *Archives of General Psychiatry, 57,* 849–859.

O'Connor, D. W., Pollitt, P. A., Roth, M., Brook, P. B., & Reiss, B. B. (1990). Memory complaints and impairment in normal, depressed, and elderly persons identified in a community survey. *Archives of General Psychiatry, 47,* 224–227.

Parmelee, P. A., Katz, I. R., & Lawton, M. P. (1989a). Depression among institutionalized aged: Assessment and prevalence estimation. *Journals of Gerontology: Medical Sciences, 44,* M22–M29.

Parmelee, P. A., Katz, I. R., & Lawton, M. P. (1991). The relationship of pain to depression in institutionalized aged. *Journals of Gerontology: Psychological Sciences, 46,* P15–P22.

Parmelee, P. A., Katz, I. R., & Lawton, M. P. (1992a). Incidence of depression in long-term care settings. *Journals of Gerontology: Medical Sciences, 47,* M189–M196.

Parmelee, P. A., Katz, I. R., & Lawton, M. P. (1992b). Depression and mortality among institutionalized aged. *Journals of Gerontology: Psychological Sciences, 47,* 3–10.

Parmelee, P. A., Lawton, M. P., & Katz, I. R. (1989b). Psychometric properties of the Geriatric Depression Scale among the institutionalized aged. *Psychological Assessment: A Journal of Consulting and Clinical Psychology, 1,* 331–338.

Pasternak, R. E., Reynolds, C. F., Schlernitzauer, M., Hoch, C. C., Buysse, D. J., Houck, P. R., & Perel, J. M. (1991). Acute open-trial nortriptyline therapy of bereavement-related depression in late life. *Journal of Clinical Psychiatry, 52,* 307–310.

Pearlin, L.I., & Schooler, C. (1978). The structure of coping. *Journal of Health and Social Behavior, 19,* 2–21.

Pearson, J., Teri, L., Reifler, B. V., & Raskind, M. (1989). Functional status and cognitive impairment in Alzheimer's disease patients. *Journal of the American Geriatrics Society, 39,* 1117–1121.

Perel, J. M. (1991). Pharmacokinetics of therapeutics, toxic effects, and compliance. In *Abstracts of consensus development conference on the diagnosis and treatment of depression in late life* (pp. 55–59). Washington, DC: National Institutes of Health.

Perel, J. M., Reynolds, C. F., & Pollock, B. G. (1989). Prospective pharmacokinetic dosing of nortriptyline for acute and maintenance treatment of elderly patients. *Clinical Pharmacology and Therapeutics, 45,* 135.

Perkins, H. W., & Harris, L. B. (1990). Familial bereavement and health in adult life course perspective. *Journal of Marriage and the Family, 52,* 233–241.

Perlick, D., & Atkins, A. (1984). Variations in the reported age of a patient: A source of bias in the diagnosis of depression and dementia. *Journal of Consulting and Clinical Psychology, 52,* 812–820.

Phifer, J. F., & Murrell, S. A. (1986). Etiologic factors in the onset of depressive symptoms in older adults. *Journal of Abnormal Psychology, 95,* 282–291.

Plomin, R., & McClearn, G. E. (1990). Human behavioral genetics of aging. In J. E. Birren & K. W. Schaie (Eds.), *Handbook of the psychology of aging* (3rd ed., pp. 67–78). New York: Academic Press.

Plotkin, D. A., Gerson, S. C., & Jarvik, L. F. (1987). Antidepressant drug treatment in the the elderly. In H. Y. Meltzer (Ed.), *Psychopharmacology: The third generation of progress* (pp. 1149–1158). New York: Raven Press.

Princeton Religion Research Center. (1982). *Religion in America.* Princeton, NJ: Gallup Poll.

Prusoff, B. Weissman, M. M., Klerman, G., & Rounsaville, B. (1980). Research diagnostic criteria subtypes of depression: Their role as predictors of differential response to psychotherapy and drug treatment. *Archives of General Psychiatry, 37,* 796–801.

Quintilliani, D., Angiullo, L., Futterman, A., Thompson, L. W., & Gallagher-Thompson, D. (1992, November). Personality factors as predictors of mental health following late-life spousal loss. Paper presented at the meeting of the Gerontological Society of America, Washington, DC.

Radloff, L. (1977). The CES-D Scale: A self-report depression scale for research in the general population. *Applied Psychological Measurement, 1*, 385–401.

Rapp, S. R., & Davis, K. M. (1989). Geriatric depression: Physician's knowledge, perceptions, and diagnostic practices. *Gerontologist, 29*, 252–257.

Rapp, S. R., Parisi, S. A., & Walsh, D. A. (1988). Psychological dysfunction and physical health among elderly medical inpatients. *Journal of Consulting and Clinical Psychology, 56*, 851–855.

Rapp, S. R., Parisi, S. A., Walsh, D. A., & Wallace, C. E. (1988). Detecting depression in elderly medical inpatients. *Journal of Consulting and Clinical Psychology, 56*, 509–513.

Rapp, S. R., Smith, S. S., & Britt, M. (1990). Identifying comorbid depression in elderly medical patients: Use of the Extracted Hamilton Depression Rating Scale. *Psychological Assessment, 2*, 243–247.

Ray, C. C., McKinney, K. A., & Ford, C. V. (1987). Differences in psychologists ratings of younger and older clients. *Gerontologist, 27*, 82–86.

Regier, D. A., Boyd, J. H., Burke, J. D., Rae, D. S., Myers, J. K., Kramer, M., Robins, L. N., George, L. K., Karno, M., & Locke, B. Z. (1988). One month prevalence of mental disorders in the United States. *Archives of General Psychiatry, 45*, 977–986.

Reifler, B. V., & Larson, E. (1989). Excess disability in dementia of the Alzheimer's type. In E. Light & B. Lebowitz (Eds.), *Alzheimer's disease treatment and family stress: Directions for research* (pp. 363–382). Washington, DC: National Institute of Mental Health.

Reifler, B. V., Larson, E., & Teri, L. (1987). An outpatient psychiatry assessment and treatment service. *Clinics in Geriatric Medicine, 3*, 203–209.

Reifler, B. V., Teri, L., Raskind, M., Veith, R., Barnes, R., White, E., & McClean, P. (1989). Double-blind trial of imipramine in Alzheimer's disease patients with and without depression. *American Journal of Psychiatry, 146*, 45–49.

Reynolds, C. F. (1992). Treatment of depression in special populations. *Journal of Clinical Psychiatry, 53*(Suppl.), 45–53.

Reynolds, C. F., Frank, E., Perel, J. M., Imber, S. D., Cornes, C., Morycz, R., Mazumdar, S., Miller, M., Pollock, B., Rifai, A. H., Stack, J. A., George, C. J., Houck, P. R., & Kupfer, D. J. (1992). Combined pharmacotherapy and psychotherapy in the acute and continuation treatment with recurrent major depression: A preliminary report. *American Journal of Psychiatry, 149*, 1687–1692.

Reynolds, C. F., Frank, E., Perel, J. M., Imber, S., Thornton, J., Morycz, R. K., Cornes, C., & Kupfer, D. (1989). Open trial maintenance pharmacotherapy in late life depression: Survival analysis. *Psychiatry Research, 27*, 225–231.

Reynolds, C. F., Kupfer, D. J., Houck, P. R., Hoch, C. C., Stack, J. A., Berman, S. R., & Zimmer, B. (1988). Reliable discrimination of elderly depressed and demented patients by electroencephalographic sleep data. *Archives of General Psychiatry, 45*, 258–264.

Reynolds, C. F., Kupfer, D. J., Taska, L. S., Hoch, C. C., Spiker, D. G., Sewitch, D. E., Zimmer, B., Marin, R. S., Nelson, J. P., Martin, D., & Moryez, R. (1985). EEG sleep in elderly depressed, demented, and healthy subjects. *Biological Psychiatry, 20*, 431–442.

Rivera, P. A., Rose, J. M., Futterman, A., Lovett, S. B., & Gallagher-Thompson, D. (1991). Dimensions of perceived social support in clinically depressed and nondepressed female caregivers. *Psychology and Aging, 6*, 232–237.

Robins, L. N., Helzer, J. E., Croughan, J. L., & Ratliff, K. S. (1981). National Institute of Mental Health Diagnostic Interview Schedule. *Archives of General Psychiatry, 38*, 381–389.

Robinson, L., Berman, J., & Neimeyer, R. A. (1990). Psychotherapy for the treatment of depression: A comprehensive review of controlled outcome research. *Psychological Bulletin, 108*, 30–49.

Rohde, P., Lewinsohn, P. M., & Seeley, J. R. (1990). Are people changed by the experience of having an episode of depression. A further test of the scar hypothesis. *Journal of Abnormal Psychology, 99*, 264–271.

Rook, K. S. (1984). The negative side of soical interaction: Impact on psychological well-being. *Journal of Personality and Social Psychology, 46*, 1097–1108.

Rose, S. (1987). *Molecules and minds.* London: Open University Press.

Rovner, B. W., Broadhead, J., Spencer, M., Carson, K., & Folstein, M. F. (1989). Depression and Alzheimer's disease. *American Journal of Psychiatry, 146*, 350–353.

Rovner, B. W., German, P. S., Brant, L. J., Clark, R., Burton, L., & Folstein, M. F. (1991). Depression and mortality in nursing homes. *Journal of the American Medical Association, 265*, 993–996.

Rush, A. J., Erman, M. K., Giles, D. E., Schlesser, M. A., Carpenter, G., Vasavada, N., & Roffwarg, H.G. (1986). Polysomnographic findings in recently drug-free and clinically remitted depressed patients. *Archives of General Psychiatry, 43*, 878–884.

Sackheim, H. (1989). The efficacy of electroconvulsive therapy in the treatment of major depressive disorder. In S. Fisher & R. P. Greenberg (Eds.), *The limits of biological treatments for psychological distress* (pp. 275–308). Hillsdale, NJ: Erlbaum.

Salzman, C. (1992). *Clinical geriatric psychopharmacology* (2nd Ed.). Baltimore: Williams & Wilkins.

Salzman, C., & Shader, R. I. (1978). Depression in the elderly: I. Relationship between depression, psychologic defense mechanisms, and physical illness. *Journal of the American Geriatrics Society, 26*, 253.

Sapolsky, R. M. (1992). *Stress, the aging brain, and the mechanisms of neuron death.* Cambridge, MA: MIT Press.

Schaie, K. W. (1965). A general model for the study of developmental problems. *Psychological Bulletin, 64*, 92–107.

Schneider, L. S. (1990). Biological markers in geriatric depression. *Psychiatric Annals, 20*, 83–91.

Schneider, L. S., Severson, J. A., & Sloane, R. B. (1985). Platelet ^{3}H-imipramine binding in depressed elderly patients. *Biological Psychiatry, 20*, 1234–1237.

Scogin, F., Jamison, C., & Gochneaur, K. (1989). Comparative efficacy of cognitive and behavioral bibliotherapy for mildly and moderately depressed older adults. *Journal of Consulting and Clinical Psychology, 57*, 403–407.

Scogin, F., & McElreath, L. (1994). Efficacy of psychosocial treatments for geriatric depression: A quantitative review. *Journal of Consulting and Clinical Psychology, 62*, 69–73.

Settin, J. M. (1982). Clinical judgment in geropsychological practice. *Psychotherapy: Theory, Research, and Practice, 19*, 397–404.

Shea, M. T., Widiger, T. A., & Klein, M. H. (1992). Comorbidity of personality and depression: Implications for treatment. *Journal of Consulting and Clinical Psychology, 60,* 857–868.

Simons, A. D., Murphy, G. E., Levine, J. L., & Wetzel, R. D. (1986). Cognitive therapy and pharmacotherapy for depression: Sustained improvement over one year. *Archives of General Psychiatry, 43,* 43–48.

Sloane, R. B., Staples, F. R., & Schneider, L. S. (1985). Interpersonal therapy versus nortriptyline for depression in the elderly. In G. D. Burrows, T. R. Norman, & L. Dennerstein (Eds.), *Clinical and pharmacological studies in psychiatric disorders* (pp. 344–346). London: John Libbey.

Smith, M. L., Glass, G. V., & Miller, T. I. (1980). *The benefits of psychotherapy.* Baltimore: Johns Hopkins Press.

Smyer, M., Zarit, S., & Qualls, S. H. (1990). Psychological intervention and the aging individual. In J. E. Birren & K. W. Schaie (Eds.), *Handbook of the psychology of aging* (3rd ed., pp. 375–403). New York: Academic Press.

Spitzer, R. L., & Endicott, J. (1978). *Schedule for Affective Disorders and Schizophrenia* (3rd ed.). New York: New York State Psychiatric Institute, Biometrics Research.

Spitzer, R. L., Endicott, J., & Robins, E. (1978). Research Diagnostic Criteria: Rationale and reliability. *Archives of General Psychiatry, 35,* 773–782.

Spitzer, R. L., Williams, J. B. W., Gibbon, M., & First, M. (1992). The Structure Clinical Interview for DSM-III-R (SCID): History, rationale, and description. *Archives of General Psychiatry, 49,* 624–629.

Stokes, P. E., & Sikes, C. R. (1991). The hypothalamic–pituitary–adrenal axis in psychiatric disorders. *Annual Review of Medicine, 42,* 519–531.

Stoudemire, A., & Blazer, D. G. (1985). Depression in the elderly. In E. E. Beckham & W. R. Leber (Eds.), *Handbook of depression* (1st ed., pp. 556–585). Chicago: Dorsey Press.

Stroebe, M. S., Stroebe, W., & Hansson, R. S. (1993). *Handbook of bereavement: Theory, research, and intervention.* Cambridge, UK: Cambridge University Press.

Stukenberg, K. W., Dura, J. R., & Kiecolt-Glaser, J. K. (1990). Depression screening scale validation in an elderly, community-dwelling population. *Psychological Assessment, 2,* 134–138.

Sunderland, T., Alterman, I. S., Yount, D., Hill, J. L., Teriot, P. N., Newhouse, P. A., Mueller, E. A., Mello, A. M., & Cohen, R. M. (1988). A new scale for the assessment of depressed mood in demented patients. *American Journal of Psychiatry, 148,* 955–959.

Teri, L., Curtis, J., Gallagher-Thompson, D., & Thompson, L. W. (1994). Cognitive-behavior therapy with depressed older adults. In L. Schneider, C. F. Reynolds, B. D. Lebowitz, & A. Friedhoff (Eds.), *Diagnosis and treatment of depression in late life* (pp. 279–291). Washington, DC: American Psychiatric Association Press.

Teri, L., Reifler, B. V., Veith, R., Barnes, R., White, E., McLean, P., & Raskind, M. (1991). Imipramine in the treatment of depressed Alzheimer's patients: Impact on cognition. *Journals of Gerontology: Psychological Sciences, 46,* P372–P377.

Teri, L., & Wagner, A. (1992). Alzheimer's disease and depression. *Journal of Consulting and Clinical Psychology, 60,* 379–391.

Thomas, C., Kelman, H. R., Kennedy, G. J., Ahn, C., & Yang, C. (1992). Depressive symptoms and mortality in elderly persons. *Journals of Gerontology: Social Sciences, 47,* S80–S87.

Thompson, L. W., Futterman, A., & Gallagher, D. (1988).

Assessment of late-life depression. *Psychopharmacological Bulletin, 24,* 577–586.

Thompson, E., Futterman, A., Gallagher-Thompson, D., Rose, J. M., & Lovett, S. B. (1993). Social support and caregiving burden in family caregivers of frail elders. *Journals of Gerontology: Social Sciences, 48,* S245–S255.

Thompson, L. W., Gallagher, D., & Breckenridge, J. S. (1987). Comparative effectiveness of psychotherapies for depressed elders. *Journal of Consulting and Clinical Psychology, 55,* 385–330.

Thompson, L. W., & Gallagher-Thompson, D. (1991, November). *Comparison of desimpramine and cognitive/behavioral therapy in the treatment of late-life depression: A progress report.* Paper presented at the annual meeting of the Gerontological Society of America, San Francisco.

Thompson, L. W., Gallagher, D., & Czirr, R. (1988). Personality disorder and outcome in the treatment of late-life depression. *Journal of Geriatric Psychiatry, 21,* 133–146.

Thompson, L. W., Gallagher-Thompson, D., Futterman, A., Gilewski, M., & Peterson, J. (1991b). The effects of late-life spousal bereavement over a 30 month course. *Psychology and Aging, 6,* 434–441.

Thompson, L.W., Gallagher-Thompson, D., Futterman, A., Gilewski, M., & Peterson, J. (1991c). The effects of late-life spousal bereavement over a 30 month interval. *Psychology and Aging, 6,* 434–441.

Thompson, L. W., Gantz, F., Florsheim, M., DelMaestro, S., Rodman, J., Gallagher-Thompson, D., & Bryan, H. (1991a). Cognitive/behavioral therapy for affective disorders in the elderly. In W. Myers (Ed.), *New techniques in the psychotherapy of older patients* (pp. 3–18). Washington, DC: American Psychiatric Press.

U.S. Bureau of the Census. (1991). *Statistical abstract of the United States* (111th ed., Tables 13, 18). Washington, DC: U.S. Government Printing Office.

Veith, R. C., & Raskind, M. A. (1988). The neurobiology of aging: Does it predispose to depression? *Neurobiology of Aging, 9,* 117–177.

Von Korff, M., Shapiro, S., Burke, J. D., Teitlebaum, M., Skinner, E. A., German, P., Turner, R. W., Klein, L., & Burns, B. (1987). Anxiety and depression in a primary care clinic: Comparison of Diagnostic Interview Schedule, General Health Questionnaire, and practitioner assessments. *Archives of General Psychiatry, 44,* 152–156.

Warshaw, M. G., Klerman, G. L., & Lavori, P. W. (1991). Further evidence for a period effect in major depressive disorder. *Journal of Affective Disorders, 23,* 119–129.

Weissman, M. M., & Klerman, G. L. (1978). Sex differences and the epidemiology of depression. *Archives of General Psychiatry, 34,* 98–111.

Williams, J. B. W. (1988). A structured interview guide for the Hamilton Depression Rating Scale. *Archives of General Psychiatry, 44,* 742–747.

Williamson, G. M., & Schulz, R. (1992a). Pain, activity restriction, and symptoms of depression among community residing elderly adults. *Journals of Gerontology: Psychological Sciences, 47,* P367–P372.

Williamson, G. M., & Schulz, R. (1992b). Physical illness and symptoms of depression among elderly outpatients. *Psychology and Aging, 7,* 343–351.

Wittgenstein, L. (1953). *Philosophical investigations.* Oxford: Oxford University Press.

Wortman, C. B., & Silver, R. C. (1989). The myths of coping with loss. *Journal of Consulting and Clinical Psychology, 57,* 349–357.

Yesavage, J. A., Brink, T. L., Rose, T. L., Lum, O., Huang, V., Addey, M., & Leirer, V. O. (1983). Development and validation of a Geriatric Depression Scale. *Journal of Psychiatric Research, 17,* 31–49.

Zeiss, A. M., & Lewinsohn, P. M. (1986). Adapting behavioral treatment for depression to meet the needs of the elderly. *Clinical Psychologist, 39,* 98–100.

Zemore, R., & Eames, N. (1979). Psychic and somatic symptoms of depression among young adults, institutionalized aged, and non-institutionalized aged. *Journal of Gerontology, 34,* 716–722.

Zisook, S. & Schuchter, S.R. (1991). Depression through the first year after the death of a spouse. *American Journal of Psychiatry, 148,* 1346–1352.

20

Epidemiology, Assessment, and Management of Suicide in Depressed Patients

DAVID C. CLARK

Suicide is the most frequently encountered emergency situation for mental health professionals. In the course of a career, for example, half of all psychiatrists and 20% of all psychologists lose a patient in treatment by suicide (Bongar, Lomax, & Marmatz, 1992). While the base rate of suicide in the general population is low, suicide remains the ninth leading cause of death in the United States. The suicide rate for psychiatric patients is about three times higher than it is for nonpatients (Babigian & Odoroff, 1969). Thus, it is sensible for mental health professionals to adopt the perspective of their medical/surgical colleagues, who know that some of their patients will inevitably die in the course of treatment. To deny this simple truth is to mislead the patient, the patient's family, and the self about the completeness of current-day knowledge about suicide and the effectiveness of available treatments for suicidal risk. To deny this simple truth is to pretend that suicides should always be understood as treatment failures.

Recognition of suicidal risk is easiest when the patient voluntarily consults with a mental health professional and complains about preoccupations with suicidal thoughts or wishes. Suicidal persons do not always seek professional help, however, or communicate their suicidal thoughts and behavior to a health professional. In the course of outpatient therapy, a patient in treatment for a different condition may develop new symptoms associated with a greater risk for death by suicide (e.g., a patient with a borderline personality disorder develops a superimposed major depressive episode, or a patient suffering from major depression begins to abuse alcohol). At this point, midstream in therapy and perhaps unknown to the treating clinician, the patient may begin to entertain suicidal thoughts. The new development may go undetected unless the clinician recognizes significant changes in the patient and initiates a new assessment for suicide risk.

Furthermore, persons suffering with psychiatric symptoms do not usually seek care in a mental health setting. Two-thirds of persons meeting diagnostic criteria for a mental disorder never make any contact with mental health services (Myers et al., 1984). Almost half of all persons who die by suicide have never seen a mental health professional in their lifetime (Barraclough, Bunch, Nelson, & Sainsbury, 1974; Beskow, 1979; Hagnell & Rorsman, 1978, 1979). While the suicide risk of some persons who never access mental health services is detected and treated in (nonpsychiatric) medical care settings, the fact remains that a large number of persons with mental disorders and suicidal thoughts receive no evaluation or treatment whatsoever for those conditions.

Yet there is evidence that persons who commit suicide have often seen a primary care physician within a few weeks or months of their death

(Barraclough et al., 1974; Seager & Flood, 1965; Vassilas & Morgan, 1993). Systematic reviews of these medical contacts show that the imminent suicide has rarely visited a physician to complain of psychiatric symptoms, depression, or suicidal impulses. The patient is more likely to visit the doctor's office with multiple, vague complaints of physical symptoms that have gone undiagnosed—symptoms often associated with major depression or alcoholism (Murphy, 1975). Thus, a patient complaining of insomnia and fatigue may present in the primary care medical setting and be treated symptomatically with sleeping pills, without consideration of the value of screening for mental disorders. In this case, the larger context is ignored, and the patient goes untreated for the underlying and more serious psychiatric problem (e.g., major depression).

Focusing on isolated physical symptoms rather than suspecting an underlying mental disorder is not the only reason why patients at risk for suicide are not recognized or evaluated appropriately. In a group of 60 suicide victims who had recently been under the care of physicians, 80% were interpreted as having depressive symptoms in reaction to situations or life events of an adverse nature (Murphy, 1975). The presence of these symptoms was accepted as a natural reaction to an upsetting life situation, and as a result, were not interpreted as symptoms of a depressive illness. The mistake that is evident in retrospect is that the physicians recognized psychological symptoms, but failed to recognize or treat a documentable psychiatric illness—because of naive theories about "normal-range stress reactions."

The problem of recognizing suicide risk is not limited to the outpatient physician's office. Prevalence rates of mental illness in prisons range from 16% to 66%, depending upon the type of facility (Gibbs, 1982; Ogloff & Otto, 1989; Teplin, 1983). The suicide rate for persons in jail is estimated to be nine times higher than that of the general population (Hayes & Rowan, 1988). Ironically, roughly two-thirds (68%) of prison suicides occur while the inmate is being held in isolation for protection and/or surveillance (Hayes & Kajdin, 1981). Another group at elevated risk for death by suicide includes patients on psychiatric inpatient units. About 1,500 suicides occur on inpatient units every year—about 5% of all suicides (Crammer, 1984). This fact probably reflects a concentration of high-risk persons in time and place by virtue of the presence of a mental disorder, the presence of a disorder of severe pro-

portions requiring hospitalization, the inability of experts to always know which subset of patients at risk for suicide are the most intent on killing themselves, and the inability of experts to always know when the suicide intent of a patient will peak.

Even when a mental health professional has an opportunity to interview the patient about suicidal thoughts and behaviors, the task of assessing suicide risk is complex. It is demonstrably impossible to predict individual cases of suicide on a consistent statistical basis, because suicide is such a rare event in any population (Rosen, 1954; MacKinnon & Farberow, 1975; Murphy, 1984; Pokorny, 1983). The best a clinician can do is determine which *groups* of persons are at greater risk for completing suicide and which persons are more likely to make nonfatal attempts. In order to detect persons at elevated risk for suicide, a complete assessment of suicide risk should include a mental status examination, a thorough assessment of psychopathology, systematic inquiry about suicidal thoughts and behavior, and application of a risk assessment formula tailored to the principal psychiatric diagnosis implicated by the diagnostic interview.

EPIDEMIOLOGY

In the United States, suicide ranks ninth as a leading cause of death, claiming more than 30,000 lives each year (National Center for Health Statistics, 1994). The suicide rate is 4 times higher for men than women, 2 times higher for whites than nonwhites, and 1½ times higher for the elderly than the young. Adolescent suicide rates have more than quadrupled since 1955, whereas elderly suicide rates (i.e., those persons 65 years and over) have decreased by a factor of 3 over a similar period. The elderly continue to evidence a higher suicide rate than youthful or middle-aged persons, although now age group differences in suicide rates are nowhere near as marked as they used to be between 1930 and 1950. Today, a person's age does not provide much useful information about statistical risk for suicide.

Other demographic markers for increased suicide risk include marital status and parental status. Young persons who have been widowed have the highest suicide rate of any marital status group (Kreitman, 1988), but death of a spouse does not help predict suicide risk much for other age groups. Parental status may contribute more directly to estimating suicide risk than marital status. Veevers (1973) first showed that responsibility for children under age 18 years is associated with a lower risk for death by suicide, which may be the underlying reason why those who are single, separated, and divorced are at elevated risk for suicide.

The demographic profile of persons who die by suicide and those who make nonfatal attempts are more different than they are alike (Linehan, 1986). About 2.9% of adults have made a suicide attempt in their lifetime (Mościcki et al., 1988). Women are three to four times more likely to make suicide attempts than men. Persons aged 25–44 make more attempts than persons at younger or older ages. Persons separated or divorced evidence a suicide attempt rate that is four times higher than persons in other marital status categories. There are no remarkable distinctions among suicide attempt rates for whites, blacks, and Hispanics. Living conditions—for example, lower income, lower educational level, adverse social circumstances, and acute life upsets—seem to play a more important role in influencing suicide attempts than suicidal deaths. Finally, personality disorders appear to be more prevalent among persons—particularly males—who make nonfatal attempts than among those who die by suicide.

It is important to try to distinguish among those who are at imminent risk for death by suicide, those who may be at long-term risk for death by suicide, and those at risk for repeated nonfatal suicide attempts. Whereas nonfatal suicidal behavior requires evaluation and prompt intervention, and chronic suicide risk requires vigilant treatment, the primary task of the clinician is to focus attention and therapeutic efforts on those who are most likely to die by suicide in the near future, and to keep the patients alive until the suicidal crisis passes. In the office, the clinic, and the hospital alike, clinicians must have access to a suicide risk prediction formula tailored to identify groups of persons at risk for *death* by suicide in the *short*-term future—a formula representing the summation of their understanding of extant scientific knowledge and their clinical experience.

INQUIRING ABOUT SUICIDAL THOUGHTS AND BEHAVIOR

Because patients evidencing psychopathology—particularly those meeting diagnostic criteria for a major depressive disorder, alcoholism, drug abuse/dependence, or schizophrenia—are at elevated risk for suicide attempts and death by suicide, explicit questions about morbid thoughts, suicidal thoughts, and suicidal behavior should be included in any assessment interview. By doing so, the clinician elicits examples of current symptoms and simultaneously alerts the patient to the idea that the interviewer will continue to be interested in hearing about morbid/suicidal thoughts if they continue, recur, or emerge *de novo*. It is important to fully explore the patient's range and depth of suicidal thoughts and behavior without interrupting to lecture, discourage, or prohibit. Premature interruptions only serve to disrupt the patient's train of thought, break empathic contact, and encourage minimization and denial of extant symptoms.

Inquiry about suicidal thoughts and behavior should always begin with the patient's description of his/her problem. By letting the patient provide an overview of the current problems in his/her own language, the interviewer has the opportunity to develop a conceptual overview of the problem and to structure inquiry for the remainder of the interview. By listening to the patient discuss current problems for 5 or 10 minutes at the beginning of the interview, the interviewer also has the opportunity to learn something about the patient's pace and style of talking.

After the patient's initial outline of his/her problems, the interviewer should inquire about dysphoric affects. Has the patient felt sad, apathetic, anhedonic, irritable, or anxious? If any of these dysphoric states have been present, the interviewer should determine their frequency, intensity, and duration. Next, the interviewer should inquire about feelings of pessimism, hopelessness, or despair by linking the predominant dysphoric affects to a view of the future: "When a person feels as sad/empty/cranky as you have been feeling for the last several weeks, he/she sometimes become discouraged, or convinced that nothing will work out well. Have you been feeling discouraged?" The frequency, intensity, and duration of any feelings of hopelessness should be explored.

The interview should next progress to thoughts of death or suicide by linking the predominant dysphoric affects and the experience of hopelessness to suicidal thoughts: "When a person feels as sad/empty/cranky as you have for the last several weeks, and feels this discouraged, he/she may begin to think about dying or even killing himself/herself. Have you?" (Endicott & Spitzer,

1978). This type of direct questioning will elicit the most complete information with the least discomfort or embarrassment. To conduct a thorough evaluation, the interviewer should allow the patient to speak freely of all suicidal plans and ideas without interruption. If the patient answers "no" to questions regarding suicide, the possibility of the patient having suicidal thoughts or having engaged in suicidal behavior should not be totally discounted. Often, a quick or firm negative response may be indicative of one of the following: (1) The patient may be reluctant to admit to his/her suicidal thoughts for any one of a number of reasons; (2) the patient may be trying to signal that he/she is not having suicidal thoughts *at this moment*; or (3) the patient may be trying to demonstrate that such thoughts are not significant because he/she would never *act* on them. In these cases, the interviewer should explain to the patient that it is important to determine whether he/she has experienced any suicidal thoughts, however fleeting or unlikely, during the current episode of illness. Further probing may be necessary to elicit this information. In addition, the patient's relatives or intimate friends should routinely be interviewed about suicidal communications if the patient is suspected of having suicidal thoughts but denies having them. Suicidal persons are most likely to share their suicidal thoughts or intentions with family members and intimates, but sometimes actively conceal their suicidal thoughts from an evaluator.

If the patient admits to having had thoughts of death or suicide, it is important to determine whether these thoughts were active or passive (e.g., "I wish I were dead" vs. "I feel like killing myself"). If the patient has had active thoughts of suicide, the interviewer should probe persistently for the specific methods of suicide that have occurred to the patient. It is best to inventory the methods considered in one fell swoop, to build an exhaustive list, because it sometimes happens that the last plan identified is the most clinically significant. After all the considered methods have been counted, we recommend that the interviewer ask how often the patient considered each plan, the degree to which each plan was rehearsed mentally, and the degree to which each plan was translated into behavior. When a patient has engaged in a great deal of mental rehearsal for a suicide, and particularly when the patient has translated some modicum of the plan into overt behavior, concern about imminent suicide risk is greatest.

If the patient denies having thought of any specific method of suicide, it is important for the interviewer to ask the patient if he/she intends to act on any suicidal thoughts in the near future and why or why not. The interviewer should not hesitate to pose these types of questions to the patient. This type of probing is not interpreted by the patient as encouragement to suicide.

A final area to explore with the suicidal patient is the question of whether he/she includes other persons in the morbid or suicidal thinking. In 3–4% of all suicides, someone else—usually a spouse, intimate, or family member—is murdered at the same time (Robins, 1981; Dorpat & Ripley, 1960; Beskow, 1979). In 5% of all homicides, the perpetrator commits suicide or makes a suicide attempt soon after the homicide (Wolfgang, 1958; Rosenbaum, 1990). About 20% of those who have killed a child later die by suicide or make a suicide attempt (Adelson, 1961; Rodenburg, 1971). Explicit questions about homicidal/suicidal thinking often help the patient to understand that these thoughts should be understood as symptoms of a current illness that can be addressed in the course of treatment.

If the patient has suicidal thoughts, or the clinician believes the patient is at more than negligible risk for suicide, the clinician will need to consider the patient's access to various instruments of suicide. If instruments (e.g., guns, medications) can easily be obtained by the patient, it is important to remove them from the patient's environment. It is wise to include family members in this discussion in order to educate them about suicide risk and suicidal communications, and to obtain complete information and, recruit their assistance.

The final step of a thorough risk assessment interview includes questioning a member of the patient's family and/or a close friend. More often than not, patients experiencing suicidal thoughts and wishes discuss these feelings with family members and/or intimates. Community-based psychological autopsy studies consistently show that more than 40% of patients who died by suicide had expressed their suicidal intentions clearly and specifically, and that another 30% had talked about death and dying, in the months preceding suicide (Barraclough et al., 1974; Beskow, 1979; Chynoweth, Tonge, & Armstrong, 1980; Dorpat & Ripley, 1960; Fowler, Rich, & Young, 1986; Hagnell & Rorsman, 1978, 1979, 1980; Rich, Fowler, Fogarty, & Young, 1988; Rich, Young, & Fowler, 1986; Robins, 1981; Robins et al., 1959a,

1959b). Mental health professionals cannot always access the same suicidal communications from their patients. In one prospective study, more than 50% of depressed psychiatric inpatients who died by suicide denied suicidal ideation or admitted to only vague thoughts of suicide when examined by an experienced clinical interviewer (Fawcett, 1988). Unfortunately, the suicidal communications directed to family members and friends are usually not interpreted as serious threats or serious intentions to suicide. Thus, it is vital that the clinician educate family members about this aspect of suicide risk and question them about the patient's morbid or suicidal thoughts.

All suicidal ideation and behavior must be taken seriously. Whereas clinicians are prone to review the psychosocial circumstances that led up to an episode of suicidal behavior to gauge the patient's "true intent" and interpret the patient's primary motives, the clinician does well to remember that the clinical value of these kinds of formulations for predicting future behavior has never been demonstrated. Litman (1964), for example, observed that intention is often ambivalent in cases of suicide—a strong wish to die and a strong wish to live can exist side by side—making decisive action appear hesitant or inconclusive.

Borderline patients can be very taxing in this regard. When a patient has shown a pattern of resorting to suicidal threats frequently in therapy as a coping strategy (e.g., as one aspect of a histrionic character style, in response to disappointments or frustrations inside or outside the therapy), the therapist may well decide that the patient has "cried wolf" one time too many and begin to discount all subsequent suicidal behavior. This can be a fatal mistake. Unless a complete strategy and context for managing chronic parasuicidal behavior has been developed in the therapy, the very next instance of self-injury may be reflexively but erroneously tagged as "manipulative," whereas this instance actually represents the first grave communication of suicide intent in a borderline patient who has just now developed a comorbid major depressive episode. The reader who is interested in promising strategies for psychotherapy with chronically parasuicidal patients is referred to the cognitive–behavioral techniques of Linehan (1993a, 1993b), who has published the favorable results of controlled trials of her techniques (Linehan, Armstrong, Suarez, Allmon, & Heard, 1991; Linehan, Heard, & Armstrong, 1993), and

the psychodynamic techniques of Maltsberger (1986).

Although a history of suicide attempts is not in and of itself a reliable index of risk for completed suicide—because half of all persons who die by suicide have never made an attempt before—it is important to question patients about each and every nonfatal attempt, since these are associated with both a higher risk for suicide and subsequent nonfatal attempts (Buglass & Horton, 1974; Morgan, Barton, Pottle, Pocock, & Burns-Cox, 1976; Kreitman & Casey, 1988; Clark, Gibbons, Fawcett, & Scheftner, 1989). Long-term follow-up studies of persons who have made nonfatal suicide attempts show that 7–10% eventually die by suicide (Ettlinger, 1964; Motto, 1965; Weiss & Scott, 1974; Cullberg, Wasserman, & Stefansson, 1988), a risk five times greater than the 1.4% lifetime risk of suicide for the U.S. general population (National Center for Health Statistics, 1992). Yet 90–93% of all nonfatal attempters will not go on to die by suicide.

THE IMPORTANCE OF ASSESSING PSYCHOPATHOLOGY

Suicide almost always occurs in the presence of major psychopathology. Findings from psychological autopsy studies and follow-up mortality studies consistently demonstrate the strong association between major psychopathology and suicide. Community-based psychological autopsy studies of 100 or more suicides in the United States, the United Kingdom, Sweden, and Australia implicate a recent major mental disorder in no less than 93% of the cases of adult suicide (Robins et al., 1959b; Dorpat & Ripley, 1960; Barraclough et al., 1974; Beskow, 1979; Chynoweth et al., 1980; Fowler et al., 1986). The diagnoses most often present in these suicide cases have been major depression (40%– 60% of cases), chronic alcoholism (20% of cases), and schizophrenia (10% of cases; Clayton, 1985; Murphy, 1986a). Persons suffering from either major depression, alcoholism, or both constitute 57–86% of all suicide cases.

Follow-up mortality studies also demonstrate the strong relationship between psychiatric disorders and suicide. The lifetime risk of suicide for patients with major affective disorder is 15%; patients with alcoholism, 3–4%; and patients with schizophrenia, 10% (Miles, 1977; Tsuang,

Woolson, & Fleming, 1980; Black, Warrack, & Winokur, 1985; Drake, Gates, Whitaker, & Cotton, 1985; Martin, Cloniker, Guze, & Clayton, 1985; Allebeck, 1989; Murphy & Wetzel, 1990) in long-term follow-up mortality studies. For this reason, it is extremely important to systematically assess symptoms of psychopathology whenever a question of suicide risk arises.

When assessing psychopathology, it is important for the clinician to consider patients meeting criteria for any psychiatric diagnosis at high risk until a second-stage evaluation can further clarify the degree of risk. Clinicians should pay special attention to persons meeting criteria for major depression, alcoholism or drug use disorders, schizophrenia, and organic brain syndromes, because these disorders are known to be associated with an elevated association with death by suicide. The second-stage evaluation is characterized by systematic inquiry about suicidal thoughts and behavior, as well as systematic inquiry about symptoms and features specifically suggestive of elevated risk among patients with the indicated psychiatric diagnosis.

RISK ASSESSMENT TAILORED TO A SPECIFIC CLINICAL DIAGNOSIS

Most "suicide risk prediction formulae" are based on studies of nonfatal suicide attempters, who can be interviewed following an attempt, and who are far more numerous than suicide completers. Most risk prediction formulae have some value for identifying nonfatal suicide attempters, repeated attempters, and attempters who make medically dangerous attempts, because these are the clinical populations to whom researchers have devoted most of their attention. If those who die by suicide are different from nonfatal attempters in important ways, then empirical profiles of nonfatal attempters may have relatively little value for identifying persons at risk for death by suicide (Clark & Horton-Deutsch, 1992). At this early stage in the science of suicide risk prediction, we think it is far more empirically sound to approach the problems of "predicting" nonfatal attempts and death by suicide as relatively independent problems; thus, we recommend that the clinician be reluctant to reduce "suicide risk" prediction to a single all-purpose formula.

Risk assessment formulations should also be tailored to the specific principal diagnosis implicated in the diagnostic interview (Clark, 1990; Clark & Fawcett, 1992). By keying the risk assessment to a single diagnostic grouping (in which the patient qualifies for one and not several mental disorders), the clinician is guided to search for features that distinguish the target patient from others afflicted with the same illness. This follows from our impression that the risk factors for suicide in major depression are different from the risk factors for suicide in alcoholism, or in schizophrenia. Inaccuracy and inefficiency would result if a single risk profile were used to gauge risk for all psychiatric patients.

Patients Meeting Criteria for a Major Depression

Major depression is the psychiatric diagnosis most commonly associated with suicide (40–60% of cases; Clayton, 1985; Murphy, 1986a). In a prospective study of patients with major depressive disorder, the following symptoms were associated with the occurrence of death by suicide within 1 year: severe psychic anxiety, severe anhedonia, global insomnia, diminished concentration, indecision, sleep disturbances, acute overuse of alcohol, and panic attacks (62% of patients in the study who committed suicide within the first year of follow-up reported panic attacks concurrent with the index episode of depression) (Fawcett et al., 1990). In the same study, a current episode of cycling affective illness, early lifetime course (i.e., one to three lifetime episodes of depression), and the absence of responsibility for children under the age of 18 years were other notable suicide risk factors to consider.

In the study of Fawcett and colleagues (1990), bipolar and schizoaffective patients did not evidence a higher risk of suicide than other patients with affective disorder. Affective disorder subtypes (e.g., psychotic, endogenous, incapacitated, agitated, primary) were not useful for predicting suicide. Thus, for example, patients qualifying for a diagnosis of major depression and simultaneously experiencing delusions or hallucinations were not more likely to die by suicide. Other characteristics that were not indicative of an elevated risk of death by suicide included family history of suicide or suicidal behavior, duration of the index episode of depression, life-stress levels as rated by a clinician, and life-stress levels as reported by the patient.

Other have reported similar findings with a similar iconoclastic favor. In a 2- to 13-year follow-up mortality study of 1,593 psychiatric inpatients admitted with a major affective disorder, for example, Black, Winokur, and Nasrallah (1988) also found no difference in suicide rates when comparing psychotic and nonpsychotic patients or comparing unipolar, bipolar, and combined subtypes. These findings are consistent with other recent retrospective (Coryell & Tsuang, 1982) reports as well. Other investigators have linked delusional depressions with increased suicide risk, but their data do not support their conclusions well. Roose, Glassman, Walsh, Woodring, and Vital-Herne (1983), for example, conducted a follow-up study of patients at one psychiatric hospital who had died while "on the hospital census" (i.e., as inpatients, on pass, or after eloping) over a 25-year period. They concluded that delusional patients with unipolar major depression were five times more likely to die by suicide than their nondelusional counterparts. But their data had three major shortcomings:

1. They only identified suicides occurring on the hospital census, neglecting to consider suicides in the same cohort occurring outside the hospital during the same period.
2. They counted "probable" cases (i.e., no evidence that the belief was fixed and unamenable to reason) as "definite" cases in their analysis.
3. Their comparison group consisted of a much lower fraction of men than did the suicide group.

For these reasons we believe their study was inconclusive.

In the Fawcett et al. (1990) study, clinical variables traditionally associated with elevated suicide risk were not so useful in the short term. The Fawcett study found that while acute suicidal ideation, history of suicide attempts, medical seriousness of prior attempts, and severe hopelessness were not associated with short-term risk for suicide, the same features were associated with death by suicide 1–5 years later.

The just-cited finding that severe hopelessness has value for predicting suicide risk 1–5 years later, but not in the imminent 6–12 months, appears to run contrary to Beck's often-replicated finding (Beck, 1987) that hopelessness is the single best clinical predictor of suicide in depressed patients. A methodological problem inherent to suicide research may resolve this

contradiction. Most studies of demographic and psychological variables that "predict" suicide in large retrospective studies have followed patients from a clinical event—for example, hospital or clinic admission—to a follow-up point 10 or 20 years later. To amass a sufficient number of suicide cases for purposes of statistical analysis, suicides occurring 1 week, 1 month, 1 year, and 10 years after the index event are lumped together and all are considered equivalent. But, as Fawcett et al. (1990) pointed out, the task of predicting suicide in the clinical situation necessarily focuses on *imminent* suicide risk—risk over a period of days or weeks, not months or years. The Fawcett findings suggest that hopelessness predicts long-term risk for suicide much better than short-term risk.

This profile of depressed patients at highest risk for suicide during the next 6 to 12 months may appear counterintuitive or iconoclastic to some. Nevertheless, the central discrimination task in the Fawcett study mimics the real clinical situation better than many other studies. When a psychiatrist or an inpatient unit has responsibility for a dozen patients with severe major depression, significant impairment in functioning, severe suicidal ideation, and a history of recent suicide attempts (i.e., all are "high-risk"), how does one begin to identify the subset at greatest risk for imminent suicide? The features that effectively discriminate suicide risk within an extremely high-risk sample of depressed patients will certainly be different from the features that discriminate risk effectively in a military physical screening setting, or in a primary medical care setting.

The clinician will find it helpful to consider this profile of depressed patients at highest risk for suicide during the next 6 to 12 months for two reasons: (1) the Fawcett study represents the only large, published clinical study in which patients were assessed in a standardized and reliable fashion prior to their suicide, so the perspective is a prospective one and the assessment data are not contaminated by hindsight bias; and (2) many of the same findings have emerged in (retrospective) long-term follow-up mortality studies of patients with a diagnosis of major depression (Black et al., 1987, 1988).

Patients Meeting Criteria for Depression and Alcoholism

The lifetime risk of suicide for persons who have had a history of inpatient treatment for alcoholism is 3.4%, and for untreated alcoholics, 1.8% (Murphy & Wetzel, 1990). Alcoholism is implicated in about 25% of all suicides in the United States. For alcoholics who have not abused other drugs, the mean duration of time from the beginning of excessive drinking to completed suicide is 19 years. For those who have abused other drugs, the mean duration is much shorter. Only one-third of alcoholics who die by suicide have ever received inpatient psychiatric treatment.

Drinking in conjunction with episodes of depression appears to play a major role in the high incidence of suicide in alcoholic patients. Suicides in a psychiatric inpatient setting are less likely to involve alcoholism than major depression or schizophrenia, probably because alcohol is difficult to obtain while the patient is hospitalized, and because depressive episodes are more likely to be detected and treated by staff.

The experience of a current or recent interpersonal loss seems to play a role in precipitating suicide among alcoholic patients in one-fourth of cases. In a study of alcoholic patients (Murphy, Armstrong, Hermele, Fischer, & Clendenin, 1979), those who died by suicide were likely to have suffered from a major depression and the effects of an interpersonal loss in the 6 months before death. The disruption of a close personal relationship as a risk factor for death by suicide appears to be specific to the diagnosis of alcoholism (Murphy et al., 1979; Murphy & Wetzel, 1990), and not characteristic of any other psychiatric disorder.

Drug abuse or dependence and imprisonment also puts alcoholic patients at a greater risk for suicide. For alcoholics who have been imprisoned, intoxication and a history of drug abuse or dependence at the time of admission to a holding cell, detention cell, jail, or prison puts the patient at an even greater suicide risk, particularly during the first 24 hours.

Persons Meeting Criteria for Depression and Schizophrenia

About 10% of persons diagnosed with schizophrenia will die by suicide in the course of a lifetime (Bleuler, 1978; Miles, 1977; Tsuang, 1978). Some evidence suggests that persons with atypical psychoses (e.g., schizoaffective disorder, schizophreniform disorder) have a parallel high lifetime risk (Buda, Tsuang, & Fleming, 1988).

The following factors are associated with elevated risk for death by suicide among schizo-

phrenic patients: periods of depressed mood and hopelessness and during periods of clinical improvement following relapse, particularly during the months following discharge from the hospital (Allebeck, 1989; Allebeck, Varla, Kristjansson, & Wistedt, 1987; Allebeck & Wistedt, 1986; Black, 1988; Drake et al., 1985; Harrow, Grinker, Silverstein, & Holzman, 1978; Roy, 1982, 1986; Westermeyer & Harrow, 1989); young age; short duration of time since onset of the illness; good premorbid history (i.e., good social and intellectual functioning prior to onset of illness); frequent exacerbations and remissions of the illness; suicidal communications; and periods when florid psychosis is minimal or mild (Drake & Cotton, 1986; Drake, Gates, Cotton, & Whitaker, 1984; Roy, 1982; Wilkinson & Bacon, 1984).

ASSESSING RISK IN THE GENERAL POPULATION

Since less than one-third of persons who die by suicide are under the care of a mental health professional at the time of their death, and since almost half of persons who die by suicide have never seen a mental health professional, mental health professionals are not provided with the opportunity to forestall the majority of deaths by suicide. General population screening for mental disorders and suicidal ideation are important avenues for reducing the suicide death toll.

When one is screening the general population for persons at high risk for suicide, it is most efficient to probe for suicidal behavior of all sorts (e.g., morbid thoughts, suicidal ideation, suicide attempts) and prevalence of the mental disorders associated with an increased risk for suicide (i.e., major depression, alcohol and drug abuse, and schizophrenia). Positive findings related to suicidal behavior or mental disorder should be a strong indication for clinical evaluation, including a thorough evaluation for suicide risk.

DECIDING THE SETTING FOR THERAPY

When the degree of suicidal risk has been estimated, the clinician must decide what type of treatment would be most suitable for the patient. In cases of acute suicidal crisis, the clinician's goal is to modify those risk features that can be modified, hoping to achieve a substantial decrease in suicide risk over a short period of time. One risk feature that can usually be modified within a period of weeks is a supervening episode of major depression. Time and resource limitations dictate that the clinician must carefully decide which patients are at most acute risk and require more intensive interventions to prevent suicide, and which patients do not require immediate and aggressive intervention (e.g., hospitalization).

If a clinician finds a patient to be at high risk for suicide, the most appropriate place for treatment is on a psychiatric inpatient unit, and the patient should be hospitalized. Suicidal patients do not always agree with this decision, however, and sometimes oppose the clinician's recommendation of hospitalization. This example of "help negation" may represent nothing more than a particularly problematic symptom of the underlying psychiatric illness—the patient may have reached a state of utter hopelessness concerning treatment and may reject all attempts at help and therapy. In this situation, it is the clinician's responsibility to initiate involuntary hospitalization procedures insofar as state mental health codes allow.

After the clinician has explained what symptoms or behaviors have led him/her to be concerned about imminent suicide risk, a relatively nonthreatening way for the clinician to raise the topic of hospitalization and involve the patient in a mutual decision is to proceed by increments—for example, "Would you wait with me while I call the hospital to find out whether there are any beds available? It will be much easier to discuss what to do next if we know all our options." Most patients will readily agree to this invitation, and it seems to pave the way for them to agree to enter the hospital voluntarily.

It is generally useful to enlist the awareness, understanding, and help of the patient's family when the patient opposes a reasonable recommendation for voluntary hospitalization. If the family is reluctant or unwilling to support this recommendation, as is often the case, the clinician must act on his/her risk formulation and best clinical judgment. If the patient requires hospitalization, he/she should be committed despite patient or family opposition, if state laws allow.

Without agreement from the patient or support from the family, committing the patient is a difficult process. Many state mental health codes and commitment laws will not allow patients to be involuntarily committed unless they have threatened or attempted suicide. Unfortunately, most persons who commit suicide have not made a prior attempt, and some patients will deny their suicidal intentions to thwart a hospitalization. The clinician acting against the wishes of the patient and the family may be subjected to the family's threats of legal retribution. However, the clinician is in far more legal jeopardy if he/she fails to hospitalize (or make every attempt to hospitalize) the patient based on the available data, and then the patient goes on to die by suicide.

One of the first steps of treatment, regardless of whether the patient has been hospitalized, is that of alleviating acute anxiety or agitation. The high prevalence rates of panic attacks and the high levels of psychic anxiety reported in depressed patients who die by suicide (Fawcett et al., 1990) suggest the possibility that acute suicide risk can be reduced by alleviating extreme levels of anxiety and fearfulness. The anxiety symptoms of depressed patients, for example, are highly responsive to brief regimens of anti-anxiety medications in the context of a superordinate treatment plan to address the prevailing major depression (i.e., the initiation of short- term psychotherapy or antidepressant medication). However, neuroleptics, which will sedate without the likelihood of inducing akathisia, should be used in treating patients who do not respond to benzodiazepines, and who may manifest anxiety as a part of depression with psychotic features. Neuroleptics can also be used safely to reduce impulsive, agitated, driven behavior until the patient can be moved to a safe place and treated for his/her suicidal crisis and underlying psychiatric illness. Electroconvulsive therapy (ECT) is another approach for managing patients with acute agitated psychosis associated with a major affective disorder, and those who are so intent on suicide that it seems unwise to wait for the beginning of a response to antidepressant medication. However, supplementary medication may still be necessary, because ECT is not entirely effective in terms of reducing anxiety immediately. ECT may also pose problems as a form of therapy because it requires the patient's informed consent at a time when the patient may not be mentally competent.

Although a hospital is preferable over the patient's home as a setting for therapy, the patient is not necessarily safe once hospitalized.

The determined patient is capable of suicide by hanging or asphyxiation, even when observed every 15 minutes for "suicide precaution" checks. Such patients need constant one-on-one supervision, with no exceptions. Adequate doses of the medications mentioned previously should be used to control the acutely suicidal patient within the hospital until the patient is sufficiently recovered to participate in verbal and other forms of psychotherapy.

Even after a patient has been discharged from the hospital, the clinician must remain extremely alert and watchful of the patient, because it is not uncommon for suicide to occur in the first 6 months following hospitalization. The current high cost of hospitalization often plays a role in pressing decisions to send patients home before they are fully stable. Discharge is also a signal to the patient that he/she will not be receiving constant supervision or attention from a physician and medical staff. The patient may experience a sense of abandonment at this abrupt change in level of care. Without close or frequent contact with a therapist, the mood fluctuations that are characteristic of recovery from depression may be misinterpreted by the patient as relapse. These misapprehensions, along with a lack of support, may cause the patient to begin thinking once again of suicide as an option to ending feelings of hopelessness and despair.

Long-term outpatient therapy is most suitable for patients who are chronically suicidal. Litman (1992) estimates that 20–25% of chronically suicidal patients will eventually die by suicide, but that in any single year the suicide rate for these patients is only 1–3%. Chronically suicidal patients feel that they lack adequate resources and optimism to overcome their problems and are often "convinced" that they will eventually die by suicide. The clinician must offer continual support, yet not to the point of feeling overwhelmed or isolated with the patient. Limits must be set with the suicidal patient who becomes demanding and intrusive. Responsibility for the patient should be shared with others, especially with the patient's family and friends who spend longer periods of time with the patient. If the clinician ever feels he/she has lost the compassionate detachment necessary to treat the patient, the clinician should transfer the patient to another clinician. But these kinds of monumental clinical decisions must be made in awareness of the possibility that the chronically suicidal patient will experi-

ence the change as a devastating abandonment and as a spur to suicide (Maltsberger, 1974).

Regardless of the setting for treatment, the clinician working with the suicidal patient should keep four considerations in mind. First, persons who have a psychiatric disorder and eventually die by suicide often do not recognize the psychological aspect of their disorder, and instead concern themselves with physical symptoms. Thus, the patient may have little insight into the circumstances of the mental disorder, may be overfocused on situational crises that "explain" current distress and morbid thoughts, and may actively oppose any psychiatric intervention.

Second, the clinician should not dismiss or minimize the possibility of elevated suicide risk in patients with major depression who are laboring under the influence of a specific, definable life stressor. One long-term follow-up study shows that those with "endogenous" or "melancholic" depression and those with "situational" depression are equally likely to die by suicide (Fawcett et al., 1990).

Third, many persons in severe and acute suicidal crisis become convinced of the logic and elegance of suicide as an option to end unbearable pain and close unresolvable problems. For a subset of extremely suicidal patients, there is deep conviction and certainty in the decision to commit suicide, which may be evident to the evaluating clinician as elaborate rationalization, justification, or mystification. Verbal interventions are no longer effective for patients in this situation, and hospitalization should be considered.

Finally, patients who have become intensely preoccupied with suicide may also evidence unshakable pessimism about the potential value of any intervention on their behalf, and so may abandon, terminate, or reject any form of treatment proffered. The treating clinician must resist temptations to comply with the decision of the hopeless, despairing patient to terminate treatment prematurely.

REFERENCES

Adelson, L. (1961). Slaughter of the innocents: A study of forty-six homicides in which the victims were children. *New England Journal of Medicine, 264,* 1345–1349.

Allebeck, P. (1989). Schizophrenia: A life-shortening disease. *Schizophrenia Bulletin, 15,* 81–89.

Allebeck, P., Varla, A., Kristjansson, E., & Wistedt, B. (1987). Risk factors for suicide among patients with schizophrenia. *Acta Psychiatrica Scandinavica, 76,* 414–419.

Allebeck, P., & Wistedt, B. (1986). Mortality in schizophrenia: A ten-year follow-up based on the Stockholm County Inpatient Register. *Archives of General Psychiatry, 43*, 650–653.

Babigian, H. M., & Odoroff, C. L. (1969). The mortality experience of a population with psychiatric illness. *American Journal of Psychiatry, 126*, 470–480.

Barraclough, B., Bunch, J., Nelson, B., & Sainsbury, P. (1974). A hundred cases of suicide: Clinical aspects. *British Journal of Psychiatry, 125*, 355–373.

Beck, A. T. (1987). Hopelessness as a predictor of eventual suicide. *Annals of the New York Academy of Sciences: Psychobiology of Suicidal Behavior, 487*, 90–96.

Beskow, J. (1979). Suicide and mental disorder in Swedish men. *Acta Psychiatric Scandinavica, 277*, 1–138.

Black, D. W. (1988). Mortality in schizophrenia—the Iowa record-linkage study: A comparison with general population mortality. *Psychosomatics, 29*, 55–60.

Black, D. W., Warrack, G., & Winokur, G. (1985). The Iowa record-linkage study: I. Suicides and accidental deaths among psychiatric patients. *Archives of General Psychiatry, 42*, 71–75.

Black, D. W., Winokur, G., & Nasrallah, A. (1987). Suicide in subtypes of major affective disorder: A comparison with general population suicide mortality. *Archives of General Psychiatry, 44*, 878–840.

Black, D. W., Winokur, G., & Nasrallah, A. (1988). Effect of psychosis on suicide risk in 1,593 patients with unipolar and bipolar affective disorders. *Archives of General Psychiatry, 145*, 849–852.

Bleuler, M. (1978). *The schizophrenic disorders: Long-term and family studies.* New Haven, CT: Yale University Press.

Bongar, B., Lomax, J. W., & Marmatz, M. (1992). Training and supervisory issues in the assessment and management of the suicidal patient. In B. Bongar (Ed.), *Suicide: Guidelines for assessment, Management and treatment* (pp. 253–267). New York: Oxford University Press.

Buda, M., Tsuang, M. T., & Fleming, J. A. (1988). Causes of death in DSM-III schizophrenics and other psychotics (atypical group). *Archives of General Psychiatry, 45*, 283–285.

Buglass, C. D., & Horton, J. (1974). The repetition of parasuicide: A comparison of three cohorts. *British Journal of Psychiatry, 125*, 168–174.

Chynoweth, R., Tonge, J. I., & Armstrong, J. (1980). Suicide in Brisbane—A retrospective psychosocial study. *Australian and New Zealand Journal of Psychiatry, 14*, 37–45.

Clark, D. C. (1990). Suicide risk assessment and prediction in the 1990s. *Crisis, 11*, 104–112.

Clark, D. C., & Fawcett, J. (1992). Review of empirical risk factors for evaluation of the suicidal patient. In B. Bongar (Ed.), *Suicide: Guidelines for assessment, management, and treatment* (pp. 16–48). New York: Oxford University Press.

Clark, D. C., Gibbons, R. D., Fawcett, J., & Scheftner, W. A. (1989). What is the mechanism by which suicide attempts predispose to later suicide attempts? A mathematical model. *Journal of Abnormal Psychology, 98*, 42–49.

Clark, D. C., & Horton-Deutsch, S. L. (1992). Assessment *in absentia*: The value of the psychological autopsy method for studying antecedents of suicide and predicting future suicides. In R. L. Maris, A. Berman, J. T. Maltsberger, & R. Y. Yufit (Eds.), *Assessment and pre-*diction of suicide (pp. 144–182). New York: Guilford Press.

Clayton, P. J. (1985). Suicide. *Psychiatric Clinics of North America, 8*, 203–214.

Coryell, W., & Tsuang, M. T. (1982). Primary unipolar depression and the prognostic importance of delusions. *Archives of General Psychiatry, 39*, 1181–1184.

Crammer, J. L. (1984). The special characteristics of suicide in hospital in-patients. *British Journal of Psychiatry, 145*, 460–476.

Cullberg, J., Wasserman, D., & Stefansson, C. G. (1988). Who commits suicide after a suicide attempt? An 8- to 10-year follow-up in a suburban catchment area. *Acta Psychiatrica Scandinavica, 77*, 598–603.

Dorpat, T. L., & Ripley, H. S. (1960). A study of suicide in the Seattle area. *Comprehensive Psychiatry, 1*, 349–359.

Drake, R. E., & Cotton, P. G. (1986). Depression, hopelessness and suicide in chronic schizophrenia. *British Journal of Psychiatry, 148*, 554–559.

Drake, R. E., Gates, C., Cotton, P. G., & Whitaker, A. (1984). Suicide among schizophrenics: Who is at risk? *Journal of Nervous and Mental Disease, 172*, 613–617.

Drake, R. E., Gates, C., Whitaker, A., & Cotton, P. G. (1985). Suicide among schizophrenics: A review. *Comprehensive Psychiatry, 26*, 90–100.

Endicott, J., & Spitzer, R. L. (1978). A diagnostic interview: The Schedule for Affective Disorders and Schizophrenia. *Archives of General Psychiatry, 35*, 837–844.

Ettlinger, R. W. (1964). Suicides in a group of patients who had previously attempted suicide. *Acta Psychiatrica Scandinavica, 40*, 363–378.

Fawcett, J. (1988). Predictors of early suicide: Identification and appropriate intervention. *Journal of Clinical Psychiatry, 49* (10, Suppl.), 7–8.

Fawcett, J., Scheftner, W. A., Fogg, L., Clark, D. C., Young, M. A., Hedeker, D., & Gibbons, R. (1990). Time-related predictors of suicide in major depressive disorder. *American Journal of Psychiatry, 147*, 1189–1193.

Fowler, R. C., Rich, C. L., & Young, D. (1986). San Diego Suicide Study: II. Substance abuse in young cases. *Archives of General Psychiatry, 43*, 962–965.

Gibbs, J. J. (1982). Problems and priorities: Perceptions of jail custodians and social service providers. *Journal of Criminal Justice, 11*, 327–338.

Hagnell, O., & Rorsman, B. (1978). Suicide and endogenous depression with somatic symptoms in the Lundby study. *Neuropsychobiology, 4*, 180–187.

Hagnell, O., & Rorsman, B. (1979). Suicide in the Lundby study: A comparative investigation of clinical aspects. *Neuropsychobiology, 5*, 61–73.

Hagnell, O., & Rorsman, B. (1980). Suicide in the Lundby study: A controlled prospective investigation of stressful life events. *Neuropsychobiology, 6*, 319–332.

Harrow, M., Grinker, R. R., Silverstein, M., & Holzman, P. (1978). Is modern-day schizophrenic outcome still negative? *American Journal of Psychiatry, 135*, 1156–1162.

Hayes, L. M., & Kajdin, B. (1981). *And Darkness Closes In . . . : National Study of Jail Suicides.* Washington, DC: National Center for Institutions and Alternatives.

Hayes, L. M., & Rowan, J. R. (1988). *National Study of Jail Suicides: Seven Years Later.* Alexandria, VA: National Center for Institutions and Alternatives.

Kreitman, N. (1988). Suicide, age, and marital status. *Psychological Medicine, 18*, 121–128.

Kreitman, N., & Casey, P. (1988). Repetition of parasuicide: An epidemiological and clinical study. *British Journal of Psychiatry, 153*, 792–800.

Linehan, M. M. (1986). Suicide people: One population or two? *Annals of the New York Academy of Sciences: Psychobiology of Suicidal Behavior, 487*, 16–33.

Linehan, M. M. (1993a). *Cognitive–behavioral treatment of borderline personality disorder.* New York: Guilford Press.

Linehan, M. M. (1993b). *Skills training manual for treating borderline personality disorder.* New York: Guilford Press.

Linehan, M. M., Armstrong, H. E., Suarez, A., Allmon, D., & Heard, H. L. (1991). Cognitive–behavioral treatment of chronically parasuicidal borderline patients. *Archives of General Psychiatry, 48*, 1060–1064.

Linehan, M. M., Heard, H. E., & Armstrong, H. E. (1993). Naturalistic follow-up of a behavioral treatment for chronically suicidal borderline patients. *Archives of General Psychiatry, 50*, 971–974.

Litman, R. E. (1964). Immobilization response to suicidal behavior. *Archives of General Psychiatry, 11*, 282–285.

Litman, R. E. (1992). Predicting and preventing hospital and clinic suicides. In R. Maris, A. T. Berman, J. T. Maltsberger, & R. I. Yufit (Eds.), *Assessment and prediction of suicide* (pp. 448–466). New York: Guilford Press.

MacKinnon, D., & Farberow, N. (1975). An assessment of the utility of suicide prediction. *Suicide and Life-Threatening Behavior, 6*, 86–91.

Maltsberger, J. T. (1986). *Suicide Risk: The formulation of clinical judgment.* New York: New York University Press.

Maltsberger, J. T., & Buie, D. H. (1974). Countertransference hate in the treatment of suicidal patients. *Archives of General Psychiatry, 30*, 625–633.

Martin, R. L., Cloninger, C. R., Guze, S. B., & Clayton, P. J. (1985). Mortality in a follow-up of 500 psychiatric outpatients: I. Total mortality. *Archives of General Psychiatry, 42*, 47–54.

Miles, C. P. (1977). Conditions predisposing to suicide: A review. *Journal of Nervous and Mental Disease, 164*, 231–246.

Modestin, J., & Kopp, W. (1988). A study of clinical suicide. *Journal of Nervous and Mental Disease, 176*, 668–674.

Morgan, H. G., Barton, J., Pottle, S., Pocock, H., & Burns-Cox, C. J. (1976). Deliberate self-harm: A follow-up study of 279 patients. *British Journal of Psychiatry, 28*, 361–368.

Mościcki, E. K., O'Carroll, P., Rae, D. S., Locke, B. Z., Roy, A., & Regier, D. A. (1988). Suicide attempts in the Epidemiologic Catchment Area study. *Yale Journal of Biology and Medicine, 61*, 259–268.

Motto, J. (1965). Suicide attempts: A longitudinal view. *Archives of General Psychiatry, 13*, 516–520.

Murphy, G. E. (1975). The physician's responsibility for suicide: II. Errors of omission. *Annals of Internal Medicine, 82*, 305–309.

Murphy, G. E. (1984). The prediction of suicide: Why is it so difficult? *American Journal of Psychotherapy, 38*, 341–349.

Murphy, G. E. (1986a). Suicide and attempted suicide. In G. Winokur & P. Clayton (Eds.), *The medical basis of psychiatry* (pp. 562–579). Philadelphia: Saunders.

Murphy, G. E. (1986b). The physician's role in suicide prevention. In A. Roy (Ed.), *Suicide* (p. 175). Baltimore: Williams & Wilkins.

Murphy, G. E., Armstrong, J. W., Hermele, S. L., Fischer, J. R., & Clendenin, W. W. (1979). Suicide and alcoholism: Interpersonal loss confirmed as a predictor. *Archives of General Psychiatry, 36*, 65–69.

Murphy, G. E., & Wetzel, R. D. (1990). The lifetime risk of suicide in alcoholism. *Archives of General Psychiatry, 47*, 383–392.

Myers, J. K., Weissman, M. M., Tischler, G. L., Holzer, C. E., Leaf, P. J., Orvaschel, H., Anthony, J. C., Boyd, J. H., Burke, J. D., Kramer, M., & Stoltzman, R. (1984). Six-month prevalence of psychiatric disorders in three communities. *Archives of General Psychiatry, 41*, 959–967.

National Center for Health Statistics. (1994). Advance report of final mortality statistics, 1992. *NCHS Monthly Vital Statistics Report, 43*(6, Suppl.), 34–35.

Ogloff, J. R., & Otto, R. K. (1989). Mental health intervention in jails. In P. Keller & S. Heyman (Eds.), *Innovations in clinical practice: A source book* (Vol. 8, pp. 357–370). Sarasota, FL: Professional Resource Exchange.

Paris, J. (1980). Completed suicide in borderline personality disorder. *Psychiatric Annals, 20*, 19–21.

Pokorny, A. D. (1983). Prediction of suicide in psychiatric patients: Report of a prospective study. *Archives of General Psychiatry, 40*, 249–257.

Rich, C. L., Fowler, R. C., Fogarty, L. A., & Young, D. (1988). San Diego Suicide Study: III. Relationships between diagnoses and stressors. *Archives of General Psychiatry, 45*, 589–594.

Rich, C. L., Young, D., & Fowler, R. C. (1986). San Diego Suicide Study: I. Young vs. old subjects. *Archives of General Psychiatry, 43*, 577–582.

Robins, E. (1981). *The final months: A study of the lives of 134 persons who committed suicide.* New York: Oxford University Press.

Robins, E. (1986). Completed suicide. In A. Roy (Ed.), *Suicide* (pp. 123–133). Baltimore: Williams & Wilkins.

Robins, E., Gassner, S., Kaye, J., Wilkinson, R. H., & Murphy, G. E. (1959a). The communication of suicidal intent: A study of 134 consecutive cases of successful (completed) suicide. *American Journal of Psychiatry, 115*, 724–733.

Robins, E., Murphy, G. E., Wilkinson, R. H., Gassner, S., & Kayes, J. (1959b). Some clinical considerations in the prevention of suicide based on a study of 134 successful suicides. *American Journal of Public Health, 49*, 888–899.

Rodenburg, M. (1971). Child murder by depressed parents. *Canadian Psychiatric Association Journal, 16*, 41–48.

Roose, S. P., Glassman, A. H., Walsh, B. T., Woodring, S., & Vital-Herne, J. (1983). Depression, delusions, and suicide. *American Journal of Psychiatry, 140*, 1159–1162.

Rosen, A. (1954). Detection of suicidal patients: An example of some limitations in the prediction of infrequent events. *Journal of Consulting and Clinical Psychology, 18*, 397–403.

Rosenbaum, M. (1990). The role of depression in couples involved in murder–suicide and homicide. *American Journal of Psychiatry, 147*, 1036–1039.

Roy, A. (1982). Suicide in chronic schizophrenia. *British Journal of Psychiatry, 141*, 171–177.

Roy, A. (1986). Suicide in schizophrenia. In A. Roy (Ed.), *Suicide* (pp. 97–112). Baltimore: Williams & Wilkins.

Seager, C. P., & Flood, R. A. (1965). Suicide in Bristol. *British Journal of Psychiatry, 111*, 919–932.

Teplin, L. A. (1983). The criminalization of the mentally ill: Speculation in search of data. *Psychological Bulletin, 94*, 54–67.

Tsuang, M. T. (1978). Suicide in schizophrenics, manics, depressives, and surgical controls. *Archives of General Psychiatry*, 35, 153–154.

Tsuang, M. T., Woolson, R. F., & Fleming, J. A. (1980). Premature deaths in schizophrenic and affective disorders. *Archives of General Psychiatry*, 37, 979–983.

Vassilas, C. A., & Morgan, H. G. (1993). General practitioners' contact with victims of suicide. *British Medical Journal*, 307, 300–301.

Veevers, J. E. (1973). Parenthood and suicide: An examination of a neglected variable. *Social Sciences and Medicine*, 7, 135–144.

Virkkunen, M. (1974). Suicide in schizophrenia and paranoid psychoses. *Acta Psychiatrica Scandinavica*, Suppl. 250, 1–305.

Weiss, J. M. A., & Scott, K. F. (1974). Suicide attempters ten years later. *Comprehensive Psychiatry*, 15, 165–171.

Westermeyer, J. F., & Harrow, M. (1989). Early phases of schizophrenia and depression: Prediction of suicide. In R. Williams & J. T. Dalby (Eds.), *Depression in schizophrenics* (pp. 153–169). New York: Plenum Press.

Wilkinson, G., & Bacon, N. A. (1984). A clinical and epidemiological survey of parasuicide and suicide in Edinburgh schizophrenics. *Psychological Medicine*, 14, 899–912.

Wolfgang, M. E. (1958). An analysis of homicide–suicide. *Journal of Clinical and Experimental Psychopathology*, 19, 208–217.

21

Women and Depression: A Comprehensive Analysis

CHRISTIANE BREMS

Twice as many women as men report depressive symptoms or diagnosable depressive syndromes in the course of their lives (McGrath, Keita, Strickland, & Russo, 1991). In fact, "one in ten women can expect to have a serious depression in her life time" (Kaplan, 1986, p. 234). This preponderance of depression in women versus men has been documented throughout recorded history concerned with mental health and has been accepted as an absolute truth by most mental health practitioners (Nolen-Hoeksema, 1990). Historically, the gender ratio differences have been attributed to women's "inferior anatomy" and the shirking of their natural feminine role (Ehrenreich & English, 1978). This chapter explores the validity of claims about gender differences in the prevalence of depression, its possible artifactual nature, and its possible explanations. Based on this investigation, treatment implications for women with depressive symptoms and syndromes are discussed briefly.

PREVALENCE RATES OF DEPRESSIVE SYMPTOMS AND SYNDROMES

Surveys of clinical populations are consistent in producing prevalence rates of depression indicating that women are more frequently diagnosed with and treated for depression than men (Nolen-Hoeksema, 1990). Women are overrepresented among mental health service agency consumers, especially single mothers between the ages of 35 and 50 (Belle, 1980). Among these single mothers, black women preponderate; white males are least likely to become clients of mental health service agencies. The rate of women treated for depressive syndromes in psychiatric facilities in the United States exceeds the rate for men across all age groups, with an average of 205.5 women versus 138 men treated for diagnosable depression per 100,000 persons in the general population (Nolen-Hoeksema, 1990). This gender ratio is not only found in clinical populations, but also holds for depression rates in the general population using community samples. Specifically, as documented by the National Institute of Mental Health (NIMH), in 1980 an average of 10.2% of the general population had diagnosable depressive syndromes; of these, 70% were women and 30% were men (Nolen-Hoeksema, 1990). Similarly, a NIMH Epidemiologic Catchment Area Study based on five communities (New Haven, CT; St. Louis, MO; Baltimore, MD; Piedmont, NC; and Los Angeles, CA) and a sample of 18,572 individuals found a mean depression rate among the general population of 3.1%, with rates ranging from 2.1% in Baltimore to 4.2% in Los Angeles. Among these depressed individuals, women were overrepresented in all communities with gender ratios from 1.5 women for every man in New Haven to 3 women for every man in Piedmont (Weissman, Leaf, Bruce, & Florio, 1988).

Similar gender ratios are found relatively consistently across the world among industrialized and urbanized nations, the only exceptions being Finland and Norway (Weissman & Klerman, 1977). Worldwide gender ratios in depression have also been deduced from suicide epidemiologies. Because 80% of all suicides can be related to depression in the victim, suicide statistics can provide further insight into depression rates among women and men (Nolen-Hoeksema, 1990). Inspection of such data indicates that the 2:1 gender ratio prevails: In the United States and many other industrialized nations, including Australia, Great Britain, and Israel, twice as many women as men attempt to kill themselves. (Completed suicides are another matter; here men tend to preponderate. See Weissman & Klerman, 1977.)

Gender ratios in depression also are interesting to investigate from an age perspective. Before puberty (i.e., among children), boys are more likely to be diagnosed with depressive syndromes in clinical and community samples (Nolen-Hoeksema, 1990). However, as soon as puberty is reached, these statistics change significantly. Among adolescents aged 14 to 18, significantly more females than males are depressed. In fact, the preponderance of females in adolescent samples is even higher than in adult samples (Kandel & Davies, 1982). Such data, in addition to age expectancies, have been used to argue that the rate of depression among the general population is on the rise (Strickland, 1988). Specifically, Strickland indicates that currently 53% of the general population is female and that this ratio will increase in the future, given that a woman's life expectancy is 78.2 years, whereas a man can expect to live only to an age of 70.9 years. The aging of the U.S. population and the subsequent increased proportion of women in the United States suggests that depression will become an increasingly critical mental health issue in the future. Interestingly, depression ratio differences almost disappear after age 65, when women and men become equally likely to show depressive symptoms (Belle & Goldman, 1980).

When the epidemiological picture of depression is summarized, several conclusions emerge (Hirschfeld & Cross, 1982). Adult women of any age are more likely to be depressed than men (particularly younger adults and individuals of lower socioeconomic status); and urban or industrialized nations' citizens are more likely to be depressed than the populations of rural or developing countries. However, it must be qualified that these differences generally apply only to unipolar depressions. Overall, bipolar disorders are not likely to show a preponderance among women (e.g., Boyd & Weissman, 1981; Rice et al., 1984), with only a few exceptions noted in the literature (cf. Clayton, 1981). However, it is noteworthy that within the category of bipolar depressions, significant gender differences do emerge, even if the overall prevalence rates for males and females are equal (Parry, 1989). Specifically, there appears to be a preponderance of women among rapid cyclers, with prevalence rates ranging from 70% women versus 30% men (Donner, Patrick, & Fieve, 1977), to 83% women versus 17% men (Cowdry, Wehr, Zis, & Goodwin, 1983), to 92% women and 8% men (Wehr, Sack, & Rosenthal, 1988). Prevalence rates for nonrapid cyclers, on the other hand, show negligible differences between female and male rates (cf. Parry, 1989). Overall, there appears to be agreement that current evidence does not suffice to conclude that gender differences hold for bipolar disorders (cf. Weissman & Klerman, 1987). Thus, the remainder of this chapter focuses on unipolar depressions only.

THE FEMALE PREPONDERANCE OF DEPRESSION AS AN ARTIFACT

Over the decades, many questions have been raised by researchers suggesting that the preponderance of depression among women may merely be an artifact of reporting biases or differential reporting styles, differential help-seeking attitudes, differential symptomatic manifestations of pathology, flawed research methodology, and poor construct validity (cf. McGrath et al., 1991). It has been argued repeatedly that women are more likely than men to admit to depressive symptoms and that, hence, the rate and severity of depression is either exaggerated among women or underestimated among men, or both (e.g., Chevron, Quinlan, & Blatt, 1978). Furthermore, rather than merely being more willing to admit depressive symptomatology in general, women have also been described as reporting trivial symptoms that tend to inflate their scores on self-report inventories as well as structured interviews (Newmann, 1984). Newmann cited literature in which gender differences in the diagnosis of depression disappeared when the persistence of symptoms was considered and held constant across women and men. She concluded that women may report more mild symptoms, but have no greater likelihood of diagnosable depression than men. However, Nolen-Hoeksema (1990) indicated that there is sufficient literature to suggest that such overreporting by women cannot be substantiated. She summarized several studies in which women were found no more or less likely than men to report depressive symptoms, either on self-report questionnaires, structured interviews, or personal interviews. Similarly, Amenson and Lewinsohn (1981) found that women and men who were matched for their depressive symptoms were equally likely to label themselves as depressed. Studies that reveal equal reporting likelihood for women and men suggest that reporting differences cannot account for the preponderance of depression among women.

O'Neil, Lancee, and Freeman (1985) have argued that although reporting differences per se may not exist, women may be more likely than men to interpret various signs or physical characteristics as symptoms of depression, and hence are more likely to admit to depression than men. However, this hypothesis has yet to be substantiated empirically. Similarly, it has been stated that women merely seek more help than men; that is, although there may not be a difference in actual severity and rate of symptomatology, women are viewed as more likely to complain. This theory has been refuted repeatedly. The same study by Amenson and Lewinsohn (1981) cited previously, also indicated that women and men with equivalent symptoms showed no differences in their likelihood to seek psychological help. Furthermore, Guttentag, Salasin, and Belle (1980) revealed that although women reported more stressors, they did not weight them differently than men. In other words, women rated the severity of an equal stressor no more highly than men (i.e., women neither complained more nor were more likely to seek help for such an event). Clancy and Gove (1974) have provided evidence against the theory that help seeking is a socially desirable behavior for women, and therefore is more likely to occur in response to minor stressors or events. They found that women had no higher need for social approval than men, and argued that if women seek more help and report more symptoms, they do so as a true reflection of higher levels of depression.

With reporting and help seeking ruled out as possible contributors to the preponderance of depression among women, several researchers turned to investigating whether depression merely manifested differently in men, and was hence neither recognized nor diagnosed as such (Nolen-Hoeksema, 1990). Nolen-Hoeksema (1987) considered the possibility that men are more likely to act out aggressively or abuse alcohol as part of their depressive symptomatology; women, on the other hand, may be more likely to be passive and cry. The fact that the female-typed symptoms are part of the nosology of depressive disorders, whereas the male-typed symptoms are not, may thus account for the increased rate of depression among women. This theory found support from investigators who revealed that in cultures where the use of alcohol is outlawed (e.g., the Amish in the United States), the rate of depression among males and females is equal (Egeland & Hostetter, 1983). Despite this evidence, however, it appears more likely that the higher rates of male alcoholism are a reflection of a completely separate disorder, perhaps one in which a male vulnerability has manifested itself (Nolen-Hoeksema, 1990). It appears possible that women and men may respond to the same circumstances with different symptoms and disorders, rather than showing different symptoms of the same disorder (Nolen-Hoeksema, 1987). The consensus that has emerged is that the preponderance of depression among women cannot be accounted for by different manifestations of the same disorder.

Because the personal variables discussed previously have not been shown to account for gender differences in depressive symptoms and syndromes, methodological issues have been explored. For instance, Golding (1988) has pointed to the possibility that the distribution of depression scores for women is highly skewed, with a few women reporting exceedingly high levels of depression. This deviation from the normal curve in measuring depressive mood (rather than relying on actual clinical diagnoses of depressive syndromes) may create artificial between-group differences. Similarly, "failure to control for the confounding of other forms of distress with a depressive syndrome" (Newmann, 1987, p. 456) may account for an overestimation of diagnosable depression among women. Poor establishment of interrater reliabilities may have resulted in noncomparable findings, both within and between studies, and questionable reliability and validity of assessment instruments has led to unclear criteria for definition of what was being measured (Belle & Goldman, 1980).

These methodological complaints have resulted in major criticisms of the validity of depression studies to date. The primary problem facing contemporary researchers is that of construct validity. Specifically, it is not clear from one study to the next what type of depression was studied and whether it represented a clinical or subclinical syndrome (Weissman & Klerman, 1977). Thus, merely the higher rate of even mild depressive symptoms may have been mistaken for the preponderance of diagnosable depression among women (Newmann, 1987). Goldman and Ravid (1980) have pointed toward the necessity for the development of better construct validity. They urge researchers to define the symptoms being measured in future research along a minimum of five dimensions: namely, intensity, pervasiveness, persistence, and interference with social or somatic functioning. Regardless of these criticisms, the fact remains that depression preponderates among women, even if not necessarily at clinical levels. Numerous epidemiological studies sampling healthy adults have provided evidence that depression is persistent, severe, and pervasive in the lives of women, more so than in the lives of men. While future studies must improve methodologically, the current methodological criticisms of existing investigations do not suffice to conclude that the gender ratio of depression is invalid or unreliable.

Weissman and Klerman (1985) concluded that there are indeed five artifacts currently present in the depression literature; however, none has to do with the preponderance rates. Instead, these investigators reveal as myths the beliefs that women are under more stress, that women weigh events as more stressful, that women are more likely to admit to symptoms, that women are more likely to seek help, and that men are more likely to manifest depression via alcohol abuse. Consequently, it is the consensus of the most prominent and prolific contemporary researchers in this area of investigation that the "female preponderance [of depression] is not an artifact" (Weissman & Klerman, 1985), but rather a reflection of reality (McGrath et al., 1991; Nolen-Hoeksema, 1990).

EXPLANATIONS FOR THE FEMALE PREPONDERANCE OF DEPRESSION

The conclusion that the preponderance of depression among women does not represent an artifact, but rather a reality, begs the question as to why this is so. If women are not simply more vulnerable to depression than men (Tennent, 1985), there must be other conditions that contribute to the development of depressive symptoms and syndromes among women. A number of explanatory hypotheses have been outlined, involving biological (e.g., genetic and endocrine), social (e.g., socioeconomic issues, social roles and support, discrimination), psychosocial/psychological (e.g., socialization and personality development, interpersonal violence), and other factors (e.g., life events such as bereavement). While these factors are discussed fairly independently of one another in the remainder of this chapter, it must be kept in mind (especially with regard to treatment) that more often than not, an interaction among variables most likely accounts for the higher prevalence rates among females. In fact, the American Psychological Association Task Force on Women and Depression has strongly recommended not ignoring any of the aforementioned factors and instead taking a biopsychosocial approach to the exploration, diagnosis, and treatment of depression among women (McGrath et al., 1991). Additionally, the Task Force suggests sensitivity to particularly vulnerable subgroups, such as ethnic minority women, women living at poverty level, single mothers, and women who are members of other minority groups, such as lesbians (Rothblum, 1990).

Biological Factors

The two primary biological factors that have been explored are derived from genetic and hormonal theories. It has been shown that "the presence of [affective] illness in a mother is more predictive of illness in an offspring of either sex than is [affective] illness in the father" (Rice et al., 1984, p. 207). While there are other possible explanations besides genetic transmission for this finding, evidence such as this has fueled interest in the possibility of genetic links to the preponderance of depression in women. Similarly, with regard to hormonal explanations, Parry (1989) indicates that the fluctuation of gonadal steroids during specific phases of the reproductive cycle may bear some relationship to the particular vulnerability of women for affective changes. The reproductive hormones could exert their effects on mood directly or indirectly by their effect in neurotransmitter, neuroendocrine, or circadian systems, all of which have been implicated in the pathogenesis of affective illness. (p. 207)

Thus, both genetic and reproductive-related possibilities must be explored in attempting to gain a better understanding of depression among women.

Genetic Theories

Genetic theories of depression have been investigated via two primary mechanisms: exploration of preponderance rates and investigation of possible X-linkage. Support for a genetic linkage of affective disorders has been derived from twin studies (Nolen-Hoeksema, 1987, citing research by Allen, 1976). Specifically, dizygotic twins (i.e., siblings who share the same uterine environment, but not necessarily identical genetic material) evidence concordance rates of 11% for affective illness. Monozygotic twins (i.e., siblings who not only share the same uterine environment, but also have identical genetic makeup) show concordance rates of 40%. Because both rates are significantly above the concordance rates of depression that would be predicted for the general population, they provide support for a genetic hypothesis in the transmission of affective illness. Similarly, there are more affectively disordered individuals among first-degree relatives of people with affective disorders than in the general population, and adoptive children of depressed biological parents are more vulnerable to developing mood disorders than adoptive children of nondepressed biological parents (Klerman & Weissman, 1980). Whereas such data support a genetic transmission, they do not explain female preponderance.

A study by Merikangas, Weissman, and Pauls (1985) was specifically designed to explore not only the likelihood of genetic transmission in general, but also a genetic explanation of female preponderance. These researchers explained that if men indeed have less genetic predisposition for the development of affective illness than women, then there should be greater genetic aberration in depressed men than in

women with the same disorder. Hence, depression in a male should result in greater likelihood of transmission to offspring than depression in a woman. In other words, in the family of a depressed mother, one would expect fewer depressed offspring than in the family of a depressed father. If such preponderance patterns among offspring of depressed parents are not found, it can be concluded that there is no genetic predisposition that accounts for the preponderance rates among women. Merikangas et al. (1985) found no such patterns and concluded that there is little evidence for a genetic "cause" of female preponderance of depression.

The evidence provided by Merikangas et al. (1985) has also been used to argue against the possibility of an X-link hypothesis for depression. The X-link hypothesis states that the genetic material that predisposes an individual for depression is located on the X chromosomes (of which a woman receives two and a man receives one from the parents). Consequently, women have a larger chance of receiving a depression-prone X chromosome than men, by mere virtue of the fact that males receive half the number of X chromosomes as females. According to this theory, all daughters of a depressed father and a nondepressed mother should be depressed (because one of their X chromosomes will come from the father), whereas no sons should be depressed (because they receive their only X chromosome from the mother). Male and female children of a depressed mother and a nondepressed father, on the other hand, would be equally likely to be depressed or not depressed (because both children have an equal chance of receiving one X chromosome from the mother). In exploring exactly such patterns, Gershon and Bunney (1976) found no evidence that would suggest X-linkage for genetic material that might predispose offspring for depression. Genetic research has thus not resulted in evidence that would support a genetic predisposition of women for depression, suggesting that explanations have to be sought elsewhere.

Reproductive-Related Theories

There are a number of reproductive-related events that clearly differentiate women and men. The fluctuation of gonadal steroids and hormones associated with the female reproductive cycle have been clearly identified and have been hypothesized to affect behavior. Furthermore, hormonal changes due to pregnancy or the end of a woman's fertile period may have an impact on her behavior. Additional changes in the hormonal environment in the female body may be related to events such as hysterectomies, abortions, or the use of oral contraceptives. Ample literature investigating reproductive-related events and their relationship to mood is available and will be reviewed briefly in an attempt to clarify the relationship these events may have with depressive symptoms and affective disorders among women.

Premenstrual Syndrome. The female menstrual cycle has been anecdotally connected with significant changes in affect, behavior, and physical functioning. In fact, in the 19th century, the disturbance due to menstrual tension was considered so severe by some physicians that they recommended bed rest for 1 week before menstruation and referred to the "monthly returns of ill health" among women (Nolen-Hoeksema, 1990, p. 51). Anecdotal physical symptoms have included reports of breast tenderness, headaches, backaches, fatigue, bloating, changes in sleep and appetite, and cramping. Affective symptoms have included supposed increases in irritability, depression, anger, anxiety, and decreases in concentration (cf. Rubinow & Schmidt, 1989). Behavioral symptoms have been reported to include loss of self-control, impulsive action, accident proneness, increased interpersonal (especially marital) conflict, changes in libido, and absenteeism from employment. These reports, although anecdotally frequently documented (usually by male physicians; see Rubinow & Schmidt, 1989), more recently have been criticized as myths that are "based on extremely faulty or limited data" (Nolen-Hoeksema, 1990, p. 51). Just how valid the historical claims of mood changes due to the menstrual cycle are has been the subject of numerous contemporary investigations.

The physical causes hypothesized as underlying the presence of affective premenstrual symptoms are twofold. First, it has been theorized that hormonal fluctuations contribute to mood changes. A strong similarity has been found among affects manifested during the premenstrual period, during menopause, and as side effects of oral contraceptives (Dennerstein, Morse, & Varnavides, 1988); this has been interpreted as lending credence to an underlying biological component for depressions that emerge during these periods in a woman's life.

However, the biochemical cause for premenstrual mood change has not received unequivocal support (cf. Rubinow and Roy-Byrne, 1984).

The second possible underlying mechanism suggests that a shift in the salt–water balance of the central nervous system, due to fluctuations in mineralocorticoids, such as aldosterone, leads to depressive symptoms. However, again, actual empirical investigations have produced only conflicting results (cf. Nolen-Hoeksema, 1990). In fact, the presence of premenstrual affective syndrome itself has been called into question by a number of researchers who have criticized research methodologies. Nevertheless, some evidence has been produced to support mood and behavior changes during the premenstrual phase.

Prevalence rates of diagnosable premenstrual affective syndrome range widely, with estimates of 20–80% of all women (McGrath et al., 1991). The prevalence of premenstrual affective symptoms in one particularly well-controlled study was even as low as 3.1% (Rivera-Tovar & Frank, 1990). Hallman (1986) reported a 72.8% prevalence rate of general premenstrual syndrome in a healthy community sample. Of these women, 7.5% had symptoms that were severe enough to require medical intervention. It was only this latter group of women who showed significant increases in depressive symptomatology during the premenstrual phase of the reproductive cycle. Similarly, in a sample of women who were selected because of complaints of premenstrual symptoms, only those with a diagnosable syndrome suffered from depression (van der Ploeg, 1989). Christensen and Oei (1989) found that whereas some women reported depressive symptomatology premenstrually, none had sufficiently severe, pervasive, or persistent symptoms to qualify for a diagnosis of mood disorder. Some women with full premenstrual syndrome (PMS) evidenced higher levels of depression and more physical symptoms during the luteal phase than at other times during the menstrual cycle, and as compared to women without a diagnosable syndrome; PMS sufferers and nonsufferers did not differ with regard to physical or affective symptoms during the follicular phase (Trunnell, Turner, & Keye, 1988).

The great variation in prevalence rates of affective symptoms in the premenstrual phase may be accounted for, at least in part, by methodological flaws of existing studies. For instance, the most commonly utilized measurement scale for PMS studies is the Moos Menstrual Distress Questionnaire (Moos, 1968). While this scale has been widely used, there are no reliability or validity data available for it. It is highly recommended that future research employ a relatively newly developed scale, the Premenstrual Assessment Form (Halbreich, Endicott, & Nee, 1983), given its superior psychometric properties. Furthermore, most PMS studies exploring the presence of affective symptoms are retrospective and rely exclusively on self-report. These procedures are likely to have created subject bias, especially because most subjects are aware of the topic of investigation. Two studies to date have carefully addressed these methodological issues and have found low prevalence rates of affective symptoms correlated with PMS in their subjects. Namely, Rivera-Tovar and Frank (1990) conducted a prospective longitudinal study in which subjects were blind to the researcher's interest in their menstrual cycle. This study resulted in a prevalence rate of only 3.1%. Similarly, Olasov and Jackson (1987) conducted a study with four experimental groups. One group received information about PMS along with information about the negative impact of this disorder on mood. A second group received the same initial information, followed by positive statements about the impact of the syndrome on mood. A third group received the same information about PMS without information about its impact on mood, and with information about circadian rhythms. A fourth group received no intervention at all. All women monitored mood and other symptoms for several weeks. The control group showed no evidence of negative mood associated with PMS, nor did the group that had received positive information about mood effects of PMS. However, both the group that had received negative mood information and the group that had received no mood information at all showed increased levels of depression. These findings clearly demonstrate that merely informing women that PMS may impact mood results in higher reports of depressive symptoms and that expectations created among women can significantly affect their experience of the menstrual cycle (Olasov & Jackson, 1987).

In addition to citing methodological flaws to account for the great variability in prevalence rates, it is also possible that the difficulty in "finding consistent evidence for various explanations of premenstrual depression is that these depressions may not represent a distinct form of depression" (Nolen-Hoeksema, 1990, p. 57). In fact, only very few women who show depressive symptoms premenstrually show these symptoms only then (Rubinow & Roy-Byrne, 1984). Instead, they show depressive symptoms across the menstrual cycle with premenstrual exacerbations. In fact, premenstrual depression appears to be linked to an underlying mild or subclinical affective disorder rather than being part of the premenstrual syndrome itself (Endicott, Halbreich, Schacht, & Nee, 1981). This conclusion is further supported by findings that 78% of women who suffer from affective syndromes during PMS also have a diagnosable affective disorder on Axis I, and 10% have an Axis II diagnosis that is consistent with at least occasional depression (Pearlstein et al., 1990). Similarly, women seeking treatment for PMS are not only more likely to have affective disorders than women not being treated for PMS, but are also more likely to have histories of sexual abuse (Paddison, Gise, Lebovits, Strain, Cirasole, & Levine, 1990). The authors concluded that other factors may result in an affective disorder that, in turn, may increase the likelihood of a premenstrual syndrome that includes depression (Endicott et al., 1981; Lahmeyer, 1984). Alternatively, PMS may exacerbate existing affective disorder, while being an independent disorder involving independent affective symptomatology only in a small number of women (Chisholm, Jung, Cumming, Fox, & Cumming, 1990).

Finally, some researchers have pointed out that for many women, depression occurs only after they have already suffered other premenstrual symptoms (physical pains and tension) for several days. The subsequent and subclinical depression that is measured in these women, therefore, is more likely to be a reactive depression to the physical symptoms of PMS than reflective of premenstrual depression caused by the hormonal environment or other biological changes secondary to the menstrual cycle (cf. Coleman, Hart, & Russell, 1988). Finally, "it does not appear that the amplitude of hormonal change necessarily correlates with the magnitude of behavior change" (Hamilton, Parry, & Blumenthal, 1988b, p. 483). Instead, it appears to be more relevant whether hormonal changes coincide with critical times, such as acute life stressors or chronic life conditions (e.g., history of sexual abuse, deprivation).

These conclusions have resulted in significant opposition to the diagnostic syndrome of premenstrual dysphoric disorder proposed for, though not included in the main text of, DSM-IV (American Psychiatric Association, 1994). It is argued that there is no current research justification for such a diagnosis because it would suggest a biological etiology, when situational factors for premenstrual depression are clearly more relevant. The implication that a "woman's reproductive biology is central to a psychiatric illness" (Nolen-Hoeksema, 1990, p. 61) would be reminiscent of the historical concept that women are vulnerable to depression because of "inferior anatomy" (Ehrenreich & English, 1978).

Menopause and Climacteric. The "climacteric," or the period during which a woman moves from reproductive to nonreproductive life, has been anecdotally associated with a climacteric syndrome that has its onset after menopause. Such postmenopausal symptoms reportedly include sleep disturbance, fatigue, irritability, mood changes, and a number of physiological symptoms, such as hot flashes and night sweats (McGrath et al., 1991). There is obvious overlap between these symptoms and diagnostic criteria for mood disorders as defined by the DSM-IV, and this has led to a common belief that climacteric results in an increase in depression among women (cf. Formanek, 1987). However, despite this anecdotally based belief, there is little empirical evidence for climacteric-caused increases in depressive symptoms among postmenopausal women.

While there is an increase in the amount of depression reported by women late in life, the same proportional increase is also observed among men (Formanek, 1987), and hence cannot be clearly related to the hormonal changes of the climacteric. Evidence to the contrary usually is based on clinical populations that clearly present for treatment because they experience symptoms and hence represent a biased sample (Lennon, 1987). Evidence from healthy community samples has shown that whereas there are indeed physical symptoms that are correlated with the climacteric, such as hot flashes and night sweats, no increase is noted in affectively relevant symptoms, such as sleep, appetite, libido, or self-confidence (Bungay, Vessey, & McPherson, 1980). This absence of depressive symptoms as related to the climacteric has been replicated time and again (e.g., Lennon, 1987; McKinlay, McKinlay, & Brambilla, 1987; Schmidt & Rubinow, 1991), and researchers

have suggested that dated findings claiming the opposite are artifacts of methodology. Researchers have pointed out that operational definitions of depression were generally missing in dated studies, that the onset of symptoms was generally not controlled for (i.e., the depression may have started premenopausally), and that findings relied solely on self-report (see Schmidt & Rubinow, 1991).

Also providing evidence against a relationship between affective symptoms and climacteric is the finding that hormonal treatment of depressed postmenopausal women reduces only physical symptoms, but has no impact on depression levels (Iatrakis, Haronis, Sakellaropoulos, Kourkoubas, & Gallos, 1986), and that premenopausal depression tends to be higher than postmenopausal depression (Ballinger, 1990). Any changes in mood that do occur late in life appear more strongly correlated with and accounted for by factors other than biological ones (McGrath et al., 1991), including sociocultural, familial, and intrapsychic ones (Ballinger, 1990). The period of life that tends to coincide with a woman's climacteric is replete with changes: Children leave home, family members and friends become ill and/or die, the spouse and the woman herself may face retirement, and physical changes may require adjustment in pastime activities (Formanek, 1987). Furthermore, societal values and stereotypes about menopause in general, fertility, and childrearing in particular, may have a negative impact on women (Formanek, 1987), although there is no current evidence that women with traditional roles and beliefs are more likely to show postmenopausal depression than nontraditional women (Lennon, 1987).

Postpartum Syndromes. The end of a pregnancy through the birth of a child is an extremely stressful event in a woman's life, both biologically and psychologically. It has been hypothesized that endocrine events after delivery—namely, the surge in gonadotropins and hormones—result in affective symptoms, even syndromes (e.g., Gitlin & Pasnau, 1989; Martin, Brown, Goldberg, & Brackington, 1989). Additionally, it has been suggested that neurotransmitter environments are affected by pregnancy and delivery, and that subsequent low levels of tryptophan (the precursor of serotonin) result in increased levels of depression (Nolen-Hoeksema, 1990). In exploring the symptoms women present postpartum, it is important to differentiate minor subclinical "blues" from diagnosable depression (Thirkettle & Knight, 1985). Whereas prevalence of postpartum blues is as high as 30–60% (even 80%; Hamilton, 1989b), postpartum depressions occur with a frequency ranging from 3–33% of all mothers (Nolen-Hoeksema, 1990). Both rates, however, indicate increases in depression beyond what would be expected in the general population, pointing toward delivery as a possible underlying factor for such affective symptoms.

In addition to the simple differentiation between postpartum blues and depression, more sophisticated nosologies have been developed, reflective of increasing severity of affective disorder postpartum. Specifically, Landy, Montgomery, and Walsh (1989) have suggested that four distinct syndromes exist. The least severe of these are postpartum blues, which usually have their onset no sooner than the third day postpartum and are marked by crying, insomnia, confusion, exhaustion, headaches, feelings of loss, anxiety, and mild depression (Hamilton, 1989b). Postpartum blues have been empirically established and are not synonymous with a diagnosable affective syndrome; rather, they are a mere collection of transitory affective symptoms (O'Hara, Zekoski, Phillips, & Wright, 1990). They generally abate within 10 days, with a peak around day 4 or 5 postpartum (Iles, Gath, & Kennerley, 1989). Next in severity is neurotic postpartum depression, which has a slow and insidious onset up to 6 months after delivery and can result in irritability, weight loss, guilt, apathy, decreased energy and initiative, and loss of self-esteem (Hamilton, 1989b; Landy et al., 1989). Third, and more severe, is borderline postpartum depression, which may become evident as late as 1 year postpartum. This type of postpartum depression is often similar to neurotic postpartum depression, but may be accompanied by occasional psychotic symptomatology (Landy et al., 1989). Fourth, the most severe form of postpartum depression is psychotic postpartum depression. This disorder is relatively rare, occurring only in approximately 2% of all mothers, and generally has its onset within the first month after birth. It is accompanied by all the symptoms described above, along with a loss of contact with reality and strong feelings of anger (Landy et al., 1989).

Whereas some type of postpartum affective reaction has thus been established with a degree of consistency in the literature, the presence of these affective disorders and symptoms cannot be mistaken as causative evidence for a endocrine or biological link between the process of pregnancy or delivery and depression. Instead, biological explanations alone are considered "clearly simplistic" (McGrath et al., 1991, p. 10), and in fact, numerous additional explanations have evolved in the literature (Nemtzow, 1987): constitutional predisposition, family history (e.g., mother's own childhood bereavement), psychosocial factors (e.g., social support, relationship with spouse, general life satisfaction), and intrapsychic factors (e.g., loss of personal freedom, loss of career, change in intimate relationships). With regard to constitutional predisposition, Kennerley and Gath (1989) have demonstrated that postpartum depression is most significantly predicted by prepartum affective symptoms. These researchers also provided support for the psychosocial hypothesis by revealing a strong relationship between the quality of the marital relationship and postpartum depression. Similarly, it has been shown not only that marital adjustment predicted postpartum adjustment, but also that unmarried, poorly educated mothers were particularly at risk (Pfost, Stevens, & Lum, 1990).

Lack of social support was identified as a risk factor by Landy et al. (1989), who also indicated that women from Western cultures were at higher risk for developing postpartum depression than women from nonindustrialized countries, where acceptance of traditional roles and familial support were higher. The change in role and identity secondary to motherhood has also been identified empirically as a predisposing factor for postpartum depressions (Nicolson, 1989). Finally, life stressors as represented by the demands of a new infant are also risk factors. This has been supported by research that has investigated mothers' expectations about infant behavior and found that the more unrealistically optimistic mothers' expectations were about infants, the more likely these mothers were to become depressed (Whiffen, 1988). Women who faced a number of additional life stressors besides pregnancy and delivery were also found to be more vulnerable (Nolen-Hoeksema, 1990).

Sufficient evidence of postpartum affective symptoms and syndromes exists to conclude that they are a reflection of reality rather than artifacts, and that women should be prepared for this possibility prepartum (i.e., stress inoculation) to facilitate coping postpartum (cf.

O'Hara et al., 1990). However, the evidence for such depression does not give credence to endocrinological explanations. Instead, other factors are much more likely to be related to and account for the affective symptoms noted postpartum. Finally, it is important to remember that the bulk of these reactions are adjustment reactions, not affective disorders. They are likely to resolve quickly and do not represent diagnosable depressions (Harris et al., 1989).

Other Reproductive-Related Events.   In addition to the reproductive-related events discussed so far, there are a few additional issues that must be addressed briefly. It has been suggested that hysterectomies, abortions, oral contraceptives, and infertility may contribute to women's preponderance of depression (McGrath et al., 1991). The endocrinological and neuroendocrinological evidence, however, for all of these factors is either negative or ambiguous. Hysterectomies have been found to be more likely to result in depression than menopause not induced by surgery (McKinlay, McKinlay, & Brambilla, 1987), but even then symptoms are short-lived (McGrath et al., 1991) or perhaps pre-existing (McKinlay et al., 1987). Furthermore, even if depression after hysterectomy is more persistent and clearly developed postmenopausally, it is more strongly related to perceived loss of femininity and grieving for the loss of fertility than to hormonal or biological factors (Roopnarinesingh & Gopeesingh, 1982). Finally, there is little evidence that hysterectomies lead to more depression than any other type of surgery (Gitlin & Pasnau, 1989).

Depression after abortion appears mediated more by preabortion coping expectations and the assessed meaningfulness of the pregnancies than the change in the hormonal environment (Major, Mueller, & Hildebrandt, 1985). Furthermore, one study found that affective symptoms were much less likely if the woman's partner was supportive and available, the decision to have an abortion was made with little ambivalence, and the woman's anger at the pregnancy was low (Shusterman, 1979). These and other recent findings indicate that interpersonal, social, and perhaps even intrapsychic factors are more important predictors of affective adjustment after abortion than biological or hormonal ones (McGrath et al., 1991).

The use of oral contraceptives has been linked to increased levels of depression for 30–50% of the women using them (Hamilton, Parry, & Blu-

menthal, 1988a). Furthermore, they are implicated in some rapid-cycling bipolar disorders (Parry, 1989). However, this presence of depression is clearly not related to the usual female endocrinological environment, because it represents an alteration of the usual balance of hormones and gonadal steroids. These findings do suggest, however, that the use of oral contraceptives must be explored by mental health service providers, because oral contraceptives may cause depressive symptoms that could be easily eliminated through the choice of alternative methods of birth control. Finally, although also not necessarily a biological cause for the female preponderance of depression, infertility is strongly related to feelings of hopelessness, helplessness, and depression among women and their partners (McGrath et al., 1991). The possibility of this factor must therefore be explored with women seeking treatment for affective symptoms.

Summary

There is literally no genetic evidence to indicate a genetic vulnerability of women toward depression. Similarly, exploration of reproductive-related depression suggests that although occasionally the hormonal environment may have an impact on a woman's mood, more often this is not the case. In fact, it appears that only atypical depressions appear to be significantly related to endocrinological and cyclical variations (Hamilton, Lloyd, Alagna, Phillips, & Pinkel, 1984), and then not to a large enough degree to account for the 2:1 female preponderance of depression in general. Rather than causing depression, reproductive-related symptoms in response to events such as menstruation, menopause, and pregnancy may serve to exacerbate existing affective symptoms and to be exacerbated by them. Additionally, social, cultural, and psychological factors appear to be more relevant to the development of affective symptoms than endocrinological, neuroendocrinological, or other biological factors. This conclusion is further supported by two studies with pubescent girls and boys. When hormonal levels were measured in adolescent females and males, no relationship was found between these endocrinological events and reported depression (Eccles et al., 1988). Similarly, when life events, development of secondary sex characteristics, and hormonal levels were measured in 10- to 14-year-old girls, no persistent relationship emerged between hormonal developments and depression, except a brief increase in depression when hormone production began, followed by a quick return to normal mood levels (Brooks-Gunn & Warren, 1989). Incidentally, however, life events were significantly correlated with these children's reported depression levels.

Social Factors

The discussion of reproductive-related events and symptoms has resulted in the conclusion that even depressive symptoms that appear to occur as part of, or subsequent to, occurrences such as menopause or pregnancy are not necessarily endocrinological or biological in origin. Instead, a number of social factors have emerged as more relevant than a woman's endocrinological environment. These social factors include issues such as support in the marital relationship, life stressors, acceptance of social roles, and socioeconomic issues. Social factors are relevant not only because of their relationship to reproductive-related depressive symptoms, but also due to their association with depressive symptoms and syndromes in general.

Socioeconomic Issues

A number of issues related to socioeconomic condition are relevant to the development and maintenance of depressive symptoms. These include, but are not limited to, poverty and socioeconomic status (SES), income, employment, and education, as well as the interaction of these variables. Depression has been found to be significantly correlated with low levels of income (e.g., Makosky, 1982), low levels of education (e.g., Radloff, 1975), and poor employment (Warren & McEachren, 1983). Financial difficulties, regardless of level of income, are similarly associated with higher levels of depression (Birtchnell, 1988; Kaplan, Roberts, Camacho, & Coyne, 1987; Ross & Mirowsky, 1988), as are job loss and unemployment (Kaplan et al., 1987). Economic stressors have been identified to be particularly likely to result in increased levels of depression for women in general and black women in particular (Dressler, 1985). Economic strain is most destructive if it encompasses low income, low education, young age of the parent, and young children in the household (Ross & Huber, 1985). In fact, poverty and lack of education appear to have an additive effect on depression (Belle, 1990). It has been hypoth-

esized that the combination of low income and low education results in increased strain and stress for parents, and thus compounds the negative effects on their mental health (McGrath et al., 1991).

The fact that these findings of the positive association (statistically speaking) of low income or poverty and depression are particularly relevant for women, especially women of color (Kessler & Neighbors, 1986), becomes clear when current population demographics are explored. The U.S. Department of Commerce (1988) has reported that 51% of all households living at or below poverty level are headed by unmarried women, as opposed to only 4.8% headed by single men. When race is considered, the special vulnerability of black women becomes evident. Of all black poverty-level households, 74.1% are headed by black women; 42% of white poverty-level households are headed by women. Almost half of all single women who have children live in poverty (namely, 46.1%). In fact, having children appears associated with increased risk of poverty, because 16.2% of all households with children live in poverty, as compared to 4.9% of all household without children. Furthermore, women have less earning power overall than men, with a median income of $16,909, as opposed to $26,008 for men. As the poverty rate increases, the educational level decreases, with 20% of all poverty-level households being headed by a person with less than an eighth-grade education.

Adding to these U.S. Department of Commerce statistics, women who divorce risk decreases of as much as 70% in earning power, as opposed to men, whose earning power after divorce tends to increase as much as 42% (Nolen-Hoeksema, 1990). Having experienced this drop in income, women are often trapped in a double bind presented by the social support system in the United States, in which women are unemployed or have low-paying jobs (Tebbets, 1982). This double bind of poverty and lack of employment compounds women's depression; a clear relationship has emerged between level of depression and inadequate employment or lack of employment (Birtchnell, 1988). Furthermore, only 60% of divorced mothers are awarded child support in divorce settlements, and of these, only 50% of the fathers actually pay (Basow, 1986). Poor living quarters, often a result of poverty, have also been shown to be related to increased levels of depression (Haellstroem & Persson, 1984). Homeless women and mothers, in addition to facing poverty and poor living conditions, are more likely to become victims of violent crimes, including rapes and battery, which in turn increase the likelihood of depression (D'Ercole & Struening, 1990; see also the section on violence). Frequent moves and social isolation, commonly associated with poverty, are highly related to increased levels of depression (Birtchnell, 1988; Kaplan et al., 1987).

Whereas employment has been correlated with increased levels of self-esteem, confidence, accomplishment, and independence, thus providing a buffer for depression (Tebbets, 1982), it also has high costs for women. The work history of women tends to be closely tied to events in their own and their family's life cycle or stage. The typical woman with a low-SES background works before marriage and until she has her first child. Once the child can walk, she usually returns to work, but switches to nighttime or home-based work when additional children are born. Divorce results in part-time work supplemented by welfare, and in associated losses in the household's earning power (Tebbets, 1982). The high cost of child care; the loss of medical assistance, Aid to Families with Dependent Children, and food stamps if income rises above welfare-approved limits; lack of education; and lack of transportation to and from work often force the most economically vulnerable women into unemployment (Tebbets, 1982). This vicious cycle is extremely unfortunate for lower-SES women, because levels of depression increase, especially with loss of employment, for this group (Birtchnell, 1988; Tebbets, 1982).

In addition to the economic hardships faced by poorly educated women of lower SES, these women are also more likely to be faced with unexpected and chronic life stressors (e.g., Dill & Feld, 1982). Such increases in life stress, in turn, are related to decreased sense of mastery, loss of a sense of control over one's life, poor coping, and helplessness in stressful situations (McGrath et al., 1991). Thus, income is not only directly, but also indirectly related to higher levels of depression via stress and its impact on mental health. Therefore, whereas hardship in and of itself has not always been found to have a differential effect on women's and men's depression (e.g., Danilewitz & Skuy, 1990; Newmann, 1986), the fact that women face more of these hardships may render them more likely to become victims of depression (Newmann, 1986).

In summary, women in the United States are faced by economic realities that empirically are highly correlated with depressive symptoms. Their greater likelihood to live at poverty level, to be poorly educated, to be under- or unemployed, and to be single parents without social supports results in life strains that make women more likely to become victims of depression. As if this were not enough, however, these social factors related to socioeconomic issues are further exacerbated by, and interact with, additional social factors that are more likely to become problematic for women than for men (i.e., restrictive, conflictual, or demanding social roles; lack of social support; and discrimination).

Social Roles and Social Support Issues

A number of theories have been developed regarding the contribution of social roles to depression. Nolen-Hoeksema (1990) reviewed three possible effects of roles in this context—namely, noxiousness of roles, paucity of roles, and overload of roles. Repetti and Crosby (1984) have suggested that nonvalued roles lead to low self-esteem and low motivation to perform well in the assigned role. These two factors, in combination, lead to depression. The housewife role has been identified as one such under- or nonvalued role (Repetti & Crosby, 1984). Additionally, if an individual perceives a limited number of roles he/she can take, the likelihood of depression increases because there are no alternative sources of gratification. Women are traditionally more likely to experience such paucity of roles, being socialized to believe that the wife and mother roles are exclusive ones for them (Nolen-Hoeksema, 1990). However, men are equally vulnerable to such a paucity of roles, and single men are often likely to be depressed, isolated, and lonely (Crosby, 1982; Radloff, 1975). Finally, and more relevant for nontraditional and contemporary women, Gove and Tudor (1973) suggest that when individuals are asked to perform more roles than they can satisfactorily complete, they are likely to despair and experience depression, because they cannot live up to expectations in all arenas of functioning. This role theory may hold for women who attempt to be full-time workers, full-time mothers, traditional wives, homemakers, and so on.

This overview of how the number of roles may contribute to the development of depression exemplifies the complexity of this approach to understanding the female preponderance of depression. This literature is fraught with ambiguities and contradictory findings, although some consistencies are beginning to emerge. Even as these consistencies are reviewed in this chapter, the need for additional research in this area is great, especially the need for sophisticated research designs that can elucidate the interactions and additive or subtractive effects thereof. Roles that need to be explored include, but may not be limited to, those related to marriage, motherhood, employment, and free time. In covering the impact of various roles, investigators must note that the number of roles in and of itself is not as predictive as the interaction between number and quality, and the effect of one's perception of the ability to fulfill one's roles (Ross & Huber, 1985).

With regard to quality, for instance, the mothering role is very highly valued among the Amish, and equally as valued as male activities that support a family economically. Among the members of this culture, there are no gender differences in depression (Nolen-Hoeksema, 1990). With regard to self-perception, Wolf (1987, as cited in Belle, 1990) found that women who perceived themselves as bad mothers were significantly more depressed than women who perceived themselves as good mothers, regardless of actual parenting skills. Belle (1990) speculated that such negative self-perceptions preponderate among women of lower SES, who tend to have less education. This, in turn, may make ultimate role fulfillment less likely, further increasing these women's depression. Similarly, it has been demonstrated that perceived control over one's roles has a negative statistical relationship with depression. Specifically, as women perceive decreased life control, and as they perceive less accomplishment and social support, their depression increases (Warren & McEachren, 1983). This perception accounts for variance in depression between groups, above and beyond the social factors covered in the previous section of this chapter.

While there appears to be a positive mediating effect of control, values, and qualities of roles, it has been suggested that the mere fact of having employment is always positive for a woman's mental health (Aneshensel, 1986; Verbrugge, 1983). However, a review of this literature shows more ambiguous findings. It does appear that homemakers are more depressed and have more dissatisfaction with their home-life than any other group of women who have employment, or any other group with other family roles (Repetti & Crosby, 1984). Homemakers' mean depression scores are significantly higher than those of their husbands, especially if the couple has a low SES (Aneshensel, Frerichs, & Clark, 1981). Working women tend to be less depressed than homemakers, especially among lower socioeconomic strata, where employment appears to function as a buffer against depression (Mostow & Newberry, 1975). The amount of income does not appear to mediate the benefit of employment; however, the mental health benefits of work for women are particularly high if their employment conditions are positive and if the demands of the family do not interfere (Kessler & McRae, 1982). The differences in level of depression between wives and husbands increase as the employment difference between the two increases (Golding, 1988). Supporting the notion that other factors, such as family demands and job conditions, may be critical to the benefits of employment, Thoits (1986) found that women and men do not differ in their levels of self-reported depression if the number of roles is held constant, unless one of the roles investigated is employment. Then, unemployed men are more depressed than unemployed women, and employed mothers are more depressed than employed fathers. Some studies have suggested that homemakers and dual-role career women are equally prone to depression (Nolen-Hoeksema, 1990). In fact, depression appears extremely common among professional women with MDs and PhDs (Clayton, Marten, Davis, & Wochnik, 1980), and career women in training anticipate more problems from combining career and family ambitions than do career men in training (Zappert & Stansbury, 1984). Career women have higher rates of depression and more health problems than career men, which may be related to the fact that career women tend to work more than career men and are more likely to be saddled with child care problems (Zappert & Stansbury, 1984). At least 50% of career women have to stay home from work at some point in time to care for ill children, as compared to 1% of career men.

The inconsistencies that have been found in the effect of women's employment roles, have been interpreted to indicate that the job role effect is mediated by other variables, such as husband's support, parental status, child care accessibility, discrimination on the job, identity conflicts, role conflicts, and other related factors (McGrath et al., 1991). The latter four variables are supported by findings that in general (i.e., for women and men), depression increases when the individual is employed in a cross-gender traditional role. For instance, female physicians, psychologists, and medical students are more depressed than their male counterparts; and male nurses are more depressed than female nurses (McGrath et al., 1991). These factors are supported by literature exploring marital and parental roles.

The transition to parenthood has a greater impact on women than on men. For new mothers, the amount of social activity decreases, social support diminishes, friendships become more limited, and demands on time and for support increase (McGrath et al., 1991). After the birth of a child, women are less likely to return to work than men, and are more likely to experience parenting and financial problems (Vanfossen, 1986). Inadequate day care has been shown to be related to increased rates of depression (Ross & Mirowsky, 1988), and may be related to the finding that there are higher rates of dysthymic mood among single female parents (Weissman, Leaf, & Bruce, 1987). The rate of depression increases with the number of children (Goldman & Ravid, 1980), at least as long as the children live in the home. On the other hand, women with an "empty nest" are less depressed than childless women or women with children in the home. Single mothers are particularly vulnerable to depression. They have to cope with economic hardships, social isolation, and parenting responsibilities by themselves—all conditions that, when held constant, increase depression in women and men alike (Pearlin & Johnson, 1977). Because these factors are more common for single mothers than for single fathers, they can account for some gender differences in depression. Additionally, family stressors have more severe consequences for women than work-related stressors, and work appears to serve as a buffer against depression related to marital stress. Parenthood, however, exacerbates occupational stress, and problems in family roles are related to the most depressions (Kandel, Davies, & Raveis, 1985).

The Kandel et al. (1985) study reveals that marriage and family roles are critical in understanding the complex configuration of women's roles in modern society. It has been suggested repeatedly that marriage in and of itself serves as a buffer against depression for men, whereas it is detrimental to women's health (Nolen-Hoeksema, 1990). This is so regardless of whether the marriage is traditional or nontraditional and regardless of the couple's employment status (Roberts & O'Keefe, 1981), and especially if the couple is under age 25 (Ensel, 1982). Similarly, men suffer more from their spouses' death than do women (Stroebe & Stroebe, 1983), and single men are more depressed than single women (Crosby, 1982). Marriage is only successful in decreasing depression in women if the relationship between the partners is satisfactory (Aneshensel, 1986), if husbands are supportive (Vanfossen, 1981), and if in the relationship there is mutual confiding (Surtees, 1980) and positive affective quality (Gove, Hughes, & Style, 1983). Furthermore, significantly more men report finding support, help, and affirmation in their marital relationships than women, which suggest that marriage is more often positive than negative for men's health (Vanfossen, 1986). Conversely, almost all women in unhappy marriages are depressed—are in fact, three times as likely as their spouses to be depressed (McGrath et al., 1991). Gove et al. (1983) suggested that this difference in adjustment to marriage may be related to the possibility that men gain "instrumentality" from marriage, even if the relationship is poor. This implies that men benefit because of having a clean house, meals waiting after work, and other conveniences secondary to their wives' efforts! Indirectly supportive of this hypothesis is the finding that women are less depressed if the marital relationship is parallel in role distribution, with husband and wife sharing household responsibilities (Ross, Mirowsky, & Huber, 1983).

The interaction between marital, parental, and employment status is also critical. Radloff (1975) found that married women were more depressed than men, except when unemployment became a factor; then men were more depressed than women. Gove and Geerken (1977) found women to be least depressed if they worked and were married, and most depressed if they were married and not employed—suggesting that it is the role value, not the number of roles, that mediates depression. Similarly, Ross and Mirowsky (1988) discovered a hierarchy of depression, with depression levels ranked from highest to lowest: (1) single mothers who work and have difficulty with child care; (2) nonworking mothers (single or married); (3) working couples with children; and (4) working mothers with supportive husbands and no child care problems. Thus, if both marital and job satisfaction are high, depression rates decrease, especially if there are no stressors secondary to parenting and if living quarters are adequate (Haellstroem & Persson, 1984).

The findings summarized here, given the realities of today's households, reveal that many women continue to exist within the types of social situations that are related to depression, and that child care and improved interactions between the genders may have preventative value. These topics are not exclusively women's issues, but rather reflect discriminatory practices that may be related to depression above and beyond the social factors that have been discussed so far.

Discrimination and Related Issues

The effects of discrimination have been thoroughly investigated and shown to be related to significant emotional stress. They lead to anger, resentment, bitterness, hurt feelings, hopelessness, and helplessness, and subsequently to depression (Steele et al., 1982). Discrimination against women is a fact of life in many aspects of women's lives, including work, marriage, and social status (McGrath et al., 1991), and hence can be viewed as a contributing factor to the female preponderance of depression. Related to discrimination are beliefs and stereotypes held about and by women that compound the effects of discrimination. For instance, a woman's beliefs about her ability to perform adequately on the job may interact with external stereotypical messages about that ability to decrease her confidence and self-esteem.

Although in the 1980s women made up more than 50% of the workforce (as compared to 31% in the late 1940s), they are still economically disadvantaged compared to men, earning only 60¢ to each dollar earned by a man in the same position. Furthermore, women are still likely to have lower status jobs than men, even with comparable education, and hence face more bias in the workplace (Nolen-Hoeksema, 1990). This bias is reflected in job statistics accumulated by Nadelson (1989). Nadelson found that fewer than 25% of university faculty members were women, and of these, proportionately more (compared to men) were in lower ranks and non-tenure-track positions, with the majority working in traditionally female fields (e.g., nursing, education). These academic women also earned less money than academic men in simi-

lar positions. In addition, Nadelson found that fewer than 16% of state legislators, fewer than 12% of mayors, fewer than 10% of judges, fewer than 5% of members of the U.S. House of Representatives, 2% of U.S. senators, fewer than 5% of middle management executives, and fewer than 2% of top management executives were women. Furthermore, women are still disadvantaged in the labor market by sex segregation on the job, less powerful positions and less power granted, and lower earnings, even if education and experience are adjusted for (LaCroix & Haynes, 1987). Of these working women, over 20 million have children under age 18, and 60% have family responsibilities (LaCroix & Haynes, 1987).

Many professional working women show high rates of depression, and this affect is often linked to prejudice against women on the job (Rothblum, 1983). Women tend to receive lower work evaluations than men, regardless of the quality of their work (Klerman & Weissman, 1980), both when they apply for employment and when they ask for promotion (Nolen-Hoeksema, 1990). This lack of relationship between performance and evaluation can be linked to feelings of learned helplessness in women, which in turn are likely to result in depression. However, more recent studies suggest that the bias in evaluation in contemporary times occurs only if the application or promotion criteria are subjective as opposed to objective (Basow, 1986). Whereas this may be the truth, Nolen-Hoeksema (1990) pointed out that most high-level positions are reached through very subjective evaluation criteria and hence may remain elusive for women. Given the data complied by Nadelson (1989; see above), there is some support for Nolen-Hoeksema's theory. In addition to being less likely to receive positive performance evaluations, women also are taken less seriously and have less influence in problem-solving situations on the job (Nolen-Hoeksema, 1987, 1990).

In addition to these direct social and discriminatory factors that impact women's employment and their subsequent emotional adjustment, attributional styles related to failure and success further result in depression for women. Women are socialized to attribute success to luck and failure to lack of ability. In contrast, men attribute success to ability and failure to bad luck (Basow, 1986). This pattern emerges particularly strongly if the position held by the individual is highly valued or traditionally masculine (the two are often one and the same thing; Basow, 1986). Also related to socialization and stereotyping is the fact that assertive women are often disliked and met with anger by both male and female colleagues (Nadelson, 1989). Socialization of women to be emotionally responsive, caring, nurturing, and passive results in direct conflict if a job requires rivalry and hard negotiation (Nadelson, 1989). The effect of socialization on women and depression is addressed more thoroughly and in a more general context later in this chapter.

Discrimination occurs not only on the job, but also in women's intimate relationships, with equally deleterious effects on women's mental health. There is a strong relationship between marital inequity and depression (Vanfossen, 1981). Because inequity continues to be a reality in most marital relationships (Basow, 1986; Nolen-Hoeksema, 1990), women are very likely to show depressive symptoms. Studies conducted as recently as 1986 (e.g., Cooper, Chassin, Braver, & Zeiss, 1986) have revealed significant inequities between husbands and wives, even among couples who express the belief or attitude that women and men should be equal. Specifically, both women and men perceive men as having more impact on joint decision making and view men as making final judgments (Peplau, 1982). In a study in which families were not informed about the actual purpose of the study (i.e., the evaluation of equity in family decision making), husbands' opinions consistently prevailed over those of their wives and children (Cooper et al., 1986).

Discrimination and stereotyping also occurs in social settings irrelevant to employment or marital status. For instance, women who depend upon welfare benefits are perceived as lazy, cheating, promiscuous, having poor character, and being dependent freeloaders (Marshall, 1982). Thus, these women face not only the negative effects of poverty, but also the added stigma and prejudice of being an undesirable member of society. Additionally, women on welfare face a lack of control over their own lives, because they often have no privacy, are not allowed free consumer choices, and have no economic security (Marshall, 1982). They often lack information that might improve their situation, which reduces their ability to make informed decisions. They are condemned to spending many hours of their lives waiting at welfare offices, waiting for applications to be processed, and waiting for checks to arrive

(Marshall, 1982). All of these conditions are perfect breeding grounds for feelings of learned helplessness, which are closely linked to depression and despair.

Summary

Numerous social factors are clearly related to high levels of depressed mood, whether of clinical or subclinical proportion. These same social factors that are related to depression—(namely, poverty, low education, under- or unemployment, role stress, etc.)—are particularly common among women. Thus, although women are clearly not any more vulnerable to depression than men because of biological differences or genetic vulnerabilities, depression preponderates among women because they are socially disadvantaged. The social and socioeconomic differences between women and men in modern society are severe, as any review of poverty, income, and educational statistics will reveal quickly. It is impossible to expect women to live up to current societally defined standards of mental health, as long as the majority of them still have to struggle for the basic survival of themselves, their children, and their families.

Psychosocial Factors

Although social and psychosocial factors are difficult to differentiate, an arbitrary decision was made in writing this chapter to facilitate organization. The psychosocial factors discussed here are relevant to the psychological adjustment of people, as well as being either relevant to their social status or influenced by it. The process of socialization is affected by the social background of children's parents and extended family. The products of socialization (behaviors, attitudes, beliefs, and identities), on the other hand, are highly likely to influence children's future social status. Psychosocial issues that are most relevant to depresion and its development are socialization, personality development, and interpersonal violence.

Socialization and Personality Development Issues

Much research reveals that adults' interactions with children are based on the children's gender (Basow, 1986; Radloff, 1980). Even very early in life—in fact, as early as infancy—children are responded to differently, depending upon whether they are male or female. Boys are handled more freely and aggressively than girls, who are more often perceived as fragile and vulnerable (Basow, 1986). By the time children reach school age, these differences in environmental responses have become exceedingly ingrained. Gurian (1987) summarized the literature and showed that teachers reward girls more for dependent behavior and proximity to the teacher, whereas boys are rewarded for actions that produce results. They react more to boys' behaviors than to girls', both positively and negatively, viewing girls as needing more protection and help, and tending to ignore girls' behaviors. They encourage boys who fail or have difficulties to try harder, whereas girls in the same situation are subtly encouraged to give up, receiving the message that their failure is due to lack in intellect.

This socialization process does not occur only in the school setting. It is also perpetuated by parents who show many of the same interactional styles with their children (Basow, 1986). Sons tend to be socialized to be more outgoing and to seek more interactions outside the home. Daughters, on the other hand, are encouraged to be dependent and close to their mothers (Gurian, 1987). Additionally, daughters are encouraged to model themselves after their mothers, and sons after their fathers—a process that solidifies stereotyped behavior as modeled by the parents.

Such "female gender role socialization [hence] produces a variety of maladaptive characteristics of styles of defining and coping with life stressors that increase the risk of developing or maintaining a depressive syndrome" (McGrath et al., 1991, p. 15). Women are socialized to be passive, dependent, helpless, and nonassertive, all personality traits that are related to depression (Rothblum, 1983). Herman (1983) concluded that depression thus has a strong cultural component. Specifically, women, the reproductive role, and feminine traits are devalued, whereas male values and traits are highly valued. The socialization process based on these cultural stereotypes results in female personality traits that overlap with symptoms of depression, and depression can be viewed as "an exaggeration of normal feminine socialization" (Herman, 1983, p. 504).

As much as the traditional feminine role has been devalued, the traditional masculine role has been overvalued. Traditional masculine traits are instrumental, active, and characteris-

tic of an approach that takes charge and control of one's life. For instance, whereas women tend to ruminate about problems, thus setting in motion a vicious cycle of lack of coping and maladjustment, men are active and distract themselves (McGrath et al., 1991). Action is related to mastery, competence, and efficacy in problem solving; rumination is related to helplessness, hopelessness, and lack of control, as well as depressive explanations of current events, and recall that is biased in favor of depressive memories while attempting to cope (Nolen-Hoeksema, 1987). Problem solving and effective coping are necessary and sufficient conditions for competence, and competence, in turn, is a necessary condition for mental health. Because women clearly are neither socialized to be competent problem solvers nor perceived as such, they are more likely to be depressed (McGrath et al., 1991). The masculine gender role has thus been identified as a buffer against mental health problems, even more so than androgyny. In fact, in a meta-analysis of existing sex role literature, Bassoff and Glass (1982) found that it is the masculine component of. androgyny that results in improved mental health, whereas the feminine component is related to emotional difficulties. The authors concluded that femininity is least, and masculinity is most conducive to emotional health (Bassoff & Glass, 1982).

Similarly, pessimistic explanatory styles are related to the maintenance of depression, as is low perceived control of one's life. Because women receive through the socialization process more feedback that they have little control, that they are not responsible for their successes, but that they are responsible for their failures, they are set up for depressive adjustment (Warren & McEachren, 1983). Persons who account for failures through self-blame (internal, stable, and global causality) and for success through luck (external, unstable, and specific causality) are more vulnerable to depression than persons who show the opposite pattern, because this attributional style is highly related to learned helplessness and giving up. Unfortunately for women, the former is more likely to be true for them and the latter is more likely to be true for men (Nolen-Hoeksema, 1987), even as young as the age of 6 (Abramson & Andrews, 1982).

In addition to being encouraged to choose stereotypically feminine solutions to problems and pessimistic explanatory styles for success and failure, women also are socialized to put relationship concerns ahead of personal concerns. Specifically, female gender role socialization includes caring for and supporting others at all times, regardless of whether a women's own needs for support are met. Women are very concerned with seeking mutuality and understanding within the confines of relationships to validate themselves and others (Kaplan, 1986). As a result, because relationships are often disappointing in their delivery of such mutuality and support, women are viewed as more vulnerable than men to experiencing loss and hence depression, especially as relational failure leads to self-blame and self-doubt (Kaplan, 1986). Such an internalized attributional style, as discussed, leads to inhibition of action and perhaps even isolation and increased loneliness, setting up a vicious cycle as the stage is set to lead the woman to feel that she is unable to fulfill her role—namely, to be in a relationship. Some authors have concluded that "women's greater 'range of caring' thus expose[s] them to a greater risk of depression" (McGrath et al., 1991, p. 23). Yet, although this conclusion is theoretically sound, no definite empirical support has been provided for it (Nolen-Hoeksema, 1987).

Related to the relationship focus of women, there is a hypothesized greater likelihood for "de-selfing" (Lerner, 1987, p. 200). Lerner, who understands depression primarily as a reaction to loss, indicates that women not only have greater likelihood of real loss as manifested by failing or dissatisfying relationships (i.e., Kaplan's [1986] position), but also of loss or sacrifice of the self. Specifically, she suggests that women frequently sacrifice the self or aspects thereof to preserve relationships. This process may begin early in life, when young girls deny their developing needs and desires to save a parental marriage, to please a struggling parent, to stabilize familial conflict, or to serve a parent's narcissistic needs (Lerner, 1987). It may be perpetuated in adulthood when a woman enters into a relationship wherein she may become economically dependent.

Additional strikes against healthy self-development and preservation have to do with women's struggle to integrate messages they received during the socialization process in childhood with messages that are given in adulthood, and the realities that become evident as they mature (Jack, 1987). Specifically, conflicts may develop between the woman's ideal self, as developed through the socialization process, and a societally approved self in adulthood. Financial dependence, as a result of following traditional gender roles, may conflict with independence needs. Unsatisfactory relationships are incompatible with positive self-esteem, because women learn when they grow up that they are not only to be relationally focused, but also are responsible for the quality and effectiveness of such relationships. Finally, traditional feminine models of goodness (e.g., a good mother should not work) are becoming increasingly incompatible with social and economic demands and realities.

In summary, socialization and personality development present numerous challenges to women in modern society. Although the socialization process continues to stress traditional roles, and results in ineffective coping patterns and negative attributional styles, these patterns are no longer compatible with the social demands of modern society. The pretense of passivity as an ideal, the reinforcement of female dependency, the role stereotypes that perpetuate helplessness and devaluation, and the encouragement to model after traditional mothers potentially serve to increase levels of depression among women (Notman, 1989). While there remains a strong need for future research in the area of socialization and personality development, it appears safe to agree with Herman (1983), who suggests that differences in depression will only disappear if cultural valuation of male and female roles and traits change, and if the socialization process becomes more equitable for children of both genders.

Interpersonal Violence Issues

A psychosocial issue that cannot be ignored in an investigation of the preponderance of depression among women is that of interpersonal violence or victimization. There is some overlap between this issue and the previous stereotypical assumptions because some interpersonal violence may not be physical or sexual in nature, but verbal. Specifically, sexual harassment, here considered an issue of interpersonal violence, is highly related to prejudice and stereotypical assumptions about women. While its consequences can be grave for the victim, they may not be as persistent and detrimental as the effects of more severe forms of violence, such as a rape, spouse abuse, and a childhood history of sexual abuse. The prevalence of rates of all of these forms of violence are significantly higher for females than males (Koss, 1990), and more often than not, males are the perpetrators. As is true for several of the economic factors, ethnicity is an important consideration in the discussion of this possible contributing factor to depression. Overall, women of color are more likely to become victims of all types of crimes than white women, and are more likely to become targets of subtle and chronic harassment and abuse (Hamilton, 1989a). For instance, black women are significantly more likely than any other group of women to become victims of rape; Hispanic women of gang rape; lower-SES women of all violent crimes, including rape; and lesbian women of violent crimes and verbal abuse (Hamilton, 1989a).

The impact of sexual assault at any time in life, whether it be in the form of childhood incest or spouse abuse, is likely to have protracted consequences resulting in a number of psychiatric diagnoses that include depression as part of their symptomatology, such as adjustment disorders, posttraumatic stress disorders, dissociative disorders, anxiety disorders, and finally mood disorders (cf. Hanson, 1990). Victimization has sequelae that are precursors of depression—namely, learned helplessness, hopelessness, negative self-esteem, self-criticism, restricted range of affect, and self-defeating behaviors (Walker, 1984). The severity of symptoms tends to vary with type and severity of symptoms and the age of molestation (Murphy et al., 1988) and more research is needed to understand cause-and-effect relationships between victimization and depression more clearly (McGrath et al., 1991). The possibility has also been suggested that emotional consequences of interpersonal violence are not purely psychological, but may have a physical component. The American Psychological Association Task Force on Women and Depression (McGrath et al., 1991) has proposed that research be conducted to explore the possibility of (perhaps subtle) neurological distress mimicking depressive syndromes, caused by closed head trauma secondary to head injuries inflicted upon women by perpetrators of abuse.

Sexual Harassment. The basic definition of "sexual harassment" is repeated, unwanted, and objectionable interpersonal interaction with sexual connotations (e.g., Cammaert, 1985). It can range from mild (e.g., a pat, ogling) to severe (e.g., explicit propositions, rape). Sexual harassment tends to occur regardless of women's

age, marital status, education and employment status, or SES; forms may vary for women of different backgrounds, but frequency does not. As such, women in high-status jobs are more likely to be targets of verbal harassment, whereas women in low-status jobs are more likely to experience physical harassment (Cammaert, 1985). Sexual harassment is extremely common, with prevalence rates from 40–88% (Cammaert, 1985). The most common forms of harassment cited in the studies reviewed by Cammaert include sexual jokes, innuendos, and suggestions; display of nude or sexual-content pictures; and touching or fondling. Nolen-Hoeksema (1990) reported prevalence rates of 40% among federal employees. One percent were victims of attempted or completed rape by a boss (according to a study by P. Mathis for the U.S. Merit Systems Protection Board, cited by Nolen-Hoeksma), and 9% ultimately quit their jobs because of the harassment.

The results of sexual harassment are many. Hamilton (1989a) reported that sexual harassment leads to increased psychological distress, decreased income (due to quitting jobs or taking demotions to evade the perpetrator), increased discrimination, and depression. Cammaert (1985) indicated that women who were sexually harassed revealed high levels of stress, were often fired or received poor job evaluations after turning down a proposition, were increasingly likely to quit their job, showed higher rates of hospitalization, and had a high likelihood of depression. Similarly, Nolen-Hoeksema (1990) summarized the literature to show that sexual harassment on the job results in decreased mental and physical health and sets up a situation that promotes the development of learned helplessness. Furthermore, it creates a double bind for women. If a woman decides to quit her job, she often has difficulty finding new employment, risking a loss of or decrease in income and social status. If she decides to stay, she continues to be subjected to an unacceptable position that taxes her self-esteem and coping ability (Nolen-Hoeksema, 1990).

Rape. According to a 1986 report by the Federal Bureau of Investigation, 90,000 women are raped every year (Nolen-Hoeksema, 1990). However, while this number appears overwhelmingly high, it is a sore *under*estimate; many rapes go unreported, especially if the rape was perpetrated by a nonstranger. In fact, Russell (1984) believes that only 10% of all rapes are actually reported. Based on face-to-face interviews, Russell and Howell (1983) estimate that 46% of all women face an attempted or completed rape in their lifetimes, and 26% become victims of completed assaults. Resick (1983) reports that of these one in four women who become victimized, all experience significant depression within the first month of the assault, whereas evidence of depression declines rapidly later. However, other problems remain, such as problems at work, fears, and difficulty in social adjustment (Resick, 1983). In contrast, other studies have provided evidence to suggest that depressions after a rape are more chronic and severe (e.g., Kilpatrick, Resick, & Veronen, 1981; Nadelson, Notman, Zackson, & Gornick, 1982; Wirtz & Harrell, 1987). Frank, Turner, and Duffy (1979) report that as many as 24% of all rape victims have a diagnosable mood disorder for some time after the assault. Acute effects include depression, self-blame, anxious mood, and helplessness; longer-term effects are only indirectly related to depression and include symptoms such as loss of a sense of control and loss of a sense of predictability in one's life (Hamilton, 1989a).

One problem that has been cited as a possible reason for the variability in these data is that many studies rely on women who seek help from rape crisis hotlines or services. This group of women may be biased, resulting in an overestimation of the depressive effect of rape. However, in a nonclinical sample that had been carefully matched with women without rape histories, 19% of rape victims reported symptoms of severe depression and 26% reported moderate depression (Ellis, Atkeson, & Calhoun, 1982). Similarly, Burnam et al. (1988), using a general community sample of over 3,000 adults, found increased levels of depression among women who reported any history of rape. A chart review of a clinical population revealed a history of sexual assault among 70% of the female clients and 27% of the male clients.

Spouse Abuse. The American Psychological Association Task Force on Women and Depression (McGrath et al., 1991) reported that, based on a review of the literature, 25–50% of married women are victimized by their spouses; marital rape has a reported prevalence rate of 12–14%. Wife abuse appears to be significantly related to depression, with 80% of victims reporting symptoms of depression, and 53% reporting symptoms sufficiently severe to warrant

a diagnosis of mood disorder (e.g., Rounsaville, 1978). More recent investigations report similar figures and confirm that depression rates increase among battered women, though not always to a diagnosable level (cf. Chapman & Gates, 1985). The effects of battery on wives have been documented repeatedly (e.g., Walker, 1984) and suggest a significant mediating factor of learned helplessness. Levels of learned helplessness have been shown to increase as the amount of abuse increases in the spousal relationship (Wilson, Vercella, Brems, Benning, & Renfro, 1992), and are likely to trap women in a vicious cycle of nonchange. Specifically, women in abusive spousal relationships often feel unable to leave because of decreased self-esteem, passive interpersonal styles, loyalty, social isolation, and the perceived stigma of divorce; these patterns and beliefs appear to increase with age (Gesino, Smith, & Keckich, 1982). Decreased self-esteem and interpersonal passivity, part of learned helplessness, create a vicious cycle, resulting in greater likelihood of victimization, which in turn increases feelings of worthlessness, contributes to depression, and continues the cycle (Hamilton, 1989a; Walker, 1984).

History of Childhood Sexual Abuse. Prevalence rates of childhood sexual abuse are as unreliable as prevalence rates of rape and spouse abuse, because underreporting is a chronic problem. However, a clear finding is that women are more likely to have been victims of childhood abuse than men (McGrath et al., 1991), as is true for other forms of interpersonal violence. Reports vary widely, with rates from 15–62% (Murphy et al., 1988). Briere and Runtz (1988) found a prevalence rate of 15% in a college sample; Bagley and Ramsay (1986) report a 22% prevalence in a community sample; and Murphy et al. (1988) found a prevalence rate of 33% among community women. Regardless of the prevalence rate, findings tend to agree that women with a history of abuse have significantly higher levels of depression (Gorcey, Santiago, & McCall-Perez, 1986; Murphy, 1988), in some studies with a frequency that was twice that of women without such a history (Bagley & Ramsay, 1986). A chart review in a psychiatric setting revealed that 90% of all abuse victims were abused by family members (Carmen, Rieker, & Mills, 1984). Severity of symptoms seems to vary widely, with college samples showing mild symptoms of dysphoria, somatization, and dissociation (Briere & Runtz, 1988), and 92% of women who have a childhood history of sexual abuse and seek treatment having diagnosable mood disorders (Jehu, 1989). Across all levels of severity, common symptoms included self-blame, guilt, and shame (e.g., Jehu, 1989; Roth & Leibowitz, 1988); low self-esteem and feelings of worthlessness (e.g., Bagley & Ramsay, 1986; Hanson, 1990; Gidycz & Koss, 1989); poor social adjustment (e.g., Hyde & Kaufman, 1984; Jackson, Calhoun, Amick, Maddever, & Habif, 1991); distorted body image, self-mutilation, or suicide (e.g., Hanson, 1990); and constricted affect (e.g., Hyde & Kaufman, 1984). Increased levels of depression were also noted, with similar symptomatology reported as a result of brother–sister incest (Laviola, 1989).

A history of sexual abuse in childhood clearly appears to predispose women to depression in adulthood. While cause and effect are for ethical reasons obviously difficult to establish experimentally, the association between the two variables is strong and consistent. The direction of the relationship appears more likely to be in the direction of the abuse preceding the depression in this case (as opposed to spouse abuse, in which the direction of the relationship could be either way), because it is less likely that only depressed girls become victims. Specifically, the prevalence figures provided previously indicate that girls are less likely to be depressed than boys; yet the figures of sexual abuse in childhood show an opposite pattern for the two genders. Thus, if depression did predispose children for victimization, boys should be the more likely target group, but they clearly are not. However, the evidence accumulated cannot rule out other factors that may mediate both depression and victimization. Wald, Archer, and Winstead (1990), for instance, found that women who were victims of childhood sexual abuse had mothers who were significantly more depressed than the mothers of nonabused children. Thus, the possibility of a third mediating factor needs further exploration.

Summary

Much evidence has been accumulated in the literature to support the notion that psychosocial factors are implicated in the female preponderance of depression. The socialization process to which children continue to be exposed at home, at school, and in society in general continues to perpetuate differential treatment of females and males. This differential treatment has resulted in personality characteristics among women that are more ineffectual in stressful situations than the coping devices reinforced among men. Similarly, it has resulted in attributional styles that leave women at a disadvantage and experiencing low self-esteem and helplessness. Other traditionally feminine interpersonal patterns also appear possibly related to depression and deserve to be investigated further.

Continued discrimination against women is evident not only in socialization, but also is relevant when exploring crime statistics. Women are at very high risk of victimization. Crimes that are perpetrated against women have been related to depressive symptoms and syndromes, as well as to other mental disorders having depressive mood as part of their clinical picture. Rape, spouse abuse, childhood history of sexual abuse, and sexual harassment are only four of the most important examples in this regard. Given the strong association between these psychosocial factors and mood disturbances, prevention will need to become a major issue in the future if this gender inequity is to cease. Behavioral and attitudinal changes among parents and teachers will need to lead the way, so that girls and boys may grow up in environments that are equally appreciative of both genders.

TREATMENT ISSUES AND IMPLICATIONS

The preceding review of the literature addressing the preponderance of depression among women has shown that there is no clear or straightforward relationship between possible predisposing factors and depression. Most studies are retrospective and correlational, and hence cannot establish a clear cause and effect. Nevertheless, a number of interesting patterns emerge, such as the mediating effects of numerous social and psychosocial factors, and the absence of evidence for a biological explanation of gender differences. Thus, it would appear that in treating women for depression, clinicians need to be more perceptive about social and psychosocial factors, as opposed to relying on physiological explanations.

Perhaps the most obvious and most important implication of the literature is that every mental health professional must be aware of these issues to engage in proper assessment and treatment planning. Misconceptions and stereotypes about women's mental health must be so labeled and replaced with empirically based conceptualizations. Before treatment implications are discussed, I will briefly detour to sensitize clinicians to their own possible biases and prejudices.

Stereotyping among Mental Health Professionals

Many researchers believe that the perpetuation of stereotypes about women among mental health professionals leads to an overuse of mood disorder labels (Klerman & Weissman, 1980), especially since six of nine such commonly endorsed stereotypes overlap with the diagnostic criteria for depression, whereas only three commonly held beliefs about men are related to depressive syndromes (Rothblum, 1983). Specifically, women are viewed as more likely to cry, more dependent, more self-deprecating, more indecisive, more socially withdrawn, and more unlikely to express anger than men; men are viewed as more nonemotional, more aggressive, and more neglectful of their personal appearance than women (Rothblum, 1983). These beliefs may explain findings showing that male psychiatrists were very likely to attach labels of depression and histrionic personality disorder to women, even if the symptoms did not match those diagnoses. The same mistakes were not made when the clients were male or when the diagnosing psychiatrists were female, suggesting a greater bias against women by males (Loring & Powell, 1986). The same beliefs that lead clinicians to overdiagnose depression in women, lead to an underdiagnosis of mood disorders among men (Lopez, 1989). Additionally, psychiatrists tended to rate women's levels of depression higher than women themselves did, suggesting a bias in assessing depression in women (Zetin, Sklanky, & Cramer, 1984).

Biases of mental health professionals not only emerge in the area of assessment and diagnosis, but also enter treatment decisions and interventions (cf. Brodsky & Holroyd, 1981). Mental health professionals continue to foster traditional gender roles for women, pushing marriage and motherhood, addressing child care and parenting issues as women's issues only, and being insensitive to career and employment issues. Furthermore, clinicians have biased expectations and

tend to devalue women's roles and characteristics, fostering dependence, criticizing assertiveness, using concepts of masochism to explain victimization, and using sexism in their language. The sexist use of psychoanalytic concepts also prevails, with mental health practitioners equating assertiveness with penis envy, and continuing to view vaginal orgasms as more sexually mature than clitoral orgasms. Finally, as their last point, Brodsky and Holroyd (1981) reveal that clinicians respond to women as sex objects, seducing female clients and excusing men's extramarital affairs as natural, while viewing women's affairs as pathological.

In summary, it is imperative that mental health practitioners take stock of their beliefs and attitudes and begin to recognize even such subtle biases as sexist language. It is time to begin questioning whether women and men should be forced into gender-specific roles, and whether social issues such as child care and parenting should continue to be women's issue (the latter bias obviously also remains a major political issue). Finally, in diagnosis and assessment, mental health professionals must become more sensitive to their own biases about what "normal" male and female behavior encompasses and how such preconceived notions can affect the labeling process. One example of this process has been mentioned earlier—namely, the proposal of a diagnostic category of premenstrual dysphoric disorder. It is inappropriate to choose labels that suggest relationships that have not been proven, and for which negative research evidence exists.

Directions for Prevention and Treatment

Once practitioners have explored their biases and familiarized themselves with the existing literature about the female preponderance of depression, treatment will clearly be affected. To date, not a single causative link has been established for depression among women. Numerous predisposing, precipitating, and even reinforcing factors have emerged, and it is imperative that treatment be tailored to those factors that appear most relevant to each individual female client. Careful and unbiased assessment must precede any diagnostic and treatment decisions, and must be multimodal, as well as thorough and far-reaching. All areas of a woman's functioning and history must be assessed, including the social, psychosocial, and biological factors explored here.

Once a thorough assessment has been completed, treatment decisions must be made based on the information that has been gleaned. For instance, if the depression appears most strongly mediated by or linked to ruminative styles, thought-stopping or distraction treatment may be implicated. If a negative explanatory style is utilized by a woman, cognitive restructuring may need to become part of her treatment. Behavioral interventions may also be of use if issues of self-assessed competence and learned helplessness emerge as critically related to a woman's depression. Self-esteem issues, lack of direction and career focus, and related matters may best be treated via an insight-oriented psychodynamic approach. If a marital or parenting conflict is at issue, family systems theory may need to be employed to tailor treatment. Sociological or social work approaches are most appropriate if a role conflict exists, or if economic issues are of great concern. Cultural or discrimination-based problems are best addressed through the utilization of feminist therapy principles. Clearly, not all therapists will choose to apply all of these methods with the same client, nor should they. Consistency of therapeutic approach is generally desirable in any treatment. However, an open mind to the special social, psychosocial, cultural, and biological issues of women is required. The truly unbiased mental health professional will recognize that for most women, interacting factors account for their depression, and the therapist will tailor a treatment approach accordingly. Clinicians who cannot shed biases are advised to discontinue their work with women.

No discussion of treatment is complete without a mention of prevention. As a number of the factors implicated in women's depression are sociocultural in nature, it is clear that social change has to be created to decrease the amount of depression noted among the women of this society. Prevention begins with one's own children in the home, and with the children of others in all social contexts, including (but not limited to) schools, church groups, Scouts, clubs, and child clients. The use of sexist language must be resisted; victimization of women must be stopped; and biases against women must be publicly identified, labeled, and denounced. In summary, the work with women must be political as much as it is healing.

CONCLUSIONS

This chapter has reviewed the literature investigating the preponderance of depressive symptoms and syndromes among women. It has provided prevalence rates and evidence to support the notion that artifacts cannot be held accountable for the gender differences in mood disorders. A number of factors, including biological, social, and psychosocial factors, have been reviewed to explain why depression preponderates among women. This review concludes that no strong, current research support exists that implicates a woman's genetic endowment or endocrinological environment as cause for the preponderance of depression. Social and psychosocial factors, on the other hand, are strongly related to depressive symptoms, and their assessment appears extremely relevant when women present for treatment. Given the specifc factors identified as most related to each individual woman's depression, treatment must be tailored to those variables that appear to have predisposed her to depressed mood, that may have precipitated her presentation for treatment, or that may perpetuate her depressive symptoms. Prevention is mentioned as a pathway to improving women's mental health.

A final word is necessary before closing this chapter. It is possible that the current standards of mental health are inherently biased against women and that the syndromes that are labeled "mood disorders" (DSM-IV; American Psychiatric Association, 1994), are not "disorders" in the true sense. Specifically, many feminist psychologists and theorists have argued that the DSM nosology is, and always has been, merely a means of perpetuating a white male Eurocentric understanding of what constitutes mental health for this world's population. Thus, it is possible that the review of the literature presented in this chapter is inherently biased by accepting the notion that depression is an unhealthy trait indicative of mental or emotional illness or disturbance. It is beyond the scope of this chapter to investigate the validity of such claims of the normality and healthy response of depressed mood. However, I feel that it is a political responsibility to at least raise the issue in the reader's mind, if only in closing.

REFERENCES

Abramson, L. Y., & Andrews, D. E. (1982). Cognitive models of depression: Implications for sex differences in vulnerability to depression. *International Journal of Mental Health, 11,* 77–94.

Amenson, C. S., & Lewinsohn, P. M. (1981). An investigation into the observed sex difference in prevalence of unipolar depression. *Journal of Abnormal Psychology*, *90*, 1–13.

American Psychiatric Association. (1994). *Diagnostic and statistical manual of mental disorders* (4th ed.). Washington, DC: Author.

Aneshensel, C. S. (1986). Marital and employment role-strain, social support, and depression among adult women. In S. E. Hobfoll (Ed.), *Stress, social support, and women* (pp. 99–114). New York: Hemisphere.

Aneshensel, C. S., Frerick, R. R., & Clark, V. A. (1981). Family roles and sex differences in depression. *Journal of Health and Social Behavior*, *22*, 379–393.

Bagley, C., & Ramsay, R. (1986). Sexual abuse in childhood: Psychosocial outcomes and implications for social work practice. *Journal of Social Work and Human Sexuality*, *5*, 33–47.

Ballinger, C. B. (1990). Psychiatric aspects of the menopause. *British Journal of Psychiatry*, *156*, 773–787.

Basow, S. (1986). *Gender stereotypes: Traditions and alternatives*. New York: Brooks/Cole.

Bassoff, E. S., & Glass, G. V. (1982). The relationship between sex roles and mental health: A meta analysis of twenty-six studies. *The Counseling Psychologist*, *10*, 105–112.

Belle, D. (1980). Who uses mental health facilities? In M. Guttentag, S. Salasin, & D. Belle (Eds.), *The mental health of women* (pp. 1–20). New York: Academic Press.

Belle, D. (1990). Poverty and women's mental health. *American Psychologist*, *45*, 385–389.

Belle, D., & Goldman, N. (1980). Patterns of diagnoses received by men and women. In M. Guttentag, S. Salasin, & D. Belle (Eds.), *The mental health of women* (pp. 21–30). New York: Academic Press.

Birtchnell, J. (1988). Depression and life circumstances. *Social Psychiatry and Psychiatric Epidemiology*, *23*, 240–246.

Boyd, J. H., & Weissman, M. M. (1981). Epidemiology of affective disorders: A re-examination and future directions. *Archives of General Psychiatry*, *38*, 1039–1046.

Briere, J., & Runtz, M. (1988). Symptomatology associated with childhood sexual victimization in a nonclinical adult sample. *Child Abuse and Neglect*, *12*, 51–59.

Brodsky, A. M., & Holroyd, J. (1981). Report of the task force on sex bias and sex-role stereotyping in psychotherapeutic practice. In E. Howell & M. Bayes (Eds.), *Women and mental health* (pp. 98–112). New York: Basic Books.

Brooks-Gunn, J., & Warren, M. P. (1989). Biological and social contributions to negative affect in young adolescent girls. *Child Development*, *60*, 40–55.

Bungay, G. T., Vessey, M. P., & McPherson, C. K. (1980). Study of symptoms in middle life with special reference to menopause. *British Medical Journal*, *281*, 181–183.

Burnam, M. A., Stein, J. A., Golding, J. M., Siegel, J. M., Sorenson, S. B., Forsythe, A. B., & Telles, C. A. (1988). Sexual assault and mental disorders in a community population. *Journal of Consulting and Clinical Psychology*, *56*, 843–850.

Cammaert, L. P. (1985). How widespread is sexual harassment on campus? *International Journal of Women's Studies*, *8*, 388–397.

Carmen, E., Rieker, P. P., & Mills, T. (1984). Victims of violence and psychiatric illness. *American Journal of Psychiatry*, *141*, 378–383.

Chapman, J. R., & Gates, M. (1985). *The victimization of women*. Beverly Hills, CA: Sage.

Chevron, E. S., Quinlan, D. M., & Blatt, S. J. (1978). Sex roles and gender differences in the expression of depression. *Journal of Abnormal Psychology*, *87*, 680–683.

Chisholm, G., Jung, S. O., Cumming, C. E., Fox, E. E., & Cumming, D. C. (1989). Premenstrual anxiety and depression: Comparison of objective psychological test with a retrospective questionnaire. *Acta Psychiatrica Scandinavica*, *81*, 52–57.

Christensen, A. P., & Oei, T. P. S. (1989). Correlates of confirmed premenstrual dysphoria. *Journal of Psychosomatic Research*, *33*, 307–313.

Clancy, K., & Gove, W. (1974). Sex differences in mental illness: An analysis of response bias in self reports. *American Journal of Sociology*, *80*, 205–216.

Clayton, P. J. (1981). The epidemiology of bipolar affective disorder. *Comprehensive Psychiatry*, *22*, 31–43.

Clayton, P. J., Marten, S., Davis, M. A., & Wochnik, E. (1980). Mood disorders in women professionals. *Journal of Affective Disorders*, *2*, 37–46.

Coleman, G. J., Hart, W. G., & Russell, J. W. (1988). Temporal sequence of symptoms in women complaining of PMS. *Journal of Psychosomatic Obstetrics and Gynecology*, *8*, 105–112.

Cooper, K., Chassin, L., Braver, S., & Zeiss, A. (1986). Correlates of mood and marital satisfaction among dual-worker and single-worker couples. *Social Psychology Quarterly*, *49*, 322–329.

Cowdry, R. W., Wehr, T. A., Zis, A. P., & Goodwin, F. K. (1983). Thyroid abnormalities associated with rapid cycling bipolar illness. *Archives of General Psychiatry*, *40*, 414–420.

Crosby, F. J. (1982). *Relative deprivation and working women*. Oxford: Oxford University Press.

D'Ercole, A., & Struening, E. (1990). Victimization among homeless women: Implications for service delivery. *Journal of Community Psychology*, *18*, 141–152.

Danilewitz, D., & Skuy, M. (1990). A psychoeducational profile of the unmarried mother. *International Journal of Adolescence and Youth*, *2*, 175–184.

Dennerstein, L., Morse, C. A., & Varnavides, K. (1988). Premenstrual tension and depression—is there a relationship? *Journal of Psychosomatic Obstetrics and Gynecology*, *8*, 45–52.

Dill, D., & Feld, E. (1982). The challenge of coping. In D. Belle (Ed.), *Lives in stress* (pp. 179–196). Beverly Hills, CA: Sage.

Dill, D., & Greywolf, E. (1982). Daily lives. In D. Belle (Ed.), *Lives in stress* (pp. 54–64). Beverly Hills, CA: Sage.

Donner, D. L., Patrick, V., & Fieve, R. (1977). Rapid cycling manic–depressive patients. *Comprehensive Psychiatry*, *18*, 561–566.

Dressler, W. W. (1985). Extended family relationships, social support, and mental health in a southern black community. *Journal of Health and Social Behavior*, *26*, 39–48.

Eccles, J. S., Miller, C., Tucker, M. L., Becker, J., Schramm, W., Midgley, R., Holems, W., Pasch, L., & Miller, M. (1988, March). *Hormones and affect at early adolescence.* Paper presented at the biennial meeting of the Society for Research on Adolescence, Alexandria, VA.

Egeland, J. A., & Hostetter, S. M. (1983). Amish study: I. Affective disorders among the Amish, 1976–1980. *American Journal of Psychiatry*, *140*, 56–61.

Ehrenreich, B., & English, D. (1978). *For her own good*. New York: Anchor Press.

Ellis, E. M., Atkeson, B. M., & Calhoun, K. S. (1982). An examination of differences between multiple- and single-incident victims of sexual assault. *Journal of Abnormal Psychology*, *91*, 221–224.

Endicott, J., Halbreich, U., Schacht, S., & Nee, J. (1981). Premenstrual changes and affective disorders. *Psychosomatic Medicine*, *43*, 519–529.

Ensel, W. M. (1982). The role of age in the relationship of gender and marital status to depression. *Journal of Nervous and Mental Disease*, *170*, 536–543.

Formanek, R. (1987). Depression and menopause: A socially constructed link. In R. Formanek & A. Gurian (Eds.), *Women and depression: A lifespan perspective* (pp. 255–271). New York: Springer.

Frank, E., Turner, S. M., & Duffy, B. (1979). Depressive symptoms in rape victims. *Journal of Affective Disorders*, *1*, 264–297.

Gershon, E. S., & Bunney, W. E. (1976). The question of X-linkage in bipolar manic–depressive illness. *Journal of Psychiatric Research*, *13*, 99–117.

Gesino, J. P., Smith, H. H., & Keckich, W. A. (1982). The battered woman grows old. *Clinical Gerontologist*, *1*, 59–67.

Gitlin, M. J., & Pasnau, R. O. (1989). Psychiatric symptoms linked to reproductive function in women: A review of current knowledge. *American Journal of Psychiatry*, *146*, 1413–1422.

Gidycz, C. A., & Koss, M. P. (1989). The impact of adolescent sexual victimization: Standardized measures of anxiety, depression, and behavioral deviancy. *Violence and Victims*, *4*, 139–149.

Golding, J. M. (1988). Gender differences in depressive symptoms. *Psychology of Women Quarterly*, *12*, 62–74.

Goldman, N., & Ravid, R. (1980). Community surveys: Sex differences in mental illness. In M. Guttentag, S. Salasin, & D. Belle (Eds.), *The mental health of women* (pp. 31–56). New York: Academic Press.

Gorcey, M., Santiago, J. M., & McCall-Perez, F. (1986). Psychological consequences for women sexually abused in childhood. *Social Psychiatry*, *21*, 129–133.

Gove, W. R. (1972). The relationship between sex roles, marital status, and mental illness. *Social Forces*, *51*, 34–45.

Gove, W. R., & Geerken, M. R. (1976). Response bias in survey of mental health: An empirical investigation. *American Journal of Sociology*, *82*, 1289–1317.

Gove, W. R., & Geerken, M. R. (1977). The effect of children and employment on the mental health of married men and women. *Social Forces*, *56*, 66–76.

Gove, W. R., Hughes, M., & Style, C. B. (1983). Does marriage have positive effects on the psychological well-being of the individual? *Journal of Health and Social Behavior*, *24*, 122–131.

Gove, W. R., & Tudor, J. F. (1973). Adult sex roles and mental illness. *American Journal of Sociology*, *78*, 812–835.

Gurian, A. (1987). Depression and young girls: Early sorrow and depressive disorders. In R. Formanek & A. Gurian (Eds.), *Women and depression: A lifespan perspective* (pp. 57–83). New York: Springer.

Guttentag, M., Salasin, S., & Belle, D. (1980). *The mental health of women*. New York: Academic Press.

Haellstroem, T., & Persson, G. (1984). The relationship of social setting to major depression. *Acta Psychiatrica Scandinavica*, *70*, 327–336.

Halbreich, U., Endicott, J., & Nee, J. (1983). Premenstrual depressive changes. *Archives of General Psychiatry*, *40*, 535–542.

Hallman, J. (1986). The premenstrual syndrome—An equivalent of depression? *Acta Psychiatrica Scandinavica*, *73*, 403–411.

Hamilton, J. A. (1989a). Emotional consequences of victimization and discrimination in "special populations." *Psychiatric Clinics of North America*, *12*, 35–51.

Hamilton, J. A. (1989b). Postpartum psychiatric syndromes. *Psychiatric Clinics of North America*, *12*, 89–103.

Hamilton, J. A., Lloyd, C., Alagna, S. W., Phillips, K., & Pinkel, S. (1984). Gender, depressive subtypes, and gender–age effects on antidepressant response: Hormonal hypotheses. *Psychopharmacology Bulletin*, *20*, 475–480.

Hamilton, J. A., Parry, B. L., & Blumenthal, S. J. (1988a). The menstrual cycle in context: I. Affective syndromes associated with reproductive hormonal changes. *Journal of Clinical Psychiatry*, *49*, 474–479.

Hamilton, J. A., Parry, B. L., & Blumenthal, S. J. (1988b). The menstrual cycle in context: II. Human gonadal steroid hormone variability. *Journal of Clinical Psychiatry*, *49*, 480–484.

Hanson, R. K. (1990). The psychosocial impact of sexual assault on women and children: A review. *Annals of Sex Research*, *3*, 187–232.

Harris, B., Johns, S., Fung, H., Thomas, R., Walker, R., Read, G., & Riad-Fahmy, D. (1989). The hormonal environment of post-natal depression. *British Journal of Psychiatry*, *154*, 660–667.

Herman, M. F. (1983). Depression and women: Theories and research. *Journal of the American Academy of Psychoanalysis*, *11*, 493–512.

Hirschfeld, R. M., & Cross, C. K. (1982). Epidemiology of affective disorders. *Archives of General Psychiatry*, *39*, 35–46.

Hyde, M. L., & Kaufman, P. A. (1984). Women molested as children: Therapeutic and legal issues in civil action. *American Journal of Forensic Psychiatry*, *5*, 147–157.

Iatrakis, G., Haronis, N., Sakellaropoulos, G., Kourkoubas, A., & Gallos, M. (1986). Psychosomatic symptoms of postmenopausal women with or without hormonal treatment. *Psychotherapy and Psychosomatics*, *46*, 116–121.

Iles, S., Gath, D., & Kennerley, H. (1989). Maternity blues: A comparison between post-operative women and post-natal women. *British Journal of Psychiatry*, *155*, 363–366.

Jack, D. (1987). Silencing the self: The power of social imperatives in female depression. In R. Formanek & A. Gurian (Eds.), *Women and depression: A lifespan perspective* (pp. 161–181). New York: Springer.

Jackson, J. L., Calhoun, K. S., Amick, A. E., Maddever, H. M., & Habif, V. L. (1990). Young adult women who report childhood intrafamilial sexual abuse: Subsequent adjustment. *Archives of Sexual Behavior*, *19*, 211–221.

Jehu, D. (1989). Mood disturbances among women clients sexually abused in childhood. *Journal of Interpersonal Violence*, *4*, 164–184.

Kandel, D. B., & Davies, M. (1982). Epidemiology of depressive mood in adolescents. *Archives of General Psychiatry*, *39*, 1205–1212.

Kandel, D. B., Davies, M., & Raveis, V. H. (1985), The stressfulness of daily social roles for women: Marital, occupational and household roles. *Journal of Health and Social Behavior*, *26*, 64–78.

Kaplan, A. (1986). The "self-in-relation": Implications for depression in women. *Psychotherapy*, *23*, 234–242.

Kaplan, G. A., Roberts, R. E., Camacho, T. C., & Coyne,

J. C. (1987). Psychosocial predictors of depression. *American Journal of Epidemiology*, 125, 206–220.

Kennerley, H., & Gath, D. (1989). Maternity blues: III. Associations with obstetric, psychological, and psychiatric factors. *British Journal of Psychiatry*, 155, 367–373.

Kessler, R. C., & McRae, J. A. (1982). The effect of wives' employment of the mental health of married men and women. *American Sociological Review*, 47, 216–227.

Kessler, R. C., & Neighbors, H. W. (1986). A new perspective on the relationship among race, social class, and psychological distress. *Journal of Health and Social Behavior*, 27, 107–115.

Kilpatrick, D., Resick, P., & Veronen, L. (1981). Effects of a rape experience: A longitudinal study. *Journal of Social Issues*, 37, 105–122.

Klerman, G. L., & Weissman, M. M. (1980). Depression among women: Their nature and causes. In M. Guttentag, S. Salasin, & D. Belle (Eds.), *The mental health of women* (pp. 57–92). New York: Academic Press.

Koss, M. P. (1990). The women's mental health research agenda: Violence against women. *American Psychologist*, 45, 374–380.

LaCroix, A. Z., & Haynes, S. G. (1987). Gender differences in the health effects of workplace roles. In R. C. Barnett, L. Biener, & G. K. Baruch (Eds.), *Gender and stress* (pp. 96–121). New York: Free Press.

Lahmayer, H. W. (1984). Premenstrual tension: An overview of its relationship to affective psychopathology. *Integrative Psychiatry*, 2, 106–110.

Landy, S., Montgomery, J., & Walsh, S. (1989). Postpartum depression: A clinical view. *Maternal–Child Nursing Journal*, 18, 1–29.

Laviola, M. (1989). Effects of older brother–younger sister incest: A review of four cases. *Journal of Family Violence*, 4, 259–274.

Lennon, M. C. (1987). Is menopause depressing? An investigation of three perspectives. *Sex Roles*, 17, 1–16.

Lerner, H. G. (1987). Female depression: Self-sacrifice and self-betrayal in relationships. In R. Formanek & A. Gurian (Eds.), *Women and depression: A lifespan perspective* (pp. 200–221). New York: Springer.

Lopez, S. (1989). Patient variable biases in clinical judgment: Conceptual overview and some methodological considerations. *Psychological Bulletin*, 106, 184–203.

Loring, M., & Powell, B. (1986). Gender, race, and DSM-III: A study of the objectivity of psychiatric diagnostic behavior. *Journal of Health and Social Behavior*, 29, 1–22.

Major, B., Mueller, P., & Hildebrandt, K. (1985). Attributions, expectations, and coping with abortion. *Journal of Personality and Social Psychology*, 48, 585–599.

Makosky, V. P. (1982). Sources of stress: Events or conditions? In D. Belle (Ed.), *Lives in stress* (pp. 35–53). Beverly Hills, CA: Sage.

Marshall, N. (1982). The public welfare system: Regulation and dehumanization. In D. Belle (Ed.), *Lives in stress* (pp. 96–108). Beverly Hills, CA: Sage.

Martin, C. J., Brown, G. W., Goldberg, D. P., & Brackington, I. F. (1989). Psychosocial stress and puerperal depression. *Journal of Affective Disorders*, 16, 283–293.

McGrath, E., Keita, G. P., Strickland, B. R., & Russo, N. F. (1991). *Women and depression*. Washington, DC: American Psychological Association.

McKinlay, J. B., McKinlay, S. M., & Brambilla, D. (1987). The relative contributions of endocrine changes and social circumstances in mid-aged women. *Journal of Health and Social Behavior*, 28, 345–363.

Merikangas, K., Weissman, M. M., & Pauls, D. L. (1985). Genetic factors in the sex ratio of major depression. *Psychological Medicine*, 15, 63–69.

Moos, R. H. (1968). The development of a menstrual distress questionnaire. *Psychosomatic Medicine*, 30, 853–867.

Mostow, E., & Newberry, P. (1975). Work role and depression in women: A comparison of workers and housewives in treatment. *American Journal of Orthopsychiatry*, 45, 538–548.

Murphy, S. M. (1988). Current psychological functioning of child sexual abuse survivors. *Journal of Interpersonal Violence*, 3, 55–79.

Murphy, S. M., Kilpatrick, D. G., Amick-McMullen, A., Veronen, L. J., Paduhovich, J., Best, C. L., Villeponteaux, L. A., & Saunders, B. E. (1988). Current psychological functioning of child sexual assault survivors. *Journal of Interpersonal Violence*, 3, 55–79.

Nadelson, C. C. (1989). Professional issues for women. *Psychiatric Clinics of North America*, 12, 25–33.

Nadelson, C. C., Notman, M.T., Zackson, H., & Gornick, J. (1982). A follow-up study of rape victims. *American Journal of Psychiatry*, 139, 1266–1270.

Nemtzow, R. (1987). Childbirth: Happiness, blues, or depression? In R. Formanek & A. Gurian (Eds.), *Women and depression: A lifespan perspective* (pp. 132–146). New York: Springer.

Newmann, J. P. (1984). Sex differences in symptoms of depression: Clinical disorder or normal distress? *Journal of Health and Social Behavior*, 25, 136–159.

Newmann, J. P. (1986). Gender, life strains, and depression. *Journal of Health and Social Behavior*, 27, 161– 178.

Newmann, J. P. (1987). Gender differences in vulnerability to depression. *Social Service Review*, 61, 447–468.

Nicolson, P. (1989). Counselling women with postnatal depression: Implications from recent qualitative research. *Counselling Psychology Quarterly*, 2, 123–132.

Nolen-Hoeksema, S. (1987). Sex differences in unipolar depression: Evidence and theory. *Psychological Bulletin*, 101, 259–282.

Nolen-Hoeksema, S. (1990). *Sex differences in depression*. Stanford, CA: Stanford University Press.

Notman, M. T. (1989). Depression in women: Psychoanalytic concepts. *Psychiatric Clinics of North America*, 12, 221–231.

O'Hara, M. W., Zekoski, E. M., Phillips, L. H., & Wright, E. J. (1990). Controlled prospective study of postpartum mood disorders: Comparison of childbearing and nonchildbearing women. *Journal of Abnormal Psychology*, 99, 3–15.

O'Neil, M. K., Lancee, W. J., & Freeman, S. J. (1985). Sex differences in depressed university students. *Social Psychiatry*, 20, 186–190.

Olasov, B., & Jackson, J. (1987). Effects of expectancies on women's reports of moods during the menstrual cycle. *Psychosomatic Medicine*, 49, 65–78.

Paddison, P. L., Gise, L. H., Lebovits, A., Strain, J. J., Cirasole, D. M., & Levine, J. P. (1990). Sexual abuse and premenstrual syndrome: Comparison between a lower and higher socioeconomic group. *Psychosomatics*, 31, 265–272.

Parry, B. L. (1989). Reproductive factors affecting the course of affective illness in women. *Psychiatric Clinics of North America*, 12, 207–220.

Pearlin, L. I., & Johnson, J. S. (1977). Marital status, life strains and depression. *American Sociological Review*, 42, 704–715.

Pearlstein, T. B., Frank, E., Rivera-Tovar, A., Thoft, J. S., Jacobs, E., & Mieczkowski, T. A. (1990). Prevalence of Axis I and Axis II disorders in women with late luteal phase dysphoric disorder. *Journal of Affective Disorders*, 20, 129–134.

Peplau, L. A. (1982). Research on homosexual couples: An overview. *Journal of Homosexuality*, 8, 3–8.

Pfost, K. S., Stevens, M. J., & Lum, C. U. (1990). The relationship of demographic variables, antepartum depression, and stress to postpartum depression. *Journal of Clinical Psychology*, 46, 588–592.

Radloff, L. S. (1975). Sex differences in depression: The effects of occupation and marital status. *Sex Roles*, 3, 249–265.

Radloff, L. S. (1980). Risk factors for depression: What do we learn from them? In M. Guttentag, S. Salasin, & D. Belle (Eds.), *The mental health of women* (pp. 93–110). New York: Academic Press.

Repetti, R. L., & Crosby, F. (1984). Women and depression: Exploring the adult role explanation. *Journal of Social and Clinical Psychology*, 2, 57–70.

Resick, P. A. (1983). The rape reaction: Research findings and implications for intervention. *The Behavior Therapist*, 6, 129–132.

Rice, J., Reich, T., Andreason, N. C., Lavori, P. W., Endicott, J., Clayton, P. J., Keller, M. B., Hirschfeld, R. M., & Klerman, G. L. (1984). Sex-related differences in depression: Familial evidence. *Journal of Affective Disorders*, 7, 199–210.

Rivera-Tovar, A. D., & Frank, E. (1990). Late luteal phase dysphoric disorder in young women. *American Journal of Psychiatry*, 147, 1634–1636.

Roberts, R. E., & O'Keefe, S. J. (1981). Sex differences in depression reexamined. *Journal of Health and Social Behavior*, 22, 394–400.

Roopnarinesingh, S., & Gopeesingh, T. (1982). Hysterectomy and its psychological aftermath. *West Indian Medical Journal*, 31, 131–134.

Ross, C. E., & Huber, J. (1985). Hardship and depression. *Journal of Health and Social Behavior*, 26, 312–327.

Ross, C. E., & Mirowsky, J. (1988). Child care and emotional adjustment to wives' employment. *Journal of Health and Social Behavior*, 29, 127–138.

Ross, C. E., Mirowsky, J., & Huber, J. (1983). Dividing work, sharing work, and in-between: Marriage patterns and depression. *American Sociological Review*, 48, 809–823.

Roth, S., & Leibowitz, L. (1988). The experiences of sexual trauma. *Journal of Traumatic Stress*, 1, 79–108.

Rothblum, E. D. (1983). Sex-role stereotypes and depression in women. In V. Franks & E.D. Rothblum (Eds.), *The stereotyping of women* (pp. 83–111). New York: Springer.

Rothblum, E. D. (1990). Depression among lesbians: An invisible and unresearched phenomenon. *Journal of Gay and Lesbian Psychotherapy*, 1, 67–87.

Rounsaville, B. J. (1978). Theories in marital violence: Evidence from a study of battered women. *Victimology*, 3, 11–31.

Rubinow, D. R., & Roy-Byrne, P. (1984). Premenstrual syndromes: Overview from a methodological perspective. *American Journal of Psychiatry*, 141, 163–172.

Rubinow, D. R., & Schmidt, P. J. (1989). Models for the development and expression of symptoms in premenstrual syndrome. *Psychiatric Clinics of North America*, 12, 53–68.

Russell, D. E. (1984). *Sexual exploitation*. Beverly Hills, CA: Sage.

Russell, D. E., & Howell, N. (1983). The prevalence of rape in the United States revisited. *Journal of Women in Culture and Society*, 8, 688–695.

Schmidt, P. J., & Rubinow, D. R. (1991). Menopause-related affective disorders: A justification for further study. *American Journal of Psychiatry*, 148, 844–852.

Shusterman, L. R. (1979). Predicting the psychological consequences of abortion. *Social Science and Medicine*, 13, 683–689.

Steele, E., Mitchell, J., Greywolf, E., Belle, D., Chang, W., & Schuller, R. B. (1982). The human cost of discrimination. In D. Belle (Ed.), *Lives in stress* (pp. 109–119). Beverly Hills, CA: Sage.

Strickland, B. R. (1988). Sex-related differences in health and illness. *Psychology of Women Quarterly*, 12, 381–399.

Stroebe, M. S., & Stroebe, W. (1983). Who suffers more? Sex differences in health risks of the widowed. *Psychological Bulletin*, 93, 279–301.

Surtees, P. G. (1980). Social support, residual adversity and depressive outcome. *Social Psychiatry*, 15, 71–80.

Tebbets, R. (1982). Work: Its meaning for women's lives. In D. Belle (Ed.), *Lives in stress* (pp. 83–95). Beverly Hills, CA: Sage.

Tennent, C. C. (1985). Female vulnerability to depression. *Psychological Medicine*, 15, 733–737.

Thirkettle, J., & Knight, R. G. (1985). The psychological precipitants of transient postpartum depression: A review. *Current Psychological Research and Reviews*, 4, 143–166.

Thoits, P. A. (1986). Multiple identities: Examining gender and marital status differences in distress. *American Sociological Review*, 51, 259–272.

Trunnell, E. P., Turner, C. W., & Keye, W. R. (1988). A comparison of the psychological and hormonal factors in women with and without premenstrual syndrome. *Journal of Abnormal Psychology*, 97, 429–436.

U.S. Department of Commerce. (1988). *Money income and poverty status in the United States: 1987*. Washington, DC: Bureau of the Census.

van der Ploeg, H. (1989). Assessment of the premenstrual syndrome. *International Psychologist*, 29, 23–30.

Vanfossen, B. E. (1981). Sex differences in the mental health effects of spouse support and equity. *Journal of Health and Social Behavior*, 22, 130–143.

Vanfossen, B. E. (1986). Sex differences in depression: The role of spouse support. In S. E. Hobfoll (Ed.), *Stress, social support, and women* (pp. 69–84). Washington, DC: Hemisphere.

Verbrugge, L. M. (1983). Multiple roles and physical health of women and men. *Journal of Health and Social Behavior*, 24, 16–30.

Wald, B. K., Archer, R. P., & Winstead, B. A. (1990). Rorschach characteristics of mothers of incest victims. *Journal of Personality Assessment*, 53, 417–425.

Walker, L. E. (1984). *The battered woman syndrome*. New York: Springer.

Warren, L. W., & McEachren, (1983). Psychosocial correlates of depressive symptomatology in adult women. *Journal of Abnormal Psychology*, 92, 151–160.

Wehr, T. A., Sack, D. A., & Rosenthal, N. N. (1988). Rapid cycling affective disorder: Contributing factors and treatment responses of 51 patients. *American Journal of Psychiatry, 145,* 179–184.

Weissman, M. M., & Klerman, G. L. (1977). Sex differences in the epidemiology of depression. *Archives of General Psychiatry, 34,* 98–111.

Weissman, M. M., & Klerman, G. L. (1985). Gender and depression. *Trends in Neurosciences, 8,* 416–420.

Weissman, M. M., & Klerman, G. (1987). Gender and depression. In R. Formanek & A. Gurian (Eds.), *Women and depression: A lifespan perspective* (pp. 3–18). New York: Springer.

Weissman, M. M., Leaf, P. J., & Bruce, M. L. (1987). Single parent women. *Social Psychiatry, 22,* 29–36.

Weissman, M. M., Leaf, P. J., Bruce, M. L., & Florio, L. (1988). The epidemiology of dysthymia in five communities: Rates, risks, comorbidity, and treatment. *American Journal of Psychiatry, 145,* 815–819.

Whiffen, V. E. (1988). Vulnerability to postpartum depression: A prospective multivariate study. *Journal of Abnormal Psychology, 97,* 467–474.

Wilson, K., Vercella, R., Brems, C., Benning, D., & Renfro, N. (1992). Levels of learned helplessness in abused women. *Women and Therapy, 13,* 53–67.

Wirtz, P. W., & Harrell, A. V. (1987). Effects of postassault exposure to attack-similar stimuli on long-term recovery of victims. *Journal of Consulting and Clinical Psychology, 55,* 10–16.

Zappert, L. T., & Stansbury, K. (1984). *In the pipeline: A comparative analysis of men and women in graduate programs in science, engineering and medicine at Stanford University* (Working Paper No. 20). Stanford, CA: Institute for Research on Women and Gender, Stanford University.

Zetin, M., Sklanky, G. J., & Cramer, M. (1984). Sex differences in inpatients with major depression. *Journal of Clinical Psychiatry, 45,* 257–259.

V

PSYCHOLOGICAL AND SOCIAL CONTEXTS

22

Life Context, Coping Processes, and Depression

RUTH C. CRONKITE
RUDOLF H. MOOS

Over the past two decades, interest in the role of contextual factors in the course of depression has been reflected by studies examining the relationship of a range of psychosocial factors to depressive symptoms. In general, numerous studies on the occurrence and course of psychological distress have shown that social factors such as life stressors and social resources, and personal factors such as sociodemographic status and coping, are important influences on psychological distress. Although these associations appear to have some generality across disorders, much of the research in this area has focused on the role of stressors and social resources in an individual's susceptibility to depression.

In this chapter, we present a conceptual framework that encompasses psychosocial processes in the course of depression. We then review and integrate the theoretical and empirical literature in this area. The framework is based on an expanded evaluation paradigm, and stress and coping theory in relation to depression. We use the framework to illustrate the interplay among the relevant domains in the process by which depressive symptoms occur and remit. We also show how the framework can be applied to examine how depressed patients' life contexts influence the treatment they receive and the outcome of treatment; in addition, we consider implications for prevention.

INTEGRATING THEORY AND EVALUATION

Whereas there has been a heritage of distinct viewpoints that emphasize personal versus social–environmental factors in explaining physical and psychological well-being, the contemporary perspective is reflected by the biopsychosocial model of health and illness, which integrates the role of biological, psychological, and social factors in the onset and course of medical and psychiatric disorders (Leventhal & Tomarken, 1987). As an example, the American Psychiatric Association (1994) has developed a multiaxial diagnostic system, DSM-IV, which considers psychosocial factors (Axis IV) along with clinical and physical factors as important aspects of psychiatric and behavioral disorders. Consequently, in addition to clinical and physical factors, patients' life context factors need to be considered when making diagnostic assessments, when planning and evaluating treatment, or when identifying individuals at risk of developing depressive symptoms or recurrent depressive episodes.

The Traditional Evaluation Paradigm

Many studies have used a "black-box" or "summative" evaluation paradigm to evaluate treatment programs for depression (Dobson, 1989; Greenberg, Bornstein, Greenberg, & Fisher,

1992; Nietzel, Russel, Hemmings, & Gretter, 1987; Steinbrueck, Maxwell, & Howard, 1983). Such a paradigm involves assessing patients at intake and at one or more follow-ups after treatment, with little attention paid to the process of treatment (the "black box") or to other factors that might influence the patient's outcome. Such evaluations may be useful for assessing the overall effectiveness of a treatment program or for comparing distinct programs and/or treatment orientations (such as psychotherapy vs. pharmacotherapy), but they reveal little about the process of treatment or about how to improve it.

Some recent evaluations have examined the process of treatment for depression and the associations between specific components of treatment and outcome (Robinson, Berman, & Neimeyer, 1990). For example, Rounsaville et al. (1987) found that high therapist activity and warmth were associated with better outcome among patients receiving interpersonal psychotherapy. These process-oriented studies are leading to new causal mediational models of the role of cognition in depression (Hollon, DeRubeis, & Evans, 1987). By identifying how specific aspects of treatment are related to outcome and the presumed mediators of outcome, such studies can suggest new ways to make treatment more effective.

Broad reviews aimed at integrating the depression treatment literature have reported a lack of consistency in the relative effectiveness of different types of treatments for depression (Robinson et al., 1990). Possible explanations for such inconsistencies include the researcher's allegiance; variations in the client populations and treatment procedures; overlap in treatment techniques; and extratreatment factors such as stressors, social resources, and coping resources. However, only a few studies have focused on how life context factors influence the initiation and length of treatment for depression or the outcome and course of depression after treatment. Stressful circumstances and a lack of social resources can obscure the benefits of treatment, especially when treatment is brief and there is a long interval between the end of treatment and follow-up. In fact, such life context factors may be largely responsible for the high rate of recurrent depressive episodes. A conceptual framework for program evaluation should consider how the interplay between treatment and life context factors can affect the process of remission and relapse in depression.

An Expanded Evaluation Paradigm

The factors that relate to the course of depressive symptoms are multiple and complex. Figure 22.1 shows the interrelationships among five sets of factors associated with depression-related outcomes. The framework depicts processes by which depressive symptoms and related functioning criteria (Panel V) are influenced by sociodemographic factors, initial functioning, and coping responses (Panel II); life context factors that occur prior to or at the time of treatment entry (Panel I); and life context factors that occur during and after treatment (Panel IV). For individuals who enter treatment for depressive symptoms, personal and life context factors influence the amount and type of treatment received (Panel III); in turn, treatment experiences affect posttreatment life context factors (Panel IV) and depression-related outcomes (Panel V).

This expanded paradigm has evolved from two current trends in program evaluation (Moos, Finney, & Cronkite, 1990). The first is an increased emphasis on the careful study of treatment, including an assessment of how well treatment is implemented and an examination of the ways in which specific treatment components are related to distinct outcome criteria. The second is the growing attention given to factors outside of treatment and the ways in which they are associated with treatment entry, treatment experiences, and treatment outcome. The paradigm illustrates the complexity of the treatment process and underscores the fact that treatment and its components are only one of several sets of factors that influence the course of depression. This expanded evaluation paradigm can help shape evaluations of pharmacological as well as psychosocial interventions and can improve our understanding of the processes involved in the course of depressive symptoms, even for those individuals who do not enter treatment.

The Dynamics of the Stress and Coping Process

All of the domains in Figure 22.1 can affect one another. Life stressors may be associated with sociodemographic conditions, lead to changes in the nature of social resources, elicit appraisal and coping responses, influence decisions about treatment, and precipitate a relapse. For example, stressful events such as losses are disrup-

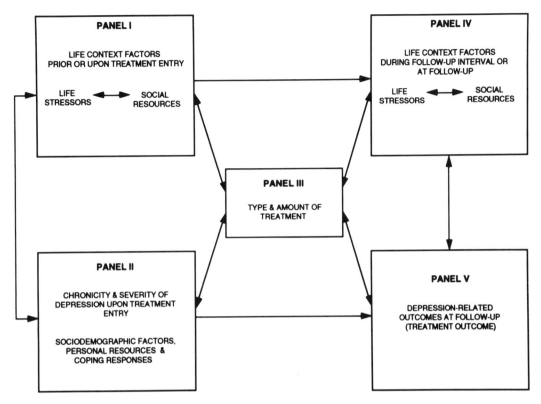

FIGURE 22.1. The relationship among life context factors, coping processes, and treatment outcome.

tions in an individual's social network that may heighten the risk of depression. Social resources may influence the occurrence of life stressors, shape appraisal and coping responses, help maintain or erode treatment gains, and affect depression-related functioning (Moos, 1991). Such interrelationships highlight the ways in which life context may affect the course of depression, and provide a rationale for the integration of stress and coping theory within an expanded evaluation paradigm.

Framework Boundaries

The expanded evaluation paradigm highlights the complexities and issues involved in the treatment and course of depression. First, it is broad enough to include several sets of factors that are beyond the scope of this chapter. Among these are developmental factors such as early parental loss (Crook & Eliot, 1980; McLeod, 1992; Tennant, 1988); personality factors (Akiskal, 1991; Akiskal, Hirschfeld, & Yerevanian, 1983; Andrews, Neilson, Hunt, Stewart, & Kilow, 1990; Boyce, Parker, Barnett, Cooney, & Smith,

1991; Duggan, Lee, & Murray, 1990; Shea et al., 1990); and attributional style (Peterson & Seligman, 1984). Because it is basically a psychosocial framework oriented toward individuals, it does not include biological markers and genetic factors (Free & Oei, 1989; Leonard, 1986; Thomas, Wilt, & Noffsinger, 1988) or macrosystem factors such as economic conditions (Catalano & Dooley, 1977). We do not discount the importance of these factors. However, as is the case with specifying any model or conceptual framework, it is important to focus on a delimited range of factors. Consequently, we focus here on the relationship of treatment, life context, and coping processes to depressive symptoms.

Second, there is considerable debate over the extent to which psychiatric symptoms, including depressive symptoms, should be categorized into distinct disorders, or whether symptoms of psychological distress can be conceptualized as varying along a continuum from less to more severe (Klerman, 1989; Mirowsky & Ross, 1989; Swartz, Carrol, & Blazer, 1989; Tweed & George, 1989; Wells, Burnam, Rogers, Hays, &

Camp, 1992). Both points of view have validity. On the one hand, any consistencies in the pattern of observed associations across distinct functioning criteria contribute toward progress in formulating conceptual frameworks that are broadly applicable to psychological distress, regardless of the specific type of disorder. On the other hand, variations in the strength of specific types of associations across apparently distinct disorders (such as unipolar depression and dysthymia, or depression and alcohol abuse) yield improved understanding of the unique aspects of the course of specific disorders. Our conceptual framework is suitable for both perspectives in that it can be applied to clinical and nonclinical populations, to psychological distress in general, or to distinct psychiatric disorders (Moos et al., 1990; Moos, 1991).

We now turn to a review of the life context and coping domains in our conceptual framework. We are primarily concerned with dimensions of life context factors and coping responses, how they relate to the course of depression, and implications for treatment.

STRESSFUL LIFE CIRCUMSTANCES

As the amount of research literature in the area of stressful life circumstances has grown, models of the stressor–depression relationship have become more complex (Aneshensel, 1985; Hammen, 1992; Monroe & Depue, 1991; Pearlin, 1989; Thoits, 1983). For example, the early unidimensional conceptualization of stressors that stimulated a great deal of research has shifted toward considering multidimensional aspects of stressors (Thoits, 1983). Likewise, the boundaries of the concept of stressors have expanded to include ongoing or chronic stressful circumstances, microstressors, nonevents, and traumas (Wheaton, 1994). Added attention has been paid to the domain or context in which a stressor occurs (Hammen, 1992; Moos, 1992; Moos & Moos, 1992; Pearlin & Turner, 1987; Swindle & Moos, 1992; Wheaton, 1994) and to whether the stressor is an antecedent, concomitant, or consequence of depressive symptoms (Barnett & Gotlib, 1988; Hammen, 1992; Monroe, Kupfer, & Frank, 1992). Finally, some research has focused on the role of stressors in the treatment process (Billings & Moos, 1984b; Monroe et al., 1992; Moos, 1990, 1991).

Life Events

Life events have long been implicated in the onset and course of depression among both clinical and nonclinical populations (Hammen, 1992; Monroe & Depue, 1991; Moos, 1991). Traditionally, "life events" have been defined as objective experiences that are sufficiently disruptive or threatening as to require a substantial readjustment on the part of the individual (Dohrenwend & Dohrenwend, 1974; Thoits, 1983). Events can vary in their severity from death of a spouse to minor violations of the law. The threat or demand for change and the subsequent readjustment process may compromise an individual's psychological well-being (Holmes & Rahe, 1967; Thoits, 1983).

Additional qualities of life events that may influence psychological distress include desirability, controllability, and the degree to which the event was expected. In general, the effects of the total number of life events (or total amount of change) on psychological distress can be attributed to the effects of undesirable events (Ross & Mirowsky, 1979; Thoits, 1983). Events that involve a significant loss to the individual—such as death of a spouse, becoming separated or divorced, death of a family member or close friend, or the loss of a job—appear to be particularly salient (Billings, Cronkite, & Moos, 1983; Aneshensel, 1985).

In addition, the association between uncontrollable events and depressive outcomes (clinical depression, depressive symptoms, and suicide attempts) is stronger than is the association between controllable events and depressive outcomes (Fava, Munari, Pavan, & Kellner, 1981; Husaini & Neff, 1980, 1981; McFarlane, Norman, Streiner, Roy, & Scott, 1980; Paykel, 1974, 1979; Streiner, Norman, McFarlane, & Roy, 1981). There is also evidence that the nonoccurrence of expected positive events or failures in settings where success is valued (such as marriage, job, or school) may be other salient dimensions of life events (Pearlin & Lieberman, 1979; Thoits, 1983).

Chronic (Ongoing) Life Stressors

Whereas the concept of life events captures one aspect of stressful life circumstances, another important aspect involves ongoing problematic conditions and difficulties in an individual's social environment or roles (Brown & Harris,

1978; Pearlin, 1983, 1989; Pearlin, Lieberman, Menaghan, & Mullan, 1981; Wheaton, 1994). Such stressful life circumstances can be differentiated into role stressors and ambient stressors (Pearlin, 1989), and along different life domains, such as finances, work, spouse/partner, child, extended family, friends, physical health, and home/neighborhood (Moos, 1992; Moos & Moos, 1992; Swindle & Moos, 1992). Role stressors encompass ongoing difficulties or problems that are associated with occupying certain roles, such as role overload (common in occupational, homemaker, and informal caregiver roles), intrarole conflict, interrole conflict (work and nonwork demands interfering with each other), role captivity (being unwillingly confined to a role such as housewife, retiree, or informal caregiver), and role restructuring (such as assuming increasing responsibility in caring for aging parents) (Klitzman, House, Israel, & Mero, 1990; Pearlin, 1983; Pearlin & Schooler, 1978). Examples of role stressors include marital, parental, or work stressors; incompatible demands across roles; or occupying a role that one does not wish to hold. Ambient stressors refer to problems that characterize the quality of life of the individual, such as disadvantageous life circumstances (financial difficulties, unsafe neighborhood) or the physical or emotional dysfunction of a family member (Moos & Moos, 1992; Wheaton, 1983).

Both role stressors and ambient stressors are associated with depressive symptoms among community and clinical samples. For example, marital and parental stressors are associated with depressive symptoms among community samples (Moos, 1992; Moos, Fenn, Billings, & Moos, 1989; Pearlin & Schooler, 1978). Work stressors characterized by role ambiguity, lack of autonomy, and work pressure are associated with psychological distress and depression among nurses, emergency medical staff, and community residents (Billings & Moos, 1982a; Golding, 1989; Holt, 1982; Murphy, 1983; Revicki & May, 1985, 1989; Revicki, Whitley, Gallery, & Allison, 1993; Schaefer & Moos, 1991). Enduring role stressors and interpersonal difficulties are also associated with depressive symptoms and recurrence of depressive episodes (Aneshensel, 1985; Avison & Turner, 1988; Moos et al., 1989). In comparisons of depressed patients and case controls, patients experience more chronic difficulties in the family and work domains (Billings et al., 1983; Moos et al., 1989).

Microstressors

Microstressors represent a level of social reality that is not usually captured by other concepts typically invoked in conceptual models of the stress process. "Microstressors" are defined as irritating, frustrating demands or minor stressors (discrete or ongoing) that characterize an individual's everyday life, such as traffic problems, too many interruptions, a home that requires a lot of maintenance or repairs, and so on (Lazarus & Folkman, 1984; Kanner, Coyne, Schaefer, & Lazarus, 1981; Wheaton, 1994).

In a community sample, Kanner et al. (1981) reported that such microstressors were better predictors of depressive symptoms than were major life events. This may be because microstressors are manifestations of life events or chronic stressors in one or more life domains. For example, too many interruptions are typically associated with the presence of one or more young children in the household, which is a risk factor for depressive symptoms among women (Brown & Harris, 1978, 1989). Consequently, it may be useful to consider the social context or life domain in which microstressors occur.

The Context of Life Stressors

Stressors occur within a social context that shapes the meaning people attach to them. Some of the relevant circumstances include stage in the life cycle, role occupancy in various life domains (marital, parental, work), commitment to a role, and socioeconomic status (Brown, 1993; Golding, 1989; Hammen, Ellicott, Gitlin, & Jamison, 1989; Pearlin & Turner, 1987). For example, the appraisal of the birth of a child may vary considerably, depending on the financial and employment status of the parents. Similarly, depending on the circumstances, retirement may be perceived as the loss of crucial elements of one's own identity (a contextual threat) or as a welcome relief and opportunity for celebration (Pearlin & Turner, 1987).

Severe events involving loss of a relationship, a cherished idea, or material resources appear to have an etiological role in clinical depression (Brown, 1993). In a comparison of depressed patients with community residents, the occurrence of fateful, disruptive loss events was substantially greater among the depressed group, suggesting that the contextual threat of such events is a potent risk factor for the onset and recurrence of depressive episodes (Shrout et al., 1989). Hammen et al. (1989) developed an individual vulnerability–life event matching model to demonstrate that individuals who depended on social relationships were more likely to become depressed when faced with interpersonal stressors, whereas achievement-oriented individuals were more likely to manifest depression when encountering frustration or failure in the achievement domain.

Stressors as Antecedents, Concomitants, and Consequences of Depression

Whereas life stressors are typically implicated as etiological factors in depression, it is difficult to empirically establish the extent to which stressors are antecedents, concomitants, or consequences of depression (Barnett & Gotlib, 1988; Hammen, 1991, 1992; Monroe et al., 1992). This difficulty is due in part to the methodological limitations of cross-sectional studies, whereby an association between stressors and depression does not imply any specific causal relationship. It is further complicated by time lags that may occur between the onset of depressive symptoms and treatment entry, in which stressors that occurred prior to treatment entry may have been generated in part by prior depressive symptoms. Moreover, the impairment and interpersonal difficulties displayed by depressed individuals may serve to generate stressful circumstances and events, which in turn may result in a higher likelihood of a recurrent or chronic course of depression (Hammen, 1991).

Recent attempts to empirically unravel the causal associations between stressors and depression have suggested that recurrently or chronically depressed people tend to experience specific patterns of stressors, such as interpersonal difficulties, unstable interpersonal and occupational contexts, and "dependent" events, which are in part a consequence of the social environment they themselves create and maintain (Hammen, 1991, 1992; Monroe et al., 1992). In a 1-year longitudinal study, Hammen (1991) reported that women with recurrent unipolar depression experienced more "dependent" events (those to which they contributed), particularly negative interpersonal events, compared to bipolar and medically ill women. Such findings suggest that depression may generate

stressful life circumstances (particularly interpersonal difficulties) that provoke further depression (Coyne et al., 1987; Hammen, 1991).

Stressors, Treatment, and Treatment Outcome

The idea that some depressive episodes may occur in response to stressors provides a rationale for Axis IV of DSM-IV, shapes clinicians' judgments about the locus of patients' difficulties, and influences decisions about treatment and predictions of treatment outcome. The often-cited clinical wisdom is that life events occurring prior to or during treatment may be a good prognostic indicator in unipolar depression, a predictor of differential response to treatment, and a risk factor for recurrent depression (American Psychiatric Association, 1994; Moos, 1991; Monroe et al., 1992). However, the empirical literature on the prognostic role of stressors in the recovery process is mixed. Some investigations have yielded results showing that stressful events occurring prior to treatment entry predicted better clinical outcomes (Monroe & Depue, 1991; Monroe, Bellack, Hersen, & Himmelhoch, 1983; Reno & Halaris, 1990), but others have not (Lloyd, Zisook, Click, & Jaffe, 1981; Monroe et al., 1992; Zimmerman, Pfohl, Coryell, & Stangl, 1987).

One reason for this inconsistency may be the nature of the stressor and/or the type of depression. For example, discrete life events may augur well for remission, but only if such events are not severe, do not generate subsequent stressors, or do not occur in social contexts that are consistently stressful. When the life events prior to treatment entry or during the early stages of treatment are severe, they predict poorer early treatment outcome and a longer time to respond to treatment for recurrent depressives (Monroe et al., 1992). If preintake stressors lead to more stressors during the treatment–posttreatment interval, then preintake stressors may predict a poorer outcome (Monroe et al., 1992; Moos, 1991). When the stressors at treatment entry take the form of ongoing difficulties, such as medical conditions or physical health problems and/or high family conflict, then they predict poorer treatment outcome and recurrent depression (Billings & Moos, 1985a; Krantz & Moos, 1988; Leff & Vaughn, 1985; Murphy, 1983; Moos, 1990, 1991; Swindle, Cronkite, & Moos, 1989).

Information about a depressed patient's level of stressors may influence attributions that clinicians make about the cause of the depression (situational vs. dispositional), and, in turn, decisions about treatment (Billings & Moos, 1984b; Fehrenbach & O'Leary, 1982; Moos, 1991). By examining predictors of treatment experiences, Billings and Moos (1984b) found that patients who experienced more negative life events and more family conflict received less treatment. These findings were stronger among outpatients, who had less severe depression, than among inpatients.

Stressful life circumstances that occur during the treatment–posttreatment interval may be better predictors of long-term treatment outcome than those that occur prior to treatment entry. Patients who experienced more negative events and chronic difficulties in the treatment–posttreatment interval improved less than expected at 1 year and 4 years, even after the severity of their symptoms at intake was controlled for (Billings & Moos, 1985a; Swindle et al., 1989). Murphy (1983) reported that negative events that occurred during the year between intake and follow-up were associated with poorer outcome among elderly depressed patients (but see Monroe et al., 1983). Similarly, Lloyd and her colleagues (1981) reported that patients who experienced negative events after initiating antidepressant treatment showed a poorer treatment response. These findings are strongest in studies focusing on the effects of personal illness stressors. Severe events and chronic difficulties have also been associated with the recurrence of depression after treatment (Surtees & Ingham, 1980), whereas a reduction in severity of difficulty was associated with improvement in chronic depressive symptoms among women (Brown, Bifulco, Harris, & Bridge, 1986).

In summary, there is substantial evidence that stressors are related to the course of depression. The stressor domain encompasses dimensions that vary in their nature from life events to ongoing stressful circumstances. They can also range in severity from minor problems to acute events and can occur in different life domains. The role of stressors in the course of depression is likely to be etiological, concurrent, and consequential. Moreover, stressors may figure in judgments that clinicians make about the nature of a patient's depression and treatment allocation. Posttreatment stressors are also associated with poorer long-term treatment outcome.

Other important considerations are the patient's social resources and coping responses, which also play a role in the dynamics of the stress and coping process, and the course of depression.

SOCIAL RESOURCES

Social resources are supportive social ties that may benefit an individual's psychological well-being by fulfilling needs for affiliation, belonging, guidance, nurturance, and self-esteem. Conceptual distinctions have been drawn between structural support, or the quantity and characteristics of social networks, and functional support, or the provision of social companionship, information, tangible help, and positive affect (for reviews, see Barrera, 1986; Cohen & Wills, 1985; House, Landis, & Umberson, 1988a; House, Umberson, & Landis, 1988b; Leavy, 1983; Moos & Mitchell, 1982; Sarason, Sarason, & Pierce, 1990; Thoits, 1986). The prominence of social support as an important psychosocial factor in psychological well-being derives from its possible role in (1) the etiology of and recovery from psychological distress, (2) the dynamics of the stress and coping process, and (3) prevention efforts and treatment. Attention has been focused on the direct relationship between social resources and psychological well-being, and the stress-buffering role of social support (Aneshensel, 1985; Cohen & Wills, 1985; Kessler, Kendler, Heath, Neale, & Eaves, 1992).

Processes by Which Social Support Influences Depression

There is consistent empirical support for an association between the lack of many facets of social support and depression in both clinical and community samples (Aneshensel & Frerichs, 1982; Barnett & Gotlib, 1988; Bell, LeRoy, & Stephenson, 1982; Billings et al., 1983; Billings & Moos, 1984a; Blazer, 1983; Dean & Ensel, 1982; Gore, 1978; Mitchell & Moos, 1984; Schaefer, Coyne, & Lazarus, 1981; Swindle et al., 1989). Such facets cover both structural and functional dimensions, ranging from the number of friends or close relationships to the perceived adequacy of existing social ties (Felton & Shinn, 1992).

The process by which social resources benefit psychological well-being, however, may differ depending on the nature of the social support (Coyne & Downey, 1991; House, 1981;

Kessler, Price, & Wortman, 1985; Kessler et al., 1992; Payne & Jones, 1987; Sarason et al., 1990; Thoits, 1982). Cohen and Wills (1985) concluded that social integration was directly related to well-being, whereas the perceived adequacy/quality of support was more likely to moderate the influence of stressors on well-being.

The degree of social integration may have a direct relationship to mental health, because it reflects the extent of one's engagement within the larger society (Cohen & Wills, 1985; Pearlin, 1989). This kind of structural integration provides a sense of belonging, mutual obligation, role occupancy, predictability, and stability to one's life context, which in turn helps to maintain psychological well-being. Such social attachments (employment, marriage, membership in organizations) may also serve to deter or reduce depression-inducing stressors such as financial problems or social isolation (Payne & Jones, 1987). Low levels of social integration characterize people who are depressed or who have a recurrent course of depression (Aneshensel, 1985; Barnett & Gotlib, 1988; Billings & Moos, 1985b; Lin & Ensel, 1984, Phifer & Murrell, 1986). In addition, the behaviors and symptoms associated with depression may detract from the formation and maintenance of social ties and social integration (Coyne & Downey, 1991; Johnson, 1991; Pearlin, 1985).

In contrast, the perceived adequacy/quality of social support can serve as a buffer by protecting persons from the detrimental effects of stressors on depression. One mechanism is by attenuation or prevention of a stress appraisal response (Kessler & McLeod, 1985; Wethington & Kessler, 1986). For example, a stressor may not be perceived as threatening or harmful when there are adequate social resources to cope with it. In addition, social support may alleviate the impact of stressors by facilitating solutions or appropriate coping responses via informational, instrumental, or esteem support. For example, the detrimental impact of financial difficulties may be reduced by instrumental support, whereas distress associated with the loss of a companion may be alleviated by social companionship (Cohen & Wills, 1985).

Whereas social support is usually beneficial, a few studies suggest that certain support attempts may be detrimental. For example, social support may have a negative influence when it involves emotional overinvolvement, excessiveness, untimeliness, inappropriateness, or an overload of emotional and other demands on the individual receiving the support (Coyne, Wortman, & Lehman, 1988; Veiel, 1993).

Given the conceptual appeal of the hypothesized stress-buffering role of social resources, it is surprising that the empirical support for this idea is relatively weak (Payne & Jones, 1987). This may in part be due to methodological issues such as (1) the prevalence of cross-sectional studies that cannot unravel causal interrelationships (Payne & Jones, 1987); (2) issues in estimating main and interaction terms to test for stress-buffering effects (Finney, Mitchell, Cronkite, & Moos, 1984); and (3) social contexts in which social support may fail (Coyne et al., 1988).

Sources of Support

Social support intrinsically involves the giving-and-receiving aspects of human relationships. Consequently, the source of social support may play a role in the association between social resources and depression. Among important sources are a spouse/partner or confidant, extended family, friends, health professionals, and supervisors and coworkers.

Confidant or Spouse/Partner Support

Depression is associated with the lack of a confiding, intimate relationship (Brown & Harris, 1978; Dean, Kolody, & Wood, 1990); with marital or family conflict (Billings & Moos, 1982b; Billings et al., 1983; Crowther, 1985; Kahn, Coyne, & Margolin, 1985; Rounsaville, Weissman, Prusoff, & Herzeg-Barron, 1979); and with a family environment that is low in cohesion and expressiveness (Billings et al., 1983). Recurrent episodes of depression are also associated with high levels of criticism by family members expressed toward the patient (Hooley, Orley, & Teasdale, 1986; Vaughn & Leff, 1976), or with an overload of emotional and other demands on the patient (Veiel, 1993). Spiegel and Wissler (1986) reported that positive family interaction, such as a willingness to discuss personal problems and express feelings openly, was associated with less rehospitalization among psychiatric patients (including depressed patients). When remitted depressed individuals are compared with normal controls, there is a tendency for continued marital dysfunction to characterize the remitted group (Merikangas, 1984; Miller et al., 1992). Overall, marital distress may be a concomitant or an enduring consequence of depression (Barnett & Gotlib, 1988). It may also serve an etiological role in depression (Menaghan & Lieberman, 1986; Monroe, Bromet, Connell, & Steiner, 1986).

Work Support

Although more research focuses on the association between work support and employee morale, several studies have examined the interconnections between work settings and their influence on individuals' adaptation and treatment outcome (for overviews, see Moos, 1984, 1985a, 1985b, 1991; Moos, Brennan, Fondacaro, & Moos, 1990). At the time of entry into treatment, depressed patients reported less work support compared to a community control group (Billings et al., 1983). These findings held for patients with and without a previous treated episode of depression (Billings & Moos, 1984c). There is also some evidence that patients with a nonrecurrent history of depression may be more responsive to work support (Billings & Moos, 1984c).

In a 1-year follow-up of depressed patients, remitted patients reported as much work support as nondepressed community controls, whereas partially remitted and nonremitted patients reported less. Even after sociodemographic characteristics and intake functioning were controlled for, work support was linked to less depression, fewer physical symptoms, and higher self-confidence (Billings & Moos, 1985a, 1985b).

Work-related support may also be provided by spouses. For example, Repetti (1987) found that understanding and supportive husbands of clerical workers helped to mitigate the effects of a stress-filled day at work. Similarly, wives often serve as a sounding board by listening to and discussing problems that their husbands are having at work (Lopata, Barnewolt, & Norr, 1980; Weiss, 1985). Moreover, for husbands, the expressive support associated with a positive marital relationship buffers the detrimental impact of a poor work-related social climate on depression (Gutek, Repetti, & Silver, 1988; Vanfossen, 1981).

Social Resources, Treatment, and Treatment Outcome

A patient's social resources may be a prognostic factor that enters into clinical judgments about the appropriate type and length of treatment. For example, a lack of social resources may suggest a need for more intensive or longer treatment. Social resources such as supportive family environments and a confidant at treatment intake are associated with better treatment outcome among depressed clients (Marziali, 1987; Moos, 1990; Steinmetz, Lewinsohn, & Antonuccio, 1983). In addition, the effect of the number of outpatient treatment sessions on outcome may depend on the quality of a relationship with a confidant. That is, clients with good confidant relationships responded better to brief treatment than to more extensive treatment, while clients with poorer relationships improved with more treatment sessions (Moos, 1990). Brief treatment may be best suited for patients who have a confidant and report low family conflict; in this situation, it may be desirable to utilize existing supportive social resources to reinforce treatment gains. In contrast, some patients may need longer treatment to establish a therapeutic alliance or to compensate for the potential erosion of treatment gains due to the lack of social resources (Koss, Butcher, & Strupp, 1986).

Social resources available during the treatment–posttreatment interval are related to treatment outcome. Surtees (1980) found that inpatients who had more close (presence of a confidant, contact with close relatives) and diffuse (contacts at work, with neighbors, at clubs or church) social resources were less severely depressed at follow-up. Compared to those who had adequate support, patients who had little or no support were more than twice as likely to remain depressed. In addition, patients who had higher levels of stressors were more likely to be remitted if they had adequate social support. At 1-year and 4-year follow-ups, patients who had more supportive posttreatment social resources showed better treatment outcome; most important were aspects of quality of support, such as the quality of a relationship with a confidant (Billings & Moos, 1985a; Swindle et al., 1989).

In summary, there is substantial empirical evidence that social support is related to lower levels of depression. The main processes involved appear to be a direct effect associated with social integration, social companionship, and stress-buffering effects associated with the perceived quality/adequacy of support. The dimensions of social support that may be salient range from structural aspects, such as the number and availability of sources of support, to perceptions of the adequacy and quality of support. The dynamics by which social support figures in the course of depression are complex; lack of social resources may both play an etiological role and be a consequence of depressive symptoms, whereas the presence and quality of social resources may contribute to attaining and maintaining remission. Social resources may also play a key role in shaping coping responses.

COPING

The domain of coping has been conceptualized in many ways, encompassing both personal coping resources, which are relatively stable dispositional characteristics, and appraisal and coping processes, which are cognitive and behavioral efforts taken by individuals to manage, reduce, or eliminate psychological distress or stressful circumstances (Moos & Schaefer, 1993). The typical hypothesized role of coping in the stress–illness relationship is that the use of more effective coping is associated with reduced psychological distress and better outcomes (Rohde, Lewinsohn, Tilson, & Seeley, 1990). Both personal and social factors may influence the use of specific coping processes, and the adaptiveness of these coping processes may depend on the context and time frame involved (Cohen, 1987; Mattlin, Wethington, & Kessler, 1990; Moos & Schaefer, 1993).

Personal Coping Resources

Personal coping resources are a complex set of personality, attitudinal, and cognitive factors that shape part of the psychological context for coping. They are relatively stable dispositional characteristics or individual styles that may influence the selection of appraisal and coping processes. Such resources include dispositional outlook (self-efficacy, dispositional optimism, and sense of coherence), cognitive styles (field dependence and independence, and information-processing styles), defense and coping styles, and problem-solving styles (for an overview, see Moos & Schaefer, 1993).

Appraisal and Coping Processes

Appraisal and coping processes are closely interrelated. According to Lazarus and Folkman (1984), primary appraisal involves people's judgments about what is at stake in a stressful encounter (perceived threat, challenge, harm, benefit), whereas secondary appraisal involves their beliefs about the viable options for coping (controllable by self or others vs. uncontrollable). Appraisals are a continuing aspect of the coping process; initial appraisals are followed by specific coping responses, and then by reappraisal and possible modification of coping strategies.

Although no single method for categorizing coping processes has yet emerged, most researchers have used one of two main conceptual approaches to classify coping processes. The first approach emphasizes the "focus" of coping: a person's orientation and activity in response to stressful situations. An individual can approach the problem and make active efforts to resolve it, and/or can try to avoid the problem and focus mainly on managing the emotions associated with it. A second approach emphasizes the "method" of coping—that is, whether a response entails primarily cognitive or behavioral efforts. A more integrated conceptualization of coping processes is to incorporate the method of coping within each of the focus domains, resulting in four basic types of coping processes: cognitive approach, behavioral approach, cognitive avoidance, and behavioral avoidance (Moos & Schaefer, 1993).

Cognitive approach coping includes logical analysis and positive reappraisal, such as paying attention to one aspect of the situation at a time, drawing on past experiences, mentally rehearsing alternative actions and their probable consequences, and accepting the reality of a situation but restructuring it to find something favorable. *Behavioral approach coping* includes seeking guidance and support, and taking concrete action to deal directly with a situation or its aftermath.

Cognitive avoidance coping consists of responses aimed at denying or minimizing the seriousness of a crisis or its consequences, as well as accepting a situation as it is and deciding that the basic circumstances cannot be altered. *Behavioral avoidance coping* covers seeking alternative rewards—that is, trying to replace the losses involved in certain crises by becoming involved in new activities and creating alternative sources of satisfaction. It also includes openly venting one's feelings of anger and despair, and adopting behaviors that may temporarily reduce tension, such as acting impulsively, going on an eating binge, and taking tranquilizers or other medications.

Folkman, Lazarus, Dunkel-Schetter, DeLongis, and Greuen (1986) identified some associations between the appraisal of a stressor and reliance on coping responses. When faced with a threat to self-esteem, for example, people tend to use more cognitive and behavioral approach coping. When people appraise situations as changeable, they tend to rely more on approach coping, such as accepting responsibility, positive reappraisal, confrontation, and problem-solving. In contrast, when people confront stressors that must be accepted, they rely more on distancing and escape/avoidance. In a sample of older problem-drinkers, stressors appraised as challenging tended to elicit more approach and less avoidance coping (Moos et al., 1990).

Type and Severity of Stressors and Coping

The type (acute vs. chronic life domain in which the stressor occurs) and severity of stressors may influence coping responses (Mattlin et al., 1990). For example, personal illness stressors tended to elicit more reliance on both approach coping (such as positive reappraisal, seeking guidance, and active behavioral coping) and avoidance coping (especially cognitive avoidance and seeking alternative rewards). In contrast, interpersonal and family stressors elicited fewer approach coping responses (especially problem solving) and more resigned acceptance and emotion-focused coping (Billings & Moos, 1981; Moos et al., 1990).

Coping responses also vary in accordance with the overall amount and chronicity of stressors. For example, depressed patients and normal controls who experienced more stressful events also tended to respond with both more approach and avoidance coping. Moreover, the patients and controls who experienced more new stressful events in a subsequent 12-month interval relied more on both approach and avoidance coping strategies, even after initial levels of coping were controlled (Holahan & Moos, 1987). More negative events and chronic stressors were also associated with less reliance on problem-solving coping and more use of avoidance coping, especially emotional discharge (Fondacaro & Moos, 1989).

Social Resources, Personal Resources, and Coping

In addition to stressful life circumstances, personal and social resources influence coping re-sponses. For example, optimistic individuals are more likely to rely on coping processes that may foster favorable outcome expectancies, more persistent coping, and better outcomes (Scheier, Weintraub, & Carver, 1986). Individuals who have more self-confidence, more perceived control, and an approach problem-solving style are more persistent and assertive, are more likely to expect success, are less anxious and depressed, have fewer health problems, and are less prone to depression when they experience a high level of stressors (Heppner, 1988; Moos & Schaefer, 1993).

Support from family and friends is associated with more reliance on information seeking and problem solving and less reliance on emotional discharge coping among both depressed patients and community controls (Billings et al., 1983). In addition, family support predicts a decline in the use of emotional discharge and avoidance coping over time (Fondacaro & Moos, 1987; Holahan & Moos, 1987). Certain characteristics of family environments are also associated with coping responses. In one study, members of cohesive, achievement-oriented, and independence-oriented families were more likely to rely on problem-focused coping responses. In contrast, members of families characterized as having high levels of conflict and control tended to rely on avoidance coping (Billings & Moos, 1982c).

Work settings and occupational experiences can also influence a person's value system and coping strategies (Kohn & Schooler, 1983). That is, occupational conditions conducive to self-direction—such as high autonomy, innovation, and support—are associated with placing a high value on self-direction and the use of approach coping processes. For example, men who experience increases in work support seek more information and support over time (Fondacaro & Moos, 1987). Similarly, Parkes (1986) found that student nurses use more approach coping responses in major stressful episodes when work support is high—that is, when the availability of supportive supervisors enables them to cope directly with major work stressors.

Coping Processes, Depression, and Treatment Outcome

Several studies have compared depressed and nondepressed individuals on the frequency and types of coping behaviors they use. Compared with nondepressed persons, depressed persons are likely to use more emotional discharge coping, wishful thinking, avoidance, and emotional support seeking, and less problem-solving coping (Billings et al., 1983; Coyne, Aldwin, & Lazarus, 1981). Rohde and his colleagues (1990) reported that escapism was associated with current and future depression; escapism also strengthened the effect of stressors on depression.

At 1-year and 4-year follow-ups of patients treated for depression, more reliance on problem solving, and less on information seeking and emotional discharge, were related to better outcome (Billing & Moos, 1985a; Swindle et al., 1989). These results are consistent with prior findings linking problem-focused coping with less severe depression, and rumination, indecisiveness, and emotional discharge coping with more severe depression (Billings et al., 1983). Similarly, Parker, Brown, and Blignault (1986) found that depressed patients who relied more on self-consolation and distraction at baseline showed poorer treatment outcome.

Reliance on avoidance coping upon entry into treatment for depression may be a significant risk factor for nonremission. Krantz and Moos (1988) found that 41% of patients who relied heavily on avoidance coping prior to treatment were nonremitted at 1 year, compared to a 26% nonremission rate among patients who did not rely on avoidance coping. In contrast, 46% of patients who relied less on avoidance coping were remitted compared to only 25% of the high-risk patients. Gaston, Marmar, Thompson, and Gallagher (1988) noted that depressed patients who rely more heavily on avoidance processes find it harder to form a positive relationship with a therapist in short-term psychotherapy. These findings suggest that a focus on decreasing the use of avoidance coping may improve treatment outcome.

In summary, appraisal and coping processes are interrelated and are influenced by personal resources, the social context and nature of stressors, and social resources. Avoidance coping processes appear to be risk factors for depression and poorer treatment outcome, while approach coping processes may facilitate stress resilience and better outcome of treatment for depression.

FUTURE DIRECTIONS

We have described a psychosocial perspective that focuses on the course of unipolar depression. The perspective integrates stress and coping theory with an expanded paradigm for program evaluation. The findings that emerge from research guided by this perspective imply that life context factors and coping processes are associated with depressive symptoms, the allocation and outcome of treatment, and the process of recovery. The conceptual framework and the findings suggest some important directions for future research and potential clinical applications.

Applications to Other Clinical and Nonclinical Populations

Life context and coping factors play an important role in a variety of psychiatric disorders. We have focused on depression here, but other research has examined the role of life context factors and coping processes in the course of psychiatric disorders such as alcohol abuse and schizophrenia, and medical conditions such as arthritis and cancer. For example, in 6-month, 2-year, and 10-year follow-ups of residentially treated alcoholic patients, we found that posttreatment stressors and lack of social resources were associated with higher levels of alcohol consumption and more depressed mood and physical symptoms. Relapsed alcoholics experienced more stressful life circumstances and fewer social resources than did their remitted counterparts and demographically matched normal-drinking controls (Moos et al., 1990).

Schizophrenic patients who relapse experience more stressors (particularly parental conflict and excessive criticism from family members) over the course of their disorder than do matched controls and schizophrenic patients who remain remitted (for a review, see Kuipers & Bebbington, 1988). However, when neuroleptic medication is combined with intensive family treatment, the prevalence of relapse is markedly reduced (Falloon et al., 1982).

Although there are common psychosocial risk factors across some psychiatric disorders, there may be variations in the relative importance of such factors and in the level of a factor that places a person at risk. For example, Leff and Vaughn (1985) showed that two or more critical comments from family members predicted relapse among depressed patients, whereas seven or more was the threshold level for schizophrenic patients. Such a finding suggests that depressed persons may be especially sensitive to criticism. The identification of risk factors common to several disorders or unique to a particular disorder, and differences in threshold levels for defining risk, can yield important refinements in our models of psychiatric disorders and their treatment.

Psychosocial models are also applicable to a range of chronic medical conditions, as well as to the well-being of healthy individuals. In one group of community married couples, stressful life events, chronic difficulties, and lack of family support were associated with depressed mood (Cronkite & Moos, 1984). In a separate group of community adults, stressful life events and lack of family support were associated with both depressed mood and physical symptoms (Holahan & Moos, 1987). The presence of common processes related to normal fluctuations in psychological and physical well-being and to clinically diagnosed disorders may help integrate community-based and clinical studies. Moreover, comparisons across groups with different disorders, and with a control group, may help yield descriptive profiles of the psychosocial risk factors that are most salient for a particular disorder. For example, alcoholic patients reported more financial and friend-related stressors and fewer financial resources compared to depressed or arthritic patients, whereas all three of these patient groups experienced more stressors and fewer social resources in some domains compared to a community control group (Moos et al., 1989).

Positive Consequences of Adversity

Some people develop depression upon encountering life stressors, but many are remarkably resilient in the face of adversity. They may emerge from a crisis with new coping skills, more maturity and self-confidence, closer relationships with family and friends, and a richer appreciation of life. Such outcomes are not unusual. When asked about the impact of life crises they have experienced, up to 50% of the people report some positive outcomes (for an overview, see Schaefer & Moos, 1992). These positive outcomes are consistent with a dialectical view of change as necessary for human development, and with the view that life crises may be "constructive confrontations" that challenge an individual and foster personal growth. We need to expand our conceptual framework to encompass the idea that life stressors can lead to more personal maturity and effectiveness, and to identify the nature and determinants of

such outcomes. An understanding of the process of personal growth under adversity may help clinicians develop intervention programs to prevent and alleviate depression in vulnerable individuals.

Implications for Clinicians and Program Evaluators

Treatment is part of an open system, in which an intervention program is only one of multiple factors that influence psychiatric disorders and other aspects of adaptation. Our expanded evaluation paradigm can help to broaden the conventional psychotherapeutic framework by incorporating life context and coping processes as factors involved in the course of a disorder such as depression. Recognizing that stressful or relapse-inducing situations inevitably occur, clinicians can help identify coping and social resources that clients can acquire and draw upon to help them deal with these situations more effectively (Holahan & Moos, 1994).

Given the mixed evidence for the prognostic role of stressors in the course of depression, clinicians should consider the nature of the stressors, the likelihood that the preintake stressors will lead to subsequent stressful circumstances, and the severity of the depressive symptoms in making decisions about the most appropriate treatment (Moos, 1991).

Most coping skills training programs emphasize behavioral problem-solving strategies; however, cognitive strategies may be just as effective in promoting well-being and preventing relapse. In fact, cognitive coping processes can be used in all kinds of circumstances, including those in which behavioral options are unavailable. They can also serve to facilitate behavioral coping. These ideas are consistent with the secondary prevention program formulated by Sanchez-Craig, Wilkinson, and Walker (1987), who noted that recovering problem drinkers relied on cognitive coping at least as much as on behavioral coping. Moreover, Lewinsohn, Hoberman, and Clarke (1989) have proposed interventions that can help people utilize both cognitive and behavioral coping strategies.

An expanded evaluation paradigm and a stress and coping perspective can also enhance the awareness of clinicians and evaluation researchers to the personal and contextual factors involved in the course of depression and other health problems, and the need to consider life context and coping processes in planning and evaluating treatment. This framework may help to explain why conceptually different interventions seem to be equally effective in alleviating depression. Because of the dynamics of stress and coping processes, changes in one domain targeted by an intervention may cause a change in one of the other domains. For example, cognitive treatment is oriented toward modifying maladaptive attributions, but it may also alter individuals' coping responses and help to enhance their social resources. Likewise, an intervention designed to strengthen problem-solving coping skills may lead to improvement in social resources, which in turn may resolve or deter some life stressors.

The planning and evaluation of treatment for depression also applies to prevention programs. Prevention efforts may be aimed at strengthening personal resources, reducing stressors and enhancing social resources, and teaching cognitive and behavioral coping skills (Munoz, 1993). With improved understanding of the interplay of these factors in the process of relapse and remission, it should be possible to design more effective prevention and intervention programs that may prevent the development of depression and help affected individuals maintain recovery.

Acknowledgments. We express our appreciation to Joan Twohey and Caryn Cohen for their assistance in literature review and manuscript preparation. This work was supported by Department of Veterans Affairs Medical and Health Services Research and Development Service research funds, and by National Institute on Alcohol Abuse and Alcoholism Grant Nos. AA02863 and AA06699. Some of the material in this chapter is adapted from Holahan and Moos (1994), Moos (1991), and Moos and Schaefer (1993).

REFERENCES

Akiskal, H. S. (1991). An integrative perspective on recurrent mood disorders: The mediating role of personality. In J. Becker & A. Kleinman (Eds.), *Psychosocial aspects of depression* (pp. 215–235). Hillsdale, NJ: Erlbaum.

Akiskal, H. S., Hirschfeld, R. M. A., & Yerevanian, B. I. (1983). The relationship of personality to affective disorders: A critical review. *Archives of General Psychiatry, 40,* 801–810.

American Psychiatric Association. (1994). *Diagnostic and statistical manual of mental disorders* (4th ed.). Washington, DC: Author.

Andrews, G., Neilson, M., Hunt, C., Steward, G., & Kiloh, L. G. (1990). Diagnosis, personality and the long-term outcome of depression. *British Journal of Psychiatry, 157,* 13–18.

Aneshensel, C. S. (1985) The natural history of depressive symptoms: Implications for psychiatric epidemiology. *Research in Community and Mental Health, 5,* 45–75.

Aneshensel, C. S., & Frerichs, R. R. (1982). Stress, support, and depression: A longitudinal causal model. *Journal of Community Psychology, 10,* 363–376.

Avison, W. R., & Turner, R. J. (1988). Stressful life events and depressive symptoms: Disaggregating the effects of acute stressors. *Journal of Health and Social Behavior, 29,* 138–149.

Barerra, M. (1986). Distinctions between social support concepts, measures, and models. *American Journal of Community Psychology, 14,* 413–436.

Barnett, P. A., & Gotlib, I. H. (1988). Psychosocial functioning and depression: Distinguishing among antecedents, concomitants, and consequences. *Psychological Bulletin, 104,* 97–126.

Bell, R. A., LeRoy, J. B., & Stephenson, J. B. (1982). Evaluating the mediating effects of social support upon life events and depressive symptoms. *Journal of Community Psychology, 10,* 325–340.

Billings, A. G., Cronkite, R. C., & Moos, R. H. (1983). Social–environmental factors in unipolar depression: Comparisons of depressed patients and nondepressed controls. *Journal of Abnormal Psychology, 92,* 119–133.

Billings, A. G., & Moos, R. H. (1981). The role of coping responses and social resources in attenuating the impact of stressful life events. *Journal of Behavioral Medicine, 4,* 139–157.

Billings, A. G., & Moos, R. H. (1982a). Work stress and the stress-buffering roles of work and family resources. *Journal of Occupational Behavior, 3,* 215–232.

Billings, A. G., & Moos, R. H. (1982b). Social support and functioning among community and clinical groups: A panel model. *Journal of Behavioral Medicine, 5,* 295–311.

Billings, A. G., & Moos, R. H. (1982c). Family environments and adaptation: A clinically-applicable typology. *American Journal of Family Therapy, 10,* 26–38.

Billings, A. G., & Moos, R. H. (1984a). Coping, stress, and social resources among adults with unipolar depression. *Journal of Personality and Social Psychology, 46,* 877–891.

Billings, A. G., & Moos, R. H. (1984b). Treatment experiences of adults with unipolar depression: The influence of patient and life context factors. *Journal of Consulting and Clinical Psychology, 52,* 119–131.

Billings, A. G., & Moos, R. H. (1984c). Chronic and nonchronic unipolar depression: The differential role of environmental stressors and resources. *Journal of Nervous and Mental Disease, 172,* 1–11.

Billings, A. G., & Moos, R. H. (1985a). Life stressors and social resources affect posttreatment outcomes among depressed patients. *Journal of Abnormal Psychology, 94,* 140–153.

Billings, A. G., & Moos, R. H. (1985b). Psychosocial processes of remission in unipolar depression: Comparing depressed patients with matched community controls. *Journal of Consulting and Clinical Psychology, 53,* 314–325.

Blazer, D. G. (1983). Impact of late life depression on the social network. *American Journal of Psychiatry, 140,* 162–166.

Boyce, P., Parker, G., Barnett, B., Cooney, M., & Smith, F. (1991). Personality as a vulnerability factor to depression. *British Journal of Psychiatry, 159*, 106–114.

Brown, G. (1993). Life events and affective disorder: replications and limitations. *Psychosomatic Medicine, 55*, 248–259.

Brown, G. W., Bifulco, A., Harris, T. O., & Bridge, L. (1986). Life stress, chronic subclinical symptoms, and vulnerability to clinical depression. *Journal of Affective Disorders, 11*, 1–19.

Brown, G. W., & Harris, T. O. (1978). *Social origins of depression: A study of psychiatric disorder in women.* London: Tavistock.

Brown, G. W., & Harris, T. O. (Eds.). (1989). *Life Events and Illness.* New York: Guilford Press.

Catalano, R., & Dooley, D. (1977). Economic predictors of depressed mood and stressful life events. *Journal of Health and Social Behavior, 18*, 292–307.

Cohen, F. (1987). Measurement of coping. In S. V. Kasl & C. L. Cooper (Eds.), *Stress and health: Issues in research methodology* (pp. 283–305). New York: Wiley.

Cohen, S., & Wills, T. A. (1985). Stress, social support, and the buffering hypothesis. *Psychological Bulletin, 98*, 310–357.

Coyne, J. C., Aldwin, C., & Lazarus, R. S. (1981). Depression and coping in stressful episodes. *Journal of Abnormal Psychology, 90*, 439–447.

Coyne, J. C., & Downey, G. (1991). Social factors and psychopathology: Stress, social support, and coping processes. *Annual Review of Psychology, 42*, 401–425.

Coyne, J. C., Kessler, R. C., Tal, M., Turnbull, J., Wortman, C. B., & Greden, J. F. (1987). Living with a depressed person. *Journal of Consulting and Clinical Psychology, 55*, 347–352.

Coyne, J. C., Wortman, C. B., & Lehman, D. R. (1988). The other side of support: Emotional overinvolvement in miscarried helping. In B. H. Gottlieb (Ed.), *Marshaling social support* (pp. 305–330). Beverly Hills, CA: Sage.

Cronkite, R. C., & Moos, R. H. (1984). The role of predisposing and moderating factors in the stress–illness relationship. *Journal of Health and Social Behavior, 25*, 372–393.

Crook, T., & Eliot, J. (1980). Parental death during childhood and adult depression: A critical review of the literature. *Psychological Bulletin, 87*, 252–259.

Crowther, J. H. (1985). The relationship between depression and marital maladjustment: A descriptive study. *Journal of Nervous and Mental Disease, 173*, 227–231.

Dean, A., & Ensel, W. M. (1982). Modelling social support, life events, competence and depression in the context of age and sex. *Journal of Community Psychology, 10*, 392–408.

Dean, A., Kolody, B., & Wood, P. (1990). Effects of social support from various sources on depression in elderly persons. *Journal of Health and Social Behavior, 31*, 148–161.

Dobson, K. S. (1989). A meta-analysis of the efficacy of cognitive therapy for depression. *Journal of Consulting and Clinical Psychology, 57*, 414–419.

Dohrenwend, B. S., & Dohrenwend, B. P. (1974). A brief historical introduction to research on stressful life events. In B. P. Dohrenwend & B. S. Dohrenwend (Eds.), *Stressful life events: Their nature and effects* (pp. 1–5). New York: Wiley.

Duggan, C. F., Lee, A. S., & Murray, R. B. (1990). Does personality predict long-term outcome in depression? *British Journal of Psychiatry, 157*, 19–24.

Falloon, I. R. H., Boyd, J. L., McGill, C. W., Razani, J., Moss, H. B., & Gilderman, A. M. (1982). Family management in the prevention of exacerbations of schizophrenia. *New England Journal of Medicine, 306*, 1437–1440.

Fava, G. A., Munari, F., Pavan, L., & Kellner, R. (1981). Life events and depression: A replication. *Journal of Affective Disorders, 3*, 159–165.

Fehrenbach, P. A., & O'Leary, M. R. (1982). Interpersonal attraction and treatment decision in inpatient and outpatient psychiatric setting. In T. A. Wills (Ed.), *Basic processes in helping relationships* (pp. 13–36). New York: Academic Press.

Felton, B. J., & Shinn, M. (1992). Social integration and social support: Moving "social support" beyond the individual level. *Journal of Community Psychology, 20*, 103–115.

Finney, J. W., Mitchell, R. E., Cronkite, R. C., & Moos, R. H. (1984). Methodological issues in estimating main and interactive effects: Examples from coping/social support field. *Journal of Health and Social Behavior, 25*, 85–98.

Folkman, S., Lazarus, R. S., Dunkel-Schetter, C., DeLongis, A., & Gruen, R. J. (1986). Dynamics of a stressful encounter: Cognitive appraisal, coping, and encounter outcomes. *Journal of Personality and Social Psychology, 50*, 992–1003.

Fondacaro, M. R., & Moos, R. H. (1987). Social support and coping: A longitudinal analysis. *American Journal of Community Psychology, 15*, 653–673.

Fondacaro, M. R., & Moos, R. H. (1989). Life stressors and coping: A longitudinal analysis among depressed and nondepressed adults. *Journal of Community Psychology, 17*, 330–340.

Free, M. L., & Oei, T. P. S., (1989). Biological and psychological processes in the treatment and maintenance of depression. *Clinical Psychology Review, 9*, 653–688.

Gaston, L., Marmar, C. R., Thompson, L. W., & Gallagher, D. (1988). Relation of patient pretreatment characteristics to the therapeutic alliance in diverse psychotherapies. *Journal of Consulting and Clinical Psychology, 56*, 483–489.

Golding, J. (1989). Role occupancy and role-specific stress and social support as predictors of depression. *Basic and Applied Social Psychology, 10*, 173–195.

Gore, S. (1978). The effect of social support in moderating the health consequences of unemployment. *Journal of Health and Social Behavior, 19*, 157–165.

Greenberg, R. P., Bornstein, R. R., Greenberg, M. D., & Fisher, S. (1992). A metaanalysis of antidepressant outcome under "blinder" conditions. *Journal of Consulting and Clinical Psychology, 60*, 664–669.

Gutek, B. A., Repetti, R. L., & Silver, D. L. (1988). Nonwork roles and stress at work. In C. L. Cooper & R. Payne (Eds.), *Causes, coping and consequences of stress at work* (pp. 141–174). New York: Wiley.

Hammen, C. (1991). Generation of stress in the course of unipolar depression. *Journal of Abnormal Psychology, 100*, 555–561.

Hammen, C. (1992). Life events and depression: The plot thickens. *American Journal of Community Psychology, 20*, 179–193.

Hammen, C., Ellicott, A., Gitlin, M., & Jamison, K. R. (1989). Sociotropy/autonomy and vulnerability to specific life events in unipolar and bipolar patients. *Journal of Abnormal Psychology, 98*, 154–160.

Heppner, P. P. (1988). *The Problem Solving Inventory Manual*. Palo Alto, CA: Consulting Psychologists Press.

Holahan, C. J., & Moos, R. H. (1981). Social support and psychological distress: A longitudinal analysis. *Journal of Abnormal Psychology, 90*, 365–370.

Holahan, C. J., & Moos, R. H. (1987). The personal and contextual determinants of coping strategies. *Journal of Personality and Social Psychology, 52*, 946–955.

Holahan, C. J., & Moos, R. H. (1994). Life stressors and mental health: Advances in conceptualizing stress resistance. In B. Avison & I. H. Gotlib (Eds.), *Stress and mental health: Contemporary issues and prospects for the future* (pp. 213–238). New York: Plenum Press.

Hollon, S. D., DeRubeis, R. J., & Evans, M. D. (1987). Causal mediation of change in treatment for depression: Discriminating between nonspecificity and noncausality. *Psychological Bulletin, 102*, 139–149.

Holmes, T. H., & Rahe, R. H. (1967). The Social Readjustment Rating Scale. *Journal of Psychosomatic Research, 11*, 213–218.

Hooley, J., Orley, J., & Teasdale, J. (1986). Levels of expressed emotion and relapse in depressed patients. *British Journal of Psychiatry, 148*, 642–647.

Holt, R. R. (1982). Occupational stress. In L. Goldberger & W. Breznitz (Eds.), *Handbook of stress: Theoretical and clinical aspects* (pp. 419–444). New York: Free Press.

House, J. S. (1981). *Work stress and social support*. Reading, MA: Addison-Wesley.

House, J. S., Landis, K. R., & Umberson, D. (1988a). Social relationships and health. *Science, 241*, 540–545.

House, J. S., Umberson, D., & Landis, K. R. (1988b). Structure and processes of social support. *Annual Review of Sociology, 14*, 293–318.

Husaini, B. A., & Neff, J. A. (1980). Characteristics of life events and psychiatric impairment in rural communities. *Journal of Nervous and Mental Disease, 168*, 159–166.

Husaini, B. A., & Neff, J. A. (1981). Social class and depressive symptomatology: The role of life change events and locus of control. *Journal of Nervous and Mental Disease, 169*, 638–647.

Johnson, T. P. (1991). Mental health, social relations, and social selection: A longitudinal analysis. *Journal of Health and Social Behavior, 32*, 408–423.

Kahn, J., Coyne, J. C., & Margolin, G. (1985). Depression and marital disagreement: The social construction of despair. *Journal of Social and Personal Relationships, 2*, 447–461.

Kanner, A. D., Coyne, J. C., Schaefer, C., & Lazarus, R. S. (1981). Comparison of two modes of stress measurement: Daily hassles and uplifts versus major life events. *Journal of Behavioral Medicine, 4*, 1–39.

Kessler, R. C., Kendler, K. S., Heath, A. C., Neale, M.S., & Eaves, L. J. (1992). Social support, depressed mood, and adjustment to stress: A genetic epidemiologic investigation. *Journal of Personality and Social Psychology, 62*, 257–272.

Kessler, R. C., & McLeod, J. D. (1985). Social support and mental health in community samples. In S. Cohen & S. L. Syme (Eds.), *Social support and health* (pp. 219–240). Orlando, FL: Academic Press.

Kessler, R. C., Price, R. H., & Wortman, C. B. (1985). Social factors in psychopathology: Stress, social support, and coping processes. *Annual Review of Psychology, 36*, 531–572.

Klerman, G. L. (1989). Psychiatric diagnostic categories: Issues of validity and measurement—an invited comment on Mirowsky and Ross. *Journal of Health and Social Behavior, 30*, 26–32.

Klitzman, S., House, J. S., Israel, B. A., & Mero, R. P. (1990). Work stress, nonwork stress, and health. *Journal of Behavioral Medicine, 13*, 221–243.

Kohn, M. L., & Schooler, C. (1983). *Work and personality: An inquiry into the impact of social stratification*. Norwood, NJ: Ablex.

Koss, M. P., Butcher, J. N., & Strupp, H. H. (1986). Brief psychotherapy methods in clinical research. *Journal of Consulting and Clinical Psychology, 54*, 60–67.

Krantz, S., & Moos, R. H. (1988). Risk factors at intake predict nonremission among depressed patients. *Journal of Consulting and Clinical Psychology, 56*, 863–869.

Kuipers, L., & Bebbington, P. (1988). Expressed emotion research in schizophrenia: Theoretical and clinical implications. *Psychological Medicine, 18*, 893–909.

Lazarus, R. S., & Folkman, S. (1984). *Stress, appraisal, and coping*. New York: Springer.

Leavy, R. L. (1983). Social support and psychological disorder: A review. *Journal of Community Psychology, 11*, 3–21.

Leff, J., & Vaughn, E. (1985). *Expressed emotion in families: Its significance for mental illness*. New York: Guilford Press.

Leonard, B. E. (1986). Neurotransmitter receptors, endocrine responses, and the biological substrates of depression: A review. *Human Psychopharmacology, 1*, 3–21.

Leventhal, H., & Tomarken, A. (1987). Stress and illness: Perspectives from health psychology. In S. V. Kasl & C. L. Cooper (Eds.), *Stress and health: Issues in research methodology* (pp. 27–55). New York: Wiley.

Lewinsohn, P., Hoberman, H., & Clarke, G. (1989). The Coping with Depression Course: Review and future directions. *Canadian Journal of Behavioral Science, 21*, 470–493.

Lin, N., & Ensel, W. M. (1984). Depression mobility and its social etiology: The role of life events and social support. *Journal of Health and Social Behavior, 25*, 176–188.

Lloyd, C., Zisook, S., Click, M. J., & Jaffe, K. E. (1981). Life events and response to antidepressants. *Journal of Human Stress, 7*, 2–15.

Lopata, H.A., Barnewolt, D., & Norr, K. (1980). Spouses' contributions to each other's roles. In F. Pepitone-Rockwell (Ed.), *Dual-career couples* (pp. 111–141). Beverly Hills, CA: Sage.

Mattlin, J. A., Wethington, E., & Kessler, R. C. (1990). Situational determinants of coping and coping effectiveness. *Journal of Health and Social Behavior, 31*, 103–122.

Marziali, E. A. (1987). People in your life: Development of a social support measure for predicting psychotherapy outcome. *Journal of Nervous and Mental Disease, 175*, 327–338.

McFarlane, A. H., Norman, G. R., Streiner, D. L., Roy, R., & Scott, D. J. (1980). A longitudinal study of the influence of the psychosocial environment on health status: A preliminary report. *Journal of Health and Social Behavior, 21*, 124–133.

McLeod, J. (1992). Childhood parental loss and adult depression. *Journal of Health and Social Behavior, 32*, 205–220.

Menaghan, E. G., & Lieberman, M. A. (1986). Changes in depression following divorce: A panel study. *Journal of Marriage and the Family, 17*, 319–328.

Merikangas, K. R. (1984). Divorce and assortative mating among depressed patients. *American Journal of Psychiatry, 141*, 74–76.

Miller, I. W., Keitner, G. I., Whisman, M. A., Ryan, C. E., Epstein, N. B., & Bishop, D. S. (1992). Depressed patients with dysfunctional families: Description and course of illness. *Journal of Abnormal Psychology, 101*, 637–646.

Mirowsky, J., & Ross, C. E. (1989). Psychiatric diagnosis as reified measurement. *Journal of Health and Social Behavior, 30*, 11–25.

Mitchell, R. E., & Moos, R. H. (1984). Deficiencies in social support among depressed patients: Antecedents or consequences of stress? *Journal of Health and Social Behavior, 25*, 438–452.

Monroe, S. M., Bellack, A. S., Hersen, M., & Himmelhoch, J. M. (1983). Life events, symptom course, and treatment outcome in unipolar depressed women. *Journal of Consulting and Clinical Psychology, 51*, 604–615.

Monroe, S. M., Bromet, E. J., Connell, M. M., & Steiner, S. C. (1986). Social support, life events, and depressive symptoms: A one-year prospective study. *Journal of Consulting and Clinical Psychology, 54*, 424–431.

Monroe, S. M., & Depue, R. A. (1991). Life stress and depression. In J. Becker & A. Kleinman (Eds.), *Psychosocial aspects of depression* (pp. 101–130). Hillsdale, NJ: Erlbaum.

Monroe, S. M., Kupfer, D. J., & Frank, E. (1992). Life stress and treatment course of recurrent depression: 1. Response during index episode. *Journal of Consulting and Clinical Psychology, 60*, 718–724.

Moos, R. H. (1984). Context and coping: Toward a unifying conceptual framework. *American Journal of Community Psychology, 12*, 5–25.

Moos, R. H. (1985a). Creating healthy human contexts: Environmental and individual strategies. In J. Rosen & L. Solomon (Eds.), *Prevention in health psychology* (pp. 366–389). Hanover, NH: University Press of New England.

Moos, R. H. (1985b). Evaluating social resources in community and health care contexts. In P. Daroly (Ed.), *Measurement strategies in health psychology* (pp. 433–459). New York: Wiley.

Moos, R.H. (1990). Depressed outpatients' life contexts, amount of treatment, and treatment outcome. *Journal of Nervous and Mental Disease, 178*, 105–112.

Moos, R.H. (1991). Life stressors, social resources, and the treatment of depression. In J. Becker & A. Kleinman (Eds.), *Psychosocial aspects of depression* (pp. 187–214). Hillsdale, NJ: Erlbaum.

Moos, R.H. (1992). Understanding individuals' life contexts: Implications for stress reduction and prevention. In M. Kessler, S. E. Goldston, & J. Joffe (Eds.), *The present and future of prevention research* (pp. 196–213). Newbury Park, CA: Sage.

Moos, R. H., Brennan, P., Fondacaro, M., & Moos, B. (1990). Approach and avoidance coping responses among older problem and nonproblem drinkers. *Psychology and Aging, 5*, 31–40.

Moos, R. H., Fenn, C, Billings, A., & Moos, B. (1989). Assessing life stressors and social resources: Applications to alcoholic patients. *Journal of Substance Abuse, 1*, 135–152.

Moos, R. H., Finney, J. W., & Cronkite, R. C. (1990). *Alcoholism treatment: Context, process, and outcome.* New York: Oxford University Press.

Moos, R. H., & Mitchell, R. E. (1982). Conceptualizing and measuring social network resources. In T. A. Wills (Ed.), *Basic processes in helping relationships* (pp. 213–232). New York: Academic Press.

Moos, R. H., & Moos, B. (1992). *Life Stressors and Social Resources Inventory—Adult Form Manual.* Palo Alto, CA: Stanford University Medical Center, Center for Health Care Evaluation/Department of Veterans Affairs Medical Center.

Moos, R. H., & Schaefer, J. A. (1993). Coping resources and processes: Current concepts and measures. In L. Goldberger & S. Breznitz (Eds.), *Handbook of stress: Theoretical and clinical aspects* (2nd ed., pp. 234–257). New York: Free Press.

Munoz, R. F. (1993). The prevention of depression: Current research and practice. *Applied and Preventive Psychology, 2*, 21–33.

Murphy, E. (1983). The prognosis of depression in old age. *British Journal of Psychiatry, 142*, 111–119.

Nietzel, M. T., Russell, R. L., Hemmings, K. A., & Gretter, M. L. (1987). Clinical significance of psychotherapy for unipolar depression: A meta-analytic approach to social comparison. *Journal of Consulting and Clinical Psychology, 55*, 156–161.

Parker, G., Brown, L., & Blignault, I. (1986). Coping behaviors as predictors of the course of clinical depression. *British Journal of Psychiatry, 146*, 287–293.

Parkes, K. R. (1986). Coping in stressful episodes: The role of individual differences, environmental factors, and situational characteristics. *Journal of Personality and Social Psychology, 51*, 1277–1292.

Paykel, E. S. (1974). Life stress and psychiatric disorder: Applications of the clinical approach. In B. S. Dohrenwend & B. P. Dohrenwend (Eds.), *Stressful life events: Their nature and effects* (pp. 135–149). New York: Wiley.

Paykel, E. S. (1979). Causal relationships between clinical depression and life events. In J. E. Barrett (Ed.), *Stress and mental disorder* (pp. 71–86). New York: Raven Press.

Payne, R. L., & Jones, J. G. (1987). Measurement and methodological issues in social support. In S. V. Kasl & C. L. Cooper (Eds.), *Stress and health: Issues in research methodology* (pp. 167–205). New York: Wiley.

Pearlin, L. I. (1983). Role strains and personal stress. In H. B. Kaplan (Ed.), *Psychosocial stress: Trends in theory and research* (pp. 3–32). New York: Academic Press.

Pearlin, L. I. (1985). Social structure and processes of social support. In S. Cohen & L. Syme (Ed.), *Social support and health* (pp. 43–60). Orlando, FL: Academic Press.

Pearlin, L. I. (1989). The sociological study of stress. *Journal of Health and Social Behavior, 30*, 241–256.

Pearlin, L. I., & Lieberman, M. A. (1979). Social sources of emotional distress. In R. Simmons (Ed.), *Research in community and mental health* (pp. 217–248). Greenwich, CT: JAI Press.

Pearlin, L. I., Lieberman, M. A., Menaghan, E. G., & Mullan, J. T. (1981). The stress process. *Journal of Health and Social Behavior, 22*, 337–356.

Pearlin, L. I., & Schooler, C. (1978). The structure of coping. *Journal of Health and Social Behavior, 19*, 2–21.

Pearlin, L. I., & Turner, H. (1987). The family as a context of the stress process. In S. V. Kasl & C. L. Cooper (Eds.), *Stress and health: Issues in research methodology* (pp. 143–165). New York: Wiley.

Peterson, D., & Seligman, M. E. P. (1984). Causal explanation as a risk factor for depression: Theory and evidence. *Psychological Review, 91,* 347–374.

Phifer, J. F., & Murrell, S. A. (1986). Etiologic factors in the onset of depressive symptoms in older adults. *Journal of Consulting and Clinical Psychology, 95,* 282–291.

Reno, R. M., & Halaris, A. E. (1990). The relationship between life stress and depression in an endogenous sample. *Comprehensive Psychiatry, 31,* 25–33.

Repetti, R. (1987). Linkages between work and family roles. In S. Oskamp (Ed.), *Applied social psychology annual: Vol. 7. Family processes and problems* (pp. 98–127). Beverly Hills, CA: Sage.

Revicki, D. A., & May, H. J. (1985). Occupational stress, social support, and depression. *Health Psychology, 4,* 61–77.

Revicki, D. A., & May, H. J. (1989). Organizational characteristics, occupational stress, and mental health in nurses. *Behavioral Medicine, 15,* 30–36.

Revicki, D. A., Whitley, T. W., Gallery, M. E., & Allison, E. J., Jr. (1993). Impact of work environment characteristics on work-related stress and depression in emergency medicine residents: A longitudinal study. *Journal of Community and Applied Social Psychology, 3,* 273–284.

Robinson, L. A., Berman, J. S., & Neimeyer, R. A. (1990). Psychotherapy for the treatment of depression: A comprehensive review of controlled outcome research. *Psychological Bulletin, 108,* 30–49.

Rohde, P., Lewinsohn, P. M., Tilson, M., & Seeley, J. R. (1990). Dimensionality of coping and its relation to depression. *Journal of Personality and Social Psychology, 3,* 499–511.

Ross, C. E., & Mirowsky, J. (1979). A comparison of life event weighting schemes: Change, undesirability and effect-proportional indices. *Journal of Health and Social Behavior, 20,* 166–177.

Rounsaville, B. J., Chevron, E. S., Prusoff, B. A., Elkin, I., Imber, S., Sotsky, S., & Watkins, J. (1987). The relation between specific and general dimensions of the psychotherapy process in interpersonal psychotherapy of depression. *Journal of Consulting and Clinical Psychology, 55,* 379–384.

Rounsaville, B. J., Weissman, M. M., Prusoff, B. G., & Herzeg-Barron, R. L. (1979). Marital disputes and treatment outcome in depressed women. *Comprehensive Psychiatry, 20,* 483–489.

Sanchez-Craig, M., Wilkinson, E. A., & Walker, K. (1987). Theory and methods for secondary prevention of alcohol problems: A cognitively based approach. In W. M. Cox (Ed.), *Treatment and prevention of alcohol problems: A resource manual* (pp. 287–331). New York: Academic Press.

Sarason, B. R., Sarason, I. G., & Pierce, G. (Eds.). (1990). *Social support: An interactional view.* New York: Wiley.

Schaefer, C., Coyne, J. C., & Lazarus, R. S. (1981). The health-related functions of social support. *Journal of Behavioral Medicine, 4,* 381–406.

Schaefer, J. A., & Moos, R. H. (1991). *Work stressors and coping among staff in long term care.* Unpublished manuscript, Center for Health Care Evaluation, Department of Veterans Affairs Medical Center. Palo Alto, CA.

Schaefer, J. A., & Moos, R. H. (1992). Life crises and personal growth. In B. N. Carpenter (Ed.), *Personal coping: Theory, research, and application* (pp. 149–170). Westport, CT: Praeger.

Scheier, M. F., Weintraub, J. K., & Carver, C.S. (1986).

Coping with stress: Divergent strategies of optimists and pessimists. *Journal of Personality and Social Psychology, 51,* 1257–1264.

Shea, M. T., Pilkonis, P. A., Beckham, E., Collins, F. J., Eldin, I., Sotsky, S., & Docherty, J. F. (1990). Personality disorders and treatment outcome in the NIMH Treatment of Depression Collaborative Research Program. *American Journal of Psychiatry, 147,* 711–718.

Shrout, P. E., Link, B. G., Dohrenwend, B. P., Skodol, A. E., Stueve, A., & Mirotznik, J. (1989). Characterizing life events as risk factors for depression: The role of fateful loss events. *Journal of Abnormal Psychology, 98,* 460–467.

Spiegel, D., & Wissler, F. (1986). Family environment as a predictor of psychiatric rehospitalization. *American Journal of Psychiatry, 143,* 56–60.

Steinbrueck, S. M., Maxwell, S. E., & Howard, G. S. (1983). A meta-analysis of psychotherapy and drug therapy in the treatment of unipolar depression with adults. *Journal of Consulting and Clinical Psychology, 51,* 856–863.

Steinmetz, J. L., Lewinsohn, P. H., & Antonuccio, E. O. (1983). Prediction of individual outcome in a group intervention for depression. *Journal of Consulting and Clinical Psychology, 51,* 331–337.

Streiner, D. L., Norman, G. R., McFarlane, A. H., & Roy, R. G. (1981). Quality of life events and their relationship to strain. *Schizophrenia Bulletin, 7,* 34–42.

Surtees, P. G. (1980). Social support, residual adversity, and depressive outcome. *Social Psychiatry, 15,* 71–80.

Surtees, P. G., & Ingham, J. G. (1980). Life stress and depressive outcome: Application of a dissipation model to life events. *Social Psychiatry, 15,* 21–31.

Swartz, M., Carrol, B., & Blazer, D. (1989). In response to "Psychiatric diagnosis as reified measurement": An invited comment on Mirowsky and Ross. *Journal of Health and Social Behavior, 30,* 33–34.

Swindle, R., Jr., Cronkite, R., & Moos, R. H. (1989). Life stressors, social resources, coping, and the 4-year course of unipolar depression. *Journal of Abnormal Psychology, 98,* 468–477.

Swindle, R., Jr., & Moos, R. H. (1992). Life domains in stressors, coping, and adjustment. In W. B. Walsh, R. Price, & K. B. Craik (Eds.), *Person environment psychology: Models and perspectives* (pp. 1–33). Hillsdale, NJ: Erlbaum.

Tennant, C. (1988). Parental loss in childhood. *Archives of General Psychiatry, 45,* 1045–1050.

Thoits, P. (1982). Conceptual, methodological, and theoretical problems in studying social support as a buffer against life stress. *Journal of Health and Social Behavior, 23,* 145–159.

Thoits, P. (1983). Dimensions of life events that influence psychological distress. In H. B. Kaplan (Ed.), *Psychosocial stress: Trends in theory and research* (pp. 33–103). New York: Academic Press.

Thoits, P. (1986). Social support as coping assistance. *Journal of Consulting and Clinical Psychology, 54,* 416–423.

Thomas, S. P., Wilt, D., & Noffsinger, A. (1988). Pathophysiology of depressive illness: Review of the literature and case example. *Issues in Mental Health Nursing, 9,* 271–284.

Tweed, D. L., & George, L. K. (1989). A more balanced perspective on "Psychiatric diagnosis as reified measurement": An invited comment on Mirowsky and Ross. *Journal of Health and Social Behavior, 30,* 35–37.

Vanfossen, B. E. (1981). Sex differences in the mental

health effects of spouse support and equity. *Journal of Health and Social Behavior, 22,* 130–143.

Vaughn, C., & Leff, J. (1976). The influence of family and social factors on the course of psychiatric illness. *British Journal of Psychiatry, 129,* 125–137.

Veiel, H. O. F. (1993). Detrimental effects of kin support networks on the course of depression. *Journal of Abnormal Psychology, 102,* 419–429.

Weiss, R. S. (1985). Men and the family. *Family Process, 24,* 49–58.

Wells, K. B., Burnam, M. A., Rogers, W., Hays, R., & Camp, P. (1992). The course of depression in adult outpatients: Results from the Medical Outcomes Study. *Archives of General Psychiatry, 49,* 788–794.

Wethington, E., & Kessler, R. C. (1986). Perceived support, received support, and adjustment to stressful life events. *Journal of Health and Social Behavior, 27,* 78–89.

Wheaton, B. (1983). Stress, personal coping resources, and psychiatric symptoms: An investigation of interactive models. *Journal of Health and Social Behavior, 24,* 208–229.

Wheaton, B. (1994). Sampling the stress universe. In W. R. Avison & I. H. Gotlib (Eds.), *Stress and mental health: Contemporary issues and prospects for the future* (pp. 77–114). New York: Plenum Press.

Zimmerman, M., Pfohl, B., Coryell, W. S., & Stangl, D. (1987). The prognostic validity of DSM-III Axis IV in depressed patients. *American Journal of Psychiatry, 144,* 102–106.

APPENDICES

APPENDIX A

Instruments for Assessing Depression in Adults

J. CHRIS NORDGREN

ATTRIBUTIONAL STYLE QUESTIONNAIRE (ASQ)

Description: The ASQ is designed to assess habitual ways that individuals construe causality. It is divided into six positive and six negative scenes for which subjects provide cause if this event were to happen to them. The cause is then rated along the dimensions of internality, stability, and globality.

Address where the test may be obtained: Martin E. P. Seligman, Department of Psychology, University of Pennsylvania, 3813 Walnut Street, Philadelphia, PA 19104.

Cost: Contact the author.

Reference

Peterson, C., Semmel, A., von Baeyer, C., Abramson, L. T., Metalsky, G. I., & Seligman, M. E. P. (1982). The Attributional Style Questionnaire. *Cognitive Therapy and Research*, 6, 287–300.

BECK DEPRESSION INVENTORY (BDI)

Description: The BDI is a 21-item, self-administered inventory that asks patients to rate how intense their experience of 21 attitudes and symptoms of depression has been over the past week. Each item has three options, which are ranked on a scale of 0 to 3 from the lowest to highest intensity, respectively. Items are written at a fifth- to sixth-grade reading level, and the inventory takes only a few minutes to complete and score.

Address where the test may be obtained: The Psychological Corporation, P.O. Box 839954, San Antonio, TX 78283.

Cost: $24.00 for a package of 25 BDI forms.

References

Beck, A. T., Rush, A. J., Shaw, B. F., & Emery, G. (1979). *Cognitive therapy of depression*. New York: Guilford Press.

Beck, A. T., Steer, R., & Garbin, M. (1988). Psychometric properties of the Beck Depression Inventory: Twenty-five years of evaluation. *Clinical Psychology Review, 8*, 77–100.

CENTER FOR EPIDEMIOLOGIC STUDIES DEPRESSION (CES-D) SCALE

Description: The CES-D Scale is a 20-item self-report scale of symptoms of depression, scaled by frequency of occurrence during the past week. It is suitable for use in general adult and older adolescent populations, and can be self-administered or scored by an interviewer.

Address where the test may be obtained: Epidemiology and Psychopathology Research Branch, Room 10C-05, National Institute of Mental Health, 5600 Fishers Lane, Rockville, MD 20857.

Cost: None.

References

Radloff, L. S. (1977). The CES-D Scale: A self-report depression scale for research in the general population. *Applied Psychological Measurement, 1*, 385–401.

Radloff, L. S., & Locke, B. Z. (1986). The Community Health Assessment Survey and the CES-D Scale. In M. Weissman, J. Meyers, & C. Ross (Eds.), *Community surveys*. New Brunswick, NJ: Rutgers University Press.

DIAGNOSTIC INTERVIEW SCHEDULE (DIS), VERSION III-R

Description: The DIS is a fully structured interview that is designed to make approximately 40 DSM-

III-R (and/or DSM-III) diagnoses, including the affective disorders. The DIS can be administered by a lay interviewer after approximately 5 days of training. It may be scored by a personal computer, and it includes three versions, allowing selection of a reduced list of disorders. The DIS 4.0, an updated version of the DIS that will include DSM-IV disorders, has been under development and may be available in 1995.

Address where the test may be obtained: Lee Robins, Department of Psychiatry, Washington University School of Medicine, 4940 Children's Place, St. Louis, MO 63110.

Cost: Contact the authors for current prices.

References

Boyd, J. H., Robins, L. N., & Burke, J. D. (1985). Making diagnoses from DIS data. In W. W. Eaton & L. G. Kessler (Eds.), *Epidemiologic field methods in psychiatry: The NIMH Epidemiologic Catchment Area Program.* New York: Academic Press.

Robins, L., & Regier, D. A. (1991). *Psychiatric disorders in America.* New York: Free Press.

GERIATRIC DEPRESSION SCALE (GDS)

Description: The GDS was specifically created for aged subjects. It was designed to be simple to administer, reliable, and valid with an elderly population. The test consists of 30 yes–no items that ask about nonsomatic symptoms and may be administered orally or in writing.

Address where the test may be obtained: T. L. Brink, 1103 North Church Street, Redlands, CA 92374.

Cost: Contact the author.

References

Brink, T. L., Yesavage, J. A., Lum, O., Heersema, P., Adey, M., & Rose, T. L. (1982). Screening tests for geriatric depression. *Clinical Gerontologist, 1,* 37–43.

Yesavage, J. A., Brink, T. L., Rose, T. L., Lum, O., Huang, V., Adey, M., & Leirer, V. O. (1983). Development and validation of a geriatric depression screening scale. *Journal of Psychiatric Research, 17,* 37–49.

PLEASANT EVENTS SCHEDULE (PES)

Description: The PES is a 320-item self-report inventory that was developed to measure the degree and frequency of enjoyment in pleasant activities for the behavioral assessment of depression. The instructions call for the subject to rate each item on two 3-point scales—one for frequency of occurrence during the last month, and the other for subjective enjoyability. The PES provides mean frequency and enjoyability scores, and a cross-product score based on the product of the frequency and enjoyability ratings for each item is computed for all the items and for various subscales.

Address where the test may be obtained: Peter M. Lewinsohn, Oregon Research Institute, 1715 Franklin Boulevard, Eugene, OR 97403.

Cost: $5.00.

References

Lewinsohn, P. M., & Amenson, C. S. (1978). Some relations between pleasant and unpleasant mood related events and depression. *Journal of Abnormal Psychology, 87,* 644–654.

MacPhillamy, D. J., & Lewinsohn, P. M. (1982). The Pleasant Events Schedule: Studies of reliability, validity and scale intercorrelations. *Journal of Consulting and Clinical Psychology, 50,* 363–380.

RASKIN THREE-AREA SCALE

Description: This scale is a clinician-rated instrument measuring depressive symptomatology in the three areas of "Verbal Report," "Behavior," and "Secondary Symptoms of Depression." Each is rated on a 5-point scale from 1 = "not at all" to 5 = very much." The three area scores are summed, producing total scores from 3–15.

Address where the test may be obtained: Allen Raskin, Department of Psychiatry, University of Maryland School of Medicine, 645 West Redwood Street, Baltimore, MD 21201.

Cost: None.

References

Raskin, A., Schulterbrandt, J. G., Reatig, N., Crook, T. H., & Odle, D. (1974). Depression subtypes and response to phenelzine, diazepam, and a placebo: Results of a nine-hospital collaborative study. *Archives of General Psychiatry, 30,* 66–75.

Raskin, A., Schulterbrandt, J. G., Reatig, N., & Rice, C. E. (1967). Factors of psychopathology in interview, ward behavior, and self-report ratings of hospitalized depressives. *Journal of Consulting Psychology, 31,* 270–278.

SCHEDULE FOR AFFECTIVE DISORDERS AND SCHIZOPHRENIA (SADS)

Description: The SADS is a procedure designed to aid in obtaining the information needed to make diagnoses of current and past episodes of mental disorder using the Research Diagnostic Criteria.

Part I of the SADS also has items that allow detailed dimensional measures of psychopathology for the current condition, including a subset of items for the week prior to evaluation. Part II has diagnostic and prognostic information for the period prior to the current condition.

Address where the test may be obtained: Jean Endicott, Department of Research Assessment and Training, New York State Psychiatric Institute, Box 123, 722 West 168th Street, New York, NY 10032.

Cost: Obtainable upon request from the address above.

References

Endicott, J. (1986). Schedule for Affective Disorders and Schizophrenia, Regular and Change versions: Measure of depression. In N. Sartorius & T. A. Ban (Eds.), *Assessment of depression*. Heidelberg: Springer-Verlag.

Endicott, J., & Spitzer, R. L. (1978). A Diagnostic interview: The Schedule for Affective Disorders and Schizophrenia. *Archives of General Psychiatry, 35,* 837–844.

STRUCTURED CLINICAL INTERVIEW FOR AXIS I DSM-IV DISORDERS (SCID VERSION 2.0)

Description: The SCID Version 2.0 is a semistructured interview for making Axis I diagnoses, including current and past mood disorders in adult patients (age 18 and over). It is for use by trained mental health professionals who are already familiar with DSM-IV criteria. The Current Major Depressive Syndrome section provides a series of structured prompts intended to elicit the necessary information for determining the patient's status on each DSM-IV major depressive syndrome criterion. This section also covers major depression subtypes and mood disorders secondary to substance abuse and general medical conditions. The SCID Version 2.0 contains other sections with diagnostic prompts for dysthymic disorder, bipolar disorders, and research criteria for mixed anxiety–depressive disorder.

Address where the test may be obtained: Division of Publications and Marketing, American Psychiatric Association, 1400 K Street N.W., Washington, DC 20005.

Cost: Contact the publisher for current prices.

References

First, M., Spitzer, L., Gibbon, M., & Williams, J. (1995a). *Structured Clinical Interview for Axis I DSM-IV Disorders (SCID Version 2.0)*. Washington, DC: American Psychiatric Press.

First, M., Spitzer, L., Gibbon, M., & Williams, J. (1995b). *User's Guide for Structured Clinical Interview for Axis I DSM-IV Disorders (SCID Version 2.0)*. Washington, DC: American Psychiatric Press.

HAMILTON RATING SCALE FOR DEPRESSION (HRSD)

Description: The HRSD was first published in the *Journal of Neurology, Neurosurgery and Psychiatry* (1960) by Max Hamilton, and several variations of the scale later followed. The 1967 version of the scale by Hamilton, published in the *British Journal of Social and Clinical Psychology*, has 21 items and is reproduced below with the permission of the British Psychological Society and The British Medical Association.

Another version of the HRSD was developed for the NIMH Early Clinical Drug Evaluation Program (ECDEU). This is a more structured version of the scale, including anchor points for rating differing levels on each item. The NIMH Treatment of Depression Collaborative Research Program used this scale with modifications to include items addressing hypersomnia, increased appetite, and weight gain. This expanded ECDEU version is reprinted below, following Hamilton's 1967 version. The most commonly used scoring approaches to the ECDEU are the 17-item version (items 1–20 as given below, excluding items 7, 14, and 19) and the 20-item scale (the 17-item version combined with items 22–24 as given below).

Hamilton did not believe that the ECDEU anchors alone constituted an adequate version of the HRSD. The ECDEU version of the scale is included here because it is widely used in research and can serve as a useful adjunct to the original scale.

The HRSD is administered in an interview format; however, it does not include specific probes for the items, and there are no universally accepted questions to probe for item information. Suggested probes have been proposed by G. L. Klerman and colleagues (1984) in *Interpersonal Psychotherapy of Depression* (New York: Basic Books) and by J. M. G. Williams (1984) in *Psychological Treatment of Depression* (New York: Free Press). Because there are so many different versions of the HRSD, research with the scale should specify which one was included.

References

Hamilton, M. (1960). A rating scale for depression. *Journal of Neurology, Neurosurgery and Psychiatry, 12,* 56–62.

Hamilton, M. (1967). Development of a rating scale for primary depressive illness. *British Journal of Social and Clinical Psychology, 6,* 278–296.

The HRSD Rating of Male Patients

1. Depression (0–4)

Depressed mood is not easy to assess. One looks for a gloomy attitude, pessimism about the future, feelings of hopelessness and a tendency to weep. As a guide, occasional weeping could count as 2, frequent weeping as 3, and severe symptoms allotted 4 points. When patients are severely depressed they may "go beyond weeping." It is important to remember that patients interpret the word "depression" in all sorts of strange ways. A useful common phrase is "lowering of spirits."

2. Guilt (0–4)

This is fairly easy to assess but judgement is needed, for the rating is concerned with pathological guilt. From the patient's point of view, some action of his which precipitated a crisis may appear as a "rational" basis for self-blame, which persists even after recovery from his illness. For example, he may have accepted a promotion, but the increased responsibility precipitated his breakdown. When he "blames" himself for this, he is ascribing a cause and not necessarily expressing pathological guilt. As a guide to rating, feelings of self-reproach count 1, ideas of guilt 2, belief that the illness might be a punishment 3, and delusions of guilt, with or without hallucinations, 4 points.

3. Suicide (0-4)

The scoring ranges from feeling that life is not worth living 1, wishing he were dead 2, suicidal ideas and half-hearted attempts 3, serious attempts 4. Judgement must be used when the patient is considered to be concealing this symptom, or conversely, when is using suicidal threats as a weapon, to intimidate others, obtain help and so on.

4., 5., 6. Insomnia (Initial, Middle and Delayed) (0–2)

Mild, trivial and infrequent symptoms are given 1 point, obvious and severe symptoms are rated 2 points; both severity and frequency should be taken into account. Middle insomnia (disturbed sleep during the night) is the most difficult to assess, possibly because it is an artifact of the system of rating. When insomnia is severe, it generally affects all phases. Delayed insomnia (early morning wakening) tends not to be relieved by hypnotic drugs and is not often present without other forms of insomnia.

7. Work and Interests (0–4)

It could be argued that the patient's loss of interest in his work and activities should be rated from his decreased performance, but it has been found too difficult to do so in practice. Care should be taken not to include fatiguability and lack of energy here; the rating is concerned with loss of efficiency and the extra effort required to do anything. When the patient has to be admitted to hospital because his symptoms render him unable to carry on, this should be rated 4 points, but not if he has been admitted for investigation or observation. When the patient improves he will eventually return to work, but when he does so may depend on the nature of his work; judgement must be used here.

8. Retardation (0–4)

Severe forms of this symptom are rare, and the mild forms are difficult to perceive. A slight flattening of affect and fixity of expression rate as 1, a monotonous voice, a delay in answering questions, a tendency to sit motionless count as 2. When retardation makes the interview extremely prolonged and almost impossible, it is rated 3, and 4 is given when an interview is impossible (and symptoms cannot be rated). Although some patients may say that their thinking is slowed or their emotional responsiveness has been diminished, questions about these manifestations usually produce misleading answers.

9. Agitation (0–4)

Severe agitation is extremely rare. Fidgetiness at interview rates as 1, obvious restlessness with picking at hands and clothes should count as 2. If the patient has to get up during the interview he is given 3, and 4 points are given when the interview has to be conducted "on the run," with the patient pacing up and down, picking at his face and hair and tearing at his clothes. Although agitation and retardation may appear to be opposed forms of behavior, in mild form they can co-exist.

10. Anxiety (Psychic Symptoms) (0–4)

Many symptoms are included here, such as tension and difficulty in relaxing, irritability, worrying over trivial matters, apprehension and feelings of panic, fears, difficulty in concentration and forgetfulness, "feeling jumpy." The rating should be based on pathological changes that have occurred during the illness and an effort should be made to discount the features of a previous anxious disposition.

11. Anxiety (Somatic Symptoms) (0–4)

These consist of the well-recognized effects of autonomic overactivity in the respiratory, cardiovascular, gastrointestinal and urinary systems. Patients may also complain of attacks of giddiness, blurring of vision and tinnitus.

12. Gastrointestinal Symptoms (0–2)

The characteristic symptom in depression is loss of appetite and this occurs very frequently. Constipation also occurs but is relatively uncommon. On rare occasions patients will complain of "heavy feelings" in the abdomen. Symptoms of indigestion, wind and pain, etc. are rated under Anxiety.

13. General Somatic Symptoms (0–2)

These fall into two groups: the first is fatiguability, which may reach the point where the patients feel tired all the time. In addition, patients complain of "loss of energy" which appears to be related to difficulty in starting up an activity. The other type of symptom consists of diffuse muscular achings, ill-defined and often difficult to locate, but frequently in the back and sometimes in the limbs; these may also feel "heavy."

14. Loss of Libido (0–2)

This is a common and characteristic symptom of depression, but it is difficult to assess in older men and especially those; e.g., unmarried, whose sexual activity is usually at a low level. The assessment is based on a pathological change, i.e., a deterioration obviously related to the patient's illness. Inadequate or no information should be rated as zero.

15. Hypochondriasis (0–4)

The severe states of this symptom, concerning delusions and hallucinations of rotting and blockages, etc., which are extremely uncommon in men, are rated at 4. Strong convictions of the presence of some organic disease which accounts for the patient's condition are rated 3. Much preoccupation with physical symptoms and with thoughts of organic disease are rated 2. Excessive preoccupation with bodily functions is the essence of a hypochondriacal attitude and trivial or doubtful symptoms count as 1 point.

16. Loss of Insight (0–2)

This is not necessarily present when the patient denies that he is suffering from mental disorder. It may be that he is denying that he is insane and may willingly recognize that he has a "nervous" illness. In case of doubt, enquiries should be directed to the patient's attitude to his symptoms of guilt and hypochondriasis.

17. Loss of Weight (0–2)

The simplest way to rate this would be to record the amount of loss, but many patients do not know their normal weight. For this reason, an obvious or severe loss is rated as 2 and a slight or doubtful loss as 1 point.

18. Diurnal Variation (0–2)

This symptom has been excluded from the rating scale as it indicates the type of illness, rather than presenting an addition to the patient's disabilities. The commonest form consists of an increase of symptoms in the morning, but this is only slightly greater than worsening in the evening. A small number of patients insist that they feel worse in the afternoon. The clear presence of diurnal variation is rated as 2 and the doubtful presence is 1 point.

The following three symptoms were excluded from the rating of symptoms because they occur with insufficient frequency, but they are of interest in research.

19. Derealization and Depersonalization (0–4)

The patient who has this symptom quickly recognizes the questions asked of him; when he has difficulty in understanding the questions it usually signifies that the symptom is absent. When the patient asserts that he has this symptom it is necessary to question him closely; feelings of "distance" usually mean nothing more than that the patient lacks concentration or interest in his surroundings. It would appear that the severe forms of this symptom are extremely rare in patients diagnosed as depressive.

20. Paranoid Symptoms (0–4)

These are uncommon, and affirmative answers should always be checked carefully. It is of no significance if the patient says that others talk about him, since this is usually true. What is important in the mild symptom is the patient's attitude of suspicion, and the malevolence imputed to others. Doubtful or trivial suspicion rates as 1, thoughts that others wish him harm [rate] as 2, delusions that others wish him harm or are trying to do so [rate] as 3, and hallucinations are given 4 points. Care should be taken not to confuse this symptom with that of guilt, "people are saying that I am wicked."

21. Obsessional Symptoms (0–2)

These should be differentiated from preoccupations with depressive thoughts, ideas of guilt, hypochondriacal preoccupations and paranoid thinking. Patients usually have to be encouraged to admit to these symptoms, but their statements should be checked carefully. True obsessional thoughts are recognized by the patient as coming from his own mind, as being alien to his normal outlook and feelings, and as causing great anxiety; he always struggles against them.

The HRSD Rating of Female Patients

The same general principles apply to the rating of women as of men, but there are special problems which need to be considered in detail.

1. Depression (0–4)

It is generally believed that women weep more readily than men, but there is little evidence that this is true in the case of depressive illness. There is no reason to believe, at the moment, that an assessment of the frequency of weeping could be misleading when rating the intensity of depression in women.

○○○○○

7. Work and Interests (0–4)

Most women are housewives and therefore their work can be varied, both in quantity and intensity, to suit themselves. Women do not often complain of work being an effort, but they say they have to take things easily, or neglect some of their work. Other members of the family may have to increase the help they give. It is rare for a housewife to stop looking after her home completely. If she has an additional job outside the home she may have to change it to part-time, or reduce her hours of work or even give it up completely. Women engage in hobbies less frequently than men. Loss of interest, therefore, may not be as obvious. Patients may complain of inability to feel affection for their families. This could be rated here, but it could be rated under other symptoms, depending upon its meaning and setting. Care should be taken not to rate it in two places. It is a very valuable and important symptom if the patient mentions it spontaneously but could be very misleading as a reply to a question.

○○○○○

11. Anxiety (Somatic Symptoms)(0–4)

These last three symptoms [i.e., attacks of giddiness, blurring of vision, and tinnitus] appear to be more common in women than in men.

○○○○○

13. General Somatic Symptoms (0–2)

It is not uncommon for women to complain of backache and to ascribe it to a pelvic disorder. This symptom requires careful questioning.

14. Loss of Libido (0–2)

In women whose sexual experience is satisfactory, this symptom will appear as increasing frigidity, progressing to active dislike of sexual intercourse. Women who are partially or completely frigid find that their customary toleration of sex also changes to active dislike. It is difficult to rate this symptom in women who have had no sexual experience or, indeed, in widows since loss of libido in women tends to appear not so much as a loss of drive but as a loss of responsiveness. In the absence of adequate information of a pathological change a zero rating should be given. Disturbed menstruation and amenorrhoea have been described in women suffering from severe depression, but they are very rare. Despite the difficulties in rating, it has been found that the mean score for women is negligibly less than for men.

ECDEU Version of the HRSD Used in the NIMH Treatment of Depression Collaborative Research Program

Instructions. Using the key beneath each symptom, please fill in the blank to the far right with the number that best describes that symptoms's severity.

1. Depressed Mood (sadness, hopeless, helpless, worthless) _____
   0 = Absent.
   1 = These feeling states indicated only on questioning.
   2 = These feeling states spontaneously reported verbally.
   3 = Communicates feeling states nonverbally—that is, through facial expression, posture, voice, and tendency to weep.
   4 = Patient reports VIRTUALLY ONLY these feeling states in his spontaneous verbal and nonverbal communications.

2. Feeling of Guilt _____
   0 = Absent.
   1 = Self-reproach, feels he/she has let people down.
   2 = Ideas of guilt or rumination over past errors or sinful deeds.
   3 = Present illness is a punishment. Delusions of guilt.
   4 = Hears accusatory or denunciatory voices and/or experiences threatening visual hallucinations.

3. Suicide _____
   0 = Absent.
   1 = Feels life is not worth living.
   2 = Wishes he/she were dead or any thoughts of possible death to self.

   3 = Suicide ideas or gesture.
   4 = Attempts at suicide (any serious attempt rates 4)

4. Insomnia Early _____
   0 = No difficulty falling asleep.
   1 = Complains of occasional difficulty falling asleep—that is, more than a half hour.
   2 = Complains of nightly difficulty falling asleep.

5. Insomnia Middle _____
   0 = No difficulty.
   1 = Patient complains of being restless and disturbed during the night.
   2 = Waking during the night—any getting out of bed rates 2 (except for purposes of voiding).

6. Insomnia Late _____
   0 = No difficulty.
   1 = Waking in early hours of the morning but goes back to sleep.
   2 = Unable to fall asleep again if he/she gets out of bed.

7. Hypersomnia _____
   0 = No difficulty.
   1 = Frequently sleeps at least one hour or more (or spends one hour or more in bed) than when not depressed.
   2 = Frequently sleeps two or more hours (or spends two or more hours in bed) than when not depressed.

8. Work and Activities _____
   0 = No difficulty.
   1 = Thoughts and feelings of incapacity, fatigue, or weakness related to activities: work or hobbies.
   2 = Loss of interest in activity: hobbies or work—either directly reported by patient, or indirect in listlessness, indecision and vacillation (feels he/she has to push self to work or activities).
   3 = Decrease in actual time spent in activities or decrease in productivity.
   4 = Stopped working because of present illness.

9. Retardation (slowness of thought and speech; impaired ability to concentrate; decreased motor activity) _____
   0 = Normal speech and thought.
   1 = Slight retardation at interview.
   2 = Obvious retardation at interview.
   3 = Interview difficult.
   4 = Complete stupor.

10. Agitation _____
   0 = None.
   1 = Fidgetiness.
   2 = Playing with hands, hair, etc.
   3 = Moving about, can't sit still.
   4 = Handwringing, nail-biting, hair-pulling, biting of lips.

11. Anxiety Psychic _____

0 = No difficulty.

1 = Subjective tension and irritability.

2 = Worrying about minor matters.

3 = Apprehensive attitude apparent in face or speech.

4 = Fears expressed without questioning.

12. Anxiety Somatic (physiological concomitants of anxiety such as: Gastrointestinal—dry mouth, wind, indigestion, diarrhea, cramps, belching; Cardiovascular—palpitations, headaches; Respiratory—hyperventilation, sighing; Urinary frequency; Sweating) _____

0 = Absent.

1 = Mild.

2 = Moderate.

3 = Severe.

4 = Incapacitating.

13. Somatic Symptoms Gastrointestinal _____

0 = None.

1 = Loss of appetite but eating without encouragement. Heavy feeling in abdomen.

2 = Difficulty eating without urging. Requests or requires laxatives or medication for bowels or medication for G.I. symptoms.

14. Increased Appetite _____

0 = Not present.

1 = Mild to moderate increase in hunger, increased eating.

2 = Hungry all the time, uncontrolled eating.

15. Somatic Symptoms General _____

0 = None.

1 = Heaviness in limbs, back, or head. Backaches, headaches, muscle aches. Loss of energy and fatigability.

2 = Any clear-cut symptom rates 2.

16. Genital Symptoms (symptoms such as loss of libido, menstrual disturbances) _____

0 = Absent.

1 = Mild.

2 = Severe.

17. Hypochondriasis _____

0 = Not present.

1 = Self-absorption (bodily).

2 = Preoccupation with health.

3 = Frequent complaints, requests for help, etc.

4 = Hypochondriacal delusions.

18. Loss of Weight _____

0 = No weight loss.

1 = Probable weight loss associated with present illness.

2 = Definite (according to patient) weight loss.

19. Weight Gain _____

0 = No weight gain.

1 = Probable weight gain associated with present illness.

2 = Definite (according to patient) weight gain.

20. Insight _____

0 = Acknowledges being depressed and ill (or no longer depressed).

1 = Acknowledges illness but attributes cause to bad food, climate, overwork, virus, need for rest, etc.

2 = Denies being ill at all.

21. Diurnal Variation

A. Note whether symptoms are worse in morning or evening. _____
   If NO diurnal variation, record "0"
   0 = No variation.
   1 = Worse in A.M.
   2 = Worse in P.M.

B. When present, mark the severity of the variation. _____
   Record "0" if NO variation
   0 = None.
   1 = Mild.
   2 = Severe.

22. Depersonalization and Derealization (such as feelings of unreality, nihilistic ideas) _____

0 = Absent.

1 = Mild.

2 = Moderate.

3 = Severe.

4 = Incapacitating.

23. Paranoid Symptoms _____

0 = None.

1 = Suspicious.

2 = Ideas of reference.

3 = Delusions of reference and persecution.

24. Obsessional and Compulsive Symptoms _____

0 = Absent.

1 = Mild.

2 = Severe.

25. Helplessness _____

0 = Not present.

1 = Subjective feelings which are elicited only by inquiry.

2 = Patient volunteers his helpless feelings.

3 = Requires urging, guidance, and reassurance to accomplish work, household, and other chores.

4 = Despite urging, does not perform necessary chores because of feelings of helplessness.

26. Hopelessness _____

0 = Not present.

1 = Intermittently doubts that "things will improve," but can be reassured.

2 = Consistently feels "hopeless" but accepts reassurance.

3 = Expresses feelings of discouragement, despair, pessimism regarding the future which cannot be dispelled.

4 = Spontaneously and inappropriately perseverrates, "I'll never get well" or equivalent.

27. **Worthlessness**—Ranges from mild loss of esteem, feelings of inferiority, self-depreciation to feelings of total worthlessness.   _____

0 = Not present.

1 = Indicates feelings of worthlessness (loss of self-esteem) only on questioning.

2 = Spontaneously indicates feelings of worthlessness (loss of self-esteem).

3 = Different from "2" by degree: patient volunteers that he/she is "no good," "inferior," etc.

4 = Expresses feelings of total worthlessness—e.g., "I'm a heap of garbage," or its equivalent.

ZUNG SELF-RATING DEPRESSION SCALE (SDS)

Description: The SDS is a widely used 20-item pencil-and-paper scale developed by W. W. Zung in 1965 and modified by him in 1974. The scale is reproduced below with permission of the author's family, and it may currently be used free of charge. Scoring of the SDS follows a simple format, with all of the items having 1–4 points possible. Half of the items are scored in a forward scheme from left to right on the scales as follows: "None or a little of the time," 1 point; "Some of the time," 2 points; "Good part of the time," 3 points; and "Most or all of the time," 4 points. Scoring for 10 scale items (questions 2, 5, 6, 11, 12, 14, 16, 17, 18, and 20) is done in a reversed format (reversed scores range from "Most or all of the time," 1 point, to "None or a little of the time," 4 points). Zung (1974) found that subject groups fell into the following score ranges: normal controls (range = 25–43; mean = 33), outpatient depressives (range = 50–78; mean = 64), and hospitalized depressives (range = 63–90; mean = 74).

References

Zung, W. W. (1965). A self-rating depression scale. *Archives of General Psychiatry*, 12, 63–70.

Zung, W. W. (1974). *The measurement of depression*. Milwaukee, WI: Lakeside Laboratories.

Zung SDS Directions: Mark the box for each item that is most applicable to you at this time.

	None or a little of the time	Some of the time	Good part of the time	Most or all of the time
1. I feel down-hearted and blue.				
2. Morning is when I feel the best.				
3. I have crying spells or feel like it.				
4. I have trouble sleeping at night.				
5. I eat as much as I used to.				
6. I still enjoy sex.				
7. I notice that I am losing weight.				
8. I have trouble with constipation.				
9. My heart beats faster than usual.				
10. I get tired for no reason.				
11. My mind is as clear as it used to be.				
12. I find it easy to do the things I used to.				
13. I am restless and can't keep still.				
14. I feel hopeful about the future.				
15. I am more irritable than usual.				
16. I find it easy to make decisions.				
17. I feel that I am useful and needed.				
18. My life is pretty full.				
19. I feel that others would be better off if I were dead.				
20. I still enjoy the things I used to.				

Instruments for Assessing Depression in Children

DIANE J. WILLIS

CHILD ASSESSMENT SCHEDULE (CAS)

Description: The CAS is a semistructured interview for the clinical assessment of children. It employs a format of standardized questions and response items. Part I contains approximately 75 items and records the child's verbal responses to clinical inquiries about school, friends, activities and hobbies, family, fears and anxieties, worries, self-image, mood, somatic concerns, expression of anger, and thought disorder symptomatology. Part II records the examiner's observations and consists of approximately 53 items that probe insight, grooming, motor coordination, activity level, other physical movement and behavior, cognitive abilities, quality of verbalization, quality of emotional expression, and quality of interpersonal interaction. For each response item, the child's responses are coded as either "yes" (presence of symptoms), "no" (absence of symptoms), "ambiguous," "no response," or "not applicable." Part III obtains information about the onset and duration of symptoms. A form for parents is available.

There is a second version of the CAS that has additional items so that it can be used with adolescents and administered by well-trained lay interviewers (referred to as the 1990 version, compared to the earlier version dated 1983/1986). The CAS yields information on presence–absence of the major DSM-III-R diagnoses and two sets of scale scores (for diagnostically related items and for topical areas, such as functioning in school, friends, family, etc.). There is a comprehensive manual detailing administration and scoring of the CAS. A companion measure to assess degree of impairment, referred to as the Child and Adolescent Functional Assessment Scale, has also been developed.

Suitable ages: 7–18 years.

Address where the test may be obtained: Kay Hodges, 537 Mark Jefferson, Eastern Michigan University, Ypsilanti, MI 48197.

Cost: $10.00.

Restrictions on availability: None.

References

Hodges, K. (1993). Structured interviews. *Journal of Child Psychology and Psychiatry, 34*, 49–68.

Hodges, K., Gordon, Y., & Lennon, M. (1990). Parent–child agreement on symptoms assessed via a clinical research interview for children: The Child Assessment Schedule (CAS). *Journal of Child Psychology and Psychiatry, 31*, 427–436.

Hodges, K., Cools, J., & McKnew, D. (1989). Test–retest reliability of a clinical research interview for children: The Child Assessment Schedule (CAS). *Psychological Assessment: Journal of Consulting and Clinical Psychology, 1*, 317–322.

Hodges, K., McKnew, D., Burbach, D. J., & Roebuck, L. (1987). Diagnostic concordance between the Child Assessment Schedule (CAS) and the Schedule for Affective Disorders and Schizophrenia for School-Age Children (K-SADS) in an outpatient sample using lay interviews. *Journal of the American Academy of Child and Adolescent Psychiatry, 26*, 654–661.

Hodges, K., Saunders, W., Kashani, J., Hamlett, K., & Thompson, R. (1990). Internal consistency of DSM-III-R diagnoses using the symptom scales of the Child Assessment Schedule (CAS). *Journal of the American Academy of Child and Adolescent Psychiatry, 29*, 635–641.

CHILD BEHAVIOR CHECKLIST (CBCL)

Description: The CBCL contains items relevant to childhood depression. On a 3-point rating scale, parents indicate the extent to which each of 113 items describes their child's behavior. The checklist yields a profile of social competence scales and problem scales scored in terms of syndromes designated as Anxious/Depressed, Withdrawn, Somatic Complaints, Social Problems, Thought Problems, Attention Problems, Delinquent Behavior, and Aggressive Behavior, plus broad-band internalizing and externalizing groups of syndromes. A Teacher's Report Form (113 items), a Youth Self-Report (112 items), and a Direct Observation Form (97 items) are also available, as well as a version of the CBCL for ages 2–3 and a clinical interview form. The 1991 editions of profiles for the parent, teacher, and self-report forms score the same syndromes for both sexes, different ages, and different informants, normed on a national sample.

Suitable ages: 4–18 years.

Address where the test may be obtained: Thomas Achenbach, University Associates in Psychiatry, 1 South Prospect Street, Burlington, VT 05401.

Cost: $8.00 for 25 forms. Manuals for each instrument are $25.00.

Restrictions on availability: None.

References

Achenbach, T. M. (1991a). *Manual for the Child Behavior Checklist and 1991 Profile*. Burlington: University of Vermont, Department of Psychiatry.

Achenbach, T. M. (1991b). *Manual for the Teacher's Report Form and 1991 Profile*. Burlington: University of Vermont, Department of Psychiatry.

Achenbach, T. M. (1991c). *Manual for the Youth Self-Report and 1991 Profile*. Burlington: University of Vermont, Department of Psychiatry.

Achenbach, T. M. (1991d). *Integrative guide for the 1991 CBCL/ 4–18, YSR, and TRF profiles*. Burlington: University of Vermont, Department of Psychiatry.

CHILDREN'S DEPRESSION ADJECTIVE CHECKLIST (C-DACL)

Description: The C-DACL assesses dysphoric mood in present state. Forms H and I each contain 34 items that include 22 depression-connoting adjectives and 12 non-depression-connoting adjectives, respectively. (The Youth Depression Adjective Checklist, described later, contains forms appropriate for adolescents.)

Suitable ages: 8–12 years.

Address where the test may be obtained: Bernard Lubin, 5319 Holmes, Kansas City, MO 64110-2499.

Cost: None.

Restrictions on availability: Available for research purposes.

Reference

Sokoloff, R. M., & Lubin, B. (1983). Depressive mood in adolescent, emotionally disturbed females: Reliability and validity of an adjective checklist (C-DACL). *Journal of Abnormal Child Psychology, 11*, 531–536.

CHILDREN'S DEPRESSION INVENTORY (CDI)

Description: The CDI is a 27-item, self-rated, symptom-oriented scale on which the child chooses the one alternative out of three presented that best describes his/her own feelings/ideas for the past 2 weeks. Alternatives reflect the nature and frequency of symptoms characteristic of childhood depression, ranging from sadness, anhedonia, and suicidal ideations to sleep and appetite disturbances. Items on the CDI have been selected to cover affective, cognitive, psychomotor, and vegetative aspects of depression.

Suitable ages: 8–17 years.

Address where the test may be obtained: Multi-Health Systems, Inc., 908 Niagara Falls Boulevard, North Tonawanda, NY 14120-2060.

Cost: $55.00 for the kit (manual and 25 scoring forms).

Restrictions on availability: Licensed mental health professional.

References

Finch, A. J., Saylor, C. F., & Edwards, G. L. (1985). Children's Depression Inventory: Sex and grade norms for normal children. *Journal of Consulting and Clinical Psychology, 53*, 424–425.

Kovacs, M. (1985). The Children's Depression Inventory (CDI). *Psychopharmacology Bulletin, 21*, 995–998.

CHILDREN'S DEPRESSION RATING SCALE—REVISED (CDRS-R)

Description: The CDRS-R is a clinician-rated scale for measuring the severity of depression. Following a structured interview, clinicians use a 7-point scale to rate the degree of symptomatology in the areas of school work, anhedonia, social withdrawal, sleep, appetite, excessive fatigue, physical complaints, irritability, guilt, self-esteem, depressed feelings, morbid ideation, suicide/ideation, weeping, depressed affect, tempo of speech, hypoactivity, and lability of mood.

Suitable ages: 6–12 years.

Address where the test may be obtained: Department of Psychiatry, Section of Child Psychiatry, Rush–Presbyterian–St. Luke's Medical Center, 1720 West Polk Street, Chicago, IL 60612.

Cost: $3.00.

Restrictions on availability: None.

References

Poznanski, E. O., Cook, S. C., & Carroll, B. J. (1979). A depression rating scale for children. *Pediatrics*, 6(4), 442–450.

Poznanski, E. O., Grossman, J. A., Buchsbaum, Y., Baneges, M., Freeman, L., & Gibbons, R. (1984). Preliminary studies of the reliability and validity of the Children's Depression Rating Scale. *Journal of the American Academy of Child Psychiatry*, 23(2), 191–197.

CHILDREN'S DEPRESSION SCALE (CDS)

Description: The CDS is a self-rated scale consisting of 66 items (48 depressive and 18 positive). Six aspects of childhood depression are measured, including affective responses, social problems, self-esteem, preoccupation with own sickness and death, guilt, and pleasure. Items are presented on cards, which the child sorts into boxes labeled "very wrong," "wrong," "don't know," "not sure," "right," and "very right." The CDS—Adult Form consists of a separate set of cards reworded for use with parents, siblings, teachers, and relatives.

Suitable ages: 9–16 years.

Address where the test may be obtained: Consulting Psychologists Press, P.O. Box 60070, Palo Alto, CA 94306.

Cost: $100.00 for the kit including manual and forms.

Restrictions on availability: None.

References

Lang, M., & Tisher, M. (1983). *Children's Depression Scale (Revised)*. Melbourne, Australia: Australian Council for Educational Research.

Tisher, M., & Lang, M. (1983). The Children's Depression Scale: Review and further developments. In D. P. Cantwell & G. A. Carlson (Eds.), *Affective disorders in childhood and adolescence: An update* (pp. 181–203). New York: Spectrum.

DEPRESSION SELF-RATING SCALE FOR CHILDREN (DSRS)

Description: The DSRS consists of 18 items found to discriminate children with major depression from nondepressed children. Children are presented with 18 statements such as "I feel very bored," or "I feel very lonely," and asked to check whether each applied "most of the time," "sometimes," or "never" over the past 2 weeks. The scale has a test–retest reliability of .80 and a split-half reliability of .86.

Suitable ages: 7–14 years.

Address where the test may be obtained: Peter Birleson, Travancore Child and Family Centre, 50 Flemington Street, Flemington, Victoria 3031, Australia.

Cost: None.

Restrictions on availability: None.

References

Birleson, P. (1981). The validity of depressive disorder in childhood and the development of a self-rating scale: A research report. *Journal of Child Psychology and Psychiatry*, 22, 73–88.

Birleson, P., Hudson, I., Grey Buchannon, D., & Wolff, S. (1987). Clinical evaluation of a self-rating scale for depressive disorder in childhood (Depression Self-Rating Scale). *Journal of Child Psychology and Psychiatry*, 28, 43–60.

DIAGNOSTIC INTERVIEW FOR CHILDREN AND ADOLESCENTS— REVISED (DICA-R)

Description: The DICA-R consists of three interviews: one for children aged 6–12 years, another for adolescents aged 13–17 years, and a parent interview that asks parents about children aged 6–17. They are semistructured interviews yielding information on the onset, duration, and severity of symptoms, including those related to depression. All three are keyed to the DSM-III-R and assess a broad range of psychopathology.

Suitable ages: 6–17 years.

Address where the test may be obtained: Wendy Reich, Washington University School of Medicine, Division of Child Psychiatry, 4940 Audubon Avenue, St. Louis, MO 63110.

Cost: $50.00 per packet (includes manual, articles, three interview scales, and scoring form).

Restrictions on availability: None.

References

Herjanic, B., & Campbell, W. (1977). Differentiating psychiatrically disturbed children on the basis of a structured interview. *Journal of Abnormal Child Psychology*, 5, 127–134.

Reich, W., & Earls, F. (1987). Rules for making psychiatric diagnoses in children on the basis of multiple sources of information: Preliminary strategies. *Journal of Abnormal Child Psychology*, 25(4), 601–616.

Reich, W., Herjanic, B., Welner, Z., & Gandhy, P. R. (1982). Development of a structured psychiatric interview for children: Agreement on diagnosis comparing child and parent interviews. *Journal of Abnormal Child Psychology*, 10, 325–336.

Welner, Z., Reich, W., Herjanic, B., Jung, D., & Amado, H. (1987). Reliability, validity, and parent–child agreement studies of the

Diagnostic Interview for Children and Adolescents (DICA). *Journal of the American Academy of Child and Adolescent Psychiatry*, 26(5) 649–653.

INTERVIEW SCHEDULE FOR CHILDREN (ISC)

Description: The ISC is a semistructured, symptom-oriented psychiatric interview covering the major symptoms of depression, anxiety, conduct problems, and a broad range of other psychopathology. Clinicians rate symptoms on degree of severity. Two parallel forms are available.

Suitable ages: 8–18 years.

Address where the test may be obtained: Maria Kovacs, Western Psychiatric Institute and Clinic, University of Pittsburgh School of Medicine, 3811 O'Hara Street, Pittsburgh, PA 15213.

Cost: $6.25.

Restrictions on availability: Licensed mental health professionals.

Reference

Kovacs, M. (1985). The Interview Schedule for Children (ISC). *Psychopharmacology Bulletin, 21*, 991–994.

KIDDIE SCHEDULE FOR AFFECTIVE DISORDERS AND SCHIZOPHRENIA (K-SADS)

Description: The K-SADS is a comprehensive–structured psychiatric interview for use with parents and children to assess major symptomatology. It records symptoms relevant to DSM-III criteria for the following diagnostic categories: major/minor depression, mania, hypomania, schizophrenia, schizoaffective disorder, autism, eating disorders, attention deficit disorder, conduct disorders, anxiety disorders, alcohol and substance abuse, and suicidal behavior. Form E assesses whether a past symptom or behavior ever occurred and whether the problem is current. Form P focuses on present episode and symptom severity.

Suitable ages: 6–16 years.

Address where the test may be obtained: Alene Harris, Western Psychiatric Institute and Clinic, Division of Child and Adolescent Psychiatry, University of Pittsburgh School of Medicine, 3811 O'Hara Street, Pittsburgh, PA 15213.

Cost: $20.00.

Restrictions on availability: None.

References

Chambers, W., Puig-Antich, J., Hirsch, M., Paez, P., Ambrosini, P., Tabrizi, M., & Davis, M. (1985). The assessment of affective disorders in children and adolescents by a semi-structured interview: Test–retest reliability of the K-SADS-P. *Archives of General Psychiatry, 21*, 696–702.

Orvaschel, H., Puig-Antich, J., Chambers, W., Tabrizi, M. A., & Johnson, R. (1982). Retrospective assessment of prepubertal major depression with the Kiddie-SADS-E. *Journal of the American Academy of Child Psychiatry, 21*(4), 392–397.

MULTISCORE DEPRESSION INVENTORY FOR ADOLESCENTS AND ADULTS (MDI)

Description: The MDI is a standardized 118-item instrument that provides an objective measure of the severity of self-reported depression. Unlike measures that produce a global depression rating, the MDI provides 10 subscales: low energy, cognitive difficulty, guilt, self-esteem, social introversion, pessimism, irritability, sad mood, instrumental helplessness, and learned helplessness. A version specific to children and adolescents is in development.

Suitable ages: 13 years and older.

Address where the test may be obtained: Western Psychological Services, 12031 Wilshire Boulevard, Los Angeles, CA 90025.

Cost: About $100.00 for a kit containing all materials pertinent to the MDI. The individual components needed for specific testing purposes can be purchased separately at lower cost.

Restrictions on availability: Users should have training and supervised experience in the use of individually administered clinical instruments.

References

Berndt, D. (1986). *Multiscore Depression Inventory (MDI): Manual.* Los Angeles: Western Psychological Services.

Berndt, D., Petzel, T., & Berndt, S. (1980). Development and initial evaluation of a Multiscore Depression Inventory. *Journal of Personality Assessment, 44*, 396–403.

PERSONALITY INVENTORY FOR CHILDREN (PIC)

Description: The PIC is a standardized instrument for the assessment of children's personality. It is completed by parents in a standard administration consisting of 280 items (a 132-item screening form and a 420-item extended form can also be administered from standard materials). There are 12 clinical scales (depression, somatic concerns, withdrawal, anxiety, psychosis, hyperactivity, delinquency, social skills, family relations, achievement, intellectual screening, and development) and three validity scales. Available computer reports also provide a clinical typology analysis and a school special service placement analyses. A self-report companion to the PIC, the Personality Inventory for Youth was published in 1994.

Suitable ages: 3–16 years.

Address where the test may be obtained: Western Psychological Services, 12031 Wilshire Boulevard, Los Angeles, CA 90025.

Cost: About $280.00 for a kit containing all materials pertinent to the PIC. The individual components needed for specific testing purposes can be purchased separately at lower cost.

Restrictions on availability: Users should have training and supervised experience in the use of individually administered clinical instruments.

References

Froman, P. K. (1971). *The development of a depression scale for the Personality Inventory for Children (PIC).* Unpublished manuscript, University of Minnesota, Minneapolis.

Kline, R. B., Lachar, D., & Gdowski, C. L. (1987). A PIC typology of children and adolescents: II. Classification rules and specific behavior correlates. *Journal of Clinical Child Psychology, 16,* 225–234.

Lachar, D. (1990). *Personality Inventory for Children (PIC): Revised format manual supplement.* Los Angeles: Western Psychological Services.

Lachar, D., & Gdowski, C. L. (1979). *Actuarial assessment of child and adolescent personality: An interpretive guide for the Personality Inventory for Children profile.* Los Angeles: Western Psychological Services.

Lachar, D., & Gruber, C. P. (1993). Development of the Personality Inventory for Youth: A self-report companion to the Personality Inventory for Children. *Journal of Personality Assessment, 61,* 81–98.

Lachar, D., & Kline, R. B. (1994). The Personality Inventory for Children and the Personality Inventory for Youth. In M. Maruish (Ed.), *Use of psychological testing for treatment planning and outcome assessment* (pp. 479–516). Hillsdale, NJ: Erlbaum.

Wirt, R. D., Lachar, D., Klinedinst, J. K., & Seat, P. D. (1990). *Multidimensional description of child personality: A manual for the Personality Inventory for Children.* Los Angeles: Western Psychological Services.

REYNOLDS ADOLESCENT DEPRESSION SCALE (RADS)

Description: The RADS is a self-report measure of the severity of depressive symptomatology in adolescents. It consists of 30 items and utilizes a 4-point response format. The RADS was developed specifically for use with adolescents. Item content reflects symptomatology specified by the DSM-III-R. The RADS manual presents psychometric data on studies with more than 10,000 adolescents, as well as normative information.

Suitable ages: 13–19 years.

Address where the test may be obtained: Psychological Assessment Resources, P.O. Box 998, Odessa, FL 33556.

Cost: $41.00 for the RADS Professional Kit (manual, scoring key, answer sheets).

Restrictions on availability: None.

References

Reynolds, W. M. (1987). *Reynolds Adolescent Depression Scale: Professional manual.* Odessa, FL: Psychological Assessment Resources.

Reynolds, W. M. (1989). Suicidal ideation and depression in adolescents: Assessment and research. In P. F. Lovibond & P. Wilson (Eds.), *Clinical and abnormal psychology* (pp. 125–135). Amsterdam: Elsevier.

Reynolds, W. M., & Coats, K. I. (1986). A comparison of cognitive–behavioral therapy and relaxation training for the treatment of depression in adolescents. *Journal of Consulting and Clinical Psychology, 54,* 653–660.

REYNOLDS CHILD DEPRESSION SCALE (RCDS)

Description: The RCDS is a self-report measure of the severity of depressive symptomatology in children. It consists of 30 items, 29 of which utilize a 4-point response format, and 1 item that consists of five smiley-type faces. The RCDS was developed specifically for use with children. Item content reflects symptomatology specified by the DSM-III-R. The RCDS manual presents psychometric data on studies with more than 2,000 children, as well as normative information.

Suitable ages: 8–12 years.

Address where the test may be obtained: Psychological Assessment Resources, P.O. Box 998, Odessa, FL 33556.

Cost: $41.00 for the RCDS Professional Kit (manual, scoring key, answer sheets).

Restrictions on availability: None.

References

Reynolds, W. M. (1989). *Reynolds Child Depression Scale: Professional manual,* Odessa, FL: Psychological Assessment Resources.

Reynolds, W. M., Anderson, G., & Bartell, N. (1985). Measuring depression in children: A multi-method assessment investigation. *Journal of Abnormal Child Psychology, 13,* 513–526.

Reynolds, W. M., & Graves, A. (1989). Reliability of children's reports of depressive symptomatology. *Journal of Abnormal Child Psychology, 17,* 647–655.

YOUTH DEPRESSION ADJECTIVE CHECKLIST (Y-DACL)

Description: The Y-DACL, a version of the Children's Depression Adjective Checklist appropriate for older children and adolescents, assesses "today" and "generally feel" versions of depressive affect. The 22 adjectives, 14 depressive and 12 nondepressive, are at or below sixth-grade reading level.

Suitable ages: Preadolescents and adolescents.

Address where the test may be obtained: Michael P. Carey, Department of Psychology, Kobacker Center, Medical College of Ohio, 3000 Arlington Avenue, Toledo, OH 43699.

Cost: None.

Restrictions on availability: Available for research purposes.

References

Carey, M. P., Lubin, B., & Brewer, D. H. (1993). Measuring dysphoric mood in preadolescents and adolescents: The Youth Depression Adjective Checklist (Y-DACL). *Journal of Clinical Child Psychology, 21*(2), 331–338.

Sung, H., Lubin, B., & Yi, J. (1992). Reliability and validity of the Koren Youth Depression Adjective Checklist (Y-DACL). *Adolescence, 27*(107), 527–533.

Index